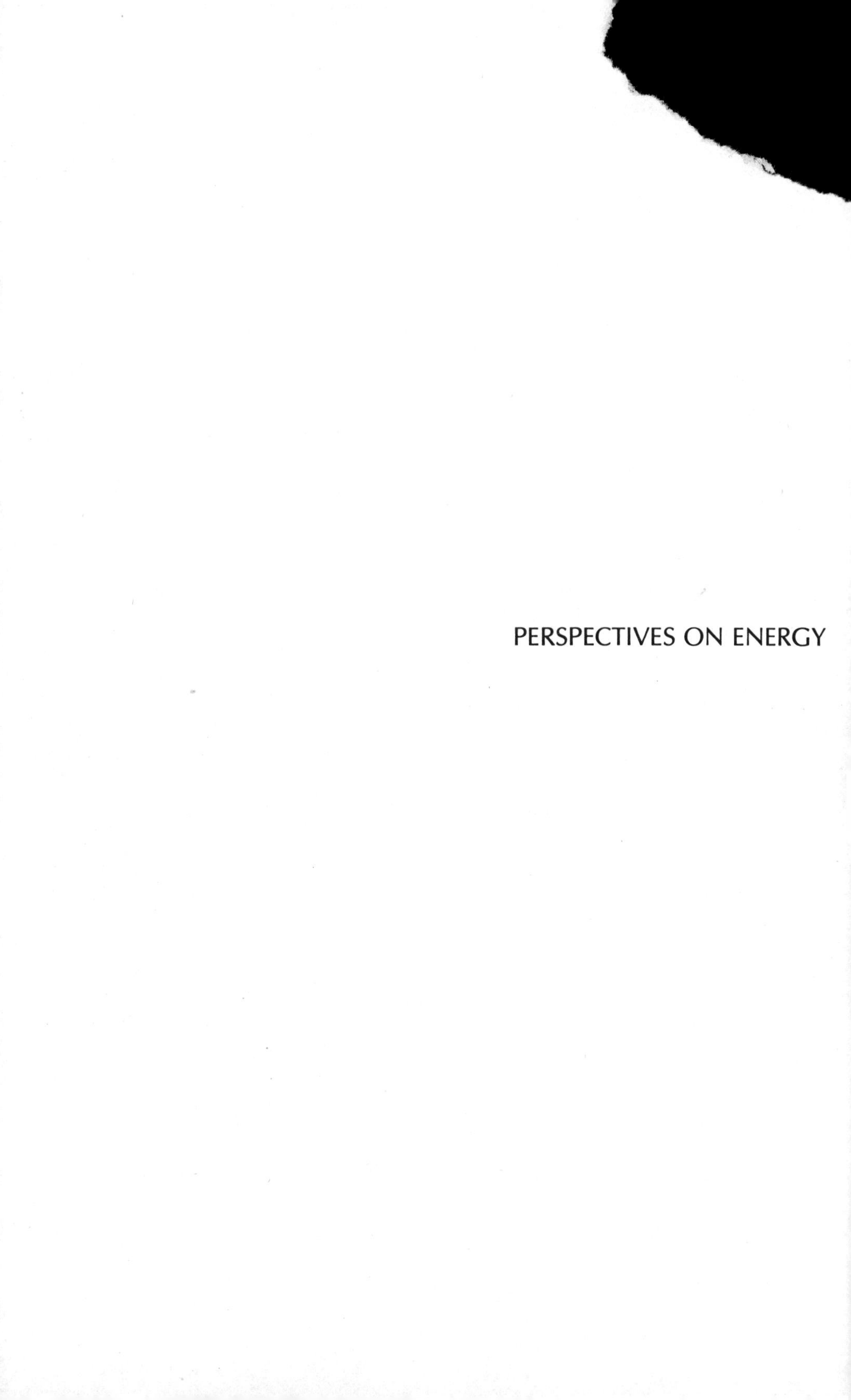

PERSPECTIVES ON ENERGY

PERSPECTIVES ON ENERGY

SSUES, IDEAS, AND ENVIRONMENTAL DILEMMAS

SECOND EDITION

Edited by
LON C. RUEDISILI
UNIVERSITY OF TOLEDO

MORRIS W. FIREBAUGH
UNIVERSITY OF WISCONSIN-PARKSIDE

NEW YORK • OXFORD UNIVERSITY PRESS • 1978

To my wife Susan, Stephen and Robert and future generations whose environment and welfare will depend upon the responsible energy decisions of our society L.C.R.

To Joyce and our children Steve and Susan, in the hope that wise energy management policies today will assure productive and rewarding lives tomorrow M.W.F.

Second printing, 1979

Printed in the United States of America

Library of Congress Cataloging in Publication Data
Main entry under title:

Perspectives on energy.

1. Power resources. 2. Power (Mechanics)
3. Energy policy. I. Ruedisili, Lon C.
II. Firebaugh, Morris W.
TJ163.2.P47 1978 333.7 77-27652
ISBN 0-19-501880-X
ISBN 0-19-501879-6 pbk.

Preface

Just as the United States had recovered from the first shock of the 1973–74 "energy crisis" and was beginning to doze off again, the second shock hit—the cold winters of 1976–78. The lessons learned in the first experience seemed to be fading as oil imports expanded, effective speed limits crept back up, and the "full-sized" car made its last bid for the allegiance of the American car buyer. Then the fuel shortage and the resulting plant and school closings, economic disruption, and unemployment reemphasized the absolutely central role energy plays in industrial societies. There is now evidence that the energy problem is grudgingly accepted as real by much of the public and is receiving official attention by the government. Thus, we are hopeful that the lessons learned recently will be incorporated into our institutions (legal and economic), thereby avoiding painful "withdrawal" experiences in the future.

The objectives and structures of the second edition are the same as those of the first. The major issues remain the finitude of our energy resources and the environmental dilemmas posed by production and use of energy. The second edition, however, has an increased emphasis in the following areas: *economics* as a tool for understanding and determining energy patterns, a better evaluation of the *relative environmental and health costs* of energy alternatives, *solar energy* as an imminent resource for heating and cooling, and serious *conservation,* including an analysis of its effect on our life-styles.

The bewilderment and confusion following the earlier crises are yielding slowly to rational analyses, several of which are included in this edition. Serious disagreement among the experts still remains on certain key issues, such as the safety of the plutonium fuel cycle, the economics of solar power, and growth versus no growth scenarios. Major studies are narrowing such differences and have even produced some consensus positions. These issues have now reached the political domain in the form of the Federal Energy Program. It is the responsibility of citizens concerned with the energy problem to become informed on the key issues. Such *informed* public opinion is essential to implement energy policy decisions that are in the public welfare. We hope this book contributes to this process.

These articles should be used with both confidence and caution, and we don't think that these terms are contradictory. They can be used with the confidence that the solutions indicated are feasible within the limitations of available science and technology. They should be used with caution because the statistics and philosophies at the date of writing may not be those of the years to come.

Again we wish to thank the many authors and publishers for permission to include their articles in the second edition. We appreciate the prompt and excellent response from authors in providing original articles on very short notice or for updating their articles. We thank our university colleagues for useful feedback on the first edition and helpful suggestions on the second. We thank Ramona Maillet and Martha Campbell for clerical and library support and the University of Toledo Department of Geology and the University of Wisconsin-Parkside Division of Science for continued support in preparing this edition. Ellis Rosenberg, Jean Shapiro, and Carol Miller of Oxford University Press continued their excellent assistance in organizational and editorial matters. Finally, special thanks must go to Susan and Stephen Ruedisili and Joyce Firebaugh for proofreading the final manuscript and seeing the book to its culmination.

University of Toledo
University of Wisconsin-Parkside L.C.R.
April, 1978 M.W.F.

Preface to the First Edition

Though the immediate impact of the "energy crisis" did not strike the American public until the winter of 1973–74, the underlying causes as well as many possible solutions have been recognized for many years. After the public clamor to "do something" to assure energy supplies and warnings of environmentalists against "rushing headlong . . . " toward various proposed solutions, the need for clear and concise information on this most confusing problem is more urgent than ever. In this book we attempt to provide such information as well as incorporate a wide spectrum of current interpretations as to its meaning and implications for public policy.

Students, and particularly students in the sciences, are accustomed to finding the "correct answer" determined by natural law. As a result, they often find the apparently contradictory statements issuing from governmental, industrial, and environmental "energy experts" both confusing and frustrating. Since the production, distribution, and utilization of energy does, in fact, involve unresolved dilemmas over which reputable authorities differ, we believe it is essential to present as wide a range of interpretation on major energy issues as feasible in one book.

The editors have attempted to present a balanced and representative analysis in areas of controversy, but we readily admit that the particular selection of articles included reflects our own interpretation of the most significant issues involved. We are attempting, in this book, to present the most current analyses in an area of rapid change and new information on both scientific and policy areas. Thus, rather than abstracting significant contributions, we have presented the material in the authors' original words in order to expedite the presentation as well as to preserve the tone and content of the more subjective interpretations. Some of the articles have been prepared specifically for this book to present a more complete picture of the dilemmas society faces in an energy age.

In the final analysis, public policy in this critical area of energy management must be determined by enlightened public opinion as it is worked out through the political process. We believe that the present generation of college students is capable of the critical "sifting and winnowing" required to reach an intelligent, informed (and, hence, effective) opinion on energy policies. We hope this book will assist them in the process.

At this point we want to acknowledge the large number of people whose fine cooperation made this book possible. First we wish to thank all the authors and publishers for permission to include their articles in this anthology. We especially appreciate the efforts of Professor Glenn T. Seaborg of the University of California, Berkeley, in preparing a very appropriate and timely Foreword. We thank Professor John S. Steinhart, University of Wisconsin-Madison, for many hours of consultation and advice on the preparation of the manuscript. We appreciate the input and advice of several of the authors included in the book as well as our Parkside colleagues and students who evaluated earlier versions of this book. The University of Wisconsin-Parkside Division of Science, the Univeristy of Wisconsin-Parkside Library-Learning Center, and the University of Wisconsin-Madison Department of Physics kindly provided valuable assistance and support in this effort for which we are grateful. Geraldine S. Covelli, Patricia E. Heckel, Nancy Lyttle, James M. Romanowski, Gail A. Tworek, and Jacqueline Willems provided the library and clerical support crucial for the successful completion of this project. Finally, we appreciate the continued assistance and encouragement of Ellis H. Rosenberg, Jean Shapiro, and Carol Miller of Oxford University Press.

University of Toledo
University of Wisconsin-Parkside L.C.R.
December, 1974 M.W.F.

Foreword

The year 1973 represented a turning point in our lives: we never again shall be in a position to take our supply of energy for granted. The energy problem took a long time in coming—even though general recognition came suddenly—and it will take a long time in going. We face difficult choices in the years to come, choices that will cut to the fabric of our way of life.

To make these choices wisely, and take the actions that will be necessary to implement them, we need not only a sense of determination, but also a coherent and realistic energy policy. Prerequisite to this is a public understanding of our dilemma and conflicting choices. In this book of readings, Professors Ruedisili and Firebaugh have assembled a spectrum of authoritative information and opinion on our energy problem. The balance of articles is sufficiently broad to stimulate and educate the reader, college student, or other interested citizen on this vital issue.

The readings make it clear that our only hope is to work on both elements of the energy problem—supply and demand. We must increase the supply and decrease the demand or at least reduce the rate of increase of the demand. At the same time, because it is all part of the same problem, we must not compromise the efforts that are under way to improve both our natural and our man-made environments and to protect the public health and safety. Our conflicting choices include those between the public goals of abundant energy and environmental quality, and these conflicts will have to be reconciled as best they can with regard to the total social welfare.

The energy technologies that can be expected to play a major role in the American energy economy in the coming decades include the use of fossil fuels, and their improvement and interconversion, nuclear fission, nuclear fusion, geothermal energy, and solar energy. These sources, and others covered in this book's readings, should be developed. It is not a question of whether geothermal energy can produce electricity, or whether solar energy is feasible, but rather how much can we expect from these sources, when and under what conditions can we expect their utilization, and, importantly, what will it cost us to ensure their development in an expenditious, timely, and safe manner.

We are in trouble because of inadequate national planning in the past, and this includes insufficient research on and development of new energy sources. The development of new technologies, where the systems are very complex, requires much basic research before they can be utilized and institutionalized. The cost of basic research is small compared with the value of the technologies it spawns, and we should not neglect the lessons of the past in this regard, even as we search for immediate solutions to our energy problems.

We are accustomed to the idea of unlimited growth from our classical theories of economics, in which supply always rises to meet demand. But unlike capital, which is a construct of man, the natural resources of our earth are finite. In fact, we are going to be faced next with a series of resource crises—metals crises (copper, aluminum, chromium, nickel, tin, manganese, and so on), a food crisis, a water crisis—if we do not plan better for the future than we have planned in the past for our future energy and material needs.

In trying to solve our energy problems, we must not neglect the questions of fragile values in our society. We need to understand more fully the role of our institutions in the resolution of specific value conflicts in order to understand how the patterns of these decisions, if there are patterns, themselves create new values and new institutions that perpetuate those values. Such questions as these should be addressed: In crises, do fragile values that are without institutional embodiment get lost, even though they may be deeply held by a substantial number of citizens? With what kind of analysis do we approach decisions involving competition and compromise between the satisfaction of present and future welfare? How is our concern for the future, itself a fragile value, concretely manifested?

The readings in this book should help in the understanding of and deliberations on all these issues.

University of California
Berkeley, California

Glenn T. Seaborg

Contents

I

BACKGROUND AND LIMITATIONS

Zepher I, a semi-submersible drilling rig, being towed into the North Sea to seek out sea-bottom oil. (Photo courtesy of Skyfotos, and Texaco, Inc.)

Use of energy in the grain wheat harvest along the Columbia River, Wasco County, Oregon. (Photo courtesy of the U.S. Department of Agriculture Conservation Service; USDA-SCS photo by G. L. Green.)

INTRODUCTION

A sound understanding of the boundary conditions applicable to energy issues is essential to the study of energy and its role in human affairs. Such limitations include the obvious physical constraints of thermodynamic laws, geological resource data, and energy flow patterns with their associated physical facilities. Less obvious, but equally important, constraints involve environmental costs, health effects, and economic factors that are inherent in various energy alternatives. Finally, we must be aware of social values and their expression in the political and legal systems. These values in conjunction with enormous social inertia are probably the most critical factor in the wise management of our energy system.

As a background for interpreting specific energy issues, we must understand the effects of these boundary conditions not only as independent constraints but also as interacting forces. For example, a change in environmental law affecting source A may cause a reduced thermodynamic efficiency, leading to a reduced economic advantage and resulting in a switch to source B, causing increased dependence on foreign sources, which may increase international tensions in times of crisis, and so on. The networks of these cause–effect relationships are very complex, and only recently have computer programs been developed to study the dynamics of such systems. As we consider the environmental, health, economic, political, and social aspects of energy, it is important to remain aware of these relationships.

The central role of energy in heating, lighting, and motive power for industrial society is obvious. There is an even more fundamental need for energy that stems from basic physical law. This law states that unless an outside agent intervenes, a given system tends to increase its entropy (e.g., disorder or randomness). For example, water in the mountains runs downhill; high and low temperature objects in contact tend to equalize their temperatures; and high quality energy, such as electricity, always ends up as low quality energy, heat. This tendency, called the "heat death of the universe" on a large scale, is apparent on a smaller scale as thermal pollution of streams and air, exhaustion of high-grade (organized) ores, and consumption of fossil fuels. In this thermodynamic analogy, many of our environmental problems stem from the increase in disorder and randomness. The outside agent that can restore order on a local basis is energy. Solar energy can lift water back to the mountains. Energy enables us to reorganize such disordered collections as solid wastes into burnable fuels and primary metals. With appropriate expenditures of energy, automobile exhausts and sulfur dioxide from coal burning power plants may be "organized" out of the environment. So although energy production and consumption is the cause of many of our problems, energy also is an important element of the solution.

In this section, Harold G. Cassidy introduces the concept of basic limitations on energy considerations in *Boundary Conditions in Energy and Ecology*. These relations are stated very simply and concisely, and yet they are often overlooked or forgotten by many who believe that our future welfare requires continued growth in all areas of society. His speculations provide a hopeful image of human nature and a helpful basis for making moral judgments on energy issues.

In *Energy and the Environment,* John M. Fowler presents an excellent historical summary of the development of energy and its flow through the social system. He discusses basic thermodynamic relations and outlines the environmental costs of various forms of energy. Several future energy options are introduced, and these are examined in greater detail later in this volume.

Cyril L. Comar and Leonard A. Sagan, in *Health Effects of Energy Production and Conversion,* discuss the environmental backlash of greatest concern to man. It is well known that all our common fuels have "bad" environmental health effects. In this article, the authors present the available data that address the more meaningful questions: "How bad?" and "Compared to what?" Before wise energy choices can be made, such questions must be answered. The authors also raise highly provocative questions on the health effects of not having enough energy and on excessive expenditures for safety equipment of questionable value for the risks involved.

John and Carol Steinhart review the enormously complex food system and its energy implications in *Energy Use in the United States Food System*. The possible failure of the energy-dependent food chain is one of the gravest concerns of many who have studied recent climatic changes. Although high energy agriculture may be necessary to carry out North America's "bread basket" mission, the Steinharts raise serious questions about the wisdom of exporting this food system to energy-poor nations.

In *The Economics of the Energy Problem,* Helmut J. Frank and John J. Schanz, Jr. examine energy issues from an economic perspective. Since economics has been shown to be the driving force in the development of energy resources, the interaction between economics and technology is examined. Price elasticity is clearly defined, and the distinction made between ''resources'' and ''reserves'' helps in an understanding of the large discrepancies between quoted energy supply figures from diverse sources. The delicate issue of the extent to which government should interfere in the *laissez-faire* free market system is raised and suggestions are offered.

The National Energy Plan—Overview and Summary is the Carter Administration's first attempt to present a coherent and comprehensive energy program. Former administrations have been severely criticized by industrialists and environmentalists alike for confusing, contradictory, or nonexistent energy policies. Much of the Carter program is administrative in nature and has already been implemented—the remainder is legislative and various provisions are in various stages of review by Congress. Whatever the outcome of this process, it is likely that this program and its subsequent modifications will be the focus of debate on the role of government in energy policy for the next several years. Since Federal energy policies are so important in shaping our energy future, it is essential that these legal boundary conditions be examined critically. Most of the issues addressed in this energy plan are examined in more detail later in this volume.

Richard J. Anderson poses both a warning and a call to action in *The Energy Situation—The Challenge*. His analysis, made several months before *The National Energy Plan,* reached essentially the same conclusions as that plan. The result is a strong call for conservation and reevaluation of our attitudes toward this vital resource. The challenge is one we cannot afford to ignore.

Boundary Conditions in Energy and Ecology 1

HAROLD G. CASSIDY 1977

Uncertainties, dilemmas, paradoxes, and the inevitable trade-offs clearly abound in the politics, economics, technology, and law related to energy and ecology. It may be helpful to restate certain fixed points that can provide boundaries for a fundamental frame of reference. What this amounts to is looking for invariant relations, relations that are not sensitive to time or place or to the observer with his own personal habitat. Because these invariant relations are persuasive they could seem trivial, were it not that they are so frequently forgotten.

Relation 1. The material Earth system is finite. Not only the great waters and land masses, but the gases above the Earth are limited. Though there is some radioactive (and other) transmutation going on, it is sufficiently correct to state that the numbers of atoms are finite with respect to each kind. This means that, given the dynamic state of the Earth, recycling must occur.

In the course of discussing large numbers, Harlow Shapley calculated the implications of such recycling.[1] In a given breath there will be 10^{19} or so argon atoms. Breathed out, these become gradually mixed with the other atmospheric argon atoms, and after awhile—perhaps a year or so—they may be well distributed over the globe. Then any day's breathing will encounter on the order of 15 of these "original" atoms. In the course of history these atoms will have passed through the lungs of innumerable persons, great and small.

Relation 2. Our world system is essentially closed in a material sense. A system may be finite, yet open. For example, a steadily burning candle-flame has finite dimensions wherever the system is bounded, yet is the seat of continuous flow as fuel burns to gases and particulate matter. Therefore we need to state the additional principle that the Earth system is closed in a material sense. We receive micro and macro meteorites, but we also surely lose some matter from the outer

Dr. Harold G. Cassidy, emeritus professor in chemistry, Yale University, is now professor-at-large at Hanover College, Hanover, Indiana 47243.

From *Bulletin of the Atomic Scientists,* Vol. 33, No. 3, pp. 31–32, March 1977. Reprinted by permission of the author and the *Bulletin of the Atomic Scientist.* This article is based on an address delivered while the author was Green Honors Chair Professor at Texas Christian University, Fort Worth, Texas.

reaches of our envelope. It is estimated that we remain in virtually a steady state with respect to matter. Some question may be raised (in connection with Relation 4) about the mass-equivalent quantity of the energy stored on the Earth. This does not appear to affect the statement of Relation 2 in any essential way.

Relation 3. The Earth is an interlinked system such that actions on one part may affect other parts. That what people do affects others has been a theme of philosophers and theologians from ancient times. We have much scientific evidence of the truth of this relation—a relation that may, indeed, be implied by Relation 2, but that needs to be stated.

It is indelicate for one to talk of rope in a house where there has been a hanging, but some time ago fallout from two Chinese atom bomb tests was registered at the Brookhaven National Laboratory in New York, a half-world away, in 9 and 14 days after the tests.[2] Water-borne and land-borne debris circulate less rapidly; but it is well known that in the 30 years or so that DDT has been widely used it has spread all over the globe, even into the remote Arctic.

Relation 4. The Earth is open to energy. The energy that bathes us ranges from radio through heat and visible and x ray to cosmic radiation (and, no doubt, beyond both these spectral "ends"). Not much is known about the ultimate disposition of the exemplars at the extremes of this range. It does appear that in respect to heat energy, the Earth exhibits a fluctuating but overall, long-range, steady-state condition. That is, within the range of fluctuations that have not been wide enough to wipe out life, the calories coming in and generated by radioactivity and volcanic and other processes balances the calories going out plus the calories stored as chemical energy.

Relation 5. There is no free good thing; there are no free lunches. All must be paid for now or later in some way. This is a free translation of the second law of thermodynamics. It is applicable to all the myriad of trade-offs that face us. In general, as many ecologists have pointed out, it is best to pay all debts promptly, since the payments tend to escalate.[3] We have perhaps thought that many things are free when the payment must come from others—other peoples, our grandchildren. The word "free" has been debased. Even banks offer "free gifts" to bring in customers. These gifts are paid for by their present customers and, to one who thinks about it, they lower the credibility of the bank as a *fiduciary* institution.

Relation 6. Organized natural resources are continually dispersed by industrialized man. Generally it is more economic to mine the richer sources of fossel fuels, metals, and inorganic materials first. When these run out one turns to less rich sources, as in the case of the move from Mesabi ore to taconite. The cost of the process for obtaining product always increases. Some industrial materials are recycled, but most are dispersed over the land or find their way into the oceans. The atoms are not lost from the Earth, but they become more elusive. The cost of developing them into an industrially useful form increases both in terms of energy and in terms of the materials needed to build the machines without which energy cannot be harnessed.

Relation 7. Constructive processes tend to be slow; destructive ones may be very rapid. Destructive processes are probably also always more rapid than the corresponding constructive ones. It takes a short time to cut down a tree that took 50 years to grow. Decay and destruction float with the stream of probabilities toward disorder. Growth and construction buck this stream, paying as they go (Relations 5 and 6).

Relation 8. Natural homeostatic systems have finite limits. It used to be that when there were fewer people inhabiting the Earth their waste products caused little irreversible pollution. Nature tended to sweep up after the polluters except in those areas where, for example, overgrazing had reduced the land to desert. Then natural reclamation became extremely slow. Today we have the power to override many natural homeostatic systems.

As an apocryphal example, the world's nuclear arsenals contain enough bombs to literally wipe out all higher (and perhaps all) life from the face of the Earth.

Relation 9 (speculative). For all that our physical world system is finite, there appears to be no limit in depth, subtlety, and creativity to human cognitive and emotional abilities. This relation is a hopeful one for human existence. This does not mean that everything whatever is possible. There is still the finite world and there are still the constraints of intransigent matter. The eight relations already stated cannot be abrogated. The capacity I speculate about has to do with humankind's creativity in the massless, spaceless (perhaps timeless) realm of the mind. If we may extrapolate from the past and present we must, I think, imagine an indefinitely increasing capability of men's minds as the future unwinds.

Relation 10 (speculative). Human survival with reasonable quality of life is one suitable criterion for judging moral issues. Good quality of life has been defined in a report prepared for the American Friends Service Committee. They said:

> In thinking through what we meant by "the quality of life," therefore, we took for granted satisfaction of these basic needs: adequate food, shelter and clothing; physical and mental health; loving and being loved, belonging, and being able to function in one's society.
>
> To Friends, a good life means much more. It means, in addition, the opportunity to develop in mind, personality, and body to one's fullest potential. It means access to education and a healthy environment. It means the chance to grow up with dignity and self-respect in a family that encourages personal and social responsibility and helpfulness to others. It means a life in which man can make responsible use of his powers—physical, intellectual, creative, social, spiritual.[4]

This is the best statement I have found of an ideal for mankind. I cannot improve upon it. Their report went on to say that for a major part of the world's people this seems an impossible dream. As a criterion, however, I believe it to be highly serviceable.

Relations 1 to 8 are valuable tools for cutting through some of the verbiage that obscures energy and ecology facts. Relation 9 gives us hope in the long run for new solutions to problems. We must accept that nature is full of surprises. We have only to remember the vast conceptual changes, based on experimental discoveries, that have occurred in physics, chemistry, and biology in the last 75 years to feel confident that more "quantum jumps" will occur. By the nature of things, of course, we do not know what these will be. But we can feel confident *that* there will be some.

Finally, Relation 10 provides criteria for moral choices that are made whenever human beings act in any way. One's moral stance may be inferred from one's actions; ethics is the theory of moral behavior; Relation 10 is a rational ethical statement.

REFERENCES

1. Harlow Shapley, *Beyond the Observatory* (New York: Charles Scribner's & Sons, 1967), chap. 2
2. G. M. Woodwell, in *Ecological Crisis. Readings for Survival,* edited by Glen A. Love and Rhoda M. Love (New York: Harcourt Brace Jovanovich, 1970), p. 49; Woodwell's article originally appeared in March 1967 issue of *Scientific American.*
3. Howard T. Odum, *Environment, Power, and Society* (New York: John Wiley and Sons, 1971), pp. 46ff
4. American Friends Service Committee, *Who Shall Live? Man's Control Over Birth and Death* (New York: Hill and Wang, 1970), pp. 52–53.

Energy and the Environment 2

JOHN M. FOWLER 1977

ENERGY: WHERE IT COMES FROM AND WHERE IT GOES

The world runs on energy, both literally and figuratively. It spins on its axis and travels in its orbit about the Sun; winds blow, waves crash on the beaches, volcanoes and earthquakes rock its surface. Without energy it would be a dead world. Energy was needed to catalyze the beginning of life; energy is needed to sustain it.

For most of life, animal and plant, energy means food; and most of life turns to the Sun as ultimate source. The linked-life patterns—the ecosystems—that have been established between plants and animals are very complex; the paths of energy wind and twist and double back, but ultimately they all begin at that star that holds us in our endless circle.

When man crossed the threshold of consciousness that separated him from animals, his uses of energy began to diversify. He, too, needed food, but poorly furred as he was, he also needed warmth. With the discovery of fire he was able to warm himself. He also found that fire could make his food digestible and thus increase its efficiency as an energy source. After a while he began to use fire to make the implements through which he slowly started to dominate nature.

Man's use of energy grew very slowly. In the beginning he required only 2,000 Calories

Dr. John M. Fowler is Director of Special Projects and Manager of Publications of the National Science Teachers Association, Washington, D.C. 20009. He directs the NSTA's Project for an Energy-Enriched Curriculum, which is providing energy-education materials for teachers and students throughout the country. Earlier, he was the Director of the Commission on College Physics (1965–1972) and was awarded the Millikan Medal by the American Association of Physics for contributions to the teaching of physics in 1969. During a tenure at Washington University, St. Louis, he helped start the Committee on Environmental Information, and the magazine *Environment.* He is currently on the Advisory Board to *Environment;* and he is a Director of the Scientist's Institute for Public Information. His publications include *Fallout: A Study of Superbombs, Strontium 90, Survival,* Basic Books, Inc. (1960), *Energy and the Environment,* McGraw-Hill (1975), and the NSTA *Energy-Environment Source Book.* He has lectured and written extensively on energy topics and this article is a revised and updated version of an article that appeared, under the same title, in *The Science Teacher.*

The original article was from *The Science Teacher,* Vol. 39, No. 9, pp. 10–22, December 1972. Reprinted by permission of the author and The Science Teacher. This article was prepared by the author for this edition in April 1977.

Table 2–1. Energy Costs for Some Foods and Fuels (Retail, Washington, D.C., April 1977).

Source	*Price per unit (dollars)*	*Energy (Cal/kg)*	*Cost per Million Calories (dollars)*
Bread	0.33/lb	2,660	273.00
Butter	1.35/lb	7,950	373.50
Sugar	0.16/lb	4,100	85.80
Sirloin steak	1.79/lb	1,840	2,140.00
Scotch	15.00/half gallon	2,580	3,840.00
Coal	79.70/ton	7,040	12.40
Fuel oil	0.47/gallon	10,660	13.40
Natural gas	2.55/Million BTU	12,450	10.10
Gasoline	0.65/gallon	12,280	20.50
Electricity	0.04/kw-hr	—	48.30

or so* per day for food; the convenience of warmth added a few thousand more Calories from easily obtainable wood. The first big jump in energy use came about four or five thousand years B.C. when man domesticated several animals and—at the cost of a little food, much of which—was able to triple the amount of energy at his service.

The waterwheel was introduced in the first century B.C. and again multiplied the amount of energy available to man. Its introduction was perhaps even more significant because it was an inanimate source of energy. For a long time the waterwheel was the most important source of energy for nascent industry. It was not until the twelfth century, more or less, that the analogy between flowing air and flowing water led to the use of windmills.

The beginning of the modern era of industry coincided with the development of the steam engine. Since that time the world's use of energy, which until then had been very nearly proportional to the number of people, began to grow in the industrial countries more rapidly than the population increased. This growth, shown in Figure 2-1 for the United States, continues.

The second historical trend, which, together with the increasing per capita use, has brought us to our present state, is the constant change in the energy mix. Wood was the dominant fuel in the 1850s but had lost all but 20 per cent of the market to coal by 1900. Coal in turn lost out after 75 years to petroleum products, which now account for 75 per cent of the energy, but they in turn will be (and *must* be as we shall see) replaced by other sources.

*We will consistently deal with Calories (kilocalories), the amount of heat energy needed to raise the temperature of 1 kilogram of water 1 degree Celsius.

Energy as a Commodity

In the early stages of man's history, energy was food, something to be found and consumed. But as life became more complex, and early barter systems were followed by a money-based economy, energy had to be bought. At first it was purchased indirectly as food or fuel. With the introduction of electricity, energy could be run directly into the house or the factory.

Energy is a commodity; it can be measured, bought, and sold. But its price depends on the form in which it is purchased—as food or fuel or electricity. Table 2-1 is an "energy shopping list." It is clear that we pay for the good taste of energy in the form of steak.

Where It Goes

The energy crisis is not a crisis caused by the "using up" or the disappearance of energy.

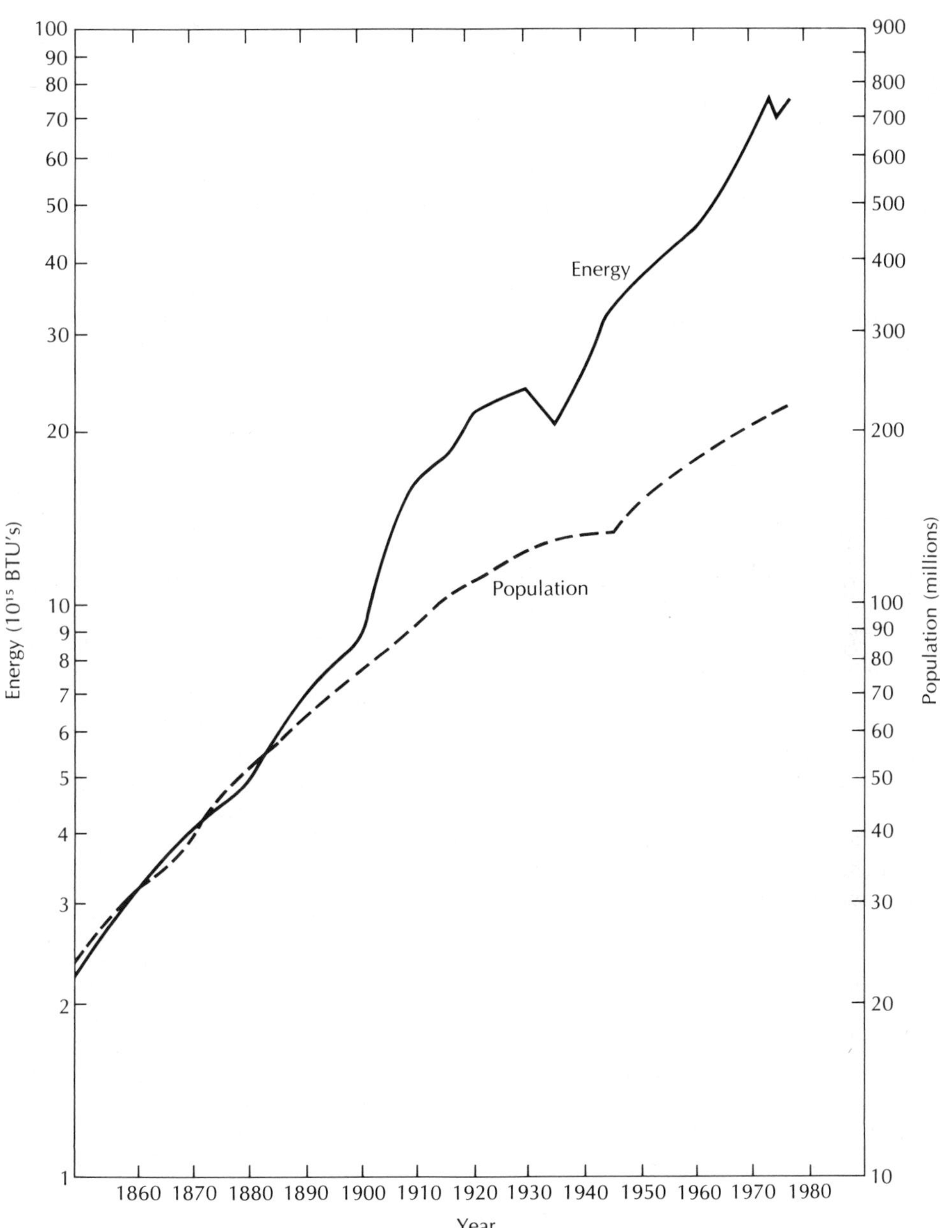

Figure 2-1. Comparison of energy and population growth, United States, 1850 to 1977.

The first law of thermodynamics assures us of that. Energy is conserved, at least in the closed system of the Universe. The crisis must then be found in the pathways of energy conversion.

We use energy, in its kinetic form, as mechanical energy, heat, or radiant energy. The form in which it is stored is potential energy. We know from physics that the potential energy of a system is increased by ΔE when we operate against a force over a distance ΔX, i.e.,

$$\Delta E = \vec{F} \cdot \vec{\Delta X}$$

In the infinite variety of the Universe we have, so far, discovered only three types of forces: gravitational, electrical, and nuclear (there seem to be two nuclear forces corresponding to the weak and the strong nuclear interaction). It follows, therefore, that there are three primary sources of energy: gravitational, electrical (chemical), and nuclear. In the phenomena of the Universe, these are the most important, and the weak one, the gravitational force, and the strong one, the nuclear force, give us the most visible effects.

At Earth's scale we choose other primary sources of energy. Solar energy, produced by the thermonuclear processes in the Sun, is the most important of these. It gives us the kinetic energy of water power and wind power, warms us, is stored as chemical energy in growing things, and is preserved in the fossil fuels.

We store the gravitational energy of lifted water in reservoirs. We also make use of some of the mechanical energy stored in the Earth–Moon system. Through the intermediary of gravitational force, this energy causes the oceans' tides.

We show these and the other important primary sources of energy in Figure 2-2. The chemical energy of fossil fuels is at present far and away the most important of these, but in addition to tidal energy there are two other nonsolar sources, geothermal energy from the earth's heated interior (originally heated by gravitational contraction and kept warm by radioactivity) and the new entrant, nuclear energy.

Excepting solar energy, the other sources are of little use to us in their primary form; they must be converted to the intermediate forms and often converted again to the end uses, which are also shown schematically in Figure 2-2.

The major source of energy in this country is the chemical energy of the fossil fuels. From them we get 93 per cent of the energy we use. They are fuels; their chemical energy is released by burning. Thus, the major energy conversion pathway is from primary chemical energy to intermediate thermal energy. In fact, most of the conversion pathways go through the thermal intermediate form.

We will look later in detail at the distribution of energy among the end uses of energy. We know in advance, however, that the major end uses are thermal (space heating, for example) and mechanical. Mechanical energy is also a major intermediate form and is converted to that most important intermediate form, electrical energy. The convenience of electrical energy shows up in its ready conversion to all the important end uses.

Conversion Efficiency

The most important conversion pathway is thus chemical→thermal→mechanical; and here we enter into the domain of the second law of thermodynamics. It is this "thermal bottleneck" through which most of our energy flows that contributes mightily to the various facets of the energy crisis. We burn to convert, and this causes pollution. We are doomed to low efficiencies by the second law and waste much of this heat energy. Let us consider the efficiency problem first.

Efficiency, the ratio of output work to input energy, varies greatly from conversion to conversion. Generally speaking, we can convert back and forth from electrical energy to other forms of energy with high efficiency, but when we convert other forms of energy to

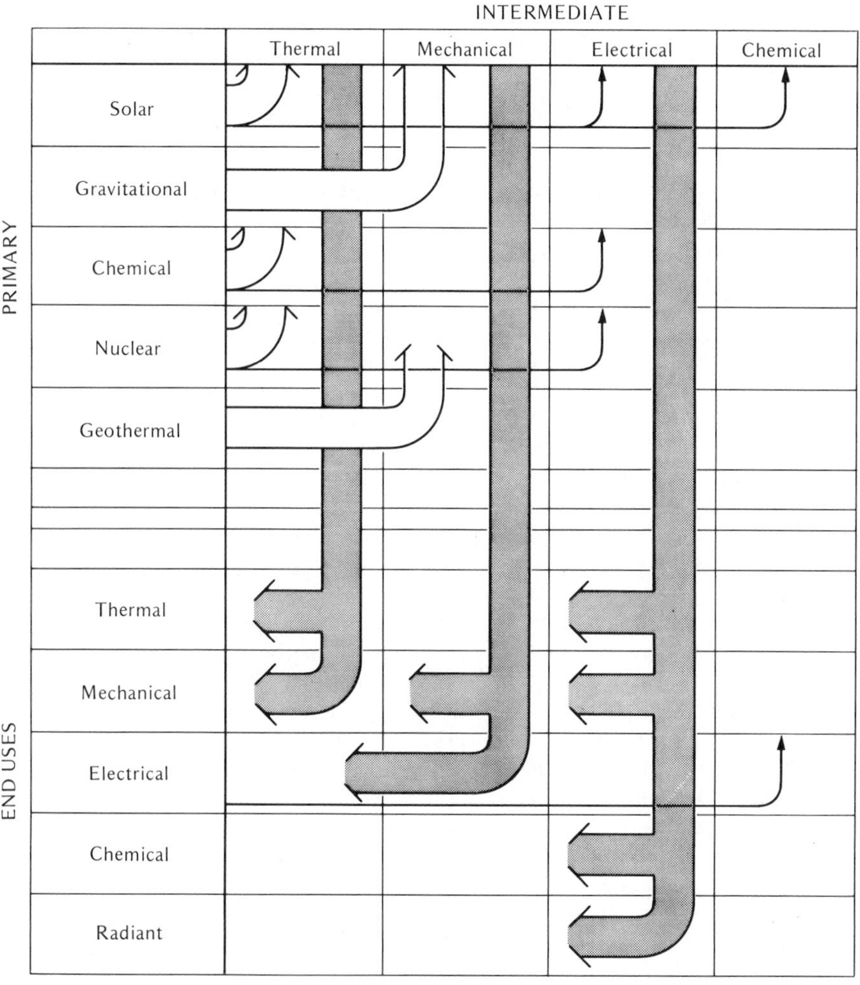

Figure 2-2. Paths of energy conversions. The shorter lines (↲) indicate relatively unimportant conversions.

heat and then try to convert heat to mechanical energy we enter the one-way street of the second law.

The efficiency of a "heat engine" (a device for converting heat energy to mechanical energy) is governed by the equation:

$$\text{Eff.} = \left(1 - \frac{T_{out}}{T_{in}}\right) 100$$

where T_{in} and T_{out} are the temperatures of intake and exhaust (in absolute degrees). This equation sets an upper limit of efficiency (it is for a "perfect" Carnot cycle). Since we are forbidden T_{out} = O K or $T_{in} = \infty$, we are doomed to an intermediate range of modest efficiencies. For example, most modern power plants use steam at 1,000 °F (811 K) and exhaust at about 212 °F (373 K), with a resulting upper limit of efficiency of 54 per cent. The actual efficiency is closer to 40 per cent. Nuclear reactors presently operate at a T_{in} of about 600 °F (623 K) and T_{out} of 212 °F

(373 K) for an upper limit efficiency limit of 40 per cent. They actually operate at about 30 per cent. In an automobile the input temperature of 5,400 °F (3,255 K) and output of 2,100 °F (1,433 K) would allow an efficiency of 56 per cent. The actual efficiency of an automobile engine is about 25 per cent.

So far we have talked about the efficiency of the major conversion process, heat to mechanical work. What is more important to an understanding of the entire energy picture, however, is the system efficiency; for example, the over-all efficiency with which we use the energy stored in the underground petroleum deposit to move us down a road in an automobile. Table 2-2 shows the system efficiency for transportation by automobile and the use of electric power for illumination. One can see that over all there are large leaks in the system and that most of the energy is lost along the way.

"Lost" does not, of course, describe precisely what happens to energy. We know what happens; it is converted to heat. The inexorable second law describes the one-way street of entropy. All energy conversion processes are irreversible; even in the highly efficient electrical generator some of the mechanical work goes into unwanted heat. The conversion of other forms of energy to heat is a highly efficient process—ultimately 100 per cent. It is a downhill run. But the reverse is all uphill; heat energy can never be completely converted to mechanical work. The potential energy available to us, whether it be chemical, nuclear, or gravitational is slowly being converted to the random motion of molecules. We cannot reverse this process, we can only slow it down. This fact has resulted in the increasing use of another measure of efficiency—the so-called second law efficiency, which is, instead of the ratio of desired output to input energy, the smallest amount of work or energy that could have been used to achieve the desired output, divided by the input energy.

This second law efficiency shows us where improvements can be made. For example, we use an oil furnace, producing air at 600 °F, to heat a room to about 70 °F. The first law efficiency of such a furnace may be 75 per cent. The same result could be accomplished with much less expenditure of energy by using a heat pump. The second law efficiency of the oil furnace is about 7 per cent.

Table 2-2. Energy System Efficiency.

Step	*Efficiency of Step (per cent)*	*Cummulative Efficiency (per cent)*
Automobile		
Production of crude oil	96	96
Refining of gasoline	87	84
Transportation of gasoline	97	81
Thermal to mechanical-engine	25–30	20–24
Mechanical efficiency-transmission (includes auxiliary systems)	50–60	10–15
Rolling efficiency	60	6–9
Electric Lighting (from coal-fired generation)		
Production of coal	96	96
Transportation of coal	97	93
Generation of electricity	33	31
Transmission of electricity	85	26
Lighting, incandescent (flourescent)	5 (20)	1.3 (5.2)

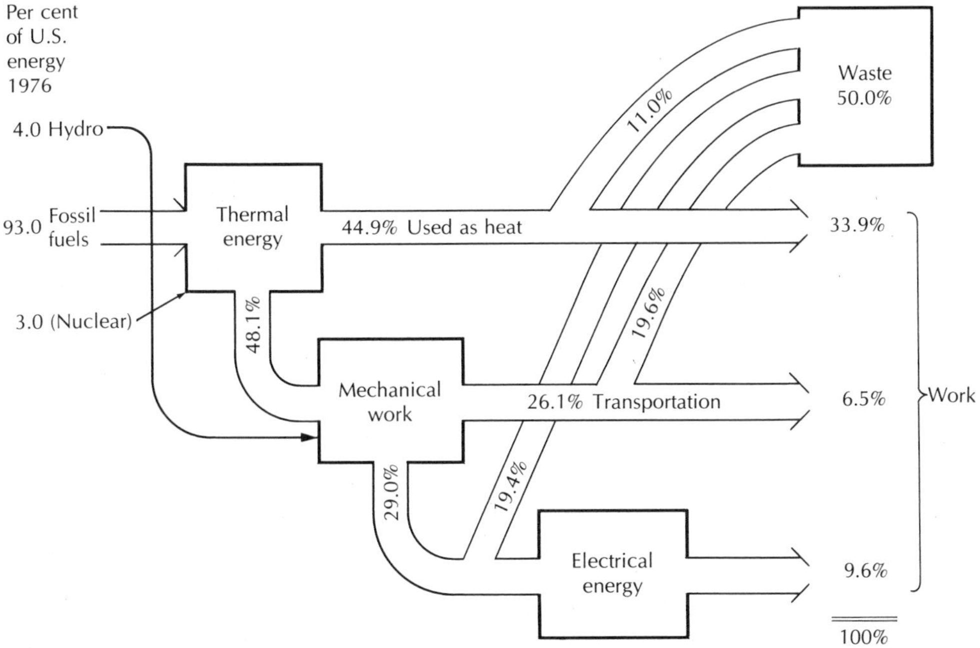

Figure 2-3. The flow of energy in the United States.

Patterns of Consumption

Ever since former President Johnson turned off the lights in the White House there has been a small (too small) but growing effort to save energy. It seems reasonable that this country and perhaps all countries will, at least for a while, have to make a real effort in this direction. The 1974 and 1975 data for the United States did show a drop in consumption to totals of 18.4 and 17.8 quadrillion Calories from the 18.8 quadrillion Calories consumed in 1973. But in 1976, consumption grew to 18.7 quadrillion Calories.

A gross flow chart of energy in our economy is shown in Figure 2-3. One sees the thermal bottleneck. Heat is the desired end product from about one-half of our energy. We do use that amount of energy efficiently. Of the one-half that goes to provide mechanical work, however, large amounts are lost in the production of electrical energy and energy for transportation. The net result is that over all our system is about 50 per cent efficient.

ENVIRONMENTAL EFFECTS OF ENERGY USE

Patterns of Consumption

The intimate connections between energy, our way of life, and the natural environment are seen in many places. The most important places are, of course, in the production of energy—in the mines and wells, refineries and generating plants—and at the place of consumption. Figure 2-3 gave a crude picture of consumption; we need to look at it in more detail.

Figure 2-4 gives both a crude breakdown and the details of the 60,526 trillion BTU of energy in each category. One sees that industry and transportation use the lion's share. The importance of space and water heating also is clear.

These data are for 1968, the only year for which we have a complete study. The lastest data for the large categories show the residential and commercial sectors combining to ac-

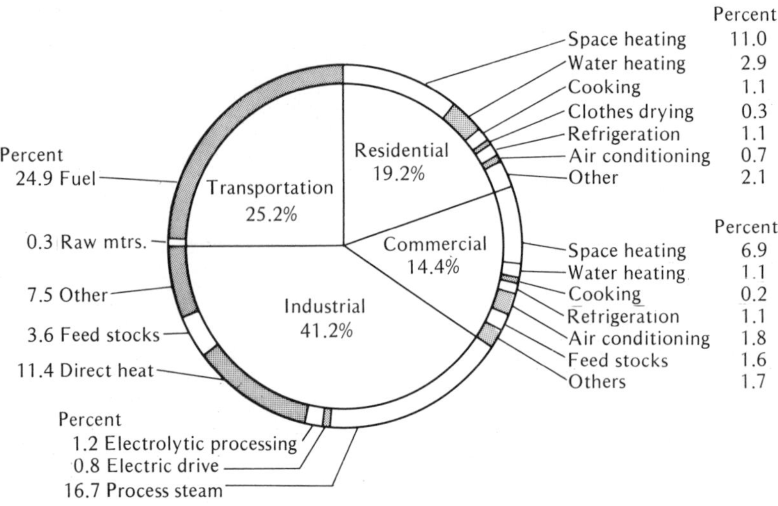

Figure 2-4. United States energy consumption, 1971 (total 60.5 x 10^{15} BTU).

count for 37.0 per cent, the industrial sector 36.6 per cent, and the transportation sector 26.1 per cent.

Electrical Energy—The People's Choice

What isn't clear in this presentation is the special case of electrical energy. It is there, contributing heavily to all categories except transportation, and it shares with transportation most of the blame for energy's role in environmental degradation.

The growth rate of electrical energy consumption, shown in Figure 2-5, has been the highest of all the various forms of energy. In discussing growth, a most useful concept is "doubling time." The energy curve of Figure 2-1 shows several different periods of growth and, therefore, several different doubling times. In the late 1800's the doubling time was about 30 years; by the early 1900's this had been cut in half, to about 16 years. The doubling time during the growth period from 1950 to 1960 was 25 years, and for the period 1960 to 1970 it dropped to 18 years.

Electrical energy can be said to have arrived commercially with the start-up of the Pearl Street Station by Thomas Edison in 1882. (The energy curve in Figure 2-1 breaks away from the "people" curve by about 1890.) The doubling time for per capita electrical energy consumption of Figure 2-5 was only 7½ years during the start-up period of 1910 to 1920, and about 14 years in the 1950's. It decreased to 10 years in the last decade. Electrical energy also shared in the decline of 1974 and 1975. It dropped by 0.9 per cent in 1974 and increased by only 0.6 per cent in 1975. In 1976, however, growth resumed by 5.6 per cent—still less than the 1973 growth rate of 6.7 per cent.

The reasons for the rapid increase in demand for electrical energy are several. Electricity is in many ways the most convenient of the forms of energy. It can be transported by wire to the point of consumption and then turned into mechanical work, heat, radiant energy, and so on.

It cannot be very effectively stored, and this has also contributed to its increasing use. Generating facilities have to be designed for peak use. In the late 1950's and early 1960's this peak came in the winter, when nights were longer and more lighting and heating

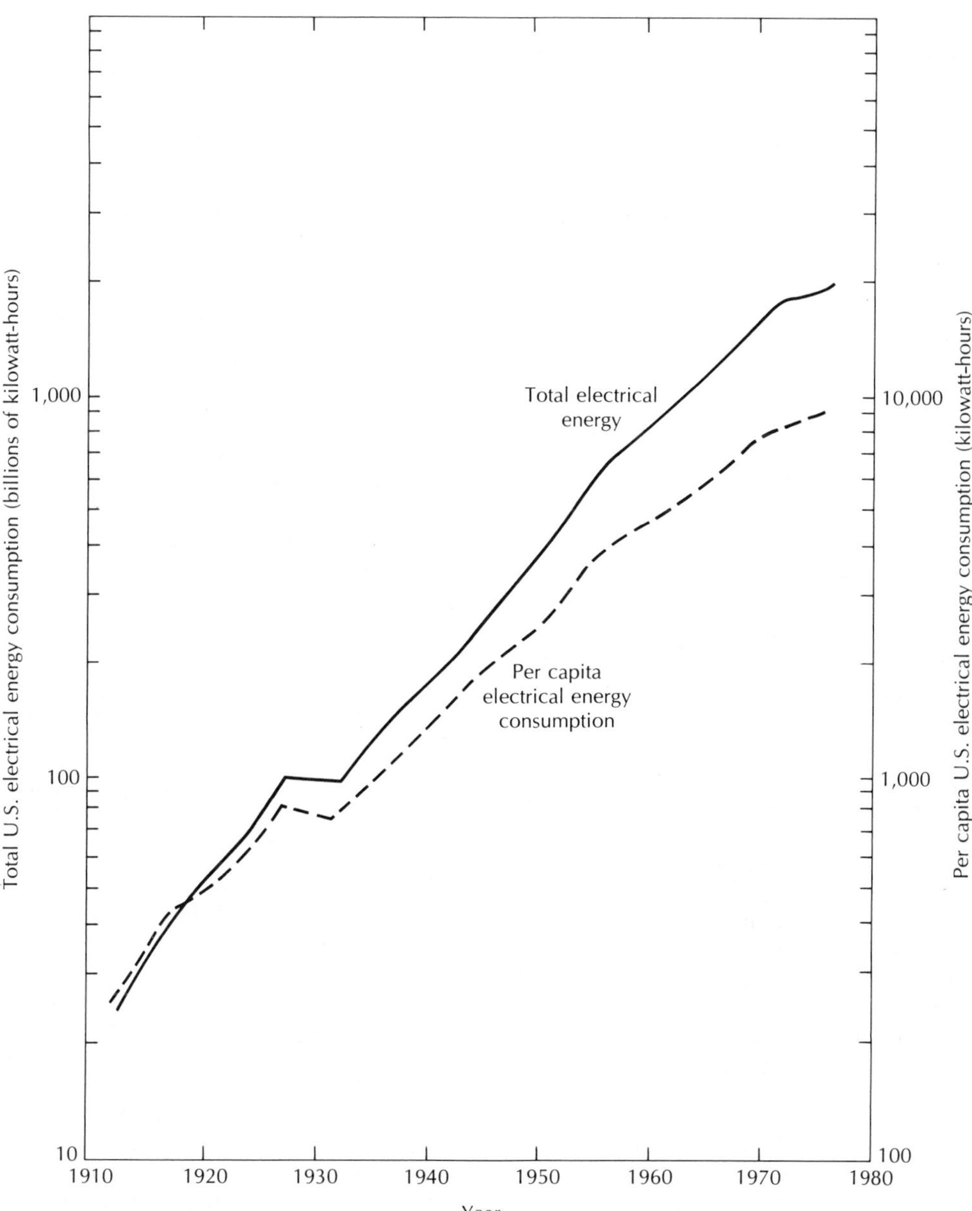

Figure 2-5. Growth rate of electrical energy consumption in the United States since 1910.

Table 2–3. Estimated Emissions of Air Pollutants by Weight Nationwide, 1974; Total 198.4 Million Tons.[a,b]

Source	*Carbon Monoxide*	*Particulates*	*Sulfur Oxides*	*Hydrocarbons*	*Nitrogen Oxides*	*Total*
Automobile	74.4(78.6)	1.5(7.8)	0.9(2.9)	12.5(41.1)	10.4(46.3)	99.7
Power plants	12.2(12.9)	5.6(28.8)	23.9(76.1)	1.9(6.1)	11.3(50.0)	54.9
Industrial	7.3(7.7)	10.9(55.9)	5.8(18.5)	3.0(10.1)	0.3(1.3)	27.3
Miscellaneous	0.7(0.8)	1.5(7.5)	0.8(2.5)	13.0(42.7)	0.5(2.4)	16.5
Total	94.6	19.5	31.4	30.4	22.5	198.4

[a]Source: *Environmental Quality*, Sixth Annual Report of the Council on Environmental Quality (Washington, D.C.), 1975.
[b]Numbers in parentheses are percentages.

were needed. It was economically sound to heavily promote off-peak use, such as summer use of air conditioners. This promotion was so effective that the summer is now the time of peak use, and the sales effort seems to be going into selling all-electric heating for off-peak winter use.

The rate structure, the so-called declining block in which each additional block of electrical energy used during a specified period is less expensive, has also contributed to demand growth.

Promotion, of course, made sense when each new generating plant was more efficient that the last one and the cost of electrical energy continued to drop. After 30 years or so of declining prices, the cost of a kilowatt-hour of electricity began to rise in 1971 and has increased each year since then. Even though the rising cost is expected to continue into the future, the electrification of the country is being accelerated and most of the new energy sources, which are discussed later, are associated with generation of electricity.

Environmental Effects: Air Pollution

Almost all airborne pollution—the increasingly familar smogs—is due to energy consumption of one form or another. We show, in Table 2-3, a breakdown of the various categories of polluters. One sees that the generation of electric power is the major source of sulfur oxides, whereas the automobile leads for three other pollutants.

It is of course not possible to determine the importance of these pollutants from their gross weight because they have very different effects. Some, like carbon monoxide, affect health in even minute concentrations, others, like the particulates, largely add to cleaning bills. This article is not the place for a detailed discussion of the effects of air pollution.* We will simply summarize the costs, which come from its effects on health and damage to crops and exposed materials and property values, by quoting the Second Annual Report of the Council on Environmental Quality, August 1971.

> The annual toll of air pollution on health, vegetation and property values has been estimated by EPA at more than 16 billion dollars annually—over $80 for each person in the United States.

Our dependence on the automobile for transportation presents us with a complex mix of problems; in addition to polluting the air, the automobile uses one-quarter of our energy total in a very inefficient way, leads to the covering of more and more of our countryside with concrete, contributes to many aspects of the problems of our cities, and takes a high toll of human life. The discussion of these problems and suggestions for solutions are fascinating and important, but cannot be undertaken here.

The generation of electric power at present depends predominantly on the burning of the fossil fuels. Sulfur oxides come from the sulfur impurities in these fuels. The burning

*See, for instance, J. M. Fowler, *Energy and the Environment*, Ch. 7. McGraw-Hill, 1975.

of these fuels also converts large amounts of carbon to carbon dioxide. This familiar gas is not a pollutant in the ordinary sense, but its steady increase in the atmosphere is a cause for concern. Carbon dioxide is largely transparent to the incoming short-wave solar radiation, but reflects the longer-wave radiation by which the earth's heat is radiated outward, producing the so-called greenhouse effect. At present about six billion tons of carbon dioxide are being added to the earth's atmosphere per year, increasing its carbon dioxide content by 0.5 per cent/year. By the year 2000 the increase could be as much as 25 per cent. Our understanding of the atmosphere is not sufficient to predict the eventual changes in climate that might be produced by this increase and by a related increase in water vapor and dust, but small changes in the average temperature could have catastrophic effects.

Nuclear Reactors—Clean Power?

In 1976, we obtained about 10 per cent of our electrical energy from nuclear power plants. At the end of that year some 64 nuclear plants, with a capacity for generating 45,455 megawatts of electricity, were in operation. We are thus well into the nuclear age.

The lightwater reactors (LWR) now in use obtain energy by fission (splitting) of the rare isotope of the heavy metal uranium, ^{235}U. The by-products of this fission are stopped in the fuel rods, heating them, and this heat is transferred by some type of heat exchanger to a conventional steam-powered electric generator.

The fission products are radioactive, dangerously so. They have many different half-lives, but the whole mess averages a half-life of perhaps 100 to 150 years. The switch to nuclear energy for the generation of electricity will be accompanied by a growing problem of disposal for this radioactive waste. It has been estimated that the 16 tons of radioactive fission products from reactors accumulated in 1970 will have grown to 388 tons by 1980 and more than 5,000 tons by the year 2000.

Nuclear reactors are carefully designed to securely contain these products, which are collected and stored for safety. But the storage problem itself is a far from negligible one, with no generally agreed-upon solution in sight. Originally, it was proposed that the most dangerous wastes be dried and stored in salt mines in Kansas. There are now indications that above-ground storage will be approved.

So far the radioactivity associated with nuclear reactors seems to have been handled safely. Any exposure to the general population from this source is in the range of present exposure from past nuclear testing. It is in all likelihood causing damage, but so are all the other forms of power generation. What really must concern us when we consider substituting uranium fission for the burning of fuel is the possibility of accident.

When discussing accidents, we are not talking about a real nuclear explosion in which a "critical mass" of fissionable material accumulates and reacts. The low enrichment densities preclude that. But since the reactor core is a witches' caldron of radioactive waste products, any accident that opens that up and spreads it over the countryside will be catastrophic. The accident that designers fear is cooling system failure. If the cooling-water somehow did not reach the fuel rods, in only a matter of seconds they would begin to melt, leaving the reactor core an uncontrollable blob of melting metal, heated internally so that it would continue to melt. The resulting steam pressure explosions could then spray the radioactive products into the environment. It is this small but troublesome chance of accident that keeps reactors away from the cities where their products, electricity and heat, are needed.

What we have said so far is specific to the LWR using ^{235}U. It has long been planned by the nuclear power industry to eventually switch to plutonium (^{239}Pu) for part of the fuel. Plutonium-239 is a man-made radioactive element; it is "bred" from the more common ^{238}U, which makes up most of the fuel in the LWR. It is also the fuel that would be provided by the so-called breeder reactors. The use of ^{239}Pu as a fuel will add much energy to our nuclear fuel stockpile, but it will also add some considerable complications. Unlike the mixtures of ^{238}U and ^{235}U of the LWR, ^{239}Pu-containing fuel is practically the raw material for nuclear bombs. The steps to separate out the ^{239}Pu are not very difficult. Entering the "Plutonium Age" will thus be dangerous and the Carter Administration has, so far, postponed our entrance.

Heat as a Pollutant

As we have earlier stressed, energy conversion is largely a one-way street: All work eventually produces heat. The "heat engines," because of their inefficiency, however, are particularly troublesome. A steam power plant, which is only 30 per cent efficient, dumps two units of heat energy for every one it converts to electricity. As our appetite for electricity grows in its apparently unbounded way, so also does the problem of heat discharged to the environment.

We can see, if we look far enough ahead, some possible problems arising from our increased release of waste heat. There are two different types of projections that make this point.

The first of these concerns the cooling-water needs. If the growth shown in Figure 2-5 continues, we will need one-sixth of the total fresh-water run-off of this country to cool our generating plants by 1990 and one-third by the year 2000. Long before we reach that point we will have to make some hard decisions about stream and river use and plant siting or change to closed cooling systems if we are to preserve inland aquatic life.

The second projection is even more serious. If we express our consumption of electricity in terms of energy released per square foot of U.S. land area, we obtain, for 1970, 0.017 watt per square foot. At the doubling time of 10 years for electric power consumption, in 100 years we would have gone through 10 doubling periods, and the energy release would be 17 watts per square foot—almost the same as the 18 or 19 watts per square foot of incoming solar energy (averaged over 24 hours). Long before we reach such a level, something will have to be changed.

These two projections only serve to emphasize what should by now be obvious: Energy use, particularly electric power use, cannot be allowed to continue to grow as it has. There are other data that reinforce this conclusion. Electricity means power plants and transmission lines; doubling consumption means doubling these. There are now about 300,000 miles of high voltage transmission lines occupying 4 million acres of countryside in the United States. By 1990, this is projected to be 500,000 miles of lines occupying 7 million acres.

All this serves to make the point that exponential growth cannot continue. But we could have learned that from nature. Exponential growth is unnatural; it occurs only temporarily when there is an uncoupling from the constraints of supply and of control. For instance, it can be demonstrated by the growth of a bacterial population with plenty of food, but it will eventually be turned over either by exhaustion of the food supply or by control from environmental processes that resist the growth of the population. We have examined some of the areas of environmental damage that may bring us to resist continued growth of energy production and consumption. What about our energy sources; Are they likely to be the controlling factor?

RESOURCES AND NEW SOURCES

Before we ask for a statement of the lavish deposits nature has made to our energy account, we must abandon our parochial view and briefly look at energy consumption as the world problem it is.

Energy and the Gross National Product

It can and will be argued that man can live happily and productively at rather low levels

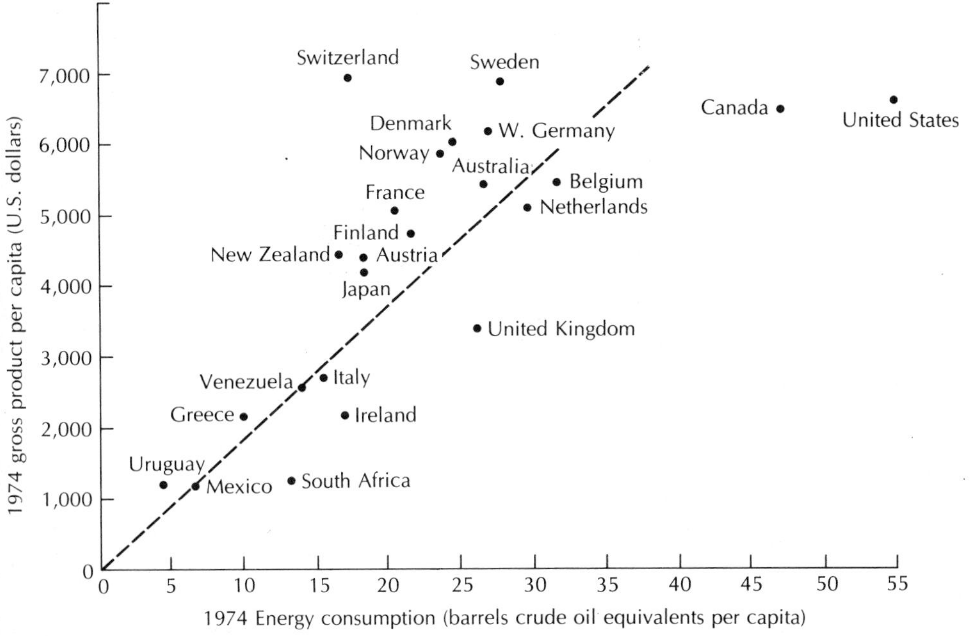

Figure 2-6. Per capita consumption of energy and gross national product for some countries of the world. (From Earl Cook, "The Flow of Energy in an Industrial Society," *Scientific American 224:* 142; September 1971.)

of energy consumption. The fact remains, however, that today per capita energy consumptions is an indicator of national wealth and influence—of the relative state of civilization as we have defined it. That this is so is seen most clearly by plotting that talisman of success, the (per capita) gross national product (GNP) against the (per capita) energy consumption shown in Figure 2-6. There appears a rough proportionality between per capita GNP and per capita energy consumption with the United States at the top, and countries like Uruguay and Mexico near the bottom. To the left of the "band of proportionality" lie the countries that manage a relatively large GNP with a relatively small energy expenditure.

Countries of this type are worthy of study and many of our present plans for industrial and other conservation strategies are suggested by practices in, for instance, West Germany and Sweden.

The United States, of course, consumes much more than its share of world energy. The United States, with 6 per cent of the world's population, uses 30 per cent of the world's energy. If we look at comparative rates of growth, we see that the U.S. per capita energy consumption is much larger (by a factor of about 30) than that of India, for instance, and is growing more rapidly. The world figure is about six times smaller but is growing a bit more rapidly than is the U.S. figure.

Even if the United States were to stabilize at the present per capita figure of 250 kilowatt-hours per day, it would take about 120 years for the world per capita average to equal it and hundreds of years for India, at its present rate of growth, to catch up. If we were to set the 1975 U.S. level of consumption as a world target for the year 2000, and if we take into account the population growth by then, the world would then be consuming 10 times as much energy as it does now. And this brings us to energy resources.

How Long Will They Last?

As someone said, "Prophecy is very difficult, especially when it deals with the future." Predicting the lifetime of energy resources is doubly difficult. Energy use curves must be projected and then unknown resource potentials guessed at. It is difficult to hope for much accuracy in either of these procedures.

The estimation of resources is based on a general knowledge of the kind of geological conditions associated with the resource and on a detailed knowledge of the distribution and extent of a resource within a favorable geological area. Coal is the easiest to work with, for it seems almost always to be found where it is predicted to be. Oil and natural gas, on the other hand, are erratic in distribution within favorable areas and are found only by exploration. In addition to coal, oil, and natural gas, there are two other sources of organic carbon compounds that are potential fuel sources, the so-called tar sands and oil shale. In the tar sands, which so far have been found in appreciable amounts only in Canada, a heavy petroleum compound (tar) binds the sands together. A Canadian refinery is currently producing oil products from this material. Oil shale is shale rock containing considerable amounts of a solid organic carbon compound (kerogen). Oil can be extracted by heating the rocks, but this process has not yet been demonstrated to be commercially feasible.

In Figure 2-7 we show the estimates of world fossil fuel resources of various types and the global distribution of these resources. The unit used to measure these resources is 10^{18} BTU. As a crude reference, it would take about 10^{18} BTU of energy to boil Lake Michigan. Perhaps more useful is the fact that U.S. total energy consumption in 1974 was about 0.07×10^{18}, whereas world consumption was 0.27×10^{18} BTU.

One sees from these data that most of the remaining fossil-fuel resources, for the United States and for the world, are in the form of coal.

Presenting data on resources does not by itself answer the question "How long will they last?" To answer that question one has to look at the rate at which the resources are being used. A simplified but very graphic way of displaying this has been adopted by M. King Hubbert of the U.S. Geological Survey. Since supplies of fossil fuels are finite, the curve tracing their production rate will be pulse-like, that is, it will rise exponentially in the beginning, turn over when the resources come into short supply, and then decay exponentially as the resources become harder and harder to find. Such data for U.S. oil and U.S. coal are presented in Figures 2-8 and 2-9.

The curve for U.S. oil is of particular interest. It shows that the actual rate of production from 1880 to the present does have roughly the predicted shape and that, in fact, we are already past the peak of production.

Although the estimate of total resources, 165 billion barrels, may be a bit pessimistic (current estimate range between 112–189 billion barrels), it is the shape of the curve that has the real lesson in it. We are on the down side of that curve and already feeling the pinch of impending shortages.

Figure 2-9 for coal is consistent with the data of Figure 2-8. We have a large amount of coal and are just started up the slope to the peak in production. The time scale is much larger, the time to produce 80 per cent of U.S. coal is on the order 300 to 400 years.

In combination, Figure 2-7, 2-8, and 2-9 give a representative view of the state of U.S. and world fossil-fuel resources. They give a qualified answer to, "How long will they last?" The answer: "Not very long," if we are talking about crude oil and natural gas; "long enough for us to find other sources," if we are talking about coal.

The answer might also have been: "Long enough for us to wreck our environment." Without much improvement in the protection we give our environment, about two more doubling periods of energy consumption may be sufficient. Each doubling not only reduces

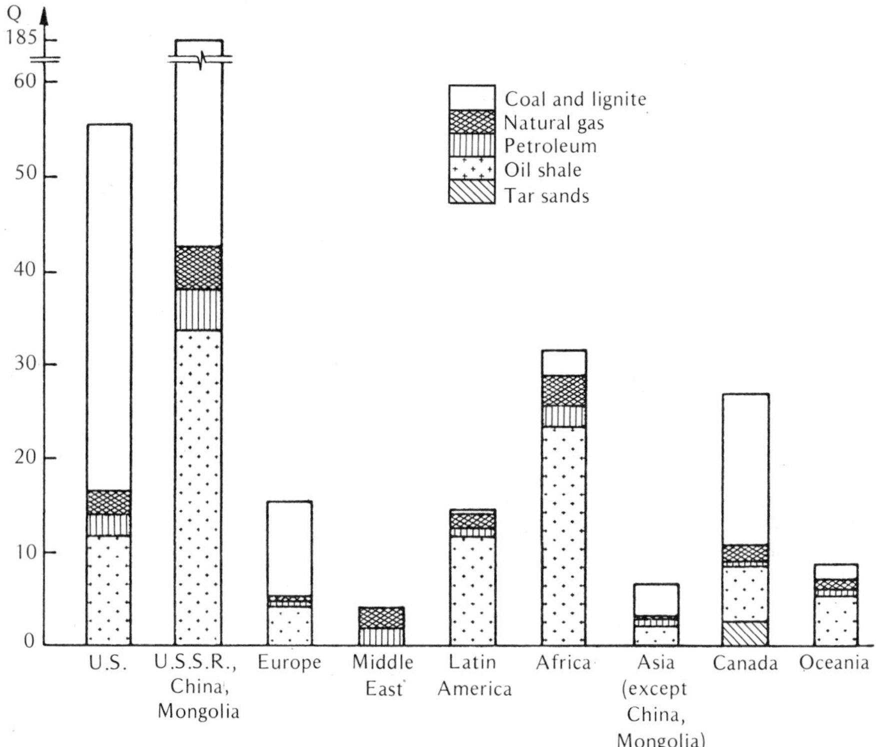

Figure 2-7. Remaining recoverable energy resources, by region. (From R. H. William and K. Fenton, "World Energy Resources: Distribution, Utilization, and Long-term Availability." Paper delivered at the Annual Meeting of the American Association for the Advancement of Science, Dec. 29, 1971)

the resources but, for instance, doubles the generating capacity (more plants), doubles (almost) the number of transmission lines, doubles coal-mining activity, doubles (unless rigid controls are implemented) the sulfur oxides and fly ash in the atmosphere, and so on.

Energy for the Future

Those of us who write about energy are no longer "prophets crying in the wilderness." The oil embargo and the cold winter of 1976–1977 have finally made believers of politicians and citizens alike. It is now clear that we are in one of those rare times of transition that mark human progress; that we are voyaging from familar shores toward an unknown future home. What kind of energy future can we expect?

One thing, at least, is certain. We must kick the fossil-fuel habit. If we are again to reach a time of energy abundance we must turn to other primary sources. In our hazy crystal ball we can only see three candidates, fission energy based largely on conversion of ^{238}U to ^{239}Pu, fusion reactions with hydrogen, and solar energy. In addition there are other smaller continuous energy sources—compared in Table 2-4—which can help.

Solar Energy

A look at Table 2-4 allows us to place the continuous energy sources in perspective. One, direct solar energy, is sufficient to prom-

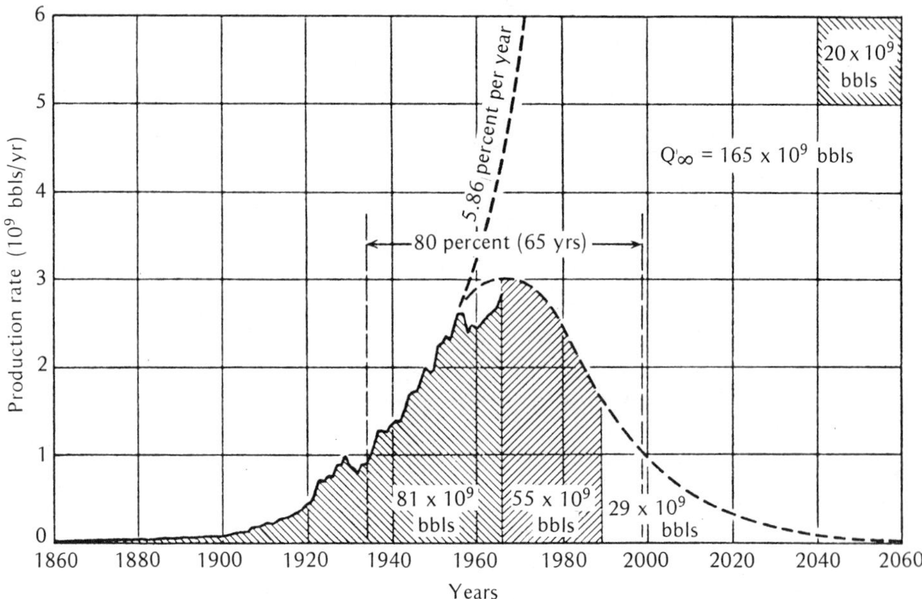

Figure 2-8. Use rate for U.S. oil resources. (From M. K. Hubbert, *Resources and Man,* W. H. Freeman, San Francisco, p. 183.)

Figure 2-9. Use rate for U.S. coal resources. (From M. K. Hubbert, *Resources and Man,* W. H. Freeman, San Francisco, p. 200.)

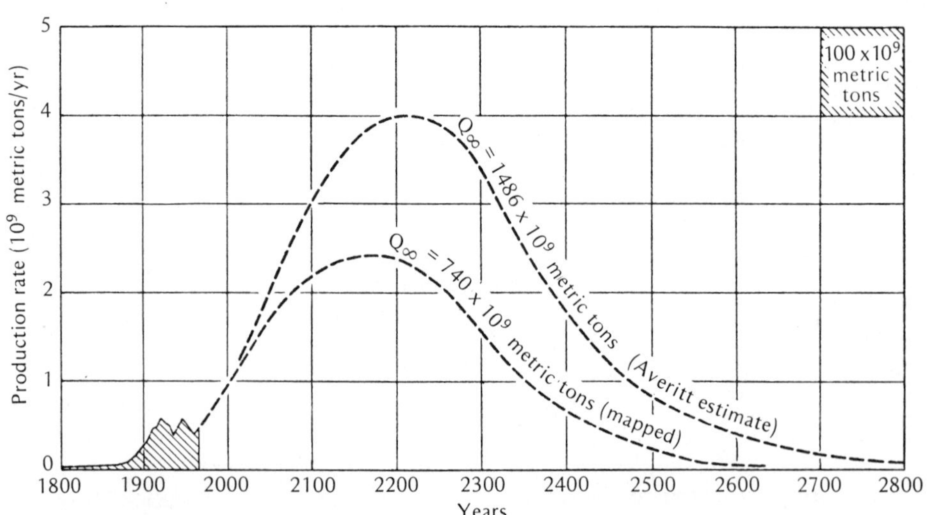

Table 2–4. Power per Acre on Continuous U.S. Land Mass.[a]

Source	*Kilowatts per acre*
Sunlight at top of clouds (day/night average)	1,420.
Sunlight absorbed at ground level (averaged)	810.
All the winds	2.8
All the tides	0.02
Natural geothermal energy (steam and hot water)	0.25
All photosynthesis	0.32
All water power	0.12
1973 U.S. Energy Consumption (average per acre)	1.1

[a]Source: Briefings before the Task Force on Energy of the Subcommittee on Science, Research, and Development, Committee on Science and Astronautics, U.S. House of Representatives, 92nd Congress, Serial Q, March 1972, p. 79.

ise future abundance. It is also clear that we must find a new method of conversion. The three existing "natural converters"—photosynthesis, water power and wind power—even at maximum utilization, would just barely meet our present needs.

Research into methods of utilizing solar energy has greatly increased during the past five years as the financial support has increased from a few thousand to 290 million dollars in Fiscal Year 1977.

This research is seeking answers in several directions. Bioconversion (use of photosynthesis) is being reexamined and even if we do not decide to deliberately grow energy crops we will probably turn to organic waste (paper, crop residues, wood waste, manure, etc.) for energy.

Solar heating and cooling should become immediately important. The technology for this more or less direct use already exists, and President Carter's Energy Message of April 1977 calls for the installation of solar space heating in 2½ million homes by 1985.

To convert solar energy to electricity will take considerably more research and development. Several methods are under investigation: photovoltaic devices (solar cells), large areas of solar collectors producing steam, mirrors focused on a boiler, and a solar sea plant, which works off of the thermal gradient between the surface layer and the deep layers of the ocean. The focusing mirrors are being given top priority, and a pilot 10-megawatt plant is under construction in New Mexico.

Nuclear Energy

The only other potentially large source of primary energy is nuclear energy. There are two possibilities here. We have pointed out earlier that the ^{235}U needed by the conventional LWR is in relatively short supply. If, however, the so-called breeder reactor were to be developed it could create a fissionable fuel, ^{239}Pu, out of the relatively abundant ^{238}U. If we were to go into this "plutonium economy" and build not only breeder reactors, but large fuel reprocessing plants to remove the ^{239}Pu from the reactor fuel, we could conceivably provide for our energy needs from known uranium supplies for 1,000 years or so.

We mentioned earlier some of the hazards of plutonium use that make this route the least attractive of the three routes to energy abundance that are open to us.

The third potential source of a large amount of energy also involves the nucleus. In fission, energy is released when a large nucleus is split in two. Energy is also released when two small nuclei are "fused" together. This is the fusion process we have been trying to master for 20 years or so.

The fuel for fusion is the heavy isotope of

hydrogen, deuterium (^2H). It is present in unimaginable abundance in the ocean; there is enough fusion fuel there to last for hundreds of thousands of years. We seem to be on the threshold of proving that the fusion process is scientifically feasible. The 1980's should see this breakthough. Beyond that, however, are the unknown problems of engineering and of demonstrating commerical feasibility.

Fusion may be a power source for the next century. It will offer the advantages of unlimited fuel and, compared to fission, much less radioactivity and essentially no explosion hazard. It is an attractive dream—but it may be only a dream.

Conclusion

Mankind is in the midst of an energy crisis. It has several dimensions. On a short time scale, we are faced with a serious shortage of natural gas and with the necessity of importing more and more oil.

On an intermediate time scale, 20 to 40 years, we are faced with the necessity of finding a substitute for the petroleum products that now dominate the energy mix.

Finally, on a larger scale of a few hundred years, we are faced with the exhaustion of fossil fuels.

What can we do? Some of the answers are obvious. We can plan more carefully and project further into the future. We can try to reduce energy expenditures and increase research and development. As concerned citizens we must demand this. We must also demand a role in the decision-making process and decide, for instance, whether we will rely most on the breeder reactor, with its dangers, or on coal and coal products (gases and liquids).

The science teachers of this country have a vital role to play in the next few years. These decisions must be based on information, and it is the science teacher who must make sure that developing citizens have access to the necessary information without bias and distortion. It is my hope that this summary, brief and sketchy as it is, can serve as a part of the foundation of that necessary effort.

SUGGESTED READINGS

Clark, Wilson, 1974, *Energy for Survival* (Doubleday, Garden City, New York), 652p.

Firebaugh, Morris W., 1977, Perspectives on Energy and the Environment, *The Physics Teacher* 15, pp. 78–85.

Fowler, John M., 1975, *Energy and the Environment* (McGraw-Hill Book Co., New York) 496p.

Fowler, John M., 1975, *Energy-Environment Source Book* (National Science Teachers Association, Washington, D.C.), 279 p.

Fowler, John M., 1976, Energy, Education, and the 'Wolf' Criers, *The Science Teacher* 43, pp. 25–32.

Library Journal, 1977, Energy *Library Journal* 102, 136 p. Reviews many energy books; lists organizations, agencies, companies, publishers, and other groups that provide energy-related information.

Romer, R. H., 1972, Energy-Resources, Production and Environmental Effects, *American Journal of Physics* 40, p. 805. A resource letter of the American Association of Physics Teachers.

———, 1971, *Scientific American* 224. The issue is devoted entirely to energy.

"The Energy Crisis," 1971, *Bulletin of the Atomic Scientists* 27. September and October issues on energy.

———, 1972, *The Science Teacher* 39. Five articles on energy.

Wilson, Richard, and Jones, William J., 1974, *Energy, Ecology, and the Environment* (Academic Press, Inc., New York), 353p.

Health Effects of Energy Production and Conversion 3

CYRIL L. COMAR AND LEONARD A. SAGAN 1976

INTRODUCTION

Historically, the development of technology has not been guided by particular concern for associated health effects. It is now becoming clear that future technological assessment will almost certainly require some prior attention to health impacts. This reflects the perception that the health effects of technology have not been internalized, i.e., they are either inadequately compensated for in the working population or are borne by segments of society not directly benefiting from the responsible industry. Black-lung disease of coal miners is an example of the former; disease produced or aggravated by industrial smogs is an example of the latter.

There are a number of compelling reasons for attempting some assessment of health effects related to energy, even though such estimates may, because of inadequate data, lack precision. The development of national energy policies and strategies, including difficult choices among fuel systems, must be guided not only by market economics but by careful consideration of health and environmental effects not necessarily reflected in pricing. Another reason for health-effects assessment is to permit rational and cost-effective safety and control procedures. Miscalculation of the risks involved can create severe dislocations, diseconomies, or hazards: for example, excessive expenditures on construction or equipment out of proportion to risk or, in the other extreme, inadequate expenditures to protect life and health. Finally, the assessment of health effects can provide guidance as to research needs and priorities.

It is important that the scientific community not only provide data and interpretations

Dr. Cyril L. Comar is professor emeritus of biology, Cornell University, Ithaca, New York, and Director of the Environmental Assessment Department of the Electric Power Research Institute, Palo Alto, California 94303. He was one of the early workers utilizing radioactive materials for biological research and has studied the biological implications of nuclear weapons fallout. He chaired the Advisory Committee on the Biological Effects of Ionizing Radiations (BEIR Report) of the National Academy of Sciences–National Research Council, Washington, D.C., 1972.

Dr. Leonard A. Sagan is associate director, Department of Environmental Medicine, Palo Alto Medical Clinic, Palo Alto, California, 94301. He has published extensively in the area of radiation and public health.

From *Annual Review of Energy,* Vol. I, pp. 581–600, 1976. Reprinted by permission of the authors and Annual Reviews, Inc., Palo Alto, California.

for policy-making bodies but also assure that the broad implications are understandable by the general public. There have been major shortcomings in the general understanding of the impacts of health effects. One of these has been the emphasis on individual energy systems treated in isolation rather than comparisons of the various systems available, each of which has its attendant risks. Knowledge of the health effects of a given type of power plant is by itself of little value. For example, if a given nuclear plant is not built, then for the near and mid-term future a coal plant must be built in its place, or a plant may not be built. (It is assumed that oil and natural gas will be in short supply and that other energy sources, such as geothermal, fusion, solar, wind, tide, etc. either have such limited application or are so uncertain that it would be highly imprudent to rely on them for the needs of the next 10–30 years. Each of these potential sources should, however, be researched as intensively as is feasible and brought into commercial production whenever possible.) It is beyond the scope of this article to consider the biological risks associated with inadequate supplies of electricity, but it is by no means certain that a coal plant or no plant at all would have less health impact that a nuclear plant.

A second shortcoming is that health effects have usually been expressed in absolute terms as numbers of either premature deaths or serious disabilities. Assessments presented in this way are most difficult to relate to the real significance they have for individuals. We propose that it would be much more helpful to convert this measure to the degree of enhanced risk to which individuals and the population are exposed. Still another technique for presentation of these risks is through conversion to a dollar cost. This concept, although particularly useful in evaluating safety expenditures, will not be developed further here. Nor will we consider abatement and control procedures or their cost-effectiveness.

The data are limited primarily to the production of electricity because of the increasing importance of this energy form in our society and because various fuel options are available. Following discussions of some basic principles in consideration of health effects, the available health-effects data are presented for fuel extraction, transport, processing, and electricity generation from the major fuel systems, with the emphasis on the major uncertainties and controversies.

HEALTH EFFECTS: THEIR NATURE AND MEASUREMENT

General

The National Academy of Sciences has recently published a report[1] that contains numerous references to support the general statements of this section; it is a perceptive treatment of what man needs to know to deal effectively with chemicals in the environment. References 2 to 6 are comprehensive reports that cover health effects of air pollution, with the emphasis on the role of fossil-fuel combustion products. The basic documentation[7–11] on the biological effects of radiation, and references 12 and 13 dealing with concepts of benefit and risk are also important.

The health consequences of technology cover a wide spectrum ranging from mere nuisance to violent death. They may be transient or permanent. They may be localized or world wide as from nuclear fallout. The noxious agents may be chemical, physical, or biological; they may be synthetic, and therefore their presence identified easily, or they may be naturally occurring and appear only as an increased concentration of a naturally occurring element, e.g., mercury, lead, arsenic. The pollutant source may be obvious, as in the case of a noisy airport, or it may be obscure, as in the case of commingled combustion products in city air. The resultant health effects may be obviously related to the cause, as with asbestos-induced lung cancer; or the relationship may be obscure, as with the London smog of 1952, which was unrecognized until identified retrospectively by a careful epidemiological analysis of mortality statistics. Acute effects (those following soon after a relatively severe exposure) are generally more easily related to their causative factors than are chronic effects. Chronic exposure to routine releases of pollutants generally has effects that are far more difficult to recognize; it often increases the frequency of a disease that occurs "naturally" in the exposed population.

There can be considerable individual variation in response to pollutants. For example, groups that appear to be more sensitive to air pollution include young children, possibly because of higher inspiratory rates, more mouth breathing, and frequent respiratory tract infection; aged persons, possibly because of decreased cardiopulmonary adaptive capacity; asthmatics; persons with preexisting chronic bronchitis and emphysema; certain occupational workers; and smokers. Generally, the fetus and the infant are more susceptible to toxic exposures than are adults. Effects from fetal exposure may also appear as congenital malformations, as from thalidomide or the virus of rubella; these agents are known as teratogens.

Probably no health effect of pollutant exposure is of greater public concern than cancer. That cancer can follow environmental exposure to chemical carcinogens has been known with some certainty ever since the eighteenth century when Sir Percival Potts recognized scrotal cancer in the chimney sweeps of London, which was undoubtedly induced by the hydrocarbons in soot. Although it is not known to what extent cancers of all organ systems are the result of exposure to chemical carcinogens, experts ascribe the majority to this source. Probably the best recognized relationship observed on a large scale in the general public is between lung cancer and cigarette smoking, but a number of agents are known or suspected to be carcinogens. One of the difficulties hindering investigators is the long latent period between exposure and the development of the cancer, which may appear decades later when occupation or exposure may have changed. Furthermore, better understanding is complicated by the possibility of synergistic or additive effects among various agents that individually may be weak carcinogens, which are difficult to identify. Although cancer is generally a "somatic" effect, i.e., occurring in the person exposed, it may be mediated by a genetic mechanism operating on the informational macromolecules at the cellular level. The implications, which are discussed later, are that since only one or a few target molecules may need to be modified to produce cancer there is some chance of harm at any exposure level above zero, although repair mechanisms may operate at low dose rates.

The classes of carcinogenic agents identified as present in products of fossil-fuel combustion and nuclear effluents are: (a) polycyclic and other aromatic hydrocarbons, (b) trace metals, and (c) radionuclides. They are often found associated with particulate matter. It must be noted that all these agents are present in routine effluents in amounts that are too small to produce detectable effects, so that there is considerable uncertainty as to their actual impact on man. Lung cancer has been studied by epidemiologists more than any other cancer that might be associated with air pollution. The evidence available does not support—nor does it deny—the conclusion that air pollution per se is a causative factor.[6]

Genetic effects, i.e., those occurring in the progeny of the exposed persons, are caused by a class of agents called mutagens. Although mutations confer on species the ability to evolve and react to new environmental conditions, most often the evolved characteristics are detrimental to the individual. Mutational changes may vary in severity from lethal effects to subtle effects not associated with mortality. Uncertainty as to how genetic effects of environmental agents will express themselves makes their recognition and quantification difficult if not impossible. In fact, no genetic effects from any agent have yet been found in human populations that can be traced with any certainty to parental exposures. Because of the great amount of research done on the genetic effects of ionizing radiation it is possible to predict the types and numbers of effects that would be produced in human populations from low levels (about natural background), even though none have been detected.

Exposure–Response Relationships

Attention is directed toward a dilemma that arises from dissemination of pollutants where there are large populations exposed to detectable levels of a contaminant known to be harmful at some high level. The outstanding example is ionizing radiation produced from nuclear weapons testing. As a result of weapons testing, it has been demonstrated that practically every living organism on the earth contains detectable amounts of man-produced radioactivity, which is definitely known to be harmful at high levels. The potential for harm has caused great amounts of money and manpower to be spent for research since the middle 1940's, and it is fair to say that we know much more about ionizing radiation and its effects than about any other agent, chemical, or drug to which man is exposed. The problem became known because of the extremely sensitive means of detection. Since that time, sensitive methods have been developed to detect chemical pollutants in the biosphere that could be potentially harmful. As a result, we are faced with concerns and public reaction to such contaminants as mercury in fish, vinyl chloride from plastics in water supplies, asbestos fibers, and chlorinated hydrocarbons in purified water, pesticides in food, and sulfur compounds, nitrogen oxides, polycyclic organic materials, and trace elements from fossil-fuel combustion. This public sensitivity understandably brings about great pressure to reduce the possible damage to zero or near-zero. To present the problem of both protecting the public welfare and persuading the public to realize that it must accept certain risks, we give a gross classification of the relationships between the level of a harmful agent and its effects (below). The solid lines represent levels of exposure ranging from high to zero; on the right are the effects caused by the corresponding level.

Level of Exposure		*Effect*
High		Death
	Range A	Clinical symptoms
	Range B	Undetectable effects at high probability
	Range C	Undetectable effects at low probability
Zero		No effects

For any pollutant, there will be some high level that will cause a large number of deaths in the population exposed. Below that will be a range of levels (Range A) in which only clinical signs in the population are observed and the percentage of deaths, if any, is much lower. These clinical symptoms, as in the case of radiation effects or a pollutant-produced persistent cough, may not themselves be long-term contributors to ill health but may denote an associated high probability of serious late effects. At still lower levels (Range B), the effects may be undetectable either directly or statistically, but they will occur at high enough probabilities that society usually decides not to tolerate them. These can be effects that are undetectable at high or low frequency because they are minor in character, or they can be serious health effects that are undetectable because they are of low frequency and occur either immediately or (with radiation, for example) at some later time or in a later generation; in this article we deal with the latter. Ionizing radiation is an agent about which enough is known so that levels in this range can be specified. At the present guidelines for radiation protection, no effects can be clinically or epidemiologically observed in exposed populations, although on the basis of radiobiological theory it is postulated that effects do or could occur. Referring again to any pollutant, at even lower levels (Range C), we find that the probabilities of effects may be so low that society is justified in accepting them if they are more than compensated by the associated benefits of the process that produces the harmful agent.

To further understand the need for risk acceptance, we must distinguish within Range C between two types of agents: the "threshold" and the "nonthreshold." For so-called threshold agents, there is some level of pollutant below which no effects occur. For nonthreshold agents, there are effects at any level of pollutant above zero. In terms of regulatory procedures, standards can be set for threshold agents that guarantee absolute safety. For nonthreshold agents, however, some level of risk must be accepted unless the agent can be completely eliminated. To protect the public and at the same time to provide the benefit of the process that produces this agent, it is desirable to establish regulations so that the population exposure falls somewhere within Range C. To do this it is usually necessary to ascertain the slope and nature of the exposure/effects relationship in the regions of interest so that public acceptance of certain levels of risk commensurate with associated benefits can be recommended.

Risks of Death

As already mentioned, health effects range from the trivial to those causing severe disability and premature death. Here we focus on the latter, mainly because they are the most important and we have no meaningful way of evaluating many of the less serious effects. It should also be noted that even premature deaths are not equivalent in their impact on individuals and society. The ethical ideal that every being has a right to be born without man-induced effects and to die from old age (the natural wearing out of the body) is fully recognized. It is obvious, however, that all early deaths do not have the same societal and personal impact. For example, the death of an early embryo before anyone even knows about it or the death of an elderly person a few months before he or she would otherwise die of old age would penalize neither the individual, the persons left behind, nor society, as would the death of a young adult, with family responsibilities, on the brink of a productive career. In addition, genetic effects can produce over a lifetime a variety of suffering and health effects, which, although they do not necessarily cause premature deaths, do constitute a social cost. At present, it is not possible in the formulation of risk values to estimate the number of person-years lost because of exposure to the agent and to weigh them so that societal and personal impacts are taken into account. In this discussion the numbers are rounded and the concepts are presented in a simple form that we hope will lead to correct interpretation as well as facilitate understanding. We are attempting primarily to assess the health consequences associated with energy in terms of effects on individuals in the general population.

In the United States, with a population of about 200 million, about 2 million people die each year from all causes, such as old age, sickness, accidents, homicide, and suicide. This means that for the population at large in the United States there is a probability of dying in a given year of 0.01 $[=(2 \times 10^6)/(200 \times 10^6)]$, or expressed another way, a risk of death in any year of 1 in 100. This risk is age-dependent, as can be seen in Table 3-1. It is usually considered that an additional man-produced risk of death per year, consciously accepted, is high if it falls in the range of 1 in 100 or less to 1 in 10,000 and low if it falls in the range of 1 in 10,000 to 1 in 1,000,000 or more.

Table 3–1. Normal Risk of Death per Year in the United States as Related to Age (1969 Data) and Comparison of High and Low Additional Risks.

Age	*Normal Risk of Death per Year (14)*
5	1 in 1,587
10	1 in 3,846
25	1 in 690
35	1 in 465
45	1 in 205
55	1 in 88
65	1 in 39
All ages	1 in 100
	Added Risk of Death per Year
High risk	1 in 100 or less to 1 in 10,000
Low risk	1 in 10,000 to 1 in 1,000,000 or more

Table 3–2. Effects of Accepting Additional Risks.

	Ten-year-old	*Fifty-year-old*
Risk of death/year	1 in 3,800	1 in 100[a]
Normal risk/year plus additional risk/year of 1 in 10,000	1.38 in 3,800	1.01 in 100
Normal risk/year plus additional risk/year of 1 in 1,000,000	1.0038 in 3,800	1.0001 in 100

[a]This corresponds to the risk faced by the U. S. population at large: 2×10^6 deaths per year/200×10^6 persons.

To convey more easily the implications of accepting additional risks, we propose that data be calculated in terms of what the enhanced risk per year from a given activity will be (Table 3-2). The 10-year-old who accepts an additional risk of 1 in 10,000 will change his over-all risk from 1 in 3,800 to 1.38 in 3,800, a considerable proportional increase (38 per cent). An older person (about 50 years of age) who accepts the same additional risk will change his over-all risk, for example, from 1 in 100 to 1.01 in 100, a change of much less significance (1 per cent). As indicated in Table 3-2, the acceptance of an additional risk of 1 in 1,000,000 produces changes of little significance regardless of age. These additional risk values can also be used to estimate the total number of individuals in an exposed population who may be affected. For example, an industrial process that imposes an additional risk per year of 1 in 10,000 on the population of the United States could cause 20,000 casualties per year [$(200 \times 10^6)/10{,}000$].

The following comparisons may be cited not to justify any additional risks, but to relate these probabilities to everyday risks. A person riding in a car in the United States has an additional probability of death per year* of about 1 in 100; this is a risk we accept, but for the 10-year-old, as an example, this represents about a forty-fold increase of normal risk. The risk of death from being struck by lightning or from being bitten by a snake is about 1 in 1,000,000 per year.

*The physical meaning of this risk estimate is confusing because of the time units; the absolute risk would be 1 in 100 if a person spent full time during the year riding in a car. The risk of death per hour while riding is 1 in 876,000, which is the same as the normal risk of death per hour of the 50-year-old person. Essentially, this means that while riding in a car, the risk of death of this person is about double.

HEALTH EFFECTS FROM ELECTRICITY GENERATION

Quantitative Data

Several published reports present estimates of health effects associated with electricity production (15–22). We have constructed Tables 3-3 and 3-4 to summarize the available estimates for each phase of the fuel cycle for each of the four fuels: coal, oil, natural gas, and nuclear fuel. By and large, the estimates relate to contemporary technology and existing circumstances. In each case the data have been adjusted to represent the number of premature deaths or occupational impairments produced per year by processes associated with a 1,000-megawatt (electric) power plant, which is roughly that required for a population of 1,000,000 people. The values given represent the lowest and highest from the cited references. The references should be consulted for an understanding of the methodology and detailed assumptions; limitations are discussed in later sections.

Consider first from Table 3-3 the effects on workers. For coal-fired plants the values range from 0.5 to 5 premature deaths per year, and for the other fuel sources the range is somewhat lower, from 0.06 to 1.3. Most of these effects are due to accidents in coal mines, to conditions that cause black-lung disease, or to activities in oil refineries, uranium mining, and nuclear fuel reprocessing.

Table 3–3. Premature Deaths per Year Associated with the Operation of a 1000-Megawatt (Electric) Power Plant (Values are Lowest and Highest Estimates from Cited References).[a]

	Coal	*Oil*	*Natural Gas*	*Nuclear Fuel*
Occupational				
Extraction				
Accident	0.45 – 0.99 (15, 17, 18, 21, 22)	0.06 – 0.21 (15–18, 22)	0.021 – 0.21 (15–18, 22)	0.05 – 0.2 (15, 17, 18, 20, 22)
Disease	0 – 3.5 (17)	—	—	0.002 – 0.1 (17, 19, 20, 22)
Transport,				
Accident	0.055 – 0.4 (15, 17, 18, 22)	0.03 – 0.1 (15–17, 22)	0.02 – 0.024 (15, 17, 18, 22)	0.002 (15, 18, 22)
Processing				
Accident	0.02 – 0.04 (17, 18)	0.04 – 1 (15–18, 22)	0.006 – 0.01 (15, 17, 18, 22)	0.003 – 0.2 (15, 17, 18, 20, 22)
Disease	—	—	—	0.013 – 0.33 (17, 19, 20, 22)
Conversion				
Accident	0.01 – 0.03 (15–18, 22)	0.01 – 0.037 (15–18, 22)	0.01 – 0.037 (15–18, 22)	0.01 (15, 17, 18, 22)
Disease	—	—	—	0.024 (20)
Subtotals				
Accident	0.54 – 1.5	0.14 – 1.3	0.057 – 0.28	0.065 – 0.41
Disease	0 – 3.5	—	—	0.039 – 0.45
Total	0.54 – 5.0	0.14 – 1.3	0.057 – 0.28	0.10 – 0.86
General Public				
Transport	0.55 – 1.3 (15, 17, 21, 22)	—	—	—
Processing	1 – 10 (17)	—	—	—
Conversion	0.067 – 100 (17, 21)	1 – 100 (17)	—	0.01 – 0.16[b] (15, 17, 19, 20, 22)
Total	1.6 – 111	1 – 100	—	0.01 – 0.16
Total Occupational and Public	2 – 116	1.1 – 101	0.057 – 0.28	0.11 – 1.0

[a]Note: Dashes indicate no data; effects, if any, are presumably too low to be observed, and no theoretical basis for prediction is available.
[b]For processing and conversion.

Table 3–4. Occupational Injuries per Year Associated with Operation of 1,000-Megawatt (Electric) Power Plant (Values are Lowest and Highest Estimates from Cited References).

Occupational Injuries	*Coal*	*Oil*	*Natural Gas*	*Nuclear Fuel*
Extraction				
Accident	22 – 49 (15, 17, 18, 22)	7.5 – 21 (15–18, 22)	2.5 – 21 (15–18, 22)	1.8 – 10.0 (15, 17, 18, 22)
Disease	0.6 – 48 (17, 21)	—	—	—
Transport				
Accident	0.33 – 23 (15, 17, 18, 22)	1.1 – 9 (15–17, 22)	1.2 – 1.3 (15–17, 22)	0.045 – 0.14 (15, 18, 22)
Processing				
Accident	2.6 – 3 (17, 18)	3 – 62 (15–18, 22)	0.05 – 0.56 (15–17, 22)	0.6 – 1.5 (15, 17, 18, 22)
Conversion				
Accident	0.9 – 1.5 (15–18, 22)	0.6 – 1.5 (15–18, 22)	0.6 – 1.5 (15–18, 22)	1.3 (15, 17, 18, 22)
Total				
Accident	26 – 77	12 – 94	4 – 24	4 – 13
Disease	0.6 – 48	—	—	—

Consider now from Table 3-3 the effects on the general population. It has been estimated that the transport of coal required for a year's operation of a 1,000-megawatt (electric) plant is responsible for 0.6 to 1.3 premature deaths by accident at railroad crossings; no estimates are available for truck or barge transport. The comparative values for the other fuel systems are insignificant.

The data so far discussed have a reasonable statistical base of past operation and are to that extent reliable. The number of premature deaths among the public from power plant operation (conversion or generation of electricity) results primarily from dissemination of air pollutants and, as discussed later, these effects are a matter of great uncertainty. The upper-limit estimates for coal and oil are about 100 premature deaths per year, compared with 1 or less for natural gas and nuclear fuel.

Table 3-4 presents data on the number of nonfatal occupational injuries per year associated with the operation of a 1,000-megawatt (electric) power plant. These have been defined as injuries serious enough to cause a loss of working time of several days or more. These effects are roughly the same for coal and oil, ranging from about 12 to 100 cases per year, and somewhat lower for natural gas and nuclear fuel. Most of these effects are associated with mining, well digging, coal transport, oil refining, and nuclear reprocessing.

Fossil Fuels

The data presented on the health effects associated with fossil fuels have certain limitations and uncertainties. First, genetic effects are not included because our present state of knowledge does not allow even an approximate estimate for such effects. Second, the data do not adequately discriminate between premature deaths that may occur early in life, such as from accidents, and those that may shorten life only slightly, as seen, for example, in increased mortality among persons hospitalized for chronic disease, who already have high mortality rates. Perhaps of greatest importance is the uncertainty about the validity of the upper estimates for the effects on the general public from burning coal and oil. Not only is there the problem of the magnitude of the effect, but lack of knowledge about the causative agents makes it difficult to institute effective control procedures.

The primary data come from epidemiological studies. Major episodes (Meuse, Donora, London, New York City, etc.) clearly showed that air pollution, sufficiently severe, could cause illness and premature death. During the 1950's and 1960's, the major issue was whether air pollution in concentrations usually existing over industrial cities would have adverse health effects. The emphasis shifted next to quantifying pollution relative to effects produced, and more recently, to the effects of low levels of pollution and interactions of pollutants.

From a methodological standpoint, epidemiological, animal, and experimental human studies are needed. Epidemiological studies are important in uncovering possible associations that can be tested under controlled conditions; they are also needed to evaluate human risks suggested by laboratory experiments. Animal studies are used to determine efficiently the sites of effects, mechanisms, and dose–response relationships, and they are more easily adapted for chronic studies than are human investigations. Because of species differences, controlled studies on humans are needed to establish specific responses and to determine the way disease or various physiological states influence the effects of pollution.

In this article, it is not possible to do more that present some general conclusions. Attention is called to a recent and comprehensive document (reference 3, Chs. 1–4) that cites about 380 articles in this subject area.

In 1970, air quality standards for selected pollutants were mandated by the United States Clean Air Amendments. Emphasis was placed on sulfur dioxide because of the evidence that ambient levels were associated with health effects of air pollution disasters. Subsequent studies indicated that sulfur dioxide by itself could not be the primary causative agent, and it was postulated that a combination of sulfur dioxide and particulates was responsible.[23–25] More recent evidence suggests that oxidation products of sulfur dioxide (i.e., sulfuric acid and particulate sulfates)—possibly acting synergistically with sulfur dioxide and other pollutants such as nitrates, particles, and ozone—are primarily the causative agents.[26–28] It must be emphasized that although suspended sulfates are now being used as an indicator of health effects and there appear to be correlations between them and such effects, there is no firm evidence as to which substance or substances in polluted air are the causative agents. Without such knowledge, air pollution control strategy based on reduction of sulfur alone does not have a valid scientific basis.

The major categories of health effects associated with air pollution are (a) chronic respiratory disease; (b) symptoms of aggravated heart–lung disease; (c) asthma attacks; (d) childrens respiratory disease; and (e) premature death. It would be most useful to understand the quantitative relationships between exposures to specific agents and these health effects in order to know how much investment is justified for control measures, to know which chemical effluents to control, and to make comparisons with the biological costs of nuclear power.

In a recent report of the National Academy of Sciences–National Academy of Engineering–National Research Council (reference 3, Ch. 13), illustrative calculations were made of the health effects associated with sulfur oxide emissions for representative power plants in the Northeast (Table 3-5). They were derived from models that related ambient levels to emissions, including factors for conversion of sulfur dioxide to sulfates; health effects from ambient levels were calculated by using dose–response curves from epidemiological data from studies of the Environmental Protection Agency (EPA). It must be emphasized that the numerical estimates of Table 3-5 are controversial, relying on limited information and numerous arbitrary assumptions, and cannot be regarded as proven results. A critique in the same document from which Table 3-5 was derived (reference 3, Ch. 4) suggests that the estimates could be low by a factor of two or high by a factor of ten. What can be concluded from Table 3-5 with reasonable assurance is that the effects listed are produced at detectable levels by factors associated with air pollution, with power plants most likely making a significant contribution. It should also be noted that a cost-benefit assessment of the data in Table 3-5 indicates that the economic impact of the nonlethal effects is much greater than that of the premature deaths.

Nuclear Power

Health risks to both the general public and occupational personnel from the nuclear fuel cycle are considerably better estimated than

Table 3–5. Health Effects Associated with Sulfur Oxide Emissions[a]

	Remote Location	*Urban Location*
Cases of chronic respiratory disease	25,600	75,000
Person-days of aggravated heart–lung disease symptoms	265,000	755,000
Asthma attacks	53,000	156,000
Cases of children's respiratory disease	6,200	18,400
Premature deaths	14	42

[a]Source: (Reference 3, Ch. 13). Illustrative calculations based on distributive models, postulated conversions of SO_2 to SO_4, and EPA epidemiological data for representative power plants in the Northeast emitting 96.5 × 10^6 pounds of sulfur per year—equivalent to a 620-megawatt (electric) plant.

those from fossil-fuel combustion. This is because (a) there is a single causative agent released from the nuclear plant—ionizing radiation—whereas there are literally hundreds of individual species released from fossil-fuel combustion; (b) since the first nuclear weapons tests in the 1940's, about a billion dollars have been spent on research on the effects of ionizing radiation; (c) radiation exposures are easily and precisely measured; and (d) there is a great body of knowledge from natural background exposure and from accidental, industrial, and military exposures of populations.

The uncertainties and limitations in regard to nuclear fuel differ somewhat from those for fossil-fuel combustion. The primary concerns cannot be completely answered by scientific evidence or technical solutions. They include such factors as (a) validity of predictions of effects and frequency of catastrophic accidents; (b) the need for long-term and adequate management of radioactive wastes; and (c) problems of malevolence. The upper-limit values quoted in Table 3-3 are most likely overestimates for reasons discussed later in connection with the report by the Advisory Committee on the Biological Effects of Ionizing Radiation (BEIR)[7] although genetic effects are not included, there are enough data to indicate that the values given for nonaccidental premature deaths would not be increased by more than about 50 per cent in the first generation or by more than several-fold after hundreds of years if genetic effects had been taken into account.

Generally speaking, the biological effects of ionizing radiation can be correlated with the dosage received. The effects on human individuals and populations can be considered most meaningful in terms of two levels of exposure:

High-Level: Acute, whole-body exposure greater than tens of rem,* which could result from nuclear warfare or from catastrophic nuclear or other radiation accidents.

Low-Level: Partial- or whole-body exposure, usually chronic and of the order of natural background (1 rem/year) or less, which could result from normal occupational exposure, fallout to date, a normally operating nuclear power industry, and miscellaneous sources such as television, jet travel, and luminous watch dials.

High-level exposures can and have produced directly observable manifestations. Acute exposures of about 1 rem can harm the fetus. Low-level exposures, as defined above, have not produced detectable deleterious effects in human individuals or populations or in other living organisms. This does not mean that such effects do not occur; it means that if they do occur, they do so at such low frequencies as to be undetectable.

High-Level Effects

High-level doses of ionizing radiation may produce both acute and delayed effects in humans or other organisms. The gross, acute effects of whole-body exposure to high-level doses are summarized in Table 3-6. Delayed effects may be noted after partial-body exposure to high-level doses; usually they are a result of hundreds to thousands of rem administered therapeutically to localized areas of the body. Such delayed effects on the reproductive organs, for example, range from decreased fertility or temporary sterility at about 25 rem to the gonads to permanent sterility at 600 rem or more.

Exposure to high levels of radiation also may produce late effects, those that may not develop until some years after the exposure. These effects can occur either in the exposed individual alone (somatic effects) or in the offspring of the exposed individual (genetic effects). (The probabilities that late somatic or genetic effects will occur can be estimated from the relationships discussed in the next section.) The principal somatic effects are the induction of leukemia and other forms of cancer. Cataracts also may develop if the lens

*Rem, a special unit of dose equivalent. This dose equivalent is numerically equal to the absorbed dose in rads multiplied by the quality factor, the distribution factor, and any other necessary modifying factors. The rem represents that quantity of radiation that is equivalent—in biological damage of a specified sort—to 1 rad of 250-kev x rays.

Table 3-6. Representative Dose-Effect Relationships in Human Beings for Whole-Body, Acute Irradiation[a]

Nature of Effect	X or gamma radiation (Rads)
Minimal dose detectable by chromosome analysis or other specialized analyses, but not by blood changes	5–25
Minimal dose readily detectable in a specific individual (e.g., one who presents himself as a possible exposure case)	50–75
Minimal dose likely to produce vomiting in about 10 per cent of people so exposed	75–125
Dose likely to produce transient disability and clear blood changes in a majority of people so exposed	150–200
Dose likely to cause death in about 50 per cent of people exposed	300

[a]Source: Reference 8.

of the eye receives a heavy dose of x rays, gamma rays, beta particles, or neutrons; neutrons are believed to be particularly damaging. In addition, research on experimental animals indicates that high-level, whole-body irradiation shortens life-spans, even when other effects do not appear. Such exposure may somehow accelerate an aging mechanism or it may weaken the body's defense mechanisms, increasing susceptibility to the usual causes of death.

Low-Level Effects

As stated earlier, low-level effects have not been observed. Nevertheless, current understanding of the mechanisms of interaction of radiation with biological systems requires that we assume that any level of radiation may be harmful to some degree. That is, we assume that there is no dosage threshold below which no damage occurs. Many have taken for granted that exposure to radiation in addition to the natural background and, of the same or lower magnitude, represents a risk so small compared with other hazards of life that any associated, nontrivial benefit gained by such exposure would far offset whatever harm resulted from it. But there has been public pressure to estimate the probabilities or frequencies of the effects of such exposure. The argument is that, since any level of radiation may cause some harm and since entire populations of nations or of the world could be exposed to additional low-level radiation, if care is not taken, the extent of the absolute harm could increase even though the damage might not be detectable.

The National Council on Radiation Protection and Measurements (NCRP)[8] has taken the view that estimates of quantitative risk are not useful and has expressed a philosophy as follows:

> In particular, it is believed that while exposures of workers and the general population should be kept to the lowest practicable level at all times, the presently permitted exposures represent a level of risk so small compared with other hazards of life, that such approbation will be achieved when the informed public review process is completed.

The BEIR committee of the National Academy of Sciences–National Research Council[7] decided, however, that there was an advantage in considering quantitative risk estimates, despite the recognized uncertainties in the data and calculations. The over-all numerical values from the BEIR report can be summarized as follows:

(1) It is estimated that exposure of the parents to 170 mrem per year (or 5 rem over the 30 years of the usual reproduction period) would cause in the first generation between about 150 and 3,600 serious genetic disabilities per year in the U. S. population, based on 3.6 million births per year.

(2) It is estimated that the same exposure of the U. S. population as above *could* cause roughly 3,000 to roughly 15,000 deaths from cancer annually, with 6,000 being the most likely number. (*Could* is used in the preceding sentence because many scientists feel that as a result of the efficiency of the body's repair mechanisms at the very low dose rates involved, the true effects might approach zero production of cancer.)

The above numerical values are in essential agreement with those reported by the International Commission on Radiological Protection[10] and the United Nations Scientific Committee on the Effects of Atomic Radiation.[11] The latter report stresses that the risk estimates are valid only for the doses at which they have been estimated (high levels), whereas the BEIR report suggests that the values are useful as upper-limit estimates in assessment of effects at low levels. In a recent NCRP report,[9] this matter is discussed critically, and it is concluded that the BEIR values have such a high probability of overestimating the actual risk that they are of only marginal, if any, value for purposes of realistic risk–benefit evaluation. At this time, we judge the consensus to be that the BEIR values are most likely overestimates by a considerable margin, but if used with that understanding, then there are important comparisons that can be made.

Other Issues

There are several issues of public concern, some of which involve technical solutions and others that are more related to institutional and sociological factors. Many of these are discussed elsewhere in this volume. It is our intention only to comment briefly on accidents because the risks can usefully be compared to those already discussed and on plutonium because the biomedical aspects have not been generally appreciated.

Accidents

The basic document in regard to reactor accidents is the "Rasmussen Report,"[29] the summary of which is included as Chapter 17 of this volume. It attempts to predict the probabilities and consequences of a total spectrum of conceivable reactor accidents. Critical reviews of this report have been made by the American Physical Society[30] and the Union of Concerned Scientists.[31] The essence of these analyses is that the Rasmussen estimates would have to be low by three to five orders of magnitude in order for the risks from catastrophic accidents to be comparable to those from normal operations of the coal, oil, or nuclear fuel cycles (see Table 3-7). It is a matter of conjecture whether the public would accept the probability, although very small, of a single nuclear event causing an immediate loss of hundreds of lives as preferable to or in place of the loss of a larger number of lives from fossil-fuel combustion occurring in driblets and therefore unnoticed.

Plutonium

Of all the radionuclides involved in the nuclear fuel cycle, plutonium has aroused the greatest public concern in regard to potential hazard. A great deal of experimental work has been done over the years on the biological effects of plutonium[32, 33]; but of course as with other toxic substances it is not possible to predict precisely the effects of low levels in the range of exposure that would produce undetectable effects.

Following is a discussion of those factors that tend to cause plutonium-239 to be hazardous, and then of those that tend to reduce its hazard. Plutonium, as any alpha-emitting radionuclide, is biologically very effective in producing cancer when it is located within the body in direct contact with living tissue. When it is inhaled it comes into direct contact with living tissue, and when it enters the blood it is deposited in such tissues as bone, liver, and lymph node; once deposited it remains for a long time during which it irradiates the tissue. Because of its long physical half-life (24,300 years) it must be regarded essentially as a permanent contaminant just as are many other stable industrial chemicals that pollute the biosphere.

Because alpha radiation will not penetrate even the dead layer of skin, plutonium is not a hazard when it is present outside the body. Contrary to popular conception, plutonium when swallowed remains essentially outside the body because it is extremely poorly absorbed, does not enter the bloodstream to a significant extent, and being mixed with in-

Table 3–7. Summary of Implications of Quantitative Assessments of Health Effects in the General Population Associated with Electricity Production (All Values Rounded).

		Coal and Oil	*Natural Gas*	*Nuclear Fuel*
Premature deaths/year/1,000-megawatt (electric) plant		2–100	0	0.01–0.2
Added risk/year[a]		1 in 10,000	0	1 in 5,000,000
Age	*Normal risk of death per year*	*Enhanced risk of death per year because of electricity production*[a]		
10	1 in 3,800	1.38 in 3,800[b]	1 in 3,800	1.0008 in 3,800
25	1 in 700	1.07 in 700[b]	1 in 700	1.0001 in 700
45	1 in 200	1.02 in 200[b]	1 in 200	1.00004 in 200
65	1 in 40	1.004 in 40	1 in 40	1.000008 in 40
All ages	1 in 100	1.01 in 100	1 in 100	1.00002 in 100
Number of premature deaths in 30 years associated with routine operation of 300 plants[c]		20,000 to 1,000,000	0	100 to 2,000
Number of deaths statistically predicted from catastrophic accidents in 30 years from 300 plants [Rasmussen estimate (29)][d]		—	—	10

[a]Upper estimates.
[b]These estimates are undoubtedly quite high because premature deaths from fossil fuel combustion products fall almost exclusively in the older age groups.
[c]This represents the total operation for a generation of power plants that would supply about 300 million people.
[d]Based on one chance in 10^6 of an accident per reactor-year causing 1,000 immediate and delayed casualties.

testinal contents, does not irradiate the surface of the intestines as it passes through the gastrointestinal tract. Plutonium does not become concentrated in the food chain. These characteristics result in large part from the low solubility of plutonium in water and biological fluids and its tendency to remain fixed in soil.

It appears that inhalation of plutonium is the most hazardous route of exposure. Because plutonium deposited in the lung may be present as small particles, a question has been raised as to whether a given amount of such radioactivity deposited in the lung would be more hazardous if present as small particles rather than being uniformly deposited. This is presently a matter of controversy. One group of workers[34] claims, on the basis of theoretical considerations, that small particles would be more hazardous (hot particle theory) and therefore that existing standards, which are based on uniform distribution, should be made more stringent. Other workers and several official groups claim that experimental data support existing concepts and that there is no reason for any drastic change of standards.[35–38]

The problem of malevolent use of plutonium cannot be logically assessed; this matter has been discussed by Cohen.[39] It appears that except for an unreasoning widespread public fear, terroristic purposes could be much more readily achieved by using other more easily available chemical or biological agents.

In general it can be stated that plutonium when inhaled is a toxic carcinogen and great care should be . .taken to prevent its access to the biosphere. Essentially none would be released from normal operation of the nuclear fuel cycle. Estimates of risks from it as a component of nuclear fuel cycles and the experience of the past 30 years indicate that they are lower than are risks from other parts of the cycle and from systems using other fuels.

DISCUSSION AND CONCLUSIONS

Certain qualitative conclusions seem justified. Occupational deaths from the use of coal are considerably greater than for the three other classes of fuel. The explanation for this is undoubtedly the very large volume of mass that must by physically extracted from the earth and the attendant risks associated with underground work. Although the extraction of ore is also required for nuclear fuel, the volume, and therefore the labor, required, is approximately 25 times less for nuclear fuel than for coal.

Premature deaths among the general public are very much more likely to result from the use of coal and oil than from the use of natural gas or nuclear fuel. The reason for this is that the use of coal and oil releases large amounts of combustion gases and particulates that cannot practically be contained, whereas gas combustion releases small amounts, and radioactive emissions from nuclear plants are relatively insignificant.

A summary of the implications of the quantitative assessments is presented in Table 3-7 using upper estimates and rounding all values.* It is noted that for nuclear fuel the added risk of death per year among the general population from electricity production is less than 0.1 per cent (e.g., 1.0008 in 3,800 compared to 1 in 3,800 for 10-year-olds). For coal and oil the added risk using upper estimates appears greater (e.g., 2 per cent at age 45), but the values for the younger age groups are undoubtedly lower than those given because no account was taken of the fact that premature death from fossil-fuel combustion products fall heavily in the older age groups. In addition to risks, values illustrative of absolute numbers of premature deaths are predicted for the operation of 300 plants for their typical lifetime of 30 years. For nuclear effects to be comparable to those of coal and oil, the upper estimates would have to be in error by a factor of about 500, with coal and oil effects having been overestimated or correctable by improved technology and/or nuclear effects having been underestimated. The issues have recently been raised of population exposures from ^{14}C produced in nuclear reactions [40] and from radon-222 from uranuim mill tailings.[41] The magnitude of these exposures and the fact that ample time is available to mitigate them if they do turn out to be important problems indicate that they would have no significant impact on the general relationships as presented.

The Rasmussen estimates of premature deaths from catastrophic nuclear accidents would have to have been underestimated by factors of 200 or 100,000 to be comparable to the upper estimates of effects of routine operations of nuclear or coal and oil systems, respectively. It should be noted that of the 10 statistical deaths from catastrophic accidents, one represents immediate fatalities and nine represent delayed cancer and genetic effects.

Because of the uncertainties in the upper estimates for coal and oil it concluded that such analyses are of little help in decision-making in a cost-effective manner for control processes or fuel selection in coal-burning plants. It is clear that large-scale expensive research to provide such evidence is justified. In our judgment, however, a satisfactory estimation of risks to health from coal and oil combustion is not likely to be available for many years because of the enormous complexity of dealing with the effects and interactions of the many chemical agents released.

Despite the uncertainties in the numerical values, they are of interest as a starting point in thinking about what risks society is willing or not willing to accept in order to avoid the acknowledged technical dkfficulties of handling nuclear power and the chance of catas-

*The estimated values of enhanced risk are calculated for illustrative purposes of comparison. They do not take into account age distribution of deaths associated with the processes dealt with and other factors and therefore should be used with care in any further calculations.

trophe, or to avoid the biological risks of inadequate electricity.

Acknowledgment

Appreciation is expressed to Dr. Ronald Wyzga for valuable assistance in the collection and interpretation of the quantitative data.

REFERENCES

1. National Academy of Sciences/National Academy of Engineering, Environmental Studies Board; Committee for the Working Conference on Principles of Protocols for Evaluating Chemicals in the Environment; National Research Council, Committee on Toxicology. 1975. *Principles for Evaluating Chemicals in the Environment,* Washington DC: Nat. Acad. Sci.
2. National Academy of Sciences/National Research Council, Assembly of Life Sciences. 1973. *Proceedings of the Conference on Health Effects of Air Pollution.* Prepared for Committee on Public Works, US Senate, Serial No. 93-15
3. National Academy of Sciences/National Academy of Engineering/National Research Council, Commission on Natural Resources. 1975. *Air Quality and Stationary Source Emission Control,* Prepared for Committee on Public Works, US Senate, Serial No. 94-4
4. National Academy of Sciences/National Academy of Engineering, Coordinating Committee on Air Quality Studies. 1974. *Air Quality and Automobile Emission Control.* Prepared for Committee on Public Works, US Senate, Serial No. 93-24
5. Electric Power Research Institute. 1975. *Conference Proceedings: Workshop on Health Effects of Fossil Fuel Combustion Products.* Rep. No. EPRI SR-11. Palo Alto, Calif: EPRI
6. Goldsmith, J. R. Friberg, L. 1976. Impact of air pollution on human health. In *On Air Pollution: A Comprehensive Treatise,* ed. A. C. Stern, Chap. 16. New York: Academic 3rd., in preparation
7. National Academy of Sciences/National Research Council, Division of Medical Sciences, Advisory Committee on the Biological Effects of Ionizing Radiations (BEIR). 1972. *The Effects on Populations of Exposure to Low Levels of Ionizing Radiation.* Washington DC: Nat. Acad. Sci./Nat. Res. Counc.
8. National Council on Radiation Protection and Measurements. 1971. *Basic Radiation Protection Criteria.* NCRP Rep. No. 39. Washington DC: Nat. Counc. Radiat. Prot. Meas.
9. National Council on Radiation Protection and Measurements. 1975. *Review of the Current State of Radiation Protection Philosophy.* NCRP. Rep. No. 43. Washington DC: Nat. Counc. Radiat. Prot. Meas.
10. International Commission on Radiological Protection. 1969. *Radiosensitivity and Spatial Distribution of Dose.* ICRP Publ. No. 14. Oxford: Pergamon
11. United Nations Scientific Committee on the Effects of Atomic Radiation. 1972. *Ionizing Radiation: Levels and Effects.* New York: United Nations
12. National Academy of Engineering, Committee on Public Engineering Policy. 1972. *Perspectives on Benefit-Risk Decision Making.* Report of a Colloquium, April 26–27, 1971. Washington DC: Nat. Acad. Eng.
13. Starr, C. 1969. Social benefits versus technological risk. *Science* 165: 1232-38
14. US Department of Commerce, Bureau of the Census. 1972. *Statistical Abstract of the United States.* 93rd ed. Washington DC: GPO
15. Argonne National Laboratory. 1973. *A Study of Social Costs for Alternative Means of Electrical Power Generation for 1980 and 1990.* Argonne, Ill: Argonne Nat. Lab.
16. Battelle Memorial Institute. 1973. *Environmental Considerations in Future Energy Growth.* Columbus, Ohio: Battelle Mem. Inst.
17. Hamilton, L. D., ed. 1974. *The Health and Environmental Effects of Electricity Generation—A Preliminary Report.* Upton, NY: Brookhaven Nat. Lab.
18. Council on Environmental Quality. 1973. *Energy and the Environment: Electric Power.* Washington DC: GPO
19. Lave, L. B., Freeburg, L. C. 1973. Health effects of electricity generation from coal, oil, and nuclear fuel. *Nucl. Saf.* 14: 409–28
20. Sagan, L. A. 1972. Human costs of nuclear power. *Science* 177: 487–93
21. Sagan, L. A. 1974. Health costs associated with the mining, transport, and combustion of coal in the steam-electric industry. *Nature* 250: 107–11
22. US Atomic Energy Commission. 1974. *Comparative Risk-Cost-Benefit Study of Alternative Sources of Electrical Energy.* Rep. No. WASH-1224. Washington DC: US AEC
23. Amdur, M. O. 1957. The influence of aerosols upon the respiratory response of guinea pigs to sulfur dioxide. *Am. Ind. Hyg. Assoc. J.* 18: 149–55
24. Amdur, M. O. 1959. The physiological response of guinea pigs to atmospheric pollutants. *Int. J. Air Pollut.* 1: 170–83
25. Amdur, M. O., Underhill, D. W. 1968. The effect of various aerosols on the response of guinea pigs to sulfur dioxide. *Arch. Environ. Health* 16: 460–68
26. Amdur, M. O., Corn, M. 1963. The irritant potency of zinc ammonium sulfate of different particle sizes. *Am. Ind. Hyg. Assoc. J.* 24: 326–33
27. Amdur, M. O. 1971. Aerosols formed by oxidation of sulfur dioxide: review of their toxicology. *Arch. Environ. Health* 23: 459–68

28. US Environmental Protection Agency. 1974. *A Report from CHESS 1970–1971*. Rep. No. 650/1-74-004, ORD, NERC/RTP. Research Triangle Park, NC: US EPA
29. US Nuclear Regulatory Commission. 1975. Reactor Safety Study: *An Assessment of Accident Risks in U.S. Commerical Nuclear Power Plants*. Executive Summary, Rep. WASH-1400, (NUREG-75/014), Washington DC: US NRC
30. American Physical Society. 1975. Report to the American Physical Society by the study group on light-water reactor safety. *Rev. Mod. Phys. Suppl.*, Vol. 47
31. Sierra Club/Union of Concerned Scientists, Joint Review Committee. 1974. *Preliminary Review of the AEC Reactor Safety Study*. Cambridge, Mass: Union of Concerned Scientists
32. Stannard, J. N. 1973. Biomedical aspects of plutonium (discovery, development, projections). In *Uranium, Plutonium, Transplutonic Elements*. New York: Springer-Verlag
33. US Atomic Energy Commission. 1974. *Plutonium and Other Transuranium Elements: Sources, Environmental Distribution and Biomedical Effects*. Rep. No. WASH-1359. Washington DC: US AEC
34. Tamplin, A. R., Cochran, T. B. 1974. *Radiation Standards for Hot Particles: A Report on the Inadequacy of Existing Radiation Protection Standards Related to Internal Exposure of Man to Insoluble Particles of Plutonium and Other Alpha Emitting Hot Particles*. Washington, DC: Nat. Resour. Def. Counc.
35. Medical Research Council. 1975. *The Toxicity of Plutonium*. London: HMSO
36. Bair, W. J., Richmond, C. R., Wachholz, B. W. 1974. *A Radiobiological Assessment of the Spatial Distribution of Radiation Dose from Inhaled Plutonium*. Rep. No. WASH-1320. Washington DC: US AEC
37. National Council on Radiation Protection and Measurements, Ad Hoc Committee on Hot Particles. 1975. *Alpha Emitting Particles in the Lung*. NCRP Rep. No. 46. Washington DC: Nat. Counc. Radiat. Prot. Meas.
38. Sanders, C. L., Dagle, G. E. 1974. Studies of pulmonary carcinogenesis in rodents following inhalation of transuranic compounds. *Symposium on Experimental Lung Cancer, Carcinogenesis and Bioassays,* June 23–26, 1974, Battelle Seattle Research Center, Seattle, Wash.
39. Cohen, B. L. 1975. *The Hazards in Plutonium Dispersal*. Oak Ridge, Tenn: Inst. for Energy Analysis
40. Magno, P. J., Nelson, C. B., Ellet, W. H. 1975. A consideration of the significance of carbon-14 discharges from the nuclear power industry. *Proc. 13th AEC Air Cleaning Conf. August 12–15, 1974,* Vol. I, CONF 740807, UC-70
41. US Environmental Protection Agency. 1973. *Environmental Analysis of the Uranium Fuel Cycle*. Pt. I (003-B), *Fuel Supply;* Pt. II (003-C), *Nuclear Power Reactors;* Pt. III (003-D), *Nuclear Fuel Processing*. EPA Rep. No. 520/9-73-003 A-D. Washington DC: US EPA

Energy Use In The United States Food System 4

JOHN S. STEINHART AND CAROL E. STEINHART 1974

In a modern industrial society, only a tiny fraction of the population is in frequent contact with the soil, and an even smaller fraction of the population raises food on the soil. The proportion of the population engaged in farming halved between 1920 and 1950 and then halved again by 1962. Now it has almost halved again, and more than half of these remaining farmers hold other jobs off the farm (1). At the same time the number of work animals has declined from a peak of more than 22×10^6 in 1920 to a very small number at present (2). By comparison with earlier times, fewer farmers are producing more agricultural products and the value of food in terms of the total goods and services of society now amounts to a smaller fraction of the economy than it once did.

Energy inputs to farming have increased enormously during the past fifty years (3), and the apparent decrease in farm labor is offset in part by the growth of support industries for the farmer. With these changes on the farm have come a variety of other changes in the United States food system, many of which are now deeply embedded in the fabric of daily life. In the past fifty years, canned, frozen, and other processed foods have become the principal items of our diet. At present, the food-processing industry is the fourth largest energy consumer of the Standard Industrial Classification groupings (4). The extent of transportation engaged in the food system has grown apace, and the proliferation of appliances in both numbers and complexity still continues in homes, institutions, and stores. Hardly any food is eaten as it comes from the fields. Even farmers purchase most of their food from markets in town.

Present energy supply problems make this growth of energy use in the food system worth investigating. It is our purpose in this article

Dr. John S. Steinhart is a professor of geology and geophysics and a professor in the Institute for Environmental Studies, University of Wisconsin-Madison, Madison, Wisconsin 53706. He also is the associate director of the University of Wisconsin-Madison Sea Grant Program.

Dr. Carol E. Steinhart, formerly a biologist with the National Institutes of Health, is now a science writer and editor.

This article is modified from *Energy: Source, Use, and Role in Human Affairs,* Duxbury Press, North Scituate, Massachusetts, 1974, and appeared in *Science,* Vol. 184, No. 4134, pp. 307–316, April 19, 1974. Reprinted with light editing and by permission of the authors, Duxbury Press, and the American Association for the Advancement of Science.

to do so. But there are larger matters at stake. Georgescu-Roegen notes that "the evidence now before us—of a world which can produce automobiles, television sets, etc., at a greater speed than the increase in population, but is simultaneously menaced by mass starvation—is disturbing" (5). In the search for a solution to the world's food problems, the common attempt to transplant a small piece of a highly industrialized food system to the hungry nations of the world is plausible enough, but so far the outcome is unclear. Perhaps an examination of the energy flow in the United States food system as it has developed can provide some insights that are not available from the usual economic measures.

MEASURES OF FOOD SYSTEMS

Agricultural systems are most often described in economic terms. A wealth of statistics is collected in the United States and in most other technically advanced countries indicating production amounts, shipments, income, labor, expenses, and dollar flow in the agricultural sector of the economy. But, when we wish to know something about the food we actually eat, the statistics of farms are only a tiny fraction of the story.

Energy flow is another measure available to gauge societies and nations. It would have made no sense to measure societies in terms of energy flow in the eighteenth century when economics began. As recently as 1940, four-fifths of the world's population were still on farms and in small villages, most of them engaged in subsistence farming.

Only after some nations shifted large portions of the population to manufacturing, specialized tasks, and mechanized food production, and shifted the prime sources of energy to move society to fuels that were transportable and usable for a wide variety of alternative activities, could energy flow be used as a measure of societies' activities. Today it is only in one-fifth of the world where these conditions are far advanced. Yet we can now make comparisons of energy flows even with primitive societies. For even if the primitives, or the euphemistically named "underdeveloped" countries, cannot shift freely among their energy expenditures, we *can* measure them and they constitute a different and potentially useful comparison with the now traditional economic measures.

What we would like to know is this: How does our present food supply system compare, in energy measures, with those of other societies and with our own past? Perhaps then we can estimate the value of energy flow measures as an adjunct to, but different from, economic measures.

ENERGY IN THE UNITED STATES FOOD SYSTEM

A typical breakfast includes orange juice from Florida, by way of the Minute Maid factory, bacon from a midwestern meat packer, cereal from Nebraska and General Mills, eggs and milk from not *too* far away, and coffee from Colombia. All of these things are available at the local supermarket (several miles each way in a 300-horsepower automobile), stored in a refrigerator-freezer, and cooked on an instant-on stove.

The present food system in the United States is complex, and the attempt to analyze it in terms of energy use will introduce complexities and questions far more perplexing than the same analysis carried out on simpler societies. Such an analysis is worthwhile, however, if only to find out where we stand. We have a food system, and most people get enough to eat from it. If, in addition, one considers the food supply problems present and future in societies where a smaller fraction of the people get enough to eat, then our experience with an industrialized food system is even more important. There is simply no gainsaying that many nations of the world are presently attempting to acquire industrialized food systems of their own.

Food in the United States is expensive by world standards. In 1970 the average annual per capita expenditure for food was about $600 (3). This amount is larger than the per capita gross domestic product of more than thirty nations of the world which contain the majority of the world's people and a vast majority of those who are underfed. Even if we consider the diet of a poor resident of India, the annual cost of his food at United States prices would be about $200—more than twice his annual income (3). It is crucial to know whether a piece of our industrialized food system can be exported to help poor nations, or whether they must become as industrialized as the United States to operate an industrialized food system.

Our analysis of energy use in the food system begins with an omission. We will neglect that crucial input of energy provided by the sun to the plants upon which the entire food supply depends. Photosynthesis has an efficiency of about 1 per cent; thus, the maximum solar radiation captured by plants is about 5×10^3 kilocalories per square meter per year (3).

Seven categories of energy use on the farm are considered here. The amounts of energy used are shown in Table 4-1. The values given for farm machinery and tractors are for the manufacture of new units only and do not include parts and maintenance for units that already exist. The amounts shown for direct fuel use and electricity consumption are a bit too high because they include some residential uses of the farmer and his family. On the other hand, some uses in these categories are not reported in the summaries used to obtain the values for direct fuel and electricity usage. These and similar problems are discussed in the references. Note the relatively high energy cost associated with irrigation. In the United States less than 5 per cent of the crop land is irrigated (1). In some countries where the "green revolution" is being attempted, the new high-yield varieties of plants require irrigation where native crops did not. If that were the case in the United States, irrigation would be the largest single use of energy on the farm.

Little food makes its way directly from field and farm to the table. The vast complex of processing, packaging, and transport has been grouped together in a second major subdivision of the food system. The seven categories of the processing industry are listed in Table 4-1. Energy use for the transport of food should be charged to the farm in part, but we have not done so here because the calculation of the energy values is easiest (and we believe most accurate) if they are taken for the whole system.

After the processing of food there is further energy expenditure. Transportation enters the picture again, and some fraction of the energy used for transportation should be assigned here. But there are also the distributors, wholesalers, and retailers, whose freezers, refrigerators, and very establishments are an integral part of the food system. There are also the restaurants, schools, universities, prisons, and a host of other institutions engaged in the procurement, preparation, storage, and supply of food. We have chosen to examine only three categories: the energy required for refrigeration and cooking, and for the manufacture of the heating and refrigeration equipment (Table 4-1). We have made no attempt to include the energy used in trips to the store or restaurant. Garbage disposal has also been omitted, although it is a persistent and growing feature of our food system; 12 per cent of the nation's trucks are engaged in the activity of waste disposal (1), of which a substantial part is related to food. If there is any lingering doubt that these activities—both the ones included and the ones left out—are an essential feature of our present food system, one need only ask what would happen if everyone should attempt to get on without a refrigerator or freezer or stove? Certainly the food system would change.

Table 4-1 and the related references summarize the numerical values for energy use in the United States food system, from 1940 to 1970. As for many activities in the past few decades, the story is one of continuing increase. The totals are displayed in Figure 4-1 along with the energy value of the food consumed by the public. The food values were obtained by multiplying the daily caloric intake by the population. The differences in caloric intake per capita over this thirty-year period are small (1), and the curve is primarily

Table 4–1. Energy Use in the United States Food System.[a]

Component	1940	1947	1950	1954	1958	1960	1964	1968	1970	References
					On farm					
Fuel (direct use)	70.0	136.0	158.0	172.8	179.0	188.0	213.9	226.0	232.0	*(13–15)*
Electricity	0.7	32.0	32.9	40.0	44.0	46.1	50.0	57.3	63.8	*(14, 16)*
Fertilizer	12.4	19.5	24.0	30.6	32.2	41.0	60.0	87.0	94.0	*(14, 17)*
Agricultural steel	1.6	2.0	2.7	2.5	2.0	1.7	2.5	2.4	2.0	*(14, 18)*
Farm machinery	9.0	34.7	30.0	29.5	50.2	52.0	60.0	75.0	80.0	*(14, 19)*
Tractors	12.8	25.0	30.8	23.6	16.4	11.8	20.0	20.5	19.3	*(20)*
Irrigation	18.0	22.8	25.0	29.6	32.5	33.3	34.1	34.8	35.0	*(21)*
Subtotal	124.5	272.0	303.4	328.6	356.3	373.9	440.5	503.0	526.1	
					Processing industry					
Food processing industry	147.0	177.5	192.0	211.5	212.6	224.0	249.0	295.0	308.0	*(13, 14, 22)*
Food processing machinery	0.7	5.7	5.0	4.9	4.9	5.0	6.0	6.0	6.0	*(23)*
Paper packaging	8.5	14.8	17.0	20.0	26.0	28.0	31.0	35.7	38.0	*(24)*
Glass containers	14.0	25.7	26.0	27.0	30.2	31.0	34.0	41.9	47.0	*(25)*
Steel cans and aluminum	38.0	55.8	62.0	73.7	85.4	86.0	91.0	112.2	122.0	*(26)*
Transport (fuel)	49.6	86.1	102.0	122.3	140.2	153.3	184.0	226.6	246.9	*(27)*
Trucks and trailors (manufacture)	28.0	42.0	49.5	47.0	43.0	44.2	61.0	70.2	74.0	*(28)*
Subtotal	285.8	407.6	453.5	506.4	542.3	571.5	656.0	787.6	841.9	
					Commercial and home					
Commercial refrigeration and cooking	121.0	141.0	150.0	161.0	176.0	186.2	209.0	241.0	263.0	*(13, 29)*
Refrigeration machinery (home and commercial)	10.0	24.0	25.0	27.5	29.4	32.0	40.0	56.0	61.0	*(14, 30)*
Home refrigeration and cooking	144.2	184.0	202.3	228.0	257.0	276.6	345.0	433.9	480.0	*(13, 29)*
Subtotal	275.2	349.0	377.3	416.5	462.4	494.8	594.0	730.9	804.0	
Grand total	685.5	1028.6	1134.2	1251.5	1361.0	1440.2	1690.5	2021.5	2172.0	

[a] All values are multiplied by 10^{12} kilocalories.

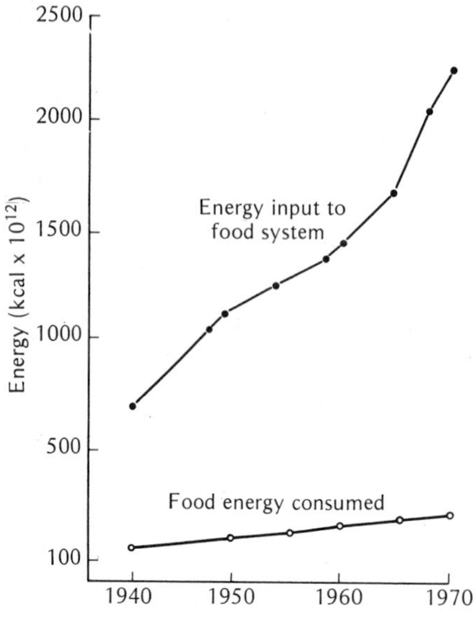

Figure 4-1. Energy use in the food system, 1940 through 1970, compared to the caloric content of food consumed.

an indication of the increase in population in this period.

OMISSIONS AND DUPLICATIONS FOR FOOD SYSTEM ENERGY VALUES

Several omissions, duplications, and overlaps have been mentioned. We will now examine the values in Table 4-1 for completeness and try to obtain a crude estimate of their numerical accuracy.

The direct fuel and electricity usage on the farm may be overstated by some amounts used in the farmer's household, which, by our approach, would not all be chargeable to the food system. But about 10 per cent of the total acreage farmed is held by corporate farms for which the electrical and direct fuel use is not included in our data. Other estimates of these two categories are much higher [see Table 4-1 (15,16)].

No allowance has been made for food exported, which has the effect of overstating the energy used in our own food system. For the years prior to 1960 the United States was at times a net importer of food, at times an exporter, and at times there was a near balance in this activity. But during this period the net flow of trade was never more than a few per cent of the total farm output. Since 1960 net exports have increased to about 20 per cent of the gross farm product (1,3). The items comprising the vast majority of the exports have been rough grains, flour, and other plant products with very little processing. Imports include more processed food than exports and represent energy expenditure outside the United States. Thus, the overestimate of energy input to the food system might be 5 per cent with an upper limit of 15 per cent.

The items omitted are more numerous. Fuel losses from the well head or mine shaft to end use total 10 to 12 per cent (6). This would represent a flat addition of 10 per cent or more to the totals, but we have not included this item because it is not customarily charged to end uses.

We have computed transport energy for trucks only. Considerable food is transported by train and ship, but these items were omitted because the energy use is small relative to the consumption of truck fuel. Small amounts of food are shipped by air, and, although air shipment is energy intensive, the amount of energy consumed appears small. We have traced support materials until they could no longer be assigned to the food system. Some transportation energy consumption is not charged in the transport of these support materials. These omissions are numerous and hard to estimate, but they would not be likely to increase the totals by more than 1 or 2 per cent.

A more serious understatement of energy usage occurs with respect to vehicle usage (other than freight transport) on farm business, food-related business in industry and commercial establishments, and in the supporting industries. A special attempt to estimate this category of energy usage for 1968 suggests that it amounts to about 5 per cent of the energy totals for the food system. This estimate would be subject to an uncertainty of nearly 100 per cent. We must be satisfied to suggest that 1 to 10 per cent should be added to the totals on this account.

Waste disposal is related to the food system, at least in part. We have chosen not to charge this energy to the food system, but, if one-half of the waste disposal activity is taken as food related, about 2 per cent must be added to the food system energy totals.

We have not included energy for parts and maintenance of machinery, vehicles, buildings, and the like, or lumber for farm, industry, or packaging uses. These miscellaneous activities would not constitute a large addition in any case. We have also excluded construction. Building and replacement of farm structures, food industry structures, and commercial establishments are all directly part of the food system. Construction of roads is in some measure related to the food system, since nearly half of all trucks transport food and agricultural items [see Table 4-1 (27)]. Even home construction could be charged in part to the food system since space, appliances, and plumbing are, in part, a consequence of the food system. If 10 per cent of housing, 10 per cent of institutional construction (for institutions with food service), and 10 per cent of highway construction is included, about 10 per cent of the total construction was food related in 1970. Assuming that the total energy consumption divides in the same way that the gross national product does (which overstates energy use in construction), the addition to the total in Table 4-1 would be about 10 per cent or 200×10^{12} kcal. This is a crude and highly simplified calculation, but it does provide an estimate of the amounts of energy involved.

The energy used to generate the highly specialized seed and animal stock has been excluded because there is no easy way to estimate it. Pimentel et al. (3) estimate that 1,800 kcal are required to produce 1 pound (450 grams) of hybrid corn seed. But in addition to this amount, some energy use should be included for all the schools of agriculture, agricultural experiment stations, the far-flung network of county agricultural agents [one local agent said he traveled over 50,000 automobile miles (80,000 kilometers) per year in his car], the U.S. Department of Agriculture, and the wide-ranging agricultural research program that enables man to stay ahead of the new pest and disease threats to our highly specialized food crops. These are extensive activities, but we cannot see how they could add more than a few per cent to the totals in Table 4-1.

Finally, we have no attempt to include the amount of private automobile usage involved in the delivery system from retailer to home, or other food-related uses of private autos. Rice (7) reports 4.25×10^{15} kilocalories for the energy cost of autos in 1970, and shopping constitutes 15.2 per cent of all automobile usage (8). If only half of the shopping is food-related, 320×10^{12} kilocalories of energy use is at stake here. Between 8 and 15 per cent should be added to the totals of Table 4-1, depending on just how one wishes to apportion this item.

It is hard to take an approach that might calculate smaller totals but, depending upon point of view, the totals could be much larger. If we accumulate the larger estimates from the above paragraphs as well as the reductions, the total could be enlarged by 30 to 35 per cent, especially for recent years. As it is, the values for energy use in the food system from Table 4-1 account for 12.8 per cent of the total United States energy use in 1970.

PERFORMANCE OF AN INDUSTRIALIZED FOOD SYSTEM

The difficulty with history as a guide for the future or even the present lies not so much in the fact that conditions change—we are continually reminded of that fact—but that history is only one experiment of the many that might have occurred. The United States food system developed as it did for a variety of reasons, many of them not understood. We would do well to examine some of the dimensions of this development before attempting to theorize about how it might have been different, or how parts of this food system can be transplanted elsewhere.

ENERGY AND FOOD PRODUCTION

Figure 4-2 displays features of our food system not easily seen from economic data. The curve shown has no theoretical basis but is suggested by the data as a smoothed recounting of our own history of increasing food production. It is, however, similar to most growth curves and suggests that, to the extent that the increasing energy subsides to the food system have increased food production, we are near the end of an era. Like the logistic growth curve, there is an exponential phase which lasted from 1920 or earlier until 1950 or 1955. Since then, the increments in production have been smaller despite the continuing growth in energy use. It is likely that further increases in food production from increasing energy inputs will be harder and harder to come by. Of course, a major change in the food system could change things, but the argument advanced by the technological optimist is that we can always get more if we have enough energy, and that no other major changes are required. Our own history—the only one we have to examine—does not support that view.

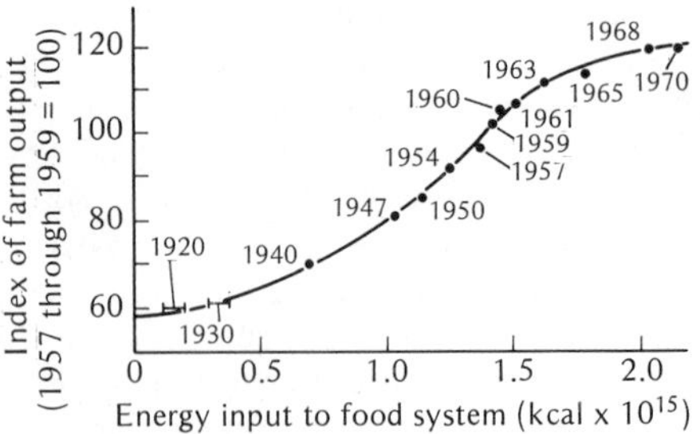

Figure 4-2. Farm output as a function of energy input to the United States food system, 1920 through 1970.

The food system that has grown in this period has provided much employment that did not exist 20, 30, or 40 years ago. Perhaps even the idea of a reduction of labor input is a myth when the food system is viewed as a whole, instead of from the point of view of the farm worker only. When discussing inputs to the farm, Pimentel et al. (3) cite an estimate of two farm support workers for each person actually on the farm. To this must be added employment in food-processing industries, in food wholesaling and retailing, as well as in a variety of manufacturing enterprises that support the food system. Yesterday's farmer is today's canner, tractor mechanic, and fast food carhop. The process of change has been painful to many ordinary people. The rural

ENERGY AND LABOR IN THE FOOD SYSTEM

One farmer now feeds 50 people, and the common expectations is that the labor input to farming will continue to decrease in the future. Behind this expectation is the assumption that the continued application of technology—and energy—to farming will substitute for labor. Figure 4-3 shows this historic decline in labor as a function of the energy supplied to the food system, again the familiar S-shaped curve. What it implies is that increasing the energy input to the food system is unlikely to bring further reduction in farm labor unless some other major change is made.

Figure 4-3. Labor use on farms as a function of energy use in the food system.

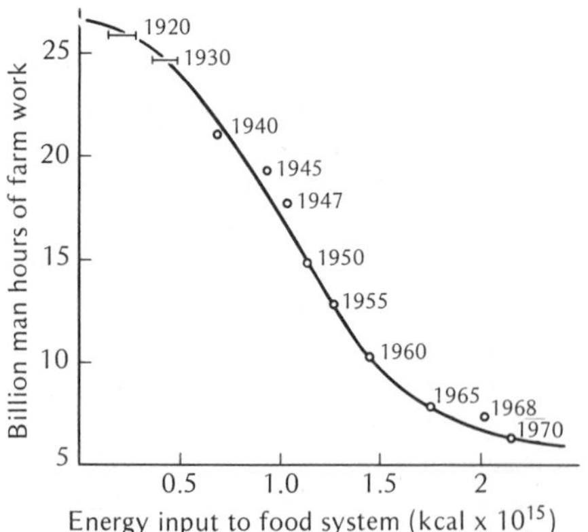

poor, who could not quite compete in the growing industrialization of farming, migrated to the cities. Eventually they found other employment, but one must ask if the change was worthwhile. The answer to that question cannot be provided by energy analysis anymore than by economic data, because it raises fundamental questions about how individuals would prefer to spend their lives. But if there is a stark choice between long hours as a farmer or shorter hours on the assembly line of a meat-packing plant, it seems clear that the choice would not be universally in favor of the meat-packing plant. Thomas Jefferson dreamed of a nation of independent small farmers. It was a good dream, but society did not develop in that way. Nor can we turn back the clock to recover his dream. But, in planning and preparing for our future, we had better look honestly at our collective history, and then each of us should closely examine his dreams.

THE ENERGY SUBSIDY TO THE FOOD SYSTEM

The data in Figure 4-1 can be combined to show the energy subsidy provided to the food system for the recent past. We take as a measure of the food supplied the caloric content of the food actually consumed. This is not the only measure of the food supplied, as the condition of many protein-poor peoples of the world clearly shows. Nevertheless, the comparison between caloric input and output is a convenient way to compare our present situation with the past, and to compare our food system with others. Figure 4-4 shows the history of the United States food system in terms of the number of calories of energy supplied to produce 1 calorie of food for actual consumption. It is interesting and possibly threatening to note that there is no real suggestion that this curve is leveling off. We appear to be increasing the energy input even more. Fragmentary data for 1972 suggest that the increase continued unabated. A graph like Figure 4-4 could approach zero. A natural

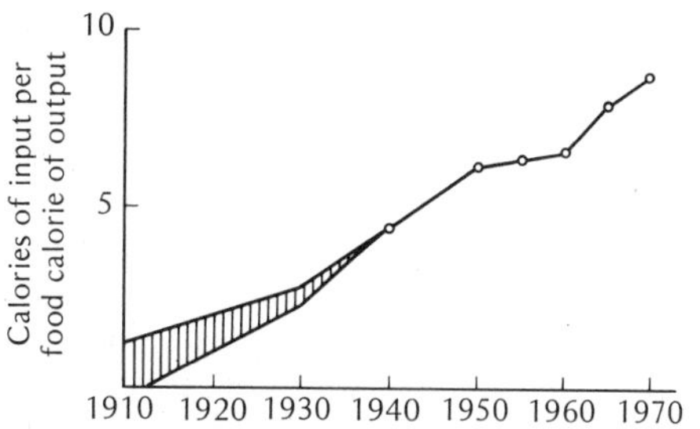

Figure 4-4. Energy subsidy to the food system needed to obtain 1 food calorie.

ecosystem has no fuel input at all, and those primitive people who live by hunting and gathering have only the energy of their own work to count as input.

SOME ECONOMIC FEATURES OF THE UNITED STATES FOOD SYSTEM

The markets for farm commodities in the United States come closer than most to the economist's ideal of a "free market." There are many small sellers and many buyers, and thus no individual is able to affect the price by his own actions in the market place. But government intervention can drastically alter any free market, and government intervention in the prices of agricultural products (and hence of food) has been a prominent feature of the United States food system for at least thirty years. Between 1940 and 1970, total farm income has ranged from $4.5 to $16.5 billion, and the national income originating in agriculture (which includes indirect income from agriculture) has ranged from $14.5 to $22.5 billion (1). Meanwhile, government subsidy programs, primarily farm price supports and soil bank payments, have grown from $1.5 billion in 1940 to $6.2 billion in 1970. In 1972 these subsidy programs had grown to $7.3 billion, despite foreign demand of agricultural products. Viewed in a slightly different way, direct government subsidies have accounted for 30 to 40 per cent of the farm income and 15 to 30 per cent of the

National Income attributable to agriculture for the years since 1955. This point emphasizes once again the striking gap between the economic description of society and the economic models used to account for that society's behavior.

This excursion into farm price supports and economics is related to energy questions in this way: first, as far as we know, government intervention in the food system is a feature of all highly industrialized countries (and, despite the intervention, farm incomes still tend to lag behind national averages) and, second, reduction of the energy subsidy to agriculture (even if we could manage it) might decrease the farmer's income. One reason for this state of affairs is that the demand for food quantity has definite limits, and the only way to increase farm income is then to increase the unit price of agricultural products. Consumer boycotts and protests in the early 1970's suggest that there is considerable resistance to this outcome.

Government intervention in the functioning of the market in agriculture products has accompanied the rise in the use of energy in agriculture and the food supply system, and we have nothing but theoretical suppositions to suggest that any of the present system can be deleted.

SOME ENERGY IMPLICATIONS FOR THE WORLD FOOD SUPPLY

The food supply system of the United States is complex and interwoven into a highly industrialized economy. We have tried to analyze this system on account of its implications for future energy use. But the world is short of food. A few years ago it was widely predicted that the world would suffer widespread famine in the 1970's. The adoption of new high-yield varieties of rice, wheat, and other grains has caused some experts to predict that the threat of these expected famines can now be averted, perhaps indefinitely. Yet, despite increases in grain production in some areas, the world still seems to be headed toward famine. The adoption of these new varieties of grain—dubbed hopefully the "green revolution"—is an attempt to export a part of the energy-intensive food system of the highly industrialized countries to nonindustrialized countries. It is an experiment, because, although the whole food system is not being transplanted to new areas, a small part of it is. The green revolution requires a great deal of energy. Many of the new varieties of grain require irrigation where traditional crops did not, and almost all the new crops require extensive fertilization.

Meanwhile, the agricultural surpluses of the 1950's have largely disappeared. Grain shortages in China and Russia have attracted attention because they have brought foreign trade across ideological barriers. There are other countries that would probably import considerable grain, if they could afford it. But only four countries may be expected to have any substantial excess agricultural production in the next decade. These are Canada, New Zealand, Australia, and the United States. None of these is in a position to give grain away, because each of them needs the foreign trade to avert ruinous balance of payments deficits. Can we then export energy-intensive agricultural methods instead?

ENERGY-INTENSIVE AGRICULTURE ABROAD

It is quite clear that the United States food system cannot be exported intact at present. For example, India has a population of 550×10^6 persons. To feed the people of India at the United States level of about 3,000 food calories per day (instead of their present 2,000) would require more energy than India now uses for all purposes. To feed the entire world with a United States type food system, almost 80 per cent of the world's annual energy expenditure would be required just for the food system.

The recourse most often suggested to remedy this difficulty is to export methods of increasing crop yield and hope for the best.

We must repeat as plainly as possible that this is an experiment. We know that our food system works (albeit with some difficulties and warnings for the future). But we cannot know what will happen if we take a piece of that system and transplant it to a poor country, without our industrial base of supply, transport system, processing industry, appliances for home storage, and preparation, and, most important, a level of industrialization that permits higher costs for food.

Fertilizers, herbicides, pesticides, and in many cases machinery and irrigation are needed for success with the green revolution. Where is this energy to come from? Many of the nations with the most serious food problems are those nations with scant supplies of fossil fuels. In the industrialized nations, solutions to the energy supply problems are being sought in nuclear energy. This technology-intensive solution, even if successful in advanced countries, poses additional problems for underdeveloped nations. To create the bases of industry and technologically sophisticated people within their own countries will be beyond the capability of many of them. Here again, these countries face the prospect of depending upon the goodwill and policies of industrialized nations. Since the alternative could be famine, their choices are not pleasant and their irritation at their benefactors—ourselves among them—could grow to threatening proportions. It would be comfortable to rely on our own good intentions, but our good intentions have often been unresponsive to the needs of others. The matter cannot be glossed over lightly. World peace may depend upon the outcome.

CHOICES FOR THE FUTURE

The total amount of energy used on United States farms for the production of corn is now near 10^3 kilocalories per square meter per year (3), and this is more or less typical of intensive agriculture in the United States. With this application of energy we have achieved yields of 2×10^3 kilocalories per square meter per year of usable grain—bringing us to almost half of the photosynthetic limit of production. Further applications of energy are likely to yield little or no increase in this level of productivity. In any case, no amount of research is likely to improve the efficiency of the photosynthetic process itself. There is a further limitation on the improvement of yield. Faith in technology and research has at times blinded us to the basic limitations of the plant and animal material with which we work. We have been able to emphasize desirable features already present in the gene pool and to suppress others that we find undesirable. At times the cost of the increased yield has been the loss of desirable characteristics—hardiness, resistance to disease and adverse weather, and the like. The farther we get from characteristics of the original plant and animal strains, the more care and energy is required. Choices need to be made in the directions of plant breeding. And the limits of the plants and animals we use must be kept in mind. We have not been able to alter the photosynthetic process or to change the gestation period of animals. In order to amplify or change an existing characteristic, we will probably have to sacrifice something in the over-all performance of the plant or animal. If the change requires more energy, we would end with a solution that is too expensive for the people who need it most. These problems are intensified by the degree to which energy becomes more expensive in the world market.

WHERE TO LOOK FOR FOOD NEXT?

Our examination in the foregoing pages of the United States food system, the limitations on the manipulation of ecosystems and their components, and the risks of the green revolution as a solution to the world food supply problem suggests a bleak prospect for the future. This complex of problems should not be underestimated, but there are possible ways of avoiding disaster and of mitigating the severest difficulties. These suggestions are not very dramatic and may be difficult to accept.

Figure 4-5 shows the ratio of the energy subsidy to the energy output for a number of widely used foods in a variety of times and cultures. For comparison, the over-all pattern for the United States food system is shown, but the comparison is only approximate because, for most of the specific crops, the energy input ends at the farm. As has been pointed out, it is a long way from the farm to the table in industrialized societies. Several things are immediately apparent and coincide with expectations. High-protein foods such as milk, eggs, and especially meat have a far poorer energy return than plant foods. Because protein is essential for human diets and the amino acid balance necessary for good nutrition is not found in most of the cereal grains, we cannot take the step of abandoning meat sources altogether. Figure 4-5 does show how unlikely it is that increased fishing or fish protein concentrate will solve the world's food problems. Even if we leave aside the question of whether the fish are available—a point on which expert opinions

Figure 4-5. Energy subsidies for various food crops. The energy history of the United States food system is shown for comparison. (Source of data: ref. 31.)

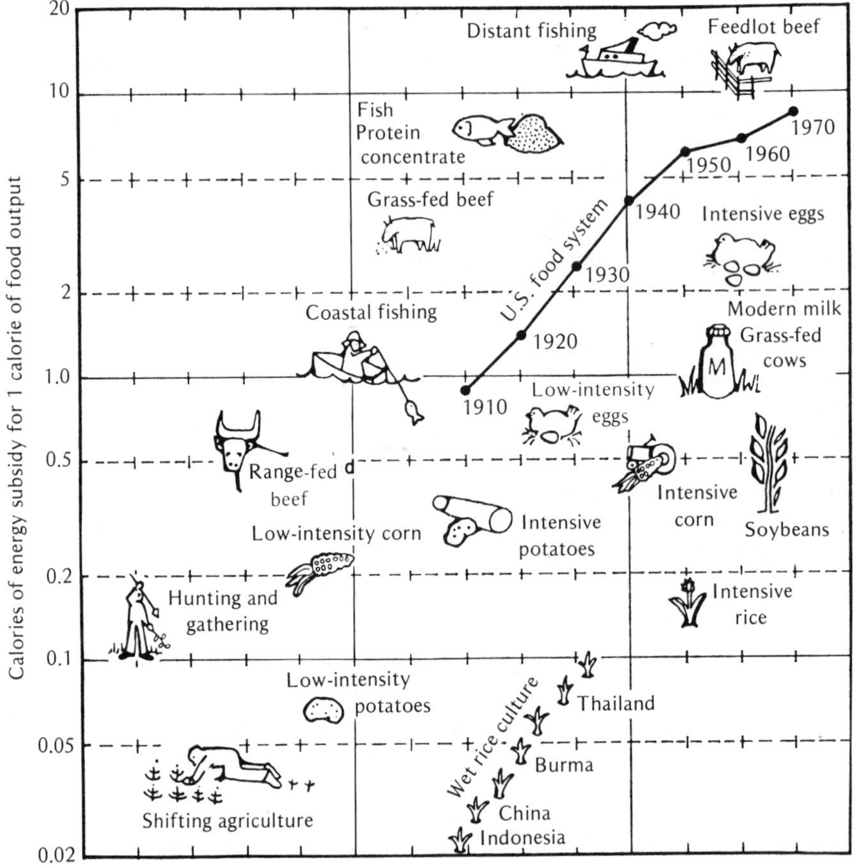

differ somewhat—it would be hard to imagine, with rising energy prices, that fish protein concentrate will be anything more than a by-product of the fishing industry, because it requires more than twice the energy of production of grass-fed beef or eggs (9). Distant fishing is still less likely to solve food problems. On the other hand, coastal fishing is relatively low in energy cost. Unfortunately, without the benefit of scholarly analysis, fisherman and housewives have long known this, and coastal fisheries are threatened with overfishing as well as pollution.

The position of soybeans in Figure 4-5 may be crucial. Soybeans possess the best amino acid balance and protein content of any widely grown crop. This has long been known to the Japanese, who have made soybeans a staple of their diet. Are there other plants, possibly better suited for local climates, that have adequate proportions of amino acids in their proteins? There are about 80,000 edible species of plants, of which only about 50 are actively cultivated on a large scale (and 90 per cent of the world's crops come from only 12 species). We may yet be able to find species that can contribute to the world's food supply.

The message of Figure 4-5 is simple. In "primitive" cultures, 5 to 50 food calories were obtained for each calorie of energy invested. Some highly civilized cultures have done as well and occasionally better. In sharp contrast, industrialized food systems require 5 to 10 calories of fuel to obtain 1 food calorie. We must pay attention to this difference—especially if energy costs increase. If some of the energy subsidy for food production could be supplied by onsite, renewable sources—primarily sun and wind—we might be able to continue an energy-intensive food system. Otherwise, the choices appear to be either less energy-intensive food production or famine for many areas of the world.

ENERGY REDUCTION IN AGRICULTURE

It is possible to reduce the energy required for agriculture and the food system. A series of thoughtful proposals by Pimentel and his associates (3) deserves wide attention. Many of these proposals would help ameliorate environmental problems, and any reductions in energy use would provide a direct reduction in the pollutants due to fuel consumption as well as more time to solve our energy supply problems.

First, we should make more use of natural manures. The United States has a pollution problem from runoff from animal feed lots, even with the application of large amounts of manufactured fertilizer to fields. More than 10^6 kilocalories per acre (4×10^5 kilocalories per hectare) could be saved by substituting manure for manufactured fertilizer (3) (and, as a side benefit, the soil's condition would be improved). Extensive expansion in the use of natural manure will require decentralization of feed-lot operations so that manure is generated closer to the point of application. Decentralization might increase feed-lot costs, but, as energy prices rise, feed-lot operations will rapidly become more expensive in any case. Although the use of manures can help reduce energy use, there is far too little to replace all commercial fertilizers at present (10). Crop rotation is less widely practiced than it was even twenty years ago. Increased use of crop rotation or interplanting winter cover crops of legumes (which fix nitrogen as a green manure) would save 1.5×10^6 kilocalories per acre by comparison with the use of commercial fertilizer.

Second, weed and pest control could be accomplished at a much smaller cost in energy. A 10 per cent saving in energy in weed control could be obtained by the use of the rotary hoe twice in cultivation instead of herbicide application (again with pollution abatement as a side benefit). Biologic pest control—that is, the use of sterile males, introduced predators, and the like—requires only a tiny fraction of the energy of pesticide manufacture and application. A change to a policy of "treat when and where necessary" pesticide application would bring a 35 to 50 per cent reduction in pesticide use. Hand application of pesticides requires more labor than machine or aircraft application, but the energy for application is reduced from 18,000 to 300 kilocalories per acre (3). Changed cosmetic standards, which in no way affect the taste or the edibility of foodstuffs, could also bring about a substantial reduction in pesticide use.

Third, plant breeders might pay more attention to hardiness, disease and pest resistance, reduced moisture content (to end the wasteful use of natural gas in drying crops), reduced water requirements, and increased protein content, even if it should mean some reduction in over-all yield. In the long run, plants not now widely cultivated might receive some serious attention and breeding efforts. It seems unlikely that the crops that have been most useful in temperate climates will be the most suitable ones for the tropics where a large portion of the undernourished peoples of the world now live.

A dramatic suggestion, to abandon chemical farming altogether, has been made by Chapman (11). His analysis shows that, were chemical farming to be ended, there would be much reduced yields per acre, so that most land in the soil bank would need to be put back into farming. Nevertheless, output would fall only 5 per cent, and prices for farm products would increase 16 per cent. Most dramatically, farm income would rise 25 per cent, and nearly all subsidy programs would end. A similar set of propositions treated with linear programming techniques at Iowa State University resulted in an essentially similar set of conclusions (12).

The direct use of solar energy farms, a return to wind power (modern windmills are now in use in Australia), and the production of methane from manure are all possibilities. These methods require some engineering to become economically attractive, but it should be emphasized that these technologies are now better understood than the technology of breeder reactors. If energy prices rise, these methods of energy generation would be attractive alternatives, even at their present costs of implementation.

ENERGY REDUCTION IN THE UNITED STATES FOOD SYSTEM

Beyond the farm, but still far from the table, more energy savings could be introduced. The most effective way to reduce the large energy requirements of food processing would be a change in eating habits toward less highly processed foods. The current aversion of young people to spongy, additive-laden white bread, hydrogenated peanut butter, and some other processed foods could presage such a change if it is more than just a fad. Technological changes could reduce energy consumption, but the adoption of lower energy methods would be hastened most by an increase in energy prices, which would make it more profitable to reduce fuel use.

Packaging has long since passed the stage of simply holding a convenient amount of food together and providing it with some minimal protection. Legislative controls may be needed to reduce the manufacturer's competition in the amount and expense of packaging. In any case, recycling of metal containers and wider use of returnable bottles could reduce this large item of energy use.

The trend toward the use of trucks in food transport, to the virtual exclusion of trains, should be reversed. By reducing the direct and indirect subsidies to trucks we might go a long way toward enabling trains to compete.

Finally, we may have to ask whether the ever-larger frostless refrigerators are needed, and whether the host of kitchen appliances really means less work or only the same amount of work to a different standard.

Store delivery routes, even by truck, would require only a fraction of the energy used by autos for food shopping. Rapid transit, giving some attention to the problems with shoppers with parcels, would be even more energy-efficient. If we insist on a high-energy food system, we should consider starting with coal, oil, garbage—or any other source of hydrocarbons—and producing in factories bacteria, fungi, and yeasts. These products could then be flavored and colored appropriately for cultural tastes. Such a system would be more efficient in the use of energy, would solve waste problems, and would permit much or all of the agricultural land to be returned to its natural state.

ENERGY, PRICES, AND HUNGER

If energy prices rise, as they have already begun to do, the rise in the price of food in societies with industrialized agriculture can be expected to be even larger than the energy price increases. Slesser, in examining the case for England, suggests that a quadrupling of energy prices in the next forty years would bring about a sixfold increase in food prices (9). Even small increases in energy costs may make it profitable to increase labor input to food production. Such a reversal of a fifty-year trend toward energy-intensive agriculture would present environmental benefits as a bonus.

We have tried to show how analysis of the energy flow in the food system illustrates features of the food system that are not easily deduced from the usual economic analysis. Despite some suggestions for lower-intensity food supply and some frankly speculative suggestions, it would be hard to conclude on a note of optimism. The world draw down in grain stocks which began in the mid-1960's continues, and some food shortages are likely all through the 1970's and early 1980's. Even if population control measures begin to limit world population, the rising tide of hungry people will be with us for some time.

Food is basically a net product of an ecosystem, however simplified. Food production starts with a natural material, however modified later. Injections of energy (and even brains) will carry us only so far. If the population cannot adjust its wants to the world in which it lives, there is little hope of solving the food problem for mankind. In that case the food shortage will solve our population problem.

REFERENCES AND NOTES

1. *Statistical Abstract of the United States* (Government Printing Office, Washington, D.C., various annual editions).
2. *Historical Statistics of the United States* (Government Printing Office, Washington, D.C., 1960).
3. D. Pimentel, L. E. Hurd, A. C. Bellotti, M. J. Forster, I. N. Oka, O. D. Scholes, R. J. Whitman, *Science* **182,** 443 (1973).
4. A description of the system may be found in: *Patterns of Energy Consumption in the United States* (report prepared for the Office of Science and Technology, Executive Office of the President, by Stanford Research Institute, Stanford, California, Jan. 1972), Appendix C. The three groupings larger than food processing are: primary metals, chemicals, and petroleum refining.
5. N. Georgescu-Roegen, *The Entropy Law and the Economic Process* (Harvard Univ. Press, Cambridge, 1971), p. 301.
6. *Patterns of Energy Consumption in the United States* (report prepared for the Office of Science and Technology, Executive Office of the President, by Stanford Research Institute, Stanford, Calif., Jan. 1972).
7. R. A. Rice, *Technol. Rev.* **75,** 32 (Jan. 1972).
8. Federal Highway Administration, Nationwide Personal Transportation Study Report No. 1 (1971) [as reported in Energy Research and Development, hearings before the Congressional Committee on Science and Astronautics, May, 1972, p. 151.]
9. M. Slesser, *Ecologist* **3** (No. 6), 216 (1973).
10. J. F. Gerber, personal communications (we are indebted to Dr. Gerber for pointing out that manures, even if used fully, will not provide all the needed agricultural fertilizers).
11. D. Chapman, *Environment (St. Louis)* **15** (No. 2), 12 (1973).
12. L. U. Mayer and S. H. Hargrove [*CAED Rep. No. 38* (1972)] as quoted in Slesser (9).
13. We have converted all figures for the use of electricity to fuel input values, using the average efficiency values for power plants given by C. M. Summers [*Sci. Am.* **224** (No. 3), 148 (1971)]. Self-generated electricity was converted to fuel inputs at an efficiency of 25 per cent after 1945 and 20 per cent before that year.
14. Purchased material in this analysis was converted to energy of manufacture according to the following values derived from the literature or calculated. In doubtful cases we have made what we believe to be conservative estimates: steel (including fabricated and castings), 1.7×10^7 kcal/ton (1.9×10^4 kcal/kg); aluminum (including castings and forgings), 6.0×10^7 kcal/ton; copper and brass (alloys, millings, castings, and forgings), 1.7×10^6 kcal/ton; paper, 5.5×10^6 kcal/ton; plastics, 1.25×10^6 kcal/ton; coal, 6.6×10^6 kcal/ton; oil and gasoline, 1.5×10^6 kcal/barrel (9.5×10^3 kcal/liter); natural gas, 0.26×10^3 kcal/cubic foot (9.2×10^3 kcal/m^3); petroleum wax, 2.2×10^6 kcal/ton; gasoline and diesel engines, 3.4×10^6 kcal/engine; electric motors over 1 horsepower, 45×10^3 kcal/motor; ammonia, 2.7×10^7 kcal/ton; ammonia compounds, 2.2×10^6 kcal/ton; sulfuric acid and sulfur, 3×10^6

kcal/ton; sodium carbonate, 4×10^6 kcal/ton; and other inorganic chemicals, 2.2×10^6 kcal/ton.

15. Direct fuel use on farms: Expenditures for petroleum and other fuels consumed on farms were obtained from *Statistical Abstracts* (1) and the *Census of Agriculture* (Bureau of the Census, Government Printing Office, Washington, D.C., various recent editions) data. A special survey of fuel use on farms in the 1964 *Census of Agriculture* was used for that year and to determine the mix of fuel products used. By comparing expenditures for fuel in 1964 with actual fuel use, the apparent unit price for this fuel mix was calculated. Using actual retail prices and price indices from *Statistical Abstracts* and the ratio of the actual prices paid to the retail prices in 1964, we derived the fuel quantities used in other years. Changes in the fuel mix used (primarily the recent trend toward more diesel tractors) may understate the energy in this category slightly in the years since 1964 and overstate it slightly in years before 1964. S. H. Schurr and B. C. Netschert [*Energy in the American Economy, 1850–1975* (Johns Hopkins Press, Baltimore, 1960), p. 774], for example, using different methods, estimate a figure 10 per cent less for 1955 than that given here. On the other hand, some retail fuel purchases appear to be omitted from all these data for all years. M. J. Perelman [*Environment (St. Louis)* **14** (No. 8), 10 (1972)] from different data, calculates 270×10^{12} kcal of energy usage for tractors alone.
16. Electricity use on farms: Data on monthly usage on farms were obtained from the "Report of the Administrator, Rural Electrification Administration" (U.S. Department of Agriculture, Government Printing Office, Washington, D.C., various annual editions). Totals were calculated from the annual farm usage multiplied by the number of farms multiplied by the fraction electrified. Some nonagricultural uses are included which may overstate the totals slightly for the years before 1955. Nevertheless, the totals are on the conservative side. A survey of on-farm electricity usage published by the Holt Investment Corporation, New York, 18 May 1973, reports values for per farm usage 30 to 40 per cent higher than those used here, suggesting that the totals may be much too small. The discrepancy is probably the result of the fact that the largest farm users are included in the business and commercial categories (and excluded from the U.S. Department of Agriculture tabulations used).
17. Fertilizer: Direct fuel use by fertilizer manufacturers was added to the energy required for the manufacture of raw materials purchased as inputs for fertilizer manufacture. There is allowance for the following: ammonia and related compounds, phosphatic compounds, phosphoric acid, muriate of potash, sulfuric acid, and sulfur. We made no allowance for other inputs (of which phosphate rock, potash, and "fillers" are the largest), packaging, or capital equipment. Source: *Census of Manufactures* (Government Printing Office, Washington, D.C., various recent editions).
18. Agricultural steel: Source, *Statistical Abstracts* for various years (1). Converted to energy values according to note (14).
19. Farm machinery (except tractors): Source, *Census of Manufactures*. Totals include direct energy use and the energy used in the manufacture of steel, aluminum, copper, brass, alloys, and engines converted according to note (14).
20. Tractors: numbers of new tractors were derived from *Statistical Abstracts* and the *Census of Agriculture* data. Direct data on energy and materials use for farm tractor manufacture was collected in the *Census of Manufactures* data for 1954 and 1947 (in later years these data were merged with other data). For 1954 and 1947 energy consumption was calculated in the same way as for farm machinery. For more recent years a figure of 2.65×10^6 kcal per tractor horsepower calculated as the energy of manufacture from 1954 data (the 1954 energy of tractor manufacture, 23.6×10^{12} kcal, divided by sales of 315,000 units divided by 28.7 average tractor horsepower in 1954). This figure was used to calculate energy use in tractor manufacture in more recent years to take some account of the continuing increase in tractor size and power. It probably slightly understates the energy in tractor manufacture in more recent years.
21. Irrigation energy: Values are derived from the acres irrigated from *Statistical Abstracts* for various years; converted to energy use at 10^6 kcal per acre irrigated. This is an intermediate value of two cited by Pimentel et al. (3).
22. Food processing industry: Source, *Census of Manufactures;* direct fuel inputs only. No account taken for raw materials other than agricultural products, except for those items (packaging and processing machinery) accounted for in separate categories.
23. Food processing machinery: Source, *Census of Manufactures* for various years. Items included are the same as for farm machinery [see note (13)].
24. Paper packaging: Source, *Census of Manufactures* for various years. In addition to direct energy use by the industry, energy values were calculated for purchased paper, plastics, and petroleum wax, according to note (14). Proportions of paper products having direct food usage were obtained from *Containers and Packaging* (U.S. Department of Commerce, Washington, D.C., various recent editions). [The values given include only proportional values from Standard Industrial Classifications 2651 (half), 2653 (half), 2654 (all).]
25. Glass containers: Source, *Census of Manufactures* for various years. Direct energy use and sodium carbonate [converted according to note (14)] were the only inputs considered. Proportions of containers assignable to food are from *Containers and Packaging*. Understatement of totals may be more than 20 per cent in this category.
26. Steel and aluminum cans: Source, *Census of Manu-*

factures for various years. Direct energy use and energy used in the manufacture of steel and aluminum inputs were included. The proportion of cans used for food has been nearly constant at 82 per cent of total production (*Containers and Packaging*).

27. Transportation fuel usage: Trucks only are included in the totals given. After subtracting trucks used solely for personal transport (all of which are small trucks), 45 per cent of all remaining trucks and 38 per cent of trucks larger than pickup and panel trucks were engaged in hauling food or agricultural products, or both, in 1967. These proportions were assumed to hold for earlier years as well. Comparison with ICC analyses of class I motor carrier cargos suggests that this is a reasonable assumption. The total fuel usage for trucks was apportioned according to these values. Direct calculations from average mileage per truck and average number of miles per gallon of gasoline produces agreement to within ± 10 per cent for 1967, 1963, and 1955. There is some possible duplication with the direct fuel use on farms, but it cannot be more than 20 per cent considering on-farm truck inventories. On the other hand, inclusion of transport by rail, water, air, and energy involved in the transport of fertilizer, machinery, packaging, and other inputs of transportation energy could raise these figures by 30 to 40 per cent if ICC commodity proportions apply to all transportation. Sources: *Census of Transportation* (Government Printing Office, Washington, D.C., 1963, 1967); *Statistical Abstracts* (1); *Freight Commodity Statistics of Class I Motor Carriers* (Interstate Commerce Commission, Government Printing Office, Washington, D.C., various annual editions).

28. Trucks and trailers: Using truck sales numbers and the proportions of trucks engaged in food and agriculture obtained in note (27) above, we calculated the energy values at 75×10^6 kcal per trucks for manufacturing and delivery energy [A. B. Makhijani and A. J. Lichtenberg, *Univ. Calif. Berkeley Mem. No. ERL-M310* (revised) (1971)]. The results were checked against the *Census of Manufactures* data for 1967, 1963, 1958, and 1939 by proportioning motor vehicles categories between automobiles and trucks. These checks suggest that our estimates are too small by a small amount. Trailer manufacture was estimated by the proportional dollar value to truck sales (7 per cent). Since a larger fraction of aluminum is used in trailers than in trucks, these energy amounts are also probably a little conservative. Automobiles and trucks used for personal transport in the food system are omitted. Totals here are probably significant, but we know of no way to estimate them at present. Sources: *Statistical Abstracts, Census of Manufactures*, and *Census of Transportation* for various years.

29. Commercial and home refrigeration and cooking: Data from 1960 through 1968 (1970 extrapolated) from *Patterns of Energy Consumption in the United States* (6). For earlier years sales and inventory in-use data for stoves and refrigerators were compiled by fuel and converted to energy from average annual use figures from the Edison Electric Institute [*Statistical Year Book* (Edison Electric Institute, New York, various annual editions] and American Gas Association values [*Gas Facts and Yearbook* (American Gas Association, Inc., Arlington, Virginia, various annual editions] for various years.

30. Refrigeration machinery: Source, *Census of Manufactures*. Direct energy use was included and also energy involved in the manufacture of steel, aluminum, copper, and brass. A few items produced under this SIC category for some years perhaps should be excluded for years prior to 1958, but other inputs, notably electric motors, compressors, and other purchased materials should be included.

31. There are many studies of energy budgets in primitive societies. See, for example, H. T. Odum [*Environment, Power, and Society* (Wiley, Interscience, New York, 1970)] and R. A. Rappaport [*Sci. Am.* **224** (No. 3), 104 (1971)]. The remaining values of energy subsidies in Fig. 4-5 were calculated from data presented by Slesser (9), Table 1.

32. This article is modified from C. E. Steinhart and J. S. Steinhart, *Energy: Sources, Use, and Role in Human Affairs* (Duxbury Press, North Scituate, Mass., 1974) (used with permission). Some of this research was supported by the U.S. Geological Survey, Department of the Interior, under grant No. 14-08–0001-G-63. Contribution 18 of the Marine Studies Center, University of Wisconsin—Madison. Since this article was completed, the analysis of energy use in the food system of E. Hirst has come to our attention [''Energy Use for Food in the United States,'' *ONRL—NSF-EP-57* (Oct. 1973)]. Using different methods, he assigns 12 per cent of total energy use to the food system for 1963. This compares with our result of about 13 per cent in 1964.

The Economics of the Energy Problem 5

HELMUT J. FRANK and JOHN J. SCHANZ, JR. 1977

INTRODUCTION

The fact that the United States at the present time consumes over 30 per cent of the world's total energy production has become a well-publicized bit of statistical information. It is probably somewhat less well known that 25 years ago the United States consumed an even higher percentage of the world's energy output and virtually all of it came from within our own borders. Throughout most of the twentieth century the United States has been a net exporter of energy, reflecting not only the quantity of the nation's energy resources, but also their quality. In the past, the American fuel producers were able to produce oil, coal, and natural gas at a relatively low cost compared to most other parts of the world and played a dominant role in world fuel prices and trade.

This long-standing historical pattern did not prepare the American public for the events that began to appear with increasing frequency in the 1970's:

—Electricity brown-outs.

—Gas utilities refusing to make new connections.

—Concern for the adequacy of heating oil supplies.

—Service station waiting lines and reduced speed limits, triggered by the 1973–1974 Middle East crisis.

—And factory and school closings for lack of natural gas in the winter of 1977.

The shortages themselves were alarming enough; but after rapid escalation, fuel prices remained high even after the immediate difficulties in deliveries seemed to ease.

The conventional wisdom growing out of these events is that the United States, while still possessing large quantities of fuel in the ground, particularly coal, may have lost the advantage it once had in the *cost* of finding and producing energy resources. The United States, as a highly industrialized and energy-intensive nation, is going to have to adjust to a

Dr. Helmut J. Frank is professor of economics at the University of Arizona, Tucson, Arizona 85721.

Dr. John J. Schanz, Jr. is a natural resources analyst with Resources for the Future, Washington, D.C. 20036.

From "The Economics of the Energy Problem," pp. 1–12, 1975 (*Economic Topic Series*). Reprinted with authors' revisions and light editing and by permission of the authors and the Joint Council on Economic Education. An accompanying teacher's guide and filmstrip for classroom use are available from the JCEE. This article was updated by the authors for this edition in April 1977.

whole new set of economic conditions. Solutions to economic and social problems that have been found in the past partly through the use of large quantities of cheap energy will no longer be available to us.

What appears to be a basic turning point in the history of American resource utilization offers a rich opportunity for us to apply the many concepts or perspectives of economics to dramatic events taking place in the real world of today. The people and government of the United States now face a series of critical choices in the face of scarcity—this is the essence of economics. Suddenly the daily news media are filled with economic terms—*demand* for gasoline, *supply* of Arab oil, or windfall *profits* for oil and gas companies. Congress is discussing the capture of *economic rents* through taxation, the *divorcement* of pipelines from *integrated* oil companies, the restoration of *marketplace competition*, or strategies to protect the consumer from an international oil *cartel*. *Market-clearing prices* and the *elasticity of demand for natural gas* are not quite household phrases, but they have a more familiar ring than in the past. Table 5-1 charts the rise in oil prices from 1960 through 1976.

We have also become aware of the fact that the energy situation is not a simple situation in which the mechanics of supply and demand will soon solve our problems. We are not dealing with the instantaneous responses and complete information assumed to exist in the classic marketplace of the economics textbook. The geologists can tell us something about the nature of our undiscovered and unrecovered energy resources, but not enough to provide an accurate picture of how much is left and how much it will cost. The engineer can inform us of new technologies available for producing some of the newer energy forms, like geothermal or solar energy, but not how much can be produced, how soon, and at what cost. The environmental scientist can warn of the health and ecological threats that producing and consuming energy involves but cannot set specific goals that balance these threats against the essential human needs for food, clothing, and shelter. The political scientist can describe the manner in which government functioned in the past but cannot tell us how we can, with any great degree of confidence, arrive at an energy policy and program implementation that will achieve the greatest public good.

Table 5-1. Changes in Oil Prices (Price of Saudi Arabian Light Crude, Dollars per Barrel).

1960–1970	$1.80
FEB. 1971	$2.18
JAN. 1973	$2.59
OCT. 1973	05.12
OCT. 1974	$10.46
OCT. 1975	$11.51
JAN. 1977	$12.09

This vista may appear discouraging. Nonetheless, it is the world of today; probably no more nor less frightening than the world of yesterday or tomorrow. Economics coupled with its companion social and physical sciences must try anew to focus as much light as possible into the dark corners of our difficulties. From this effort we may forge, not the perfect answer, but one that is perhaps a bit more rational and offers a greater chance of success than might have been possible otherwise.

ENERGY SUPPLY

Definition

Energy represents the ability to do work. This capability can be employed in many ways, and energy can be found in many forms. The potential of energy for work may be found chemically in carbon-bearing substances, such as food and the fossil fuels, or physically in the atomic structure of matter. Or it may depend upon its position, such as water located on a high plateau or behind a dam. These forms of *potential* energy can be transferred into *kinetic* energy when they are put into motion. Thus we have many kinds of flowing energy—light, sound, heat, and electricity. The various forms of energy provide us with a variety of ways to transmit energy from one place to another, to transform it from one form to another, and eventually to use it to accomplish work. In some cases, the energy flow itself is the manner in which the energy initially becomes available to us—as sunlight, tides, wind, or waterfall.

Until now, humans have relied most heavily on the advantages nature has provided in stored energy. But the volumes so stored are, of course, limited, and increasing usage is causing a decline in the quality as well as in the size of the remaining stock. A rise in the relative cost of energy can result from this condition.

How We Use Energy

How we intend to use energy is important in our choice of the form of energy we will try to obtain or how we might alter its form before final use. The uses of energy fall into three categories: work, comfort, or process. For the most part we have found that work is accomplished best by using compact, transportable petroleum liquids and gases or by converting the raw energy into efficient, flexible electricity. Thus we find that all modern, industrial societies have seen the demand for electricity, for light petroleum products and for gas gradually take on a dominant role in energy supply. This explains in part why we may convert energy for work from its original form to either electricity or to a liquid hydrocarbon, even though there may be a cost or an expenditure of energy in the process.

In the case of comfort uses, where energy warms or cools our bodies, we are less concerned about the physical form of the raw energy, since we convert it to circulating warm or cold air or liquids. We tend to be more concerned about the cost and convenience of the heating or cooling units themselves than the cost and form of the energy used.

The form of energy used for processing may or may not be critical. In this case, heat is used to bring about a physical or chemical change. If we are melting materials it may not be important what form the energy takes as long as it does the job at least cost. In some of the more delicate material-processing activities, however, such as in the glass industry, the purity and controllability of the combustion of the fuel is very important. In some cases, the energy is both a heat source and a part of a chemical reaction as in producing pig iron in the blast furnace. Here coke produced from coal is preferred. We could cook using kerosene, wood, or coal stoves, but obviously the cleanliness and controllability of gas or electricity are attractive to both the home and commercial energy user.

The combination of the form of the energy, the type of use, and the level of our technology has been the controlling factor in the particular energy supply that has been important in the various ages of human existence. Early cave dwellers obtained simple comfort and heat from an energy supply readily available and requiring little technology. Obviously fuel wood was an ideal solution to cave-dwelling society. Early industrial society, however, needed a more potent package of heat for stationary uses and for producing iron and steel. Coal filled the bill. A more mobile society with sophisticated processes and better controls turns quite naturally to oil, gas, and electricity.

As this progression of choices continues into the future it seems reasonable to expect that we will become less dependent upon the form in which nature provides our initial energy and more capable and desirous of converting it into any form that is more suitable to a particular end-use as well as more acceptable environmentally. As in the past, the future will be limited by our technology and what we can afford to expend in the way of human effort and physical resources.

Units of Measurement

Since energy comes in solids, petroleum liquids, gases and flows, we have to contend with a whole variety of units of measurement such as tons, barrels and cubic feet. In the United States, for measuring heat-producing capacity we customarily use the British thermal unit (BTU), which represents the quantity of heat required to raise the temperature of 1 pound of water 1°F. (The counterpart in metric system countries is the calorie. See Appendix for more detail.)

Mechanical power is usually defined in terms of horsepower, or the force required to lift 33,000 pounds 1 foot per minute. The preferred unit for electrical energy is the watt, which is 1/746 horsepower. The expenditure of force over a period of time is usually measured in kilowatt-hours or horsepower-hours.

Compared to the more familiar physical units of tons or barrels, BTUs and kilowatt-hours are hard to visualize. So it is quite common to convert statistically the various forms of energy into equivalent tons of coal or barrels of oil (42 gallons per barrel).*

Reserves and Resources

If we examine a map of the world in which those areas with known coal beds or sedimentary basins favorable for the accumulation of petroleum and natural gas are outlined, we find that the United States, both onshore and offshore, has a generous share of the earth's crust considered likely to hold deposits of fossil fuels. If we estimate the total fuel content of these vast volumes of rock, we arrive at numbers having impressive magnitudes compared to the amount of oil and gas we annually consume in the United States. From these kinds of calculations were derived such recent government agency resource estimates as 3 trillion tons of coal, 3 trillion barrels of oil, or 6 quadrillion cubic feet of natural gas.** These numbers are only estimates, but they seem to be very reassuring since they represent perhaps several hundred years of consumption of fossil fuels at present U.S. rates.

*The conversion factors commonly used for this purpose are 5.8 million BTU per barrel of oil, 1,031 BTU per cubic foot of gas, and 25 million BTU per ton of coal. There are 3,413 BTU per kilowatt-hour of electricity, but some analysts prefer to convert electricity to its coal equivalent on the basis of the pounds of coal required to produce 1 kilowatt-hour in a steam electric power plant. This approximately triples the fossil fuel equivalent represented by hydroelectric or nuclear power production.

**P. K. Theobald et al., *Energy Resources of the United States*. U.S. Geological Survey Circular 650 (1972), p. 1. Some economists question the size of these estimates, considering them to be exceptionally high.

Unfortunately, these numbers are estimated measurements of the U.S. *resource base*, or total endowment of the nation. They had not been tempered by estimates of the technical capability to find and produce the energy nor of the quality of energy. Much of the oil included in estimates of this type may never be found, and what *is* found may not be recoverable. At the present time, well over half the oil we discover is being left behind—clinging tenaciously to the grains of sand in the reservoir or flowing so slowly, and in such small quantities, that we cannot afford to bring it to the surface. So it must be recognized that any estimate of our petroleum resource base includes hundreds of billions of barrels of oil undiscovered, unrecoverable, or left behind in old fields.

At the other extreme, we see oil and gas reserve estimates that are much smaller, 39 billion barrels of oil or 228 trillion cubic feet of natural gas.* These numbers are measurements of the *proven reserves* of the United States and are only ten or eleven times current U.S. annual production. Proven reserves are our most conservative estimates and include only the recoverable portion of oil and gas that has actually been discovered and is producible from existing wells during their remaining lifetimes, ranging from a few more months to 50 years or more.

Obviously, the actual cumulative future production of oil and gas in the United States will fall somewhat between these two extremes. The proven reserves are the working inventory of the oil- and gas-producing industry. The process of further developing old fields and discovering new fields is a continuous one, which constantly through time adds to our proven reserves of oil and gas. In effect, we transfer barrels of oil and cubic feet of gas from a potential to a more certain classification.

* American Gas Association, American Petroleum Institute, Canadian Petroleum Association, *Reservgs of Crude Oil, Natural Gas Liquids, and Natural Gas in the United States and Canada and United States Productive Capacity as of December 31, 1975*, Volume 30 (May 1976), p. 1.

There are other dynamic features in the process of providing energy for the future. As our population increases and our economy expands, the amount of energy that constitutes an *adequate* quantity of proven reserves increases. At the same time, holding an inventory for future use is expensive. With capital costs at historic highs, business firms may want to keep investment in working inventories at a minimum. Finally, if the price of oil, gas, or coal falls or rises, the quantities that are recoverable from existing wells or mines with existing technology also diminish or expand.

Thus, the kind of ton of coal, barrel of oil, or cubic feet of gas that can qualify technically and economically as part of our proven or developed fuel reserve will change through time. The total of known reserves recoverable at present and those we can reasonably expect to discover and become recoverable through time represents the real domestic energy supply of the United States. How big a reserve might that be? One clue is that the United States, in 1970, passed its peak of oil production, and this peak may never be reached again, even with the contribution of the large new supply from the Alaskan North Slope. By now, we have attained an all-time cumulative production total of some 112 billion barrels. It may logically follow that the size of our remaining oil supply is approximately equivalent to that produced to date. Another approach, based on extensive geological studies and on statistical concepts, estimates the sum of reserves plus undiscovered recoverable oil resources to range between 112 billion and 189 billion barrels, with a mean of 144 billion barrels.* Whether or not we ultimately fall short of, fall within, or exceed this range of oil reserves in the United States depends upon future petroleum technology and price. More important, the cost at which other forms of energy—that is, natural gas, coal, shale oil, nuclear power, solar energy, and geothermal energy—can be made available will place an upper limit on how much we could or should pay for energy in the form of crude oil.

* Betty M. Miller et al., *Geological Estimates of Undiscovered Recoverable Oil and Gas Resources in the United States*, U.S. Geological Survey Circular 725 (1975), p. 4.

Energy Supply

Converting underground resources into usable supplies involves a complicated mixture of incentives, effort, skill, and just plain luck. Investors will not risk their money by financing the exploration and development of energy resources if they can get a greater return elsewhere at no greater risk. It is hard to say, in advance, precisely what incentives will be needed to convince investors to undertake energy resource development. The profit currently being earned by a company will not be an incentive, because this profit reflects past costs and successes, current prices, and other conditions. More important is the amount of earnings expected in the future from the new investments, possible future prices, and other factors. These expected earnings must also be compared with the returns that would be obtained from other investment opportunities in the energy industries and in other industries, both in the United States and abroad. Furthermore, expected returns in different investments must be measured against risks, as viewed by the investor. Moreover, prices, costs and earnings are all heavily affected by a wide range of governmental policies, including price controls, tax measures, public land policies, environmental regulations, controls over energy imports, and support of domestic operations.

The known world reserves and sources of energy that are not yet exploitable are quite impressive both in relation to past as well as current production. From this kind of information it is believed that the world has the potential to continue to supply itself with fossil fuels until it is technically and economically possible to shift to some of the other types of energy.

There are two immediate points to keep in mind: the world has become heavily dependent on petroleum and, in large part, the Middle East provides that petroleum. The United States, which produced approximately one-third of the world's oil in 1960, by 1976 provided only 14 per cent, whereas the nations of the Middle East supplied 38 per cent, as against 25 per cent in 1960.

This isn't hard to understand. Until late in 1973 the Middle East was an extremely attractive source of energy. The United States has about 600,000 wells and an average production of less than 20 barrels per day per well. The entire Middle East has only several hundred wells, but an average production up in the thousands of barrels per day. In Saudi Arabia, a single well may produce over 10,000 barrels per day.

As a consequence, after the initial investment is made in drilling equipment, transportation, and storage, the direct cost of producing a barrel of oil in the Middle East is only a few cents. To this "lifting" cost (as it is known in the industry) must be added the costs of the capital, transportation charges, and royalty and tax payments to the country where the oil is produced. Before the large increases in payments to the "host" governments, this meant that crude oil could be delivered on the East coast of the United States for $2 to $3 per barrel, and less in Europe. It is not too surprising that the world turned to the Middle East for energy. In recent years, however, the petroleum-exporting nations have been able to take advantage of their new position in world energy supply by rapidly escalating the payments they expected for their energy resources as well as gradually taking over ownership of the operations. Delivered crude oil prices, as a result, now are in the $13 to $14 per barrel range.

The world's energy consumers must now face the reality that the petroleum-exporting nations wish to: (a) exercise control over their own resources; (b) increase the returns from the production of those resources; (c) limit the levels of production to maintain the price levels; and (d) extend the useful lifetime of their nonrenewable resources. The proper implementation of these goals should lead to a maximum present value of their petroleum supplies. Consumers, as a result, are stimulated to turn their attention to those other forms of energy that have not been fully exploited. This is particularly attractive to the United States because of the magnitude of her energy holdings, particularly of coal and shale oil.

The world's remaining resource base of energy is very large relative to current levels of consumption. The bulk of these resources, however, is locked in solid material such as coal and oil shale. Our solid fossil fuels present us with an array of problems. First it is necessary to move large masses of solid rock to recover much of the fuel. This is unavoidably labor-intensive* and costly and leaves scars on the landscape. The solid fuels carry with them contaminants and noncombustible materials, which must be disposed of as solid waste (ash or spent rock) or discharged into the atmosphere. To do this in a fashion that minimizes the environmental damage is also costly. Second, as emphasized previously, we may find the physical form of the energy unattractive so we may go through the process of changing it from solid to liquid, liquid to gas, or chemical to electrical. Again costs are added, further increasing the price level at which gases and liquids made from coal, oil shale, or tar sands become "commercial." We have very little experience in the United States with large-scale production of these supplementary forms. Until we do, we cannot judge very precisely either their true cost or their environmental impact. Moreover, because of the requirements of large capital investments, approaching 1 billion dollars per plant, and the long construction periods required, these are not quick solutions to our need to escape our reliance on foreign oil supplies.

The nonchemical, more exotic forms of energy, are attractive on several counts. The total supply through time is large and we can avoid some environmental problems, e.g., using solar energy does not require the physical laceration of the earth's surface. But they are not without their own special impacts.

* That is, it requires a great deal of human labor as opposed to the type of production that can be carried out largely with capital equipment, such as machines.

Geothermal heat extracted from hot fluids that contain dissolved salts presents a disposal problem. There are other limiting factors. We sometimes overlook the fact that solar, geothermal, wind, tidal, and nuclear energy are all producers of electricity, which is currently less than 30 per cent of our total use of energy. For some uses, such as in our auto, truck, and plane transportation systems, or for certain kinds of processes, it is just not feasible to shift very quickly to electricity. In other cases, conversion is possible but will require time and large investments of labor, energy, and materials to convert such things as our extensive space-heating systems to greater use of electricity.

Perhaps an even greater limitation is the relatively primitive state of our technology in these areas. After 30 years of massive governmental effort, nuclear power is providing only 3 per cent of U.S. energy and is still harassed by problems of siting, safety, waste disposal, and threats to public health. Some of these may be more imaginary than real; others have still not been handled to our satisfaction. There are a number of geothermal plants, including one in California. France has a tidal power plant, and windmills have been producing electricity for many years. But these sources to date depend upon unique local circumstances; also we have limited capability to construct many installations. A nationwide network of large windpower towers is easy to imagine, but do we have the facilities to construct many towers in the near future without sacrificing our ability to meet some other national need?

Solar energy has become a favorite of the editorial writer and the concerned citizen. We have outfitted space stations with solar power, can manufacture solar equipment using thin silicon wafers, and know how to build a functioning solar home. But solar space and hot water heating can meet only a very small part of our total energy needs, whereas solar batteries and small power plants are still an extremely expensive source. We have never built a solar power plant that will occupy thousands of acres with its collector surfaces and heat transfer equipment.* Nor do we have an industry that builds solar power plants. In essence, solar power (except for a few specialized opportunities) is now in a position comparable to that of nuclear plants 25 years ago.

We have much to do, and *soon*, in examining these energy alternatives. But this involves a different order of research magnitude from that which enabled us to put a man on the moon. We can probably accelerate the development of the technology and the engineering needed for these newer energy forms. But time measured in decades will be needed to put enough of them into operation to be of any real significance.

Critical Issues

This paints a rather gloomy picture for the United States. The student of U.S. energy history might be inclined to note that the country has passed through energy shortages a number of times. In these past cases, after a few years of limited supplies and high fuel prices, the United States would find that oil, gas, and coal producers, spurred on by the unsatisfied demands and the resultant high prices, would scurry around and generate new supplies. In fact, more often than not, these shortages would be followed by long periods of abundant and extremely low-cost energy. It is reasonable to ask whether or not we are just in another one of these cyclical swings.

There is evidence that supply conditions could improve in the future. For example, some think that the shortage of natural gas is largely the result of very tough regulation of field prices. Relaxation of these controls might stimulate supply and induce consumers, especially those who use gas only because it has been underpriced, to shift to other forms of energy.

Whether corrections of such policies, alone, will reverse basic market conditions is doubtful. The lowest cost domestic oil and

* The first such plant will be built near Barstow in the California desert. Its capital costs will be some ten times those of conventional fossil-fuel or nuclear power plants.

gas reserves have probably been found; future discoveries will be in areas and strata where costs will be much greater. General inflation continues to increase the costs incurred by oil and gas producers and refiners.

Supplementary sources of oil and gas—whether from shale, coal, or Arctic oil fields—are all high in cost; in some cases much higher than the highest cost of conventional sources. Therefore, even if the amount demanded can be reduced because of conservation efforts and in response to higher prices, recurrence of significant surpluses is unlikely. Appropriate government policies call for coping with an indefinite period during which heavy dependence on imports of oil and, to some extent, gas appears unavoidable. But the political and security risks of relying too greatly on supplies from unstable sources may make such reliance unacceptable to the nation once alternatives become feasible. Imported fuel is no longer cheap; its cost is likely to stay relatively high. Development of a variety of domestic energy sources may be desirable for economic, as well as security, reasons. Prospects for expanded supplies of crude oil and natural gas are not too favorable; only a prevention of further declines or, at best, modest increases appear attainable even with much greater efforts. However, United States reserves of shale and coal are vast; by the late 1980's, these could begin to provide growing volumes of liquid and gaseous hydrocarbons. In the still more distant future, new technology may open up such sources as the breeder reactor, solar and geothermal power, and possibly, nuclear fusion. Meanwhile, our reliance must be placed on measures that promise quick results: greater direct use of coal, especially in electric power plants; emergency oil storage as protection against interruption of imports; and efforts to restrain increases in energy demand.

A critical question is by what means do we stimulate the necessary changes. Accelerated, broadened private research and development, supported by a wide range of appropriate government efforts, is one obvious avenue. Beyond that, the country must choose, according to its subjective value and political judgments, an appropriate mix of administrative actions concerning rules, regulations, prohibitions, subsidies, and taxes. But perhaps most important, we must decide when and how we will rely upon the pricing mechanism. Unless we decide to make some major alterations in our economy, price, despite its admitted shortcomings, is the most efficient mechanism to be employed if we wish to avoid government intervention every step of the way. If we do follow that route, we must let price show us how to make rational choices among our energy alternatives and environmental necessities. At this point in our history of energy supply, gradually rising prices appear to be the most effective way to deal with the current shortage of deliverable energy.

ENERGY DEMAND

In a recent report, the Joint Economic Committee of Congress termed energy "the ultimate raw material which permits the continued recycle of resources into most of man's requirements for food, clothing and shelter" and stated that "the productivity (and consumption) of society is directly related to the per capita energy available."

If there is indeed such a close relationship between energy consumption and economic well-being, then a growing scarcity of energy (whether caused by supply problems, environmental concerns, or faulty policies) could eventually endanger the material progress of American society, thereby, perhaps, denying large segments of society an opportunity to improve their economic circumstances.

To shed light on this critical issue, it is useful to examine current patterns of energy usage, historical trends, and projections of demand into the future. This highlights the role of economic forces in energy consumption and demonstrates the options open to policy-makers and the public in their efforts to cope with the long-term energy problem.

Table 5–2. 1976 U.S. Energy Consumption Mix (Quadrillion BTU).[a]

Fuel	*Residential and Commercial*	*Industrial*	*Transportation*	*Electric Generation*	*Miscellaneous Unaccounted*	*Total Consumption*
Coal	0.3	3.8	—	9.7	—	13.8
Oil	6.3	6.2	18.7	3.5	0.2	34.9
Gas	8.1	8.4	0.6	3.1	—	20.2
Hydro	—	0.03	—	3.0	—	3.0
Nuclear	—	—	—	2.0	—	2.0
Total Primary	14.7	18.4	19.3	21.3[a,b]	0.2	73.9
Electric Usage	4.1	2.8	0.02	14.4	—	14.4[a,b]
Total	18.8	21.2	19.3	6.9[a,b]	0.2	59.5

[a]Source: U.S. Department of the Interior, Bureau of Mines, News Release, March 14, 1977.
[b]Of the 21.3 primary energy input, 14.4 became generation losses and 6.9 were distributed to the use sectors.

Current Pattern of Energy Use

In 1976, the residential–commercial sector accounted for one-fifth of the direct consumption of primary energy (coal, oil, gas, and so forth) in the United States. Transportation and industrial usage required one-quarter each, and electricity generation accounted for the remainder, nearly 30 per cent (Table 5-2). The residential–commercial sector utilized large volumes of both oil and natural gas; industry met nearly half of its energy needs with gas but also utilized large quantities of oil and coal (about half for coking to make steel); transportation depended almost entirely on oil. Electricity is generated by hydroelectric plants, nuclear power reactors, and mostly, by burning fossil fuels (led by coal) in steam-power plants.

A more revealing pattern emerges if the electric power actually generated is distributed to the remaining sectors. Note that two-thirds of the energy is lost in conversion and distribution and must be deducted from the total. This recognizes that electric power is only an intermediate step in the transfer of the original form of energy from its source to its final use in the other sectors. Residential–commercial uses then represent about 31 per cent of the total end-use of energy, transportation 32 per cent, and industry 36 per cent.

A still more useful way of looking at energy consumption is by function served. Although our data are not complete nor as recent as we

Table 5–3. Estimated 1973 U.S. Energy-Use Pattern[a,b]

Use Area	*Percentage of National Use*	*Quadrillion BTU*
Transportation	25	17.6
Space heating	18	12.8
Process steam	16	11.5
Direct heat	11	7.7
Electric drive	8	5.4
Lighting	5	3.9
Water heating	4	2.9
Feedstocks	4	2.6
Air conditioning	3	2.2
Refrigeration	2	1.4
Cooking	1	0.7
Electrolytic processes	1	0.9
Other	2	1.7
Total	100	71.4

[a]Source: National Academy of Engineering, *U.S. Energy Prospects: An Engineering Viewpoint,* Washington, D.C., 1974, p. 26.
[b]Developed by extrapolating 1960–1968 relative trend data by use area and applying to total estimated energy consumption in 1973 (converted from million barrels oil-equivalent per day).

would like, they demonstrate rather clearly that large energy uses are very few (Table 5-3). Transportation accounts for 25 per cent of the total, space heating for 18 per cent, and three major industrial uses (process steam, direct heat, and electric drive) for another 35 per cent. Adding lighting (5 per cent) raises the total of these six categories to five-sixths (83 per cent) of all energy consumed. Clearly, any major efforts at energy conservation must be directed chiefly at these six sectors, or at making use of the two-thirds of the energy input now wasted in the process of making electricity.

Energy and Economic Growth

Between the end of World War II and the mid-1960's, U.S. energy consumption increased at a rate of about 3.5 per cent per year; energy usage doubled every 20 years. In the mid-1960's, the rate rose to 4.5 per cent, implying a doubling every 15 years.

The increases in energy consumption were much more rapid than the growth of population. For example, between 1960 and 1968, the U.S. population increased by 11 per cent, while energy consumption rose 38 per cent in the transportation sector, 45 per cent in the residential, and 52 per cent in the commercial. And, although the rates of increase in the rest of the world exceed those of the United States, this country, with but 6 per cent of the world's population and 6 per cent of the world's continental area, consumes a full one-third of the world's energy. Until very recently the energy consumed by the United States has been obtained from within the country's own borders. Most other advanced industrialized countries managed on a fraction of the 359 million BTU per capita we consumed in 1973—Europe with one-half or less, Japan with a mere one-quarter.

Historically, increases in energy consumption and increases in "real" income (and hence material well-being) are closely related. For many years, energy consumption in most industrial countries, including the United States, rose 0.8 to 0.9 per cent for every 1 per cent increase in "real" GNP.* The acceleration in energy growth after 1965 gives rise to questions regarding how rigid the relationship between the two may be. If there are factors that can cause energy consumption to grow more rapidly than GNP, perhaps there are also conditions under which appropriate policies could reverse the situation so that energy usage would grow more slowly without seriously hurting our economic well-being.

Close examination of trends since the mid-1960's is revealing. A portion of the accelerated growth in energy usage compared to our GNP was caused by more rapid increases in electricity use (such as air conditioning) which requires a larger input of BTUs per unit of final consumption. Other factors included greater utilization of inefficient plants and equipment, which increased conversion losses, and the initial impact of environmental controls, which tended to raise energy consumption in many instances (for example, in automobiles and power plants). All these factors together, however, explain only about one-half of the acceleration in energy growth. The clear implication is that another force was at work. The most likely candidate turns out to be the price of energy.

Energy prices in "real terms," i.e., relative to prices of other things, underwent a marked long-term decline until the sudden sharp increases in late 1973. Between 1951 and 1971, "real" coal prices fell 15 per cent, petroleum prices 17 per cent, and electricity rates no less than 43 per cent. Moreover, the decreases accelerated continuously during the period, as Table 5-4 indicates.

Admittedly, consumers have a limited capability of adapting to changing energy prices in the short run (months or a few years). The reason is that energy is really not a final

* GNP, the Gross National Product, is the nation's output of goods and services during a particular period of time (usually one year). GNP is usually expressed in terms of its money value, such as $1,384 billion in 1974. "Real" GNP refers to the actual output of goods and services without reference to current money value. or to the money value adjusted to account for price changes. Thus, if prices in 1974 had been the same as in 1958, the GNP for 1974 would have been about $827 billion.

Table 5-4. Index of Energy Prices, 1950–1973 (Annual Rates of Change)[a]

Period	*Yearly Change (percent)*
1950–55	−.62
1955–60	−.75
1960–65	−1.31
1965–70	−1.73
1970–mid-73[b]	−1.87

[a]Source: Edward J. Mitchell, *U.S. Energy Policy: A Primer*, Washington, D.C., American Enterprise Institute for Public Policy Research (1974), p. 82.
[b]Preliminary.

product but an intermediate good suitable for operating a piece of equipment, which provides the desired utility. We enjoy the mobility a car provides us, not the gasoline it burns. We value electricity because it makes our TV and air conditioner run, and we buy fuel oil or natural gas because they stoke the furnace that heats the house. Once we have invested in equipment or appliances, typically expensive items with a long life, we are pretty well locked into a given energy consumption level. So long as we use them, we could drive the car more or fewer miles, run the TV more or fewer hours, adjust the thermostat for more or less heating or cooling. But realistically the degree of discretion is rather limited unless we are willing to put the equipment "on ice" because fuel costs have risen. The price of fuel is only a . .small portion of the total cost of owning and using the item. Financial charges, depreciation, and maintenance and repair costs are more important. Letting energy prices be the primary determinant of our level of utilization would not make much sense.

It does, however, make a great deal of sense to consider energy consumption and costs when the time for deciding on a new car or home appliance is at hand. We find, then, that in the long run, i.e., beyond the life of existing energy-using equipment, the price of energy, relative to that of other things (especially capital), can make a substantial difference in energy growth. In addition, supplementary factors, such as better consumer knowledge and governmental regulation, can also have an effect. Therefore, the notion that there is some fixed amount of energy required to support a given level of economic activity is unacceptable to an economist. Professor Dale Jorgenson describes this as "engineering thinking," which equates the behavior of our economy with the functioning of physical mechanisms.

Energy and the Price Mechanism

Most economists consider price to be the best mechanism for allocating resources. This does not imply that the price system always provides socially ideal (or even politically acceptable) results; but because it leaves buyers and sellers free to make voluntary decisions, many feel that it increases the likelihood that we will approach the highest level of economic well-being. Alternative methods all involve a degree of governmental regulation, which requires one group of people to make judgments as to the preferences or needs of other individuals. Traditionally, most economists of the Western world have felt that this method is subject to abuse and may be less likely to achieve the optimal results that individuals would have reached through purely voluntary transactions.

Utilizing the price mechanism to allocate resources between energy and other inputs and among various energy forms does not require complete *laissez-faire* by any means. A strong case can be made for government to become involved in free market decisions in three important ways:

(1) Providing energy users and potential suppliers with information essential to reaching sound decisions.

(2) Modifying energy prices to include the damage that energy production and consumption inflict on the "free" social goods (air, water, space, etc.), which the market does not normally take into account unaided.

(3) Altering any socially unacceptable income distribution stemming from free market prices by redistribution measures (e.g., eas-

ing the burden of high gasoline prices on the poor through credits against their income taxes, or, if necessary, cash payments; or increasing the tax on large "windfall" profits made by owners of oil and gas lands.)

"How much would energy prices rise, relative to prices of other goods, if all restraints currently imposed were removed?" is a logical question at a time of limited deliveries of fuel. Good numerical answers are not available, in part because little research has been devoted in the past to such questions. But the "spot" market in coal and the intrastate market in gas give us some clues. When serious shortages became imminent, about 1972, this need was recognized. Large econometric models,* like the Project Independence Evaluation System (PIES) model of the Federal Energy Administration (FEA), and the Hudson–Jorgen model of Data Resource, Inc. (DRI) began grinding out results in 1974, but early results were necessarily tentative. (The FEA has now completed its third forecast, and model techniques have been substantially improved over the first effort.) The general impression is that price *elasticities* (the percentage decrease in the quantity bought in response to a 1 per cent increase in price, all other things being equal) are quite low in the short run. A doubling of the price may lead to only a 5 or 10 per cent reduction in consumption. With the passage of time, however, rising real energy rrices will reduce the long-term growth of energy use from the historical average of 3.4 per cent per year, without necessarily lowering the rate of economic growth significantly. Recent forecasts indicate that the annual growth rate of energy consumption will be in the range of 2.5 to 2.8 per cent, even if no further conservation measures are enacted. Stronger policies should permit additional savings, though it is difficult to anticipate just how large these may be.

To a considerable extent, the reduced energy growth rates represent a response to recent events, primarily sharply rising energy prices already in effect and those anticipated for the future. Compare, for example, the DRI projections, made for the Ford Foundation's Energy Policy Project published in 1974, with the most recent (1977) forecast by the FEA (Table 5-5). The DRI forecast for 1985 was 116 quadrillion BTU, 55 per cent above the 1973 level, assuming no changes in historical growth trends and energy policies. The FEA 1977 "Reference Case," which assumes no further policy changes or additional changes in real energy prices, projects 1985 consumption at 91 quadrillion BTU, only 21 per cent higher than in 1973. Some 4 quadrillion of the difference represent conservation measures already enacted, such as scheduled increases in automobile efficiency; most of the balance takes into account voluntary savings in energy use made since the crisis, plus additional ones expected to occur during the next several years. Significantly, the latest FEA forecast for 1985 is nearly 9 quadrillion BTU below that made only a year earlier, and projects a level of usage no higher than the Ford Foundation's "Technological Fix," which was based on an extensive list of conservation measures. The FEA further projects that 1985 energy consumption with accelerated conservation policies (presumably akin to those proposed by the Carter Administration) will be no higher than the Ford Foundation's "Zero Energy Growth," which would have entailed major changes in the life-style of the average American.

Where would these savings be made and what would they entail for energy users? Substantial reductions in energy use can be achieved merely by consumers being conscious of the fact that energy is a "scarce" commodity, i.e., that its cost is significant and likely to rise in the future. During the energy "crisis" induced by the Arab embargo, in the winter of 1973–1974, there was

* *Econometric models* combine economic theory with real-life economic events, and employ mathematical analysis in trying to measure relationships between or among such events. For example, an econometric model might be established to try to determine the relationship between rising energy prices and changes in energy use.

Table 5-5. U.S. Energy Consumption Projections under Alternative Assumptions (Quadrillion BTU).[a]

	1973	*1976*	*1985*	*2000*
Actual (i)	75	74		
Ford Foundation (ii)				
Historical growth			116	187
Technical fix			91	124
Zero energy growth			83	100
Federal Energy Administration (iii)				
Reference case			91	
Low Growth			83	
No conservation			95	
Accelerated conservation			88	

[a]Sources
i. U.S. Bureau of Mines.
ii. *A Time To Choose* (Ballinger, 1974).
iii. *1977 National Energy Outlook* (NEO-77) (based on preliminary draft).

a decline in energy use. People made fewer unnecessary car trips, lowered their thermostats, turned off unneeded lights, and used appliances less frequently. Many industries achieved savings of 10 to 15 per cent or more by improved maintenance, tracking down leaks in heating systems, and so forth. The federal government reduced its energy consumption by no less than 30 per cent in the first three months of 1974, compared to the first three months of 1973.

Most of these economies were one-shot affairs that cannot contribute much toward reducing the rate of energy growth in future years. To accomplish this, energy users must take rising relative energy costs into account when making decisions regarding replacements of cars, appliances, homes, machines, and plants. Higher gasoline prices will induce potential car buyers to consider models that are lighter and have smaller engines. Heating and cooling units vary widely in efficiency, and rising energy costs will tend to result in more careful purchase decisions. The same holds for many standard household appliances; for example, how many buyers of refrigerators weigh the convenience of frost-free units against a 50 per cent increase in energy usage? (The decision may still be in favor of higher energy consumption, but it should be a conscious, rational one.) Industrial users will tend to scrap old, energy inefficient equipment sooner and replace it with pieces having smaller energy needs, even if acquisition costs, and perhaps labor requirements, are somewhat greater.

Rising energy prices will tend to dampen the growth of energy consumption over time, but they require supplementary measures to be fully effective. Thus, sound energy decision-making can be greatly aided if consumers are provided with adequate, reliable information on energy needs of alternative models and sizes. The requirement that auto dealers post the average miles-per-gallon performance of each size and weight class, although far from perfect, is helpful. So is information on the efficiency (kilowatt or fuel consumption for a given output) of heating and cooling equipment and all types of household appliances. A full-fledged "Truth in Energy Law" would require builders of homes and apartments to provide potential purchasers with reliable data on monthly or annual energy operating costs (and thus induce sellers to compete in constructing energy-saving dwellings).

If the price is to be an effective allocator of energy supplies it must incorporate all costs of producing, transporting and consuming. Subsidies to particular energy producers, like the recently removed depletion allowance (and other special tax incentives for oil and gas producers) prevent market prices from reflecting the true cost of the resources used. (These tend to lower energy costs to consumers, but do not change oil and gas company profits.) Tax advantages for owners of private houses permit them to deduct from their adjusted gross incomes the interest they pay on mortgages and their property taxes, when determining their federal income tax. (People who own apartments through condominium or housing cooperative arrangements have similar advantages.) Unattached dwellings consume substantially more energy per unit of usable space than apartments. Thus, some feel that tax provisions that favor owners of unattached houses should be removed. Preferences given to highway transportation over rail transportation under current methods of financing might also be dropped. "Full cost pricing" requires that environmental damage caused by the strip-mining of coal, spillage from oil tankers, and the burning of hydrocarbons (to the extent that it is avoided by stack abatement or other devices) be fully reflected in the prices users will pay for energy.

An essential feature of correct energy pricing is that electric and gas rates be differentiated between peak and off-peak usage—so called "peak load pricing." This rests on the fact that peak energy users are responsible for the construction of additional plant capacity by the utility, whereas off-peak users are not. Also, facilities designed to supply additional volumes for short peak periods (like gas turbines or propane-air gasification units) are typically more energy intensive and costly to operate than base-load plants. Rate schedules should be designed to reflect at least some of these cost differentials, i.e., electricity rates in warm climates should be higher in summer, when air conditioners cause usage to soar, whereas natural gas rates should be higher during the heating season. Homeowners would then have an added incentive to install improved insulation, adjust thermostats, purchase efficient equipment, or take vacations during the hottest time of the year. It should be noted that this is a major change in utility marketing strategy, which in the past has sought to induce people to use more energy in the "valleys" rather than to use less energy during the "peaks."

Further refinements of the peak load concept would distinguish between daily peak and off-peak hours. This would provide housewives with incentives to run discretionary appliances (e.g., washers, dryers, or dishwashers) late in the evening or early in the day, rather than in mid- or late-afternoon when system peak loads typically occur. But much more elaborate and more costly metering would be required to bring about hourly peak load pricing. In addition, a shift from average to marginal costs (i.e., the cost of the last unit bought, which is generally above average cost) would tend to raise profits of utility companies above the generally accepted "fair return" on investment. Revised rate structures, an excess profits tax, or some other offsetting device would be needed to bring them down to what the public considers acceptable for the regulated monopoly sector.

Other Demand-modifying Measures

The slowing down of energy consumption growth in response to full-cost pricing does not mean that it will be easy to accomplish other overriding national objectives, such as limiting our dependence upon foreign energy sources or achieving environmental goals. For example, even a perfectly clean solar power plant in the desert would still take up space, and its transmission lines could block scenic views. There is increasing support for the view that energy growth should be held to a fraction of its historic rate—perhaps 2 per cent per year or even less. This would require that the market mechanism be supplemented by specific governmental actions designed to effect additional energy savings.

The Ford Foundation's "Technical Fix" growth option would imply an annual average increase of 1.7 per cent, about one-half the historical rate. By the year 2000, energy consumption would be 35 per cent below what it would be if we followed the historical growth pattern. This could be accomplished under certain conditions without reducing our economic well-being, and without significant changes in life-style. It would, however, require such measures as greater reliance on smaller, more efficient cars; increased load factors for aircraft; shifts of intercity freight hauls from trucks to rail; more efficient production of steam in industry; greater recycling of metals; improved building design; and use of energy-saving heating and cooling systems (heat pumps and solar heating/cooling). The price mechanism would still play a key role in fostering these changes, but it would have to be supplemented by government-supported research and development, changes in taxation, and some new forms of regulation (e.g., stricter building codes).

The Ford Foundation's "Zero Energy Growth" option would reduce the average energy growth rate somewhat more sharply during the next 25 years to 1.2 per cent; but more important, the rate of growth would be stable by the end of the century. This, too, would not mean that *economic* growth would have to cease. Average real income per capita would be greater than today and no group would be condemned to remaining in poverty for lack of energy. But a significant change in life-style would be required. Cities and transportation systems would have to be redesigned to stress energy conservation; energy-intensive products (like plastics) would be deemphasized; services (e.g., health and education) would grow in relative importance, while the supply of material goods would shrink. None of this could happen overnight; in fact, the ZEG path could begin to diverge significantly from the Technical Fix pattern only after 1985. Long-term planning would be necessary; wide public support essential; and further regulation required, as well as shifts in taxation and government subsidies. The purpose of these exercises is not to predict the future but to demonstrate that we do have choices available to us for the future if we act promptly.

POLICY ISSUES

In determining energy policy, we must be fully aware of the economic forces at work. The effects of changes in energy costs and availability are felt by every homeowner, driver, employer, and worker. The firms supplying energy are typically among the giants of American industry (although many small ones also participate), and their behavior and performance are constantly in the limelight. And because the United States imports large amounts of oil and many American firms have large-scale operations outside the country, energy policy critically affects our relations with the rest of the world. Energy is truly a subject where economics and politics are intertwined—a prime case of political economy.

Any brief survey can touch on only a few of the issues falling under the heading of "energy policy," and it can do no more than skim the surface of these. One way to gain insight into the complex web of energy policy questions is to ask which group carries what degree of responsibility for the "energy problem" with which we are currently confronted—industry, environmentalists, consumers, or government. All are being charged with having contributed in various ways to aggravating, if not bringing on, the current shortages.

Oil Industry

The charges against the energy suppliers (primarily the large integrated oil companies) are many. The critical one is that the "energy crisis" was deliberately caused by them, by holding back supplies so as to force the public to accept higher prices. Once accomplished, supplies would be permitted by the companies to become ample again, industry profits would skyrocket, and the public would grumble but have no choice but to accept the outcome.

There is enough plausibility to this accusation to give it widespread appeal. During the 1973–1974 energy crisis, oil company profits soared—and acute shortages soon gave way to much easier supply conditions. But the prudent energy analyst must consider the counterarguments:

The structure of the oil industry can be

described as *oligopolistic*,* reflecting the importance of a number of large companies. The four largest companies in 1973 held 31 per cent of crude production and 33 per cent of refinery output compared to an average market share of the four largest firms for all U.S. manufacturing (in 1966) of 39 per cent.

There is no evidence that new entry into the oil industry was blocked artificially, a situation that can gradually stifle innovation and competition. For example, in 1972, there were 31 refineries with a capacity of 50,000 barrels per day or more, compared with 20 in 1951. Nine of the 31 were not in the refining business in 1950.

Some of the oil companies are industrial giants with multi-billion dollar assets and annual sales. Most are also highly integrated vertically, operating from the well to the gas pump. But energy is a large, capital-intensive business.** There are sound business reasons why most raw materials firms find it advantageous to intergrate in this fashion. But, we expect the giants to compete among themselves and with the smaller "independents" who remain a part of the industry. If they do not, then we must question how well the Antitrust Division of the Department of Justice and the Federal Trade Commission are doing their job.

Oil company profits did soar, but they started from a point well below the average of American industry and were only slightly above it after prices increased. Most of the increase stemmed from such temporary factors as profits from inventory valuation and exchange rates, which are "once-and-done" gains.

Supply conditions have improved since 1974, not because U.S. production was increased by the companies (it can't be, in the short run) but because less is consumed at the higher prices, and the normal flow of oil from the Arab states was restored—in fact, it sharply increased.

It is apparent that the oil industry did not develop domestic energy resources adequate to the demands of the American economy. But the reasons may lie chiefly with the failure of policy-makers to create the necessary economic climate and to make firm policy commitments. No "conspiracy theory" is needed to explain the energy shortage, only a recognition that in the face of uncertainty about future political conditions, or lack of access to resources, even the largest of our industries may be unable to make decisions or act positively. Moreover, when they do act, it is expected that their decisions must reflect the interests of their stockholders.

Environmentalists

The charge against environmental groups is that they are opposed to just about every proposal to expand energy supplies: offshore drilling for oil and gas; construction of the Alaska pipeline; development of new oil refineries and superports; strip-mining of coal; approval of nuclear power plants; emissions of fossil-fueled plants; and so on.

The cumulative weight of the circumstantial evidence is certainly formidable, and there are no doubt extremists who have attempted, and will continue to attempt, to block every energy-related project, in an effort to stop economic growth which they consider undesirable per se. On closer examination, though, the charges turn out to be exaggerated in terms of actual quantitative impact. Offshore leasing could have proceeded more rapidly in areas where the danger of spillage is less than in the Santa Barbara Channel or the Gulf of Alaska; refineries could have been built in Louisiana and Mississippi if not New Hampshire or Delaware; the Alaska pipeline could have been started

* An *oligopoly* is an industry dominated by a few large firms; a monopoly exists when there is only one firm selling a product or service. Oligopoly is often measured by the *ratio of concentration*—the percentage of sales (or output) accounted for by the four largest firms in the industry. During one recent year the four largest firms in the tire and tube industry accounted for 70 per cent of the sales.

**A capital-intensive business is one in which relatively large amounts of capital equipment (machinery, tools, and plants) are used in relation to businesses in which labor is relatively more important. For example, in petroleum refining and pipeline transportation, the value of capital invested per production worker is about twenty-five times as great as it is in the apparel industry.

once the need for appropriate environmental safeguards (like preventing permafrost damage) was recognized by industry and implemented. The causes of delays are more complex than merely environmental concerns. Moreover, environmental damage has been largely ignored for much too long, and greater efforts to minimize this through charging the resulting social costs to energy users have been long overdue. Rational ecological concern need not block energy development unduly, but can and should be reflected in the planning and costing of energy projects from the start.

Energy Consumers

Americans have been called ''energy gluttons'' who drive overweight cars at excessive speeds, live in overheated (or overcooled), underinsulated houses, and use inefficient manufacturing processes. The charge is true, from what we consider to be the ''engineering'' point of view, in that we have not been motivated to be physcially efficient in our use of energy. But it is false if it is meant to imply that consumers have been ''wasting'' resources in the economic sense. With energy prices low and falling over long periods, consumers acted perfectly rationally and in accord with expected economic behavior by substituting energy for other inputs, such as saving time and labor at the expense of using energy. Europeans drive smaller cars and insulate their houses better than Americans, not necessarily because they are naturally more prudent than Americans, but because energy costs are higher relative to the cost of other things. If U.S. energy prices continue rising, Americans should be expected to become increasingly ''European'' in conserving energy.

Government Policies

Prior to the energy crisis and the establishment of a Federal Energy Adminsitration there were over 70 federal agencies concerned with various aspects of energy policy. Their responsibilities ranged from energy development (Interior Department and Atomic Energy Commission) to import restriction (Oil Import Administration) to regulating prices (Federal Power Commission). With so many agencies oriented toward different objectives, and serving the interests of different groups of ''clients,'' it is not surprising that their efforts frequently clashed. Examples abound, but two will suffice:

Special tax advantages designed to encourage exploration and development have been enjoyed by oil and gas producers for many years. Yet price controls on natural gas since 1954 and on oil since 1971 have tended to discourage investment in exploration and development.

Mandatory oil import controls were enacted in 1959 to stem the inflow of low-cost foreign supplies. But these controls and other government price and resource policies did not seem to create enough incentive for an adequate development of domestic supplies.

One would hope that the realization that energy will never again be cheap will bring in its wake not only a short-term effort to deal with acute crises after they have broken out, but a long-range program with policies and implementing machinery designed to achieve reasonable goals that deserve wide public support. One set of criteria is contained in the report of the Ford Foundation:

(1) Assuring reliability of energy supply.

(2) Achieving the lowest cost to society for energy.

(3) Avoiding economic and regional inequities.

(4) Safeguarding the quality of the environment.

(5) Minimizing international problems due to energy.

In the opinion of the authors the study of economic aspects of energy contributes this important lesson: Energy policy should rely primarily on market forces to provide incentives to suppliers and signals of real costs to consumers. Market forces require supplemental action in areas in which they cannot operate, such as environment and national defense. Society may also wish to modify the resulting income distribution but should do so by income transfers, not interference with price mechanism. Perhaps most important of all, any policy requires a well-informed and enlightened public and open, candid decisions by industry and government if it is to have more success in the future than it has to date.

A CHALLENGE

The study of energy economics and energy policy provides an experience that is at once frustrating and rewarding. It is frustrating because the energy-related problems the United States as a country and the American people as a society face are complex—the choices are few and hard ones and consensus will be difficult to attain. And, whatever course is selected, progress will be slow and the cost high.

On the other hand, the rewards from considering energy questions in some depth are many: gaining an understanding of economic concepts in action (the role of choice, cost, demand and supply elasticities, prices, and profits are a few); the interplay of economic and political forces; the key importance of social and institutional constraints on economic policy; the interdependence of the United States with the rest of the world; and the close linkage between resource development, economic growth, and the preservation of a healthy environment. The authors hope that this introduction to our national energy problem will stimulate the reader to study topics such as these, which are among the most challenging facing this and future generations of Americans.

SUGGESTED READINGS

American Academy of Political and Social Science, 1973, The Energy Crisis: Reality or Myth, *The Annals*, November.

Edison Electric Institute, 1976, *Economic Growth in the Future, the Growth Debate in National and Global Perspective* (McGraw-Hill).

Energy Policy Project for the Ford Foundation, 1974, *A Time to Choose: America's Energy Future* (Ballinger).

Energy Research and Development Administration, 1975, A National Plan for Energy Research, Development and Demonstration: Creating Energy Choices for the Future, ERDA-48, Vol. 1, U.S. Government Printing Office.

Eppen, Gary D, ed., 1975, *Energy: The Policy Issues* (University of Chicago Press).

Exxon Company, 1977, *U.S.A.'s Energy Outlook, 1977–1990*, January.

Federal Energy Administration, 1977, *1977 National Energy Outlook,* U.S. Government Printing Office.

Fisher, John C., 1974, *Energy Crises in Perspective* (John Wiley).

Grayson, Leslie E., ed., 1975, *Economics of Energy: Readings on Environment, Resources, and Markets* (Darwin).

Hollander, Jack M., and Simmons, Melvin K., ed., 1976, *Annual Review of Energy*, Vol. 1 (Annual Reviews, Inc.).

Huettner, David A., 1976, Net Energy Analysis: An Economic Assessment, *Science 192*, pp. 101–104.

Institute for Comtemporary Studies, 1975, *No Time to Confuse, A Critique of the Final Report of the Energy Policy Project of the Ford Foundation* (Institute for Contemporary Studies).

Mancke, Richard B., 1977, *Providing for Energy, Report of the Twentieth Century Fund Task Force on United States Energy Policy* (McGraw-Hill).

Mitchell, Edward J., 1974, *U.S. Energy Policy: A Primer*, National Energy Project (American Enterprise Institute, Washington, D.C.), June.

National Academy of Engineering, 1974, *U.S. Energy Prospects: An Engineering Viewpoint*, a report prepared by the Task Force on Energy.

Organization for Economic Co-operation and Development, 1977, *World Energy Outlook*.

Schurr, Sam H., ed., 1972, *Energy, Economic Growth, and the Environment* (Johns Hopkins Press for Resources for the Future, Baltimore).

———, 1974, *Science* (Energy Issue) *184,* April 19.

Stanford Research Institute, 1972, *Patterns of Energy Consumption in the United States*, Office of Science and Technology, Executive Office of the President, January.

Steinhart, Carol, and Steinhart, John, 1974, *Energy Sources, Uses, and Role in Human Affairs* (Duxbury Press, N. Scituate, Mass.).

U.S. Congress, Joint Economic Committee, 1973, *The Energy Outlook for the 1980's* (W. N. Peach), December 17, 1973.

U.S. Department of the Interior, 1975, *United States Energy through the Year 2000*, revised December.

The National Energy Plan—Overview and Summary 6

EXECUTIVE OFFICE OF THE PRESIDENT 1977

OVERVIEW

The diagnosis of the U.S. energy crisis is quite simple: demand for energy is increasing, while supplies of oil and natural gas are diminishing. Unless the United States makes a timely adjustment before world oil becomes very scarce and very expensive in the 1980's, the nation's economic security and the American way of life will be gravely endangered. The steps the United States must take now are small compared to the drastic measures that will be needed if the United States does nothing until it is too late.

How did this crisis come about?

Partly it came about through lack of foresight. Americans have become accustomed to abundant, cheap energy. During the decades of the 1950's and 1960's, the real price of energy in the United States fell 28 per cent. And from 1950 until the quadrupling of world oil prices in 1973–1974, U.S. consumption of energy increased at an average annual rate of 3.5 per cent. As a result of the availability of cheap energy, the United States developed a stock of capital goods—such as homes, cars, and factory equipment—that uses energy inefficiently. (See Figure 6-1.)

The Nature of the Problem

The most critical increase in demand has been for oil, the most versatile and widely used energy resource. To meet that growing demand, the United States has turned increasingly to imports. In January and February of 1977, the United States imported about 9 million barrels of oil per day, half of total domestic oil consumption. By 1985, U.S. oil consumption could equal 12 to 16 million barrels per day.

United States domestic oil production has been declining since 1970. New production from Alaska, the deep Outer Continental Shelf, and new recovery methods should reverse the decline, but will be unable to satisfy the projected growth in U.S. demand. Other major additions to domestic oil supply are unlikely.

The principal oil-exporting countries will not be able to satisfy all the increases in demand expected to occur in the United States and other countries throughout the 1980's. In 1976, the 13 OPEC countries exported 29 million barrels of oil per day. If world demand continues to grow at the rates of recent years, by 1985 it could reach or exceed 50 million

This article includes the "Overview" and "Summary" sections of *The National Energy Plan,* a 100-page document issued by the White House. This document describes the Carter Administration's energy proposal presented April 20, 1977, and is available from the U.S. Government Printing Office.

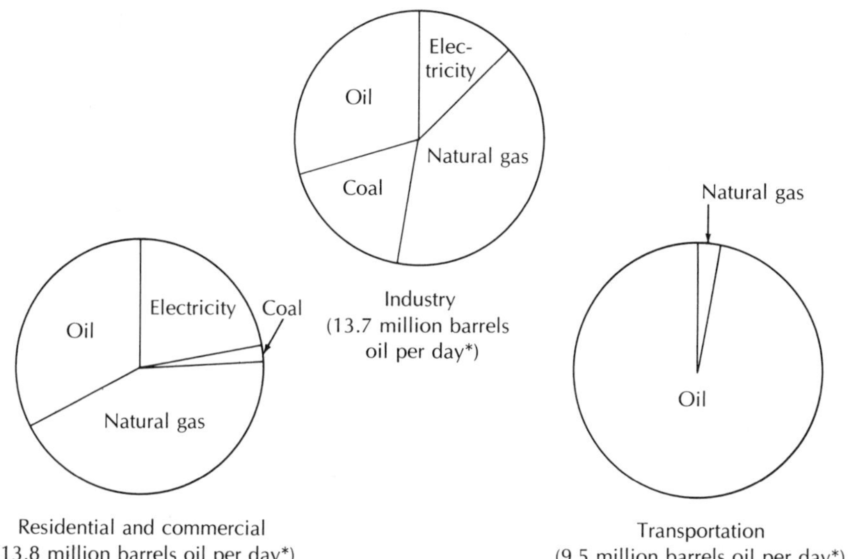

Figure 6-1. United States energy consumption by sector, 1976. (Source: Federal Energy Administration.)

barrels per day. However, many OPEC countries cannot significantly expand production; and, in some, production will actually decline. Thus, as a practical matter, over-all OPEC production could approach the expected level of world demand only if Saudi Arabia greatly increased its oil production. Even if Saudi Arabia did so, the highest levels of OPEC production probably would be inadequate to meet increasing world demand beyond the late 1980's or early 1990's.

There are physical and economic limits on the world's supply of oil. A widely used geological estimate of total recoverable world oil resources, past and present, is about 2 trillion barrels. More than 360 billion barrels have already been consumed. Current proved crude reserves are 600 billion barrels. World consumption of oil has grown at an average annual rate of 6.6 per cent since 1940, and it grew by as much as 8 per cent annually during the 1960's. (See Figure 6-2.)

If it could be assumed that world demand for oil would grow at an annual rate of only 3 per cent, and if it were possible (which it is not) that production would keep pace with that rate of growth, the world's presently estimated recoverable oil resources would be exhausted before 2020. At a conjectural growth rate of 5 per cent, those resources would be exhausted by 2010. Despite some uncertainty about the exact size of recoverable world oil resources, and about the rate of increase of productive capacity, this fundamental fact is clear: *within about four generations, the bulk of the world's supply of oil, created over hundreds of millions of years, will have been substantially consumed.*

Of course, actual physical exhaustion of oil resources will not occur. Even today, well over half the oil in existing fields is being left in the ground because additional recovery would be too expensive. As production by conventional methods declines and oil becomes more scarce, its price will rise and more expensive recovery methods and novel

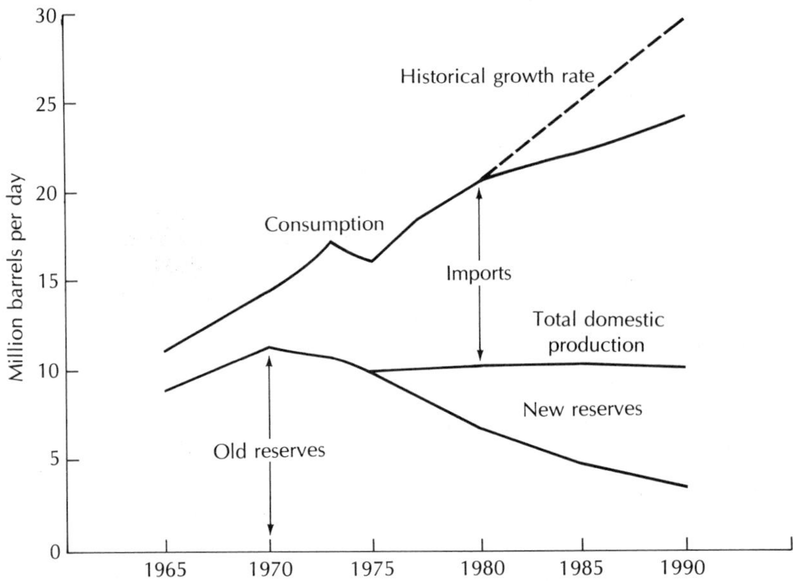

Figure 6-2. United States oil consumption, including natural gas liquids, without the National Energy Plan. (Source: U.S. Bureau of Mines and Federal Energy Administration.)

technologies will be used to produce additional oil. As this process continues, the price of oil will become prohibitive for most energy uses. Eventually the nations of the world will have to seek substitutes for oil as an energy source, and oil will have to be reserved for petrochemical and other uses in which it has maximum value.

The world now consumes about 20 billion barrels of oil per year. To maintain even that rate of consumption and keep reserves intact, *the world would have to discover another Kuwait or Iran roughly every three years, or another Texas or Alaska roughly every six months*. Although some large discoveries will be made, a continuous series of such finds is unlikely. Indeed, recent experience suggests that, compared to world oil consumption, future discoveries will be small or moderate in size, will occur in frontier areas, and will yield oil only at very high cost. Obviously, continued *high rates of growth* of oil consumption simply cannot be sustained.

Natural gas supplies are also limited. In the United States, natural gas constitutes only 4 per cent of conventional energy reserves, but supplies 27 per cent of energy consumption. Gas consumption grew about 5.7 per cent per year between 1960 and 1970. From 1970 to 1974, however, consumption dropped 1.3 per cent. (See Figure 6-3.) The demand for gas is considerably higher than the amount that can be supplied. Hence, gas is rationed by prohibitions on hook-ups for new homes in many areas.

Gas is not only in short supply, but its allocation across the country is distorted, and its distribution among end-uses is unsatisfactory. Federal regulation of the wellhead price of natural gas in interstate commerce has discouraged its distribution from gas producing states to other states and has encouraged consumption of this premium fuel for less essential uses. Industry and utilities currently consume almost 60 per cent of U.S. natural gas, despite the fact that other fuels could be used in a majority of cases.

During the 1973–1975 period, only 19 per cent of new gas reserve additions were made available to the interstate market, and much of

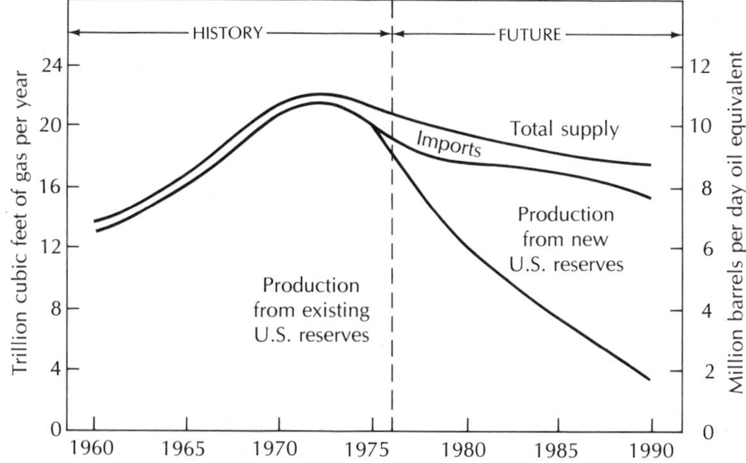

Figure 6-3. United States gas supply. The effect of the National Energy Plan is not included. (Source: Federal Energy Administration.)

that gas was from the Federal domain. Since the price of intrastate gas is not regulated, there are strong economic incentives to sell gas within the producing states. *The existing distinction between intrastate and interstate sales has given intrastate users first claim to natural gas.*

Strategies and Objectives

The United States has three overriding energy objectives:

—As an immediate objective that will become even more important in the future, to reduce dependence on foreign oil and vulnerability to supply interruptions.

—In the medium term, to keep U.S. imports sufficiently low to weather the period when world oil production approaches its capacity limitation.

—In the long term, to have renewable and essentially inexhaustible sources of energy for sustained economic growth.

The United States and the world are at the early stage of an energy transition. Previous energy transitions in the United States were stimulated by new technologies, such as the development of the railroad and the mass production of automobiles, which fostered the use of coal and oil, respectively. The latest transition springs from the need to adjust to scarcity and higher prices.

To make the new transition, the United States should adhere to basic principles that establish a sound context for energy policy and provide its main guidelines. The energy crisis must be addressed comprehensively by the Government and by a public that understands its seriousness and is willing to make necessary sacrifices. Economic growth with high levels of employment and production must be maintained. National policies for the protection of the environment must be continued. Above all, the United States must solve its energy problems in a manner that is fair to all regions, sectors, and income groups.

The salient features of the National Energy Plan are:

—Conservation and fuel efficiency.

—Rational pricing and production policies.

—Reasonable certainty and stability in Government policies.

—Substitution of abundant energy resources for those in short supply.

—Development of nonconventional technologies for the future.

Conservation and fuel efficiency are the cornerstone of the proposed National Energy Plan. Conservation is cheaper than production of new supplies, and is the most effective means for protection of the environment. It can contribute to international stability by moderating the growing pressure on world oil resources. Conservation and improved efficiency can lead to quick results. For example, a significant percentage of poorly insulated homes in the United States could be brought up to strict fuel-efficiency standards in less time than it now takes to design, build, and license one nuclear power plant.

Although conservation measures are inexpensive and clean compared with energy production and use, they do sometimes involve sacrifice and are not always easy to implement. If automobiles are to be made lighter and less powerful, the American people must accept sacrifices in comfort and horsepower. If industry is required to make energy-saving investments and to pay taxes for the use of scarce resources, there will be some increases in the cost of consumer products. These sacrifices, however, need not result in major changes in the American way of life or in reduced standards of living. Automobile fuel efficiency can be greatly improved through better design and use of materials, as well as by producing lighter and less powerful cars, without inhibiting Americans' ability to travel. With improved energy efficiency, the impact of rising energy prices can be significantly moderated.

Energy conservation, properly implemented, is fully compatible with economic growth, the development of new industries, and the creation of new jobs for American workers. Energy consumption need not be reduced in absolute terms; what is necessary is a slowing down in its rate of growth. (See Figure 6-4.) By making adjustments in energy consumption now, the United States can avoid a possibly severe economic recession in the mid 1980s.

The United States has a clear choice. If a conservation program begins now, it can be carried out in a rational and orderly manner over a period of years. It can be moderate in scope, and can apply primarily to capital goods, such as homes and automobiles. If, however, conservation is delayed until world

Figure 6-4. A lower growth rate can make a large difference in energy requirements. (Source: U.S. Bureau of Mines.)

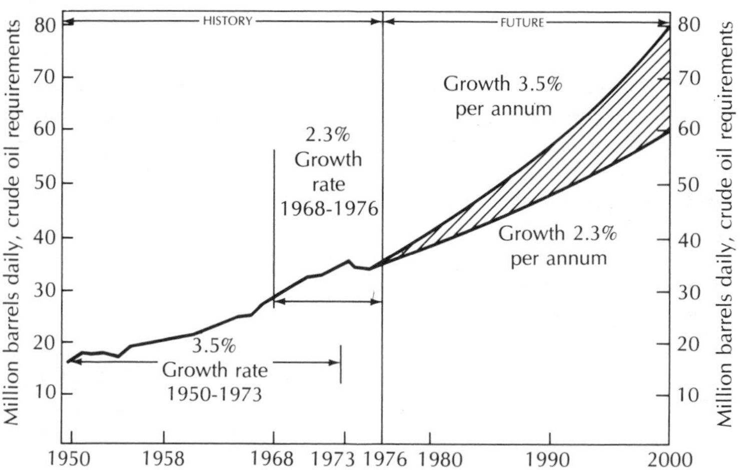

oil production approaches its capacity limitation, it will have to be carried out hastily under emergency conditions.

It will be sudden, and drastic in scope; and because there will not be time to wait for incremental changes in capital stock, conservation measures will have to cut much more deeply into patterns of behavior, disrupt the flow of goods and services, and reduce standards of living.

Pricing policies should encourage proper responses in both the consumption and the production of energy, without creating any windfall profits. *If users pay yesterday's prices for tomorrow's energy, U.S. resources will be rapidly exhausted. If producers were to receive tomorrow's prices for yesterday's discoveries, there would be an inequitable transfer of income from the American people to the producers, whose profits would be excessive and would bear little relation to actual economic contribution.*

Currently, federal pricing policy encourages overconsumption of the scarcest fuels by artificially holding down prices. If, for example, the cost of expensive foreign oil is averaged with cheaper domestic oil, consumers overuse oil, and oil imports are subsidized and encouraged. Consumers are thus misled into believing that they can continue to obtain additional quantities of oil at less than its replacement cost.

Artificially low prices for some energy sources also distort interfuel competion. The artificially low price of natural gas, for example, has encouraged its use by industry and electric utilities, which could use coal, and in many areas has made gas unavailable for new households, which could make better use of its premium qualities.

These misguided Government policies must be changed. But neither Government policy nor market incentives can improve on nature and create additional oil or gas in the ground. From a long-term perspective, prices are an important influence on production and use. As long as energy consumers are misled into believing they can obtain energy cheaply, they will consume energy at a rate the United States cannot afford to sustain. Their continued overuse will make the nation's inevitable transition more drastic and difficult.

A national energy policy should encourage production. The energy industries need adequate incentives to develop *new* resources and are entitled to sufficient profits for exploration for *new* discoveries. But they should not be allowed to reap large windfall profits as a result of circumstances unrelated to the marketplace or their risk-taking.

The fourfold increase in world oil prices in 1973–1974 and the policies of the oil-exporting countries should not be permitted to create unjustified profits for domestic producers at consumer's expense. By raising the world price of oil, the oil-exporting countries have increased the value of American oil in existing wells. That increase in value has not resulted from free market forces or from any risk-taking by U.S. producers. *National energy policy should capture the increase in oil value for the American people.* The distribution of the proceeds of higher prices among domestic producers and consumers must be equitable and economically efficient if the United States is to spread the cost fairly across the population and achieve its energy goals.

The pricing of oil and natural gas should reflect the economic fact that the true value of a depleting resource is the cost of replacing it. An effective pricing system would provide the price incentives that producers of oil and natural gas need by focusing on harder to find new supplies. The system should also moderate the adjustment that households will have to make to rising fuel costs. It should end the distortions of the intrastate–interstate distinction for new natural gas, which is a national resource. It should also promote conservation by raising the ultimate price of products made by energy-intensive processes.

Reasonable certainty and stability in Government policies are needed to enable consumers and producers of energy to make investment decisions. A comprehensive national energy plan should resolve a wide range of uncertainties that have impeded the orderly development of energy policy and projects.

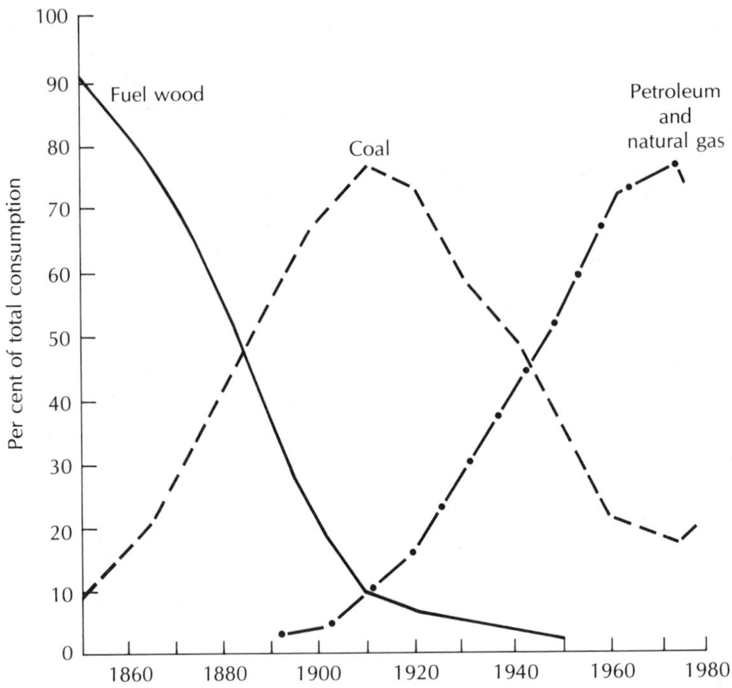

Figure 6-5. The United States has shifted to different fuel use patterns. (Source: U.S. Bureau of Mines and Federal Energy Administration.)

Some uncertainties are inherent in a market economy, and Government should not shelter industry from the normal risks of doing business. But Government should provide business and the public with a clear and consistent statement of its own policies, rules, and intentions so that intelligent private investment decisions can be made.

Resources in plentiful supply should be used more widely as part of a process of moderating use of those in short supply. Although coal comprises 90 per cent of U.S. total fossil-fuel reserves, the United States meets only 18 per cent of its energy needs from coal. Seventy-five per cent of energy needs are met by oil and natural gas, although they account for less than 8 per cent of U.S. reserves. This imbalance between reserves and consumption should be corrected by shifting industrial and utility consumption from oil and gas to coal and other abundant energy sources. (See Figure 6-5.)

As industrial firms and utilities reduce their use of oil and gas, they will have to turn to coal and other fuels. The choices now for electric utilities are basically coal and nuclear power. Expanding future use of coal will depend in large part on the introduction of new technologies that permit it to be burned in an environmentally acceptable manner, in both power plants and factories. Efforts should also be made to develop and perfect processes for making gas from coal.

Light-water nuclear reactors, subject to strict regulation, can assist in meeting the U.S. energy deficit. The 63 nuclear plants operating today provide approximately 10 per cent of U.S. electricity, about 3 per cent of total energy output. That contribution could be significantly increased. The currently projected growth rate of nuclear energy is substantially below prior expectations due mainly to the recent drop in demand for electricity, labor problems, equipment delays, health and safety problems, lack of a publicly accepted waste disposal program, and concern over nuclear proliferation. The Government should ensure that risks from nuclear power are kept as low as humanly possible, and should also establish the framework for resolving problems and removing unnecessary delays in the nuclear licensing process.

To the extent that electricity is substituted for oil and gas, the total amounts of energy used in the country will be somewhat larger due to the inherent inefficiency of electricity generation and distribution. But conserving scarce oil and natural gas is far more important than saving coal.

Finally, *the use of nonconventional sources of energy must be vigorously expanded*. Relatively clean and inexhaustible sources of energy offer a hopeful prospect of supplementing conventional energy sources in this century and becoming major sources of energy in the next. Some of these nonconventional technologies permit decentralized production, and thus provide alternatives to large, central systems. Traditional forecasts of energy use assume that nonconventional resources, such as solar and geothermal energy, will play only a minor role in the U.S. energy future. Unless positive and creative actions are taken by Government and the private sector, these forecasts will become self-fulfilling prophecies. Other technologies that increase the efficiency of energy use should also be encouraged, such as cogeneration, simultaneous production of industrial process steam and electricity.

A national energy plan cannot anticipate technological miracles. Even so, nonconventional technologies are not mere curiosities. Steady technological progress is likely, breakthroughs are possible, and the estimated potential of nonconventional energy sources can be expected to improve. Some nonconventional technologies are already being used, and with encouragement, their use will grow. Because nonconventional energy sources have great promise, the Government should take all reasonable steps to foster and develop them.

The National Energy Plan is based on this conceptual approach. It contains a practical blend of economic incentives and disincentives as well as some regulatory measures. It strives to keep Government intrusion into the lives of American citizens to a minimum. It would return the fiscal surpluses of higher energy taxes to the American people.

Finally, the Plan sets forth goals for 1985, which, although ambitious, can be achieved with the willing cooperation of the American people. These goals are:

—Reduce the annual growth of total energy demand to below 2 per cent.

—Reduce gasoline consumption 10 per cent below its current level.

—Reduce oil imports from a potential level of 16 million barrels per day to 6 million, roughly one-eighth of total energy consumption.

—Establish a Strategic Petroleum Reserve of 1 billion barrels.

—Increase coal production by two-thirds, to more than 1 billion tons per year.

—Bring 90 per cent of existing American homes and all new buildings up to minimum energy efficiency standards.

—Use solar energy in more than 2½ million homes.

The Plan would reverse the recent trend of ever-rising oil imports and ever-increasing American dependence on uncertain foreign sources of supply. It would prepare the United States for the time when the world faces a limitation on oil production capacity and consequent skyrocketing oil prices. It would achieve substantial energy savings through conservation and increased fuel efficiency, with minimal disruption to the economy, and would stimulate the use of coal in a manner consistent with environmental protection.

The United States is at a turning point. It can choose, through piecemeal programs and policies, to continue the current state of drift. That course would require no hard decisions, no immediate sacrifices, and no adjustment to the new energy realities. That course may, for the moment, seem attractive. But, with each passing day, the United States falls farther behind in solving its energy problems. Consequently, its economic and foreign policy position weakens, its options dwindle, and the ultimate transition to scarce oil supplies and much higher oil prices becomes more difficult. If the United States faces up to the energy problem now and adopts the National Energy Plan, it will have the precious opportunity to make effective use of time and resources before world oil production reaches its capacity limitation.

The energy crisis presents a challenge to the American people. If they respond with understanding, maturity, imagination, and their traditional ingenuity, the challenge will be met. Even the "sacrifices" involved in conservation will have their immediate rewards in lower fuel bills and the sense of accomplishment that comes with achieving higher efficiency. By preparing now for the energy situation of the 1980's, the United States will not merely avoid a future time of adversity. It will ensure that the coming years will be among the most creative and constructive in American history.

SUMMARY OF THE NATIONAL ENERGY PLAN

Conservation

In the transportation sector, the Plan proposes the following major initiatives to reduce demand:

—A graduated excise tax on new automobiles with fuel efficiency below the fleet average levels required under current legislation; the taxes would be returned through rebates on automobiles that meet or do better than the required fleet averages and through rebates on all electric automobiles.

—A standby gasoline tax, to take effect if total national gasoline consumption exceeds stated annual targets; the tax would begin at 5 cents per gallon, and could rise to 50 cents per gallon in 10 years if targets were repeatedly exceeded by large or increasing amounts; the tax would decrease if a target were met; taxes collected would be returned to the public through the income tax system and transfer payment programs; states would be compensated for lost gasoline tax revenues through sources such as the Highway Trust Fund.

—Fuel efficiency standards and a graduated excise tax and rebate system for light-duty trucks.

—Removal of the Federal excise tax on intercity buses.

—Increase in excise tax for general aviation fuel, and elimination of the existing Federal excise tax preference for motorboat fuel.

—Improvement in the fuel efficiency of the Federal automobile fleet, and initiation of a vanpooling program for Federal employees.

To reduce waste of energy in existing buildings, the Plan proposes a major program containing the following elements:

—A tax credit of 25 per cent of the first $800 and 15 per cent of the next $1,400 spent on approved residential conservation measures.

—A requirement that regulated utilities offer their residential customers a "turnkey" insulation service, with payment to be made through monthly bills; other fuel suppliers would be encouraged to offer a similar service.

—Facilitating residential conservation loans through opening of a secondary market for such loans.

—Increased funding for the current weatherization program for low-income households.

—A rural home conservation loan program.

—A 10 per cent tax credit (in addition to the existing investment tax credit) for business investments in approved conservation measures.

—A Federal grant program to assist public and nonprofit schools and hospitals to insulate their buildings.

—Inclusion of conservation measures for state and local government buildings in the Local Public Works Program.

The development of mandatory energy efficiency standards for new buildings will be accelerated. In addition, the Federal Government will undertake a major program to increase the efficiency of its own buildings.

The Plan proposes the establishment of mandatory minimum energy efficiency standards for major appliances, such as furnaces, air conditioners, water heaters, and refrigerators.

The Plan proposes to remove major institutional barriers to cogeneration, the simultaneous production of process steam and electricity by industrial firms or utilities, and to provide an additional 10 per cent tax credit for investment in cogeneration equipment. Encouragement will also be given to district heating, and the Energy Research and Development Administration (ERDA) will undertake a study to determine the feasibility of a district heating demonstration program at its own facilities.

To promote further industrial conservation and improvements in industrial fuel efficiency, an additional 10 per cent tax credit for energy-saving investments would be available for certain types of equipment (including equipment for use of solar energy) as well as conservation retrofits of buildings.

The Plan also contains a program for utility reform, with the following elements:

—A phasing out of promotional, declining block, and other electric utility rates that do not reflect cost incidence; declining block rates for natural gas would also be phased out.

—A requirement that electric utilities either offer daily off-peak rates to customers willing to pay metering costs or provide a direct load management system.

—A requirement that electric utilities offer customers interruptible service at reduced rates.

—A prohibition of master metering in most new structures.

—A prohibition of discrimination by electric utilities against solar and other renewable energy sources.

—Federal authority to require additional reforms of gas utility rates.

—Federal Power Commission (FPC) authority to require interconnections and power pooling between utilities even if they are not now subject to FPC jurisdiction, and to require wheeling.

Oil and Natural Gas

Government policy should provide for prices that encourage development of new fields and a more rational pattern of distribution; but it should also prevent windfall profits. It should promote conservation by confronting oil and gas users with more realistic prices, particularly for those sectors of the economy where changes can be made without hardship. To promote these ends, the Plan proposes a new system for pricing oil and natural gas.

The proposal for oil pricing contains the following major elements:

—Price controls would be extended.

—Newly discovered oil would be allowed to rise over a 3-year period to the 1977 world price, adjusted to keep pace with the domestic price level; thereafter, the price of newly discovered oil would be adjusted for domestic price increases.

—The incentive price for "new oil" would be applicable to oil produced from an onshore well more than 2½ miles from an existing well, or from a well more than 1,000 feet deeper than any existing well within a 2½-mile radius; the incentive price would be applicable to oil from Federal offshore leases issued after April 20, 1977.

—The current $5.25 and $11.28 price ceilings for previously discovered oil would be allowed to rise at the rate of domestic price increases.

—Stripper wells and incremental tertiary recovery from old fields would receive the world price.

—All domestic oil would become subject

in three stages to a crude oil equalization tax equal to the difference between its controlled domestic price and the world oil price; the tax would increase with the world price, except that authority would exist to discontinue an increase if the world price rose significantly faster than the general level of domestic prices.

—Net revenues from the tax would be entirely returned to the economy: residential consumers of fuel oil would receive a dollar-for-dollar rebate, and the remaining funds would be returned to individuals through the income tax system and transfer payment programs.

—Once the wellhead tax is fully in effect, the entitlements program would be terminated, along with certain related activities, but would be retained on a standby basis.

The proposal for natural gas pricing contains the following major provisions:

—All new gas sold anywhere in the country from new reservoirs would be subject to a price limitation at the BTU equivalent of the average refiner acquisition cost (before tax) of all domestic crude oil.

—That price limitation would be approximately $1.75 per thousand cubic feet (Mcf) at the beginning of 1978; the interstate-intrastate distinction would disappear for new gas.

—New gas would be defined by the same standards used to define new oil.

—Currently flowing natural gas would be guaranteed price certainty at current levels, with adjustments to reflect domestic price increases.

—Authority would exist to establish higher incentive pricing levels for specific categories of high-cost gas, for example, from deep drilling, geopressurized zones, and tight formations.

—Gas made available at the expiration of existing interstate contracts or by production from existing reservoirs in excess of contracted volumes would qualify for a price no higher than the current $1.42 per Mcf ceiling; gas made available under the same circumstances from existing intrastate production would qualify for the same price as new gas.

—The cost of the more expensive new gas would be allocated initially to industrial rather than residential or commercial users.

—Federal jurisdiction would be extended to certain synthetic natural gas facilities.

—Taxes would be levied on industrial and utility users of oil and natural gas to encourage conservation and conversion to coal or other energy sources.

The Plan contains the following additional proposals for oil and natural gas:

—To encourage full development of the oil resources of Alaska, Alaskan oil from existing wells would be subject to the $11.28 upper tier wellhead price and would be treated as uncontrolled oil for purposes of the entitlements program; new Alaskan oil finds would be subject to the new oil wellhead price.

—Production from Elk Hills Naval Petroleum Reserve would be limited to a ready reserve level at least until the west-to-east transportation systems for moving the surplus Alaskan oil are in place or until California refineries have completed a major retrofit program to enable more Alaskan oil to be used in California.

—The Outer Continental Shelf Lands Act would be amended to require a more flexible leasing program using bidding systems that enhance competition, to assure a fair return to the public, and to assure full development of the OCS resources.

—Shale oil will be entitled to the world oil price.

—The guidelines established by the Energy Resources Council in the previous administration would be replaced by a more flexible policy: projects for importation of liquified natural gas (LNG) should be analyzed on a case-by-case basis with respect to the reliability of the selling country, the degree of American dependence the project would create, the safety conditions associated with any specific installation, and all costs involved; imported LNG would not be concentrated in any one region; new LNG tanker docks would be prohibited in densely populated areas.

—Federal programs for development of

gas from geopressurized zones and Devonian shale would be expanded.

—The Administration hopes to eliminate gasoline price controls and allocation regulations in the fall of 1977; to maintain competition among marketers, it supports legislation similar to the pending "dealer day in court" bill.

—As part of the extension of oil and natural gas price controls, the Adminstration would urge that independent producers receive the same tax treatment of intangible drilling costs as their corporate competitors.

—A Presidential Commission will study and make recommendations concerning the national energy transportation system.

To provide relative invulnerability from another interruption of foreign oil supply, the Strategic Petroleum Reserve will be expanded to 1 billion barrels; efforts will be made to diversify sources of oil imports; contingency plans will be transmitted to the Congress; and development of additional contingency plans will be accelerated.

Coal

Conversion by industry and utilities to coal and other fuels would be encouraged by taxes on the use of oil and natural gas.

The Plan also contains a strong regulatory program that would prohibit all new utility and industrial boilers from burning oil or natural gas, except under extraordinary conditions. Authority would also exist to prohibit the burning of oil or gas in new facilities other than boilers. Existing facilities with coal-burning capability would generally be prohibited from burning oil and gas. Permits would be required for any conversion to oil or gas rather than to coal. By 1990, virtually no utilities would be permitted to burn natural gas.

While promoting greater use of coal, the Adminstration will seek to achieve continued improvement in environmental quality. A strong, but consistent and certain, environmental policy can provide the confidence industry needs to make investments in energy facilities. The Administration's policy would:

—Require installation of the best available control technology in all new coal-fired plants, including those that burn low sulfur coal.

—Protect areas where the air is still clean from significant deterioration.

—Encourage states to classify lands to protect against significant deterioration within 3 years after enactment of Clean Air Act amendments.

—Require Governors to announce intent to change the classification of allowable air quality for a given area within 120 days after an application is made to construct a new source in that area.

—Require states to approve or disapprove the application within 1 year thereafter.

Further study is needed of the Environmental Protection Agency's policies allowing offsetting pollution trade-offs for new installations. A committee will study the health effects of increased coal production and use, and the environmental constraints on coal mining and on the construction of new coal-burning facilities. A study will also be made of the long-term effects of carbon dioxide from coal and other hydrocarbons on the atmosphere.

The Administration supports uniform national strip-mining legislation.

An expansion is proposed for the Government's coal research and development program. The highest immediate priority is development of more effective and economic methods to meet air pollution control standards. The program will include research on:

—Air pollution control systems.

—Fluidized bed combustion systems.

—Coal cleaning systems.

—Solvent refined coal processes.

—Low BTU gasification processes.

—Advanced high BTU gasification processes.

—Synthetic liquids technology.

—Coal mining technology.

Nuclear Power

It is the President's policy to defer any U.S. commitment to advanced nuclear technologies that are based on the use of plutonium while the United States seeks a better approach to the next generation of nuclear power than is provided by plutonium recycle and the plutonium breeder. The United States will defer indefinitely commercial reprocessing and recycling of plutonium. The President has proposed to reduce the funding for the existing breeder program, and to redirect it toward evaluation of alternative breeders, advanced converter reactors, and other fuel cycles with emphasis on nonproliferation and safety concerns. He has also called for cancellation of construction of the Clinch River Breeder Reactor Demonstration Project and all component construction, licensing, and commercialization efforts.

To encourage other nations to pause in their development of plutonium-based technology, the United States should seek to restore confidence in its willingness and ability to supply enrichment services. The United States will reopen the order books for U.S. uranium enrichment services, and will expand its enrichment capacity by building an energy-efficient centrifuge plant. The President is also proposing legislation to guarantee the delivery of enrichment services to any country that shares U.S. nonproliferation objectives and accepts conditions consistent with those objectives.

To resolve uncertainties about the extent of domestic uranium resources, ERDA will reorient its National Uranium Resources Evaluation Program to improve uranium resource assessment. The program will also include an assessment of thorium resources.

The United States has the option of relying on light-water reactors to provide nuclear power to meet a share of its energy deficit. To enhance the safe use of light-water reactors:

—The Nuclear Regulatory Commission (NRC) has already increased the required number of guards at nuclear plants and the requirements for the training that guards receive.

—The President is requesting that the NRC expand its audit and inspection staff to increase the number of unannounced inspections and to assign one permanent Federal inspector to each nuclear power plant.

—The President is requesting that the Commission make mandatory the current voluntary reporting of minor mishaps and component failures at operating reactors.

—The President is requesting that the NRC develop firm siting criteria with clear guidelines to prevent siting of nuclear plants in densely populated locations, in valuable natural areas, or in potentially hazardous regions.

The President has directed that a study be made of the entire nuclear licensing process. He has proposed that reasonable and objective criteria be established for licensing and that plants that are based on a standard design not require extensive individual licensing.

To ensure that adequate waste storage facilities are available by 1985, ERDA's waste management program has been expanded to include development of techniques for long-term storage of spent fuel. Also, a task force will review ERDA's waste management program. Moreover, improved methods of storing spent fuel will enable most utilities at least to double their current storage capacity without constructing new facilities.

Hydroelectric Power

The Department of Defense (Corps of Engineers), together with other responsible agencies, will report on the potential for installation of additional hydroelectric generating capacity at existing dams throughout the country.

Nonconventional Resources

America's hope for long-term economic growth beyond the year 2000 rests in large measure on renewable and essentially inexhaustible sources of energy. The Federal Government should aggressively promote the development of technologies to use these resources.

Solar Energy

Solar hot water and space-heating technology is now being used and is ready for widespread commercialization. To stimulate the development of a large solar market, a tax credit is proposed. The credit would start at 40 per cent of the first $1,000 and 25 per cent of the next $6,400 paid for qualifying solar equipment. The credit would decline in stages to 25 per cent of the first $1,000 and 15 per cent of the next $6,400. The credit would be supported by a joint Federal–state program of standards development, certification, training, information gathering, and public education. Solar equipment used by business and industry would be eligible for an additional 10 per cent investment tax credit for energy conservation measures.

Geothermal Energy

Geothermal energy is a significant potential energy source. The tax deduction for intangible drilling costs now available for oil and gas drilling would be extended to geothermal drilling.

Research, Development, and Demonstration

An effective Federal research, development and demonstration program is indispensable for the production of new energy sources. The Federal Government should support many research options in their early stages, but continue support into the later stages only for those that meet technical, economic, national security, health, safety, and environmental criteria. Research and development should be accompanied by preparation for commercialization so that successful projects can rapidly be put to practical use.

Additional research, development, and demonstration initiatives are proposed, with emphasis on small, dispersed, and environmentally sound energy systems.

An Office of Small-Scale Technologies would be established to fund small, innovative energy research and development projects. The office would enable individual inventors and small businesses to contribute to the national energy research and development effort.

Information

A three-part energy information program is proposed. A Petroleum Production and Reserve Information System would provide the Federal Government with detailed, audited data on petroleum reserve estimates and production levels. A Petroleum Company Financial Data System would require all large companies and a sample of small firms engaged in crude oil or natural gas production to submit detailed financial information to the Federal Government. Data required from integrated companies would permit evaluation of the performance of their various segments by providing vertical accountability. An Emergency Management Information System would provide the Federal and state governments with information needed to respond to energy emergencies.

Competition

Effective competition in the energy industries is a matter of vital concern. The Undersecretary for policy and evaluation in the new Department of Energy would be responsible for making certain that policies and programs of the Department promote competition. Although at this time it does not appear necessary to proceed with new legislation for either horizontal or vertical divestiture of the major oil companies, their performance will be monitored. The proposed information program would greatly assist that effort.

A present anomaly in the availability of the tax deduction for intangible drilling costs within the oil industry would be removed as part of the program for extending oil and natural gas price controls.

Emergency Assistance for Low-income Persons

Existing emergency assistance programs are deficient in assisting low-income persons to meet sharp, temporary increases in energy costs due to shortages or severe winters. A redesigned program will be completed promptly and submitted to the Congress.

The Energy Situation—the Challenge 7

RICHARD J. ANDERSON 1977

Like ants on a log, floating steadily downstream, just above a precipitous waterfall, the American public continues to ignore the desperate energy supply situation. Each month, the domestic production of petroleum continues to shrink, while imports continue to rise. Our consumption of petroleum products is now at an all-time high—over 19 million barrels per day. Over half of this enormous flow comes from abroad, at a cost of more than 4 million dollars per hour.

The coldest winter in many years has speeded the decline in the nation's natural gas reserve. Curtailment of gas to industrial users is reaching into more and more regions as gas supplies are reserved for the highest priority category—the residential consumer. Most of us live in houses in which half-hearted attempts at insulation have been made or in which there is no insulation whatsoever.

Most states make no serious attempt to enforce the 55-mile per hour speed limit. Small car sales here dropped off, and two of the major automobile producers are pushing their largest cars into production. "In our '77 models," boasts one popular maker, "luxury comes first!"

While we continue to ignore the fuel-supply situation, other nations have taken drastic steps to reduce their production of petroleum and natural gas, chiefly by limiting exports. Canada, for many years one of our largest suppliers of both petroleum and natural gas, has begun a cutback schedule calling for a stop to exports to the United States by 1982. Already, the flow has been reduced by 50 per cent.

Venezuela, once our largest overseas source of oil, has nationalized its petroleum industry, and has ordered cutbacks in exports to the United States. These reductions in exports have shifted Saudi Arabia to the position of the major oil supplier to the United States, with all the attendant hazards of a Middle East source.

The American press, almost daily, contains

Richard J. Anderson is editor of *Energy Perspectives*, a periodic publication of the Battelle Energy Program, and until recently, he was associate director of Education and Information for this program at Battelle, Columbus Laboratories, Columbus, Ohio 43201. During his 28 years with Battelle, he has participated in a wide range of research projects, including energy-resource evaluations, regional economic-development studies, and industrial raw material inventories.

items concerning new sources of energy, each expected to solve the energy supply problem. Electric cars, methane from manure, new wind-driven turbines, solar-heated homes, the list goes on and on. Ignored or at best unappreciated, is the miniscule energy contributions of such inventions, which, if successful, would not make even a tiny dent in the total energy demand for years to come. And most are deemed to be unsuccessful. Strangely enough, there is no follow-up. We never read that a solar-heated house has been a success, only that one is "going to be built." And electric cars, states a major TV network announcer, "use no energy at all(!)."

The Federal government continues to make substantial investments in developing techniques to produce synthetic natural gas or synthetic liquid fuels from coal. The press announcements of these moves usually omit the boring details as to how long a period of research is required, and if successful, how long it will take before the new technique can be put into practice. At present, no commercial-sized gas-from-coal, or oil-from-coal plant is in production, and none are expected to enter the supply picture before the 1990's.

Oil shale, as a source of refinery feedstock, will not be available in commercial quantities until the late 1980's at the earliest. Solar heating systems for residences are currently priced in the $4,000 to $8,000 range, and are economically attractive only in regions with a high percentage of clear *winter* days. It will be 1985 or later before enough houses can be equipped with solar heating systems to justify including solar energy in the national energy budget.

In summary, there appears to be no help coming in the short term. All indicators point to the conclusion that petroleum, natural gas, coal, hydroelectric facilities, and nuclear-fueled power, the principal energy sources of today, will continue to play major roles for another decade. Today's national energy budget looks like this: petroleum, 47 per cent; natural gas, 27 per cent; coal, 19 per cent; hydroelectric power, 4 per cent; nuclear power, 2.8 per cent; and miscellaneous, 0.2 per cent.

Some changes are expected to affect the contributions of the major energy sources to the national budget in the 1990's, and by the year 2000, the budget could look something like this: petroleum (natural), 30 per cent; "synthetic" liquid fuel, 4 per cent; natural gas, 5 per cent; synthetic natural gas, 10 per cent; hydroelectric power, 4 per cent; coal, 35 per cent; nuclear power, 10 per cent; and solar energy, 2 per cent.

The above is not necessarily a desirable budget, and the economic consequences, let alone the economic requirements of such a budget, can only be imagined. Twenty-some years is not much time in which to build synthetic natural gas plants in such numbers as to jointly contribute 10 per cent of our energy requirement. Similarly, twenty years is scarcely long enough to nearly double coal production, increase nuclear reactors four- to fivefold, and to construct facilities to treat millions of tons of coal and oil shale to yield significant quantities of "synthetic" oil or refinery feedstocks. And finally, thousands of buildings (including hotels, residences, churches, apartment houses) would have to be equipped with solar heating systems before solar energy could reach 1 per cent, let alone 2 per cent, of the national budget.

If the new construction and increased production outlined here are not realized for any one of several reasons, then we are facing an economic decline more fearsome than the Great Depression of the 1930's. As we approach the year 2000, the world demand for petroleum will exceed the world's ability to provide petroleum, and the final slide will begin.

Deposits of natural gas by the year 2000 will have been so depleted as to force the use of this precious resource only for purposes for which no other economically viable raw material is available.

The development of economically viable fusion, magnetohydrodynamics, breeder reactors, all are long range goals, *not* present-day realities. To expect these to become sources of energy soon, is to ignore completely the difference between scientific hypothesis and commercial fact. If fusion ever is mastered as a "power plant" phenomenon, it will not be until after the year 2000, perhaps 2050. Similar long waiting periods are expected for other "new," and as yet untested, sources of energy.

If then, there is no help coming to us in the short term, and the long term holds little promise until close to the year 2000, the question is–"How do we survive between now and 1999?" There can only be one answer–"Reduction in energy consumption, *now*!"

Energy consumption can be reduced many ways. Here are only a few:

(1) Install insulation to prevent the escape of calories in winter and to reduce absorption of the sun's heat in summer.

(2) Reduce automobile weight, to make possible smaller engines, lower fuel consumption.

(3) Enforce speed limits.

(4) Redesign appliances to consume less energy.

(5) Substitute spark igniters for pilot lights.

(6) Discontinue the use of natural gas and petroleum as boiler fuels.

(7) Discontinue automobile racing.

(8) Limit lighted signs to traffic and safety uses only.

(9) Close service stations on Sunday.

(10) Ban decorative gas lights and flares.

Each of you can add many more ways to reduce your own consumption of energy.

Recently Americans have been in an indictment mood. Based on the Watergate syndrome, the public has the impression that any problem, or shortage, has no basis in fact, but is the product of a foul plot to "rip-off" the consumer. All we have to do, therefore, is to find the culprit, indict him, find him guilty, and throw him in jail, then all will be "right" again. Although there may be scoundrels in the energy industry, the shortage that faces America is based on fact, and when the "crooks" are identified and removed from the scene, the shortage will still be there.

The grim facts are these:

(1) America is the largest consumer, and the greatest waster of energy, of any nation on earth.

(2) Once we supplied all of our energy requirements from domestic deposits; today we cannot.

(3) America has been blessed with abundant energy resources for 200 years. We have consumed these resources as though they were inexhaustible; they are not.

(4) Although we are not at the end of our energy resources, the end of our oil and our natural gas is in sight. Only coal remains in apparently plentiful supply, but its life is also finite. Even our coal will not last forever.

(5) Because our energy resources were abundant, the cost to the consumer was low. We enjoyed "cheap" energy. "Cheap" energy is now on its way out; it will not return during the lifetime of most living Americans, if ever.

(6) The task, then—the enormous task that lies before us—is to develop, with all the skill and genius at our command, *new* sources of energy, to replace those sources that are nearing exhaustion. To do this will take time, and it will require that all Americans admit not only that the problem we face is real, but that all of us, each and everyone, is partly responsible for the problem in the first place, and therefore has a share in finding a solution.

(7) To "buy" time, we *must* reduce our consumption of energy. By reducing our "draw down" of petroleum and natural gas, we will stretch what is left a few more years. In those few years, if we pursue the search with the same kind of dedication that characterized the Manhattan Project in the 1940's, or Project Apollo in the 1960's, it can be hoped that we *will* develop substitute energy sources, and that we *will* survive.

(8) If we do not reduce our energy consumption and we persist in following our

present course, a collision with reality is not far off. The consequences of such a "crash" can only be imagined, and even our imagination is inadequate. Our nation depends on huge amounts of energy easily available on demand. What if they are not? Think about it.

SUGGESTED READINGS

Benedict, Manson, 1976, U.S. Energy: The Plan that can Work, *Technology Review 78,* pp. 52–59.

Christiansen, Bill and Clack, Jr., Theodore H., 1976, A Western Perspective on Energy: A Plea for Rational Energy Planning, *Science 194*, pp. 578–584.

1976, Energy: The U.S. at the Crossroads, *Environmental Science and Technology 10,* pp. 854–859.

Lapp, Ralph E., 1973, The Chemical Century, *Bulletin of the Atomic Scientists 29,* pp. 8–14.

McKelvy, V. E., 1972, Mineral Resource Estimates and Public Policy, *American Scientist 60,* pp. 32–40.

Starr, Chauncey, 1973, Realities of the Energy Crisis, *Bulletin of the Atomic Scientists 29,* pp. 15–20.

FOSSIL FUEL ENERGY SOURCES

Dotting the Texas-Louisiana coast are hundreds of oil rigs, which help meet U.S. energy demands. (Photo courtesy of the Federal Energy Administration.)

Typical oil tanker unloading at a Texaco Company refinery. (Photo courtesy of Ray Maurer, Texaco, Inc., and the American Petroleum Institute.)

A stripping shovel operator's view of the Peabody Coal Company surface pit, Sinclair Mine, Kentucky. The dipper of this big shovel holds 125 cubic yards of earth and rock. The loading shovel in the background scoops coal into 135-ton trucks. (Photo courtesy of the National Coal Association.)

An underground miner operates his longwall machine under the protection of movable steel roof supports. Whirling cutters move back and forth along the face, slicing off the coal. The coal falls on a conveyer below the machine and is moved to the haulageway. The roof supports are advanced as the miner works into the coal seam, and the roof behind him is permitted to fall. This longwall mining, a technique imported from Europe, did not gain attention until the 1960's. (Photo courtesy of the National Coal Association.)

TVA's Bull Run steam plant, Oak Ridge, Tennessee. This large, coal-fired unit has a capacity of 950 megawatts (electric), burning over 5 tons of coal a minute. (Photo courtesy of the Tennessee Valley Authority.)

INTRODUCTION

The period 1900–2000 has been accurately called the Chemical Century. In spite of all the discussion, pro and con, of fission, fusion, and solar energy, fossil fuels still dominate the energy supply picture with over 90 per cent of the market. Because of the enormous social inertia, which was discussed in Chapter I, all energy futures predict that this dominance will continue to the end of our century. So it is essential that we understand these energy sources and the role they play in society.

The inevitable dilemmas surrounding fossil fuels involve the finite nature of the resources and the environmental impact of their use. From a long-term perspective, these dilemmas will be resolved. When we have consumed all the economically accessable oil and gas, their production, transportation, and consumption will no longer pose any environmental hazards. Since we are, in fact, over the peak in U.S. production and approaching the peak in consumption of oil and gas, it is fair to say that at most we can only do as much additional environmental damage as we've already done. As recently enacted environmental legislation is implemented, the environmental insult per unit of fossil fuel consumption should dramatically decrease.

Diseases such as black lung, the ravages of strip mining, and oil pollution of our beaches are obvious social and environmental costs imposed by society's demand for energy. One of the most serious environmental impacts of the utilization of fossil fuels is that on health, which was analyzed in Chapter I. Less apparent are such unexpected phenomena as the "acid rain" resulting from adding smoke precipitators and taller stacks on coal burning plants. Sulfur dioxide, which was once neutralized by the alkaline particulate matter from "dirty stacks," is an even more serious problem after such particulate pollution is eliminated. Taller stacks now disperse sulfur dioxide over a larger area and rain then precipitates it out as sulfuric acid; there is evidence that this leaches out soil nutrients and destroys coniferous forests over wide areas.

Even less well understood and potentially much more serious are fossil fuel combustion-related climatic changes such as the "greenhouse effect," a change in the heat balance of the earth resulting from the unavoidable carbon dioxide production. Some scientists feel this may melt the polar ice caps, flooding most of the major coastal cities of the world; and others claim we are entering a new ice age with its attendant human misery and mass starvation. Although the direction of this man-made climatic change is unclear, there is little doubt as to its possibility. Carbon dioxide production is intrinsic to fossil fuel combustion—no technological fix exists.

In this chapter, an enlightening perspective on the role of fossil energy in human affairs is presented by M. King Hubbert in *Survey of World Energy Resources*. Our fossil fuel consumption is seen as a mere blip on the time scale of human history. But although this event is transient, it has had a tremendous impact on mankind. Just as the rise of fossil fuel use has paralleled the rise in living standards, the eventual decline in fossil fuel use will have profound social consequences. In this article, he presents the best current estimates of the nature of this rise and fall for each of the fossil fuels. This is best described by the bell-shaped curves that apply to the production of all finite resources. Important concepts such as culmination time (peak production) are easily seen from these curves, and they help explain why our natural resources will never "run out" but rather only "fade away." The startling fact is that we passed the culmination time for domestic gas and oil production in the early 1970's.

The largest single source of energy in the United States is petroleum with about 47 per cent of the market. In *Facts About Oil* by the American Petroleum Institute, a wealth of information on the history, production, transportation, and uses of petroleum products is presented. The great versatility, low cost, and ease of using this resource, primarily as a fuel, have resulted in its assumption of a central role in industrial society. The sobering consideration is that this valuable resource on which we are most dependent is one of the least abundant, domestically. As with many chemical addictions, life appears beautiful while under the influence, but the withdrawal symptoms are very painful—as we notice each cold winter.

Natural gas is the second largest source of energy, providing for 27 per cent of domestic demand, and is probably the finest fuel available from an environmental point of view. In the Federal Energy Administration document *The Natural Gas Story*, we take a closer look at this natural resource that is both clean burning and easily handled. These attractive features, in combination with the artificial price structure imposed by the government, have resulted in demand for natural gas far exceeding available supplies. This article traces the history of such regulation and strongly recommends a policy of deregulation. Again, we note the irony of energy management policies that have resulted in excessive consumption of one of our scarcest resources.

Finally we turn to coal, our "warm but dirty friend," whose once waning star is on the rise again. In the article *Coal—Meeting the Energy Challenge* the National Coal Association outlines the role that coal can play. After peaking with about 80 per cent of the energy market in 1910, coal steadily lost ground to oil and natural gas until its recent low point of 18 per cent, although production itself remained relatively constant during this period. Now, driven by economic factors and government policies, which are discussed in this article, coal seems destined to regain much of its former market. The blessings of its much touted abundance must, however, be continually balanced against the very serious environmental costs of its extraction, transportation, and use.

The most promising methods of utilizing coal in an environmentally acceptable fashion and simultaneously achieving the versatility of oil and gas are by gasification and liquefaction. Several processes of proven technical feasibility are described by Harry Perry in his article, *Coal Conversion Technology*. Although many pilot plant operations are well under way, the chief obstacle to widespread implementation of these processes is one of economic feasibility. We should also emphasize that such conversion processes provide no *new* energy sources but simply a cleaner and more convenient method of burning our present coal resources, much of which exceeds government standards for sulfur content. This improvement in utilization, however, is not achieved without a price. These conversion processes range from 50 to 70 per cent in their thermal efficiences (i.e., the heat content of the product is much less than that of the original coal). Thus, for a given end-use power requirement, we must mine 43 to 100 per cent more coal if we are to burn the synthetic oil or gas product. In order to improve the environmental quality of our air, we would sacrifice the environmental quality of land overlying coal beds and the water required in conversion plants.

The harsh choices forced on us by such expanded production of coal are brought home forcefully in *Agony on the Northern Plains* by Alvin M. Josephy, Jr. The President's call to increase coal production by two-thirds by 1985 must be set against this background of personal anguish, displacement, and environmental degradation. Recent federal environmental protection legislation should reduce the disruption to grazing and tribal lands, thereby minimizing the bitter confrontations described in this article, while still allowing the coal production generally considered essential for "the public good."

The ecological balance of nature is at the same time both delicate and sturdy. Man in his ignorance or greed may abuse his natural habitat, causing enormous short-term damage, but nature is resilient and will generally recuperate in the long run. Abuses in fossil-fuel production and consumption, the most severe environmental disruptions, will certainly disappear—the question is simply when and how. Will it be sooner, through responsible human decisions, or later, through the total depletion of available resources or zonal climatic changes? As one wit has observed, ''Nature always bats last.''

Fossil fuels are still the mainstay of our energy economy and will certainly remain so for the midterm future. As such they must serve as benchmarks for the benefit and environmental cost analysis; we will measure the alternative energy sources against them in the following chapters.

Survey of World Energy Resources 8

M. KING HUBBERT 1973

INTRODUCTION

By now, it has become generally recognized that the world's present civilization differs fundamentally from all earlier civilizations in both the magnitude of its operations and the degree of its dependence on energy and mineral resources—particularly energy from the fossil fuels. The significance of energy lies in the fact that it is involved in everything that occurs on the earth—everything that moves. In fact, in the last analysis, about as succinct a statement as can be made about terrestrial events is the following. The earth's surface is composed of the 92 naturally occurring chemical elements, all but a minute radioactive fraction of which obey the laws of conservation and of nontransmutability of classical chemistry. Into and out of this system is a continuous flux of energy, in consequence of which the material constituents undergo either continuous or intermittent circulation.

The principle energy inputs into this system are three (Figure 8-1):

(1) $174{,}000 \times 10^{12}$ thermal watts from the solar radiation intercepted by the earth's diametrical plane;

(2) 32×10^{12} thermal watts conducted and convected to the earth's surface from inside the earth; and

(3) 3×10^{12} thermal watts of tidal power from the combined kinetic and potential energy of the earth-moon-sun system. Of these inputs of thermal power, that from solar energy is overwhelmingly the largest, exceeding the sum of the other two by a factor of more than 5,000.

Of the solar input, about 30 per cent, the earth's albedo, is directly reflected and scattered into outer space, leaving the earth as short-wavelength radiation; about 47 per cent

Dr. M. King Hubbert has served as a research geophysicist with the U.S. Geological Survey, Washington, D.C. His scientific work has included geophysical and geological exploration for oil, gas, and other minerals; structural geology and the physics of earth deformation; the physics of underground fluids; and the world's mineral and energy resources and the significance of their exploitation in human affairs. He has published 65 technical papers and is author or coauthor of several texts.

Originally presented during the Plenary Session of the 75th Annual General Meeting of the CIM, Vancouver, April 16, 1973, and subsequently published in *The Canadian Mining and Metallurgical Bulletin,* Vol. 66, No. 735, pp. 37–54, July, 1973. Reprinted by permission of the author and *The Canadian Mining and Metallurgical Bulletin* published by the Canadian Institute of Mining and Metallurgy.

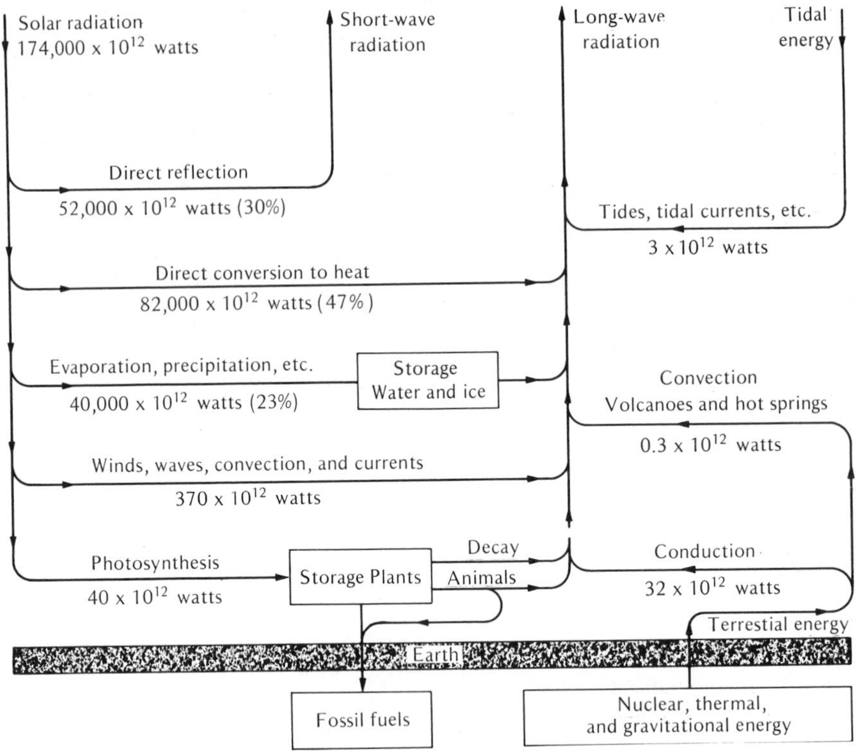

Figure 8-1. World energy flow sheet.

is directly absorbed and converted into heat; and about 23 per cent is dissipated in circulating through the atmosphere and the oceans, and in the evaporation, precipitation, and circulation of water in the hydrologic cycle. Finally, a minute fraction, about 40 × 10^{12} watts, is absorbed by the leaves of plants and stored chemically by the process of photosynthesis whereby the inorganic substances, water and carbon dioxide, are synthesized into organic carbohydrates according to the approximate equation:

$$\text{Light energy} + CO_2 + H_2O \rightarrow [CH_2O] + O_2$$

Small though it is, this fraction is the energy source for the biological requirements of the earth's entire populations of plants and animals.

From radioactive dating of meteorites, the astronomical cataclysm that produced the solar system is estimated to have occurred about 4.5 billion years ago and microbial organisms have been found in rocks as old as 3.2 billion years. During the last 600 million years of geologic history, a minute fraction of the earth's organisms have been deposited in swamps and other oxygen-deficient environments under conditions of incomplete decay, and eventually buried under great thicknesses of sedimentary muds and sands. By subsequent transformations, these have become the earth's present supply of fossil fuels; coal, oil, and associated products.

About 2 million years ago, according to recent discoveries, the ancestors of modern man had begun to walk upright and to use primitive tools. From that time to the present, this species has distinguished itsglf by its inventiveness in the progressive control of an ever-larger fraction of the available energy supply. First, by means of tools and weapons, the invention of clothing, the control of fire, the domestication of plants and animals, and use of animal power, this control was principally ecological in character. Next followed the manipulation of the inorganic world, including the smelting of metals and the primitive uses of power of wind and water.

Such a state of development was sufficient for the requirements of all premodern civilizations. A higher-level industrialized civilization did not become possible until a larger and more concentrated source of energy and power became available. This occurred when the huge supply of energy stored in the fossil fuels was first tapped by the mining of coal, which began as a continuous enterprise about nine centuries ago near Newcastle in northeast England. Exploitation of the second major fossil-fuel supply, petroleum, began in 1857 in Romania and two years later in the United States. The tapping of an even larger supply of stored energy, that of the atomic nucleus, was first achieved in a controlled manner in 1942, and now the production of nuclear power from plants in the 1,000-megawatt range of capacity is in its early stages of development.

In addition to increased energy sources, energy utilization was markedly enhanced by two technological developments near the end of the last century: the development of the internal-combustion engine, utilizing petroleum products for mobile power, and the development of electrical means for the generation and distribution of power from large-scale central power plants. This also made possible for the first time the large-scale use of water power. This source of power derived

Figure 8-2. World production of coal and lignite (Hubbert, 1969, Figure 8.1).

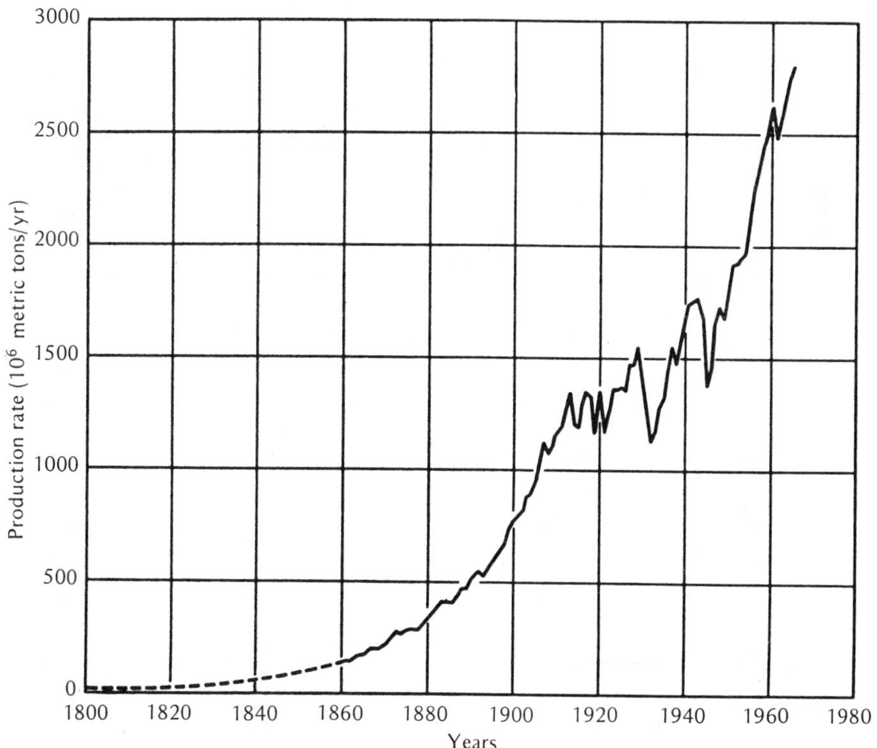

from the contemporary flux of solar energy has been in use to some degree since Roman times, but always in small units—units rarely larger than a few hundred kilowatts. With electrical generation and distribution of hydropower, first accomplished at Niagara Falls about 1895, progressively larger hydropower stations have been installed with capacities up to several thousand megawatts.

ENERGY FROM FOSSIL FUELS

To the present the principal sources of energy for industrial uses have been the fossil fuels. Let us therefore review the basic facts concerning the exploitation and utilization of these fuels. This can best be done by means of a graphical presentation of the statistics of annual production.

World Production of Coal and Oil

Figure 8-2 shows the annual world production of coal and lignite from 1860 to 1970, and the approximate rate back to 1800, on an arithmetic scale. Figure 8-3 shows the same data on a semilogarithmic scale. The significance of the latter presentation is that straight-line segments of the growth curve indicate periods of steady exponential growth in the rate of production.

Annual statistics of coal production earlier than 1860 are difficult to assemble, but from intermittent earlier records it can be estimated that from the beginning of coal mining about the twelfth century A.D. until 1800, the average growth rate of production must have been about 2 per cent per year, with an average doubling period of about 35 years. During the eight centuries to 1860 it is estimated that cumulative production amounted to about 7 ×

Figure 8-3. World production of coal and lignite (semilogarithmic scale) (Hubbert, 1971, Figure 4).

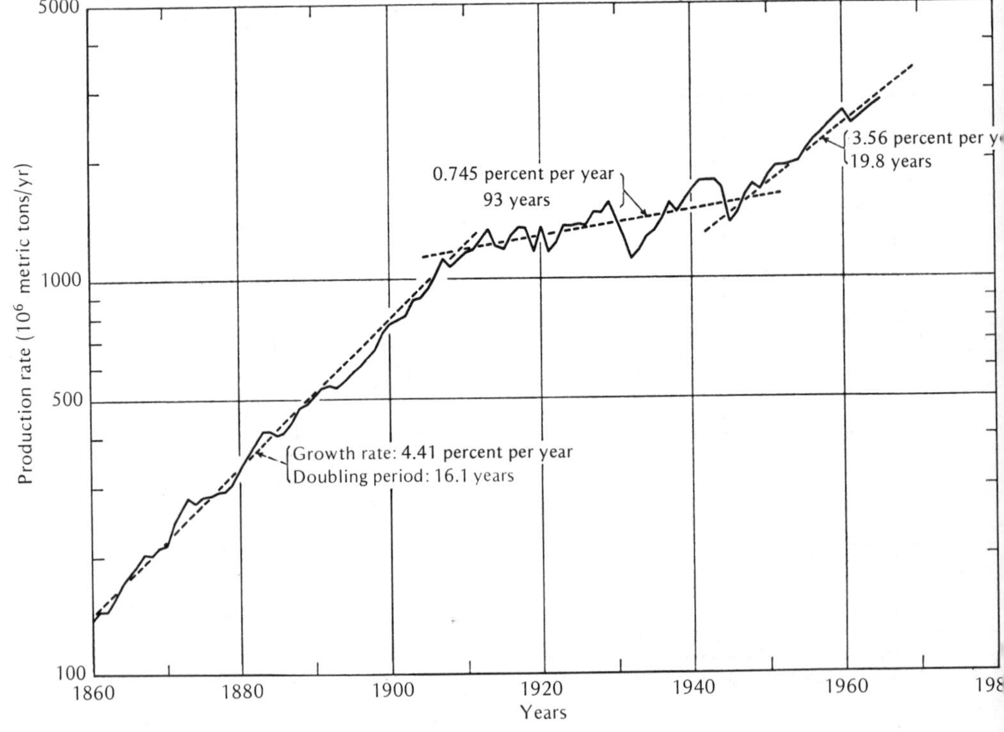

10^9 metric tons. By 1970, cumulative production reached 140×10^9 metric tons. Hence, the coal mined during the 110-year period from 1860 to 1970 was approximately 19 times that of the preceding 8 centuries. The coal produced during the last 30-year period from 1940 to 1970 was approximately equal to that produced during all preceding history.

The rate of growth of coal production can be seen more clearly from the semilogarithmic plot of Figure 8-3. The straight line segment of the production curve from 1860 to World War I indicates a steady exponential increase of the rate of production during this period at about 4.4 per cent per year, with a doubling period of 16 years. Between the beginning of World War I and the end of World War II, the growth rate slowed down to about 0.75 per cent per year and a doubling period of 93 years. Finally, after World War II a more rapid growth rate of 3.56 per cent per year and a doubling period of 19.8 years was resumed.

Figure 8-4 shows, on an arithmetic scale, the annual world crude-oil production from 1880 to 1970. Figure 8-5 shows the same data plotted semilogarithmically. After a slightly higher initial growth rate, world petroleum production from 1890 to 1970 has had a steady exponential increase at an average rate of 6.94 per cent and a doubling period of 10.0 years. Cumulative world production of crude oil to 1970 amounted to 233×10^9 barrels. Of this, the first half required the 103-year period from 1857 to 1960 to produce, the second half only the 10-year period from 1960 to 1970.

When coal is measured in metric tons and oil in United States 42-gallon barrels, a direct comparison between coal and oil cannot be made. Such a comparison can be made, however, by means of the energy contents of the two fuels as determined by their respective heats of combustion. This is shown in Figure 8-6, where the energy produced per year is expressed in power units of 10^{12} thermal watts. From this it is seen that until after 1900 the energy contributed by crude oil was barely significant as compared with that of coal. By 1970, however, the energy from crude oil had

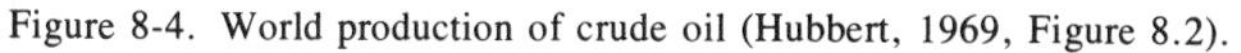
Figure 8-4. World production of crude oil (Hubbert, 1969, Figure 8.2).

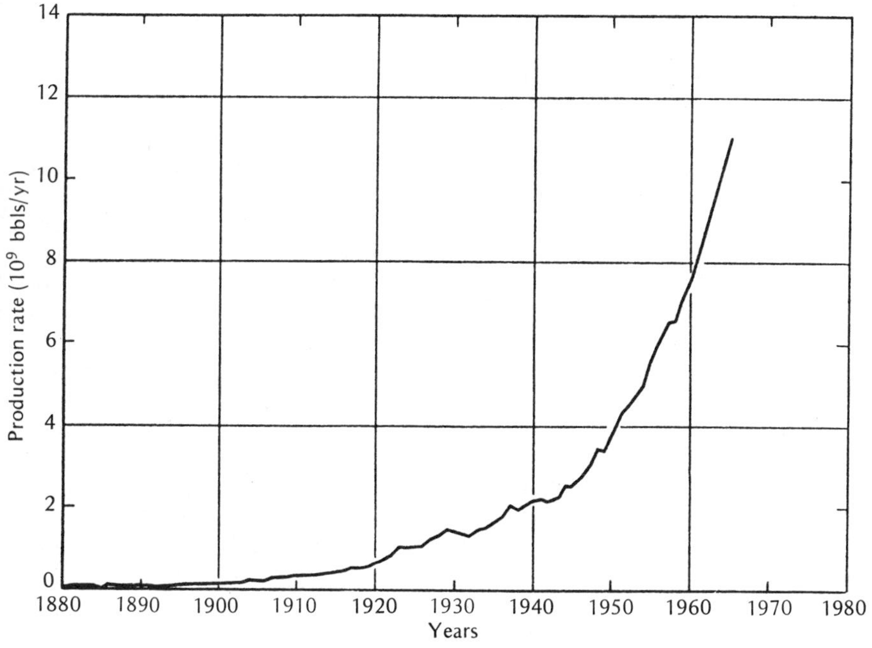

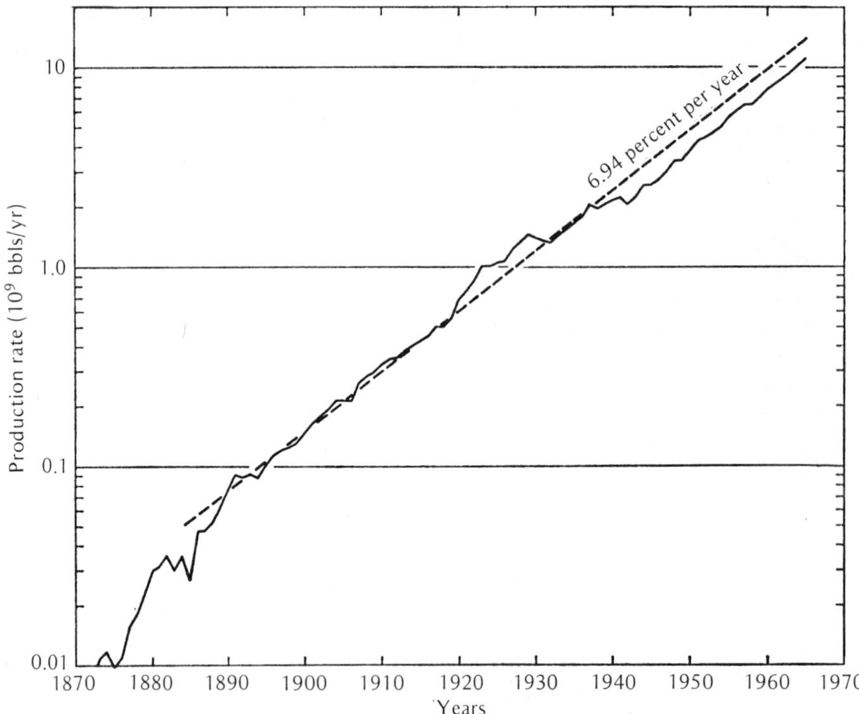

Figure 8-5. World production of crude oil (semilogarithmic scale) (Hubbert, 1971, Figure 6).

increased to 56 per cent of that from coal and oil combined. Were natural gas and natural-gas liquids also to be included, the energy from petroleum fluids would represent about two-thirds of the total.

United States Production of Fossil Fuels

The corresponding growths in the production of coal, crude oil, and natural gas in the United States are shown graphically in Figures 8-7 to 8-9. From before 1860 to 1907 annual United States coal production increased at a steady exponential rate of 6.58 per cent per year, with a doubling period of 10.5 years. After 1907, due largely to the increase in oil and natural-gas production, coal production fluctuated about a production rate of approximately 500 × 10^6 metric tons per year. After an initial higher rate, United States crude-oil production increased steadily from 1870 to 1929 at about 8.27 per cent per year, with a doubling period of 8.4 years. After 1929, the growth rate steadily declined to a 1970 value of approximately zero. From 1905 to 1970 the United States production of natural gas increased at an exponential rate of 6.6 per cent per year, with a doubling period of 10.5 years.

Finally, Figure 8-10 shows the annual production of energy in the United States from coal, oil, natural gas, and hydroelectric and nuclear power from 1850 to 1970. From 1850 to 1907, this increased at a steady growth rate of 6.9 per cent per year and doubling every 10.0 years. At about 1907, the growth rate dropped abruptly to an average value from 1907 to 1960 of about 1.77 per cent per year, with a doubling period of 39 years. Since 1960, the growth rate has in-

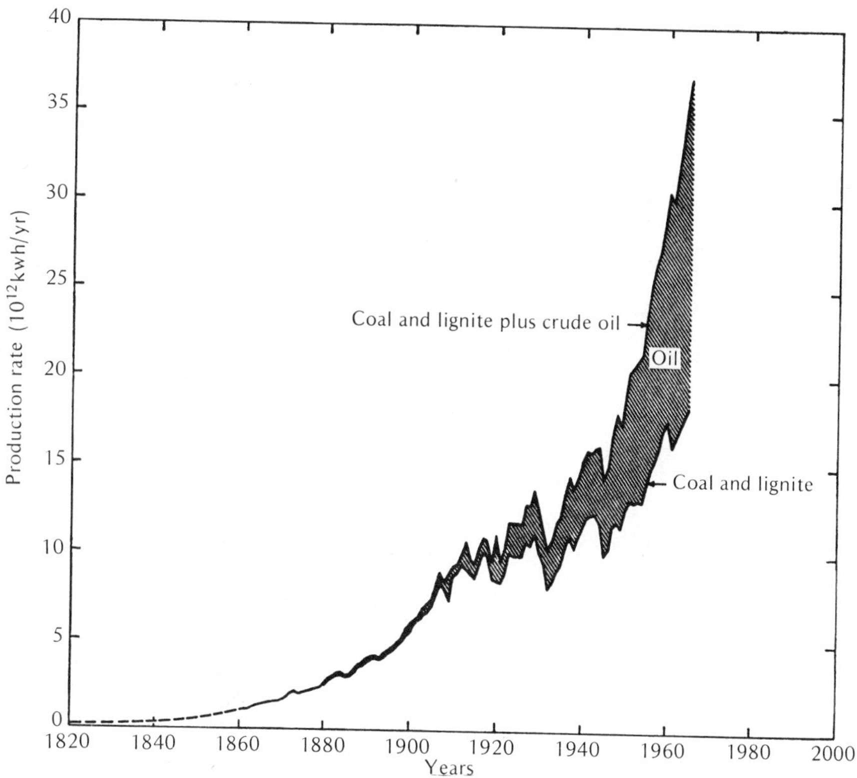

Figure 8-6. World production of thermal energy from coal and lignite plus crude oil (Hubbert, 1969, Figure 8.3)

creased to about 4.25 per cent per year, with the doubling period reduced to 16.3 years.

DEGREE OF ADVANCEMENT OF FOSSIL-FUEL EXPLOITATION

The foregoing are the basic historical facts pertaining to the exploitation of the fossil fuels in the world and in the United States. In the light of these facts we can hardly fail to wonder: How long can this continue? Several different approaches to this problem will now be considered.

Method of Donald Foster Hewett

In 1929, geologist Donald Foster Hewett delivered before the American Institute of Metallurgical Engineers one of the more important papers ever written by a member of the U.S. Geological Survey, entitled "Cycles in Metal Production." In 1926, Hewett had made a trip to Europe during which he visited 28 mining districts, of which half were then or had been outstanding sources of several metals. These districts ranged from England to Greece and from Spain to Poland. Regarding the purpose of this study, Hewett stated: "I have come to believe that many of the problems that harass Europe lie in our path not far ahead. I have therefore hoped that a review of metal production in Europe in the light of its geologic, economic and political background may serve to clear our vision with regard to our own metal production."

In this paper, extensive graphs were pre-

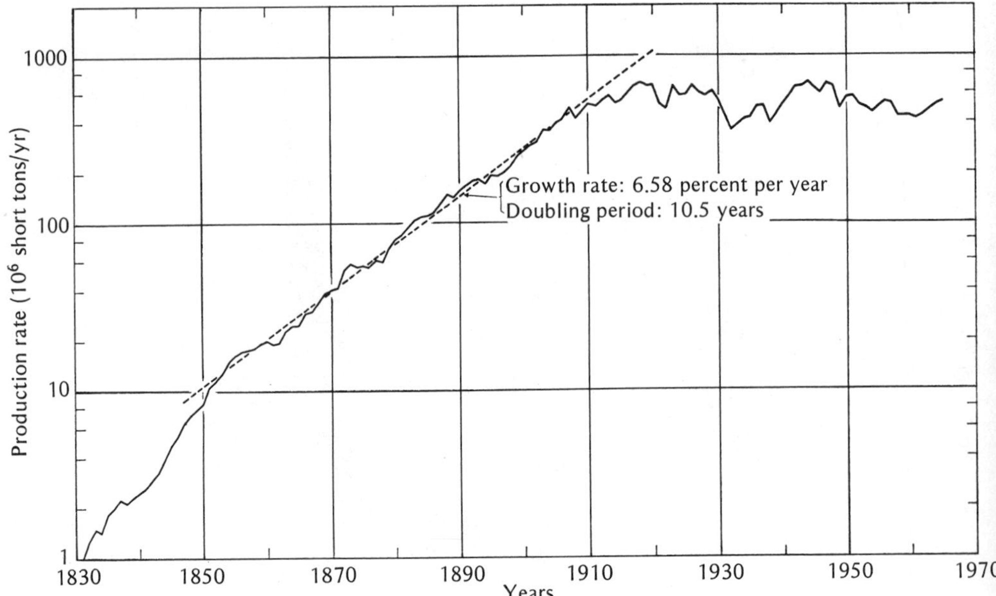

Figure 8-7. United States production of coal (semilogarithmic scale).

Figure 8-8. United States production of crude oil, exclusive of Alaska (semilogarithmic scale).

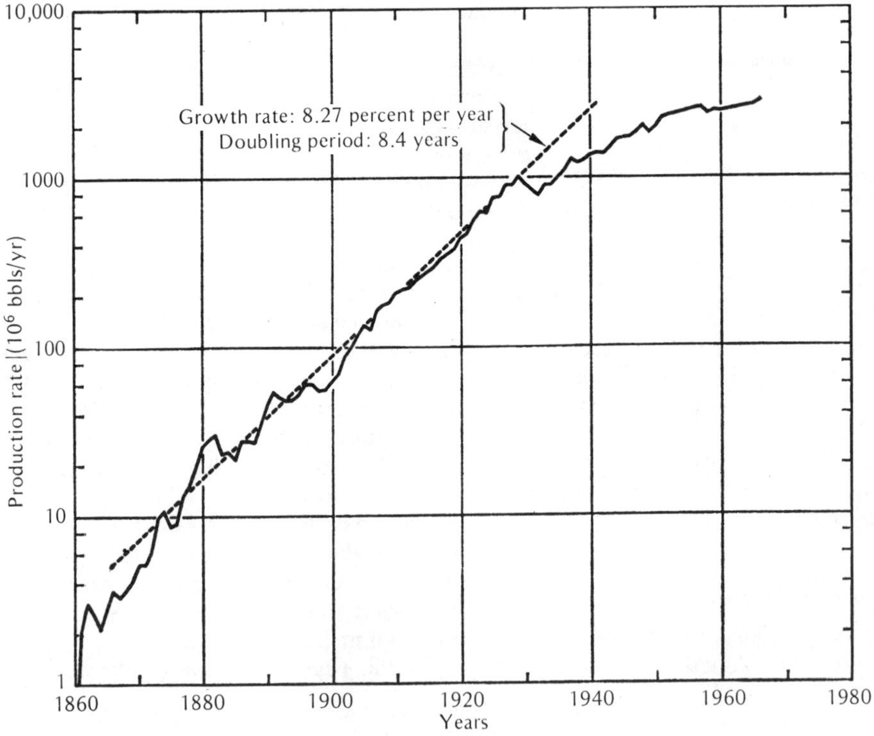

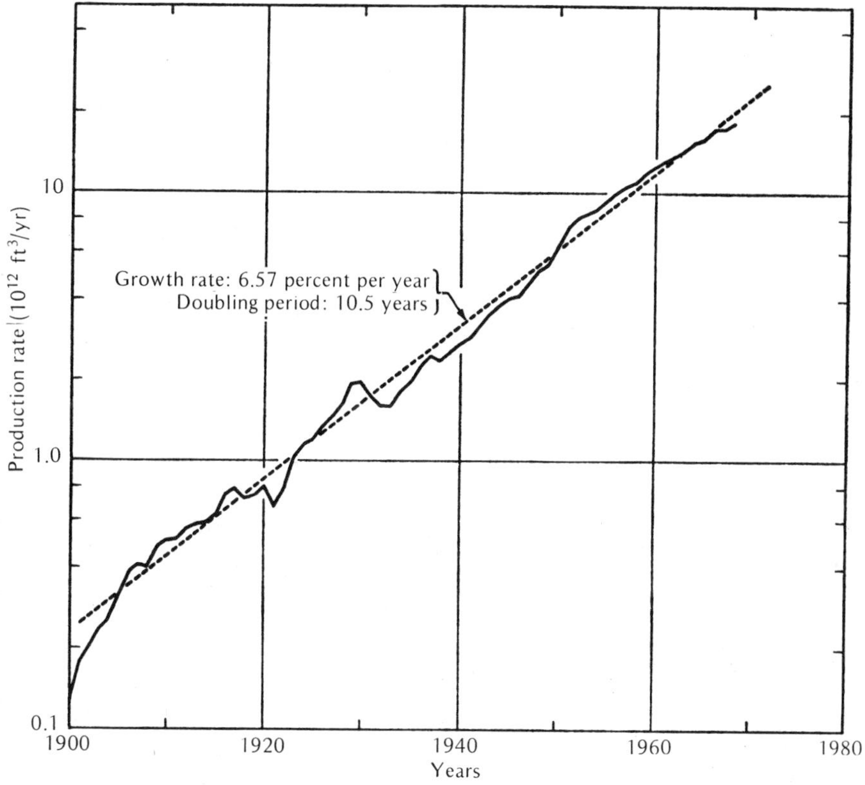

Figure 8-9. United States net production of natural gas (semilogarithmic scale).

sented of the production of separate metals from these various districts showing the rise, and in many cases the decline, in the production rates as the districts approached exhaustion of their ores. After having made this review, Hewett generalized his findings by observing that mining districts evolve during their history through successive stages analogous to those of infancy, adolescence, maturity and old age. He sought criteria for judging how far along in such a sequence a given mining district or region had progressed, and from his study he suggested the successive culminations shown in Figure 8-11. These culminations were:

(1) the quantity of exports of crude ore;
(2) the number of mines in operation;
(3) the number of smelters or refining units in operation;
(4) the production of metal from domestic ore; and
(5) the quantity of imports of crude ore.

Although not all of Hewett's criteria are applicable to the production of the fossil fuels, especially when world production is considered, the fundamental principle is applicable—namely, that like the metals, the exploitation of the fossil fuels in any given area must begin at zero, undergo a period of more or less continuous increase, reach a culmination and then decline, eventually to a zero rate of production. This principle is illustrated in Figure 8-12, in which the complete cycle of the production rate of any exhaustible

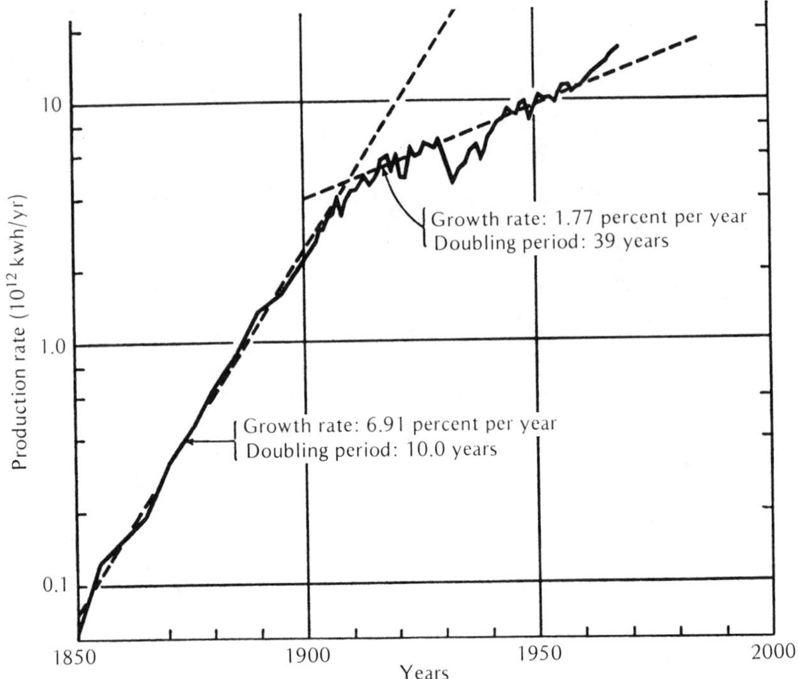

Figure 8-10. United States production of thermal energy from coal, oil, natural gas, water power, and nuclear power (semilogarithmic scale).

resource is plotted arithmetically as a function of time. The shape of the curve is arbitrary within wide limits, but it still must have the foregoing general characteristics.

An important mathematical property of such a curve may be seen if we consider a vertical column of base Δt extending from the time axis to the curve itself. The altitude of this column will be the production rate

$$P=\Delta Q/\Delta t$$

at the given time, where ΔQ is the quantity

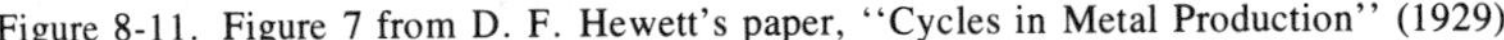

Figure 8-11. Figure 7 from D. F. Hewett's paper, "Cycles in Metal Production" (1929).

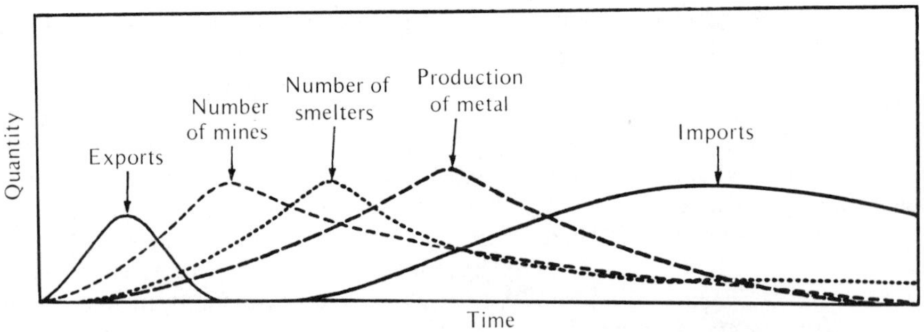

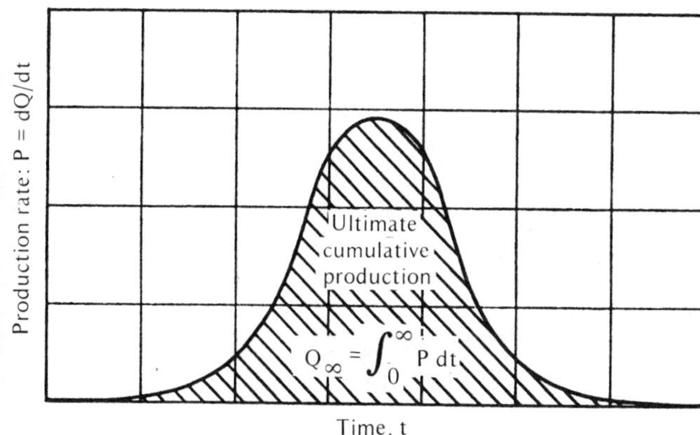

Figure 8-12. Mathematical relations involved in the complete cycle of production of any exhaustible resource (Hubbert, 1956, Figure 11).

produced in time Δt. The area of the column will accordingly be given by the product of its base and altitude:

$$P \times \Delta t = (\Delta Q/\Delta t) \times \Delta t = \Delta Q.$$

Hence, the area of the column is a measure of the quantity produced during the time interval Δt, and the total area from the beginning of production up to any given time t will be a measure of the cumulative production up to that time. Clearly, as the time t increases without limit, the production rate will have gone through its complete cycle and returned to zero. The area under the curve after this has occurred will then represent the ultimate cumulative production, Q_∞. In view of this fact, if from geological or other data the producible magnitude of the resource initially present can be estimated, then any curve drawn to represent the complete cycle of production *must be consistent with that estimate*. No such curve can subtend an area greater than the estimated magnitude of the producible resource.

Utilization of this principle affords a powerful means of estimating the time scale for the complete production cycle of any exhaustible resource in any given region. As in the case of animals where the time required for the complete life cycle of, say, a mouse is different from that of an elephant, so in the case of minerals, the time required for the life cycle of petroleum may differ from that of coal. This principle also permits a reasonable accurate estimate of the most important date in the production cycle of any exhaustible resource, that of its culmination. This date is especially significant because it marks the dividing point in time between the initial period during which the production rate almost continuously increases and the subsequent period during which it almost continuously declines. It need hardly be added that there is a significant difference between operating an industry whose output increases at a rate of 5 to 10 per cent per year and one whose output declines at such a rate.

Complete Cycle of Coal Production

Because coal deposits occur in stratified seams which are continuous over extensive areas and often crop out on the earth's surface, reasonable good estimates of the coal deposits in various sedimentary basins can be made by surface geological mapping and a limited amount of drilling. A summary of the current estimates of the world's initial coal resources has been published by Paul Averitt (1969) of the U.S. Geological Survey. These estimates comprise the total amount of coal (including lignite) in beds 14 inches (35 centimeters) or more thick and at depths as great as 3,000 feet (900 meters), and in a few cases as great as 6,000 feet. Averitt's estimates as

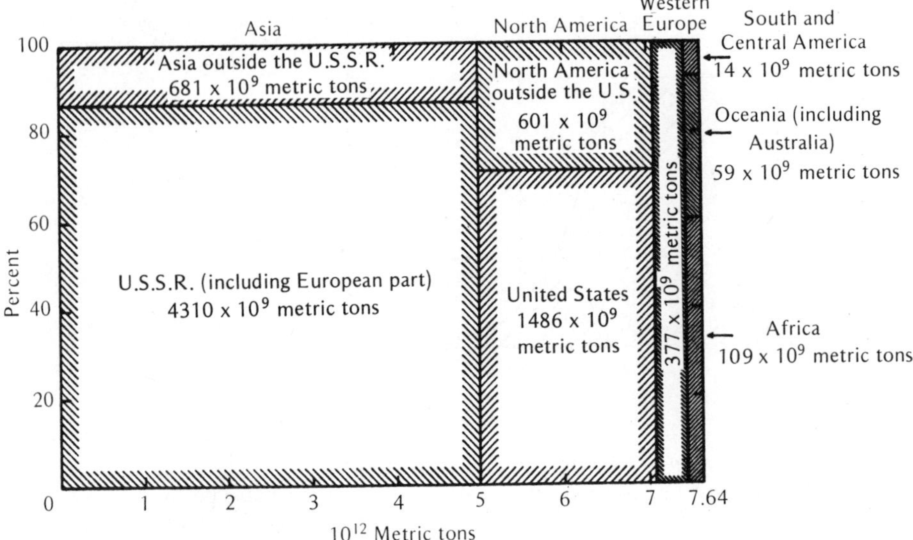

Figure 8-13. Averitt (1969) estimate of original world recoverable coal resources (Hubbert, 1969, Figure 8.24).

of January 1, 1967, for the initial producible coal, allowing 50 per cent loss in mining, are shown graphically in Figure 8-13 for the world's major geographical areas. As seen in this figure, the original recoverable world coal resources amounted to an estimated 7.64 $\times 10^{12}$ metric tons. Of this, 4.31 $\times 10^{12}$, or 56 per cent, were in the U.S.S.R., and 1.49 $\times 10^{12}$, or 19 per cent, in the U.S. At the other extreme, the three continental areas, Africa, South and Central America, and Oceania, together contained only 0.182 $\times 10^{12}$ metric tons, or 2.4 per cent of the world's total.

Figure 8-14 shows two separate graphs for the complete cycle of world coal production. One is based on the Averitt estimate for the

Figure 8-14. Complete cycle of world coal production for two values of Q_∞ (Hubbert, 1969, Figure 8.25).

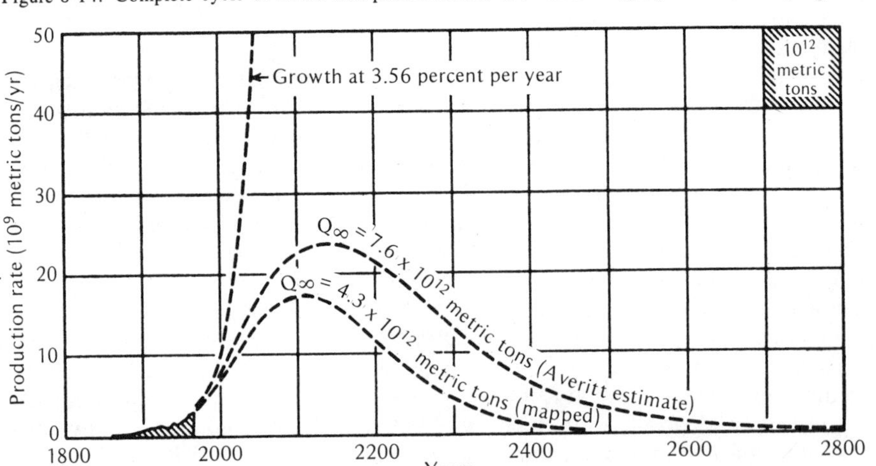

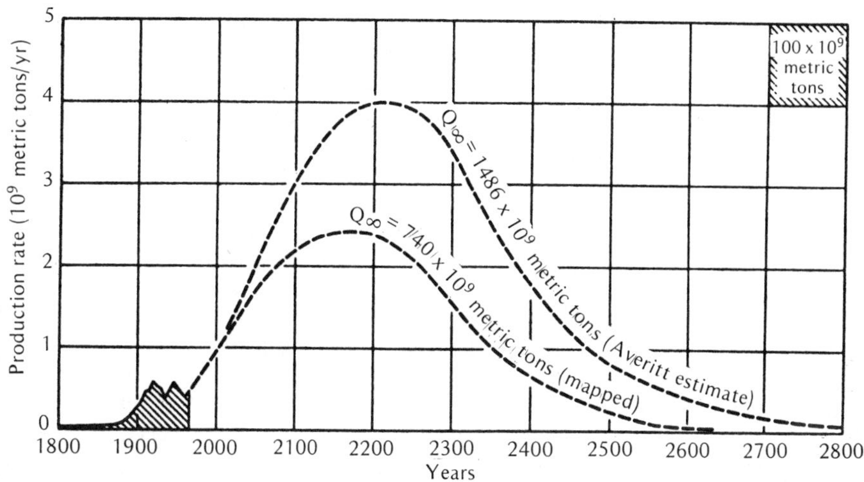

Figure 8-15. Complete cycle of United States coal production for two values of Q_∞ (Hubbert, 1969, Figure 8.26).

ultimate production of 7.6×10^{12} metric tons. These curves are also based on the assumption that not more than three more doublings, or an eightfold increase, will occur before the maximum rate of production is reached. The dashed curve extending to the top of the drawing indicates what the production rate would be were it to continue to increase at 3.56 per cent per year, the rate that has prevailed since World War II. For either of the complete-cycle curves, if we disregard the first and last ten percentiles of the cumulative production, it is evident that the middle 80 per cent of Q_∞ will probably be consumed during the three-century period from about the years 2000 to 2300.

Figure 8-15 shows the complete cycle of United States coal production for the two values for Q_∞, $1{,}486 \times 10^9$ and 740×10^9 metric tons. Here too the time required to consume the middle 80 per cent would be the 3 or 4 centuries following the year 2000.

A serious modification of the above coal-resource figures has been given by Averitt (cited in Theobald, Schweinfurth, and Duncan, 1972). Here, Averitt, in February 1972, has given an estimate of the amount of coal remaining in the United States that is recoverable under present economic and technological conditions. This comprises coal in seams with a minimum thickness of 28 inches and a maximum depth of 1000 feet. The amount of coal in this category is estimated to be 390×10^9 short tons or 354×10^9 metric tons. Adding the 37×10^9 metric tons of coal already produced gives 391×10^9 metric tons of original coal in this category. This amounts to only 26 per cent of the 1486×10^9 metric tons assumed previously. Of this, 9.5 per cent has already been produced. If we apply the same ratio of 26 per cent to the previous world figure of 7.6×10^{12} metric tons, that is reduced to 2.0×10^{12} metric tons. Of this 0.145×10^{12} metric tons, or 7.2 per cent, has already been produced.

Revisions of Figures 8-14 and 8-15 incorporating these lower estimates of recoverable coal have not yet been made, but in each instance the curve for the reduced figure will encompass an area of only about one-quarter that of the uppermost curve shown, and the probable time span for the middle 80 per cent of cumulative production will be cut approximately in half.

Estimates of Petroleum Resources

Because oil and gas occur in limited volumes of space underground in porous sedimentary rocks and at depths ranging from a few hundred feet to five or more miles, the estimation of the ultimate quantities of these fluids

Table 8–1. Petroleum Estimates by Geological Analogy: Louisiana and Texas Continental Shelves (crude oil, 10^9 barrels).

	U.S. Geological Survey Estimates, 1953	*Cumulative Discoveries to 1971*
Louisiana	4	ca. 5
Texas	9	Negligible

that will be obtained from any given area is much more difficult and hazardous than for coal. For the estimation of petroleum, essentially two methods are available: (a) estimation by geological analogy and (b) estimation based on cumulative information and evidence resulting from exploration and productive activites in the region of interest.

The method of estimating by geological analogy is essentially the following. A virgin undrilled territory, Area *B*, is found by surface reconnaissance and mapping to be geologically similar to Area *A*, which is already productive of oil and gas. It is inferred, therefore, that Area *B* will eventually produce comparable quantities of oil and gas per unit of area or unit of volume of sediments to those of Area *A*.

Although this is practically the only method available initially for estimating the oil and gas potential of an undrilled region, it is also intrinsically hazardous, with a very wide range of uncertainty. This is illustrated in Table 8-1, in which the estimates made in 1953 for the future oil discoveries on the continental shelf off the Texas and Louisiana coasts are compared with the results of subsequent drilling.

In 1953, the U.S. Geological Survey, on the basis of geological analogy between the onshore and offshore areas of the Gulf Coast and the respective areas of the continental shelf bordering Texas and Louisiana, estimated future discoveries of 9 billion barrels of oil on the Texas continental shelf and 4 billion on that of Louisiana. After approximately 20 years of petroleum exploration and drilling, discoveries of crude oil on the Louisiana continental shelf have amounted to approximately 5 billion barrels; those on the continental shelf off Texas have been negligible.

The second technique of petroleum estimation involves the use of various aspects of the Hewett criterion that the complete history of petroleum exploration and production in any given area must go through stages from infancy to maturity to old age. Maturity is plainly the stage of production culmination, and old age is that of an advanced state of discovery and production decline.

In March 1956, this technique was explicitly applied to crude-oil production in the United States by the present author (Hubbert, 1956) in an invited address, "Nuclear Energy and the Fossil Fuels," given before an audience of petroleum engineers at a meeting of the Southwest Section of the American Petroleum Institute at San Antonio, Texas. At that time the petroleum industry in the United States had been in vigorous operation for 97 years, during which 52.4 billion barrels of crude oil had been produced. A review of published literature in conjunction with inquiries among experienced petroleum geologists and engineers indicated a consensus that the ultimate amount of crude to be produced from the conterminous 48 states and adjacent continental shelves would probably be within the range of 150 to 200 billion barrels. Using these two limiting figures, the curves for the complete cycle of United States crude-oil production shown in Figure 8-16 (Hubbert, 1956) were constructed. This showed that if the ultimate cumulative production, Q_∞, should be as small as 150×10^9 barrels, the peak in the rate of production would probably occur about 1966—about 10 years hence. Should another 50×10^9 barrels be added, making $Q_\infty = 200 \times 10^9$ barrels, the date of the peak of production would be postponed by only about 5 years. It was accordingly predicted on the basis of available information that the peak in United States crude-oil production would occur within 10–15 years after March 1956.

This prediction proved to be both surprising and disturbing to the United States petroleum industry. The only way it could be

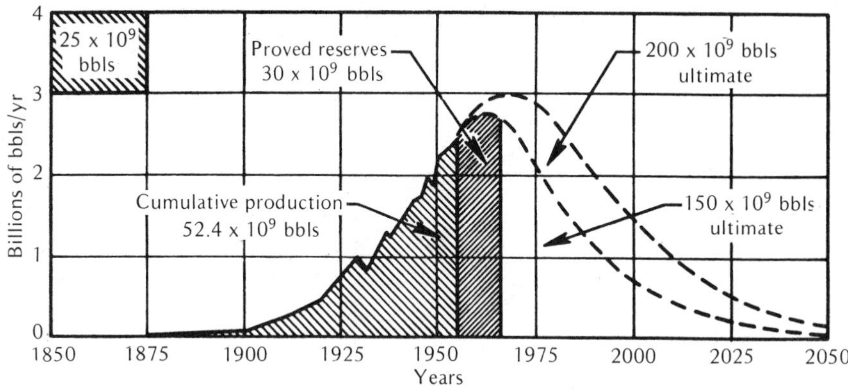

Figure 8-16. 1956 prediction of the date of peak in the rate of United States crude oil production (Hubbert, 1956, Figure 21).

avoided, however, was to enlarge the area under the curve of the complete cycle of production by increasing the magnitude of Q_∞. As small increases of Q_∞ have only small effects in retarding the date of peak production, if this unpleasant conclusion were to be avoided, it would be necessary to increase Q_∞ by large magnitudes. This was what happened. Within the next five years, with insignificant amounts of new data, the published values for Q_∞ were rapidly escalated to successively higher values—204, 250, 372, 400 and eventually 590 billion barrels.

In view of the fact that values for Q_∞ used in Figure 8-16 involved semisubjective judgments, no adequate rational basis existed for

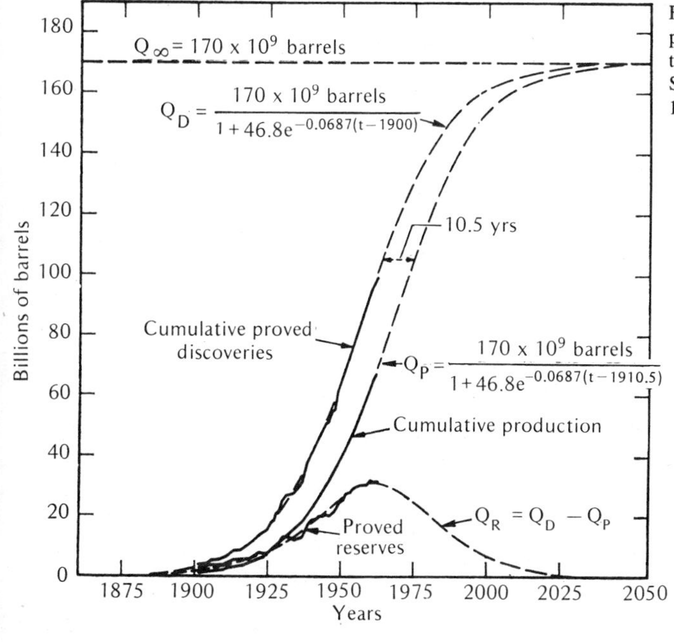

Figure 8-17. Curves of cumulative proved discoveries, cumulative production and proved reserves of United States crude oil as of 1962 (Hubbert, 1962, Figure 27).

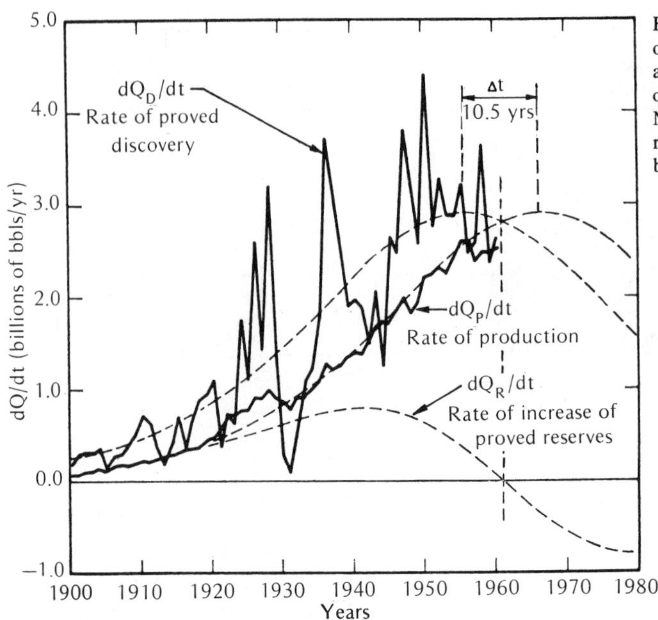

Figure 8-18. Curves showing the rates of proved discovery and of production, and rate of increase of proved reserves of United States crude oil as of 1961. Note prediction of peak of production rate near the end of 1960 decade (Hubbert, 1962, Figure 28).

showing conclusively that a figure of 200 × 10^9 barrels was a much more reliable estimate than one twice that large. This led to the search for other criteria derivable from objective, publicly available data of the petroleum industry. The data satisfying this requirement were the statistics of annual production available since 1860, and the annual estimates of proved reserves of the Proved Reserves Committee of the American Petroleum Institute, begun in 1937. From these data cumulative production from 1860 could be com-

Figure 8-19. 1962 estimates of the dates of the peaks of rate of proved discovery, rate of production, and proved reserves of United States natural gas (Hubbert, 1962, Figure 46).

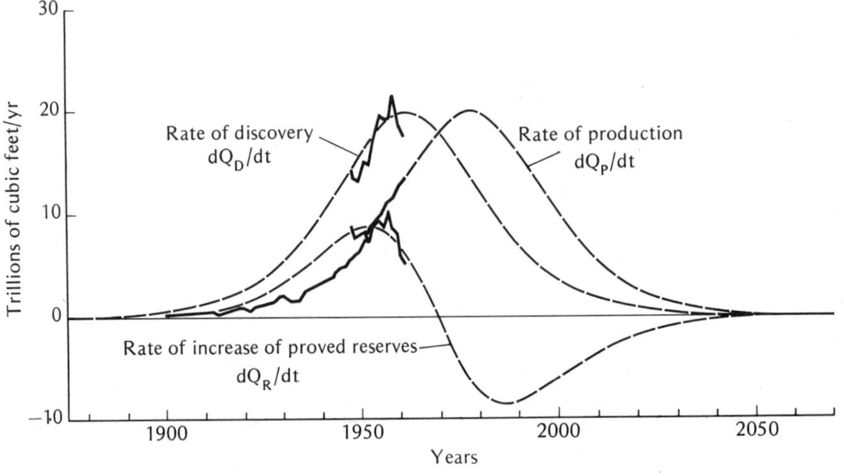

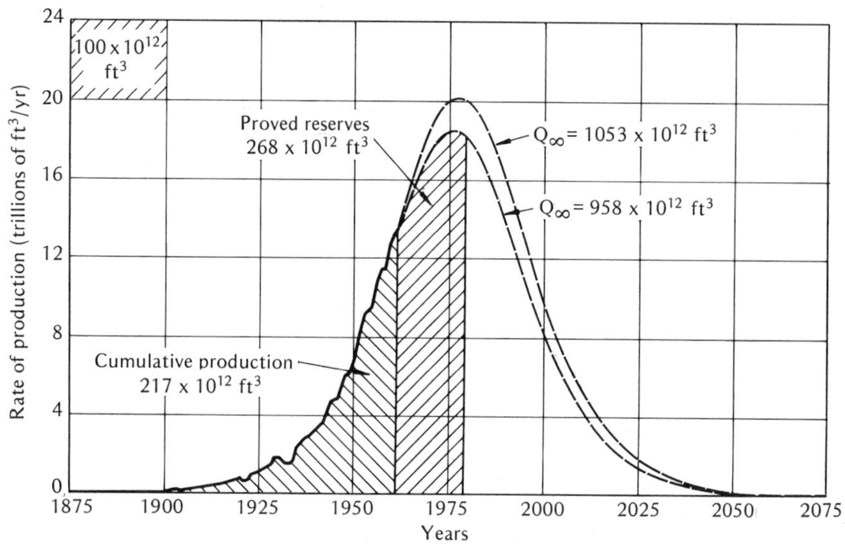

Figure 8-20. 1962 estimates of ultimate amount of natural gas to be produced in conterminous United States, and estimates of date of peak production rate (Hubbert, 1962, Figure 47).

puted, and also cumulative proved discoveries defined as the sum of cumulative production and proved reserves after 1937.

This type of analysis was used in the report, *Energy Resources* (Hubbert, 1962), of the National Academy of Sciences Committee on Natural Resources. The principal results of this study are shown in Figures 8-17 and 8-18, in which it was found that the rate of proved discoveries of crude oil had already passed its peak about 1957, proved reserves were estimated to be at their peak in 1962, and the peak in the rate of crude-oil production was predicted to occur at about the end of the 1960 decade. The ultimate amount of crude oil to be produced from the lower 48 states and adjacent continental shelves was estimated to be about 170 to 175 billion barrels.

The corresponding estimates for natural gas are shown in Figures 8-19 and 8-20 (Hubbert, 1962). From these figures it will be seen that the rate of proved discoveries was estimated to be at its peak at about 1961. Proved reserves of natural gas were estimated to reach their peak ($dQ_r/dt=0$) at about 1969, and the rate of production about 1977.

At the time the study was being made, the U.S. Geological Survey, in response to a presidential directive of March 4, 1961, presented to the Academy Committee estimates of 590×10^9 barrels for crude oil and 2,650 trillion cubic feet for natural gas as its offical estimates of the ultimate amounts of these fluids that would be produced from the lower 48 states and adjacent continental shelves.

These estimates were, by a wide margin, the highest that had ever been made up until that time. Moreover, had they been true, there would have been no grounds for the expectation of an oil or gas shortage in the United States much before the year 2000. These estimates were cited in the Academy Committee report, but because of their wide disparity with any available evidence from the petroleum industry, they were also rejected.

As only became clear some time later, the basis for those large estimates was an hypothesis introduced by the late A. D. Zapp of the U.S. Geological Survey, as illustrated in Figure 8-21 (Hubbert, 1969). Zapp postulated that the exploration for petroleum in the United States would not be completed until

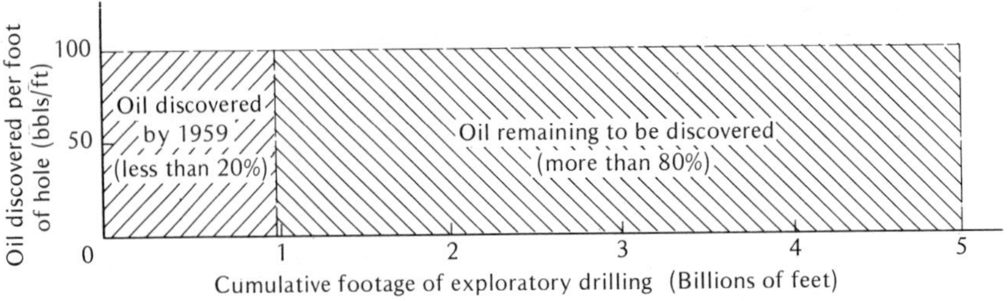

Figure 8-21. Zapp (1962) hypothesis of oil discoveries per foot versus cumulative footage of exploratory drilling for conterminous United States and adjacent continental shelves (Hubbert, 1969, Figure 8.18)

exploratory wells with an average density of one well per each 2 square miles had been drilled either to the crystalline basement rock or to a depth of 20,000 feet in all the potential petroleum-bearing sedimentary basins. He estimated that to drill this pattern of wells in the petroliferous areas of the conterminous United States and adjacent continental shelves would require about 5 × 10^9 feet of exploratory drilling. He then estimated that, as of 1959, only 0.98 × 10^9 feet of exploratory drilling had been done and concluded that at that time the United States was less than 20 per cent along in its ultimate petroleum exploration. He also stated that during recent decades there had been no decline in the oil found per foot of exploratory drilling, yet already more than 100 × 10^9 barrels of oil had been discovered in the United States. It was implied, but not expressly stated, that the ultimate amount of oil to be discovered would be more than 500 × 10^9 barrels.

This was confirmed in 1961 by the Zapp estimate for crude oil given to the Academy Committee. At that time, with cumulative drilling of 1.1 × 10^9 feet, Zapp estimated that 130 × 10^9 barrels of crude oil had already been discovered. This would be at an average rate of 118 barrels per foot. Then, at this same rate, the amount of oil to be discovered by 5 × 10^9 feet of exploratory drilling should be 590 × 10^9 barrels, which is the estimate given to the Academy Committee. This consitiutes the "Zapp hypothesis." Not only is it the basis for Zapp's own estimates, but with only minor modifications it has been the principal basis for most of the subsequent higher estimates.

The most obvious test for the validity of this hypothesis is to apply it to past petroleum discoveries in the United States. Has the oil found per foot of exploratory drilling been nearly constant during the past? The answer to this is given in Figure 8-22 (Hubbert, 1967), which shows the quantity of oil discovered and the average amount of oil found per foot for each 10^8 feet of exploratory drilling in the United States from 1860 to 1965. This shows an initial rate of 194 barrels per foot for the first unit from 1860 to 1920, a maximum rate of 276 barrels per foot for the third unit extending from 1929 to 1935 and then a precipitate decline to about 35 barrels per foot by 1965. This is approximately an exponential decline curve, the integration of which for unlimited future drilling gives an estimate of about 165 × 10^9 for Q_∞, the ultimate discoveries.

The superposition of the actual discoveries per foot shown in Figure 8-22 on the discoveries per foot according to the Zapp hypothesis of Figure 8-21 is shown in Figure 8-23 (Hubbert, 1969). The difference between the areas beneath the two curves represents the difference between the two estimates—an apparent overestimate of about 425 × 10^9 barrels.

To recapitulate, in the Academy Committee report of 1962, the peak in United States proved crude-oil discoveries, excluding Alaska, was estimated to have occurred at about 1957, the peak in proved reserves at

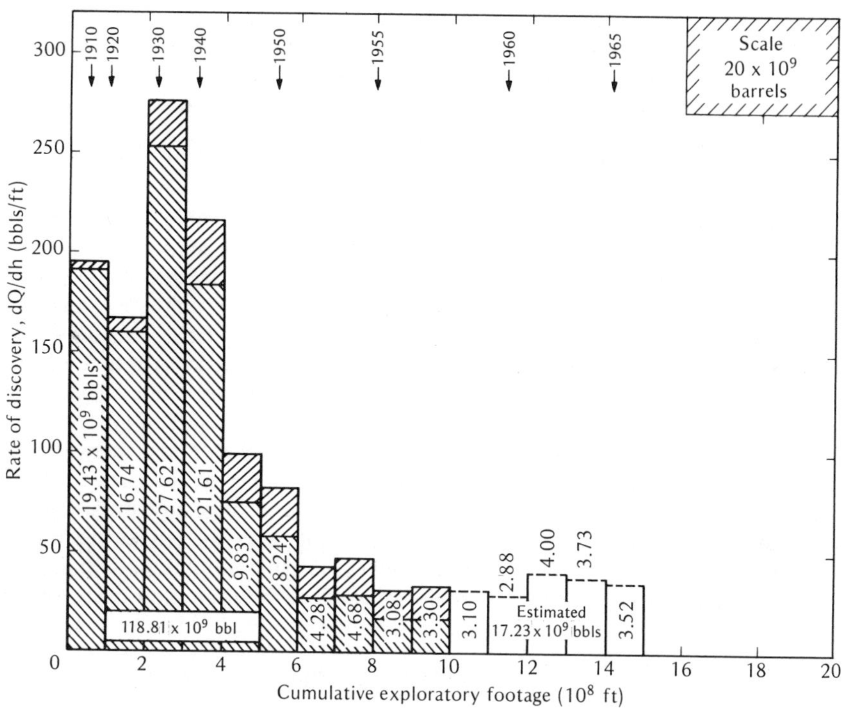

Figure 8-22. Actual United States crude-oil discoveries per foot of exploratory drilling as a function of cumulative exploratory drilling from 1860 to 1965 (Hubbert, 1967, Figure 15).

Figure 8-23. Comparison of United States crude oil discoveries according to Zapp hypothesis with actual discoveries. The difference between the areas beneath the two curves represents an overestimate of about 425 billion barrels (Hubbert, 1969, Figure 8.19).

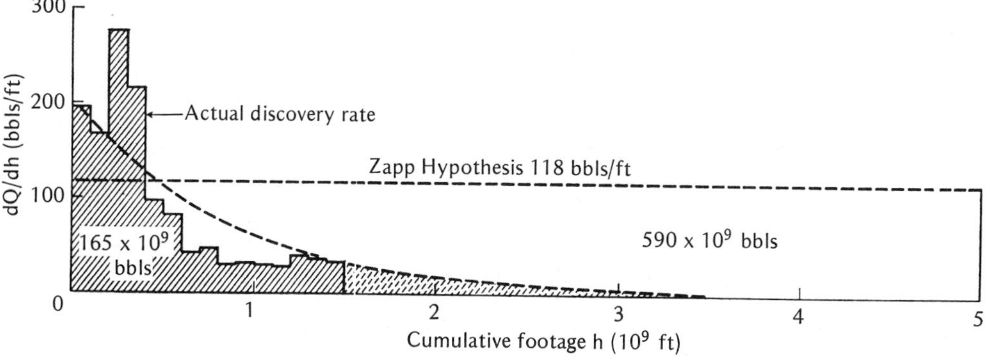

about 1962 and the peak in production was predicted for about 1968–1969. The peak in proved reserves did occur in 1962, and the peak in the rate of production occurred in 1970. Evidence that this is not likely to be exceeded is afforded by the fact that for the six months since March 1972, the production rates of both Texas and Louisiana, which together account for 60 per cent of the total United States crude-oil production, have been at approximately full capacity, and declining.

As for natural gas, the Academy report estimated that the peak in proved reserves would occur at about 1969 and the peak in the rate of production about 1977. As of September 1972, the peak of proved reserves for the conterminous 48 states occurred in 1967, two years ahead of the predicted date, and it now appears that the peak in the rate of natural-gas production will occur about 1974 to 1975, two to three years earlier than predicted. In the 1962 Academy report, the ultimate production of natural gas was estimated to be about $1{,}000 \times 10^{12}$ cubic feet. Present estimates by two different methods give a low figure of $1{,}000 \times 10^{12}$ and a high figure of $1{,}080 \times 10^{12}$, or a mean of $1{,}040 \times 10^{12}$ cubic feet.

Because of its early stage of development, the petroleum potential of Alaska must be based principally on geological analogy with other areas. The recent Prudhoe Bay discovery of a 10-billion-barrel field—the largest in the United States—has been a source of excitement for an oil-hungry United States petroleum industry, but it still represents less than a three-year supply for the United States. From present information, a figure of 30×10^9 barrels is about as large an estimate as can be justified for the ultimate crude-oil production from the land area of Alaska, although a figure greater than this is an admitted possibil-

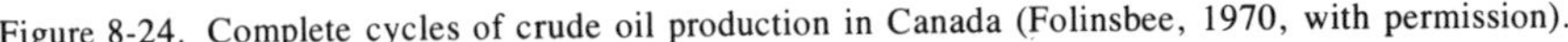
Figure 8-24. Complete cycles of crude oil production in Canada (Folinsbee, 1970, with permission).

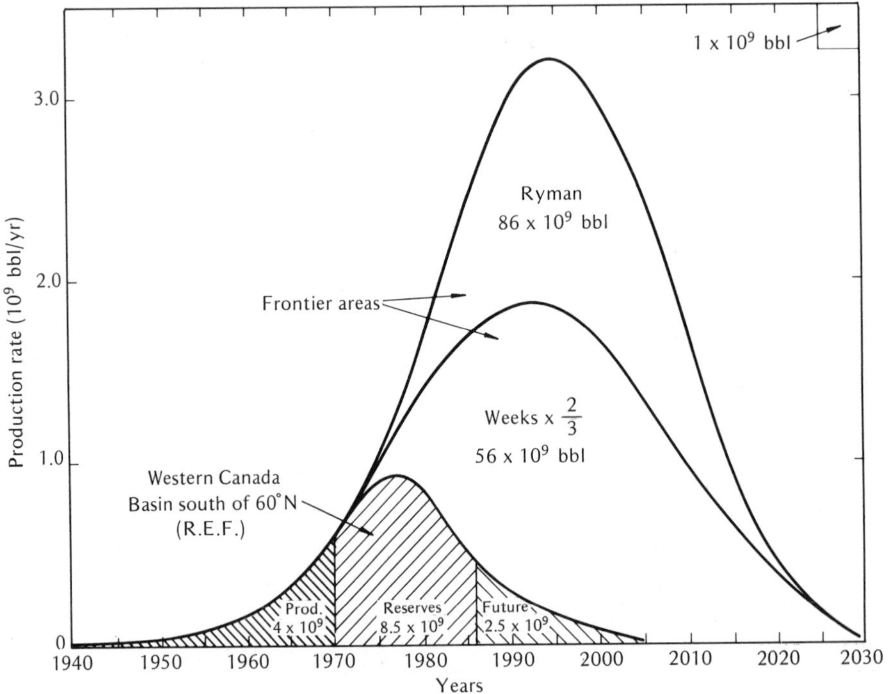

ity. Adding this to a present figure of about 170 × 10^9 barrels for the conterminous 48 states gives 200 × 10^9 as the approximate amount of crude oil ultimately to be produced in the whole United States.

Canada's Resources

For this article, it has not been possible to make an analysis of the oil and gas resources of Canada. However, Figure 8-24, from R. E. Folinsbee's Presidential Address before the geological section of the Royal Society of Canada (1970), provides a very good appraisal of the approximate magnitude of Canadian crude-oil resources. According to this estimate, the ultimate production of crude oil from western Canada south of latitude 60° will be about 15 × 10^9 barrels, of which 12.5 × 10^9 have already been discovered. The peak in the production rate for this area is estimated at about 1977. This figure also shows a maximum estimate of 86 × 10^9 barrels of additional oil from the frontier areas of Canada. Should this be exploited in a systematic manner from the present time, a peak production rate of about 3 × 10^9 barrels per year would probably be reached by about 1995.

As of 1973, however, the proved reserves for Canadian crude oil and natural-gas liquids both reached their peaks in 1969; those for natural gas in 1971. Therefore, unless development and transportation of oil and gas from the frontier provinces begins soon, there may be a temporary decline in total Canadian production of oil and gas toward the end of the present decade.

World Crude Oil Production

In this brief review, only a summary statement can be made for the petroleum resources of the world as a whole. Recent estimates by various major oil companies and petroleum geologists have been summarized by H. R. Warman (Warman, 1971) of the British Petroleum Company, who gave 226 × 10^9 barrels as the cumulative world crude-oil production and 527 × 10^9 barrels for the proved reserves at the end of 1969. This totals 753 × 10^9 barrels as the world's proved cumulative discoveries. For the ultimate recoverable crude oil, Warman cited the following estimates published during the period 1967–1970:

Year	*Author*	*Quantity (10^9 barrels)*
1967	Ryman (Esso)	2,090
1968	Hendricks (USGS)	2,480
1968	Shell	1,800
1969	Hubbert (NAS-NRC)	1,350–2,100
1969	Weeks	2,200
1970	Moody (Mobil)	1,800

To this, Warman added his own estimate of 1,200–2,000 × 10^9 barrels. A recent unpublished estimate by the research staff of another oil company is in the mid-range of 1,900–2,000 × 10^9 barrels.

From these estimates, there appears to be a convergence toward an estimate of 2,000 × 10^9 barrels, or slightly less. The implication of such a figure to the complete cycle of world crude-oil production is shown in Figure 8-25 (Hubbert, 1969), using two limiting values of 1,350 × 10^9 and 2,100 × 10^9 barrels. For the higher figure, the world will reach the peak in its rate of crude-oil production at about the year 2000; for the lower figure, this date would be about 1990.

Another significant figure for both the United States and the world crude-oil production is the length of time required to produce the middle 80 per cent of the ultimate production. In each case, the time is about 65 years, or less than a human lifetime. For the United States, this subtends the period from about 1937 to 2003, and for the world, from about 1967 to 2032.

Another category of petroleum liquids is that of natural-gas liquids, which are produced as a by-product of natural gas. In the United States (excluding Alaska), the ultimate amount of natural-gas liquids, based on an ultimate amount of crude oil of 170 × 10^9 barrels, and 1,040 × 10^{12} feet of natural gas, amounts to about 36 × 10^9 barrels. Corre-

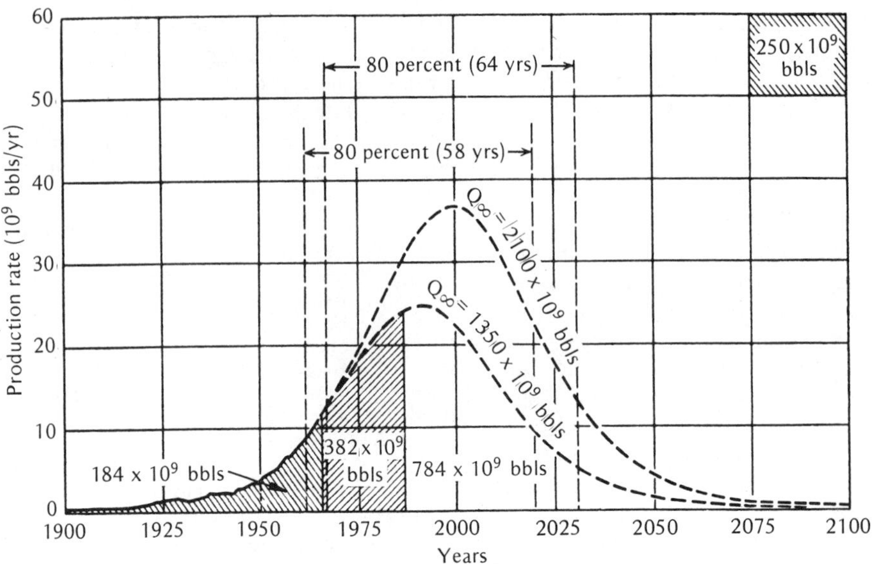

Figure 8-25. Complete cycle of world crude-oil production for two values of Q_∞ (Hubbert, 1969, Figure 8.23).

sponding world figures, based on an estimate of 200 × 10^9 barrels for crude oil, would be about 400 × 10^9 barrels for natural-gas liquids, and 12,000 cubic feet for natural gas.

Other Fossil Fuels

In addition to coal, petroleum liquids and natural gas, the other principal classes of fossil fuels are the so-called tar, or heavy-oil, sands and oil shales. The best known and probably the largest deposits of heavy-oil sands are in the "Athabasca Tar Sands" and two smaller deposits in northern Alberta containing an estimated 300 × 10^9 barrels of potentially producible oil. One large-scale mining and extracting operation was begun in 1966 by a group of oil companies, and others doubtless will follow as the need for this oil develops.

Unlike tar sands, the fuel content of which is a heavy, viscous crude oil, oil shales contain hydrocarbons in a solid form known as *kerogen,* which distils off as a vapor on heating and condenses to a liquid on cooling. The extractible oil content of oil shales ranges from as high as 100 United States gallons per short ton for the richest grades to near zero as the grades diminish. When all grades are considered, the aggregate oil content of the known oil shales is very large. However, in practice, only the shales having an oil content of about 25 gallons or more per ton and occurring in beds 10 feet or more thick are considered to be economical sources at present. According to a world inventory of known oil shales by Duncan and Swanson (1965), the largest known deposits are those of the Green River Formation in Wyoming, Colorado and Utah. From these shales, in the grade range from 10 to 65 gallons per ton, the authors estimate that only 80 × 10^9 barrels are recoverable under 1965 economic conditions. Their corresponding figure for oil shales outside the United States is 110 × 10^9 barrels.

The absolute magnitude of the world's original supply of fossil fuels recoverable under present technological and economic conditions and their respective energy contents in terms of their heats of combustion are

Table 8–2. Approximate Magnitudes and Energy Contents of the World's Original Supply of Fossil Fuels Recoverable under Present Conditions.

		Energy Content		
Fuel	*Quantity*	*10^{21} Thermal Joules*	*10^{15} Thermal Kilowatt-Hours*	*Per Cent*
Coal and lignite	2.35×10^{12} metric tons	53.2	14.80	63.78
Petroleum liquids	$2{,}400 \times 10^{9}$ barrels	14.2	3.95	17.03
Natural gas	$12{,}000 \times 10^{12}$ cubic feet	13.1	3.64	15.71
Tar-sand oil	300×10^{9} barrels	1.8	0.50	2.16
Shale oil	190×10^{9} barrels	1.1	0.31	1.32
Totals		83.4	23.20	100.00

given in Table 8-2. The total initial energy represented by all of these fuels amounted to about 83×10^{21} thermal joules, or 23×10^{15} thermal kilowatt-hours. Of this, 64 per cent was represented by coal and lignite, 17 and 16 per cent, respectively, by petroleum liquids and natural gas, and 3 per cent by tar-sand and shale oil combined. Although the total amount of coal and lignite in beds 14 or more inches thick and occurring at depths less than 3,000 feet, as estimated by Averitt, are very much larger in terms of energy content, than the initial quantities of oil and gas, the coal practically recoverable under present conditions is only about twice the magnitude of the initial quantities of gas and oil in terms of energy content. Therefore, at comparable rates of production, the time required for the complete cycle of coal production will not be much longer than that for petroleum—in order of a century or two for the exhaustion of the middle 80 per cent of the ultimate cumulative production.

To appreciate the brevity of this period in terms of the longer span of human history, the historical epoch of the exploitation of the fossil fuels is shown graphically in Figure 8-26, plotted on a time scale extending from 5000 years in the past to 5000 years in the future—a period well within the prospective span of human history. On such a time scale, it is seen that the epoch of the fossil fuels can be only a transitory or ephemeral event—an event, nonetheless, which has exercised the most drastic influence on the human species during its entire biological history.

Figure 8-26. Epoch of fossil-fuel exploitation in perspective of human history from 5,000 years in the past to 5,000 years in the future (modified from Hubbert, 1962, Figure 54).

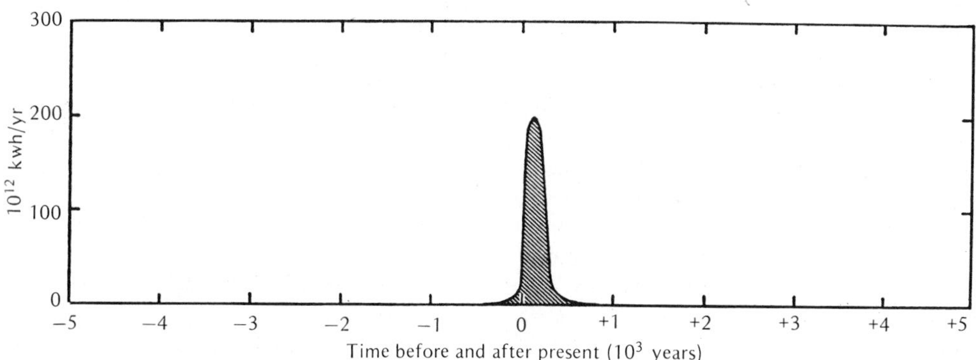

OTHER SOURCES OF INDUSTRIAL ENERGY

The remaining sources of energy suitable for large-scale industrial use are principally the following.

1. Direct use of solar radiation
2. Indirect uses of solar radiation
   (a) Water power
   (b) Wind power
   (c) Photosynthesis
   (d) Thermal energy of ocean water at different temperatures
3. Geothermal power
4. Tidal power
5. Nuclear power
   (a) Fission
   (b) Fusion

Solar Power

By a large margin, the largest flux of energy occurring on the earth is that from solar radiation. The thermal power of the solar radiation intercepted by the earth, according to recent measurements of the solar constant, amounts to about $174{,}000 \times 10^{12}$ thermal watts. This is roughly 5,000 times all other steady fluxes of energy combined. It also has the expectation of continuing at about the same rate for geological periods of time into the future.

The largest concentrations of solar radiation reaching the earth's surface occur in desert areas within about 35 degrees of latitude north and south of the equator. Southern Arizona and neighboring areas in the southwestern part of the United States are in this belt, as well as northern Mexico, the Atacama Desert in Chile, and a zone across northern Africa, vhe Arabian Peninsula, and Iran. In southern Arizona, the thermal power density of the solar radiation incident upon the earth's surface ranges from about 300 to 650 calories per square centimeter per day, from winter to summer. The winter minimum of 300 calories per square centimeter per day, when averaged over 24 hours, represents a mean power density of 145 watts per square meter. If 10 per cent of this could be converted into electrical power by photovoltaic cells or other means, the electrical power obtainable from 1 square kilometer of collection area would be 14.5 megawatts. Then, for an electrical power plant of 1,000 megawatts capacity, the collection area required would be about 70 square kilometers. At such an efficiency of conversion, the collection area required to generate 350,000 megawatts of electrical power—the approximate electric-power capacity of the United States at present—would be roughly 25,000 square kilometers or 9,000 square miles. This is somewhat less than 10 per cent of the area of Arizona.

Such a calculation indicates that large-scale generation of electric power from direct solar radiation is not to be ruled out on the grounds of technical infeasibility. It is also gratifying that a great deal of interest on the part of technically competent groups in universities and research institutions has arisen during the last five years over the possibility of developing large-scale solar power.

Hydroelectric Power

Although there has been continuous use of water power since Roman times, large units were not possible until a means was developed for the generation and transmission of power electrically. The first large hydroelectric power installation was that made at Niagara Falls in 1895. There, ten 5,000-horsepower turbines were installed for the generation of alternating current power, which was transmitted a distance of 26 miles to the city of Buffalo. The subsequent growth of hydroelectric power in the United States is shown in Figure 8-27 and that for the world in Figure 8-28.

In the United States, by 1970, the installed hydroelectric power capacity amounted to 53,000 megawatts, which is 32 per cent of the ultimate potential capacity of 161,000 megawatts as estimated by the Federal Power Commission. The world installation, by 1967, amounted to 243,000 megawatts, which is 8.5 per cent of the world's estimated

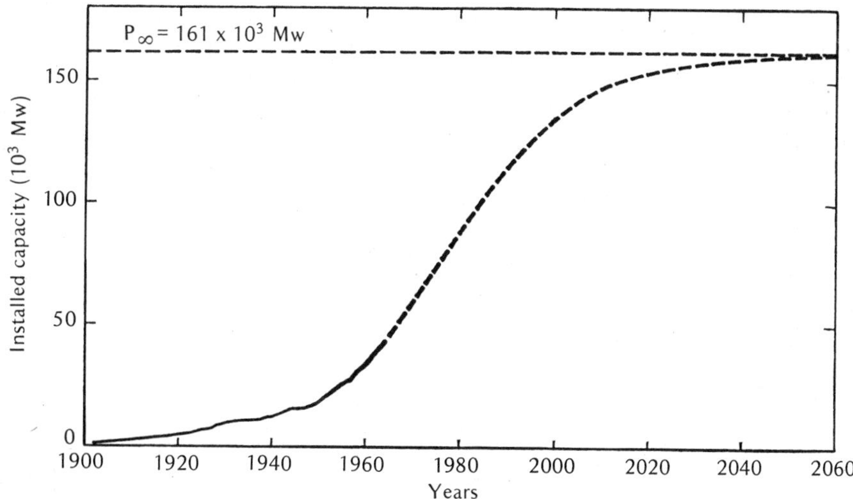

Figure 8-27. Installed and potential hydroelectric-power capacity of the United States (Hubbert, 1969, Figure 8.28).

potential hydroelectric power of 2,860,000 megawatts. Most of this developed capacity is in the highly industrialized areas of North America, Western Europe, and the Far East, especially Japan.

The areas with the largest potential water-power capacities are the industrially underdeveloped regions of Africa, South America, and Southeast Asia, where combined capacities represent 63 per cent of the world total.

The total world potential water power of approximately 3×10^{12} watts, if fully developed, would be of about the same mag-

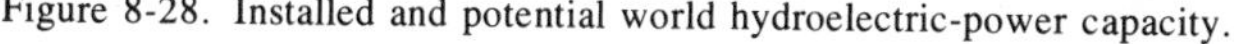

Figure 8-28. Installed and potential world hydroelectric-power capacity.

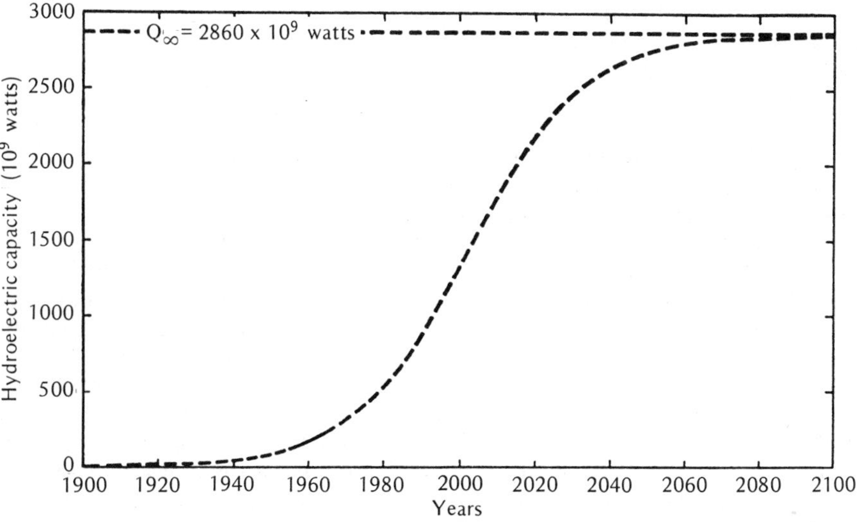

nitude as the world's present rate of utilization of industrial power. It may also appear that this would be an inexhaustible source of power, or at least one with a time span comparable to that required to remove mountains by stream erosion. This may not be true, however. Most water-power developments require the creation of reservoirs by the damming of streams. The time required to fill these reservoirs with sediments is only two or three centuries. Hence, unless a technical solution of this problem can be found, water power may actually be comparatively short lived.

Tidal Power

Tidal power is essentially hydroelectric power obtainable by damming the entrance to a bay or estuary in a region of tides with large amplitudes, and driving turbines as the tidal basin fills and empties. An inventory of the world's most favorable tidal-power sites gives an estimate of a total potential power capacity of about 63,000 megawatts, which is about 2 per cent of the world's potential water power capacity. At present, one or more small pilot tidal-power plants of a few megawatts capacity have been built, but the only full-scale tidal plant so far built is that on the Rance estuary on the English Channel coast of France. This plant began operation in 1966 with an initial capacity of 240 megawatts and a planned enlargement to 320 megawatts.

One of the world's most favorable tidal-power localities is the Bay of Fundy region of northeastern United States and southeastern Canada. This has the world's maximum tides, with amplitudes up to 15 meters, and a combined power capacity of nine sites of about 29,000 megawatts. Extensive plans have been made by both the United States and Canada for the utilization of this power, but as yet no installations have been made.

Geothermal Power

Geothermal power is obtained by means of heat engines which extract thermal energy from heated water within a depth ranging from a few hundred meters to a few kilometers beneath the earth's surface. This is most practical where water has been heated to high temperatures at shallow depths by hot igneous or volcanic rocks that have risen to near the earth's surface. Steam can be used to drive steam turbines. At present, the major geothermal power installations are in two localities in Italy with a total capacity of about 400 megawatts, the Geysers in California with a planned capacity by 1975 of 500 megawatts, and at Wairakei in New Zealand with a capacity of 160 megawatts. The total world installed geothermal power capacity at present is approximately 1,500 megawatts.

What may be the ultimate capacity can be estimated at present to perhaps only an order of magnitude. Recently, a number of geothermal-power enthusiasts (many with financial interests in the outcome) have made very large estimates for power from this source. However, until better information becomes available, an estimation within the range of 60,000 to 600,000 megawatts, or between 2 and 20 per cent of potential water power, is all that can be justified. Also, as geothermal-power production involves "mining" quantities of stored thermal energy, it is likely that most large installations will also be comparatively short lived—perhaps a century or so.

Nuclear Power

A last major source of industrial power is that of atomic nuclei. Power may be obtained by two contrasting types of nuclear reactions: (a) the fissioning of heavy atomic isotopes, initially uranium-235; and (b) the fusing of the isotopes of hydrogen into heavier helium. In the fission process, two stages are possible. The first consists of power reactors which are dependent almost solely on the rare isotope, uranium-235, which represents only 0.7 per cent of natural uranium. The second process is that of breeding whereby either the common isotope of uranium, uranium-238, or alternatively thorium, is placed in a reactor initially fueled by uranium-235. In response to neutron bombardment, uranium-238 is converted into plutonium-239, or thorium-232 into uranium-233, both of which are fissionable. Hence by means of a breeder reactor, in principle, all of the natural uranium or thorium can be converted into fissionable reactor fuel.

Uranium-235 is sufficiently scarce that, without the breeder reactor, the time span of large-scale nuclear power production would probably be less than a century. With complete breeding, however, it becomes possible not only to consume all of the natural uranium or thorium, but to utilize low-grade sources as well.

The energy released by the fissioning of a gram of uranium-235 or plutonium-239 or uranium-233 amounts to 8.2×10^{10} joules of heat. This is approximately equivalent to the heat of combustion of 2.7 metric tons of bituminous coal or 13.4 barrels of crude oil. For the energy obtainable from a source of low-grade uranium, consider the Chattanooga Shale, which crops out along the western edge of the Appalachian Mountains in eastern Tennessee and underlies, at minable depths, most of several midwestern states. This shale has a uranium-rich layer about 16 feet or 5 meters thick with a uranium content of 60 grams per metric ton, or 150 grams per cubic meter. This is equivalent to 750 grams per square meter of land area. Assuming only 50 per cent extraction, this would be equivalent in terms of energy content to about 1,000 metric tons of bituminous coal or to 5,000 barrels of crude oil per square meter of land area, or to one billion metric tons of coal or 5 billion barrels of oil per square kilometer. In this region, an area of only 1,600 square kilometers would be required for the energy obtainable from the uranium in the Chattanooga Shale to equal that of all the fossil fuels in the Untied States. Such an area would be equivalent to that of a square 40 kilometers, or 25 miles, to the side, which would represent less than 2 per cent of the area of Tennessee.

The fusion of hydrogen into helium is known to be the source of the enormous amount of energy radiating from the sun. Fusion has also been achieved by man in an uncontrolled or explosive manner in the thermonuclear or hydrogen bomb. As yet, despite intensive efforts in several countries, controlled fusion has not been achieved. Researchers, however, are hopeful that it may be within the next few decades.

Should fusion be achieved, eventually the principal raw material will probably be the heavy isotope of hydrogen, deuterium. This occurs in sea water at an abundance of 1 deuterium atom to each 6,700 atoms of hydrogen. The deuterium-deuterium, or D-D, reaction involves several stages, the net result of which is

$$5\,{}^{2}_{1}\mathrm{D} \rightarrow {}^{4}_{2}\mathrm{He} + {}^{3}_{2}\mathrm{He} + \mathrm{H} + 2n + 24.8\ \mathrm{Mev}$$

or, in other words, 5 atoms of deuterium, on fusion, produce 1 atom of helium-4, 1 atom of helium-3, 1 atom of hydrogen, and 2 neutrons, and in addition release 24.8 million electron volts, or 39.8×10^{-13} joules.

It can be computed that 1 liter of water contains 1.0×10^{22} deuterium atoms, which upon fusion would release 7.95×10^{9} joules of thermal energy. This is equivalent to the heat of combustion of 0.26 metric tons of coal or 1.30 barrels of crude oil. Then, as 1 cubic kilometer of sea water is equivalent to 10^{12} liters, the heat released by the fusion of the deuterium contained in 1 cubic kilometer of sea water would be equivalent to that of the combustion of 1,300 billion barrels of oil or 260 billion tons of coal. The deuterium in 33 cubic kilometers of sea water would be equivalent to that of the world's initial supply of fossil fuels.

ECOLOGICAL ASPECTS OF EXPONENTIAL GROWTH

From the foregoing review, what stands out most clearly is that our present industrialized civilization has arisen principally during the last two centuries. It has been accomplished by the exponential growth of most of its major components at rates commonly in the range of

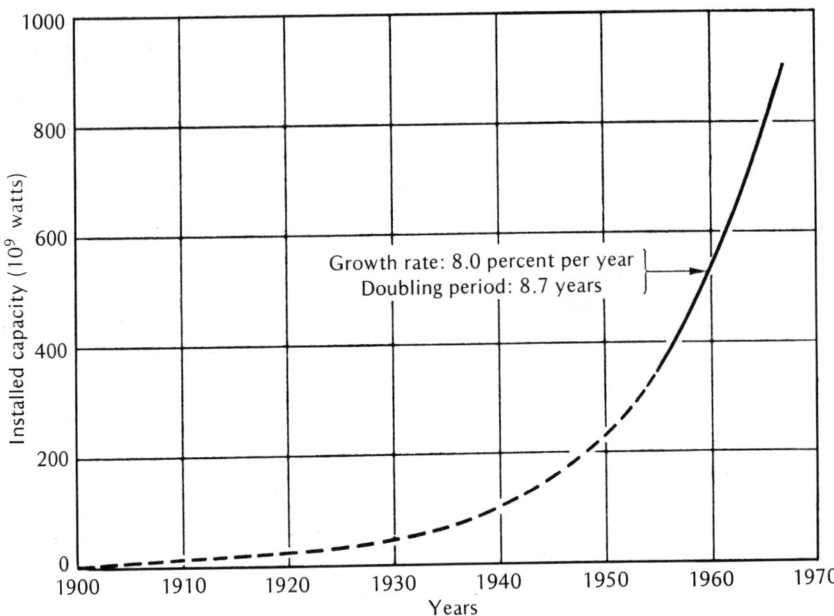

Figure 8-29. World electric generating capacity as an example of exponential growth (Hubbert, 1971, Figure 2).

Figure 8-30. Growth of human population since the year 1000 A.D. as an example of an ecological disturbance (Hubbert, 1962, Figure 2).

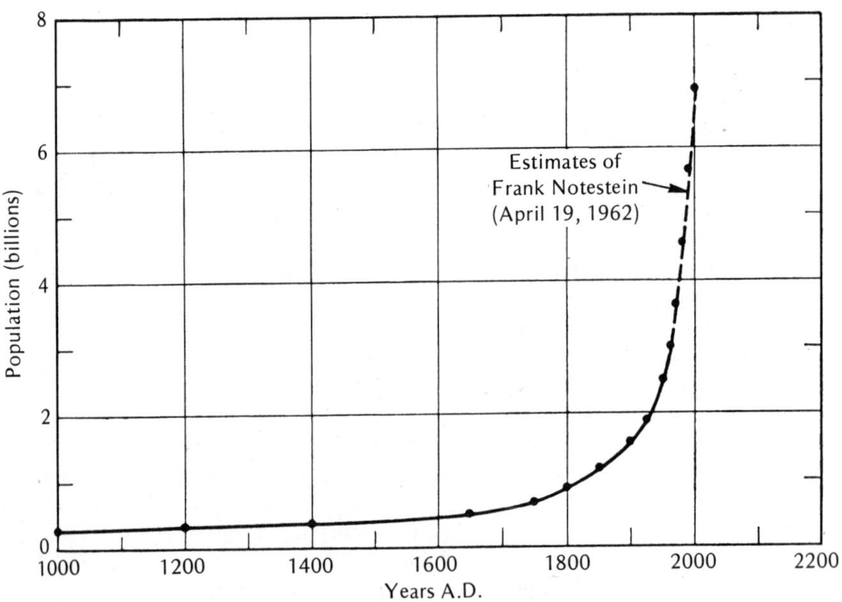

4 to 8 per cent per year, with periods of doubling from 8 to 16 years. The question now arises: What are the limits to such growth, and what does this imply concerning our future?

What we are dealing with, essentially, are the principles of ecology. It has long been known by ecologists that the population of any biologic species, if given a favorable environment, will increase exponentially with time; that is, that the population will double repeatedly at roughly equal intervals of time. From our previous observations, we have seen that this is also true of industrial components. For example (Figure 8-29), the world electric power capacity is now growing at 8 per cent per year and doubling every 8.7 years. The world automobile population and the miles flown per year by the world's civil aviation scheduled flights are each doubling every 10 years. Also, the human population is now doubling in 35 years (Figure 8-30).

The second part of this ecological principle is that such exponential growth of any biologic population can only be maintained for a limited number of doublings before retarding influences set in. In the biological case, these may be represented by restriction of food supply, by crowding or by environmental pollution. The complete biologic growth curve is represented by the logistic curve in Figure 8-31.

Figure 8-31. The logistic growth curve showing both the inital exponential phase and the final slowing down during a cycle of growth.

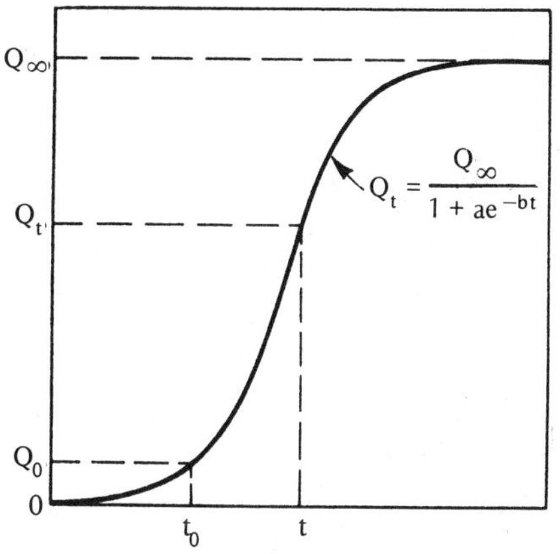

That there must be limits to growth can easily be seen by the most elementary arithmetic analysis. Consider the familiar checkerboard problem of placing 1 grain of wheat on the first square, 2 on the second, 4 on the third, and doubling the number for each successive square. The number of grains on the nth square will be 2^{n-1}, and on the last or 64th square, 2^{63}. The sum of the grains on the entire board will be twice this amount less one grain, or $2^{64} - 1$. When translated into volume of wheat, it turns out that the quantity of wheat required for the last square would equal approximately 1,000 times the present world annual wheat crop, and the requirement for the whole board would be twice this amount.

It follows, therefore, that exponential growth, either biological or industrial, can be only a temporary phenomenon because the earth itself cannot tolerate more than a few tens of doublings of any biological or industrial component. Furthermore, most of the possible doublings have occurred already.

After the cessation of exponential growth, any individual component has only three possible futures:

(1) it may, as in the case of water power, level off and stabilize at a maximum;

(2) it may overshoot and, after passing a maximum, decline and stabilize at some intermediate level capable of being sustained; or

(3) it may decline to zero and become extinct.

Applied to human society, these three possibilities are illustrated graphically in Figure 8-32. What stands out most clearly is that our present phase of exponential growth based on man's ability to control ever larger quantities of energy can only be a temporary period of about three centuries' duration in the totality of human history. It represents but a brief transitional epoch between two very much longer periods, each characterized by rates of change so slow as to be regarded essentially as

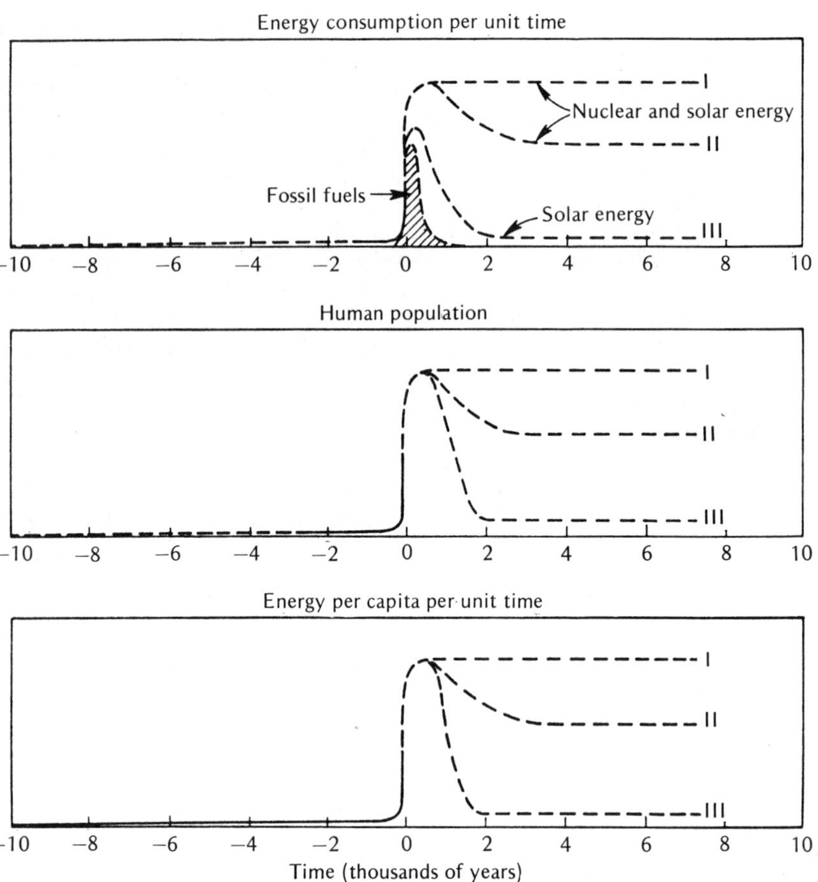

Figure 8-32. Epoch of current industrial growth in the context of a longer span of human history (Hubbert, 1962, Figure 61).

a period of nongrowth. Although the forthcoming period poses no insuperable physical or biological difficulties, it can hardly fail to force a major revision in those aspects of our current culture, the tenets of which are dependent on the assumption that the growth rates which have characterized this temporary period can somehow be sustained indefinitely.

REFERENCES

Averitt, Paul, 1969, Coal resources of the United States, January 1, 1967: *U.S. Geological Survey Bulletin 1275,* 116 p.

Duncan, D. C., and Swanson, V. E., 1965, Organic-rich shale of the United States and world land areas: *U.S. Geological Survey Circular 523,* 30 p.

Folinsbee, R. E., 1970, Nuclear energy and the fossil fuels: *Trans. Royal Society of Canada, Fourth Series,* Vol. 8, pp. 335–359.

Hewett, D. F., 1929, Cycles in metal production: *AIME Tech. Pub. 183,* 31 p.; Trans. 1929, pp. 65–93; discussion pp. 93–98.

Hubbert, M. King, 1956, Nuclear energy and the fossil fuels: *American Petroleum Institute, Drilling and Production Practice* (1956), pp. 7–25.

Hubbert, M. King, 1962, Energy resources: *National Academy of Sciences—National Research Council, Publication 1000-D,* 141 p.

Hubbert, M. King, 1967, Degree of advancement of petroleum exploration in United States: *American*

Assoc. of Petroleum Geologists Bulletin, Vol. 51, pp. 2207–2227.

Hubbert, M. King, 1969, Energy resources, *Resources and Man,* a study and recommendations by the Committee on Resources and Man of the Division of Earth Sciences, National Academy of Sciences. National Research Council: San Fransisco, W. H. Freeman, pp. 157–242.

Hubbert, M. King, 1971, Energy resources for power production, *Environmental Aspects of Nuclear Power Stations:* Vienna, International Atomic Energy Agency, pp. 13–43.

Theobald, P. K., Schweinfurth, S. P., and Duncan, D. C., 1972, Energy resources of the United States: *U.S. Geological Survey Circular 650,* 27 p.

Warman, H. R., 1971, Future problems in petroleum exploration: *Petroleum Review,* Vol. 25, No. 291, pp. 96–101.

Zapp, A. D., 1962, Future petroleum producing capacity of the United States: *U.S. Geological Survey Bulletin 1142-H,* 36 p.

SUGGESTED READINGS

Hubbert, M. King, 1974a, U.S. energy resources, a review as of 1972, part I, in A national fuels and energy policy study: U.S. 93rd Congress, 2nd Session: Senate Committee of Interior and Insular Affairs, Serial No. 93-40 (92-75), Washington, US Government Printing Office (Stock No. 527002419, $2.15), 267 p.

Hubbert, M. King, 1974b, World energy resources, in Proceedings of Opening Ceremony and Plenary Sessions of Tenth Commonwealth Mining and Metallurgical Congress, Ottawa, Canada, pp. 24–106.

Hubbert M. King, 1976, Energy resources: A scientific and cultural dilemma: *Bulletin of the Association of Engineering Geologists,* Vol. 13, No. 2, Spring, pp. 81–124.

Hubbert, M. King, 1977, World oil and natural gas reserves and resources, part IV, B, in U.S. Energy demand and supply, 1975–1990: Congressional Research Service of the Library of Congress.

Facts About Oil 9

AMERICAN PETROLEUM INSTITUTE 1977

OIL HISTORY

Since prehistoric days, man has sought to convert earth's resources to his own use—to bring him warmth, cook his food, and ease his workload. When he first began to use petroleum remains a secret of the ages. However, seepages of crude oil and natural gas are thought to have furnished fuels for the "sacred" fires of primitive peoples, who ascribed divine powers to the flames.

Both the Babylonian and Judaic versions of the Great Flood record that pitch—a natural form of asphaltic petroleum—was used to caulk the vessels that saved Utnapishtim and Noah. Pitch was also used to grease the axles of the Pharoahs' chariots in ancient Egypt. And the Greeks record the destruction of a Scythian fleet, when oil was poured on the water and set afire.

Ancient Chinese used both oil and gas. In fact, they actually drilled for oil as early as the third century B.C. Using bamboo tubes and bronze bits, they successfully reached depths of over 3,000 feet. This was long before Western civilization began to search underground for oil.

The Early Years

The oil industry in the United States had its beginning at Titusville, Pennsylvania, on August 27, 1859. On that date, the first well drilled specifically for the purpose of finding oil was successful. Oil, however, was not new to the North American continent.

White men exploring the area of New York and Pennsylvania found Indians using crude oil for medicinal purposes. The Indians obtained the oil by skimming it from the springs and streams where it appeared as a thick scum. George Washington described a spring on his property, which was probably seeping natural gas, as "of so inflammable a nature as to burn freely as spirits."

In Washington's lifetime, and even in the first half of the nineteenth century, Americans had only tallow candles and whale oil for light. Whaling became a major industry as New England ships combed the seas. But the hunting was too good, for over the years the supply of whales became scarcer.

The Stage Is Set

At the same time, other forces were working to provide a new source of illumination. In

This article is an abbreviated version of the latest edition of *Facts About Oil* prepared by The American Petroleum Institute, 2101 L Street, N.W., Washington, D.C. 20037. It was provided through the courtesy of James E. Champagne and reprinted by permission of The American Petroleum Institute.

America and in Europe during the 1850's, some illuminating oils were being distilled from coal and from petroleum skimmed off ponds and streams. Although the amounts of oil that could be gathered in this way were extremely limited, the stage was set for the industry's birth. Americans needed and wanted a plentiful source of oil for light. And far-sighted men were beginning to see the possibilities of petroleum to fill this need.

The Drake Well

Armed with a favorable report on petroleum as an illuminant, which was written by Yale University Professor Benjamin Silliman, a group of businessmen led by James M. Townsend formed the Pennsylvania Rock Oil Company, which later became the Seneca Oil Company. Their objective was to recover petroleum in large quantities by drilling for it just as men drilled for salt.

Townsend and his associates hired Edwin L. Drake, a retired railroad conductor, to undertake drilling operations on the banks of Oil Creek at Titusville, Pennsylvania, near an old oil spring. By the time Drake and his men had struck rock below the 30-foot level, their drilling rig—an old steam engine and an iron bit attached by a rope to a wooden windlass—had won the title "Drake's Folly." And when the rock slowed drilling to 3 feet a day, even Townsend became discouraged.

Drake and his men persisted, however, and late one summer afternoon in 1859, after the bit had been withdrawn from the well at 69½ feet, a dark green liquid rose to a few feet below the top. The drillers were jubilant. They had struck oil.

The events leading to the first shout of "We've struck oil!" were of vast significance, because they proved to the Western world that it was sound and practical to drill for oil.

The Oil Boom

The immediate results of Drake's success were dramatic. An oil boom, which took on many aspects of California's gold rush a decade before, began. The Pennsylvania hills echoed to the sound of thousands of drill bits pounding their way into the earth. Towns mushroomed.

As the trickle of oil became a stream, facilities for storage and transportation became a pressing problem. Coopers worked overtime making barrels for crude oil. Thousands of teamsters churned roads into quagmires as they lurched and splashed toward the nearest railroad. Rafts laden with barrels of oil were floated down Oil Creek.

In 1861, the first refinery went into operation in the oil region. Like other early refineries, it produced kerosine* and little else. There were some local markets for greases and lubricating oils, but refiners concentrated on producing a kerosine that was a virtually odorless and smokeless illuminant.

To supply refineries at a distance, railroads built spurs into the producing region. At first, the barrels of oil were transported in flatcars. Then, in 1865, a railroad tank car was developed especially for carrying crude oil. A primitive forerunner of modern tank cars, it was a flatcar on which two vertical wooden tanks had been built.

That same year, the first oil pipeline was laid. It brought crude oil five miles from Pithole City to the Oil Creek Railroad, impressing producers with its efficiency. And in 1879, the first major pipeline was completed. It extended 110 miles across the Allegheny Mountains to Williamsport, Pennyslvania, and was regarded as the engineering marvel of the age.

The Comming of the Automobile

The opening years of the twentieth century witnessed an event that was to give the petroleum industry its greatest impetus—the development of a practical internal combustion engine.

*This spelling is preferred by certain technical authorities and used by the American Petroleum Institute to conform to the spelling of gasoline.

Inventors had experimented with "horseless carriages" for many years. But it was not until 1892 that the first American gasoline-powered automobile was built by Frank and Charles Duryea. Although in 1900, many people still thought that steam or electricity would power the automobile of the future, it turned out that gasoline proved to be the most practical fuel for automotive transportation because, when it burns, it delivers direct power in the form of a high amount of heat energy in relation to its weight and leaves almost no ash.

The oil industry had a growing outlet for what was previously a useless by-product. Until the development of the automobile, gasoline had been a waste product in the distillation of crude oil. Gasoline-filling stations began to appear; several cities claim to have had the first.

Meanwhile, the search for new oil fields continued. Oil was found in West Virginia (1860), Colorado (1862), Texas (1866), California (1875), Ohio and Illinois (1880's), Oklahoma (1905), Louisiana (1906), and Kansas (1916).

The Need for More and Better Fuels

As the number of automobiles increased and the demand for more and better motor fuels grew, it became necessary to find more oil and to improve refining processes. Only so much gasoline, however, could be obtained from crude oil by straight distillation. It became apparent that even the tremendously increased production of crude oil would not be enough to meet the rising demand for motor fuels.

A young chemist, Dr. William M. Burton, stepped into the breach with a significant new application of chemistry and engineering. He developed the thermal cracking process that was patented in 1913. By applying intense heat and pressure to the heavier fuels, Dr. Burton found that their larger molecules broke up into smaller molecules of lighter fuels, including gasoline.

Cracking units were soon put into commercial operation. Within a few decades, improved cracking processes more than doubled the yield of gasoline from crude oil. Equally important, cracking produces a product far superior in antiknock characteristics—its ability to burn properly in an engine—than the "straight-run" gasoline produced from the primary distillation process. This permitted the development of higher compression ratio engines with greatly improved efficiency.

Later Developments

In 1937, the catalytic cracker was introduced, increasing substantially the quality and yield of gasoline from each barrel of crude oil.

By cracking, adding tetraethyl lead, and making other improvements in the refining process, the antiknock characteristics of gasoline were increased.

At the same time, automotive engineers were improving engines to use the higher quality fuels. Thus, fuel and automobile engine improvements went hand in hand. And hundreds of other new and improved products began to appear during this period as a result of this research.

Between the wars, the farmer also took to oil. New highways, surfaced with petroleum asphalt, got him "out of the mud" and gave him a ready means of delivering his produce to market.

More and more rapidly, mechanized farm equipment replaced the horse and mule. As it did, agricultural productivity took giant strides forward.

During World War II, the petroleum industry proved its ability to meet sudden demands for specialized products. Huge quantities of oil were produced and converted to motor and high octane aviation gasoline, lubricants, butadiene (for synthetic rubber), toluene (for TNT), medicinal oils, and an expanding number of other critically needed products.

Despite the tremendous wartime needs, peace brought even greater demands for petroleum products. Americans, no longer faced with wartime rationing of gasoline, took to the roads in droves. Motor vehicle registrations increased by one-half during the five years following the war. The number of domestic oil burners doubled, and farm tractors increased by almost 50 per cent. Consumption of all petroleum products rose to record levels, jumping from 1.8 billion barrels (a barrel equals 42 gallons) in 1946 to 2.4 billion barrels in 1950 and 6.4 billion barrels in 1976.

Natural gas also came into its own after World War II. Transmission pipelines were constructed, linking remote producing areas to large population centers, and natural gas established itself as a major fuel for industry and home heating and as a feedstock in making glass and other products.

So tremendous was the increase in oil and natural gas consumption, that in 1946, for the first time, petroleum supplied more of our nation's energy needs than coal. By 1950, when the Korean War broke out, oil and natural gas were supplying 57.8 per cent of our energy requirements. Today, petroleum supplies three-fourths of our energy needs.

Functions of the Industry

Today's oil industry is engaged not only in finding oil and gas and getting them out of the ground, but also in transporting oil, making it into useful products and marketing and delivering these products to other industries and to private consumers.

The *production* branch of the industry is concerned with the science and mechanics of exploring for new oil and gas fields, drilling wells and bringing oil and gas to the surface.

Once crude oil is above ground, the *transportation* branch must deliver it to refineries in large volume often over long distances. From the refinery, oil products must then be delivered to bulk depots, to distributors, and finally to consumers. Pipelines, ocean-going tankers, canal and river barges, railroad tank cars, and highway tank trucks are all part of the petroleum transportation network. Transportation and distribution of gas is generally independently handled by the gas industry.

The oil industry's *manufacturing* branch concentrates on refining and petrochemical processing. At the refinery, crude oil is separated by a complex series of processing methods into gasolines, fuel oils, lubricants and many other products. Petrochemical plants process the gaseous by-products of refining into many useful chemicals.

The *marketing* end of the oil business sells and distributes oil products to consumers who range from industrial users to homeowners. Sales departments of oil companies, independent jobbers or wholesalers, service station operators, and fuel oil dealers are all engaged in marketing activities.

Performing these diverse functions are several thousand companies, ranging from small one-man businesses, such as the consulting geologist or the single-truck fuel oil dealer, to large integrated firms that operate throughout the world.

Integrated firms are engaged in all aspects of the industry's operations, from exploration to marketing. There are over 50 integrated U.S. oil companies.

By far the larger number of companies are those that are engaged in one, and sometimes two or three, of the industry's operating functions. Many companies work exclusively in the production of crude oil and gas; others transport oil exclusively. There are separate refining companies and various types of marketers. When a company is engaged in production and transportation; refining and marketing; or production, transportation, and refining, it is referred to as a "semi-integrated" company.

Oil Installations

In the more than 115 years since the birth of the U.S. oil industry, oil companies have had to develop and expand their facilities to supply the vast amounts of energy required by our highly industrialized society.

As a consequence, the oil industry is no longer the localized business it was in the early years. Oil and/or natural gas are now produced in 30 states. The leading oil producing states are Texas, Louisiana, California, Oklahoma, Wyoming, New Mexico, Kansas, and Alaska. Some states that produce oil do not produce natural gas. Nevada, for example, produces oil but has no commercial natural gas production. Maryland, on the other hand, produces natural gas only.

In 1859, the year of Colonel Drake's pioneer well, total United States production of crude oil was about 2,000 barrels. In 1976, 3.0 billion barrels of crude oil and condensate were produced in this country from more than 503,000 wells.

The United States was for many years the leading oil-producing country in the world. It is now third behind the Soviet Union and Saudi Arabia in production. Our 1976 production represented 14.2 per cent of the estimated 21 billion barrels produced throughout the world.

Of the world's other major oil-producing nations, the Soviet Union ranked first in 1976 with an output of 3.8 billion barrels. Iran with 2.2 billion barrels and Venezuela with 0.8 billion barrels ranked fourth and fifth.

Processing our nation's output of crude oil is the task of 268 refineries that currently operate in 41 states and Puerto Rico. In the aggregate, these refineries have a capacity to process more than 15.5 million barrels of crude oil every day. This capability represents 21.6 per cent of the total world refining capacity.

The petroleum transportation network in the United States is both vast and complex. Today, more than 223,000 miles of pipeline network, along with thousands of petroleum tank cars, tank trucks, ocean tankers, and barges, serves to carry petroleum and its products quickly and economically from producer to consumer.

Petroleum marketing is also a large-scale operation. The wholesale distribution of petroleum products is handled, for the most part, by about 15,000 jobbers. These companies operate many of the more than 25,000 bulk plants and terminals in the country. Their job is to fill the bulk orders for petroleum products from service stations, commercial consumers, public utilities, transportation companies, factories, and rural farms.

At the retail level, there are approximately 13,700 fuel oil and liquefied petroleum gas establishments and about 186,000 gasoline service stations. More than 80 per cent of these service stations are owned or operated by local people.

Supply and Demand

The United States is not only one of the world's greatest producers and refiners of crude oil, it is also the greatest consumer of petroleum products. In 1976, it consumed about 6.4 billion barrels of petroleum or approximately 29.7 per cent of the total world demand.

U.S. production that year totaled 3.56 billion barrels—2.97 billion barrels of crude oil and 587 million barrels of natural gas liquids. The balance was supplied by imports of crude oil and oil products.

Oil companies also invest heavily in research. The 1975 annual combined research budget was $669 million.

Major energy consumers in the U.S. can be divided into four major sectors—household and commercial, industrial, transportation, and electric power generation. It is estimated that in 1976 the household and commercial sector consumed 17.4 per cent of the U.S. demand for petroleum products. The industrial market consumed 18.4 per cent and the transportation sector 54.8 per cent. Generation of electric power used the remaining 9.4 per cent.

In 1976, oil accounted for 47.2 per cent of all U.S. energy needs and natural gas accounted for 27.3 per cent. Coal, on the other hand, contributed 18.6 per cent and water power 4.1 per cent. Nuclear power is, at present, a minor factor in the total energy picture—contributing only 2.8 per cent.

Supplying petroleum energy not only requires specialized facilities, but also vast amounts of capital. Here are some examples: The new Trans-Alaska pipeline is 48 inches in diameter and 789 miles long and, when it was put in operation in mid-1977, it had cost more than $7.7 billion. A 100,000-barrel refinery can cost more than $200 million. A complete drilling rig in Alaska may represent an investment of over $2.8 million. And an offshore installation can cost over $100 million.

Comparable high capital costs are faced throughout the petroleum industry. During the past decade, about 80 per cent of all oil company expenditures has come from cash earnings. In 1975 alone, they earmarked an estimated $45.4 billion for world-wide capital expenditures to maintain, replace, and expand their production, refining, transportation, and marketing facilities. This is an increase of over 280 per cent of what they invested ten years earlier.

An illustration of the large sums that oil companies have had to set aside for property, plants, and equipment is the industry's ratio of assets to employees. In 1975, oil companies invested $196,927 per employee. Average assets invested per employee in the manufacturing industry generally were $37,929.

Petroleum's Employees

Petroleum companies and dealer-operated service stations employ approximately 1.5 million people. This provided a source of personal income for one out of every 62 persons in the U.S. civilian labor force. Wages paid by the petroleum industry are among the highest paid by industry in general.

SEARCHING FOR OIL

The science of exploring for oil and natural gas starts with geology and geophysics. It is based on theories of the origin of oil and on its behavior underground.

The petroleum we use today has been in the earth for millions of years. Since it was formed long before men appeared on our planet, we can only theorize about its origins.

In Drake's time men had strange ideas about oil. Some thought it ran in a vast underground river from Pennsylvania to Texas. A few even protested that oil drillers were removing the oil that kept the earth's axle greased.

Today, the "organic" theory of petroleum's origin is the one most widely accepted. This theory holds that crude oil and natural gas are organic minerals formed by the decay and alteration of the remains of prehistoric marine animals and plants.

Oil is most often found in sediments laid down in ancient ssea. These seas once covered much of the continental land area we now know. According to the organic theory, oil began with the remains of countless tiny creatures and plants that lived in the sea or washed down into it with mulch and silt from streams. This residue settled to the bottom of the ancient seas and accumulated there, layer by layer.

As the old layers were buried deeper and deeper, they were compressed by the tremendous weight of the sediments above them. Under this pressure, heat was generated. This heat, along with chemical and bacterial activity and radioactivity, gradually reformed the organic matter into the compounds of hydrogen and carbon we know as petroleum.

Through geologic ages, the sands, marine forms, and silts that settled to the ocean floor were transformed into sedimentary rocks. These loose particles, cemented into solid masses, are now called sandstone, limestone, and shale.

Some of these sedimentary rock layers were too dense to permit easy penetration by gases or liquids. Others were more loosely compacted and porous enough to let the newly formed oil and gas migrate slowly through them.

Since gas and oil are lighter than water, they tended to rise upward through the water that filled the porous spaces when the sedimentary formations were laid down.

Where a formation of dense, nonporous rock lay above a porous layer, the migration stopped, and there oil and gas collected. Lightweight gas filled the small voids present in the upper parts of the porous rock layer. Oil settled beneath the gas. And the heavier water remained in the lower areas.

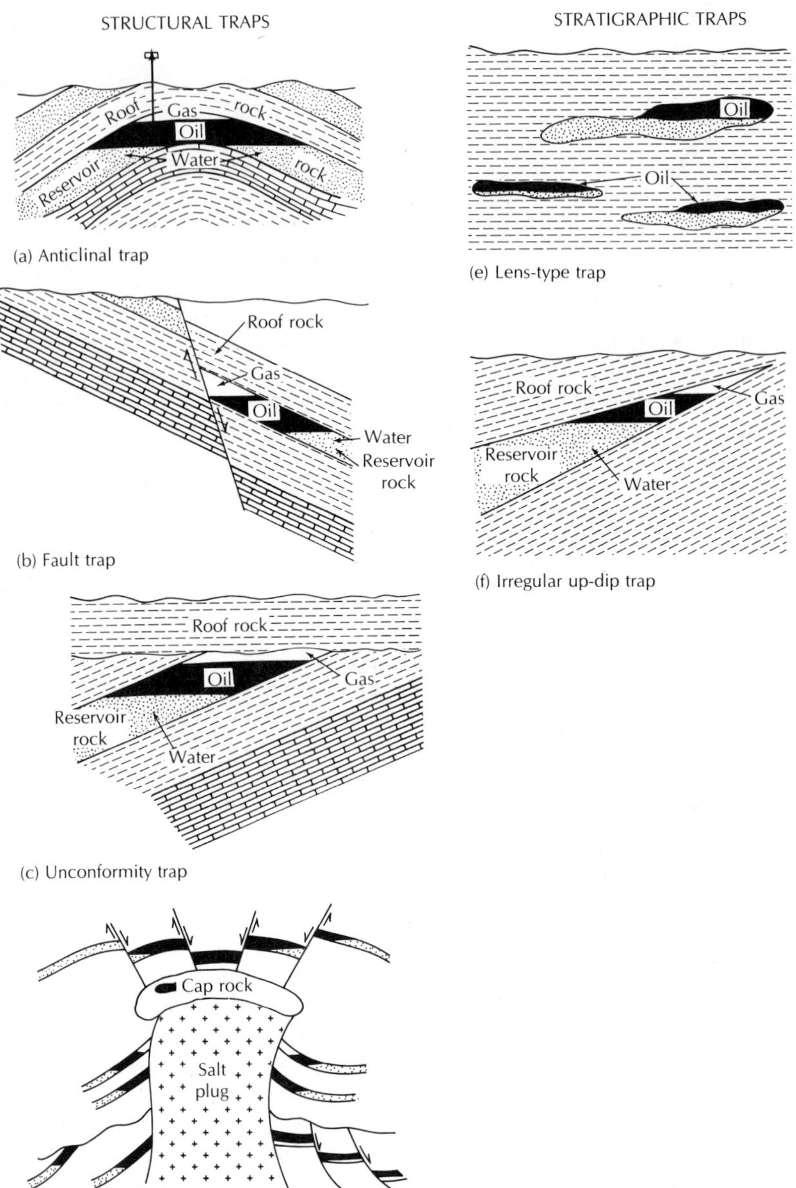

Figure 9-1. Idealized sections through various types of petroleum traps: a, b, c, and d are structural traps; e and f are stratigraphic traps. Gas (white) overlies oil (black) that floats on water (stippled), which saturates the reservoir rock and is sealed by roof rock (shale or clay). Gas and oil fill only the void (pore) spaces of the rock.

Originally, the deposits laid down on the sea floors were nearly horizontal. But through the centuries, movements and strains in the earth's crust folded or disrupted them. Seas shifted and land areas formed. Mountain ranges appeared and ancient sea bottoms became dry land.

These upheavals often caused shifts or breaks in the rock layers to create traps that collected migrating gas and oil.

The most common types of oil and gas traps are called structural traps (e.g., unconformities, faults, anticlines, salt domes) and stratigraphic traps (e.g., lens-type, irregular up-dip) (Figure 9-1).

An *anticline* is an arch-like upward fold in the earth's strata.

A *fault* is a fracture in the earth's crust that vertically shifts a nonporous layer next to a porous one, cutting off the porous layer.

Oil and natural gas are frequently found adjacent to, or on top of, an underground *salt dome*. This type of structure results from the upward thrust of a great mass of salt far below the earth's surface. Sometimes the salt enters the overlying strata. When a salt dome rises through a layer of oil-bearing sedimentary rock, oil may be trapped above the salt dome or in structures similar to faults along its flanks.

An *unconformity* is a break in the geologic sequence and is marked by a surface of erosion, or a period of nondeposition, separating two groups of strata.

A *stratigraphic trap* is one in which there are lateral changes formed as a result of rock types rather than structural deformation.

Exploring for Oil and Gas

The men who searched for oil during the first decades after Drake's well knew little about underground rock formations and potential oil traps. But as more and more oil was discovered, oil geology became a more precise science.

Geologists learned to take careful notes on underground structures and formations where oil was found. And they learned to categorize and compare them. In time, new scientific accomplishments helped geologists develop various instruments for mapping underground rock formations more accurately.

Today, oil geologists use many tools when they set out to find a new area for exploration. First, they do some preliminary work in the office and library checking records and data. Since most of the oil fields developed to date are located in the world's great sedimentary basin regions, they begin with maps of these basins, which are fairly well documented for most of the world.

One of these regions is the intercontinental basin of the Western Hemisphere, including the U.S. Gulf Coast, Mexico, and the Caribbean area.

Another is in the Middle East area, including the oil fields of southern Russia, Iraq, Iran, and the countries of the Arabian peninsula.

Still another is in the countries of northern and western Africa.

A new region, just discovered in 1968, is the North Sea Field. Scientists predict it contains from 10 to 40 billion barrels of oil and 26 trillion cubic feet of natural gas.

New oil discoveries in Indonesia, both offshore and onshore, are occurring with increasing frequency.

Lands surrounding the Arctic waters are also known to have great potential for the discovery of oil. The Prudhoe Bay Field, discovered in 1968 on Alaska's North Slope, has estimated proved recoverable reserves of 9.6 billion barrels of crude oil and 26 trillion cubic feet of natural gas.

Geophysical surveys suggest that sedimentary formations underlying the Georges Bank, Baltimore Canyon, and Blake Plateau troughs in the U.S. Atlantic Outer Continental Shelf may also contain oil and gas reserves.

When the geologists have selected a particular area, they check local geological offices for maps showing rock formations. They look at the data obtained from wells already drilled in the area for clues about the underlying strata. They are looking primarily for records of sandstone and limestone, for this is where oil and gas are most likely to be found.

When they have pinpointed an area that appears favorable, the geophysicist enters the picture. His tools, the magnetometer, gravimeter, and seismograph, provide a more detailed picture of subsurface formations.

The *magnetometer* measures variations in the earth's magnetic field. Sedimentary rocks generally have low magnetic properties compared to other rocks, particularly basement rocks, which are much denser and contain a higher concentration of iron and other magnetic materials. Thus, the magnetometer gives geophysicists a clue to their location. The "flying magnetometer" is trailed on a cable from a surveying plane. It records the varying magnetic intensities of the earth as the plane flies overhead.

The *gravimeter* measures minute differences in the pull of gravity at the earth's surface. Because large masses of dense rock increase the pull of gravity, gravimeter readings at a number of surface points provide a key to the underlying structures.

The *seismograph,* originally developed to record earthquakes, is now also widely used as an oil prospecting tool. An explosive is set off in a shallow, small-diameter hole. The waves from the explosion travel downward where they strike successive rock formations and are reflected back to the surface. As these waves return, geophones (detectors) pick up and record the impulses. By correlating wave intensity and the time intervals required for them to travel down and back, the geophysicist learns the general characteristics of the underground structure.

Newer developments in seismic survey on land include the use of vibratory or percussion devices, which do away with the drilling of holes and the use of explosives. Vibratory devices are used to provide more accurate information and minimize environmental damage. In water, they send out pulses in the form of electrical discharges or contained explosions of propane gas or air so marine life is not harmed.

Satellites moving above the earth can also be used to provide large-scale pictures of landforms that might lead to areas rich in oil and gas.

The oil explorer has still another tool. Often he drills a well, known as a stratigraphic test, near a likely site to get a core of the rock strata. Geologists can then examine these core samples for traces of oil and gas. And paleontologists can study the core for fossils that might indicate the ages of various strata.

But even if all the preliminary reports are favorable, they simply indicate the possibility of finding oil. There is no sure way to know whether the oil is there until a drill has actually found it. And the odds are ten to one against the possibility that the driller of an exploratory well in a new field will find any oil or natural gas, and 50 to one that the petroleum will be found in commerical quantity.

The next step is to secure permission to drill on the property. Under most agreements, both the surface and mineral rights to the property are leased for a stipulated period. The landowner is usually given an initial "bonus" and an annual rental fee for the term of the lease, or until production is begun. Once production commences he receives a percentage royalty on any oil or gas that may be produced.

Oil companies spend approximately $826 million each year in the United States for geological and geophysical exploration and lease rentals. In addition, payments to individual landowners and federal and state governments in the form of royalties, including Outer Continental Shelf lease sale bonuses, can amount to several billion dollars a year.

There is little chance of environmental pollution from exploratory operations, prior to actual drilling into the earth for oil and gas. But numerous safety devices and techniques are used to minimize the risk of pollution-causing incidents during the production, refining, and marketing stages.

DRILLING FOR OIL AND GAS

Before drilling can start, a great deal of work must be done. In remote or rough and swampy terrain, site preparation alone is a major engineering job. The land must be surveyed, cleared, and graded.

Often, roads must be built to move in derricks and other drilling equipment, fuel, and supplies. Roadbuilders must follow environmental requirements in locating these roads. For example, they must respect game trails in woodland areas.

A constant power source must be provided for operating the on-site equipment and provisions must be made for a constant supply of water, both for the workers and the drilling operation. If the site is far from a town, a camp may have to be built to house the workers. And sometimes, temporary fences must be built to keep out inquisitive animals.

Finally, the drilling rig is brought to the site. Two basic types of drilling equipment, a rotary tool and a cable tool, are used today.

In both cases, machinery is set up and a derrick is erected for handling the tools and pipe that go down into the well. Most rigs now use a portable hinged or "jackknife" derrick or mast that can be raised and lowered intact rather than steel girder "standard" derricks that must be erected and dismantled, piece by piece. Standard derricks, however, are still used for some very deep wells and in other special situations.

Cable Tool Drilling

Of the two drilling methods, the cable tool is much older; it is seldom used today. Five centuries before Christ, the Chinese invented a cable drilling method essentially similar to early American techniques.

A cable tool rig is made up of machinery and gear that raise and drop a "string" of tools, consisting of a bit and stem on the end of a cable. The heavy bit pounds its way into the earth, pulverizing soil and rock. At intervals, the string of tools is removed, the hole is flushed, and the resulting "slurry" of drilling cuttings is removed. Periodically the hole is lined with steel casing to prevent caving in and to protect underground fresh strata encountered during drilling.

The cable tool rig is used today primarily to drill shallow water wells. Most petroleum wells are now drilled by the rotary method.

Rotary Drilling

In rotary drilling, a bit is attached to the lower end of a string of pipe, called "drill pipe." Bits range in size from less than 4 inches to more than 22 inches in diameter. They are made of very hard steel and may cost thousands of dollars. Some bits have two or three rotating cones covered with sharp teeth for grinding through rock. Others have industrial diamonds embedded in them.

The bit and pipe pass vertically through a turntable on the derrick floor. As the pipe is turned and lowered into the earth, the bit bores a hole deeper and deeper. As the hole deepens, the drilling crew adds new lengths of drill pipe.

When a bit becomes dull, the entire length of drill pipe must be removed, disconnected in stands of two or three joints each, and stacked in the derrick. After a new bit is attached, the drilling crew reconnects the stands of pipe one at a time and runs the drillstring into the hole again. This operation demands skill, speed, and precision and must by repeated many times in drilling a deep well.

Extreme care must be taken during the entire drilling operation to avoid having the string of drilling tools part and drop to the bottom of the hole. If this happens, it could mean the loss of the well. At the very best, it becomes a costly "fishing" operation to retrieve whatever has been dropped.

Drillers must also take great care not to let the drilling tools get stuck in the hole. To lessen the chances of this happening, and for other reasons, rotary drilling follows a nonstop schedule seven days a week.

A mixture of water, clay, and chemical additives called drilling mud is pumped under pressure down through the drill pipe during rotary drilling. When it reaches the bottom, it is forced out through openings in the bit, and returns to the surface outside the drill pipe.

This constantly circulating fluid cools and cleans the bit and transports cuttings from the well. It also cakes the sides of the hole, preventing cave-ins and, by its weight, controls the pressure of any gas, oil, or water that may be encountered by the drill bit.

Setting casing is an important job in drilling wells. Casing is run in the hole to shut off water-permeated sands and high pressure gas zones, prevent cave-ins, and protect fresh water strata. The casing consists of a number of lengths of heavy steel pipe joined together, usually by threaded couplings.

After the casing has been lowered to the desired point, it must be securely sealed to the walls of the hole. This is done by pumping a cement slurry through the string of casing and forcing it out through the bottom, so that it rises to fill the space between the outside of the casing and the walls of the hole.

Blowout Prevention

The casing and drilling muds normally keep the flow from the well under control, but other safeguards are provided. After the surface casing is placed in the well, further drilling is protected by one or more large valves, called blowout preventers, which are attached to the top of the casing in what is known as a stack.

These valves can be closed to seal off the well bore so the gases and liquids under pressure in the hole can be controlled. The blowout preventers in a stack vary in size, design, and number. There are usually from four to seven on a deep well.

One commonly used control is the bag-type blowout preventer. It uses an inflatable bag to close the area between the casing and the drill pipe in an emergency. Hydraulic fluid is forced into the bag, expanding it and sealing off any flow from the well outside the pipe.

Another frequently used control is the ram type. Hydraulic pressure activates piston-like rams, causing them to close in the well. Rams are designed either to close around drill pipe (pipe rams) or to completely shut in the well (blind rams). These rams can be reopened, tested, and set again by reversing the fluid pressure.

While a well is being drilled, instruments measure and record critical aspects of the drilling operation, what is occurring within the well, and the behavior of the drilling machinery. Any unexpected change indicating the threat of a blowout triggers an automatic alarm. Crews immediately close the blowout preventer, adjust the weight of the drilling mud, or take other steps to control the flow of fluids.

Drilling Facts

Most of the wells drilled in the early days were relatively shallow. Drake's well, which was 69½ feet deep, took about 12 to 15 drilling days.

Today's wells average nearly 5,000 feet. And many go beyond 15,000 feet. The world's deepest well, drilled in Oklahoma, was 30,050 feet. Drilling time now commonly ranges from a few days to a few months, with some wells taking longer than a year to drill.

Today, drilling an oil well involves large quantities of equipment and supplies as well as substantial capital investment. As one example, the cost of drilling a single well may range from an average of $150,200 for an onshore well to over $1 million for an offshore well. Ten years ago, costs ranged from $51,200 to $412,558.

PRODUCING OIL

Between the time the bit drills into a formation containing oil and/or natural gas and the time the well begins to produce, several operations, called "completing the well," take place. During this period of completion and testing, the pressure of the drilling fluid and the use of special surface equipment restrict and control the flow from the well.

First, the drill pipe and bit are removed. Cementing operations then set the final string of casing. Next, a special instrument, containing sockets holding either shaped explosive charges or bullets similar to those used in a gun, is lowered into the well. This perforating instrument fires charges or bullets by electric impulse through the casing into the producing formation to open passages through which the oil and natural gas can flow into the well bore. Tubing is installed inside the casing and the oil and natural gas flow through it to the surface.

To control the flow, a set of valves and control equipment is put in place at the top of the well. In oil country, this mechanism is called a "Christmas tree" because of its many branchlike fittings. It controls the flow of oil and natural gas from the moment the well starts producing.

Other safety devices in the production system may include automatic and manually operated valves, surface and subsurface alarms, and monitoring and recording equipment.

Sometimes in drilling a well, more than one commercially productive formation is found. In such cases, a separate tubing string is run inside the casing for each productive formation. Production from the separate formations is directed through the proper tubing strings and is isolated from the others by packers that seal the annular space between the tubing strings and casing. These are known as multiple completion wells.

When the oil and natural gas reach the surface, they are separated. The gas is sent to a gas processing plant; once the water and sediment are removed from the oil, it is transported to a refinery.

Wells that are primarily natural gas producers are of two types. If they produce gas containing dissolved liquids, they are called wet gas wells. These natural gas liquids are taken out before the gas is delivered to a pipeline company for transmission. Other wells produce only "dry" gas, that is, gas composed of hydrocarbons that cannot easily be liquefied. Since natural gas moves easily through porous and permeable rock, it can be produced simply and efficiently under its own pressure.

Life of an Oil Well

The life of a producing well begins with the first barrel of oil brought to the surface. It ends when the well is abandoned as uneconomical, because the cost of producing the oil is greater than the price received for it. The life of a well varies greatly from field to field. A small pool may be in production for only a few years. Others may produce for 75 years or more.

The recovery of oil is basically a displacement process. Oil alone does not have the ability to expel itself from the reservoir. It must be moved from the rock formation to the well bore by a displacing agent. Fortunately, oil has two natural displacement agents that usually occur with it—gas and water.

The varying pressures and drives of the natural displacement agents provide a general basis for the different phases of a well's producing life. These phases are commonly called the flush, artificial lift, and stripper periods of production.

Flush production refers to the phase during which the rate of flow is governed by natural pressure within the reservoir. It is usually the first stage in a well's life, although not always, and occurs when the drill taps an oil-bearing formation that has enough natural pressure to enable the petroleum to flow by itself. With variations, three types of "drives" can generate this force.

(1) *Dissolved Gas Drive*. In virtually all oil accumulations, gas is found dissolved in the oil. Under certain conditions of pressure, all the gas is dissolved in the oil. When the formation is penetrated, the gas can expand and drive the mixture to the surface. In principle, this condition is similar to the action of gas dissolved in soda pop; it expands when the bottle is opened.

(2) *Gas Cap Drive*. In many reservoirs the pressure is such that a considerable cap of gas is trapped above the oil in addition to the gas dissolved in the oil. When the rock is penetrated, this gas (both dissolved gas and cap gas) expands and exerts enough pressure on the oil to move it toward the only escape hatch available—the well bore leading to the surface.

(3) *Water Drive*. In many oil reservoirs, there is water under hydrostatic pressure beneath the oil. When a drill penetrates the

reservoir, the resulting release of pressure drives the oil to the well bore and, in some cases, upward to the surface. As the natural water pressure in the reservoir is reduced by oil production, water from the surrounding porous rock tends to flow into the reduced pressure zone, displacing the oil and driving it toward the well bore.

Artificial lift methods are applied when the initial pressure of a flush well expends itself. At this point, the well is usually put on pump. There are several varieties of pumps. One kind of surface pump connects the power source by means of a rocker arm assembly to a rod extending into the well, which is attached to a valved plunger. Submersible electric pumps can be lowered into the well. The gas lift method uses pressurized gas to raise the fluids up the well bore. Many wells never flow naturally and must be pumped from the start. Others drop in flow rate shortly after production begins, and go on artificial lift fairly early in their lives.

Stripper or marginal production exists when a well reaches the point when it can be produced only intermittently. Stripper wells are usually older wells that produce only a few barrels of oil a day, but are kept in production because their output is marginally above the costs of operation. Many are pumped intermittently to allow the oil to accumulate in the well bore.

Today there are more than 367,800 stripper wells in this country. Their slow but sure production gives us 12.9 per cent of our total domestic production.

In 1975, stripper wells added over 394 million barrels of crude oil to the nation's energy supply. During the 10-year period, 1966–1975, oil produced from stripper wells totaled more than 4.4 billion barrels. Thus, although production per stripper well is slow, these wells play a significant part in meeting our energy demands.

Abandoning a Well

Under current practice, when an oil or gas reservoir is depleted, the site is cleaned up and the well abandoned. The hole is plugged with cement to protect all underground strata, prevent any flow or leakage at the surface, and protect water zones. Salvageable equipment is removed, pits used in the operations are filled in, and the site is regraded. Where practical, the ground is replanted with grass or other kinds of vegetation.

TRANSPORTING OIL AND GAS

To make products from petroleum, tremendous quantities of crude oil—more than 10 million barrels daily—are moved from producing fields in the United States to refineries. A large part of this volume must be transported over long distances. The output of refineries, in turn, must be delivered wherever petroleum products are used. Every branch of the petroleum industry depends upon economical and efficient transportation facilities.

Crude oil and petroleum products are moved by five major means of transportation: pipelines, tankers, barges, highway tank trucks, and railroad tank cars.

Each method was devised and developed to meet the unique problems of petroleum transportation. No other industry is required to move such enormous volumes of liquids and gases over such long distances.

In its movement from the oil field to the refinery, and on to the consumer, a petroleum product may use any combination of these methods of transportation. Today, not counting gathering lines, domestic crude oil and products movement is about 47 per cent by pipeline, 29 per cent by tank truck, 22 per cent by water, and 1 per cent by railroad.

Oil and Gas Move by Pipeline

Buried underground, pipelines move great volumes of crude oil, oil products, and natural gas across the nation so silently and efficiently that few people are aware of their existence. They are the largest single movers of oil, carrying 920 million tons annually. Pipelines rank third among all types of domestic freight carriers in tonnage handled.

Most crude oil travels at least partway to a refinery by pipeline. It is carried from producing wells to field storage tanks by flow lines. Gathering lines connect these tanks to trunk pipelines. Trunk lines are the long distance arteries that usually end at a refinery or at waterside terminals. From the refinery, oil products begin their journey to consuming centers, also by pipeline.

There is now a vast network of more than 223,000 miles of crude oil and products pipelines serving 50 states and the District of Columbia. Today about 25 per cent of all intercity freight (including coal and food) moves by pipeline.

With the tremendous expansion of natural gas use after World War II, the mileage of our natural gas pipelines system had grown to a total of 980,044 miles by the end of 1975.

Modern pipelines vary in diameter from small, 2-inch flow or gathering lines to large, 48-inch trunk lines. Until World War II, very few pipelines were larger than 12 inches in diameter. With heavy wartime demands, pipeliners came up with a technological innovation, the "big inch" pipe.

As a result, pipelines have become one of the most economical means of transporting petroleum. It now costs little more than one cent to ship a gallon of oil by large diameter pipeline from Texas to New York. Sending a postcard that distance costs nine times as much.

Pipelines are constructed to meet safety standards set by industry specifications and government regulations. These standards include pipewall thickness, welds, testing procedures, and pipe placement. Valves are installed along the line as needed to lessen spill damage in the event of an accident and to isolate the pipeline from storage and pump facilities.

To lay a pipeline, a ditch is dug deep enough to ensure adequate cover over the pipe for safe operation. Then various lengths of pipe are joined by welding. They are scrubbed clean, and corrosion-resistant coverings are applied around the outside. The line is laid in the ditch by hoists mounted on tractors called "side-booms," and the ditch backfilled to provide firm support for the pipe. Once the trench is filled with earth, the right of way is cleaned up and regraded. The pipeline may be further protected by the application of a low external voltage that keeps the pipe relatively free of corrosion almost indefinitely.

Although most pipelines are made of steel, there has been a marked increase in the use of plastic pipe in recent years. They are primarily used for small-diameter gathering lines, saltwater disposal lines, and water injection lines in oil and gas fields.

Pipelines go almost anywhere, through swamps and forests, across desert wastes, and even over mountain ranges. Sometimes the ditch must be dug through solid rock or, in some cases, the line may lie on the surface. Frequently, pipeliners must contend with other obstacles, such as rivers, lakes, and other large bodies of water. They may have to build spans to carry pipelines over streams or highways. Or, they may have to weight the pipe so that it will lie in a trench beneath the bed of a lake, a river, or an ocean.

Building a pipeline is a costly venture. For example, the Colonial Pipeline laid between the Texas Gulf Coast and New York cost over $370 million. Construction was begun in 1971 on an additional 461 miles of 36-inch loop line and 128 miles of 10-inch spur lines, plus pump stations and modifications of existing stations for an estimated cost of $113.8 million. The nearly 800-mile crude oil pipeline across Alaska cost more than $7.7 billion.

Oil and Gas Transport by Water

Many pipelines end at water terminals, where crude oil is transferred to tankers or barges for the second phase of its long journey to refineries. And refined products from refineries or coastal storage centers are often sent on their way to consuming centers by tanker or barge.

The tanker, a special type of merchant vessel, has a hull divided into compartments for carrying liquid cargoes. The largest modern tankers are more than 1,300 feet in over-all length, with capacities of 1.75 to 3.50 million barrels of crude oil or petroleum products. Their cruising speeds average 15 knots.

At the end of 1975, the U.S. tanker fleet consisted of 293 vessels. Specially designed tankers, capable of transporting liquified natural gas (LNG) at subfreezing temperatures, are now in operation. When the temperature of the gas is lowered to −260 °F, it occupies 1/600th the volume it would under normal temperatures. This permits the shipment of greater quantities of gas in these tankers.

Most of the American tanker fleet operates in coastal and intercoastal trade. The most frequent run is between the Gulf Coast producing areas and the Atlantic seaboard, because eastern refineries depend primarily on tankers for their supplies. Most of the crude oil and heavy fuel oil supplying east coast refineries is imported by tanker, primarily from points in South America and the Middle East.

On a world-wide basis, waterborne traffic is also a vital factor. The world tankship fleet of approximately 5,092 tankers, flying the flags of many countries, currently carries petroleum from producing nations to those that must import part or all of the oil they require. Our country must import more than 40 per cent of its petroleum, and nearly all that oil comes by tanker.

On any given day, about 750 million barrels of crude oil and products, 31.5 billion gallons, are in transit in tankers on the high seas. A large, modern-day tanker costs about $100 million.

Oil Moves by Tank Truck and Railroad

Tank trucks are a major means of transporting oil products from bulk plants to consumers. Direct deliveries from the refiner to large bulk consumers are also frequently made by tank truck. At one point or another, between the refinery and its final destination, probably every oil product is carried by tank truck.

Today there are approximately 158,000 tank trucks of all kinds in operation. Some are built for long-distance hauls, others for local deliveries.

Trucks roll from refineries, terminals, and bulk plants to farms, factories, service stations, and homes. They supply more than 13 million households with more than 23 billion gallons of heating oil a year. They supplied 190,000 service stations and other outlets across the nation with almost 107 billion gallons of gasoline in 1976.

Most over-the-road tank trucks operate on diesel fuel, which is more economical than gasoline for long hauls. Modern tank trucks are lighter and stronger than their forerunners, because their compartments are now made of aluminum alloys, stainless steel, and reinforced fiber glass. They are also larger. Today, tank trucks capable of carrying up to 13,000 gallon loads are not uncommon.

Railroad tank cars carry a smaller volume of oil but are nevertheless important. There are some 165,000 privately owned railroad tank cars in operation, excluding those owned by the railroads themselves. These tank cars range in carrying capacity from 4,000 to 60,000 gallons. Some are specifically designed to transport particular products.

Each Method Has Its Advantages

When large volumes of crude oil or products must be moved overland, pipelines are usually the most economical means of transportation, despite the large initial investment they require.

Over long distances that are nearly equal by land or sea, large ocean tankers are usually more economical than pipelines. If volume is relatively small and distance great, barge transportation offers advantages when points of origin and destination are near inland water routes.

If pipelines or water routes are not available, shipment by tank truck and railroad tank car, which are the most expensive modes of transport, may be necessary.

With distance, volume, and many other factors in mind, oil transportation experts must not only select the most efficient means of transportation for a particular shipment, but also the most economical. In a business as highly competitive as oil, each company realizes the importance of saving even a fraction of a cent on every gallon it ships.

REFINING AND PETROCHEMICALS

There were 265 refineries owned by 133 different companies operating in the United States on January 1, 1976. Refineries range in size from small plants, capable of processing only 150 barrels of crude oil daily, to modern complex giants, with daily crude capacities of more than 445,000 barrels. At the beginning of 1977, the total crude oil capacity of all U.S. operating refineries amounted to more than 16.1 million barrels daily.

Many factors influence the choice of a refinery location. Some refineries are built close to oil fields; others are constructed near large consuming areas. Frequently a controlling factor is easy access to water transportation.

To understand some of the processes of modern refining, it is necessary to know something about the nature of crude oil.

Crude oil, as it is delivered to the refinery, is a mixture of thousands of different hydrocarbons—compounds of hydrogen and carbon. The mixture varies widely from one oil field to another. Not all hydrocarbons are present in every crude oil.

The assortment of hydrocarbons in a crude oil and the proportions in which they are mixed determine its particular character and type. Crude oils are generally classified into three basic types. *Paraffin base* crude oils contain a high degree of paraffin wax and little or no asphalt. Besides wax, they yield large amounts of high-grade lubrication oil. *Asphalt base* crude oils contain large proportions of asphaltic matter, and *mixed base* crude oils contain quantities of both paraffin wax and asphalt.

This is why crude oils do not always look alike. Some are almost colorless and some are pitch black. Others may be amber, brown, or green. They may flow like water or creep like molasses. Some crude oils containing over 1 per cent of sulfur and other mineral impurities, are called sour crudes. Crude oils having a sulfur content below 1 per cent are called sweet crudes.

Crude oil's basic unit is a molecule of one carbon atom linked with four hydrogen atoms. This is the molecule of methane or marsh gas. Millions of variations of carbon–hydrogen pairing are possible, and millions of different hydrocarbon compounds can be formed.

This is where the petroleum chemist steps in. His job is to rearrange and juggle the number of atoms to make new combinations that can open up a whole new world of products.

The refining process performs on a large scale what the chemist has already done in the laboratory. By a series of processes, crude oil is separated into various hydrocarbon groups. These are then combined, broken up, or rearranged, and perhaps other ingredients are added.

Among the several refining operations known today, the three major processes are *separation, conversion,* and *treatment.*

Separation

The most common separation processes are solvent extraction, adsorption, crystallization, and the most important, fractional distillation.

In *solvent extraction,* different components of a mixture are separated from one another by a liquid solvent that dissolves certain compounds but not others. *Adsorption* is quite similar to solvent extraction. The important difference is that a solid, rather than a liquid solvent is used.

The solid substance must be porous in order to adsorb, or hold, the undesired petroleum components on its surface. In *crystallization,* cooling the mixture causes some of its compounds to solidify or crystallize and separate out of the liquid.

Fractional distillation is the fundamental process of refining. In distillation, volatility characteristics of hydrocarbons are particularly important. Volatility refers to the ease with which a liquid vaporizes. It depends on the boiling points of the various hydrocarbon compounds of crude oil. Hydrocarbon boiling points range from below minus 250 °F up to several hundred degrees above zero. Some crudes contain a significant amount of material boiling above 1,300 °F. Because different hydrocarbons compounds have different boiling points, they condense at different temperatures.

In modern refineries, crude oil is pumped through rows of steel tubes inside a furnace, where it is heated to as much as 725 °F depending on the type of crude. The resulting mixture of hot vapors and liquid passes into the bottom of a closed, vertical tower, sometimes as high as 100 feet. This is a fractionating or "bubble" tower.

As the vapors rise, they cool and condense at various levels in the tower. The liquid "residue" is drawn off at the bottom of the tower to be used as asphalt or heavy fuel. Higher up on the column, lubricating oil is drawn off at a lower temperature. Next come fuel oils, including gas oil, light heating oil, and light diesel fuel at still lower temperatures. Kerosine condenses still higher in the column and gasoline condenses at the top. Those gases that do not condense are carried from the top of the column.

The condensed liquids are caught by a number of horizontal trays, placed one above the other, inside the tower. Each tray is designed to hold a few inches of liquid and the rising vapors bubble up through the liquids. At each condensation level, the separated fractions are drawn off by pipes running from the sides of the tower. The fractions obtained by this distillation process are known as "straight run" products.

Conversion

At the beginning of the twentieth century, the market for petroleum products began to change radically. Automobiles became popular, and the demand for gasoline increased. But only a relatively small amount of gasoline can be distilled from the average crude oil. So refiners had to find some way of producing more gasoline from each barrel of crude processed. This problem was overcome by the development of conversion processes that enabled refiners to produce gasoline from groups of hydrocarbons that are not normally in the gasoline range.

These basic conversion processes are *thermal cracking, catalytic cracking, and polymerization.*

Thermal Cracking

Two American chemists, William M. Burton and Robert E. Humphreys, introduced the thermal cracking process in 1913. With this process, the less volatile heating oil fractions are subjected to higher temperatures under increasing pressure. The heat puts a strain on the bonds holding the larger, complex molecules together, and causes them to break up into smaller ones, including those in the gasoline range.

With this discovery, refiners also found that cracking not only increased gasoline *quantity* per barrel of crude oil processed, but also produced a substantial improvement in its *quality*. The product obtained by thermal cracking was found to be far superior in antiknock characteristics than the gasoline obtained by straight distillation.

Catalytic Cracking

Thermal cracking awakened refiners to what could be done by altering the petroleum molecule. This led to extensive probing into the physical and chemical properties of hydrocarbons.

Catalytic cracking was the next great advance. It was brought to the United States in 1937 by Eugene Houdry of France.

Catalytic cracking does essentially the same thing as thermal cracking, but by a different method. A catalyst is a substance that causes or accelerates chemical changes without itself undergoing change. Unfinished heating oils are exposed to a fine granular catalyst and the result is the breakup of these heavier hydrocarbons into light fractions, including gasoline. The catalyst enables this breakup to be accomplished under only moderate pressure.

Catalytic cracking produces a gasoline with an even higher octane (antiknock) rating. This became extremely important in meeting the special needs of World War II. Today there are many versions of this process, in which catalysts in the form of beads, powders, or pellets are used. Such catalysts range from aluminum and platinum to acids and processed clay.

Polymerization

Polymerization is the reverse of cracking. Developed during the 1930's independently by two American companies to utilize refinery gases, which were often wasted or burned as fuel, it is a method of combining smaller molecules to make larger ones.

These refinery gases are subjected to controlled high pressures and temperatures in the presence of a catalyst. This forces them to unite or polymerize, and form liquids called polymers. Polymers are essential components of high-octane motor and aviation fuels.

Other refining methods that alter the structure of hydrocarbons are also widely used today. *Alkylation, isomerization, catalytic reforming,* and *hydrocracking* are four such methods that rearrange petroleum molecules to form high-octane products.

As a result of these advances, refinery efficiency has increased substantially. In 1920, the gasoline yield from each 42-gallon barrel of crude oil refined was only 11 gallons. Today, refiners obtain an average of 19 gallons from each barrel of crude. Far higher yields could be obtained if market demand called for more gasoline in relation to fuel oil and other petroleum products.

If no improvements had been made in gasoline processing techniques since 1920, refiners would have to run over 3.5 billion barrels of additional crude oil per year to meet our gasoline requirements today.

PETROLEUM PRODUCTS AND THEIR USES

At the turn of the century, it was relatively simple to pinpoint the major markets of the petroleum industry. Grease was the major lubricant. Kerosine was used for illumination. Coal, the major energy source, was used for heating. Today, petroleum supplies the power for our transportation network and our factories and farms; the heat for our homes and large buildings; the lubricants to keep the wheels of industry turning; the material with which much of our highway, road, and street network is paved; and a host of products derived from petrochemicals.

Product Quality Assessment

Approximately 3,000 products are currently produced wholly or in part from petroleum, in addition to 3,000 or so petrochemicals. The companies that manufacture these products and the customers who purchase them want to have some general idea of their properties, quality, and performance. In the early days of the industry, each customer and each major supplier had his own methods of assessing performance of quality, and disagreement was widespread over these various proprietary methods. In more recent years, the excellent programs of such organizations as the American Society for Testing and Materials, Society of Automotive Engineers, National Lubricating Grease Institute, the Acid Processors Association, Coordinating Research Council, Inc., Department of Defense, National Bureau of Standards, Bureau of Mines, and others have led to the development of technology that permits the writing of tests. Once these standardized tests have been agreed upon, it is possible to come up with specifications. The lead taken by U.S. institutions in this area of petroleum testing is being followed by the rest of the world through the work of such international organizations as the International Organization for Standardization (ISO).

Petroleum Fuels

Among the products derived from petroleum are the fuels that now supply three-quarters of all the energy consumed in the United States. Petroleum energy provides the power for supersonic jet aircraft, the fuel for small space heaters, and a multitude of uses in between.

Gasoline

Motor and aviation gasolines are blends of straight-run gasoline (obtained by primary distillation), natural gasoline (one of the liquids processed out of natural gas), cracked gasoline, reformed gasoline, polymerized gasoline, and alkylate.

To these gasoline blends, refiners add a wide variey of chemicals, called additives, to further improve the quality of the fuel.

Antiknock compounds are one such gasoline additive. Their purpose is to reduce or eliminate the "knock" or "ping" that occurs when the fuel is not being properly burned in the engine. The measure of gasoline's resistance to engine knock is its octane number. This is determined by comparing a gasoline with fuels of known composition and knock characteristics under specified conditions. Two different types of tests conducted in a single-cylinder laboratory engine yield antiknock measures called Research or Motor Octane Number. When the test is run in a test car, it is called Road Octane Number.

Because of emission control devices and regulations on motor vehicles, refiners are now producing gasolines that contain little or no lead-based antiknock additives. Instead, they use hydrocarbon compounds as antiknock additives.

Over the years, the octane numbers of gasoline have increased as automotive engineers have developed cars with higher compression ratios. In 1935, regular-grade gasoline had a Research Octane Number of 72. By 1974, it had risen to 94. Premium gasolines rose during the same period from a Research Octane of 78 to almost 100.

Gasoline is the petroleum industry's principal product. Some 107 billion gallons were consumed by motor vehicles in this country during 1976. Of this total, about 75 per cent was used in automobiles alone. Trucks, buses, and motorcycles accounted for the rest. A passenger car consumes, on the average, about 712 gallons of gasoline yearly. The average truck uses 1,227 gallons of motor fuel a year and the average commerical bus, an estimated 5,896 gallons.

Aviation Gasoline

After the war, research on ways to develop increased power without enlarging the size of the airplane engine continued. Researchers realized that the key was a standardized fuel with high antiknock characteristics. Refiners went to work and developed an aviation gasoline with an octane number of about 87. In 1934, an aviation fuel of 100 octane was developed. The engine's size remained the same, but its power output was considerably increased.

Commercial aviation came into its own as Americans took to the air after the war. Mail and all kinds of freight were carried by air. Private aviation surged upward, as more and more business organizations bought and maintained their own airplanes. Small plane flying became popular, and aircraft became important to farmers for seeding, dusting, and spraying their crops and defoliating and fertilizing.

During the 1950's, commercial airlines began to switch over to the faster jets. Even though the private use of piston-engine aircraft continued to increase steadily, the demand for aviation gasoline began to slacken. There is still a substantial market for it, however—over 560 million gallons in 1976.

Jet Fuels

When research first began on jet fuels, commercially available kerosine was used because of its relatively low volatility—an important jet fuel requirement. Today's commerical jet airliners still depend on a highly refined kerosine for most of their fuel supply.

Military jets require a somewhat more complex fuel to withstand the severe conditions of supersonic flight. To meet the military's jet fuel requirements, scientists have developed carefully compounded blends of kerosine and gasoline.

Jet aircraft consume enormous amounts of fuel. Some of the jumbo-sized jets now in operation consume an average of 3,335 gallons of fuel during each hour of flight. Their fuel tanks can hold up to 47,210 gallons of fuel.

The extent of the changeover from pistons to jets by the military and by commerical airlines is evidenced by the rapid rise in jet fuel consumption during the last 16 years. In 1959, U.S. jet fuel consumption totaled 4.4 billion gallons. By 1976, it had risen to over 15.2 billion gallons.

Kerosine

In the early days of the petroleum industry, kerosine was the refiners' principal product. Once used primarily as a illuminant, kerosine is now used mostly for cook stoves, space heaters, farm equipment, and jets.

But this product also has many other uses. It is an ingredient in insecticides, paints, polishes, and cleaning and degreasing compounds. On farms, kerosine not only powers tractors and other equipment, but also provides the fuel for heaters used in the curing of tobacco.

Total consumption of kerosine in 1976, exclusive of its use as jet fuel, amounted to more than 62 million barrels.

Diesel Fuels

Diesel engines are fundamentally different from gasoline engines. A diesel engine is ignited by the heat of compressed air in a cylinder, not by a spark plug, as is the case in a gasoline engine.

Early diesel engines were massive, built to withstand tremendous heat and pressure. At first, they served primarily as stationary power sources in factories and ships, and they used almost any oil as fuel.

Large diesel engines are still important stationary power sources, but through the years, diesels have gradually been adapted for other uses. Today, they provide economical power for heavy road equipment, such as trucks, buses, and tractors. In recent years, railroads have turned to diesel engines for locomotives and they now represent a large market for diesel fuels.

Just as modern diesel engines have become specialized, the diesel fuels that run them are highly refined for their specialized uses. Modern diesel fuels are manufactured in several grades, ranging from heavy oils to light kerosine-type oils.

Fuel Oils

Today, fuel oils are designed to meet the needs of residential and commerical heating, manufacturing processes, industrial steam and electrical generation, and marine engine and many other uses.

Fuel oils are generally classified as distillates or residuals.

Distillates are the lighter oils, some of which are used in space heating, water heating, and cooking. But the major market for distillates is in the automatic central heating of homes and smaller apartment houses and buildings.

One of the big advances in home heating has been the development of the Degree Day—the system worked out by oil companies to determine just when each customer's oil tank needs filling. This system practically eliminates the possibility of an oil-user finding himself without oil an a cold morning.

Total distillate consumption (including diesel fuel) in 1976 amounted to 1.1 billion barrels.

Residuals are the heavier, high-viscosity fuel oils that usually must be heated before they can be pumped and handled conveniently. Gas and electric utilities are the major market for residual oil. Industry is the second largest consumer of oils. It uses them to fire open-hearth furnaces, steam boilers, and kilns. Large apartment and commercial buildings make up the third largest residual oil market.

The total market for residual oil during 1976 amounted to over 1.0 billion barrels.

Petroleum Coke

Petroleum coke is almost pure carbon. As such, it has many useful properties. It burns with little or no ash, conducts electricity, is highly resistant to chemical action, does not melt, and is an excellent abrasive.

Coke is invaluable in the manufacture of electrodes for electric furnaces and in electrochemical processes. Carbon, or graphite, often made from petroleum coke, is used in flashlight and radio batteries. Sandpaper and knife-sharpening whetstones are made by fusing sand and coke.

But petroleum coke is primarily a fuel, valuable in refining aluminum, nickel, special steels, and chemicals. The fact that it is almost pure carbon reduces the chance of contaminating the metals or chemicals being refined.

Liquefied Petroleum Gas (LPG)

Familiar to many as "bottled gas," LPG consists primarily of propanes and butanes, highly volatile gases that are extracted from refinery and natural gases. It has a unique characteristic. Under moderate pressure, LPG becomes liquid and can be easily transported by pipelines, railroad tank cars, or trucks. Released from its storage tank, LPG reverts to vapor form, burning with a clean flame to provide high heat value.

Part of the growing demand for LPG is as fuel for internal combustion engines, primarily those used in buses, tractors, forklift trucks, and in-plant equipment. A principal use for the fuel is in the manufacture of petrochemicals.

Liquefied petroleum gas is also used extensively in the home—for stoves, refrigerators, water heaters, space heaters, and furnaces. At present, cooking is the predominant household use for LPG, with clothes drying and air conditioning gaining in importance.

On farms LPG heats incubators and brooders, sterilizes milk utensils, dehydrates fruit and vegetables, prevents frost damage, and controls weeds by flame weeding. In industry, it is used in metal cutting and welding.

Total consumption of liquefied petroleum gases (excluding those amounts used in the production of gasoline) reached the 20.4 billion-gallon level in 1975.

Lubricants and Greases

Lubricating Oils

All equipment with moving parts require lubrication. Finished lubricating oils range from the clear thin oil that is placed by a hypodermic needle on tiny compass bearings to the thick dark oil that is poured into the massive gears of giant machines.

As the needs of industry have become more complex, lubricating oils have become more specialized. American companies manufacture hundreds of different oils to exacting specifications. Industrial lubricating oils must maintain their friction-fighting properties without thickening or coagulating for thousands of hours between shutdowns. Lubricating oils for automotive engines are designed to show a relatively small change in viscosity with temperature, neither thinning out unduly in searing heat nor thickening excessively in below-zero winter weather. They are designed to prevent formation of excessive carbon, corrosive acids, or sticky deposits. The addition of chemical detergents enable these oils to hold in suspension harmful matter that would otherwise accumulate on engine parts.

Greases

The essential ingredients of grease are lubricating oil base stocks, soaps that act as thickening agents, additives to improve performance and stability, and fillers to increase wearability. Technologists have developed greases in hundreds of consistencies to meet innumerable performance needs. Some greases must resist the pounding heat of steel rolling mills or the subzero temperatures encountered by high-altitude aircraft. Others must withstand acids or water or stand up to the grinding friction of railroad roller bearings.

Waxes

The two types of wax derived from petroleum, paraffin and microcrystalline, are extracted from lubricating oil fractions by chilling, filtering, and solvent washing.

Paraffin wax is a colorless, more or less clear crystalline substance, without odor or taste, and is slightly greasy to the touch. Microcrystalline waxes do not crystallize like paraffin, because they are composed of finer particles.

Wax is used for the most part in packaging. It waterproofs and vapor-proofs such articles as milk containers and wrappers for bread, cereals, and frozen foods. Wax is also used in casting intricate parts and components of machinery, jewelry, and dentures.

Asphalt

For centuries, men obtained asphalt from natural deposits, or "lakes," where it remained as residue after the air and sun had evaporated the lighter petroleum fractions from it. Solid or semi-solid at normal temperatures, asphalt liquefies when it is heated. It is a powerful binding agent, a sticky adhesive, and a highly waterproof, durable material.

Today, asphalt is an important petroleum product, extracted as a refining residue or by solvent precipitation from residual fractions. By careful selection of crude oils, controlled air oxidation, and blending, modern asphalt is given several added properties such as inertness to most chemicals and fumes, weather and shock resistance, toughness, and flexibility over a wide temperature range.

There are a multitude of uses for asphalt. It is a major road-paving material. It also surfaces sidewalks, airport runways, and parking lots. It goes into such products as floor coverings, roofing materials, protective coatings for pipelines, and underbody coatings for automobiles.

Petroleum's Total Market

All told, a level of 6.4 billion barrels of petroleum products were consumed in the United States during 1976—a 45 per cent increase over demand 10 years ago. This works out to be an average of 1,246 gallons per person—or more than 95 gallons per week for an average family of four. Much of this, of course, would be in the form of petroleum products used by industry and transportation to provide the goods and services that such a family requires.

The major portion of petroleum's total market is accounted for by gasoline—over 2.5 billion barrels in 1976. Petroleum's second largest market is the fuel oils, the distillates and residuals, which were consumed at a rate of over 2.1 billion barrels. Jet fuel demand totaled 361 million barrels, while kerosine, once the industry's prime product, accounted for 62 million barrels.

The remaining 1.4 billion barrels were accounted for by LPG, asphalt, lubricating oils and greases, and many other products.

ENERGY AND THE ENVIRONMENT

The petroleum industry is well aware of the damage that petroleum and its products could do to the environment. That is why the industry has for many years conducted extensive research on the problems of atmospheric wastes and industrial water pollution.

The ever-growing need for energy in this country, with a rising population, more automobiles, and the universal desire to raise living standards, signals the need for petroleum companies to expand operations. At the same time, environmental quality is a major concern.

The cost to the oil industry during the last ten years for pollution abatement has been more than $9.2 billion. During 1975 alone, it is estimated that oil companies' capital investment to combat pollution was nearly $1.4 billion.

While exploring for and producing oil, the industry is careful that its operations do not contaminate the environment. Seismic crews in many situations replace explosives with air guns to produce acoustical waves during exploration. Oil well blowouts, almost a trademark of early days in the industry, almost never happen today, thanks to advances in petroleum technology.

No longer are natural gases burned off or wells drilled side by side to relieve the natural underground pressure. Wells are carefully spaced far apart, and production is controlled to conserve reservoir energy for maximum recovery before pumps are used.

The industry has also improved the design of oil field equipment, including oil-water separators and remote emergency equipment and the cement plugging of abandoned wells, all in the interest of conservation and the environment.

Ocean-going tankers bring to our shores nearly one-half the oil used in the United States. Pipelines, railroad tank cars, barges, and trucks move tremendous quantities across the country every day, rarely disturbing the environment. Each transportation phase is prepared to prevent and clean up oil spills quickly and efficiently.

Oil pollution at sea results from discharges of bilge and waste, spills from tanker accidents, and discharges of dirty water from tanker washings. Over four-fifths of the world's tankers no longer discharge dirty water at sea, but store it and either offload it at the next port for processing in refinery oil-water separators or make it part of the next crude oil cargo without any of the oil being spilled. New techiques have been developed for use at sea and on beaches for the cleanup of possible oil spills. The American Petroleum Institute was instrumental in the founding of a school at the Texas Engineering Extension Service where oil company personnel learn the skills of oil-spill cleanup.

Three-fourths of American crude oil and almost one-third of our refinery products move around the country in pipelines, with minor amounts of leakage—about six-thousandths of 1 per cent of the volume moved annually. Safety devices that help prevent pollution include ultrasonic leak detectors, corrosion preventives, automatic shutdown techniques that go into operation in case of a leak, and regular pipeline inspections. Computerized control of the pipelines helps make possible the safe movement of batches through the lines.

When a new pipeline is laid, construction crews work to restore the right of way to its original form, with almost no perceptible change in the environment.

Although refineries in years past contributed to the pollution of air and water, tremendous changes have taken place. Noxious emissions of fumes and odors have been eliminated to a great extent. A refinery uses great quantities of water for cooling and processing, usually from a river, and that water is now purified in multiple-stage effluent treatment to remove oil and other wastes. The water is then returned to rivers in the same state of purity and at about the same temperature at which it was removed. Air is replacing water as a coolant in some systems, with a resultant decrease in thermal pollution.

Refineries are now better neighbors, with steps taken to reduce the light and noise of refining by shielded, smokeless flares and by equipment silencers. In all, refiners have spent billions of dollars to stop air and water pollution, and additional millions have been spent in fuel and process research. In building new refineries or chemical faciltiies, the advice of environmental consultants is carefully heeded.

Automobile Emissions

A decrease in automobile emissions has taken place, with improvements in automobile systems. According to EPA estimates, there have been reductions of 83 per cent in carbon monoxide emissions, and emissions of nitrogen oxides have declined 43 per cent. The automobile industry's estimates run even higher, and figure a reduction of over 90 per cent in hydrocarbon emissions, an 84 per cent reduction in carbon monoxide emissions, and a 63 per cent reduction in emissions of nitrogen oxides.

Lead-free gasoline is now made by refiners throughout the industry and is available at service stations in every state. In addition, lead emissions from leaded grades of gasoline are going down and will go down even further because of the recently ordered lead phasedown in gasoline by the EPA.

ENERGY CONSERVATION

The petroleum industry strongly supports and favors the wise and efficient use of energy. But public acceptance of a conservation ethic has been painfully slow.

Most Amercians, accustomed to low-cost energy, continue to consume it as they did in the pre-OPEC days, while imports of oil, much of it from OPEC countries, have risen to approximately one-half of U.S. oil consumption.

The American refining industry is one of six energy-intensive industries selected to cooperate in the first federal voluntary conservation program. It has pledged to reduce its energy use 15 per cent by 1980, from the 1972 base year.

By 1976 refiners had achieved a 13.6 per cent reduction, more than two-thirds of the way to their voluntary goal. Over 94 per cent of the refining capacity in the United States are taking part in this voluntary reporting program, which was shaped by the American Petroleum Institute in cooperation with the Federal Energy Administration and the Commerce Department. Refining's conservation rate was the highest of six high-energy users chosen to cooperate in the program.

The refining industry has invested over 1 billion dollars in conservation equipment, much of it in computers to control the efficient firing of furnaces and heaters. It has also installed improved heat exchangers and turbines to capture and use the energy from surplus pressure.

The International Energy Agency, critical of the recent American oil consumption rate, ranked the United States 14th among its 18 members in energy conservation. Overall, the U.S. energy picture remains one of shocking waste. It is estimated that one-half the energy this nation uses, which amounts to more than the fuel consumed by two-thirds of the world's population, could be saved through conservation.

Nearly every other developed country except the United States uses taxes on petroleum to restrict demand. Such a "user" tax would be very unpopular in this country. The alternative is voluntary conservation—careful observance of the 55 mile per hour speed limit; smaller and more efficient automobiles; better insulation of homes; lower thermostat settings and other procedures for which the technology is already available.

If the conservation ethic could become popular in the United States, as the environmental ethic has, tremendous gains in energy-saving could come about. Public participation in energy conservation would affect the whole energy future of the nation and indeed, the world.

PETROLEUM AND THE FUTURE

As goes the growth of the U.S. economy in the remainder of this century, so go the energy industries. The two are inseparably bound in modern industrial society.

Of course, it is impossible to predict the growth of the nation's economy with complete accuracy. But energy companies must look to the future. Long lead times are needed to bring an oil or gas field into production, to build refineries, and to construct pipelines. Months, even years, can be spent developing innovative technology such as that needed to solve the problems of Arctic weather in constructing the Trans-Alaska pipeline or designing new drilling machinery to enable companies to drill for oil in deeper water off our country's shores. Each company can but calculate the risks and cost involved, plus other factors, then figure out how they are to deal with them.

How Much Energy?

The Federal Energy Administration (FEA) points out that the world oil price between now and 1985 will greatly influence both energy demand in the nation and the economic feasibility of producing various high-cost alternate sources of energy.

In the three years since OPEC raised the world price of oil some 366 per cent, that cartel has shown its ability to keep the price high, even in the face of substantial decline in demand through 1975, because of the high price and a general world economic slump.

Taking the prediction of continued high prices into account, the FEA estimates that U.S. energy demand should increase from 72.9 quadrillion BTU in 1974, to 98.9 in 1985 (Figure 9-2).

Energy demand in this country grew at a rate of 3.6 per cent in the 20 years before the 1973 embargo. As a result of the sharp, OPEC-inspired, world price increase in oil, the energy-demand growth rate will be much lower than the historic growth rate, even with continued economic expansion.

The largest reductions in energy growth, the FEA predicts, will be the household, commerical, and transportation sectors, which will respond most sharply to higher energy prices (Figure 9-3).

Meeting Growing Energy Demands

Between now and 1985, the FEA forecasts, the United States will increase its supply of energy more than 40 per cent. Coal production could increase to over 1 billion tons from the current levels of 640 million tons. Oil production could reach 13.9 million barrels per day, if oil is found near areas of the Outer Continental Shelf and if market prices prevail.

Natural gas production may reach 22.3 trillion cubic feet, if field prices are deregulated; otherwise, a figure of 17.9 trillion cubic feet is predicted under current regulations.

Nuclear power has experienced significant delays, but it could grow from current levels of less than 10 per cent to about 26 per cent of electricity generation by 1985.

Emerging technologies, such as the conversion of coal into oil or gas, and solar and geothermal energy, are predicted to be impor-

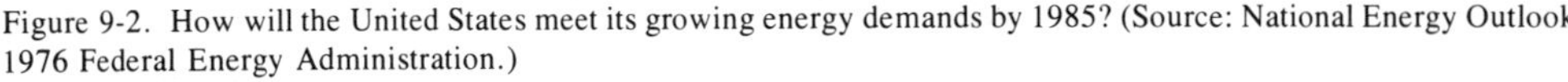
Figure 9-2. How will the United States meet its growing energy demands by 1985? (Source: National Energy Outlook 1976 Federal Energy Administration.)

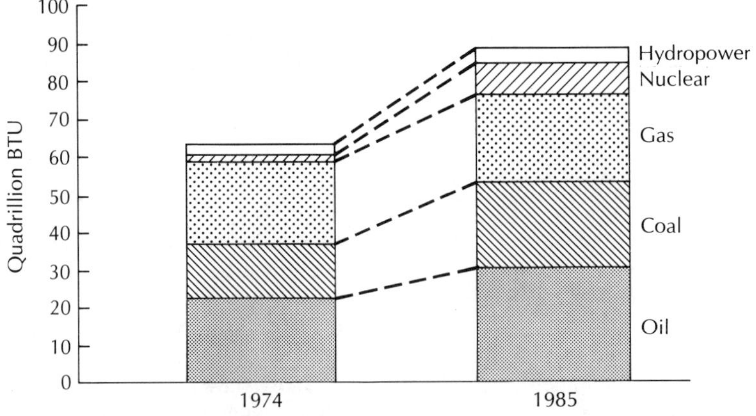

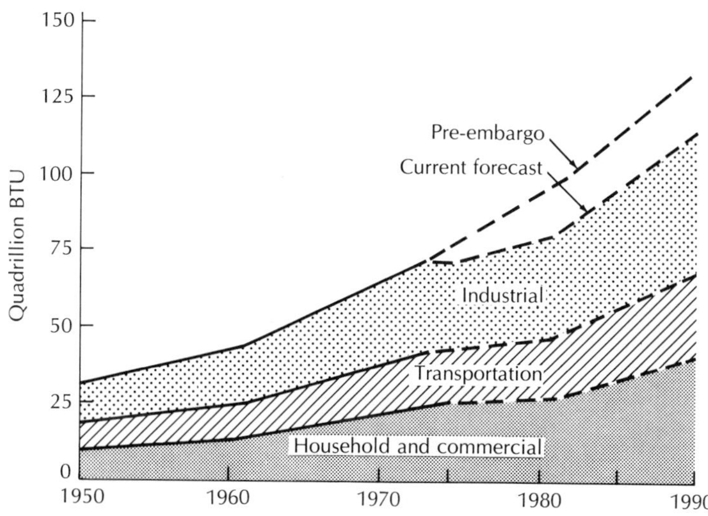

Figure 9-3. How much energy will the nation consume? (Source: National Energy Outlook 1976 Federal Energy Administration.)

tant after 1985, but not before that time, according to the FEA.

Moving into Alternate Energy Sources

American oil companies, looking far to the future in their corporate planning, are doing active research and development in preparation for the time when oil and natural gas reserves in the United States begin to peter out. Well aware that the United States has been called "the Saudi Arabia of coal reserves," oil companies have moved into coal as an alternate energy source. With their expertise, they have introduced new mining methods and machinery and are doing research and development in coal gasification, coal liquefaction, and transportation of the mineral by coal slurry pipeline.

Oil companies are also investigating oil shale, tar sands, geothermal, solar, and other possible energy sources. And they are developing technology for them, often based on their know-how from oil and gas engineering methods.

The FEA predicts that the major contribution from solar and geothermal energy and synthetic fuels will not be felt until after 1990. The technology for these sources exists, but must be proved economically viable on a commercial scale. Unless commercial-sized plants are started now and prove economical by 1985, according to the FEA, it will not be possible for these new sources to replace dwindling supplies of gas and oil by 1985.

Oil Imports

With oil imports in 1976 at more than 40 per cent of total U.S. consumption, the FEA makes some prediction about oil imports in America's future. It sees no way to cut imports in the next year or so, although conserving energy and increasing U.S. production of oil and natural gas would help (Figure 9-4).

Gradual deregulation of oil and gas prices, the FEA says, and a continuation of current world oil prices could result in a drop to 5.9 million barrels per day of imported oil, slightly below today's level, by the year 1985. If this nation's supply of petroleum were to increase and all-out conservation practices were to go into effect, imports would decrease to one-third of what they are

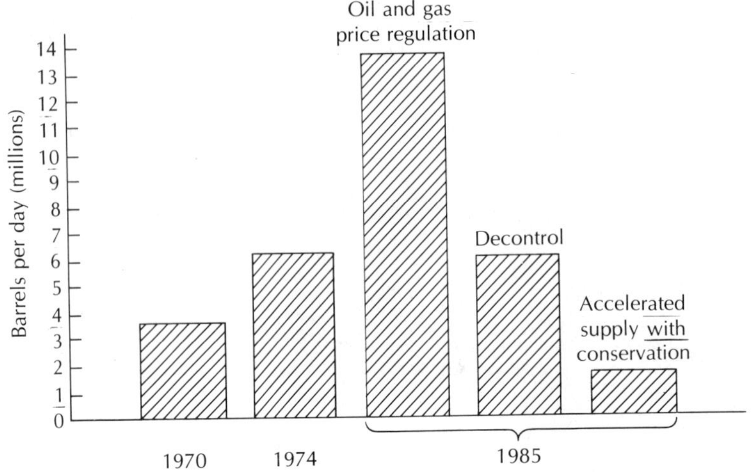

Figure 9-4. What will oil imports be by 1985? (Source: National Energy Outlook 1976 Federal Energy Administration.)

now by 1985. The FEA estimates that if oil and gas prices are regulated so that domestic production is discouraged, by 1985 oil imports may reach 13.5 million barrels per day—more than twice the amount we now import.

SUGGESTED READINGS

Blumer, Max, 1971, Scientific Aspects of the Oil Spill Problem, *Environmental Affairs 1,* pp. 54–73.

Federal Task Force on Alaskan Oil Development, 1972, Final Environmental Impact Statement, Proposed Trans-Alaska Pipeline: U.S. Dept. of the Interior, Washington, D.C. (Vols. 1–6).

Hodgson, Bryan, 1976, The Pipeline; Alaska's Troubled Colossus, *National Geographic 150,* November, pp. 684–717.

Livingston, Dennis, 1974, Oil on the Seas, *Environment 16,* September, pp. 38–43.

Meyerhoff, Arthur A., 1976, Economic Impact and Geopolitical Implications of Giant Petroleum Fields, *American Scientist 64,* pp. 536–541.

———, 1976, *Technology Review 78,* February, A special issue on offshore petroleum production.

Travers, William B., and Percy R. Luney, 1976, Drilling, Tankers, and Oil Spills on the Atlantic Outer Continental Shelf, *Science 194,* pp. 791–795.

Zaffarano, Richard F., and William B. Harper, 1975, Petroleum, in *Mineral Facts and Problems,* 1975 Edition of Bureau of Mines, pp. 793–817.

The Natural Gas Story 10

FEDERAL ENERGY ADMINISTRATION 1975

The importance of natural gas to the development of the United States cannot be overstated. Natural gas is our most widely used *domestic* energy resource. It supplies over one-quarter of our energy needs compared with about 47 per cent supplied by crude oil and other liquid petroleum products; 18 per cent supplied by coal; 4.2 per cent supplied by water power; and 2.8 per cent supplied by nuclear energy. It also is the primary source of energy for American industry and supplies about 47 per cent of its needs.

EARLY HISTORY OF NATURAL GAS

Natural gas is believed to have issued from the ground at Delphi in ancient Greece and to have been used in temples that were erected there. In Burma and China, natural gas from shallow wells was piped in bambo tubes and used for lighting and in the production of salt from seawater about 2,400 years ago, but it did not become popular for general use.

The first natural gas transported by pipeline (hollow logs) in the United States was at Fredonia, New York, in 1821. The use of gas for industrial purposes dates from 1863 when a well at East Liverpool, Ohio, was put into operation. The first metal pipeline—made of cast iron—was built in 1862 to supply Titusville, Pennsylvania, from a well located 5 miles away. Steel was first used in gas pipelines in 1887. The early developments of natural gas were in western New York and Pennsylvania, eastern Ohio, West Virginia, and northern Kentucky. Other gas fields were discovered later, many of them while producers were drilling for oil. Some of the most important of these were the Monroe and Richland parish fields in Louisiana; the Panhandle field in Texas; the Hugoton field in Kansas; the fields in Oklahoma; and the Kettleman Hills, Button Willow, and Ventura fields in California.

FORMATIONS IN WHICH NATURAL GAS IS FOUND

Natural gas and crude oil are often found together underground. Both are derived from plant and animal life that existed millions of years ago and that subsequently was covered by prehistoric oceans that once covered much of the Earth's present land area. Natural gas and crude oil are found in similar geological formations in structural or stratigraphic traps.

This article is taken from a booklet issued by the Federal Energy Administration, Washington, D.C. 20461, October 1975.

These traps usually contain porous rock or sand, and the oil and gas are found in the minute pores in the rock and between the grains of sand. In some cases, the gas is trapped above the oil deposit.

EARLY HISTORY OF MANUFACTURED GAS

The manufactured gas industry was developed and flourishing long before the commerical use of natural gas. In 1609, John Baptist van Helmont of Brussels first produced gas by combustion, fermentation, and the action of acids on limestone. About 200 years after his discovery, the substance was harnessed to practical purpose.

On the Continent, Phillippe Lebon was the first to make gas commerically by distilling coal. In 1801, he lighted his home and gardens in Paris. Three years later, William Murdock built a gas works of 900 burners in London. In 1812, the London and Westminster Gas Light and Coke Company was formed. On December 31, 1813, Westminster Bridge was lighted with manufactured gas to the amazement of the people of London. When Napoleon heard of the idea, he dismissed it as "one big foolish act." By 1820, however, Paris streets were lighted with manufactured gas.

Baltimore, in 1816, was the first city in the United States to light its streets with manufactured gas. In 1855, Robert Wilhem von Bunsen, a German chemist, invented the blue flame burner. Between 1865 and 1875, the use of manufactured gas for home lighting began to make progress. Carl Auer, an Austrian chemist, developed the incandescent mantle for which he was awarded the title "von Welsbach."

NATURAL GAS CHARACTERISTICS

Natural gas is a clean, efficient, and versatile fuel. It can produce a flame temperature of 3,800 °F, which is essential to furnace operations of the glass, steel, and other industries. In addition to its use as a fuel, natural gas is a major feedstock for the manufacture of ammonia, which is used to produce fertilizer; and it is a source of such other feedstocks as propane and ethane, which are used extensively in the petrochemical industry and for fuel in rural areas.

Natural gas has additional advantages over other fuels:

—It is more efficient to use.
—It is cleaner—it contains no sulfur and, if properly burned, produces, no soot, smoke, or ash.
—It enables close control of temperature at the point of use.
—It does not require storage by users.

Dry natural gas can be used in the same form as it flows from the ground, since it is essentially methane. No costly refining is required as in the case of crude oil. However, most natural gas is processed to recover such valuable by-products as propane, butane, and other natural gas liquids and to remove such inert substances as carbon dioxide and hydrogen sulfide.

TYPES OF GAS

There are three general types of gas:

(1) *Natural gas*. The major component of natural gas is methane (CH_4). Components, which appear in relatively smaller amounts, are ethane (C_2H_6), propane (C_3H_8), butane (C_4H_{10}), and some heavier, more complex hydrocarbons. Other components such as water, sulfur, nitrogen, and carbon dioxide are removed at the processing plants.

(2) *Synthetic* or *substitute natural gas (SNG)*. This gas is made synthetically from coal or from such petroleum liquids as naphtha.

(3) *Liquefied petroleum gas (LPG)*. This gas is propane, butane, or a mixture of these gases. It is obtained primarily by extraction from natural gas or as a by-product of refining crude oil.

Before 1940, much natural gas was wasted in the Southwest by being flared into the air. Many gas wells were shut-in for lack of a market. Producers sold gas at the low price of 4 to 5 cents per thousand cubic feet. All of this was changed with improvements in technology. Development of a high-strength steel pipe that has a thin wall permitted transportation of natural gas over long distances under high pressure. The development of underground storage facilities near market centers also helped make long-distance transmission of natural gas more practicable economically.

During the 1950's, metallurgical technology was developed for the transport of liquefied natural gas (LNG) at extremely low temperatures (−259 °F) in specialized, refrigerated ocean-going tankers. Liquefied natural gas, for example, is now being shipped from Algeria to the United States.

COMPONENTS OF TOTAL GAS SUPPLY

Domestically produced natural gas is by far the largest component of our total gas supply. Less than 5 per cent of our natural gas is imported. However, increased imports of LNG are expected to help alleviate the gas shortage. Only a small amount of SNG is presently being produced and this from petroleum liquids. The cost of both LNG and SNG is relatively high when compared with present prices for natural gas produced from domestic sources.

STRUCTURE OF THE GAS INDUSTRY

The natural gas industry has three main segments: production, transmission, and distribution. The industry includes many companies that are engaged only in producing, transporting, or distributing gas. However, the increasing shortage of natural gas has led some natural gas pipeline and distribution companies to engage more extensively in exploration, development, and production—either on their own or with oil and gas producers. Many of the larger pipeline and distribution companies also have made advance payments to producers for exploration and development. These payments give the companies priority over other companies to purchase natural gas that might be discovered.

STATE REGULATION OF UTILITIES

The marketing of natural gas to end-users in the United States is performed mainly by public utilities, which are subject to regulation by state agencies or commissions.

The legal concept of regulating public utilities is fairly ancient. Early Roman law, for example, gave recognition to the special obligation of a common carrier of goods. Three centuries ago, in British law, Lord Chief Justice Hale made the distinction between business "charged with a public interest" and other forms of enterprise not subject to regulation.

In the United States, the pattern of public regulation was worked out by the states before federal commissions arrived on the scene. What is that pattern? Public utility regulation is the expression of the right of the public, through the state, to obtain adequate service at reasonable rates from a public utility, in return for a grant of authority or a charter to the utility to operate in a given territory. The pattern to establish the public utility agency has three components: First, the monopoly factor; second, the duty to serve; third, the obligation to maintain reasonable rates. The basic reason for regulation is that the operations of utility companies are monopolistic in character.

In a landmark case, *Smyth v. Ames,* decided in 1898, the United States Supreme Court laid down standards of fairness for fixing rates that the states would have to observe to assure that neither the public suffered from rates that were too high, nor the public utility owner suffered from rates that were too low. The same balance between interests of the consumer and those of the investor continues to be a prerequisite of fair regulation.

FEDERAL REGULATION OF NATURAL GAS

The Federal Power Commission (FPC) was created by Congress in 1920 to administer the Federal Water Power Act. Its early activities were confined to the issuance of licenses for hydroelectric projects.

The Commission had no jurisdiction over the gas industry until 1938, when the Natural Gas Act was enacted. This Act gave the FPC jurisdiction over the *inter*state transportation and sale of natural gas for resale. The Commission regulates rates to be charged, accounting practices of natural gas companies, and the issuance of certificates authorizing construction of pipelines and other related facilities. It has control over the abandonment of facilities and expired contracts, it investigates the impact on the environment of proposed new facilities, and it publishes some natural gas industry statistics and reports. The FPC also regulates rates for the export and import of natural gas.

In the early 1930's, many cities (led by the U.S. Conference of Mayors and the Municipal Leagues of Ohio and Wisconsin) sought antitrust action against the major gas holding company groups and urged federal regulation of the interstate natural gas companies on the basis of testimony developed in an investigation by the Federal Trade Commission. This testimony showed: (a) the waste of gas in the producing fields, (b) an urgent need for natural gas by industries in the Midwest, (c) the monopolistic control of interstate pipelines by major oil and gas producers or utility holding companies, and (d) excessive wholesale natural gas rates to the distribution companies.

The Natural Gas Act was approved by Congress in 1938 without a single dissenting vote in either House. The concept was that the Federal Power Commission would regulate the *inter*state pipelines and the states would continue to regulate the *intra*state gas distribution companies.

Natural gas producers normally sell the "dry" gas that they produce to pipeline companies, which take the gas from the field and transport it to large industrial users and to gas distributing companies. The price at which the producer sells the gas in the field is frequently referred to as the wellhead price. Gas contracts between producers and pipeline companies are frequently of long duration—for 10 years, 20 years, or for the life of the dedicated gas reserves.

Before 1954, wellhead prices charged by producers were unregulated. On June 7 of that year, in a case involving *Phillips Petroleum* v. *the State of Wisconsin,* the U.S. Supreme Court decided that the Federal Power Commission had a mandate to regulate the wellhead price of gas sold by producers to interstate pipelines. However, the court did not indicate how much regulation was to be carried out.

On two occasions, Congress has passed legislation specifically to exempt wellhead prices from FPC regulation—the Kerr bill in 1950 and the Harris bill in 1956. The Kerr bill was vetoed by President Truman, who said that regulation of field prices was necessary because of a lack of effective competition among sellers. President Eisenhower vetoed the Harris bill because of the high-pressure lobbying tactics on behalf of the bill.

Between 1938, when the Natural Gas Act became law, and the 1954 Supreme Court decision in the Phillips case, the FPC held that it had no jurisdiction over independent producers.

IMPACT OF FEDERAL REGULATION

During the 1950's and since, the gas industry expanded rapidly. One of the prime reasons for the rapid increase in demand was the relatively low price of natural gas compared with the price of competing fuels, such as oil and coal, and, more recently, its environmental desirability.

In 1950, the annual consumption of natural gas in the United States was about 6 trillion cubic feet. By 1973, consumption was 22.6 trillion cubic feet and dropped for the first time in 1974 by 5 per cent to 21.6 trillion cubic feet. From 1950 to 1973 the rate of growth averaged 5.9 per cent per year. At the same time energy consumption of all fuels in the United States increased at the rate of only 3.4 per cent per year.

After World War II, proved recoverable reserves of natural gas increased steadily year after year, and reached a peak in 1967. (Proved reserves are estimated quantities of natural gas that analysis of geological and engineering data demonstrates with reasonable certainty to be recoverable from known oil and gas fields under existing economic and operating conditions.) Since 1967, natural gas reserves have declined with the exception of 1970, when the Prudhoe Bay field reserves in Alaska were added to the inventory. Reserve additions of natural gas in the lower 48 states (except for 1970) have been less than annual production since 1968. By 1974, natural gas reserves had fallen 25 per cent below the 1967 peak.

At the end of 1974, proved U.S. reserves were estimated to be 237.1 trillion cubic feet of which 205.2 trillion were located in the lower 48 states and the rest in Alaska. Between 1967 and 1974, annual reserve additions averaged 11.3 trillion cubic feet for the lower 48, but average annual production was 21.1 trillion cubic feet. Thus, the decline in proved reserves for the lower 48 states averaged about 10 trillion cubic feet annually during the period.

Natural gas shortages have developed in the systems of major interstate pipeline companies, and wintertime curtailments (primarily to industrial customers) have increased each year since the winter of 1970–1971. Even greater curtailments occurred in the winter of 1976–1977.

The growing shortage of natural gas has been attributed to federal control of prices at the wellhead—prices that the FPC is required to hold down by law. These relatively low prices fail to provide adequate incentives for exploration, development, and production of new natural gas. At the same time, the low prices encourage greater consumer demand and inefficient use. As of September 1975, the national area ceiling rate established by the FPC for new gas was 51 cents per 1,000 cubic feet at the wellhead. The FPC also has offered other price incentives to encourage the sale of natural gas in the interstate market. (With applicable adjustments, the wellhead price for new gas averages about 58 cents.) If the wellhead price were permitted to rise to a competitive level with other fuels, there is every reason to believe that more gas could be found and developed from domestic gas resources. In addition, many consumers would curtail or stop using natural gas for less essential purposes, and some large industrial or electric utility plants would be more inclined to convert from natural gas to other more plentiful fuels, such as coal.

EXPANSION OF THE NATURAL GAS INDUSTRY

During the 1930's, the natural gas industry began to expand at an accelerating rate. This expansion took place mainly because natural gas was plentiful and less costly than the manufactured gas it replaced. Moreover, new technology made it possible to transport gas over distances exceeding 1,000 miles.

In 1937, natural gas accounted for 10.6 per cent of the total energy supply in the United States and by 1946, 15.7 per cent.

The steady growth of the natural gas industry was constrained during World War II to conserve scarce supplies of steel, compressors, valves, and manpower. As a result, a large pent-up demand developed, which could not be served until the war ended. The demand for natural gas was so great that it was necessary for state regulatory commissions to establish priorities for new service connections, and the backlog of requests was not eliminated until 1950. Consumers quickly caught on to the disparity between the prices of natural gas and other fuels. There was a virtual "run on the bank" to secure natural gas.

Natural gas supply was abundant and adequate to assure the successful financing of new interstate pipelines. By 1973, the national network of the gas utilities industry consisted of nearly 1 million miles of gas pipelines and mains. Of this total, distribution mains serving local customers accounted for

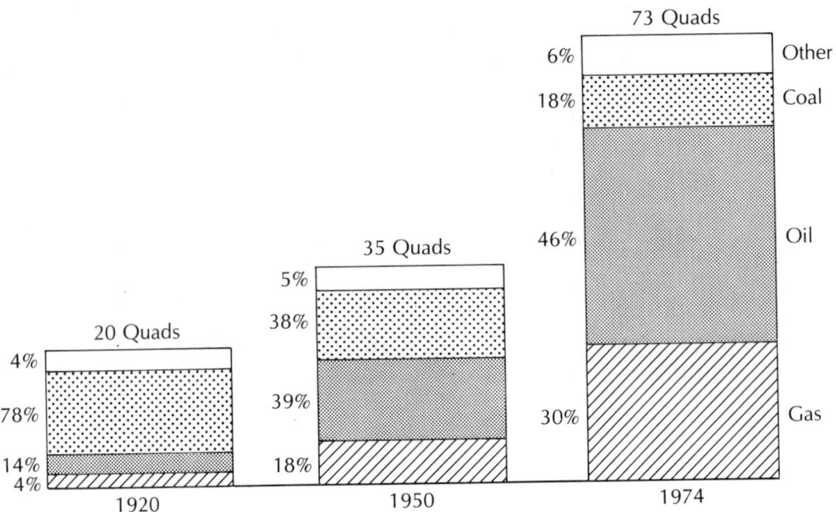

Figure 10-1. Growth in U.S. natural gas consumption, 1920–1974.

634,000 miles, long-distance transmission pipelines 265,000 miles; and field and gathering lines 68,000 miles.

In 1974, the number of consumers served by the gas industry was about 43.3 million, and sales by gas utility industry amounted to 16.0 trillion cubic feet. That year natural gas accounted for 30 per cent of domestically produced U.S. energy. Figure 10-1 indicates the growth of natural gas consumption from 1920 to 1974.

Natural gas is vital to the American economy. It supplies about one-half of the energy needs of our manufacturing industries; and the gas utility industry serves some 40 million residential customers.

THE APPROACHING GAS CRISIS

The increasing shortage of natural gas to meet the needs in some areas of the United States is reaching crisis proportions. The shortage is most severe in nonproducing states that receive gas from interstate pipelines. The regulation of the wellhead price of gas sold by producers to interstate pipelines has been a major cause of the decline in the availability of new gas supplies to the interstate market. If a producer has the opportunity, he naturally will sell his gas to a customer in his own state, because the price he receives on intrastate sales is not subject to FPC regulation. In recent years, intrastate sales of new gas have been made at prices three to four times the fixed interstate base price, which is still lower than the relative cost of an alternate fuel.

Following the 1954 Phillips decision, the FPC estimated that the court ruling would result in the regulation of over 5,000 independent producers as compared with about 100 interstate pipeline companies. In fiscal year 1955, the FPC received 10,978 filings from independent producers. The Commission then started regulating producers on a case-by-case basis.

It also applied a cost-of-service formula to each individual producer and later tried to establish rates on an area-wide basis and other regulatory procedures.

GAS DEREGULATION SUPPORTED BY FPC

The FPC supports the concept of limited natural gas deregulation as set forth in the Administration's recommendations to Congress. The 1974 FPC Annual Report stated that:

—The price of natural gas at the wellhead has lagged behind the price changes in other fuels.

—Workable competition exists in the natural gas production industry.

—Controlled deregulation of the producer segment of the gas industry is the most important measure the Congress can take to alleviate present natural gas shortages.

CONSERVATION AND CONVERSION

The FPC has jurisdiction over the operations and curtailment practices of interstate pipeline companies. The Federal Energy Administration (FEA) has been concerned with the problems arising from the existing and expected natural gas shortages because of its authority to allocate crude oil and petroleum products and its responsibility for ensuring efficient utilization of our available natural energy resources.

The FEA has worked closely with the FPC to achieve a coordinated program aimed at minimizing shutdown of industrial plants and corresponding unemployment and economic dislocation due to natural gas curtailment. The FPC's curtailment policy gives priority to residential customers and other essential users over industrial customers. Industrial customers usually have the financial means to convert from gas to alternate fuels, but similar conversion would impose serious economic hardship on residential customers. Because of this policy, the shortage of natural gas most severely affects the industrial sector and, in some regions of the country, threatens to disrupt production and employment.

Thus, in 1975, the FEA sent out a comprehensive questionnaire to all major fuel-burning installations, including both electric utility and industrial users of natural gas. The purpose of this questionnaire was to determine the expected amount of interruption of gas supplies and the type and quantity of alternative fuel that would be needed by natural gas consumers to maintain production schedules and employment.

The FEA also is engaged in a continuing effort to enlist the support of the American people in conserving energy and eliminating wasteful use of electricity, natural gas, oil, and other fuels. Several Presidents have stressed repeatedly to Congress and the American public the need to reduce our dependence on imports of oil. One of the quickest and easiest ways to accomplish this task is through simple practices of energy conservation—turning thermostats down in the winter and up in the summer; maximum use of insulation to prevent heat loss; and substitution of more efficient gas engines, appliances, and gas-fired equipment for less efficient ones.

The FEA, other government agencies, and industry have prepared many publications that give detailed suggestions on how homeowners, stores, and factories can reduce their use of energy without sacrificing comfort or production efficiency.

The FEA has issued directives requiring the conversion of several dozen large utility power plants from natural gas and oil to coal. The FEA also has requested authority for mandatory conversions of utility and industrial power plants from natural gas to oil. This conversion program is intended to save natural gas reserves for higher priority use and to reduce our imports of crude oil and petroleum products.

In May 1975, at the direction of President Ford, the Federal Energy Administration was given the responsibility of coordinating a special interagency Natural Gas Task Force. This task force was established to assess the magnitude and potential economic impact of the natural gas shortage and to recommend policy options to ease the impact.

In September 1975, President Ford announced legislative and administrative initatives designed to minimize the adverse effects of natural gas shortages during the following winter. Among the administrative actions was the establishment of a Natural Gas Task Force within FEA to provide a continuing liaison with government officials and the public and to coordinate legislative and contingency planning activities.

Even with effective conservation and conversion measures, the only long-term solution to the natural gas crisis is to increase the supply of natural gas. The most effective way to do this is for Congress to deregulate the price of new natural gas at the wellhead. And, even with deregulation of new gas, the shortage will not be alleviated in the near future. It will take three to seven years before any substantial amount of new gas supplies is available to the interstate market—following decontrol.

OTHER GAS SOURCES

With the increasing shortage of natural gas, many industrial users have turned to propane and other petroleum products as substitutes to be used during periods of natural gas curtailment. However, these light petroleum products are likely to be in short supply during the winter when natural gas curtailments become more severe and more widespread. Shifting from natural gas to alternate fuels will provide only limited relief.

Another alternative is to convert from natural gas to fuel oil, but this option has many disadvantages.

Such conversions would require new investment by the consumer for oil storage and utilization equipment. The price of fuel oil to the residential, commercial, and industrial user is much higher today than the price of natural gas. Existing natural gas users would be far better off economically to pay the higher price of deregulated new supplies of natural gas than to be compelled to shift over to fuel oil. Futhermore, a shift from natural gas produced from domestic fields to fuel oil that must be imported would increase our dependency on foreign supplies and prevent the attainment of our goal of greater self-sufficiency.

One supplemental source of gas being considered by several large pipelines and gas distribution companies is liquefied natural gas (LNG). Some LNG is being sent to the east coast from Algeria. Other projects contemplate transportation of LNG from Alaska, Indonesia, and other areas. But the present cost of LNG landed at a United States port is about 2 to 2½ times the wholesale price of domestic interstate gas.

Another supplementary source of gas is synthetic natural gas (SNG). Several SNG plants designed to use liquid hydrocarbons have already been constructed. Because of the high cost of the feedstock used by these plants, the synthetic gas produced is expected to cost between $3 and $4 per million BTU, depending upon the plant size and contract price. This is much higher than the present cost of domestic natural gas delivered to major consuming areas, but equal to the cost of an increment of heating oil from foreign crude oil. Some SNG plants are used seasonally to handle winter demands. Others are operated year-round to supply baseload requirements. Most of these plants are located on the east coast where utilities have access to imported petroleum feedstocks.

COAL GASIFICATION

Increased use of the nation's vast coal supplies will be needed to meet future energy demand. Gas companies, in cooperation with federal and state governments, are trying to develop commercial-scale plants to convert coal to synthetic gas. This conversion will use both existing processes and more advanced techniques that are now being developed.

United States gas pipeline and distribution companies have announced plans for the construction of several commercial and demonstration coal gasification plants. All the plants are designed to convert coal into high-BTU gas. These coal gasification complexes will use coal reserves located in New Mexico, North Dakota, Colorado, Montana, Wyoming, Illinois, southwestern Pennsylvania, and western Kentucky.

One proposed coal gasification plant to be built in northwest New Mexico, would deliver supplemental gas to California and the

Midwest. This plant will be the first large commercial plant in the United States capable of producing gas comparable to conventional natural gas.

Capital requirements for construction of coal gasification plants run into the hundreds of millions of dollars. For example, the capital cost of one plant scheduled to be built in the late 1970's in New Mexico, with an average daily capacity of 260 million cubic feet, is estimated at $1 billion.

Because of the large capital investment required and the inherent risks of technological change and environmental constraints, it will be exceedingly difficult for the gas industry to finance these projects by the conventional methods of issuing new stocks and bonds. The gas industry has presented testimony to Congress urging consideration of measures to supplement private investment. Recommended measures include increased investment tax credits; direct loans or grant assistance; and loan guarantees comparable to those provided for construction of ships in U.S. yards under the Merchant Marine Act of 1936.

An important factor needed to facilitate financing of coal gasification projects is stability of fuel prices in the marketplace.

GAS FROM THE SEA

The natural gas industry recently has made a considerable financial investment in support of research directed toward the use of marine biomass as a source of methane. The objective of this project is to develop a system for large-scale, commercial production and harvesting of seaweed in the open ocean, and conversion of the seaweed to methane and valuable by-products, such as food and fertilizer.

ACCOMPLISHING OUR ENERGY GOAL

The United States can and must begin now to regain its energy independence. Neither conservation of energy nor development of new energy supplies alone can minimize our dependence on imported petroleum. But a combination of sound energy conservation practices and a national energy policy designed to encourage the rapid development of our extensive domestic energy resources can reduce our energy vulnerability to near zero within 10 years.

To meet our long-term energy requirements, the nation will need new technology to create efficient and economical systems to use solar, tidal, and wind power, as well as the massive energy potential of nuclear power. For the short term, though, we must depend largely on proven conventional energy sources—natural gas, oil, and coal.

To attain our goal of energy independence, we must have a comprehensive national energy policy that encourages exploration for new oil and natural gas supplies and provides for the production and utilization of existing energy sources in ways consistent with our aim of preserving and improving the environment. At the same time, that policy must provide for the development of the non-traditional energy sources that will meet our energy requirements in the longer term, after our reserves of fossil fuels are depleted.

To forestall that day, however, we must learn to use all of our energy resources more efficiently, particularly natural gas—our cleanest and most efficient fuel.

SUGGESTED READINGS

Anderson, Richard J., 1973, Natural Gas, *Energy Perspectives,* No. 2, September, 4p.

Koelling, Gordon W., and Ronald F. Balazik, 1975, Natural Gas, in *Mineral Facts and Problems,* 1975 Edition of Bureau of Mines, pp. 715–732.

Coal—Meeting the Energy Challenge 11

CARL E. BAGGE 1977

Aside from the discomfort and disruption it created, the Arab oil embargo of 1973 drove home a crucial lesson once and for all. It made the American public, business, and government realize the extent to which the nation is dependent on oil and natural gas to maintain its refined standard of living. Even more important, the embargo underscored the fact that the age of almost limitless, inexpensive energy is at an end.

Oil and natural gas currently provide about three-quarters of the total energy produced in the United States each year, but account for just 7 per cent of the nation's energy reserves. These circumstances, combined with a 4 per cent annual increase in the country's energy demand, have resulted in the United States being dependent on imported crude and refined petroleum for nearly half of its total oil supply.

Since it accounts for 80 per cent of our fossil fuel energy reserve, coal is the one resource certain to be available to meet the nation's near-term energy needs. President Carter emphasized this fact when he called for a two-thirds increase in annual coal production to 1.1 billion tons by 1985. The significance of coal, therefore, makes its extraction, production, and transportation a matter of national importance.

UNITED STATES COAL—AN OVERVIEW

As the world's second largest coal producer, the United States possesses an extensive and varied coal industry. Identified U.S. coal reserves are approximately 1.5 trillion net tons of coal, including beds down to 3,000 feet below the surface. Additionally, it is estimated there are 1.3 trillion short tons of coal in unmapped and unexplored areas throughout the United States.

About 34 of the 50 states of the United States have significant reserves of coal, with mining operations underway in about 25 of these states. In 1976, the country produced 665 million tons of coal.

Coal mines in the United States average less than 300 feet in depth and have relatively level and thick seams, with most of the coal

Original article by Carl E. Bagge. Mr. Bagge is president and chief executive officer of the National Coal Association, Washington, D.C. 20036. He is also a member of NCA's Executive Committee and Board of Directors and the Executive Committee and Board of Directors of Bituminous Coal Research, Inc., NCA's research affiliate in Monroeville, Pa. Before joining NCA in 1971, Mr. Bagge was a member of the Federal Power Commission and served as vice chairman in 1966 and in 1969.

mined from beds that are 2½ to 8 feet thick. Some beds in areas west of the Mississippi River, however, are as thick as 100 feet.

The chief U.S. coal fields are spread over several wide areas, classified as the Eastern Province (from Alabama north to Pennsylvania and Ohio); Interior Province, eastern region (including Illinois, Indiana, and western Kentucky); Interior Province, midwestern region (Iowa, Missouri, Kansas, and Oklahoma); Interior Province, southwest region (Texas); Northern Great Plains Province (North and South Dakota, northern Wyoming, and Montana); Rocky Mountain Province (southern Wyoming, Colorado, Utah, New Mexico, and Arizona); and the Pacific Coast Province (Washington).

About 80 per cent of the coal mined in the United States comes from fields east of the Mississippi, but eastern reserves make up only 45 per cent of the nation's total. Western coal, on the average, has a much lower sulfur content—some of it 0.6 to 0.7 per cent—than eastern coal, much of which is in the 2 to 4 per cent sulfur range. Eastern coal, however, usually has a higher BTU content than western coal. But western coal is currently in increasing demand because it allows utilities and industrial users to more easily meet U.S. government air quality standards, which limit sulfur emissions.

UNDERGROUND MINING

In U.S. underground mines, also called deep mines, highly specialized machines have replaced the traditional pick and shovel of years gone by. Conventional and continuous underground mining follow a "room-and-pillar" plan, resulting in intersecting tunnels 14 to 20 feet wide. Currently, to develop a new deep mine in the two million-tons-per-year category with a 20- to 30-year life-span can require five to seven years and an investment of $60 million or more. Mine expansion is similarly time-consuming and costly.

A major factor in this expenditure of time and money is shaft and entry development. A large number of entries have to be driven and shafts sunk to meet stringent U.S. government ventilation requirements as well as provide access for men and materials. Thus, new equipment is now being developed that will permit the high-speed boring of tunnels and main entries. These machines permit tunneling rates in excess of 100 feet per day, compared with an advance of 250 to 300 feet per month by present excavation methods.

About 60 per cent of all U.S. coal mined underground is produced by continuous mining machines, which can cut coal from the face at a rate of 4 to 15 tons per minute. Although these machines are a big improvement over the pick and shovel, research is being conducted to develop even more sophisticated systems. An example is an automated extraction system that will completely control the mining cycle, including machine movement and coal transfer onto continuous-haulage equipment to move the mined coal from the face to the surface.

The longwall technology developed in Germany is now being used in an increasing number of U.S. mines where geology and conditions permit, although it currently accounts for less than 5 per cent of the total amount of U.S. coal mined underground. The first modern longwall system employing powered roof supports was installed in the United States in 1960. By 1975, a total of only 50 longwalls were operating in this country. One reason for this sluggish growth is the thick, easily accessible, and generally horizontal U.S. coal seams, which are mined efficiently by room-and-pillar methods. However, the high production and recovery potential of longwall has made the mining industry realize that such equipment can be adapted to the broad spectrum of American coal beds.

Another technique receiving considerable attention from U.S. coal companies is the shortwall system, in which a continuous miner cuts and loads from the open end of a rectangular panel of coal while self-advancing roof supports provide protective cover. The characteristics of such shortwall systems include panel lengths of 2,000 to

4,000 feet and face widths of 100 to 200 feet; positive or one-way ventilation; face operations under steel canopies; and an over-all recovery of about 85 per cent. Factors restricting the use of this system include friable roof conditions and, depending on the haulage method, seam height.

Other areas in which extensive research relating to underground mining is underway include using jets of water to cut coal; recovering and utilizing methane prior to mining; and using continuous haulage systems.

SURFACE MINING

About one-half of all coal produced in the United States is obtained by surface mining from seams lying fairly close to the earth's surface. In this method, earth and rock above the coal seam—the overburden—are removed and placed to one side. The exposed coal is then broken up, loaded into trucks, and hauled away. The overburden is then regraded to the desired shape, planted with vegetation or young trees, and restored to productive use as pastures, farmland, or recreation areas.

The machines used in surface mining range in size from ordinary bulldozers and front-end loaders, common to construction projects, to gigantic power shovels and draglines, which are the largest land machines in the world. Since the specialized machinery used for this process is so large and expensive, the huge power shovels and draglines are chiefly used in the U.S. Midwest and West, where coal seams at strippable depths extend for miles. In these mines, the large machines may work in the same general vicinity for years and even decades.

In the eastern United States, surface mining is not as extensive; the coal is generally worked with smaller, more mobile equipment, such as bulldozers, front-end loaders, and highway-sized trucks.

Some of the new surface mining equipment being developed and tested in the United States include a forward-rotating bucket conveyor to dig and load coal, foam-filled tires for excavation machinery, and new mining shovels to provide digging forces not available in current shovels. In addition, techniques more familiar to the European mining industry, such as a continuous materials-handling system and large hydraulic excavators with a front shovel arrangement, are now being tested in the United States.

Surface mining has proved fast and efficient, with over 90 per cent of the coal being recovered. However, the correction of the surface disturbance has long been a concern of both the government and the coal industry. American coal companies have developed many ways of reclaiming strip-mined areas, including replacement and grading of overburden, and revegetating the land into useful pastures, farmland, or recreation areas. Many states have had laws for some time to regulate the reclamation process closely and to minimize its impact on the environment. Congress recently passed a federal bill to set minimum standards for reclamation of surface-mined areas.

In addition, research has concentrated on developing tools that will move large volumes of spoil and reduce reclamation costs without requiring a large capital investment. Among new types of reclamation tools being examined are a 40-foot angle blade used in conjunction with two bulldozers; a 24-foot vee-type plow mounted on a dozer designed to make the initial cuts of spoil bank ridges; a 30-foot grading bar mounted on a dozer and used for smoothing rough-graded land prior to revegetation; and a 60-foot lateral earth-moving blade for leveling spoil banks. Also, the new mining methods being evaluated, such as haul back and mountaintop removal, offer reduced reclamation costs and more versatile end land uses.

PREPARATION

As it leaves the mine, coal may contain bits of rock and other impurities, which were imbedded in the seam or picked up in the mining process. About one-half of the coal produced in the United States goes through a crushing, sizing, washing, drying, and treatment process at the preparation plant, which is usually at the mine mouth. However, many coal customers find it more economical to use run-of-mine coal, particularly if they have boilers designed to burn raw coal and are permitted to do so.

There has been a resurgence of interest in improved preparation technology in the United States in recent years, with the goal of producing even cleaner coal at maximum yields. With the national concern over clean air, there is a growing emphasis on finding ways to remove substantial quantities of sulfur from coal during the preparation steps. Also, techniques are under study to develop continuous haulage of coal from the mine face to the preparation plant.

HEALTH AND SAFETY

Health and safety conditions are of paramount concern to the U.S. coal industry. State and federal laws and regulations, such as the Coal Mine Health and Safety Act, as well as company rules, impose elaborate safety rules and regulations on every phase of mining. Company supervisors make health and safety inspections daily. In addition, federal and state agencies conduct extensive inspections. Federal officers made more than 63,800 inspections at some 5,500 coal mines in 1976.

One area in which the industry has made remarkable progress is the reduction of coal dust levels in mines to safe concentrations. The air in each underground working areas is tested regularly for dust level and each miner must wear a personal air sampler at regular intervals. The Mining Enforcement and Safety Administration has reported that 63.5 per cent of nearly 5,000 working sections in underground mines had dust levels in 1976 of no more than 2 milligrams per cubic meter of air.

Accidents are always a concern to the U.S. mining industry. A recent Bureau of Mines study estimated that every lost-time injury mishap in an underground coal mine in America, regardless of magnitude, costs the government, the miner's family, and the coal company an average of more than $3,700, with the coal company bearing 41 per cent and the injured miner bearing 47 per cent of the total financial loss caused by the accident.

United States coal mines today are safer places to work than they ever have been. The number of fatal accidents have fallen each year since 1970, and last year they occurred at the rate of 0.34 per million man-hours worked, the lowest rate ever recorded. Despite this progress, coal operators, miners, and government officials continue to seek means to reduce hazards from roof falls, equipment operation, and the safe handling of supplies and materials and to improve the working environment of the nation's coal mines.

THE FUTURE OF COAL IN THE UNITED STATES

With the decline of oil and natural gas reserves, the environmental and safety problems of nuclear power, and the undeveloped technology of solar energy, it has become increasingly clear that more use of coal is the secure, logical course to take to help meet U.S. energy needs for the immediate future.

In the last six years, coal-generated electricity in the United States has increased from 44.4 per cent of the total production to 46.5 per cent. The amount of coal used to produce power during the same period increased from 328 million to 448 million tons. A recent study on national energy predicted that coal's share of the total U.S. energy production will grow from the present 19 to 25 per cent by 1990, and total consumption will be nearly 1.5 billion tons.

In his recent proposals for a rational energy policy, President Carter suggested massive U.S. efforts at not only increasing the production but the use of coal on a much wider scale to generate electricity. He also called for an increase in federal funding for coal research, particularly gasification.

Indicators such as these underscore the importance of finding processes and techniques for not only making it possible to burn coal more cleanly, but to make feasible the conversion of coal into more usable forms of energy, such as synthetic gas and oil. Gasification, liquefaction, and techniques permitting the more direct burning of high-sulfur coal are all being studied in great detail at present and all hold some promise for the future.

The U.S. coal industry does have its problems, with the need for more miners, better production methods, increased financing, and improved pollution control processes among the most prominent. But the industry is seeking equitable solutions to these problems. President Carter has made a strong commitment to greatly increased coal use as part of his national energy program. Coal's one unmatchable asset is that it is the country's only plentiful reservoir of raw energy—over 80 per cent of America's fossil fuel energy reserve—at a time when the United States needs more energy than ever before. By solving its problems and utilizing its assets, the coal industry can assume the vital role it seems destined to play in the U.S. energy picture before the turn of the century.

SUGGESTED READINGS

———. 1976, Clean Coal: What Does It Cost at the Busbar?, *Electric Power Research Institute Journal,* November, pp. 6–13.

Naill, Roger F., Meadows, Dennis L., and Stanley-Miller, John, 1975, The Transition to Coal, *Technology Review 78,* No. 1, October-November, pp. 18–29.

Nephew, Edmund A., 1973, The Challenges and Promise of Coal, *Technology Review 76,* No. 2, December, pp. 21–29.

———, 1977 Outlook for Coal: Bright, but with Problems, *Chemical and Engineering News 55,* pp. 24–31.

Price, Robert V., 1976, The Role of Coal in Future U.S. Energy Development, *Bull. of the Assoc. of Engineering Geol. XIII,* pp. 105–136.

Schmidt, Richard A., and George R. Hill, 1976, Coal: Energy Keystone, *Annual Review of Energy, 1,* pp. 37–63.

Young, Gordon, 1975, Will Coal be Tomorrow's "Black Gold"?, *National Geographic 148,* No. 2, August, p. 234–259.

Coal Conversion Technology 12

HARRY PERRY 1974

Even before the Arab oil embargo of fall, 1973, it was obvious that indigenous oil and gas resources could not satisfy the burgeoning United States demand for fuel much longer. Petroleum had become a dominant force in the economy, but it was far too vulnerable.

Increases in the absolute amounts of petroleum consumed per year were even more indicative of the supply problems that were certain to occur at some future time. In 1956, the peak year of exploration, the United States consumed 2.93 billion barrels of oil and 10.1 trillion cubic feet of gas. By 1973, this had increased to 6.3 billion barrels of oil and 22.8 trillion cubic feet of gas.

At the same time, the contribution of oil and gas to the total energy supply increased from 67 to 75 per cent. Nearly all of this growth was at the expense of coal. Because it is more difficult to handle than the other fuels, leaves a residue that must be disposed of, and creates dust and dirt during its use, coal was displaced in the residential and commercial markets first by oil and then by gas.

Traditional coal markets were lost one by one. Following World War II, the coal industry lost a large market when the railroads converted their inefficient, coal-burning steam locomotives to more efficient diesel engines. The remaining coal markets were for the production of coke as a fuel, for the rapidly growing electric utility market, and for large industrial users such as cement mills. By 1973, the electric utility industry consumed 69 per cent of all the coal used in the United States.

Prices of bituminous coal remained relatively static between 1948 and 1969, ranging only from $5.08 per ton to $4.39 per ton, the lower price generally prevailing at the end of the period. In the face of inflation during this period, real prices for coal declined signifi-

Harry Perry has been a consultant working part time for the National Economic Research Associates, Inc. and for Resources for the Future, 1755 Massachusetts Ave., N.W., Washington, D.C., since 1973. He is former director of coal research for the U.S. Bureau of Mines (1940–1967), research advisor to the assistant secretary of the interior for mineral resources (1967–1970) and senior specialist for energy in the environmental policy division of the Congressional Research Service of the Library of Congress (1970–1973). His experience has been in mining, combustion, carbonization and gasification of coal, the abatement of air pollution, and the large-scale production of helium.

From *Chemical Engineering,* Vol. 81, No. 15, pp. 88–102, July 22, 1974. Reprinted by permission of the author and *Chemical Engineering.*

cantly. Starting in 1973, there were a number of adverse economic developments: inflation picked up; the field price allowed for natural gas escalated sharply; steep price rises in imported oil were imposed by the Organization of Petroleum Exporting Countries (OPEC) nations; and productivity declined in the underground coal mines. The result: eastern United States bituminous coal prices also increased sharply, from an average mine price of \$4.99 per ton in 1969 to \$7.66 per ton in 1972, and an estimated \$8.50 per ton in 1973. During the energy shortage in the spring of 1974, spot prices were as high as \$25 to \$35 per ton. Prices in the 1975 to 1978 period have stabilized at around \$20 per ton.

FOUR CONVERSION TECHNIQUES

Such price volatility indicates a great turnabout for coal. But this time, interest is centering on converting the mineral into liquid and gas products to substitute for oil and gas.

Four distinct conversion routes are possible. These include: pyrolysis, solvation, hydrogenation, and production of synthesis gas. The amount and type of products made by each of these methods depend upon the coal properties and process conditions.

In pyrolysis, the coal is heated in some manner to break it down into solids, liquids, and gases. Higher heating rates yield greater amounts of liquids and gases.

In solvation, the coal is dissolved and, with the addition of small amounts of hydrogen, can be filtered and converted into an essentially ash- and sulfur-free solid or liquid, depending upon the degree of hydrogenation.

In hydrogenation reactions, coal and hydrogen are reacted together directly. If this is done in the presence of a catalyst at 850°F and at elevated pressures, a liquid product can be made. If a catalyst is not present, the coal can react directly with hydrogen at even higher temperatures (1,500–1,800°F) and pressures to form methane.

In the production of synthesis gas (carbon monoxide and hydrogen), coal is usually reacted with an oxidizing agent and steam. However, the heat for the steam-carbon reaction can be supplied in ways other than by using an oxidizing agent (see discussion on coal gasification). The synthesis gas produced can then be used to make a high-BTU gas by reacting the purified synthesis gas over a nickel catalyst. The purified gas can also be used as the raw material for production of alcohols, ammonia, synthetic gasoline, and a variety of other petrochemicals. The product obtained depends on the raw materials, processing conditions, and the catalyst used.

GASIFICATION—BACKGROUND

Gas was first made from coal by heating the coal in the absence of air. The gas was distributed in many cities for lighting streets, homes, and buildings. Late in the nineteenth century, the major market for gas shifted to cooking as the lighting market was replaced by electricity.

As the gas market grew, it became necessary to find ways to supplement the low yield from coal distillation. Over 70 per cent of the coal remains as a solid when it is heated, and this portion had to be sold if the price were to be competitive. When slot-type ovens for making coke for the steel industry became widely used, coke-oven gas—the composition of which is similar to that of distillation gases—was used as a supplement.

Other methods that used all of the coal rather than just the distillation products were devised to further supplement coal-gas supplies. The most widely used process made a gas known as "water gas" or "blue gas." The process was cyclic. First, a bed of anthracite or coke was heated by burning a part of the carbon in the bed with air. The evolving hot gases heated the rest of the carbon. The basic reaction was

$$C + O_2 + 4N_2 \rightarrow CO_2 + 4N_2$$

As the carbon in the upper part of the bed became heated, the reverse reaction started to occur:

$$CO_2+C+4N_2 \rightarrow 2CO+4N_2$$

When the CO value in the existing gas became too high to be acceptable, the air blast was stopped and the hot bed of carbon reacted with steam according to the reaction

$$C+H_2O \rightarrow CO+H_2$$

The heat for this endothermic reaction was supplied by the hot carbon. When the carbon bed cooled to the point at which rate of steam and carbon reaction were too low, the steam flow was stopped and the "blow" cycle repeated, using air.

Gas produced during the steam period ("run gas") had a heating value of 300 BTU per cubic foot and had to be enriched to make it compatible with the other gases being distributed by the gas utilities. The enrichment was also carried out in a cyclic process. Gases from the last part of the "blow" cycle, which contained CO, were burned to heat a vessel filled with refractory bricks. When the refractory was sufficiently hot, the gas was shut off and an oil was introduced onto the hot bricks, where it was "cracked" into lower-molecular-weight hydrocarbons, which were then mixed with the "run" gas to adjust the heating value to the desired level.

The "water gas" process had many limitations. Cyclic processes are always expensive and are troublesome to maintain and operate. The process required coke or anthracite, both noncoking sources of carbon. Over-all efficiency of the process was low, the oil used for enrichment greatly increased cost, and the operation was inevitably dirty.

To avoid some of these problems, the "producer gas" process was used at industrial plants needing a clean source of fuel but for which the cost of transport and distribution of the gas was not important (the gas was consumed at the point of manufacture). In this process, the bed of carbon was reacted continuously with a mixture of air and steam. The simultaneous reactions were

$$C+O_2+4N_2 \rightarrow CO_2+4N_2$$

$$C+CO_2 \rightarrow 2CO$$

$$C+H_2O \rightarrow CO+H_2$$

The product was a mixture of CO, H_2, CO_2, N_2, and whatever distillation gases remained in the final gas product. Heating value was 135 to 150 BTU per cubic feet. Despite its low heating value, producer gas was much less costly per unit of heat than was water gas.

In the United States, manufactured gas played a major role in supply to markets far from natural-gas fields but near coal fields. The residential gas market in the eastern United States was supplied mainly with manufactured gas as late as 1932. With the introduction of long-distance natural-gas pipelines during World War II, however, natural gas rapidly became more widely distributed, and by the end of the war it was supplying nearly 90 per cent of the heating value of gas being sold. The last year for which data were reported for manufactured gas was 1968, and by then the amount was too inconsequential to matter.

Although interest in new coal-gasification technology disappeared in the United States as a result of the shift to natural gas, interest continued high in petroleum-short Europe, where coal remained the chief source of energy supplies. Mixtures of carbon monoxide and hydrogen (synthesis gas) also became increasingly important as the basic raw material for ammonia and a whole range of organic chemicals needed to supply the exploding markets for plastics.

In the past several years, a relatively large number of United States firms have announced plans to construct commercial coal-gasification plants, using proven foreign technology, but none are yet under construction.

MEDIUM- AND HIGH-BTU GAS

Most of the interest in coal gasification has centered on medium- or high-BTU gas that could be piped economically over long distances. High-BTU gases might even substitute for natural gas.

Table 12–1. Coal Gasification Processes for Production of Medium- and High-BTU Gas.

Process	Reactor Bed Type	Gasifying Medium	Nature of Residue	Pressure (atmospheres)	Temperature (°F)	Capacity (tons per day)
Commercial						
Lurgi gasifier	Fixed	Oxygen-steam (air being tested)	Dry ash	30–35	500–800 (top), <2,000 (bottom)	1,000
Koppers-Totzek	Entrained	Oxygen or limited oxygen-steam (air being tested)	Dry ash	1	1,750–2,350	850
Winkler	Fluidized	Oxygen-steam and air-steam	Dry ash	1	1,500–1,800	100
Small Demonstration						
Hygas[a] (Institute of Gas Technology)	Fluid	Hydrogen in hydro-gasifier	Dry char	75–100	1,200–1,500 first stage 1,700–1,800 second stage	80
Carbon dioxide acceptor	Fluid	Air in regenerator, steam in the gasifier	Dry ash	10–20	1,575	30
Pilot Plants						
Synthane	Fluid	Oxygen-steam	Dry char	40–70	1,100–1,450 first stage 1,750–1,850 second stage	75
Bigas	Entrained	Oxygen-steam	Slag	70	2,700 first stage 1,700 second stage	120
Cogas	Fluid	Steam in gasifier	Dry ash	1–3	1,600–1,700	50
Carbide-Battelle	Fluid	Steam in gasifier	Dry ash	6	1,600–1,800	25
Institute of Gas Technology-electrothermal	Fluid	Steam in gasifier	Dry char	75–100	1,900	25
Institute of Gas Technology-steam-oxygen	Fluid	Steam-oxygen	Dry ash	100	1,500	25
Institute of Gas Technologyo-steam-iron	Fluid	Steam in oxidizer	Dry ash	100	1,500	25
Hydrane	Fluid	Hydrogen in hydro-gasifier	Dry char	70	1,600–1,700	0.25

[a]The Hygas process is a hydrogasification route. Three alternative methods to produce the hydrogen required have been proposed. These are: electrothermal, steam-oxygen and steam-iron processes; they are described under "Pilot Plants."

The state of these processes and some of their major characteristics are shown in Table 12-1. Most use oxygen instead of air, and all except one (the electrothermal gasifier) use some form of heat carrier to supply heat for the endothermic steam-carbon reaction.

Three types of gas-solid contact have been used: fixed, fluid, and entrained beds. Fixed-bed processes require a sized coal and have been operated smoothly only on noncoking or weakly coking coals. These techniques tend to preserve the methane and other distillation products of the fresh coal, and thus have a decided advantage over fluid and entrained processes for making high-BTU gas—unless carried out in two stages, in which case the distillation products are consumed by the gasifying media. On the other hand, entrained processes can use all sizes and any kind of coal, and will produce fewer pollutants. The fluid-bed processes have operating characteristics that are intermediate to the fixed and entrained beds. In fixed-bed processes, the gases leave at low temperatures in the range of 500 to 800°F; in fluid processes, they leave at intermediate temperatures (1,500 to 1,800°F); while in entrained routes (unless staged), the gases exit at over 2,000°F.

HIGH-BTU GAS

Lurgi Process

This is a fixed-bed process. As shown in Figure 12-1, sized noncoking coal is fed by lock hoppers into a pressure gasifier having a diameter of up to 12 feet. Steam and oxygen are introduced below the grate at the bottom of the gasifier in amounts that will cool the grate and prevent clinkering of the ash. The grate is rotated and the ash is collected in a lock hopper, from which it is removed periodically. The coal is spread evenly over the entire bed by a distributor located near the top of the gasifier. Raw gases leave the top at about 850°F and are scrubbed and cooled before further treatment.

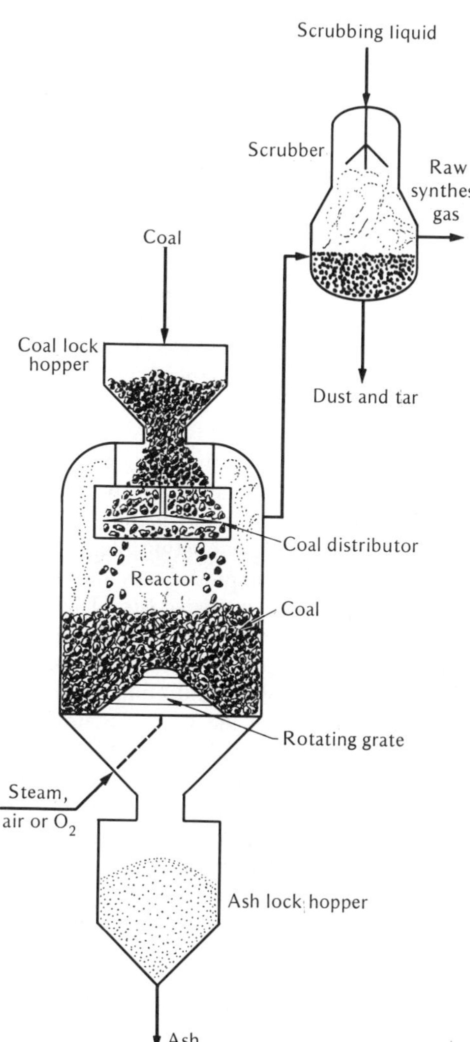

Figure 12-1. The Lurgi gasifier uses a rotating grate underneath the coal bed for feeding oxygen and steam.

One of the advantages of this process is that the countercurrent flow of reactants in a fixed-bed reactor allows the efficient use of the heat released during the oxidation of the coal near the base of the gasifier. The hot gases transfer a large part of this heat to the incoming coal as they pass through the coal in the upper levels of the gasifier. This results in a smaller oxygen consumption per unit of gas produced, and—since the gases distilled from the coal leave the gasifier with the raw product gas—in a higher-BTU-content raw gas. This makes it a more desirable feedstock for further upgrading to high-BTU gas, but less desirable if synthesis is wanted.

Another advantage of the Lurgi method is that it operates under pressure (unlike the other two commercially available processes). This leads to significant over-all process economies, because in most cases the gas will be processed further at elevated pressure. Over-all thermal efficiences of the Lurgi method are said to be in the order of about 70 per cent.

The disadvantage of the Lurgi route is that it requires a sized coal. Fines produced in mining must either find suitable outlets in other parts of the gasification plant or they must be briquetted to produce a suitable sized feed, which adds to coal costs. The Lurgi gasifier, as it is presently designed and used, can only handle noncoking (or very weakly coking) coals. This would eliminate its use with virtually all of the United States coals east of the Mississippi River. Finally, the fixed-bed gasifiers are basically low-throughput devices that require a large number of gasifiers occupying a large area. This, in turn, requires more complex and costlier piping than if fewer gasifiers were needed. One way to reduce the number and reduce piping would be to increase the diameter of the individual gasifiers, but this would require extensive development work.

Koppers-Totzek Process

As shown in Figure 12-2, the Koppers-Totzek process reacts the coal, steam, and oxygen in an entrained state at atmospheric pressure. Most of the ash leaves the gasifier with the raw product gas, but a portion leaves as a slag and is collected in a receiver at the bottom of the gasifier. Commercial gasifiers use either two or four opposing burners, and the four burners can handle up to 850 tons per day.

Because of the entrained mode of operation, the raw gases leave the gasifier at very high temperatures (up to 3,300°F) so that the consumption of oxygen per unit of product gas is significantly higher than for fixed-bed operations. Another disadvantage when compared to the Lurgi unit is the atmospheric operation of the Koppers-Totzek process. There appears to be no reason why the Koppers-Totzek unit should not be capable of pressure operation, although this would require developing a low-cost, reliable method to feed fine coal into a pressure vessel, and modification in the design of the slag-removal system.

The Koppers-Totzek gasifier, however, can use all of the coal, including the fines, and

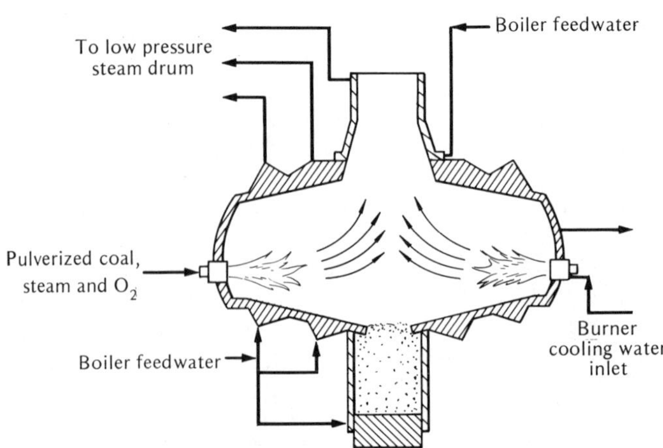

Figure 12-2. The Koppers-Totzek reactor contains an entrained bed of reactants. Gas flows out top; ash to bottom.

can gasify any type or rank of coal. Moreover, it has fewer environmental problems because the tars, phenols, and light oils collected during operation of the Lurgi gasifier are never produced at the higher temperature of the process. Over-all thermal efficiencies are said to be about 77 per cent.

Winkler Process

This process is an atmospheric fluid-bed route in which the gasifying media are oxygen and steam. The fluid bed operates at 1,500 to 1,850°F, and most of the ash is carried over with the product gas. The unreacted carbon that is also carried out of the bed is reacted with additional steam and oxygen in the disengaging space above the fluid bed. To prevent slagging of the ash, the gases are cooled by a radiant boiler section in the upper portion of the gasifier. The process was constructed at 16 plants in a number of countries, using a total of 36 generators. These plants are still operating, with the largest having a capacity of 1.1 million standard cubic feet per hour. The last installation was in 1960.

Like the Koppers-Totzek process, the Winkler route can handle the entire size range of coal, but without pretreatment it would be difficult, if not impossible, to operate with a strongly coking coal. Oxygen consumption is intermediate between that of the fixed-bed Lurgi and the entrained Koppers-Totzek process. Though the Winkler does not produce the tars, phenols, and light oils that the Lurgi does, this process like Koppers-Totzek, has been operated commercially only at atmospheric pressure. Studies of estimated results under conditions of 1.5 atmospheres pressure have been made. Over-all thermal efficiencies are said to be about 75 per cent.

Hygas Process

The Hygas process is one of the two large pilot plants that have been constructed under contract with the Office of Coal Research and which are being tested at the present time. Hydrogen (produced in another process step) is reacted directly with coal at 1,000 to 1,500 pounds per square inch to make a high-BTU gas. The hydrogasifier is operated in a countercurrent fashion with coal being fed into the top and hydrogen at the bottom. It consists of two fluid beds in series; the upper bed is operated at about 1,200°F and the lower bed at 1,700°F. Operating in this fashion optimizes the process with respect to reaction rate and the amount of methane at equilibrium in the product gas. The easily gasified part of the coal reacts in the upper zone, the more refractory portion in the lower zone, and the most refractory part of the coal is removed and used to prepare the hydrogen for the hydrogasification reaction.

Three methods to produce the hydrogen required for Hygas have been proposed by the Institute of Gas Technology: electrothermal, Institute of Gas Technology steam-oxygen, and Institute of Gas Technology steam-iron. The characteristics of these three processes are shown in Table 12-1. The Hygas pilot plant is still in the early stages of operation.

Carbon Dioxide-acceptor Process

This is the second of the two fully constructed, Office of Coal Research-supported, large pilot plants for producing high-BTU gas. The flow sheet is shown in Figure 12-3. Coal is fed into the top of the gasifier, and after being devolatilized, the char is reacted with steam in a fluid-bed gasifier operating at 150 to 300 pounds per square inch, into which hot dolomite also has been introduced. The dolomite provides the reaction heat in two ways—by the sensible heat that it brings into the gasifier (obtained during calcination) and by the heat released when the calcium oxide reacts with part of the CO_2 made in the gasifier by the char-steam reaction.

The product gas leaves at the top of the gasifier, and a steam of spent dolomite and unreacted char is removed from the bottom. These solids are introduced into a second vessel, where the unreacted carbon is burned with air and the heat produced calcines and regenerates the dolomite.

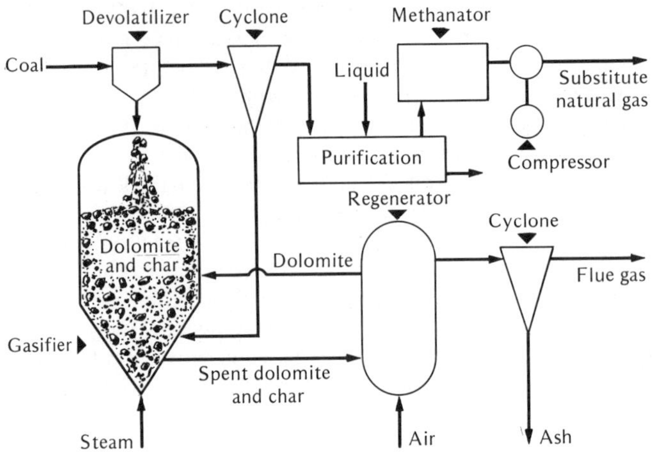

Figure 12-3. The carbon dioxide acceptor process operates from air instead of pure oxygen because of the dolomite regeneration loop.

The major advantage of the process is that it avoids the use of oxygen—a relatively expensive raw material. The major disadvantage is that it can probably only be utilized successfully with reactive coals such as lignite, and may not be suitable for higher rank coals.

The pilot plant is still in the early stages of operation.

Synthane Process

This process, as with the balance of high-BTU gas processes that will be described, has only been operated in a small pilot plant, although a 70-ton-per-day plant has been built at Bruceton, Pennsylvania.

The Synthane process, shown in Figure 12-4, is a two-stage pressurized gasifier developed by the Bureau of Mines, in which the coking properties of the coal are destroyed with oxygen and steam, either in a free-fall stage or in a fluid bed. The coal then enters a carbonization zone and is finally gasified in a lower zone using steam and oxygen. Char and ash are removed from the bottom of the gasifier and raw product gas (containing the effluent gas from the pretreater) leaves at the top. The upper part of the fluid bed is operated

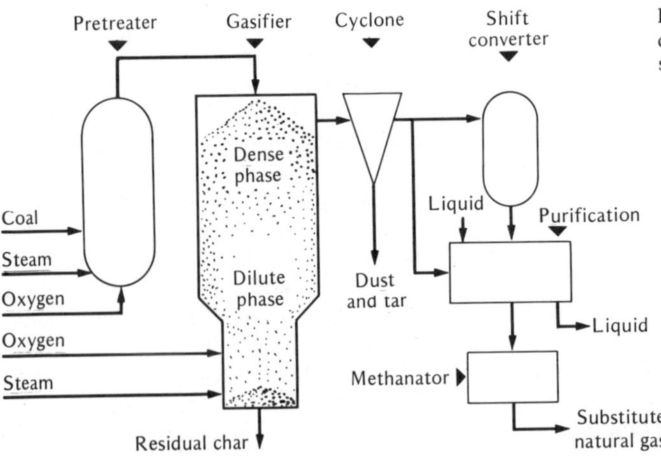

Figure 12-4. The Synthane route requires a pretreated feed to prevent slagging in the reactor.

at about 1,100°F and the lower part at 1,750 to 1,850°F.

Bigas Process

This route is a two-stage entrained, superpressure method developed by Bituminous Coal Research, Inc. The basic design data were obtained in a 100-pounds-per-hour unit, and a 120-tons-per-day plant has been built at Homer City, Pennsylvania. It started operation in late 1975.

Coal is introduced into the upper section of the gasifier, where it is heated by the hot gases produced in the bottom of the unit. The coal is carbonized, and the distillation gases leave the gasifier with the gases produced in the lower section of the vessel. Part of the char leaves with the raw gas and is recirculated to the lower section, where it reacts in an entrained state with steam and oxygen to produce synthesis gas. The bottom stage is operated at 2,800°F and the upper stage at 1,400 to 1,700°F.

Cogas Process

The Cogas process is a privately funded research and development effort, supported by a consortium of six companies. No detailed flow sheets or cost estimates have been released, but it has been reported that two different types of pilot plants are being investigated, neither one of which uses oxygen for the gasification step. One pilot plant is at Princeton, New Jersey, and the other is in England. Gasification occurs in a fluid bed, and ash is removed either dry or as a slag. In April 1974, the first successful run was reported on the British pilot plant. Construction of the Princeton plant was recently completed.

Union Carbide-Battelle Process

This is a two-stage fluid bed system. In one stage, part of the carbon is burned with air in a fluid-bed combustor, during which the coal ash agglomerates to form a heat barrier. These hot pellets are circulated to a second vessel into which coal and steam are introduced to provide the heat for the gasification reaction between steam and carbon. Part of the heat carrier is separated from the char, returned to the first vessel and reheated. The balance of the heat carrier is removed as ash from the gasifier. The process is operated at 100 pounds per square inch. As with the Cogas process, the Union Carbide-Battelle process does not require oxygen. Construction of a 25-ton-per-day development unit was started in late 1973.

Hydrane Process

This is the Bureau of Mines version of the hydrogasification step incorporated in the Hygas pilot plant. It is a two-stage countercurrent process. Coal is introduced at the top of the first stage, where it is devolatilized in a dilute phase to destroy its coking properties using hot gas produced in the hydrogasification section at the bottom of the vessel. Here the char produced in the upper section is reacted at 1,650°F with hydrogen (produced in a separate vessel), using the residual unreacted char remaining from the hydrogasification operation. The method, which is expected to be used to make hydrogen, is similar to that for the Synthane process and is a pressurized fluid-bed gasifier using steam and oxygen as the reactants.

Bench-scale tests have been completed and currently a small 10-pounds-per-hour pilot plant is being operated.

Several other processes have been investigated. These include the Molten Salt process of the Kellogg Co., the Atgas reactor of the Applied Technology Corp., and the nuclear coal gasification process of Stone and Webster-Gulf General Atomics. In addition, a limited number of commercial plants using other types of gasifiers were constructed abroad for a period following World War II, and large-scale pilot tests were run on several different types of gasifiers in the United States in the late 1940's and early 1950's.

The molten salt process was studied on a

small scale some years ago but was discontinued because of problems arising from the corrosive nature of the salt. Currently a corrosion resistant design is being tested for its long-term effectiveness. The early version of the process used two vessels. In the first, steam and coal were reacted in a molten bath of sodium carbonate to make synthesis gas. The unburned carbon and sulfur in the coal were discharged with the circulating molten carbonate solution. In the second vessel, the residual carbon in the salt was burned with air to reheat the sodium carbonate, which was recirculated.

In a more recent development, M. W. Kellogg Co. has reported investigation of a single-vessel molten carbonate gasification system using two different methods of operation. In one, the molten carbonate moves between two sides of a divided vessel. On one side, steam and carbon are reacted to make synthesis gas while on the other, the oxidation reaction—formerly carried out in the second vessel—occurs. In the other variation of the single-vessel process, steam and oxygen are introduced into the molten bath of carbonate, where both the steam-carbon reaction and the carbon-oxygen reaction occur simultaneously.

The Atgas process, also in the laboratory stage, uses a molten iron bath to carry out the reaction in a single vessel. The process operates at low pressures, and either air or oxygen can be used as the oxidizing medium. Limestone is injected into the bath to control the sulfur compounds that would otherwise appear in the product gas. When air is used, the product gas is a sulfur-free, low-BTU gas (195 BTU per cubic foot); with oxygen, the product is a medium- or high-BTU gas, depending upon how much subsequent upgrading is used.

As a result of a favorable study of the State of Oklahoma on the possibility of adapting the nuclear high-temperature gas-cooled reactor to coal gasification, Gulf General Atomics and Stone and Webster are cooperating on a joint program to develop this process. The over-all concept involves making both liquid products and pipeline gas. The hydrogen for the process is made by reforming a part of the product methane with steam. The heat required for the steam-methane reforming reaction is supplied by a hot stream of helium from the gas-cooled reactor.

A number of private firms have announced that they have pilot-plant studies under way. General Electric is investigating a fixed-bed atmospheric gasifier using moderately coking coals. The unit will eventually be used to make synthesis gas, but is now running with air (see section on low-BTU gas). Exxon has recently completed a $40-million pilot plant for production of 20 billion BTU per day of medium-BTU gas (about 400 BTU per cubic foot) from 500 tons of coal. The gas is then piped to an Exxon refinery and used as fuel there. The plant was completed in late 1976.

A consortium of American companies has been formed to test a slagging, fixed-bed gasifier at the Westfield gasification plant of the Scottish Gas Board. A bottom section will be added to one of the existing Lurgi gasifiers so that it can be operated in a slagging mode. This work will be an extension of a series of experiments conducted several years ago by the British Gas Council at Solihull.

METHANATION STUDIES

Although at least three commercial processes exist for the production of synthesis gas or medium-BTU gas from coal, the methanation step required to make a high-BTU gas has never been operated on a commercial scale. In making a gas of pipeline quality, it will be necessary to use a methanator to upgrade the gases that are produced in any of the commercially proved gasifiers.

A wholly owned subsidiary of the Continental Oil Co. has joined with 15 other industrial firms to demonstrate the purification and methanation steps on a large scale. The tests are being conducted at the Westfield plant of the Scottish Gas Board. The output of a single Lurgi generator, approximately 10 million cubic feet per day of medium-BTU gas, is purified and then methanated in a fixed-bed reactor to produce 2.6 million cubic feet per day of high-BTU gas.

The tests were started in 1973 and are continuing. No detailed reports have been issued, but published data suggest that, although the investigation is not complete, the program has achieved a degree of success. High yields of methane have been produced at 85 to 90 per cent of designed capacity.

CCI has been operating a small methanation pilot plant for several years with private sponsorship. This plant is able to produce about 150,000 cubic feet per day of pipeline-quality gas. It consists of several fixed-bed reactors. Temperature control for the very exothermic process is achieved by recycling part of the hot gases. Much of the effort has been devoted to developing improved catalysts that can function over a wide range of operating conditions and that can recover from short periods of unbalanced operation.

Other projects include a fixed bed being studied at the Institute of Gas Technology Hygas plant, a liquid-phase methanator that will be built on a small, skid-mounted scale by Chem Systems (under contract from Office of Coal Research), and a fluid-bed unit constructed by Bituminous Coal Research. No results have yet been reported for the fluid-bed method.

The Bureau of Mines has a project going to study the use of Raney nickel catalysts that are flame sprayed on tubes and plates. Two types are being tested on a small scale: in one, the catalyst is sprayed on steel plate over which the synthesis gas is passed. Temperature control is obtained by recycling cold product gas. In the other reactor, the catalyst is sprayed on the inside of the tubes, which are surrounded by a boiling liquid that removes the heat of the methanation reaction.

LOW-BTU GAS

The process steps involved in the manufacture of low-BTU gas from coal are similar to those for high-BTU gas through the gasification step, except that in low-BTU gas, air is substituted for oxygen. The product gas is diluted with the nitrogen in the air, producing a gas with a heating value in the range of 135 to 200 BTU per cubic foot, depending on how much of the gases distilled from the raw coal are retained in the product.

The manufacture of low-BTU gas is less complicated and thus less expensive than making high-BTU gas. The shift conversion is not needed, and a simpler gas cleanup system can be used because there is no need to clean the gas for the protection of the methanation catalyst. The methanator is also eliminated, thus increasing the over-all thermal efficiency significantly.

If the major societal objective was to make a clean fuel from coal for heating purposes, methods to produce low-BTU gas should have been investigated first. However, the opposite actually occurred. High-BTU gas investigations are conducted many years in advance of low-BTU gas studies. The reasons are understandable: The gas transmission and distribution companies—with large capital investments of their facilities—were concerned, at an early date, that supplies of indigenous gas would be insufficient to keep their pipelines operating at high capacities. They needed a substitute natural gas, not just a clean gas from coal, since the cost of transporting and distributing low-BTU and even medium-BTU gas to most of their customers would have been prohibitive. Moreover, a return to a significantly lower-BTU gas would require replacement of millions of gas burners. These companies were willing to support a high-BTU gas at an early date.

Unfortunately, there has been little research on processes to make clean, low-BTU gas from coal using air as an oxidant. Of the processes in Table 12-1, only those of Lurgi and Winkler have actually operated in a full-scale gasifier using air. The Lurgi is just completing the experimental operations stage. The stirred fixed-bed and the General Electric processes listed in Table 12-2 have also been operated on a reasonable scale using air to produce a low-BTU gas. In addition to these four, the Atgas process has been tested on a small scale using air to produce a 190-BTU-per-cubic-foot gas.

The balance of the processes shown in Table 12-2 are now under study, but there are no operating pilot plants. The Office of Coal Research has awarded contracts for preliminary design of the low-BTU gasifiers to Combustion Engineering, Westinghouse, and Pittsburg & Midway Coal companies. The Institute of Gas Technology is actively seeking support for its "U-gas" project.

The large difference between the state of development of high-BTU and low-BTU gasification processes is shown by comparing Tables 12-1 and 12-2. A large number of processes have been extensively tested for high-BTU gas while most of the new low-BTU gas processes have yet to be operated—construction on some has not even been started. The fiscal-year-1975 federal coal research and development budget attempted to correct this imbalance by increasing the low-BTU gas budget to $49 million, compared to only $31.8 million for the high-BTU gas budget. Five atmospheric-pressure and five high-pressure, low-BTU projects are to be supported.

Air-blown Winkler Generator

A number of the commercially installed Winkler generators were operated using air instead of oxygen to supply the heat. No special problems with air operation have been reported. Costs per million BTU are estimated to be about 20 per cent lower for gasification of United States lignite with air rather than with oxygen.

Air-blown Lurgi Gasifier

An air-blown Lurgi gasifier has been operated intermittently for several years at a German power plant designed to use the make-gas in a combined gas-steam-turbine plant. The coal is gasified with air at 20-atmospheres pressure. The exit gases leave the gasifier at about 1,000°F and are scrubbed to remove tar and dust. Hydrogen sulfide would be removed at this stage, if necessary. The gases are expanded in a turbine and then burned in a pressurized boiler. The exhaust gases from the boiler are again expanded in a gas turbine and then used to heat the feedwater to the steam turbine.

After modification to correct some design

Table 12–2. Coal Gasification Processes for Production of Low-BTU Gas.

Process	*Reactor Bed Type*	*Nature of Residue*	*Pressure (atmosphere)*	*Temperature (°F)*	*Capacity (tons per d*
Commercial					
Winkler	Entrained	Dry ash	1	Approx. 1,500	2,000
Demonstration					
Lurgi	Fixed	Dry ash	20	1,000	2,000
Pilot Plants					
Stirred fixed producer (U.S. Bureau of Mines)	Fixed	Dry ash	20	1,000	20
General Electric fixed bed	Fixed	Dry ash	8	1,000	0.25
Combustion Engineering-Consolidated Edison gasifier	Entrained	Slag	1	>2,100	180
Westinghouse Electric Corp. gasifier	Multiple fluid beds	Dry ash	10–16	1,300–1,700 and 2,000	15
Pittsburg-Midway gasifier	Entrained (two-stage)	Slag	4–35	>2,100	1,200
Institute of Gas Technology U-gas	Fluid bed	Dry ash	20	1,900	30–50

deficiencies, testing was resumed in late 1973 and is continuing.

Commonwealth Edison Co., in cooperation with the Electric Power Research Institute, is planning to operate an air-blown Lurgi gasifier. It would process 60 tons per hour of coal to supply a boiler fuel for a 70-megawatt generating unit. The tars made during gasification would be used to form briquettes of the fine coal produced in mining that is unsuitable as a Lurgi feed. Original plans called for construction of the Lurgi to begin in late 1974, and operation to begin in 1976.

Stirred Fixed-bed Producer

The fixed-bed gasifier of the Bureau of Mines, shown in Figure 12-5, has an inner diameter of 3.5 feet and is 24 feet long. The gasifier is equipped with a stirrer to break up any coke that is formed in the upper section. The stirrer both rotates on the shaft and moves vertically in the gasifier.

Unlike any other previously tested fixed-bed gasifier, it was found possible to gasify highly-coking coals using this stirrer. Additional research is to be directed toward higher pressure operation and to gas cleanup at high temperatures and pressures.

General Electric Fixed-bed Producer

General Electric has studied the gasification of strongly coking coal in a small-diameter fixed-bed gasifier operated at atmospheric pressure. The coal is fed by extrusion into the gasifier and is shaped into uniform cylinders. A larger gasifier, 2 feet in diameter, is being designed to operate at 20 atmospheres and gasify 12 tons per day.

The unique feature of the process is the extrusion feeding system. It would simplify feeding of fine coal into a pressure vessel by eliminating lock hoppers.

The following four processes are still in the design and construction stage and no operating data are available.

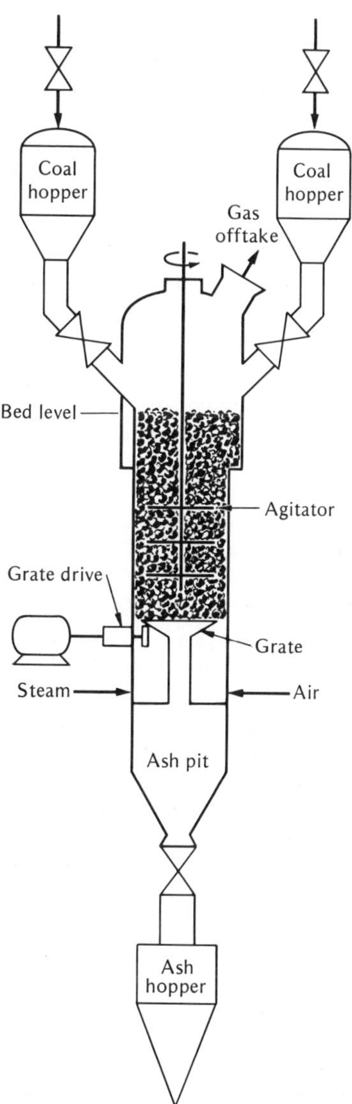

Figure 12-5. Another Bureau of Mines development, the stirred fixed-bed producer, can gasify highly coking coals.

Combustion Engineering

This is an entrained process supported by the Office of Coal Research, which will be operated in the range of 1 to 10 atmospheres. It will produce a clean, low-BTU gas suitable for steam/gas combined-cycle electric plants.

The experimental pilot plant is designed to handle 120 tons per day—the equivalent of the heat requirements of a 10-megawatt power plant. The plant is thought to be large enough so that, if successful, design of a full-scale plant would follow.

Westinghouse Electric Corp.

This is also supported by the Office of Coal Research and is being directed by a five-member government/industry team. The process selected for study consists of two fluid-bed gasifiers in series. In the first fluid bed, operating at 1,300 to 1,700°F, the dried coal is devolatilized, desulfurized, and partially hydrogasified with gas produced in the second fluid bed. The fresh coal is prevented from coking by contacting it with very large streams of hot recycled char and lime absorbent from the second vessel. Fresh limestone is added to the vessel and a stream of spent limestone removed. The char carried out with the spent limestone is stripped from it and returned to the system. The product gas leaving the first vessel is separated from carryover char and consists of a clean, low-BTU gas suitable for gas turbine use. The overflow char from the first fluid bed is then reacted in a second vessel with air and steam. Gasification of the char occurs in the upper section of the fluid bed in the second vessel at 1,800 to 2,000°F. The heat for the gasification reaction is generated by the combustion (at 2,100°F) of part of the char in the lower section of the gasifier. At this temperature, the ash agglomerates and settles to the bottom of the combustor where it can be removed.

Pittsburg and Midway Coal Mining

This program is cosponsored by the Office of Coal Research and four industrial companies, and is designed to develop an entrained type, two-stage, slagging pressure gasifier. The process is fashioned after the two-stage Bigas process. The fresh coal is devolatilized and partially gasified in the upper stage of the gasifier as it comes into contact with the hot gases produced from the combustion of char with air in the lower section. Char carried over with the product gas is separated and reinjected into the bottom part of the gasifier. The exit temperatures are sufficiently high so that they contain no tars or oils.

IGT-U Gas Process

This is a fluid-bed pressurized gasifier developed by the Institute of Gas Technology to produce a clean gas with a heating value of about 140 BTU per cubic foot. The process is designed to be able to use coking and high-sulfur coals. If it is necessary to destroy coking properties, the coal would be pretreated with air at 800°F in a separate vessel, and the heat released during pretreatment would be recovered as steam. The pretreated coals and the gas produced flow into the gasifier vessel. The char reacts with steam and air at temperatures at which the ash agglomerates, then settles to the bottom and can be removed from the char-ash fluid bed (similar to the Westinghouse ash-removal method). The gas leaving the fluid bed has a residence time above the bed of 10 to 15 seconds at 1,500 to 1,900°F, in order to crack the tars and oils that may have been formed. Eliminating the tars and oils will reduce heat exchanger fouling and simplify gas cleanup. The gas will then be cleaned using a new process that is said to be capable of removing sulfur and particulates at high temperatures and pressures. The Institute of Gas Technology worked with the Ralph Parsons Co. to prepare a cost estimate for a demonstration plant large enough to permit direct scaleup to a commercial size.

UNDERGROUND GASIFICATION OF COAL

The idea of gasifying coal without mining can be traced back as far as 1868. However, it was not until after World War II that world-wide interest developed in the technique, and experimental work was conducted until about

1960 in at least eight countries. The main advantage of underground gasification is that the heat in the coal could be extracted with little or no underground manpower required and with limited mining costs. Moreover, it might be possible to extract energy from coal seams that are either too thin or of too poor a quality to be mined by conventional methods.

The only commercial applications of underground gasification have been in the Soviet Union, where production in 1956 was reported to be 116 billion cubic feet of fuel having an average heating value of 85 BTU per cubic foot. This represents less than 0.05 per cent of United States demand for gas in 1972.

Because of the enormous potential for increasing safety and reducing extraction costs, underground gasification is again receiving attention in the United States. In the spring of 1973, the Bureau of Mines initiated a small-scale underground gasification experiment in a subbituminous coal seam in Wyoming. Before the experiment was initiated, the direction of the maximum natural permeability of the bed was determined. It was found that this permeability coincided with the natural fractures of the seam. A number of holes were drilled from the surface to the coal seam and the natural permeability of the bed was increased by various fracturing methods. The system was ignited using foward burning, and some combustible gas has been produced. The experiment is still underway, and continuous operation for one year was achieved in March 1974. Coal consumption had been 15 tons per day, and the product gas reached an output of 3 million cubic feet per day at a heating value of 140 to 170 BTU per cubic foot.

COAL LIQUEFACTION—BACKGROUND

In the past, the degree of interest in liquefaction technology has largely depended on estimations of the adequacy of proved oil reserves, both domestic and worldwide.

Extensive liquefaction research was conducted in Germany in the 1920's and 1930's. In the absence of indigenous liquid fuel supplies, Germany had to convert its large coal resources to remain a major power.

In the United States, the Bureau of Mines conducted small-scale feasibility studies of German technology in the 1930's, but the effort was largely moot because of the huge east Texas oil discoveries in 1930. During World War II, interest revived in the United States, and in 1944 Congress passed the Synthetic Liquid Fuels Act that provided $60 million in funds until the program's expiration in 1955. Then, just as in 1930, another big oil discovery killed interest in coal liquefaction—this time the discovery was in the Middle East.

Until recently, liquefaction research has concentrated on producing a substitute refinery feedstock. Now the emphasis is on getting the maximum amount of low-cost, clean fuel suitable for direct use in boilers.

COAL TO REFINERY FEEDSTOCKS

The Bergius Process

The Bergius process is one of the two processes used industrially during World War II. This route produced about 85 per cent of all synthetic liquid fuels made in Germany. It is a hydrogasification reaction. Coal is first ground to a fine size and mixed with a hydrocarbon liquid, which has been produced by the process itself, and with a catalyst. This mixture is reacted with hydrogen (produced by the gasification of coal) at 10,000 pounds per square inch at 850°F. The products from the first reactor are separated into light, middle, and bottom fractions. The middle fraction is further treated over a catalyst in a vapor phase and under relatively mild conditions to produce petroleum-like products. The bottom fraction is filtered to remove solids (unreacted coal, catalyst, ash), and the remaining liquid is used to mix with the fresh coal being processed in the first reactor.

The extreme operating conditions in the

primary reactor (resulting from the poor quality of the catalysts available) and the large volume of hydrogen consumed, which was expensive to produce from coal using existing technology, made the liquid products very expensive. Over-all process efficiency was about 55 per cent. No commercial Bergius plants are currently operating.

The Fischer-Tropsch Process

The Fischer-Tropsch process was the other one used in World War II by the Germans to produce industrial quantities of synthetic hydrocarbon liquids. It is a synthesis gas process. The major difference in the products resulting from the Bergius and Fischer-Tropsch processes was that the coal hydrogenation oil was aromatic whereas the Fischer-Tropsch was paraffinic (with cobalt) or highly olefinic (with iron catalysts).

Coal is first gasified completely to synthesis gas. The ratio of the hydrogen to carbon monoxide can be adjusted to produce different final products for use with different types of catalysts. The purified gas is passed over a catalyst at temperatures of 570 to 640°F at pressures of about 450 pounds per square inch. A mixture of straight-chain paraffinic and olefinic products are made that can be further refined to give synthetic liquid fuels.

Whereas the Fischer-Tropsch process as used in Germany avoids the extreme processing conditions of the Bergius method, the complete gasification of coal and its reconstitution to liquid products gives an over-all conversion efficiency of only 38 per cent. One small industrial Fischer-Tropsch plant has been in operation in South Africa since about 1955. It uses fixed-bed Lurgi gasifiers to make the synthesis gas and two different methods of contacting the purified gas with catalyst: a modified fixed-bed German process and an entrained circulating-bed catalyst. The major engineering problem is the removal of the large volumes of heat that are released when the gas is converted to a liquid by the catalyst.

The plant produces a wide range of hydrocarbons from methane to light oils. In recent years the methane and other lighter weight hydrocarbons have been used increasingly as a pipeline gas substitute.

Numerous alterations have been made in the plant since it was first designed, and plant management now believes that the use of the historical data to calculate costs is misleading. With larger plants and improved design, costs of liquid and gaseous fuels from a Fischer-Tropsch process are said to be similar to other conversion processes.

REFINERY FEEDSTOCKS—DEVELOPMENTAL

Several projects are underway to test new technology, or at least untried technology. Ambitious feasibility studies are in progress to determine the economics of methanol production from gasified coal. The methanol would be used as fuel in boilers, and possibly as a gasoline extender in automobiles. A typical process scheme would couple a gasification route (yielding synthesis gas) with existing methanol production technology.

Processes under investigation to produce nonalcoholic hydrocarbon fuels include the COED process (FMC Corp.), Project Gasoline (developed by Consolidation Coal Co.), and the H-Coal process (developed by Hydrocarbon Research, Inc.). In addition, there is the Synthoil process of the Bureau of Mines, which is still in the experimental stage.

The COED Process

Though the liquid produced by this process can be used as a refinery feedstock, the process is basically a pyrolysis method aimed at removing valuable liquids from the coal before it is burned. The amount of liquid and char produced will vary with both the coal used and processing conditions, but in all cases the char is the major product. As a result, COED must be viewed as a way to supplement supplies of liquids from coal and not as a primary coal liquefaction process, unless methods to liquefy the char are found.

The process consists of a series of fluidized, low-temperature, carbonization reactors. The number of reactors and the processing conditions necessary to optimize liquid yields will vary for different coals. Typically, four stages operating at 600, 850, 1,000, and 1,600°F are used. Heat for the process is generated by burning char in the fourth stage and by using the hot gases and hot char to supply the heat for the other stages. Some medium-BTU gas is produced during the carbonization, but the two major products are a hot char and liquids. The oil is filtered to remove solids and hydrotreated at pressure to make a synthetic crude oil. Hydrotreating tests have been conducted with favorable results.

A number of coals have been tested in a small unit with a capacity of 100 pounds per hour. A few coals have been tested in a larger pilot plant with a capacity of 1.5 tons per hour, and there are plans to test additional coals in this pilot plant. A western Kentucky coal has been successfully carbonized, and even more strongly coking coals were tested in fiscal years 1975 and 1976.

The usefulness of the COED process as a source of liquids from coal will depend on the successful development of a method for using the char in an environmentally acceptable way. If the over-all economics justify it, there should be no major problems in engineering and constructing a large commercial plant.

Project Gasoline

Following successful laboratory tests, this process was to have been tested on a 1-ton-per-hour scale, but the plant constructed at Cresap, West Virginia, was plagued with a large number of engineering difficulties, only some of which were directly related to the hydrogenation process itself. Moreover, operations were handicapped by labor unrest so that only a limited amount of experimental data was obtained from the pilot plant before work was terminated.

In the process, which uses both solvation and catalytic hydrogenation, the coal is first partially converted to liquid by a hydrogen-transfer recycle solvent. Then solids are separated, and the liquid product is treated with hydrogen in a fluid-bed catalyst reactor. The solvent (which is recycled) must then be separated from the product, which is a satisfactory refinery feedstock. The solids separation has been one of the most persistent engineering problems encountered. The hot filters originally used have never operated satisfactorily. When hydrocyclones were used for solid-hot liquid separation they gave a product somewhat higher in ash and sulfur than desired.

The maximum amount of liquids is produced at an extraction temperature of 810 to 815°F, but to reduce the sulfur content to the levels desired, operations must be conducted under conditions that yield more gas and distillates while consuming more hydrogen. The residue from the extraction step can be utilized to generate the hydrogen and to rehydrogenate the solvent.

Standard Oil of Ohio, which still retains some interest in the background patents of Project Gasoline, has proposed that a 900-ton-per-day pilot plant be erected, supported by 15 or more energy companies. The plant is expected to produce 500 tons per day of clean solid fuel and 400 barrels per day of low-sulfur distillates. Total capital costs of the project are estimated at $70 million.

H-Coal Process

This process has been under study by Hydrocarbon Research, Inc. and represents a modification of their H-Oil process of catalytic hydrogenation—which is being used commercially—so as to be able to handle coal.

Coal is mixed with a recycle oil and fed into a hydrogenator containing a granular catalyst of cobalt molybdate, which is maintained in an ebullient state by the flow of the liquid-solid mixture and hydrogen. The product is first treated in a hot atmospheric flashdrum and the bottoms stream is further treated to produce a bottoms slurry product, part of which is used for the recycle stream. A number of coals have been tested in an 8-inch-diameter reactor handling 200 pounds per hour of coal. The catalyst can be added or removed continuously as required. A high yield of low-sulfur liquids is produced that are suitable for a refinery feedstock. Tests have also been made to produce a low-sulfur boiler fuel rather than a refinery feedstock. Because of its high cost, the catalyst that is attrited must almost all be recovered from the unconverted coal and coal ash.

As with Project Gasoline, one of the major problems has been solids separation. Several methods have been investigated, including the use of a hydroclone, centrifuge, magnetic separation and filtering. Hydroclones removed only two-thirds of the solids, centrifuges were too expensive, and the results of magnetic separation were not encouraging. Filteration rates were not as cost effective as treating the solid-liquid mixture by vacuum distillation, followed by coking.

Construction of a larger plant to hydrogenerate 300 to 700 tons per day of coal has been proposed to the Office of Coal Research for financing. Three years will be required for design and construction, and a two-year operating program is believed to be required.

Synthoil Process

This particular process has been under development by the Bureau of Mines for the past three years. The key feature of this one-step hydrodesulfurization process is the use of rapid, turbulent flow of hydrogen to propel a coal slurry through an immobilized bed of cobalt-molybdate catalyst pellets. The reactor is operated at 2,000 to 4,000 pounds per square inch and 800°F, and with an excess of hydrogen (which is recycled). The slurry vehicle for conveying the coal is a recycled portion of its own product oil. The combined effect of the hydrogen, turbulence, and catalyst is to liquefy and desulfurize the coal at high yields and high throughput. Sulfur is removed as hydrogen sulfide, which is converted into elemental sulfur for sale or storage.

Both a low-sulfur liquid suitable for boiler fuel use and a refinery grade feedstock have been produced from five different high-sulfur, high-ash coals. The nature of the product, whether it is to be a boiler fuel oil or refinery feedstock, depends upon the pressure and residence time to which the coal is exposed.

Operations with 100-pound-per-day and 0.5 ton-per-day development units have proven long-term operability. The smaller reactor was 5/16 inches in diameter and 68 feet long; the larger is 1 inch in diameter and 14 feet long, both containing a fixed bed of 1/8-inch catalyst pellets. Coal reaction residence time is only 2 minutes.

The process can be operated to produce a gasoline at much less severe operating conditions (4,000 versus 10,000 pounds per square inch) than the Bergius process because of improved catalysts (cobalt, molybdenum on alumina) that have been developed, and because of the rapid reaction rates obtained through the use of a highly turbulent regime. Thus, it should be much less costly than feedstock made by the Bergius process.

An 8-ton-per-day pilot plant is currently being designed.

Other Research Programs

Although no details have been revealed, it has been reported that at least three oil companies now have coal liquefaction processes currently under study, and other companies were known to have had programs in the past. Gulf Oil Co. is said to be investigating on a relatively small scale at least one, and possibly two, different coal hydrogenation technologies. Exxon has said that it has at least one process under study, in which a donor solvent is used to transfer hydrogen to the coal in one vessel, followed by catalytic hydrogenation in a second vessel. The pilot plant operated until 1973.

The Oil Shale Corp., which has developed

a retort for producing oil from oil shale, has also tested coal in that unit. The process involves low-temperature pyrolysis of coal using an inert heat carrier. Tests have been conducted on subbituminous coals, and liquid product yields of 13 to 22 gallons per ton have been obtained. Gas yields varied between 1,250 and 1,650 standard cubic feet per ton. The higher liquid and gas yields were at a retorting temperature of 970°F and the lower yields were at 800°F. The chars produced have the same bulk density as the raw coal, but because their heating value is higher (12,000–13,000 BTU per pound for chars compared to 7,200–9,500 BTU for the coals), they can be transported at a much lower cost per million BTU. The chars have been evaluated by several boiler manufacturers who have indicated the material can be used satisfactorily as a fuel.

Tests will also be conducted for the Office of Coal Research on a zinc chloride catalyst designed to produce a 90-octane (lead-free) gasoline from coal. Earlier tests on a small scale have been successful, with the only major problem being recovery of the catalyst. In addition, a new type of reactor—a centrifugal one—will be tested. It should provide a more rapid and direct contact of the gas and solids and promote a more rapid reaction rate. In this way, a very short contact time can be used, and this prevents the repolymerization of the product and favors the production of a high yield of lighter products.

RESEARCH AND DEVELOPMENT: LOW-ASH, LOW-SULFUR FUELS

A certain parallel exists between research and development paths followed by gasification and liquefaction investigators: in gasification, the premium, high-BTU gas was sought first; in liquefaction, the refinery feedstock has been the first choice. A more widely useful liquid product would be a low-ash, low-sulfur one that could be used directly as fuel.

While all of the liquefaction processes already discussed may be able—with modifications—to produce a low-sulfur boiler fuel from coal at lower cost than a refinery feedstock, only the Synthoil and the H-Coal processes have reported the results of such experiments. In addition, extensive experimental work has been carried out on the Pamco process, which makes a low-sulfur boiler fuel that solidifies at ambient temperatures, although it can be modified to also make a low-sulfur liquid product.

Pamco Process

As originally conceived, fine coal is dissolved in a recycled stream, hydrogenated with small quantities of hydrogen at modest pressures (1,000 pounds per square inch), and filtered to remove the solids. These process steps eliminate part of the sulfur and add some hydrogen to the coal. The product is a relatively low-sulfur, low-ash material, solid at room temperature but liquid at 350°F. It could be burned in a boiler, either as a solid or as a liquid, if it is first heated. With more stringent processing conditions, or with a second step involving catalytic hydrogenation of the product, a satisfactory refinery feedstock can be produced.

After a number of years of small pilot operations, a 75-ton-per-day coal pilot plant was completed in late 1973, and testing on this scale is in progress. Another smaller pilot plant using essentially the same process is being tested at Wilsonville, Alabama by the Edison Electric Institute and Southern Electric Generating Co.

Synthoil to Low-sulfur Boiler Fuel

This process, described earlier for producing a liquid fuel from coal in a fixed-bed turbulent reactor, has also been operated so as to make a low-sulfur, low-ash boiler fuel. Coals with a sulfur content of as high as 5.5 per cent have been treated at pressures of 2,000 pounds per square inch and temperatures of 840°F. Oils with sulfur contents in the range of 0.2 to 0.4 per cent have been produced. Production of 3

Table 12–3. Studies of Plant Costs for Various Substitute Fuels Processes (1973 prices).[a]

Study	Output Fuel (billion BTU/ day)	Daily Plant Output	Total Capital Investment ($ million)	Annual Operating Costs ($ million)	Capital Charge 15 per cent per year (¢/million BTU)	Operating Cost (¢/million BTU)	Coal Cost (¢/million BTU)	Product Cost (¢/million BTU)
Coal Gasification								
FPC[1b] Lurgi-bituminous	237.2	250 million cubic feet pipeline gas	347	23.1	66.5	29.5	54.1	150.1
FPC New-bituminous	240.0	250 million cubic feet pipeline gas	296	16.2	56.1	20.5	53.1	129.7
FPC Lurgi-Western	238.8	250 million cubic feet pipeline gas	313	24.6	59.6	31.2	26.1	116.9
FPC New-Western	240.0	250 million cubic feet pipeline gas	261	16.1	49.4	20.3	26.5	96.2
NPC[2c] Lurgi-bituminous	243.0	270 million cubic feet pipeline gas	285	20.8	53.3	25.9	47.1	126.3
NPC Lurgi-Western	243.0	270 million cubic feet pipeline gas	241	18.6	45.1	23.2	23.6	91.9
NAE[3,4d] Lurgi	235.0	240 million cubic feet pipeline gas	318		61.5			
Fluor[5] Lurgi-Western	252.1	257 million cubic feet pipeline gas	427		77.0	24.5	28.5	130.0
Coal Liquefaction								
NPC[2] H-Coal-bituminous	240.0	30,000 barrels syncrude 60-billion BTU fuel-gas	260	26.8 excluding coal	49.2	33.9	43.2	126.3
NPC PAMCO-bituminous	180.0	30,000 barrels "de-ashed product"	187	13.4 excluding coal	47.2	22.6	42.7	112.5
Amoco, COED-bituminous	405.0	29,175 barrels syncrude 250 million cubic feet pipeline gas	500	53.8 excluding coal	56.0	40.0	56.0	152.0
Foster-Wheeler,[6] CONSOL A-Bit	358.8	284.3 billion BTU liquid 74.5 billion BTU gas	309	36.0 excluding coal	39.1	30.4	45.1	114.6
Foster-Wheeler, CONSOL B-Bit	421.0	282.1 billion BTU liquid 138.9 billion BTU gas	405	43.3 excluding coal	43.7	31.2	47.8	122.7
Low-BTU Gas from Bituminous Coal								
NAE[4] low-to-intermediate-BTU gas	235.0		165–210		31.9–40.6		40.0–45.7	110–125
FPC[1] low-BTU gas	235.0		189–191		36.6–36.9		20.0–22.9	
Methanol from Coal								
ORNL[7e]-bituminous	391	20,000 tons methanol	416	58.4 excluding coal	48.4	45.3	47.8	141.5

[a]Source: "Project Independence: An Economic Evaluation," MIT Energy Laboratory Policy Study Group, Mar. 15, 1974. Printed in *Technology Review*, May 1974. Reprinted by permission.
[b]FPC—Federal Power Commission.
[c]NPC—National Petroleum Council.
[d]NAE—National Academy of Engineering.
[e]ORNL—Oak Ridge National Laboratory.

1. "Final Report—The Supply-Technical Advisory Task Force–Synthetic Gas-Coal" National Gas Survey, Federal Power Commission, Apr. 1973.
2. "U.S. Energy Outlook—Coal Availability" Report of the Fuel Task Group on Coal Availability, National Petroleum Council Committee, 1973.
3. "Evaluation of Coal Gasification Technology, Part I, Pipeline Quality Gas," National Academy of Engineering, 1972.
4. "Evaluation of Coal Gasification Technology, Part II, Low- and Intermediate-BTU Fuel Gases," National Academy of Engineering, 1973.
5. Moe, J. M., "SNG from Coal via the Lurgi Gasification Process," Symposium on "Clean Fuels Firm Loaf," Institute of Gas Technology, Chicago, Ill., Sept. 10–14, 1973.
6. Foster-Wheeler Corporation, "Engineering Evaluation and Review of Consol Synthetic Fuel Process," R&D Report No. 70, Office Coal Research, Feb. 1972.
7. Methanol from Coal for the Automotive Market, ORNL Feb. 1974.
8. Wen, C. Y., "Optimization of Coal Gasification Processes," R&D Report No. 66, Office of Coal Research, 1972.
9. Siegel, H. M., and T. Kalina, "Technology and Cost of Coal Gasification," *Mech. Engr.*, May 1973, pp. 23–28.
10. Shearer, H. A., "The COED Process Plus Char Gasification," *Chem. Engr. Prog. 69*, No. 3, 43 (1973).
11. Michel, J. W., "Hydrogen and Synthetic Fuels for the Future," 166th Nat. Mec. Amer. Chem. Soc., Div of Fuel Chem Preprints 18 No. 3, 1, Aug. 1973.

barrels per ton of low-sulfur oil has been achieved using only 3,000 cubic feet of hydrogen per barrel of product. Over-all energy conversion efficiencies of 75 to 78 per cent have been obtained.

H-Coal Process

This route can also produce a low-sulfur boiler fuel rather than a refinery feedstock by changing operating conditions. These modifications result in a major increase in reactor space velocity and a greatly reduced hydrogen consumption per ton of coal processed—both of which result in lower product costs. Low-sulfur boiler fuel (0.5 per cent sulfur) has been produced from an Illinois No. 6 coal containing 5.0 per cent sulfur, using only two-thirds the amount of hydrogen required when making a synthetic crude oil from the same coal.

COSTS

In giving any estimate of the costs of synthetics from coal it must be recognized that they are just that—estimates. No commercial plant of any kind is currently in operation in the United States, so that none of the published cost data is based on actual plant operation.

There are a number of other caveats that need to be stressed in making meaningful comparisons among cost data. *First,* in a period of rapidly escalating capital costs, the date of the estimate and the method used (if any) to inflate costs during construction must be known. *Second,* the source of the estimate must be identified, since the promoters of a new process tend to be optimistic and those with competitive processes pessimistic about both capital and operating costs. *Third,* in comparing different estimates, the cost of the coal should be the same, or the effect of any differences in coal costs on product price should be known. *Fourth,* the degree to which the estimate has included the costs of meeting environmental standards must be described. *Fifth,* even the best and most careful estimates tend to increase as one approaches the actual construction of the facility. *Sixth,* the early estimates of product costs are now known to have been grossly understated, and there is still no way to be certain that present estimates, although much higher, may not still be too low. *Finally,* even the most careful estimates by firms using commercially available technology have been sharply escalated. For example, the cost of a Lurgi plant was estimated at under $300 million in the spring of 1971. The latest estimate for the same size plant filed with the Federal Power Commission by El Paso Natural Gas in the fall of 1973 was just under $500 million.

The available information on various synthetic processes with costs computed to 1973 prices is presented in Table 12-3. Published capital investments were converted to 1973 dollars. No changes were made in the contingencies or off sites claimed on the original paper, but all coal costs were standardized at 32¢ per million BTU for bituminous coal ($8 per ton) and 25¢ per million BTU for western coal ($3 per ton).

The hazards noted earlier of using published data are illustrated in Table 12-3, in which four different estimates for a Lurgi plant using the same available commercial technology give capital costs ranging from $214 to $427 million, and all of them are lower than the latest estimate of nearly $500 million.

Table 12-4 presents in condensed form the data from Table 12-3, adjusting all the plants to the same size—250×10^9 BTU per day. For high-BTU gas this is equivalent to 250 million cubic feet per day, for hydrocarbon liquids it is equivalent to 40,000 barrels per day, and for methanol it is equivalent to 12,500 tons per day. The scaling factor used to calculate investment costs for the common-sized plant was the 0.9 power of capacity. The investment was also standardized to include on sites, auxiliaries and off sites. The figures also include 15 per cent for contingency, 5 per cent for startup, 7.5 per cent for working capital and 15 per cent interest on construction loans. A plant stream factor of 90 per cent, labor costs of $5.50 per hour, 2.5 per

Table 12–4. Plant Costs for 250 Billion BTU per Day of Product.[a]

Process Type	Input Fuel (tons per day)	Thermal Efficiency (per cent)	Total[b] Capital (1973) ($ million)	Annual Operating Cost ($ million)	Costs (¢/million BTU) (330 days per year onstream)			
					Capital (at 15 per cent per year)	Operating Costs	Coal Cost	Total Cost
Gasification (Lurgi, gasifier)								
Bituminous coal[c]	14,700–17,900	56–68	334–390	21.4–22.2	60.7–70.9	25.9–26.9	47.1–54.1	135–150
Western coal[d]	19,600–23,800	56–68	290–390	19.5–23.0	52.7–70.9	23.6–28.5	23.6–28.5	100–127
Liquefaction	13,200–17,500	60–75	233–373	22–35	43.4–67.8	26.7–35.0	42.7–56.0	112–166
Low BTU Gas								
Bituminous[c]	12,500–14,300	70–80	195–208	—	35.5–37.8	—	40–45.7	110–125
Western[d]	16,700–19,000	70–80	195–208	—	35.5–37.8	—	20–22.7	90–105
Methanol								
Bituminous[c]	14,900	60–67	279–364	44	50.7–66.2	—	53.4	158–174

[a] Source: "Project Independence: An Economic Evaluation," MIT Energy Laboratory Policy Study Group, Mar. 1974.
[b] Includes on sites, off sites, auxiliaries, 5 per cent startups, 15 per cent interest during construction, 7.5 per cent working capital.
[c] 32¢/million BTU, 25 million BTU per tons, $8 per ton.
[d] 16¢/million BTU, 18.75 million BTU per ton, $3 per ton.

cent of plant investment for taxes and insurance, and 4.5 per cent for plant maintenance were all assumed.

Cost of high-BTU gas made from bituminous coal in a Lurgi generator is estimated at \$1.35 to \$1.50 per million BTU, and at \$1.00 to \$1.27 per million BTU using western coals. Low-BTU gas ranged from \$1.10 to \$1.25 per million BTU using bituminous coals and from \$0.90 to \$1.05 per million BTU using western coals.

Estimates of liquids made from coal range from \$1.12 to \$1.66 per million BTU (\$6.40–\$9.60 per barrel). The lower values are for a low-sulfur boiler fuel and the higher values are for a refinery feedstock. Methanol made from a bituminous coal was estimated at \$1.58 to \$1.74 per million BTU or the equivalent of \$9.15 to \$10.10 per barrel of oil.

All of these values are probably lower than what will actually result when plants are constructed and operated. This will be the result partly of continuing inflation in construction costs and partly from the other reasons already given. For example, if the most recent Lurgi capital cost estimates are used, the costs of high-BTU gas shown in Table 12-4 are about 25¢ too low. On the other hand, some of the newer gasification and liquefaction processes now in the pilot plant stage, if successful, might result in lower product costs.

These tables, even with all the uncertainties about the accuracy of the calculated values, demonstrate that if we decide to rely on synthetics from coal, the price of energy will increase sharply. The well-head price of oil used to be about \$3.25 per barrel before the Organization of Petroleum Exporting Countries price rises. The estimates for making it from coal would increase this price two or three times. To the consumers of gasoline this would mean that, if the increased cost of syncrude were simply allowed to be passed along, an increase in price from the former retail price of 35¢ per gallon (when crude oil was \$3.25 per barrel) to 47 to 59¢ per gallon would result.

High-BTU gas prices for a residential consumer in Washington, D.C., would increase from about \$1.70 per million BTU to \$2.95 per million BTU (on a pass-along basis) if all of the gas were produced from synthetics. For gasoline, the increase in retail price to the consumer would be 35 to 70 per cent (assuming gasoline taxes did not change), and for the residential gas consumer in Washington, D.C., an increase of 70 per cent.

Since the higher priced gas and liquids would be "rolled in" slowly with existing lower cost supplies as synthetic plants were constructed, prices would increase slowly, and it would be a number of years before the maximum values indicated above would be reached.*

REFERENCES

A.E.C., Sr. Management Comm., "Synthetic Fuels From Coal," Feb. 1974.

Institute for Gas Technology, "Clean Fuels From Coal," Symposium, Sept. 10–14, 1973.

Perry, H., "The Gasification of Coal," *Scientific American 230,* No. 3, March, 1974, pp. 19–25.

Perry, H., "Coal Liquefaction," *Physics and the Energy Problem—1974,* American Institute of Physics Conf. Proceedings, No. 19, Feb. 1974, pp. 43–56.

"Project Independence: An Economic Evaluation," M.I.T. Energy Laboratory Policy Study Group, Mar. 15, 1973.

"Synthetic Fuels," Cameron Engr., Mar. 1974.

U.S. Dept. of the Interior, Office of Coal Res., Energy Res. Program, Feb. 1974.

SUGGESTED READINGS

Alpert, S. B., and R. M. Landberg, 1976, "Clean liquids and gaseous fuels from coal for electric power," *Annual Review of Energy,* Vol. 1, pp. 87–99.

Linden, H. R., W. W. Bodle, B. S. Lee, and K. C. Vyas, 1976, "Production of high-Btu gas from coal," *Annual Review of Energy,* Vol. 1, pp. 65–85.

Siegel, H. M., and T. Kalina, 1973, "Technology and Cost of Coalgasification," *Mechanical Engineering 95,* May, pp. 23–28.

Squires, Arthur M., 1974, "Clean Fuels from Coal Gasification," *Science 184,* pp. 340–346.

*Editors' Note: The OPEC price of crude oil has remained relatively firm at about \$12 to \$13 per barrel and has resulted in gasoline prices somewhat higher than those quoted above.

Agony of the Northern Plains 13

ALVIN M. JOSEPHY, JR. 1973

In October 1971, a "Coordinating Committee," composed of the U.S. Bureau of Reclamation and 35 major private and public electric power suppliers in 14 states from Illinois to Oregon, issued a dramatic document. Innocuously titled the "North Central Power Study," it stunned environmentalists throughout the country and sent waves of horror among the ranchers, farmers, and most of the townspeople of the northern plains. Rushed through in a little over a year (the project was initiated in May, 1970 by the then Assistant Secretary of the Interior for Power and Water Development, James R. Smith), and reflecting the goals and points of view of utility interests that were in business to sell electricity, the study proposed a planned development and employment of the coal and water resources of some 250,000 square miles of Wyoming, eastern Montana, and western North and South Dakota for the generation of a vast additional power supply for the United States.

The scope of the proposal was gargantuan—rivaling the grand scale of the region itself. One of the most serene and least spoiled and polluted sections of the nation, it averages about 4,000 feet above sea level and stretches below the Canadian border roughly from the Badlands and Black Hills in the east to the Bighorn Mountains in the west. It is a huge, quiet land of semiarid prairies, swelling to the horizon with yellow nutritious grasses; rich river valleys, lined with irrigated farms; low mountains, buttes, and rimrock ridges dark with cedar and ponderosa pine; open, wind-swept plains covered with sagebrush, greasewood, and tumbleweed; and hundreds of meandering creeks edged with stands of cottonwoods. The rains average only 12 to 14 inches a year, the topsoil is thin and fragile, easily eroded and blown or washed away, and the vegetation in most places must struggle for life. Towns and cities are small and few and far between, and distances measured along the infrequent highways and ribbons of railroad track are great. For almost a hundred years the natural grasses and irrigated hay fields have sustained big flocks of sheep and herds of cattle, and the region has been one

Alvin M. Josephy, Jr. is a leading authority on American Indian affairs and western American history and his most recent book is *Red Power: The American Indians' Fight for Freedom*. He has served as a consultant to the President, the Secretary of the Interior, the Public Land Law Review Commission, and the National Congress of American Indians. Presently he is vice-president of American Heritage Publishing Company.

CANA
FORT PECK RESERVATION
Missouri R.
Fort Peck Reservoir
Great Falls
MONTANA
Yellowstone
BITTERROOT RANGE
Hamilton
Anaconda
Butte
ROCKY
MOUNTAINS
Roundup
BULL MTS.
Hysham
Miles City
BURLINGTON NORTHERN R.R.
Billings
Hardin
Colstrip
Sarpy
WOLF MTS.
Tongue R.
NORTHERN CHEYENNE RESERVATION
CROW RESERVATION
Lodge Grass
Birney
Otter
Powder R.
Wyola
Decker
Yellowstone R.
Yellowtail Reservoir
ABSAROKA RANGE
BIGHORN MTS.
Sheridan
L. DeSmet
Buffalo
Gillette
IDAHO
Shoshone R.
BIGHORN BASIN
Bighorn R.
Boysen Res.
WIND RIVER RANGE
WIND RIVER BASIN
Lander
WYOMING
Casper
Glenrock
Snake R.
GREAT DIVIDE BASIN
HANNA BASIN
LARAMIE RANGE
MEDICINE BOW MTS.
UNION PACIFIC R.R.
Rock Springs
Laramie
FRONT RANGE
COLORA
Seattle
Spokane
Portland
FORT UNION FORMATION
Twin Cities
Des Moines
Omaha
Kansas City
St. Louis

Bituminous and sub-bituminous coal deposits
Lignite coal deposits
Thermal generation plants
10,000 megawatts
5,000 megawatts
3,000 megawatts
1,000 megawatts
Pumped storage generation
Proposed reservoirs
Major water conveyance conduits
Transmission lines
Land-grant railroads
Source: North Central Power Study, Oct 1971
Minot
Garrison Reservoir
FORT BERTHOLD RESERVATION
NORTH DAKOTA
Bismarck
Oahe Reservoir
Cheyenne R.
Pierre
SOUTH DAKOTA
Rapid City
BADLANDS
Missouri River
NEBRASKA
KANSAS
0 50 100 150 Miles

essentially of large, isolated ranches and farms, whose owners have fought endlessly against blizzards, drought, high winds, and grasshoppers—and have treasured their independence and the spaciousness and natural beauty of their environment.

Ominously for them, the surface of their part of the country sits atop the Fort Union Formation (in the Powder River Basin of Wyoming and Montana and in the western part of the Williston Basin of Montana and the Dakotas), containing the richest known deposits of coal in the world. There are at least 1.5 trillion tons of coal within 6,000 feet of the surface, and perhaps more than 100 billion tons so close to the surface—in seams 20 to 250 feet thick—as to be economically recoverable today by the relatively cheap modern techniques of strip mining. This is, staggeringly, 20 per cent of the world's total known coal reserves and about 40 per cent of the United States' reserves. (The total national figure would be able to supply the country for an estimated 450 to 600 years should the present use trend continue.) But perhaps even more significantly, in view of recent environmental concerns, the sulfur content of these deposits of high-quality subbituminous coal in Montana and Wyoming and lesser-grade lignite in northeastern Montana and North Dakota is low enough to meet the new air pollution standards for coal-burning power plants in urban areas.

In the past, very little of the northern plains coal has been mined, principally because of its comparatively lower BTU heat content and its distance from major markets, which made it less desirable competitively than eastern coal. But by May 1970 the need for low-sulfur coal in the cities was hurrying a change in that thinking. In addition, an energy panic was in the offing—a panic concerned more with sources of future supplies of conventional fuels than with conservation, realistic planning and pricing, dampening of demand, and the development of alternative, nonpolluting fuels. A large-scale (though little-publicized) rush to acquire exploration permits and leases for the low-sulfur coal in the northern plains—together with plans on how to maximize short-term and long-range profits from the enormous deposits—was already stirring the energy industry. It appeared evident that national policy, guided by the industry, would inevitably encourage the exploitation of the western states' coalfields as an answer to the apparently diminishing supplies of fuels from elsewhere, the threat of growing dependency on the oil-producing nations of the Middle East, and power-plant pollution in the cities. So, strict over-all government planning and regulation were necessary if the imposition of coal-based industrialization on the traditional farming-ranching economy and environment of the north central states was not to bring disaster to the area and its people.

Viewing this as a mandate, the Department of the Interior and the 35 cooperating utilities launched their study. There were few persons in the affected region who were not already aware of the increasing attention being given to their coal; indeed, many landowners were already being subjected to the pressures of lease brokers, speculators, and coal companies. But the threat to the region as a whole was not yet visible, and the implications of the stupendous changes that the coal reserves would bring to the lives and environment of the people were not even dreamed of. The release of the North Central Power Study shattered that innocence.

Together with an accompanying document that dealt with the utilization of the region's water resources for the proposed coal development, the study suggested the employment of strip mines in Montana, Wyoming, and North Dakota to supply massive amounts of coal to fuel mine-mouth power plants, which by 1980 would produce 50,000 megawatts of power, and by the year 2000 approximately 200,000 megawatts. The power would be sent east and west over thousands of miles of 765-kilovolt transmission lines to users in urban areas. The study located sites for 42 power plants—21 in eastern Montana, 15 in Wyoming, 4 in North Dakota, and 1 each in South Dakota and Colorado. Their suggested sizes were mind boggling. No fewer than 13 of them would generate 10,000 megawatts each (about *14 times as much* as the original capacity of the Four Corners plant in New Mexico, much criticized as the world's worst polluter, and almost five times more than the 2,175 megawatts which that plant is now capable of generating.) Other plants would range from a 1,000- to 5,000-megawatt capacity. In addition, 10 of the proposed giant 10,000-megawatt plants would be concentrated in a single area, 70 miles long by 30 miles wide, between Colstrip, Montana, and Gillette, Wyoming; another group, with a combined capacity of 50,000 megawatts, was targeted for another compact area close by.

To supply some 855,000 acre-feet of cooling water (an acre-foot is enough to cover one acre with one foot of water) which would be needed each year by the plants at the 50,000-megawatt level, the study proposed a huge diversion of water from the rivers of the Yellowstone Basin, requiring a large system of dams, storage reservoirs, pumping heads, and pipeline aqueducts to be built by the Bureau of Reclamation. As if that were not enough, the water resources document went further, envisaging—with great realism, as it has turned out—the construction of immense coal gasification and liquefaction plants and petrochemical complexes, located near the strip mines and power plants, and raising the need for water to at least 2,600,000 acre-feet a year.

Once they got over their shock at the stupendous dimensions of what was being proposed, environmentalists set to work dissecting the study. It was entirely oriented to the producer of electricity and dealt scarcely, or not at all, with such overwhelming problems as air, water, and noise pollution, strip mining and the reclamation of ravaged land, the diversion of major rivers and resultant conflicts over water rights in the semi-arid country, the degradation of the human and natural environments, the disruption of the region's economy, soil erosion, the destruction of fish and wildlife habitat, and the explosive influx of population with attendant social and economic strains and dislocations that would follow the carrying out of the project's individual schemes. Dr. Ernst R. Habicht, Jr. of the Environmental Defense Fund found the plan almost unbelievable, pointing out that it called for the generation of "substantially more electricity than is now produced either in Japan, Germany, or Great Britain (and would be exceeded only by the present output of the United States or the Soviet Union)." The 855,000 acre-feet of water needed annually, just for the 50,000-megawatt goal, Habicht noted, was more than half of New York City's annual water consumption, and if the need rose to the proposed 2,600,000 acre-feet, it would exceed "by 80 per cent the present municipal and industrial requirements of New York City (population 7,895,000)." Moreover, in wet years, the mammoth diversion would reduce the flow of the Yellowstone River by one-third, and in dry years by about one-half. "Water use of this order of magnitude in a semiarid region . . . will have significant environmental impacts," the scientists warned. "Extreme reduction in river flows and the transfer of water from agricultural use will drastically alter existing agricultural patterns, rural life styles, and riverine ecosystems."

All of this the study had, indeed, overlooked, but there was more. Analysis showed that coal requirements for the 50,000-megawatt level in 1980 would be 210 million tons a year, consuming 10 to 30 square miles of surface annually, or 350 to 1,050 square miles over the 35-year period, which the study proposed for the life of the powerplants. At the 200,000-megawatt level, the strip mines would consume from 50,000 to 175,000 square miles of surface during the 35-year period. In addition, each coal gasification plant, producing 250 million cubic feet of gas per day, would use almost 8 million tons of coal a year, eating up more land, as well as 8,000 to 33,000 acre-feet of water (estimates vary widely) and 500 megawatts of electric power.

The astronomical figures continued. At the

50,000-megawatt level nearly 3 per cent of the tristate region would be strip-mined, an area more than half the size of Rhode Island. The transmission lines would require approximately 8,015 miles of right-of-way, which, with one-mile-wide multiple-use corridors, would encompass a total of 4,800 square miles, approximately the size of Connecticut. Power losses over the network of lines would exceed 3,000 megawatts, greater than the present average peak demand requirements of Manhattan, and would raise a serious problem of ozone production.

A population influx of from 500,000 to 1,000,000 people might be expected in the tristate area. (The present population of Montana is 694,000; Wyoming, 332,000; and North Dakota, 617,000.) Half a million newcomers would mean a 500 percent increase in the present population of the coal areas and would result in new industrial towns and cities, putting added pressures on the states for public services and increased taxes. The quality of life, as well as the environment, would change drastically. At the 50,000-megawatt level, the proposed plants, even with 99.5 per cent ash removal, would fill the air with more than 100,000 tons of particulate matter per year, detrimental to visibility and health. The combustion of the coal would introduce dangerous trace elements like mercury into the atmosphere; and the plants would emit at least 2,100,000 tons of sulfur dioxide (yielding, in turn, sulfurous and sulfuric acids that would be deposited by the wind on farms, ranches, communities, and forests) and up to 1,879,000 tons of nitrogen oxides per year. Though the story ignored the prospect, living in the Colstrip-Gillette area, with ten 10,000-megawatt powerplants, not to mention an unspecified number of coal gasification plants as neighbors, could be lethal.

If the simplistic report, blithely ignoring the need for scores of impact studies, bewildered environmentalists, it sent peals of alarm among many of the people of the three states. The powerful energy companies and utilities of the country, with the encouragement of the federal government, were going to turn them into an exploited and despoiled colony, supplying power to other parts of the nation. Far from planning the orderly development of their region, the study had considered only the needs of industry and, without publicity, without public hearings, without representation from, or accountability to, those who would be affected, had shown a green light to the devastation of life on the Great Plains.

Throughout the region, individuals were soon comparing notes and discovering that a coal rush of gigantic proportions was, indeed, already under way. Lease brokers, syndicate agents, and corporate representatives—many of them from places like Louisiana, Texas, and Oklahoma, with a long experience of wheeling and dealing in gas and oil rights—had been swarming across the plains country, and more coal lands than anyone had dared imagine were already locked away in exploration permits and leases. Ranch owners found out with a start that neighbors had already signed agreements, and that a strip mine and power plant might soon be disturbing their cattle or destroying their range. Irrigation farmers learned of corporations from Pennsylvania, Ohio, and Virginia buying options on the limited supplies of water, and worried about their own water rights. The areas of busiest activity matched the study's proposed sites for development, and rumors multiplied of industrial plans and commitments being made so fast that they could not be stopped. In half a dozen districts in Montana and Wyoming that seemed most threatened, ranchers and farmers hastily organized landowners' associations, which banded together as the Northern Plains Resource Council—a loose federation based with volunteer officers and staff in Billings, Montana—to pool their information, pledge landowners to hold out against the strippers, and contest the coal interests in the courts and the state capitals.

From the start, opposition to the coal development was hobbled by a lack of reliable knowledge of what was going on. In the first place, it soon became evident that the coal and energy companies that were buying up the land and making plans to exploit the region had rejected the proposals of the North Central Power Study even before the document had been made public, and were proceeding, instead, on a voracious, every-developer-for-himself basis. Alarming as the suggestions of the Bureau of Reclamation and the utilities had been, they had nevertheless reflected the federal government's desire to guide development according to a comprehensive and orderly plan. Even the critical environmentalist groups had recognized that, if coal development was inevitable, the study was something with which to work—a plan susceptible to detailed examination and protective actions and modifications that would ensure a minimal degradation of the human and natural environments.

Now the study was nothing but a check list of some—but far from all—of the opportunities for the fastest corporations with the most dollars. Aside from alerting the region's people to the scope of the calamity they faced, the study's effect was to draw additional attention in Wall Street and elsewhere to the possibilities of the immense coal fields and accelerate what was becoming a frantic, modern-day version of the California Gold Rush. By October 1972 the guideline aspects of the study were dead, and Secretary of the Interior Rogers C. B. Morton, aware of the concern in the region over the chaotic exploitation taking place, announced the formation of an interagency federal-state task force and the launching of a Northern Great Plains Resource Program to assess the social, economic, and environmental impacts of the coal development, and hopefully, "coordinate on-going activities and build a policy framework which might help guide resource management decisions in the future."

It was pretty much a case of locking the barn door after the horse was stolen. The 1971 study had been issued well after the coal rush had started, and the new study group—which was criticized because it did not provide fully enough for the participation of the public—would not release its final report until December 1975, although results were expected to be "incorporated into regional planning and decision-making by the end of the first year," or October 1973. In view of the rapid developments taking place, even this seemed too late. Regional planning by then would be almost impossible.

Meanwhile, other factors were adding to the confusion. Without the over-all guidance, planning, or authority of any federal or state agency, it became difficult for anyone, including state officials, to assemble accurate and comprehensive information about who was acquiring what rights and where, and what they intended to do with them. The roster of those who were buying coal deposits read like a who's who of the energy industry: Shell Oil, Atlantic Richfield, Mobil, Exxon, Gulf, Chevron, Kerr-McGee, Carter Oil, Ashland Oil, Consolidation Coal (Continental Oil), Peabody Coal (Kennecott Copper), Westmoreland Coal, Reynolds Metals, North American Coal, Kewanee Oil, Kemmerer Coal, Concho Petroleum, Island Creek Coal (Occidental Petroleum), Cordero Mining (Sun Oil), Arch Minerals, Hunt Oil, Pacific Power & Light, Valley Camp Coal, Penn Virginia Corporation, National Gas Pipeline (Star Drilling), Farmers Union Central Exchange, Cooper Creek, and Western Standard.

They were all there, but so, also, were subsidiaries, subsidiaries of subsidiaries, fronts for bigger names, syndicates, partnerships, speculators, and lease brokers. Rights were acquired by a firm named Meadowlark Farms, suggesting to the public the bucolic image of dairy cows and buttercups rather than a coal strip mine. The company was a subsidiary of Ayrshire Coal Company, formerly Ayrshire Collieries Corporation, which with Azure Coal Company was owned by American Metal Climax's Amax Coal Company. The world-wide construction firms of Peter Kiewit Sons in Omaha, Nebraska, and Morrison-Knudsen Company in Boise, Idaho, also held rights; the former, moving into Montana in a big way, owned the Big Horn and Rosebud Coal companies and half of Decker Coal Company, and the latter held 20 per cent of Westmoreland Resources. There were names relatively unfamiliar to the public: Temporary Corporation, Tipperary Resources, Pioneer Nuclear, J & P Corporation, Ark Land Company, Badger Service Company, Allied Nuclear Corporation, BTU Inc., as well as dozens of individuals like Violet Pavkovich, Fred C. Woodson, E. B. Leisenring, Jr., Billings attorney Bruce L. Ennis, and lease brokers Jase O. Norsworthy and James Reger.

All of them, to a greater or lesser extent, were engaged competitively, and the securing of permits and leases and the making of plans and commitments for exploitation were done with great secrecy. But the necessity to conceal activities and intentions from rivals also frustrated interested officials and the public, who were kept in the dark about plans for such projects as strip mines, power plants, new railroad spurs, water purchases, and coal gasification plants—all of which would affect their environment and lives—until the companies were prepared to announce them. By that time, commitments had been made, and though clues to some of the projects—like the number of companies or the amount of capital involved, the large size of a water pipeline, or the required tonnage of coal—implied immense undertakings with serious impacts on the people and environments of large areas, questioners had to grapple for detailed and meaningful information and were at a disadvantage.

Perhaps the greatest confusion stemmed from the complex ownership rights to the coal and the land surface above it. Some of the coal is owned by the federal government and is administered by the Bureau of Land Management. Some is owned by the states; some by the Union Pacific or Burlington Northern railroads (though their legal rights to the coal, acquired originally with the railroad land grants of the last century, are being questioned by certain congressmen and organizations); some by Indian tribes (the Crow, Northern Cheyenne, and Fort Peck reservations in Montana and the Fort Berthold reservation in North Dakota); and some by private owners. A purchaser may secure an exploration permit or lease for the coal; but to get at it, he also has to deal with the owner of the surface—which frequently produces a problem. The surface rights, again, might be owned by the federal government, the states, the railroads, the Indians, or private owners. Where the same interest owns both the surface and the coal and is willing to part with them, there is no complication. But more often than not, private ranchers own or lease land above coal that does not belong to them. In the past, they or their forebears might have gotten their land from the federal government (under the various Homestead Acts) or from the railroads, but in both cases the government and the railroads reserved the mineral rights, including the coal, for themselves. Similarly, when the Crow Indians ceded some of their land to the government in 1904 and the government opened it to white settlers, the government retained the mineral rights. But in 1947 and 1948 it returned those rights to the Crows, creating a situation of Indian tribal ownership of coal under white-owned ranches.

Strip mining was not a concern when the original homesteaders bought their lands. If the coal were ever to be mined, they and the sellers undoubtedly envisioned deep mining, which would have disturbed only a small part of the surface. A strip mine is a different matter, for it eats away the pasture, range, farmland, and buildings that constitute one's home and means of livelihood. The question of the surface owner's rights versus the rights of the purchaser of the coal beneath his land is a matter of contention and will inevitably be tested in the courts. But the necessity of acquiring separate items of coal rights and surface rights from different owners (and sometimes—when trying to create a large compact block of coal—from several different adjoining owners of both the coal and the surface) introduced bitter conflict and more confusion to the harassed region.

In Montana, a surface condemnation law that favored the coal purchasers made the situation worse. Under the influence of the

Anaconda Company, which had wished to condemn land for copper mining at Butte, that state in 1961 had declared mining a "public use" and had given mineral companies the right of eminent domain. Speculators, lease brokers, and the agents of corporations acquiring coal rights—sometimes even before they had bought the coal—now abused that law. They frightened many Montana landowners into signing exploration permits and leases or selling their lands on the purchaser's terms ("better than you'll get from any court"), and threatened condemnation proceedings against those who resisted. Episodes of angry confrontation and near violence multiplied as the purchasers—nervously eyeing the progress of competitors and aware of large secret corporate plans that depended on timely acquisitions—pressured the landowners.

The unpleasantness visited on the Boyd Charter family in the Bull Mountain region north of Billings is typical of many small, human agonies. The Bull Mountain area is a particularly fragile one, a grassy parkland with irregular topography that includes rimrock walls and picturesque hills covered with dense growths of ponderosa pine. Because coal seams are exposed on the rock walls and outcrop on the hillsides, contour stripping—the most destructive of all open-cut techniques—probably would be necessary, and reclamation to restore the present natural beauty and scenic values would be virtually impossible. A Montana Coal Task Force, established by the state government in August 1972, urged that no strip mining be permitted there unless a severe national coal shortage occurred in the future (an unlikely event for half a millennium), and Montana's Senator Mike Mansfield singled out the area as one district of the state in which strip mining should be banned outright.

Nevertheless, the Bull Mountain area contains approximately 130 million tons of coal, the rights to which were quietly purchased by Consolidation Coal Company in permits and leases from Burlington Northern railroad and the State of Montana. Owned by Continental Oil Company (whose chairman, John G. McLean, also head of the National Petroleum Council, has been in the forefront of industry leaders warning of an energy crisis and advocating governmental encouragement of western coal development), Consol, as the coal company is known, plans an $11.5 million strip mine in the Bull Mountains, to be worked over a 25-year period. Its initial production would be about two million tons a year, but the figure would rise. For the present, there are no plans for a mine-mouth power plant, and there is not enough coal to sustain a coal gasification development. Most of the coal would be shipped by train to customers in the upper Mississippi Valley, and a total of some 3,500 acres of the Bull Mountains would be subject to mining for those distant users, with additional acreage being disturbed by roads, installations, and the operations of the miners.

Though Consol officials recently made verbal promises to reshape the stripped land "to a contour similar to and compatible with its virgin contour, to save and replace topsoil, to revegetate, fertilize, and continue reclamation work, with as many replantings as necessary, until reclamation is successful," the company's leases, reflecting a traditional looseness in state and federal regulations, bound them to no such obligations. For instance, a lease made with Montana on June 3, 1970, for 640 acres of state-owned coal in the Bull Mountains merely obliged Consol "so far as reasonably possible" to "restore the stripped area and spoil banks to a condition in keeping with the concept of the best beneficial use," adding vaguely that "the lessee may prescribe the steps to be taken and restoration to be made." A $1,000 bond accompanied the lease, considered hardly enough to guarantee the reclamation of one acre in that area.

In 1970 Consol set about purchasing the surface rights necessary to make exploration drillings and mine the Bull Mountain coal. Many of the people in the nearest town, Roundup (population 2,800), welcomed the development. Small-scale deep mining had been done for many years in the Bull

Mountains; Tony Boyle, the former United Mine Workers president, had come from the area; and the townspeople, without landholdings at stake, saw prosperity for themselves in Consol's promise to spend $1,400,000 each year in the region and employ 80 men, whose needs, said the company, would generate 240 other jobs. To the Boyd Charters and other ranchers, however, plans for the strip mine became a nightmare.

Originally from western Wyoming, the Charters and their three sons and a daughter ran cattle on approximately 20 sections of land, 10 of which they owned and the rest leased from the Burlington Northern. Without warning, they were visited one day by a land agent from Consol, who told them that the company had bought the coal beneath their land from the federal government and the railroad and now wanted to drill exploratory core holes preparatory to mining. He produced a form for them to sign, offering one dollar to release the company from any damages done to their property by the drilling. When the Charters refused to sign, the agent left them and made a tour of other ranches, relating, according to the word of one ranch owner, that the Charters had signed, and thus winning the agreement of a few of them.

The company thereafter began harassing the Charters. Higher officials, including a Consol regional vice-president from Denver and company attorneys, began showing up at their home, increasing the pressure on them, and gradually driving the family frantic with worry. After numerous sessions the visits stopped, and the Charters wondered if condemnation proceedings, under the Montana law, were to be instituted against them. Then, one morning, they heard a racket near their house. They ran out, discovered a Consol crew drilling core holes on a deeded part of their land, and ordered them to stop. A fat man, according to Boyd Charter, came over to them, threatening a fist fight. "I got as much goddamn right on this land as you," he said. The infuriated Charters finally drove the crew off the property, and they have heard nothing more since then from Consol. But the company has tested all around the Charter ranch, it can get Burlington Northern to break the lease for its part of Charter's holdings, and it still intends to strip-mine the Bull Mountains in the near future. Far down the line from Continental Oil's national policy planner, John McLean, this small Montana ranching family is one of his victims.

Many similar conflicts have occurred elsewhere. Almost 150 miles by road southeast of the Bull Mountains, the Billings firm of Norsworthy & Reger helped Westmoreland Resources (a partnership of Westmoreland Coal, Kewanee Oil, Penn Virginia, Kemmerer Coal, and Morrison-Knudsen) assemble a package of rights to about one billion tons of very rich coal deposits at the head of Sarpy Creek for a huge strip mine and at least one coal gasification plant. The area, a beautiful basin under the pine-covered Wolf Mountains in southeastern Montana, encompassed land ceded by the Crow Indians. White ranchers now owned the surface, but the tribe still owned the coal. In a series of transactions, Norsworthy & Reger and E. B. Leisenring, Jr., a director of the Fidelity Bank in Pennsylvania, won permits for approximately 34,000 acres of Crow coal—apparently paying the Indians an average of $7.87 per acre and a royalty of 17.5 cents a ton for the first two years of production and 20 cents a ton for the next eight years—and then assigned their rights to Westmoreland Resources.

Surface rights still had to be won from the ranchers. Under threat of condemnation, some of them sold, but others resisted, including the family of John Redding. Westmoreland and its agents became desperate for the Reddings' signatures. The company had plans to begin stripping in March 1974; a giant 75-cubic-yard walking dragline was under construction; contracts were being made to sell 76.5 million tons of coal over a 20-year period to four Midwestern utilities (Wisconsin Power and Light, Iowa's Interstate Power Company, Wisconsin's Dairyland Power Cooperative, and Minnesota's Northern States Power Company to fuel a 1,600-megawatt generating plant near Henderson, Minnesota); and a 10-year option agreement for the delivery of a whopping 300 million tons of coal had been signed with Colorado Interstate Gas Company, which was planning to build up to four coal gasification plants in the region.

Moreover, the abundant and rich coal deposits guaranteed enormous growth potential in the value of the area. Consol was acquiring coal and surface rights nearby, with leases in which the language implied coal gasification plants and a large-scale industrialization of its own; and just to the east was still another huge developing coal-and-power center at Colstrip, where Montana Power Company was building new power-plant units, two transmission lines of which would come through the Sarpy district to Hardin, Montana. The region was going to become one of the principal new coal-based industrial centers in the northern plains, with a city of perhaps 25,000 people, and Westmoreland's plans and needs to assemble and invest capital required the combining of their package of coal and surface rights as quickly as possible.

On February 25, 1972, Billings attorney Bruce Ennis served written notice on the Reddings that unless they agreed to sell the entire, or necessary, portion of their ranch to Westmoreland at $137 an acre within one week, Westmoreland would begin condemnation proceedings against them. John Redding had come to Sarpy 56 years before, had lived in a tent, then a cabin, and finally had established a home, a family, and a 9,000-acre ranch. Through good years and lean, fighting the elements and the Depression, the Reddings had reflected the tradition of Westerners who treasured the place they lived because they could "stand tall and breathe free," and they now proved tougher than the coal company. Calling Ennis' bluff, they stood firmly over their property with gun in hand, and the company eventually backed away. "We've gotten enough people to agree that, at least for the time being, we don't have to go the condemnation route," Westmoreland's president, Pemberton Hutchinson, announced. "We needed to settle with eight landowners, and we settled with six—and that's enough." (Actually, at last count, there were still three holdouts, including one who claimed that a Westmoreland agent had told her, "You'll be down on your knees begging to sell." The lands of the holdouts are so strategically located as to split the coal company's surface rights and limit initial operations to a comparatively small tract.)

In four instances in a different area, but one connected with the Sarpy Creek development, landowners actually had condemnation proceedings instituted against them, but by Burlington Northern railroad, which is building a 37-mile spur line from its main tracks at Hysham, Montana, up Sarpy Creek to take out coal from the new Westmoreland mine. Ranchers and other landowners opposed the railroad's demands for right-of-way easements, often through the best parts of their land, and the conflicts became angry and tense. One woman, harassed by the railroad, suffered a nervous breakdown. Another, Mrs. Montana Garverich, 67 years old, a widow with 14 grandchildren and 8 great-grandchildren, who had lived on her land since 1912 and still operated her 4,000-acre ranch with the help of some of the children, fended off attempts to take her bottomland and was hauled into a U.S. District Court by the railroad. When the court found in favor of the Burlington Northern, Mrs. Garverich announced she would appeal, and the railroad, not relishing further action and its attendant publicity, rerouted its line in several places and dropped its suits.

As might be expected, hundreds of landowners in the three states, willingly or unwillingly, have already leased or sold their surface rights. Some, getting on in years and tired of a strenuous, often harsh, existence on the plains, did so happily, taking what they could get and planning on retirement to an easier life somewhere else. Others became frightened, were cajoled, or failed to understand what was involved, and signed whatever was asked of them, while still others hired lawyers, dickered back and forth, and finally felt they had outsmarted the purchaser and had gained a good deal for themselves. On the whole, the negotiated terms differed from one lease to another, depending on how badly a company wanted a particular right and how resistant the owner was. One rancher may have given up all his rights for a dollar an acre, while his neighbor received more than $100 an acre and a small percentage royalty on each ton of coal taken from beneath his surface. The operations of the land buyers inevitably stirred up jealousies and divisions within families and among old friends and neighbors, some of whom wanted to sell out while others hoped for a united show of resistance against the purchasers. At Sarpy Creek, at Otter, and elsewhere, distrust and defensiveness soured relationships that had existed happily for decades.

A division of opinion also affected those who did not have land at stake. Like the townspeople of Roundup, many citizens in all three states regard the coal-field development as an economic boon to the region and, not sharing the torment that such a point of view visits on a Montana Garverich or a John Redding, agree with the comment of Los Angeles financier Norton Simon, a development-minded director of the Burlington Northern: "For a state like Montana to have only 700,000 people is cockeyed." But others enjoy living on the northern plains precisely because of the small population and are fearful of pollution, the degradation of the environment, higher taxes, a change in life style, and other unfavorable impacts that the development will have on their part of the country and their lives.

Meanwhile, the absence of hard information concerning exactly what the impacts will be, and when they will start to be felt, has become something of a scandal. Despite all the developments that have occurred, not a single meaningful impact study has yet been made of any one of them; nor will an in-depth study be available for the region as a whole, or for any one of the affected states, until Secretary Morton's resource program report is finished at the end of 1975. It has been estimated that more than 5.5 million acres of federal- and Indian-owned land have already been let out in coal permits and leases. More acreage has been let out by the states, the railroads, and private individuals. In Montana, the Northern Plains Resource Council, checking documents on file in many of the counties, estimates that at least 1.7 million acres, more than half of that state's surface covering economically strippable reserves, are already signed away. The figures in Wyoming and North Dakota are believed to be far greater. But such information, lacking the addition of anything but occasional and very brief and bare corporate announcements on how a certain quantity of coal at some particular locality is to be utilized, has only increased the sense of helplessness.

In Wyoming, with strippable coal reserves of 23 billion tons in seven major coal areas, only a few of the mammoth projects that are certainly in store for the use of the resource have yet been described with any detail. Near Rock Springs, the $300 million, 1,500-megawatt Jim Bridger power plant is being constructed by Pacific Power & Light and Idaho Power Company, threatening an even worse degradation of Wyoming's air quality than is already caused by Pacific Power's offending 750-megawatt Dave Johnston plant at Glenrock on the North Platte River. And near Buffalo, Reynolds Metals has proposed the organization of a consortium of companies to build and operate a uranium enrichment plant requiring, according to Reynolds, "millions of kilowatts" of power. Coal for the power plant to supply electricity to the $2.5 billion project would come from a strip mine at the site, utilizing deposits of more than two billion tons owned by Reynolds. To provide the large amount of water that would be required, Reynolds has bought nearby Lake De Smet and has dammed Piney Creek for the diversion of its water into the lake, causing fears already among ranchers and farmers in that semiarid area of limited water. The uranium plant, the first one to be privately owned, might export some of its product to Japan; similarly, coal producers are known to be shopping for customers outside the United States. This raises the question of how valid is the exploitation of Western coal as an answer to the so-called energy crisis.

The Sierra Club, the Sheridan County Action Group, and several other Wyoming citizens' bodies, together with editor Tom Bell of the crusading *High Country News* in Lander, Wyoming, have tried to ring the alarm bells in that state. Very much a specter to them is the North Central Power Study's suggestion that ten 10,000-megawatt plants could be built in the Gillette area. That possibility is made more real by the knowledge that the massive, 100-mile-long Wyodak beds, all in Campbell County, contain more than 62 billion tons of coal—the national high for a county—and that a single township contains 2.87 billion tons in spectacular seams averaging about 70 feet in thickness and lying within 500 feet of the surface. A number of energy companies have paid record prices—as high as $505 an acre—for the Campbell County coal, but although the Black Hills Power & Light Company has been stripping some 500,000 tons of coal annually from the area for years, only one new development has yet occurred. In May, 1973, American Metal Climax's Amax arm opened the Belle Ayr mine to strip 6 million tons a year from its 6,000-acre holdings. Kerr-McGee, Exxon, Atlantic Richfield, Ark Land Company, Mobil and Cordero Mining (Sun Oil) are among the other large lease holders in the area, all capable of opening additional strip mines and building polluting complexes.

Moreover, the State of Wyoming generally, its governor and junior senator, and a majority of the members of the state legislature are development-oriented, welcoming the coal industrialization as a boost to the state's economy, and showing little appetite for conducting significant studies or enacting sufficiently strong reclamation and other laws that would give protection to the state but, at the same time, irritate and impede the energy companies.

In Montana, where large-scale coal mining is a new fact of life, the reverse is true, and state officials and agencies have, if anything, been ahead of many of the people in evidencing genuine concern over the uncontrolled character of the coal exploitation. On March 9, 1971, the state passed an Environmental Policy Act, which among other things, created a 13-member Environmental Quality Council, headed by George Darrow, a Billings geologist and state representative who had been one of the chief architects of the act. Fletcher E. Newby, another concerned Montanan, became executive director of the council, the functions of which include watchdogging the environmental problems in the state, recommending protective actions, and furthering state environmental impact statements. On August 2, 1972, on the recommendation of the council, the state created a Coal Task Force to watch the developing coal situation, identify problems, and recommend needed legislation or other action.

Both Montana bodies have tried to gather adequate information for laws necessary to protect the state, but cooperation from the federal level has been sorely missed. Aware of the regional character and the enormity of what was just beginning, the governor and state officers, from December 1971 on, appealed to the Environmental Protection Agency and various federal officials for a coordinated federal-state study of the total regional and state impacts of the coal development, but until the launching of the Interior Department's long-range study in late 1972, they were told that reviews could only be made of impact statements on individual projects. This was ironic, in view of the fact that the regulations requiring the filing of such statements were, themselves, not being enforced.

By the fall of 1972, the every-man-for-himself development in Montana, occurring without meaningful impact statements or regulations strong enough to provide protection to the environment, was becoming alarming. A study made by Thomas J. Gill for the state Environmental Quality Control, and based on data supplied by various state agencies, pointed out that total strip-mined coal production in Montana would jump from 1.5 million tons in 1971 to 16 million tons in 1973 and to 75 to 80 million tons in 1980. At the 16 million-ton level in 1973, 275 to 520 acres of Montana land would be disturbed by the mines. Four strip mines were already in operation in the state: at Colstrip, the Rosebud Mine of Western Energy, owned by Montana Power, was producing 5.5 million tons a year and in five years would raise the figure to 11.5 to 13 million tons, disturbing 240 to 350 acres annually. Also at Colstrip, Peabody Coal Company's Big Sky Mine was producing 2 million tons a year and would double the production in five years, disturbing 100 acres a year. In addition, Peabody was writing a mining plan for a new mine at Colstrip on 4,306.5 acres leased on April 1, 1971, without a preliminary environmental impact statement, from the Bureau of Land Management. At Decker, Montana, where Decker Coal Company, owned by Peter Kiewit and Pacific Power & Light, possessed 1 billion tons of strippable coal, the company had startled long-time ranchers in the area by disrupting a large part of the peaceful countryside within a matter of months, building a 16.5-mile-long railroad spur line, rerouting the main road, and beginning operations on a huge strip mine committed to ship 4 million tons of coal annually to the Midwest. The fourth mine, a smaller one operated by Knife River Coal Company, produced about 320,000 tons a year and disturbed 20 acres annually. The state also expected the big Westmoreland mine at Sarpy, the Consol mine in the Bull Mountains, and another Peabody mine on the Northern Cheyenne Indian Reservation to begin operations within a couple of years.

Reclamation of the mined land was only one of the problems posed by the increased stripping in the state. Neither federal nor state regulations written into the leases carried any guarantees that the lands would be successfully restored, and railroad, private, and Indian leases were so deficient that they almost guaranteed that there would be no reclamation. For anyone concerned about the preservation of the land, Montana Governor Thomas L. Judge pointed out to Congress early in 1973, "the lease agreements make sinister reading." One contract, for instance, gave a company the "right to use and/or destroy so much of said lands as may be reasonably necessary in carrying out such exploration and mining." Reclamation experiments were being carried out by Big Horn Coal Company and at Colstrip, but they were inconclusive. The best estimates were that it would take many years and successive replantings with much fertilizer and large amounts of water, and would cost upward of $500, perhaps as much as $5,000, per acre, before one could tell if reclamation had truly worked in that dry and fragile land of thin topsoil. Yet the leases carried no bonds, or ridiculously low ones, usually less than would be required to pay for the restoration of a single acre. A company could make a try at reclamation, then walk away, forfeiting the bond and leaving it to the state or someone else to struggle with reclamation problems.

In addition, there was little information available about water problems that would result from the strip mines. Some of them would seriously disturb patterns of drainage and surface runoff; at Decker, aquifers that lie among the coal deposits would disappear. The implications for the entire region's future water supply, especially as it felt the impact of increased demand for industry, were great, but no meaningful hydrological studies existed.

The power-plant problem in Montana, Gill's study showed, was still a relatively small cloud in the sky, but already an ominous one. On a 50-50 ownership basis with Puget Sound Power & Light Company, Montana Power was constructing two 350-megawatt units of a new plant at Colstrip, and had announced two more units of 700-megawatts each, with Puget Sound owning 75 per cent of them. The first units were to be completed in 1975 and 1976, and the next two in 1978 and 1979. An initial environmental impact study, based on data supplied by Montana Power, was submitted by the State Department of Health's Division of Environmental Sciences, but was deemed inadequate and deficient on many counts. Fears of ineffective emission controls; widespread pollution harmful to vegetation, trees, and livestock; degradation of the quality of the air; and disruption of the ecosystem of a large region all seemed justified to many of those who analyzed the study. A final, 400-page version was more complete, but failed to still the fears. Alarm was heightened, moreover, by the prospect that additional polluting power plants and otjer industrial installations were already being planned for the same area. In its own notice of appropriation for Yellowstone River water in 1970, Montana Power had indicated it planned to run a 31-mile-long, 60-inch pipeline, capable of conveying 250 cubic feet of water a second, from the river to Colstrip. This was more water than the power plant units would need, would divert from downstream users about one-eighth of the Yellowstone's water at low flow in an average year, and suggested a future use for something else, perhaps a coal gasification plant, at Colstrip.

As to water, the study noted that the state's total existing and potential supply from the rivers of the Yellowstone Basin was 1,735,000 acre-feet a year; yet energy companies (possibly planning gasification and liquefaction plants) had already received options from the Bureau of Reclamation for 871,000 to 1,004,000 acre-feet per year and had requested or indicated interest in another 945,000 acre-feet per year from those streams! Where this would ultimately leave farmers, ranchers, towns, Indian tribes, and others with claims on the water was not stated, but Gill suggested that "it seems safe to assume that a supply of water sufficient to accommodate the coal developments would require complete development of the area's water resources," including more dams, as well as the interbasin and interstate transportation of water via a network of aqueduct pipelines, built by the Bureau of Reclamation.

As if to underscore the pressures that were already building for water, Gill noted an intention of the HFC Oil Company of Casper, Wyoming, to construct two or more gasification plants in Dawson County, Montana; the proposed Colorado Interstate Gas plant at Sarpy, and another one near Hardin; and Consol's plan to build a complex of four of them on the Northern Cheyenne Indian Reservation in Montana. Since a three-plant complex would require 50,000 to 75,000 acre-feet a year, the total water needs, he suggested, would probably limit the number of complexes in Montana "to 12 or less," an observation that, in fact, focused on the one definitive limit (outside of the vast total coal supply) to the ultimate coal-field development of the entire region. In other words, he who gets the water can build, and after the water is all taken, there can be no more users.

Gill's study also dealt with looming problems of transmission line corridors. Much of the power generated at Colstrip would be transmitted to consumers in the Pacific Northwest, requiring corridors for new lines across central and western Montana as well as Idaho. Conflict was already breaking out with landowners over rights-of-way for a new 40-mile-long corridor in the Bitterroot Valley in the western part of the state, and it was only the forerunner of what was sure to be a mass of angry confrontations as more plants were built and more corridors were sought to carry power east and west to distant consumers.

The report finally mentioned problems of air pollution, the increase in population, and changes in the human environment. All were matters of pressing concern to the state, but in the absence of over-all planning and controls, none of them could be discussed intelligently until plans for each project were made public. Then the impacts would have to be assessed on an *individual* project basis—a sure formula for the rapid deterioration of the human and natural environment.

Montana's growing distress over these problems was reflected when the state legislature convened early in 1973. Numerous regulatory bills were introduced, and by April several significant ones had become law. Coal was eliminated from the condemnation statute, and operators were prohibited from prospecting or mining until they had secured the permission of the owners of the surface rights. Both measures came too late to help all those who had already sold their surface under threat, but they took some of the pressure off the many Boyd Charters and John Reddings who were still holding out. Ahead, however, lay legal battles over the rights of coal purchasers versus those of the landowners. The companies, claiming that other state and federal statutes gave them rights, felt that they still had ways of getting the surface rights they needed. The legislature also passed a strong reclamation law that spelled out required reclamation procedures in detail, increased sharply the state tax on coal, set up a Resource Indemnity Trust Fund to rectify damage to the environment caused by the extraction of nonrenewable natural resources, established a centralized system for water rights, and created a power facility siting mechanism, giving the state's Department and Board of Natural Resources and Conservation authority to approve the location of generation and conversion plants, transmission lines, rail spurs, and associated installations.

Still missing, at that late date, was convincing evidence of concern or commitment on the part of agencies of the federal government. A major portion of the coal lands in the northern plains is public domain, administered by the Bureau of Land Management of the Department of the Interior. Every aspect of the bureau's practices in the granting of federal coal permits and leases has been severely criticized in Congress and by the General Accounting Office. In March 1972, the General Accounting Office focused on the question of whether the United States was receiving a fair price for its coal, and concluded that it probably was not.

In the past, the lack of competition for western coal had permitted the securing of permits and leases for bonuses and royalties so low as to constitute a virtual steal in present-day terms. But the agreements ran for twenty years before they could be adjusted, and many of them still have long periods to run before the royalty can be raised. So the "steals" on those leases continue. Moreover, even the prices paid to the government today can be questioned. Permits and leases are awarded to applicants who pay the highest bonus in competitive bidding. But the royalty rate which the applicant must pay the government for each ton of coal produced is recommended to the Bureau of Land Management by the U.S. Geological Survey and is set as a fixed term or percentage for a specified number of years. Of late, the figures have usually been 17.5 cents for subbituminous coal and 15.5 cents for lignite—considered by many critics to be too low, in view of actual market conditions. In non-Bureau of Land Management deals, for example, producers have revealed with uninhibited realism the extent of their ravenous appetite for coal lands by offering higher royalties and letting speculators who assign them their rights tack on increased tonnage royalties for themselves. Moreover, companies who have leased the coal are now asking the federal government to do research that will establish the value of the coal—something which, if done before the leasing, might have gotten the government a higher price for it.

The General Accounting Office was even more critical on other points. Speculators could buy rights cheaply, hold onto them for long periods of time with no plans to mine the coal, then sell the rights at a large profit in the rising market. Reclamation and environmental requirements were almost nonexistent in older leases, and the Bureau of Land Management was ignoring this deficiency, waiting for each lease to come up for renegotiation on the twentieth year after the lease had been made. Newer leases had stiffer requirements, but they were not being enforced. In August 1972 a second General Accounting Office report spelled out its criticisms on this score more sternly, aiming its charges also at the Bureau of Indian Affairs, which was administering the leases of coal owned by Indian tribes. Technical examinations of environmental effects were not being conducted by either agency; coal operators were permitted to proceed with exploration and mining without approved plans; compliance and performance bonds covering the requirements, including reclamation, were not being obtained—or, if in some cases they were, the amounts were insufficient to cover estimated reclamation costs; required reports were not being received from operators; and procedures did not exist for the preparation of environmental impact statements, so they were not being made.

The criticisms pinpointed numerous violations of federal laws and the code of federal regulations by both the Bureaus of Land Management and Indian Affairs. The Department of the Interior made no meaningful response, and in October and November 1972, both Russell E. Train, chairman of the Council on Environmental Quality, and William D. Ruckelshaus, then administrator of the Environmental Protection Agency, urged the department to undertake remedial actions. Train particularly recommended an environmental impact statement on the overall coal leasing program. Except for directives to the field for a minor tightening up of enforcement procedures, silence in Washington continued, presumably because of a desire not to do anything until President Nixon's national energy policy could be prepared and made public or the Northern Great Plains Resource Program study could issue a report.

Meanwhile, Secretary of the Interior Morton refused to uphold a resolution passed by the United States Senate on October 12, 1972, calling for a moratorium on further coal leasing of federal lands in Montana for one year or until the Senate could act on strip-mining legislation. Senators Mike Mansfield and Lee Metcalf of Montana and Frank E. Moss of Utah wrote angrily to Morton, terming his decision "arrogance of the executive branch" and "unconscionable," and criticizing his statement that the Senate could rely on the regulations of the Interior Department to guarantee "environmentally acceptable mining."

Actually, after April 1971, the Bureau of Land Management had held up the approval of all federal coal permits and leases in the northern plains until it could assess how much coal was already under lease and ascertain the demand and need for additional coal. It was conducting a study of the coal-rich Birney-Decker area in the Tongue River Basin of southeastern Montana, where many applicants hoped to secure rights to deposits of some 11 billion tons, and it used the study as one of the excuses for the unofficial moratorium. But the study was released (angering the coal companies by proposing the mining of only a limited strip, two townships wide, just north of the Montana-Wyoming border—"leaving out the best coal and including only the poorest area," according to one operator), and still no new Bureau of Land Management leases were approved. But now, according to Secretary Morton, the department would proceed "cautiously on a case-by-case basis," suggesting to the companies that even the desired part of the Birney-Decker region would soon be opened to them.

In a Senate speech on January 12, 1973, Mansfield called attention to what the energy crisis was doing to his state, complaining that the individual landowner was being treated "shabbily," attacking the utilities and coal companies for "approaching this situation with little compassion and regard for the future of this part of our nation," and asserting that "if we cannot have orderly and reasonable development of the vast coal resources in Montana and the west, there should be no strip mining of coal."

Meanwhile, if the federal government was not protecting the non-Indian people of the region, it was actually selling out the Indians. The General Accounting Office criticisms of the Bureau of Indian Affairs merely scratched the surface of the derelictions of government trust obligations to the tribes. Indian lands in Montana contain approximately one-third of the state's total 30 billion tons of strippable coal reserves. Some of it is owned by the Fort Peck Indian Reservation in northeastern Montana, but the largest and most valuable deposits underlie the entire Crow and Northern Cheyenne reservations in the southeastern part of the state, roughly in the heart of the prized Colstrip-Gillette area. Beginning in 1966, the Bureau of Indian Affairs—which as legal protector of Indian resources must approve all tribal permits and leases—brought coal companies to the Northern Cheyenne tribal council, encouraging that body ultimately to sign a total of eleven exploratory permits for the tribe's land. Uninformed of the ramifications of strip mining and of the omissions and deficiencies of Bureau of Indian Affairs coal leases (the terms and regulations of which adhered pretty closely to those of the Bureau of Land Management), the tribal council put its trust in the Bureau of Indian Affairs, one of whose officials was quoted as saying as late as 1972, "There are indications coal will be a salable product for only a few years." Encouraged to take money while the taking seemed good (bonuses, rentals with a floor of 1 dollar an acre, and royalties of 17.5 cents a ton), the tribe let out to Peabody, Amax, Consol, Norsworthy & Reger, and Bruce Ennis a total of 243,808 acres—a startling 56 per cent of the reservation's entire acreage!

The permits were loosely worded as to reclamation and other environmental considerations; and, like Bureau of Land Management and most other permits, gave the operators the right to exercise lease options which were appended as part of the original agreements and which set forth the monetary and other terms of the leases. Thus, a permit holder could explore for the coal, discover its value, then secure it without the seller being able to negotiate for the really true value of the coal. The leases, in turn, gave the purchaser the right to use the Indian land for all manner of buildings and installations necessary for the production, processing, and transportation of the coal, opening the way for the construction of power, conversion, and petrochemical plants, railroad lines, associated industrial complexes, and new towns of non-Indians, whose numbers would submerge the approximately 2,500 Northern Cheyennes and turn the reservation quickly into an industrialized white man's domain.

Most members of the tribe were uninformed about the terms of the leases, but when Peabody and Amax exploration crews appeared, drilling among Indian burial grounds and disrupting the Indians' lives, friction and unrest developed rapidly. Fearful for the future of the reservation, their culture, and the tribe itself, a number of Indians, mostly those who held allotments of their own land on the reservation, formed the Northern Cheyenne Landowners' Association to oppose the coal development. At almost the same time, Consol entered negotiations with the tribal council for another 70,000 acres of the tribe's land (which would have brought the total acreage held by permittees to 72 per cent of the reservation). Consol's proposal, which was not made public to the tribal members, offered $35 an acre and a royalty of 25 cents a ton (7.5 cents above what the federal government was getting for Bureau of Land Management coal and what the Indians had received in all previous leases).

To the startled Indians, Consol explained that it intended to invest approximately $1.2 billion in an industrial complex that would include four coal gasification units and that implied a city of perhaps 30,000 non-Indian people on the small reservation. The company was in a rush to get the permit signed. It urged the Indians to forgo the usual practice of asking for competitive bids (it would mean "the loss of several months'" income to them), and it offered the tribe $1.5 million toward the cost of a new health center (needed badly by the Indians, but also by the non-Indian industry, the white employees of which would, according to a clause in the proposed agreement, have access to the facility—inevitably becoming the center's major users). It also tried to pressure the Indians with a threat: "If Consol cannot conclude negotiations with the Northern Cheyenne tribe at an early date, Consol will be forced to take this project elsewhere . . . this project will be lost to the Northern Cheyenne, and it may be a long time before a project of this magnitude comes again, if ever."

But the company, which had prospective customers of its own for the coal, needed the deal more than the Indians did. Word of the proposal leaked out to the Northern Cheyenne Landowners' Association, and public meetings were held, cautioning the tribal council to go slowly. The higher price offered by Consol for the coal started some new thinking. Gradually, the tribal council could recognize problems with all the permits. The exercise by Peabody of its options to lease raised the question of whether the coal company should have had to negotiate anew, treating the leases as separate documents and letting the tribe ask for a fairer price for the coal. The company's activities also were causing many resentments among the Indians; the terms of the Peabody lease were now seen to be too loose for the protection of the reservation; the enforcement of strip-mining procedures in the code of federal regulations was not being observed by the Bureau of Indian Affairs; and the possibility that corporations would erect gasification plants and other installations on Peabody's leased land posed a fearful threat to the Indians' future. The same questions were raised about Amax's permit, while in connection with a third permit, given to Bruce Ennis, the Billings lawyer, and then assigned by him to Chevron, the Indians wondered if this had been speculation with their property and if Ennis had received a royalty from Chevron on top of their own 17.5 cents—which would have been illegal.

After more public meetings and deliberations, the Northern Cheyennes called in an attorney of the Native American Rights Fund in Boulder, Colorado, for advice and to write an environmental code that would protect the reservation. Other attorneys were consulted, and on March 5, 1973, postponing further consideration of the Consol proposal, with its threat of gasification plants, the Northern Cheyennes demanded that the Bureau of Indian Affairs declare null and void all their existing coal permits and leases. At the same time, the tribe implied that if the agency refused to undertake such action, the Northern Cheyennes would consider suing the federal government for not having protected the tribe and its resources, either in the drawing up and approval of the agreements or in the observance of provisions in the code of federal regulations. The tribal council indicated, moreover, that the Indians might prefer to mine and market their own coal themselves, drawing on independent expertise and, with the advice of competent environmental scientists, protecting the reservation with proper planning, regulations, and controls.

While the tribe's demand was being pondered by solicitors of the Interior Department, the coal companies' plans went forward. On March 21, 1973, Peabody announced it would supply 500 million tons of coal from its Northern Cheyenne strip mine to the Northern Natural Gas Company of Omaha and the Cities Service Gas Company of Oklahoma City, which jointly would build four gasification plants, at a cost of $1.4 billion, presumably in the vicinity of the mine. Each plant would employ up to 600 people (meaning an influx of many more non-Indians), and construction of the first plant would start in 1976. Peabody's coal, moreover, would only fuel two of the giant plants; the gas companies would need another 500 million tons from a second mine, which the Indians guessed would be opened by one of the other permit holders.

Somewhat similar events were transpiring, meanwhile, on the Crow Indian Reservation, which abuts that of the Northern Cheyennes. The Crows had let out permits for 292,680 acres, including rights to the coal in the off-reservation Sarpy area, the surface of which the Crows no longer owned. Some of the rights to that coal had been bought from them for 17.5 cents a ton by Norsworthy & Reger, which had then assigned the rights to Westmoreland. In view of the situation on the Northern Cheyenne Reservation, the Crows began to question the 17.5 cents-a-ton price they had received, as well as a 5 cents-a-ton overriding royalty that Westmoreland had paid Norsworthy & Reger, making it clear that Westmoreland had actually been willing to pay at least 22.5 cents for the coal.

In addition, when making the original deal, Norsworthy & Reger had persuaded the Crows that they could not sell their coal unless they also handed over rights to 30,000 acre-feet of water a year (which would be needed for gasification plants). Unknowledgeably, the Crows obliged, transferring one of their water options from agricultural to industrial use and turning it over to Norsworthy & Reger. Altogether, in fact, the Crows gave away to the different coal companies valuable options for 140,000 acre-feet of water per year without a penny of payment. Testimony by James Reger to the Montana Water Resources Board in Helena on May 20, 1971, relating how he had maneuvered the water from the Crows, angered the Indians when, almost two years later, it came to their attention. Again, the tribe felt that the Bureau of Indian Affairs had not offered protection, and now, as with the Northern Cheyennes, violations were noted in all the permits, and fears were raised for the people's future. Early in 1973, lease options were exercised by Gulf and Shell for reservation lands. A report was circulated that a non-Indian city of up to 200,000 people was being considered for the neighborhood of Wyola or Lodge Grass on the reservation. Sentiment for canceling all the tribe's leases spread rapidly, and the tribal chairman, meeting with attorneys and Montana environmental experts, indicated that the Crows might take actions paralleling those of the Northern Cheyennes.

The resentments of the two tribes could seriously threaten some of the major projects being planned for the heart of one of the principal coal fields. As such, they would prove a significant impediment to the federal government's encouragement of the full-scale exploitation of the western coal. But there is a greater threat inherent in the indictment that Indians, once again, were defrauded by their trustee, the Bureau of Indian Affairs, which, abetting the coal companies, opened the reservations to an exploitation marked by unfair terms, lack of protection, and deceit. Throughout the country, other Indians are coming to recognize that the massive nature of the coal developments means the end of the Crow and Northern Cheyenne reservations as they have been, and, with it, the almost certain extinction of those peoples as tribal groups. As a result, the situation has a growing significance to all Indians and bids fair to become another source of explosive confrontation between Native Americans and the federal government.

The lack of impact statements, the nonobservance of regulations, and the many violations of laws that have characterized the first years of the coal rush throughout the region have provided concerned environmentalists with opportunities for numerous lawsuits. The Natural Resources Defense Council, the Environmental Defense Fund, the Sierra Club, and other organizations, consulting with attorneys, scientists, landowners, and environmental advocates like William L. Bryan, Jr. in the region, are currently preparing a number of cases which may attack some of the worst evils, bring about tighter controls and a modicum of order, and slow the headlong exploitation. In addition, an independent committee of twelve prominent natural scientists headed by Dr. Thadis W. Box, dean of the College of Natural Resources at Utah State University in Logan, was formed in April 1973 under the auspices of the National Academy of Sciences and the National Academy of Engineering. The committee reviewed the ecological and environmental consequences of the coal and power operations, and its report was completed in July 1973. Meanwhile, each week new projects are announced, the hurried pattern of development grows more chaotic, and the threat to the northern plains increases.

In Wyoming, Tipperary Resources, holder of 1 billion tons of coal, announces that it will build a 1,200-megawatt power plant near Buffalo, using water from 58 wells in the dry country; a new Atlantic Richfield strip mine will ship 10,000 tons of coal a day to Oklahoma; Wyodak Resources Development Corporation will build a 200- to 300-megawatt plant near Gillette, using 1 to 1.5 million tons of strip-mined coal a year; and the total

Wyoming coal production will jump from 10.9 million tons in 1972 to 30 million tons in 1976. In Montana, Basin Electric Power Cooperative will build a generating plant to send power to eight states; coal will be shipped to two 600-megawatt plants that will be built in Oregon; a new Montana Power transmission line is planned to run from Anaconda to Hamilton, another from Billings to Great Falls, small parts of an eventual great new network.

In North Dakota, more than 2 million acres of land are believed already leased for strip mines; companies holding rights to 1 billion tons of coal in Hettinger County will build 4 large-scale power plants; the Michigan Wisconsin Pipe Line Company, arranging for the purchase of 1.5 billion tons of strip-mined lignite from the North American Coal Corporation, asks for 375,000 acre-feet of water per year from Garrison Reservoir on the Missouri River, enough for no less than 22 gasification plants; still another company wants water for 8 more gasification plants. And so it goes.

The horrors conjured up by the North Central Power Study in 1971 are coming true even faster than that document proposed—without the focus for planning and control which its blueprint provided. Is it, then, all over for the northern plains? Will they inevitably become another Appalachia? On the Tongue River near Birney, Montana, where strip mines, power plants, gasification plants, and other industrial installations threaten the land, air, water, and quality of life of the Irving Alderson, Jr. family, fifth-generation owners of the Bones Brothers Ranch, Mrs. Alderson gives voice to a desperate, last-ditch courage that says there is still time to save the region:

"To those of you who would exploit us, do not underestimate the people of this area. Do not make the mistake of lumping us and the land all together as 'overburden' and dispense with us as nuisances. Land is historically the central issue in any war. We are the descendants, spiritually, if not actually, of those who fought for this land once, and we are prepared to do it again. We intend to win."

SUGGESTED READINGS

Box, Thadis, W. et al., 1973, Potential for Rehabilitating Land Surface—Mined for Coal in the Western United States: National Science Foundation—National Academy of Engineering.

Caudill, Harry M., 1963, *Night Comes to the Cumberlands,* Boston: Atlantic-Little, Brown.

Caudill, Harry M., 1973, Farming and Mining, *Atlantic Monthly,* September 13, 1973, pp. 85-90.

Conaway, James, 1973, "The Last of the West: Hell, Strip It!," *Atlantic Monthly,* September 13, 1973, pp. 91-103.

Frank, Robert, 1972, Biological Effects of Air Pollution: *AAAS/CEA Power Study Group,* Section 1, Chapter 2, pp. 31-49.

Gillette, Robert, 1973, Western Coal: Does the Debate Follow Irreversible Commitment?, *Science 182,* pp. 456-458.

Strip and Surface Mine Study Policy Committee, 1967, Surface Mining and Our Environment: U.S. Dept. of Interior, Washington, D.C., 124 p.

Wolf, Anthony, 1972, Showdown at Four Corners: *Saturday Review,* June 3, 1972, pp. 29-41.

NUCLEAR FISSION AS AN ENERGY SOURCE

The San Onofre nuclear generating station near San Clemente, California. It provides 430 megawatts (electric), enough to supply well over a half a million users. The sphere houses a pressurized water reactor. (Photo courtesy of the Southern California Edison Company.)

View of the exterior Westinghouse turbine and generator at the San Onofre nuclear generating station. (Photo courtesy of J. R. Lennartson, Westinghouse Electric Corporation.)

The control room of the San Onofre nuclear generating station. Any one of approximately 60 types of malfunction will shut down the plant automatically. (Photo courtesy of the Southern California Edison Company.)

Fueling the San Onofre nuclear generating station. Note the bundle of fuel rods making up this fuel assembly. (Photo courtesy of the U.S. Atomic Energy Commission.)

The Experimental Breeding Reactor II at Argonne National Laboratory's Idaho site. The power plant is at the left, the reactor containment shell, center, and the fuel cycle facility, behind the stack. (Photo courtesy of Argonne National Laboratory.)

INTRODUCTION

Nuclear power is emerging as perhaps the most controversial and bitterly contested issue thrust into the public arena by the declining production of conventional fossil fuels. Unfortunately, the level of the public debate has often suffered from an excess of dogmatism and emotion and a paucity of information and analysis. Certainly, no major energy resource poses the dilemmas surrounding its utilization in quite as stark and dramatic a fashion as does nuclear power. Recently, however, many of these issues have been analyzed in depth by both public and private studies. In this chapter, we present both basic information on nuclear fission itself and analyses of the most serious problems involved in harnessing nuclear energy.

Proponents of nuclear energy point to the relatively pollution-free power to be obtained (compared to coal plants), the relative economic advantage of fission over fossil energy, the impeccable safety record of the commercial nuclear industry, and the large potential resource, particularly with the breeder program. Opponents warn of the environmental risks of radiation emission in the nuclear fuel cycle, uncertainties inherent in the analysis of catastrophic reactor accidents, the lack of fully tested and implemented radioactive waste storage procedures, and the increased risks of nuclear proliferation and terrorism implicit in a "plutonium economy." Certainly all who have studied nuclear energy recognize the imperatives of keeping nuclear wastes out of the biosphere and nuclear materials out of the hands of terrorists. Differing perspectives on nuclear power arise from differing evaluations of the feasibility of satisfying these imperatives.

Since nuclear fission does pose such severe dilemmas for society, it is essential that its risks and benefits be widely understood. Public policy is determined as much by *perceptions of the truth* as by *the truth* itself. Hence, we present here both factual information on the characteristics of nuclear fission energy and a range of interpretations on the implications of nuclear energy for the social system.

In *The Impact of Technical Advice on the Choice for Nuclear Power,* John Steinhart recounts the development of national policies on nuclear power and describes the personalities that helped shape them. While the article places no blame for past nuclear energy decisions, it does raise an interesting question on how different the history of energy development might have been had experts from other energy fields been represented in the decision-making process. The strong impetus for the development of nuclear energy is interpreted as a natural result of the emergence of the nuclear physicists and chemists from the Manhattan Project as the leading government science advisors. This thesis is further substantiated by the relatively reduced emphasis on nuclear power given by the new generation of science advisors, which is gradually replacing that described in this article.

James Duderstadt presents a comprehensive survey of fission reactor technology, ranging from the basic fission process itself through advanced reactor design concepts, in *Nuclear Power Generation*. The wealth of material includes a description of reactor operations, the nuclear fuel cycle, and safety and environmental aspects, and then introduces concepts on the economics and reliability of nuclear power plants. The article concludes with a concise introduction of the issues involved in nuclear energy, with a perceptive analysis of the conscious and subconscious factors underlying the nuclear debate.

Nuclear fission would certainly be an ideal energy source if it were not for two serious associated risks: (a) the radioactive by-products of the nuclear fuel cycle, which are dangerous to living things, and (b) the basic fuel in the proposed plutonium fuel cycle, which is bomb-grade material. The first of these problems is analyzed in considerable depth by Bernard Cohen in *Impacts of the Nuclear Energy Industry on Human Health and Safety*. The data on routine emissions, risks of major accidents, problems of transportation and waste disposal, and plutonium toxicity are considered together with the known biological effects of radiation to calculate the detrimental effects on human health. Although the author in no way suggests ignoring the potential hazards posed by each of these aspects of nuclear power generation, he does suggest that a more realistic perspective on these risks involves comparing them with the risks involved in other human activities.

The next five articles assess in detail the most serious issues concerning fission energy. Representing as they do the authors' personal perspectives, these articles illustrate the wide range of interpretations held by reputable authorities on these crucial issues.

More details on the techniques used in evaluating the risks of catastrophic accidents are provided in the *Reactor Safety Study: An Assessment of Accident Risks in United States Commercial Nuclear Power Plants*. In this study, the U.S. Nuclear Regulatory Commission presents the conclusions of an intensive three-year study by a group of over 50 scientists and engineers headed by Professor Norman Rasmussen of the Massachusetts Institute of Technology. Although funded by the federal government, this report provides an independent assessment of the risks of catastrophic accident in commercial reactors. Using "event and fault tree analysis" techniques, the report concludes that the danger of accident from 100 commercial reactors is roughly comparable to that posed by meteor impact.

Proposals for dealing with the troublesome problem of the disposal of radioactive fission by-products are presented in *Alternatives for Managing Post-Fission Nuclear Wastes,* by A. M. Platt and J. W. Bartlett. This condensation of the much more detailed ERDA-76-43 report summarizes the major waste management proposals now under consideration and presents useful data on the quantities of wastes resulting from each stage of the fuel cycle process. Although the report makes no recommendations as to which of the alternatives is the most desirable, it does indicate that there is a range of feasible options for solving this problem. The eventual choice of a particular alternative will involve social and political factors, some of which are discussed in the following articles.

In *Toxicity of Plutonium and Some Other Actinides,* John Edsall discusses the dangers posed by the primary fuel and by-product of the proposed breeder reactor "plutonium economy." Evidence from studies that question the present standards for maximum permissible dose is presented, and the disturbing possibility is suggested that the "linear hypothesis" may not be the most conservative hypothesis after all. Some studies indicate that a given amount of radiation at low rates of exposure may be more dangerous than the same amount delivered over a shorter period of time. Professor Edsall concludes that the advantages offered by plutonium as a fuel are not worth the uncertain risks involved.

The second major risk intrinsic to the plutonium economy, that of diversion of bomb-grade materials, is analyzed by Harold Feiveson and Theodore Taylor in *Security Implications of Alternative Fission Futures.* The widespread distribution of plutonium required by a plutonium-based breeder reactor system would greatly increase the likelihood of nuclear weapons proliferation and terrorism. The thorium-232, uranium-233 breeder cycle, on the other hand, provides substantially less risk, since expensive isotope separation facilities would be required to obtain material for bomb production. The article proposes very thoughtful safeguard principles to which any eventual nuclear fuel cycle should conform, to replace our past policy of trying to tack adequate control measures onto established technologies.

One aspect of nuclear power that has been much debated, but poorly understood, is that of its economics. David Montgomery and James Quirk discuss the forces shaping the nuclear economics picture in *Cost Escalation in Nuclear Power.* The history of the growth of the commercial reactor industry is traced and correlated with the affect of federal support and "turnkey" contracts from reactor manufacturers. The role of capital cost inflation, labor cost increases, interest rate increases, and stiffer licensing and regulation procedures are indicated for several periods of reactor development. Interestingly enough, although nuclear power costs were seriously underestimated by both utilities and manufacturers, the authors conclude that "utility decisions to adopt nuclear power were probably reasonable at the time and correct after the fact." Since the economics of nuclear power will clearly play a determining role in its future, this economic history is important.

Since the social implications of nuclear power are so profound and far reaching, several organizations have undertaken independent assessments of various aspects of the nuclear energy industry. *Policy Studies of Nuclear Futures* by Carol Steinhart summarizes the findings and recommendations of several of the more important studies. The major issues of safety, environmental and health effects, waste management, weapons proliferation, and terrorism are clearly delineated and the findings of each study group is analyzed. The decision as to which alternative nuclear future we will pursue is a momentous one, and the independent evaluations summarized here deserve the attention of everyone involved in making the decision. The recent change in emphasis in the U.S. breeder program indicates that these studies are getting attention at the highest levels of government.

In the next two chapters, we present energy alternatives available from such sources as solar energy and nuclear fusion energy and by energy conservation, all of which are highly desirable and should be pursued with the greatest urgency. The fact remains, however, that the only realistic options presently available to electric utilities for meeting increased demand are coal- or uranium-fueled plants. These restraints raise some very real dilemmas that must be faced by environmentalists and hard-line "growth" addicts alike. They include:

(1) The human and social costs of not having enough energy. The law now requires environmental impact statements for every new power plant, and in the case of nuclear plants, stringent licensing and regulation procedures. In addition, most utilities are, in fact, under legal requirement to meet the increased demand. Perhaps the role of the environmental impact statement should be broadened to include the social consequences (such as possible equipment burnout, plant shutdowns, unemployment, lower standard of living, and the resulting decline in human health and happiness) of the decision not to build the plant.

(2) The relative environment impacts of coal versus nuclear power. This is an issue addressed directly by Comar and Sagan in Article 3 and again by Cohen in Article 16, but it is one that is usually completely ignored by both electric utilities and environmentalists for different reasons. Historically, coal has not faced the rigorous environmental scrutiny applied to nuclear reactors. If environmental concern were proportional to presently recognized hazards to human welfare, coal power would receive orders of magnitude more opposition than nuclear power.

Instead, it seems to be receiving tacit, if not overt support, by environmentalists opposed to nuclear power.

(3) Appropriate and cost-effective investments in safety. For an extra 10 to 20 per cent increase in the cost, nuclear plants could be built deep enough underground to provide the safety margin to satisfy the harshest nuclear safety critic. This expenditure of some $200 million would reduce the risk from about the 0.06 fatalities expected per year to virtually zero. Air travel, however, is 3,000 times as dangerous as the whole nuclear power industry, and motor vehicle transportation 75,000 times as dangerous. If our concern were truly for human health and welfare, would it not be the more socially responsible investment to spend this money to alleviate the really serious risks?

(4) The shifting sands of nuclear opposition. The history of the opposition to nuclear power can be classified into fairly clearly defined periods. The early period was the "30,000 annual deaths from routine emissions" period and lasted from the late 1960's to the early 1970's. As this threat faded in the light of actual operating data, we entered the "catastrophic accident" period of 1971 through 1975, which closed as the Rasmussen and subsequent reports were issued. We then went through a brief "impossible to manage those nuclear wastes" period and now are in the midst of the "terrorism and nuclear proliferation" period. This is the most durable of the issues yet proposed because of our inability to quantify the risks. This issue certainly deserves the attention of policy-makers, and the tightened security at reactor installations and changes in the construction schedule for the breeder program indicate that it is getting such attention.

(5) Implications of the fission economy. The problems implicit in the use of fission energy are very real, and although they may have technological solutions, the impact on society of implementing these solutions will be significant and perhaps severe. Already, "improvements in plant security" have resulted in eliminating civilian tours of reactor facilities and arming guards with automatic weapons. If the plutonium breeder reactor program is carried out, such security restrictions will increase manyfold. How much freedom are we willing to sacrifice to buy the security essential for the safe use of this source?

The whole reactor program itself is, in a sense, in a precarious position. If a relatively serious (10 to 100 deaths) reactor accident did occur, even though its likelihood is small, there could be a huge public uproar with calls for investigations and demands to close down all reactors until it was proven that this could never happen again. Since such proof is impossible, such an event could eliminate over 10 per cent of our installed electrical capacity. And a similar public reaction could result from an international incident involving the hijacking of nuclear material and the use of a crude nuclear bomb. Serious questions may be raised about the wisdom of relying so heavily on such a vulnerable energy source.

(6) The symbolic aspect of nuclear power. Many of the really emotional social concerns of former years are now gone. The Vietnam War is over,

minorities and women have achieved formal legal protection of their rights, and even the environment has received some legal protection and is improving in many instances. This leaves nuclear power as the lightening rod which attracts much of the alienation and discontent present in any free society. Nuclear power symbolizes bigness, impersonal corporate policies, and complex technology that many who long for the simple life see as the root of all evil. On the other hand, to those more technologically inclined, nuclear power is a gleaming symbol of man's desire to ''beat their swords into plowshares'' and provide a clean, nearly inexhaustible supply of energy. An appreciation of these symbolic aspects of nuclear power will help interpret many of the more subjective sections of the following material.

The Impact of Technical Advice on the Choice for Nuclear Power 14

JOHN S. STEINHART 1974

In 1954, the first nuclear-powered electric generating plant was placed in service near Moscow. That same year the United States launched the first nuclear submarine, *Nautilus*. At the time these developments appeared promising. If there was some nagging worry that, as a military ship, the *Nautilus* represented another step in an arms race, it also might be a step toward the widespread economical nuclear-powered transportation that many hoped for. The accomplishment of the Soviet Union seemed to show that our own hopes for cheap nuclear electric power were possible.

This kind of tangible achievement must have been welcome to politicians as well as the public, because the 1954 budget assigned more than 1.2 billion dollars to the Atomic Energy Commission, and the Atomic Energy Commission had been spending about 1 in every 7 research dollars expended from the public purse. Nor were these expenditures new. By then more than $6 billion of public funds had been invested in nuclear reactor research and development.[1] If the long-promised peaceful uses of nuclear energy did not come to fruition, we would have been left with the most terrible weapons of war ever devised as the principal result of the vast expenditure of public funds and technical talent. It would not have seemed like much of a bargain in those days of the politics of "brinkmanship."

By 1957, when the first United States nuclear power station was put into service in Shippingport, Pennsylvania, the commitments of public funds and the efforts of many of our finest scientists had continued for more than a decade. It is a fair question to ask: What forces carried this commitment forward for so long, at such public expense, without more in the way of practical results? Clearly, our society made a decision to pursue nuclear energy as a power source. It is my purpose to

1. U.S. Bureau of the Census, Historical Statistics of the United States, Colonial Times to 1957, Washington, D.C., 1960.

Original article by Dr. John S. Steinhart. Dr. Steinhart is professor of geology and geophysics and environmental studies at the University of Wisconsin-Madison. He has engaged in extensive science advisory work, having served in the Office of Science and Technology, Executive Office of the President, 1968–1970. He is associate director of the Marine Studies Center at the University of Wisconsin-Madison and coauthor of a recent book, *Energy: Source, Use, and Role in Human Affairs*.

examine the circumstances and machinery under which this decision was made.

Two disclaimers seem necessary at the outset. First, the desirability or hazards of a nuclear powered future have been discussed elsewhere in this volume in considerable detail. I do not propose to enter this argument, nor to pass final judgment on the merits of the case. It is sufficient to note that there is a real dispute among competent, sober analysts. Second, since the following discussion often must examine the performance of a scientific advisory apparatus made up of real people, I must state that hindsight may reveal things not obvious at the time, and that these advisors (many of whom are colleagues, acquaintances and friends) are, as far as I know, honest and able persons of good intentions.

The question is this: How have we embarked on a nuclear-powered future, what mechanisms have continued the commitment in the face of the dispute about the decision, and how may future policy for energy be affected by this history? In a larger sense, these questions could and should be asked for any technical decision that may be made in a democratic society. If we are unable to anticipate the consequences of our technical decisions with the institutional machinery at hand, we stand continually vulnerable in a society increasingly shaped by technological change.

THE EARLY DAYS OF TRAGEDY AND EUPHORIA

On August 7, 1945 the atom bomb exploded in the air over Hiroshima. The grisly results may have been exaggerated by the press that day, but subsequent radiation deaths and genetic damage produced a toll that is still being counted. It is not that the results were quantitatively unprecedented, for one massive fire bomb raid on Tokyo produced as much or more death and tragedy, but, thought most of us, "a single bomb from a single plane. . . ." In a different way the bomb burst upon the American people and most of the elected officials in Washington. Awe at the technical achievement, horror at the human suffering, optimism about the imminent end of the trauma of World War II, and just plain bewilderment underlay the talk at the corner tavern and in congressional cloakrooms. German nuclear physicists, interned in England, at first refused to believe it. Among them, Otto Hahn (who later received a Nobel Prize for the discovery of fission) considered suicide.[2] The American pilot of the plane that dropped the bomb in Hiroshima went slowly and publicly mad.

In the years just following World War II, the awe won out among these conflicting emotions, at least in the government of the United States. Scientists fresh from the wartime technical successes were summoned before the Congress and sought out as evening speakers or special attractions at Washington meetings. David Lilienthal, who became the first chairman of the Atomic Energy Commission, described the situation this way:

> The scientist's mastery of nature, as so dramatically evidenced by the Atom, was expected to lead to the conquest of hunger, of poverty, and of the greatest of human ills: war. As "Master of the Atom," the scientist had transformed the world. His views on all subjects were sought by newspapermen, by Congressional committees, by organizations of all kinds; he was asked in effect to transfer his scientific mastery to the analysis of the very different questions of human affairs: peace, world government, population control, military strategy, and so forth. And his authority in these nonscientific areas was, at least at first, not strongly questioned.[3]

Almost all the scientists were strongly affected by their wartime experiences. Much has been written about the wartime scientific projects of the Office of Scientific Research and Development, and especially about the building of the bomb.[4] The paths of a number

2. Jungk, Robert, *Brighter Than a Thousand Suns,* Harcourt Brace Jovanovich, Inc., New York, 1958, p. 220.
3. Lilienthal, D. E., *Change, Hope and the Bomb,* Princeton Univ. Press, Princeton, N.J., 1963, p. 64.
4. Among the numerous accounts of the building of the bomb, three especially illuminating and well-written ones are: Jungk, Robert, *op. cit.;* Laurence, W. L., *Men and Atoms,* Simon & Schuster, New York, 1962, 319 p.; Davis, N.P., *Lawrence and Oppenheimer,* Simon & Schuster, New York, 1968, 384 p.

of extraordinarily intelligent physicists had been crossing and recrossing from early days at Gottingen and elsewhere. They and their teachers restructured physics almost completely. These dizzy heights of discovery and achievement were lived out in the presence of (but separate from) the gathering storm of World War II. Then, increasingly, their private lives were uprooted as European colleagues fled to Britain and the United States. Colleagues in the Soviet Union became silent and were sometimes imprisoned.

As World War II began, these scientists shared with almost everyone else, an overwhelming sense of the morality of the Allied cause and the grimness of the Axis threat. When they were mobilized into the projects of the Office of Scientific Research and Development, many found a cause for their concern and conviction—as well as one for their talents.

In the next few years these scientists worked in relative isolation from the society around them. The Office of Scientific Research and Development laboratories—the Chicago Metallurgical Laboratory, the Massachusetts Institute of Technology's Rad Lab, Los Alamos, and several others—were a heady and purposeful atmosphere, especially for the young scientists that became the post-war advisors to the government. It was like living and working amid a continual meeting of the world's finest physical scientists. No university, before or since, could match the concentration of talent. Budgets, too, were almost unlimited if one could convince the group that an idea was worth pursuing. Many participants later spoke of these times with a fondness reserved for the great adventures of life.

It is not that there were no doubts or second thoughts. As the bomb neared completion and testing (and as it became clear that the Germans had not succeeded in developing a fission bomb), protests were heard. In June of 1945, the Franck petition was forwarded to Secretary of War Henry Stimson opposing the military use of the bomb. Among its signers was Glenn Seaborg—later Chairman of the Atomic Energy Commission—then just turned 33. When the successful bomb test was detonated at Alamagordo, the heady feeling of accomplishment was joined by forebodings of what the risks for civilization might be. Oppenheimer distilled the feeling for many: "There floated through my mind a line from the Bhagavad-Gitā in which Krishna is trying to persuade the Prince that he should do his duty: 'I am become death, the shatterer of worlds.' I think we all had this feeling more or less."[4]

Against this background a new estate in public affairs, the science advisors, were catapulted into government circles at the end of the war.

THE NEW-OLD PRIESTHOOD

Not all the wartime scientists and engineers involved themselves in public affairs at the end of World War II. The leaders of the successful proximity fuse project returned to their research in physics—some even abjuring the use of government funds. Some left physics altogether and made important contributions to the field that later became molecular biology. Yet another group of the wartime scientists involved themselves in the public debates about nuclear arms control without entering the growing government science advisory apparatus. Leo Szilard, for example, coauthor of the famous Einstein letter that had begun the bomb project (and author of the Franck petition opposing its use in 1945), devoted a substantial portion of his remaining years to the search for controls to nuclear weapons. Before he died in 1963, Szilard founded the Council for a Livable World, which continues the search for an end to nuclear arms.

The group that became the government science advisors were thus largely self-

An account of all the major technical achievements of the Office of Scientific Research and Development during World War II is: Baxter, J. P., 3rd, *Scientists Against Time*, Little, Brown, 1946, MIT Press, Boston, 1968, 473 p. Personal memoirs of these events have been written by many of the participants (see Davis *op. cit.*, for an extensive bibliography).

selected. Those who moved to other fields, whether in search of new challenges or seeking escape from the horror of their creation of the bomb, removed themselves. Those who chose the public forum for opposition to governmental nuclear weapons policies were not invited into the inner circles. Known pacifists, like Einstein, were rarely consulted by the new scientific advisors about anything.

But what has all this about bombs and their builders to do with energy policy? It is one of my principal theses that, to the extent scientific advice played any role in creating the momentum that carries us into a nuclear power based future, the scientists that provided this advice (and still do) were a very special and biased subset of the scientific community. They had these things in common: (a) they were drawn from a narrow set of specialties in the physical sciences (nuclear physics or chemistry and related fields); (b) they shared a set of intensely moving experiences during World War II; (c) they were not among those who objected to weapons work or whose values dictated that they leave the field; (d) they were born between 1890 and 1920 (suggesting a common generational bias); (e) they had enough liking or tolerance for the quasi-political world of science advising to be extensively involved in the heady atmosphere of deliberating on crucial public issues at the highest levels of government. These men, and their self-selected successors have run the science advisory apparatus ever since.

None of this is news to the participants themselves. Harvey Brooks, a long time member of the inner circles, writes:

> The advisory role tends to become self-perpetuating, and constitutes a kind of sub-profession within the scientific professions. Certain administrative skills and some degree of political sophistication are factors almost as vital as scientific competence and reputation in the selection of members for top committees. Experience in one of the major wartime laboratories, especially the MIT Rad Lab and the laboratories of the Manhattan (bomb) Project, or an apprenticeship on one or more of the military 'summer studies,' still appears to be a useful qualification for scientific advising. There is as yet little sign of a change in generations that would affect this pattern. Even the relatively few younger scientists that have filtered into the higher level advisory committees are often students of one of the wartime giants like Rabi, Teller, Oppenheimer, or Fermi.[5]

What is this "political sophistication" that is so valuable? It cannot be a sophistication born of the experience of elective politics, for none of these men is known to have stood for elective political office. With few exceptions, none is known to have particpated in the scholarly study of political science. Brooks' statement suggests that "political sophistication" is, in part, a shared world view with those already there. This view includes a center or slightly left-of-center political posture. Neither the radical or extreme liberal scientists nor the politically conservative scientists are invited into the self-perpetuating apparatus of science advising (although such scientists are sometimes summoned to testify before congressional committees by elected officials of similar political views).

One article of faith among those who hold centrist or liberal political views—whether scientists or not—has been that reasoned discussion will produce a consensus plan that will solve both technical and social problems. Similarly, this group has shown a consistent preference for, and faith in, technological remedies for problems rather than politically negotiated ones. Eugene Wigner, Nobel Laureate in Physics, asked "why scientists so consistently overestimate the realizibility of what appears to them the rational solution? It is, in my opinion," he continued, "because they are not sufficiently aware of the phenomenon of the conflict of desires."[6] As long as the self-perpetuating scientific advisors share a common political position on the political spectrum, as well as a common background, officials receiving advice from this group can be deluded into believing that there is

5. Brooks, Harvey, "The Scientific Advisor," in R. Gilpin and C. Wright, eds., *Scientists and National Policy-Making*, Columbia Univ. Press, New York, 1964, pp. 73–96.
6. Wigner, E. P., as quoted in Lilienthal (3) *op cit*.

genuine consensus among the technical community.

In a larger sense, many students of politics conclude that for a decision-maker adequate representation of conflicting viewpoints is more useful in choosing among alternatives than is the "platitudinous consensus"[5] that is often the result of the present system. Yet the faith in reason to resolve all political and value differences is so strong that Brooks justifies exclusion of some dissenters on the grounds that:

> People with very strong viewpoints which are impervious to rational argument or compromise merely tend to lead to a hung jury which does not help the decision-maker. A majority vote is much less useful than a well-reasoned consensus in providing scientific advice.[5]

Yet Walter Heller, writing from the experience as Chairman of the Council of Economics Advisors, concludes that value judgments are "inescapable" and "obligatory."[7] At the very least, it is hard to see how the elimination of contradictory views from the scientific advisory apparatus improves the quality of government decisions.

WHO IS IN AND WHO IS NOT

It has already been mentioned that the World War II leaders of the scientific advisory apparatus represent a narrow collection of specialties. By looking at the composition of the President's Scientific Advisory Committee, the extent of this concentration may be easily seen. Between its origin in 1951 and 1966,[8,]* there were 65 members of the President's Scientific Advisory Committee. Of these 32 are physicists, 8 are from closely related fields of physical chemistry, nuclear chemistry, biophysics, or nuclear engineering, and 5 others are veterans of the World War II Manhattan projects (though they identify themselves as practitioners of other disciplines). The next-largest grouping are physicians and biologists, together including 10 members. The same analysis performed on the General Advisory Committee of the Atomic Energy Commission, not surprisingly, reveals even more concentration.

Since the special interest here is in energy and, particularly, the choice of nuclear energy, it is important to note who has not been in these advisory councils. There has never been a geologist or a resource expert on the President's Scientific Advisory Committee.** When the National Aeronautics and Space Administration and the National Science Foundation assembled a panel of solar energy experts, it was clear that none had ever been on the President's Scientific Advisory Committee. Other fields in the sciences and social sciences have been similarly not represented (economics, ecology, and the agricultural sciences come immediately to mind), but they are of less immediate interest to the subject of this essay.

It is quite true that when the President's Scientific Advisory Committee undertook studies, experts relevant to the question under study were sought out, but the makeup of this group usually determined the questions that led to such studies. In any case, it is not surprising that the scientific advisory apparatus favored nuclear energy as a power source for society. To put it bluntly, if you ask an economist for a solution to the problems of society, he will propose an economic solution in most cases—and if you ask a nuclear physicist about energy sources, do not be surprised if nuclear power is suggested.

It can be argued that much of this is beside the point. After all, nuclear power does work,

7. Heller, W. W., "Economic Policy Advisors," in T. E. Cronin and S. D. Greenberg, eds., *The Presidential Advisory System*, Harper and Row, New York, 1969, pp. 29–39.

8. U.S. Government, *The Office of Science and Technology*, A report to the Committee on Government Operations, House of Representatives, U.S. Government Printing Office, 1967.

*The President's Science Advisory Committee obtained that title in 1957, when the office of President's Science Advisor was created. A somewhat less influential committee, the Science Advisory Committee, was set up in 1951 in the Executive Office of the President. This analysis considers members of both committees.

**There have been two members of the President's Scientific Advisory Committee from the related field of geophysics, but neither of them has ever claimed to be geologists, nor are they regarded as geologists or resource experts by the geological profession.

in the sense that the heat generated by a reactor does supply electric power (although up to 1972 we had still supplied more energy to the nuclear power program than we had obtained from it). What is more, the arguments displayed later in this book show that the risks of nuclear power are under active discussion. The question of energy sources for society, however, is never a qualitative question. Many sources of energy—sun and wind, for example—have been demonstrated to work centuries ago, but are little used today. The question of advantage or risk associated with the choice of an energy source can only be dealt with if one asks: In comparison to what? Such comparative discussions must involve economic, health, and environmental considerations as well as technical ones. Usually a good many aesthetic and value considerations are important as well. With the advantage of hindsight it is clear that these discussions did not take place. Meanwhile, public money has been heavily committed to nuclear-power development. Would things have been different if a broader mix of backgrounds had characterized the scientific advisory apparatus? That question cannot be answered directly, but a retracing of the steps in the decision may help readers make their own estimates.

THE DECISION FOR NUCLEAR POWER

It would be all too easy to credit or blame scientists solely for the decision to pursue nuclear power. History is much more complex than that. The overwhelming impact of the atomic bomb on the public has made many forget that the romance of "splitting the atom" and the possible results of doing so had, even in 1945, a long history in the popular press. Magazines like *Popular Mechanics* and *Popular Science* had frequent articles on both peaceful and weapons uses of nuclear power all through the 1930's. Ernest O. Laurence's experiments with the early cyclotron led to newspaper headlines like "DEATH RAY" and "POSSIBLE CURE FOR CANCER" in 1934, and it was written in the *New York Times* that "transmutation [of the elements] and the release of atomic energy are no longer mere romantic possibilities."[9]

After World War II, the public notice was much intensified. David Lilienthal wrote that:

> . . . it is well to recall the temper of those early days of the Atom. No predictions seemed too fantastic, whether of the doom of civilization through nuclear holocaust or of a world beneficently transformed through the peaceful use of this great new source of energy. Men were convinced that they were living in a world in which only the Atom counted, and man was almost incidental.[3]

Writing of the 1955 International Conference on the Peaceful Uses of Atomic Energy, W. L. Laurence (easily the most knowledgeable journalist in the field at that time) listened to "one scientific report after another, presented by world authorities in the field" and concluded that "it thus became clear . . . that man was on the eve of the greatest industrial, social and economic revolution in the millions of years of his evolution on earth. From a civilization limited and controlled by scarcity, he is about to emerge into the green pastures of a civilization built upon plenty."[10] Laurence quoted the confident predictions of scientists that the power of the hydrogen bombs would be tamed "possibly no more than twenty years from now." The twenty years have now elapsed, and fusion power is expected in twenty years—or never.

The bureaucracy of nuclear power had somehow acquired similar ideas. The leaders of Congress's powerful Joint Committee on Atomic Energy made rosy predictions, and Lewis Strauss, chairman of the Atomic Energy Commission, said in 1954 that "it is not too much to expect that our children will enjoy in their homes electrical power too cheap to meter, will know of great periodic regional famines in the world only of matters of history. . . ." Now we struggle to produce nuclear electric power at prices even competitive with other methods, and stand on the brink of world famine.

The past is littered with many foolish predictions about the future—on many subjects.

9. Davis, N. P., *op. cit.*, p. 63.
10. Laurence, W. L., *op. cit.*, p. 243.

The point here is that the unfulfilled predictions were based on what scientists said, or did not deny, and they are the very same scientists who have occupied central positions in the scientific advisory apparatus ever since.

It is often said that science has become the secular religion of our time. Despite this it comes as no surprise to most that scientists on political and ethical matters are right or wrong with about the same frequency as everyone else, but Brooks says that "scientists are often in a position to exercise their political and ethical judgments as citizens in a more realistic and balanced manner than other citizens."[5] Less often understood is the fact that scientists are, occasionally, completely wrong on technical and scientific matters. In a celebrated case, Lord Rutherford, pioneer leader in studies of atomic physics, asserted near the end of his life in 1936 that nuclear fission was a long way off and probably impossible. The following year Hahn, Strassman, and Meitner achieved fission. To add to the irony, fission had already been obtained in 1934 by Fermi and his co-workers, but he failed to identify the results of his own experiment. Fermi was, by common agreement, among the greatest physicists of the twentieth century, yet he did not recognize his achievement, even after a German chemist, Ida Noddack, pointed out the result in a paper of the time.[11]

In a more recent, and less well-known, case in 1962, a British astronomer objected to a planned high-altitude nuclear explosion (named Starfish) on the grounds that it would disrupt the Van Allen radiation belts. In the resulting dispute, the Atomic Energy Commission and the Department of Defense assembled a panel of distinguished scientists who concluded that, "these planned U.S. explosions in the upper atmosphere will not greatly disturb conditions for the magnetic orbits of the particles of the Van Allen belt. Perturbations produced on the inner belt will be minor if detectable at all." James Van Allen, discoverer of the radiation belts, agreed with the panel. In the face of these reassurances, President Kennedy told a news conference that his advisors had deliberated carefully and that "Van Allen says it is not going to affect the belt and it is his."[12] Nevertheless, when the bomb went off, on July 9, 1962, the resulting trapped electrons seriously damaged five United States satellites and Britain's first satellite, Ariel. Clearly, committees as well as individuals in the scientific community can be very wrong.

None of the foregoing should be interpreted as a veiled implication the scientists are always wrong—quite the reverse. Because most good scientists are right most of the time about matters within their field, they have little experience, or expectation, of having events prove them wrong. The best clue an outsider to a scientific dispute can use is that disagreement among qualified and serious men is likely to signal that the answers are uncertain. Unfortunately, simple observations such as the foregoing have never penetrated to some of our political leaders. Richard Nixon, upon awarding the National Medals of Science, May 21, 1971, said that he had read the citations accompanying the awards and went on: "I have read them, and I want you to know that I do not understand them, but I want you to know, too, that because I do not understand them, I realize how enormously important their contributions are to this nation."[13]

If this attitude prevails, and the government credits the inside science advisors more heavily than others—rather than struggle to understand the facts of the case—we are always open to the admittedly rare colossal blunder.

THE MOMENTUM FOR NUCLEAR POWER

By the late 1950's or the early 1960's, expansion of nuclear power plants was well underway. The most visible and powerful advocates of nuclear power were no longer the

11. Segre, E., *Enrico Fermi: Physicist,* Univ. of Chicago Press, Chicago, 1970, 273 p.

12. Cox, D. W., *America's New Policy Makers,* Chilton Books, Philadelphia, 1964, 298 p.

13. Reported in Science and Government Report, Vol. 1, No. 9, June 1971, Washington, D.C., p. 3.

research and development scientists. Political figures on Congress's Joint Committee on Atomic Energy welcomed supporters of expanded nuclear power and treated those expressing doubts about the nuclear power program as hostile witnesses in an adversary court proceeding. By 1971, in authorizing hearings for the budget of the Atomic Energy Commission, Congressman Holifield suggested that the only work in radiation safety worth considering was that of the Atomic Energy Commission, and went on to say that "there is nothing else for them [the environmentalists] to lean on unless they want to lean on the fairy tales that are sold to *Esquire, Look,* and a few other of our popular magazines."[14] The statement is startling partly because it ignores the long and detailed dispute in technical books and journals, and partly because none of these critics of nuclear policy was called to testify before the committee that year.

In elementary mechanics momentum is defined as mass times velocity. These remarks suit that definition well. The mass in this case is composed of three parts: (a) a well established government bureaucracy including the Joint Committee on Atomic Energy and the Atomic Energy Commission with a total budget of more than $2 billion; (b) the electric utility industry with vastly larger sums already spent or committed to nuclear electric-generating plants; and (c) the oil industry, the entry of which into all aspects of nuclear fuel supply and processing and to reactor manufacture has been documented elsewhere.[15] The political lobbyists of the oil industry have been the most powerful in Washington for decades. The analogue of velocity in nuclear energy development arises from the times required to provide solid, unchallenged results about medical risk, safety of fuel transport, and storage as compared to the rate of expansion of nuclear generating plants. Thus, we are building new nuclear power plants even though the Atomic Energy Commission has announced that there is not yet a satisfactory way to store nuclear wastes.

The decision for nuclear power is, for most of these vested interests, a closed issue. Money, jobs, prestige, and political power provide a momentum that overshadows mere scientific uncertainty. It is no surprise, then, that many outsiders, who feel the commitment to nuclear power is a mistake, seek to apply political pressure to gain their ends. In the absence of some abrupt catastrophe, the reversal of the nuclear power commitment on the basis of some suggested technical risk seems very unlikely.

CONCLUSION: WHO DECIDED WHAT?

Scholarly analyses of scientists effect on public decisions emphasize the enormous differences in impact, depending upon what is being decided. In a carefully reasoned study, Schooler[16] concludes that scientists have had greatest impact in governmental "entrepreneurial" programs for which atomic energy and the space program are typical. These programs are seen initially as largely technological, and provide growing benefits to special groups (who in turn become advocates for the program) and do not, at first, challenge any vested interests. Haberer[17] emphasizes the ambivalence of scientists concerning responsibility for applications of their scientific results and the "prudential acquiescence" of the leaders of science to political pressure.[17]

In the unique setting of the weapons successes of post World War II we found a public and a government in awe of the physical scientists. The prospect of harnessing nuclear energy seemed attractive indeed and even a

14. U.S. Government, *AEC Authorizing Legislation, Fiscal Year 1972,* hearings before the Joint Committee on Atomic Energy, U.S. Congress, Part 1, Feb. 3, 4, and March 2, 1971. U.S. Government Printing Office, 1971.

15. Steinhart, C. E. and J. S., *Energy: Sources, Use and Role in Human Affairs,* Duxbury Press, North Scituate, Mass., 1974, 362 p.

16. Schooler, D., Jr., *Science, Scientists and Public Policy,* Free Press, New York, 1971, 338 p.

17. Haberer, J., *Politics and the Community of Science,* Van Nostrand Reinhold, New York, 1969, 337 p.

political conservative like Enrico Fermi wrote in 1945, without thinking it needed justification: "A few remarks about the peaceful possibilities of atomic energy. There is little doubt that the applications both to industry and to sciences other than physics will develop rapidly."[11] At that time, few asked the question, that became relevant later: "What other options than nuclear power have we, and how do they compare with nuclear power?"

As the 1950's began and wore on, there were more nuclear weapons developments, but the peaceful applications failed one by one. After $1.1 billion, the nuclear airplane was given up, partly at the recommendation of the science advisors. The nuclear cargo ship *Savannah* was launched with great fanfare about a new age in commercial shipping, only to be put quietly into mothballs a few years later. It was not competitive commercially. Schemes to increase natural gas flow, extract oil from shale and tar sands, and create underground storage reservoirs from underground nuclear explosions have had modest-scale tests and even some mixed success, but met increasing resistance from local residents. Plans for creating new harbors and canals from nuclear bomb excavation are seldom even spoken of anymore. Medical and research uses of radioactive isotopes continue, but, by the 1960's, had taken a place among other tools and treatments. The glittering promise of a "cure for cancer" did not materialize.

We have seen a generation of brilliant scientists thrust into a position of prominence that they did not seek. Those who tolerated the role, or liked it, have spent a large portion of their lives ever since advising the government.[18,*] Always living with their part in creating the bomb, the advisor scientists must have noted the peaceful uses slipping away or falling far short of the rosy hopes of the 1940's. Finally, only nuclear generation of electric power is left. We should not be surprised if the old guard of advisors cling to the hopes for this peaceful use, even in the face of doubts.

Alvin Weinberg, bomb project physicist and former White House energy advisor, is forthright about the choice. Admitting some disadvantages of nuclear power to be weighed against the advantages, he calls the choice a "Faustian bargain" for society and urges for nuclear power. But, according to the legend of Faust, such a bargain must be made by each person with Mephistopheles. When the technical issues raised in this book are understood we must each make a choice. The momentum that now drives the expansion of nuclear power has removed the decision from the hands of the scientists, however; if and when the disputes are settled among technical people, or even if the disputes are not settled, the choice of society's energy source will be sought out in the political and economic arenas. If the cost of nuclear electric power continues to increase as it has in recent years, still more public subsidy will be required. The breeder-reactor and fusion programs will require public money. The machinery for making these choices and commitments has not always been responsive.

As for the technical advisory machinery of government, the President's Scientific Advisory Committee, President's Science Advisor, Office of Science and Technology mechanism was dismantled by the Nixon administration. Many scientists, not among the insiders, had already become disillusioned with that machinery. Paul Ehrlich, for example, says that "these Washington committees also seem to wind up having an impact that's zero . . . or bad."[19] Yet the same group and their hand picked successors have been until recently in control of the advisory apparatus.

18. Atomic Energy Commission, *In the Matter of J. Robert Oppenheimer*, Transcript of hearing before the Personnel Security Board, April 12 through May 6, 1954, U.S. Government Printing Office, 1954, p. 451.

*I. E. Rabi noted in the Oppenheimer hearings that he spent 120 days a year on advisory committees. Allowing some nonworking time and a little time for homework for these advisory services, 120 days must represent more than half his working time. Such commitments of time are not unusual among the inside advisors.

19. Interview with Paul Ehrlich, *Mother Earth News*, No. 28, July 1974, p. 12.

With a tenure longer than all but four of the Supreme Court Justices in the history of the United States, they recommend, in a recent National Academy of Sciences report,[20] a reestablishment of the old system with minor cosmetic changes. Eugene Skolnikoff, a long-time student of the scientific advisory apparatus, concludes sadly that "the report . . . reflects the attitudes and arguments of the 50's and 60's, and rather obstinately refuses to recognize some of the important lessons of OST and PSAC."[21] The scientific advisory apparatus, like most human institutions, seems to find self-criticism and reform difficult.

The history recalled in this essay suggests that, though scientists must bear a fundamental share of the praise or blame for the choice of nuclear power, there is no nefarious conspiracy to be found. Many scientists still work—as this volume shows—to clarify the advantages and risks in our choice of energy sources. From a world-wide point of view, it is not too late to end the race toward a nuclear-powered future, but, with the commitment and momentum now driving the choice, it will become more difficult each year to change.

20. National Academy of Sciences, *Science and Technology in Presidential Policy-making: A Proposal,* Report of the ad hoc Committee on Science and Technology, National Academy of Sciences, Washington, D.C., June, 1974.
21. Skolnikoff, E., Science and the President: A New Debate with Old Solutions, *Public Science,* Vol. 5, No. 6, 1974, pp. 1–9.

Nuclear Power Generation 15

JAMES J. DUDERSTADT 1977

Since that moment over 30 years ago when Fermi achieved the first nuclear fission chain reaction, a massive international effort has been directed toward harnessing the enormous energy contained within the atomic nucleus for the peaceful generation of power. Nuclear reactors have evolved from embryonic research tools into the mammoth units that drive hundreds of central-station electrical generating plants throughout the world today. The impending shortage of fossil fuels has made even more significant the role that nuclear power must play in meeting man's future energy requirements.

For roughly a decade now, electrical utilities have been ordering and installing nuclear plants in preference to fossil-fueled units. Such plants (see Table 15-1) are truly enormous in size, typically generating over 1 billion watts of electrical power (one gigawatt, enough to supply the electrical power needs of a city of half a million people) and costing as much as $1 billion per generating unit. It is estimated[1] that some 500 nuclear power plants installed in the United States alone by the year 2000 will have an electrical generating capacity of 550 gigawatts (electric) and represent a capital investment of more than $600 billion, with this pattern being repeated throughout the world. The motivation for such a commitment involves a number of factors that include not only the very significant economic and operational advantages and substantially lower environmental impact exhibited by nuclear plants compared to conventional sources of power, but the resources of fuel (particularly of domestic origin) available for nuclear power generation as well.

In this article, we will concern ourselves with a discussion of nuclear power generation, ranging from the fundamental concepts involved in nuclear fission chain reactions through descriptions of the principal types of nuclear power systems being utilized throughout the world today, to advanced nuclear reactor concepts such as the fast breeder reactor. We will also summarize several operational aspects of nuclear power plants, including their safety, environmental impact, and associated nuclear fuel cycle. Finally, we conclude with a brief catalog of the various

Original article by Dr. James J. Duderstadt. Dr. Duderstadt is professor of nuclear engineering, The University of Michigan, Ann Arbor, Michigan 48105. He is the author or coauthor of over 44 technical publications in the areas of nuclear reactor theory, radiation transport, statistical mechanics, plasma physics, and computer simulation; as well as a text titled *Nuclear Reactor Analysis,* John Wiley & Sons (1976), 650 p.

Table 15–1. Status of Nuclear Power Plant Commitments (1976).

Status	*Number (U.S.)*[a]	*Number (non-U.S.)*[a]
Operable	64 (45)	112 (36)
Under construction	92 (97)	117 (85)
On order or planned	70 (79)	225(222)
Total	226(222)	454(343)

[a] Numbers in parentheses are gigawatts (electric) generated.

"pros" and "cons" (both real and imagined) expressed in the continuing debate over the role nuclear power should play in our society (and leave it to the subsequent articles in this volume to present these topics in more detail).

INTRODUCTORY CONCEPTS OF NUCLEAR FISSION CHAIN REACTORS

The term *nuclear reactor* is used to refer to devices in which controlled nuclear fission chain reactions can be maintained. In such a device, neutrons are used to induce nuclear fission reactions in the nuclei of such heavy metals as uranium or plutonium. These nuclei fission into lighter nuclei (fission products) with the release of energy plus several additional neutrons. These fission neutrons can then be utilized to induce still further fission reactions and thereby propagate a chain of fission events. In a very narrow sense, then, a nuclear reactor is simply a sufficiently large mass of appropriately "fissile" material (e.g., the isotopes uranium-235 or plutonium-239) in which such a controlled *fission chain reaction* can be sustained. Indeed, a small sphere of ^{235}U metal slightly over 8 cm in radius could support such a chain reaction and could be called a nuclear reactor.

But a modern power reactor is a considerably more complex beast. It must not only contain a lattice of very carefully refined and fabricated nuclear fuel, but it also must cool this fuel during the course of the chain reaction as fission energy is released, while maintaining the fuel in a very precise geometrical arrangement with appropriate structural materials. Furthermore, the chain reaction must be controlled, the surroundings must be shielded from the intense nuclear radiation generated during the fission reactions, and the nuclear fuel assemblies must be replaced when the fission chain reaction has depleted the amount of fissile nuclei present. If the reactor is to produce power in a useful fashion, it must also be designed to operate economically, reliably, and safely. Such engineering constraints make the actual configuration of a nuclear power reactor quite complex indeed.

Fission Chain Reactions and Nuclear Criticality

In order to understand the principal concepts underlying nuclear reactor operation, we need to look in more detail at the fission chain reaction process.[2] To maintain a stable fission chain reaction, a nuclear reactor must be designed so that, on the average, exactly one neutron from each fission will induce yet another fission reaction. That is, the production of neutrons from fission reactions must be balanced against their loss by either leakage from the reactor or by their absorption in non-productive nuclear reactions.

To illustrate how this might be accomplished, suppose that, in a particular nuclear system, more neutrons are lost by leakage and absorption than are produced in fission. Then a self-sustaining chain reaction cannot be achieved—we say the system is *subcritical*. One way to alter the system so that there is a more favorable balance between production and destruction is simply to make it bigger. Then the probability that a neutron will leak out before being absorbed by a nucleus is decreased (the average neutron has to travel farther to leak out—hence it will suffer more collisions on the way). An alternative approach would be to increase the relative concentration of fissile nuclei. By adjusting the fuel concentration and size of the reactor, we can balance neutron production versus loss and achieve a self-sustaining chain reaction, a *critical* system.

Actually, it is appropriate to dismiss neutron leakage and reactor size from further consideration, since most modern power reactors are so large that very few neutrons leak out (usually less than 3 per cent). In fact, the size of a power reactor is determined not by the desire to minimize neutron leakage, but rather to provide enough space for coolant flow to adequately remove the enormous amount of heat produced by fission reactions. In reactor design, one first determines how large the reactor must be built to accommodate adequate cooling for a desired power output, and then one determines the fuel concentration that will make a reactor of this size critical.

Suitable Fuels for Fission Chain Reactors

The necessary fuel concentration is sensitive to the fuel type. Nuclear engineers characterize the suitability of a material for sustaining a fission chain reaction by a parameter denoted by the Greek symbol eta:

η = Average number of neutrons produced (by fission) per neutron absorbed by fuel nucleus

This parameter not only characterizes the relative propensity of a fuel nucleus to fission, but its ability to produce further neutrons in the fission process, which can be used to sustain the chain reaction. Evidently, if the fission chain reaction is to be self-sustained, we must utilize fuels that are characterized by values of η greater than one (since some neutrons will always leak out or will be absorbed in nonfuel materials in the reactor).

There are very few heavy nuclei with values of η sufficiently in excess of one to be suitable candidates for nuclear reactor fuel. These *fissile* materials include the isotopes of uranium, ^{233}U and ^{235}U, and plutonium, ^{239}Pu and ^{241}Pu. Unfortunately, only the isotope ^{235}U occurs in nature, and then only as a very small percentage (0.711 per cent) of naturally occurring uranium (which is primarily ^{238}U). To effectively utilize uranium as a reactor fuel, it is usually necessary to increase the concentration of ^{235}U, to "enrich" the uranium in this isotope, using very elaborate and expensive isotope separation methods.

The other fissile isotopes can be produced artificially by bombarding certain materials with neutrons. For example, ^{238}U and thorium-232 can be transmuted into the fissile isotopes ^{239}Pu and ^{233}U, respectively, by exposing them to neutrons in a reactor. In fact, there are usually a sufficient number of "excess" neutrons produced in a fission chain reaction (since η is greater than one) so that *fertile* materials such as ^{238}U can be transmuted into fissile isotopes such as ^{239}Pu as the reactor operates. Actually, this conversion of fertile material into fissile material occurs in all modern power reactors (although it is not their primary function), since they contain substantial amounts of ^{238}U, which will be transmuted into plutonium during normal operation. For example, a light water reactor will contain a fuel mixture of roughly 3 per cent ^{235}U and 97 per cent ^{238}U in freshly loaded fuel assemblies. After a standard operating cycle (usually three years), this fuel will contain roughly 1 per cent ^{235}U and 1 per cent ^{239}Pu, which can then be separated out of the spent fuel and refabricated into fresh fuel elements for reloading (plutonium "recycling").

These considerations suggest that it might be possible to fuel a reactor with ^{239}Pu and ^{238}U and thus directly produce the fuel (^{239}Pu) needed for future operation. Indeed, it might even be possible to produce more ^{239}Pu than is burned—that is, to "breed" new fuel—if η were large enough. To be more precise, one can introduce the concept of the *conversion ratio:*

CR = av. rate of fissile nuclei production/ av. rate of fissile nuclei consumption

From this definition, it is apparent that consuming N atoms of fuel during reactor operation will yield $CR \cdot N$ atoms of new fissile isotopes. For example, most modern light water reactors are characterized by a conversion ratio about 0.6. By way of contrast, gas-cooled reactors have somewhat higher conversion ratios of 0.8 and are sometimes referred to as "advanced converter" reactors. For breeding to occur, we require that the conversion ratio be greater than one—in which case we rename it the *breeding ratio*—$CR = BR > 1$. Of course for this to happen we must have $\eta > 2$, since slightly more than one fission neutron is needed to maintain the chain reaction (accounting for neutron leakage or parasitic capture), whereas one neutron will be needed to replace the consumed fissile nucleus by converting a fertile nucleus into a fissile nucleus.

To achieve this we take advantage of the fact that the parameter η depends not only upon fuel type, but upon the average kinetic energies (speeds) of the neutrons sustaining the chain reaction as well. In general, η becomes larger as the neutron energy increases. Since the average energy of fission neutrons is quite large ("fast" neutrons), one can maximize the value of η and hence the breeding ratio by simply designing the reactor so that these neutrons do not slow down during the chain reaction. Reactors that attempt to optimize the breeding of new fuel by utilizing fast neutrons are known, naturally enough, as *fast breeder reactors*. A more careful comparison of η for various fissile isotopes[3] makes it apparent that the optimum breeding cycle for fast reactors would utilize ^{238}U as the fertile material and ^{239}Pu as the fissile fuel. Breeder reactors can be designed to achieve breeding ratios of 1.3 to 1.5 based on this cycle.

But there is a very significant drawback to such a reactor. The probability of a neutron inducing a fission reaction decreases with increasing energy, so that it is easiest to sustain a chain reaction (although not to breed new fuel) with low energy or "slow" neutrons. For this reason, most power reactors are designed so that the fast fission neutrons are slowed down or "moderated" to enhance the probability that they will induce fission reactions. In such reactors, materials of low mass number (such as water or graphite) are interspersed among the fuel elements. Then as the fission neutrons collide with the nuclei of these "moderator" materials, they rapidly slow down to energies comparable to the thermal energies of the nuclei in the reactor core—which explains the term *thermal reactors,* which is used to describe such designs. Most nuclear power plants utilize thermal reactors, since these systems require the minimum amount of fissile material for fueling and are the simplest reactor types to build and operate, even though they cannot achieve a net breeding gain (aside from a modest conversion).

It should be noted that it is possible—at least in theory—to achieve breeding even in thermal reactors if a thorium-232/uranium-233 fuel cycle is used.[4] Unfortunately, the maximum breeding ratio one can achieve appears to be only slightly greater than one ($BR \sim 1.02$). Although this marginal breeding ratio would lead to a more effective utilization of nuclear fuel (at least compared to such conventional thermal reactors as the light water reactor), it would not produce a sufficient amount of additional fissile material (^{233}U) to fuel new reactors (particularly when the material losses associated with fuel reprocessing are taken into account).

Nuclear Reactor Operation

The final parameter of interest in fission reactor design is the fuel concentration, which can be adjusted to alter the balance between neutron production (fission) and loss (leakage and absorption) processes. The fuel concentration can be adjusted to enrich the fuel (i.e., the percentage of fissile material in the fuel), the density and geometry of the fuel, and the quantity of nonfuel materials in the core. The amount of fissile material required to achieve a critical fission chain reaction is the *critical mass* of the fuel. This amount depends upon the particular composition and geometry of the fuel. For example, the critical mass characterizing a sphere of pure ^{235}U metal is only 17 kg. By way of contrast, the fuel loading required for a modern light water reactor is roughly 100 tons of 3 per cent enriched uranium.

It should be noted, however, that a nuclear power reactor is always loaded with much more fuel than is required to achieve criticality only. The extra fuel is included to compensate for those fuel nuclei destroyed in fission reactions during power production. Since most modern reactors are run roughly a year before refueling, a sizable amount of excess fuel is needed to compensate for fuel burnup and to facilitate changes in the reactor power level.

To compensate for this excess fuel, that is, to alter the balance between neutron production and loss, one introduces materials into the reactor that absorb neutrons from the chain reaction, thereby "canceling" out the excess fuel. These absorbing materials can then slowly be withdrawn as the fuel burns up. They can also be used to adjust the criticality of the nuclear reactor in order to control the chain reaction. This might be accomplished in a variety of ways. For example, the neutron absorber might be fabricated into rods, which can then be inserted into or withdrawn from the reactor at will to regulate the power level of the reactor. That is, one can withdraw the absorber or *control rods* to make the reactor slightly supercritical so that the chain reaction builds up. Then when the power level has reached the desired level, the rods can be re-inserted to achieve a critical or steady-state chain reaction. Finally, the rods can be inserted still further into the reactor to shut down the chain reaction.

The longer term changes in fuel concentration due to burnup are usually compensated for by neutron absorber fabricated directly into the fuel (which then burns up as the fuel burns up) or dissolved in the coolant. Eventually, enough fuel will be burned up so that the reactor can no longer be made critical even by withdrawing all the control absorbers; the reactor must then be shut down and refueled.

A very important facet of reactor operation concerns the stability of the reactor. It happens that the probabilities for various neutron interactions (fission or absorption) depend upon the temperature and therefore upon the power level of the reactor. Nuclear reactors are always designed with "negative feedback" so that increasing power and therefore temperature "brakes" the chain reaction, thereby decreasing power again. The most significant feedback mechanisms involve the decrease in moderator density (and therefore in moderation) with increasing temperature, which occurs in thermal reactors and the enhanced tendency of nonfissile material to absorb neutrons with increasing temperature (the Doppler effect in all types of reactors). These mechanisms are so effective that a reactor tends to operate in a very stable fashion. Power reactors are quite incapable of operating significantly above their designed power level. That is, if somehow the reactor was inadvertantly made supercritical (e.g., a control rod was accidently withdrawn while the reactor was operating at full power), the power level of the reactor (and hence the reactor temperature) would increase only slightly before negative feedback would return the reactor to a critical (or subcritical) state by slowing down the chain reaction. Such inherent feedback mechanisms eliminate any possibility of a runaway chain reaction and remove the concern about certain nuclear accidents (i.e., those involving the chain reaction itself) from nuclear power reactor design and operation.

NUCLEAR POWER GENERATION

Nuclear power reactors are designed to produce heat, which can then be used to generate electrical energy, usually by way of a steam thermal cycle. In this sense, a reactor

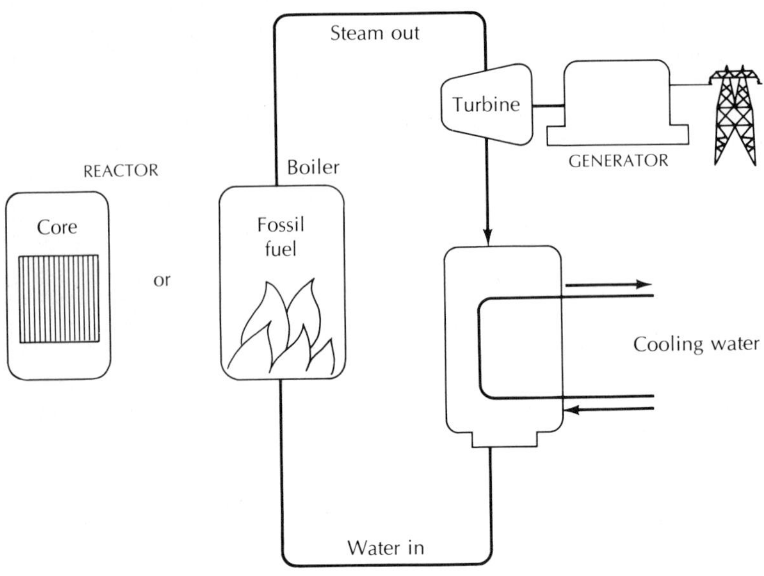

Figure 15-1. Components of electrical generating plants.

functions primarily as an exotic heat source to turn water into steam. Aside from the nuclear reactor and its associated coolant system, nuclear power plants are remarkably similar to large fossil-fuel-fired power plants (see Figure 15-1). Only the source of the heat energy differs—nuclear fission versus chemical combustion. Most of the components of large central station power plants are common to both nuclear and fossil-fueled units.

Current generated by power plants is by a steam cycle in which the heat generated by combustion or fission is used to produce high temperature steam. This steam is then allowed to expand against the blades of a turbine. In this way, the thermal energy of the steam is converted into the mechanical work of turning the turbine shaft. This shaft is connected to a large electrical generator that converts the mechanical turbine energy into electrical energy that can be distributed over an electrical power grid. The low pressure steam leaving the turbine must be recondensed into liquid in a steam condensor so that it can be pumped back to the steam supply system to complete the cycle. The condensor is cooled by large quantities of ambient temperature water, which is usually obtained from artificial cooling ponds or cooling towers.

The Nuclear Steam Supply System

At the center of a nuclear power plant is the *nuclear steam supply system* (NSSS), which produces the steam used to run the turbine generator. The NSSS consists of three major components: (a) the *nuclear reactor,* which supplies the fission heat energy, (b) several *primary coolant loops* and pumps, which circulate a coolant through the nuclear reactor to extract the fission heat, and (c) heat exchangers or *steam generators,* which use the heated primary coolant to turn feedwater into steam. The NSSS in a modern nuclear power plant is completely enclosed within a containment structure designed to prevent the release of radioactivity to the environment in the event of a gross failure of the primary coolant system. This nuclear island within the plant is analogous to the boilers of a fossil-fueled unit.

At the heart of the NSSS is the nuclear reactor. Far from being just a simple "pile" of fuel and moderator à la Fermi, a modern power reactor is an enormously complicated system designed to operate under the most severe conditions of temperature, pressure, and radiation. The energy released by nuclear fission reactions appears primarily as kinetic energy of the various fission fragment nuclei. The bulk of this fission product energy is rapidly deposited as heat in the fuel. This heat is then extracted by a primary coolant flowing between the fuel elements and transported (convected) by this coolant to the steam generators.

A number of possible coolants can be used in the primary loops of the NSSS. Indeed, nuclear reactor types are usually characterized by the type of coolant they use, such as "light water" reactors or "gas-cooled" reactors. There are also a number of possible NSSS configurations. For example, the steam may actually be produced in the reactor itself. Or a single-phase primary coolant, such as water or helium, may be used to transfer the fission heat energy to a steam generator. In the "liquid metal-cooled" fast breeder reactor NSSS, an intermediate coolant loop is used to isolate the steam generator from the very high induced radioactivity of the primary coolant loop passing through the reactor (see Figure 15-2).

The most common coolant used in power reactors today is ordinary water, which serves both as a coolant and a moderating material. There are two major types of *light water reactors* (LWR)[5]: *Pressurized water reactors* (PWR) and *boiling water reactors* (BWR). In a PWR, the primary coolant is water maintained under very high pressure (~ 155 bar) to allow high coolant temperatures (300 °C) without steam formation within the reactor. The heat transported out of the reactor core by the primary coolant is then transferred to a secondary loop containing the working fluid (the steam system) by a heat exchanger known as a steam generator, since it is within this component that the inlet feedwater is converted into steam (see Figures 15-3 and 15-4). Such systems typically contain from two to four primary coolant loops and associated steam generators. A surge chamber or pressurizer is added into the primary coolant loop to maintain the very high primary system pressure as well as to accommodate coolant volume changes in the primary loop. The primary loop also contains coolant pumps, as well as auxiliary systems to control coolant purity and to inject new makeup water or to control absorption.

In a boiling water reactor, the primary coolant water is not only the moderator and coolant, but also the working fluid, since the system pressure is kept low enough (~ 70 bar) so that appreciable boiling and steam formation can occur within the reactor. In this sense, the reactor itself serves as the steam generator, thereby eliminating the need for a secondary loop and heat exchanger. Also, since there is an appreciable steam volume in the primary loop, a pressurizer tank is not required to accommodate pressure surges.

The coolant water rising to the top of the BWR core is a very wet mixture of liquid and vapor. Therefore, moisture or steam separators must be used to separate off the steam, which is then piped outside the reactor pressure vessel to the turbine, and then through the condensor, before it is pumped back into the core as liquid condensate. The saturated liquid separated off by the moisture separators flows downward around the core and mixes with the return condensate. This natural recirculation is assisted by pumps.

In both the PWR and BWR, the nuclear reactor itself and the primary coolant are contained in a large steel pressure vessel designed to accommodate the high coolant pressures and temperatures. In a PWR, this pressure vessel must be fabricated with thick steel walls to contain the primary coolant, which is under very high pressure. By way of contrast, the BWR pressure vessel need not be so thick, but it must be much larger to contain both the nuclear reactor and the steam moisture separating equipment.

CONTAINMENT STRUCTURE
Steam generator
Control rods
Steam
Generator
Turbine
Water
Water
Core
Condenser
Cooling water
Water
Reactor pressure vessel
Secondary water pump
Primary water pump

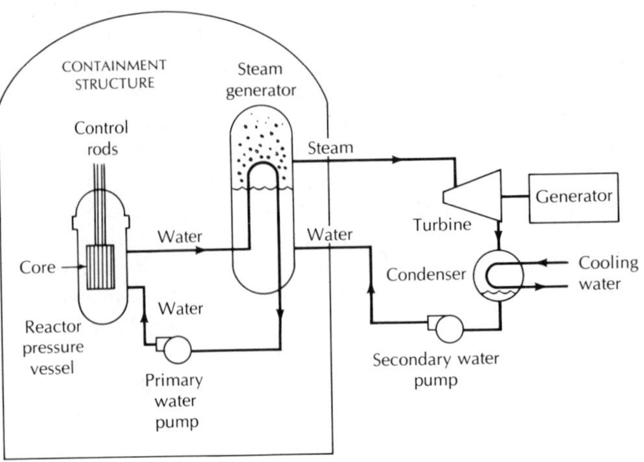

(a) Pressurized-water reactor

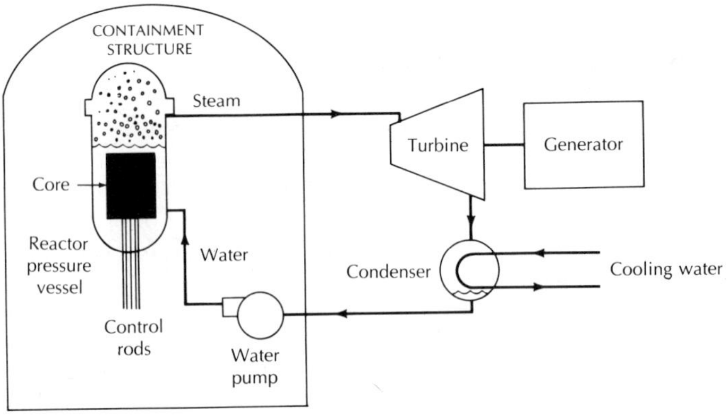

CONTAINMENT STRUCTURE
Steam
Turbine
Generator
Core
Reactor pressure vessel
Water
Condenser
Cooling water
Control rods
Water pump

(b) Boiling water reactor

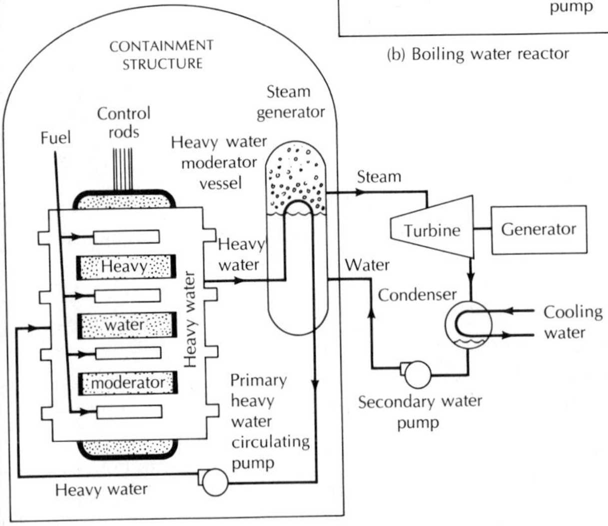

CONTAINMENT STRUCTURE
Steam generator
Control rods
Fuel
Heavy water moderator vessel
Steam
Turbine
Generator
Heavy water
Heavy
water
moderator
Heavy water
Water
Condenser
Cooling water
Primary heavy water circulating pump
Secondary water pump
Heavy water

(c) Heavy-water reactor

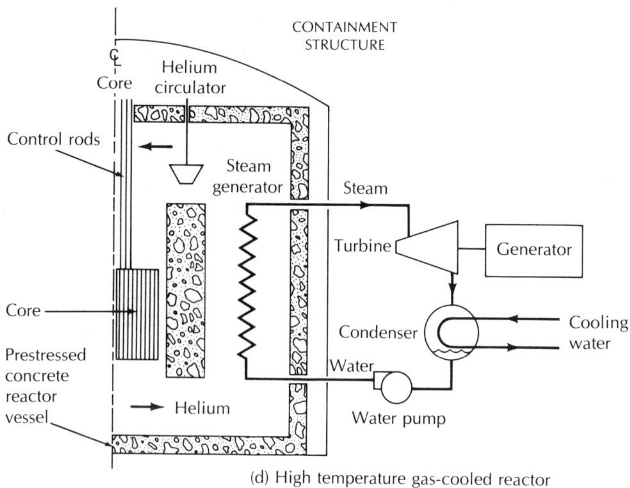

(d) High temperature gas-cooled reactor

(e) Liquid metal fast breeder reactor

Figure 15-2. Principal types of nuclear steam supply systems (NSSS) (ref. 20). Schematic diagrams of: (A) pressurized-water reactor; (B) boiling-water reactor; (C) heavy-water reactor; (D) high temperature gas-cooled reactor; (E) liquid metal fast breeder reactor.

The BWR direct cycle does present one major disadvantage. Since the working fluid actually passes through the reactor core before passing out of the containment structure and through the turbine, one must be particularly careful to avoid radiation hazards. For example, the primary coolant water must be very highly purified to avoid impurities that might be converted to radioactive compounds upon exposure to the high neutron fluxes in the core. Even so, the primary coolant will exhibit significant induced radioactivity, and therefore the turbine building must be heavily shielded; this increases construction costs and complicates maintenance activities.

A closely related class of reactors uses heavy water, D_2O, as moderator and either D_2O or H_2O as primary coolant.[6] The most

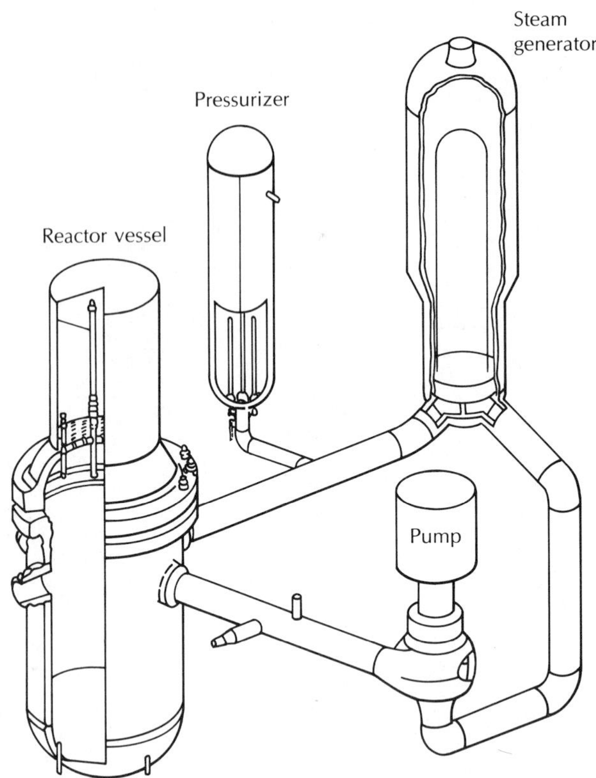

Figure 15-3. A nuclear steam supply system (NSSS) including a nuclear reactor, a coolant loop, and a steam generator. (Systems Summary of a Westinghouse PWR Nuclear Power Plant, G. Masche, 1971.)

popular type of such heavy water reactors is the Canadian CANDU-PHW reactor. This reactor uses a pressure tube design in which each coolant channel in the reactor is designed to accommodate the primary system pressure, thus eliminating the need for a pressure vessel. As with a PWR, the primary coolant thermal energy is transferred via a steam generator to a secondary loop containing light water as the working fluid. One major advantage exhibited by heavy water reactors is their ability to utilize natural uranium (with only a 0.711 per cent ^{235}U assay) as fuel due to the superior neutron-moderating properties of deuterium. More recently, a heavy water pressure tube reactor has been designed [the CANDU-BLW or the steam generating heavy water reactor (SGHWR)] which is similar to a BWR, producing H_2O steam directly in the core.

Gas-cooled nuclear reactors have been used for central station power generation for many years. The earliest such power plants were the Magnox reactors developed in the United Kingdom; they used carbon dioxide as the coolant for a natural uranium-fueled, graphite-moderated core. More recently, interest has shifted toward the high temperature gas-cooled reactor (HTGR), which uses high pressure helium to cool an enriched-uranium/thorium core moderated with graphite.[7] To date, all such reactors have been operated with a two-loop steam thermal cycle similar to that of a PWR, in which the primary helium coolant loop transfers its thermal energy via steam generators to a secondary

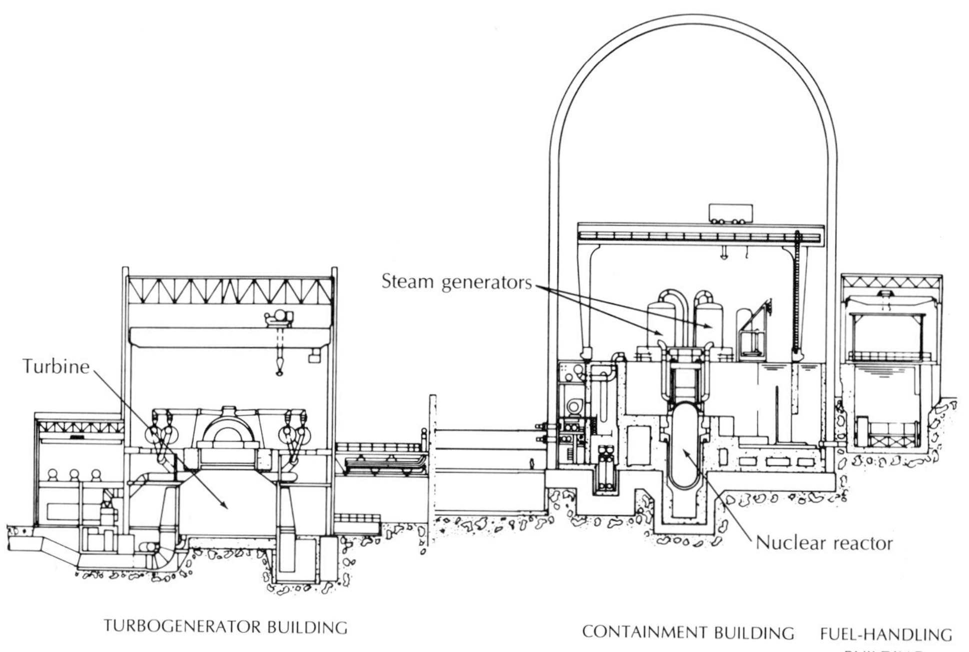

Figure 15-4. A schematic diagram of a nuclear power plant. (G. Masche, Westinghouse Systems Summary, 1971.)

loop containing water as the working fluid. The HTGR can operate at relatively high temperature, thereby producing high temperature (400 °C), high pressure (60 bar) steam, with an attendant increase in thermodynamic efficiency and an easing of turbine requirements. Moreover, the HTGR has the potential of being run in a direct cycle configuration, in which high temperature helium is used directly to drive a gas turbine (with thermal efficiencies approaching 50 per cent).

The HTGR has several other advantages. For example, it can be operated using a thorium/uranium-233 fuel cycle. The use of helium as a coolant not only allows higher operating temperatures at moderate pressures, but provides flexibility in the selection of optimum coolant temperature, pressure, and flow rate conditions. It also effectively eliminates that scourge of all reactor designers, the loss-of-coolant accident. Since the coolant always remains in the same phase, the worst that can happen in the event of a rupture of the primary coolant loop is a loss of pressure. And in a HTGR, even the natural circulation of helium at atmospheric pressure is sufficient to remove the radioactive decay heat given off by the core following shutdown.

But the gas coolant also implies low power densities and hence large reactor sizes. Furthermore, since the fissile material in such reactors is highly enriched ^{235}U (93 per cent), the HTGR presents a rather major problem from the viewpoint of the proliferation of strategic nuclear materials. Nevertheless, these reactors have been under extensive development in the United States and in West Germany.

Gas coolants have also been proposed for use in fast breeder reactors, the gas-cooled fast reactor (GCFR). Because of the very high power density required by such reactors, extremely high coolant flow rates would be required. Nevertheless, the large breeding ratios ($BR \sim 1.5$) obtainable by in the GCFR make it appear a very promising alternative to other fast reactor designs that utilize liquid metals, such as sodium, as the primary coolant.

Although sodium could be used in thermal reactors if alternative moderation were provided, its primary use is in fast breeder reactors[8] that require a primary coolant with low moderating properties and excellent heat transfer characteristics. We have noted that the NSSS for the liquid-metal-cooled fast breeder reactor (LMFBR) actually is a three-loop system, since an intermediate sodium loop must be used to separate the highly radioactive sodium in the primary loop from the steam generators (see Figure 15-2).

Nuclear Reactor Components

To introduce the general components and design of a nuclear power reactor, we will consider the specific example of a modern large pressurized water reactor. The reactor proper consists of a *core* (see Figures 15-5 and 15-6) containing the fuel, coolant channels, structural components, control elements, and instrumentation systems. In this particular example, the core is a cylindrical lattice, roughly 350 cm in diameter by 370 cm in height, consisting of long *fuel assemblies* or *bundles*. Each fuel assembly is composed of several hundred long metal tubes, the *fuel elements,* which contain the small ceramic fuel pellets of uranium oxide. Most modern power reactors utilize such ceramic fuels to facilitate high temperature operation—either as an oxide (UO_2), a carbide (UC), or a nitride (UN). The fuel element tube or cladding is either stainless steel or a zirconium alloy, which is designed not only to provide structural support for the fuel but to retain any radioactivity produced in the fuel during operation. The primary coolant then flows up through the fuel assembly between the fuel elements to extract the heat of fission. Fuel is

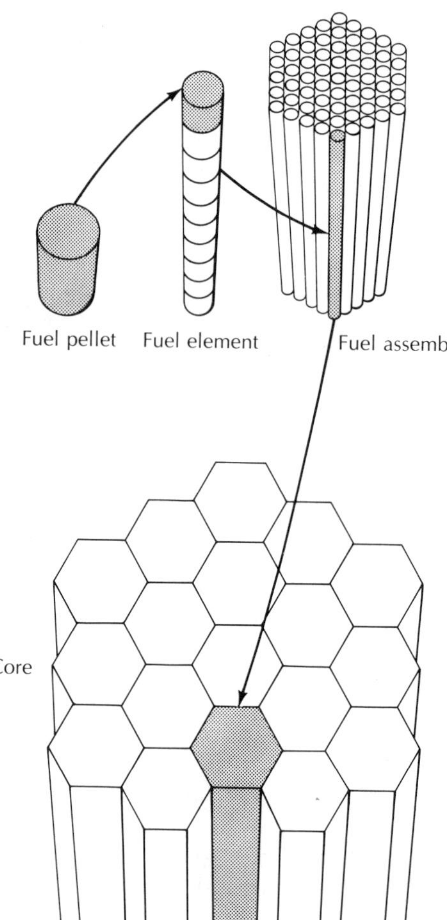

Figure 15-5. Fuel arrangement in a reactor core.

loaded into a reactor core or replaced one fuel assembly at a time. A typical power reactor core will contain several hundred such fuel assemblies.

The reactor core itself, the structures that support the core fuel assemblies, control assemblies, coolant circulation channels, and radiation shields are all contained in a reactor *pressure vessel,* which is designed to withstand the enormous pressures of the coolant and to isolate the reactor core from the rest of the NSSS. The pressure vessel is designed with inlet and outlet nozzles for each primary coolant loop. The cap or head of the vessel is

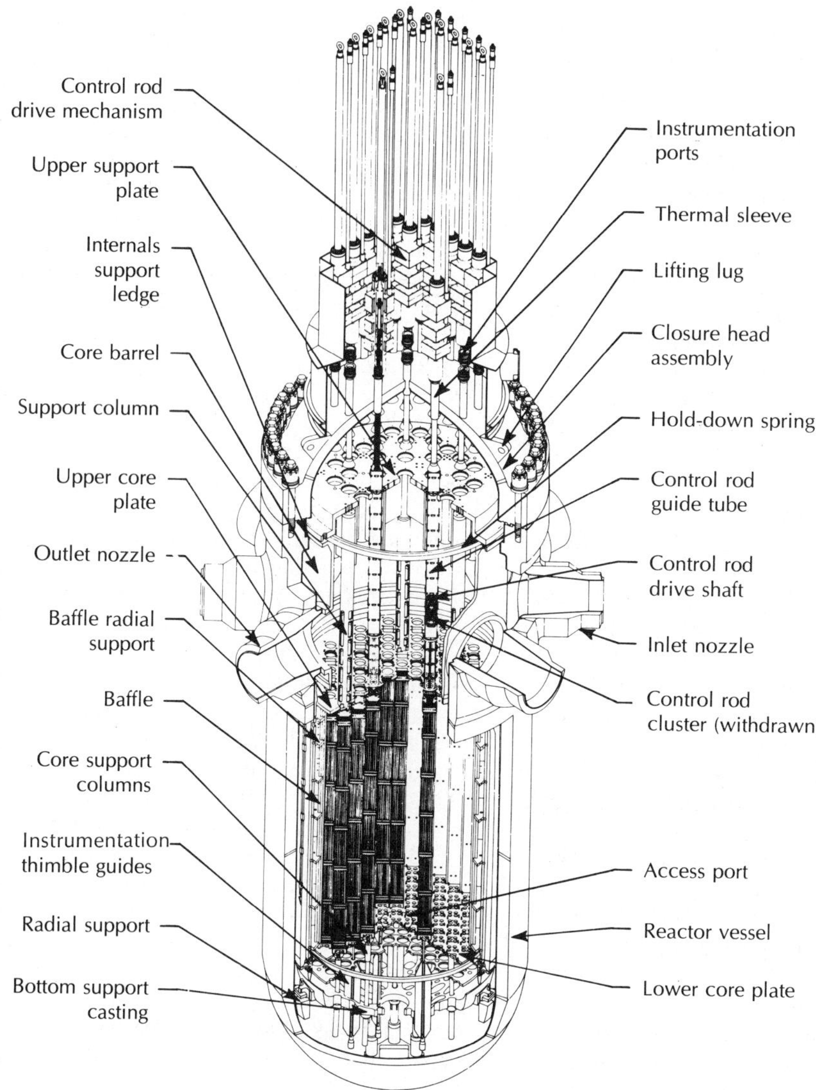

Figure 15-6. A pressurized water reactor (Westinghouse).

designed so that it can be removed for refueling and maintenance. The vessel, of low alloy carbon steel, is designed to accommodate the high coolant pressures and temperatures and to withstand damage from the radiation generated in the core.

Nuclear Reactor Safety

We now turn our attention to situations in which a nuclear power plant may be subjected to abnormal operating conditions caused, for example, by component malfunction, operator error, or a host of other possible events that could lead to a nuclear reactor accident. We should first note that the principal safety problems inherent in nuclear reactor operation do *not* arise because of the possibility of a nuclear explosion. A nuclear reactor cannot explode like an atomic bomb because it is fundamentally a very different kind of device. Nuclear explosives require that highly concentrated uranium-235 or plutonium be very rapidly assembled into a supercritical configuration. In a nuclear reactor, however, the fuel concentration is far too dilute (amounting to 3 per cent fissile enrichment in light water reactors and roughly 15 per cent in fast breeder reactors). Furthermore, we have noted that reactors possess a number of inherent mechanisms that act to shut off the chain reaction automatically if the power level increases substantially.

Rather, the principal concern in nuclear reactor safety is the large inventory of radioactive fission products that accumulates in the reactor fuel during operation. As long as the radioactive fission products remain in the fuel, they represent no hazard. Should they be released and transported (by wind, for example) to populated areas, however, significant damage could occur. Nuclear reactors must be designed so that under no credible—or even incredible—operating situation could such radioactive material be released from the core. To achieve this guarantee, not only must the nuclear reactor and coolant system be carefully designed against every imaginable accident situation, but in addition, auxiliary systems must be incorporated into the design to ensure core integrity in the event that such accidents should occur.

The containment of radioactive fission products is accomplished by designing into a nuclear power plant a series of physical barriers that inhibit or prevent the release of fission products.[9,10] The first line of defense is the ceramic fuel pellet itself, which entrains most of the nongaseous fission products and greatly inhibits the diffusion of gaseous fission products out of the fuel. The fuel pellets are contained in metallic tubes or cladding, which are designed to retain even the gaseous fission products that build up in the gap between the fuel pellet surface and the cladding tube. The fuel elements are contained within a 20-centimeter thick steel pressure vessel, which serves as yet a third barrier. The primary coolant loop piping is some 8 to 10 centimeters thick, and the coolant water itself is continuously circulated through traps to filter out any radioactive material. The pressure vessel is surrounded by 2- to 3-meter thick concrete shielding and is located within a containment structure that consists of 1-meter thick concrete walls lined with a 10-centimeter thick, leak-tight steel shell, which is designed to prevent the release of radioactivity in the event of a major rupture of the primary coolant system. The plant itself is contained within an exclusion area over which the operating utility controls access and which separates the plant from the public.

Nuclear plants are equipped with highly redundant and diverse safety systems designed to prevent the occurrence of abnormal operating conditions. Furthermore, the plants encompass engineered safeguards systems designed to protect against the consequences of highly unlikely, but potentially catastrophic accidents (e.g., a loss-of-coolant accident in which the fission product decay heat could lead to fuel melting unless auxiliary cooling were provided, equipment failures, human error, and severe natural events, such as earthquakes, tornados, or floods). This approach to nuclear plant safety is sometimes referred to as "defense in depth." [9,10] It implies that nuclear engineers must do everything possible to prevent accidents from happening, through conservative design and safety systems. Then to cover the possibility that some of these systems will not work as intended, they must add engineered safeguards systems to minimize the consequences of any accident that might occur. All these features are then augmented by complete and detailed testing and inspection procedures for the various systems in the plant. The success of this approach is reflected in the exceptional safety record of the nuclear power industry in which, after some 300 reactor years of commercial reactor operating experience, there has never been a single incident in which a member of the public has been injured or in which damage to private property has occurred.

Environmental Impact of Nuclear Power Plants

The major source of environmental impact of any power plant is caused by the types of discharges that such plants release to the environment.[11] We need only glance up at the stack towering above a fossil-fueled power plant to realize that such plants discharge substantial quantities of combustion products in both gaseous and solid forms directly into the atmosphere, as well as waste materials into adjacent bodies of water. Although nuclear plants are not characterized by such combustion product releases and therefore are environmentally far superior to fossil-fueled units from this perspective, they do release minute quantities of radioactive materials into the environment (see Tables 15-2, 15-3, and 15-4). Furthermore, all large power plants discharge significant quantities of waste heat to the environment, either directly into adjacent bodies of water or into the atmosphere.

Any electrical power plant based upon a thermal cycle will inject some 60 to 70 per cent of the thermal energy it produces directly into the environment as waste heat. To be more specific, a 1,000-megawatt (electric) nuclear plant will typically discharge 2,000 megawatts of waste heat into the environment. A comparable sized fossil-fueled plant, because of its somewhat higher efficiency, will discharge 1,250 megawatts. Hence, although thermal discharge problems are not unique to nuclear power plants, they are somewhat more significant in this type of generating unit. Most modern nuclear plants are therefore designed with closed cooling cycles, usually based upon natural draft cooling towers (which discharge waste heat directly into the atmosphere).

As noted, nuclear plants inevitably release small quantities of radioactive material into the environment (since it is impossible to achieve zero release of pollutants from fossil-fueled plants or any other process, for that matter). Nuclear power plants, however, must be designed so that these releases are kept far below not only those levels that might have a significant effect on public health, but be, in addition, "as low as practicable" (as the federal regulations put it).[12] In practice, this means that the radioactivity released from nuclear plants is restricted so that the increased exposure to an individual in the vicinity of the plant is less than 1 per cent of the exposure he would receive from natural sources (cosmic radiation or radioactivity

Table 15-2. Occupational Health and Safety of Electric Power Plants (Nuclear Power and the Environment, American Nuclear Society, 1976).

	Plant Fuel[a]			
	Coal	*Oil*	*Natural Gas*	*Nuclear*
Occupational health (man days lost per year)	600	Unknown	Unknown	480
Occupational safety fatalities (deaths per year)	1.1–4	0.17–0.35	0.08–0.2	0.1–0.15
Nonfatal injuries (number per year)	46.8	13.1	5.3	6.0–7.0
Total man days lost per year	3,770[b]–9,250[c]	1,725–3,600	780–1,990	270–1,000

[a]Based on 1000-MW(e) power plants operating 75 per cent of the time.
[b]Surface strip-mined coal.
[c]Deep-mined coal.

Table 15–3. Public Health Effects from Coal, Oil, and Nuclear Power Plants.

Plant Type	*Pollutant*	*Relative Hazard Index*[a]
Coal	Sulfur dioxide	32,000
	Particulates	1,100
	Nitrogen oxides	4,530
Oil	Sulfur dioxide	11,960
	Particulates	176
	Nitrogen oxides	4,450
Nuclear		
Pressurized water reactor	Krypton-85 and xenon-133	1
	Iodine-131	19
Boiling water reactor	Krypton-85 and xenon-133	1
	Iodine-131	20

[a] As an example, a relative hazards index of 4,450 from the nitrogen oxide emitted from an oil-fired plant means that the nitrogen oxide emissions from an oil-fired plant should have 4,450 times the public health impact of the krypton-85 and xenon-133 emissions from the same-sized nuclear plant.

from the natural environment). Indeed, the exposure from nuclear plants is less than the fluctuations in this natural background level of exposure. Members of the public living some distance from the plant would receive far lower exposures. Experience has shown that nuclear power plants generally operate far below even these very low levels.

The Licensing of Nuclear Power Plants

The responsibility for nuclear power plant safety and environmental impact rests with the Nuclear Regulatory Commission (NRC), which has the authority to issue permits to construct and licenses to operate nuclear power plants. An application for a construction permit must contain a detailed description of the plant, its site characteristics, the utility's financial and technical qualifications for constructing and operating the plant, a justification for the new plant, and two voluminous reports: a Preliminary Safety Analysis Report (PSAR) consisting of ten to twenty volumes of analysis of the safety of the proposed power plant and an Environmental Impact Report (EIR) consisting of five to ten volumes evaluating the impact of the plant upon the environment. These documents are examined in great detail by the staff of the NRC as well as by outside consultants. The evaluation of the application for a construction permit will typically take about two years. During this time there will be several public hearings at which members of the public can present testimony before the Atomic Safety and Licensing Board within the NRC and may intervene by cross-examining the testimony of others.

Usually the evaluation process is one of iteration, in that the NRC will return to the applicant with a number of questions concerning the PSAR and EIR, and the applicant must then respond satisfactorily to these questions, frequently by agreeing to implement changes in the proposed design or possibly changing the location of the proposed site.

If the amended application is found to be acceptable, the NRC issues a construction permit to the applicant who then proceeds with construction of the plant. As the construction proceeds, a second major safety report, the Final Safety Analysis Report (FSAR) and an updated EIR are prepared with changes that were made in the original PSAR and EIR; they essentially document the final design of the plant. The review process then begins once again, utilizing both the internal staff of the NRC and outside consultants while allowing for public hearings. If the

Table 15–4. Fuel Consumption and Waste—1,000-Megawatt Power Plant.

	Hourly	*Daily*	*Annually*
Fuel Consumption			
Coal	690,000 pounds	8,300 tons[a]	2,300,000 tons
Uranium	0.3 pounds	7.4 pounds	About 1 ton
Waste Production			
Coal (ash)	69,000 pounds	830 tons[b]	230,000 tons
Uranium (total)	2.7 pounds	64 pounds	11.6 tons
High-level fission product waste	0.26 pounds	6.1 pounds	1.1 tons
Other waste	2.4 pounds	58 pounds	10.5 tons

[a]Equivalent to a 100-car trainload every day.
[b]Equivalent to a 33-car trainload every day (not including airborne wastes).

application is approved, then an operating license is issued.

But the NRC's responsibility is not ended at this point, for it must maintain continual onsite inspection to ensure that the plant is operating in a manner consistent with its operating license. As nuclear technology evolves, the NRC may require that the utility retrofit the plant to upgrade safety systems or operating procedures. Hence, the safety design of the plant should not be considered as fixed, but rather as a continually evolving process that must always be brought up to date.

THE NUCLEAR FUEL CYCLE

It is important to recognize that nuclear fuels are totally different from fossil fuels in several very important respects. Nuclear fuel (e.g., uranium) requires a number of sophisticated and expensive processing operations before it is inserted into the reactor core. It is then "burned" in the reactor for several years before being removed. Even after several years of use in the reactor, the fuel still possess a significant concentration of fissile material. Therefore, it can be removed from the reactor core, reprocessed, and refabricated into new fuel elements. The by-product waste from the reprocessed fuel is highly radioactive, and its disposal requires great care.

The operations involved in the extraction of uranium ore and the preparation, utilization, and reprocessing of nuclear reactor fuels are referred to as the nuclear fuel cycle.[13] The various stages (see Figure 15-7) of the fuel cycle can be identified as:

(1) *Mining*. Most of the uranium ore mined in the United States comes from the sedimentary sandstone and mudstone deposits of the Colorado Plateau and the Wyoming Basin and yields from 0.1 to 1 per cent U_3O_8. Both underground and open pit techniques are used to mine uranium ore in a manner similar to that used in other low grade ore mining. There is some uncertainty (and much disagreement) about the extent of our domestic uranium ore reserves. For example, the most recent ERDA estimates project that domestic reserves of relatively high concentration uranium ore are sufficient to fuel some 300 gigawatts (electric) of nuclear plant capacity[1] for the projected plant lifetimes of 40 years—which also happens to be the projected installed capacity by the year 2000 (see Figure 15-8). But the reserves of lower concentration are considerably larger. Furthermore, the significance of such estimates of uranium reserves depends greatly upon the reactor type. If plutonium recycling is allowed, these reserves can be extended by some 40 per cent.[14] Furthermore, if breeder reactors could be introduced, then the resource base becomes essentially infinite (or at least equivalent to thousands of years of fuel supply), since these reactors can utilize some

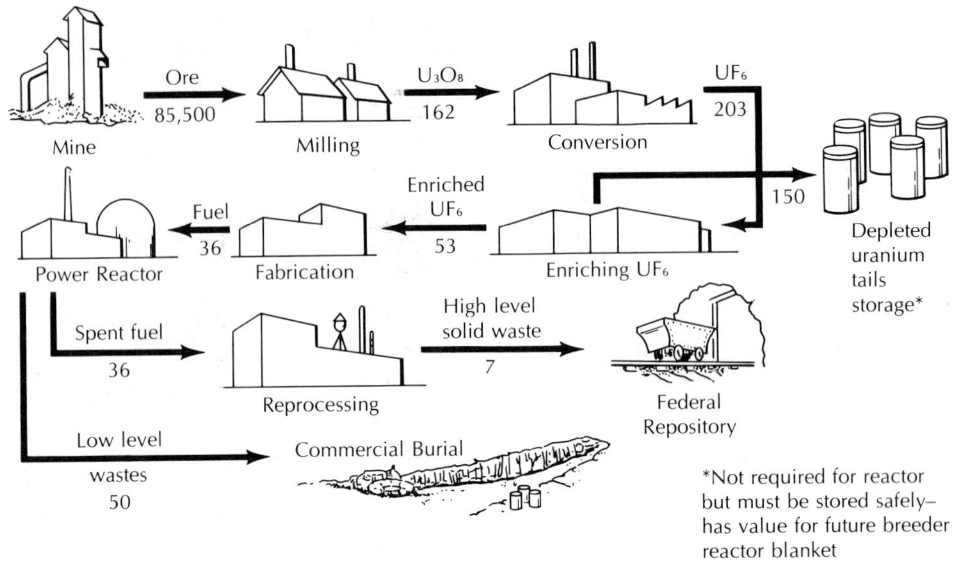

Figure 15-7. Annual quantities of fuel material required for routine (equilibrium) operation of 1,000-megawatt light water reactor. (The Nuclear Industry, USAEC Report WASH-1174-73, 1973.)

70 per cent of natural uranium and thorium reserves (in contrast to the 1 to 2 per cent utilization of light water reactors) and furthermore would make it economically attractive to utilize very low concentration ores.

(2) *Milling*. Milling is necessary to extract and concentrate uranium from the raw ore. The ore is first pulverized and then solvent extraction is used to produce *yellowcake*, a crude oxide containing some 70 to 90 per cent U_3O_8. It should be noted that concern has recently been voiced about the piles of residue or tailings from the milling process; these release small quantities of radon-222, a radioactive gas (although the public exposure from this source is estimated to be extremely small).[15] This problem is discussed and a solution suggested in Article 16 of this volume.

(3) *Conversion and Enrichment*. Essentially all power reactors (with the exception of heavy water reactors or the early gas-cooled, graphite-moderated reactors) utilize enriched uranium, that is, uranium with higher than the natural 0.711 per cent concentration of ^{235}U. The enrichment of uranium is a very difficult and expensive process, since it involves separating two isotopes, ^{235}U and ^{238}U, with very little mass difference and essentially no chemical difference. A variety of separation techniques have been used or proposed:

(i) Electromagnetic separation: Huge mass spectrometers were used for isotope separation during the Manhattan Project, but this scheme was rapidly replaced by the gaseous diffusion technique.

(ii) Gaseous diffusion: Since the diffusion coefficient for a gas to pass through a porous membrane is inversely proportional to the square root of its mass, one can first convert U_3O_8 into a gaseous compound, uranium hexaflouride (UF_6), and then pass this gas through thousands of porous barriers to separate the UF_6 (^{235}U) from the UF_6 (^{238}U).

(iii) Ultracentrifuges[16]: This simply involves the use of very high speed gas centrifuges or nozzle devices to separate the two isotopic forms of UF_6.

(iv) Laser photochemistry[17]: Of more recent interest are schemes that use high-

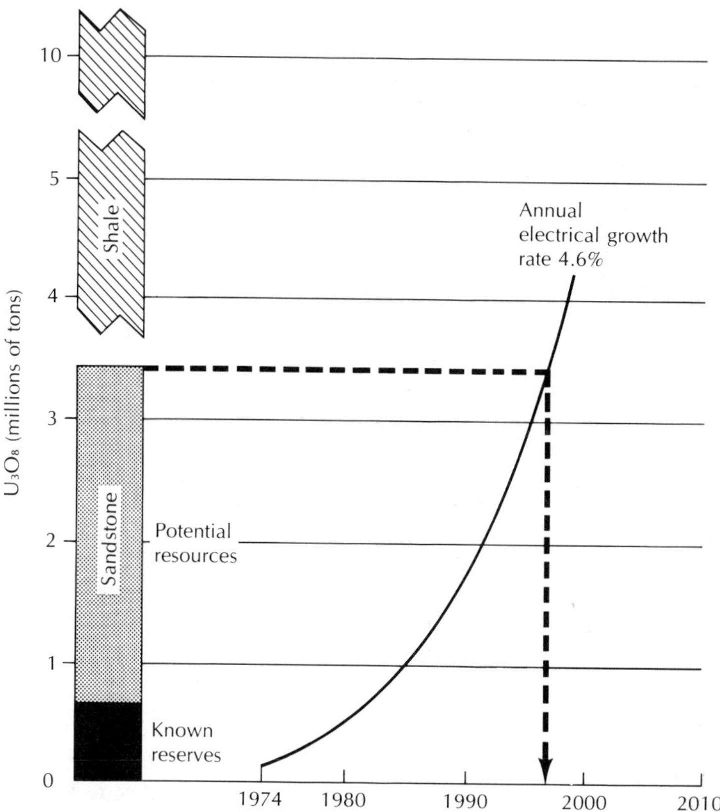

Figure 15-8. Uranium ore requirements for committed nuclear power plants (40 year lifetime) versus uranium ore reserves (domestic).

powered lasers to selectively excite ^{235}U in uranium vapor of UF_6 (^{235}U) by tuning the laser wavelength to distinguish between the isotopic mass shift in the electronic or vibrational energy levels of the mixture and selectively exciting (i.e., "tagging") one isotopic species. Then standard physical or chemical separation techniques can be used to skim off the excited species.

At present, gaseous diffusion continues to be the most common method used for uranium enrichment, although both centrifuge and nozzle separation plants are under construction, and laser photochemical methods hold great promise for the near future. It is likely, however, that enrichment will remain an extremely expensive process (presently accounting for some 30 per cent of nuclear fuel costs).

(4) *Fuel Fabrication*. Following enrichment, the UF_6 is then chemically converted into a ceramic powder, such as UO_2 or UC, and compacted into small pellets. These are loaded into metallic tubes, which are then bundled into fuel assemblies.

(5) *Fuel Burnup in the Reactor Core*. The fuel assemblies are loaded into the reactor core for power production. The assemblies are typically irradiated in the core for a period of several years. The fuel lifetime is limited by either criticality considerations (i.e., the fissile concentration drops too low to sustain a

chain reaction) or by radiation damage sustained by the fuel elements during operation.

(6) *Spent Fuel Storage and Decay*. After being irradiated in the reactor core, the fuel is intensely radioactive due to fission product buildup. The spent fuel is removed from the core and stored in water pools for several months to allow the short-lived fission products to decay. It is then loaded into heavily shielded and cooled casks for shipping to reprocessing facilities by either truck or rail. The shipping containers are carefully designed to ensure their integrity in the event of any conceivable type of shipping accident.

(7) *Spent Fuel Reprocessing*. The spent fuel discharged from a nuclear power reactor contains a significant quantity of unused uranium and plutonium, which can be extracted and reloaded into fresh fuel elements. Reprocessing of the spent fuel is also necessary to concentrate the radioactive fission product wastes into small volumes for eventual disposal. The principal scheme available for commercial recovery of uranium and plutonium from low enrichment LWR fuels is the hybrid aqueous-fluorination or Purex[18] process, which has been used on a commercial basis throughout the world for almost two decades.

Recently, it has been suggested that such reprocessing may pose a severe threat to world peace due to the nuclear weapons proliferation potential of plutonium, and therefore all efforts to recycle nuclear fuel should be abandoned in favor of a throwaway fuel cycle.[19, 20] On the surface, a throwaway fuel scheme would not appear to significantly increase the cost of nuclear fuel, since the direct cost savings anticipated with plutonium recycling (although they would amount to some $3 billion by the year 2000)[20] are only a small fraction of over-all nuclear fuel costs. But the real motivation for plutonium recycling involves the significant savings in uranium ore feed requirements, which would be reduced by 40 per cent.[14] Furthermore, such reprocessing and recycling will be required in any event if the fast breeder reactor is to be deployed.

(8) *Radioactive Waste Disposal*. Most public attention concerning the nuclear fuel cycle has been directed toward the disposal of high-level radioactive waste produced by nuclear power reactors. Such reactors build up an inventory of radioactive fission products during their operation. Although most of this radioactivity will decay quite rapidly following reactor shutdown and removal of spent fuel elements from the reactor core, a significant fraction of the high level radioactivity induced in the fuel is due to fission products such as radioactive strontium (^{90}Sr) and cesium (^{137}Cs), which are characterized by half-lives of roughly 30 years and which will decay to harmless levels only after several hundred years. But spent fuel will also contain trace amounts of such heavy radioactive elements (actinides) as plutonium, neptunium, and americium, which have half-lives of thousands of years. Therefore, radioactive wastes will have a residual radioactivity for a much longer period. The magnitude of this very slowly decaying component, however, is usually rather small. For example, the processed high-level radioactive wastes from a nuclear power plant will decay to essentially the same radiotoxicity level as natural uranium ore after several hundred years.[21]

The current procedure for treating high-level radioactive wastes is to first store them as a liquid waste solution following fuel reprocessing for up to five years in underground storage tanks to allow the bulk of the fission product activity to decay. Then, the liquid waste solution is converted into a stable form—either glass or cement—and encapsulated in a water-impervious inert container and shipped to a federal waste depository. The most promising scheme for permanent disposal of these wastes (i.e., permanent isolation from the environment so that no further surveillance or other monitoring or processing efforts are required) is to bury them deep beneath the earth in rock formations that exhibit exceptional geological stability. The hazard of such buried wastes, even when human intervention is taken into account (e.g., inadvertant drilling into the depository), is estimated to be extremely small.[22]

The Fast Breeder Reactor

The present generation of light water fission reactors can effectively utilize only about 1 per cent of our uranium ore resources. Hence, the resource base available to this type of reactor is rather limited, being of the same magnitude as the domestic reserves of petroleum and natural gas. Although these reserves should prove sufficient to fuel several hundred of these power plants for their operating lifetimes, it is apparent that this type of nuclear reactor must be regarded as only an interim, relatively short range energy source (see Figure 15-9).

A far more attractive reactor concept is the breeder reactor, which can utilize as much as 70 to 80 per cent of the available uranium (or thorium) reserves by converting ^{238}U (^{232}Th) into plutonium (^{233}U), which could then be reprocessed into fuel for either the original or other breeder reactors. The reserves of high grade uranium and thorium ores are sufficient to supply a fast breeder reactor economy for thousands of years. In fact, we have already stockpiled over 200,000 tons of ^{238}U as the "waste" products of the uranium enrichment plants used in the LWR plants. Furthermore, sufficient plutonium has been produced in LWR's to provide the initial fuel charge for several breeder reactors.

The fast breeder reactor occupies a rather unique position among our long-range energy options, since its scientific and technical feasibility and, to some extent, its commercial viability have already been established (in

Figure 15-9. Available energy from recoverable domestic resources. (Leonard J. Koch, in Conference on Magnitude and Deployment of Energy Resources, Oregon State University, 1975, p. 160.)

Available energy in quads (10^{15} BTU) shown graphically by area

Total U.S. energy consumption in 1974 was 73 quads

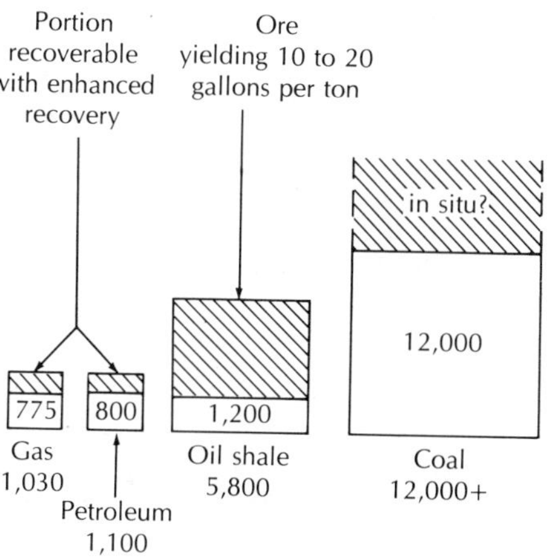

sharp contrast to other options such as solar, geothermal, or nuclear fusion energy). Fast breeder reactors have been built in this country and abroad for the past two decades. Indeed, France, the United Kingdom, and the Soviet Union have been successfully operating demonstration breeder reactor power plants for several years. Furthermore, the French have under construction a commercial prototype breeder reactor (Super Phenix)[8] rated at 1,250 megawatts (electric) and expect to market commercial fast breeder reactors by the early 1980's.

But there are major hurdles that must be overcome if we are to realize even a small fraction of the enormous potential of this energy source, and unfortunately, the most serious of these barriers to successful deployment of the breeder reactor are of a social and political (and perhaps psychological) rather than of a technical or an economic nature. Foremost among these barriers is the reluctance of the public to support breeder reactor development because they perceive such reactors as inherently more dangerous than light water reactors. (The term "fast" conveys an impression that such reactors might be harder to control.) But, in fact, the safety and environmental impact of a breeder reactor power plant is quite similar to that of more conventional nuclear plants.

A more serious problem involves the fuel cycle of the breeder reactor that utilizes larger amounts of plutonium as fuel than does the light water reactor. This poses a serious problem from the viewpoint of the proliferation of strategic nuclear weapons material—a problem that is similar in nature but considerably more serious than that posed by plutonium recycling in light water reactors.[20]

CONCLUDING REMARKS

As the nuclear power industry has matured—as nuclear power has passed from Fermi's demonstration of scientific *feasibility* to the present status of economic *viability* (and perhaps to the future status of technological *inevitability*)—so too has grown the public controversy over the role nuclear power

Table 15–5. The Pros and Cons of Nuclear Power.

Pros	*Cons*
	Popular press
Cheaper	Concern over nuclear reactor safety
Safer	Radiation release
Cleaner	Environmental impact
Available now	Radioactive waste disposal
Necessary to meet demand	Sabotage and nuclear theft
	Nuclear weapons proliferation
Sizable fuel reserves	Economics, reliability, energy payback
	Subconscious
	Legacy of Hiroshima (guilt complex)
	Nuclear = strange, new, invisible
	A means to force conservation
	Natural suspicion of technology
	Anti-establishment
	Real problems
	Public acceptance
	Lack of federal energy policy
	Complexities of federal regulations
	Financing all types of energy development
	International aspects (proliferation)

should play in our society. It is difficult these days to pick up a newspaper or turn on a television set without being confronted with some aspect of this controversy.

To illustrate the issues that arise in this rather heated debate, we have listed in Table 15-5 several of the more popular "pros" and "cons" involving nuclear power. Many of these topics will be examined in detail in subsequent articles in this chapter. A few comments are in order at this point, however.

In the "pro" column we have listed the contentions that nuclear power is *cheaper, safer,* and *cleaner* than other current viable alternatives and that it is available for immediate massive implementation (as evidenced by the fact that some 10 per cent of our electrical capacity is nuclear). The proponents of nuclear power note further that the past decade of nuclear plant operation has actually *demonstrated* these advantages. Nuclear plants have proven, by actual operation, to generate electrical power significantly more cheaply than have fossil-fueled fired plants (see Table 15-6). During their operation there is essentially no release of waste material (such as combustion products) to the environment. Furthermore, in two decades of nuclear power experience, there has never been a single instance of public injury or damage to private property from a nuclear plant accident. The proponents will furthermore claim that nuclear power is necessary if we are to meet the electrical demands of our society during the next several decades in the face of diminishing fossil fuel reserves, that sufficient domestic uranium reserves are available to make the present type of light water reactor a viable source of energy until well after the turn of the century, and with the introduction of the fast breeder reactor, nuclear power will become essentially an unlimited source of energy.

Table 15–6. Electrical Generating Costs (mills per kilowatt-hour).[23]

Plant type	*1975*	*1985*
Oil	33.45	55.1
Coal	17.54	42.0
Nuclear	12.27	38.3

A Breakdown of Electrical Generating Costs for the Year 1985

	Oil	*Coal*	*Nuclear*
Capital cost	13.7	20.8	25.2
Fuel cost	39.7	17.0	10.0
Operating and maintenance cost	1.7	4.2	3.1
Total	55.1	42.0	38.3

But balanced against these considerations is a rather imposing list of arguments commonly voiced against nuclear power. We have chosen to separate these arguments into three different classes. Most of the items in the first grouping have received intense public exposure in the media. These include concern over nuclear reactor safety and low level radiation releases; the environmental impact of both nuclear plants and their associated fuel cycle; the disposal of the radioactive waste produced by such plants; possibilities of sabotage of nuclear power plcnts and the theft of nuclear materials that might be suitable for nuclear weapons; the degree to which nuclear power accentuates the international proliferation of nuclear weapons; and concerns about the economics, reliability, and the energy efficiency of nuclear power (see Table 15-7).

But there are also a number of subcon-

Table 15–7. Reliability of Electrical Power Plants for 1975.[24]

	Nuclear	*Oil*	*Coal*	*Oil/Coal*
Availability factor	73.8%	70.3%	79.5%	76.4%
Capacity factor	64.4%	42.5%	54.8%	49.7%
Forced outage rate	13.7%	26.9%	11.1%	15.2%

scious elements involved in the nuclear power debate. Certainly, nuclear power continues to be burdened by the legacy of Hiroshima. Many in our society continue to be driven by a suppressed guilt complex engendered by the role our nation played in the development and military use of nuclear weapons. Their opposition to nuclear power may be, in part, a manifestation of their deep-rooted horror about and revulsion to nuclear weapons. They approach nuclear as if, by dismantling the nuclear power industry, they can return us to a world without the bomb, without the possibility of nuclear war. (But, unfortunately, the nuclear genie is out of the bottle, and there is very little that unilateral actions in this country can do to cram him back into it again.)

Certainly, too, the overwhelming emphasis of the early atomic energy program on military applications contributed to the public view of all nuclear technology as a mysterious and sinister force with a destructive potential that probably far outweighed any peaceful applications. Although this emphasis has certainly changed during the past decade as the peaceful atomic energy industry has matured, the aura of the military's nuclear weapons program remains, and nuclear power is far more likely to trigger the image of a mushroom cloud in the public mind than that of a clean, efficient power plant generating much needed electrical energy.

There are other subconscious elements involved in the opposition to nuclear power. There is, undoubtedly, a small number of people in the anti-nuclear movement who view any technology with great suspicion, and their real goals are to force our society back to a simpler way of life in which dependence on technology is minimized. This natural suspicion of technology is present not only in laymen, but in many scientists as well. In this sense one must be careful to distinguish the scientist, who usually studies fundamental scientific principles, from the engineer, who must deal with the highly complex applications of science and technology in society. Since few scientists have experience or training in engineering design or application, they frequently find it difficult to accept that *anyone* can deal with the technical problems, the conflicting goals, and the real and complex systems that are required in the practical applications of nuclear power routinely dealt with by the engineer.

But we certainly cannot dismiss the opposition to nuclear power simply as an emotional manifestation of suppressed fear or guilt concerning nuclear weapons or as a general reaction against technology. There are some very real problems that must be overcome if we are to realize the potential of nuclear power. Certainly, public acceptance, or the lack of it, presents the major barrier to the massive deployment of nuclear power, both in this country and abroad. Moreover, the processes by which nuclear power is regulated, licensed, and controlled continue to flounder in an unwieldy mass of red tape and bureaucratic delay. The rapid escalation of the already staggering cost of central station power plants—both nuclear and fossil fueled—may very well exceed the ability of our society to finance such construction from the private sector. Certainly, too, the international aspects associated with the spread of nuclear technology—particularly that associated with the nuclear fuel cycle—are intimately related to the proliferation of nuclear weapons capability and require immediate and serious attention.

REFERENCES

1. R. C. Seamans, *Transactions of the American Nuclear Society 24,* 6 (1976).
2. A variety of low level introductions to nuclear power engineering are available and include:
   J. R. Lamarsh, *Introduction to Nuclear Engineering* (Addison-Wesley, Reading, 1975).
   A. R. Foster and R. L. Wright, *Basic Nuclear Engineering* (Allyn & Bacon, Boston, 1976), 3rd Ed.
   S. Glasstone and A. Sesonske, *Nuclear Reactor Engineering* (Van Nostrand, New York, 1977), 2nd Ed.
3. J. J. Duderstadt and L. J. Hamilton, *Nuclear Reactor Analysis* (Wiley, New York, 1976), p. 69.
4. A. M. Perry and A. M. Weinberg, *Annual Review of Nuclear Science 22,* 317 (1972).
5. G. Masche, Systems Summary of a Westinghouse

Pressurized Water Reactor Nuclear Power Plant (Westinghouse Electric Corporation, Pittsburgh, 1971).
6. H. C. McIntyre, *Scientific American 233,* 17 (October, 1975).
7. H. Stewart et al., *Advances in Nuclear Science Technology 4,* 1 (1968).
8. G. A. Vendryes, *Scientific American 236,* 26 (1976).
9. Reactor Safety Study, U.S. Nuclear Regulatory Commission Report WASH-1400 (1976).
10. American Physical Society Reactor Safety Study, *Review of Modern Physics 14,* Suppl. *1,* 546 (1975).
11. G. G. Eichholz, *Environmental Aspects of Nuclear Power* (Ann Arbor Science Publishers, 1976).
12. Admendments to Title 10, Code of Federal Regulations, Part 50, Appendix I 40, Federal Register 19439 (May 5, 1975).
13. D. M. Elliot and L. E. Weaver, eds., *Education and Research in the Nuclear Fuel Cycle* (Oklahoma University Press, Norman, 1970).
14. B. Spinrad and E. Evans, *Transactions of the American Nuclear Society 24,* 10 (1976).
15. R. O. Pohl, Nuclear Energy: Health Effects of Th-230 (Cornell University Physics Report, 1975); B. Cohen, *Bulletin of the Atomic Scientist 32* (February, 1976), p. 61.
16. D. Olander, *Advances in Nuclear Science Technology 6* (1972).
17. R. N. Zare, *Scientific American 236,* 86 (1977).
18. W. P. Beggington, *Scientific American 235,* 30 (1976).
19. F. Ilke, *Bulletin of the Atomic Scientists* (October, 1976), p. 15; B. Feld, *Physics Today* (July, 1975), p. 23.
20. *Nuclear Power Issues and Choices* (Ford Foundation—MITRE Report) (Ballinger, Cambridge, 1977).
21. J. Hamstra, *Nuclear Safety 16,* 2 (1975).
22. C. F. Smith and W. E. Kastenberg, *Nuclear Engineering and Design 34,* 293 (1976).
23. L. Reichle, Ebasco Services, Inc., Presented to the New York Society of Security Analysts, 1975.
24. AIF Survey on 1975 Economics and Performances, Atomic Industrial Forum, Washington, 1976.

SUGGESTED READINGS

Benedict, Manson, 1971, Electric Power from Nuclear Fission, *Technology Review 74,* pp. 32–41.

Bethe, H. A., 1976, The Necessity of Fission Power, *Scientific American 234,* pp. 21–31.

Inglis, David R., 1973, *Nuclear Energy: Its Physics and Social Challenges* (Addison-Wesley, Reading, Mass.), 395p.

Rose, David J., 1974, Nuclear Electric Power, *Science 184,* pp. 351–359.

Spinrad, Bernard I., 1973, The Case for Nuclear Energy, *Ambiente-Environment 1,* No. 2.

Impacts of the Nuclear Energy Industry on Human Health and Safety 16

BERNARD L. COHEN 1976

Although many people believe that the effects of radiation on human health are poorly understood, at least the upper limits of these effects are well known from incidents in which people have received large doses of radiation. The data have been analyzed in reports by two prestigious groups of radiation biomedical experts—the National Academy of Sciences-National Research Council Committee on Biological Effects of Ionizing Radiation (BEIR)[1] and the United Nations Scientific Committee on Effects of Atomic Radiation (UNSCEAR).[2] In addition, there is continuing surveillance of the information by the International Commission on Radiological Protection (ICRP) and the National Council on Radiation Protection and Measurements (NCRP), groups mainly concerned with setting standards for maximum permissible exposure. Their conclusions will be used here to estimate the effects on human health of radioactivity released into the environment by various aspects of the nuclear energy industry.

The principal health effects of radiation are acute radiation sickness, cancer, and genetic defects. Acute radiation sickness, which can be fatal in a matter of days, results from exposures in excess of 100 rem (1 *r*oentgen-*e*quivalent-*m*an = energy deposit per unit mass of tissue, in units of 100 ergs per gram, times relative biological effectiveness). Gamma-ray exposures of about 500 rem (as it enters the body) without medical treatment and of 700 to 1,400 rem with various levels of treatment[3] have a 50 per cent probability of causing death. If death does not result, the patient recovers after several weeks. There have been seven fatalities (none since 1961) from acute radiation sickness in the United States—all of them workers on nuclear projects where something went wrong.

Cancer induction by radiation is a much broader threat, and there is a rather substantial

Dr. Bernard L. Cohen, an experimental nuclear physicist, is a professor of physics and the Director of the Nuclear Physics Laboratory at the University of Pittsburgh, Pittsburgh, Pennsylvania 15260. For the past five years, he has been active in research on environmental impacts of nuclear power, especially regarding plutonium and waste problems. He is past chairman of the American Physical Society Division of Nuclear Physics, and a member of the National Council of American Association of Physics Teachers, the Health Physics Society, and the American Nuclear Society.

From *American Scientist*, Vol. 64, No. 5, pp. 550–559, September-October 1976. Reprinted by permission of the author and Sigma Xi, The Scientific Research Society of North America.

body of data on human victims. The largest single source is the Japanese atomic bomb survivors. About 24,000 people were exposed to an average of about 130 rem, and more than a hundred excess cancer deaths have resulted. Almost 15,000 people in the United Kingdom who were treated with heavy doses of x ray for ankylosing spondylitis, an arthritis of the spine, received an average whole-body exposure of almost 400 rem, which resulted in more than a hundred excess deaths. Among 4,000 uranium miners who received average doses to the lung approaching 5,000 rem from radon inhalation, deaths have also exceeded that toll. Several situations have caused about 50 excess cancer deaths, including those involving 775 American women employed in painting radium numerals on watch dials between 1915 and 1935, almost 1,000 German victims of ankylosing spondylitis treated with ^{224}Ra, and fluorspar and metal miners exposed to radon gas. Several other situations that led to ten or so excess deaths have also been studied.

In assessing these data, it is usually assumed that the cancer risk is proportional to the total exposure in rem. This "linear–no threshold" hypothesis involves a very large extrapolation; it assumes, for example, that the probability of cancer induction by 1 millirem (mrem) which is typical of most exposures of interest, is 10^{-5} times the probability of induction by 100 rem, which is the region for which most data are available. For a number of reasons, however, this assumption seems more likely to overestimate than to underestimate the effects of low dosage. That there are mechanisms in the body for repairing radiation damage is well established[4]: chromosomes broken by radiation have been observed under a microscope to reunite, and 1,000-rem doses that are lethal to mice in a single exposure have little effect when distributed over several weeks. Rapidly multiplying cells are more susceptible to radiation injury than normal cells because there is less time for repair between cell divisions—this is the basis for cancer radiation therapy. In addition, cancer induction by radiation is known to be a multi-event process: if cancer were caused by a single hit on a single cell, the risk would be proportional to the number of cells, and a given exposure would be much less effective on small animals like mice. Good evidence exists that the latent period before cancers develop (15 years for large exposures) increases with decreased exposure, and for small exposures it may well exceed life expectancy. For these reasons, all four of the monitoring groups mentioned above have acknowledged that the linear–no threshold hypothesis is highly conservative, and although they all accept it as a basis for setting exposure standards, only the BEIR Committee condones its use for estimating risks; UNSCEAR pointedly refuses to do so, and NCRP has been highly critical of it.

The linear–no threshold hypothesis greatly simplifies calculations, making total effects proportional to the population dose in "man-rem," the sum of the exposures in rem to all those exposed. I shall use it here with the understanding that it yields upper limits for radiation effects. In particular, I shall use the BEIR estimate of 180×10^{-6} cancer deaths per man-rem[5], which means that for every rem of radiation a person receives to his whole body, his probability of ultimately dying of cancer is increased by 1.8 parts in ten thousand above the normal probability (16.8 per cent for the average American). On this basis, 1 rem of whole-body radiation reduces life expectancy by a little more than one day[6]. For perspective, it may be noted that the life expectancy reduction from smoking a single cigarette is equivalent to that of 5 mrem.

If radioactive material enters the body, exposures of individual organs are more of a problem than whole-body exposure, and the BEIR Report gives the risks separately. For example, the number of cancer deaths per million man-rem exposure to bone is 6; to thyroid, 6; to lungs, 39; and to the gastrointestinal tract, 30. Studies of the survivors of the Japanese atomic bombings show no evidence that the incidence of diseases other than cancer is affected by radiation.[7]

Genetic defects, which normally occur in

about 3 per cent of all live births[2], number about 100,000 per year in the United States; they are generally caused by spontaneous mutations in the sex cells. Because there is no evidence from human data for genetic defects in offspring from radiation received by parents, all estimates of such damage are based on animal data. Averaging the BEIR and UNSCEAR estimates gives 150×10^{-6} eventual genetic defects per man-rem exposure of the entire population[5]. The defects range from color blindness or an extra finger or toe (usually removed by simple surgery shortly after birth) to serious deformities that make life very difficult, and include diseases that develop much later in life. Studies of the Japanese survivors of the atomic bombings[8] have yielded no evidence for excessive genetic defects among offspring—a result that virtually ensures that the above estimate is not too small—and a recent reassessment indicates that it may be an order of magnitude too large.[9]

ROUTINE EMISSIONS FROM NUCLEAR INSTALLATIONS

A light water reactor consists of long, thin rods of UO_2 (fuel pins), enriched to about 3 per cent in ^{235}U, submerged in water. In the proper geometry, this arrangement permits a chain reaction in which a neutron striking a ^{235}U nucleus induces a fission reaction, which releases neutrons, some of which induce other fission reactions. Each fission reaction releases energy (about 200 MeV), which is rapidly converted to heat, warming the surrounding water. The reactor therefore serves as a gigantic water heater; as water is pumped through at a rate of thousands of gallons per second, it is heated to 600 °F. The hot water may then be converted to steam either in the reactor (boiling water reactor, BWR) or in an external heat exchanger (pressurized water reactor, PWR); the steam then drives a turbine which turns a generator to produce electric power.

The fuel is in the form of UO_2 ceramic pellets about 1.5 centimeter long by 1 centimeter in diameter. About 200 of these pellets are lined up end to end inside a zirconium alloy tube (cladding), which is then sealed by welding. The reactor fuel consists of about 40,000 of these fuel pins, or a total of about 8 million pellets.

When a ^{235}U nucleus is struck by a neutron and undergoes fission, the two pieces into which it splits are ordinarily radioactive—this is the principal source of radioactivity in the nuclear energy industry. The pieces fly apart with considerable energy (about 80 per cent of the 200-million electron volt energy release is in their kinetic energy), but they are stopped after traveling only about 0.02 millimeter, so nearly all the radioactivity remains very close to the site of the original uranium nucleus inside the ceramic fuel pellet. The same is true for the second most important source of radioactivity, the neutrons captured by the uranium to make still heavier radioactive nuclei—neptunium, plutonium, americum, and curium—called actinides.

Although nearly all the radioactive nuclei remain sealed inside the ceramic pellets, a few of the fission products have a degree of mobility, and some small fraction of them eventually diffuse out of the pellets but remain contained inside the cladding. During the operation of the reactor, about one or two per thousand of the fuel pins develop tiny leaks in the cladding, releasing the radioactive material that has diffused out of the pellets into the water. Chemical cleanup facilities remove the radioactive material from the water, but they do not remove the gaseous fission products, which include krypton and xenon isotopes and iodine. The iodine is so volatile that, in spite of elaborate equipment for trapping it out, a fraction of 1 per cent of it comes off with the gases. These gases, including also small fractions of 1 per cent of a few other volatile fission products, are held for some time within the power plant to allow the short half-life activities to decay. Eventually they are released into the environment. This is one way in which the public is exposed to radiation by routine operation of a nuclear plant.

Nuclear Regulatory Commission regulations require that no member of the public, including those living closest to the plant, receive a radiation dose from these emissions larger than 5 mrem per year to the whole body, or 15 mrem per year to the thyroid. It is estimated that if all the electric power now used in the United States (approximately 400 million kilowatts) were produced by light water reactors, the average American would receive an average annual exposure from the krypton and xenon of about 0.05 mrem per year.[10] The iodine released yields exposures to human thyroids of the same order of magnitude,[11] mostly due to the concentration in cow's milk of material settling on grass; but this does considerably less harm because it is less effective in inducing cancer.

Another source of routine emissions of radioactivity is tritium (^3H). In about one fission reaction out of 500, the uranium nucleus splits into three parts (ternary fission) rather than two, and in about 5 per cent of these cases (once in 10,000 fissions) one of the three pieces is ^3H. Other sources of ^3H in reactors are neutron reactions in boron and ^2H. The difficulty with ^3H is that it mixes with the ordinary hydrogen in the water and cannot be separated from it; thus, when water is released from the plant, it releases some ^3H into a nearby river, lake, or ocean. The Nuclear Regulatory Commission regulations require that no member of the public be exposed to more than 5 mrem per year of whole-body radiation from this water, and that value is calculated on the assumption that a person derives all his drinking water and fish from the plant discharge canal and swims in it for an hour a day. It is estimated that, if all our power were nuclear, the average American would receive less than 0.01 mrem per year from this source.[12]

When as much of the fuel in a reactor has been burned up as consistent with proper operation, it must be removed from the reactor and replaced with fresh fuel (typically one-third of the fuel is replaced in one such operation per year). The spent fuel is stored for about 6 months in the power plant to allow short half-life radioactivity to decay away, and it is then shipped to a fuel reprocessing plant. There the fuel pins are cut into pieces of manageable size and dissolved in acid, and the solution is chemically processed to remove the uranium, which is useful for making fresh fuel, and the plutonium, which may be used for making future fuels. Everything else is classified as "waste"—including all the fission products that contain the vast majority of the radioactivity, the uranium and plutonium that escaped removal in the chemical processing (typically 0.5 per cent with current technology), and the other actinides produced. The eventual disposal of this waste is an important topic that will be discussed below.

When the fuel pins are dissolved, the gases once again present a problem. Since xenon has no long half-life isotopes, no radioactive xenon is present, but krypton-85 has a 10-year half-life, and in current technology all of it is released to the atmosphere from a tall stack. The tritium is released as water vapor in the same way. It is estimated that if all our present electric power were nuclear, the average American would be exposed to 0.02 mrem per year from the krypton-85 and 0.15 mrem per year from the tritium.[13] In addition, people in other countries would be exposed to 0.02 mrem per year from krypton-85 produced in the United States. Active and advanced development programs are in progress for greatly reducing the emissions of krypton-85, but reducing the tritium emissions is a much more difficult problem.

When these exposures are added to the 0.05 mrem per year from the power plants, we see that the exposure to the average American from routine emissions if all our power were nuclear would be about 0.23 mrem per year. If we compare this average exposure with other radiation we experience,[14] we find that it is less than 1/500 of our exposure from natural radiation (U.S. average = 130 mrem per year) and about 1/300 of our exposure from medical and dental x rays. Natural radiation varies widely, from an average of 250 mrem per year in Colorado and Wyoming to

100 mrem per year in Texas and Louisiana. In parts of India and Brazil, where average exposures are 1,500 mrem per year from monazite sands rich in thorium and uranium, studies of the population have revealed no unusual effects. Even within a single city exposures may vary considerably: the radiation level is 10 mrem per year higher[15] in Manhattan (built on granite) than in Brooklyn (built on sand). Building materials such as brick and stone also contain significant quantities of radioactive material. Living in a typical brick or stone house (rather than a wooden one) adds about 30 mrem per year and in eight months causes more exposure than a lifetime of all-nuclear power. The 0.23 mrem per year from routine emissions if all our power were nuclear is substantially exceeded by even such minor sources of radiation[14] as luminous-dial watches (1 mrem per year) and airplane flights (0.7 mrem per year at 30,000 feet), and is comparable to the average child's dosage from watching television (0.3 mrem per year from x rays).

The consequences of 0.23 mrem per year of whole-body radiation to the average American may be readily calculated using the risk estimates given in the previous section: 8.3 additional cancer deaths per year and 7.0 additional genetic defects. Uranium and its daughters are released from various other elements of the nuclear fuel cycle besides the power plant and fuel reprocessing facilities, but because these involve alpha-particle emitters, which do their damage to a few specific organs following inhalation, the effects cannot be expressed in terms of whole-body radiation. The numbers of deaths caused by these agents if all our power were nuclear are[16]: uranium ore mills, 0.16 per year; conversion facilities, 0.09 per year; enrichment facilities, 0.01 per year; fuel fabrication plants, 0.03 per year; transportation, 0.08 per year. Adding these effects to the 8.3 deaths per year from power plants and fuel reprocessing gives a grand total of 8.7 deaths per year.[17] This is the first entry in Table 16-1.

The preceding estimates are based on steady production of 400 million kilowatts for

Table 16–1. Annual Cancer (Plus Acute Radiation Sickness) Deaths due to Radiation from Aspects of a U.S. Nuclear Energy Industry Generating 400 Million Kilowatts of Electricity[a]

Source	*Deaths per year*
Routine emissions	8.7
Reactor accidents	10.0 (600)[b]
Transportation accidents	0.01
Waste disposal	0.4
Plutonium (routine release)	0.1
Total	20.00 (600)[b]

[a]Does not include effects of long half-life radioactivities, sabotage, or terrorism.

[b]Numbers in parentheses represent worst claim by critics of the nuclear energy industry.

a period long enough to bring the effects of krypton-85 and ^3H into equilibrium with their decay, which would be a few decades. However, no such equilibrium can be achieved with long half-life radionuclides like carbon-14 (5,600 years) and radon-222, which is a granddaughter of thorium-230 (8×10^4 years), and their effects would grow linearly with time. At present and for the near future, because they contribute to population exposure in a very minor way, control of their emissions is not considered to be an urgent matter and is receiving little attention. However, unless the linear–no threshold theory of biological effects of radiation is abandoned, action on these matters cannot be long delayed.

The issue of carbon-14 was first raised in mid-1974. Carbon-14 is produced by neutron reactions on the rare oxygen isotope oxygen-17 and nitrogen-14 impurities in the fuel and coolant. If all our power were from light water reactors, about 4,000 curies per year would be released from these plants, and an additional 8,000 curies per year would be discharged from fuel reprocessing plants with current technology.[18] The discharge will presumably mix with the carbon in the biosphere, and if its effects are integrated to infinity with populations remaining constant, on the linear–no threshold theory it would eventually cause 20 cancer deaths in the United States plus a proportionate number in the rest of the world. However, it seems likely that equipment now being developed to freeze out the krypton-85 in reprocessing plants will simultaneously remove the carbon-14, thus eliminating two-thirds of the effects.

When uranium is separated from the mined ore in the ore processing mill, the residue containing radium and its precursor, thorium-230, is accumulated in large piles, typically 1 kilometer square in area × 5 meters deep. The radon gas emitted from the tailings piles resulting from one year of all-nuclear power (2.5 piles of the above dimensions) is estimated[19] to cause 0.8 lung cancers per year in the United States (my estimate, ref. 20, is an order of magnitude smaller)—but this situation will continue for tens of thousands of years if it is not remedied. Mill tailings have caused local problems, for example, in Grand Junction, Colorado, where they were used for building construction[21] and in Salt Lake City, where there is a large pile within the city limits. As a result, the problem has been under intense investigation, and plans are being made to remove or cover the piles.[22] For example, a half-inch of asphalt protected by a few feet of earth cover stabilized by rock would reduce the emissions by a factor of 500 and would cost about $3.5 million per year if all U.S. power were nuclear[23]—only 0.01 per cent of the value of the electricity. For perspective it might be pointed out that if nothing were done about the piles, the tailings from one year of all-nuclear power would increase the natural radon background by only one part in 6,000 and would contribute less radon than is currently being released by phosphate mining. The whole problem would, of course, be grossly reduced with breeder reactors and one might question the validity of equating health effects tens of thousands of years in the future with those of the present day.[23]

It is difficult to deal with emissions of carbon-14 and radon-222 in Table 16-1. If nothing is done about them and their entire potential cost in human lives is eventually realized, they would be dominant contributors in that table, but if they are properly handled, they will be of minor importance. The NRC policy[24] requiring emission control devices in power plants where the cost is less than $1,000 per man-rem exposure avoided, which corresponds to $6 million per life saved, leads us to expect the latter. Since these problems are so recently discovered, are doing little harm as yet (radon emissions from mill tailings begin only after the mill is closed and the pile dries out), and are being actively worked on, it does not now seem reasonable to include them in Table 16-1.

POWER PLANT ACCIDENTS

In routine operations in the nuclear industry, nearly all the radioactivity produced in reactors ends up as waste at the fuel reprocessing plant, which, as we shall see, is not difficult to dispose of safely. However, the danger exists that, due to some sort of accident in the reactor, an appreciable fraction of this radioactivity will be released into the environment at the power plant. If this should happen, the potential for damage is very great.

Because essentially all the radioactivity produced is sealed inside the UO_2 ceramic fuel pellets, the only way for it to be released is for these pellets to be melted. Thus any reactor accident of large consequences must involve a "melt-down." Since the melting temperature of UO_2 is over 5,000 °F, whereas normal operating temperatures are near and below 1,000 °F, a melt-down cannot result from small abnormalities. One possible cause of a melt-down might seem to be a large reacvivity excursion produced by withdrawing control rods too far and too fast. Several mitigating effects would follow, however: initially, the power level would escalate rapidly, but as a result the reactor would heat up. As the temperature increases, uranium-238 captures more neutrons in the "resonance region" (due to Doppler broadening of resonances) leaving fewer neutrons to be slowed down to thermal energies where they induce fission in uranium-235; moreover, as the temperature increases, water becomes a poorer moderator (in a BWR, more water boils into steam, which is essentially an elimination of the moderator). Hence, these reactors have a large "negative temperature coefficient of reactivity" which works powerfully against large reactivity excursions. In addition, the emergency insertion of control rods (called "scram") is such a simple operation that it would rarely fail. Because it depends only on gravity (PWR) or on stored fluid pressure (BWR), it does not require electric power.

These safety features are challenged rather frequently. About once a year on the average, a generator is suddenly taken off-line because of some abnormal electrical occurrence, and when this happens, the turbine that drives it can no longer accept steam. The resulting back pressure causes the steam bubbles to collapse in a BWR, thereby suddenly increasing the reactivity, which greatly increases the reactor power. If the emergency control rods should fail to insert, the pressure would build up dangerously. This accident is called ATWS (*a*nticipated *t*ransient *w*ithout *s*cram), and in many reactors the scram system is the only defense against this once-a-year challenge. A backup "poison-insertion system," which would inject boron solution (a strong neutron absorber), would be another defense, but there has been strong resistance to this because, if it were to be activated unnecessarily, it would keep the reactor shut down for many hours.

Safety experts agree that the most likely cause of a reactor fuel melt-down is not a reactivity excursion but a loss of coolant accident (LOCA) resulting from a large leak in the cooling water system. The water temperature in these reactors is about 600 °F (high temperatures produce high efficiencies), and to prevent or control boiling, the pressure must be very high, about 1,000 pounds per square inch in the BWR and 2,200 pounds per square inch in the PWR. If there were a rupture in the high-pressure system, the water would flash into steam and escape at a tremendous rate (this is called a "blow-down"), leaving the reactor core without coolant. Loss of the water moderator would immediately shut down the chain reaction, but it would not, of course, halt the radioactivity decay process.

The power generated by the radioactivity in the fuel pellets immediately after the chain reaction stops is very substantial—about 6 per cent of the full power level of the reactor—and it is easily enough to eventually melt the fuel. In the PWR, if the fuel were left without coolant for 45 seconds (possibly even for 30 seconds), the temperature would get so high that bringing in water might do more harm than good; at high temperatures, water reacts chemically with the zirconium fuel cladding in an exothermal reaction, which would raise the temperature still more. Thus, if cooling is not restored within about 45 seconds, the reactor may be doomed to melt-down (in a BWR, this critical time is about 3 to 5 minutes), releasing the radioactive material. Complete melt-down of the fuel would take about 30 minutes, and after an hour or so the molten fuel would melt through the reactor vessel. An appreciable fraction of the radioactivity would at this point come spewing out in the form of a radioactive dust or gas.

A great deal of engineering effort has been expended to minimize the probability of a LOCA, to reduce the chance that a LOCA would lead to a melt-down, and to mitigate the consequences of a melt-down if it should occur. Quality standards on materials and fabrication methods match or exceed those in any other industry, and rarely is expense an issue in this regard. A very elaborate program of inspections is maintained during the fabrication stage, including x raying of all welds, magnetic particle inspections, and a very elaborate series of ultrasonic tests aimed at detecting imperfections that might lead to failures of materials. Once the reactor comes into operation, periodic shutdowns are scheduled for extensive ultrasonic and visual inspections. (It was in these visual inspections that the hairline pipe cracks in a few BWR's were discovered in early 1975).

Since large leaks develop from small leaks,

the next line of defense is in systems for detecting small leaks if they should occur. Since the water is at high temperature and under high pressure, any leak would release steam, which would increase the humidity. Two types of systems, based on different physical principles, are used to detect increases in humidity around the high-pressure system. Because radioactivity in the water would emerge with the steam, two particularly sensitive types of systems capable of detecting increases of airborne radioactivity are also used.

If, in spite of these precautions, a LOCA should occur, the next line of defense is the emergency core cooling system (ECCS), an elaborate arrangement for injecting water back into the system to reflood the reactor core (because all pipes enter the reactor vessel above the core, reflooding is possible unless the rupture is in the lower part of the reactor vessel itself; the latter is of very thick, high-quality steel, and its rupture is orders of magnitude less probable than breaks in piping or in external components). The ECCS is a highly redundant system, and simple failures of pumps or valves would not prevent its operation. All estimates indicate that it is about 99 per cent certain of delivering water in the event of a LOCA.

Nevertheless, there has been extensive controversy over whether the ECCS will prevent a melt-down in the event of a large LOCA. By the time the water from the ECCS fills the reactor vessel up to the bottom of the fuel pins, the latter are quite hot, and the water flashes into steam. The steam exerts a back pressure that retards flooding to a rate not much more than 1 inch per second, and there is a period during which the heat transfer is principally by water droplets entrained in steam. This type of heat transfer is not well understood, and there is considerable uncertainty about cooling by the water-steam mixture during the initial blow-down. In order to assess these problems, engineers conducted experiments with full-length electrically heated fuel-pin mock-ups and developed empirical "theories" to explain their observations. They then used these empirical theories in computer codes to calculate the operation of the ECCS. This procedure is highly inaccurate, and the engineering approach to such a situation is to apply a factor of safety.

In 1971, the Union of Concerned Scientists (UCS) headed by Henry Kendall studied these matters and declared that they did not consider the factor of safety adequate. In the controversy that followed, the Atomic Energy Commission (AEC) organized hearings that lasted more than a year to consider the question, and several AEC safety experts came forward to support Kendall's contention. As a result of the hearings, the AEC increased the factor of safety and some reactors were forced to reduce their power levels until fuel pins with smaller diameters could be installed. The AEC safety experts who had supported Kendall said (according to an AEC statement) that they were now satisfied that the precautions are adequate, but Kendall is still far from convinced. Very elaborate tests to develop further understanding of the problem began in 1977, using a reactor especially constructed and instrumented for the purpose.

If a LOCA should occur and the ECCS should fail to perform its function, there would be a melt-down. In order to mitigate the consequences, the entire system is enclosed in a "containment," constructed of very thick, heavily reinforced concrete lined with steel plate (the most common type is tested to withstand an internal pressure of 5 atmospheres). The containment is strong enough to repel a wide variety of external threats, including missiles a tornado might hurl at it (automobiles, trees, etc.) and conventional explosives and bombs. The function of the containment in a melt-down accident is to contain the radioactive dust for a time. Inside it are systems for pumping the air through filters to remove the dust and sprays for removing iodine. Because the walls are relatively cool, many of the radioactive materials would plate out on them. Thus, if the containment held for at least a few hours, most of the airborne radioactivity would be removed and the consequences of the accident to the public would not be serious.

The situation could be much more serious if

the containment should fail shortly after the molten fuel melts through the reactor vessel. This could happen immediately as a result of a very violent (but highly improbable) explosion as the molten fuel drops into water, or relatively early as a result of high steam pressure if the water sprays designed to condense the steam inside the containment should fail to function. In such situations, the airborne radioactive dust would be released into the environment, and the results would then depend on weather conditions. Ordinarily, the radioactivity would be widely dispersed and cause little obvious damage,[25] but if there were a strong temperature inversion the radioactive cloud would be concentrated close to the ground—anyone it passed would be exposed externally and would inhale radioactive dust. There could be thousands of fatalities.

Among the many surveys of the probabilities and consequences of reactor accidents, the most elaborate is the recent study financed by the AEC and directed by Norman Rasmussen of the Massachusetts Institute of Technology. This project involved 60 man-years of effort and cost $4 million; its results were published in draft form in August 1974, and, after extensive criticism and revision, in final form in November 1975 as the multivolume document WASH-1400. If one is willing to accept the Rasmussen study, answers are immediately available to a wide variety of questions. For example, there would be a melt-down about once in 20,000 reactor-years; if all our power were nuclear (400 reactors), we might expect an accident every 50 years on an average. The average annual consequences (1/50 the average consequence per melt-down) would be 0.2 deaths from acute radiation sickness plus 10 eventual cancer deaths (see Table 16-1), and $6 million in damages, mostly in cleanup and evacuation costs. The frequency of accidents of varying severity (as indicated by the number of fatalities) is shown in Table 16-2 and a summary of this study is presented in Article 17 of this volume.

The consequences of the worst possible

Table 16–2. Severity Distribution of Accidents.

	Frequency^{-1} (Average Years between Accidents)		
Number of Fatalities	*Nuclear*	*Other Man-caused*[a]	*Natural Disasters*
>100	100	1.5	2
>1,000	300	25	8
>10,000	10,000	500	50

[a]Includes dam failures, airplane crashes in crowded areas, fires, explosions, releases of poison gas, etc.

accident are estimated to be 3,500 fatalities from acute radiation sickness plus 45,000 later cancer deaths. An accident of this magnitude is predicted to occur about once in a million years in the United States if all our power were nuclear. This catastrophe would do little property damage, but other accidents, especially those accompanied by widespread heavy rainstorms, would cause few fatalities but would contaminate large areas and require extensive evacuation and clean-up. In the worst accident of this type, expected once in a million years, these would cost $14 billion.

Although it is often said that the worst nuclear accident would be much more terrible than any other accident connected with man's production of energy, this is by no means correct. There are hydroelectric dams whose failure could cause over 200,000 fatalities, and such failures are estimated to be much more probable than a very bad nuclear accident.[26] Gas explosions, especially those connected with the transport of liquified natural gas, which have been envisioned, could cause 100,000 fatalities. Moreover, unlike these situations, the great majority of the fatalities from the nuclear catastrophe would be essentially unnoticed, arising from a slight increase in cancer occurrence many years later.

The critics of nuclear power have not accepted the Rasmussen report. Perhaps their most concrete objection has been to the emergency core cooling system, as discussed above; if they are correct on this matter, the probability of a melt-down would be increased threefold to one in 6,000 reactor-years. They have also objected to the general approach of the Rasmussen group to predicting the probability of a melt-down ("fault-tree analysis"). Although they have never offered a numerical estimate of this probability, they would be hard put to justify a number larger than one in 2,000 reactor-years, 10 times the WASH-1400 estimate. Naval reactors, which have all the same problems and potential dangers, have already operated 2,000 reactor-years without a melt-down, and civilian reactors of this type have operated 250 reactor-years without a significant LOCA (there can be no doubt that the ECCS would prevent a melt-down in the great majority of LOCA's, which would be relatively small and slow in developing).

On the other basic element, the consequences of a melt-down, WASH-1400 is open to criticism in that it did not use the linear–no threshold dose-effect relationship recommended by the BEIR Report[1] but introduced a dose-reduction factor recommended by its prestigious advisory panel on health effects. This reduces its cancer estimates by a factor of two. The critics also object to the assumptions about evacuation and claim that WASH-1400 underestimates the consequences of accidents by about a factor of six.[27] Combining this with the factor of 10 disagreement on probability of accidents, the critics could claim that WASH-1400 underestimates the average number of fatalities from reactor accidents by a factor of 60, giving an annual average of 600 fatalities per year from all-nuclear power. This number is shown in parentheses in Table 16-1.

TRANSPORTATION ACCIDENTS

When spent fuel is shipped from the power plant to the fuel reprocessing plant, there is a possibility of an accident in transit that would release radioactivity to the environment. Several features differentiate such releases from those in power plant accidents. First, only a very small fraction of the fuel in a reactor is involved in any one shipment. Second, the fuel is stored in the plant for about 6 months before shipment to allow the short half-life radioactivity to decay away; this reduces the potential danger by two orders of magnitude. Third, and most important, the highest temperatures that would ordinarily be encountered in a transport accident are those of a gasoline or an organic solvent fire—about 1,500 °F, far below the 5,000 °F temperature to melt the UO_2 ceramic fuel pellets. Thus, since nearly all the radioactivity remains trapped in the pellets, the major danger is that the cladding tubes will be ruptured, releasing the small fraction of the radioactivity that had migrated out of the pellets to become trapped inside the tubes. This radioactivity is principally krypton-85, which is destined to be released from the fuel reprocessing plant under more controlled conditions. In addition, it is sometimes assumed that, in some unspecified way, a very small fraction of the solid fission products are released.[28,29]

In order to minimize the danger of such releases, spent fuel is shipped in casks costing about $2 million each, designed and prototype-tested to withstand, without release of radioactivity, a 30-mph crash into a solid and unyielding obstacle, envelopment in a gasoline fire for 30 minutes, submersion in water for 8 hours, and a puncture test. It seems reasonable to expect a high degree of protection against accident damage from such an elaborate effort.

The same precautions are also taken with the waste glass to be shipped from the fuel reprocessing plant to a burial site. Moreover, by the time the glass is shipped, radioactivity has decayed by another factor of six, and the glass is enclosed in a thick stainless steel container, which is far stronger than the fuel pin cladding. Thus, the risk in waste glass transport is considerably less than in spent fuel transport.

Studies of the problem, including estimates of releases and their consequences from all types of waste transport accidents, indicate that if all U.S. power were nuclear there would be an average of less than one fatality per century due to radioactivity releases in these accidents.[30] There would, of course, be orders of magnitude more fatalities from the traffic aspects of these accidents, but coal-fired power requires a hundred times more transport and hence would cause a hundred times as many transport accident fatalities.

RADIOACTIVE WASTE DISPOSAL

At present, the high-level wastes that accumulate in fuel reprocessing plants are kept in solution and stored in large tanks. There is currently 600,000 gallons of this waste from nuclear power plants, and more than 100 times that much from government operations, principally the production of plutonium for weapons. The plans for waste from civilian power are very different. The Nuclear Regulatory Commission regulations require that it be converted to a suitable solid form (as yet unspecified) within 5 years and delivered to a government repository within 10 years. The first deliveries may be expected in the late 1980's (the little waste that has already been generated is exempted from this schedule by a "grandfather" clause). Plans for the repository are not yet final, but the waste will be buried in some suitably chosen geological formation about 600 meters underground. Probably it will be in the form of glass cylinders 0.3 meters diameter × 3 meters long (0.2 cubic meters volume); a typical power plant would produce about ten of these per year.

I have evaluated the hazard from these buried wastes previously in both a summary[31] and a detailed paper,[32] and so I review the situation only very briefly here. The principal danger once the material is buried is that it might be contacted by ground water, be leached into solution, move through aquifers with the water, and, eventually reach the surface, contaminating food and drinking water. The ingestion hazard from the waste generated in one year if all our present electric power were from light water reactors is shown in Table 16-3.

The material must be isolated from our environment for a few hundred years; before worrying about longer times one should consider some of the other chemical and biological poisons in the earth and those produced by man. For example, a lethal dose of arsenic (As_2O_3) is 3 grams, and we import ten times as much of it into our country each year as we would produce radioactive waste if all our power were nuclear. This arsenic is not buried deep underground; in fact much of it is scattered on the surface as herbicides in regions where food is grown.

The requirement that radioactive waste be isolated for hundreds of years seems alarming to some because few things in our environment last that long. Deep underground, however, the time constants for change are in the range 10^7 to 10^8 years. The following factors provide additional protection against release during the few-hundred-year critical period: (a) The material will be buried in a geological formation that has been free of ground water for tens of millions of years and in which geologists are quite certain there will be no water for some time into the future. (b) If water should get into the formation, the rock would have to be leached or dissolved away before water could reach the waste. Even if the rock were salt, dissolution would typically require thousands of years. (c) Once the water reached the waste glass, the latter

Table 16–3. Ingestion Hazard from Waste Generated in One Year if All U.S. Electric Power Were from Light Water Reactors.

	Years after Reprocessing							
	0	*100*	*200*	*300*	*500*	*1,000*	*10^6*	*10^8*
Grams ingested for 50 per cent cancer risk	0.025	0.25	2.5	25	150	400	4,000	25,000

would be leached at a rate of only about 1 per cent per century. (d) Ground water flows through aquifers rather slowly, requiring typically 1,000 years to reach surface waters from a depth of 600 meter. (e) Most of the radioactive materials would be held up by ion exchange processes, traveling 100 to 10,000 times slower than water.

A quantitative evaluation of the hazard from the waste throughout its existence may be obtained using a model in which the waste is buried at random locations throughout the United States but always at a depth of 600 meters. It is assumed that an atom of buried waste is no more likely to reach the surface and get into a person than is an atom of radium in the rock or soil above it. The probability for an atom of radium is easily estimated because we know the amount of radium in the top 600 meters of the United States and the amount of radium in people (from measurements on corpses). For radium the probability is 4×10^{-13} per year. When this probability is applied to the waste, the number of fatalities expected annually from one year's waste may then be calculated as a function of time and integrated over time to yield the ultimate consequences. If the integration is extended over a million years, the result is 0.4 eventual fatalities from the waste generated by 1 year of all-nuclear power (see Table 16-1).

By comparison, burning up the uranium to produce this waste would save about 50 fatalities due to radon emissions. Thus, on any long-time scale, nuclear power must be viewed as a method for *cleansing* the earth of radioactivity. It should be noted that this estimate is based on no surveillance, since there is no surveillance of the radium with which it is compared in the model. Also, the model is a conservative one: random burial offers less security than careful choice of a burial site based on geological information, and the average radium in the top 600 meters includes material near the surface where most erosion takes place and where it is thus more likely to be accessible for ingestion than material buried 600 meters below.

Estimates were made of the fatalities that would result from releases as airborne particulates and as gamma-ray emissions from the surface of the ground, and from releases by natural cataclysms and human intrusion, but all of these predicted fewer fatalities than the ground-water-ingestion pathway considered above.

HAZARDS FROM PLUTONIUM TOXICITY

One of the radioactive materials produced in reactors—plutonium—is too valuable to be buried with the waste, since it can be used as a fuel in future reactors. However, plutonium has received a great deal of bad publicity because of its toxicity and its potential as a material for nuclear bombs. I have considered the problems arising from plutonium toxicity extensively in another paper[33] and will treat them only very briefly here. Claims of great harm resulting from plutonium toxicity are commonly based on the assumption that all the plutonium under consideration will find its way into human lungs and the acceptance of the "hot particle" theory of alpha-particle carcinogenesis, in which it is assumed that concentration of alpha-particle emitters in a relatively few particles causes a few cells of the victim to be exposed to much more than the average amount of radiation and consequently to a greatly increased risk of cancer. The "hot-particle" theory has now been studied and rejected by many prestigious official groups, including the NCRP, the NRC, the AEC, the British Medical Research Council, a committee of the National Academy of Sciences, and the United Kingdom Radiological Protection Board. In addition, the ICRP and the U.S. Environmental Protection Agency have inferentially rejected it by not changing their standards on allowable exposure to plutonium. No prestigious or official group has accepted the "hot particle" theory.

If the usual procedures accepted by these groups are used and if normal meteorological dispersion is assumed, dispersal of reactor-plutonium (six times more radioactive than plutonium-239) in a large city would typically result in about 25 eventual cancers per pound dispersed. Seventy per cent of these would result from exposure to the cloud of dust generated by the initial dispersal, and nearly all the rest from resuspension of the dust by winds within the first few months after it first settles on the ground. Less than 3 per cent of the effects are due to exposures during the tens of thousands of years during which the plutonium remains in the soil.

Radium is about 40 times per curie more dangerous than plutonium as a component of soil, and there is as much radium in every 18 centimeters of depth of the earth's crust as there would be plutonium in the whole world if all the world's electric power were derived from fast breeder reactors. About 10,000 pounds of plutonium has been dispersed in bomb tests, whereas it is expected that about 0.01 pounds per year would be released from an all-fast-breeder nuclear power industry. About 0.1 fatalities per year (Table 16-1) are expected as a consequence of these releases.

THEFT OF PLUTONIUM

Widespread concern has been expressed that plutonium may be stolen from the nuclear energy industry by terrorists for fabrication of nuclear bombs. While this threat cannot be quantified for use in Table 16-1, it cannot be ignored in assessing the environmental impacts of nuclear power.

The principal protection against this threat is to prevent plutonium from becoming available to prospective terrorists. The method for keeping track of it since the 1940's has been to weigh all plutonium entering and leaving a facility, but errors in weighing leave substantial room for undetectable losses. It is not impossible that enough plutonium has already been diverted to make many bombs. On the other hand, there is no evidence that plutonium has ever been stolen in quantities as large as 1 gram.

The AEC has long conducted programs for improving security, but in . . 1973, T. B. Taylor, a former bomb designer, became disenchanted with the slow progress in these programs and "blew the story open" in a remarkable series of articles in the *New Yorker* magazine and a book[34] in which he gave information on how to make nuclear bomb. As a result of the publicity he received, plutonium safeguard procedures were greatly tightened and new regulations are constantly being added. (See a review of this concern in Article 20 of this volume).

Clearly, the issue of terrorism should have been considered in the 1950's, before the nuclear industry began. It seems almost irresponsible to raise the problem after so much money and effort has been expended on the industry and we need its product so badly. Nevertheless, the threat of terrorism has continued to escalate in importance, and it is now one of the principal points of contention in the nuclear power controversy.

A number of factors should be considered in evaluating the risk of terrorism. First, stealing plutonium would be very difficult and dangerous under present safeguards. Taylor has estimated[35] that a group of thieves would have much less than a 50 per cent chance of escaping with their lives. Fabrication of a bomb from stolen plutonium would also be very difficult, expensive, time-consuming, and dangerous. Estimates vary considerably, but a rough median of the opinions of experts indicates that it would require three people highly skilled in different technical areas a few months and perhaps $50,000 worth of equipment to develop a bomb with a 70 per cent chance of doing extensive damage, and that the people involved would have a 30 per cent chance of being killed in the effort.

Terrorist bombs would be "block-busters," not "city-destroyers." Taylor's principal scenario[34] is that an explosion of this sort could blow up the World Trade Center in New York, killing the 50,000 people that building can contain. Of course, there are many much easier ways to kill as many people (e.g., introducing a poison gas into the ventilation system of the World Trade Center). Terrorists have always had many options for killing thousands of people, but they have almost never killed more than a few dozen.

And, of course, plutonium and highly enriched uranium, which would be much more suitable for the making of bombs, could be obtained from sources that have no connection with nuclear electric power.

Safeguards in the United States are constantly being improved, and even what Taylor considers to be a very adequate system would add only 1 per cent to the cost of nuclear power. On the other hand, safeguards are generally less stringent in foreign countries than in the United States, and only if we maintain our involvement with nuclear power can we influence international regulations.

SOME STATISTICALLY COMPARABLE RISKS

Table 16-1 reveals that estimates based on the acceptance of WASH-1400 predict that an all-nuclear energy economy would result in about 20 deaths per year; critics of nuclear energy claim that the number is about 600. I shall now attempt to put these estimates in perspective. Since cancer is delayed by 15 to 45 years after exposure, the average loss of life expectancy per victim is 20 years. The loss of life expectancy for the average American from these 20 deaths per year is then (20 $\times$ 20 man-years lost/2 $\times$ 10^8 man-years lived) = 2 $\times$ 10^{-6} of a lifetime = 1.2 hours.

Some of us subject ourselves to many other risks that reduce our life expectancy, such as smoking cigarettes. One pack per day (3.6 $\times$ 10^5 cigarettes) reduces life expectancy by about 8 years,[36] which, assuming linearity, corresponds to 12 minutes loss of life expectancy per cigarette smoked; thus the risk of nuclear power is equivalent to that of smoking six cigarettes in one's lifetime, or one every 10 years.

Statistics show that life expectancy in large cities is 5 years less than in rural areas.[37] This phenomenon may be explained in part by differences in racial makeup, but it is believed to be largely due to the strains of city life. If linearity is assumed, the risk of nuclear power (1.2-hour loss of life expectancy) is equal to the risk of spending 16 hours of one's life in a city.

Traveling in an automobile subjects us to a death risk of 2 $\times$ 10^{-8} per mile, or if 35 years of life are lost in an average traffic fatality, loss of life expectancy is 7 $\times$ 10^{-7} years per mile traveled. The risk of nuclear power is then equal to that of riding in automobiles an extra 3 miles per year. Riding in a small rather than a large car doubles one's risk[38] of fatal injury, so the 1.2 hours loss of life expectancy from all nuclear power is equivalent to the risk of riding the same amount as at present, but 3 miles per year of it in a small rather than a large car.

Another risk some of us take is being overweight. If we assume loss of life expectancy to be linear with overweight, the 1.2-hour loss from all-nuclear power is equivalent to the risk of being 0.02 ounces overweight.[39] However, Pauling[40] has shown that the data are better fit by a quadratic dependence, and if this is accepted the risk of all-nuclear power is equivalent to that of being 0.3 pounds overweight.

All these estimates are based on the government agency projection of 20 deaths per year. If we instead accept the critics' estimate of 30 times as many deaths, the risk of nuclear power is equivalent to the risks of smoking three cigarettes per year, spending 20 days of one's life in a city (one day every 3 years), riding in automobiles an extra 100 miles per year, riding in automobiles the same amount as at present but 100 miles of it per year (1 per cent) in a small rather than a large car, or being 0.6 ounces overweight on the linear hypothesis or 1.6 pounds overweight on the quadratic hypothesis.

Additional perspective may be gained by comparing the effects of an industry deriving electric power from coal by present technology. The most important environmental impact of coal-fired power is air pollution, which, it is estimated, would cause about 10,000 deaths per year,[41] at least an order of magnitude more than even the critics estimate would be caused by nuclear power. In addition, this air pollution would cause[41] about 25 million cases per year of chronic respiratory disease, 200 million person-days of aggravated heart-lung disease symptoms, and about $5 billion worth of property damage; there are no comparable problems from nuclear power. Mining of coal to produce this power would cause about 750 deaths[42] per year among coal miners, more than 10 times the toll from uranium-mining for nuclear power, and the uranium figure would be reduced about 50-fold with breeder reactors. Transporting coal would cause about 500 deaths per year,[43] two orders of magnitude more than would be caused by transportation for the nuclear industry.

It is important to point out that the numbers in Table 16-1 (and the perspective I have put them in) are based on annual averages. As the critics are constantly reminding us, if their estimates are correct, there might be an accident every 10 years with several thousand deaths and every 50 years with tens of thousands of decths. It is not difficult to make this prospect seem extremely dismal. On the other hand we should not envision these accidents as producing stacks of dead bodies; the great majority of fatalities predicted are from cancer that would occur 15 to 45 years later. In nearly all cases, the affected individuals would have only about a 0.5 per cent increased chance of getting cancer. The average American's risk of cancer death is now 16.8 per cent; typically it would be increased to 17.3 per cent. For comparison, the average risk varies from 18.4 per cent in New England to 14.7 per cent in the Southeast, but these variations are rarely noticed.

If an area were affected by a nuclear accident and authorities revealed that, as a result, the average citizen's probability of eventually dying of cancer was increased from 16.8 to 17.3 per cent, it would hardly start a panic. We have had some experience with a similar but much more serious situation: when reports first reached the public of the risk in cigarette-smoking, tens of millions of Americans were suddenly informed that they had accrued a 10 per cent increased probability of cancer death, 20 times larger than the effects from a nuclear accident. Even that story did not stay in the headlines long, and it produced very little counteraction.

Critics often raise the point that the risks of nuclear power are not shared equally by all who benefit but are disproportionately great for people who live close to a nuclear power plant. This, of course, is true for all technology, but let us put it in perspective. The risk is 10^{-6} per year if we accept the WASH-1400 accident estimates, or equal to the risk of riding in an automobile an extra 50 miles per year or 250 yards per day.

Thus if moving away from a nuclear power plant increases one's commuting distance by more than 125 yards (half a block), it is safer to live next to the power plant. If one prefers the estimates we attribute to the critics (20 times larger), it does not pay to move away if doing so increases commuting distances by more than 1.5 miles per day. Even with the critics' estimates, living next to a nuclear power plant reduces life expectancy by only 0.03 years, which makes it 150 times safer than living in a city.

REFERENCES

1. Committee on Biological Effects of Ionizing Radiation (BEIR). 1972. The effects on populations of exposure to low levels of ionizing radiation. National Academy of Sciences—National Research Council.
2. United Nations Scientific Committee on Effects of Atomic Radiation (UNSCEAR). 1972. Ionizing radiation: Levels and effects. NY: United Nations.
3. U.S. Nuclear Regulatory Commission. 1976. WASH-1400, Reactor safety study. Appendix VI.
4. NCRP. 1975. Review of the current state of radiation protection.
5. B. L. Cohen. 1976. Conclusions of the BEIR and UNSCEAR reports on radiation effects per man-rem. *Health Phys*. 30:351.
6. One rem gives 180×10^{-6} probability of cancer death which, on an average, causes 20 years loss of life; thus it reduces life expectancy by $3{,}600 \times 10^{-6}$ years, which is 1.3 days. Smoking one pack of cigarettes per day (about 4×10^5 cigarettes) reduces life expectancy by about 7.5 years (calculated from Surgeon-General's Report on effects of cigarette smoking, 1962) or 2,700 days. Assuming linearity, one cigarette then reduces life expectancy by 7×10^{-3} days. This is equal to the effect of $(7 \times 10^{-3}/1.3)$ rem, or about 5 mrem of radiation.

7. Data from Atomic Bomb Casualty Commission are tabulated in B. L. Cohen, 1974, *Nuclear Science and Society* (NY:Doubleday), p. 64.
8. J. V. Neel, H. Kato, and W. J. Shull. 1974. Mortality of children of atomic bomb survivors and controls. *Genetics* 76:311.
9. H. B. Newcombe. Mutation and the amount of human ill health. Paper presented at Int. Congress of Radiation Research, Seattle, 1974.
10. Environmental Protection Agency. 1973. Report EPA 520/9-73-003, pt. C, pp. 135, 137. The cheapest noble gas hold-up systems that are capable of limiting site boundary doses to the required 5 mrem/year are no system at all for a PWR with a population dose of 89 man-rem per year for twin reactors and charcoal adsorption for BWR with an annual population dose of 27 man-rem. Averaging these yields 58 man-rem/yr, or, for the 200 required sites exposing 2×10^8 people, 0.058 mrem/yr to the average person. Actually, most PWR plants use physical hold-up for more than 60 days, reducing their population dose by a factor of ten.
11. Ibid., pt. C, pp. 141, 142; the cheapest iodine control systems that reduce site boundary doses to below the required 15 mrem/yr give annual population doses to the thyroid of about 7 man-rem for elemental iodine and 13 man-rem for organic iodine; the average exposure is thus of the order of 10 man-rem $\times$ 200 sites/ 2×10^8 people, or about 0.01 mrem/yr to the thyroid.
12. Ibid., pt. C, p. 130.
13. Ibid., pt. D, p. 10. ^{85}Kr from a plant capable of reprocessing 5 metric tons per day would yield an average dose commitment in the U.S. of 520 man-rem/yr. Because such a plant would service about 50 reactors, about 8 plants would be needed, yielding a total of 4,200 man-rem. Dividing this by a population of 2×10^8 gives an average dose of 0.02 mrem/yr. For tritium, the result is larger, in the ratio of 3,700/520. The ^{85}Kr exposure is worldwide, but the tritium exposure is largely limited to the U.S.
14. Environmental Protection Agency. Estimates of ionizing radiation doses in the United States, 1960–2000. Report ORP/CSD 72-1.
15. M. Eisenbud. 1970. Standards of radiation protection and their implications for the public health. In *Nuclear Power and the Public,* ed. H. Forman. U. Minnesota Press.
16. EPA Report 520/9-73-003, pt. B, pp. 39, 88, 109, 128, 146.
17. Several other estimates deviate widely in the detailed contributions of noble gases and tritium, but the overall result is always close to this. See International Atomic Energy Agency (Vienna), Nuclear power and the environment, quoting EPA estimates for 1971; EPA, 1974, Environmental radiation dose commitment: An application to the nuclear power industry, EPA-520/4-73-002; and ref. 14 above.
18. R. O. Pohl. 1976. Nuclear energy: Health impact of carbon-14. Preprint from Physics Dept., Cornell University.
19. W. H. Ellett (EPA), pers. comm., 2 July 1975.
20. The meteorology in refs. 16 and 19 is not given in sufficient detail to be followed, but according to ref. 16 (and other sources) a standard pile 1 km^2 in area emits 500 pCi/m^2-sec, and 2.5 such piles per year would be accumulated if all our power were nuclear, whereas the 7×10^6 km^2 of soil in the U.S. emits an average of about 1 pCi/m^2-sec. Thus, natural radon exceeds the annual increase from tailings piles by a factor of $7 \times 10^6/2.5 \times 500 = 6{,}000$. Ref. 19 estimates 4,000 deaths per year from natural radon in the U.S.—which at first seems reasonably consistent with their estimate of effects from tailings piles. However, we give here two alternative calculations of deaths from natural radon which circumvent the rather uncertain meteorology. Ref. 2 gives 0.15 rem/yr as an average exposure to the tracheobronchial tree which, multiplied by 39×10^{-6} cancer deaths per man-rem from ref. 1 and the 2×10^8 population, gives 1,200 deaths per year. As another approach, one "working level" (WL) is 150 $\times 10^3$ pCi/m^3 and BEIR gives 0.5 rem to lung per WL-"month" where one working "month" is 170 hours or 0.02 years; these combine to give 5,000/150 $\times 10^3 \times .02 = 1.6$ mrem/yr per pCi/m^3. (This is 2.5 times smaller than the value used in ref. 16, but more significant than this discrepancy is the fact that the BEIR value was used in assessing lung cancer incidence in miners, which was instrumental in determining the value 39×10^{-6} lung cancers per man-rem). From ref. 2, the average ^{222}Rn level in the U.S. is about 120 pCi/m^3 which (when multiplied by the above 1.6) gives an average dose of 190 mrem/yr to the lung. Multiplying this by 39×10^{-6} cancers/ man-rem and 2×10^8 population gives 1,500 deaths per year from natural radon, in agreement with our above estimate of 1,200. Since radon from tailings piles is 6,000 times smaller, these would give 0.20–0.25 deaths per year from the latter. However, the latter radon originates in sparsely populated regions and must travel about 1,500 miles to reach populous regions; since, during this travel more than half of the ^{222}Rn (3.6-day half-life) would decay away, the average toll would be no more than 0.1 death per year from each year of all-nuclear power.
21. EPA Office of Radiation Programs. 1974. Summary report on Phase I: Study of inactive uranium mill sites and tailings piles. Phase II, which involves remedial action, began in 1975.
22. M. B. Sears et al. 1975. Oak Ridge National Laboratory Report ORNL-TM-4903, vol. 1. Correlation of radioactive waste treatment costs and the environmental impact of effluents in the nuclear fuel cycle.
23. B. L. Cohen. 1976. Environmental impacts of nuclear power due to radon emissions. *Bull. Atomic Scientists,* Feb., p. 61.
24. *Federal Register* 40:19441, 5/15/75.
25. USAEC. 1957. WASH-740: Theoretical consequences of major accidents in large nuclear power

plants. Washington, D.C.
26. P. Ayyaswamy, B. Hauss, T. Hseih, A. Moscati, T. E. Hicks, and D. Okrent. 1974. Estimates of the risks associated with dam failure. UCLA Report ENG-7423.
27. H. Kendall. Testimony before Udall Committee on Energy and the Environment, 28 April–2 May 1975. Factors are corrected to those in the final version of WASH-1400.
28. USAEC. 1972. WASH-1238: Environmental survey of transportation of radioactive materials to and from nuclear power plants. See also L. B. Shappert et al., 1973, *Nuclear Safety* 14:597.
29. M. Ross has proposed that a rather large fraction of the ^{137}Cs might be released in an accident (*Proc. Int. Symp. on Packaging and Transportation of Radioactive Materials,* Miami Beach, 1974, USAEC doc. CONF-740901, p. 830). However, recent studies by G. Parker and L. B. Shappert (pers. comm., letter to U.S. Energy Research and Development Agency, and testimony before Atomic Safety Licensing Board, docket numbers STN50-483, STN50-486) indicate that Ross's estimates were far too large. Far smaller amounts were found to migrate out of the fuel pellets and the Cs was found to be in nonvolatile forms.
30. U.S. NRC document NUREG-0034. The transportation of radioactive material by air and other modes, March 1976. Other studies giving much lower results are C. V. Hodge and A. A. Jarrett, 1974, EPA Report NSS-8191.1, Transportation accident risks in the nuclear power industry, 1975–2020; and USAEC, 1975, WASH-1535: Environmental impact statement for the liquid metal fast breeder reactor, sec. 4.5.
31. B. L. Cohen. 1976. Environmental hazards in radioactive waste disposal. *Physics Today,* Jan. 1976, p. 9.
32. B. L. Cohen. 1977. High-level radioactive waste from light water reactors. *Rev. Mod. Phys. 49,* Jan., pp. 1–20.
33. B. L. Cohen. 1977. Hazards from plutonium toxicity. *Health Phys. 32,* May, pp. 359–379.
34. J. McPhee. 1974. *The Curve of Binding Energy.* NY: Farrar, Strauss, and Giroux.
35. T. B. Taylor, at Hearings of Joint Committee on Atomic Energy, June 1975.
36. U.S. Surgeon-General. 1962. Report on cigarette smoking.
37. E. Teller and A. L. Latter. 1958. *Our Nuclear Future.* NY: Criterion Books, p. 124.
38. Insurance Institute for Highway Safety, vol. 10, no. 12 (9 July 1975), gives 24.6 fatalities per 100,000 vehicle years registered for small cars and 11.3 for large cars. A similar conclusion is obtained from National Safety Council, *Accident Facts-1965* (Chicago).
39. Being overweight by 25% (about 40 lb for the average adult male) reduces life expectancy by about 5 years (L. I. Dublin and H. H. Marks, 1952, *Mortality among Insured Overweights in Recent Years.* NY: Metropolitan Life Insurance Co.). Since 1.2 hours is 1.4×10^{-4} years, a linear hypothesis gives the risk to be that of 8 lb/yr $\times\ 1.4 \times 10^{-4}$ yr = 1.2×10^{-3} lb = 0.02 oz.
40. L. Pauling. 1958. *Proc. Nat. Acad. Sci.* 44:619.
41. U.S. Senate Committee on Public Works, 1975, "Air quality and stationary source emission control," gives values for an urban plant (p. 631) and a remote plant (p. 626); we use the average of these and multiply by 400 for the number of plants. A larger number of deaths is estimated by R. Wilson, paper presented at Energy Symposium, Boulder, CO, June 1974.
42. B. L. Cohen. 1974. *Nuclear Science and Society.* NY: Doubleday-Anchor. pp. 139, 140.
43. L. Sagan. 1974. *Nature* 250:109.

SUGGESTED READINGS

———, 1976, *Bulletin of the Atomic Scientists 32,* entire issue on the plutonium economy.

Cohen, Bernard L., 1974, Perspectives on the Nuclear Debate, *Bulletin of the Atomic Scientists XXX,* pp. 35–39.

Dukert, Joseph M., 1976, Nuclear Power and the Environment: Energy Research and Development Administration, 88p.

Geesaman, Donald P., and Dean E. Abrahamson, 1974, The Dilemma of Fission Energy, *Bulletin of the Atomic Scientists 30,* pp. 37–41.

Task Force, 1977, The Unfinished Agenda: The Citizen's Policy Guide to Environmental Issues, Rockefeller Brothers Fund.

von Hippel, Frank, and Robert H. William, 1976, Energy Waste and Nuclear Power Growth, *Bulletin of the Atomic Scientists 32,* pp. 18–21, 48–56.

Weinberg, Alvin M., 1977, Is Nuclear Energy Acceptable?, *Bulletin of the Atomic Scientists 33,* pp. 54–60.

Reactor Safety Study: An Assessment of Accident Risks in United States Commercial Nuclear Power Plants 17

U.S. NUCLEAR REGULATORY COMMISSION ("Rasmussen Report") 1975

INTRODUCTION AND RESULTS

The Reactor Safety Study was sponsored by the U.S. Atomic Energy Commission (AEC) to estimate the public risks that could be involved in potential accidents in commercial nuclear power plants of the type now in use. It was performed under the independent direction of Professor Norman C. Rasmussen of the Massachusetts Institute of Technology. The risks had to be estimated, rather than measured, because although there are about 50 such plants now operating, there have been no nuclear accidents to date resulting in significant releases of radioactivity in U.S. commercial nuclear power plants. Many of the methods used to develop these estimates are based on those that were developed by the Department of Defense and the National Aeronautics and Space Administration in the last 10 years and are coming into increasing use in recent years.

The objective of the study was to make a realistic estimate of these risks and, to provide perspective, to compare them with non-nuclear risks to which our society and its individuals are already exposed. This information may be of help in determining the future reliance by society on nuclear power as a source of electricity.

The results from this study suggest that the risks to the public from potential accidents in nuclear power plants are comparatively small. This is based on the following considerations:

(1) The possible consequences of potential reactor accidents are predicted to be no larger, and in many cases much smaller, than those of non-nuclear accidents. The consequences are predicted to be smaller than people have been led to believe by previous studies that deliberately maximized estimates of these consequences.

(2) The likelihood of reactor accidents is much smaller than that of many non-nuclear accidents having similar consequences. All non-nuclear accidents examined in this study, including fires, explosions, toxic chemical releases, dam failures, airplane crashes, earth-

This final report of the Executive Summary of the Reactor Safety Study (WASH-1400) was directed by Professor Norman C. Rasmussen of the Massachusetts Institute of Technology. The work, originally sponsored by the U.S. Atomic Energy Commission, was completed and published in October 1975 under the sponsorship of the U.S. Nuclear Regulatory Commission, which came into being on January 19, 1975. This report was provided through the courtesy of Saul Levine, Project Staff Director of the Reactor Safety Study, U.S. Nuclear Regulatory Commission.

quakes, hurricanes, and tornadoes, are much more likely to occur and can have consequences comparable to, or larger than, those of nuclear accidents.

Figures 17-1, 17-2, and 17-3 compare the nuclear reactor accident risks predicted for the 100 plants expected to be operating by about 1980 with risks from other man-caused and natural events to which society is generally already exposed. The following information is contained in the figures:

(1) Figures 17-1 and 17-2 show the likelihood and number of fatalities from both nuclear and a variety of non-nuclear accidents. These figures indicate that non-nuclear events are about 10,000 times more likely to produce large numbers of fatalities than accidents in nuclear plants.*

(2) Figure 17-3 shows the likelihood and dollar value of property damage associated with nuclear and non-nuclear accidents. Nuclear accidents are about 1,000 times less likely to cause comparable large dollar value accidents than other sources. Property damage is associated with three effects:

(i) The cost of relocating people away from contaminated areas.

(ii) The decontamination of land to avoid overexposing people to radioactivity.

(iii) The cost of ensuring that people are not exposed to potential sources of radioactivity in food and water supplies.

In addition to the over-all risk information in Figures 17-1 through 17-3, it is useful to consider the risk to individuals of being fatally injured in various types of accidents. The bulk of the information shown in Table 17-1 is taken from the 1973 *Statistical Abstracts of the U.S.* and applies to the year 1969, the latest year for which these data were tabulated when this study was performed. The predicted nuclear accident risks are very small compared to other possible causes of fatal injuries.

In addition to fatalities and property damage, a number of other health effects could result from nuclear accidents. These include injuries and long-term damage to health, such as cancers, genetic effects, and thyroid gland illness. The early illness expected in potential accidents would be about 10 times higher than the fatalities shown in Figures 17-1 and 17-2; for comparison, 8 million injuries occur annually from other accidents. The number of cases of genetic damage and long-term cancer fatalities is predicted to be smaller than their normal incidence rate. Even for a large accident, the small increases in these diseases would be difficult to detect.

Thyroid illnesses that might result from a large accident are mainly the formation of nodules on the thyroid gland; these can be treated medically and rarely have serious consequences. For most accidents, the number of nodules caused would be small compared to their normal incidence rate. The number that might be produced in very unlikely accidents would be about equal to their normal occurrence in the exposed population. These would be observed over a period of 10 to 40 years following the accident.

Although the study has presented the estimated risks from nuclear power plant accidents and compared them with other risks that exist in our society, it has made no judgment on the acceptability of nuclear risks. The judgment as to what level of risk is acceptable should be made by a broader segment of society than that involved in this study.

*The fatalities shown in Figures 17-1 and 17-2 for the 100 nuclear plants are those that would be predicted to occur within a short period of time after a reactor accident. This was done to provide a consistent comparison to the non-nuclear events that also cause fatalities in the same time frame. As in potential nuclear accidents, there also exist possibilities for injuries and longer term health effects from non-nuclear accidents. Data or predictions of this type are not available for non-nuclear events and so comparisons cannot easily be made.

QUESTIONS AND ANSWERS ABOUT THE STUDY

This section presents more information about the details of the study than was covered in the introduction. It is presented in question and answer format for ease of reference.

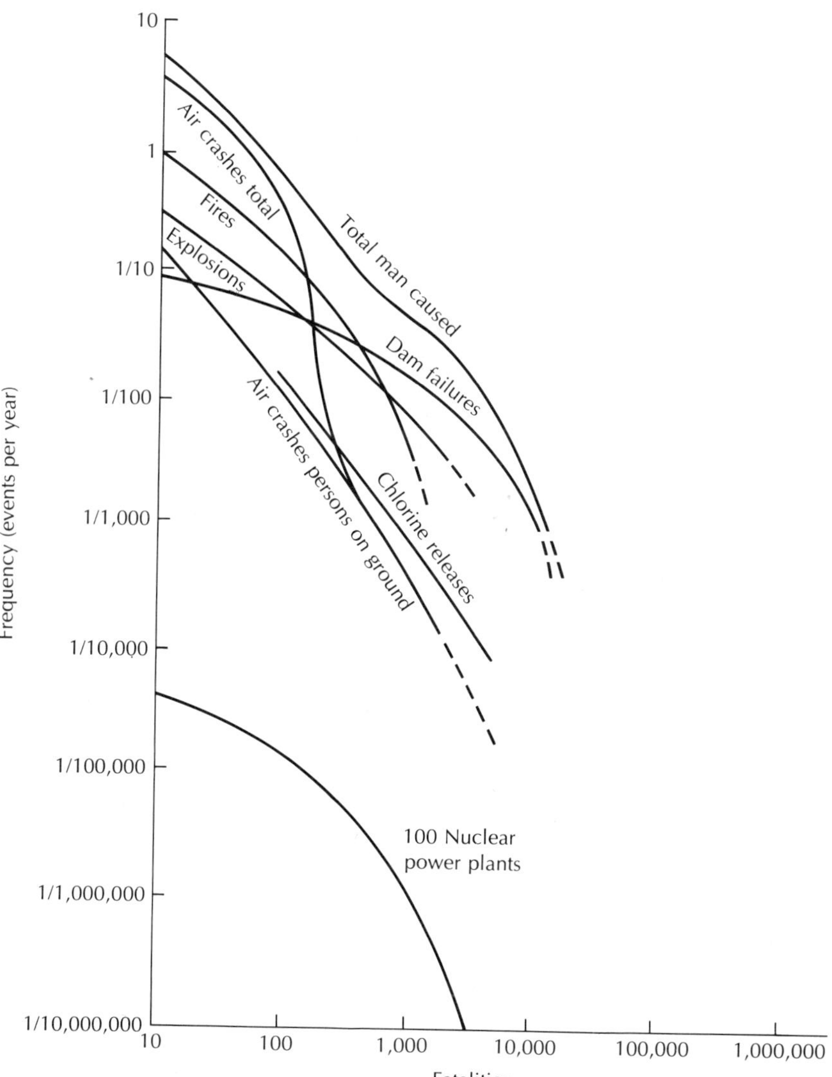

Figure 17-1. Frequency of fatalities due to man-caused events.
Notes:

1. Fatalities due to auto accidents are not shown because data are not available. Auto accidents cause about 50,000 fatalities per year.

2. Approximate uncertainties for nuclear events are estimated to be represented by factors of 1/4 and 4 on consequence magnitudes and by factors of 1/5 and 5 on probabilities.

3. For natural and man-caused occurrences the uncertainty in probability of largest recorded consequence magnitude is estimated to be represented by factors of 1/20 and 5. Smaller magnitudes have less uncertainty.

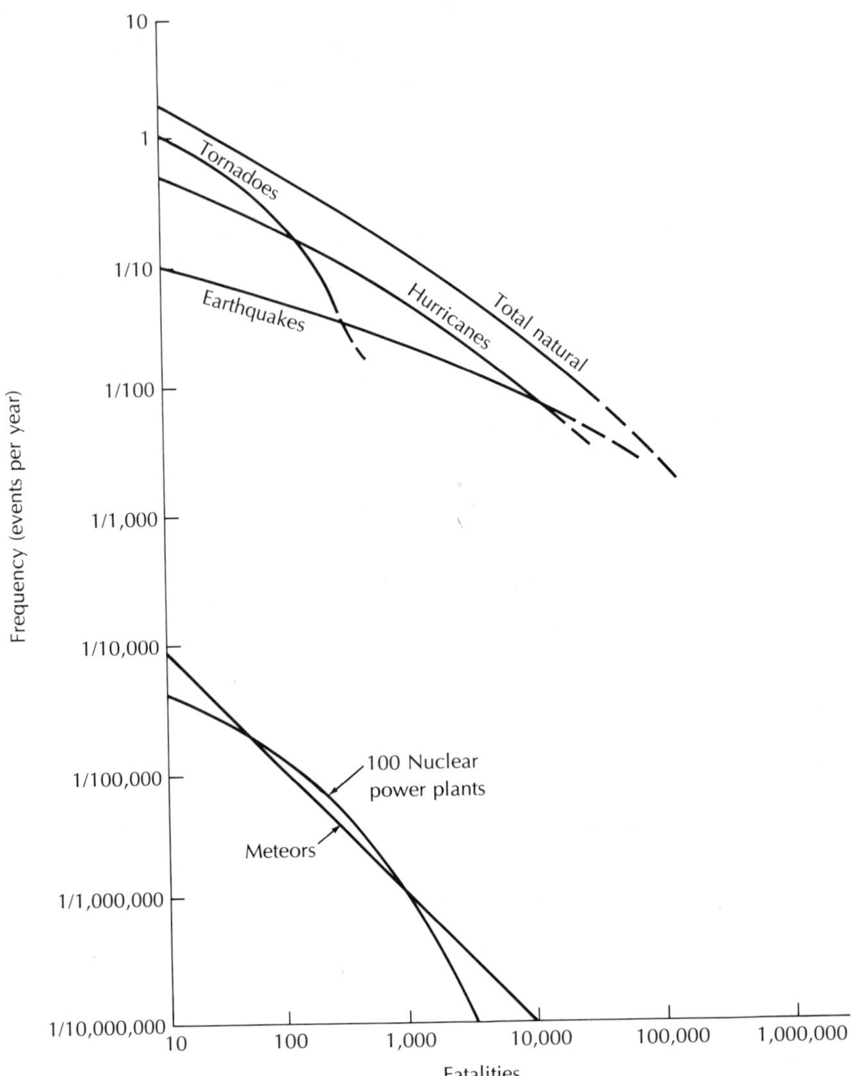

Figure 17-2. Frequency of fatalities due to natural events.
Notes:

1. For natural and man-caused occurrences the uncertainty in probability of largest recorded consequence magnitude is estimated to be represented by factors of 1/20 and 5. Smaller magnitudes have less uncertainty.
2. Approximate uncertainties for nuclear events are estimated to be represented by factors of 1/4 and 4 on consequence magnitudes and by factors of 1/5 and 5 on probabilities.

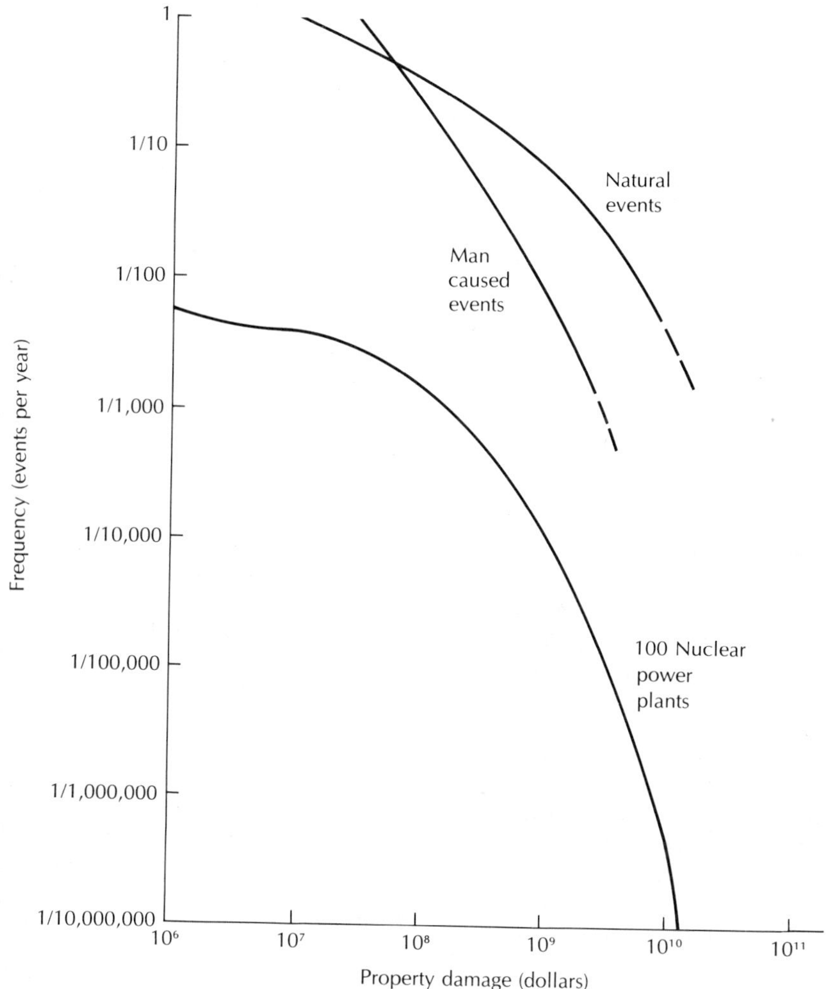

Figure 17-3. Frequency of property damage due to natural and man-caused events.
Notes:

1. Property damage due to auto accidents is not included because data are not available for low probability events. Auto accidents cause about $15 billion damage each year.
2. Approximate uncertainties for nuclear events are estimated to be represented by factors of 1/5 and 2 on consequence magnitudes and by factors of 1/5 and 5 on probabilities.
3. For natural and man-caused occurrences the uncertainty in probability of largest recorded consequence magnitude is estimated to be represented by factors of 1/20 and 5. Smaller magnitudes have less uncertainty.

Table 17–1. Average Risk of Fatality by Various Causes.

Accident Type	*Total Number*	*Individual Chance per Year*
Motor vehicle	55,791	1 in 4,000
Falls	17,827	1 in 10,000
Fires and hot substances	7,451	1 in 25,000
Drowning	6,181	1 in 30,000
Firearms	2,309	1 in 100,000
Air travel	1,778	1 in 100,000
Falling objects	1,271	1 in 160,000
Electrocution	1,148	1 in 160,000
Lightning	160	1 in 2,000,000
Tornadoes	91	1 in 2,500,000
Hurricanes	93	1 in 2,500,000
All accidents	111,992	1 in 1,600
Nuclear reactor accidents (100 plants)	—	1 in 5,000,000,000

Who Did this Study and How Much Effort Was Involved?

The study was done principally at the AEC headquarters by a group of scientists and engineers who had the skills needed to carry out the study's tasks. They came from a variety of organizations, including the AEC, national laboratories, private laboratories, and universities. About 10 people were AEC employees. The Director of the study was Professor Norman C. Rasmussen of the Department of Nuclear Engineering of the Massachusetts Institute of Technology, who served as an AEC consultant during the course of the study. The Staff Director who had the day-to-day responsibility for the project was Mr. Saul Levine of the AEC. The study was started in the summer of 1972 and took three years to complete. A total of 60 people, various consultants, 70 man-years of effort, and about $4 million were involved.

What Kind of Nuclear Power Plants Are Covered by the Study?

The study considered large power reactors of the pressurized water and boiling water type being used in the United States today. Reactors of the present generation are all water cooled, and therefore the study was limited to this type. Although high temperature gas-cooled and liquid metal fast-breeder reactor designs are now under development, reactors of this type are not expected to have any significant role in U.S. electric power production in this decade; thus, they were not considered.

Nuclear power plants produce electricity by fissioning (or splitting) uranium atoms. The nuclear reactor fuel in which uranium atoms fission is in a large steel vessel. The reactor fuel consists of about 100 tons of uranium. The uranium is contained within metal rods about 1/2 inch in diameter and about 12 feet long. These rods are formed into fuel bundles of 50 to 200 rods each. Each reactor contains several hundred bundles. The vessel is filled with water, which is needed both to cool the fuel and to maintain the fission chain reaction.

The heat released in the uranium by the fission process heats the water to form steam; the steam turns a turbine to generate electricity. Similarly, coal and oil plants generate electricity, using fossil fuel to boil water.

Today's nuclear power plants are very large. A typical plant has an electrical capacity of 1,000,000 kilowatts or 1,000 megawatts. This is enough electricity for a city of about 500,000 people.

Can a Nuclear Power Plant Explode Like an Atom Bomb?

No. It is impossible for nuclear power plants to explode like a nuclear weapon. The laws of physics do not permit this because the fuel contains only a small fraction (3 to 5 per cent) of the special type of uranium (uranium-235) that must be used in weapons.

How Is Risk Defined?

The idea of risk involves both the likelihood and consequences of an event. Thus, to estimate the risk involved in driving an automobile, one would need to know the likelihood of an accident in which, for example, an individual could be (a) injured or (b) killed. Thus there are two different consequences, injury or fatality, each with its own likelihood. For injury, an individual's risk per year is about one in 130 and for fatality, it is about one in 4,000. This type of data concerns the risk to individuals and can affect attitudes and habits individuals have toward driving.

However, from an over-all societal viewpoint, different types of data are of interest. Here, 1.5 million injuries per year and 55,000 fatalities per year due to automobile accidents represent the kind of information that might be of use in making decisions on highway anf automobile safety.

The same type of logic applies to reactors. From the viewpoint of a person living in the general vicinity of a reactor, the likelihood of being killed in any one year in a reactor accident is one chance in 5 billion, and the likelihood of being injured in any one year in a reactor accident is one chance in 75,000,000.

What Causes the Risks Associated with Nuclear Power Plants?

The risks from nuclear power plants are due to the radioactivity formed by the fission process. In normal operation, nuclear power plants release minute amounts of this radioactivity under controlled conditions. In the event of a highly unlikely accident, larger amounts of radioactivity could be released and could cause significant injuries or fatalities.

The fragments of the uranium atom that remain after fission are radioactive. These radioactive atoms are called fission products. They distintegrate further with the release of nuclear radiation. Many of them decay away quickly, in a matter of minutes or hours, to non-radioactive forms. Others decay away more slowly and require months, and in a few cases, many years to decay. The fission products accumulating in the fuel rods include both gases and solids. Included are iodine, gases like krypton and xenon, and solids like cesium and strontium.

How Can Radioactivity Be Released?

The only way potentially large amounts of radioactivity could be released is by melting the fuel in the reactor core. The fuel that is removed from a reactor after use and stored at the plant site also contains considerable amounts of radioactivity. However, accidental releases from such fuel have been found to be quite unlikely and small compared to a potential release of radioactivity from the fuel in the reactor core.

The safety design of reactors includes a series of systems to prevent the overheating of fuel and to control potential release of radioactivity from the fuel. Thus, for an accidental release of radioactivity to the environment to occur, there must be a series of sequential failures that would cause the fuel to overheat and release its radioactivity. There would also have to be failures in the emergency systems designed to remove and contain the radioactivity.

The study has examined a very large number of potential paths by which radioactive release might occur and has identified those that determine the risks. This involved defining the ways in which the fuel in the core could melt and the ways in which systems to control the release of radioactivity could fail.

How Might a Core Melt Accident Occur?

It is significant that in some 200 reactor-years of commercial operation of reactors of the type considered in the report there have been no fuel melting accidents. To melt the fuel requires a failure in the cooling system or the occurrence of a heat imbalance that would allow the fuel to heat up to its melting point, about 5,000 °F.

To those unfamiliar with the characteristics of reactors, it might seem that all that is required to prevent fuel from overheating is a system that would promptly stop, or shut down, the fission process at the first sign of trouble. Although reactors have such systems, they alone are not enough, since the radioactive decay of fission fragments in the fuel continues to generate heat (called decay heat) that must be removed even after the fission process stops. Thus, redundant decay heat removal systems are also provided in reactors. In addition, emergency core cooling systems (ECCS) are provided to cope with a series of potential but unlikely accidents, caused by ruptures in, and loss of coolant from, the normal cooling system.

The Reactor Safety Study has defined two broad types of situations that might potentially lead vo a melting of the reactor core: the loss-of-coolant accident (LOCA) and transients. In the event of loss of coolant, the normal cooling water would be lost from the cooling systems and core melting would be prevented by the use of the emergency core cooling system (ECCS). However, melting could occur in a loss of coolant accident if the ECCS were to fail to operate.

The term "transient" refers to any one of a number of conditions that could occur in a plant and that would require the reactor to be shut down. Following shutdown, the decay heat removal systems would operate to keep the core from overheating. Certain failures in either the shutdown or the decay heat removal systems also could cause melting of the core.

What Features Are Provided in Reactors To Cope with a Core Melt Accident?

Nuclear power plants have numerous systems designed to prevent core melting. Furthermore, there are inherent physical processes and additional features that come into play to remove and contain the radioactivity released from the molten fuel should core melting occur. Although there are features provided to keep the containment building from being damaged for some time after the core melts, the containment would ultimately fail, causing a release of radioactivity.

An essentially leak-tight containment building is provided to prevent the initial dispersion of the airborne radioactivity in the environment. Although the containment would fail in time if the core were to melt, until that time the radioactivity released from the fuel would be deposited by natural processes on the surfaces inside the containment building. In addition, plants are provided with systems to contain and trap the radioactivity released within the containment building. These systems include such things as water sprays and pools to wash radioactivity out of the building atmosphere and filters to trap radioactive particles prior to their release. Since the containment buildings are essentially leak-tight, the radioactivity is contained as long as the building remains intact. Even if the building were to have sizable leaks, large amounts of the radioactivity would likely be removed by the systems provided for that purpose or would be deposited on interior surfaces of the building by natural processes.

Even though the containment building would be expected to remain intact for some time following a core melt, eventually the molten mass would be expected to eat its way through the concrete floor into the ground below. Following this, much of the radioactive material would be trapped in the soil; however, a small amount would escape to the surface and be released. Almost all of the non-gaseous radioactivity would be trapped in the soil.

It is possible to postulate core melt accidents in which the containment building would fail by overpressurization or by missiles created by the accident. Such accidents are less likely, but they could release a larger amount of airborne radioactivity and have more serious consequences. The consequences of these less likely accidents have been included in the study's results shown in Figures 17-1 through 17-3.

How Might the Loss-of-coolant Accident Lead to a Core Melt?

Loss-of-coolant accidents are postulated as resulting from failures in the normal reactor cooling water system, and plants are designed to cope with such failures. The water in the reactor cooling systems is at a very high pressure (between 50 to 100 times the pressure in a car tire) and if a rupture were to occur in the pipes, pumps, valves, or vessels that contain it, then a "blowout" would occur. In this case, some of the water would flash to steam and blow out of the hole. This could be serious, since the fuel could melt if additional cooling were not supplied within a rather short time.

The loss of normal cooling in the event of a LOCA would stop the chain reaction, so that the amount of heat produced would drop very rapidly to a few per cent of its operating level. However, after this sudden drop, the amount of heat being produced would decrease much more slowly and would be controlled by the decay of the radioactivity in the fuel. Although this decrease in heat generation is helpful, it would not be enough to prevent the fuel from melting unless additional cooling were supplied. To deal with this situation, reactors have emergency core cooling systems (ECCS) whose function is to provide cooling for just such events. These systems have pumps, pipes, valves, and water supplies that are capable of dealing with breaks of various sizes. They are also designed to be redundant so that if some components fail to operate, the core can still be cooled.

The study has examined a large number of potential sequences of events following LOCA's of various sizes. In almost all of the cases, the LOCA must be followed by failures in the emergency core cooling system for the core to melt. The principal exception to this is the massive failure of the large pressure vessel that contains the core. However, the accumulated experience with pressure vessels indicates that the chance of such a failure is small. In fact, the study found that the likelihood of pressure vessel failure was so small that it did not contribute to the over-all risk from reactor accidents.

How Might a Reactor Transient Lead to a Core Melt?

The term "reactor transient" refers to a number of events that require the reactor to be shut down. These range from normal shutdown for such things as refueling to such unplanned but expected events as loss of power to the plant from the utility transmission lines. The reactor is designed to cope with unplanned transients by automatically shutting down. Following shutdown, cooling systems would be operated to remove the heat produced by the radioactivity in the fuel. There are several different cooling systems capable of removing this heat, but if they all should fail, the heat being produced would be sufficient to eventually boil away all the cooling water and melt the core.

In addition to the above pathway to core melt, it is also possible a core melt would result from the failure of the reactor shutdown systems following a transient event. In this case it would be possible for the amounts of heat generated to be such that the available cooling systems might not cope with it and core melt could result.

How Likely Is a Core Melt Accident?

The Reactor Safety Study carefully examined the various paths leading to core melt. Using methods developed in recent years for estimating the likelihood of such accidents, the study determined a probability of occurrence for each core melt accident identified. These probabilities were combined to obtain the total probability of melting the core. The value obtained was about one in 20,000 per reactor per year. With 100 reactors operating, as is anticipated for the United States by about 1980, this means that the chance for one such accident is one in 200 per year.

What Is the Nature of the Health Effects a Core Melt Accident Might Produce?

It is possible for a potential core melt accident to release enough radioactivity so that some fatalities might occur within a short time (about 1 year) after the accident. Other people might be exposed to radiation levels that would produce observable effects requiring medical attention but from which they would recover. In addition, some people might receive even lower exposures, which would produce no noticeable effects but might increase the incidence of certain diseases over a period of many years. The observable effects that occur shortly after the accident are called early, or acute, effects.

The delayed, or latent, effects of radiation exposure could cause some increase in the incidence of such diseases as cancer, genetic effects, and thyroid gland illnesses in the exposed population. In general these effects would appear as an increase in these diseases over a 10- to 50-year period following the exposure. Such effects may be difficult to observe because the expected increase would be small compared to the normal incidence rate of these diseases.

The study has estimated the increased incidence of potentially fatal cancers over the 50 years following an accident. The number of latent cancer fatalities are predicted to be relatively small compared to their normal incidence. Thyroid illness refers mainly to small lumps or nodules of the thyroid gland. The nodules are treated by medical procedures that sometimes involve simple surgery, and these are unlikely to have serious consequences. Medication might also be necessary to supplement gland function.

Radiation is recognized as one of the factors that can produce genetic effects that appear as defects in a subsequent generation. From the total population exposure caused by an accident, the expected increase in genetic effects in subsequent generations can be estimated. These effects would be small compared to their normal incidence rate.

What Are the Most Likely Consequences of a Core Melt Accident?

As stated, the probability of a core melt accident is, on the average, one in 20,000 per reactor per year. The most likely consequences of such an accident are given in Table 17-2.

How Does the Average Annual Risk from Nuclear Accidents Compare to Other Common Risks?

Considering the 15 million people who live within 25 miles of current or planned U.S. reactor sites, and based on current accident rates in the United States, the annual numbers of fatalities and injuries expected from various sources are shown in Table 17-3.

What Is the Number of Fatalities and Injuries Expected as a Result of a Core Melt Accident?

A core melt accident is similar to many other types of major accidents, such as fires, explosions, dam failures, in that a wide range of

Table 17–2. Most Likely Consequences of a Core Melt Accident.

	Consequences
Fatalities	<1
Injuries	<1
Latent fatalities per year	<1
Thyroid nodules per year	<1
Genetic defects per year	<1
Property damage[a]	<$1,000,000

[a]This does not include damage that might occur to the plant or costs for replacing the power lost by such damage.

Table 17–3. Annual Fatalities and Injuries Expected among the 15 Million People Living within 25 Miles of U.S. Reactor Sites.

Accident Type	*Fatalities*	*Injuries*
Automobile	4,200	375,000
Falls	1,500	75,000
Fire	560	22,000
Electrocution	90	—
Lightning	8	—
Reactors (100 plants)	2	20

consequences is possible depending on the exact conditions under which the accident occurs. In the case of a core melt, the consequences would depend mainly on three factors: the amount of radioactivity released, the way it is dispersed by the prevailing weather conditions, and the number of people exposed to the radiation. With these three factors known, it is possible to make a reasonable estimate of the consequences.

The study calculated the health effects and the probability of occurrence for 140,000 possible combinations of radioactive release magnitude, type of weather, and population exposed. The probability of a given release was determined from a careful examination of the probability of various reactor system failures. The probability of various weather conditions was obtained from weather data collected at many reactor sites. The probability of various numbers of people being exposed was obtained from U.S. census data for current and planned U.S. reactor sites. These thousands of computations were carried out with the aid of a large digital computer.

These results showed that the probability of an accident resulting in 10 or more fatalities is predicted to be about 1 in 3,000,000 per plant per year. The probability of 100 or more fatalities is predicted to be about 1 in 10,000,000, and for 1,000 or more, 1 in 100,000,000. The largest value reported in the study was 3,300 fatalities, with a probability of about one in 1 billion.

These estimates are derived from a consequence model that includes statistical calculations to describe evacuations of people out of the path of airborne radioactivity. This evacuation model was developed from data describing evacuations that have been performed during non-nuclear events.

If a group of 100 similar plants are considered, then the chance of an accident causing 10 or more fatalities is 1 in 30,000 per year. For accidents involving 1,000 or more fatal-

Table 17–4. Average Probability of Major Man-Caused and Natural Events.

Type of Event	*Probability of 100 or More Fatalities*	*Probability of 1,000 or More Fatalities*
Man-Caused		
Airplane crash	1 in 2 years	1 in 2,000 years
Fire	1 in 7 years	1 in 200 years
Explosion	1 in 16 years	1 in 120 years
Toxic gas	1 in 100 years	1 in 1,000 years
Natural		
Tornado	1 in 5 years	Very small
Hurricane	1 in 5 years	1 in 25 years
Earthquake	1 in 20 years	1 in 50 years
Meteorite impact	1 in 100,000 years	1 in 1,000,000 years
Reactors		
100 plants	1 in 100,00 years	1 in 1,000,000 years

ities the number is 1 in 1,000,000 per year. Interestingly, this value coincides with the probability that a meteor would strike a U.S. population center and cause 1,000 fatalities.

Table 17-4 can be used to compare the likelihood of a nuclear accident to non-nuclear accidents that could have the same consequences. These include man-caused as well as natural events. Many of these probabilities are obtained from historical records, but others are so small that no such event has ever been observed. In the latter cases, the probability has been calculated using techniques similar to those used for nuclear plants.

In regard to injuries from potential nuclear power plant accidents, the number of injuries that would require medical attention shortly after an accident is about 10 times larger than the number of fatalities predicted.

What Is the Magnitude of the Latent, or Long-term, Health Effects?

As with the short-term effects, the incidence of latent cancers, treatable latent thyroid illness, and genetic effects would vary with the exact accident conditions. Table 17-5 illustrates the potential size of such events. The first column shows the consequences that would be produced by core melt accidents, the most likely of which has one chance in 20,000 per reactor per year of occurring. The second column shows the consequences for an accident that has a chance of 1 in a million of occurring. The third column shows the normal incidence rate.

In these accidents, only the induction of thyroid nodules would be observable, and this only in the case of larger, less likely accidents. These nodules are easily diagnosed and treatable by medical or surgical procedures. The incidence of other effects would be low and not discernible in view of the high normal incidence of these two diseases.

What Type of Property Damage Might a Core Melt Accident Produce?

A nuclear accident would cause no physical damage to property beyond the plant site but might contaminate it with radioactivity. At high levels of contamination, people would

Table 17–5. Incidence per Year of Latent Health Effects Following a Potential Reactor Accident.

	Probability per Reactor per Year		*Normal[b] Incidence Rate in Exposed Population per Year*
Health Effect per Year	*One in 20,000[a]*	*One in 1,000,000[a]*	
Latent cancers	<1	170	17,000
Thyroid illness	<1	1,400	8,000
Genetic effects	<1	25	8,000

[a]The rates due to reactor accidents are temporary and would decrease with time. Most of the cancers and thyroid modules would occur over a few decades, and the genetic effects would be significantly reduced in five generations.
[b]This is the normal incidence that would be expected for a population of 10,000,000 people who might receive some exposure in a very large accident over the time period in which the potential reactor accident effects might occur.

have to be relocated until decontamination procedures permitted their return. At levels lower than this, but involving a larger area, decontamination procedures would also be required, but people would be able to continue to live in the area. The area requiring decontamination would involve a few hundred to a few thousand square miles. The principal concern in this larger area would be to monitor farm produce to keep the amount of radioactivity ingested through the food chain small. Farms in this area would have their produce monitored, and any produce above a safe level could not be used.

The core melt accident having a likelihood of one in 20,000 per plant per year would most likely result in little or no contamination. The probability of an accident that requires relocation from 20 square miles is one in 100,000 per reactor per year. Eighty per cent of all core melt accidents would be expected to be less severe than this. The largest accident might require relocation from 290 square miles. In an accident such as this, agricultural products, particularly milk, would have to be monitored for a month or two over an area about 50 times larger until the iodine decayed away. After that, the area requiring monitoring would be very much smaller.

What Would Be the Cost of the Consequences of a Core Melt Accident?

As with the other consequences, the cost would depend upon the exact circumstances of the accident. The cost calculated by the Reactor Safety Study included the cost of moving and housing people who were relocated, the cost caused by denial of land use, the cost associated with the denial of use of reproducible assets such as dwellings and factories, and costs associated with the cleanup of contaminated property. The core melt accident having a likelihood of one in 20,000 per reactor per year would most likely cause property damage of less than $1,000,000. The chance of an accident causing $150,000,000 damage would be about one in 100,000 per reactor per year. The probability would be about one in 1,000,000 per plant per year of causing damage of about one billion dollars. The maximum value would be about 14 billion dollars, with a probability of about 1 in 1,000,000,000 per plant per year.

This property damage risk from nuclear accidents can be compared to other risks in several ways. The largest man-caused events are fires. In recent years, there have been an average of three fires with damage in excess of 10 million dollars every year. About once every two years there is a fire with damage in the 50- to 100-million dollar range. There have been four hurricanes in the last 10 years that caused damage in the range of 0.5 to 5 billion dollars. Recent earthquake estimates suggest that a 1-billion dollar earthquake can be expected in the United States about once every 50 years.

A comparison of the preceding costs shows that, although a serious reactor accident would be very costly, the costs would be within the range of other serious accidents experienced by society and the probability of such a nuclear accident is estimated to be smaller than that of the other events.

What Would Be the Chance of a Reactor Meltdown in the Year 2000 if We Have 1,000 Reactors Operating?

One might be tempted to take the per plant probability of a particular reactor accident and multiply it by 1,000 to estimate the chance of an accident in the year 2000. This is not a valid calculation, however, because it assumes that the reactors to be built during the next 25 years will be the same as those being built today. Experience with other technologies, such as automobiles and aircraft, for example, generally shows that, as more units are built and more experience is gained, the over-all safety record improves in terms of fewer accidents occurring per unit. The plants now being constructed appear to be improved as compared to the plants analyzed in the study.

How Do We Know that the Study Has Included All Accidents in the Analysis?

The study devoted a large amount of its effort to ensuring that it covered those potential accidents of importance to determining the public risk. It relied heavily on over 20 years of experience in the identification and analysis of potential reactor accidents. It also went considerably beyond earlier analyses by considering a large number of potential failures that had never before been analyzed. For example, the failure of reactor systems that can lead to core melt and the failure of systems that affect the consequences of core melt have been analyzed. The consequences of the failure of the massive steel reactor vessel and of the containment were considered for the first time. The likelihood that various external forces, such as earthquakes, floods, and tornadoes, could cause accidents was also analyzed.

In addition there are further factors that give a high degree of confidence that the important and significant accidents affecting risk have been included. These are: (a) the identification of all significant sources of radioactivity at nuclear power plants, (b) the fact that a large release of radioactivity can occur only if the reactor fuel were to melt, and (c) knowledge of the physical phenomena that can cause fuel to melt. This type of approach led to the screening of thousands of potential accident paths to identify those that would essentially determine the public risk.

Although there is no way of proving that all possible accident sequences that contribute to public risk have been considered in the study, the systematic approach used in identifying possible accident sequences makes it unlikely that an accident that would significantly change the over-all risk was overlooked.

What Techniques Were Used in Performing the Study?

Methodologies developed over the past 10 years by the Department of Defense and the National Aeronautics and Space Administration were used in the study. As used in the study, these techniques, called event trees and fault trees, helped to define potential accident paths and their likelihood of occurrence.

An event tree defines an initial failure within the plant. It then examines the subsequent course of events as determined by the operation or failure of various systems that are provided to prevent the core from melting and to prevent the release of radioactivity to the environment. Event trees were used in this study to define the thousands of potential accident paths that were examined to determine their likelihood of occurrence and the amount of radioactivity they might release.

Fault trees were used to determine the likelihood of failure of the various systems identified in the event tree accident paths. A fault tree starts with the definition of an undesired event, such as the failure of a system to operate, and then determines, using engineering and mathematical logic, the ways in which the system can fail. Using data covering (a) the failure of components such as pumps, pipes, and valves; (b) the likelihood of operator errors; and (c) the likelihood of maintenance errors, it is possible to estimate the likelihood of system failure, even when no data on total system failure exist.

The likelihood and the amount of radioactive releases from potential accident paths were used in combination with the likelihood of various weather conditions and population distributions in the vicinity of the reactor to calculate the consequences of the various potential accidents.

SUGGESTED READINGS

———, 1975, *Bulletin of the Atomic Scientists 31*, entire issue on nuclear reactor safety.

Hendrie, J. M., 1976, Safety of Nuclear Power, *Annual Review of Energy 1*, pp. 663–683.

Hohenemser, Christoph, Roger Kasperson, and Robert Kates, 1977, The Distrust of Nuclear Power, *Science 196*, No. 4285, April, pp. 25–34.

von Hippel, Frank, 1977, Looking Back on the Rasmussen Report, *Bulletin of the Atomic Scientists 33*, No. 2, February, pp. 42–47.

Webb, Richard E., 1976, *The Accident Hazards of Nuclear Power Plants* (University of Massachusetts Press, Amherst, Mass.), 228 p.

Alternatives for Managing Post-Fission Nuclear Wastes 18

A. M. PLATT AND J. W. BARTLETT 1976

This article presents an overview and synopsis of the alternatives from the back end of the commercial LWR fuel cycle. The basis for the information is the so-called technical alternatives document (TAD) published as ERDA 76-43.[1] It is available from the National Technical Information Service, Springfield, VA 22151. Approximately two hundred professionals participated in writing the document.

The basic scope of TAD includes:

(1) Overview characterization of three alternative fuel cycle and waste management systems:

—Operation without fuel reprocessing (''throwaway'' fuel cycle).

—Recycle of uranium, storage of plutonium, and use of available waste management technology.

—Recycle of uranium and plutonium; use of available waste management technology.

(2) Identification and characterization of wastes from the back end of the commercial LWR fuel cycle.

(3) Projection of waste quantities.

The alternative waste management technologies are discussed in terms of four basic waste management activities:

(1) *Treatment,* which converts the wastes from their as-generated form to forms needed for handling, transportation, and final disposition of the wastes. As-generated wastes are termed ''primary wastes''; wastes that emerge from treatment operations are ''secondary wastes.''

(2) *Interim storage,* which provides retention of primary and secondary wastes while they are in man's environment and subject to subsequent management activities such as treatment or transportation.

(3) *Transportation,* which is applied to movement of waste materials between sites.

Dr. A. M. Platt is manager of the Nuclear Waste Technology Programs of Battelle Pacific Northwest Laboratories, Richland, Washington 99352.

Dr. J. W. Bartlett is manager of the Advanced Waste Management Program of Battelle Pacific Northwest Laboratories.

This is Battelle Pacific Northwest Laboratories' Report BNWL-SA-5835, December 1976, 13 p. Reprinted by permission of the authors and Battelle Pacific Northwest Laboratories.

(4) *Final isolation or disposal,* which provides final disposition of wastes. The basic alternatives are isolation in geological media or elimination of the wastes from the earth.

We identify three technology classifications: commercialized, available, or under development. Commercialized technology is in routine use in the nuclear industry. Technology is said to be "available" if design, construction, and verification testing of full-scale commercial facilities can be initiated on the basis of present knowledge. Technologies under development range from early concept testing in the laboratory to nearly available. These technologies anticipate benefits such as reduced environmental impact, simplified procedures, and reduced costs but are unproven and not available.

FUEL CYCLE OPERATIONS

Characteristics and quantities of wastes produced in the back end of the LWR fuel cycle will depend on technologies and logistics used for fuel cycle and waste management operations. Overview characterizations were developed for three basic alternatives, each of which was assumed to use available waste management technology:

—No recycle of uranium or plutonium.
—Uranium recycle only (plutonium is stored).
—Recycle of uranium and plutonium.

Waste management requirements for these alternatives differ in detail. The two recycle options are, within the framework of assumptions used, similar with respect to impact on waste management: both require fuel reprocessing and its comparatively great impact on waste quantities and characteristics. Recycling of plutonium, in addition to uranium, involves addition of mixed-oxide fuel fabrication plants to the fuel cycle; such operations have a minor effect on waste quantities. The "throwaway" fuel cycle (no recycling of plutonium or uranium) minimizes waste quantities but maximizes inventories of long-lived, alpha particle-emitting nuclides in the wastes. Detailed comparative assessments of these alternatives have not been made and are not within scope of the TAD document.

Figure 18-1 summarizes some of the information on the types, quantities, and activi-

Table 18–1. LWR Fuel Cycle Comparison.

	Clad + High-level Waste	*Discard Fuel*
Mass, (metric ton per gigawatt electric-year)		
Plutonium	0.006	0.35
Uranium	0.20	43
Total	16	65
Heat (kilowatt per gigawatt electric-year)		
1 year cooled	350	410
10 year cooled	60	40
Activity (megacurie per gigawatt electric-year)		
1 year cooled	75	100
10 year cooled	10	15
Self-fission (10^9 neutrons per gigawatt electric-year)		
1 year cooled	160	4
10 year cooled	110	2.5

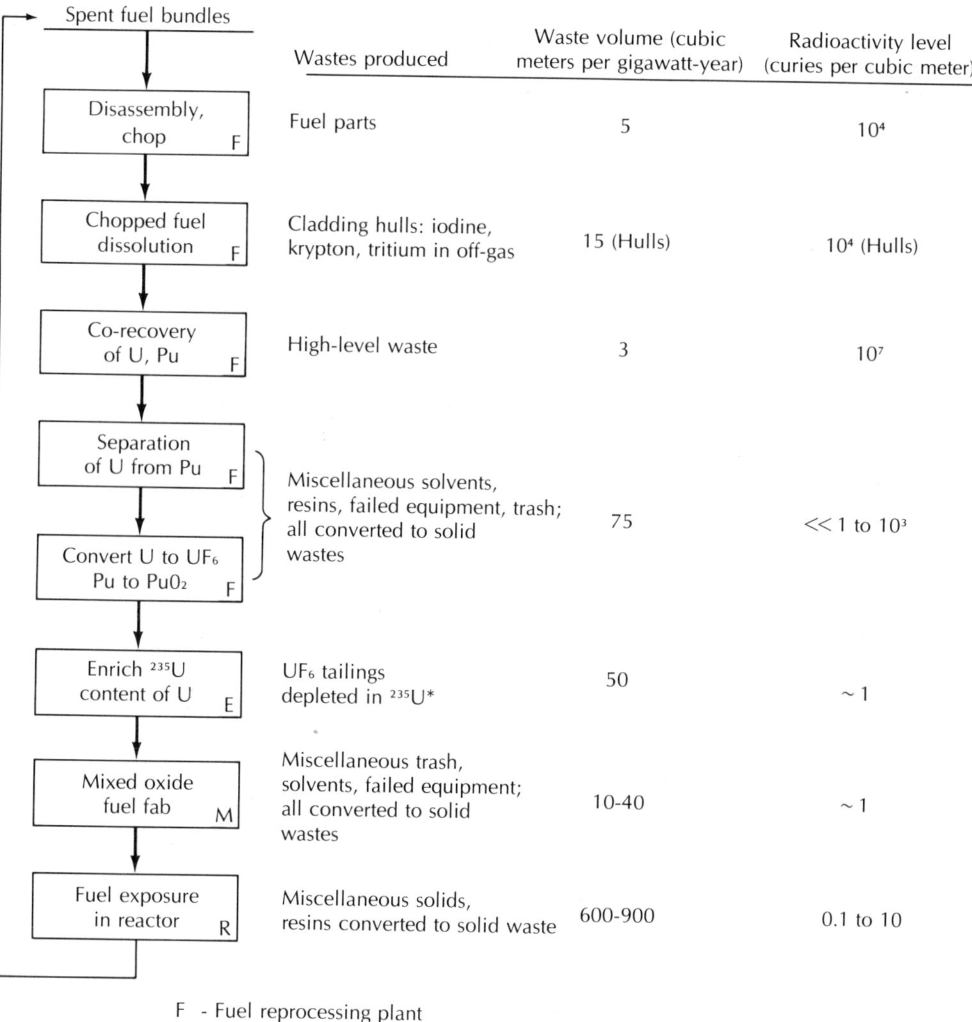

Figure 18-1. Process operations and wastes in the light water reactor fuel cycle.

ties of the wastes produced by a fuel cycle reutilizing both plutonium and uranium.

The principal effects of the fuel cycle operational mode on waste management are shown in Table 18-1. Perhaps the most significant factor is an increase in actinide content by a factor of 50 in spent fuel as compared to that in the wastes from a closed cycle.

We consider now the status of technology

for the four basic waste management activities identified earlier, i.e., treatment, interim storage, transportation, and final isolation or disposal of the various types of wastes.

IRRADIATED FUEL

The technology is available and in use for interim storage and transportation of irradiated LWR fuel. If the irradiated fuel becomes a waste, i.e., if the uranium and plutonium in spent fuel are not returned to the fuel cycle, then the fuel assemblies can be stored or managed as a waste, e.g., by placing them in containers and filling the void space with metal. Such technology is available but has not been used.

CHOP-LEACH FUEL BUNDLE RESIDUES

The chop-leach fuel bundle residues are solid wastes comprising short lengths of fuel cladding, fuel bundle support rods, poison rods, massive end fittings, fuel support grids, assorted springs, and spacer elements. Between 0.05 and 0.5 per cent of the original fuel material remains with these wastes as an insoluble residue. The available technology is to store these wastes without treatment. The small amount of chop-leach bundle residue wastes generated in the United States to date, at the Nuclear Fuel Services Plant, was packaged in steel containers and placed in shallow geological isolation (burial grounds).

Advanced technology is being developed to decontaminate and/or consolidate these wastes by mechanical compaction, by melting, or by chemical reaction.

HIGH-LEVEL WASTE

Table 18-2 shows the many available technologies to treat the high-level liquid waste. This treatment operation has received intensive development throughout the world. Most of these developments are now aimed toward the production of silicate glasses as the primary product.

Most of the processes are considered ready or available for commercialization. The remaining minor technical questions can be answered in parallel with the design/construction activities.

COMBUSTIBLE SOLIDS

The basic treatment options available for combustible solids are shown in Figure 18-2.

Table 18–2. High-level Waste Immobilization.

	Concentrator		*Calciner*		
Product Concept	None	Other	Rotary kiln	Fluid bed	Spray
Calcine			US-BNL	US-INEL; US-GE	
Glass in-can	Harvest Fingal United Kingdom	Drum drier Pamela FRG	US-PNL	US-PNL	
Glass metallic melter	Piver France	Phosphate US-BNL	AVM France		VERA FRG
Glass ceramic melter		Wiped film US-PNL			
Metallic matrix				Stirred bed Lotes FRG/Belgium	Coated pellets US-PNL

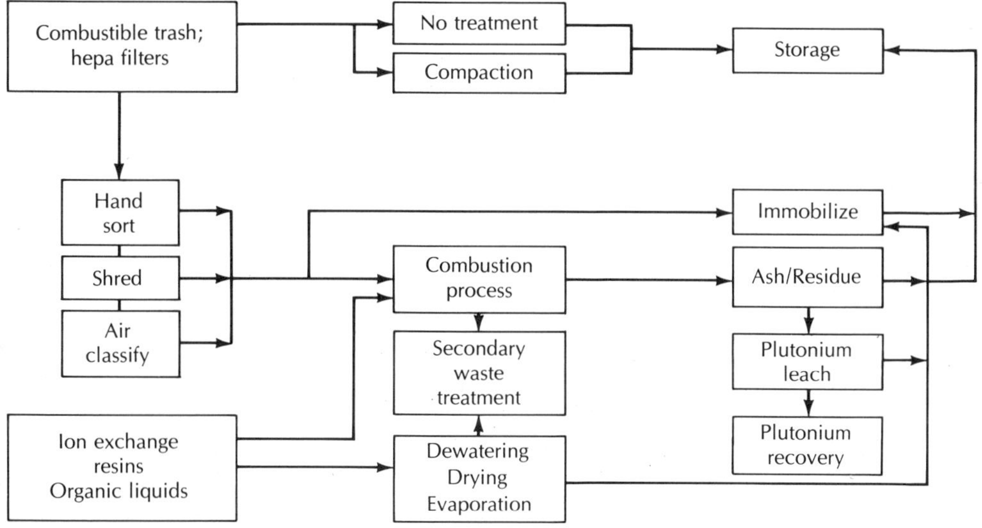

Figure 18-2. Treatment options for combustible radioactive wastes.

In most cases, the preferred path is combustion or oxidation of the waste to reduce its volume and its ignition capability.

Combustible solid radioactive wastes include a large variety of items, such as paper, rags, plastic sheeting, protective clothing, gloves, rubber shoes, wood, organic ion exchange resins, and filter aids. Much of the waste material is collected as general trash, which usually is a mixture of combustible and noncombustible items. Therefore, treatment options generally include sorting prior to treatment of the wastes.

A wide range of combustion/oxidation technologies are available.

NONCOMBUSTIBLE SOLID WASTES

Figure 18-3 shows the options available for treatment of noncombustible solid waste. There is no sharp line of distinction between technologies available and those requiring further development. In most cases, the development required is the engineering necessary for the technique to be employed in radioactive service.

The primary constituent of these solid wastes is metal, but other noncombustibles, such as glass and concrete, are also present. Incidental quantities of combustible material, such as grease, plastic, and floor sweepings, can also be included with the noncombustible waste.

Most failed or obsolete process equipment eventually becomes noncombustible waste. It is normally flushed and decontaminated prior to removal from service, and its combustibles are removed whenever it is practical to do so. Typical large items from a fuel reprocessing plant may consist of dissolvers, columns, and concentrators, which might be up to 3 meters in diameter and 10 meters in height. Disassembly may be required for movement beyond the confines of the reprocessing facility. Such wastes are typical of decommissioning operations.

IMMOBILIZATION OF NON-HIGH–LEVEL WASTES

Essentially all the treatment processes just described for liquids and solids result in dispersable liquid concentrates or solids.

There are many alternative technologies for

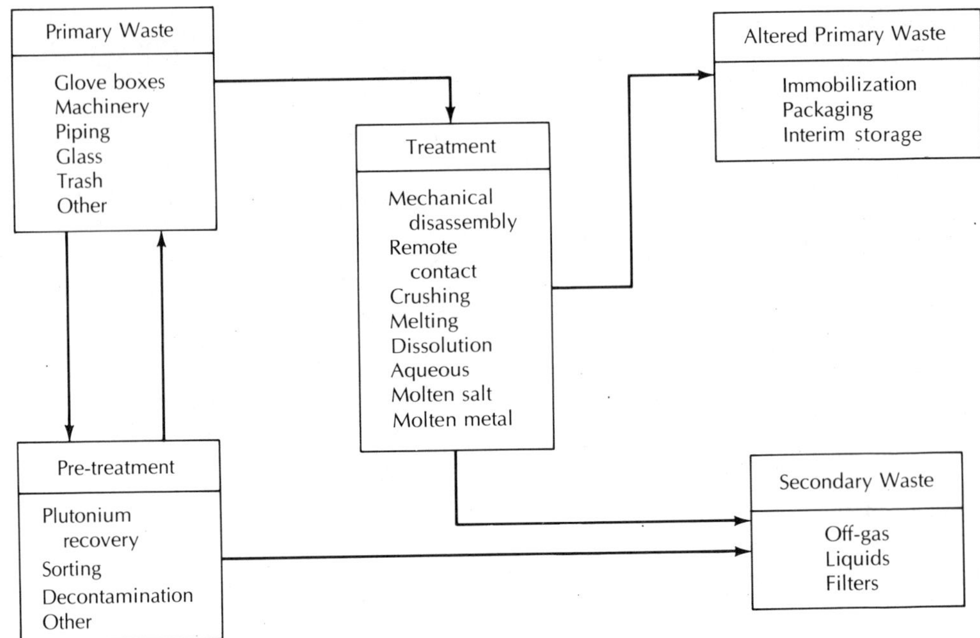

Figure 18-3. Noncombustible solid waste flow diagram.

immobilizing these wastes. Without going into detail, Table 18-3 lists the principal technologies.

The technologies under development are designed primarily to improve the leach resistance of the solidified products. Foremost in this field are the vitrification processes, which yield glass products with leach rates of 5×10^{-5} gram per square centimeter-day or less

Table 18–3. Immobilization Alternatives.

Technologies in Use	*Technologies under Development*
Absorbents	Aluminosilicate minerals (clay)
Salt matrix	Glass/ceramics
Urea-formaldehyde resins	Pelletization/ compaction
Cement/concrete	Polyethylene and other organic polymers
Bitumen (asphalt)	Metal matrix

for the more leachable components. Pelletization processes produce ceramic or cermet pellets that should have equally high leach resistance. The leach resistances of polyethylene products are comparable to those for bitumen products, whereas the leach resistances of the aluminosilicate mineral salt-fixation products are approximately comparable to those for cement products. The leach rates for rare-earth and actinide elements are several orders of magnitude lower than the leach rates for alkali and alkaline-earth elements.

GASEOUS WASTE

The current generation of reprocessing plants releases krypton-85 and tritium and recovers iodine-131 and iodine-129. Consideration is currently being given to whether or not this practice should or need be changed. However, technical work on all three gaseous wastes is underway, primarily because of

Table 18–4. Gaseous Waste Treatment.

Iodine	
Caustic scrubbing	Technology available
Mercuric nitrate scrubbing	Technology available
Nitric acid scrubbing—iodox	Technology under development
Chemisorption	
silver loaded	Technology available
metal loaded	Technology under development
Krypton	
Cryogenic distillation	Technology available
Liquid fluorocarbon	Technology under development
Tritium	
Voloxidation	Technology under development
Pyrochemical	Technology under development

potential need in non-LWR fuel cycles. A summary of this work is shown in Table 18-4. Technology is available for capture of krypton and iodine, but further development is required for tritium.

INTERIM STORAGE

The basic options that exist for interim storage are shown in Table 18-5. Considerations such as radiation levels, heat generation rates, and allowable temperature limits are key factors in the selection of the most appropriate packaging and interim storage technology for a particular waste. The most practical and effective choice among the many basic interim storage alternatives is to minimize the number of packaging, handling, and transportation steps between the generation of the waste and terminal storage.

Table 18–5. Interim Storage Alternatives.

Storage Alternative	*Heat Removal*	*Corrosion Control*	*Maintenance Requirements*
Water basin	Forced circulation of basin water	Packaged in inert or noncorrosive medium	High
Air-cooled vault	Natural circulation of air	Packaged in inert or noncorrosive medium	Low
Concrete surface silo	Natural circulation of or conduction to air	Packaged in inert or noncorrosive medium	Low
Near-surface heat sink	Conduction to earth	Packaged in inert or noncorrosive medium	Low

GEOLOGICAL ISOLATION

Most of the nations now using nuclear power are considering geological isolation as the means for the final disposition of commercial nuclear power wastes. The other basic option for final disposition is to eliminate the isotopes from the earth. This might be done by extraterrestrial ejection or by transmuting the isotopes into other elements. At present, however, there is no practical technology for these elimination options.

Four candidate geological isolation environments can be identified: sediments or basement rock of the sea floor, ice sheets, shallow continental geological formations, and deep continental geological formations. The focus of effort throughout the world is to use deep geological formations within national borders to isolate high-level and other transuranic wastes. Low-level and nontransuranic wastes would be placed in shallow geological formations (burial grounds) or the sea floor.

The United States (lower 48) has numerous geological formations that are potentially suitable for deep isolation of transuranic wastes. These include the Michigan and Permian basins (bedded salt), the salt domes of the Gulf Coast region, and igneous rock formations in the northcentral and northwestern states. The various formations are described in Volume 5 of ERDA-76-43.

The process of selecting a site for a geological repository is one of proceeding from the general to the specific. The formations cited above are generally suitable; through a process of geological characterization and evaluation of other factors such as ecology, climate, and availability of services, site-specific candidate repository locations will be identified. System designs reflecting the characteristics of the candidate site and the wastes to be emplaced would then be developed and evaluated. Emplacement of wastes into the geological formation would be expected to be by conventional mining technology.

A major part of evaluating a geological repository concept is the consideration of maintaining a long-term isolation of the wastes. The process actually starts with the site selection procedures, since the particular site is selected on the basis of past stability and expected future stability of the geology. Basic geological stability must be anticipated (e.g., freedom from faulting or water intrusion) or a site will not be a candidate for a repository.

Evaluation and design to assure long-term maintenance of waste isolation go beyond selection of highly stable geological formations. One concept used is that of multiple barriers between the waste and the biosphere. The first such barrier is the waste form itself, which is selected to be highly resistant to degradation and leaching. The second barrier consists of engineered structures (e.g., waste canister containers or vault liners), if used, between the waste form and the surrounding geology, which serves as the third barrier. Loss of isolation would then require that disruption of all barriers occur in such a manner that pathways and mechanisms to transport the wastes from the repository to the biosphere are created.

Although such disruptions are not expected, studies have been made to estimate the consequences if they should occur. The studies fall into four categories:

(1) Sudden natural events such as meteorite impact.

(2) Geological processes such as faulting or ice ages.

(3) Changes in local geology caused by creating the repository and introducing thermal and radiation sources.

(4) Human intrusion.

Studies completed in the past are reported or discussed in several documents.[1-4] There have been evaluations in each of the above categories.

Past studies have used evaluation techniques such as risk analysis, probability assessment, consequence analysis, and hazard indices. All results to date show that loss of isolation is highly improbable and/or the consequences are insignificant. Additional evaluations are needed, however, to expand the scope of conditions considered and to provide as much confidence as possible in the validity of results, which can never be subjected to experimental verification. Additional generic studies are under way, and specific evaluations will be made for each candidate repository site.

REFERENCES

1. ERDA-76-43, *Alternatives for Managing Wastes from Reactors and Post-Fission Operations in the LWR Fuel Cycle,* U.S. Energy Research and Development Administration, May 1976.
2. BNWL-1900, *High-Level Radioactive Waste Management Alternatives,* Battelle, Pacific Northwest Laboratories, May 1974.
3. BNWL-1927, *Incentives for Partitioning High-Level Waste,* Battelle, Pacific Northwest Laboratories, November 1975.
4. NUREG-0116, *Environmental Survey of the Reprocessing and Waste Management Portions of the LWR Fuel Cycle,* U.S. Nuclear Regulatory Commission, October 1976.

SUGGESTED READINGS

Bebbington, William P., 1976, The Reprocessing of Nuclear Fuels, *Scientific American 235,* pp. 30–41.

Carter, Luther J., 1977, Radioactive Waste: Some Urgent Unfinished Business, *Science 195,* pp. 661–666, 704.

Cowan, George A., 1976, A Natural Fission Reactor, *Scientific American 235,* pp. 36–47.

Dau, Gary, and Robert Williams, 1976, Secure Storage of Radioactive Waste, *Electric Power Research Institute Journal,* July-August, pp. 6–14.

Dukert, Joseph M., 1975, High-level Radioactive Waste: Safe Storage and Ultimate Disposal, Energy Research and Development Administration, 23 p.

Kubo, Arthus S., and David J. Rose, 1973, Disposal of Nuclear Wastes, *Science 182,* pp. 1205–1211.

Rippon, Simon, 1976, Reprocessing—What Went Wrong? *Nuclear Engineering International 21,* pp. 21–31.

Rochlin, Gene I., 1977, Nuclear Waste Disposal: Two Social Criteria, *Science 195,* pp. 23–31.

Rueth, Nancy, 1977, Wrapping Up the Nuclear Fuel Cycle, Part 2—A Permanent Home for Nuclear Waste, *Mechanical Engineering 99,* pp. 20–27.

Zebroski, E., and M. Levenson, 1976, The Nuclear Fuel Cycle, *Annual Review of Energy 1,* pp. 101–130.

Toxicity of Plutonium and Some Other Actinides 19

JOHN T. EDSALL 1976

Decisions on policy regarding the large-scale development of nuclear energy inevitably involve judgments concerning the hazards of plutonium and other actinides. The major hazards involve the toxicity of these substances and the risk that plutonium from reactors can be made into nuclear weapons. My concern here is only with the former problem.

Everyone agrees that plutonium is highly poisonous, but there has been sharp disagreement as to just how great a risk it does represent, if produced and used on a large scale in nuclear reactors, and processed in the various steps of the nuclear fuel cycle. The problem would become crucially important in large breeder reactors and in the associated reprocessing and shipping operations. A 1,000-megawatt breeder might contain something of the order of 3 metric tons (3,000 kilograms) of plutonium. Even in the current light water reactors, however, the problem of plutonium is important, especially if the high-level wastes from the reactors are reworked so as to extract the plutonium, and return it as fuel to the reactors. Moreover, the problem of the ultimate disposal of both high-level and low-level wastes involves the handling of substantial amounts of plutonium.

As part of our legacy from atmospheric testing, plutonium is present everywhere, especially in the Northern Hemisphere—in soils, plants, animals, and human beings. The amounts in any one organism are very small, but not necessarily insignificant. In addition, some plutonium from the nuclear fuel cycle will inevitably leak into the environment, no matter how effective containment may be. The problem of toxicity, therefore, inevitably involves the behavior of plutonium in the environment.

Our knowledge of all these matters is still preliminary and incomplete. Important decisions will soon be thrust upon us, regarding the future of nuclear energy; and they must be made with full awareness of the scope, and of

John T. Edsall, M.D. is emeritus professor of biochemistry at the Biological Laboratories of Harvard University, Cambridge, Massachusetts 02138. He has been an active member of the National Academy of Sciences, editor of the "Journal of Biological Chemistry" (1958–1967), and President of the American Society of Biological Chemists (1957–1958).

From *Bulletin of the Atomic Scientists,* Vol. 32, No. 7, pp. 27–37, September 1976. Reprinted by permission of the author and the *Bulletin of the Atomic Scientists*.

the uncertainty, of our knowledge of the magnitude of the risk from plutonium and other actinides. The primary focus of concern in this discussion will be on plutonium (element 94), but I will refer briefly to americium and curium (elements 95 and 96, respectively), which give rise to problems similar to those connected with plutonium.

THE PLUTONIUM ISOTOPES*

Plutonium is toxic because it emits alpha radiation; this seems to be generally agreed upon. The specific chemical properties of plutonium and its compounds are of importance only insofar as they determine its uptake by plants and animals from the environment, and the manner of its distribution within living organisms.

Alpha particles are helium nuclei, with an electric charge twice as great as that of a proton. Their mass is four times as great as that of a proton or neutron, and several thousand times that of an electron (a beta particle is an electron, released from certain radioactive atoms). Because alpha particles are so massive, and are emitted with high energy in radioactive disintegration, they release large amounts of energy as they travel through any resisting medium, including living tissues. They are thus high in what is commonly called linear energy transfer (abbreviated as LET). Alpha particles ionize neighboring molecules extensively as they travel through tissue, producing chemical alterations, which may be drastic, in such sensitive substance as nucleic acids, proteins, and other biological molecules. The range of alpha particles is short; they discharge their energy, and come to a stop, over a short path length of the order of 40 micrometers (0.04 millimeters) in a dense tissue.

Beta particles have a much lower LET, but a longer range, in living tissue. Gamma rays, which are essentially x rays of very short wavelength, are also a form of low-LET radiation. Gamma rays penetrate tissue through much greater distances than either alpha or beta particles. The short range and the very high ionizing power of alpha particles set them apart in a distinctive fashion from low-LET beta and gamma radiations.

Reactor plutonium is a mixture of isotopes. The predominant isotope plutonium-239 has a half-life of 24,390 years and emits energetic alpha particles, most of them with energies of 5.11 to 5.16 million electron volts. The product of plutonium-239 decay is uranium-235, which is also an alpha emitter with a half-life of 710 million years. Reactor plutonium also contains smaller, but important, amounts of other isotopes of plutonium, namely plutonium-238 (86.4 years), plutonium-240 (6,600 years), plutonium-241 (13.2 years) and plutonium-242 (390,000 years). The half-lives are indicated in parentheses. All are alpha emitters, with energies in the range of 5 to 6 million electron volts, except plutonium-241 which emits beta radiation, with the half-life indicated above, and is thereby converted to americium-241.

Americium-241 is an alpha emitter with a half-life of 458 years. In the course of some 30 to 50 years, it will become a major source of alpha radiation, comparable in importance

Some definitions and standards. The unit of radioactivity used in this paper is the nanocurie. One nanocurie denotes 37 radioactive disintegrations per second. For plutonium-239, and most other isotopes of plutonium, this means that 37 alpha particles are shot off each second. One nanocurie of plutonium-239 equals 16.3 nanograms. One nanogram equals 10^{-9} gram, a quantity much too small to weigh: a good standard analytical balance can weigh, if used with care and skill, to about 10^{-5} gram, or 10,000 nanograms. Radioactivity measurements are far more sensitive. The mixture of plutonium isotopes from a reactor gives off alpha particles about five times as rapidly as the same mass of plutonium-239, and is therefore about five times as hazardous.

The International Commission on Radiation Protection (ICRP) and the National Council on Radiation Protection (NCRP) have set the permissible body burden of plutonium as 40 nanocuries for workers in contact with plutonium, who are constantly monitored for exposure to radioactivity. For members of the general public, who are not monitored, the permissible body burden is set lower, by a factor of 10 (in other words, at 4 nanocuries). These values are based on the assumption that bone is the critical organ, in which cancers from plutonium are most likely to develop, and on certain other assumptions discussed here.

The maximum permissible deposit in lung is officially 16 nanocuries for occupational exposure, and 1.6 nanocuries for the general public. See, for instance, the references to Morgan[4] and to Bair and Thompson[5]. Several workers in the field, including Morgan, believe that these limits do not provide sufficient protection, and should be lowered by a substantial factor. Their views are discussed in this article.

to the plutonium isotopes, and with somewhat different chemical properties. There are indications that compounds of americium may be taken up by plants from the soil more readily than those of plutonium. In any case, the radioactivity from americium-241 represents a biological hazard comparable to that of similar amounts of plutonium.

Curium, especially curium-242 and curium-244, is also found in important amounts in reactors. These two isotopes have half-lives of 163 days and 18.1 years, respectively. Any consideration of the total hazards from alpha emitters must take into account americium and curium, and probably some of the higher actinides also. This discussion, however, will focus on plutonium.

All the isotopes mentioned above, except plutonium-242, have considerably shorter half-lives than plutonium-239. This means that the rate of alpha emission from the mixture derived from the reactor, and therefore its toxicity, is greater than that of pure plutonium-239 by a factor that varies for different types of reactors, but is of the order of five.[1, 2]

IN MAN AND ANIMALS

Plutonium can be taken in by ingestion, absorption from the skin, or inhalation. The latter route is the most important. Ordinarily plutonium entering the digestive tract is nearly all excreted. According to Bair (Ref. 3, Table I), studies in rats show that the amount of ingested plutonium absorbed from the gut varies from 0.03 per cent for plutonium-238 nitrate to 0.0001 per cent for plutonium-239 oxide. The latter compound is highly insoluble. For newborn rats, however, the absorption is much greater, 2 per cent for plutonium-238 nitrate, and 0.3 per cent for plutonium-239 nitrate. The reason for the difference between the isotopes is not clear.

Fortunately, we have as yet no knowledge of what the corresponding figures for human subjects would be. Presumably, however, a similar difference between the newborn and the adult would hold. In any case we must allow for the possibility that some diseases might significantly increase the uptake of plutonium from the gut. Americium and curium isotopes, which will become important in reactor discharge fuels pass through the food chains more readily than plutonium, and are appreciably absorbed from the gut.

Absorption of plutonium through normal skin is likewise very small, of the order of 0.05 to 0.3 per cent of plutonium-239 nitrate being absorbed internally, over 5 to 15 days, after application to the skin in rats or rabbits (Ref. 3, Table II). In wounds or abrasions, however, absorption may be much greater and may have grave consequences. Morgan has written (Ref. 4, p. 572): "There is no question that epithelial cells of the skin are very radiosensitive and local doses such as are produced by microgram quantities of plutonium-239 in wounds are very carcinogenic." However, the reports of carcinogenesis by plutonium in skin are still extremely few, and more evidence on this point is needed.

The respiratory tract is the major port of entry of plutonium in man and other mammals. The most extensive studies of inhaled plutonium have been on beagles at Battelle's Pacific Northwest Laboratories in Richland, Washington, by W. J. Bair and his associates.

The dogs were exposed to aerosols of plutonium-239, with depositions ranging from less than 1,000 to more than 50,000 nanocuries. About 80 per cent of the plutonium initially deposited in the alveolar region of the lung was still present in the bodies of the surviving dogs 10 years after exposure. The lungs still retained 10 per cent; 40 per cent was in the thoracic lymph nodes, 15 per cent in liver, and about 5 per cent both in the abdominal lymph nodes and the skeleton.[5]

At the higher doses (100 to 1,000 nanocuries per gram of lung), most of the dogs died of pulmonary fibrosis within 1 to 2 years. At lower doses, there were also deaths from fibrosis after periods as long as 6 years. Dogs exposed to lower doses (3 to 20 nanocuries per gram of lung) developed malignant tumors after periods of 6 to 13 years (Ref. 5, Figure 5). As Bair and Thompson[5] noted, "The incidence of tumors was essentially 100 per cent at the lowest dose of plutonium dioxide tested." They concluded, very tentatively, that a dose of more than 1 nanocurie of plutonium-239 per gram could cause premature death from a lung tumor in beagles; and it seems clear that cancer might occur at still lower doses.

Plutonium will reach the blood from the lung, the gastrointestinal tract, or surface wounds. Extensive studies have been made at the University of Utah on plutonium injected directly into the bloodstream of beagles. Plutonium tends to hydrolyze under physiological conditions and form colloidal polymeric aggregates. These disappear rapidly from the blood and are chiefly deposited in the liver. "Soluble" plutonium, complexed with citrate or some other complex-forming ion, stays in blood much longer and is largely deposited in bone. For further discussion, and many more details, one may consult the important review by Bair and Thompson.[5]

Plutonium in bone gives rise to malignant tumors, chiefly osteosarcomas, which have been observed in the beagle studies at the University of Utah. For instance, in a table of data reproduced by Bair and Thompson,[5] nine out of 13 beagles, each injected with 48 nanocuries of plutonium-239, developed bone sarcomas over a period that averaged 8.5 years. Extensive studies on rats in the Soviet Union[6] have given similar results, when the plutonium was administered by inhalation, injection, or other ways.

Significant amounts of administered plutonium find their way to male and female gonads. As reported in a review by Richmond and Thomas,[7] the fraction of administered plutonium found in the gonads of five species of animals (mouse, rat, pig, dog, and rabbit) was around 0.0003 per cent, with variations of only a factor of 10 between the lowest and the highest values. The concentration of plutonium from fallout in human autopsies averaged close to 0.0005 nanocuries per gram of tissue in gonads. This figure was substantially higher than the concentration in lung or vertebrae, though less than in liver, and much less (by a factor of six) in thoracic lymph nodes. Because of the possible implications for genetic damage, the presence of plutonium in gonads clearly deserves much more study than it has apparently received up to now.

PRESENT STANDARDS FOR MAXIMUM PERMISSIBLE DOSE

The International Commission, and the National Council, on Radiation Protection (ICRP and NCRP) agreed, nearly a quarter century ago, on a maximum permissible body burden of 40 nanocuries of plutonium-239 for workers occupationally exposed to plutonium; the permissible dose for the general public was set at one-tenth of this value. We note that 1 nanocurie of plutonium-239 equals 16.3 nanograms (1 nanogram = 10^{-9} grams); for the mixed isotopes of plutonium from a reactor, the mass corresponding to a given number of curies would be less by a factor of about five. Note that a nanogram of any material is an almost invisible speck; even 100 nanograms is an amount too small to weigh on a standard analytical balance of high sensitivity.

Since direct evidence on the toxicity of plutonium in man is extremely scanty, the choice of the value of 40 nanocuries depended heavily on the extensive studies of production of malignant tumors in human bone by radium-226, and on the fact that both radium-226 and plutonium-239 are bone-seekers. The Utah studies on beagles indicated that plutonium-239 is more dangerous than radium, by a factor of five to 10, because it deposits on the bone in a more hazardous location.

As Bair and Thompson have pointed out, three major assumptions are involved in the officially permissible limit of 40 nanocuries of plutonium:

(i) that comparison with the limit of 100 nanocuries for radium is acceptable as a standard; (ii) that bone, which is the critical organ for radium, may also by considered the critical organ for plutonium and (iii) that comparative effects of radium and plutonium on the bone of animals can be meaningfully extrapolated to man (Ref. 5, p. 720).

The data on the effects of radium in man are as well established as any that are known. However, it is not clear that bone is necessarily the critical organ for plutonium; liver, lung, and lymph nodes, at least, would have to be considered also. Bair and Thompson suggest that the 40-nanocurie limit for plutonium may be several fold "less safe" than the 100-nanocurie limit for radium.

Recently, Spiers and Vaughan[8] have calculated the "maximum risk" to skeletal contents for radium-226 and plutonium-239 and concluded that the value of maximum permissible body burden of 40 nanocuries of plutonium-239 is not in need of any major revision, as far as bone is concerned. They conclude: "A maintained skeletal burden of plutonium-239 of 0.04 microcuries [40 nanocuries] would lead, on our calculations, to possibly two cases of leukemia and 13 cases of bone sarcoma per 1,000 persons over about 50 years" (Ref. 8, p. 534).

This may be compared with a recent calculation by Bair and Thomas[9] based on comparison with the data on rats for inhaled insoluble alpha-emitters, that one case of lung cancer per eight persons might develop for individuals with a lung burden of 16 nanocuries of plutonium—if human beings are as susceptible to plutonium-induced lung cancer as rats. Calculations based on human exposures to other alpha emitters (none of them actinides) gave an estimated risk about nine times less than the above figure. In spite of many uncertainties, Bair and Thomas considered the inferences from the animal data to be probably the more reliable as a basis for judgment.

These estimates of risk are based on the present officially accepted maximum permissible body burden. Whether such risks are acceptable is a matter of social rather than scientific judgment, to which I will return later. Critics of the present standards hold that the risk is actually much larger than these estimates indicate.

ARE PRESENT STANDARDS STRICT ENOUGH?

Recently, several critics have proposed that the maximum permissible concentration of plutonium should be lowered by a substantial factor. The arguments advanced by various critics differ considerably, and I will try to explain them briefly here. First, however, we should be clear about certain definitions concerning the energy delivered to cells and tissues by radiation.

The unit of absorbed dose, the rad, is by definition equal to 0.01 joule per kilogram of medium, in any medium. The mean energy of an alpha particle from plutonium-239 is close to 5.15 million electron volts $= 8 \times 10^{-13}$ joule. If we know the specific activity of the plutonium present, in curies (1 curie $= 3.7 \times 10^{10}$ disintegrations per second), the total energy produced in t seconds is directly calculable. However, to translate this energy into rads we must know the effective mass of the medium that is exposed to radiation.

It has generally been conventional to assume that the radiation is distributed continuously throughout the medium (for example, lung tissue). This is a good approximation for beta and gamma radiation. However, bombardment from the massive alpha particles is in fact by no means continuously distributed. The particle discharges its energy and comes to a stop, over a short path length of the order of 40 micrometers in a dense tissue; the path length may be several times greater in a tissue such as lung with many open spaces between the layers of tissue.

Calculation of radiation damage on the assumption of a continuous distribution has usually been justified on the ground that such a distribution would do at least as much biological damage as the more particulate distribution actually found. Therefore it is held to be a conservative procedure to calculate rads on this basis. Some recent challenges to this view are discussed below.

We must note that the relative biological effectiveness (RBE) in producing damage is much greater for the massive (high LET) alpha particles than for x rays, gamma rays, or beta particles (low LET). Therefore we must multiply the dose in rads by an appropriate factor to convert from rads to rems; the rem is the biologically significant unit of radiation. The value of this conversion factor for alpha radiation is still in some dispute; but it is of the order of 10 except for the special case of plutonium in bone, where 1 rad is taken as equivalent to 50 rem (Ref. 5, p. 40) because plutonium is considered particularly hazardous in bone.

"Hot Particle" Hypothesis

The hypothesis claims that alpha radiation in a tissue, such as the lung, if concentrated in small particles within a specified range of size and activity, is far more likely to induce cancer than the same amount of radiation distributed uniformly throughout the tissue. This hypothesis was proposed by Tamplin and Cochran[10] in 1974 and has given rise to sharp controversy. Tamplin and Cochran based their argument on earlier studies of radiation damage to rat skin by R. C. Albert and his associates.

Qualitatively, the hot particle hypothesis states that "when a critical tissue mass is irradiated at a sufficiently high dose, the probability of tumor production is high."[11] More specifically, Tamplin and Cochran[10] proposed that a plutonium-containing particle, in deep respiratory tissue, active enough to expose the immediately surrounding lung tissue to a dose of at least 1,000 rem per year, represents a unique carcinogenic risk. They estimated the risk of cancer induction from such a particle as of the order of 1 in 2,000. In their first report, they calculated, from this assumption, that the maximum permissible body burden of plutonium should be reduced by a factor somewhat greater than 100,000. In a later discussion,[11] they made a less drastic claim, but still concluded that the present permissible body burden should be lowered by a factor of 2,000.

The hot particle hypothesis was severely criticized in a report by Bair, Richmond and Wachholz,[12] by a Committee of the British Medical Research Council, and also in a recent MCRP report.[13] No brief summary can do justice to the arguments involved.

Bair et al. (Ref. 12, pp. 16–23) review a large number of animal experiments in which plutonium was inhaled in particulate form into the lungs of animals, or instilled so as to form finer dispersions. They concluded that the evidence available did not indicate an increased hazard from particulates, and that if anything the danger of cancer was greater when a given dose was more finely dispersed. They also considered data on human workers who had taken in small amounts of plutonium at Los Alamos in 1944–1945, and others who were exposed later, in the plutonium plant at Rocky Flats, Colorado. None of these workers has developed cancer, but they concluded that a number of cancers would have appeared if the hot particle hypothesis were correct.

Most of the cells close to a hot particle will be killed by the intense radiation. Dead cells do not give rise to cancer. This would suggest that uniformly diffused radiation is more dangerous than the same amount of radiation concentrated in hot particles. Tamplin and Cochran hold, however, that the damage done to certain critical architectural features of the tissue by the intense alpha radiation is the essential feature in cancer induction. Most of their critics, however, favor the view that some form of non-lethal damage to cells by the radiation is the critical event. This might involve two or more mutational events in the cell, in order to transform it to malignancy. Certainly, a continuous distribution of a given total amount of radiation in the tissue will ensure that more cells will receive non-lethal hits than if the radiation is concentrated in a smaller number of hot particles. In fact, of course, we still do not know what the mechanism of carcinogenesis is.

The hot particle hypothesis assumes that cancer production *by this mechanism* requires a particle that will administer a dose of at least 1,000 rem per year to the surrounding tissue. Below this threshold the risk is considered to fall to zero, although the hypothesis leaves open the possibility that cancer may be induced by other mechanisms—by ouch smaller particles or by individual atoms of plutonium.

Most investigators in recent years have assumed, in disagreement with the hot particle hypothesis, that damage from low-level radiation is a linear function of dose, with no threshold, and that this is a conservative assumption. (I consider this question below.)

Recently Mayneord and Clarke[14] have explored the hot particle hypothesis mathematically, assuming both linear and non-linear dose-response functions. They conclude that the linear assumption can be very conservative for small numbers of alpha or beta emitters, and that at worst the linear assumption is not likely to underestimate risks by more than a factor of about five, even in the most unfavorable cases. They conclude that: "The circumstances in which the 'hot particles' are relatively more dangerous are those in which the absolute risks are low" (Ref. 14, p. 539).

My own views will hardly satisfy either side in the controversy. I conclude, from evidence such as that presented in (Refs. 12 and 13) that the hot particle hypothesis is quite likely to be incorrect, but also conclude that it has not been rigorously disproven. Indeed, a rigorous disproof will probably be very difficult indeed. A recent exchange of views between the Nuclear Regulatory Commission and Cochran and Tamplin has apparently left the issues still unresolved (See Ref. 12).

Implications from Studies on Polonium-210 in Tobacco Smoke

Another line of evidence concerning the damage done by alpha radiation comes from studies of radioactivity in tobacco smoke. In this instance, the radiation comes not from plutonium but from polonium-210, which is a product of a chain of radioactive disintegrations, from radium-226 and its daughter radon-222, through several relatively rapid steps to lead-210 and thence by two steps of beta emission to polonium-210. Radford and Hunt[15] in 1964 were the first to note the presence of polonium-210 as a volatile element in tobacco smoke, and a series of later researchers in the same laboratory have explored the biological effects of radioactivity extensively.

In the most recent paper, Little and others[16] have reported studies on hamsters exposed to polonium-210 at levels comparable to those found in human subjects who have been heavy smokers for years. The polonium-210 was instilled into the lungs of the animals, either in solution or in a suspension, absorbed on fine particles of solid. The results were similar in both cases. Hamsters virtually never developed spontaneous lung tumors, but in the presence of polonium-210—to take one fairly typical example from the numerous data—at doses as low as 15 rads, averaged over the whole lung, 11 out of 83 hamsters developed malignant tumors. Control animals showed none.

Studies on hamsters exposed to plutonium, at the Battelle Laboratories in Richland, Washington, and at the Lovelace Foundation in Albuquerque, New Mexico, indicate that these animials are far less susceptible to induction of tumors by inhaled plutonium-238 and plutonium-239 than they are to polonium-210.

Radiation pneumonitis and pulmonary fibrosis were observed in many of the animals who received the higher doses of plutonium; but very few cancers appeared, even though hundreds of hamsters were studied over their lifetimes. This was true at much higher doses than those that Little[16] had found to induce large numbers of malignant tumors in their polonium experiments. These findings,[17] which are not yet published, emphasize the difficulty of drawing inferences concerning the effects of one alpha emitter from studies on another, even in the same species of animal. The greater uncertainties in extrapolating toxicity data from one species to another are of course well known.

E. A. Martell has worked extensively on radioactivity in tobacco smoke, and has summarized his conclusions in a recent review.[18] He stresses the importance of lead-210, with its half-life of 22 years, as a reservoir of radioactivity that gives rise to a continuing release of polonium-210 after the radioactive particles from the tobacco smoke have become implanted in the respiratory tissue.

Martell proposes that cancer induction arises from multiple mutations in the exposed cells; a hypothesis already put forward by other workers. Two successive mutations may be sufficient. A period of cell proliferation is assumed to follow the first mutation; a subsequent hit by an alpha particle may then induce cancer in any one cell, of the resulting clone of proliferated cells. Thus, the carcinogenic radioactivity must be low enough not to kill the cells, but intense enough to produce successive mutations. If Martell's hypothesis is correct, low-level radiation can be more dangerous than is generally assumed. The hypothesis should be susceptible to experimental test, though such experiments will be difficult to design.

Martell thus favors the hypothesis that alpha radioactivity is the primary cause of lung cancer in smokers, and that other chemical carcinogens play only an auxiliary role in enhancing the risks from the radioactivity. Most workers in the field would probably disagree, and would hold other chemical carcinogens to be fully capable of producing cancer, whether or not radioactive material is present.[19]

Martell's hypothesis is certainly controversial. Nevertheless, in view of the work of Little[16] on hamsters, in which polonium-210 was the only known carcinogen, we must take seriously the possibility that such radioactivity is an important factor in producing lung cancer (and possibly other cancers) in human smokers.

All this is clearly relevant to the hazards of inhaled plutonium; indeed Martell's concern with the effects of polonium-210 in smokers arises primarily from his work on plutonium in the environment[2] and his continuing concern with it. All of us, and particularly the inhabitants of the Northern Hemisphere, carry some plutonium in our lungs and other organs, since some 340 kilocuries of plutonium (predominantly plutonium-239) were distributed over the world by atmospheric weapons testing.[20]

The total average amount, in the bodies of individuals in the Northern Hemisphere, has been estimated as of the order of 0.042 nanocuries (Refs. 7, 21). Martell, in a personal communication, estimates the alpha activity of plutonium in the lungs, for the general population, as around 5 to 10 per cent of the polonium-210 alpha activity in the lungs of heavy smokers. This plutonium from fallout is present in all of us, including those who were infants at the time of heavy atmospheric testing. The deposit of plutonium from fallout has of course been gradually declining since the Test Ban Treaty of 1963, in spite of the French and Chinese tests.

Gofman[22] believes that this inhaled plutonium has already induced about 100,000 cases of lung cancer in the United States alone, and that perhaps 10,000 persons per year in the whole Northern Hemisphere may be dying from this cause. Since cancers due to plutonium cannot be distinguished from other cancers, there is no way of verifying this by direct observation on the patients.

The general calculations of Gofman are given in the first of the two papers cited,[22] he calculated a "lung cancer dose," which is the amount of plutonium that, when introduced into a population, will induce one extra death from lung cancer. For non-smokers he estimates the lung cancer dose as about 450 nanocuries. This corresponds to 73,000 nanograms of plutonium-239, or 1,400 nanograms of "reactor plutonium" (1 nanogram = 10^{-9} gram).

These figures are, within a factor of four or less, in agreement with the data of Bair[5] on the carcinogenicity of plutonium in beagles. Gofman assumes that cigarette smokers are about 100 times as susceptible as non-smokers to cancer induction by plutonium.

He thus gives the "lung cancer dose" for smokers as 3.6 nanocuries. This estimate is considered exaggerated by many other experts.

The dispute depends largely on the estimate of the time that foreign particles, such as insoluble plutonium compounds, spend in the lungs and bronchi. Clearance mechanisms, in a normal lung, largely remove such particles from the lung into lymph nodes and other tissues in a relatively short time. Gofman holds that these clearance mechanisms are drastically impaired in smokers, at least in heavy smokers, and estimates that in such cases half the plutonium initially present may still be in the lung after a period as long as 500 days. The longer the plutonium stays in the lung, of course, the greater the chance that a cancer will develop there. Others hold this 500-day estimate to be far too long, on the basis of available evidence.

There is indeed good evidence that exposure to radioactivity—for instance among uranium miners—increases the extra risk of lung cancer for smokers by a considerable factor. Most researchers, however, would probably put the increase in the risk factor as something like five to 10, rather than the factor of 100 that Gofman assumes. On this basis, Gofman's estimates of death due to plutonium from fallout would be substantially reduced; but even this lowered estimate is still disturbingly high.

The Calculations of Karl Z. Morgan and of C. W. Mays

Morgan[4] recently concluded on different grounds that the maximum permissible body burden of plutonium-239 should be reduced by a factor of 240, from 40 nanocuries to 0.17 nanocuries. He made no use of the hot particle hypothesis in reaching this conclusion, although he regards the validity of the hypothesis as still an open question. In his argument, Morgan considered four factors that he believes call for revision:

(1) He took the biological effectiveness of plutonium-239, relative to radium-226, as 15 rather than the previously employed factor of five.

(2) He corrected for the difference in the surface:volume ratio of trabecular bone for dog and man. The factor here is two.

(3) The rate of turnover (burial), of the alpha emitters by apposition of new bone, is about 10 times as great in dog as in man. This would give a correction factor of 10, for greater hazard in man than in dog.

(4) He noted that studies on baboons exposed to plutonium-239 suggested that they are about four times as radiosensitive as dogs. Since baboons are more like humans than dogs are, he held that it was appropriate to apply this correction factor in man. Thus the total correction factor became $3 \times 2 \times 10 \times 4 = 240$.

C. W. Mays, of the University of Utah, one of the leaders in a long series of studies on plutonium in beagles has recently given a detailed estimate of risks of human bone cancer (sarcoma) from plutonium. His figures are fairly close to those deduced from the maximum permissible dose values of the ICRP and NCRP, but in a discussion of Morgan's paper he concluded that the permissible limits of exposure to plutonium might be appropriately reduced by a factor of about nine. He held Morgan's factor of 240 to be much larger than the evidence justified, and among other things concluded that the data on baboons did not provide relevant evidence.[23]

INFLUENCE OF TOTAL DOSE AND DOSE RATE ON TOXICITY

Is the Linear Hypothesis Conservative Enough? Studies on radiation damage in animals must be done at radiation levels that are high enough to obtain statistically significant differences between the irradiated animals and the controls. Our concern about the radiation damage, however, extends to much lower radiation levels, for which the number of animals needed to obtain significant results and the time required for the experiments would become impracticably large. Here we enter the realm of what Alvin Weinberg has called "trans-science," where we can ask scientifically meaningful questions, but cannot get experimental answers today, or perhaps ever. Nevertheless we must make decisions, on matters of radiation protection, that require this extrapolation into the realm of trans-science.

It has long been a matter of debate whether there is a threshold level of radiation, below which no damage occurs if the dose rate is low enough, or whether a given dose, administered at very low rate over a long period of time, still produces as much damage as if it were administered rapidly. The latter assumption is known as the linear hypothesis: that is the damage produced is assumed to be a linear function of the total dose, regardless of rate.

The National Academy of Sciences Report on the biological effects of ionizing radiation, commonly known as the BEIR Report,[24] adopted this hypothesis as the basis for its calculations; but the authors carefully qualified their estimates when it came to extrapolating from statistically significant data to hypothetical radiation effects at extremely low dose rates. A recent discussion of these problems by the NCRP suggested that the linear hypothesis might well be overconservative, especially for beta and gamma radiation and for x rays.[25] For alpha radiation, with which we are here concerned, they concluded that the linear hypothesis was more probable, in the light of all the evidence.

There appears to be a basic difference between the effects of dose rate on genetic damage and on somatic damage, including cancer induction. Genetic damage for a given total dose, administered at a low level over a long period of time, is less than if it is given rapidly. Studies on mice at Oak Ridge also indicate that, in this species at least, females are much less susceptible than males to genetic damage by radiation. There are mechanisms for enzymatic repair of the genetic material (DNA) that operate quite effectively if the rate of damage is low, but cannot restore the damage adequately at high dose rates. This does not mean, however, that the effect of a given dose must approach zero as the dose rate approaches zero. For such a relation to hold, the genetic repair mechanisms would have to be 100 per cent effective at very low dose rates; a hypothesis that seems unlikely.

In contrast to the genetic effects, there is now evidence that cancer induction, and other forms of somatic damage, may be greater if a specified total dose is given at a low level over a long period of time than if it is given rapidly. The evidence comes from a number of publications, only a few of which can be mentioned here.

The studies of Little[16] on hamsters exposed to polonium-210 appear to indicate that the ratio of induced tumors to rads is substantially higher at the lowest dose rates employed than it is at the higher dose rates. In personal discussion, Little has pointed out to me that many different experiments were involved, and that conditions were not always comparable. Therefore at present he does not want to draw any conclusions on this point until other experiments, now under way, have been completed. He agrees, however, that the available data appear to point to a greater carcinogenic effect, for a given dose, at low dose rates.

Sanders[26] found that rats exposed to very low doses of plutonium-238 showed a sharp rise in the incidence per rad of lung tumors and other types of tumors at low total doses, the effect leveling off at higher doses. The sensitivity to damage at low doses was 50 to 100 times greater than would have been expected from earlier work at higher intensity.

Morgan[4] has recently emphasized the same conclusion. He writes:

> Frequently in the literature it is stated that the linear hypothesis is a very conservative assumption. During the past few years, however, many studies have indicated that this probably is not true in general and that at low doses and dose rates somatic damage per rad (and especially that from alpha irradiation) probably is usually greater than would be assumed on the linear hypothesis.

Morgan points out several possible reasons why this should be so. Although the mechanism of cancer induction is still obscure, it is rather likely that it may involve two or more somatic mutations, whereby a normal cell may become potentially cancerous. At low intensities of radiation, there is a better chance that such successive events may happen in a given cell. High intensity radiation may simply kill the cell and thus it cannot become cancerous. The assumption of such a mechanism is, of course, in contradiction to the hot particle hypothesis.

There is also good evidence that individuals differ widely in their sensitivity to radiation. For instance, Bross and Natarajan[27] found that children of age 1 to 4 who suffered from asthma had 3.7 times as much risk of developing leukemia as did normal children. For asthmatic children who had also had intrauterine x-ray exposure, the risk of leukemia was 24.6 times as great as for the normal controls. Any sound policy for radiation protection must allow for the presence of such susceptible individuals in the populations.

Whatever the explanation, the extra risk of radiation damage at low levels of intensity appears to be an established finding for a number of experimental studies. Therefore, we must view the possible effects of low-level radiation with more concern than would have appeared necessary to most of us a few years ago.

To see the problem in perspective, however, we must remember that all of us are exposed to the natural background radiation, at a level of the order of 100 millirems per year. This varies from place to place, being about twice as great in high mountain country as at sea level. Medical x rays, for an average person in the United States, may account for another 50 to 70 millirems per year.[24]

Exposure to plutonium is at present very small indeed, by comparison, for the vast majority of people. What it may be in future depends on decisions to be made on the development of nuclear power and the control of nuclear weapons, and on a multitude of other factors that are exceedingly difficult to estimate.

IN SOIL, WATER, AND AIR

The effects of plutonium and other actinides on living organisms naturally depend on the distribution and mobility of these elements and their compounds in soil, water, and air. There is already an extensive literature on this subject, and numerous further reports were presented at a 1975 Symposium of the International Atomic Energy Agency in San Francisco. A useful survey of the earlier work has been given by Martell.[2] Here I can merely mention a few recent findings.

Under some circumstances plutonium can apparently remain *in situ,* where it is formed, over very long periods. This appears to be true, for instance, for the "natural nuclear reactor" recently discovered in the Gabon Republic in West Africa. A metallic ore in that region has been found to contain much uranium (10 to 60 per cent) with about 15 per cent water. About 1.8 billion years ago the concentration of uranium-235 was about 3 per cent, similar to that in a typical light water reactor of today. Thus, like such a reactor, this uranium-rich ore formed plutonium-239 from uranium-235. The interesting aspect, from an environmental point of view, was that the plutonium did not move as much as a millimeter during its half-life of 24,000 years (Bethe[28]).

This situation is not to be regarded as typical. We may consider, for instance, findings in two places where man-made plutonium has been released in substantial quantities, in the one case by accident, in the other by design. The accidents have occurred at the plutonium processing plant at Rocky Flats, Colorado, about 16 miles northwest of Denver. As a result of two fires in the plant (1957 and 1969), of a spill of plutonium-contaminated oil, and perhaps of other spills, several curies of plutonium-239 have been released into the environment and carried, largely by wind, over many miles.

Poet and Martell,[29] who studied the resulting contamination in detail, reported that the plutonium in the soil at the east side of the plant was about 1,300 times that from fallout. The plutonium was largely concentrated in a thin surface layer of soil. They reported that in central Denver the plutonium concentration was several times that from fallout. The concentration of americium-241 in the soil was already appreciable in 1972, with alpha activity of the order of 3 to 15 per cent of that of the plutonium. In another 30 to 50 years its activity will be comparable with that of the plutonium. This is of biological significance, since americium is taken by plants from the soil more readily than plutonium.

A recent study by Krey[30] gives, in general, considerably lower values than those of Poet and Martell for the plutonium contamination from the Rocky Flats plant. Krey estimates that 3.4 ± 0.9 curies of plutonium were deposited in the surrounding area, outside the plant itself.

In the semiarid region around Rocky Flats, the mobility of plutonium, as it spreads out into the surrounding areas, is apparently due primarily to transport by wind, largely in dust particles. A quite different patvern has been reported by Meyer[31] for the migration of plutonium at Maxey Flats, in northeastern Kentucky, where approximately 104,000 cubic meters of solid "low level" radioactive wastes were buried in trenches, between 1963 and 1974. These wastes contained approximately 80 kilograms of plutonium-239 and large, undetermined amounts of other plutonium isotopes.

Measurements of the distribution of plutonium in the region around the trenches indicate that, in the course of some 10 years, substantial amounts have migrated tens and even hundreds of meters from the original burial sites. Analysis of the relative quantities of the various plutonium isotopes indicates that this material comes from the buried plutonium in the trenches, not from atmospheric fallout.

The climate of Maxey Flats, unlike that of Rocky Flats, is humid, and the forest soil is acid. Migration is presumably through water channels, aided by the geological character of the region, and perhaps by the formation of relatively soluble chelate complexes of plutonium by reaction with substances naturally present in the soil. Meyer's report, though quite detailed, is preliminary, and we need to know much more about this situation before we can judge all its implications.

This is merely a brief look at some of the problems of plutonium in the environment. Obviously, our ignorance is great, and we need to know vastly more in order to make sound decisions for the future.

FINAL COMMENTS AND PERSONAL CONCLUSIONS

Plutonium and some higher actinides, being alpha emitters, are extremely powerful poisons. The official maximum permissible body burden—40 nanocuries of plutonium-239—is equivalent to 0.65 micrograms of this isotope, and to about 0.13 micrograms of the mixed plutonium isotopes from a reactor. Such a dose is already close to the lower limits of reliable measurement. If we were, for instance, to follow Morgan's recommendation[4] and reduce the permissible body burden by a factor of 240, we would pass below the limits of present detectability. This would certainly complicate the enforcement of protective standards, but obviously the need for maintenance of standards cannot be limited by the present limitations of analytical techniques.

Plutonium has sometimes been compared in toxicity with some of the very powerful biological toxins, such as those of botulinus or tetanus. The latter are somewhat more deadly, weight for weight; moreover they kill their victims rapidly, in a day or two or three. They are, however, unstable like most proteins; boiled in solution, they lose activity in a few minutes, and even in the dry state they can be inactivated by ultraviolet light and other agents.

Plutonium-239, on the other hand, remains a hazard for periods up to some 20 times it half-life, or nearly half a million years—more than one Ice Age may come and go before its dangers disappear. Unlike the bacterial toxins, plutonium acts slowly; small carcinogenic doses in the lungs may not produce cancer for 10, 20, or 30 years—sometimes longer.*

Cohen[32] has argued that plutonium is less dangerous than most people have supposed. (See Article 18, this volume.) For instance he has calculated, on various assumptions, that an attempt by terrorists to intimidate people by scattering, say, 15 grams of powdered plutonium over a crowd, or in the air circulation system of a large office building, would probably result in only one death, since only a very small fraction of the plutonium would actually be inhaled. This calculation has been further publicized by Bethe.[28] I have not tried to check Cohen's calculations. All of us hope, of course, that such an experiment will never be tried. The calculation may perform a useful service if it helps to discourage potential terrorists from using plutonium as a terror weapon. It might produce widespread fear and anxiety; but it would kill very few people, and those probably only after many years.

In general, however, I do not find Cohen's calculations reassuring. The situation is so full of complexities that are imperfectly understood, and the known toxicity of plutonium is so high, that I would not wish to base far-reaching policy decisions about plutonium on such preliminary calculations.

The hazards from plutonium must be viewed in the light of the general concept of acceptable risk.[33] Consider that in the United States some 50,000 people die from automobile accidents each year, and about a million are injured, including many who are crippled for life. In industry, job-related injuries number about 2.2 million per year, with some 14,000 deaths. About 100,000 deaths per year are attributed to occupational disease.[34] Our society accepts these facts, not perhaps with complacency, but without any widespread or urgent demand to alter drastically the conditions that bring them about. If society accepts such risks in return for mobility of travel and cheaper industrial production, why not accept the risks of plutonium in return for the proffered benefits of nuclear energy?

Let me say at once that I regard the present toll of death and injury from automobile and industrial accidents totally unacceptable. I do not regard the existence of these disasters as justification for them or for anything else.

As to the risk of plutonium, Bair and Thomas[9], as already mentioned, have estimated that one person in eight, carrying a "permissible" lung burden of 16 nanocuries of plutonium over many years, might ultimately develop lung cancer as a result, if humans are as susceptible as rats. If plutonium were, for example, a food additive, such a risk would certainly be considered inadmissible.

An advisory Panel to the Food and Drug Administration, on food additives and pesticides, wrote in its report: "No one would wish to introduce an agent into a human population for which no more could be said than that it would probably produce no more than two tumors per 1,000".[35] Evidently they regarded this conclusion as axiomatic. Instead they asked how much testing would be

**Cancer in workers exposed to plutonium.* It has often been stated that there is no clear evidence of cancer induced by exposure to plutonium in human subjects (see, for instance, Ref. 13). This view has recently been challenged by Dr. Sidney M. Wolfe, of the Public Citizen's Health Research Group in Washington, D.C., in a letter submitted to *Lancet*. Dr. Wolfe makes use of data from the U.S. Transuranium Registry in Richland, Washington, established by the U.S. Atomic Energy Commission in 1968. The Registry is accumulating data on the uptake, distribution, and retention of plutonium and other transuranium elements among AEC employees whose work has exposed them to these substances.

Of some 5,800 workers identified under this program, 819 have agreed to be autopsied. The results of the first 30 autopsies have been reported[39], and the authors of this report inferred nothing unusual in the resulting pattern of deaths. Dr. Wolfe, however, making use of the same data, noted that 11 of the 30 subjects had cancer or leukemia, whereas the predicted number of such cases, in a sample of individuals with the same age distribution, drawn from the general public, would have been just over 6.

The difference appears highly significant, in spite of the smallness of the sample. Moreover, only one of the 11 subjects was found to carry a body burden of plutonium greater than the officially permitted maximum of 40 nanocuries. One of the others was just above 1 nonocurie, and the values for the rest were far below this. Wolfe concluded that these data offered a powerful argument for reducing the permitted body burden for plutonium, perhaps by a factor of 1,000.

required to establish that there would be no more than two tumors per million animals exposed. In contrast, the figure of one tumor per 8 persons, calculated by Bair and Thomas, would be 125 per thousand; even their alternative calculation (one tumor per 71 persons) gives a figure of 14 per 1,000. Some of the critics of present radiation standards, as we have seen, would wish to put the risk a good deal higher. Clearly, the prevailing standards of acceptable risk for plutonium are far more tolerant that those for food additives or pesticides. Does it make sense to maintain such widely divergent standards for different kinds of hazardous substance?

There is also the still largely unevaluated risk of genetic damage from plutonium; this needs far more attention than it has received. In an entirely different area, not discussed here, there is the risk of spread of nuclear weapons, and increased international instability from plutonium theft.

The compelling argument put forward for accepting such risks, of course, is that of necessity, as illustrated by the title of a recent article of Hans Bethe: "The Necessity of Fission Power."[28] Nuclear energy, he and others hold, is essential if our society is to avoid a disastrous energy shortage during the coming generation. It is far outside the scope of this discussion to debate these large issues here. I reject the argument from necessity, and hold that preferable alternative solutions to energy problems are available.

The consequences of introduction of plutonium into the environment, on the very large scale required by an intensive nuclear power program, may be even more dangerous than we can now perceive. For material with a 25,000 year half-life, they will certainly be irreversible. I believe that it is the part of wisdom, and of our due responsibility to the generations who will follow us, to resist making such commitments.

I have argued these issues of energy policy elsewhere[36]; and there are other and more searching studies leading to similar conclusions, of which I cite two (Refs. 37 and 38). I believe that the vigorous pursuit of these alternatives is far preferable to the risk of irreversible contamination of the environment that may well result from an economy heavily dependent upon plutonium and on the other actinides that would accompany it.

REFERENCES AND NOTES

1. For the actinide isotopes, see for instance the "Table of Isotopes" in any recent edition of the *Handbook of Physics and Chemistry* (Cleveland, Ohio: CRC Press).
2. The distribution of actinide isotopes in reprocessed material from various types of reactors is given in Table II of E. A. Martell, "Actinides in Environment and Their Uptake by Man," NCAR-TN/STR-110 (Boulder, Colo.: National Center for Atmospheric Research, May 1975), 49pp. I refer to this paper later, in other connections.
3. W. J. Bair, "Recent Animal Studies on Deposition, Retension and Translocation of Plutonium and Other Transuranic Compounds," IAEA-SR-6/101, paper presented at 1975 IAEA Symposium in Vienna.
4. K. Z. Morgan, "Suggested Reduction of Permissible Exposure to Plutonium and Other Transuranium Elements," *American Industrial Hygiene Association Journal,* 36 (1975), 567–575.
5. W. J. Bair and R. C. Thompson, "Plutonium: Biomedical Research," *Science,* 183 (1974), 715–722.
6. Y. I. Moskalev, "^{239}Pu: Problems of its Biological Effect," *Health Physics,* 22 (1972), 723–729.
7. C. R. Richmond and R. L. Thomas, "Plutonium and Other Actinides in Gonadal Tissue of Man and Animals," *Health Physics,* 29 (1975), 241–250. See also D. Green et al., "Localization of Plutonium in Mouse Testes," *Nature,* 255 (1975), 77.
8. F. W. Spiers and J. Vaughan, "Hazards of Plutonium with Special Reference to Skeleton, *Nature,* 259 (1976), 531–534.
9. W. J. Bair and J. M. Thomas, "Prediction of Health Effects of Inhaled Transuranium Elements from Experimental Animal Data," IAEA-SM-199/58, paper presented at 1975 IAEA Conference in San Francisco.
10. A. R. Tamplin and T. B. Cochran, "Radiation Standards for Hot Particles" (Washington, D.C.: Natural Resources Defense Council, 1974), 52pp., with two appendices.
11. A. R. Tamplin and T. B. Cochran, "The Hot Particle Issue: A Critique of WASH-1320 As It Relates to Hot Particle Hypothesis" (Washington, D.C.: Natural Resources Defense Council, Nov. 1974). For WASH-1320, see n. 12 below. See also, for a discussion of the issues in the debate, *New Scientist,* 66 (1975), 497–506, with a defense of the hot particle hypothesis by Cochran and Tamplin and a highly critical reply by R. H. Mole.

12. W. J. Bair, C. R. Richmond and B. W. Wachholz, "A Radiobiological Assessment of Spatial Distribution of Radiation Dose from Inhaled Plutonium," WASH-1320 (Washington, D.C.: U.S. Atomic Energy Commission, Sept. 1974).

In April 1976 the Nuclear Regulatory Commission issued a statement criticizing the hot particle hypothesis along similar lines. Tamplin and Cochran in their reply point out that the NRC is attacking positions which in fact they do not now hold, and that the NRC is not addressing the issues that they have raised.

13. Medical Research Council, "The Toxicity of Plutonium," London: Her Majesty's Stationery Office, 1975: and National Council on Radiation Protection and Measurements, "Alpha Emitting Particles in Lungs," NCRP Report No. 46 (Washington, D.C.: NCRP, Aug. 15, 1975).

14. W. V. Mayneord and R. H. Clarke, "Quantitative Assessment of Carcinogenic Risks Associated with 'Hot Particles,'" *Nature,* 259 (1976), 535–539.

15. E. P. Radford, Jr., and V. R. Hunt, "Polonium-210: A Volatile Radioelement in Cigarettes," *Science,* 143 (1964), 247–249.

16. J. B. Little, A. R. Kennedy and R. B. McGandy, "Lung Cancer Induced in Hamsters by Low Doses of Alpha Radiation from Polonium-210," *Science,* 188 (1975), 737–738.

17. See Inhalation Toxicity Research Institute, Annual Report, 1974–1975 (Albuquerque, N.M.: Lovelace Foundation, 87115). Also R. C. Thompson, et al., Pacific Northwest Laboratory, Annual Report, 1975. (Richland, Wash.: Battelle Pacific Northwest Laboratories, Jan. 1976).

18. E. A. Martell, "Tobacco Radioactivity and Cancer in Smokers," *American Scientist,* 63 (1975), 404–412.

19. There is a vast literature on chemical carcinogenesis. See, for instance, the series of recent papers from the laboratory of B. N. Ames on carcinogens as mutagens; the latest of these is by J. McCann, et al., "Detection of Carcinogens as Mutagens in Salmonella? Microsome Test: Assay of 300 Chemicals," *Proceedings of National Academy of Science,* 72 (1975), 5135–5139.

20. E. P. Hardy, P. W. Krey and H. L. Volchok, "Global Inventory and Distribution of Fallout Plutonium-238 in Rat," *Radiation Research,* 56

21. In addition to the references cited in n. 7, others are cited by Gofman in n. 22.

22. J. W. Gofman, "The Cancer Hazard from Inhaled Plutonium," CNR report 1975-1R; and Gofman, "Estimated Production of Human Lung Cancers by Plutonium from Worldwide Fallout," CNR report 1975-2. (Yachats, Oregon: Committee for Nuclear Responsibility, P. O. Box 332, 97498).

23. C. W. Mays et al, in *The Health Effects of Plutonium and Radium,* (papers presented at Symposium on Health Effects of Plutonium and Radium, Sun Valley, Idaho, 1975), edited by W. S. S. Jee (Salt Lake City, Utah: J. W. Press, 1976); see also C. W. Mays, "Estimated Risk from ^{239}Pu to Human Bone, Liver and Lung," paper presented at 1975 IAEA Symposium in Chicago. Comments by Mays on Morgan's calculations are in the discussion following this paper.

24. National Academy of Sciences, "The Effects on Populations of Exposure to Low Levels of Ionizing Radiation," BIER report (Washington, D.C.: The Academy, Nov. 1972).

25. National Council on Radiation Protection and Measurements, "Review of the Current State of Radiation Protection Philosophy" (Washington, D.C.: The National Council, Jan. 1975).

26. C. L. Sanders, Jr., "Carcinogenicity of Inhaled Plutonium-238 in Rat," *Radiation Research,* 56 (1972), 540–553.

27. I. D. J. Bross and N. Natarajan, "Leukemia from Low-Level Radiation: Identification of Susceptible Children," *New England Journal of Medicine,* 287 (1972), 107–110; and Bross and Natarajan, "Risk of Leukemia in Susceptible Children Exposed to Preconception, *in* Utero and Postnatal Radiation," *Preventive Medicine,* 3 (1974), 361–369.

28. H. A. Bethe, "The Necessity of Fission Power," *Scientific American,* 234 (1976), 21–31.

29. S. E. Poet and E. A. Martell, "Plutonium-239 and Americium-241 Contamination in Denver Area," *Health Physics,* 23 (1972), 537–548.

30. P. W. Krey, "Remote Plutonium Contamination and Total Inventories from Rocky Flats," *Health Physics,* 30 (1976), 209–214.

31. G. L. Meyer, "Preliminary Data on Occurrence of Transuranium Nuclides in Environment at Radioactive Waste Burial Site, Maxey Flats, Kenvucky," paper presented at 1975 IAEA Symposium in San Francisco. Office of Radiation Programs, U.S. Environmental Protection Agency, Washington, D.C.

32. B. L. Cohen, "The Hazards in Plutonium Dispersal," Institute for Energy Analysis (Oak Ridge, Tenn.: Oak Ridge Associated Universities, 1975).

33. W. W. Lowrance, "Of Acceptable Risk: Science and Determination of Safety" (Los Altos, Ca.: William Kaufman, 1976).

34. For the industrial figures, see U.S. Departments of Labor and Health, Education and Welfare, *President's Report on Occupational Safety and Health* (Washington, D.C.: GPO, May 1972), p. 111; cited by D. H. Wegman in *New England Journal of Medicine,* 294 (1976), 653.

35. U.S. Food and Drug Administration, Advisory Committee on Protocols for Safety Evaluation, "Panel on Carcinogenesis Report on Cancer Testing in Safety Evaluation of Food Additives and Pesticides," *Toxicology and Applied Pharmacology,* 20 (1971), 431. Quoted by Lowrance [33, p. 63].

36. J. T. Edsall, "Hazards of Nuclear Fission Power and Choice of Alternatives," *Environmental Conservation,* 1 (1974), 21–30; "Further Comments on Hazards of Nuclear Power and the Choice of Alter-

natives,'' *Environmental Conservation,* 2 (1975), 205–212.

37. Ford Foundation Energy Project, ''A Time to Choose: America's Energy Future'' (Cambridge, Mass.: Ballinger Publishing Co., 1974). See also Denis Hayes, ''Energy: the Case for Conservation,'' Worldwatch Paper 4 (Washington, D.C.: Worldwatch Institute, 1976).
38. A. B. Lovins, ''World Energy Strategies: Facts, Issues and Options,'' *Bulletin of Atomic Scientists,* May and June 1974; a later expanded version was published by Ballinger Pub. Co. in 1975.
39. W. E. Norwood and C. E. Newton, Jr., ''U.S. Transuranium Registry: Study of Thirty Autopsies,'' *Health Physics,* 28 (1976), 609–675.

Security Implications of Alternative Fission Futures 20

HAROLD A. FEIVESON AND THEODORE B. TAYLOR 1976

The world-wide rapid growth of civilian nuclear power is exposing a rising and potentially staggering amount of plutonium to the risk of its diversion to nuclear weapons by nations or criminals. In the often heated controversy over the future of nuclear power, it is this risk that appears to be the one most intractable to technical resolution and, as well, most insistently fundamental to the way people feel about nuclear power. It is the issue that should, in our view, most determine the character of the next stage in the development of nuclear power in the United States and abroad.

The information and non-nuclear materials needed to make fission explosives are now widely distributed and available to the general public. Dozens of nations have or could acquire the skills and facilities required to design and build reliable, lightweight, and efficient fission explosives, using plutonium diverted from their civilian nuclear power systems. Although crude, inefficient, and unpredictable, such devices would nonetheless be highly destructive. Fission explosives small enough to be transported by automobile could be designed and built by small groups of people, even conceivably by individuals working alone, if they somehow managed to acquire the needed dozen kilograms or so of plutonium. Under some conditions, the manufacturing could be done in an ordinary home workshop, using equipment and materials that are easily available world wide.

When thinking about these risks it is important to bear in mind that there can be various milestones on the path to possession of nuclear weapons. Most people seem to worry about what is traditionally called the "proliferation" of nuclear weapons, that is, the

Dr. Harold A. Feiveson, a political scientist, is assistant professor of public and international affairs in the Woodrow Wilson School of Public and International Affairs, and a member of the Center for Environmental Studies, Princeton University, Princeton, New Jersey 08540.

Dr. Theodore B. Taylor, a nuclear physicist and founder of International Research and Technology Corporation, is a lecturer in the Aerospace and Mechanical Sciences Department, Princeton University. He is co-author, with Dr. Mason Willrich, of *Nuclear Theft: Risks and Safeguards* (1974), Ballinger Publishing Company, Cambridge, Massachusetts.

From *Bulletin of the Atomic Scientists*, Vol. 32, No. 10, pp. 14–18, 46–48, December 1976.

demonstrated acquisition of usable nuclear weapons by nations or criminals. But there is potentially a continuous spectrum of degrees of drift or purposeful action toward the actual possession of nuclear explosives. We use the phrase "latent proliferation" to include that part of the spectrum that falls short of actual diversion of nuclear materials from civilian nuclear facilities, but which facilitates a possible future decision to acquire nuclear weapons.

There are wide variations in the time and resources required to make the transition from a condition of latent to one of demonstrated proliferation. Inadequately controlled stockpiles of concentrated plutonium separated from spent fuel, combined with the knowledge of how to design and fabricate a nuclear explosive, and the possession of tested non-nuclear components of nuclear weapons, can allow a nation or a criminal group to have nuclear weapons within days or even hours after diverting or overtly stealing a dozen kilograms or so of plutonium. This situation can be contrasted with that of a nation that has nuclear power plants but no facilities for enriching uranium or separating plutonium from nuclear reactor fuel. Such a nation would be much further away from actually having nuclear weapons, and inherently much better protected from theft of plutonium by criminals.

Fortunately, nearly all the plutonium associated with nuclear power throughout the world is not yet in forms directly usable in nuclear explosives because it is not yet separated from spent reactor fuel. Nuclear technology is now dominated by the deployment of essentially two reactor technologies: the light water reactors, developed in the United States and now also being produced by industrial combines in France, West Germany, Japan, Sweden, and the Soviet Union and the heavy water CANDU reactor, produced for domestic and export markets by a joint industry-government venture in Canada.

Both the light water and the CANDU reactors currently use the "once-through" fuel cycle leading from the uranium mine to the uranium enrichment plant (a step that is skipped in the CANDU cycle) to the fabrication plant to the reactor to spent fuel storage. The reactors and spent fuel are the only parts of this fuel cycle in which there are materials from which nuclear weapons can be made without requiring the costly and, at present, very difficult process of isotope enrichment. But the plutonium made in the reactors is dilute and mixed with extremely radioactive fission products. The fresh fuel is unenriched or slightly enriched uranium (up to a few per cent uranium-235 mixed with uranium-238). This mixture of uranium isotopes cannot be used for making nuclear explosives.

This once-through fuel cycle cannot form the basis for an enduring nuclear industry, however. If the growth rate of nuclear power is suitably modest, a once-through system could probably be designed to last many decades. But, in the long run, it is a system that is resource limited, capable of using only a small fraction of the available uranium. For this reason, the long-term vitality of fission power, as it reaches its second and mature stage, is generally believed to depend on the introduction of "breeder reactors," which are able to convert the abundant fertile isotopes, uranium-238 or thorium-232, into the chain-reacting materials, plutonium or uranium-233. Such conversion could expand the resource base for nuclear fission by over 100 times.

The path on which the nuclear industry world wide appears bent is to separate plutonium from spent reactor fuel and to recycle it as fresh fuel first into light water reactors and later into fast plutonium breeders. Commercial reprocessing of spent reactor fuel will soon be possible in several countries: the United Kingdom, France, West Germany, India, Japan, the Soviet Union, and the United States. Still other countries have announced plans to deploy reprocessing plants, including Argentina, Brazil, Italy, Pakistan, Spain, and Yugoslavia.

The United Kingdom, France, West Germany, Japan, the Soviet Union, and the United States also have significant programs of breeder development underway, all of them focused on a single technology, the liquid-metal fast breeder reactor based on the uranium-238–plutonium cycle. Without significant new governmental and international intervention, it appears likely that in another decade several countries will be engaged in substantial recycle of plutonium, with plutonium thus becoming a staple of nuclear commerce, routinely separated, fabricated, traded, and stockpiled.

These developments have been little constrained by considerations of purposeful abuse of nuclear materials. The fuel cycle configurations that promise to dominate the worldwide nuclear industry in the future have been conceived with virtually no significant attention given to their impact on the risks of proliferation and criminal diversions. It is time, we believe, to place safeguards against these risks at the forefront of our thinking and to inquire whether it is possible to shape a nuclear fuel cycle that is consistent with principles of effective safeguards instead of, as now, letting the technology develop first, with control measures tagging along afterward. From our preliminary inquiry, we conclude that alternatives to the present course of nuclear power development should be thoroughly assessed before irreversible commitments are made to the plutonium economy.

The objectives of an effective safeguard system can, we believe, be usefully formulated as the set of guiding principles we set forth below. The first two principles focus on the problem of criminal diversions, the last three on the problem of nuclear proliferation.

(1) *All fixed sites and transport links should be effectively protected against criminal theft or diversion of weapons-grade materials, using techniques that are open to inspection and assessment by all interested nations.*

Here, we insist that national systems of physical security over materials that, without isotope enrichment, can be used for making nuclear explosives (that is, weapons-grade material) should be monitored by the international community. International safeguards as now structured, by contrast, permit commerce in weapons-grade material unencumbered by physical security arrangements other than those imposed by individual nations. There are no existing measures that translate the international community's clear interest in every nation's physical security system into concrete international arrangements.

(2) *Internationally managed physical security safeguards should not be required at national facilities.*

Here, we recognize the generally strong resistance of countries to any actions that suggest infringement of national sovereignty over internal law enforcement. Since reactors are both by far the most numerous of nuclear facilities, and the fuel cycle components that countries are most reluctant to site outside their boundaries, the principle suggests that reactors should be designed to minimize the problem of physical security at and en route to reactor sites.

(3) *All nuclear materials for civilian use, and from which weapons-grade materials can be derived, should be kept within authorized channels defined by specific physical boundaries. An International Atomic Energy Agency (IAEA) or equivalent international safeguards system should be able promptly to detect and report any transfers of strategic quantities of these materials outside these boundaries.*

Here, the primary objective of the current international safeguards system to *detect*, rather than directly *prevent* diversion of nuclear materials for unauthorized purposes. But we have added the provision that any diversions should be *promptly* detected. Present IAEA safeguards are primarily based on materials accounting procedures that, even if perfectly accurate, would not actually reveal any significant diversions of material for weeks or even months afterward.

A further difficulty is that inherent limits of accuracy of materials accounting procedures at facilities that process bulk quantities of nuclear materials, such as chemical reprocessing or fuel fabrication plants, are often too wide to detect losses of sufficient quantities of weapons-grade material to make at least several nuclear weapons. Application of our principle, on the other hand, would require that present international safeguards be extended to include means for essentially immediate detection of very small flows of strategic quantities of nuclear materials from places where they are authorized to be to places where they are not.

(4) *The activities intrinsic to civilian nuclear programs within a country should be kept as starkly distinct as possible from efforts by that country to acquire nuclear weapons.*

This principle emerges from consideration of the process of "latent proliferation" that we referred to above. If civilian nuclear power is not developed in accordance with this principle, nations could come close to having a nuclear weapons capability without even making an explicit decision to do so. Furthermore, it is to be expected that some countries may purposely wish to reduce the time and cost needed to convert some parts of their civilian programs to weapons production, without clearly being perceived as having done so. Thus, countries may, purposely or not, gradually shorten the necessary time between decision and weapon and thereby, we believe, hasten a decision to make nuclear weapons.

We are convinced that, if a country is determined to acquire nuclear weapons, there are no practical technical controls on nuclear power programs that can prevent it from doing so. It can be done either *directly* through the construction of a plutonium production reactor and reprocessing plant and/or isotope separation facility, or *indirectly* through diversion of weapons-grade material from its civilian power program. However, this stark reality, far from proving that safeguards and limitations on civilian programs are therefore useless, suggests instead the importance of devising and implementing policies that add to the time and the technical and political costs a country would have to expend to acquire nuclear weapons.

In general, we would expect a government to be far less likely to launch a weapons program that might not reach fruition during a time when that government is still in power, than to do so when the critical nuclear material is already at hand and the necessary resources already expended. We think it would also discourage proliferation if countries were not in a position to acquire nuclear weapons quickly, in response to some external event that threatened their security or, perhaps, in response to a perceived prestige value of having nuclear explosives.

(5) *All safeguards, measures, and restrictions on access to specific civilian nuclear technologies should be equitably applied to all countries.*

We believe it illusory to suppose that a safeguards system can persist long if it denies some aspects of *civilian* nuclear technology to certain countries, while permitting them to others, or otherwise imposes safeguards obligations inequitably. Beyond the asymmetric safeguard obligations that now exist under the Non-Proliferation Treaty between the nuclear-weapon states and the non-nuclear weapons states, there are increasing international efforts to discriminate between classes of non-nuclear countries.

Several of the industrialized countries with the strongest indigenous programs of civilian nuclear power hope to deny technologies that they themselves plan to develop (such as reprocessing plants) to as many other countries as possible. Moreover, these nuclear suppliers have sometimes sought (or have felt obliged because of past commitments) to make distinctions on a country by country basis. The United States, for instance, partly because of a perceived burden of past bilateral agreement, is willing to have Spain reprocess spent fuel from U.S. supplied reactors, but has seemed unwilling to enter into new agreements with countries, such as Iran, that would permit them to do so. The United States has been willing to provide nuclear systems to India and South Africa, which are non-signatories of the NPT, but evidently is not prepared to do so with some countries that are parties to the Treaty, such as Libya. These distinctions are not necessarily unreasonable as a short-term expedient, but they do not form a basis for a long-term stable policy. They will seem unfair and unpersuasive to other supplier countries as well as to the countries denied assistance.

There is a deep inequity intrinsic to any non-proliferation strategy, between the countries that already have nuclear weapons and the countries that are to be denied them. In the long run, we doubt that any strategy to impede proliferation can succeed without confronting directly this fundamental inequity. We do believe, however, that an equitable system of controls of civilian nuclear power that establishes a significant reliance on international institutions will provide useful bridges to the more far-reaching international arrangements that are urgently required for dealing with stockpiles of nuclear weapons themselves.

ALTERNATIVE FISSION FUTURES

A Plutonium Economy

Set against these safeguard principles, the current world-wide move toward a plutonium economy looks unwise. The recycle of plutonium in low enrichment uranium reactors and, eventually, in national fast breeder reactors will, as we have noted, force weapons-grade plutonium free of fission products to circulate widely in the nuclear fuel cycle, *whether or not fuel reprocessing and fabrication are restricted to a few regional, multinationally operated centers*.

Reactors, which are likely to remain predominantly under national control for the indefinite future, require substantial stockpiles of fresh fuel containing plutonium and frequent shipments of the fuel to the power plant sites. Under such conditions, the physical security objectives distilled in the first two principles could be met only with the utmost difficulty. Even if most countries had the technical ability to safeguard plutonium and other weapons-grade material effectively, at reasonable costs, the institutional and political problems of achieving effective physical security for weapons-grade material in all countries would be immense. Plutonium recycle does exactly the wrong thing: it focuses the physical security burden at and en route to national reactors, the most numerous components of nuclear fuel cycles.

The potential impact of plutonium recycle on latent proliferation is especially striking. By involving countries in the separation, fabrication, transport, and stockpiling of weapons-grade material, the plutonium economy would obscure irretrievably much of the existing distinction between activities intrinsic to civilian nuclear power production and those required to produce nuclear weapons. Countries would be in a position to move rapidly to nuclear weapons, either through the seizure of "civilian" stockpiles of plutonium, or through a direct route made easier by the prior construction of "civilian" reprocessing and plutonium fabrication facilities.

These characteristics of plutonium recycle are apparent and have more or less been recognized by the countries now contemplating reprocessing and recycle. Some of these, such as the United States, hope therefore to restrict these activities to only a few industrialized countries—through agreement if possible and through export conditions imposed by nuclear suppliers if necessary. But we believe it extremely unlikely that it will be possible to restrict the use of plutonium to selected classes of countries permanently. Argentina, Brazil, India, Iran, and Pakistan have hardly indicated a disposition to accept such distinctions. Export restrictions may be, in our view, a potentially useful first step toward effective international control of nuclear power, but cannot be an alternative to such control.

A Once-through Fuel Cycle

The development of a plutonium economy looks to us imprudent, not only in its own terms, but also in comparison with other possible fission futures. One such future would involve a continued reliance on a once-through fuel cycle, a path that eventually must lead to a long-term phase-out of fission power altogether, but perhaps on a time scale such that high-grade uranium resources would not be used up before alternative non-fission energy sources (such as solar power) are commercially developed and deployed. As we have noted, a once-through fuel cycle has the intrinsic safeguards advantages of minimizing (or even eliminating) the need for commerce in weapons-grade material that is separated from highly radioactive fission products.

For this reason, we think it may be possible in a once-through cycle to devise a safeguard system consistent with our principles, although the task will be difficult. Above all, it will be critical to develop a system to dispose of the plutonium in the spent fuel, copious amounts of which will be produced in many parts of the world in the next decades. There are some who argue, both on security and safety grounds, that the chemical separation of the constituent parts of the spent fuel is necessary for the safe disposal of radioactive wastes. It is not obvious to us whether this is so or not. However, such separation certainly need not be done immediately; and, in the long run, if separation before disposal is called for, it could be accomplished at a very few sites under international auspices, and thus in a manner consistent with our safeguards principles.

An International Thorium Cycle

Despite the attractions of the once-through system, if the growth of nuclear power and availability of uranium resources are such that a once-through system cannot be maintained sufficiently long to permit the development of alternative energy sources, it may be necessary to develop a fission breeder system. In this case, we believe that a fuel cycle based on breeding from thorium, which, like natural uranium, is abundant, may offer a significant security advantage over one focused on fast plutonium breeders. The fissile material uranium-233 bred from the thorium can be diluted with the naturally abundant isotope uranium-238 to such an extent as to make the mixture unsuitable for weapons without isotope separation—currently a technology available only to a few nations. In contrast, no comparable isotopic "denaturant" exists for plutonium. This distinction, which to our knowledge has not been systematically explored for its safeguards implications, may permit a breeder fuel cycle in which no weapons-grade material need be handled (except in the dilute, highly radioactive spent fuel) under national control.

In principle, at least, one can visualize a thorium fuel cycle of this kind that is compatible with all of our guiding safeguards principles. At maturity, the system (schematically presented in Figure 20-1) would consist of two classes of facilities: national reactors and a few international fuel cycle support centers.

The *national* reactors could be slightly modified versions of today's light water or heavy water reactors or they could be new reactor types. These reactors would operate on a fresh fuel mix of something like one part uranium-233, six parts uranium-238, and 10 to 60 parts thorium. The 6 to 1 ratio of uranium-238 to uranium-233 would probably be sufficient for practical purposes to denature the uranium-233, so that the denatured uranium, both in the fresh fuel assemblies and in the spent fuel, would not be suitable weapons material. There would be some plutonium in the spent fuel, produced by neutron capture in the uranium-238 dilutant, but only somewhere between one-fifth and one-tenth as much as in plutonium breeder fuel, for the same amount of power.

The *international* fuel cycle support centers would reprocess all the spent fuel from the national reactors and would undertake all the fabrication and denaturing of fresh fuel assemblies to be sent to the national plants. Since it is unlikely that current types of nuclear power plants could breed sufficient amounts of uranium-233 to allow them to be self-sustaining on a thorium cycle if the recycled uranium-233 is denatured with uranium-238, the internationally controlled

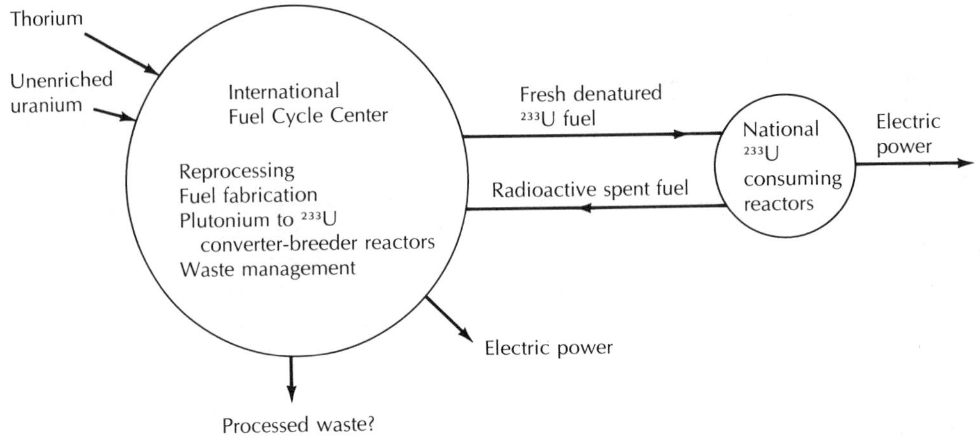

Figure 20-1. The mature denatured uranium-thorium fuel cycle.

centers at which the fuel is reprocessed would also have to provide some additional source of uranium-233.

One possibility is fast breeder reactors that use plutonium extracted from the converter reactor fuels in their cores and thorium as the fertile materials in their breeding blankets. Such reactors could produce more uranium-233 than the plutonium they consume. All recycled plutonium could in this fashion be consumed on-site at the centers, avoiding the need for any national access to plutonium free from fission products. Another, more speculative future possibility is to use fusion reactors as a source of neutrons at the regional centers. "Makeup" uranium-233 produced by the capture of excess neutrons in thorium blankets could keep the entire nuclear power system self-sustaining.

The support center would, of course, have to be under considerably greater international control than the outlying national power plants, with its physical security system subject to international standards and review procedures. The entire complex would also be subject to international safeguards designed to prompt detection of any unauthorized removal of nuclear materials from the complex.

An important measure of the practicality of this system, both in mature equilibrium and perhaps even more so in the period of conversion to the thorium cycle, will be the ratio of required plutonium consuming, uranium-233 producing reactors in the international center to the number of national reactors. The greater the number of national reactors that can be serviced by a given size fuel center, the more reasonable the system will appear. This ratio depends on a very large number of detailed reactor characteristics, and should be the subject of considerable further study. But it is clear that during a transition period it would depend sensitively on the rate of nuclear power growth and on the timing of the changeover from the present to the new fuel cycle.

In general, the transition seems far more practical for low than for high rates of nuclear growth. In a rapidly expanding nuclear economy, the international centers may have to produce several times as much power as all the national reactors they are servicing, just to be able to make large quantities of uranium-233 for starting up new reactors. If the growth rate is slow enough so that most of the uranium-233 produced at the international centers is used to keep existing reactors self-sustaining, the power produced by the national reactors can be several times greater than that of international centers. Of course, if the growth is relatively slow, fission energy might also be phased out before any types of breeders are required.

Very little uranium-233 (perhaps a few hundred kilograms) now exists. If it were decided to shift from the present type of fuel cycle to the thorium cycle, there are several alternatives. One could be to start by using uranium-235 in place of uranium-233 (that is, uranium enriched to about 15 to 20 per cent in uranium-235), mixed with thorium, and gradually shifting to uranium-233 as more of it becomes available. This would provide the safeguards advantages of the mature thorium-uranium-233 cycle during the transition period, since no weapons-grade material would be present in fresh fuel, and much more uranium-233 than plutonium would be produced in the reactors.

Another possibility would be to use the large stockpiles of plutonium made before the changeover in contemporary reactors, for conversion to uranium-233 in regional, internationally controlled reactors. These reactors would not necessarily have to breed at least during the transition period of a decade or more. In any case, we think it unrealistic that conversion of substantial numbers of national power plants to the thorium cycle would start in less than about a decade, and it would probably take at least another decade to reach maturity. This would provide considerable time for determining and implementing the best specific type of mature fuel cycle.

The thorium cycle permits a fuel cycle in which no weapons-grade fuel unmixed with highly radioactive fission products need ever be placed under national control, nor ever be fabricated or stockpiled except at a few international centers. Nations could, of course, physically take possession of the denatured fuel and undertake the isotopic separation necessary to produce highly concentrated uranium-233, or similarly appropriate the spent fuel and separate out the contained plutonium. But there would be no legitimate commerical reason to engage in such activities. There would be little ambiguity if a country so set out to acquire weapons-grade material; and the absence of stockpiles of weapons-grade material would ensure that the diversion of weapons-grade material in this manner would also take some time. With respect to the problem of criminal diversion, the thorium scheme preserves the intrinsic safeguard advantage of the once-through system—that no weapons-grade material exist within a country except in highly radioactive spent fuel.

We do not view either of these fuel cycle alternatives to the plutonium economy as a complete solution to the problem of nuclear proliferation. We do not think that there is any technical fix, much less a simple one, to prevent nuclear proliferation. One cannot expect a non-proliferation strategy to succeed if it does not grapple with the political and security incentives for countries to acquire nuclear weapons and the political constraints to doing so. One cannot wave the magic wand of a thorium cycle or some other technical innovation to turn an essentially political problem into a technical one.

More fundamentally, we do not believe that, in the long term, proliferation can be significantly impeded while one class of countries (the nuclear-weapon states) act as if nuclear weapons are politically useful things to have and insist on the special privilege of possessing them while denying the weapons to others.

Nor will any of the alternatives be easy to implement. A long-term dependence on a once-through fuel cycle will probably eventually require a concomitant dramatic expansion in the use of solar energy, a development that will certainly require substantial technological and institutional innovation. The international thorium cycle path will also require some technical innovation and, most markedly, it will require a considerable expansion of international institutions in the nuclear area. But we do not believe that these difficulties and "impracticalities" are insurmountable. Any energy future will be difficult and painful, whether or not it includes a phase-out of nuclear power.

The plutonium economy is consistent with current industry plans and may seem therefore less impractical than the alternatives. But we think this is deceptive. Systematic and effective safeguarding of plutonium, to the extent that it is even possible, would involve as fully complex a set of institutional arrangements as any alternative future energy path.

Although our discussion of the once-through and the thorium alternatives for fission power is quite preliminary, these alternatives appear at this stage to be sufficiently attractive from a security point of view to warrant that the present world-wide plans for the future of fission power be thoroughly reexamined before irreversible commitments are made to the plutonium economy. We must not stumble unwittingly into the plutonium economy.

We recommend that, until all nations have assessed more clearly several energy options, plutonium should not be separated from spent fuel from civilian reactors anywhere in the world. It is after all the *long-term* future of fission power that is at issue. It would be foolhardy indeed to foreclose possible attractive future paths through precipitate decisions on reprocessing and recycle.

SUGGESTED READINGS

Bulletin of the Atomic Scientists 32, 1976, entire issue on the plutonium economy.

Bulletin of the Atomic Scientists,33, 1975, pp. 59–69. Six different views on atomic energy.

Flood, Michael, 1976, Nuclear Sabotage, *Bulletin of the Atomic Scientists 32*, pp. 29–36.

Gilinsky, Victor, 1977, Plutonium, Proliferation and Policy, *Technology Review 79*, pp. 58–65.

Cost Escalation in Nuclear Power 21

W. DAVID MONTGOMERY AND JAMES P. QUIRK 1977

INTRODUCTION

Rarely in the history of United States industry has there been a rags-to-riches-to-rags story as dramatic as that of the nuclear power industry. Just 20 years ago, the AEC was subsidizing the construction and operation of small research reactors, pursuing a goal mandated for it by the Atomic Energy Act of 1954, to promote a viable nuclear power industry. By the early 1960's, the technical capabilities of nuclear power had been demonstrated, but it was generally agreed within industry and by the government that nuclear power would not be economically competitive with fossil fuel until the 1970's. Then between 1963 and 1966, the two major reactor manufacturers, General Electric and Westinghouse, promoted nuclear power through fixed-price (turnkey) contracts at capital costs that made nuclear power competitive with coal for much of the nation. Orders for nuclear units soared during 1966 and 1967, followed by a trough in 1969. A second wave of orders hit the reactor manufacturers in the early 1970's, peaking in 1973. Since 1974, there has been a falling off of orders to the point that only two units were announced in 1976, and there is a rather general feeling that nuclear power might no longer be the "energy source of the future"; it may, instead, be replaced by coal.

Nuclear power has always been controversial. In the mid-1960's, the expansion of the nuclear power industry coincided with the

Dr. W. David Montgomery is an assistant professor of economics at the California Institute of Technology, Pasadena, California 91125. His publications include "Markets in Licenses and Efficient Pollution Control Programs," *Journal of Economic Theory* (1972); "Artificial Markets and the Theory of Games," *Public Choice* (1974); "Separability and Vanishing Externalities," *American Economic Review* (1976).

Dr. James P. Quirk is a professor of economics at the California Institute of Techology, Pasadena, California 91125. His publications include *Introduction to General Equilibrium Theory and Welfare Economic* (1968); "Qualitative Problems in Metric Theory" (with J. Maybee), *SIAM Review* (1969); "Complementarity and the Stability of the Competitive Equilibrium," *American Economic Review* (1970); *Intermediate Microeconomics,* 1976.

This original article is based on research supported in part by a grant from the National Science Foundation; APR-75-16566AOI, and the California Energy Commission. The authors also acknowledge the assistance provided by the Environmental Quality Laboratory at Caltech as well as that provided by the Jet Propulsion Laboratory. This article is reprinted with light editing and permission of the authors.

growth of the environmental movement, leading to confrontations between utilities and intervenors in the nuclear licensing process. Safety issues and anti-trust questions dominated the hearings up to the late 1960's. Then environmental issues came to the fore, leading to a restructuring of the licensing process following the Calvert Cliffs decision in 1971. But recently, an even more fundamental problem has hit the industry. Environmentalists and many neutral observors alike argue that even if nuclear units are safe, and even if nuclear power meets environmental standards, nonetheless nuclear units should not be built because they are simply too expensive relative to other alternatives, particularly coal-fired power plants. It is this issue of the cost of nuclear power that is the central topic of this article.

The basic economic advantage of nuclear power has always been low fuel costs relative to fossil fuel units. The economic viability of nuclear power is currently under attack on the ground that other costs of nuclear power undercut this fuel cost advantage. Specifically, it is argued that:

(1) Escalation of capital costs for nuclear units over the past 10 years will, if it continues, more than offset the inherent fuel cost advantage of nuclear power.

(2) The operating performance of the new large [1,000-megawatt (electric) and over] nuclear units has been poor, resulting in low plant availability factors and high maintenance costs. Coupled with high capital costs per kilowatt-hour of electricity generated, the result is a total cost per kilowatt-hour greater for nuclear units than for coal units in much of the country.

Most of our discussion is concerned with the escalation of nuclear capital costs, which is well documented in the data available. The operating performance of large nuclear units is still a matter of considerable controversy, in large part because only two or three years of operating experience are available for the typical large unit. In any case, however the argument concerning operating performance is resolved, escalation of capital costs remains a central issue so far as the economics of the nuclear industry is concerned.

Our approach here is historical, documenting the course of development of the nuclear power industry and examining some of the leading explanations for that course of development. Based on previous unsuccessful attempts by the Atomic Energy Commission (AEC) and others to predict the future course of the industry, it might be well to point out that we do not attempt any such predictions here. Instead, we feel that there is a contribution to be made simply by recounting what has happened and attempting to understand that.

We examine in detail the two basic explanations that have been offered for capital cost escalation in nuclear power, first, the argument that cost increases are related to the activities of intervenors in the nuclear licensing process, and second, the argument that cost increases reflect bottleneck problems in construction and equipment supplying industries and in the licensing process. As will be discussed later, capital cost increases in the nuclear industry far exceed those that would have resulted simply from inflation of the general price level, or even inflation of the construction industry price level. Hence, an explanation of the differential rate of escalation of nuclear costs must ultimately rest on characteristics specific to the nuclear industry.

Our general conclusions are these: in the early years of commercial development of the nuclear power industry (1966–1970), bottleneck problems accounted for most of the cost increases that occurred; but since 1970, although bottleneck problems still occur, the procedural and substantive effects of intervention in the licensing processes have dominated the cost picture. We draw these conclusions in the course of a narrative description of the economic history of the industry, rather than an attempt at an explicit statistical treatment aimed at identifying the quantitative importance of these two underlying hypotheses. Data problems relating to small sample size, site specific characteristics of nuclear units, serial correlation and autocorrelation, and other related issues argue against the reliability of sophisticated statistical models in the analysis of the cost escalation problem.

The period from the early 1960's to the present has been one of dramatic changes in the technology and costs of power generation, not only in the nuclear industry, but also in the coal, oil, and natural gas industries. Moreover, it has been a period during which the federal government has played an increasingly important role in influencing investment decisions by electric utilities. Thus, in our analysis of the development of the nuclear power industry, we place special emphasis on the information available to decision-makers at the time that decisions were made, and on how that information was used, rather than on judgments as to whether the decisions make sense from the point of view of informed hindsight. With one or two notable exceptions, a rather consistent picture of the period can be constructed using the usual model of the economist, namely that decision-makers, whether utilities or reactor manufacturers, tended to make profit maximizing choices based on the best data available and that the market for nuclear units was relatively responsive to changes in information.

To develop these points, we begin with a brief description of the pattern of growth in nuclear generating capacity and changes in nuclear costs. Then we turn to a detailed description of the economic decisions that created those patterns.

BACKGROUND: THE GROWTH OF NUCLEAR POWER

Table 21-1 summarizes the statistics on the growth of the nuclear power industry over the

Table 21–1. Growth of Nuclear Power[a]

	NSSS Orders		*Units Attaining Commercial Status*		*Installed Capacity*	
Year	*No.*	*MWe*[b]	*No.*	*MWe*[b]	*No.*	*MWe*[b]
1955	5	776	—	—	—	—
1956	2	33	—	—	—	—
1957	2	76	—	—	—	—
1958	3	122	—	—	—	—
1959	1	72	—	—	—	—
1960	—	—	1	200	1	200
1961	1	50	1	175	2	375
1962	1	575	1	265	3	640
1963	4	2,560	2	140	5	780
1964	—	—	3	50	8	830
1965	7	4,624	1	72	9	902
1966	20	16,603	1	90	10	992
1967	30	25,673	1	40	9	1,004
1968	14	12,903	2	1,025	10	2,007
1969	7	7,203	2	1,260	12	3,267
1970	14	14,266	3	1,796	15	5,063
1971	15	15,122	6	3,615	21	8,678
1972	31	34,652	8	5,673	29	14,351
1973	36	40,812	7	4,513	36	18,864
1974	23	27,058	11	9,527	46	28,351
1975	4	4,100	10	8,837	56	37,188
1976	1	1,200	3	2,627	59	39,815

[a]Source: *Status of Central Station Nuclear Power Reactor, Significant Milestones*, ERDA-30, July 1976.
[b]MWe, megawatts (electric).

period 1955 to 1976. The term NSSS refers to "nuclear steam supply system," the heart of the nuclear unit. As indicated by the column headed "NSSS orders," units ordered up through 1961 were mainly small research reactors [capacity of less than 100 megawatts (electric)], but beginning in 1962, commercial size reactors dominate the picture. The history of the industry has been characterized by a rapid growth in unit size, the typical unit under order being in the 600-megawatt range in the mid-1960's in contrast to a typical size of 1,000 megawatts (electric) and over in the mid-1970's. Except for a handful of large coal units, only nuclear plants are built in the 1,000-megawatt (electric) and over range, even today.

Construction and operation of a nuclear plant requires licenses from the AEC, now the Nuclear Regulatory Commission (NRC). The licensing process involves four basic stages: applying for and receiving a construction permit; building under a construction permit until construction is far enough along so that the design can be finalized, at which time an operating license application is filed; applying for and receiving an operating license; testing under the operating license until approval is received for operating the plant commercially, under full power. The second pair of columns in Table 21-1 list the number and capacity of units attaining commercial status for each year in the 1955–1976 time span. Finally, in the last two columns of the table are listed the installed capacity of the nuclear power industry, figures that reflect both the commissioning of new units and the decommissioning (or shutdown) of older units.

There is a pronounced cyclic character to orders for NSSS, a feature common to all capital goods industries. This leaves it at least open to question whether the recent falling off of orders is simply a hiatus before a new cyclical revival or whether the decline signals a permanent bottoming out of orders.

The rate of growth in installed capacity has been impressive, with capacity doubling approximately every two years over the 1966–1976 period. Moreover, it is clear that whatever the long-term economic picture for nuclear power is, the units that are already underway will result in large increases in installed capacity for a number of years to come. By the end of 1976, there were 59 nuclear units operating to produce power in the United States; and by July 1976, there were 134 units (with an average size perhaps 50 per cent larger than the average of installed units) in the construction-licensing stage. Thus, the units already underway would increase the nuclear generating capacity over its present level by something on the order of 300 per cent, over the next 5 to 10 years. About half of those units are still awaiting construction permits, and others are in early stages of construction. Units in the early stages of licensing and construction can be, and have been, canceled or deferred. Consequently the backlog is not an irreversible commitment to nuclear power, although the construction of many units is so far advanced that outright cancellation is unlikely.

The increase in the cost of nuclear power plants has been as dramatic as the growth of the nuclear industry. Units coming on line in the late 1960's had costs in the range of $150 per kilowatt; by 1976, costs for units coming on line had increased to $560 per kilowatt. Thus, capital costs (dollars per kilowatt) of nuclear units increased by approximately 300 per cent over the 1968–1976 period, whereas the general price index increased by "only" 67 per cent.* To identify the factors responsible for increasing costs, and to explain how the nuclear power industry continued to grow for a time in the face of such astonishing cost increases, a more detailed account of the economic history of nuclear power is required. We begin with a discussion of the turnkey period, during which construction of the first large (over 400 megawatts) commercial reactors commenced.

*Moreover, the rate of increase in costs of nuclear units coming on line underestimates the true rate of cost increases, since for any cohort of plants, the cheapest tend to come on line earliest, as has been pointed out by Bupp.[1]

THE TURNKEY ERA, 1963–1966

The Atomic Energy Act of 1954 provided a mandate for the AEC to develop and regulate a commercial nuclear power industry. The first stage in this effort was a program of research and development designed to identify commerically viable reactor types. This program, designated the Power Reactor Demonstration Program (PRDP), involved a partial AEC financing (in collaboration with utilities) of a number of small reactors between 1955 and 1961. By 1962, the LWR (light water reactor) had been established as the most immediately promising of the reactor types, with the breeder reactor and gas-cooled reactor still at the development stage.

The problem with the LWR was that capital costs for the small units that had been constructed under the PRDP were too high to provide competitive generating costs relative to fossil fuel power plants. Commercialization of the LWR required a move to larger capacity units, say in the 200- to 400-megawatt (electric) and over range, where capital costs per kilowatt were expected to show a sizable drop. But utilities were not willing to undertake the risks of financing such plants, and when the AEC showed no inclination to subsidize plants of this size, orders for reactors simply stopped. At this point, in 1962, the Joint Committee for Atomic Energy stepped into the picture by specifically earmarking $20 million of previously appropriated AEC funds for design and research and development assistance to subsidize construction of commercial size LWR's.

Two reactors were financed, in part by the AEC, under this new authorization, the last two LWR's to receive government assistance—Connecticut Yankee (NSSS order in December 1962) and San Onofre 1 (NSSS order in January 1963). Both of these units were built by Westinghouse, and both were built under so-called "turnkey" contracts. Turnkey contracts were contracts under which the builder of the reactor took on all of the responsibility for designing and building the unit, including any actions required to meet regulatory guidelines. After the plant had passed through the licensing process, including testing to attain commercial status, the plant was then turned over to the utility for operation. The typical turnkey contract also provided a financial guarantee in the form of a fixed price for the unit, this price to cover all the costs of construction and licensing, exclusive of interest during construction.

San Onofre and Connecticut Yankee were contracted for at prices to the utility (after deducting the AEC subsidy) of around $180 per kilowatt. This still left a competitive advantage to coal power plants, with capital costs in the $110 to $160 per kilowatt range. Then, in December 1963, came the dramatic announcement that General Electric had agreed to build the Oyster Creek unit for Jersey Central at a turnkey price of $132 per kilowatt, with no AEC subsidy. Added to the known fuel cost advantages of nuclear units, this capital cost was so low that nuclear power was actually cheaper than coal power at Oyster Creek, the first instance of a nuclear unit being built on the basis of economic advantages alone.

For the next two and one-half years, General Electric, Westinghouse, and several of the small reactor manufacturers (including General Atomics and Allis-Chalmers) offered turnkey contracts at fixed prices at or near the Oyster Creek level. In all, 13 plants were contracted for on a turnkey basis between December 1962 and mid-1966.** Then, in June 1966, General Electric announced that it

**There is some confusion in the literature concerning the number and identification of the turnkey plants. Mooz[2] lists 13 plants built by General Electric and Westinghouse, all contracted for between 1962 and 1966, as turnkey units: Dresden 2, 3, Connecticut Yankee, San Onofre 1, Ginna, Oyster Creek, Millstone 1, Point Beach 1, 2, Robinson 1, Monticello, and Quad Cities 1, 2. ERDA lists an additional 12 units as turnkey, for a total of 25: Big Rock Point, Dresden 1, Yankee Rowe, Humboldt Bay, Peach Bottom 1, Pathfinder, Piqua, Genoa, Fort St. Vrain, Indian Point 2, 3, Northcoast Power. Of these, all except the last four were development reactors built before 1962, and Northcoast Power was later canceled. Further, in WASH-1345, Indian Point 2 is listed as one of 13 turnkey units, but Connecticut Yankee is not listed as a turnkey. Generally, we have used Mooz' classification.

Table 21–2. Costs[a] of Turnkey Units as Reported by Utilities and Estimated in WASH-1345.[b]

Turnkey Units	*Reported Cost*	*WASH-1345 Estimated Cost*	*Estimated Loss*
General Electric			
Oyster Creek	91	170	79
Dresden 2, 3	230	413	183
Millstone	97	182	85
Quad Cities 1, 2	250	448	198
Monticello	105	168	63
Totals	773	1,381	608
Westinghouse			
San Onofre	97	131	34
Ginna	83	161	78
Robinson	78	179	101
Point Beach 1, 2	128	329	201
Connecticut Yankee	92	149	57
Totals	478	949	471
Combined totals	1,251	2,330	1,079

[a]In millions of dollars.
[b]Source: *Power Plant Capital Costs*, WASH-1345, AEC, October 1974.

would no longer offer complete nuclear power plants on a firm-price (turnkey) basis in the United States (turnkey contracts are still available for foreign orders). As a practical matter, Westinghouse also pulled out of the turnkey business at about the same time, although a formal announcement to this effect was not made until 1971.†

The initial response of the utility industry to the Oyster Creek announcement was one of cautious skepticism; only two nuclear units were announced in 1964 and six in 1965. But in 1966, a flood of 23 announcements were made, most after June and most on a non-turnkey basis. This continued into 1967, with 27 more announcements. Whatever else can be said about the turnkey era, it is a fact that for the nuclear power industry it represented a transition from a period of being a heavily subsidized stepchild of the AEC to a period of being a vigorous competitor with fossil fuels for base-load power plants.

From all reports, the turnkey contracts signed by General Electric and Westinghouse turned out to be first-class financial disasters for the two companies. Mooz[2] cites correspondence with executives of the two companies that indicate combined losses in the range of $1 billion, and there is corroboration of this estimate from the CONCEPT cost model developed by United Engineers and discussed in WASH-1345. Specifically, the comparisons between reported costs (by the utilities) of turnkey units and the WASH-1345 estimated costs (to the contractor) are summarized in Table 21-2.

The estimated losses presented in Table 21-2 should be viewed as at best educated guesses, in part because estimates of capital costs prepared by United Engineers for the

†Although General Electric and Westinghouse ceased to offer fixed price contracts for nuclear units in mid-1966, both continued to offer fixed price contracts for nuclear fuel. Westinghouse's problems with its fuel contracts are well known; General Electric followed a less ambitious program, but for certain units (including Oyster Creek and Browns Ferry) guaranteed fuel price contracts for periods up to 12 years of plant operations were signed. The major difference between General Electric and Westinghouse was that General Electric followed the practice of covering its fuel commitments through forward purchases, whereas Westinghouse generally remained in an unhedged position.

AEC have not proven to be particularly accurate in the past.††

Whatever the exact figures, there seems little doubt that General Electric and Westinghouse lost substantial amounts of money on the turnkey contracts of the 1963–1966 period. And, because the turnkey era was pivotal in the history of the nuclear power industry, it is important to try to understand the motivations of reactor manufacturers and utilities at that time, and how market forces in the nuclear power industry might have operated.

One version of the history of the turnkey era goes something like this.§ General Electric negotiated the Oyster Creek contract at a time when the nuclear power industry was at a standstill. General Electric engineers expected to take a loss on Oyster Creek, but acted in the expectation that if two other such units could be built, the learning curve would lower construction costs enough so that General Electric could at least break even on three units. Westinghouse was forced to offer contracts at or near the Oyster Creek price by the competitive pressures applied by General Electric. But as construction proceeded, it became clear both to General Electric and Westinghouse that costs would far exceed original estimates, at which point turnkey contracts were withdrawn from the market. The effect of the turnkey period on utilities, however, was to create expectations that non-turnkey units would come in at costs near the turnkey prices, so that orders continued to come in for reactors even after the turnkey option was phased out. Whether intended or not, the turnkey era produced the kinds of results associated with a "loss leader" strategy, in terms of expanding demand for nuclear units. As it turned out, the non-turnkey units came on line 6 to 8 years later at costs two to three times higher than turnkey prices, so that both the reactor manufacturers (on turnkey contracts) and the utilities (on non-turnkey contracts) suffered losses deriving from their overly optimistic expectations as to costs.

The main problem with this story of the turnkey era is the clear evidence that cost problems with the turnkey units stemmed largely from the post-turnkey period. The reasons cited for cost overruns by Westinghouse in Mooz' study[2] were (a) a dramatic change in labor costs (annual rate of increase of 30 per cent from 1967 on versus a rate of increase of about 5 per cent before 1967); (b) the birth of the environmental movement; (c) increases in licensing costs; (d) decreases in labor productivity. All these factors came to the fore only *after* 1966, that is, only after turnkey contracts had been withdrawn. And there is no evidence of special sources of information available to General Electric and Westinghouse concerning these general economic trends that were not also available to utilities planning nuclear units.

An alternative to the "loss leader" argument as an explanation for the growth in nuclear orders following the turnkey era is as follows. There are certain advantages to utilities from nuclear power that make it a desirable investment even if generating costs are slightly higher for nuclear relative to fossil fuel plants. First, there is a spreading the risk argument: given that a utility is already using coal, oil, and/or natural gas units, adding a nuclear unit reduces the vulnerability of a utility to fossil fuel price increases or availability. Second, nuclear fuel is a high capital cost, low operating cost power source. Nuclear units increase the rate base of the regulated utility more than alternative power sources do, and hence, increases allowed profits for any given level of output. Third, at

††Moreover, in Mooz' discussion[2] of the turnkey era, an executive of Westinghouse is quoted to the effect that San Onofre "came in under budget, on time, and made a good profit," whereas Connecticut Yankee "also returned a modest profit." In contrast, the WASH-1345 estimates show Westinghouse losing $91 million on these two units.

§This is a highly simplified version of Mooz' view of the turnkey era. The same viewpoint was expressed at the time by Philip Sporn, president of American Electric Power: "Competitive levels of nuclear plants may not be quite so low as initial announcement had seemed to indicate. One of the effects of competition might be to induce a manufacturer to risk somewhat greater uncertainty in the costs behind his turnkey price than might be tolerable repeatedly." (*Electrical World*, August 17, 1964).

the time, nuclear power was regarded as a "clean" fuel, and hence would be less subject to problems of siting and pollution control.

These inherent advantages of nuclear power were offset before the turnkey era by uncertainties as to capital costs and the technical feasibility of large nuclear units. The reactor manufacturers had strong incentives to prove the technology of large reactors in the mid-1960's. They did this, in effect, by engaging in privately financed demonstration projects, subsidizing the building of the turnkey plants. As construction progress was reported on San Onofre and Connecticut Yankee, the concerns of the utilities as to technological risks diminished. Moreover, by the end of the turnkey era, capital costs of coal plants were increasing at the rate of 15 per cent or more per year, and there was a general expectation that coal prices would increase in the future, an expectation that was realized in the wake of the mine safety legislation of 1969. Finally, reported costs on the turnkey units under construction (and on non-turnkey units such as Nine Mile Point) were favorable. The point is that there were a number of factors, over and above estimated capital costs of nuclear units, that encouraged utility investments in nuclear units, even after the turnkey era had ended.

As noted earlier, capital costs to electric utilities for the non-turnkey units contracted for in the immediate post-turnkey era were badly underestimated. But even in the face of those underestimates, it can be argued that, from hindsight, utilities going nuclear at that time might well have made the correct decision. Development of alternative fuels, especially coal, acted in part to offset the underestimates of nuclear capital costs.

It seems to us that the turnkey era can only be understood in terms of the distinction between technological risks and cost risks. Although the reactor manufacturers had incentives to establish the technological feasibility of large nuclear units, the utilities appear to be in a better position to bear cost risks. Turnkey contracts are rare in the history of United States utilities for that very reason. As a permanent fixture of the contracting process, the price quoted for a turnkey contract would have to incorporate an actuarially sound insurance premium against cost increases. The withdrawal of turnkey contracts once utilities were convinced of the technological feasibility of large nuclear units can be interpreted as a return to the historical practices of the industry, with the utility bearing cost risks, because self-insurance against such risks was preferable to the "contingency" premium that would have been built into future turnkey contracts.

There are several reasons for this. In the first place, the utilities are regulated monopolies, able to pass through cost increases to customers through rate increases, whereas the reactor manufacturers were operating in a competitive environment, competing with fossil fuel units and less able to absorb such cost increases. Moreover, there are moral hazards in turnkey-type contracts. The utility is interested in obtaining the lowest total cost of electricity possible for its base-load plants, but a turnkey contract only provides a guarantee as to the capital cost of the plant. To the extent that there is the possibility of substitution between low capital cost components and low operating cost components, the incentives for the contracting firm under a turnkey contract are to opt for the low capital cost component. Thus, there might well be sound economic reasons for a utility to prefer a non-turnkey contract to a turnkey contract, even if the capital cost of the non-turnkey unit is greater than that of the turnkey unit.

We can of course only speculate on the forces that were at work during the turnkey era. One thing is clear, however—by the end of the era, the nuclear industry had established itself as a major force in the future development of electric power in the United States.

THE COMMERCIAL SUCCESS OF NUCLEAR POWER, 1966–1970

As the turnkey era ended, commercialization of nuclear power was an accomplished fact.

In 1966, twenty plants were ordered, six on turnkey contracts. The remaining reactors, and almost all reactors ordered after 1966, were built by utilities under normal financial arrangements involving contracting with architect-engineers. During 1967, 30 reactors were ordered, but only one was on a turnkey basis. In 1968 and 1969, orders dropped off to fourteen and then seven reactors; by 1970 orders were back up to fourteen reactors.

Nuclear Costs in Contemporary Perspective

Construction of the reactors ordered in 1966 and 1967 on a non-turnkey basis did not begin until at least 12 months after the orders were announced, because of the time required for various licenses to be granted. Consequently, the inital surge of decisions to build nuclear plants occurred when there was little experience with the construction of large nuclear reactors under normal utility contracting procedures. Nevertheless, a mood of general optimism about total nuclear costs—both capital and operating—appears to have pervaded this industry. *Electrical World* quoted Dr. Alvin Weinberg as saying that reactors ordered during 1966 would produce electricity at a cost of 25 per cent less than that of coal, and in mid-1967, TVA Board member Frank Smith described nuclear power as having a clear but somewhat smaller advantage in the TVA area.

There were, however, some warnings that turnkey quotations were unreliable bases for projections of nuclear costs. General Electric's annual report issued in 1967 stated that "earlier commitments made to win customer acceptance of the new [nuclear] technology continue to affect earnings." Stephen F. Dunn, president of the National Coal Association, said that General Electric's annual report illustrated that coal was a more competitive fuel than turnkey prices implied.

The trend in actual and estimated nuclear capital costs is apparent from Figure 21-1. Three time series are plotted in that figure:

(1) The average estimated capital costs of all plants ordered in the previous year.

(2) The average of updated capital cost estimates for all plants still under construction during the previous year (and ordered in years prior to the previous year).

(3) The average actual capital cost of all plants completed in the previous year.

During 1966 and 1967, estimates of nuclear costs appear to have been based on the price quotations for turnkey plants. During 1967, updated estimates of the cost of non-turnkey plants under construction became available. They indicated that actual costs would exceed initial estimates, but not by a large margin.

Estimates of the cost of newly ordered plants did increase from year to year between 1968 and 1971, rising from about \$150 per kilowatt in 1968 to \$220 per kilowatt in 1971. They rose more rapidly than interim estimates of the cost of plants under construction, but perhaps no more than was necessary to incorporate the additional inflation that would affect plants with later completion dates.

Licensing Delays

Between 1967 and 1970, problems in licensing and constructing nuclear plants began to emerge. With a total of 50 new commitments to deal with during 1966 and 1967, AEC processing of applications showed signs of strain.

By the fall of 1967, licensing delays were apparent throughout the industry, and by the end of 1967, 26 plants were caught in the construction permit process alone. Table 21-3 reveals that the time required to obtain a construction permit for a reactor ordered in 1968 was 14 months longer, on the average, than it had been for a reactor ordered in 1966. Between 1968 and 1970, the situation worsened, when the time required to obtain a construction permit increased by another 15 months.

During the 1966–1970 period, intervenors such as environmental groups, states, and municipalities, entered the licensing process.

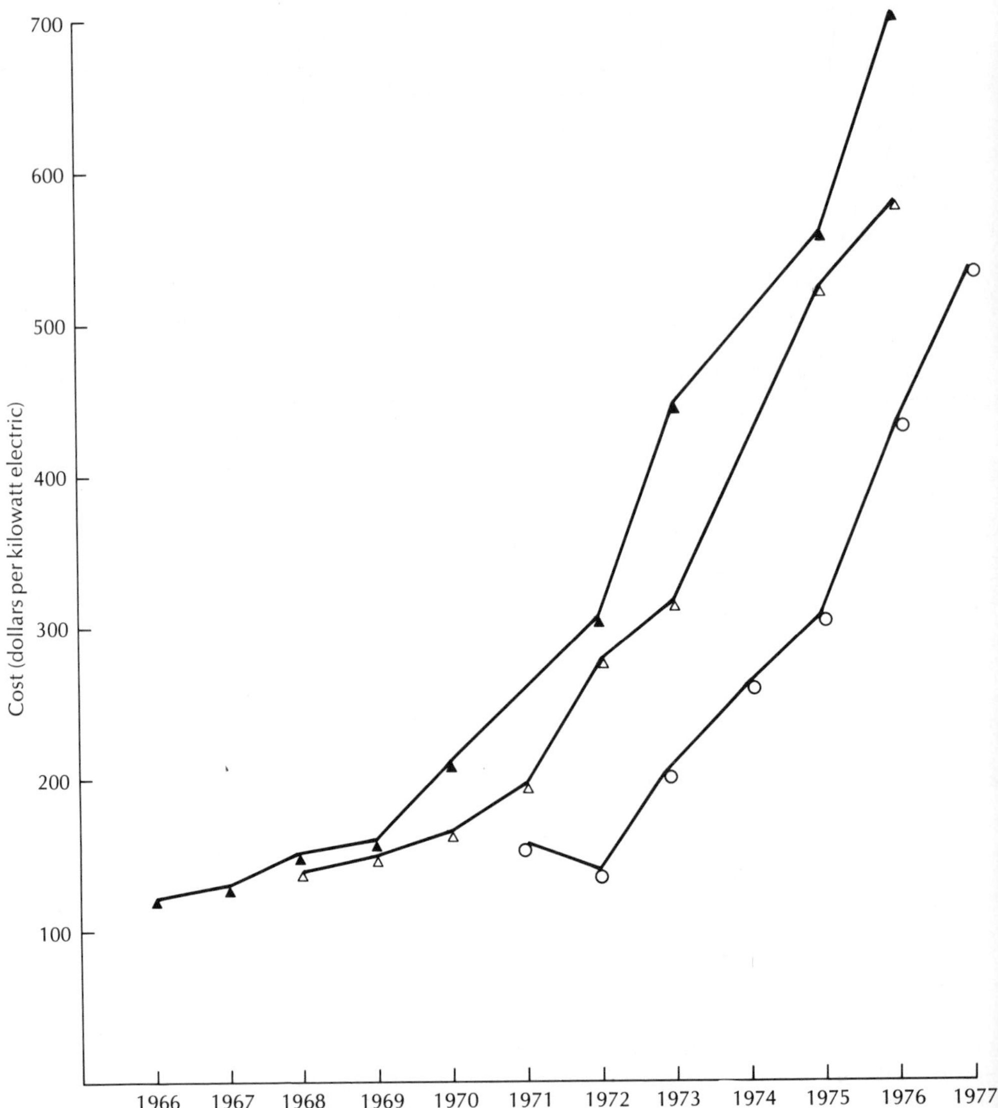

Figure 21-1. Estimated and actual capital cost, 1966–1976 (data missing on estimated costs for 1974). ▲, initial cost; △, interim estimate on all prior plants; ○, final report.

There were a few well publicized cases in which the activities of intervenors resulted in a lengthening of the licensing process.

There is clear evidence, however, that a major part of the increase in regulatory delay was due to bottleneck problems involving the staff and the Advisory Commission on Reactor Safety (ACRS). In 1966, uncontested applications could be processed in 10 months or less; by 1970, it took a year and one-half or more simply to perform the staff and ACRS review that preceded the announcement of the

Table 21–3. Permit and Licensing Delays, 1966–1979.[a,b]

1966 CP Application

7/66	CP application	
7/67	CP issuance	12 months
7/69	OL application	24 months
5/73	OL issuance	46 months
9/73	Commercial status	4 months
		86 months

(Average time, CP application to commercial, 7 years, 2 months)

1968 CP Application

			Change from 1966 (Months)
7/68	CP application		
9/70	CP issuance	26 months	+14
3/73	OL application	30 months	+ 6
?/77	OL issuance		
?/77	Commercial status		

(Average time, CP application to commercial, over 8 years)

1970 CP Application

			Change from 1966 (Months)	*Change from 1968 (Months)*
7/70	CP application			
12/73	CP issuance	41 months	+29	+15
1/76	OL application	36 months	+12	+ 6
?/79	OL issuance			
?/79	Commercial status			

(Average time, CP application to commercial, over 9 years)

[a]Source: *Status of Central Station Nuclear Power Reactors, Significant Milestones*, ERDA-30, July 1976.
[b]CP, construction permit; OL, operating license.

establishment of a licensing board and the scheduling of prehearing conferences. This increase, it might be noted, occurred before the expansion of the scope of the construction permit review process to handle anti-trust and environmental matters. No doubt, a part of this bottleneck problem was indirectly related to intervention; it simply takes more staff time to prepare answers to issues that might be raised by intervenors in a contested hearing than in an uncontested hearing.

Delays in Construction

Licensing requirements were not, however, the only source of delay or of increasing costs. The Joint Committee on Atomic Energy warned in 1967 that manufacturers might have problems delivering equipment on time and meeting performance and safety standards. To keep up with nuclear demands, General Electric announced in October 1968, a major expansion of two manufacturing divisions. Another NSSS manufacturer, Babcock and Wilcox, was reported to be having problems meeting delivery dates because of insufficient capacity.

One contemporary study§§ found the following reasons for delays in bringing nuclear units on line:

(1) Labor trouble, 28 plants
(2) Licensing delays, 25 plants
(3) Late delivery of pressure vessels, 21 plants
(4) Public opposition, 16 plants
(5) Construction problems, 16 plants
(6) Scheduling problems, 6 plants

Labor trouble, late delivery, construction and scheduling problems can all be interpreted as evidence of bottlenecks resulting from a too rapid expansion of the demand for nuclear plants. The authorities recognized that equipment problems were epidemic, but favored the bottleneck hypothesis. The president of Westinghouse Power Systems, for example, claimed that "much of the delay being experienced by some utilities is simply the result of the large influx of orders experienced in 1966–1967. Once this is behind us, plants should consistently come on line with five year lead time from order to operation" (*Electrical World,* September 1, 1970).

The Relation between Estimated and Actual Costs: 1966–1970

Although licensing and construction delays were recognized in the nuclear industry, their implications for nuclear costs were not apparent until after 1970. Between 1968 and 1971, estimates of nuclear capital costs were made by utilities on the basis of historical experience: inflation and rising interest rates that appeared late in the 1960's were not anticipated, delays were seen largely as a transitory phenomenon resulting from the great influx of orders in 1966 and 1967, and an increase in the size of the nuclear power units was expected to provide the economies of scale that had in the past been obtained by building larger fossil fuel plants. It was not until 1972 and later that it became widely apparent that estimates of the capital costs of nuclear power plants were grievously in error, and that the 50 per cent increase in estimates between 1966 and 1970 fell far short of the trend in realized costs.

The AEC's first commissioned study of nuclear power costs in March 1968 was based on March 1967 data (WASH-1082). It estimated that a 1,000-megawatt plant would cost about $135 per kilowatt, a figure lower than 1968 estimates by electric utilities. The procedures used were seriously flawed—the bill of materials was underestimated, the design of the plant was poorly defined, an unrealistically low interest rate was used, and zero inflation was assumed.

In a second report, published in June 1969 (WASH-1150), an attempt was made to determine the causes of the obvious increase in estimated cost. The WASH-1150 estimate of $250 per kilowatt actually exceeded the current utility estimates. The reasons cited for cost increases were:

(1) Higher direct costs, due to a revised description of the plant—including additional safety systems—and higher prices of factor inputs.
(2) Higher indirect costs (which included some construction costs), contingency reserves, and interest rates.
(3) Escalation of construction and manufacturing labor rates.

In January 1971 a new estimate of $350 per kilowatt was recorded (WASH-1230). The increase was attributed to "latest safety requirements, codes, and standards . . ., environmental protection and licensing criteria." WASH-1230 also assumed an additional year of construction time and a higher interest rate. Utility estimates of nuclear costs lagged behind WASH-1230; the average reported during 1971 was only $300 per kilowatt.

In Table 21-4 original estimates and actual realized costs of plants ordered in each year

§§Sources: *Electrical World,* March 2, 1970.

Table 21-4. Comparison of Initial Estimates to Actual Costs of Nuclear Plants by Year of Order.[a]

Year of NSSS Order	*Initial Estimate*	*Cost of Plants Complete by 1/77*
1965	120	240
1966	125	240
1967	150	365
1968	155	460
1969	205	
1970	220	

[a]Source: *Central Station Nuclear Plants*, AEC and ERDA 1968–1976.

from 1965 to 1970 are compared. As Bupp[1] has pointed out, not all these plants have been completed, and estimates of costs for plants still in the operating license process when the data were assembled exceed the actual cost of completed plants.

The 1965 and 1966 cohorts were completed at an average cost that was twice the estimated cost. Costs of completed plants in the 1967 and 1968 cohorts range from two and one-half to three times the initial estimate.

But it must be emphasized that these retrospective comparisons could not be made by utilities considering nuclear power plants in 1970 or 1971. They had only the historical experience of the utility industry with construction of fossil fuel power plants and four years of nuclear construction experience to rely on. Moreover, such plants as Connecticut Yankee or San Onofre had been completed on time and, to all appearances, under budget.

A TIME OF CHANGE, 1971–1976

During the 1970's initial estimates of the cost of newly ordered plants increased rapidly, from $200 per kilowatt in 1970 to almost $700 per kilowatt in 1975. The fact that information on the actual costs of completed plants became available at almost exactly the time that new estimates shot up (see Figure 21-1) suggests that utilities were learning from experience. From 1971 on, year to year changes in updated estimates of the eventual costs of plants under construction increased at about the same pace as the initial estimates.

But the actual costs of completed plants also increased rapidly during the 1970's. During 1970 and 1971, many of the turnkey plants ordered before 1967 were completed; average reported costs in those years were about $125 per kilowatt. Through 1974, reported costs increased at an average of $50 per year. Plants completed in 1975 and early 1976 provided the real shock; the average cost of plants completed during 1975 was $425 per kilowatt, compared to $300 per kilowatt during 1974. And plants completed during 1976 cost on an average $560 per kilowatt.

These changes in real—as opposed to estimated—costs were the result of changes in the regulatory process and of external events that changed the whole environment in which utilities operated.

The Regulatory Process

Events in the regulatory process tend to increase capital costs in two general ways. First, regulation can increase costs through mandated changes in the design and construction of plants when regulatory guidelines are strengthened or extended; such added costs reflect the *substantive* impact of regulation. Second, regulation can increase costs by imposing delays on the construction process, even when no changes take place in the design or construction of the plant; such costs represent the *procedural* effects of regulation. The most important procedural effects arise from changes in the length of time required to complete the licensing process. As that time increases, interest payments on prior expenditures accumulate and inflation drives up the cost of later procurements.

Table 21-3 revealed that the length of time spent in construction permit processes alone was 29 months longer for a plant ordered in 1970 than for one ordered in 1966. The primary reason for licensing and construction delays from 1970 on was undoubtedly increasing attention to environmental and safety issues, much of which stemmed from intervenor activities in the licensing process.

The Calvert Cliffs decision introduced a new dimension of environmental concern into licensing procedures. In 1971, the United States District Court ruled that the National Environmental Policy Act of 1969 required the AEC to consider all environmental impacts of a nuclear plant in its decision to issue a construction permit or operating license. During 1971, the AEC began to implement this ruling, which required preparation of new environmental impact statements for all plants not yet in operation. By October 1972, *Electrical World* estimated that 48 plants had suffered construction delays since the effects of the Calvert Cliffs decision on schedules had become apparent.

Throughout the 1970's, the AEC issued increasingly stringent standards regulating environmental impacts and safety of nuclear plants under construction; additional delays resulted from AEC rulings that applied new standards to all nuclear plants. On June 15, 1971, *Electrical World* reported that five plants would be delayed in construction because of a new study of the emergency core cooling system that would result in imposition of new requirements, adding $4 million to the cost of a typical reactor. Another example of a substantive effect of nuclear regulation is the estimated increase of $12 million in costs per plant for water intake structures, noise abatement measures, and so on, mandated by the AEC in the 1971–1973 period.

It should be noted that there is some evidence (Indian Point 2, Surrey 1) that delays and costs of rebuilding nuclear plants were due to inadequate initial design, as well as to the regulatory requirements.

During 1973, the AEC admitted that "increases in reported power plants costs [have] continued to exceed expectations. Essentially all power plants under construction . . . show large costs overruns. . . ." The AEC identified the causes of cost overruns as:

(1) Additional engineering, safety, and environmental factors.

(2) Increased costs of all types.

(3) Increased escalation and interest due to longer project time.

Responses to Changing Circumstances

During the early 1970's, utilities became aware of the serious underestimation of costs in early expectations about nuclear power.

From 1971 on, the year to year increase in cost estimates for new plants ranged from $75 to $150 per kilowatt. The average of reported costs showed a smaller annual increase, of $50 per kilowatt, until 1975. Interim estimates of costs of plants under construction increased at about the same pace as initial estimates.

Estimates of the cost of plants ordered during 1975 reached an average of $700 per kilowatt—a figure that will still be low unless there is a sizable fall in historical escalation rates.

Despite the rising estimates of nuclear costs, orders for nuclear plants rose from 1970 until 1973, and then fell off precipitously. Only two plants were ordered in 1976. As early as 1972, some cancellations and deferrals were, however, reported. Two factors can be identified as explanations for the surge of nuclear orders in the early 1970's. First, air quality regulations made construction of fossil fuel plants appear expensive, not feasible, or at least, antisocial in many areas of the country. Second, during the 1970's, coal-fired power plants—the most attractive alternative to nuclear power given the limitation on oil and gas supplies that developed after 1970—were also increasing in costs, and coal prices were rising as well.

Table 21-5 presents data on coal and nuclear capital costs between 1968 and 1976 (1974 for coal). New non-turnkey nuclear units coming on line in 1972 had capital costs that were 70 per cent higher than those for new coal units, with the differential reduced to roughly 50 per cent higher in 1973–1974. Whereas nuclear capital costs for units coming on line show a high rate of escalation (between 25 and 30 per cent per year over the past few years), there has also been a marked

Table 21–5. Historical Capital Cost Data, 1968–1976, Nuclear and Coal Power Plants.

	Number of New Units[a]			Average Megawatts (Electric) per New Unit[a]			Capital Cost[b]			Range Capital Cost[b]		
Year	Nuclear Non-turnkey	Nuclear Turnkey	Coal	Nuclear Non-turnkey	Nuclear Turnkey	Coal	Nuclear Non-turnkey	Nuclear Turnkey	Coal	Nuclear Non-turnkey	Nuclear Turnkey	Coal
1968	—	2(N)	9(N) 17(A)	—	525(N)	344(N) 360(A)	—	164	117(N) 132(A)	—	153– 180	72– 184
1969	1(N)	1(N)	13(N) 17(A)	620(N)	550(N)	382(N) 486(A)	262(N)	163	140(N) 114(A)	262	163	79– 192
1970	—	2(N) 1(A)	13(N) 10(A)	—	520(N) 810(A)	488(N) 472(A)	—	151(N) 114(A)	157(N) 113(A)	—	114– 161	83– 205
1971	1(N)	2(N) 2(A)	11(N) 11(A)	812(N)	615(N) 785(A)	693(N) 507(A)	181(N)	170(N) 115(A)	128(N) 120(A)	181	101– 193	96– 216
1972	4(N) 1(A)	1(N) 2(A)	7(N) 14(A)	712(N) 760(A)	879(N) 701(A)	665(N) 556(A)	274(N) 143(A)	121(N) 129(A)	174(N) 160(A)	143– 353	121– 136	115– 244
1973	4(N) 3(A)	—	8(N) 14(A)	765(N) 873(A)	—	562(N) 652(A)	293(N) 184(A)	—	204(N) 157(A)	161– 393	—	115– 307
1974	5(N) 6(A)	—	10(N) 10(A)	811(N) 914(A)	—	565(N) 693(A)	354(N) 285(A)	—	230(N) 172(A)	181– 498	—	136– 312
1975	7(N) 3(A)	—	NA	875(N) 905(A)	—	NA	436(N) 408(A)	—	NA	251– 518	—	NA
1976	3(N)	—	NA	914(N)	—	NA	560(N)	—	NA	415– 692	—	NA

[a]Number of new units, coal, is the number of new coal units reported in *Steam Electric Plant Construction Cost and Annual Production Expenses*, FPC, 1968–1974. Nuclear units, non-turnkey and turnkey are from *Central Station Nuclear Plants*, AEC and ERDA, 1968–1976. (N) and (A) in the new units columns refer to new plants and additions to existing plants, respecitvely.

[b]Capital cost is in dollars per kilowatt. Capital cost, for coal, are FPC figures, 1968–1974; nuclear data are from *Central Station Nuclear Plants*.

rate of escalation in coal capital costs as well. As noted earlier, due to the long and variable gestation period for nuclear units, data on units coming on line tend to understate the average capital costs for any cohort of plants, so that as dramatic as are the cost changes shown, in fact capital costs were escalating even more rapidly than indicated. Offsetting this was the increase in capital costs for coal, coupled with technological and cost uncertainties as to the new environmental controls (scrubbers, cooling towers, etc.) that were beginning to be applied to coal units.

Moreover, after remaining almost constant for many years, coal fuel prices began to rise dramatically during the late 1960's. At first, the rise in prices was driven by increasing labor costs in mining coal, which were the result of new standards protecting miners' health and safety. The rise in coal prices played an important role in the continued viability of nuclear power through 1973. Then a strike reduced mine output during 1973 at the same time that rising oil prices led some utilities to increase their demand for coal. There was a 300 per cent increase in spot prices during 1974; many utilities were cut off from coal promised under long-term contracts as suppliers diverted coal to the more profitable spot market.

By 1975, coal prices had stabilized at a level about twice that reached in the mid-1960's. Coal remained at about one-half the price (per million BTU heating value) of oil, and supplies were adequate to meet utility demand.

On net balance, developments through the early 1970's apparently favored expansion of nuclear capacity for base-load plants. But as early as 1972, there were indications that the rate of escalation of nuclear capital costs was beginning to tip the scales in favor of coal.

In 1972, several utilities cited nuclear cost increases and construction delays as reasons for reversing earlier decisions and choosing coal over nuclear (Florida Power & Light, Iowa Power & Light). During 1972, three nuclear units were canceled, one in favor of a coal-fueled facility. During 1973, another reason for cancellations and deferrals became apparent—rising costs and inadequate revenues were making utilities unable or unwilling to finance capacity expansion. On March 1, 1973, Georgia Power & Light deferred two nuclear units because of financial strains resulting from the denial of a request for a rate increase. The seven outright cancellations reported in 1973 were attributed, at least in part, to environmental opposition.

In 1974, still a third reason for cancellations and deferrals became apparent—the unprecedented slowdown in electricity demand growth that resulted from rising energy prices, recession, and mild weather. *Electrical World* stated that throughout the industry, "Rescheduling of generating additions approaches landslide proportions as U.S. utilities move to align capital expenditures with lower than expected load growth." Generating capacity was projected to grow faster than load through 1976, despite announced cutbacks.

Because of their high capital cost and long lead times, nuclear plants were particularly vulnerable to financing problems and cutbacks due to inadequate demand. *Electrical World* estimated that 36 per cent of all nuclear units under construction had their schedules set back during 1974. A few were reported to be plants suffering construction delays, but most were reported to be victims of "utility ordered stretchouts averaging two years."

As utility financial problems eased during late 1975 and 1976, general construction plans recovered, but nuclear orders did not. It is difficult to say whether this represented a temporary legacy of the low demand and financial difficulties of 1974 and 1975 or a permanent shift away from nuclear power.

CAUSES FOR NUCLEAR CAPITAL COST

It might be well to place the cost history of nuclear power reactors in perspective through comparisons with other indicators for the 1967–1976 period. Table 21-6 shows that the Gross National Product (GNP) implicit price index increased by 69 per cent between 1967

Table 21-6. Price Indices and Interest Rates, 1967–1976.[a]

	GNP Price Index (1972 = 100)		*Construction Price Index (1967 = 100)*			
Year	*Index*	*Change (%)*	*Index*	*Change (%)*	*Net Yield Moody's AAA Corp. Bonds*	*Change in Kilowatt Cost of New Nuclear Units (%)*
1967	79.0	+2.9	100.0	+1.2	5.51	—
1968	82.6	+4.5	104.9	+4.9	6.18	—
1969	86.7	+5.0	110.8	+5.9	7.03	+19.7
1970	91.4	+5.4	112.6	+1.7	8.04	+4.1
1971	96.0	+5.1	119.7	+6.3	7.39	+4.0
1972	100.0	+4.1	126.2	+5.4	7.21	+10.9
1973	105.8	+5.8	136.7	+8.4	7.44	+28.9
1974	116.4	+10.0	161.6	+18.2	8.57	+20.2
1975	127.3	+9.3	176.4	+9.2	8.83	+35.5
1976	133.8	+5.1	187.9	+6.5	8.43	+30.9
1967–1976		+69.4		+87.9	1968–1976	+294.4

[a]Source: GNP price index, construction price index, and yields from the *Economic Report of the President*, January 1977; change in cost of nuclear units is taken from Table 21-2, using WASH-1345 estimates of costs for turnkey units.

and 1976, and the construction price index increased by 88 per cent. Capital cost per kilowatt for new or additional nuclear units rose by 294 per cent between 1968 and 1976, assuming that the early turnkey units had cost as much as the estimates from WASH-1345. Between 1967 and 1976, the interest rate on AAA bonds rose from 5.51 to 8.43 per cent, an increase of roughly 53 per cent.

If construction costs for nuclear units had risen at the average rate for the construction industry as a whole, and if interest costs (roughly 17 per cent of total costs for a nuclear unit, according to WASH-1345) had risen simply to reflect the increase in interest rates, then the cost of a nuclear unit would have roughly doubled between 1967 and 1976, rather than quadrupled, as indicated by the last column of Table 21-6. The difference is accounted for by several factors:

(1) Nuclear units being built in the 1970's were different from those being built in the 1960's, because of new safety and environmental requirements.

(2) The time required to complete the licensing-construction process for new units coming on line increased from five years in 1967 to nine years in 1976, and will be even longer for units still to come.

(3) Rising interest rates interacted with delays to increase interest charges.

(4) Because of bottleneck problems, labor and material cost increased much more in nuclear construction than in construction in general.

(5) Licensing costs rose substantially over the period.

The leading study that had addressed itself to analyzing the relative importance of these factors is the study by Bupp.[1] Bupp's work has been complemented by studies undertaken by the AEC.[3]

Bupp found that one driving factor in cost increase was the increase between 1965 and 1975 in manpower and raw material requirements of nuclear power plants.[||] Bupp inter-

[||]Bupp[1] estimated that the cost per kilowatt of plants completed before 1975 increased at a rate of $49 per year when the effects of gross geographical and design differences between plants completed in different years are statistically controlled, and $27 when they are not. These estimates cannot be compared directly to Figure 21-1, because Bupp deflated all costs using the Handy-Whitman index of construction costs. We suspect that such

preted this increase to be ''obviously a consequence of more stringent nuclear safety and environmental design criteria,'' but asserted that the increase in reactor construction time is thought to be more important.

Bupp divided total project length into licensing time (the time between application for and issuance of the construction permit) and on-site construction time (the interval between beginning of site preparation and operation of the reactor). He found that ''an increase in the licensing time has a strong effect on total cost,'' but that the relationship between total costs and on-site construction time was insignificant.

Bupp gave two reasons why increases in the licensing period might increase total costs: (a) the length of the licensing period measures the stringency of design changes and safety features that are required; (b) long licensing periods lead the utility to speed construction to make up for licensing delays, with consequent increases in costs. Bupp observed that this may also explain the lack of correlation between on-site construction time and costs.

In summary, Bupp identifies the major factor behind the differential rate of increase in nuclear costs to be the activities of intervenors; he concludes that the nuclear licensing process has been used by opponents of nuclear power as a vehicle for raising the private cost of nuclear power to the perceived level of social cost.

WASH-1345, published by the AEC in October 1974,[3] represents an alternative approach to the nuclear cost issue. Rather than an attempt to identify underlying causal factors, WASH-1345 is a retrospective study of cost increases between 1966 and 1974 in which costs are estimated, by categories, for nuclear units coming on line during those periods. Escalation of labor and material costs and increases in interest during construction were identified as the major components of cost increase between 1966 and 1974. In addition, the study found that direct construction costs more than doubled over the period, with about $90 million in cost of a hypothetical 1,000-megawatt plant ordered in 1973 ($90 per kilowatt) being due to environment and safety-related changes in plant design mandated between 1971 and 1973.

Because the approaches are different, there is no necessary conflict between conclusions of these two studies; and because nuclear units are so site specific in characteristics and so lacking in standardization, neither study can be said to represent a definitive answer to the question of the source of cost increases between 1966 and 1974. That licensing problems represent a major source of cost increases from 1970 on is clearly correct, and that bottleneck problems have been present throughout the history of the industry is also true. But Bupp's conclusion that intervenors are to be assigned the major role in the explanation of cost increases deserves further comment.[1]

Intervention in the licensing process became the normal pattern from 1969 on; prior to that time, uncontested licensing hearings were as common as hearings in which intervenors appear. Table 21-7 gives data on construction permit (CP) applications between 1966 and 1970.

The average time required to complete the CP process rose from 10.5 months in 1966 to 37.7 months in 1970, and the number of uncontested hearings dropped noticeably between those dates. But the average time required for an uncontested hearing rose from 8.7 month in 1966 to 28.3 months for plants applying for a CP in 1970, which strongly suggests that intervention was not the only factor lengthening the licensing time. Contested hearings, on average, required more time than did uncontested hearings; intervention is associated with time delays. But bottlenecks in the licensing process and changes in rules and regulations unrelated to intervention also clearly played a role in regulatory delays, especially prior to 1971.

Intervenors can lengthen the licensing process by increasing the number and scope of issues before a licensing board, thus increas-

deflation is inappropriate: the Handy-Whitman index is based, in part, on nuclear plant costs. Consequently, some cost changes that should be explained vanish because of the deflator Bupp uses.

Table 21-7. Construction Permit Applications, 1966–1970.[a]

	Total Number		Uncontested		Contested	
	No.	Average Time (Months)	No.	Average Time (Months)	No.	Average Time (Months)
1966	13	10.5	7	8.7	6	13.8
1967	21	13.2	10	13.7	11	13.0
1968	9	22.8	5	16.0	4	31.3
1969	9	26.5	1	41.0	8	25.0
1970	12	37.7	3	28.3	9	40.8

[a]Source: *Status of Central Station Nuclear Power Reactors, Significant Milestones*, ERDA-30, July 1976.

ing the number and time-duration of prehearing conferences and hearings; but often those or related issues are also the subject of some disagreements within the AEC and might have caused delays even in the absence of intervention. Appeals after a CP has been issued have no effect on delaying construction unless a stay is granted, a relatively rare occurrence. Thus, there have been cases of very active intervention, involving many appeals and many issues, but producing relatively short time delays in the utility obtaining a CP.

Aside from causing delays, intervenors had little discernible effect on the licensing process before 1970. Intervention never resulted in denial of a license and rarely succeeded in changing the location of a reactor or challenging the safety and/or environmental features associated with construction; but there were several cases in which conditions were imposed on licenses to take into account issues raised by intervenors. Intervenors probably did increase the costs of constructing a reactor, by imposing time delays and informational costs on a utility.

The primary success of intervenors has been generic rather than specific to individual plants. For example, contested hearings in 1966–1968 often involved the issue of "practical value" of nuclear units, with small utilities and municipalities attempting to intervene to force anti-trust hearings. This led to Congressional action in 1970, mandating an anti-trust review of all units entering the nuclear licensing process. Similarly, environmental issues raised in the later 1960's led finally to the incorporation of an environmental review as a part of the CP issuing process. No doubt anti-trust review and environmental review can, in certain cases at least, take into account the complaints of intervenors. But these reviews also increase the over-all time delays associated with licensing and hence the cost of reactors, so that they also play a role in decreasing the economic advantages of nuclear power.

The history of the 1966–1970 period was not simply one of intervenors entering the licensing process and imposing delays on plant licensing. But after 1970, the success of intervenors on generic issues led to substantial cost increases to meet new design and safety requirements. Moreover, the Calvert Cliffs decision led to major time delays in preparing environmental impact statements and in hearings on such statements.

OPERATING COSTS OF NUCLEAR AND COAL UNITS

Finally, some comments should be made about the total costs of generating electricity using nuclear units as compared to coal units. Cost-benefit analyses of nuclear units have typically assumed an 80 per cent plant factor (output to capacity) for these baseload plants, and the AEC has historically employed comparably high plant factors in its comparisons of costs between coal and nuclear units. The higher the plant factor, the lower the capital costs per unit of output, so that high plant factors lead to a more favorable cost comparison for nuclear units relative to coal units.

As early as the mid-1960's, some utility managers were expressing skepticism concerning the assumption that nuclear units could operate in the 80 per cent range.

In a recent study by Komanoff,[4] it was found that capacity factors deteriorated with the increasing scale of new plants, as a result of equipment malfunctions and difficulty in making repairs. Deterioration was found to be so rapid that capital costs per kilowatt-hour generated actually *increase* with increasing scale above about 800 megawatts. Komanoff also found that coal plants had a somewhat better performance than nuclear plants when an optimum-size coal plant is compared to a nuclear plant of optimum size (optimum being defined as the size at which capital costs per kilowatt-hour are minimized, with the reduced cost due to scale economies in construction being just balanced by the increased cost due to poorer operating performance).

Komanoff's conclusions are based on a relatively small data base and are disputed by utility spokesmen and reactor manufacturers, who argue that the shakedown period for large reactors has not yet been completed in the reactors currently operating and that higher plant factors and lower costs will be observed in future years.

Federal Power Commission data on nuclear and coal units coming on line between 1968 and 1973 indicate that although nuclear units have not met the 80 per cent plant factor goal, nonetheless, operating costs and total costs (including capital cost) per unit of output were less on average for nuclear fuel than for coal.

Coal units coming on line in 1968 operated at a plant factor of roughly 55 per cent between 1969 and 1974, while nuclear units had an average plant factor of roughly 70 per cent. In 1974, operating cost per kilowatt-hour for 1968 coal units was 5.87 mills, for 1968 nuclear units, 2.74 mills; for 1969 plants, the costs were 7.02 mills per kilowatt-hour for coal versus 5.12 per kilowatt-hour for nuclear fuel. A similar operating cost advantage applies for later units.

The basis for the observed cost advantage for nuclear units is low fuel cost, which is not completely offset by higher capital costs for nuclear units than coal units. Using a 16 per cent fixed charge rate together with the observed plant factors for coal and nuclear units of 1972 and 1973, total cost (mills per kilowatt-hour) in 1974 was 13.43 for 1972 coal units and 12.49 for 1972 nuclear units; total cost in 1974 was 18.42 mills per kilowatt-hour for 1973 coal units versus 14.56 mills per kilowatt-hour for 1973 coal units. Thus, as of 1974, the most recent year for which FPC coal capital cost data are available, new nuclear units were producing electricity more cheaply than new coal units.[‖‖]

REFERENCES

1. I. Bupp, J. Derian, M. Donsimoni, R. Treitel, 1974, Trends in Light Water Reactor Capital Costs in the United States: Causes and Consequences, CPA 74-8, December, Center for Policy Alternatives, Massachusetts Institute of Technology, Cambridge, sachusetts Institute of Technology, Cambridge, Mass.
2. W. Mooz, 1976, A Cost History of the Light Water Reactor, WN-9494-NSF Rand, November.
3. Atomic Energy Commission, 1974, Power Plant Capital Costs: Current Trends and Sensitivity to Economic Parameters, WASH-1345, Washington, October 1974.
4. C. Komanoff, 1976, *Power Plant Performance: Nuclear and Coal Capacity Factors And Economics* (Council of Economic Priorities, New York).

SUGGESTED READINGS

Bupp, I., J. Derian, M. Donsimoni, R. Treitel, 1975, The Economics of Nuclear Power, *Technology Review,* February, pp. 15–25.

Hammond, Allen L., 1976, Uranium: Will There Be a Shortage or an Embarrassment of Enrichment, *Science 192,* pp. 866–867.

Lieberman, M. A., 1976, United States Uranium Resources—an Analysis of Historical Data, *Science 192,* pp. 431–436.

McCaull, Julian, 1976, The Cost of Nuclear Power, *Environment 18,* pp. 11–16.

‖‖ It had, however, taken longer to complete the nuclear units. If substitute power were required because of nuclear delays, its cost could have reduced the nuclear advantage. Nuclear and coal units announced in the same year cannot be compared because of lack of cohort data on coal.

Policy Studies Of Nuclear Futures 22

CAROL E. STEINHART 1977

Prometheus is here again, offering the blessings and curses of fire in the form of nuclear energy. Where optimists see a glowing future with unlimited energy, pessimists see only a world-wide nuclear calamity.

A major issue in any energy policy is what form our nuclear future will take—or whether we should have a nuclear future at all. This issue transcends national boundaries, creating an unprecedented situation. Never before have nations so intensely debated a new technology and its control. From the furor have emerged a number of thoughtful policy studies, several of which are summarized in the following pages (see references). Some of the recommendations of these studies have already been incorporated into President Carter's energy program, and they influenced discussions between the President and European heads of state in May 1977.

BACKGROUND—HOW WE GOT HERE

The United States has had a nuclear energy policy of sorts since the end of World War II, but nuclear programs have enjoyed an independence unrelated to an over-all energy policy—except for vague promises that the desert would bloom and electricity would be too cheap to meter. The privileged place of nuclear technology resulted from the creation of the Atomic Energy Commission (AEC), a civilian agency with a mission to search out, promote, and supervise peaceful uses of the atom. At the same time, recognizing the danger of world-wide spread of nuclear weapons, the United States maintained strict secrecy regarding nuclear technology.

But secrecy and monopoly did not last long. Other countries developed their own nuclear programs and the United Kingdom and the Soviet Union tested nuclear weapons. A sharp change in policy came with Eisenhower's ''Atoms for Peace'' proposal in December 1953 and the revised Atomic Energy Act of 1954. If the United States were no longer sole possesser of the secret, then it would cooperate with other nations and have a voice in determining the direction of nuclear technology. It supported the activities of the

Original article by Dr. Carol Steinhart. Dr. Steinhart is project specialist in the Biometry Division, Department of Human Oncology, University of Wisconsin School of Medicine, Madison, Wisconsin 53706. She has authored or co-authored numerous articles ranging from plant metabolism to energy policy. Her publications include *Blowout: A Case Study of the Santa Barbara Oil Spill* (1972), *Energy: Sources, Use and Role in Human Affairs* (1974), *Human Ecology* (1975), and *The Fires of Culture: Energy Yesterday and Tomorrow* (1975), all published by Duxbury Press.

new International Atomic Energy Agency (IAEA), while vigorously promoting development of civilian nuclear power at home and abroad. During this period, the government's science advisers were drawn largely from men who had worked on the bomb project (see Article 14, this volume). The enthusiasm with which world-wide nuclear power was promoted stemmed from optimistic estimates of development schedules and economic benefits given by these advisers and the budding nuclear industry.

Further international attempts to encourage beneficial uses of nuclear energy while discouraging destructive uses resulted in the negotiation of the Limited Test Ban Treaty and the Treaty on the Non-Proliferation of Nuclear Weapons (NPT) during the 1960's. During this period, projections of the electric power industry showed nuclear energy taking over an ever larger share of the utility market.

During the 1970's, the government of the United States began to acknowledge the contradictions in its nuclear policy and moved to resolve them. In 1974, the AEC was abolished, largely because of the dilemmas arising from the same body trying both to promote and to regulate nuclear energy. The regulatory functions of the old AEC were assumed by the new Nuclear Regulatory Commission. The rest of the AEC's mission was absorbed into the Energy Research and Development Agency, whose jurisdiction also encompasses the other energy technologies. The Carter administration further consolidated energy-related agencies, creating a Department of Energy at the cabinet level.

Now the world stands on the brink of commitment not only to a nuclear future but to a nuclear future based on plutonium. Policy studies in the United States and abroad seriously question the wisdom of such a commitment. The issues discussed in the following pages are: (a) reactor safety, (b) environmental and health effects of production of nuclear power, (c) management of radioactive wastes, (d) proliferation of nuclear weapons, (e) nuclear terrorism, and (f) alternative, longe-range energy sources and strategies, including "proliferation-resistant" nuclear fuel cycles. Problems involved with fuel reprocessing and plutonium recycling pervade most of these issues and are considered with them. The policy studies discussed generally show an awareness that the problems are not merely economic and technological (although experts from the utilities and nuclear industry appear to think they are), but social and political as well. In fact, the technological problems may be the easiest to solve, hence the unquenchable optimism of technologists.

REACTOR SAFETY

Nuclear reactors contain enormous amounts of radioactivity in the fuel itself, in fission products, and in materials made radioactive by intense neutron bombardment. Concern about reactor safety involves two questions: If a potentially dangerous situation arises, can the reactor be shut down quickly? Can the intense heat generated by radioactive decay be removed to prevent meltdown of the reactor core? An accident serious enough to affect the public must rupture the containment structure enclosing the reactor, allowing radioactive materials to escape to the environment. The steps leading to such an accident are somewhat different in a light water reactor and a liquid-metal fast breeder reactor.

Most reactors operating today are light water reactors, which contain water at high temperature and pressure. A sudden drop in pressure would cause the heat from short-lived fission product decay to release large amounts of steam and cause loss of cooling ability. This loss-of-coolant accident (LOCA) is considered one of the most dangerous accidents in a water-cooled reactor. In the event of such a accident, buildup of heat in the reactor could melt the core. The molten core might then sink through the floor of the reactor, or high pressure or steam explosions might rupture the containment vessel. After failure of containment, radioactive material would be dispersed throughout the atmosphere.

Because of the form of its fuel, a light water reactor could never explode like a bomb. In contrast, the fast breeder uses fuel in highly concentrated form, which, in a loss-of-coolant accident, might "go critical" and explode. The explosion would not be of the proportions of that of a nuclear weapon, but it could rupture the containment vessel and allow large amounts of radioactivity to escape.

There are three lines of defense against catastrophic accidents. The first is careful design, construction, operation, and maintenance of the entire system. This includes engineering for proper performance in the event of transients—large and rapid fluctuations in temperature, pressure, or rate of fission, for example. The second line of defense includes safety features to shut down the reactor and remove the heat if malfunction occurs. The third is another set of safety features designed to prevent or to minimize harmful consequences should the primary safeguards fail.

An important feature of safety design is redundancy, so that if one component or subsystem fails another will operate. A persistent problem has been common mode failures, in which one failure affects more than one part of the system so that the expected redundancy turns out not to exist. In a complex system, it is extremely difficult to identify all possible common mode failures.

Another way to increase the margin of safety is in the selection of reactor sites. There are strong arguments for locating reactors underground. Locating them far from population centers makes sense from the standpoint of safety, but it precludes utilization of waste heat and requires expensive, wasteful transmission facilities.

After understanding the nature of reactor accidents and designing safety features to prevent them or to mitigate their effects, there remains the problem of safety analysis. Because our cumulative experience with nuclear reactors is still relatively small and the reactors have had a good safety record so far, we must rely on estimated probabilities of everything that could conceivably go wrong and of how much damage would result if these things did go wrong. Many estimates are based on design and performance standards, although some accidents have been simulated and actual experiments are being carried out on a few other types of accidents. But drawing board conditions are rarely met in the real world, and we do not always think of every possibility for engineering failure or human error. The unanticipated failures that plagued and finally aborted the Apollo 13 space mission give an example of a serious weakness in a system designed, built, and tested with meticulous care.

We have little experience with the reliability of emergency systems because they are rarely called upon. A case in point is the emergency core cooling system (ECCS), designed to take over in event of a loss-of-coolant accident. In the past, the effectiveness of this system was checked by computer calculations. But people asked if the system would *really* work. As it turned out, certain designs would not, being subject to the very common mode failure that caused the accident in the first place. Now full-scale experiments on the emergency core cooling system are being conducted.

One way of putting the hazards of nuclear power into perspective is to compare them with such other man-made and natural hazards as dam failures, air crashes, and earthquakes (see Article 17, this volume). Viewed in this way, nuclear power seems safe enough. But two studies, one by a British Royal Commission[3] and one by the Ford Foundation/MITRE Corporation,[4] emphasize the problem with this sort of comparison. For most hazards, there are firm data based on many years of experience or large numbers of cases. For nuclear hazards, we have no such experience. The British report criticizes the concept of the "maximum credible accident," asking how people decide whether a theoretically possible accident is credible or incredible and pointing out that incredible things do happen. Even statistics based on firm data can be falsely reassuring. According to graphs in the British report, an airplane crash on the ground such as the one that killed nearly 600 people in the Canary Islands early in 1977 is expected to occur about once in 1,000 years. It happened during the first half-century of commercial flying.

The studies by the Royal Commission, Ford/MITRE, and the American Physical Society (APS)[5] are, with certain qualifications, unanimous in their conclusions that light water reactors are sufficiently safe. The APS report is the most sanguine of the three. The panel feels that the safety outlook is good, and no insurmountable problems remain. It recommends continued research in all areas related to safety, emphasizing human engineering to reduce chances of human error, and automation of controls wherever possible. It sees a need for improvements in containment of an accident and in minimizing its consequences. It points to the need of resolving uncertainties in estimating risks and consequences. Rather than the current practice of imagining the worst possible accident and then designing against it (which sometimes smacks of a public relations job to convince people the reactor is safe), the APS recommends realistic assessment of a reactor's behavior in abnormal circumstances and allowance of a generous margin of safety.

The Ford/MITRE and British reports, in which the fast breeder as well as light water reactors are considered, are more reserved in their endorsement of safety. They point to special hazards of the fast breeder, especially the use of highly (chemically) reactive liquid sodium as coolant and the stringent demands placed on the structural materials of the reactor by the relentless bombardment of fast neutrons. The British report recommends that commercial development of the fast breeder be restricted until it is convincingly established that accidents can be controlled, since effects of an accident could be from ten to more than on hundred times more severe than the effects of a comparable accident in a light water reactor.

The Ford/MITRE study stresses that the organizations and procedures for ensuring reactor safety must be improved. Especially, at all stages of design, construction, and operation, safety authority must remain independent so that safety is never sacrificed to expediency. The study criticizes the Rasmussen report (see Article 17, this volume) for certain methodological defects and for underestimating uncertainties. It suggests that the fatality rate from accidents proposed by the Rasmussen report may be as much as 500 times too low. Even so, Ford/MITRE concludes that, for light water reactors, (a) the toll from expected accidents compares favorably with the toll from competing technologies,* (b) consequences of an extremely severe accident would not be greater than other major catastrophes (fire, flood, etc.) our society has handled without long-term impact, and (c) the probability of the worst credible accident is acceptably low. On this basis, they conclude that the risks associated with the light water reactor are acceptable. The fast breeder presents problems that have not yet been resolved, but the panel sees no obvious technical barriers to developing a fast breeder reactor that is as safe as a light water reactor.

The British report, too, stresses that uncertainties about the consequences of an accident are so great that the true toll could be ten times higher or lower than predicted. It concludes, however, that hazards from nuclear accidents are not great enough to suggest abandoning nuclear power on these grounds alone. But risks exist, they must be recognized, and they should be weighed carefully in making decisions on nuclear development.

ENVIRONMENTAL AND HEALTH EFFECTS OF PRODUCTION OF NUCLEAR POWER

Exposure to radiation affects all living things in similar ways. Energetic rays and particles

*By "competing technologies," Ford/MITRE means coal. Despite recent estimates (see Article 34, this volume), the panel does not consider solar and other technologies as economically competitive with nuclear energy and coal.

emitted from radioactive materials cause ionization and disrupt chemical bonds in living matter. If the dose is very large, it kills cells or entire organisms outright. Nonlethal doses sometimes cause changes in DNA, the informational material of the cell, which are passed on when the damaged cell divides. If the affected cell is a sex cell, a mutant offspring will be produced which, if it survives, can transmit faulty information to *its* offspring, and so on indefinitely. Exposure of body cells to nonlethal doses of radiation may cause cancer or leukemia. Prenatal exposure sometimes causes developmental abnormalities, such as cleft palate, as well as various cancers and leukemias. (See Articles 3 and 16, this volume.)

Radioactive materials escape into the environment at every stage of the production of nuclear power, from the mining and milling of uranium to the decommissioning of an old power plant. During the mining of uranium, gaseous radon-222 is released. It decays to polonium-210 and lead-210, which can be inhaled or can enter the human food chain by deposition on crops. This is one of the largest sources of radiation in the entire fuel cycle. After the ore has been milled, radioactive tailings often lie exposed to wind and water, providing another significant source of exposure. Even covering the tailings does not significantly reduce the long-term exposure. At the power plant itself, radioactive gases are vented to the atmosphere and cooling water becomes slightly radioactive. If plutonium recycling becomes widespread, chemical reprocessing facilities will contribute a major portion of the radioactive pollutants related to the fuel cycle.

Normally, however, nuclear power production subjects the general population to radiation equivalent to only a few per cent of the average background radiation. In comparison, the average rate of medical exposure approaches 50 per cent of background, and occupational exposures occasionally range up to 50 times background.

Standards for doses of man-made radiation have been revised repeatedly since the first occupational limits were set in England more than 50 years ago. Today, the International Commission on Radiological Protection recommends standards. Each nation can act on these recommendations as it chooses. In the United States, the National Council on Radiation Protection also recommends standards. The Environmental Protection Agency establishes and enforces standards for environmental quality. The Nuclear Regulatory Commission establishes and enforces standards for occupational exposure, and exposure of the general public, and for maximum emission levels for various facilities. Implicitly or explicitly, both the Royal Commission and Ford/MITRE panels express confidence in the existing standards and in the institutional arrangements for establishing and enforcing them.

There are glaring uncertainties, however, in predicting the consequences of radiation on which such standards are based. It is senseless to speak of "radiation" in general as if we were bathed in radiation as we are bathed in the light of the sun. Each isotope presents its individual hazards related to its half-life, the nature of the products to which it decays, how it enters the body, and what parts of the body it affects. Exposure to a given amount of radiation from one isotope might be harmless; of another, deadly. Questions also persist about the long-term effects of low doses of radiation and whether dose-response thresholds exist in all cases (see Article 19, this volume.) Most serious are the uncertainties about how radioactive substances are distributed and accumulate in the environment and become concentrated in food chains upon which man depends. Pollutants sometimes return to haunt us in surprising ways. What may be harmless levels of release today could become damaging as radioactivity accumulates and use of nuclear energy increases.

One of the APS reports[6] recommends increased efforts to measure and minimize the collective occupational dose and to develop new standards for occupational exposure. The Ford/MITRE and British reports are cautiously optimistic in their conclusions about emissions standards and health risks. The British report concludes that current standards, if met, give adequate protection against dangers of radioisotopes including plutonium. Ford/MITRE compares the health effects of nuclear energy to those of coal, which they say is the only major alternative source of electricity in this century. Both technologies will produce a certain number of immediate and delayed deaths, as well as illness and discomfort. In the balance, Ford/MITRE concludes that, in the absence of accidents, nuclear energy has less adverse impact on health than has coal. But accidents must be considered, and here nuclear energy presents much greater hazards than coal. Resolution of the uncertainties in relative health risks could tip the scale in favor of either coal or nuclear energy. Therefore, Ford/MITRE believes that consideration of health costs should not be a factor in choosing between the two in the present state of knowledge.

Environmental problems of nuclear power include effects of radiation, waste heat, and land use. Ford/MITRE does not consider radiation damage to species other than man. The British report concludes that populations of most organisms can probably survive increased incidence of tumors and decreased fertility due to radiation, although populations that are already under environmental stress may be lost. It recommends monitoring areas that receive higher levels of radiation.

Waste heat is a potentially serious problem in any large-scale use of energy. In the generation of electricity, it is most notorious for its effects on aquatic ecosystems. But the British report and Ford/MITRE warn that the possible impact on global climate is the most serious consequence of generating increasing amounts of electricity. Any climatic change has potentially disastrous implications for agriculture and natural ecosystems. The critical level of heat release is estimated to be a few per cent of an area's solar energy flux. In many places, waste heat release already exceeds 1 per cent of the solar flux, and in a few places (such as Fairbanks, Alaska) it is greater than the solar flux during winter. No one is certain how waste heat might change the climate or if the change, over all, would be "bad" or "good." It would almost certainly be more complicated than a simple warming of average temperatures.

In weighing the impact of energy on land use, Ford/MITRE concludes that coal is more disruptive than uranium. Larger areas of land are involved in mining and storage of coal, and acid mine drainage pollutes rivers and lakes. The report states that much coal underlies productive regions. (This claim is questionable. The coal fields of Appalachia and the arid West, where most of our coal resources lie, are marginally productive at best.) Uranium mining and milling, however, releases radioactivity to the atmosphere and waterways; and whatever advantage uranium has over coal at present with respect to mining will diminish as lower grade ores are mined.

A comparison between coal and nuclear power must also take into account the environmental effects of air pollution. In addition to health problems, extensive damage to property and to crops and other plant life results from emissions of coal-fired power plants. It is possible (though expensive) to burn coal cleanly, avoiding all the troublemakers but one: carbon dioxide. By increasing the level of carbon dioxide in the atmosphere we are virtually certain to affect global climate. Ford/MITRE suggests that if and when we determine what effect increased carbon dioxide is having on climate, this effect could be the deciding factor in a decision between coal and nuclear power. Again, the report fails to consider solar energy as an option in this century and to compare its much smaller adverse health and environmental effects with those of coal and nuclear fuel.

The British report sums up its remarks on environmental effects of nuclear energy this way: "There are substantial environmental objections to a nuclear power programme on the scale envisaged in official projections."

MANAGEMENT OF RADIOACTIVE WASTES

Any nuclear fuel cycle generates gaseous, liquid, and solid wastes including large amounts of radioactive trash. Our experience with management of this waste has not been good. There have been recurrent problems with environmental contamination from intentional dumping, surface storage facilities, and shallow burial sites. It is not surprising, then, that many people are unconvinced that adequate technology for waste disposal is available when all they see are the mistakes of the past.

The Ford/MITRE and APS[6] reports view problems from existing wastes as a result of previous poor judgment and shortsightedness, largely in the nuclear weapons program. To date, waste management has been characterized by split and misplaced responsibilities and improper substitution of short- for long-term goals. This is one of many cases in which the social and institutional aspects of a problem are as real as and more difficult than the technical ones. The fact is that waste management techniques are well developed in theory, but not in practice. The state of waste technology is discussed by Platt and Bartlett (Article 18, this volume).

At the root of the problem has been the assumption that nuclear wastes would one day be reprocessed to recover plutonium. Large amounts of waste have not been disposed at all, merely stored pending decisions on reprocessing. It has been widely thought, particularly abroad, that reprocessing is necessary to decrease the long-term hazards of wastes, as well as for economic reasons. The Ford/MITRE and British studies question this idea. They point out that the economic benefits of reprocessing are marginal at best and that management of spent fuel is much easier and safer than management of wastes from reprocessing. In fact, they conclude that whatever benefits for long-term safety are derived from reprocessing are small compared to the hazards of reprocessing and the plutonium fuel cycle.

The status of waste management in the rest of the world, is about as uncertain as it is in the United States. West Germany has advanced technology for disposal in salt beds, but other countries have not yet decided on long-term solutions to the problem of waste. Many countries require or anticipate recycling of plutonium, which increases the complexity of waste management. It is likely that international agreements must be made to aid countries with small nuclear programs or with unsuitable geology for permanent waste disposal.

Because the size and the complexity of future management problems depend partly on the fuel cycles chosen, with plutonium recycling increasing the range and difficulty of the problems, the Ford/MITRE report recommends: (a) postponing recycle to gain time for demonstration technology and to make institutional arrangements and management decisions; (b) retrievable storage of spent fuel in the same geological formations that would be used for permanent storage, pending decisions on recycling; and (c) integration of military and civilian waste programs. Although the report expresses confidence in our ultimate ability to handle wastes safely, it emphasizes the need for demonstration of waste disposal technology before its intensive use.

The British report is less confident, warning that "There should be no commitment to a large programme of nuclear fission power until it has been demonstrated beyond reasonable doubt that a method exists to ensure the safe containment of long-lived, highly radioactive waste for the indefinite future." It questions the wisdom of ocean dumping as it is practiced by a group of European nations according to international guidelines. It recognizes two reasonable options for permanent disposal of vitrified wastes, geological formations and below ocean beds, but believes that neither has been sufficiently studied or demonstrated. It expresses concern about the future impact of the radioactive gases that are currently vented to the atmosphere and suggests developing techniques to control them.

In sharp contrast to the skepticism of the Royal Commission, the APS report[6] categorically asserts that for all light water reactor fuel cycles, technologies exist or can easily be developed for the management of wastes and the control of effluents. It points out, however, that technical choices cannot be made without further decisions on policy. In contradiction to the Ford/MITRE and British studies, the APS report concludes that the decision to reprocess nuclear fuel does not depend significantly on waste management considerations. Its principal recommendations include (a) setting a high priority for completion of Federal regulations and standards; (b) completing and demonstrating the technology for interim storage and long-term disposal of spent reactor fuel; (c) continuing research on other suggested technologies as future alternatives to geological disposal as now envisioned; (d) reevaluating management of uranium mill tailings; and (e) perfecting technology for the control of radioactive gases.

None of the reports considers that protection of disposal sites from intrusion by people with nefarious intentions or by future, unsuspecting generations poses any technical or social problems.

PROLIFERATION OF NUCLEAR WEAPONS

One consequence of nuclear power that dominates all others is the accompanying increase in the number of nations that will have access to the materials and technology for nuclear weapons. In 1974, India exploded a "peaceful nuclear device," and with it she also exploded the belief that there is a practical distinction between peaceful and military uses of nuclear energy. The grim reality is that almost any nation with civilian nuclear power can build a bomb if it so chooses. Table 22-1, derived from the Royal Commission Report, documents the growth of nuclear power in the world and suggests the scope of the proliferation problem that confronts us.

The dangers of proliferation have been widely recognized for many years. Most nations at least pay lip service to the ideal of non-proliferation, whether or not they are parties to the NPT. But the decision not to acquire nuclear weapons is not irrevocable. It is a commitment that must be constantly renewed, and there is nothing, under present international agreements and controls, to prevent a nation from fabricating all the separate parts of a nuclear weapon while maintaining its non-weapon status in the eyes of the NPT and the IAEA. Any nation can terminate its commitment to the NPT on three months' notice, after which a bomb could be assembled within hours. So much for the power of a signed piece of paper, in the absence of good faith among nations and in the presence of domestic and international instability and stress.

Policy studies are in general agreement as to how the problem of proliferation should be

Table 22–1. Countries Operating or Expecting to Operate Commercial Nuclear Reactors above 100 Megawatt, with their Status under the NPT.

Period	*Cumulative Total*	*Countries*[a]
1955–1959	2	United States (r); United Kingdom (r)
1960–1964	5	Soviet Union (r); Italy (r); France (—)
1965–1969	11	Japan (r); West Germany (r); Canada (r); India (—); Spain (r); Switzerland (r)
1970–1974	19	Pakistan (—); Czechoslovakia (r); Netherlands (r); Argentina (—); East Germany (r); Belgium (r); Sweden (r); Bulgaria (r)
1975–1979	25	Korea (r); Taiwan (r); Finland (r); Austria (r); Mexico (r); Brazil (—)
1980–1984	32	Yugoslavia (r); Iran (r); Hungary (r); South Africa (—); Philippines (r); Egypt (s); Israel (—)

[a] s, signed; r, ratified.

attacked: (a) weaken incentives for proliferation (by, for example, working to resolve international conflicts peacefully and reducing the prestige associated with nuclear weapons); (b) strengthen the disincentives for proliferation (by political and economic sanctions, for example); and (c) improve international safeguards. There is also agreement that world-wide reprocessing of fuel and recycling of plutonium would make the problem of proliferation much worse or, some say, intractable.

In a somber appraisal, the British report observes that the proliferation problem is very serious and will not go away by our refusing to acknowledge it. It points out that although the possession of large nuclear arsenals by the United States and the Soviet Union may have been a strong mutual deterrent to their use, it is absurd to conclude that proliferation would similarly lead to balance and restraint among all nations. With respect to plutonium, the report states: "It appears to us that the dangers of the creation of plutonium in large quantities under conditions of increasing world unrest are genuine and serious. For this reason we think it remarkable that none of the official documents we have seen . . . convey any unease on this score. The management and safeguarding of plutonium are regarded as just another problem arising from nuclear development, and as one which can certainly be solved given suitable control arrangements. Nowhere is there any suggestion of apprehension about the possible long-term dangers to the fabric and freedom of our society. Our consideration of these matters, however, has led us to the view that we should not rely for energy supply on a process that produces such a hazardous substance as plutonium unless there is no reasonable alternative."

One reason for the strange lack of doubt that proliferation problems can be solved may be that advice on nuclear matters is commonly sought from scientists and technologists. These people are trained to develop rational answers that may be tested and verified with confidence because of the inviolable "laws" of nature. If they can provide rational solutions to proliferation, they reason, these solutions should work. But the problems are no longer in the realm of physics and engineering. They are in the realm of the sometimes irrational, unpredictable, and unlawful behavior of people and nations. As the British report warns, the unquantifiable effects of the security measures that might become necessary in a plutonium economy must be a major consideration in decisions on substantial nuclear development. This issue requires wide public debate and understanding.

The Ford/MITRE study takes a more operational approach to the problem of proliferation than does the British. Pointing out that for many countries, nuclear weapons offer dubious advantages and considerable risk, it analyzes the advantages and disadvantages of such weapons and the situations in which the balance between the two might shift in the perception of the nation involved. It stresses that the programs and policies of the United States that are designed to constrain proliferation can be only partially effective without broad international cooperation and effective international arrangements. A broad spectrum of foreign policy issues is involved, many of which do not relate to nuclear power. They include a commitment to long-term international peace, security, and stability (goals the British report considers unattainable); security commitments to reduce the perceived need of other nations for nuclear weapons; use of influence to discourage apparent moves toward nuclear weapons status; arms limitation and disarmament agreements; deemphasis of nuclear weapons in military policy; and cooperation in international development of the full range of energy resources. Nowhere does the report question whether the programs listed are or will necessarily remain in the over-all best interests of our foreign policy or whether it is desirable to have foreign policy tightly constrained by problems related to energy.

With direct regard to nuclear power, Ford/MITRE recommends seeking out the most "proliferation resistant" fuel cycles and working to strengthen and improve arrangements for controlling the fuel cycle. It expresses the belief that a decision by the United States to go ahead, full speed, with the fast breeder and plutonium recycling would probably encourage world-wide movement toward a plutonium economy. But it is uncertain whether a policy to forgo the breeder and plutonium recycling would have the opposite effect.

The study by Cochran and Tamplin[1] documents numerous loopholes and weaknesses in the NPT, the IAEA, and other international arrangements to constrain proliferation. The authors express concern (with some factual support) about the weapons intentions of certain nations including Brazil, Israel, and Taiwan. These considerations have convinced them that, in the future development of nuclear power, all economic and technical considerations must be secondary to the objective of obtaining a high degree of separation between nuclear power and nuclear weapons technologies. In particular, they urge an unequivocal rejection of plans to reprocess nuclear fuel at any time in the foreseeable future, either here or abroad. Similar concerns are expressed by a minority report of the LMFBR Review Steering Committee.[2] (The majority report was unavailable at this writing. However, it was favorable to the breeder reactor and its associated fuel cycle, and concluded that the fast breeder research and development should be carried out with some urgency.) In presenting the minority view, the committee members recommend (a) nonproliferation objectives must take precedence over economic benefits; (b) nonproliferation criteria must be established to govern fission energy activities; (c) use of any energy technology must leave a nonweapon state no closer to a nuclear weapons capability than it would be if all its nuclear power came from low-enriched uranium fueled reactors operating without reprocessing and with verified spent fuel storage in secured international facilities; and (d) the United States' breeder research and development program should be converted to one aimed at preserving nuclear fission as an energy option for the long term in a manner consistent with nonproliferation objectives. This last recommendation precludes commercialization of the plutonium fast breeder reactor and its associated fuel cycle.

NUCLEAR TERRORISM

The use of nuclear power inevitably brings an unquantifiable but real danger of nuclear blackmail and sabotage from terrorists, extremists, criminals, and lunatics. If a worldwide plutonium industry develops, theft of plutonium—or even growth of an international black market in plutonium—seems likely. Cochran and Tamplin[1] report that during the period from 1968 through 1975 in the United States, there were 99 reported threats and acts of violence directed against licensed nuclear facilities, 76 against unlicensed nuclear facilities, and 28 involving nuclear materials. In 1973, a guerrilla group occupied a reactor in Argentina, and in two separate incidents in 1975, bombs were detonated in French nuclear plants. Clearly, the threat of terrorism is serious and has international ramifications. Neither terrorists nor clouds of radioactivity are stopped by political boundaries. The safety of nuclear facilities everywhere is of concern to each nation.

It would be possible for a knowledgeable group of armed terrorists to seize a nuclear power plant and damage the reactor so as to cause a meltdown and release of radioactivity. This act might claim the lives of those perpetrating it, but it would have the same consequences as a serious reactor accident. At the least, the group could count on damaging the reactor enough to cause significant economic loss and to have a great psychological impact. The Royal Commission Report further warns of attacks on nuclear installations during a war (even a conventional one). If nuclear power had been widespread at the time of World War II, it points out, some areas of central Europe would probably still be uninhabitable because of contamination by cesium-137.

Construction of a nuclear bomb would present formidable difficulties for and dangers to any group attempting it. Nevertheless, the equipment required is not very elaborate, and the necessary information on principles of bomb construction, properties of explosives, and the physics and chemistry of uranium and plutonium is available in the open technical literature. The yield of a terrorist bomb is very uncertain, as much a matter of good luck as of good judgment. Even in a well-planned effort, there is a good chance that the bomb would fail to detonate or that the group would suffer fatal accidents during its construction. The most likely yield of a successful bomb would be equivalent to a few tons of TNT; with exceptional luck it might equal 100 tons of TNT or more. But any explosion would be damaging, and regardless of the odds, the threat to explode such a weapon would place a government in an appalling dilemma.

The hazards of plutonium arise not only from its explosive properties but from its extreme radiotoxicity. Dispersed into the atmosphere by conventional explosives, a small quantity of plutonium could cause an indeterminate number of deaths from lung cancer or fibrosis of the lung. In any case, the psychological impact of such a situation would be profound, normal activity in the affected area would be disrupted, and decontamination could be very expensive.

The reports by the Royal Commission, Ford/MITRE, and Cochran and Tamplin are unanimous in the conclusion that existing national and international security measures could not prevent sabotage of a nuclear facility or theft of nuclear materials by a determined group. Cochran and Tamplin go so far as to say that adequate protection is impossible, short of turning nuclear facilities into heavily armed camps. The weakest point in the system is transport. Nuclear weapons and nuclear materials owned by the Energy Research and Development Administration are transported under strict security. But commercial nuclear materials are transported by procedures similar to those used by carriers of any highly valuable cargo. We know from experience that criminals and terrorists can circumvent these precautions.

The Ford/MITRE study considered security measures at both the technical and the institutional levels. Possible technical measures for increasing security include improvements in communications and inventory systems. The practice of radioactive "spiking" to facilitate detection of lost or stolen nuclear materials is not recommended because spiking itself produces an additional radiation hazard.

Ford/MITRE finds industry and different levels of the government poorly prepared to deal with acts of terrorism because the responsibilities of various groups have not been defined clearly. In the federal government alone, numerous agencies would be involved, including Civil Defense, Federal Bureau of Investigation, the Nuclear Regulatory Commission, and the Department of Energy. Over all, Ford/MITRE finds that measures to strengthen security at the local, national, and international levels need to be carefully developed and vigorously carried out. Federal regulation and training of security forces are seen as essential.

The Ford/MITRE panelists feel that improved security measures can be introduced without endangering civil liberties, although they recognize some potential problems. They compare nuclear terrorism with airline terrorism, suggesting that all nations are mutually dependent and have a common interest in preventing both. When airplane hijacking became commonplace, "modest increases in security bought a lot." Perhaps, they reason, similarly modest improvements would substantially decrease the likelihood of terrorism at nuclear facilities.

Three areas of concern with regard to civil liberties are (a) safeguarding rights of employees, (b) safeguarding rights of the general public, and (c) the widespread disturbance that would be caused by a search for stolen nuclear materials. Ford/MITRE considers 30,000 nuclear employees that would be subjected to security clearance insignificant compared to the 5,000,000 people already subject to such clearance, and believes that adequate legal protection for the rights of employees already exists. Domestic surveillance poses more of a problem. Targets for surveillance would include criminals, terrorists, and "possibly domestic dissidents," both U.S. citizens and foreign nationals. In event of an actual or a threatened crisis, civil liberties would be subjected to greater pressure. Should a terrorist act occur, public reaction might demand that steps be taken to ensure that such an event could not recur. Ford/MITRE also sees some risk that tactics employed during a crisis might be carried over into routine operations or extended to other law enforcement problems.

The British and Cochran and Tamplin reports express a great deal more concern over the erosion of civil liberties than does Ford/MITRE. They point out that where known or suspected members of extremist or terrorist groups, or employees with undesirable contacts, are concerned, security procedures would involve some combination of informers, infiltrators, wire tapping, checking on bank accounts, and opening of mail. This comes at a time when people are expressing indignation at the extent to which surveillance of private citizens is already carried on. Although the United States is in the process of setting limits on the activities of federal investigative agencies, threats of nuclear terrorism would require creation of a federal police force with wide powers. Should a theft of plutonium occur, attempts at recovery would involve no-knock search, search and interrogation without warrant, area search, preventive detention, press censorship, and community evacuation. In the event of nuclear blackmail, Cochran and Tamplin believe that martial law would be likely.

The British report warns of an insidious growth in surveillance in response to increased amounts of plutonium and familiarity with it. A serious incident in the future might precipitate oppressive (but by then unavoidable) security measures. Although they feel serious risks from terrorism probably lie well into the future, the British panel warns that we dare not wait until problems actually arise because by then it will be too late to worry about the effects of needed safeguards on civil liberties.

All the reports present a pessimistic view of prospects for effective international safeguards. Although the IAEA has published guidelines for security at nuclear facilities, they are only advisory. Ford/MITRE urges the United States to propose that security be included in all future international agreements on nuclear energy. At the same time, analyzing the small to nonexistent economic and resource advantages of the fast breeder reactor and plutonium recycling, the report concludes that it has not been shown that suggested international security measures would reduce risks to a level commensurate with the questionable benefits of the breeder and of fuel reprocessing. Social considerations argue strongly against the plutonium fuel cycle. Therefore, the panel asserts, reprocessing should be deferred indefinitely, the United States should not subsidize completion or operation of existing facilities and should seek alternatives to a world-wide plutonium economy.

Cochran and Tamplin are also skeptical that any future system of safeguards would effectively prevent terrorism. Such a system would have to operate on a world-wide scale, and the authors see no reason to believe that international cooperation on the necessary scale is possible. Their conclusion is that we should therefore unequivocally reject the idea that plutonium should ever be reprocessed and thereby removed from the protection of the intensely radioactive spent reactor fuel. The British report expresses a reluctance to count on any nation's stability or political system for as far into the future as would be necessary to ensure reliability of security agreements.

Alvin Weinberg** has postulated a future "nuclear priesthood," a dedicated, self-perpetuating technological elite, entrusted

**Alvin Weinberg. Social Institutions and Nuclear Energy, *Science 177* (4043):27, 1972.

through the generations with the task of protecting society from the hazards of nuclear energy. It is nothing less than this kind of future that must be weighed in today's policy decisions on plutonium and nuclear power.

ALTERNATIVE LONG-RANGE ENERGY SOURCES AND STRATEGIES

Nuclear energy policy decisions should be based on the widest possible analysis of alternative futures, not on the most expedient way to realize the projections of the utility industries. The major studies considered here agree that it is desirable to keep a variety of energy options open and to either postpone commercial development of the fast breeder indefinitely or forgo it entirely. Beyond that, there are sharp differences in the approaches and biases of the panels.

The LMFBR Steering Committee minority report points out that the economy of the United States is relatively insensitive to energy intensity over the long term and concludes that energy efficiency and conservation are more in the national interest than is the growth expected by the electric utilities. In any case, growth in electricity use must level off early in the next century because there is a limit to the degree of electrification possible.

The timetable for development of fission will depend on trends in demands for electricity and size of uranium resources. Recent growth in electricity use has been much slower than expected, and the LMFBR panel thinks that all but the lowest projections for future growth are "absurd." Knowledge of ultimate uranium resources is uncertain. Some recent reports express the doubt that more than one-half of the postulated high-grade ore will ever be found, whereas others point out that exploration for uranium has been limited and that the total resource base is probably much larger than we now think. The panel concludes, however, that as long as growth of fission power continues to be as slow as now appears likely, not even the most pessimistic estimates of uranium supplies justify commercial development of the fast breeder—especially since a number of proliferation-resistant and resource-conserving alternatives to the plutonium cycle exist. (These fuel cycles are discussed in Article 20, this volume.)

A study prepared for the Joint Economic Committee of Congress[7] concludes that uranium resources are probably much greater than suggested by early estimates; supplies seem assured until well into the twenty-first century; growth in electricity use is reaching a plateau and, beyond 1980, will be nearer 2 per cent than the past rate of 7 per cent; the days of declining energy prices are over; and the economic benefits of the plutonium fuel cycle are marginal. These conclusions argue for a close look at alternatives to the official energy strategy of the recent past.

The Ford/MITRE panel analyzes the dependence of the economic future of the United States on the cost and supply of energy using various assumptions based on the rate of development of nuclear power and reliance on fossil fuels, and largely ignoring alternative energy sources. The panel concludes that energy costs within the range foreseen are not critical in determining the economic or social future. They assert further that neither scarcity nor cost of energy will force fundamental changes in social and economic structure or in life-styles. This is a very surprising conclusion that leaves one wishing that the panel would say what it considers a fundamental change. Both theory and experience with systems show that change in one part has ramifications throughout the whole. In a culture, as in any other system, "everything is related to everything else." Surely something as basic as patterns of energy use has profound influence on social and economic structure and life-style. Consider the impact of the automobile on society. Future changes in transportation brought about by energy cost and supply will have similarly large and pervasive effects.

In asserting that coal and nuclear energy are the only real choices for the rest of this century, the Ford/MITRE panelists recommend

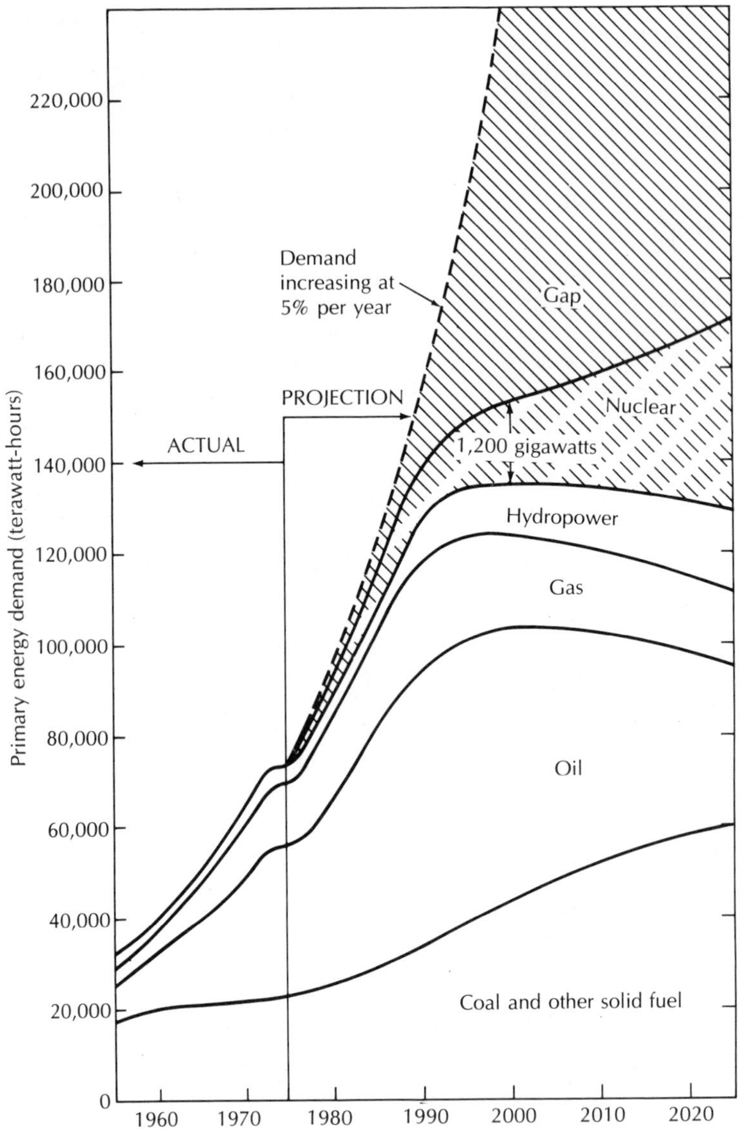

Figure 22-1. World energy demands, and a possible means of supply, projected to 2025. (Ref. 3.)

that a broad study of other energy sources be undertaken while avoiding premature commercialization before the alternatives are economically competitive. Here, their conclusions are based only on economics, which may not be justified, just as economic considerations are not the major criteria for choosing a nuclear fuel cycle.

But even on purely economic grounds, some of the panel's analyses are questionable. The panel seems unaware of the large literature on the technology, applications, and potential of wind and solar energy. Assuming 100 mills per kilowatt-hour as an achievable cost of solar electric power, they declare solar electricity noncompetitive. But Honeywell and Black and Veatch have designed a solar electric plant that they believe will produce electricity at a cost of 35 to 50 mills per kilowatt (1974 dollars). This overlaps the cost range for nuclear power, and it is no environmentalist's fantasy but the estimate of a group that proposes to build such a plant. As for wind power, the panel quotes "untried advanced designs, if successful" at "as low as $1,000 per peak kilowatt," and then assumes that they will put out no more than one-fifth to one-third this much useful energy. But existing and widely used "off-the-shelf" models from Switzerland and Canada already cost as little as $840 per peak kilowatt, and in favorable sites their performance is much better than that assumed by Ford/MITRE. Truly advanced designs have capital costs estimated at $400 to $500 per peak kilowatt.†

In contrast to energy use in industrialized nations, world energy use must continue to grow rapidly until well into the next century, as developing countries seek to improve their economic condition. But the world will soon reach the peak of petroleum production, after which severe shortages are expected.[3] Figure 22-1, from the Royal Commission report, shows one suggested mix of world energy sources projected to the year 2025. The graph shows realistic limitations on the availability of energy from conventional sources and projects the huge gap between supply and demand if major alternative sources of energy are not developed. The British panel does not predict whether the energy gap will materialize or whether nuclear power will be able to fill it. They note, however, that to fill the gap with nuclear power an average of three large reactors would have to be commissioned each week for the rest of the century—something that is clearly not going to happen. In addition, large nuclear plants are inappropriate for most needs of most developing countries. Fortunately, many such countries are so situated that wind, solar, and water power could fill a major portion of their energy needs, with conventional fuels supplying the rest.

The Royal Commission report emphasizes that a wise energy strategy must match the source to the need. The basic needs are for low temperature heat (primarily for space heating), high temperature heat (for industrial processes), mechanical power, transportation, and specifically electric applications (which are actually few in number but include lighting and electronics). The panel recommends making use of waste heat in district heating systems and using central boilers rather than power plants. The trend toward total electrification and centralized power production is seen as wasteful and undesirable, on economic and environmental grounds.

In supporting their recommendation to develop a variety of energy sources and keep open as many options as possible, the British panel shows the striking contrast between "official" energy strategy and one of the many possible alternative strategies, illustrated in Figures 22-2 and 22-3. The official strategy shows the result of depending heavily on nuclear energy in terms of inefficiency and the total primary energy produced. The alternative strategy delivers the same amount of useful energy, but much more efficiently. It utilizes a wide range of energy sources, with only minor dependence on nuclear fission. It might work and it might not, and if it worked for the United Kingdom, it would not necessarily be optimal or even possible for the United States or the rest of the world. But it illustrates that skepticism may be in order when the official strategists decide what will be necessary to meet energy needs of the future. Whether or not solar, wind, geothermal, and other energy sources will provide substantial amounts of energy in the future depends on decisions that are being made now, just as the present favored position of nuclear energy depended on decisions (and vast expenditures) made during the 1950's.

†Bent Sorensen, 1976, Dependability of wind energy generators with short-term energy storage, *Science 194*, 26 November.

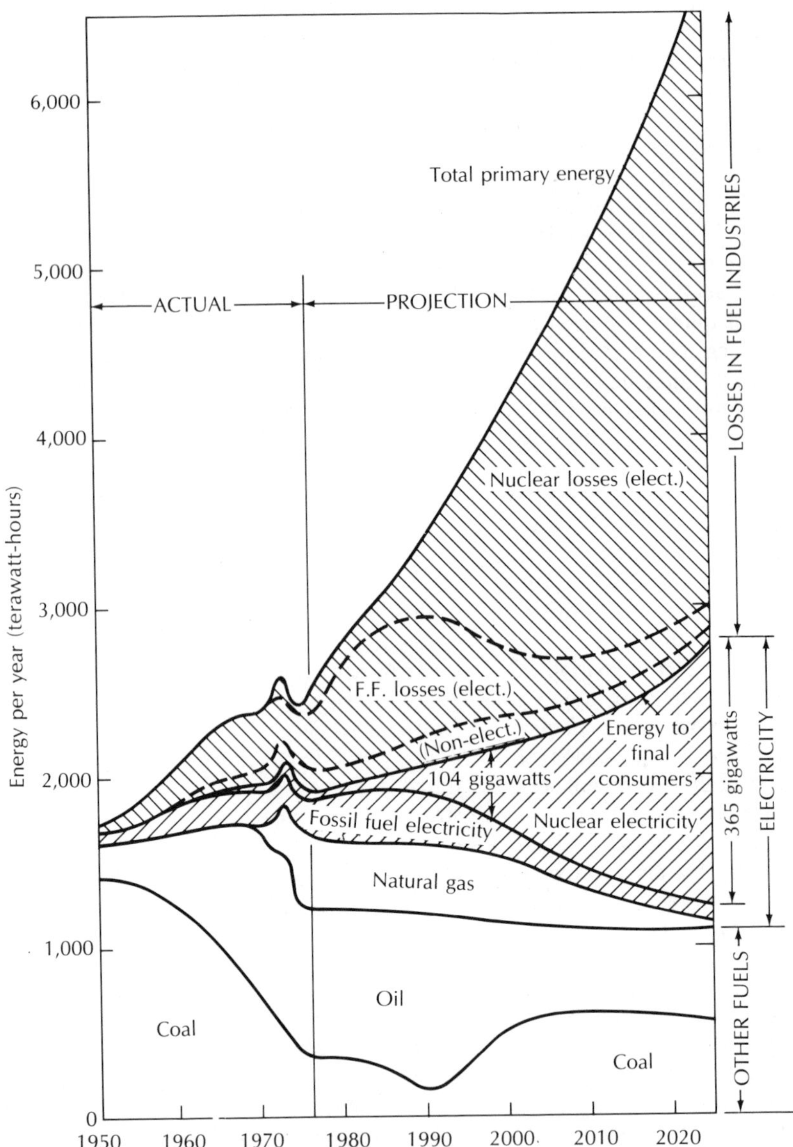

Figure 22-2. The provision of energy for the United Kingdom, projected to 2025, on the "official strategy." (Ref. 3.)

In their recommendations on future energy supply, the Royal Commission urges an increased emphasis on conservation and on alternative energy sources including nuclear fusion. It stresses the importance of comprehensive exploration and assessment of alternative strategies, encouraging freedom and originality of thought *unfettered by institutional pressures and the need to justify existing policies*.

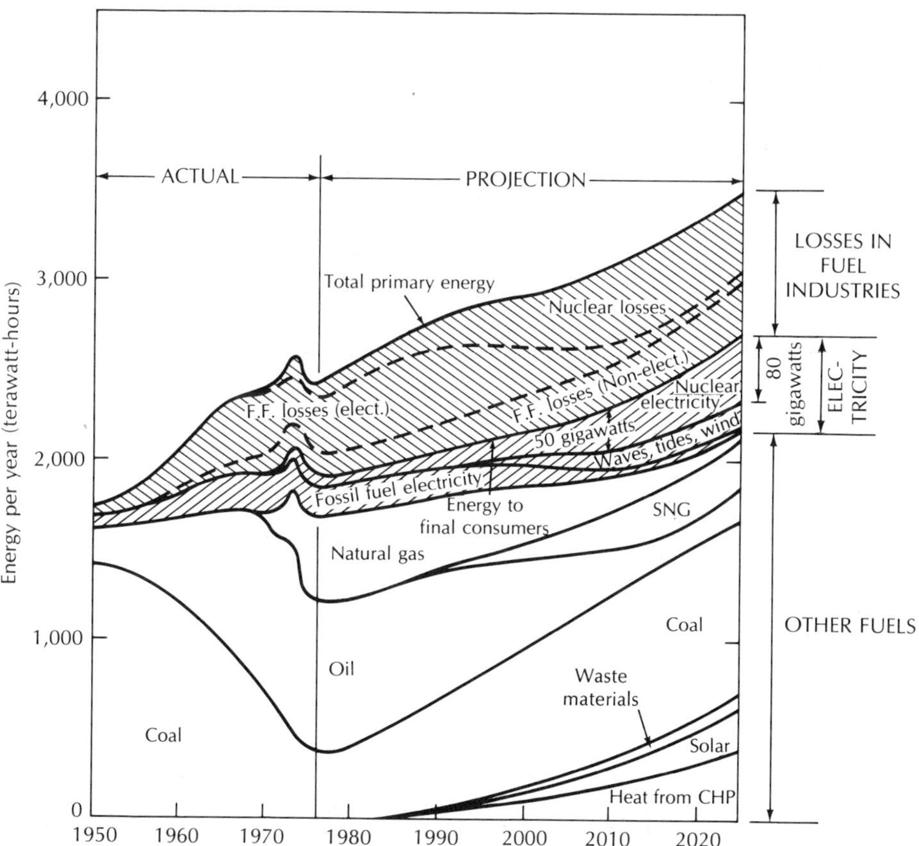

Figure 22-3. The provision of energy for the United Kingdom, projected to 2025, on the "alternative strategy." (Ref. 3.)

Policy studies reveal many things about the individuals who made the study—about their personal areas of expertise, but more importantly, about their visions, hopes, and fears for the future. This is probably as it should be, because any policy must be directed at achieving some goal. Perhaps we are doing it backwards. Perhaps we should first think more carefully about our goals for the future and then seek an energy policy that is compatible with them.

REFERENCES

1. Thomas B. Cochran and Arthur R. Tamplin, Nuclear Weapons Proliferation—The State Threat and the Non-State Adversary. Position paper for the National Resources Defense Council, Inc. (1977).
2. Thomas B. Cochran, Russell E. Train, Frank von Hippel, and Robert H. Williams, Proliferation Resistant Nuclear Power Technologies: Preferred Alternatives to the Plutonium Breeder (Minority report of the LMFBR Review Steering Committee, 1977).
3. Nuclear Power and the Environment (Report of the Royal Commission on Environmental Pollution, London, 1976).
4. Report of the Nuclear Energy Policy Study Group, Nuclear Power, Issues and Choices. Ford Foundation/MITRE Corporation (Ballinger, Cambridge, Mass., 1977).
5. Report to the American Physical Society by the Study Group on Light-water Reactor Safety. *Reviews of Modern Physics 47,* Suppl. No. 1., Summer (1975).

6. Report to the American Physical Society by the Study Group on Nuclear Fuel Cycles and Waste Management, 1977.
7. The Fast Breeder Reactor Decision: An Analysis of Limits and the Limits of Analysis. A Study Prepared for the Joint Economic Committee Congress of the United States (U.S. Govt. Printing Office, Washington, D.C., April 1976).

SUGGESTED READINGS

Campana, Robert J., and Sidney Langer, Eds, 1976, Questions and Answers, Nuclear Power and the Environment, American Nuclear Society.

Forbes, I. A., M. W. Goldsmith, A. C. Kadak, J. B. Muckerheide, J. C. Tarnage, and G. J. Brown, 1976, The Nuclear Debate: A Call to Reason (Energy Research Group, Inc.), 17 p.

Murphy, Arthur W., Ed., 1976, *The Nuclear Controversy* (Prentice-Hall, Englewood Cliffs, New Jersey), 185 p.

Schmidt, Fred H., and David Bodansky, 1976, The Energy Controversy—The Fight over Nuclear Power (Albion Publishing Co., San Francisco, California), 154 p.

Stauffer, T. R., H. L. Wyckoff, and R. S. Palmer, 1977, To Breed or Not To Breed?, *Mechanical Engineering 99*, pp. 32–41.

Willrich, Mason, 1976, International Energy Issues and Options, *Annual Review of Energy 1*, pp. 743–772.

IV

ALTERNATIVE ENERGY SOURCES

Scyllac, the Atomic Energy Commission's recent experiment in fusion. The goal of the Controlled Thermonuclear Research Program at the Los Alamos, New Mexico, Scientific Laboratory is to develop this process as a cheap, clean source of energy, particularly electricity. (Photo courtesy of the Los Alamos Scientific Laboratory.)

The Solar Residence Laboratory, Colorado State University, Ft. Collins, Colorado. Top, a solar-heated, three-bedroom house, used as offices. Note that the roof panels are flat-plate collectors. Bottom, data-recording apparatus and plumbing for solar heating in the basement. (Photo courtesy of the Solar Energy Applications Laboratory.)

The Sunpak™ solar energy collector developed by Owens-Illinois, Inc. Top, these Sunpak™ collectors are mounted on a grid system that spans the courtyard and main entrance of the Terraset Elementary School in Reston, Virginia. Nationally recognized for its innovative design, the school won the 1975 Energy Conservation Award from Owens-Corning Fiberglas Corporation. Bottom, the glass tubular collector uses air or liquid to absorb solar energy. Each collector tube consists of a small feeder tube (pulled out, above), which distributed fluid throughout the system; an absorber tube, in which the fluid is heated; and a clear outer tube, which is evacuated to cut down heat loss. (Photos courtesy of John E. Hoff, Owens-Illinois, Inc.)

Wind power, once used extensively in rural America, is again being considered as an alternative to our fossil fuel supply. (Photo courtesy of the Federal Energy Administration.)

The Great Canadian Oil Sands, Ltd., LMG bucketwheel excavator, the Athabasca Oil Sands, Fort McMurray, Alberta, Canada. This 4.6 million-dollar excavator can dig 54,000 tons of sand daily, yielding 50,000 to 55,000 barrels of oil. (Photo courtesy of J. Perehinec, Public Relations Department, Great Canadian Oil Sands, Ltd.)

The Geysers Steam Field, Sonoma County, California. This is the largest geothermal power development in the world, generating 502,000 kilowatts (electric) from 10 power plant units. (Photo courtesy of C. C. Newton, Public Information Department, Pacific Gas and Electric Company.)

Feedlot of the Nebraska Feeding Company, Omaha, Nebraska, in 1968. About 6,000 cattle can be fed here at one time. Such feedlots may be prime locations for facilities that convert certain organic wastes, i.e., cattle manure, into methane gas to be used as a source of energy. (Photo courtesy of the U.S. Department of Agriculture, Office of Information; USDA photo.)

INTRODUCTION

Although the fossil fuels and uranium will continue to dominate the energy picture through the end of this century, they both fall into the "finite resource" category and must eventually be replaced by alternative energy sources. In this chapter, we examine some of the most promising alternatives and try to understand some of the technical, economic, and environmental factors that are affecting their implementation. Once these factors are appreciated, the development of these energy alternatives can be seen in a more natural historical perspective, and less justification remains for various "conspiracy theories" to explain the present pattern of energy research and development.

With the exception of fusion energy (whose technical feasibility has not even been proven) and geothermal energy (whose technical and economic feasibility are both well established), the main theme underlying the discussion of most alternative energy sources is the following: *This alternative is now somewhat more expensive than conventional fuels, but as the cost of such fuels escalate and as mass production is applied to the alternative, it will surely become competitive*. This argument was proposed in the 1950's and 1960's for nuclear fission and verified in the early 1970's. It was proposed in the 1960's and early 1970's for solar energy, which, as the discussions in this chapter indicate, is on the verge of economic feasilility. The petroleum resources in shales and tar sands require only a guarantee of the present price structure or a modest increase in OPEC oil prices to make them commercially feasibile, and some fusion optimists are even estimating that the cost per installed kilowatt for fusion power plants will be comparable to that estimated for breeder reactors.

This argument, in conjunction with the finitude of our conventional energy resources, makes it imperative that we press research and development efforts on all energy alternatives that show promise of making a significant contribution. Some critics of fossil fuel and fission energy oppose new plant construction because "if we can just get along with present facilities for a little while longer, solar or fusion energy will come to our rescue." Here, the history of the fission energy program itself provides a useful lesson on the time frame for the introduction of any new, large-scale energy technology. The "proof of principle" for nuclear reactors occurred in 1942, the first commercial reactor came on line in 1957, and the effect of nuclear energy was not even visible on any energy picture until 1970. Even now, over 35 years after its feasibility was proven, it contributes only somewhat over 10 per cent of our electrical energy. Because of the development and enormous capital investments involved, there will simply be no "quick and easy" energy alternative to bail us out of our energy crisis.

An important distinction should be made in studying energy alternatives—that between *new primary energy sources* (e.g., fusion and solar energy) and *improvements in energy utilization and interconversion techniques* (e.g., coal gasification and hydrogen production). Both fusion and solar energy promise virtually unlimited supplies of clean energy. The interconversion alternatives promise increased ease of utilization and environmental acceptability of present nonrenewable fuels but often with a severe loss of over-all efficiency.

We turn now to *The Prospect for Fusion* by David Rose and Michael Feirtag. In this article, the authors give an intuitive explanation of the basic fusion process, the plasma physics conditions required, and the awesome engineering problems that must be solved before fusion devices produce more energy than they consume. Several techniques for harnessing fusion energy are described, and the Tokamak is shown to be the device most likely to succeed. The authors present a rather somber assessment of the chances of overcoming the extremely difficult problems involved and some good insight on the broader aspects of optimizing the research and development process itself. The prospect of an essentially unlimited energy supply (literally "oceans full of fuel") is too promising to ignore.

Next, we present a series of articles describing solar energy, the energy alternative that has been "waiting in the wings" for years and that is now entering a period of extremely rapid expansion as the price increases of other energy sources make it an economically feasible option. First, we present an overview of solar energy including its variants, wind energy and ocean temperature gradients, followed by a more detailed analysis of the use of solar energy for heating and cooling (the first application to become economically competitive), and finally, a proposal for converting solar energy into electricity by collecting it in space and beaming it to earth via microwaves, thus overcoming the main objections to solar energy based on its intermittent nature.

In his article, *Solar Energy*, William Eaton surveys the historical development of solar energy, the range of applications that have been proposed and implemented, and the role solar energy may play in the future. In addition to the heating and cooling application and conversion to electricity, which we will examine in detail later, he describes several interesting proposals such as using ocean thermal gradients (a form of stored solar energy) and living plants to process and store solar energy. An ironic aspect of solar energy is that, although we tend to think of it as the energy source of the future, it was actually one of the earliest forms of inanimate energy used by man. Farmers have used solar energy from prehistoric times for the drying of crops, windmills have been used in Europe and China for centuries, and even the "advanced" ocean thermal gradient proposal originated with D'Arsonval, a French physicist, in 1881. In the longer historical perspective, the trend has certainly been toward expanded use of solar energy with the only interruption being our century-long flirtation with oil and natural gas.

As the price of natural gas and oil continues to climb, the first economically attractive application of solar energy is the direct thermal applications described by John Duffie and William Beckman in their article *Solar Heating and Cooling*. They describe several experimental solar heating systems that are now operational, the simulation program being used to model the behavior of such systems, and the sensitivity of the economics of home heating systems to such parameters as the collector area. The final economic feasibility of solar heating systems is shown to depend not only on the initial capital costs and on interest rates, but also on public policies such as deregulation of natural gas prices and tax incentives for the installation of solar systems. President Carter's energy program ties the price of natural gas to the equivalent oil price and includes tax incentives for the installation of solar equipment. Such policies will certainly help reach the goal of 2½ million solar homes by 1985.

Two characteristics of terrestrial solar energy are its low intensity and intermittent nature. These problems are largely eliminated by the intriguing proposal by Peter Glaser in his *Solar Power from Satellites*. By collecting sunlight in space, the intensity is increased by a factor of seven over the average intensity on earth, and by using geostationary satellites and microwave transmission, a continuous energy supply is achieved (except for occasional short eclipses). The design study shows a remarkable 55 per cent efficiency for the over-all process of converting solar cell electricity on the satellite to microwaves, beaming it to earth, collecting in there, and reconverting it back to direct current electricity on earth. The environmental implications appear completely manageable, no major breakthroughs in space technology are necessary, and even the economics appear to be in the same range as the costs projected for the breeder reactor and fusion reactor programs. So the fascinating possibility exists that a really "practical" (and unexpected) benefit of the multibillion dollar space program will be this harnessing of solar energy to produce electricity.

Next we turn to two sources of energy that may extend our supplies of petroleum considerably, but which, until recently, have not been economically feasible. These are the oil shales, primarily those of the famous Green River Formation in the western United States and the oil sands from the Athabasca Formation of Alberta, Canada.

In *Oil Shale and the Energy Crisis*, Gerald U. Dinneen and Glenn L. Cook outline the nature of the Green River reserves and the two basic techniques for extracting oil from shale under investigation. An interesting problem in both oil-shale and oil-sand mining is that the mine "tailings" occupy more space than the original "ore." The disposal of such tailings poses serious environmental questions. Since the mining, crushing, and retorting of the shale constitute 60 per cent of the expense of extracting oil, *in situ* processing techniques are being given considerable attention. No oil shale is being mined commercially now, but the results of pilot projects in Colorado, Utah, and Wyoming are being analyzed to determine the optimum system for tapping this vast source of future oil.

A. R. Allen tells of the struggle of his company, the Sun Oil Company, in *Coping with the Oil Sands*. This operation, the Great Canadian Oil Sands, now produces over 55,000 barrels of crude oil per day. Many of the problems unique to oil sands, such as handling vast quantities of this wet, sticky, quick-freezing ore, however, have been met and apparently overcome. The complex nature of the oil-sand particles themselves, the large temperature range over which mining takes place, and the mining location (a muskeg swamp) all complicate this economically marginal operation. It is obvious after reading this article why "synthetic crude" has not made larger inroads on the oil market before now. But with the upward trend in foreign oil prices, the future of such operations seems assured, and two more ventures are planned for the near future.

One of the alternative energy sources that is, in fact, now in commercial operation is that of geothermal energy, and it shows promise for alleviating energy shortages, at least locally. This energy resource is described by L. J. P. Muffler and D. E. White in their article, *Geothermal Energy*. Various geothermal operations are discussed, and the natural conditions giving rise to geothermal reservoirs are shown to occur in geologically active regions. Though geothermal energy was produced as early as 1904, there is still no consensus among geologists as to the potential impact it could have on the energy budget. Estimates presented here indicate it could supply up to 10 per cent of the electrical power demand.

Finally, we present an energy "resource" that was largely ignored during the period of cheap energy prices. This is the technique of *Processing Energy from Wastes* as reported by E. Milton Wilson and Harry M. Freemen. This technique offers partial answers to two major problems—solid waste management and energy shortages. Here, the pioneering efforts of several municipalities, led by St. Louis, are described, and the authors estimate that up to 3 per cent of the nation's energy could be provided by such waste disposal techniques. In addition to supplying this significant portion of our energy requirement, this technique greatly reduces the volume of wastes to be managed and often recovers valuable metal or glass by-products as well. For all these environmentally sound reasons, this process should grow to become the standard method of municipal waste processing.

In conclusion, we offer the following observations:

(1) All the energy alternatives discussed have definite advantages that justify continued research and development.

(2) They all have some intrinsic problems of a technological, environmental, or economic nature that have prevented them from contributing significantly to the energy picture to date.

(3) A wise energy policy will include a balanced research and development program to assure the optimum deployment of each of these energy alternatives. Any other policy risks the pitfalls of "all the eggs in one basket," which many observers feel represented the U.S. fission reactor program during the last 20 years. With such a balanced program we spread the risks, and if one approach, for instance fusion, should prove intractable, the emphasis can easily be shifted to other promising alternatives. Although this approach is more expensive than the policy of "picking the best alternative and sticking with it," it represents the most conservative and safest long range policy.

Although the energy alternatives presented do not completely exhaust the list of proposals, they certainly include the most promising alternatives and those with the greatest capacity for sizable energy production.

The Prospects For Fusion 23

DAVID J. ROSE AND MICHAEL FEIRTAG 1976

Designing a nuclear fusion reactor in 1977 is a little like planning to reach heaven: theories abound on how to do it, and many people are trying, but no one alive has ever succeeded. Also, the challenge is too important to be ignored—in fusions's case because we are running out of energy. In the short term, for perhaps 25 years, there will be oil. For 50 to 100 years after that, we could fight over the last available drops of oil and burn increasing quantities of coal, probably at great environmental cost. But after that—and preferably before—humankind will have to turn to one or more of the long-term options that nature holds before us. There are only three. One is solar power. A second is nuclear fission—or, more specifically, since rich fissionable material also grows scarce, the development of a so-called breeder reactor that creates more fissionable fuel than it consumes. The third is nuclear fusion. At present, none of these options is sure to work. Each possesses remarkable and perverse difficulties. To bring any one of them to a point at which society can decide whether or not to adopt it as a principal energy resource will cost 10 to 20 billion dollars. To develop alternatives within an option (an alternative breeder, for example) will cost an additional 1 or 2 billion dollars for each new possibility. In short, we are compelled to play a desperate poker game against nature in which each betting chip costs tens of billions of dollars, and thus far we fear to buy the chips. After all, one can imagine the spending in this game of 60 to 100 billion dollars if we are to back all three possibilities, and that is an awesome amount of money—or it seems awesome until it is compared to the capital investment the United States must make by the year 2000 to provide what energy it needs and transform its patterns of use to match new supplies. Even without much

Dr. David J. Rose is a professor in the Nuclear Engineering Department, Massachusetts Institute of Technology, Cambridge, Massachusetts 02139. He is presently a member of the National Academy of Sciences' Committee on Nuclear and Alternate Energy Systems, which is preparing a study on energy strategies for the Energy Research and Development Administration. He is also a consultant to Congress's Office of Technology Assessment.

Michael Feirtag is a member of the *Technology Review* Board of Editors.

From *Technology Review*, Vol. 79, No. 2, pp. 21–43, December 1976. Reprinted with light editing and by permission of the authors and *Technology Review*.

growth in energy demand, and even with prodigious energy conservation, that investment will be about 1 trillion dollars, with much more to follow in the twenty-first century. Since the social cost of having *no* energy options in the year 2000 is incalculable, there seems no alternative but to pursue all three long-term options, reassessing them all the while, until we know enough to narrow the choices.

It is in this spirit that we approach controlled nuclear fusion. The subject has a vast scientific literature, and a growing technological literature. There are, however, few public explanations; we will attempt to lessen the imbalance. It is a good time to do so, for during the past few years the pursuit of controlled nuclear fusion has led to a number of so-called "reference designs" for large fusion reactors; later in this article we will give some examples. Far from being blueprints for any fusion reactor, the reference designs were started (in 1967) and carried through for almost the opposite purpose—they were meant to ensure that those pursuing controlled nuclear fusion would have to face every problem associated with a given reactor concept. Thus the designs were problem-finders, not problem-solvers, and as such they were spectacular successes. From the tortured and sometimes bizarre schemes to which the researchers were compelled to resort, long lists emerged of scientific and technological areas needing attention: more radiation-resistant alloys, different systems for cooling the reactor, higher energy-handling ability per unit area of reactor wall, and so forth. Their purpose being accomplished, the current reference designs are now being discarded as their makers turn to the critical problems, and new reference designs in due course should appear. The making of reference designs that uncover problems, and the development of technologies that solve them, are activities that proceed more or less continuously; and if, years from now, the fusion program succeeds, designs will appear for a practical fusion reactor probably unlike anything now envisaged.

But will it succeed? Is civilization mad to persist in a search that seems so complex, so uncertain? The science and some of the technology have progressed to a point where many questions of a decade ago—for example, "Is controlled fusion scientifically feasible?"—now appear obsolete; they have been answered affirmatively as a by-product of the race to develop ever larger experiments. On the other hand, the technological and engineering difficulties are now known to far surpass any original estimates; still another decade or two will be needed to resolve them, and decide about fusion, pro or con. In the meantime, fusion's expanding success coupled with its increasingly evident difficulty will remain a hard mixture to manage; it could easily inspire false optimism or false pessimism—and, either way, wrong judgments. Responsibility for keeping a proper sense of perspective falls primarily upon the Department of Energy, the patron of controlled fusion research in the United States—it costs so much that no organization but the federal government can afford to sponsor it. DOE's inclinations, coupled with the prospect of support, could stimulate its clients, the National Laboratories and other research organizations, to adopt a sycophantic, or at least a neutral, stance. When false certainty grows, so critical judgment withers. The true development effort suffers.

How might it happen? The answer is: bit by bit, and with the best of intentions. Administrators, overcome by the temptation of so much to administer, may mistake vision for reality. Engineers, meanwhile, may become expert at their task, and neglect to maintain constructively critical attitudes. After all, it is human nature to assume that some fault in a grand conception will be solved by future ingenuity, and it is easy to allow a design to become a neat assemblage of what engineers call black boxes. In these ways, an inadequate design becomes the accepted design, and finally the official program, attracting to itself all the support and funding that exists. The public is led to believe that technological salvation is imminent. It then develops that the design is unworkable and the program ends in disaster. An exemplar exists of this sort of calamity. Several years ago, development of the liquid-metal fast breeder reactor was almost halted by administrative rigidity and money—not because that breeder reactor is a bad (or a good) idea, and certainly not because those in charge of the program planned it that way. It just happened. . . . And whether the same thing may now be happening to controlled nuclear fusion is a topic we will turn to at the end of this article.

ENERGY TECHNOLOGY FOR THE TWENTY-FIRST CENTURY

Strategies to supply future energy are varied: new coal technology, solar energy, perhaps local geothermal energy, accelerated and advanced nuclear fission technology, fusion. All have a long leadtime, both for development and deployment, and most could last for relatively long periods of time if they are deployed at all. New technologies that are expected to be extensively deployed early in the next century must be fully developed by the end of this century; thus the main technological lines should be clear and the main difficulties resolved by 1985 or 1990. Advanced fission power systems, including breeder reactors, are being developed in approximate accord with this schedule. Because of fission's cost advantage (relative to fossil-fuel electric power) in most locations, even if uranium prices should rise several-fold, arguments of resource limitation will not apply to nuclear power unless an acceptable breeder reactor cannot be developed by the early twenty-first century. Thus, barring a public decision against it, nuclear power plants could be well developed and installed before the end of the century.

Against this specific situation and on this time scale, fusion must offer some real advantage if it is to supplant advanced fission systems. What then are the benefits? Part of the fuel for a fusion reactor will be tritium—a radioactive isotope of hydrogen. Fortunately, tritium is vastly less hazardous than uranium fission products or than plutonium, per unit of energy produced by nuclear reactions or simply per unit weight. Exactly how much less depends upon the particular route by which the radioactive material is imagined to invade the human body—whether it enters by ingestion, inhalation, and so on. Analysts speak of it being a factor of a thousand or ten thousand less hazardous. Countering that is the fact that such hazards are not solved by merely stating them in simplistic terms. One can imagine a fusion reactor that would work perfectly well, in the technological sense of giving out energy, but that was equivalent in hazard to a fission reactor because its loss rate of fuel, although still microscopically small, was ten thousand times higher than that of a fission reactor. That sort of question can be resolved only on the basis of fairly specific designs.

Some other social advantages of fusion are more certain. First, tritium is no blackmail weapon. Though it can be used in H-bombs, an A-bomb is needed to set one off, so a terrorist would have to already own a fission weapon. Second, a fusion reactor would contain no equivalent of the highly concentrated radioactive fuel used in fission reactors. Thus, a meltdown accident, the most serious calamity possible in a fission reactor, would be impossible in most fusion-reactor designs (the concentrated energy source just wouldn't be there) and exceedingly small in others. To be sure, the structure of a fusion reactor would itself become radioactive, to an extent, depending on the materials used to build it. This radioactivity would surely complicate operation and maintenance; and the reactor's cold hulk might remain radioactive for many decades after its operating life had ended. Still, current estimates rate this aspect of radioactivity as much less severe than the difficulties arising from concentrated fuel in fission. Over all, fusion should be "cleaner." If its advantages could be coupled with a cost advantage and an engineering study that demonstrates feasibility, an energy-hungry society would have a very good option.

This debate brings us to the timetable for

fusion development. To offer a meaningful alternative to fission, fusion should aim for approximately the same time scale—principal engineering problems seen to be resolvable before 1990, say. That is a very short time for a task so large, too short for scientific, technological, and economic feasibilities to be established in conventional and orderly sequence. The various stages must partly overlap and coalesce, so that technology and engineering known to be needed are worked on now. This is the rationale for the reference designs: groups persistently try to design fusion reactors, based on the latest science and technology, then analyze the designs to uncover their shortcomings. From that activity, clues appear about the next set of problems to be studied and also about what decision large experiments should take. If all the problems prove to be tractable, the whole effort will culminate in a well-worked-out fusion concept by the late 1980's, ready for trial on a grand scale.

This leads us to the question: How to do the job? Development of any difficult modern technological devices, including fusion reactors, tends to suffer from excessive disciplinary reductionism: any single group concerned with only one phase of the work tends to use up all the design flexibility to solve its own problems, thus leaving impossible tasks for everyone else. Each discipline appropriates to itself all the available option space, so to speak. In illustrative exaggeration, we note that the development of fusion concepts has been mainly in the hands of physicists until almost the present time, so controlled fusion has been looked upon mainly as a research problem—specifically, as a matter of confining a plasma (a gas of charged particles). Such physics-oriented research was conducted under the naïve assumption that technology (the development of new materials and processes) and engineering (the application of technology to socially desirable purposes) could do anything necessary to make a plasma that precisely suited the plasmologist's fancy. But technology and engineering cannot be conjured up at will; and in fact, they are usually very expensive to extend in new directions. Thus the need for balance from the start. The three major constraints of "plasma dynamics," technology, and engineering must be jointly satisfied if there is to be a happy outcome to the search for fusion.

ENERGY FROM THE NUCLEUS

The idea of controlled nuclear fusion is not new. Ever since the 1930's, when the sun's nuclear cycle was first worked out in detail, people have speculated about its possibility. However, nothing was accomplished until World War II, when the Manhattan Project was set up to build what is commonly called an "atomic bomb," a name that is somewhat misleading. It should be called a nuclear bomb, for "atomic" refers to the whole atom—that is, to the nucleus and the surrounding electrons. An atom may be ionized (it loses one or more of its electrons and thereby becomes positively charged), but the energies involved are modest, on the order of a few electron volts.

Interactions within the nuclei are vastly more energetic; the Manhattan Project developed bombs operating on the principle of breaking up, or fissioning, the nuclei of uranium or plutonium. The energy released by each such fissioning is about 50 million times greater than the energies associated with the outermost electrons in the atom.

Why does fission work at all? In one parlance, it is because the heaviest elements have "excess mass"—more mass than the sum of the atoms into which they fission—so that when their nuclei break up, this mass difference becomes energy, in accordance with Einstein's law, $E = mc^2$. Looking at Figure 23-1, we are not surprised to find that uranium undergoes fission if mass is added to it, such as one more neutron. The facts that ^{238}U can be turned fairly easily into ^{239}Pu, which is useful for fission, and that ^{232}Th can become ^{233}U, are additional evidence of the general instability of very heavy elements.

Inspection of the curve shows immediately that the middle-weight nuclei are most stable,

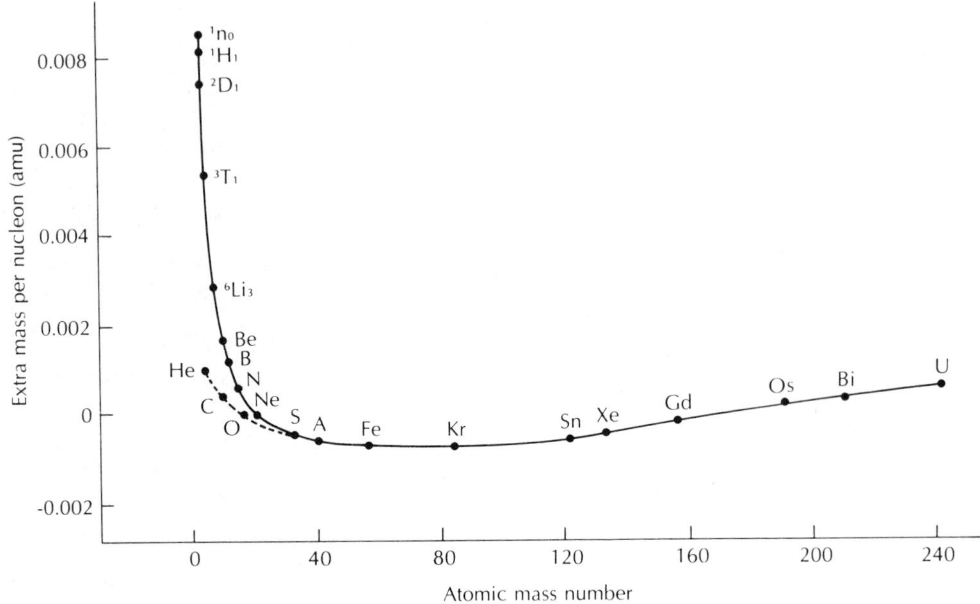

Figure 23-1. The mass of a nucleon—a neutron or a proton—in the nuclei of the various chemical elements. By convention, the ^{16}O nucleus is taken to have a mass of 16 atomic mass units, and other nuclei are then compared with it. It is found that free neutrons ($^1n_0$ in the chart) and free protons ($^1H_1$ nuclei) have more mass than any neutrons and protons bound within nuclei. This means that when the chemical elements formed, mass disappeared. It became energy, in accordance with $E = mc^2$. The nucleons in the middle-atomic-weight elements—iron (Fe) and krypton (Kr), for example—lost the most mass. Such elements are therefore the most stable: any rearrangement of their nucleons requires energy. On the other hand, breaking up the heaviest nuclei into lighter ones releases energy; this is nuclear fission. So does the combination of the lightest nuclei into heavier ones; and this is nuclear fusion.

and that a second possibility exists: combining the lightest nuclei, and releasing energy in that way—by nuclear fusion. Hydrogen is the lightest element—its nucleus is simply a proton—but the element also has two heavier isotopes: deuterium, in which the proton is joined by one neutron, and tritium, in which it is joined by two. The Sun works mainly on a hydrogen fusion cycle, using two protons to make a photon, a positron (a positively charged electron), a deuterium nucleus (called a deuteron), and energy. The reaction rate is very slow, fortunately for us, in that the Sun has lasted several billion years, and much of it is still there. But the energy crisis demands reactions that run quicker. The deuterium-deuterium combination is much better, but best of all is combining deuterium and tritium. This reaction produces ordinary helium, a neutron, and 17.6 million electron volts. Eighty per cent of the energy, or 14.1 million electron volts, emerges with the velocity of the neutron, and 3.5 million electron volts with the velocity of the helium nucleus (also called an α- particle).

Deuterium is in plentiful supply; it constitutes one part in 7,000 of the hydrogen in ordinary water. Since there are some 150×10^6 cubic miles of water in the oceans, the amount is prodigious, enough in fact to last for billions of years, even at the highest rate at which we can use energy without overheating our environment. The problem comes with tritium: it is radioactive, with a half-life of 12.3 years, so it does not occur in nature. Fortunately, the two isotopes of lithium can be used to make it. High-energy neutrons (above 2.5 million electron volts) can react with ^{7}Li:

$$^7\text{Li} + \text{n[fast]} \rightarrow {}^4\text{He} + {}^3\text{T} + \text{n [slow]}$$

and ^{6}Li absorbs neutrons (the slower they are, the better the absorption) with great appetite:

$$^6\text{Li} + \text{n} \rightarrow {}^4\text{He} + {}^3\text{T} + 4.8 \text{ million electron volts}$$

Thus we have a generation scheme for tritium. Note the parallel with a fission *breeder*. A fusion reactor is, in fact, a breeder: it uses deuterium and lithium as raw fuels and breeds tritium as an intermediate product that is burned in the reaction. Because only a single neutron appears per fusion event, one might imagine that fusion cannot work: the losses would not let the tritium reproduce itself. Not so, because the two lithium reactions can, in principle, proceed sequentially, using the same initial neutron. On the other hand, other materials in the reactor compete for the neutrons. The result is that fewer than two tritons (tritium nuclei), on average, can be created for each triton destroyed. Still, tritium can be more than replenished.

A second problem now appears. Fission is easy (given some fissionable material) because a neutron is electrically neutral, so it can enter the positively charged nucleus without encountering any repulsive force. Thus, uranium and neutrons can be at room temperature, and yet the uranium will fission, atom by atom, and the fission energy can be turned into heat, say, to boil water. In fact, a water solution of some uranium salts, in which the uranium is suitably enriched with ^{235}U, will go critical—that is, a self-sustaining chain reaction will occur—if the container is large enough. This is not the case with fusion for a simple reason: the reacting particles are all nuclei, all positively charged. They are therefore all mutually repulsive. Rather than approaching to within a few times 10^{-15} meters of each other so that fusion can occur, a deuteron and a triton are far more likely to repel each other while large distances separate them. Forcing a close approach requires high energy, which requires high temperature—as we shall see, temperature on the order of 10^8 K. All this was well known and applied by nuclear physicists in the late 1940's. The idea of building an "H-bomb" that fuses isotopes of hydrogen occurred to them, as well as a way to attain the high temperature: explode a fission bomb in the middle of a hydrogen-isotope mixture. If the bomb is made large enough or is surrounded by heavy material, then inertia alone will keep it together for the microsecond or so the reactions require.

Clearly that scheme will not do for controlled fusion in a power plant. Gravity will not work either, for only on the scale of the Sun (or more precisely on about the scale of Jupiter) would it be strong enough to force the nuclei together. What is left? The reacting particles are fully ionized—they are nuclei with all the electrons stripped from them. Since they are charged, perhaps magnetic forces will confine them.

Thus arose the first epoch in controlled fusion research, starting in the early 1950's. In summary, it was characterized by four realizations. First came measurements of reaction energies and rates between hydrogen isotopes and other light elements, which showed that under proper conditions large energy releases would be possible. Second, the well-known laws of single-particle physics seemed to show how an assembly of high-energy ions and electrons could be confined in magnetic fields long enough to establish the proper conditions. Third, the radioactive isotopes and by-products of fusion were known to be much less hazardous than those associated with nuclear fission: therefore fusion reactors would be simpler and safer than fission reactors. Fourth, deuterium was known to be in plentiful supply. Only the first of these realizations is a prerequisite for making H-bombs. The combination of all four captured the imagination of a sizable and very competent fraction of the physics community. The ensuing search for controlled fusion—the ultimate energy source, the source that powers the stars—has sometimes taken on a moral character, possibly as a reaction to the darker uses to which nuclear energy has been put. Whatever the reason, the efforts exerted by some were like those lavished on Mt. Everest—and a good thing, too, for the 1953 workers had anticipated very few of the complexities in both science and technology that had to be overcome before controlled fusion could reach even today's half-way stage. The whole field of plasma physics—the physics of ionized gases—had yet to be invented at that time; superconducting magnets—absolutely essential for most fusion concepts—were not even contemplated. A controlled fusion reactor seemed simple; but, in fact, it is not. Developing one, assuming that it can be developed, will be scientifically and technologically more difficult than developing a fission reactor in roughly the measure that a fission reactor is more difficult to develop than a coal-burning power plant.

THE DESIGN OF A FUSION REACTOR

It is possible to describe many of the design requirements for a fusion reactor using only simple physical principles and a little common sense. Consider first a deuteron and a triton that are supposed to fuse, and consider also a "target area" associated with one of the particles. The other particle must pass within this area if the two particles are to interact—that is, combine, disintegrate, or even just scatter. The target area will have a different size for each type of reaction; and for a fusion reaction it will grow larger if the incoming particle is more energetic—that is, if it has higher velocity—up to a limit that does not concern us here. The target area is called a reaction cross section, and is measured in units of "barns," as in the familiar taunt, "You couldn't hit the broad side of a barn." One barn is 10^{-24} square centimeters.

Figure 23-2 shows several fusion cross sections for reactions among light nuclei. We see that no reactions involving protons as fuel have usefully large cross sections. Not shown at all is the two-proton reaction by which the Sun is burning hydrogen. That reaction has a cross section about 10^{-20} of the deuterium-tritium reaction; accordingly, as we noted, the Sun takes billions of years to consume its hydrogen—a time suitable for stars, but not for the fusion reactors we have in mind.

Several lithium reactions are shown; they have smaller cross sections than deuterium, tritium, or ^{3}He reactions because of the higher repulsive force between the particles. Thus, lithium is good for breeding tritium but not for the fusion reaction itself, and we apparently must consider deuterium, tritium, or helium. In fact, the choice is more limited. It will turn out that producing more energy than is consumed will be a significant problem in fusion reactors: the constituents must be heated to the reaction temperature, and even then only a small fraction of the hot fuel will react in one pass through the reactor. Power will also be needed for other purposes. This energy-balance difficulty pertains even to the deuterium-tritium reaction, but noting that the deuterium-deuterium and deuterium-^{3}He reactions have cross sections that are smaller by factors of 30 to 100, we concluded that deuterium-tritium is the fuel of obvious choice, despite the need for tritium breeding and the problems of radioactivity.

Thus, from the illustration, we wish to extract a typical energy and cross section for deuterium-tritium fusion. Although 150 thousand electron volts and 5 barns seem ideal, it turns out that the associated temperatures and pressures are too high for many fusion schemes. Let us consider lower energies, say 20 to 50 thousand electron volts, so that the average cross section for the reacting particles will be about 1 barn—a convenient number to use in our discussions. A gas at 20 thousand electron volts has a temperature of about 2.3×10^8 K, a value far surpassing any temperature ordinarily found on Earth. It is exceedingly hot—about 10 times the temperature of the Sun's core. Will the reacting particles be neutral atoms or will they be ions at this temperature? The question is easily an-

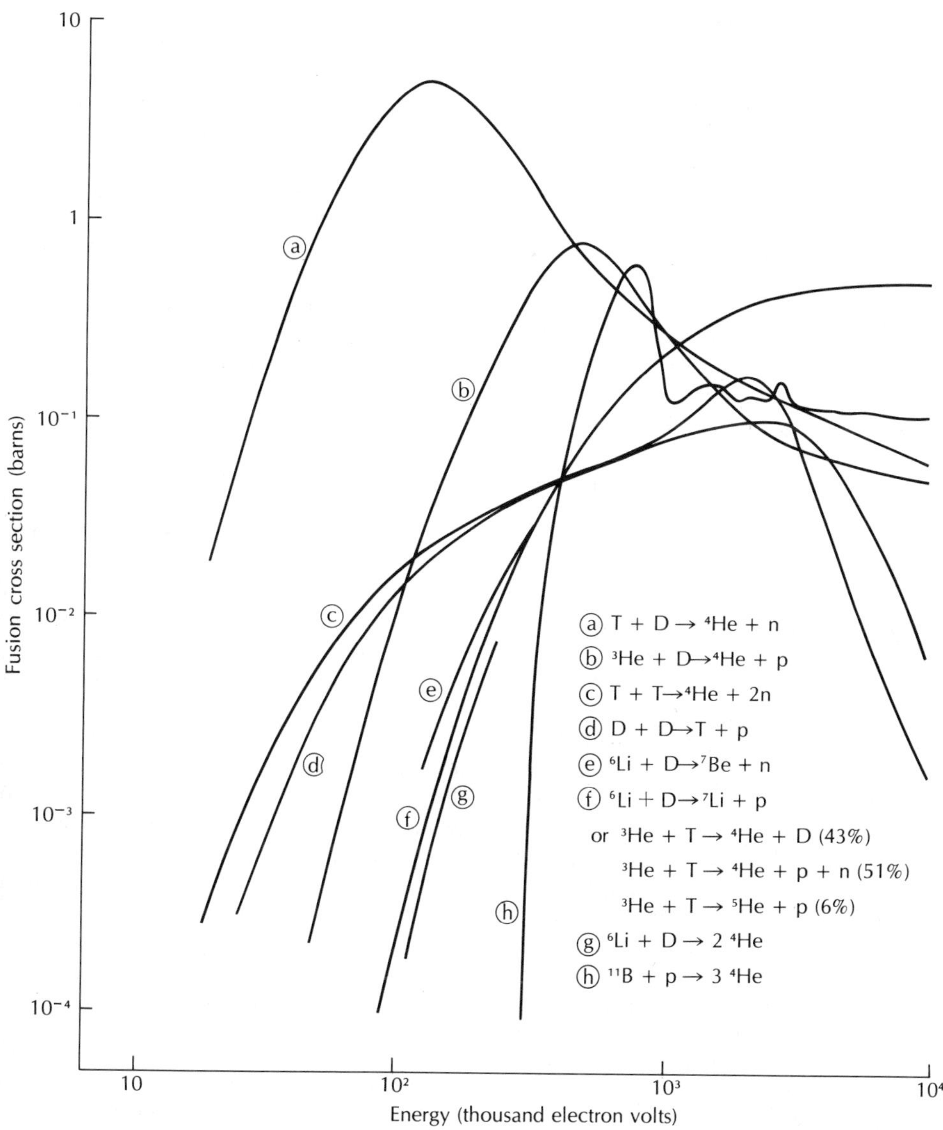

Figure 23-2. Several fusion reactions of interest to an energy-hungry society. The horizontal axis plots particle energy, in electron volts. The vertical axis plots the so-called reaction cross section, a measure of how close two nuclei must come in order to fuse. For the vertical axis, the units are "barns," where each barn is 10^{-24} square centimeter. The fusion of deuterium and tritium is easiest to manage: 20-kev (20 thousand electron volts) deuterium and tritium nuclei have, from the chart, a fusion cross section of about 0.1 barn. However, a gas with an average energy per particle of 20 thousand electron volts includes a considerable number of more energetic particles, and their fusion cross sections (up to 5 barns) raise the average for the whole group to about 1 barn. It follows that the deuterium and tritium nuclei in a fusion plasma at 20 thousand electron volts must approach to within a distance of 10^{-12} centimeter (the radius of a circle 10^{-24} square centimeter in area). One other reaction on the chart—that of boron-11 with a proton—is noteworthy, for it produces no radioactivity and also no neutrons to pass through a reactor wall to damage outside structures. But a million electron volts is required to start the reaction, making boron-proton fusion remote in humanity's future.

swered by comparing some orders of magnitude. The energy required to ionize a hydrogen atom—that is, to remove its sole electron—is 13.6 electron volts. The energy required to split the two-atom hydrogen molecule into individual atoms is even lower. Thus, an assembly of 20 thousand electron volts molecules will decompose into ionized nuclei and free electrons. And at these very high energies, the electrons will not recombine with the ions.

Moreover, these dissociation and ionization processes will occur rapidly. Cross sections for reactions of this sort are typically about the size of the atoms themselves, say 10^{-20} square meters, which is 10^8 times the fusion cross section. Thus, a collection of deuterium and tritium atoms at fusion temperatures will turn into a plasma containing, in this case, deuterium and tritium ions, and an equal number of free electrons, in a time very short compared to the time the assemblage would require to undergo appreciable fusion. By this reasoning we can also conclude that a chance neutral atom injected into the fusion plasma will have a very short lifetime. This is not to say that a fusion plasma fully ionizes an arbitrary amount of neutral gas in the vicinity; the task requires energy, so the plasma cools, and the addition of too much neutral gas will depress the temperature to uninterestingly low values. Also, a truly fearsome atomic-type reaction called charge exchange can take place wherein low-energy atoms (say at room temperature, with corresponding energy of about 0.03 electron volts) enter the plasma and exchange their charge with a high-energy (20 thousand electron volts) ion; they become fast atoms that leave the plasma, perhaps to strike and damage the surrounding walls.

Another major question concerns scattering of the ions by each other before they come sufficiently close to fuse—a phenomenon we have mentioned briefly. For 20 thousand electrons volt ions, the scattering cross section is about 2×10^{-26} square meters, which is 200 times larger than the fusion cross section; and if the energy were less, there would be even more scattering. The implication of this is that the assembly will become randomized: any given initial distribution, even of carefully focused ion beams, will take on the properties of a gas after each ion has been scattered by its neighbors a few times. Accordingly, temperature, pressure, density, and other concepts useful in thinking about ordinary gases will also be useful here. By considering the fusion plasma as a gas, we can derive various combinations of temperature, density, and confinement time that are required if a substantial fraction of the fuel is to undergo fusion. One combination, assuming a plasma temperature of about 10^8 K, is a density of about 10^{14} particles per cubic centimeter and a confinement time of about 1 second. That density is rather low (by comparison, the density of the air around us is about 3×10^{19} particles per cubic centimeter), so the plasma approximates a good vacuum. But the product of density and temperature is a measure of a gas's pressure, and in this example, the plasma's pressure turns out to be 10 atmospheres. That is not fortuitous. Though large structures can be built to withstand pressures one order of magnitude greater, the extra order of magnitude must be saved to withstand the stresses that arise from high magnetic fields, soon to be described. For now, we note that as far as the physics is concerned, it doesn't matter whether one achieves high density and short confinement time, or low density and long confinement time, at a given temperature; this trade-off can be a matter of technological and engineering convenience. The fractional burn-up of nuclear fuel will be the same.

We have discovered that the reactor contains a deuterium-tritium gas, confined in some way yet to be determined, for some period of time, inside an evacuated chamber—the vacuum being necessary in order to keep the plasma hot and pure. Thus we will need a vacuum wall. Now recall that 3.5 million electron volts, or one-fifth of the energy created by deuterium-tritium fusion, appears in the velocity of the helium ion created in the reactions; and 14.1 million electron volts, or four-fifths, appears in the velocity of a neutron. We can imagine the charged particles being slowed down within the reacting plasma itself by electrical forces. On the other hand, the neutrons will not be affected by electromagnetic fields, nor will they be stopped by collisions within any reasonable length of the tenuous gas. They must pass through the vacuum wall into a surrounding "blanket" region of some sort, in which their velocity will be slowed and their energy converted into extractable heat. That was the reason for building the reactor. Moreover, it is in this region that the neutrons must breed tritium as they slow down and are captured in lithium. Our rudimentary fusion reactor now starts to take shape; it is shown in Figure 23-3. The major missing component is a mechanism for plasma confinement, to be discussed shortly.

How thick must the blanket region be? Assume it is made of solid or liquid moderators, absorbers, and so on, all of whose density is typically about 5×10^{28} particles per cubic meter. The cross section for a 14 million electron volt neutron colliding with a nucleus inside such materials is about 2×10^{-28} square meters, or 2 barns, and the corresponding mean penetration distance before the first collision is about 0.1 meter. But the blanket must be much thicker than that in order to stop all but a negligible fraction of the fast neutrons, and moderate the energy neutron so that the neutrons can be absorbed in lithium. Calculations show that the blanket must be about 10 times as thick, or about 1 meter; and even then further shielding may be required outside.

Almost intuitively, we foresee that the fusion blanket will be a high-technology item, and hence, expensive. Compounding this cost problem will be the vacuum wall itself, called in the trade the "first wall." Every 14 million electron volt neutron must pass through it before it regenerates tritium—a circumstance in sharp and important contrast to that in fission reactors, where most of the energy appears with fission fragments, which are stopped in the fuel itself. It takes no great insight to see that material damage via irradiation by 14 million electron volt neutrons will be one of the most severe problems in fusion reactor design. In the first place, some of the neutrons, and all of the x rays and other radiation from the plasma, will give up energy at the vacuum wall. Calculations of permissible heat transfer show that the total energy incident cannot be allowed to average much more than a few megawatts per square meter, and possibly less. In the second place, one wishes to limit the number of neutrons penetrating all the way through the blanket, so as to minimize damage to outside apparatus, which will doubtless be expensive. (This requirement will certainly be true if we consider putting expensive superconducting magnetic windings outside the blanket, as is contemplated in almost all fusion schemes, for reasons we shall consider shortly.)

All these factors—the need for low values of neutron and energy flux per unit area of vacuum wall, coupled with the high cost of the reactor's technology—together dictate that the reactor must be large. How large? If the vacuum wall surrounds a sphere whose radius is 2 meters, the power created will be about 50 megawatts if the first-wall neutron loading is to be kept at 1 megawatt per square meter. In fact, the power per reactor is liable to be much larger, because of considerations not yet discussed. Some are geometrical ones, such as the circumstance that most fusion concepts work not with a spherical plasma region, but only with a toroidal or donut-shaped one. Thus Figure 23-3 would represent a cut through a torus. If the minor radius to the vacuum wall will be 2 meters, the major radius will be 5 meters or more, the total vacuum-wall area will be 400 square meters or more, and the reactor power will be comparable with that produced by large present-day power plants.

SCHEMES FOR PLASMA CONFINEMENT: LASER FUSION

Last, we consider how to confine the plasma. The only physical confinement principles that exist are:

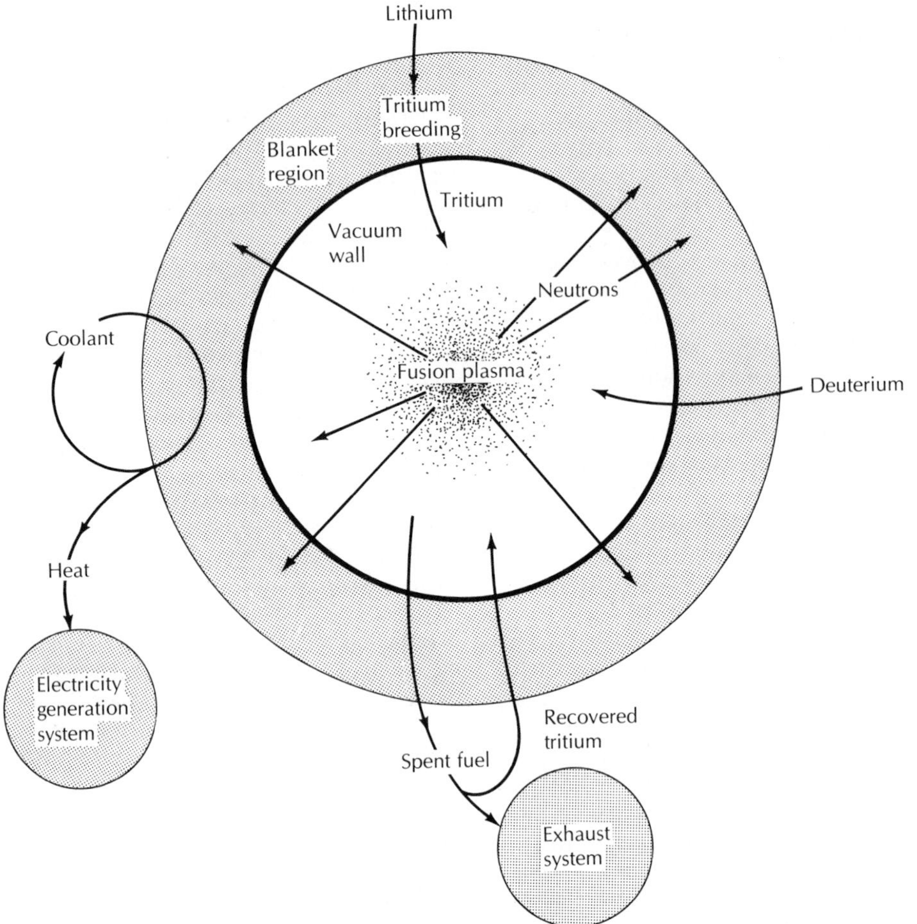

Figure 23-3. Conceptual design of a fusion reactor. At the center of its reaction chamber, gaseous deuterium and tritium are heated to a temperature of 10^8K, by some mechanism that isn't shown—or even suggested—in the drawing. The gas, now a plasma, is confined at that temperature long enough for fusion to occur—again, by a mechanism that the drawing fails to suggest. Neutrons are freed by the fusion reaction. They speed through the so-called vacuum wall and into a blanket region, where their energy is somehow transferred to electricity-generating apparatus—conventional steam-driven turbines, perhaps. Also in the blanket region, tritium is bred from lithium. Meanwhile, spent fuel is somehow removed from the reactor, unburned tritium is somehow recovered, and fresh fuel is somehow injected.

(1) Gravity, which won't work on Earth. It can work on the Sun due only to that body's mass.

(2) Material walls, which are self-defeating: it isn't that the plasma would melt the walls, but more likely the plasma's ions and electrons would lose their energy and cool on their first encounter with their container.

(3) A surrounding colder gas, which is not entirely unfeasible, but suffers from several problems, among them energy loss by collision with material walls.

(4) Static electric fields, which are impossible, not only because oppositely charged particles—nuclei and electrons—must both be confined, but also because the fields re-

quired to confine either species would be huge.

(5) High-frequency electromagnetic fields, which have been seriously studied; but the prognosis is poor, partly because of the undesirable electrically driven particle motions and partly because the power required for the scheme is very great.

Two principles remain: inertia and magnetic fields. We turn first to the simplest idea of all—inertia, as in the H-bomb itself. Here, nothing confines the plasma; it is heated to a sufficient temperature so rapidly that it fuses before the particles can go anywhere. The idea is to cause fusion to occur in a very small deuterium-tritium pellet, so that the explosion will be very small by nuclear standards, and it can be managed by a simple mechanical system. The pellet is to be heated by a giant laser pulse. Every atom in it is to reach (say) 10 thousand electron volt of energy, and a corresponding speed of about 10^6 meters per second. Under these conditions, a pellet 2 centimeters in diameter will disintegrate in about 10^{-8} second. But in that time, and under ideal circumstances, it will fuse about one-tenth of its fuel, and release more than 10^{11} joules of energy.

This explosion, however, is unacceptably large: it is equivalent to the detonation of many tons of TNT. What to do? Just decreasing the pellet diameter won't work, because the pellet will disintegrate quicker (i.e., each particle will travel a distance equal to the pellet's diameter in a shorter time), and not enough of the fuel will undergo fusion. In principle, there is a way out, based on the fact that the fusion reaction rate increases as the square of the pellet's density. This is the key: smaller pellets will work if compressed by the laser pulse itself. The pulse is to be very short and very intense; it is to evaporate the outer layers of the pellet so rapidly that the momentum change of the material leaving the surface creates a compressive force in the remaining core. The pellet's density will then rise well above that of the original solid, and fusion can now occur with a smaller total amount of fuel. A 1,000-fold compression of the pellet is planned, not only to ensure that the pellet burns well, but also to heat it to the initial fusion temperature. At high density (4×10^{31} particles per cubic meter), the pellet will undergo fusion in about 10^{-11} second.

We now have a fair picture of laser fusion. We imagine a mighty laser, with many beams impinging on the pellet to ensure even illumination, and thus that the pellet will compress. If the illumination were uneven, part of the plasma would spurt out where the intensity of the impinging light is even slightly lower.

Why won't this work? We see at least three reasons. First, the laser necessary to implode the pellet must produce a 1 million-joule pencil of light in a pulse lasting a billionth of a second; and it must do so with high efficiency, or else it will consume more energy than the fusion reactor can generate. Such a laser does not now exist, and its science remains very unclear. Although there have been remarkable advances in lasers, they have come mainly by extension of well-known scientific principles. Even then, they have come at a very high cost.

Second, laser fusion necessarily implies a pulsed reactor, one that produces nuclear heat in bursts perhaps a fraction of a second apart, but the unfortunate fact is that pulsed reactors must operate under far less internal stress than steady-state reactors, because cyclic stress tends to fatigue materials. Consider the reactor's vacuum wall, and suppose that laser fusion is proceeding in pulses next to it. The vacuum wall is first heated by the fusion-released energy, and then cooled by the coolant flowing behind the wall. Thus the temperature throughout the wall cyclically rises and falls to different levels at different depths within it; and because metal expands when it is heated, the result is a cyclic stress in the wall. That stress can be calculated, and both the calculations and the experiments made to date suggest that the laser-fusion schemes thus far proposed will fail from thermal stress alone, unless the walls are placed so far from the pellet that the thermal stress becomes negligible. But in that case, the device becomes too huge and too expensive for the small amount of energy that can be captured—a circumstance that will not please the stockholders.

The third problem may be the worst. Imagine that the fuel starts out as a 1-millimeter pellet, and that the laser light shining upon it creates an inward force on its surface that compresses the pellet by a factor of 1,000, to a final diameter of 100 microns. Throughout this compression, all the light of the 1 million-joule laser must remain focused upon it. Now the light must come from large optical surfaces—mirrors, probably—of most remarkable quality, most carefully placed, for no ordinary searchlight mirror will focus all its energy down on a 100-micron spot. There will be perhaps 10 or 20 such mirrors, each 1 meter in diameter, surrounding the little pellet, which compresses and undergoes fusion in 10^{-11} second, and releases about 10^8 joules—the energy content of a satchel full of dynamite. But that amount of nuclear heat is worth about 5 cents, even at today's inflated prices, and so the explosion must cause very much less than 5 cents' worth of damage and disalignment to the optical surfaces, considering all the other costs of building and operating the reactor.

SCHEMES FOR PLASMA CONFINEMENT: MAGNETIC MIRRORS

Evidently the little pellets that can be fried so cavalierly in computor simulations cannot so easily be fried in a fusion reactor. The final possibility is magnetic confinement of a plasma. We therefore turn to an examination of magnetic forces.

Most people have seen iron filings sprinkled on a sheet of paper with a bar magnet placed underneath; it is a ritual of adolescence practiced in high school science classes. A tap of the paper, and the filings arrange themselves into a pattern that suggests a set of curved lines looping from the north pole of the magnet to the south. The lines bunch most closely near the poles, and are most widely spaced far from the magnet. These are the so-called magnetic field lines. They are a way to represent a magnetic field which is otherwise an ethereal thing. Its presence cannot be seen until the iron filings line up and reveal it.

For us, the feature of paramount importance about magnetism is that in a straight and uniform magnetic field—that is, in a field that can be represented by evenly spaced, parallel field lines—a charged particle is constrained to follow a circular path around a field line. If an arbitrary constant velocity along the magnetic field is also imparted to the particle, then its trajectory will be a corkscrew with its axis along a field line. In short, the charged particle's trajectory will be tied to the line. Moreover, if the line is slightly curved, the particle will *almost* remain tied. (The importance of the qualification "almost" will appear later, when we describe tokamaks.)

The particle's bondage suggests a scheme for plasma confinement that is most easily understood if we build it up in two stages. The top drawing in Figure 23-4 shows a single magnet coil carrying a current. The resulting magnetic field lines are also shown, and we have no trouble in seeing that the field is strongest in the plane of the coil, where the field lines bunch together, and progressively weaker at increasing distance from the coil, even on or near the axis. Now imagine two such coils, as in the second drawing. Each carries a current in the same direction. If the coils are suitably far apart, some of the diverging field lines from one coil will be "caught" by the other and will pass through it; accordingly the field's strength will be greatest in the throat of each coil, and less in the space between.

This is a simple magnetic mirror. The name describes a charged particle's motion in the field that the two coils create. Consider Figure 23-5, which is an abstracted and idealized view of the field lines as they approach and pass through the right-hand coil. Imagine that a positive ion is gyrating about the axial field line and that it has some velocity toward the right-hand coil. Now the magnetic force on the ion is always perpendicular to the field line and to the particle's orbit. Therefore it

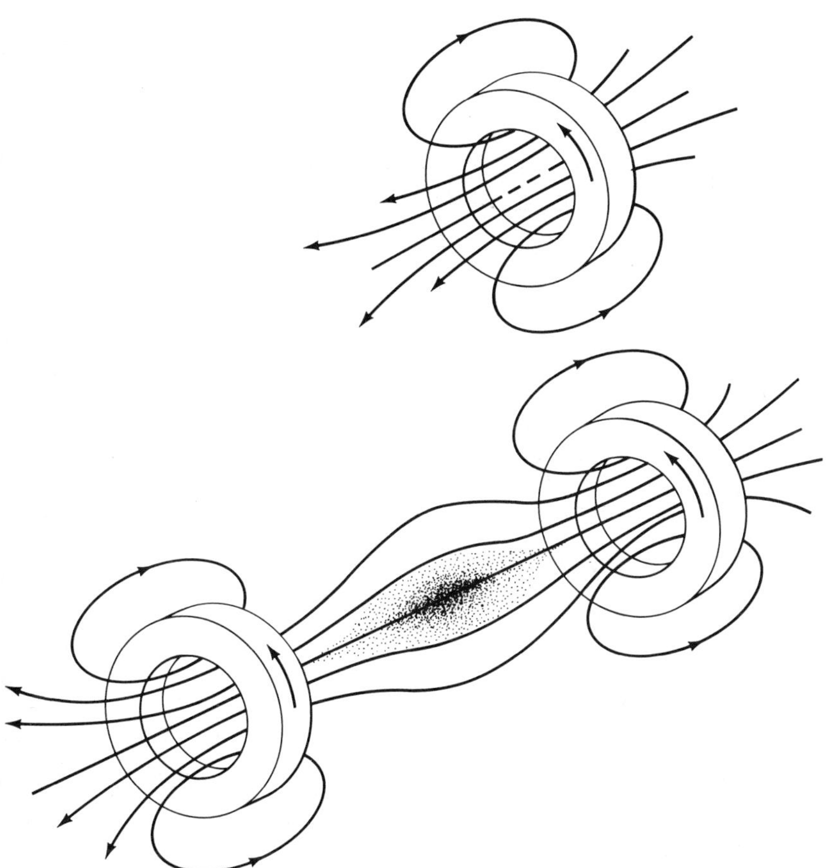

Figure 23-4. The magnetic mirror scheme for confinement of a fusion plasma. In the top drawing, current flows through a single coil. The resulting magnetic field is shown. In the bottom drawing, a second coil is added. Again, the magnetic field is shown. The bottom drawing suggests that plasma can be trapped between the coils of the device. It can, but this simplest mirror configuration is too leaky for a workable fusion reactor.

points toward the axis; this is what makes the particle gyrate around it. But because the field lines converge—because they are not parallel and evenly spaced—a component of the magnetic force also pushes the ion away from the high-region. Accordingly, the ion's progress toward the coil is slowed, but because the magnetic field is unchanging, the ion's total energy remains constant—its loss in axial energy is offset by an increase in rotational energy. In the figure, the ion spirals toward the coil until it loses all its axial velocity, and then it spirals back. When it reaches the other magnet coil, it will be reflected there as well. Thus it will remain inside the magnetic cage more or less indefinitely, unless some other phenomenon intervenes. Seemingly, we need only heat up a fusion plasma and maintain it between two magnetic mirrors, and we will have a fusion reactor.

How can the plasma be heated? Present ideas call for large particle accelerators to produce ion currents totaling thousands of amperes at a voltage of (say) 100 thousand

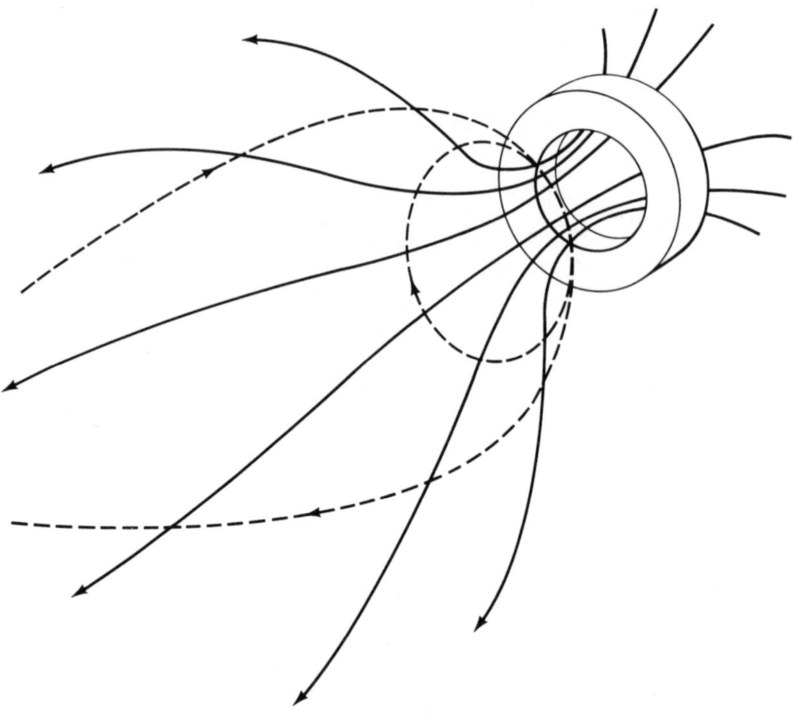

Figure 23-5. The trajectory of a charged particle approaching the right-hand coil of the magnetic mirror device shown in Figure 23-4. At first, the particle spirals toward the mirror region, but its axial velocity progressively decreases. Finally, it is reflected back toward the left. Some particles, however, are not reflected. Those traveling too directly toward the mirror's throat pass through the ends of the device.

electron volts. The ions, as such, would not be able to cross the magnetic field and enter the confinement region; therefore they must be reconverted to neutral atoms before injection. Once inside, the plasma already present will re-ionize them and they will promptly become trapped on magnetic field lines. In sum, the injection process, as now envisaged, proceeds from neutral gas in a storage tank to energetic ions emerging from the accelerator to energetic neutral particles at the entrance to the fusion chamber and, finally, to energetic ions within the fusion plasma—surely a very roundabout method. Yet it has been tried with good success on a moderate scale, producing, for example, beams of 20 amperes at 50 thousand electron volt energy.

Do we now have a workable fusion reactor? Not yet. Notice that the magnetic field, in its confining effect on charged particles, acts as if it exerted a pressure: where the field strength is high, the pressure pushing against the charged particles is high. On axis in a magnetic-mirror device, the field strength—and thus pressure—reaches a relative minimum between the two coils, just as one would hope, seeing that a high-energy plasma is to be confined there long enough to undergo fusion. But unfortunately, the field strength also falls off as one moves radially outward, away from the axis. This means that the plasma is unstable: if too much gas is injected between the mirrors, the plasma will pop, like a bicycle tire with too much air pumped into

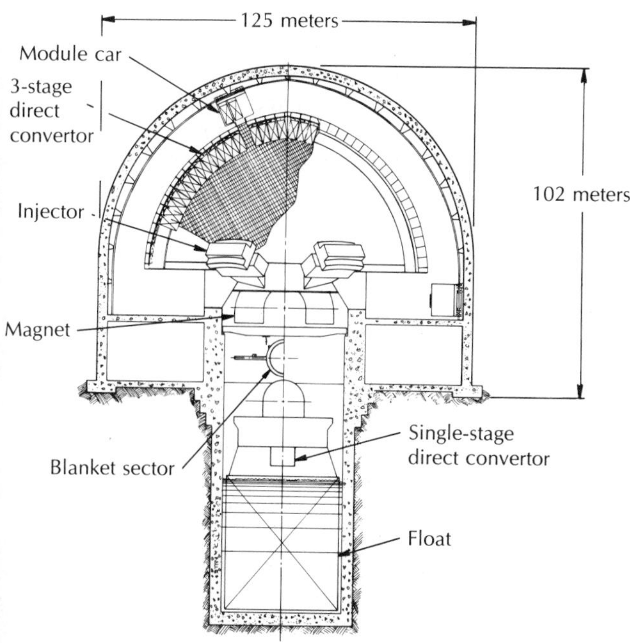

Figure 23-6. A magnetic mirror reference design, as envisaged by the Lawrence Livermore Laboratory. The plasma itself is about 6 meters in diameter. By contrast, the power plant around it is longer than a football field in every dimension. (In most fission power plants, incidently, the reaction chamber is similarly dwarfed by the reactor superstructure.) The plasma lies within a blanket more than 1 meter thick; heat- and tritium-recovery mechanisms are not shown. As in Figure 23-4, the plasma is confined by two magnet coils. Here, however, both have a complicated shape, and both are superconducting. The lower magnet is underground. It rests on a float so that it can be lowered for maintenance of the blanket. This magnet is more powerful than the upper; thus, particles tend to escape toward the top. Escaping particles—above and below the reaction chamber—make the innate efficiency of the reactor very low. They must be recaptured, and their energy reconverted to electricity, by so-called direct convertors—ion accelerators run backward. The ones at the top are to be more complicated and more efficient, but the design of any direct convertor remains problematic. A "module car" is provided in the design for servicing the upper convertors. Finally, a pair of "injectors" are shown; the design calls for several. They inject high-energy neutral atoms, which are re-ionized by the plasma, and thus sustain it.

it. The problem can be cured by causing the magnetic field to have a true minimum in the middle of the device. But there is a cost: the magnetic field and the coils that produce it become very complicated (see Figure 23-6).

Having modified the design, do we *now* have a fusion reactor? Still no, for a second problem remains, and it is far more serious: If an ion between the mirror regions happens to be traveling straight along a magnetic field line, or nearly in such a direction, the axial decelerating force acting upon it will be weak. Thus, ions with velocities directed more or less axially will not be reflected. Instead, they will pass through the high-field region, and escape from the ends of the device. We conclude that the magnetic mirror is leaky. But how leaky? The calculations show that each scattering of an ion is fairly likely to send it flying out the end of the magnetic mirror. This means that the ion is unlikely to stay in the device long enough to undergo fusion because, as we found earlier, even a 20 thousand electron volt ion is likely to scatter many times before it fuses. For this reason, it appears that the energy released by fusion in a magnetic mirror will be approximately equal to the energy that was required to heat the plasma to fusion temperature in the first place. Now the released energy must be converted, at some loss, from heat to electricity. Moreover, energy is required to maintain the steady-state magnetic field that confines the plasma, however poorly, between the mirror regions. In sum, the device seems to be an energy-loser, not an energy-maker.

Immense efforts are now underway to solve the energy-balance problem by developing a way to recover energy from the plasma not only in the form of heat but also directly, as electric power. The idea is to have particles that scatter out the end of the reaction chamber pass immediately into a so-called direct converter—in essence, an ion accelerator run backward. Here, the ions are made to decelerate. Their kinetic energy, lost in this way, reappears in an external electric circuit as delivered power. Valiant attempts to ameliorate the basic problem have been made—the confinement quality of the magnetic mirror itself—by placing subsidiary mirrors at each end, by injecting ions in artful ways, and so on. Whether these various projects will succeed is still unclear. Yet the magnetic-mirror scheme will be successful in at least some of them if its energy balance is to be made attractive.

We can end this account of magnetic mirrors by noting that nature successfully deploys enormous mirrors above our heads. High-energy ions are produced in space by solar flares or by cosmic rays. They may be trapped by the earth's magnetic field, which looks much like the field of a bar magnet. If trapped, they follow corkscrew trajectories around a field line until they near the north or south magnetic pole, and there, where the field lines close in and the field strength rises, they are reflected. The space around earth is thus occupied by charged particles shuttling back and forth between mirrors at the polar regions. The heavenly mirrors, however, are no fusion devices. Indeed, they are no better at confining a plasma than their earthly namesakes. Particles almost continuously escape and rain down into the upper atmosphere, where they create the aurora borealis in the Northern Hemisphere, the aurora australus in the Southern Hemisphere. When solar flares modulate the solar wind, and rattle the configuration of magnetic field lines far out in space, the aurorae become more spectacular.

SCHEMES FOR PLASMA CONFINEMENT: THETA-PINCHES

A second fusion device employing magnetic plasma confinement is shown in schematic diagram in Figure 23-7. Its principle of operation seems to be fairly simple: Electric current is made to flow around a cylinder. In so doing, it creates a magnetic field whose field lines (within the cylinder, at least), are parallel to the cylinder's axis. If cold, dilute plasma initially lies within the cylinder, an immediate increase in the magnetic field strength will compress the plasma initially into a rodlike region at the cylinder's axis; and if this increase is sufficiently rapid, the compression can also shock-heat the plasma—sufficiently, perhaps, so that it will start to undergo fusion. The device is called a theta-pinch because the direction in which current flows around the cylinder, by world-wide convention among fusion researchers, is labeled by the Greek letter theta.

Compressing and heating a plasma requires energy. Doing it quickly requires that the energy come quickly—in other words, that the power be high. Accordingly, theta-pinches will require enormous power supplies, of two sorts. First of all there must be a source of electric current that peaks on the order of microseconds (millionths of a second). It induces a magnetic field that comprgsses and shock-heats the gas to a temperature of about 10^7 K, or about 1 thousand electron volts per particle—approximately 100 times the ionization energy. Then a second power supply, cut in by suitable switching, takes over. It furthers heats and compresses the plasma, this time on the order of milliseconds (thousandths of a second). Pre-

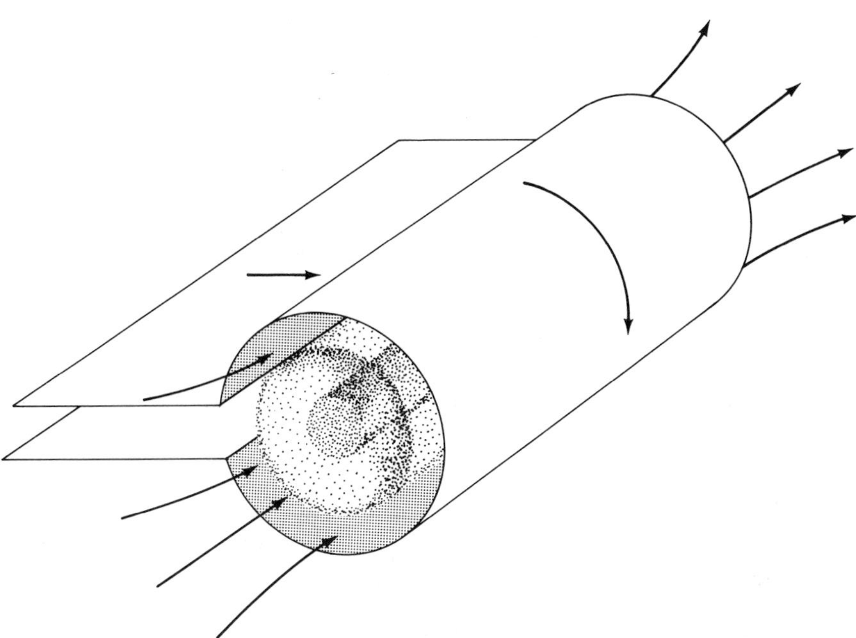

Figure 23-7. The theta-pinch scheme for plasma confinement. Current is made to flow abruptly around a cylindrical surface. This induces a magnetic field that compresses and heats a deuterium-tritium mixture contained with the cylinder. For reasons given in the article, two power supplies and associated switching mechanisms are required, and the larger supply, used for plasma compression, must be superconducting, or the reactor will lose energy, not make it. The power supply's design remains to be invented. One major fault of this schematic drawing: if the cylinder in a real theta-pinch reactor were straight, it would have to be several kilometers long, or the plasma being compressed would spurt out its ends before fusion could occur. Actual designs call for the cylinder to be bent so that its ends meet, obviating the problem. But other problems persist.

sumably fusion now occurs. Two stages of heating and compression are necessary because of the differing time scales. To supply energy on the order of microseconds, capacitors must be used, and capacitors are expensive. To supply energy on the order of milliseconds, cheaper equipment will work. It could be managed, for example, by rotating machinery—a so-called homopolar generator that contains elements that spin at a high rate of speed. When it is slowed, an appreciable fraction of its rotational energy is converted to electrical energy.

Why won't *this* confinement scheme, which worked so well at the plasma-physics stage, work for a commercially interesting reactor? The first problem is that the theta-pinch, like laser fusion, requires a pulsed reactor, with a consequent cycle of thermal stress. Each spurt of fusion in a theta-pinch reactor will last 10^{-2} second, not 10^{-9}, but failure of the vacuum wall through cyclic overstressing will still be a problem. Experiments suggest that only 10^5 to 10^6 cycles can be withstood by a vacuum wall, and thus, with 1 pulse per second, as the proponents of the theta-pinch hope, the reactor will have an operating life of under 2 weeks. Dismal as this sounds, the true stress problem may be even worse, for in the theta-pinch reactor, the metallic cylinder through which current flows will experience a force that arises because the current sheet lies within the very magnetic field that it creates. This is the familiar force that turns electrical machinery. Here, in the cylindrical geometry of a theta-pinch reactor, it will be equivalent to a pressure coming from within. Because the current comes in pulses, so does the pressure, and the cyclic stress problems is exacerbated.

The second problem is energy balance: in this case, the amount of energy delivered by the power supply as compared with the amount of energy produced by fusion. Consider a 1-meter length of theta-pinch reactor. An input of energy approaching 200 megajoules is required to shock-heat and compress the plasma column contained therein; an output of fusion-released heat approaching 6 megajoules is the result. The reactor, then, is a sure loser, unless the power supply's energy can be recycled with incredible efficiency. But doing so will require superconducting pulsed magnets, and superconducting switches as well. The former are now made in small sizes; however, a design for larger versions is hard to foresee and still harder to develop. The need for these devices suggests that the cost of a theta-pinch will be frightening, if only because the cost of a system often relates fairly closely to the amount of energy it must handle.

Problem number three: Suppose that all the other problems have been solved. The fusion reaction proceeds. At the end of each pulse cycle, the magnetic field must drop, in preparation for the succeeding cycle. In consequence, the remaining plasma re-expands to fill the original cylinder volume. Even if fusion no longer proceeds within it, that plasma is still close to fusion temperature. It will damage any material surface it hits, and on the time scale of operation envisaged for a theta-pinch reactor—a fraction of a second per cycle—no way is known by which to protect the vacuum wall from its onslaught. To keep the plasma from hitting the wall, the magnetic field lines would have to change their configuration suddenly at the end of each cycle in such a way that gas nearing the wall would be guided into some receiving area where it could be cooled. The alteration of the magnetic field must be interfaced with the rest of the cycle, and moreover, it must not interfere with the onset of the succeeding cycle. Considering the device's rapid pulsing, its awful energy balance, its precarious technology, and its cost, that feat seems impossible.

One non-magnetic scheme to save the vacuum wall of a theta-pinch reactor has been explored. The hope was to have thousands of little pipes perforating the vacuum wall. At the end of each cycle, puffs of gas would enter the reaction chamber by way of these pipes, and a cooling gas blanket would be created around the plasma. The idea cannot work, because the cooling gas obeys the kinetic theory of gases, according to which some atoms in that gas will have higher velocities than others; and they will reach the plasma first. Here many of them will exchange their charge with ions in the plasma, in the fearsome type of reaction we noted much earlier in this article, and become marauding atoms. Thus, one way or another, high-energy particles will smash into the vacuum wall before the slower particles can enter and erect a gaseous shield (see Figure 23-8).

SCHEMES FOR PLASMA CONFINEMENT: TOKAMAKS

In searching for another magnetic scheme by which to confine a plasma, we begin again with the basic configuration of a theta-pinch; a long, straight cylinder with current circling through it. Assume that the current travels through windings coiled around the cylinder, as in a solenoid—a helix of electrical conductor. Now the cylinder can be gently bent until it has a circular shape. The cylinder becomes a torus, a donut. Not only do its ends meets, but so do the ends of the field lines within: they are closed loops now.

It might be imagined that the confinement problem is solved—just pump in plasma, and at a suitably impressive magnetic field strength it will remain confined at high temperature and density long enough for fusion to occur. In reality, there are difficulties. The principal one is that the plasma ions cannot be kept from drifting to the sides of the torus,

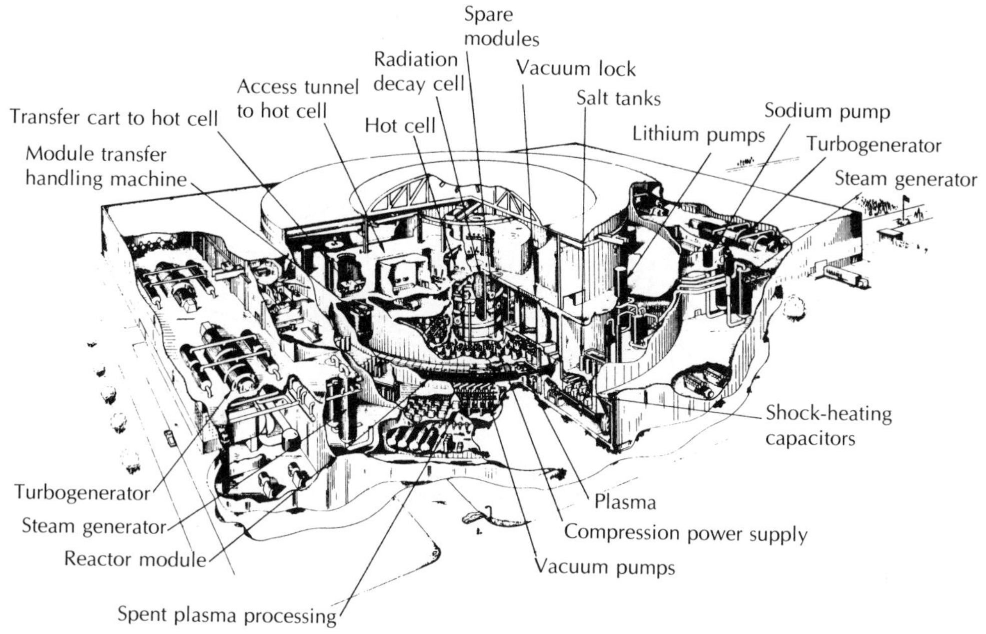

Figure 23-8. A theta-pinch reference design proposed by Los Alamos Scientific Laboratory and Argonne National Laboratory. It suffers from several problems, as described in the article. The reaction chamber is a ring of modules, each working on the principle schematized in Figure 23-7. It is thought that each can be removed for servicing, first to a "radiation decay cell" where, in perhaps a day, it will lose much of its radioactivity, and thence to a "hot cell," where maintenance and repair is to be conducted. Power supplies occupy much of the remaining space around the reaction chamber. Even so, their size may have been underestimated. The reactor is cooled by a series of systems interconnected by heat exchangers. Lithium and lithium salts remove heat from the reactor. Their heat is removed by sodium, which then surrenders it to steam in an exchanger much like the one proposed for the liquid-metal fast breeder reactor. Finally, the steam generates electricity in turbogenerators at either side of the mammoth building.

because curved field lines in fact yield not the perfect gyration circles we have considered thus far, but almost-circles that gradually drift across the magnetic field. These drifts cause ions and electrons to be lost in opposite directions, since they are oppositely charged; and the separation of positive and negative charges by means of these drifts gives rise to *electric* fields, which cause profound plasma motions. The result is impact of the plasma on the confining vacuum walls in times that are short compared to the desired confinement time. The heart of the trouble, expressed in another way, is that a plasma inside the torus experiences a larger magnetic pressure on its inner periphery than on its outer periphery. Thus, it is basically unstable against motion radially outward—motion toward the outer torus wall.

Fortunately, this ill seems curable. The illustration in Figure 23-9 shows the torus in perspective. The windings that wrap around the cylinder are present as before: they induce the magnetic field whose field lines run lengthwise through the donut. But note that the primary coil of a transformer has been added to the device. The secondary coil is the plasma itself. Now a pulse of current sent through the primary coil of any transformer induces a pulse of current in the secondary coil. Here, it induces current in the plasma; and also, it causes the plasma to heat up, just

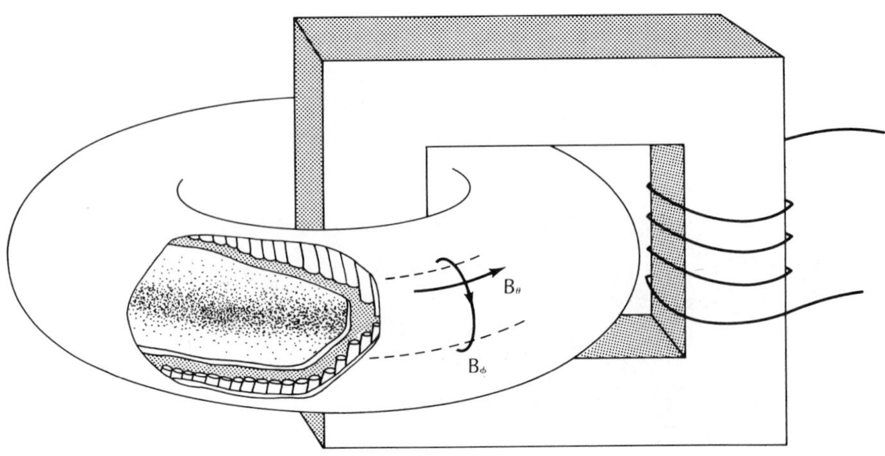

Figure 23-9. The tokamak scheme for plasma confinement. The reaction chamber is toroidal—that is, donut-shaped. Within it, two magnetic fields confine the plasma. The first (B_θ) is induced by current that flows through coils looped around the torus. The second (B_ϕ) is required to correct particle drifts toward the outer torus wall. It is induced by currents in the plasma iteslf, and those currents are induced by current flowing through the primary coil of a transformer. At present, the tokamak is the main repository of American hopes for fusion.

as current sent through a resistor causes the resistor to heat up. The crucial point is that a new magnetic field is created by the plasma's motion. Its field lines circle the plasma in the same way as the windings for the first magnetic field circle the torus cylinder. This second field corrects the separations of positive and negative charges because particles can now flow from the top of the plasma column to the bottom as they gyrate around the new field lines. The result is that the plasma tends to have a uniform electromotive potential. No voltages build up, and in first approximation the plasma is stable. There is a drawback: the unavoidable use of a transformer to generate the second magnetic field means that this device, like a theta-pinch or a laser-fusion reactor, will necessarily be operated in pulses. Here, however, it will be possible to have each pulse last many seconds—perhaps even minutes—and so, while there may still be a thermal-stress problem, it will be much ameliorated. Moreover, the lengthwise magnetic field, which is by far the largest, will not be pulsed at all. It will be steady state, so it may prove possible, using superconducting coils, to make the energy loss from the main confining system negligible. There will, of course, be losses elsewhere—notably losses from the second, pulsed magnet system—but the over-all energy balance may not be the serious problem for this device that it seems to be for the other schemes we have examined. Indeed, it appears at present that the energy balance can be favorable, perhaps by one order of magnitude, which is as good a performance as conventional generating systems can manage today.

The device we are now discussing is the so-called tokamak, first conceived in the Soviet Union and liberally described by the Soviets throughout the mid-1960's, but neglected by the United States until early in 1969, when the late Academician Lev Artsimovich gave a series of lectures on the subject at the Massachusetts Institute of Technology. It is currently the principal vehicle by which the United States hopes to realize its fusion ambitions. To some extent, and at the present time, this hope seems justified. For one thing, Alcator, a small device with a tokamak configuration built at MIT's National Magnet

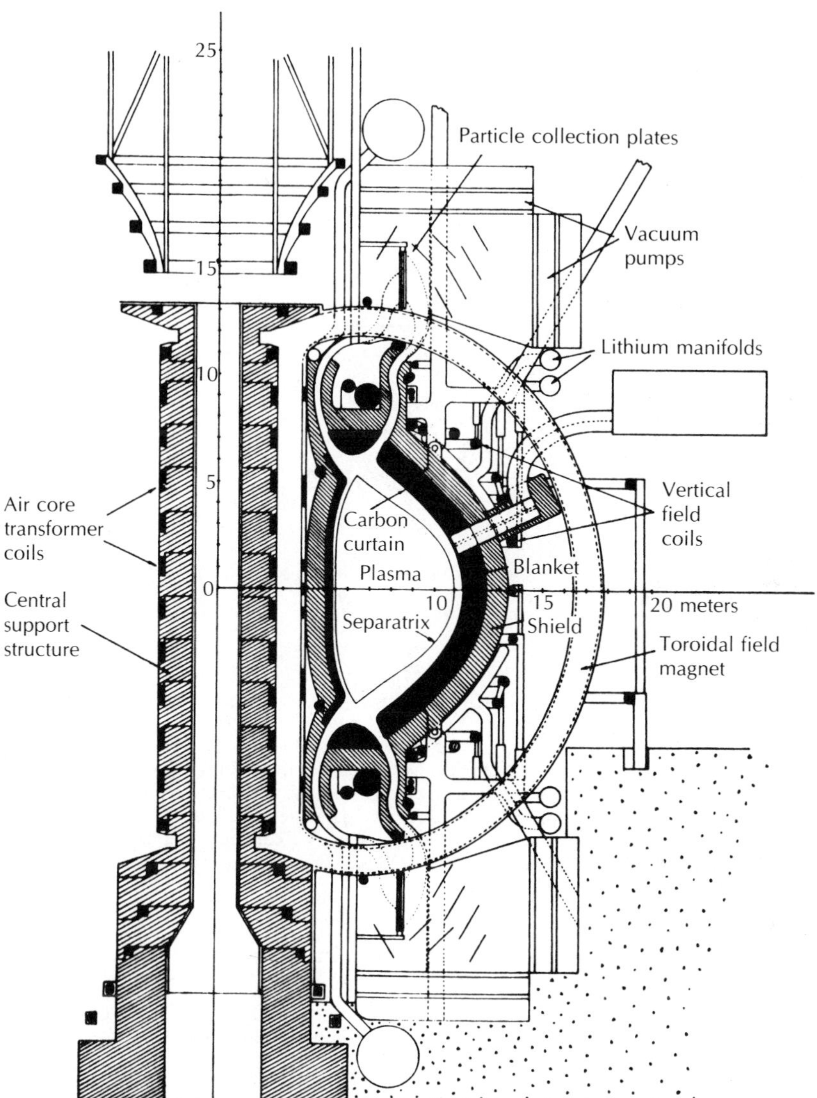

Figure 23-10. Cross section of UWMAK-III, a reference design for a tokamak prepared at the University of Wisconsin. The main magnetic field is induced by a "toroidal field magnet" looping around the reaction chamber. The secondary magnetic field is induced by current in the plasma, and that current is induced by "transformer coils" in the "central support structure." A third field, not mentioned in the article, is produced by "vertical field coils." Like the second field, it corrects particle drifts, and its magnitude is relatively small. The three fields act together to confine a plasma. One field line is shown—the so-called separatrix. Ideally, plasma within that line is confined, while plasma outside it is guided to "particle collecting plates" above and below the reaction chamber. Other details of the UWMAK-III design: The "blanket" contains a lithium-aluminum compound. The lithium is there only to breed tritium, not to cool the reactor. (Cooling is to be accomplished with helium.) The "shield" provides additional protection to outside structures; the blanket alone is deemed insufficient. The vacuum wall has a graphite curtain, intended to protect the wall from radiation and plasma particles. But graphite will trap atmospheric gases during construction and maintenance, and then pollute the vacuum during reactor operation.

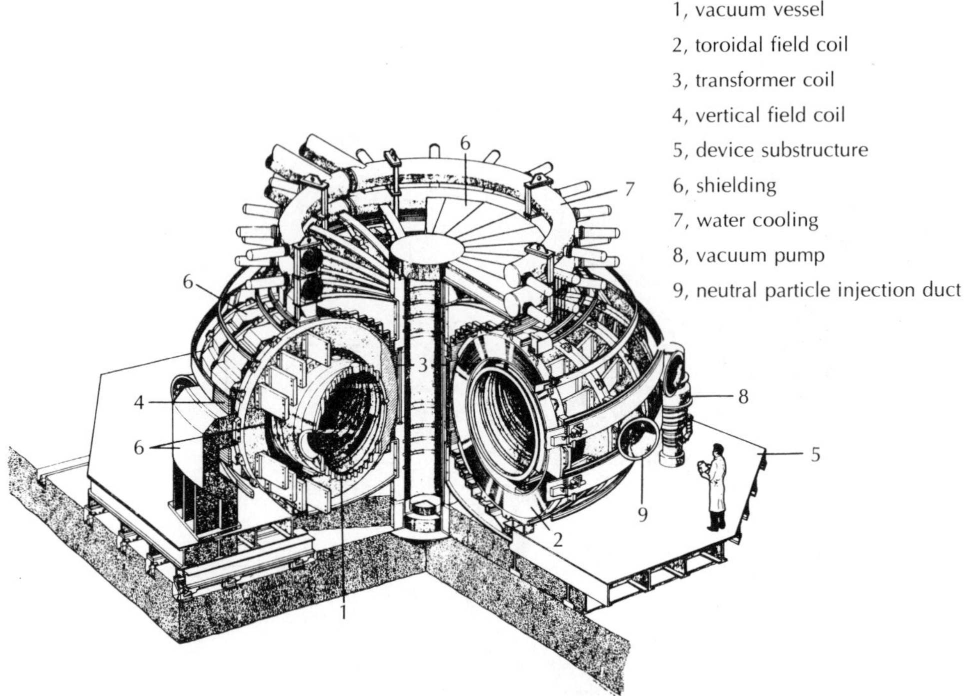

Figure 23-11. The Tokamak Fusion Test Reactor (TFTR), to be constructed at Princeton University's Plasma Physics Laboratory. Over $200 million will be spent to build the device, with its associated facilities; and roughly the same amount will be spent on operating costs through the mid-1980's. The device is not a reactor; it represents an opportunity to create and experiment with a fusion plasma. ''Neutral particle injection ducts'' will continually introduce hot particles into the torus. Initially only light hydrogen will be used; toward the end of the experiment's life, a deuterium-tritium mixture may be tried.

Laboratory, has produced the best plasma confinement the world has yet known: the plasma's density was more than 10^{14} particles per cubic centimeter, which is adequate for fusion. The other confinement parameters, however, were not adequate: the plasma's temperature was not 100 million degrees, but only 10 to 15 million, and the confinement time was not 1 second, but only one-twentieth of that. Still, these numbers are limited by the size of the device, and Alcator performed roughly as hoped for—well enough to permit new experiments to be conducted on the physics of plasmas. The Magnet Laboratory is building a bigger one.

In tokamaks, the opportunity may exist to solve, or at least bypass, some of the problems unearthed by the other conceptions. Some of the solutions will come at the cost of increased complexity, but at least the researcher has the chance to move on and discover what else lies ahead in fusion development. Consider the problem of plasma hitting the vacuum wall. Although a tokamak may run at almost a steady state for many seconds, the problem persists because plasma confinement inevitably will be imperfect. Even if it magically were perfect, the spent fuel would have to be removed and fresh fuel added. Thus, there is a need for a plasma pump—in practice, a region near the walls of the torus from which the magnetic field lines peel off into a receiving area, carrying plasma with them and keeping it off the vacuum wall.

Provision for such a pump is included in the tokamak reference design called UWMAK III, prepared at the University of Wisconsin and shown in Figure 23-10. Here, the simple conceptual design of a tokamak has grown into an immense and immensely complicated structure; the regions at the top and bottom of the plasma are the pump or graveyard regions, actually called divertors. Spent plasma arriving there will have a temperature not much below that in the main part of the plasma, so the pump's surfaces will probably have to be replaced periodically. Still, the damage occurs where it can be planned for, and not at the main vacuum wall.

FUSION'S SHOPPING LIST

Will a tokamak ultimately be the basis for a successful fusion reactor? Notice that our discussion of the device, and the remarkably uncluttered illustration (Figure 23-9), lack all of the following: An injector of fresh fuel; a neutron-moderating blanket; a heat-removal apparatus for the blanket; an arrangement for tritium recovery and tritium breeding; mechanical support for the magnets; thermal isolation of the magnets—they must be kept below 20 K (perhaps less) if they are to be superconducting, while the nearby plasma must be kept at 100 million degrees (perhaps more); any method of heating the plasma to an initial fusion temperature, other than with the transformer (and it can be shown that the resistance heating of the plasma by transformer-induced current is by itself insufficient); any arrangements for safety, access, or repair. In fairness to tokamaks it should be said that many of these problems are design-independent: they and others will apply in some form to any fusion reactor. Here is our shopping list:

Plasma Engineering

Ionized gas is not enough. It must have the right density and the right temperature in the right places. Moreover, it must be pure, in part for reasons we touched upon earlier: impurities cool the plasma and may, after charge-exchange reactions, damage the vacuum wall. An additional reason is that scattering of the plasma's particles by the massive particles typical of impurities leads to loss of energy from the plasma by electromagnetic radiation—for example, by the so-called *Bremmsstrahlung* (literally braking radiation), created by the deceleration of electrons. Keeping impurities out of a plasma is very difficult. The laws of physics assure us that the boundaries of the plasma will be fuzzy; the best we can hope for is a density that is high in the middle and that tapers at the sides. But then the hydrogen isotopes in the plasma will tend to diffuse outward, while other particles—perhaps heavy niobium or molybdenum atoms freed from the vacuum wall—will tend to diffuse inward. Such phenomena portend future needs for plasmas whose temperature and density gradients are controlled for engineering objectives. Plasma physics will have to become plasma engineering and related to specific fusion systems.

Entrances and Exits

Over $2 billion has been spent around the world on plasma confinement. But how is the plasma to be injected into the vacuum region? And when part of the plasma has fused, how are the helium and the unburnt gas to be removed? In discussing tokamaks, we mentioned divertors to remove the spent plasma; they are a necessary invention for any practical fusion reactor. What about plasma injection? That problem also looks fierce. A neutral beam of deuterium and tritium won't work in a large device; the atoms will be ionized before they get deep enough into the plasma to suit the plasma engineers. Can injection be accomplished with chunks of fuel the size of a grain of rice, or of a pea? The problem resembles in some ways the reentry problem for a space vehicle nearing the earth's atmosphere, but it is harder to solve. Ignoring it is like proposing an internal combustion engine that contains only a combustion chamber, and lacks intake valves.

Materials

They must be resistant to an immense flux of radiation, neutrons, and heat and also to strange kinds of corrosion and immense pressures; if the reactor operators had to replace the insides once a week, even if it could be done quickly, the reactor would soon be an economic loser. It will take years to find and develop new materials—longer, probably, than the optimists think, and the administrators in Washington proclaim. The vacuum wall, for example, faces an environment that is unimaginably hostile—an energy flux that is higher than anything else ever made, except a nuclear weapon in the process of exploding. There is a serious danger that the vacuum wall will sputter away when high-energy particles hit it, dislodging heavy atoms that will contaminate the plasma. One might conclude that the vacuum wall will have to be outrageously thick if it is to survive many years of operation. On the other hand, thick walls give poor heat transfer and also capture large numbers of neutrons where they should not be captured. Developing a material suitable for the vacuum wall and similar critical locations will be one of the most difficult problems of controlling fusion.

Progress, however, is being made. High-nickel stainless steels developed at Oak Ridge National Laboratory are much more radiation-resistant than any structural metals known a few years ago. Such alloys suggest that the energy flux in the reaction area could safely be increased, and that, in consequence, the reactor could be made smaller for the same power output. If it could be made smaller still, perhaps normally conducting coils could be used instead of superconducting ones, with a vast reduction in engineering complexity. But it might then have disastrously poor net power output. The true direction of progress is still uncertain.

Reliability, Repair, and Accessibility

None of the present schemes is credible from this aspect, and in general, the larger and more complex systems are less credible. Again, the most critical item is integrity and possible repair of the vacuum wall. Recall that reactor operation will make it radioactive. The problem cannot be wished away until a fusion demonstrator stage: experience with acceptance of fission reactors shows that the efforts made to develop fusion reactors must include work on these matters, too, or power companies will not be interested.

Plasma Confinement

It appears that simple magnetic mirrors will not work as fusion reactors, nor will fast-pulsed devices such as theta-pinches and systems using lasers. The tokamak configuration remains, but whether it is truly workable as a fusion reactor is not certain either. Fortunately, other ideas are appearing. One, still in its earliest stages of investigation, is the so-called bumpy torus, made by taking a set of coils such as those used in magnetic mirrors, and arranging them in a ring, like hoops in a circular croquet game. The plasma confined by this array takes on the shape of a string of sausages. It appears that a bumpy torus may correct the radial instabilities found in a single magnetic mirror, for the stability of a plasma depends on the average history of the particles within it—on the changing strength and orientation of the magnetic field sampled by the particles as they move. Moreover, particles would not be lost out the ends of a bumpy torus, since it has no ends. Finally, a bumpy torus could operate continuously, without pulsing, in the manner of a single magnetic mirror. The scheme is only one of a whole class of steady-state toroidal devices, most of them inadequately explored.

Tritium

The fact that tritium does not occur in nature received little attention until about 1960, because it had been a tacit assumption that, as we reported, one could always make tritium by using fusion's leftover neutron in a reaction with lithium. But this means that the fusion reactor must be a complicated breeder reactor from the start. The need for tritium (with its radioactivity) is lamentable, but the cross sections for fusion reactions involving other light nuclei are far smaller than the cross section for the deuterium-tritium reaction. Therefore, far greater values of density, temperature, and confinement time would be required to make the other reactions proceed at an appreciable rate. We noted all this earlier.

Now it may be that only 1 gram of tritium will be reacting in a 50,000-ton fusion reactor at any one time. However, the burnup of nuclear fuel for each pass through the reactor will be only a few per cent, so the reactor will likely contain several kilograms of tritium, most of it being separated from the spent plasma and then recycled—all by a process not yet worked out. Perhaps some of the details are yet to be discovered, for controlling tritium is exceedingly difficult. The isotope is a form of hydrogen, and hydrogen diffuses through almost all metals useful for the reactor structure. Those metals that can contain hydrogen include platinum, which is too soft; tungsten, which is almost impossible to machine; and gold.

Lithium

Will there be enough deuterium and tritium to run a fusion-powered economy of the future? Deuterium, at least, is plentiful, as we have seen. To provide an environment in which tritium can be created, every fusion reactor will be surrounded by a lithium-containing blanket in which the lithium-neutron reactions will occur. Therefore we turn to the question of lithium availability.

For the year 2000, it is estimated that an electric generating capability of up to 1,000,000 megawatts will be needed in the United States. No megawatts in that year will be generated by fusion, but let us imagine similar energy demand at some later time. The potential world reserves of lithium are estimated at 2×10^7 metric tons, enough for 2.8×10^{14} megawatt-hours of electric power production. This is approximately a 30,000-year supply, seemingly enough to last through a long technological age. However, there are complications. First, the inventory of lithium in a fusion reactor must be fairly high, if the lithium reactions are to occur before the neutrons are absorbed elsewhere, perhaps by the structural material of the reactor. Second, liquid lithium (or a molten salt that contains lithium) may also be required to remove nuclear heat from the reactor. One might conclude that lithium will be in short supply for fusion reactors. One estimate is that about 9×10^5 metric tons will be required to begin operation of 1,000,000 megawatts worth of fusion reactors; this is a large drain on lithium resources, but could probably be met by a determined effort.

The lithium reserves quoted above do not include the lithium in sea water (approximately 2 parts per million by weight), which is much larger but so far is very expensive to extract. Yet past experience shows that when a serious attempt is made to locate new reserves of previously ignored minerals, more will probably appear. Plainly, the lithium resources could permit vastly more energy generation than petroleum ever did or coal ever will, before heroic measures need be undertaken to exploit dilute lithium deposits. Since complex civilizations have been built on fossil fuel, lithium availability should not be a barrier to fusion development; the supply is short only compared with the essentially endless supply of deuterium.

In view of all the difficulties, we ask again: Are we mad to pursue controlled nuclear fusion? And are all the moribund concepts—laser fusion, simple magnetic mirrors, theta-pinches—a sign of the expensive folly? The answer to the second question is easy, and it is definitely no. By such trials and errors, we have come as far as we have. The experiments have taught us about high-density, high-temperature plasmas, about plasma instabilities, about the damage that high-energy particles and radiation cause in various materials. In any event, the work typifies the way the development of high technology must proceed.

As fusion schemes come and go, it is hard to distinguish between a valuable stepping-stone that lets us advance, and a corner-stone of the final fusion edifice. How does one tell when the final concept arrives—the one upon which all further efforts ought to be focused? One cannot know in an absolute sense. Judgment must enter in. In our view, the field is still open; the best fusion concept has yet to be recognized. Meanwhile, however, the Energy Research and Development Administration made a long-range plan for fusion, and at first gave the impression that it knew pretty well what a fusion reactor will look like. The drafts included trial plans describing in inappropriate detail the development of an "experimental thermonuclear reactor"—an extrapolation, evidently, of current reference designs. "Start fabrication of magnet coils"; "Complete installation of magnet coils"; "Start test"—this last step in July of 1989! Taken literally, the ERDA exercise suggested to some that the fusion program is fixed in direction through the late 1980's, and this generated vigorous comment in the scientific literature.

Of course, extrapolation of current reference designs would lead to fusion monstrosities: structures 50 meters in diameter, cooled by liquid lithium flowing behind 1 acre of wall 1 millimeter thick, magically maintained by remote machinery. The superconducting magnets that surround the reaction region, as presently designed, would make it inaccessible for any kind of servicing by an electric utility company. The minimum feasible size of such a reactor might be 10,000 megawatts, too much in one unit for any electric utility. If fusion reactors look like that, officials of the utilities are saying, then we don't want them.

The plans more recently presented by ERDA show a welcome flexibility, and no fixed view of what a real fusion reactor will look like. Indeed, the first page points out in effect that such plans are meant to be self-destructing: five years from now we hope to know much more than we do now, just as now we know much more than we did five years ago. So we live in hope.

THE PROSPECT FOR FUSION

The growth of nuclear power fluctuated greatly in the period preceeding the early 1970's. Because of hopes for cheap nuclear power, a flurry of orders for fission reactors came in during the mid-1960's, at very low quoted prices—one figure was $130 per kilowatt of installed generating capacity. Reality soon caught up with both the utilities and the reactor manufacturers; it was realized that nuclear power would be more expensive, and that all the faults had not been eliminated. (See Article 21, this volume). Then the orders declined. They picked up again only as fossil-fuel power began to look more expensive, partly because in the early 1970's it came under increasingly strict environmental regulation; virtually every coal-fired electric power plant in the Northeast either closed down or switched to low-sulfur oil. Finally, in 1973, the predictions of fossil-fuel difficulty became known to all, and about 50,000 megawatts of nuclear power-generating capacity were ordered. Continuing fossil-fuel price rises in 1974 reinforced the trend to nuclear power. However, the plants now cost up to $1,000 per kilowatt, in 1980's money, for 1980's delivery. The electric utility industry is in real danger of economic collapse; the commitments to new nuclear plants (180 gigawatts, more or less) could break it.

Nuclear fission has had a number of successes and a number of failures. Some of the failures have been organizational in nature—there has been insufficient self-criticism and insufficient internal responsibility. Don't rock the boat, various committees seem to have decided. Give us the money and we'll get around the problems somehow, but let's handle it secretly. This strategy doesn't work in the long run: criticism will come anyway, and when it does, people will grumble even more, asking, "Why didn't you tell us that before?" Surely it must be possible for a society to face a difficult problem, knowing that an effort must be made though a happy outcome is uncertain. Each citizen seems perfectly able to understand the situation. But when people become members of committees, they don't dare say those things that committee members should say to one another.

In efforts to control fusion, some of these problems have already appeared. For example, fusion research was sold for years on the basis that fusion reactors were just around the corner. In the 1950's, engineers were making designs of fusion reactors that employed copper coils and steam pipes instead of the very exotic materials that we now know will have to be developed. At Princeton, researchers planned to build four models of the Stellerator—a fusion device of olden days. They proposed Models A, B, C, and D, each bigger than the one before, and they spent $30 million on C. Model D was to have been the industrial demonstrator, but it was never built, because Model C led to a new plasma science, not to a confirmation of the old. In that way, these expensive experiments showed researchers that an entire field—plasma physics—had yet to be developed. It took about 10 years, and great credit accrues to the plasma physicists for managing the feat—in essence, for showing how to contain a Promethian fire. After all, confining a plasma is like taking all the air in a room, forcing it into the center of the room without touching it, and heating it to a temperature of several million degrees. A principal difficulty was expecting and predicting too much too soon. Bit by bit, realism now works its way in. Princeton now plans to build the TFTR—the tokamak fusion test reactor—at a cost of $228 million. It is meant to be operational in 1981 or 1982, but it will have no engineering for energy recovery. Still, it will (one hopes) confine a plasma well enough for fusion to occur, were it fueled with a deuterium-tritium mixture. (Doing that, however, would cause the TFTR to become radioactive after very few test firings) (see Figure 23-11).

The design that currently gets the most money is the tokamak, which has many problems. But at least the difficulties seem to be evenly spread: the confinement time, the divertors that pump the plasma in and out, start-up, access, wall damage, repairability. . . .

Many things must be done, and failing to do any principal one could kill the entire effort. Consider this fable: If you, as the director of an energy utility in the twenty-first century, had a fusion reactor constructed according to 1977 designs, and a pinhole puncture developed in its vacuum wall, you'd have to move to Antarctica, and you'd be pursued, not necessarily by radiation but surely by outraged investors. Technological problems such as vacuum-wall integrity may yet be the critical ones in controlling fusion.

SUGGESTED READINGS

Booth, Lawrence A., David A. Freiwald, Thurman G. Frank, and Francis T. Finch, 1976, Prospects of Generating Power with Laser-driven Fusion, *Proceedings of the IEEE 64*, pp. 1460–1482.

Energy Research and Development Administration, 1976, Fusion Power by Magnetic Confinement: Program Plan, Division of Magnetic Fusion Energy, U. S. E. R. D. A., Washington, D.C. 02545. Five parts, but its "Executive Summary" and "Volume One: Summary" are useful as an overview.

Glasstone, Samuel, 1974, Controlled Nuclear Fusion, Energy Research and Development Administration, 88 p.

Hirschfeld, Fritz, 1977, The Future with Fusion Power, *Mechanical Engineering 99*, pp. 22–31.

Kulcinski, Gerald L., 1974, Fusion Power: An Assessment of its Potential Impact in the United States, *Energy Policy Journal 2*, pp. 104–125.

Lidsky, Lawrence M., 1972, The Quest for Fusion Power, *Technology Review 74*, pp. 10–21.

Metz, William D., 1976, Fusion Research (II): Detailed Reactor Studies Identify More Problems, *Science 193*, pp. 38–40, 76.

Post, R. F., 1976, Nuclear Fusion, *Annual Review of Energy 1*, pp. 213–255.

Post, R. F., and F. L. Ribe, 1974, Fusion Reactors as Future Energy Sources, *Science 186*, pp. 397–407.

Solar Energy 24

WILLIAM W. EATON 1976

INTRODUCTION

Solar energy—the energy received by the Earth from the Sun—has provided, directly or indirectly, almost all the sources of energy for the Earth since its creation.

Sunshine consists of a wide variety of electromagnetic waves that are similar in many ways to radio and TV waves. Its three main components are invisible heat waves, visible light rays of various colors, and invisible ultraviolet rays. Most of the ultraviolet portions are absorbed by the Earth's atmosphere.

This energy travels from the Sun through space at a speed of 300,000 kilometers (186,000 miles) per second, and for practical purposes, it is inexhaustible.

For millions of years, sunlight has been captured by photosynthesis in plants. Through the slow action of heat, pressure, and aging, plant substances have turned into coal, petroleum, and natural gas—the fossil fuels—which now provide over 93 per cent of the energy used by industrial man.

The human race, and indeed all animal and plant life upon the earth, has always depended for existence on the Sun's energy. Most importantly, the Sun's rays provide the heat necessary to maintain the temperature required for human, animal, and plant survival. Photosynthesis enables sunlight to provide the energy needed to convert atmospheric carbon into organic forms, which animals use as food, and is a key element in the ecological balance of nature. Solar radiation also produces combustible materials—chiefly wood—that provide heat for cooking and other uses.

The amount of energy reaching the Earth's surface is so vast as to be almost incomprehensible. Two examples may make this clear. On a global scale, the solar energy that arrives in one to two weeks is equivalent to the fossil energy stored in all the Earth's known reserves of coal, oil, and natural gas. In the United States, the solar energy that reaches one-five hundredth of the country—an area smaller than that of Massachusetts— could, if

Dr. William W. Eaton is an independent consultant and a registered professional engineer with extensive experience in industrial research and development. He has served as Deputy Assistant Secretary for Science and Technology, U.S. Department of Commerce, and has headed several studies on environmental effects of nuclear power plants. He holds several patents and has written widely in energy-related fields.

From the booklet *Solar Energy*, 1976, 49 p. Reprinted with light editing and by permission of the author and the U.S. Energy Research and Development Administration, Office of Public Affairs, Washington, D.C. 20545.

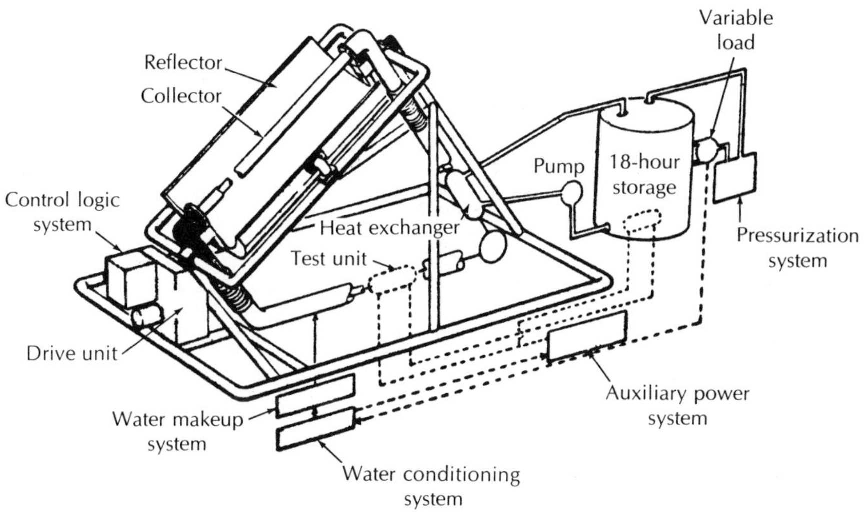

Figure 24-1. The highly reflective curved metal plates on this solar collector cause the sun's rays to converge on the glass tube in the center. Water or another suitable fluid in the tube is heated by the sun, circulated through the tubes of the heat exchanger, and recirculated to pick up more heat. The heat is transferred in the heat exchanger to another fluid that is pumped to the storage tank where it can be used to produce electricity, provide air conditioning, and furnish hot water and heat for homes and other buildings. The work at ERDA's Sandia Laboratories in New Mexico is typical of research under way in university, industry, and national laboratories throughout the United States.

converted at 20 per cent efficiency, satisfy all our present needs for electrical power.

But there are two disadvantages of solar energy. One is that the Sun's energy is *diffuse,* i.e., it is spread out very thinly. It must therefore be collected by some means because only a small amount arrives at one place. The second problem is that it is *intermittent.* The Sun shines only by day and is often obscured by clouds. Thus its energy must be stored until it is needed. Figure 24-1 shows how solar energy is collected and stored for short periods of time.

Sunlight arriving at the edge of the Earth's outer atmosphere carries energy at an approximately constant rate of 1.36 kilowatts per square meter (130 watts per square foot) of area covered. In terms of heat, this is equivalent to 428 British thermal units (BTU) per square foot per hour. (One BTU will raise 1 pound of water 1 °F.)

Measurements in various locations all over the United States have shown that, on the average, over an entire year (including night and day, winter and summer, cloudy and clear conditions) about 13 per cent of the sun's original energy arrives at ground level. (The actual amount at any particular spot at any given moment ranges from much higher to much lower than this average value. See Figure 24-2.) This average is equivalent to about 177 watts per square meter (16.4 watts or 58.5 BTU per square foot) per hour.

If arrangements can be made to collect even this diffuse energy over a relatively large area, tremendous quantities can be made available. For example, the average rate at which solar energy falls on just 0.4 hectare (1 acre) is equivalent to about 710 kilowatts (950 horsepower).

To deal with the other basic problem—the intermittent characteristic of solar energy at ground level—inexpensive techniques are required to store large quantities of energy. The cost of storage is usually a significant fraction of the cost of operating a solar energy installa-

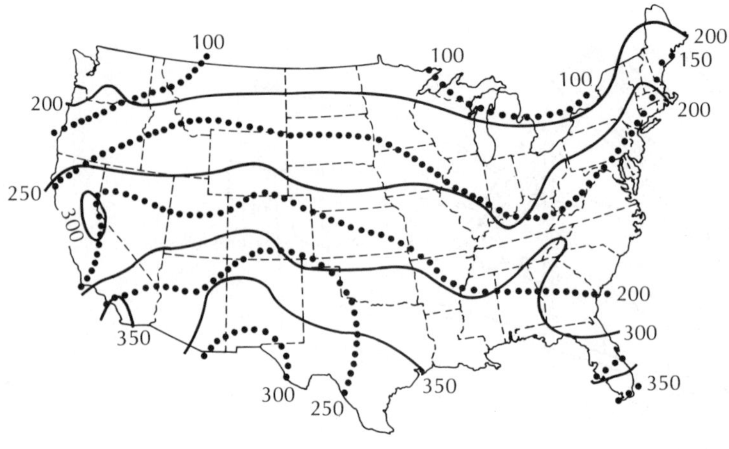

January

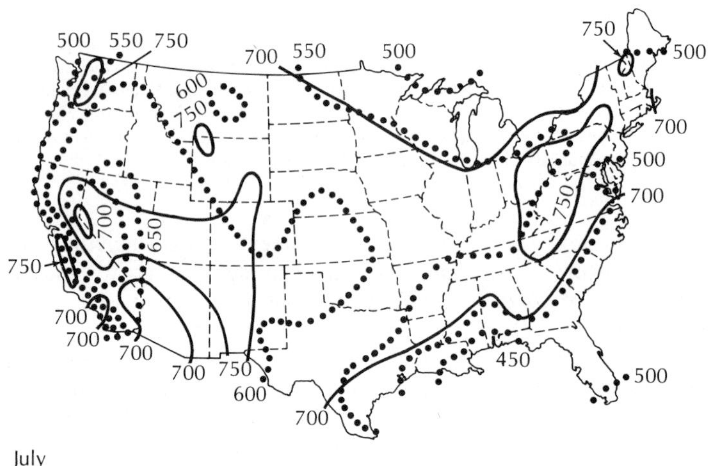

July

Figure 24-2. Lines of equal total daily solar energy at the ground on cloudless days (solid lines) and on days of average cloudingss (dotted lines) in January and July. Units are calories per square centimeter per day. The annual average for the United States is 377, corresponding to 13 per cent of the original energy of the sun. Expressed in American units, this is 58 BTU per square foot per hour.

tion. Thus, major efforts are under way in energy storage research and development.

Of course, mankind has used solar energy for thousands of years. The winds, produced by unequal amounts of solar energy falling in different geographical locations, have been an important tool since earliest recorded history.

Winds that moved ships around the globe were the main source of energy for transportation for many centuries. Windmills are also an ancient way of harnessing solar energy. Even though windmills in many parts ot the world have given way slowly to other kinds of energy sources, there is considerable interest now in reviving them as a supplementary source of energy.

The Sun's energy has also been used extensively by man simply as heat for a wide variety of applications. Solar energy can be used to generate electricity and to produce high quality fuels.

All these solar energy applications have a number of advantages in common: sunlight is inexhaustible compared with almost all other known available energy sources; it is constant as it arrives in the vicinity of the Earth, even if the amount reaching the ground varies; and it is clean. The only environmenval impact of significance to initial applications is aesthetic, i.e., there is a need to design solar energy facilities that are attractive.

One other advantage of solar energy is that the cost of the "fuel"—the rays of the Sun—is zero. But that is counterbalanced by the initial cost of installing the equipment. Thus, for example, a homeowner using solar energy for heating will save on his bills for oil, gas, coal, or electricity. But this saving may be more than counterbalanced by the payments on the bank loan needed to pay for the installation of the solar heating plant. Nevertheless, the energy is there and, in a time of national and world energy supply problems, the United States has undertaken programs to harness it.

The purpose of this article is to present some basic information about the various applications of solar energy and the developments in technology that will be needed to use it more effectively for the benefit of mankind. Since our supplies of oil and natural gas are being rapidly depleted, it is necessary to develop other possible sources of energy—solar, nuclear, coal, geothermal, and so on. Accordingly, this article covers what is being done in solar energy research, development, and demonstration programs under the leadership of a new agency of the federal government, the Energy Research and Development Administration (ERDA), which was formed in 1975. The activities of ERDA were absorbed by the newly created Department of Energy in 1977.

[In this article, metric units are given first, followed by U.S. units in parentheses. For example, 61 meters (200 feet). Please note that all the units have in general been rounded off to the same number of significant figures.]

SOLAR ENERGY USED AS HEAT

Aside from the more obvious uses of the Sun's direct heat, such as drying food and warming people, the most common method of using solar energy directly has been in a greenhouse, which is principally a glass structure that provides a controlled climate for growing plants.

Although nothing could be much simpler than a greenhouse, it is a surprisingly effective method of converting and trapping the Sun's radiation in the form of heat. This is largely because ordinary glass can transmit the shorter wavelength, visible portions of sunlight and at the same time prevent the passage of longer wavelength, invisible heat waves.

The greenhouse effect is based on this specific property of common glass. A large portion of the visible energy of the sunlight enters the greenhouse through the glass. When it is absorbed by the plants, ground, and fixtures of the interior, it is changed to longer wavelength heat waves that are retained by the glass and raise the temperature of the greenhouse interior. The principle operates on cloudy as well as sunny days and accounts for the effectiveness of this kind of building.

In order to capture the Sun's energy for household and hot water heating, the same basic idea has been applied in the simple solar heat collector unit shown in Figure 24-3. A substantial part of the Sun's energy passes through the glass cover plate, but after it is absorbed by the black background material, it cannot escape and heats the water circulating through the tubes. The heated water is then piped to storage tanks or radiators.

This type of collector unit, which can yield water with temperatures of 38 to 93 °C (100 to 200 °F), depending on conditions, has been employed extensively to supply domestic hot

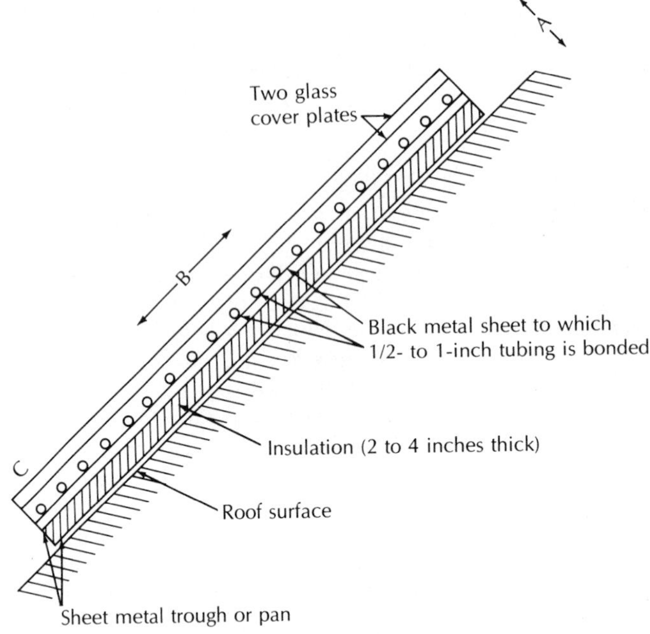

Figure 24-3. Basic design of a solar collector for residential heating and cooling.

water in many portions of the world where sunlight is prevalent. Units of this kind are manufactured and sold in Australia, Israel, Japan, Russia, and to a very limited extent in the United States.

Roughly one-quarter of all U.S. energy consumption is related to space heating, water heating, and air conditioning. As U.S. energy supply demands have grown in recent years, interest has developed in the potential use of devices such as these to supply space heating needs as well as hot water. Several major experiments were carried out in 1974, and planning and construction work is under way on others.

In January 1974 the federal government issued contracts for the installation of solar heating to augment the conventional heating plants in four public schools. The first of these was completed in 6 weeks at the Timonium Elementary School in Timonium, Maryland, near Baltimore. The others were in operation before the end of the winter heating season of 1974 at the Grover Cleveland Junior High School in Boston, Massachusetts; the Fauquier County High School in Warrenton, Virginia; and the North View Junior High School in Brooklyn Park, a suburb of Minneapolis, Minnesota.

All the systems, using different kinds of

collectors and with different capacities to store heat energy, worked satisfactorily. During the 1974 to 1975 heating season, extensive data were collected on the operation and costs of the four systems.

The recent widespread use of air conditioning in the United States has focused attention on using solar energy for cooling instead of heating. Solar cooling, which is another important use of this resource, uses absorption refrigeration equipment of the type employed in gas-burning refrigerators and air conditioners. The solar heat simply substitutes for the gas flame.

For solar cooling, the engineering design challenge is somewhat greater than for solar heating. Whereas lower temperatures are satisfactory for heating, cooling requires that the working fluid must be raised to a temperature of between 88 to 93 °C (190 to 200 °F). Solar air conditioners have been tested and operated at various locations for many months, and tests indicate that they are quite effective. Air conditioning appears to be an attractive use of solar energy because cooling requirements for buildings are apt to be highest during the daylight hours and in the summer, when available solar energy is at its peak, and so there is not as great a need to store heat as there is when solar energy is used for winter heating.

If the design and production problems can be worked out successfully, the use of sunlight for both heating and cooling in a single installation seems to offer the greatest ultimate economic benefit. Such a system is shown in Figure 24-4.

Another important experiment, which was begun in 1974, uses a solar heating and cooling system and instruments to measure solar radiation. This equipment is carried from place to place in two large trailers that join into a single structure at each location. By mid-1975, this laboratory had gathered data in a dozen states in the southwestern, southern, and Atlantic coastal regions of the United States, and was scheduled to cover the entire country by 1976.

Major significant solar cooling experiments were also begun in 1975. A cooling system was added to the school in Timonium, Maryland, and a combined solar heating and cooling system was installed at the Towns Elementary School in Atlanta, Georgia. These were the first tests of solar energy air-conditioning units of commercial size. The rated capacity of the Timonium unit is 126 kilocalories per second (150 tons) and that of the Atlanta unit 84 kilocalories per second (100 tons). Thus far, these absorption cooling units cannot be run at full capacity with solar power.

Congress and the Executive Branch of the federal government have begun to examine the problems of establishing the necessary industrial capacity for rapidly expanding the use of solar energy for heating and cooling. The first result, called "The Solar Heating and Cooling Demonstration Act of 1974", became law in September 1974, and ERDA is working in cooperation with other federal agencies to implement it. This legislation calls for two major demonstrations of the practical use of solar energy on a large scale as follows:

(1) Solar heating technology within 3 years.

(2) Combined solar heating and cooling technology within 5 years.

There is more to do, however, than merely solve design and production problems. Ways must be found to establish conditions under which banks and other lending institutions will provide funds for the purchase of equipment, both to be installed in new buildings and to be retrofitted onto existing ones. Architects, builders, and heating and cooling engineers have to learn to use this new technology and to keep up with developments. Local building codes need to be studied to determine whether changes are needed. There is a need to consider whether laws should protect a building owner against the possibility that someone may build a high-rise just to the south that cuts off his supply of solar energy. Architects face a challenge in

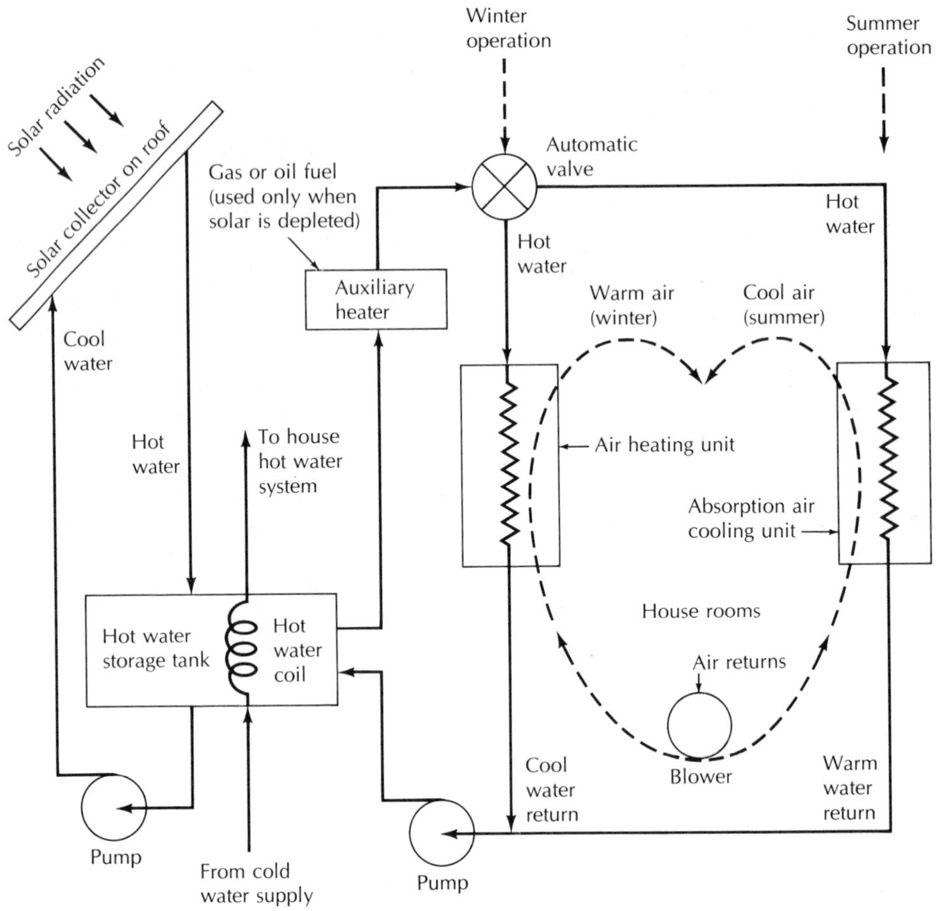

Figure 24-4. This diagram shows a system that combines residential heating and cooling with solar energy.

designing building modifications and buildings that are sufficiently attractive to potential residents as well as to neighbors.

CONVERTING SOLAR ENERGY TO ELECTRICITY

There are a number of different methods, direct and indirect, for converting solar energy into electricity (see Figure 24-5). This section will concentrate on four different techniques that have not been used extensively but which show promise of expanded application as a supplement or a possible replacement for other resources that produce electricity. (Plants and synthetic fuels produced by solar energy could quite possibly be used to generate electricity as well as to produce heat for other purposes. But since the primary objective in these processes involving photosynthesis is to produce general purpose fuels, rather than electric power as such, they are treated separately in the next section.)

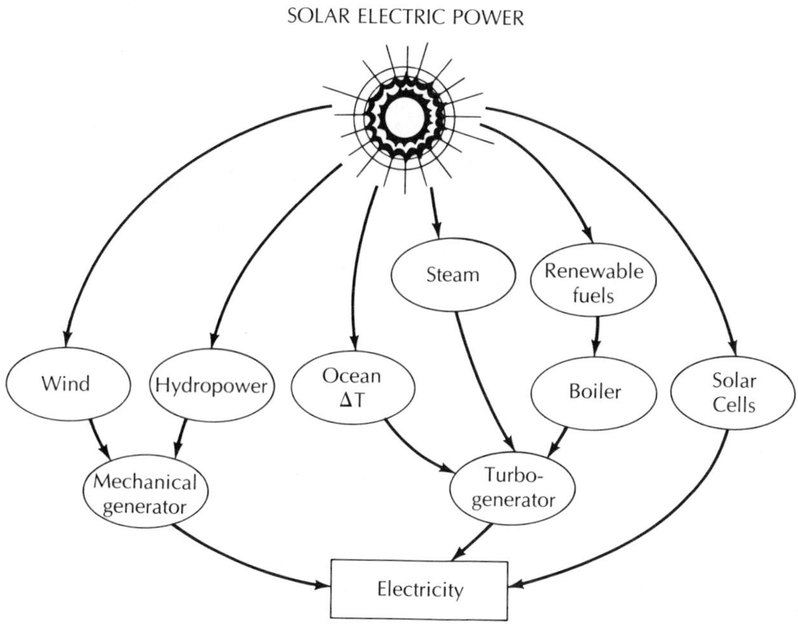

Figure 24-5. This diagram shows the various routes by which solar energy can be converted to electricity.

Wind Energy

It is hard to believe that the fury and destruction of a tornado are the result of anything so benign as sunlight. However, the unequal heating of the Earth's surface produces air masses of differing heat content and density (reflected in the pressure on a barometer) and creates a simple atmospheric heat machine that drives the winds. The problem is how to use them, since the winds are highly variable in place, time, and intensity.

Windmills were extensively used in Europe from the twelfth to the eighteenth centuries, mainly for pumping water and operating machinery. They were eventually replaced by steam and diesel engines.

As the United States grew in the nineteenth century, windmills again became popular, at first for pumping water and later for generating electric power.

Thus, there is nothing really new about using the wind to generate electricity or other useful forms of energy. The main reason windmills have been out of style for some time is that other energy sources, particularly centrally generated electricity now distributed to over 98 percent of U.S. farms, became relatively cheap.

Recent attempts to construct windmills of larger size to produce greater quantities of electricity have not been economically successful. In Denmark in 1915, wind power generated over 134,000 horsepower (100 megawatts), but cheaper hydroelectric power eventually became too competitive. In the United States in the 1940's, a 1,675-horsepower (1.25-megawatt) machine in Vermont became inoperable because of structural failure, and it was never restored to full operation. Again, the primary deterrent to restoration was an economic one.

A large wind-powered electric generator under the joint sponsorship of NASA and

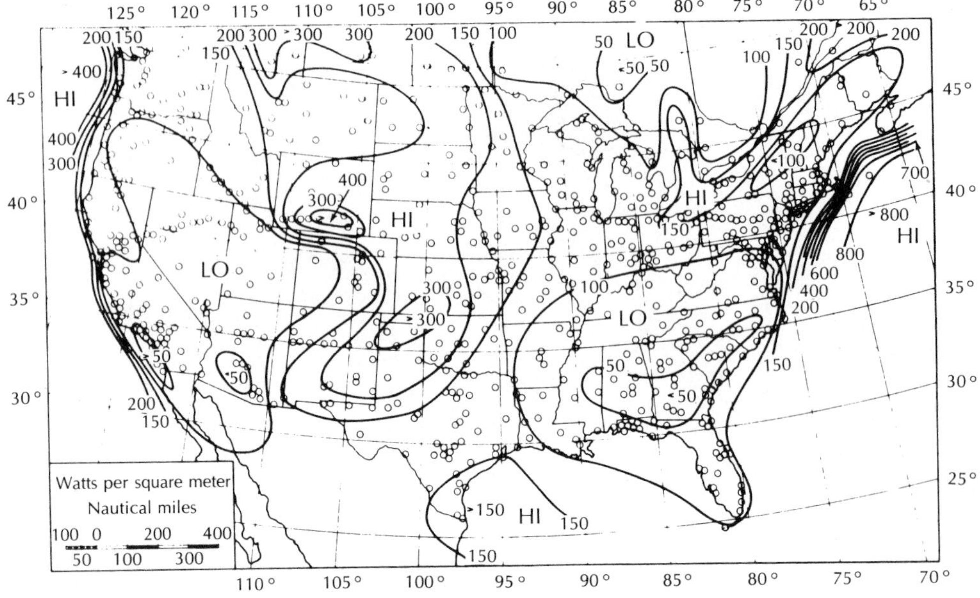

Figure 24-6. Annual average of available wind power.

ERDA has been built at the Sandusky, Ohio, site of the Government's Lewis Research Center. A 38-meter (125-foot) diameter rotor blade mounted on top of a 38-meter tower is designed to generate 134 horsepower (100 kilowatts) of power. Work is also under way on a much larger machine that will use blades up to 61 meters (200 feet) in diameter. In addition, researchers in university, industrial, and national laboratories throughout the United States are carrying out a wide range of studies and experiments in wind energy conversion technology, wind characteristics, mission analyses, applications and systems analyses, as well as large wind energy systems for various purposes. (See Figure 24-6.)

It remains to be seen how much of the total available wind power can really be utilized. Much depends on the size and number of windmills and their location. The challenge to proponents of wind energy is to design systems that work effectively with existing power distribution networks. As other energy sources become relatively scarce and more expensive, there could be a significant return to this ancient power source with its variable but often predictable output integrated with more common means of generating electricity.

Solar Thermal Conversion

Since lenses or mirrors can focus the Sun's rays so as to set combustible materials on fire, it seems logical that the same method could also be used to create steam and produce mechanical forces. This is the basis for the concept involving the concentration of solar radiation by lenses, curved mirrors, or other collectors so that high enough temperatures can be reached to produce steam for a turbogenerator that produces electricity. To obtain sufficient energy for such purposes the solar collectors must be distributed over a broad area. This energy is brought together by one of two approaches: Either the energy is reflected from the field of collectors to a single receiver or a working fluid carries it

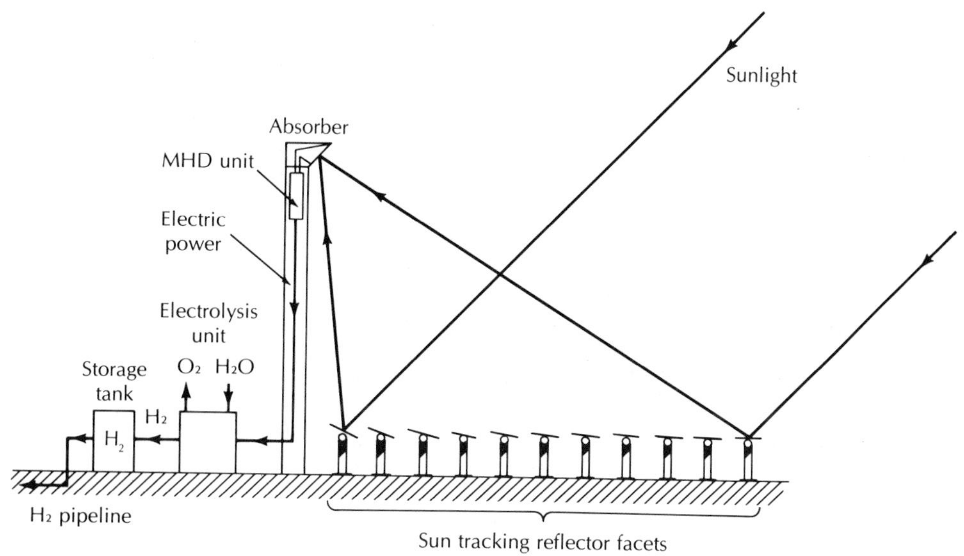

Figure 24-7. If solar heat can be used to drive a magnetohydrodynamic (MHD) power generator, the system might look like this. A two-axis concentrator consisting of a large number of movable reflectors focuses energy at extremely high temperatures to operate a magnetohydrodynamic power unit. Energy from the power unit is used to produce hydrogen (H_2) by electrolysis, the hydrogen then to be supplied directly to consumers or placed in storage for use when solar energy is not available. (From *Technology Review 76,* pp. 30–42, December, 1973. Courtesy of W. E. Morrow, Jr.)

through an insulated heat pipe to the location where it is utilized. Figure 24-7 shows one concept for a central receiver.

There are no basic technical limitations in this method. The main questions are over-all efficiency and economics. As long ago as 1913, a solar power plant built in Egypt used a curved reflecting mirror to focus the Sun's rays on a pipe carrying water. The steam thus generated operated a 37-kilowatt (50-horsepower) steam engine.

With the use of high temperature selective coatings developed in the space program, temperatures can now be reached that make possible the use of standard steam turbogenerators. This makes it practical to use lower precision—and hence less expensive—lens and mirror systems for concentrating the Sun's heat. Researchers in university, industrial, and national laboratories throughout the country are investigating a wide variety of imaginative approaches to this problem.

Solar thermal conversion systems have the following basic elements: (a) A concentrator to focus the Sun's rays; (b) a receiver to absorb the radiant energy; (c) a means for transmitting the heat to either a storage facility or directly to the turbogenerator; (d) a means for storing the heat for use at night and while the Sun is not shining; and (e) a turbogenerator that converts the heat energy of the steam into mechanical energy and, in turn, electricity.

There are many variations of this concept. One of the objectives in all such systems is to produce steam at as high a temperature as possible. When steam is used to produce mechanical work, the higher the initial steam temperature, the more efficient will be the conversion of heat to work.

As mentioned earlier, sunlight is diffuse

and must be collected over a wide area. It is estimated that in the southwestern part of the United States, approximately 26 square kilometers (10 square miles) would be needed to operate a 1,340,000-horsepower (1000-megawatt) plant working at an average capacity of 60 percent. (This is enough power to supply a city of 1 million people.) The initial cost of such a system would be several times that of a conventional power plant, but, as in all solar energy utilization schemes, the "fuel" (sunshine) is free. The principal aim of the research and development in process is to find ways to build such systems that will operate reliably at costs low enough to make them economically attractive.

Substantial technical progress has been made in materials that reflect and absorb solar energy (items a and b above) and in developing heat transfer technology (item c), but there is no present economically attractive solution to the storage problem (item d). Turbogenerator technology (item e) is well developed. The ERDA program includes demonstrations of technical feasibility by small solar thermal pilot plants, which will also help determine the economic feasibility of these concepts.

The environmental aspects of this method are generally favorable. The main environmental problem would be the proper disposition of the heat given off by the condensers of the steam turbines, which is an important problem for all steam-electric plants. The ERDA program includes the design and demonstration of total energy systems in which this "surplus" heat would be used for the heating and cooling of buildings and for industrial purposes.

Photovoltaic Conversion (Solar Cells)

For millions of years, the solar energy in the winds has been creating electricity indirectly in the form of lightning, but it has only been since man has gone into space that he has developed the technology for converting the Sun's radiation directly into electricity on a significant scale. The basic units that accomplish this are called solar cells.

In certain substances, the absorption of light creates an electrical voltage that can be used to generate electric current in an external circuit without any additional power source. This process is called the photovoltaic effect. At the present time, the materials that are used commonly are silicon, cadmium sulfide, cadmium telluride, and gallium arsenide.

The most familiar applications to date for solar cells have been in the space program and in photographic light meters. These cells have supplied most of the electricity for a variety of space vehicles, which could not have operated without them.

Solar cells also have important potential applications on earth in such diverse applications as remote-sensing devices, harbor and buoy lights, fire telephones, and microwave repeater stations, where in most cases they are connected to batteries that store the electrical energy for use when the Sun is not shining. The size and type of the solar-cell panel and battery needed depend on the power required, the sunlight available, and the geographical location.

To make large central installations of solar cells economically attractive, the cost must be reduced very substantially. At present, an array of silicon solar cells measuring 25 centimeters (10 inches) square and costing about $50 would be needed to generate 1 watt. It is generally considered that this cost must be reduced by at least a factor of 100 before solar cells could compete for widespread use as substantial producers of electricity. However, research has produced significant improvements in manufacturing methods and quality control, and the outlook seems good for further progress. Hopes for lowering the cost of solar collectors were raised when recent experiments showed that continuous ribbons of crystalline silicon could be produced routinely in large quantities if more automated equipment were adapted to a mass production system.

If the cost of solar cells is sufficiently

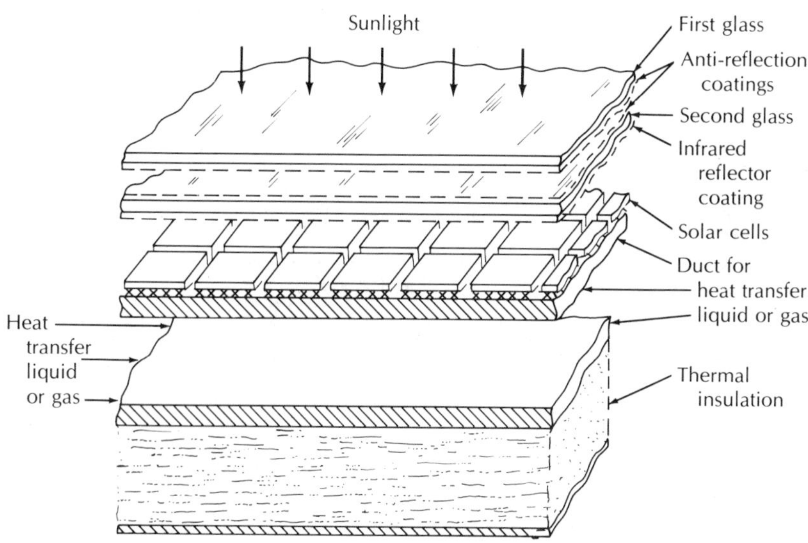

Figure 24-8. Combination collector arrangement to extract both electrical energy and heat from sunlight.

reduced and economical storage techniques become available, solar cells could be used on a large scale, either as elements in the central power system of a utility network or as on-site power supplies to meet the requirements of individual residences and other buildings. For example, a 6 × 9 meter (20 × 30 foot) panel of solar cells operating at an efficiency of only 10 per cent and with a peak output capacity of about 6 horsepower (5 kilowatts) at midday in the northeastern United States, would yield an average of approximately 1 kilowatt over the entire year. This is more than the electrical consumption of the average house. However, since it is unlikely that it will be economically attractive to store electricity on a large scale to make up for the variations in available sunlight throughout the year, auxiliary electricity sources would probably also be required.

Looking to the future, however, when heat and electric storage technology is improved and the cost of solar cells is sharply reduced, the concept of a combination solar battery and heat collector for an individual residence or other building offers attractive possibilities.

A combination thermal-photovoltaic solar collector is shown in Figure 24-8. Under favorable conditions of cost and technology, a panel or array of such collectors mounted on the roof or in some other place would be able to supply the total power requirements of the interior of a house. This would eliminate the need for many electrical transmission lines and central power generating stations with their environmental problems and large fuel requirements. It is estimated that such combination cells could extract as much as 60 per cent of the incident solar energy.

A schematic presentation of the over-all arrangement visualized in this concept is shown in Figure 24-9.

Included for completeness are such features as auxiliary power connections, the possibility of using organic wastes, the use of an electric vehicle, and the provision for air conditioning as well as heating functions.

The system described above represents a fully integrated combination of a number of different subsystems. Such a complex arrangement would not be necessary, however,

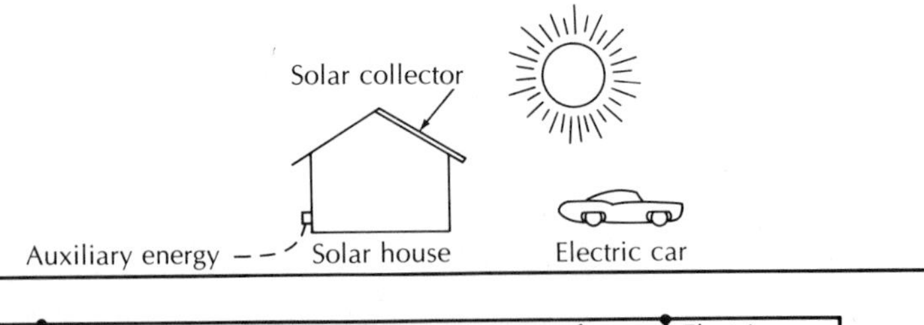

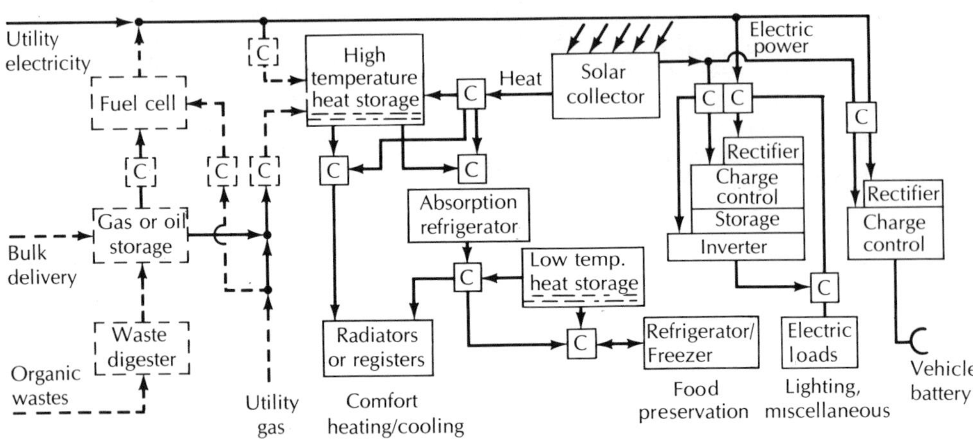

Figure 24-9. System for comprehensive utilization of solar energy in a residential building.

to use solar cells on a more limited basis to produce electricity for localized use in buildings of various kinds to supplement other sources.

The ERDA program also includes wide-ranging studies and experimentation aimed at large-scale, low-cost generation of electricity by photovoltaic means.

Energy from Tropical Ocean Temperature Differences

A large portion of the total solar energy received by the earth is absorbed in the waters of the tropical oceans, and thus the surface temperature of these oceans is maintained at about 28 °C (82 °F).

At the bottom of these oceans, however, are the much colder waters, which are produced by the partial melting of the northern and southern polar ice caps during their respective summers. Thus, beneath 58 million square miles of tropical ocean, there is a continuously replenished supply of water at 1 to 3 °C (35 to 38 °F). Much of this is as close as 610 meters (2,000 feet) below the surface level of the warm water described above. Both the warm and cold water layers are replenished continually by the direct or indirect effects of solar energy. The problem is to find a way of using this 27 °C (45 °F) temperature difference to operate a heat engine, even at low efficiency.

It was suggested in 1881, and shown experimentally in 1930, that significant amounts of heat could be converted to electricity by using the warm surface water of the sea as a heat source and the cold water pumped from the depths as a heat sink.

This thermal energy can be converted to electrical energy by using the open or closed cycle methods. In the open cycle, sea water is used as the working fluid. The warm water is flash-evaporated in partial vacuum, the water

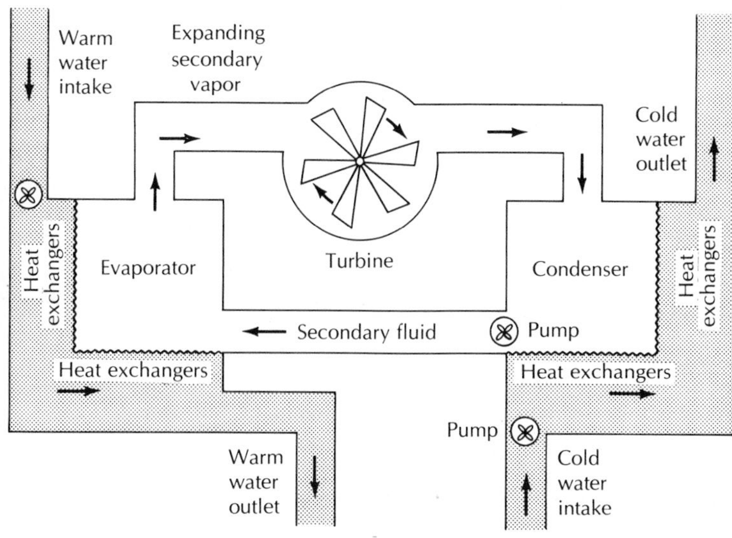

Figure 24-10. Diagram of a closed cycle ocean thermal power plant.

vapor runs a turbine, and the vapor is cooled in a condenser with cold water. In the closed cycle, a working fluid, such as ammonia or propane, is vaporized by the warm water, the vapor propels a turbine, and the vapor is cooled in a condenser using cold water. This cycle, shown in Figure 24-10, resembles a refrigeration cycle and is the one that will probably be used when ocean thermal plants are built. These plants will be incorporated in a floating hull containing heat exchangers, one or more turbines, generators, and pumps.

Large floating power plants, located close to populated areas, could extract large quantities of ocean thermal energy and transmit electrical energy to shore via a submarine cable. A likely outgrowth of this research would be the development of land-based ocean thermal power plants. However, there are a limited number of suitable locations for these plants because of a scarcity of shorefront land with a steep off-shore gradient and an adequate year-round thermal energy resource. The thermal energy resource of the oceans is thus available mainly at sea in the tropical and temperate latitudes.

CONVERTING SOLAR ENERGY TO PLANTS AND FOSSIL FUELS

The "magic" action of sunlight in stimulating the growth of plants is one of the most fascinating phenomena of nature. This process, called photosynthesis, occurs when sunlight interacts with chlorophyll, water, and carbon dioxide to produce the great variety of organic materials seen in plants.

As pointed out in the Introduction, the conversion of solar energy into organic plant materials and their subsequent transformation in prehistoric times into natural gas, petroleum, and coal, has provided the world with its fossil-fuel energy supply.

In addition to using solar energy to produce direct heat or electricity, there is the possibility of providing large additional supplies of high-quality concentrated fuels through the managed production of various kinds of plant tissue formed by photosynthesis. These materials would include trees, grasses, and various water plants, such as kelp, water hyacinths, and microscopic algae.

These plant materials, which, it would be

hoped, could grow under conditions in which solar energy is used more efficiently than it is under natural conditions, have a relatively low heat content per unit of weight. An essential part of the whole process, as now conceived, would be to devise methods of converting these basic plant materials into higher heat content fuels, such as gases, liquids, and solids, which would be similar in many ways to the natural fossil fuels found in the earth.

Theoretically, it has been calculated that the entire electrical needs of the country could be met by the large-scale cultivation of plants over a moderate portion of the land and water in the United States, particularly if efficiencies of solar energy conversion could be achieved that are greater than those now common in agriculture. Although some of the resulting substances could be used directly as fuels in power plants, they could alternatively be converted into more concentrated fuels of higher quality, by drying, heating, fermentation, thermal conversion, or chemical reduction. Chemical feedstocks for industry could also be derived.

The over-all concept includes the feasibility of applying conversion processes to other available organic materials, particularly solid wastes (agricultural, animal, industrial, and urban), which are now causing serious environmental problems and a loss of valuable energy resources.

A schematic diagram showing the production of fuels by these various methods is shown in Figure 24-11.

The amount of energy available from the total quantity of animal and urban wastes now being produced (assuming that collection of these materials could be economically accomplished) has been calculated to represent about 6 per cent of present energy requirements for generating electric power. The pyrolysis (high-temperature decomposition) of organic wastes to produce various fuels has already been demonstrated in several countries, including the United States. Laboratory experiments have also established the feasibility of thermal-chemical treatment of organic fuels to produce liquid fuel, such as methanol, and biological treatment to produce methane gas, simple sugars, and ethyl alcohol. (See Article 30, this volume).

Also under investigation is the possibility of producing hydrogen gas by photosynthetic processes as applied to plants or algae. Such a process has been demonstrated in small-scale laboratory experiments. The advantages of hydrogen as a clean fuel and a means of generating electricity through fuel cells makes the idea attractive. Substantial additional research, pilot plant operations, and economic studies will be required, however.

Still another concept is the idea of converting various organic materials to methane—which is a clean, high heat content fuel—by fermentation or similar processes. One proposed process is shown in Figure 24-12.

It has been calculated that if the entire amount of economically recoverable solid organic waste (agricultural, animal, industrial, and urban) could be subjected to such a fermentation process, it would represent about 5 per cent of the current yearly consumption of methane in the United States. Technical feasibility has already been established, and the next logical step is to evaluate the economic aspects of the process.

There are many different variations and possibilities for producing much larger quantities of fuel by the improved use of solar energy and the application of photosynthetic and various other chemical processes, but these require much further technical and economic study. The collection and processing of all the various materials involved, even assuming they could be grown and processed efficiently, constitutes a substantial challenge, and there are also other difficulties. A program of this kind can succeed only if the economic and other nontechnical problems are solved. Current estimates indicate that about 15 per cent of the projected energy requirements of the United States could easily be satisfied within the next 30 to 35 years by energy sources resulting from bioconversion to fuels.

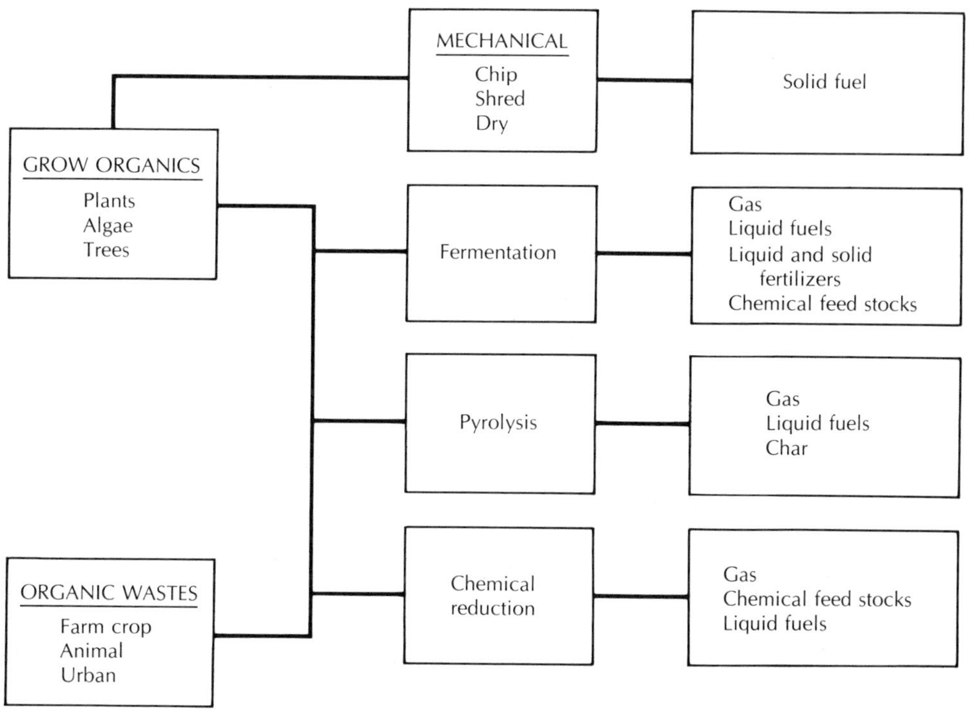

Figure 24-11. Various methods of producing different kinds of fuels from solar energy.

ENERGY PLANNING FOR THE FUTURE

The basic problem of energy planning for the nations of the world is to provide for future energy supplies on a planet that is rapidly depleting its limited deposits of oil and natural gas while demanding constantly increasing amounts of energy.

This article has attempted to show the role for solar energy by outlining facts about various possibilities and technical challenges for its more efficient use in the future.

The fact that our fossil fuels were indirectly formed by solar energy is interesting historically but does not help much in solving future energy supply problems. The production of fossil-like fuels to meet out mounting needs would probably require devoting such extensive land areas to energy-related plant growth that other vital land uses would be severely and unacceptably affected.

However, the total solar energy falling upon the earth is very much greater than current or projected demands by mankind. The challenge is how to use even a small fraction of this vast energy resource effectively and economically.

In trying to meet this challenge, the following over-simplified but objective summary of the good and bad news about solar energy may help to develop a balanced view regarding its future potential.

The good news is that solar energy is free, clean, and inexhaustible. The bad news is that it is intermittent, undependable in many locations, and diffuse. Many solar energy applications involve the use of techniques that need to be improved and made more economical

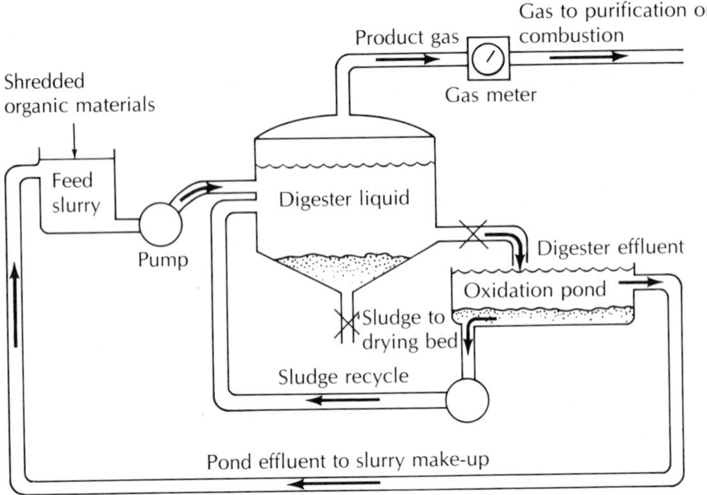

Figure 24-12. Concept of a unit for continuous conversion of organic material to methane by anaerobic fermentation (without oxygen).

through research, development, and demonstrations.

With regard to current U.S. energy use, it would be reasonable to describe our present situation as a kind of "fossil" economy, since about 93 per cent of the energy we use comes from fossil fuels. There is also little doubt that our overwhelming dependence on these limited fuels must soon give way to other sources. Since no single source is certain to provide for all of our needs in fully acceptable fashion, several different alternative energy sources are being explored. A partial solution is to use nuclear fuel, whose contribution to electric power generation has already grown from 2 per cent in 1970 to 10 per cent in 1977 and is expected to continue to increase. Another new and growing source is geothermal energy, the natural heat of the earth, which, if it can be tapped and distributed economically, will also provide significant quantities of heat and electricity.

A complete picture of the projected energy flow in the United States in 1970, including the major inputs and outputs, is shown in Figure 24-13.

The generation of electricity in the United States has roughly doubled every decade for the last half century. Only 6 per cent of the world's population lives in the United States, yet we generate and use one-third of all the electric power in the world. The main reasons for this continued rise have been:

(1) The steady population growth, although this is now at a much lower rate.

(2) The increased use of electricity in the average household for labor-saving and convenience equipment and devices, especially air conditioning.

(3) The extension of the benefits of electricity to a wider segment of the population (for example it now goes to 98 per cent of all farms) and particularly to those at lower income levels.

This steady uninterrupted growth of the generation and use of electricity has led to the idea that we are entering an era that could be called an "electric economy," which might eventually become distinct and different from the fossil economy.

Today, about one-fourth of all energy resources are consumed in the generation of

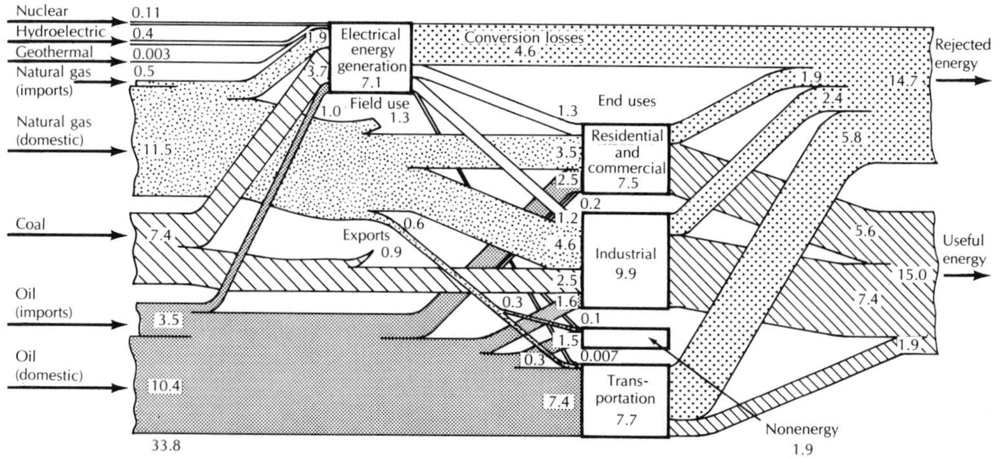

Figure 24-13. United States energy flow, 1970. Units: million BBLS/day oil equivalent.

electricity. In the preceding sections of this article, we have seen how solar energy can also be applied in many different ways, directly and indirectly, so that its utilization in the future can be flexible and varied. If machinery to convert solar energy into electricity can be produced at competitive prices, a substantial and useful total contribution to the electric economy will result.

If much improved electricity storage techniques are developed, the utility of solar conversion units would be still further enhanced, and they could take over, for instance, a significant portion of the electricity requirements of individual households.

In the future, solar energy might also play an important part in what has been called the hydrogen economy, a term that describes the situation that might develop in the future as a kind of alternative to the electric economy. The hydrogen economy would be based on the large-scale distribution, storage, and varied end use of hydrogen as an intermediate and final energy source. Conceivably, hydrogen could be the end product of central nuclear, fossil, geothermal, and solar power plants. Thus, hydrogen may be a solution to the problem of storing solar energy.

It therefore seems evident that solar energy utilization would have a role to play in either an electric or a hydrogen economy. It is still too early to predict which of these conditions might develop or whether the outcome would involve some combination of the two.

It is reasonable to hope that the solar energy programs will succeed and that this alternative will indeed be used much more effectively for mankind in the foreseeable future. To the extent that solar energy can substitute for fossil and nuclear fuels, their depletion will be reduced and the associated environmental problems alleviatgd.

CONCLUSION

Of the various solar applications, heating and cooling is the one that can make the most immediate impact. (See Article 25, this volume). The widespread use of energy from the Sun to heat and cool buildings and to supply energy for commercial applications would have a significant effect on the nation's supply and consumption of energy. If only 1 per cent of the buildings in the United States were now equipped with solar heating and cooling systems, about 30 million barrels of oil would be saved annually. In general the problem is to stimulate the production and marketing of reliable, low-cost solar heating and cooling systems. Wind energy and production of fuel by bioconversion processes also give promise of relatively near-term benefits.

In the total energy picture, solar energy is one of the major alternative sources and offers the promise of making significant and long-range contributions to the solution of our energy problems. Therefore, it is essential to move ahead in research, development, and demonstration of potential solar applications.

SUGGESTED READINGS

Caputo, Richard S., 1977, Solar Power Plants: Dark Horse in the Energy Stable, *Bulletin of the Atomic Scientists 33,* pp. 46–48, 50–56.

Chalmers, Bruce, 1976, The Photovoltaic Generation of Electricity, *Scientific American 235,* pp. 34–43.

Edmondson, William B., Ed., *Solar Energy Digest*—a monthly publication of new developments in solar energy.

Faltermayer, Edmund, 1976, Solar Energy is Here, But It's Not Yet Utopia, *Fortune XCIII,* pp. 103–106, 114, 116.

Faltermayer, Edmund, 1976, The New Business of Harvesting Sunbeams (A Portfolio), *Fortune XCIII,* pp. 107–111.

Glaser, Peter E., Editor-in-chief, *Journal of Solar Energy*—a bimonthly publication on all aspects of solar energy for the International Solar Energy Society.

Goodenaugh, J. B., 1976, The Options for Using the Sun, *Technology Review 79,* pp. 62–71.

Hamilton, Roger, 1975, Can We Harness the Wind?, *National Geographic 148,* pp. 812–829.

Heronemus, William E., 1975, Wind Power: A Near Term Partial Solution to the Energy Crisis in Ruedisili and Firebaugh (eds.), *Perspectives on Energy* (1st Ed.), pp. 364–376.

Hirshberg, Alan S., Public Policy for Solar Heating and Cooling, *Bulletin of the Atomic Scientists 32,* pp. 37–45.

McCaull, Julian, 1973, Windmills, *Environment 15,* pp. 6–17.

Merriam, M. F., 1977, Wind Energy for Human Needs, *Technology Review 79,* pp. 28–39.

Morrow, Walter E., Jr., 1973, Solar Energy: Its Time Is Near, *Technology Review 76,* pp. 30–42.

Morse, Frederick H., and Melvin K. Simmons, 1976, Solar Energy, *Annual Review of Energy 1,* pp. 131–158.

O'Neill, Gerard K., 1975, Space Colonies and Energy Supply to the Earth, *Science 190,* pp. 943–947.

Sorensen, Bent, 1976, Wind Energy, *Bulletin of the Atomic Scientists 32,* pp. 38–45. The 9th article in a series on solar energy.

Swann, Mark, 1976, Power from the Sun, *Environment 18,* pp. 25–31.

Wade, Nicholas, 1974, Windmills: The Resurrection of an Ancient Energy Technology, *Science 184,* pp. 1055–1058.

Wilhelm, John L., 1976, Solar Energy, the Ultimate Powerhouse, *National Geographic 149,* pp. 380–397.

Solar Heating and Cooling 25

JOHN A. DUFFIE AND WILLIAM A. BECKMAN 1976

Thermal energy for buildings, supplied at temperatures near or below 100 °C, constitutes an important segment of the U.S. energy economy and accounts for about one-quarter of the nation's energy use. Energy at these temperatures can readily be delivered from flat-plate solar energy collectors, and the solar energy incident on most buildings is more than adequate to meet these energy needs. Flat-plate collectors are manufactured and sold on a small but growing scale in the United States; they have been in use for more than a decade in heating water for buildings in Australia, Israel, and Japan. We expect that solar heating and cooling for buildings, with energy collected by flat-plate collectors, will be the first large-scale application of solar energy.

The basic problem with solar heating and cooling has been that the energy could not, except in special cases, be delivered at costs competitive with costs of energy from other sources. This situation is rapidly changing, and interest in solar energy is increasing almost daily as fuel costs rise. In areas where new natural gas connections are no longer available, where oil is not distributed, and where electrical resistance heating is the only alternative among conventional sources, solar heating is economically attractive.

In addition to technical and economic considerations, several social factors will influence the course and pace of developments. Two examples are worth examining. First, architectural constraints are imposed by the need for collectors to be oriented within rather narrow limits. This will make it difficult to fit solar heating systems to many existing buildings; thus new residential construction will be the easiest starting place for conversion in solar heating. Solar cooling may first be installed in existing low-rise, flat-roof buildings such as schools and shopping centers, where cooling is usually more important than heating. Second, tax policy is important. Today the installation of solar heating or cooling systems brings an increase in property valuation in most states, and a corresponding

Dr. John A. Duffie is professor of chemical engineering and Dr. William A. Beckman is professor of mechanical engineering at the University of Wisconsin-Madison, Madison, Wisconsin 53706. They are directors of the Solar Energy Laboratory at the University of Wisconsin-Madison.

From *Science*, Vol. 191, No. 4223, pp. 143–149, January 16, 1976. Reprinted by permission of the authors and the American Association for the Advancement of Science.

modest increase in real estate taxes. Government encouragement to invest in solar energy systems in the form of tax write-offs or other inducements (as are provided for investments by other energy producers) could very rapidly change the competitive position of solar energy in relation to conventional energy sources.

In all buildings, intelligent practices for energy conservation are worth following. The basic advantages of reducing energy needs by good thermal design apply whether buildings are supplied with solar or conventional energy. If solar energy costs the same as an alternative energy source, the value of energy conservation techniques, such as extra glazing on windows and doors or added insulation, is the same whether solar energy or the alternative is being used.

SOLAR RADIATION

The solar constant, that is, the intensity of solar radiation outside of the Earth's atmosphere at the mean distance between the Earth and the Sun, has been determined by measurements from satellites and high altitude aircraft to be 1.353 kilowatts per square meter[1]. This extraterrestrial radiation, which corresponds closely to that of a black body at 5,762 K, is 7 per cent in the ultraviolet range (wavelength less than 0.38 μm) and 47 per cent in the visible range (wavelengths from 0.38 to 0.78 μm), with the balance in the near infrared (largely with wavelengths of less than 3 μm).

Solar radiation is depleted as it passes through the atmosphere by a combination of scattering and absorption; the radiation that reaches the ground—the raw material of this energy source—can vary from almost none under heavy cloud cover to 85 to 90 per cent of the solar constant under very clear skies. Energy rates on surfaces normal to the radiation during good weather are not very high, and are typically about 1 kilowatt per square meter (a little more than 1 horsepower per square yard). Solar radiation on the ground consists of a diffuse component that has been scattered by molecules and particulate matter in the atmosphere and, when the atmosphere is sufficiently clear, a beam component that is unchanged in its direction of propagation from the Sun. Its spectral distribution is altered in a manner dependent on atmospheric composition, with the major changes due to absorption of ultraviolet radiation by ozone and infrared radiation by water vapor.

There are several sources of solar radiation data. The National Oceanic and Atmospheric Administration weather service measures total (beam diffuse) radiation on a horizontal plane at more than 100 stations. Some stations report daily values, and some report hourly values. These data are available from the National Climatic Data Center.[2] Monthly averages of daily radiation on horizontal surfaces are available for many locations.[3] Daily integrated energy quantities at particular locations vary widely during the year. In Madison, Wisconsin, on a clear January day, energy on a horizontal surface is typically 3 kilowatt-hours per square meter, and July clear-day energy is typically 9 kilowatt-hours per square meter, the corresponding monthly averages of daily radiation on the horizontal surface are 1.8 kilowatt-hours per square meter and 6.2 kilowatt-hours per square meter. Flat-plate collectors sloped toward the south in Madison, with a slope equal to the latitude, will have incident on them an average daily radiation of 3.4 kilowatt-hours per square meter in January and 5.6 kilowatt-hours per square meter in July. These data illustrate the gains to be obtained by orienting a collector in a favorable manner.

Although solar energy intensity is low, integrated energy quantities may be large. For ezample, in Madison the annual average solar energy incident per day on an acre of ground is the equivalent of about 10 barrels of oil, and on a 200-square meter house is equivalent to about 25 gallons, which is far more than enough to meet the needs of the building for thermal energy.

CURRENT STATUS

Two major reasons may be cited for the failure of solar energy to be a serious competitor in the energy market in past years. First, the costs of delivering solar energy have been substantially higher than those of other energy sources. Solar energy has not been able to be a competitor to inexpensive natural gas or petroleum. Second, there was no constituency pressuring for solar energy development in a manner similar, for example, to that of the nuclear industry that existed at the close of World War II and gave a substantial impetus to the development of peacetime uses of nuclear energy. The environmental movement of the last 5 years, the realization that the United States is dependent to an undesirable degree on foreign energy sources, and increasing fuel costs have served to establish a broad base of interest in developing solar energy.

The contrasts between the development of nuclear energy and solar energy are striking. After the destruction wrought by the atomic bombs in World War II, a large, concerned constituency, backed by the nation at large, pushed for development of peaceful uses of atomic energy. The result was a program supported by billions of dollars of federal funds over the course of three decades. Solar energy, in contrast, had no such support and it was only the persistence of a few individuals that kept interest in solar energy alive. Outstanding in this group was Farrington Daniels, who, through his publications[4] as well as through his support of the struggling International Solar Energy Society, served as an elder statesman for solar energy.

During the 1960's, support for solar energy research for applications in the United States was essentially nonexistent. However, one program resulted in economic studies that have become part of the current interest in solar energy. Tybout and Löf, with support from Resources for the Future, developed a series of cost analyses of solar energy for heating and cooling.[5] They indicated that solar heating could be competitive with conventional energy sources in high energy cost areas in 1968. They also showed that the combination of solar heating and cooling, which results in higher use factors on the solar energy equipment, is, in most places, more economical than heating or cooling alone. Their two studies were based on optimistic projections of the cost of solar energy equipment ($20 and $40 per square meter of flat-plate collector), but also on 1968 and 1970 energy costs. Later and more detailed studies of cost and thermal performance, based on more realistic collector and energy costs, bear out the same general conclusion that solar heating can now compete with expensive fuels.

By 1972, several dozen solar-heated residences or small laboratory buildings had been constructed and operated. A few of these have been studied, evaluated, and reported.[6] The few air conditioning experiments were confined largely to experimental operation of 3-ton lithium bromide-water absorption machines or analytical studies of system performance.[7] In contrast, the manufacture and sale of solar water heaters to provide hot water for residences and some institutional buildings (hotels, dormitories, and the like) has been a commercial enterprise in Australia, Japan, and Israel for more than a decade. Perhaps a million solar water heaters are in use in these countries.

During the past 3 years, the availability of funds for experimental programs from the NSF Research Applied to National Needs (RANN) program and the Energy Research and Development Administration (ERDA), coupled with private and industrial investment, has led to many new experiments and applications of solar heating and cooling in the United States. Public buildings, schools, and a variety of residential buildings with heating or combined heating and air conditioning capacity are being planned and built. Quantitative information is now beginning to come in from these new experiments.[8] The Solar Heating and Cooling Demonstration

Act of 1974 should lead to many new solar buildings. In addition to research and development activities, there are now a few sales of solar heating systems that are installed as operating heat delivery systems rather than as experiments.

SOLAR BUILDING ARCHITECTURE

Several approaches to solar building architecture are evident. A solar-heated house and school are illustrated at the beginning of this chapter. The basic problem faced by architects and engineers is to integrate collectors into or onto the building in such a way that thermal performance is adequate, while obtaining an esthetically satisfactory structure. In this context, the major variable is the area of collector that must be integrated into the building. Collector area is central to the fraction of heating loads to be carried by solar energy and, ultimately, to cost.

The solutions are mixed. Some collectors have been mounted above flat-roof buildings. To obtain structural or esthetic advantages, other collectors have been built into vertical walls in higher latitudes or placed flat on horizontal roofs in lower latitudes. In addition, collectors have been integrated into the envelopes of buildings at orientations that are near optimum for the best thermal performance.

SOLAR ENERGY SYSTEMS

Systems for producing service hot water, space heating, and cooling are based on the concept of the flat-plate collector. This unique heat exchanger uses a black absorber plate to absorb solar energy. Ducts or tubes carry air or liquid that remove energy from the plate. Layers of air provide transparent insulation between plates and their covers (usually made of glass) and thus reduce upward heat loss. Conventional insulation is provided on the backs and edges of the plates. The collectors are mounted in a fixed position according to the desired use of the energy. Figure 25-1 shows cross sections of air and water heaters.

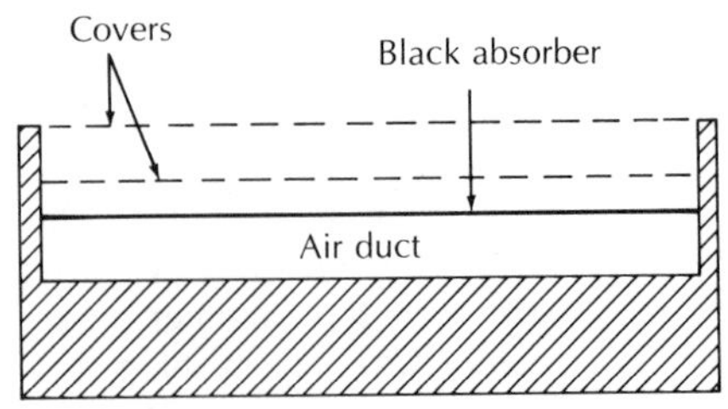

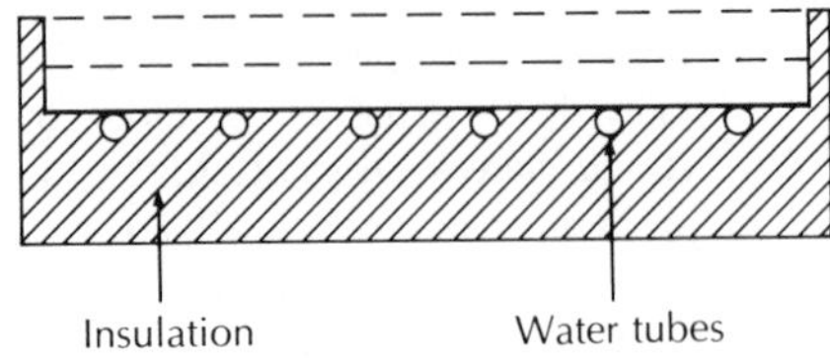

Figure 25-1. Cross sections of a solar air heater and a solar water heater.

The other major component in the system is the energy storage unit, which is designed to accumulate solar energy when it is obtainable and make it available to meet energy needs at other times. Liquid systems usually use insulated water tanks for storage, and air systems usually use pebble beds. A third method of storage takes advantage of the latent heat of a phase transition, and has been the object of considerable study.[9] Early work on house-heating applications concentrated on hydrated sodium sulfate ($Na_2SO_4 \cdot 10H_2O$), which undergoes a phase transition when heated at 32 °C. Because phase separation of this hydrate occurs on cycling, other chemical systems that can undergo thousands of cycles without loss of storage capacity are being sought.

Schematic diagrams of liquid and air solar heating systems are shown in Figure 25-2. Both show an auxiliary energy source, which is included in most solar energy systems. In climates in which a high degree of reliability is required of a heating system, the auxiliary source must be capable of carrying the full heating load of the building. If auxiliary energy is added in parallel with solar energy,

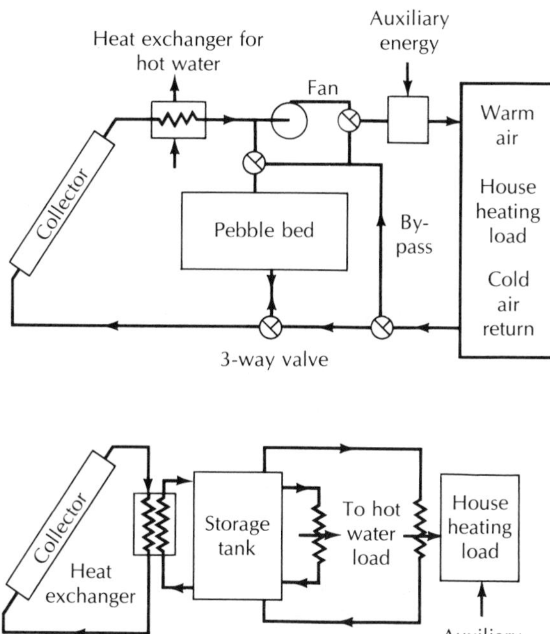

Figure 25-2. Schematic diagrams of solar heating systems based on air and liquid heat transfer media.

then the maximum amount of energy can be obtained from the solar system and the balance from auxiliary. Other methods are possible.

For the liquid system, the heat exchanger between collector and storage tank allows the use of an antifreeze solution in the collector loop, which is one of the methods to avoid freezing and reduce boiling problems. The diagram shows an additional heat exchanger to transfer heat to the building, and another to provide service hot water. The technology of solar liquid heaters is very well established, and most of the systems built recently have used liquids for heat transfer.

Air systems avoid boiling and freezing problems in the collector. In most air systems energy is stored as sensible heat in a pebble bed. A well-designed pebble bed has good heat transfer between air and pebbles, a low loss rate, and a high degree of stratification. Mechanical energy for pumping air can be a significant item of cost, and care is required to design for minimum pressure drops. The design of air systems and the balancing of good heat transfer characteristics against pressure drop are problems that are now receiving adequate attention.

Many of the scores of solar-heated buildings that have been constructed so far have provided reduced fuel bills as well as satisfaction to their owners. The performance of a few of these has been carefully measured, and provides a firm base of data on long-term thermal performance. Experiments up to 1961 were very well reported in papers presented at the U.N. Conference on New Sources of Energy in 1961 and summarized by Löf.[6]

Massachusetts Institute of Technology (MIT) house IV, built in 1959, was the last in a series of experiments carried out by H. C. Hottel and his colleagues and represented a cooperative effort of architects and engineers to develop a functional, energy-conserving home with a major part of the energy for space

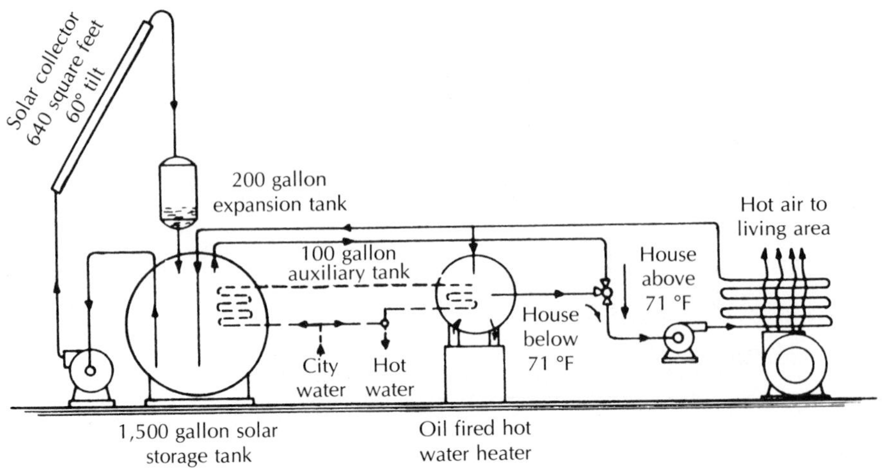

Figure 25-3. Schematic diagram of the heating system in MIT house IV. (Adapted from Engebretson, Ref. 6.)

heating and water heating to be supplied from the flat-plate collector. Figure 25-3 from Engebretson,[6] is a schematic diagram of the heating and hot water system. The collector had an area of 60 square meters for the 135-square meter floor area, two glass covers, and a flat, black paint, energy-absorbing surface. To avoid freezing, collectors were designed to drain into an expansion tank. The main storage tank capacity was 5,700 kilograms. Means were provided for adding auxiliary energy, extracting hot water for household needs, and transferring heat to air that was circulated to the rooms. This solar heating system was operated for three seasons, during which its performance was carefully measured. Data for the first 2 years are summarized in Table 25-1, which shows how energy requirements for space heating and water heating were met by solar or auxiliary energy. During the first two heating seasons solar energy supplied 52 per cent of the energy for hot water and heating.

The Denver solar house, built by Löf[6] in 1958, uses air as the heat transfer medium and a pebble-bed storage unit. The ratio of collector area to house area is about one to five, a proportion much smaller than that of MIT house IV. This house has served as the Löf family residence since its construction, and the equipment has been routinely operated with only nominal maintenance. The system performance was measured in 1959 to 1960, and again in 1974 to 1975. For the period from December to April, 22 per cent of the heating and hot water loads were carried by

Table 25-1. Performance Data for MIT House IV for Two Heating Seasons (Summarized from Engebretson, Ref. 6).[a]

Item	*1959 to 1960*	*1960 to 1961*
Space heating		
Demand	72.5	70.7
From solar energy	33.6	40.2
Water heating		
Demand	14.7	17.6
From solar energy	8.4	9.7
Total heating		
Demand	87.1	88.3
From solar energy	41.9	49.9
Per cent from solar energy	48.1	56.6

[a]Units are gigajoules.

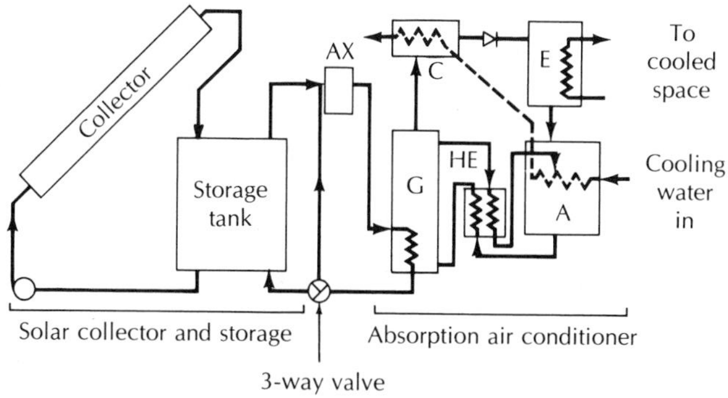

Figure 25-4. Schematic diagram of a solar-operated absorption air conditioner. AX, auxiliary energy source. The cooler components are as follows: G, generator; C, condenser; E, evaporator; A, absorber; HE, heat exchanger to recover sensible heat (Ref. 18.)

solar energy during the earlier season, and 20 per cent during the later season.

Solar air-conditioning technology is not as advanced as the heating process, since an additional thermodynamic process is needed for cooling. Several current experiments use absorption cooling cycles that are operated by heat from flat-plate collectors. These coolers are the analogs of the gas-fired refrigerators used in campers, but due to the lower temperature of fluid from the collectors (compared to a gas flame), water cooling is required rather than air cooling. Figure 25-4 shows a diagram of a solar-operated absorption cooling system. The same collector and storage units that provide winter heating thus can provide summer cooling.

Colorado State University (CSU) house I (which serves as an office building) uses a heating system that differs in some details from that of the MIT house, and also includes an absorption air conditioner. A glycol-water solution is used in the collector to avoid freezing problems and permit collector operation at higher temperatures. A heat exchanger is used to transfer solar heat into the water storage tank, and additional heat exchangers serve for heat transfer from the tank to hot water and the building. Thus, the collector supplies energy for three purposes: space heating, water heating, and air conditioning. A gas furnace provides auxiliary energy for both heating and cooling. The experiments started in August 1974,[10] and for the first 6 months of the heating season 86 per cent of the space heating loads and 68 per cent of the hot water loads were met from solar energy. Integrated performance statistics of a summer's air-conditioning operation are not yet available.

A mobile laboratory[11] developed by Honeywell under NSF-ERDA sponsorship includes a heating and absorption air conditioning system similar to that of CSU house I. In addition, solar heat can be used to vaporize a fluorohydrocarbon, which then expands through a turbine to drive a mechanical air conditioner. Thus, solar energy is converted to mechanical energy, which is used to provide cooling by conventional means. The mobile laboratory is being operated in several locations to gather data and provide a public demonstration.

In addition to closed cycle absorption cooling, open cycles are of potential interest for solar technology. For example, desiccants can be used to absorb water vapor from room air, which can then be evaporatively cooled; the desiccant is regenerated and recycled. Löf suggested the use of triethylene glycol as the desiccant, with solar-heated air for regeneration;[12] this system is now being evaluated for use on the Citicorp Building in New York. Dunkle has designed a cycle with rotary beds of silica gel and rotary heat exchangers.[13] In the Munters (M.E.C.) system lithium chloride is used as the desiccant; the system is being adapted for solar operation.[14]

It is also possible to use a collector as an energy dissipater by designing it to lose heat by convection and by radiation to clear night sky. To accomplish this, the collector must have opposite properties to those needed for efficient collection; thus compromises are necessary or movable insulation must be used. Hay designed such a system for a clear, mild California climate. He achieves combined collector-radiator-storage capabilities in the horizontal roof of the building with movable insulation, and thereby provides heating in the winter and cooling in the summer. This system was evaluated for a year,[15] and kept conditions inside the house within acceptable ranges throughout the period.

Another class of systems combines solar collectors and heat pumps. The heat pump can serve as an independent (auxiliary) source of heating energy, or the collector-storage system can serve as the energy source for the evaporator of the heat pump. The latter system has the apparent advantages of lowering mean collector temperature and raising the mean evaporator temperature of the heat pump (thus improving the performance of each). Systems of this type have been studied experimentally.[16] A simulation study by Freeman compares these methods in one climate, and indicates little choice between them,[17] but there remain many unanswered questions on how these combined systems should best be constructed and operated.

PERFORMANCE CALCULATIONS

The general approach to calculating the thermal performance of solar energy systems is to write the equations that describe the performance of each of the components in a system (including collector, storage, controls, pumps, and the like, as well as the building itself), and simultaneously solve the equations, usually hour by hour. Meteorological data for the location in question, which affects both collector and building heating and cooling loads, are used as forcing functions. The solutions are time-dependent temperatures and energy rates. The energy rates can be integrated to give energy quantities over the period of the stimulation. The amount of energy a system is expected to deliver over a year can then be the basis for an economic analysis. These procedures are outlined by Duffie and Beckman.[18]

The most criticali and unique component is the collector. Thanks to pioneering studies of collectors by Hottel and his colleagues, beginning almost 40 years ago and carried on by others since,[19] methods of predicting collector performance are well established. Based on a detailed analysis, the useful gain of most collectors can be written as

$$
\begin{aligned}
Q_U &= A_c F_R S - U_L[(T_{f,in} - T_a)]^+ \\
&= \dot{m} C_p (T_{f,out} - T_{f,in})
\end{aligned}
$$

where F_R is equal to the ratio of actual energy gain to gain if the whole plate were at the fluid inlet temperature, $T_{f,in}$, and accounts for the material properties and configuration of the plate. This collector heat removal factor takes into account fluid flow rate and temperature gradients along and across the plate and enables the calculation to be made on the basis of $T_{f,in}$ (a very convenient variable). Also, A_c is the collector area, a major design parameter; S equals the absorbed radiation per unit area of collector. It is the product of incident radiation on the plane of the collector, the transmittance of a cover system, and the absorptance of the plate for solar radiation. It is a function of the orientation of the collector, the number of covers, and the properties of the covers and plate for solar radiation. The thermal loss coefficient U_L is a function of the number of covers, cover and plate properties for longwave (thermal) radiation, wind speed, and temperatures. Correlations and charts are available to determine this coefficient.[18,19,20] Finally, $T_{f,out}$ is the outlet fluid temperature; T_a is ambient air temperature; and $\dot{m}C_p$ is the product fluid of mass flow rate and heat capacity. The plus sign on the bracket indicates that only positive values are taken. This simulates a controller that turns on the pump or blower whenever useful energy is to be gained from the collector, that is, when the fluid outlet temperature is higher than the inlet temperature.

Included in the equation are a wide range of design parameters and materials properties. For example, the effects of selectivity of the energy-absorbing surface, that is, the absorptance of the surface for solar radiation and emittance for longwave radiation, are implicit in S and U_L.

The equation also illustrates an important determining factor in solar energy system performance. As the collector temperature ($T_{f,in}$) rises, the thermal loss term approaches the absorbed radiation term and collector output diminishes. For most practical designs today, zero output collector temperatures are typically 150 to 175 °C above ambient, and normal operating temperature ranges are less than 75 °C above ambient. So, collectors are uniquely sensitive to temperature and must be designed to operate at minimum temperatures above the levels required.

New collector developments are aimed at increasing absorbed radiation S and reducing thermal losses. Extensive efforts have gone into development of selective surfaces with low longwave emittances to reduce U_L.[21] The practical problem has been to maintain desirable combinations of properties over very extended periods (20 years or more) in oxidizing atmospheres. Many of the surfaces studied are metal substrates with semiconductor coatings, for example, chrome oxide on a bright nickel base. Another approach to control of thermal losses is to evacuate the space between the absorbing surface and the cover, thus reducing or eliminating convection and conduction across the gap. This is done by enclosing the absorbing surface in tubes;[22] elimination of convection and conduction coupled with selective surfaces of low emittances results in very low loss coefficients and allows energy delivery from collectors at substantially higher temperatures than from conventional designs.

Equations based on standard energy and materials balances, rate equations, and equilibrium relationships are available for energy storage, heat exchangers, heating and cooling loads, controls, and other components of solar energy systems. Although the models of some components can be based on physical principles, it may be necessary to fall back on empirical models of coolers, heat pumps, and other complex equipment. The combination of the models of each component provides the basis for system performance calculations.

SIMULATIONS

Physical experiments on solar heating and cooling are indispensable. However, numerical experiments, such as simulations, can yield much of the same kind of information quickly and inexpensively. The effects on long-term system performance of changes in system configuration, materials properties, and component design can readily be assessed in a way that is not practical in experiments. Simulations are also useful in understanding the dynamics of systems (which never operate at steady state) and in selecting and planning experiments. We have developed a modular solar process simulation program, TRNSYS, in our laboratory, and other simulation programs have been described.[23]

The two most obvious design variables of a solar heating system for a particular building are collector area and storage size. To see the effects of these parameters on energy delivered to a building, let us consider the following example. A house in Madison, Wisconsin, is to be provided with solar heating and hot water, from a system similar to that of the CSU experiment. The house is a typical, moderate size house with a heat loss rate corresponding to a floor area of 180 square meters and with conventional insulation. A liquid heating collector has two glass covers, a high-absorptance, flat black paint for absorption of solar energy, and is sloped toward the south with a slope equal to the latitude.[24] The storage tank is to be located within the building so that losses from the tank are uncontrolled gains to the building. Hot water demands are typical for a family of four or five.

The results of simulations of this system, with forcing functions of hourly weather data for an average Madison year and a fixed ratio of storage mass to collector area of 75 kilograms per square meter, are shown in Figure 25-5. Incident radiation, total loads, and the load carried by solar energy for two collector areas are shown by months. Monthly collector efficiencies are the ratio of solar energy delivered to the building to incident solar energy on the collector; these are high when heating loads are high relative to the size of the collector, and low when loads are low. Thus, these systems tend to be overdesigned

Figure 25-5. Month-by-month performance of heating systems of two collector areas on a Wisconsin house with a floor area of 182 square meters. Incident radiation on the collector is shown by the heavy broken lines. Total heating and hot water load is indicated by the bars; the shaded portion represents the load met by solar, and the unshaded portion, the load met by auxiliary; GJ, gigajoule.

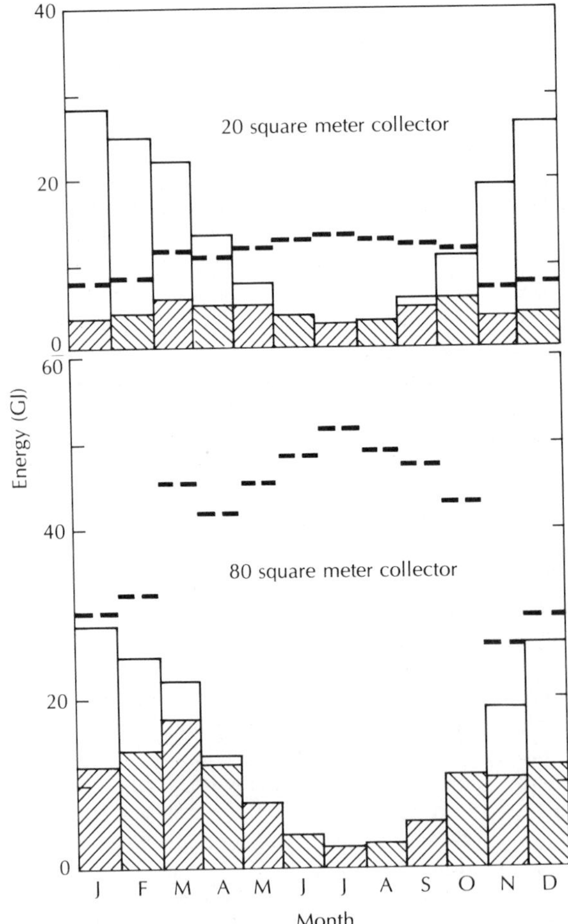

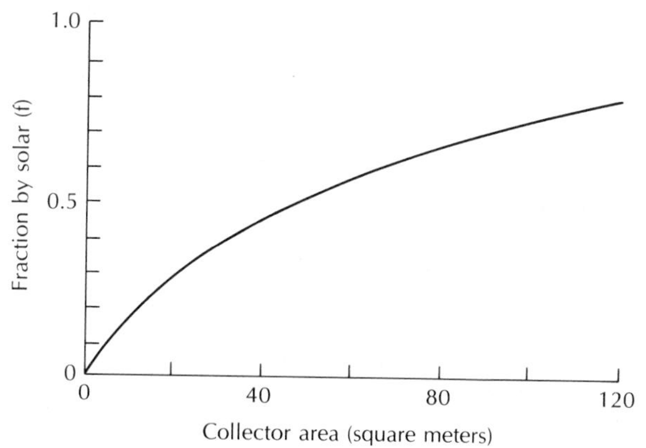

Figure 25-6. Variation of the fraction of the annual total load carried by solar energy with collector area for the Wisconsin example.

for part of the year and underdesigned for part of the year.

Annual performances, expressed as the fraction of loads supplied by solar energy, are shown in Figure 25-6. Since the total loads are nearly independent of collector size, these data also indicate the total amount of solar energy delivered. These numbers are useful in deciding how much collector area should be used on the house, and indicate that very large collector areas (relative to the heating loads on the house) are needed to approach 100 per cent solar heating. In other words, the larger the solar energy system, the larger the fraction of the year that it is overdesigned.

What should the storage capacity be? Figure 25-7 shows the effects of storage capacity on annual performance of this system. Below about 50 kilograms per square meter, system capacity drops off rather sharply as tank size decreases. Above 100 kilograms per square meter, there is a slow increase in annual performance as tank size increases. Cost studies by Tybout and Löf,[5] and others, which take into account the cost of tanks as a function of their size, indicate that a slight cost penalty is incurred on going beyond about 100 kilograms per square meter.

There remains a question of seasonal storage from summer to winter. If very large storage systems were used (probably with a volume of roughly the same size as that of the heated space if heat-capacity storage is used) smaller collectors might be possible.

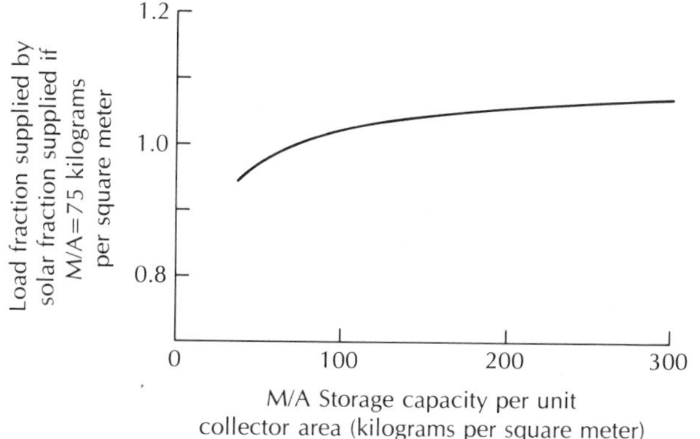

Figure 25-7. Variation of the fraction of the annual total load carried by solar energy with storage capacity for water storage tanks.

Speyer,[25] in 1959, concluded that this is uneconomical; reexamination of this possibility with simulation methods would be of interest.

ECONOMICS

Solar energy processes are generally capital-intensive; large investments are made in equipment to save operating costs (that is, fuel purchases). The essential economic problem is balancing annual cost of the extra investment (interest and principle, based on reasonable estimate of lifetime) against annual fuel savings. Thermal performance predictions, with estimated equipment and fuel costs, show the effects of major design decisions on annual costs.

An example of annual savings as a function of collector area, on the basis of the performance calculations noted in the previous section, is shown in Figure 25-8. We assume two collector costs, \$60 and \$100 per square meter, and two conventional energy costs, \$5 and \$15 per gigajoule. Delivered energy costs in the United States today range from less than \$2 per gigajoule for natural gas in the South-

Figure 25-8. Annual savings as a function of collector area for the Wisconsin example. Two collector costs and two conventional energy costs are plotted. C_F, cost of fuel; C_C, cost of collector. Curve A: C_F = \$15 per gigajoule; C_C = \$60 per square meter. Curve B: C_F = \$15 per gigajoule; C_C = \$100 per square meter. Curve C: C_F = \$5 per gigajoule; C_C = \$60 per square meter. Curve D: C_F = \$5 per gigajoule; C_C = \$100 per square meter.

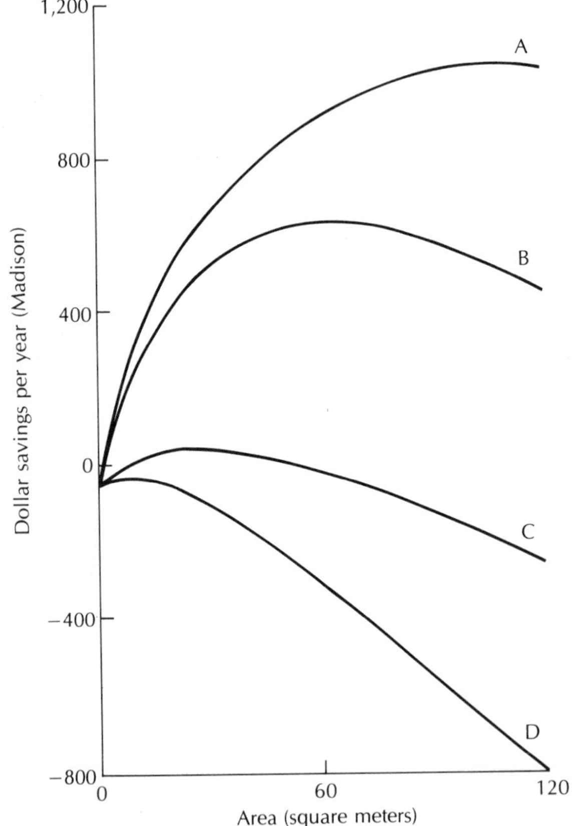

west to more than \$15 per gigajoule for demand electric resistance heating in some parts of the Northeast. The collector cost is the major investment and is proportional to collector area. Storage cost depends only slightly on collector area, and there are other equipment costs that are essentially independent of collector area. Here we have used \$500 for the storage and other equipment costs and an annual charge on investment of 12 per cent, corresponding to 10 per cent interest over 20 years.

The curves show distinctly different behavior, with the maximum "savings" at small collector areas for the expensive collector and cheap fuel, and at a collector area of 100 square meters for the \$60 per square meter collector and expensive fuel. The savings for the collector cost of \$60 per square meter and the fuel cost of \$15 per gigajoule are positive over a range of collector areas from 10 to 50 square meters. Significant deviations from the optimum values do not greatly affect savings; thus the selection of a precise value for collector area is not very critical.

There are many assumptions inherent in these curves. Costs of taxes, maintenance, and insurance have not been included. Conventional energy costs were assumed to be fixed over the lifetime of the system. The nature of the equipment for supplying auxiliary energy (as indicated in Figure 25-2) is assumed to be independent of the amount of auxiliary required during a year, whereas in fact it may change substantially. Costs associated with the time dependence of auxiliary energy needs are ignored; this implies that the auxiliary energy source is stored on site, since utilities could be subjected to unacceptable peak loads by large numbers of solar buildings that draw on them simultaneously only during periods of bad weather.

Nevertheless, some generalizations can be drawn from these analyses. As fuel costs rise and as supplies of low-cost natural gas become increasingly more difficult to obtain, solar energy will become more competitive and optimum fractions of annual loads to be carried by solar energy will increase. As collector and other solar energy system costs decrease as a result of mass production, by improved technology, or by users "doing it themselves," similar improvements in the relative economics of solar energy will occur.

Finally, political decisions may be made that will affect the extent to which solar energy can be competitive. Deregulation of natural gas prices or further increases in the cost of imported oil will increase their costs to consumers and make solar energy more competitive. Tax incentives, such as write-off of investments in solar energy-producing equipment, could make an incremental improvement in solar energy economics.

SUMMARY

We have adequate theory and engineering capability to design, install, and use equipment for solar space and water heating. Energy can be delivered at costs that are competitive now with such high-cost energy sources as much fuel-generated, electrical resistance heating. The technology of heating is being improved through collector developments, improved materials, and studies of new ways to carry out the heating processes.

Solar cooling is still in the experimental stage. Relatively few experiments have yielded information on solar operation of absorption coolers, on use of night sky radiation in locations with clear skies, on the combination of a solar-operated Rankine engine and a compression cooler, and on open cycle, humidification-dehumidification systems. Many more possibilities for exploration exist. Solar cooling may benefit from collector developments that permit energy delivery at higher temperatures and thus solar operation of additional kinds of cycles. Improved solar cooling capability can open up new applications of solar energy, particularly for larger buildings, and can result in markets for retrofitting existing buildings.

Solar energy for buildings can, in the next decade, make a significant contribution to the national energy economy and to the pocket-book of many individual users. Very large aggregate enterprises in manufacture, sale, and installation of solar energy equipment can result, which can involve a spectrum of large and small businesses. In our view, the technology is here or will soon be at hand; thus the basic decisions as to whether the United States uses this resource will be political in nature.

REFERENCES AND NOTES

1. See, for example, M. P. Thekaekara, *Sol. Energy 14,* 109 (1973).
2. Radiation and related weather data are available from the National Climatic Data Center, Asheville, N.C.
3. B. Y. H. Liu and R. C. Jordan, in *Low Temperature Engineering Applications of Solar Energy* (American Society of Heating, Refrigerating, and Air Conditioning Engineers, New York, 1967); G. O. G. Löf, J. A. Duffie, C. O. Smith, *Univ. Wis. Eng. Exp. Stn. Rep. No. 21* (1966).
4. The best example is F. Daniels, *Direct Use of the Sun's Energy* (Yale Univ. Press, New Haven, Conn., 1964).
5. R. A. Tybout and G. O. G. Löf, *Nat. Resour. J. 10,* 268 (1970); G. O. G. Löf and R. A. Tybout, *Sol. Energy 14,* 253 (1973); *ibid. 16,* 9 (1974).
6. C. D. Engebretson, in *Proceedings of the U.N. Conference on New Sources of Energy* (United Nations, New York, 1964), vol. 5, p. 159; G. O. G. Löf, M. M. El-Wakil, J. P. Chiou, *ibid.*, p. 185; R. W. Bliss, *ibid.*, p. 148; G. O. G. Löf, *ibid.*, p. 114.
7. R. Chung, J. A. Duffie, G. O. G. Löf, *Mech. Eng. 85,* 31 (1963); J. A. Duffie and N. R. Sheridan, *Mech. Chem. Eng. Trans. MC-1,* 79 (1965). The NH_3-H_2O cycles have also been studied; six papers at the International Solar Energy Society (ISES) meetings concerned NH_3-H_2O systems.
8. The July 1975 ISES meetings also included 12 papers on performance of solar heating and cooling systems.
9. M. Telkes, in *Solar Energy Research,* F. Daniels and J. A. Duffie, Eds. (Univ. of Wisconsin Press, Madison, 1955); final summary report to NSF-RANN on *Conservation and Better Utilization of Electric Powgr by Means of Thermal Energy Storage and Solar Heating* (National Center for Energy Management and Power, University of Pennsylvania, Philadelphia, 1973).
10. D. S. Ward and G. O. G. Löf, annual report to NSF-RANN on *Design, Construction and Testing of a Residential Solar Heating and Cooling System* (Colorado State University, Fort Collins, 1975).
11. Honeywell report to NSF-RANN, *Design and Test Report for Transportable Solar Laboratory Program* (Minneapolis, Minn., 1974).
12. G. O. G. Löf, in *Solar Energy Research,* F. Daniels and J. A. Duffie, Eds. (Univ. of Wisconsin Press, Madison, 1955). The triethylene glycol system is used in commercial, fuel-fired air conditioning equipment.
13. R. V. Dunkle, *Mech. Chem. Eng. Trans. MC-1,* 73 (1965).
14. W. F. Rush, J. Wurm, L. Wright, R. Ashworth, paper presented at International Solar Energy Society meeting, Los Angeles, 1 August 1975.
15. P. W. Niles, *ibid.*
16. F. H. Bridgers, D. D. Paxton, R. W. Haines, *Heat. Piping Air Cond. 29,* 165 (1957).
17. T. L. Freeman, thesis, University of Wisconsin, Madison (1975).
18. J. A. Duffie and W. A. Beckman, *Solar Energy Thermal Processes* (Wiley, New York, 1974).
19. H. C. Hottel and B. B. Woertz, *Trans. Am. Soc. Mech. Eng. 64,* 91 (1942); H. C. Hottel and A. Whillier, in *Transactions of the Conference on the Use of Solar Energy* (Univ. of Arizona Press, Tucson, 1958), vol. 2, part 1.
20. S. A. Klein, *Sol. Energy 17,* 79 (1975).
21. For example, see H. Tabor, in *Low Temperature Engineering Applications of Solar Energy* (American Society of Heating, Refrigerating, and Air Conditioning Engineers, New York, 1967).
22. E. Speyer, *J. Eng. Power 86,* 270 (1965); D. C. Beekley and G. R. Mather, paper presented at International Solar Energy Society meeting, 28 July 1975; U. Ortabassi and W. Buehl, *ibid.*
23. S. A. Klein *et al., Univ. Wis. Eng. Exp. Stn. Rep. No. 38* (1975); see also S. A. Klein, P. I. Cooper, T. L. Freeman, D. M. Beekman, W. A. Beckman, J. A. Duffie, *Sol. Energy 17,* 29 (1975).
24. As a rule a solar collector should be sloped toward the equator with a slope of latitude $+10°$ for winter use, a slope of latitude $-10°$ for summer use, and with a slope equal to latitude for year-round use. Deviations of 5° or 10° usually make little difference in annual performance.
25. E. Speyer, *Sol. Energy 3* (No. 4), 24 (1959).

Solar Power from Satellites 26

PETER E. GLASER 1977

Various alternative energy sources have been proposed in the last few years. The recognition that no one of these energy sources will, by itself, meet all future power needs, together with the large uncertainties inherent in the achievement of full potential for each of them, has led to what might appear the most daring proposal so far: large-scale solar-energy conversion in space with a satellite solar-power station located in synchronous orbit around Earth—that is, at an altitude of 22,300 miles above the surface.

The satellite power station could use one or more of several methods to convert solar energy to electricity on a nearly continuous schedule. This electricity could be fed to microwave generators incorporated in a transmitting antenna in the satellite, and the antenna would direct a microwave beam to a receiving antenna positioned in a direct line of sight on Earth. There the microwave energy could be reconverted safely and efficiently to electricity and fed into conventional power-transmission networks. With additional satellite systems, power could be delivered almost anywhere on Earth.

Technical and economic feasibility studies of such systems already indicate that they could provide an economically viable, and environmentally and socially acceptable, option for power generation on a scale substantial enough to meet a significant portion of future world energy demands.

Solar-energy conversion in synchronous orbit has many advantages over ground-level conversion. These include:

(1) A satellite in synchronous orbit is exposed to between four and 11 times the solar energy available in those areas on Earth that receive copious sunshine.

(2) The solar energy in orbit is available nearly continuously—the only "blackout" is at short periods around the equinoxes when the satellite is in shadow for a maximum of 72 minutes each day (near midnight at the receiv-

Peter E. Glaser is vice-president of Arthur D. Little, Inc., Cambridge, Massachusetts 02139. He was the first proponent of the use of solar power satellites and holds patents in this area. He has written and spoken extensively on this subject.

From *Physics Today*, Vol. 30, No. 2, pp. 30–38, February 1977. Reprinted by permission of the author and *Physics Today*. Copyright 1977 by the American Institute of Physics. This article is adapted from a talk presented at the annual meeting of the Optical Society of America in Tucson, Arizona, October 1976.

ing antenna site, when power demands are lowest). Averaged over a year, shadowing by the Earth results in only a 1 per cent energy reduction compared with continuous irradiation.

(3) Zero gravity and the absence of wind and rain at the satellite's location would permit the building and use of structures with large area and light weight. The vacuum of space makes unnecessary the evacuated enclosures around microwave generators and other components that are required on Earth.

(4) Because the satellite in synchronous orbit (or, more precisely but less familiarly, "geostationary" orbit) would be stationary with respect to points on Earth, the microwave beam could be directed to receiving antenna sites conveniently close to most major power users—so substantially reducing the length of transmission lines.

(5) The environmental effects of the proposed system are expected to be within acceptable limits. All waste heat associated with solar energy conversion and microwave generation could be rejected to space; no waste products would be generated; the microwave beam densities could be designed to meet international safety standards, and the thermal pollution entailed in the reconversion of microwaves directly to electricity at the receiving antenna would be about one-fourth that of conventional power plants. Furthermore, the receiving antenna would be substantially transparent to solar radiation and open enough for rain to reach the land below it, thus providing opportunities for multiple land use.

Following the original broad concept of the satellite solar-power station, about 8 years ago, detailed feasibility and design studies are currently in progress at NASA, Jet Propulsion Laboratory, Boeing, Econ, and Rockwell. The industry team working with Arthur D. Little, Inc. was responsible for different segments of the design: Grumman Aerospace Corp. for structure and transportation; the Raytheon Company for microwave components, and Spectrolab Inc. for solar cells.

The current position is that, whereas the broad outline of the design is beginning to be defined, many options remain within the major areas. Let us look now at the the state of development of the technology within each of these major areas, and the options that have been considered.

CONVERTING SOLAR ENERGY IN SPACE

As originally conceived, the satellite solar-power station could use any of several current options for solar-energy conversion[1]—thermionic, thermal electric, photovoltaic, and others that may be developed in the future. Photovoltaic energy conversion, however, appeared to be the most useful starting point because of the widespread experience with solar cells in the space program. The current "base-line" design uses this approach. There are other advantages, too, to the selection of photovoltaic conversion: ERDA's National Photovoltaic Program has as its objective the development of low-cost, reliable photovoltaic systems; and the reduced maintenance requirements of the passive photovoltaic process (as compared to active conversion processes) should lead to increased reliability during the desired 30-year operational lifetime of each solar-power station.

The alternative methods include thermal-electric conversion, where focused solar energy operates a heat engine.[2] Lightweight solar concentrators could focus solar radiation into a cavity receiver, where the heat could be absorbed by a circulating fluid or a gas (say, helium) and transmitted to a heat engine, which would, in turn, drive an electric generator. For reasonable operating efficiencies, the over-all system would need radiators to reject waste heat to space.

The potential of such a system, particularly one with a Brayton-cycle engine, is sufficient that it is being investigated as an alternative solar-energy converter for the satellite power station.[3] The difficulties, however, appear to be formidable, particularly with the need to provide a large waste-heat radiator (about 1 square kilometer in one design) and with the design of the solar concentrators (about 50 square kilometers to drive 48 turbogenerators with an output of 14,000 megawatts in space).

TRANSMITTING THE POWER TO EARTH

Power generated within the satellite solar-power station could conceivably be transmitted to Earth, 22,300 miles below, either by a microwave beam or a laser beam, or simply by using mirrors to focus sunlight down to Earth.

Of these options, the microwave method alone uses achievable, demonstrated technology to obtain high efficiency in generation, transmission, and rectification. In addition, it promises to satisfy environmental requirements and safety considerations. The mass production of more than 1 million microwave devices, serving an annual market of half a billion dollars in the United States alone, indicates the degree of commercialization of the technology.

Among the optional transmission methods, the laser beam is not acceptable because of the low efficiencies associated with the conversion of electricity into laser power and to eventual reconversion of laser power into electricity, and because of optical limitations. The absorption of laser beams by the atmosphere and by clouds would reduce the overall efficiency even further, to an unacceptable level, and the risks involved to the general public should the beam-direction control system fail are too great. The third option, concentrating sunlight with mirrors placed in synchronous orbit to overcome the diurnal variation of solar energy on Earth, is equally unacceptable—in part because of the large area of mirrors that would be required in orbit for a reasonable concentration factor at a location on Earth, and in part because of the losses from absorption in clouds. In addition, serious ecological problems might arise from an interference with the diurnal cycle if this scheme were employed.

THE CURRENT DESIGN CONCEPT

The design study to be described here represents the present stage of evolution of a series of theoretical, technical, and economical studies—which are still in progress. This design[4] uses silicon solar cells in combination with solar reflectors to convert solar energy into electricity, and it has the potential for large-scale power generation, delivering from 2,000 to 15,000 megawatts to Earth. The lower end of this range represents a satellite power station that could be used to meet incremental capacity demands, and the upper end one that would eventually replace conventional power plants.

Present silicon solar cells are about 200 microns thick and have efficiencies up to 15 per cent. The current design uses silicon cells mounted on rigid substrates with cover glasses bonded to the solar cell for radiation shielding. Flexible substrates with printed circuits to which solar cells can be soldered or welded are being developed for other space applications and may prove superior.

The efficiency of silicon solar cells has been steadily increasing, due to such techniques as shallow diffusion to increase ultraviolet response, non-reflecting . .solar-cell surfaces, antireflective coatings to improve ultraviolet resistance, reduction of current-conductor size to increase the active area, and doping to reduce the degradation of performance induced by energetic solar radiation. The best present-day technology suggests a weight-to-power ratio of about 14 kilograms per kilowatt, but projections based on improvements expected in the next 10 years indicate that 1.4 kilograms per kilowatt may be achievable. These figures are for designs that incorporate solar concentrators with reflective-film mirrors coated to divert solar radiation onto the cells and filter out undesirable portions of the solar spectrum.

Exposure to the space environment will degrade the silicon solar cells logarithmically, with about 6 per cent of the original efficiency being lost after the first 5 years. For the 30-year lifetime of a satellite power station, calculations suggest that 1 per cent of the cells will be affected by micrometeorite impacts.

The present stage of evolution of satellite solar-power station design studies is represented in Figure 26-1. This shows two solar collector panels, each 5.92 × 4.93 kilometers, together producing a power output of about 9,300 megawatts (resulting in an effective power output at the receiving antenna on Earth of about 5,000 megawatts). Rigidity of this double array is provided by a central mast 100 meters in diameter and a stiffened skeletal structure running through the assembly. Between the two panels is a microwave-transmitting antenna; the panels will face the Sun continuously while the microwave antenna rotates once a day (with respect to the panels) to face the receiving station. Only the rotating joints necessary for antenna orienta-

Figure 26-1. *Geometry and dimensions.* The two solar collector panels shown here would together produce about 9,300 megawatts (about 5,000 megawatts available power output at the receiving antenna before the power interface). The central mast, 100 meters in diameter, and the stiffened skeletal structure provide rigidity for the flexible solar-cell substrate. The transmitting antenna must rotate once each day (relative to the satellite structure) to remain oriented toward the receiving antenna while the solar-cell array is facing the Sun to within 1 degree.

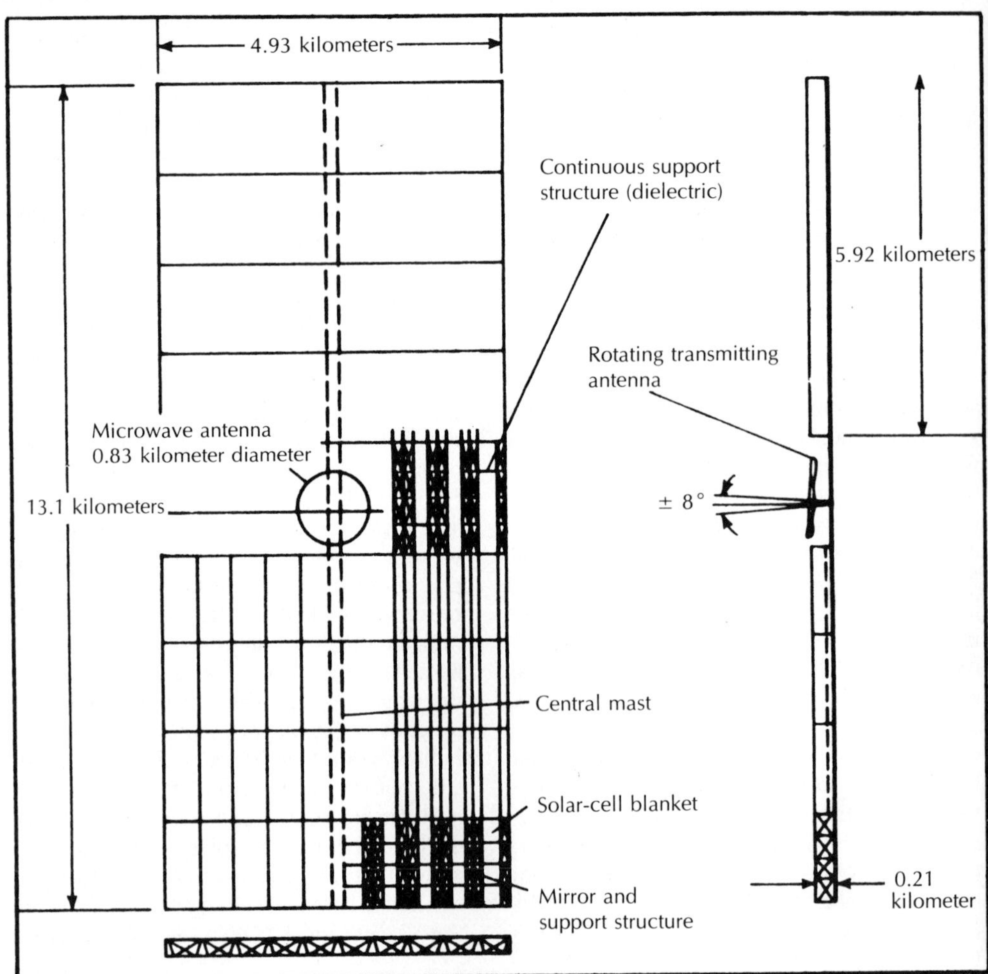

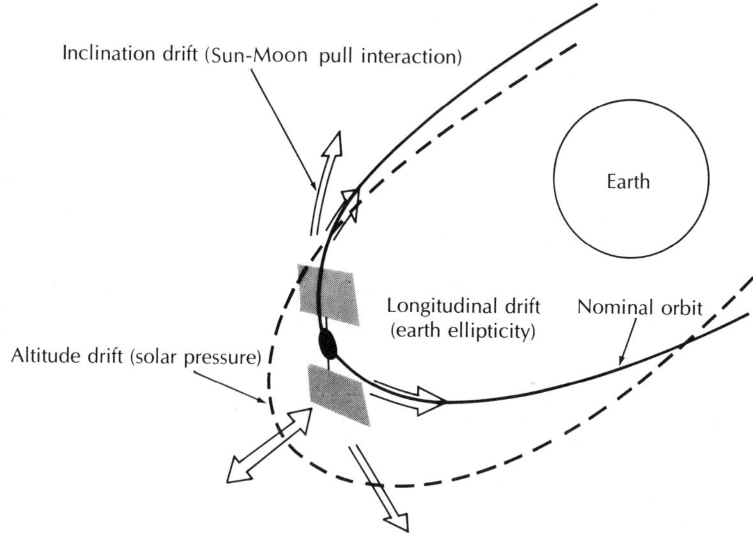

Figure 26-2. *Orbit perturbations.* The satellite must remain fixed in its geostationary orbit despite perturbations that threaten to move it from its nominal position. This drawing shows three perturbations: *longitudinal drift* around the synchronous orbit, due to the ellipticity of the Earth's equatorial plane; *altitude drift,* due to solar radiation pressure, which would change the eccentricity of the orbit, and *orbit inclination drift,* caused by the gravitational gradient arising from the pull of the Sun and Moon, which would alter the orbital plane. Stationkeeping and attitude control could be maintained by ion engines, possibly fueled by argon.

tion are "active" in what is otherwise a passive satellite.

The entire structure is subject to thermal stresses and distortions induced by thermal gradients during the equinoctial eclipses when the satellite passes through Earth's shadow. The longest eclipse lasts 72 minutes. For such a large structure, oscillations caused by this thermal exposure could be a problem. Fatigue effects might shorten its service life. Structural-design approaches that would minimize the effect have been identified, but more detailed evaluation of the problem is still necessary.

Obviously, the satellite must remain fixed in its geostationary orbit at all times, despite the orbital perturbations (some of which are identified in Figure 26-2) that threaten to move it from the desired spot. Ion engines, possibly fueled by argon, will be needed to keep the power station in the appropriate orbit and to maintain orientation of the solar panels toward the Sun and the microwave antenna toward the receiving antenna on Earth. The quantity of propellant required for this stationkeeping and attitude control is around 50,000 kilograms per year.

The total mass of such a power station (delivering 5,000 megawatts at the receiving antenna) amounts to 18.2×10^6 kilograms, not including consumables. Most of this mass, 12.4×10^6 kilograms, is in the solar arrays with the transmitting antenna adding 5.5×10^6 kilograms and the remainder being made up by the control system and the rotary joint. The weight to power efficiency ratio of 3.6 kilograms per kilowatt is remarkably low, compared with that of terrestrial systems, and demonstrates the advantages to be gained by placing the solar energy conversion system in synchronous orbit.

MICROWAVE POWER TRANSMISSION

Free-space transmission of power by microwaves is a relatively new technology, but

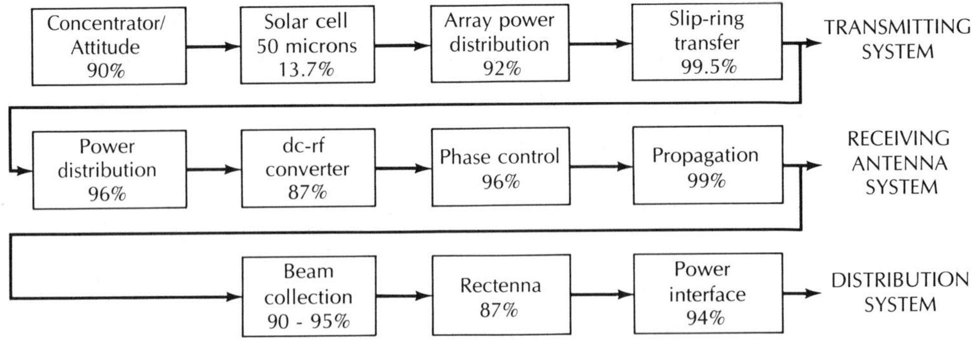

Figure 26-3. *Efficiency chain* of the elements that make up the entire system. The figures quoted here are efficiency goals for each stage. For the solar cells, the quoted efficiency, 13.7 per cent, is for a two-panel system, 5 years into its projected 30-year life-span.

it has advanced rapidly and can already show system efficiencies of 55 per cent including the interconversion between dc power and microwave power at both terminals.[5] Figure 26-3 is a block diagram of the system designed for the satellite solar-power station,[6] with the efficiency goals of each stage.

For converting the dc voltage output from the solar cells to rf power at microwave frequencies either an amplitron or a klystron may eventually be selected. The amplitron[6,7] is a cross-field amplifier with a cold platinum cathode operating by secondary emission to achieve a very long life. The amplitron requires 20 kilovolt dc voltage. The weight of the unit can be low enough for this satellite application if special materials are used in its construction—samarium cobalt for the permanent magnet and pyrolitic graphite for the space radiators. The specific weight and cost of the amplitron are optimum at a frequency in the industrial microwave band 2.40 to 2.50 gigahertz and at a power output around 5 kilowatts.

The klystron, a linear beam device, differs from the amplitron in being a high-gain device with an efficiency only modestly high (70 to 80 per cent), in contrast to the low-gain amplitron efficiency of perhaps 90 per cent. Klystrons have low noise properties, whereas the amplitron's noise behavior is still unknown in this application.

In terms of cost and weight, the klystron is both more expensive and heavier than the amplitron. But fewer and higher-powered klystrons (such as solenoid-focused units with outputs greater than 50 kilowatts instead of the conventional low-powered, permanent-magnet-focused klystrons) could simplify the orbital assembly task.

Space is an ideal medium for the transmission of microwaves; an efficiency of 99.6 per cent is thought to be possible for propagation from the point at which the beam leaves the transmitting antenna to a point above the upper atmosphere. To ensure high efficiency in transmission for the lowest cost, the geometric relationships between the two antennas[7,8] indicate that the transmitting antenna should be about 1.0 kilometers in diameter and the receiving antenna about 10 kilometers in diameter.

The transmitting antenna is designed as a circular, planar active phased array, divided into a large number of subarrays, each approximately 20 square meters. Much emphasis has been placed in the design study[9,10] on the phasing control system to ensure high efficiency, good pointing accuracy, and safe operation of the microwave beam.

Absorption, refraction, and scattering effects in the ionosphere are expected to be negligible at the low microwave power densities being considered.

Down on the ground, the receiving antenna will be, according to the current design study, an array of elements to absorb and rectify the incident microwave beam; in each element will be a half-wave dipole, an integral low-pass filter, a diode rectifier, and a bypass capacitor. The dipoles will be dc-insulated from the ground plane and appear as rf absorbers to the incoming microwaves. The design study shows the dipoles spread about 0.6 wavelength apart, arranged in a triangular lattice about 0.2 wavelength from the ground plane. This distance can be adjusted (within limits) until there is a good match between the specific dc load impedance and the incoming microwave beam. This match can approach 100 per cent; reflection losses of less than 1 per cent have been achieved experimentally. Tests on the entire "rectenna" element in its current state of development show an efficiency of 90 per cent.

The power density at the receiving point will always be a maximum at the middle of the beam, decreasing with distance from the center. The over-all size of the receiving array will be determined by the radius at which the collection and rectification of the power becomes marginally economical. It can be made 80 per cent transparent, so that the land underneath could be put to other uses. Heat generated during the rectification stage (in Schottky barrier diodes made from gallium arsenide material) will amount to less than 15 per cent of the incoming microwave radiation—a source of thermal pollution lower than that of any known thermodynamic conversion process.

The JPL Venus antenna site at Goldstone, California was the location of tests[10] in summer, 1975 of a 24-square meter array of microwave rectifier elements constructed according to this design study. The transmitting antenna for these tests, an 86-foot diameter dish, was about 1 mile from the receiving array. At a radiated frequency of 2,388 megahertz, incident peak intensities of up to 170 milliwatt per square centimeter yielded as much as 30.4 kilowatts of dc power output from the array. This represents a combined collection and rectification efficiency under these conditions of more than 82 per cent.

TRANSPORTATION, ASSEMBLY, MAINTENANCE

So far we have discussed efficiency and economics only for a satellite power station fully assembled, in working order and "on station" in its geostationary orbit. But obviously the components have to be transported from Earth to that position, they have to be assembled into the operating array, and the working power station will presumably need maintenance from time to time during its 30-year life. The costs of these operations will clearly have a great impact on the economic feasibility of the project.

As currently foreseen, transportation will be a two-stage process—one stage to low Earth orbit and a second delivering partially assembled components into synchronous orbit.[11] The first stage, as presently considered, will utilize either a modification of the space shuttle, which is already well along in its development, or a new heavy-lift launch vehicle. The cost for a modified space shuttle capable of lifting payloads of 80,000 kilograms to low Earth orbit is projected to be \$200 to 400 per kilogram; with a specially designed heavy-lift launch vehicle these costs could fall to \$40 to 120 per kilogram (Figure 26-4).

Each complete satellite power station will need from 60 to 100 individual flights of heavy-lift launch vehicles. The limits on lifting capability may be set more by the available volume than by the weight-lifting performance of each flight; although some deployment of prefabricated structures (such as the transmitting antenna) at low Earth orbit is desirable, there is a limit to the amount of folding and compressing that can be achieved.

After assembly in low Earth orbit, the satellite power station could be lifted to synchronous orbit by ion propulsion. The many chal-

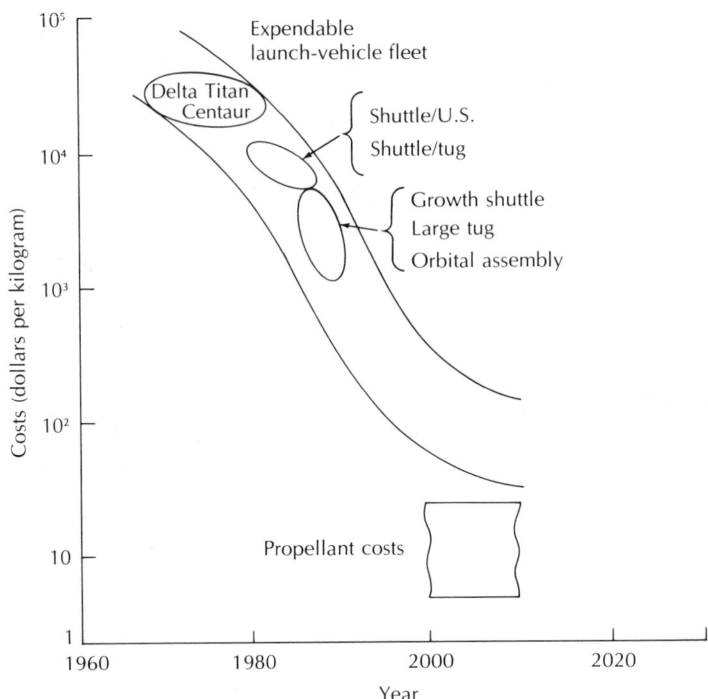

Figure 26-4. *Payload delivery costs* to synchronous orbit in 1975 dollars. The space shuttle is already well along in its development; if this is eventually replaced by a specially designed launch vehicle (perhaps by the year 2000) delivery costs would fall from $200 to 400 per kilogram to $40 to 120 per kilogram. (Source of data: NASA Johnson Space Flight Center, Houston, Texas.)

lenges inherent in the development of a low-cost, heavy-lift space transportation system for this stage are currently being explored.[12]

To assess maintenance costs before experience is gained with a working satellite power station is obviously difficult, depending as it does on a knowledge of the reliability of the entire system. The costs can be reduced by using a large number of identical components (for example, the solar cells) for redundancy. Also the cost of performing repairs must be compared with the "cost" of delaying repairs and a potential loss of revenue. The eventual goal, of course, is the evolution of a maintenance-free system.

One option that must be considered under the general heading of "assembly" is that certain components could well be actually manufactured in space.[13] For example, silicon crystals suitable for solar-cell manufacture could be grown in the space station from purified silicon produced on Earth, thereby obviating degradation during passage through the Van Allen belt. Fabrication and assembly of structural components could be done in orbit from appropriately prepared flat-rolled stock.[14] These and similar techniques would ease the transportation problem because the materials would be lifted into orbit in their most compact form, so reducing the number of orbital flights required. NASA's present study[13] of the role of the space stations is the logical first step in the establishment of such space manufacturing activities.

ENVIRONMENTAL IMPLICATIONS

The benefits of this (or, indeed, any) large-scale power generation system must be weighed against potential dangers to human health, destruction of valued natural resources, and intangible effects that might influence the "quality of life." Failure to take these steps is demonstrated by the difficulties met by such counter-examples such as the supersonic transport aircraft, nuclear power, and interstate highways.

The major social costs of environmental impacts of the satellite solar-power stations appear to lie in: resource allocations (land management, energy requirements for both construction and operation, etc.); environmental degradation (waste heat disposal, interactions with the upper atmosphere, environmental modifications, etc.), and public safety (long-term exposure under normal operations, effects on communications, safety under accident or abnormal situations, continuity of power generation, effects of interrupted operations, etc.).

Specific examples of environmental impacts are:

(1) *Waste heat* released at the receiving antenna site could be limited to 15 per cent of the rectified power, which is, as stated above, much less than from the alternative power-generation methods.

(2) *Land despoilment.* Land use per power station would be about 270 square kilometers; but as stated earlier the receiving antenna would be about 80 per cent transparent to sunlight, impervious to rain, and no barrier to the productive use of the land beneath it. There need be no microwave radiation beneath the antenna, and transportation of supplies to the site (and maintenance operations) would be infrequent, compared with conventional power plants. Offshore locations could be considered as antenna sites.

(3) *Resource consumption.* The materials necessary for construction are largely those in plentiful supply, such as silicon and aluminum. Each satellite power station would need less than 2 per cent of the yearly supply of critical materials, such as platinum, available to the United States.

(4) *Energy consumption.* The energy required to produce the materials for power-station construction and the propellants to place each satellite into orbit would be regenerated in about 3 years of operation.

(5) *Atmospheric pollution.* Space vehicles using liquid-hydrogen and liquid-oxygen propellants are expected to add primarily water vapor to the atmosphere. Heating of the atmosphere would be very small.

(6) *Ionospheric interactions.* At a microwave power density of 20 milliwatts per square centimeter or less within the beam no interactions are expected with the ionosphere. Changes in electron density caused by power densities greater than 20 milliwatts per square centimeter and frequencies higher than 2.45 gigahertz, however, need to be investigated for possible effects on other users of the ionosphere.

(7) *Microwave exposure* can be controlled by providing suitable enclosures for the maintenance crew working on the receiving antenna. Beyond 10 kilometers from the beam center, the microwave power density would meet the lowest international standards for continued exposure to microwaves. If the microwave-beam pointing system were to fail, the coherence of the beam would be lost, the energy dissipated, and the beam spread out so that the energy density would approximate communication-signal levels on Earth. The effects on birds and on aircraft flying through the beam are projected as negligible, but they should be experimentally determined.

(8) *Radiofrequency interference* by the fundamental microwave frequency and its harmonics, turn-on and shut-down sequences, random background energy and other superfluous signals emanating from the microwave-generation devices could be controlled by filters, choice of frequency, and narrow-band operation. The effects on radioastronomy, shipborne radar, and communication systems should be determined before specific frequency allocations can be made. It appears very possible, for example, that amateur sharing, state-police radar, and high-power defense radar will suffer substantial interference if 3.3 gigahertz is chosen as the fundamental frequency.

ECONOMIC IMPLICATIONS

The results of investigations[15] made to compare the economics of the satellite solar-power station with those of the other alternatives show that an operational 5,000-megawatt power station would cost about $7.6 billion, or about $1,500 per kilowatt. Figure 26-5 shows the breakdown of this total. Note that the largest cost element is for space transportation, which indicates that improvements in efficiency and in weight reductions would be significant.

For an operational life of about 30 years, the cost of power at the bus bar would be 27 mills per kilowatt-hour. Expected life-cycle revenues will be about $35 billion for each satellite power station, whereas operating costs will amount to $4.2 billion for the same period.

Of course the development program will be expensive—say $20 billion for the power-station technology and another $24 billion for the transportation system and related matters—but these costs would be repaid if 60 satellite solar-power stations were operating by the year 2014 (assuming that the cost of generating electricity by alternative means averages 35 mills per kilowatt-hour). This number of satellite power stations would provide at least 10 per cent of incremental installed generation capacity in the United States.

Figure 26-6 compares the range of projected generation costs for fossil-fueled and terrestrial solar-power systems with those of the satellite solar-power system. A 5,000-megawatt operational satellite power station will be cost-effective with fossil fuels at the projected bus-bar cost of 27 mills per kilowatt-hour. Between 1995 and 2025, coal prices are projected to rise by as much as 50 per cent because of increased production costs and the additional cost of pollution-control equipment. The relative price rise of oil is expected to be more pronounced; indeed, it is unlikely to be available at any price after 2000 for large-scale power-generation purposes.

The development program for this project, by any measure a major program ranking with nuclear fission and fusion or satellite telecommunications in scale of effort, will demand careful planning. The best route appears a three-phase program: a first phase of technology verification, largely carried out on Earth, and culminating in an orbiting test

Figure 26-5. *Breakdown of unit cost* of a 5,000-megawatt satellite solar power station. Costs shown are in units of 1974 dollars × 10^9. This breakdown shows clearly that space transportation is by far the largest cost element, and therefore represents the area in which improvements in efficiency and weight reduction would have the most significant effect.

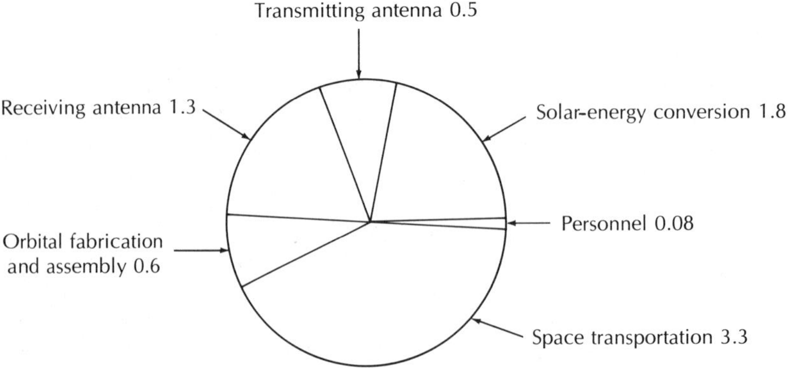

Total cost $7.6 × 10^9 (approx. $1,500 per kilowatt)

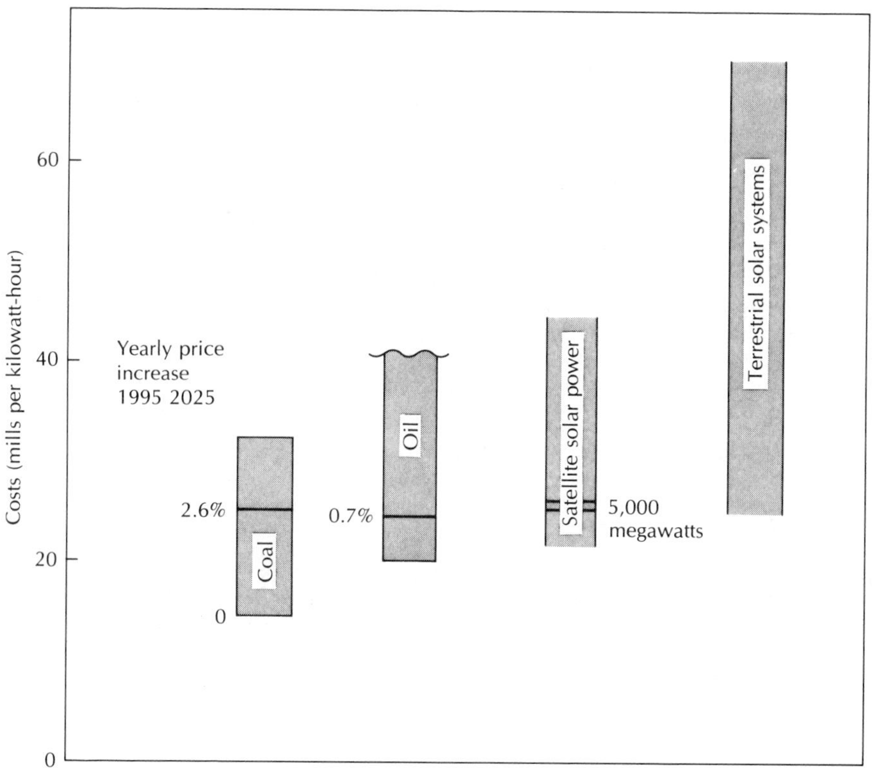

Figure 26-6. *Range of power-generation costs* over the period 1995 to 2025 compared for coal, oil, and both terrestrial and satellite-based solar power systems. A 5,000-megawatt satellite power station would be competitive with fossil fuels at the projected cost of 27 mills per kilowatt-hour. Both coal and oil prices are expected to rise in this period. Costs shown are based on 1974 dollars. (Source of the data is Econ., Inc. 1975—see Ref. 15.)

facility; a second stage leading to a prototype system (say 200 to 750 megawatts), and finally the mass production of full-size units with the goal of at least a hundred 5,000-megawatts stations by 2025.

Since the concept was first proposed in 1968, academic, industrial and government groups in the United Svates and abroad have been assessing the feasibility of the satellite solar-power station. These studies find the concept to be promising, both technically and economically, and environmentally acceptable. They also find that critical developments in technology needed for the satellite power stations would be useful contributions to other worthwhile developments in space and on Earth—and, conversely, developments already being studied for advanced space-transportation systems, solar energy conversion systems, and other related programs could be of help to satellite power-station technology.

This undertaking, because of its magnitude, world-wide implications on energy availability, and potential for the industrial use of space, could benefit many countries. Agreements on such matters as frequency assignments, launch sites and receiving-antenna locations would then become areas of international concern, and decisions would need to be made in the common interest as we look forward to a new era of world-wide energy resource development.

REFERENCES

1. P. E. Glaser, "Method and Apparatus for Converting Solar Radiation to Electrical Power," United States Patent, 3 781 647, 25 December 1973.
2. G. R. Woodcock, D. L. Gregory, "Derivation of a Total Satellite Energy System," AIAA Paper 75-640, AIAA/AAS Solar Energy for Earth Conference, Los Angeles, California, April 1975.
3. Boeing Aerospace Company, "Space-Based Power Conversion and Power Relay Systems," Contract No. NAS8-31628.
4. Arthur D. Little, Inc., "Feasibility Study of a Satellite Solar Power Station," NASA CR-2357, NTIS N74-17784, February 1974.
5. R. M. Dickinson, W. C. Brown, "Radiated Power Transmission System Efficiency Measurements," Tech. Memo 83-727 Jet Propulsion Laboratory, California Institute of Technology, 15 May 1975.
6. Raytheon Company, "Microwave Power Transmission System Studies," NASA CR-134886, ER 75-4368, December 1975.
7. W. C. Brown, *Proc. IEEE 62,* 11 (1974).
8. G. Goubau, J. *Microwave Power 5,* 223 (1970).
9. W. C. Brown, "Adapting Microwave Techniques to Help Solve Future Energy Problems," *IEEE Transactions on Microwave Theory and Techniques,* December 1973, pp. 755–763.
10. R. M. Dickinson, "Evaluation of a Microwave High-Power Reception-Conversion Array for Wireless Power Transmission," Technical Memorandum 33-741, Jet Propulsion Laboratory, September 1975.
11. R. Kline, C. A. Nathan, "Overcoming Two Significant Hurdles to Space Power Generation: Transportation and Assembly," AIAA Paper 75-641, AIAA/AAS Solar Energy for Earth Conference, Los Angeles, California, April 1975.
12. Boeing Aerospace Company, "System Concepts for STS Derived Heavy Lift Launch Vehicles Study," NASA-14710, Mid-Term Review, 2–6 February 1976.
13. NASA, "Space Station Systems Analysis" (studies being performed under contract for Johnson Space Flight Center, Houston, Texas by McDonnell Douglas and for Marshall Space Flight Center, Huntsville, Alabama by Grumman Aerospace Corporation).
14. Grumman Aerospace Company studies "The Development of Space Fabrication Techniques" for NASA/MSFC and "Orbital Assembly Demonstration Study" for NASA/JSC.
15. Econ, Inc., "Space-Based Solar Power Conversion and Delivery Systems," NASA/MSFC Contract No. 8-31308.

Oil Shale and the Energy Crisis 27

GERALD U. DINNEEN and GLENN L. COOK 1974

The oil shales of the United States are a potential source of vast quantities of liquid fuels. These sedimentary rocks contain solid organic material that can be decomposed by heat into an oil resembling petroleum, gases, and a carbonaceous residue. Although the shales are widely distributed, only those of the Green River Formation in Colorado, Utah, and Wyoming have received appreciable attention, because these shales are particularly rich in organic material.

Many attempts have been made, since early in this century, to develop commercial utilization of the Green River oil shale. These have typically involved underground mining, with processing in above-ground equipment. This approach is still the most likely to be utilized for developing those portions of the deposit that crop out along cliffs or that are accessible to surface mining. However, an alternative approach—*in situ* processing—has received increased attention during recent years. This approach may be applicable to deposits of various grades and thicknesses of shale, and it has the additional advantage of avoiding the problem of disposing of large amounts of spent shale.

Although past efforts have not resulted in an oil-shale industry in the United States, the current status of oil-shale technology and economics in the context of the country's need for new energy sources breeds optimism for future development.

OIL SHALE IN THE GREEN RIVER FORMATION

The Green River Formation covers an area of about 17,000 square miles of Colorado, Utah, and Wyoming in four principal basins: The

Gerald U. Dinneen has been research director of the U.S. Bureau of Mines, Laramie Energy Research Center, since 1964. He has concentrated his research on the composition and reactions of shale oil.

Glenn L. Cook, a long-time member of the Laramie Energy Research Center, is supervisor of a research group studying the characterization of oil shale and shale oil. He has worked on identifying the components of oil shales with spectroscopic and nuclear magnetic resonance techniques.

From *Technology Review,* Vol. 76, No. 3, pp. 26–33, January, 1974. Reprinted with light editing and by permission of the authors and *Technology Review*. This article is adapted from a paper presented at the 1972 annual meeting of the American Society of Mechanical Engineers.

Figure 27-1. The western oil shales, rocks containing up to 10 to 15 per cent organic matter, occur in the Green River Formation in the area where Utah, Wyoming, and Colorado join. The Piceance Creek basin in Colorado (1)—though a small fraction by area of the Green River Formation—contains most of the richest shale and 80 per cent of the total recoverable oil, and it is the area of greatest current interest and potential activity. Other areas which contribute to the total of 600 billion barrels of recoverable oil include the Uinta Basin (2) in Utah (90 billion barrels) and the Green River (3) and Washakie (4) Basins in Wyoming and Colorado with some 30 billion barrels. (Map redrawn from map © 1963 National Geographic Society.)

Piceance Creek Basin of Colorado, the Uinta Basin of Utah, and the Washakie and Green River Basins of Wyoming. (See Figure 27-1). If only shale at least 10 feet thick and yielding at least 25 gallons of oil per ton is considered, the potential oil yield in place in the three states has been estimated at 600 billion barrels. If learner shale is included, the oil potential is increased substantially.

The shales of the Green River Formation were laid down during the Eocene geologic period, some 50 million years ago, as sediments of living organisms and precipitates of minerals at the bottoms of lakes. Deposition continued over a period of several million years. Compaction of the sediments with the elimination of water preserved the organic material, and the high organic content is an indication of the prolific production of living organisms that must have been characteristic of the lakes.

The small area of the Piceance Creek Basin (about 10 per cent of the area covered by the Green River Formation) contains about 80 per cent of the potentially recoverable oil. Some of the shale crops out in cliffs along the southern edge of the basin, where the Mahogany Zone, the best known interval of the Green River Formation, is about 75 feet thick. In the center of the Piceance Creek Basin continuous sections of oil shale averaging more than 25 gallons of oil per ton are several hundred feet thick but are generally under several hundred feet of overburden. In Utah and Wyoming the sections of rich shale are not as thick, and in Wyoming they are often interspersed with alternating beds of lean shale. Piceance Creek Basin shales were used to develop most of the current technology; they are a resource of tremendous size, and it is probable that they will be the first raw materials utilized in a developing shale-oil industry.

Mineralogically, the oil shales range in composition from rocks composed of illite clay through those containing dawsonite, nahcolite, and potash feldspars as the principal minerals, to those made up of calcite and dolomite. The organic matter is fairly high in hydrogen, so that heat converts about 65 per cent of it to oil, 10 per cent to gas, and 25 per cent to carbonaceous residue. Although shales in the Mahogany Zone have an average oil yield of 25 to 30 gallons per ton the zone is made up of material with yields ranging from about 5 to 75 gallons per ton. This heterogeneity is an important factor that must be considered in developing processes for recovering oil from the Green River Formation.

Oil shale in the Mahogany Zone is a highly consolidated organic-inorganic system with no significant micropore structure, pore volume, permeability, or internal surface. The mineral constituents consist of fine particles with 99 per cent by weight having diameters of less than 44 microns. Only the lower-grade shales typically show any appreciable porosity; and, although there is some variation among the shales of different oil yields, all raw shales are strong rocks.

As would be expected, heating to 950°F to remove the organic matter produces appreciable porosity, which is roughly proportional to the grade of shale. Further heating to decompose the carbonates produces some additional porosity. After heating, leaner shales retain high compressive strengths, but richer shales lose much of their strength. These characteristics will have to be taken into consideration in recovering the energy values from the shales.

Two general approaches to the recovery of shale oil from the Green River Formation have been proposed: mining, crushing, and above-ground retorting, and *in situ* processing. The first is the traditional approach that has been used in various parts of the world for over 100 years and will probably be used for the first development of the Green River Formation. The second has received serious consideration only in the last few years, but it has potential advantages that make efforts to develop a feasible method worthwhile. Because of the wide variations in conditions under which oil shales are found in the Green River Formation, the two approaches are complementary rather than competitive.

SHALE OIL FROM MINED SHALE

Many attempts have been made during more than the last half-century to mine the Green River oil shale and retort it—treat it by heat—to separate the hydrocarbons from their associated inorganic minerals. Notable among these are the extensive investigations conducted during the past thirty years by the Bureau of Mines under the Synthetic Liquid Fuels Act, by a group of six oil companies utilizing Bureau of Mines facilities, by the Union Oil Co. of California, and by the Colony Development Co. (See Tables 27-1 and 27-2.)

The Bureau of Mines in 1944 opened a demonstration mine near Rifle, Colorado, to

Table 27–1. Shale-Oil Deposits in the Green River Formation.[a]

	Billions of barrels of oil in place			
	Colorado	*Utah*	*Wyoming*	*Total*
Intervals 10 feet or more thick averaging 25 gallons per ton or more of oil	480	90	30	600
Intervals 10 feet or more thick averaging 10 to 25 gallons per ton of oil	800	230	400	1,430
Total: intervals 10 feet or more thick averaging over 10 gallons per ton	1,280	320	430	2,030

[a]Over 2 trillion barrels of oil are locked in known shale oil deposits in the Green River Formation, but less than one-third of this is in reasonably thick deposits which average more than 25 gallons of oil per ton of shale; only these are generally regarded as potentially exploitable.

Table 27–2. Mahogany Zone Oil-Shale Deposits.[a]

	Per Cent	*Weight Per Cent*
Mineral matter:		
Content of raw shale		86.2
Estimated mineral constituents:		
Carbonates, principally dolomite	50	
Feldspars	19	
Illite	15	
Quartz	10	
Analcite and others	5	
Pyrite	1	
Organic matter:		
Content of raw shale		13.8
Ultimate organic composition:		
Carbon	80.5	
Hydrogen	10.3	
Nitrogen	2.4	
Sulfur	1.0	
Oxygen	5.8	

[a]The richest oil shales occur in the Mahogany Zone of Colorado (the Piceance Creek Basin near Rifle) and adjacent portions of Utah. Even here the organic matter represents less than 15 per cent of the total shale content; one ton of shale may yield as much as 75 gallons of crude oil, but the average even in this richest shale deposit is more nearly 25 to 30 gallons per ton.

tap a 73-foot minable section of the Mahogany Zone, and by 1956 it had been shown with fair assurance that low mining costs and high recovery in a conventional room-and-pillar underground mining operation were possible. The research also indicated that petroleum technology would be adaptable to refining shale oil produced in any of the several retorts studied.

The most promising results were achieved with a gas combustion retort—a vertical, refractory-lined vessel through which crushed shale moves downward by gravity. Recycled gases enter the bottom of the retort and are heated by the hot retorted shale as they pass upward through the vessel. Air is injected into the retort at a point approximately one-third of the way up from the bottom and is mixed with the rising, hot recycled gases. Combustion of the gases and some residual carbonaceous material from the spent shale heats the raw shale immediately above the combustion zone to retorting temperature. Oil vapors and gases are cooled by the incoming shale and leave the top of the retort as a mist. The manner in which retorting, combustion, heat exchange, and product recovery are carried out gives high production and thermal efficiency. The process does not require cooling water, an important feature because of the semiarid regions in which the shale deposits occur. The process appeared to offer the possibility of large-scale operation. (See Figure 27-2.)

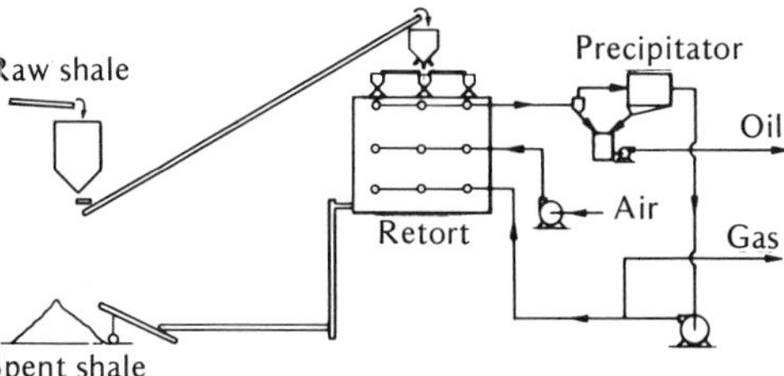

Figure 27-2. Crude oil will be recovered from mined oil shale by some version of a retorting process of which this is a basic flow diagram. Quarried shale, broken into pellets and heated to just under 1,000 °F in a retort, gives off gas and vaporized crude oil; from this mixture the crude oil is condensed and the remaining gas is returned to fuel the retort. Spent shale and a carbonaceous residue accumulate at the bottom of the retort and are moved to a disposal site; the latter may be the mine from which the original shale came, except that the volume of the spent shale is somewhat larger than that of the original material, so the mines are inadequate to accommodate all of the solid waste which accumulates. (Drawing: Savage, Holt, and Sims from the *Colorado School of Mines Quarterly*, October, 1968.)

From 1964 to 1968 the Bureau of Mines facilities were leased by the Colorado School of Mines Research Foundation, which operated them under a research contract with six oil companies. The first phase of this research, which lasted approximately two years, was devoted primarily to studying the gas combustion retorting process in two small pilot plants (nominal capacities of 6 and 24 tons per day) that had been constructed by the Bureau. Mining research involved extension of the room-and-pillar method used by the Bureau of Mines with somewhat smaller pillars. Work on retorting in the largest gas-combustion process pilot plant at the facilities showed that oil yields in excess of 85 per cent of the standard assay could be obtained using feed rates of 500 pounds per hour for each square foot of bed area. This was about double the rate previously achieved by the Bureau of Mines, with only a relatively small decrease in oil yield. Although the results indicated a material advance in processing technology, some of the operating problems associated with the scale-up in the size of the plant were not fully resolved.

Meanwhile, a retort developed by Union Oil Co. of California was tested between 1956 to 1958 on a demonstration scale of about 1,000 tons per day, and at the conclusion of the project it was announced that the process could be commercialized whenever energy demand and economic conditions warranted. This retort, also a vertical, refractory-lined vessel, operates on a downward gas flow principle; the shale is moved upward by a charging mechanism usually referred to as a "rock pump." Heat is supplied by combustion of the carbonaceous residue remaining on the retorted shale and is transferred to the oil shale, as in the gas combustion retort, by direct gas-to-solids exchange. The oil is condensed on the cool, incoming shale and flows over it to an outlet near the bottom of the retort. This process, like that of the Bureau of Mines, does not require cooling water.

A third group—the Colony Development Co., representing Standard Oil Co. of Ohio, Oil Shale Corp., Cleveland Cliffs Iron Co., and more recently Atlantic Richfield Oil Co. as project manager—has for several years been investigating the TOSCO II retorting process, based on a rotary kiln utilizing ceramic pellets heated in external equipment to accomplish retorting. Shale ground into particles not exceeding 0.5 inch is preheated and pneumatically conveyed through a vertical pipe by flue gases from the pellet-heating furnace, entering the rotary retorting kiln with the heated pellets; here it is brought to a retorting temperature of 900 °F by conductive and radiant heat exchange with the pellets. Passage of the kiln discharge over a trommel screen permits recovery of the pellets from the shale dust for recycling and reheating. The spent shale is routed to disposal by a screw conveyer. The oil is recovered by condensation from the gases leaving the retort. High shale through-put rates were reported, and considerable research was also done on environmental aspects of oil-shale operations, particularly in regard to handling spent shale deposits. On a commercial scale the system would yield some 50,000 barrels of oil per day.

PROCESSING THE SHALE IN THE MOUNTAIN

Because mining, crushing, and retorting make up about 60 per cent of the cost of producing shale oil by above-ground techniques, recovery of oil from shale by *in situ* processing has received attention during the past 20 years. This approach is attractive because it may be applicable to deposits of various thicknesses, grades of shale, and quantities of overburden. Also, it eliminates the necessity to dispose of large quantities of spent shale.

One concept of *in situ* processing envisions a five-step process: drilling a predetermined pattern of wells into the oil-shale formation, fracturing to increase permeability, igniting the shale at one or more centrally located wells, pumping compressed air down these ignition wells to support combustion of the oil shale and force the hot combustion gases through the fractured rock to convert the solid organic matter to oil, and recovering the oil thus generated through other wells. Research on the *in situ* technique is in the early stages and has so far been devoted to the development of fracturing techniques and methods of underground heating. The fracturing might be achieved by relatively conventional methods, such as hydraulic pressure or chemical explosives, or by unconventional methods, such as a nuclear explosive. Heating may be achieved either by underground combustion or by forcing previously heated gases or liquids through the formation.

One of the earliest investigations of *in situ* processing was by Sinclair Oil and Gas Co., now a part of Atlantic Richfield Co., which conducted a study in 1953 and 1954 at a site near the southern edge of the Piceance Creek Basin. This work confirmed that communication between wells could be established through induced or natural fracture systems, that wells could be ignited successfully, and that combustion could be established and maintained in the shale bed. More recently, over a period of several years in the mid-1960's, Sinclair conducted field research at a site near the center of the Piceance Creek Basin where the shale is much deeper and thicker. The results of this experiment were not promising; the fracturing techniques used apparently did not produce sufficient heat transfer surfaces for successful operation.

Another experiment of particular interest has been conducted by Equity Oil Co., in which hot natural gas was injected into an oil shale formation in order to achieve retorting. This presumably is especially advantageous from the point of view of the type of oil produced.

Two major *in situ* research projects are now in progress, one by the Bureau of Mines and the other by Garrett Research and Development Co. The Bureau's program involves laboratory studies, pilot scale simulation of underground operations, and field experiments. In the field experiments near Rock Springs, Wyoming, several methods of fracturing—hydraulic pressure, chemical explosives, and electricity—are being tested on an oil-shale bed that is 20 to 40 feet thick and under 50 to 400 feet of overburden. Using hydraulic pressure, four horizontal fractures have been produced over a vertical interval of about 35 feet at a depth of approximately 400 feet; tests indicate that these fractures extend at least 200 feet from the injection well. Chemical explosives have also been used—in the liquid form for detonation after being forced into naturally occurring or artificially created fractures, and in pelletized solid form for detonation in well bores. (See Figure 27-3.)

The combination of hydraulic pressure and liquid chemical explosive was used for a test of *in situ* processing of shale in a formation less than 100 feet beneath the surface. Fracturing was completed in a small five-spot pattern, and the shale was then ignited for a combustion test in which about 190 barrels of oil were produced. Preparations for a similar, but larger, underground recovery test are in progress.

The Garrett project utilizes a combined mining and explosive fracturing technique to prepare the oil shale for *in situ* processing. In

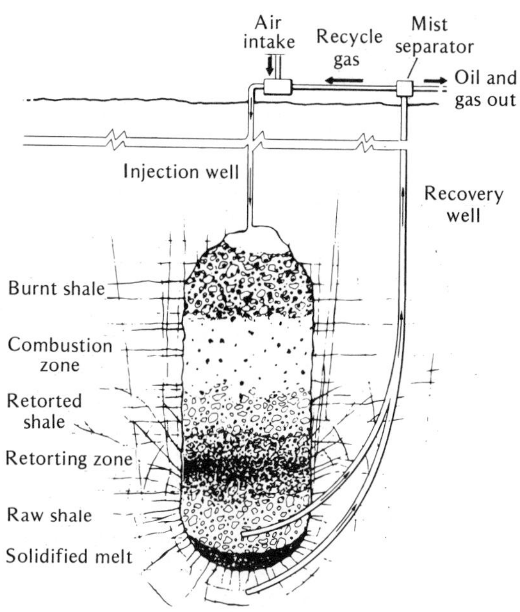

Figure 27-3. This method for *in situ* recovery of crude from oil shale was proposed by D. B. Lombard of the Lawrence Radiation Laboratory and H. C. Carpenter of the U.S. Bureau of Mines in 1968: a nuclear explosive detonated in the oil shale layer creates a "nuclear chimney" with fracturing through the adjacent shale deposits. Air forced into the "chimney" supports combustion, the hot combustion gases move through the fractures to convert the solid organics to liquids and gases, and these products are then drawn off for condensation and—in the case of the gas—to support further combustion. Efficient *in situ* recovery depends on effective fracturing of the shale; the nuclear explosive was unsatisfactory in this (and other) respects, and the method is not presently under active development. But the same general principles of fracturing (by conventional explosives), combustion, and product recovery figure in current *in situ* recovery concepts. (Drawing: Lombard and Carpenter from the *Journal of Petroleum Technology,* June, 1967.)

this approach shale is mined from the lower part of a room to provide porosity when the shale above this mined portion is collapsed into it. The broken shale in the room is then retorted from the top down. The present field experiment on the southwestern edge of the Piceance Creek Basin was started in 1972. The company has indicated that preliminary results are encouraging. As the project progresses, it should answer many of the questions concerning the feasibility of processing large quantities of broken shale *in situ*.

HOW TO REFINE CRUDE SHALE OIL

The fuels and chemicals normally produced from petroleum can also be obtained from shale oil. However, an adaptation of petroleum technology based on the properties peculiar to shale oil is required. Shale oil produced by retorting oil shale from the Green River Formation is usually a dark, viscous material with a relatively low sulfur content but a high pour point (high viscosity) and high nitrogen content; indeed, the pour point is so high that viscosity reduction is necessary before the oil is amenable to pipeline transportation. The high nitrogen content complicates the refining process. At present, it appears that special treatment of shale oil will be required to lower the nitrogen content before it is acceptable for such refining methods as catalytic cracking. The Bureau of Mines has recently demonstrated that a premium refinery feedstock can be made from *in situ* shale oil by a processing sequence suggested by the National Petroleum Council.

With the present emphasis on *in situ* processing, there is considerable interest in how the composition of oils produced in this way may compare with those from above-ground retorting. Recent research suggests that the specific gravity, pour point, viscosity, and contents of heavy gas oil and residuum will be lower in oil produced *in situ;* the content of naphtha, light distillate, and light gas oil will apparently increase under these conditions. The nitrogen and sulfur contents of the oils do not seem to vary systematically with the retorting variables. On the basis of these results, it seems that shale oil produced *in situ* may be more valuable than that produced in above-ground retorts.

THE ENVIRONMENTAL IMPACT OF A SHALE OIL INDUSTRY

Can the production of shale oil be done without significant environmental degradation? The environmental effects directly associated with oil-shale processing are expected to be from retorted or burned shales, contaminated waters, and gases. The present emphasis on *in situ* processing is partly because this technique would obviate the necessity of disposing of large quantities of retorted or burned shale. However, before *in situ* processing is finally proved feasible, the effect of leaching of the in-place retorted shale on ground waters will have to be determined. A start toward investigating this problem has been made by drilling a series of wells at the Bureau's experimental site near Rock Springs to compare hydrologic conditions in the area before and after an *in situ* processing experiment.

As indicated earlier, some portions of the Green River deposit appear to be most amenable to mining and above-ground processing. For this reason, and because of the unresolved technical problems confronting *in situ* processing, both industry and the Bureau of Mines are investigating problems associated with disposal of retorted or burned shales. The Colony group has done substantial research on the vegetation of retorted shale and has shown that this can be accomplished.

Retorting oil shale produces water from the combustion of fuel used to heat the shale and from decomposition of the organic matter in the shale. Because these retorting waters have been in contact with shale oil, they contain substantial amounts of organic materials in addition to the usual inorganic compounds. Experiments to treat water from gas combustion retorting and from the *in situ* retorting experiment near Rock Springs indicate that nearly complete removal of the inorganic ions can be achieved from water from the gas combustion process, but slightly less complete removal was obtained from water from the *in situ* process.

Gases generated by the combustion inherent in oil-shale processing are expected to be amenable to gas treating methods developed for other industries.

THE ECONOMICS OF SHALE OIL

Predictions of the probable cost of producing shale oil must be based on engineering estimates; data on plants of the size required to produce commercial quantities of oil are not available. Recent estimates—including those by the Bureau of Mines, the National Petroleum Council, and the Oil Shale Corp.—vary widely. Without extensive discussion of the assumptions involved in the different estimates, comparison of them is impossible. However, all estimates agree that to construct a plant to produce about 100,000 barrels per day of shale oil (about 0.6 per cent of our present petroleum demand) will involve a capital investment of several hundred million dollars, and the oil will have to yield a reasonable return on investment.

CAN WE BEGIN A HIGH-RISK NEW INDUSTRY?

Green River oil shale represents an immense potential source of energy, and there is now mounting evidence that the political and economic climate may be favorable for a modest beginning of a new industry—the winning of the energy values from the oil shales of the Green River Formation of Colorado, Utah, and Wyoming. However, the development is contingent on the willingness of industry to commit substantial sums of money to what must still be termed a high-risk venture; among the costs will be the necessary techniques of environmental control to prevent the degradation of air, water, and land in an area that is still largely in the state in which it was created by nature.

SUGGESTED READINGS

Burwell, E. L., T. E. Sterner, and H. C. Carpenter, "Shale Oil Recovery by *In Situ* Retorting, a Pilot Study," *J. Petrol. Technol. 22,* December 1970, p. 1520–1524.

Duncan, Donald C., and Vernon E. Swanson, "Organic-Rich Shale of the United States and World Land Areas," U.S. Geological Survey Circ. 523, 1965, 30 p.

East, J. H., Jr., and E. D. Gardner, "Oil Shale Mining, Rifle, Colorado, 1944–56," *U.S. Bureau of Mines Bulletin* 611, 1964.

Matzick, A., R. O. Dannenberg, J. R. Ruark, J. E. Phillips, J. D. Lankford, and Boyd Guthrie, "Development of the Bureau of Mines Gas-Combustion Oil-Shale Retorting Process," *U.S. Bureau of Mines Bulletin* 635, 1966.

Rattien, Stephen and David Eaton, 1976, "Oil Shale: The Prospects and Problems of an Emerging Energy Industry." *Annual Review of Energy,* Vol. 1, pp. 183–212.

Schramm, L. W., 1975, "Shale oil," *Mineral Facts and Problems,* 1975 Edition of Bureau of Mines, pp. 963–983.

U.S. Dept. of the Interior, 1973 "Final Environmental Impact Statement for the Prototype Oil Shale Leasing Program," U.S. Dept. of the Interior, Washington, D.C., (Vol. 1–6).

Van West, Frank P., 1972 "Green River Oil Shale," *Geologic Atlas of the Rocky Mountain Region, U.S.A.* Denver: Rocky Mountain Association of Geologists,.

Coping with the Oil Sands 28

A. R. ALLEN 1974

The reserves of readily available liquid hydrocarbons have been predicted with reasonable accuracy over the last five years, the production capability has been analyzed, and the consumption rate has followed the expected trend. Everyone has been nervous about the vulnerability of our economy to the international behavior of the Organization of Petroleum Exporting Countries from which we have been purchasing ever-increasing amounts of hydrocarbons. These concerns have now been amply justified.

Though this awareness has existed in the minds of the producers and the enlightened economists, the oil companies have been bombarded with irrational accusations of price fixing, gouging the public, excess profits, and lethargy in developing new sources.

Many, many millions of dollars are being spent each year in looking for oil and gas. Although the success rate has been very low, oil is being found in the less accessible regions of our continent and further and further offshore. Some oil companies have also devoted a great deal of money to examining the economic potential for hydrocarbon production out of oils sands, oil shales and coal.

One such company, Sun Oil Company, after some years of research and pilot-plant work embarked upon a commercial scale of operations to produce 55,000 barrels of synthetic crude oil per day from Athabasca Tar Sands. This operation lies near the center of the Athabasca Tar Sand region* at latitude 57° north and longitude 111° west in the province of Alberta. (See Figure 28-1.)

This article deals mainly with the solids handling and some related problems encountered in producing oil from the tar sand. A quick look at the dimensions involved will help one to have a more complete grasp of the whole picture. The ultimate reserves of bitu-

*Editors' note: The Athabasca Tar Sands cover an area of about 30,000 square miles and contain an estimated reserve of 300 billion barrels of recoverable crude oil—an amount closely approximating the world's total known reserve of conventional oil. Commercial recovery of oil from the oil sands are currently being accomplished by open-pit mining the sands and transporting the sand to a separation plant. However, this process will only recover 35 to 36 billion barrels of this estimated reserve. It is anticipated that recovery of bitumens from the sands in place (*in situ* mining) will become technically and economically feasible in the future.

A. R. Allen is Director of Operation for Great Canadian Oil Sands Limited, Fort McMurray, Alberta, Canada.

Reprinted with light editing and by permission of the author. This article is based on an address delivered at the American Chemical Society, 167th National Conference, Los Angeles, California, April, 1974.

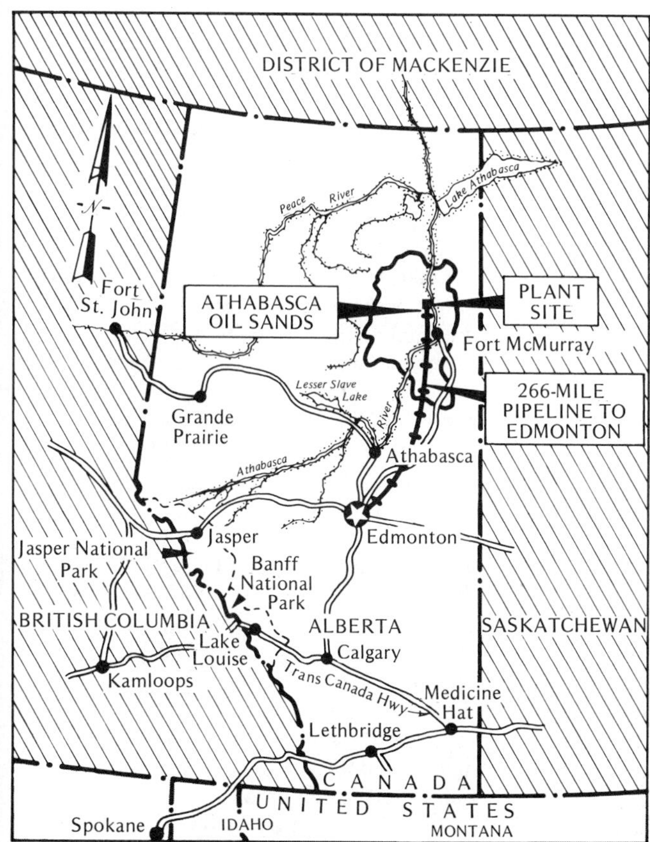

Figure 28-1. Athabasca tar sand location, Alberta, Canada.

men in the Athabasca Tar Sands have been estimated at about 700 billion barrels. The sands are discontinuous, erratic both in thickness and depth below the land surface, and highly variable in terms of oil saturation and particle size. The most important factors affecting economic development of the tar sands are the depth below surface, thickness of the ore body, and bitumen saturation. Figures 28-2 and 28-3 show roughly how these factors apply to the Athabasca region.

Recovery may be affected by two methods, by mining the sands and transporting the sand to a separation plant, or by using ways to recover bitumen from the sands in place.

The recoveries which might be anticipated before processing the sand, are estimated to conform roughly to Table 28-1. The restraints

Figure 28-2. Athabasca tar sands overburden thickness.

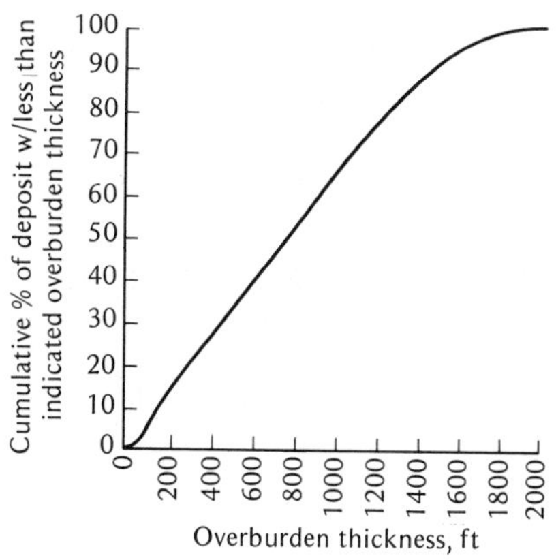

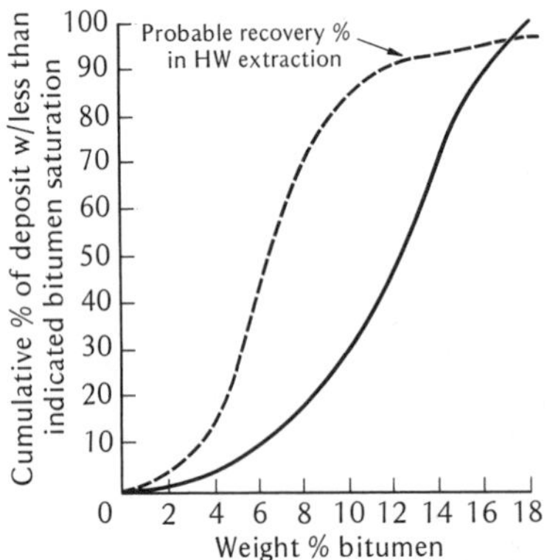

Figure 28-3. Athabasca tar sands bitumen saturation and probable recovery rate.

applied to these guesses are that only one open pit mining operation has been attempted on a large scale, and it has encountered many problems; underground mining may be completely uneconomic at any scale due to high gas concentrations and mobility of tar sand and aquifers above and below the tar sands beds; *in situ* processes have been under investigation for many years and produce high-cost oil, and early assessments may have been overly-optimistic.

The figures mentioned are generalized. However, when an operation is to be undertaken, the data required for the decision to invest over a billion dollars a plant must be specific. The changes in depth, thickness and grade of tar sand can be very abrupt and unless carefully evaluated in detail before beginning an operation, could result in financial disaster. All of the money has to be spent before a drop of oil is produced.

Table 28–1. Ore Recovery Estimates before Sand Processing.

Method	*Depth to Top of Ore*	*Recovery Per Cent of Ore*
Open-pit mining	0–150	85–90
Underground mining	>300	50–60
In situ extraction	>600	20–30

With this in mind, look again at Figure 28-2 and realize that at the present price structure for oil it is unlikely that more than 10 per cent of the bitumen in this vast reserve will be recovered by open pit mining methods. This would represent about 43 billion barrels of synthetic crude oil and would take about 100 years to produce from 12 plants each handling up to 400,000 tons a day of solids.

Let us now examine the Great Canadian Oil Sands operation. The lease of 4,000 acres of this area contained about 700 million barrels of recoverable bitumen. The operation now produces 55,000 barrels of synthetic crude oil per day. This entails production from one open-pit mine of around 140,000 tons of tar sand and 130,000 tons of overburden per stream day of these activities. The temperature varies between 90 °F down to −50 °F, and to add a local touch of geography much of the area is covered by muskeg swamp, a semifloating mass of decaying vegetation.

This is not a conventional strip mining operation. The restraints imposed by environmental considerations, administrative regulation, confining boundaries, weather, and the nature of the materials to be handled create severe limitations.

All overburden and tailings must be confined within the operators lease and must not be placed on recoverable tar sand within the lease. The overburden and tailings occupy a considerably larger volume after the oil has been removed than they did before being disturbed; also, space is required in the pit for excavators, conveyors, and other equipment. Accordingly, much long-term planning is required to permit progressive dumping of overburden and tailings without hindering the subsequent mining operations.

The initial tailings pond was constructed on the river flat with a starter dyke of overburden and subsequent sand dyke construction to allow the mine to progress unhindered. While this is going on, the overburden is being used to prepare a second tailings pond inside the mined-out portion of the pit by the time the initial tailings pond is filled.

In order to accommodate the volume increase and allow space for conveyors the terminal or new land surface must be at least 70 feet above the original land surface.

OVERBURDEN REMOVAL

The sequence of operations prior to the actual mining of the tar sand involves an unusually long time span. The first step is to clear off the scraggly growth of tamarack and black spruce trees that grow in the muskeg. This and the preparation for muskeg removal can only be done efficiently when the muskeg is frozen deeply enough to support equipment. Early operations tended to concentrate more on the retrieval of sunken equipment than removal of material. So, being thus restricted to the coldest part of the winter keeps people pretty well on their toes. The hours of daylight are short, the time period is limited, visibility is restricted by fogs, and exposure conditions for men are at their worst. Morale and efficiency require a lot of attention under these conditions.

In order to remove the muskeg, drainage networks are blasted to run off as much water as possible during the summer periods. Ideally, two years drainage are needed prior to muskeg excavation—even then, muskeg material can only be handled efficiently in winter. Different methods have been tried—finally settling down to two-pass ripping for fragmentation and frost penetration followed by the combined efforts of fifteen yard front-end loaders and 150-ton trucks. By working a long muskeg face it is possible to maintain a trafficable frozen bottom on which the vehicles operate. Icing up and freezing of the damp fibrous material in the loader buckets is a nuisance affecting efficiency but more tolerable than the previous difficulties with different equipment arrays.

The frozen muskeg cannot be used in constructing the tailings dykes and so has to be piled up in special dumps. When the muskeg piles thaw, a mobile, liquid, stringy mess results. Earth dams are constructed to keep the material under control. Muskeg dumps, as shown in Figure 28-4, are up to 100 feet high.

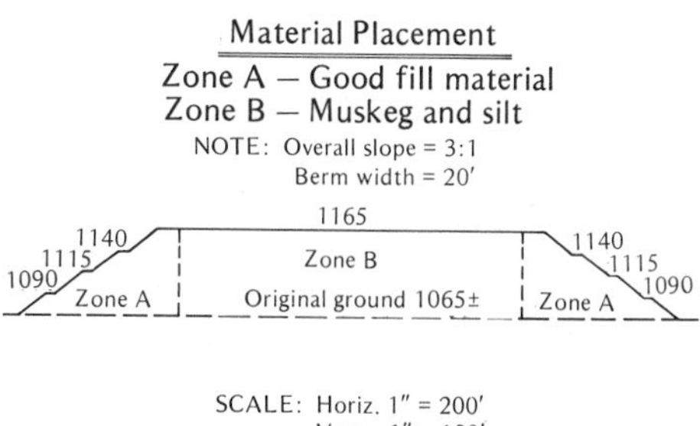

Figure 28-4. Typical section of muskeg dump.

The bulk of the overburden, removed after the muskeg operation, is used to build the earth dams inside the floor of the pit after the tar sand has been mined. The material consists of various kinds of sand, clay, boulders and low-grade tar sand. The distribution of these members is determined and the excavation sequence must be planned to conform to the civil engineering requirements of the massive 300-foot-high dams. Figure 28-5 shows a typical cross section of the overburden dams.

The amount of overburden that must be removed varies greatly with location. The minimum objective is to have one year of "prepared" tar sand available for mining at the end of the stripping season; with additional room for maneuvering the stripping fleet. The overburden dams can only be built using unfrozen material; hence, this job also has a time restraint of about 8 months in the year.

Figure 28-5. Typical section of overburden dyke.

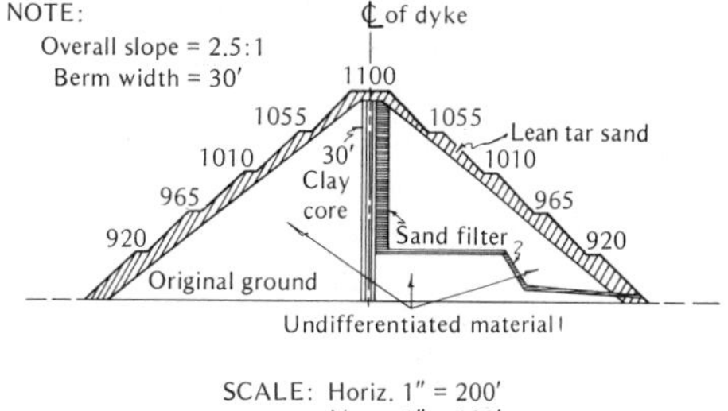

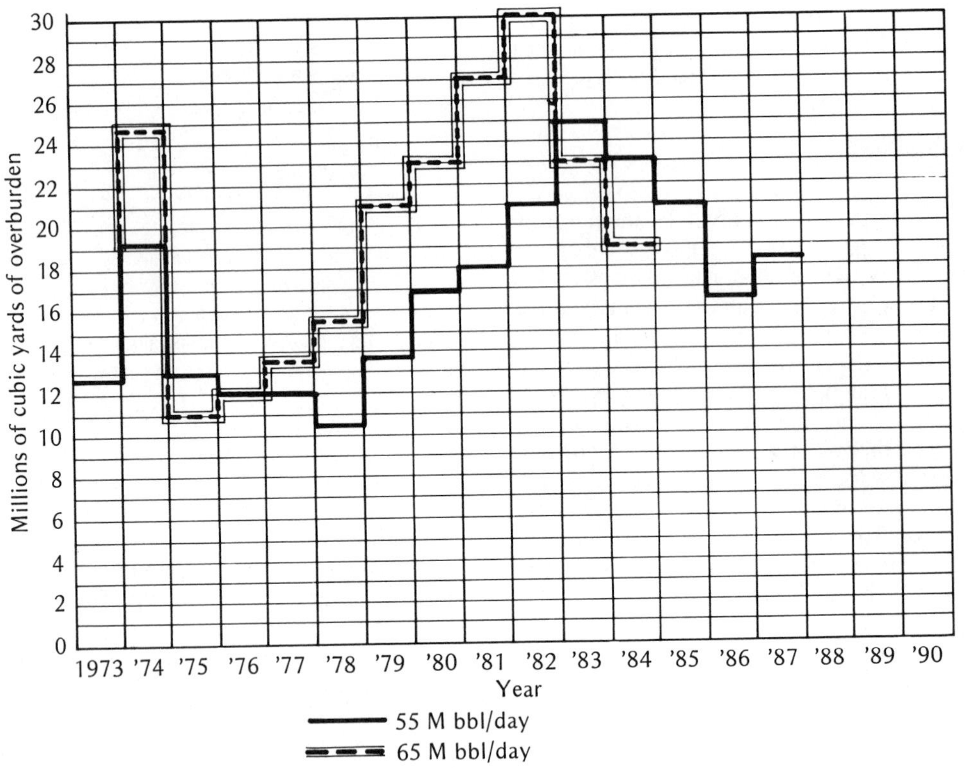

Figure 28-6. Overburden stripping to meet the mining requirements year by year.

Figure 28-6 shows the actual amount of cover to be removed and the "average line" to meet the long-term requirements of a stable work force and fleet size.

In the overburden removal, again several methods have been tried, many more have been studied. Some of the overburden members are very wet fine silts. The base of overburden is tar sand. The major problems associated with the job are the scarcity of road building material, and very poor soil-bearing properties. Trafficability both on the burrow floors and the dyke being constructed is poor. Long hauls, big boulders, ground moisture, and compaction difficulties make this an expensive operation.

The present method of removing overburden uses seven 15-cubic yard front-end loaders, twenty-one 150-ton rear dump trucks, graders, bulldozers, and compactors. For five months out of the eight, the operation is supplemented by the loading capability of a Bucyrus-Erie bucket wheel—in all, $10 million worth of mobile equipment. Round trips are about 3 miles: 14 million cubic yards, or 24 million tons should be moved each year, from here on; in 8 months of elapsed time per year. Rain and silts are our worst enemies.

MINING OPERATION

Nothing quite like this material has ever been mined before in such quantities, and this operation will probably be the smallest of its kind—the next two operations will be at least twice the size of the Great Canadian Oil Sands operation.

The average thickness of the tar sand in the lease now being mined is about 140 feet. It varies from about 90 to 220 feet. The mine is designed to extract the tar sand in two parallel benches up to 75 feet in height with a trailing bench of varying depth. The floor of the mine is limestone, but it is often not possible to run the main excavating machinery on the limestone base due to the pronounced rolling shape of the floor and the travel-grade limitations of the machinery.

The bucket-wheel excavators deliver the tar sand via traveling conveyors to a shiftable face conveyor. These conveyors discharge to collector belts feeding the extraction facility. The excavators are of German manufacture and have a theoretical digging capacity of about 5,000 tons per hour each. Service factors are below 80 per cent, and they are in a chain of apparatus, each one having an individual service factor. The two systems are barely capable of supplying the plant. Feed capability is supplemented by a smaller wheel and trucks, loaders and trucks, or in special cases, scrapers.

The logistics of large bins or surge piles with this kind of material are a special kind of nightmare—and so not in the design. This means that with the 30- to 40-minute surge coupling, which is designed through the extraction plant feed bin, all phases of the bitumen production step are tightly interdependent. Operators and supervisors throughout must be in close communication and constantly alert to the operating conditions and delays which might cause a set of problems upstream or downstream. The domino effect rules with an iron fist.

The tar sand is difficult stuff to deal with; its properties are not constant and these properties vary with particle size, oil saturation, moisture content, temperature, and, as it seems sometimes, even with the time of day. Figure 28-7 shows the typical arrangement of the components of tar sand.

The problems of temperature variation are of immense importance in the mining operations. The bitumen viscosity varies from 35,000 centistokes at 90 °F to 10^6 centistokes at 40 °F. At 0 °F we have a solid—but not quite. The sand particles are quartz with a mohs hardness of about 5.5 to 6.0. When these particles are bound together with the bitumen matrix at low temperatures, extremely high pressures are required to penetrate the formation. The teeth of the digging apparatus take the brunt of the punishment. On undisturbed tar sand in wintertime a 100-pound alloy tooth can be worn out in less than 8 hours—each of the bucket wheels has 120 of these cutting teeth. This was indeed part of the initial experience—teeth were being airlifted to the operation from anywhere in the world they could be obtained. It was obvious something had to be done about this, and it has now been done. Another early problem was related to the large dimension of the jointing planes—blocking out of huge frozen chunks of tar sand, which cascaded from the crest—occasionally wiping out the digging heads on the machines; and yet another—that minute water envelope around the grains of sand. After penetrating the 8 feet of frozen material the tar sand in place averages 40 °F; at this temperature the shear strength is much lower—and the water is not ice—but on exposure to the metal surface of buckets and transfer chutes or the cold surface of conveyor belts it promptly freezes, then stays there. As the newly planted frozen surfaces continue to cool, more sand builds up until openings of 20 square feet or more, designed to handle the passage of 10,000 tons an hour become completely closed off.

The resulting mass of frozen bitumen, water, and sand is far worse than concrete to remove. Many frigid hours have been spent trying to break, burn, drill, or scrape this out of chutes. Obviously, something had to be done about this too—and has been.

Then comes the summertime and occasional thunderstorms. Tar sand in summer can only be described as smelly and sticky; it hangs on with appalling tenacity to everything it touches. The material on the floors of the working benches no longer has the confin-

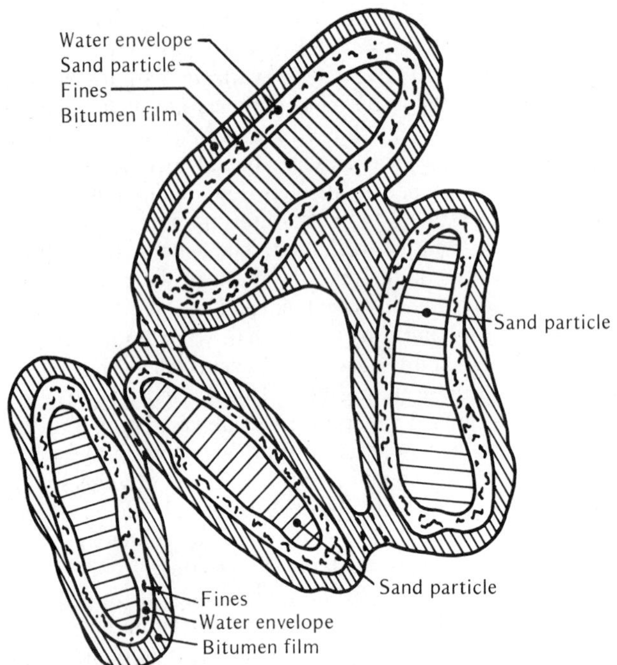

Figure 28-7. Typical arrangement of tar sand particles.

ing stress of the load it once bore, it is black, and the ground surface of exposed tar sand has a temperature higher than the air temperature. Some gas escapes from the tar sand. Within minutes of a freshly cut surface being exposed, the surface becomes noticeably softer and in the rich sands the surface will bleed bitumen and crumble to a sticky mess. The trafficability of the softened skin is very poor and the resistance to forward motion extremely high. Repeated passes of equipment cause the thickness of the softened layer to increase and the muckiness of the surface to intensify. Equipment is rapidly bogged down. This thixotropic characteristic of the tar sand disappears with the cool weather—but a sponginess remains until the frost penetrates deep into the floor. Throughout this period of each year there are some problems with equipment. In addition to the continuous cleaning load on mobile equipment (a 4,000-pound pickup truck will weigh in empty at 6,000 pounds), there are occasional incidents due to differential settlement under the tracks of the 1,800-ton bucket wheels. One further problem associated with getting tar sand to the extraction plant in summertime is the conveying systems. The bitumen sticks to the conveyor belts, and partly transfers itself to the idlers and drive pulleys carrying with it some sand. This causes tremendous vibration, differential slip on drives, rapid wear of shells, failure of bearings, ripping of belts, and summer madness in the maintenance staff. Again the cleaning problems have enormous dimensions. We have managed to solve some of these problems to a degree: the cost is unbelievably high and we still have a long way to go.

THE EXTRACTION OF BITUMEN FROM TAR SAND

Bitumen extraction is accomplished by a very simple process which is sometimes difficult to control. Figure 28-8 is a simplified flow sheet. Tar sand is removed from the 5,000-ton surge bin, which it does not want to leave, by eight pan feeders, which deliver in pairs to four parallel belt conveyors. The plant has four parallel processing lines each one capable of handling about 2,300 tons of tar sand per hour. The fundamental steps in processing are feed conditioning, separation of the bitumen, waste disposal, and cleaning bitumen concentrate.

Conditioning is done in a very short period of time by mixing feed with water and caustic soda at 180 °F. The vessel used is a slowly rotating drum into which live steam is sparged below the slurry surface. In this process the tar sand disintegrates liberating bitumen from sand and clay particles. The sand is water-wetted in its natural state and stays water wet, allowing fairly clean separation of bitumen in the next process. The clays in the feed report largely as layers interbedded with the tar sand. These clay layers do not ablate or disintegrate as completely as the tar sand does, but remain intact as lumps or balls of clay. In addition to clays, large pieces of rock are encountered in the feed that also remain as competent chunks. The slurry leaving the conditioning drum is passed over a vibrating screen. The unablated clays and the rocks are eliminated by this screening process. All screen-undersize material drops into a sump pump and is delivered by 18-inch pumps into separation cells.

In the separation process the sand particles settle quickly to the bottom of the cell, which has fast thickener type rakes for conveying the sand to spigots controlled by three large air-operated valves. The bitumen floats to the surface of the cell, and in between the bitumen and the sand layer is a layer wherein separation is taking place. This layer consists predominantly of clays. In order for the process to be effective, the temperature of the cell must be controlled. This control is achieved in the conditioning process: the density caused by the presence of clay suspended in water must also be controlled so that there is an effective differential between the density of warm bitumen and the density of the clay slurry, and last, the viscosity of the clay suspension in the middle of the cell is important. Control of viscosity is achieved by managing the pH with caustic soda. This control is also effected in the conditioning cell.

The bitumen flows from the top of the cell, whence it is further heated and pumped into the upgrading plant for removing the last water and mineral particles from the bitumen

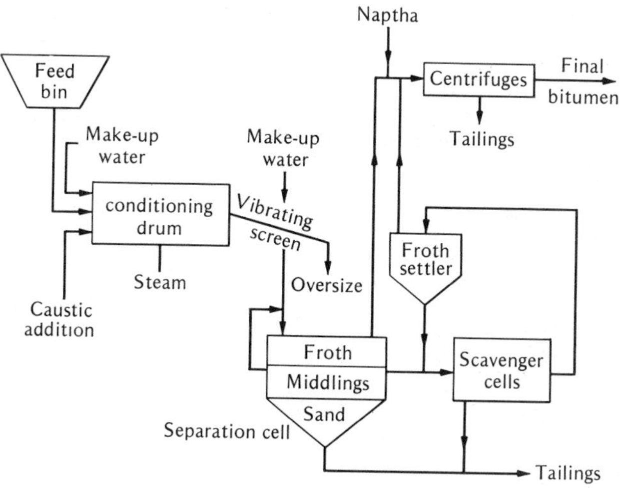

Figure 28-8. Schematic flow diagram of the primary extraction process.

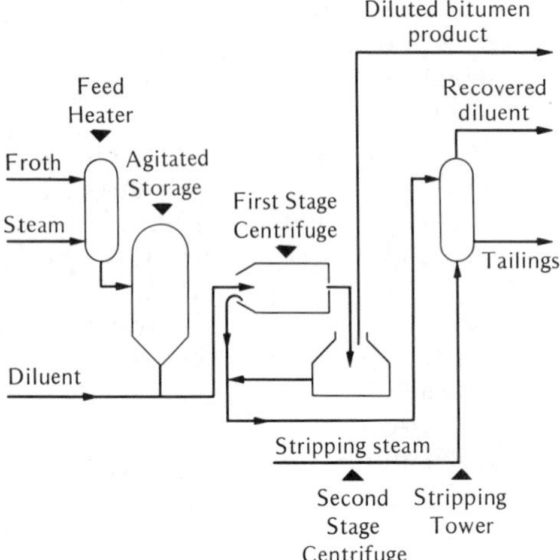

Figure 28-9. Schematic flow diagram of the final extraction process.

froth. The layer in the center of the cell is tapped from the side of the cell and this side stream containing clay, silty particles, and minute droplets of bitumen that cannot make it through this medium is then delivered to banks of standard sub-'A' flotation cells where ordinary air flotation is used to scavenge the minute portions of bitumen. The concentrate from the scavenger cells is delivered along with the primary bitumen froth from the separation cell into the centrifuge plant.

The bitumen from primary separation is delivered first into a holding tank where is it deaerated. The deaerated heated slurry is then mixed with a diluent and fed to primary centrifuges (scroll type). In Bird centrifuges the coarse mineral load is removed from the diluted bitumen along with some of the water. The concentrate from the Bird centrifuging operation is then passed into several banks of Westfalia separators. These are high speed centrifuges which take out most of the remaining water and the clay particles. The Westfalia concentrate, now containing about 0.5 per cent of mineral particles and 2 or 3 per cent water, is pumped into diluted bitumen storage tanks, whence it is fed to the refining process.

Figure 28-9 shows the schematic flow in the centrifuge plant. The tailings from the two-stage centrifugation of bitumen are delivered into the tailings pond separately from the main tailings stream. The entire centrifuge plant is a separate building compartmented for protection against fire and operated with very strict rules because of the dangerous atmospheres that could accidentally be generated by a leak of the light hydrocarbons.

TAILINGS DISPOSAL

The tailings stream, about 24,000 gallons per minute, is delivered to the pond by pumps in a separate building from the main extraction plant. These are multistage installations of centrifugal pumps. In the tailings area the coarse fraction of the tailings sand is used to build the dyke while the slimes portion flows into the center of the pond. There are four lines across the top of the tailings dyke. Construction of the dyke by decantation methods and compacting can be carried out simultaneously in three locations. Normally, only three banks of pumps are needed to handle the flow. Because of the final purpose of the tailings dyke, the quality of construction is monitored in considerable detail and supervised in general by a consultant in soils mechanics. The

Figure 28-10. Relationship between the rate of construction of the dyke and the rate of rise of the water level contained by the dyke.

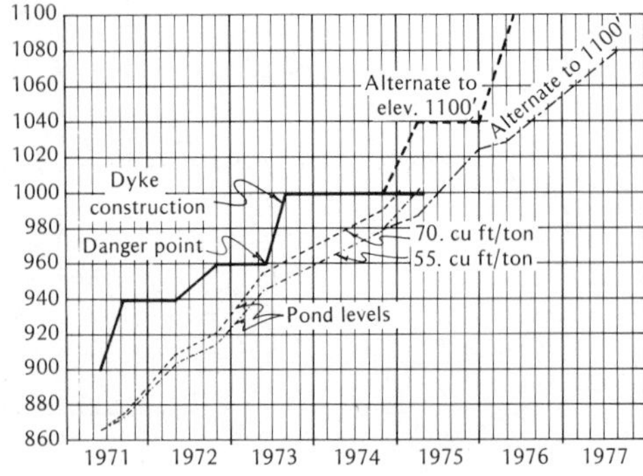

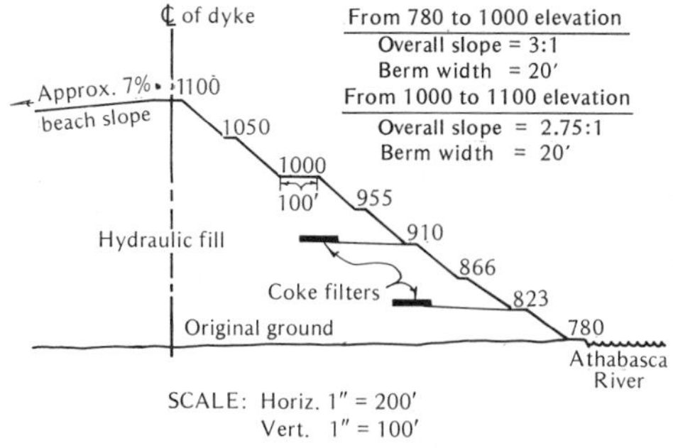

Figure 28-11. Typical section of sand dyke.

top layer of the liquid portion of the pond is recycled to the extraction plant for use in the processing. There is a slight imbalance in water management due to the fact that the clays will not settle, and also that there is a small amount of bitumen floating on the pond. Certain controls must be imposed upon the quality of the water recycled because prior to its use it must pass through several tubular heat exchangers. Figure 28-10 shows the relationship between the rate of construction of the dyke and the rate of rise of the water level contained by the dyke. Figure 28-11 shows a typical section through the dyke.

LAND RECLAMATION

This topic, if dealt with in proportion to the number of words uttered over the past two years would fill a library and take seven hours to discuss. This article can only touch on the highlights at the Great Canadian Oil Sands operation.

The climate for the growth of government departments and controlling agencies is far more favorable than the climate we have for the rapid reestablishment of fields and forests. Research studies are in progress to define the chemical, physical, mineralogical, and microbiological properties of tailings deposits. Concurrent, but dragging somewhat, are field studies to determine how tailings can be treated to improve their quality by addition of topsoil, leaching experiments, and the use of synthetic fibers and muskeg and manure. Field revegetation experiments and "high-speed" laboratory growth experiments are in progress. The quality of supernatant waters is being scrutinized to determine its effect upon migratory birds, fish populations, and thermal regimes with adjustment possibilities for the development of aquatic life systems. Then more general over-all conditions must be brought into the picture so that some direction may be given to the operators.

Great Canadian Oil Sands began its program of rehabilitation in 1971, sloping the dyke walls and establishing grasses and shrubs, and is now into the experimental stages of tree growth. In this work several thousand trees of different kinds, in different areas, and with different early life support, are under observation. The cooperation and assistance we have received from research councils, government departments and universities has been excellent. It is not easy to set the pace for a regional program which will later affect all producers in this area; but with the number of people living in this region twenty years from now, their recreational needs, and the desired quality of their surroundings, one cannot leave these matters to settlement by chance or public pressure. A well-designed and carefully planned future must be mapped out now.

SUMMARY

In summary, Great Canadian Oil Sands Ltd. is the only "synthetic oil" production installation of its type in the world. It is the largest single investment ever made by Sun Oil Company. Production of oil from mined tar sand is inherently a high cost method of producing oil, both capital and labor intensive. Tar sands are an extremely low-valued, nonhomogeneous ore requiring very careful investigation. The cost of overburden removal is high relative to the value of the tar sands beneath.

These characteristics make profitability highly dependent upon careful evaluation, and the soundness of a number of both long term and short term mining decisions. The extraction process is new and continuously improving.

There is a great deal of interest in the detail of these works and the techniques of evaluation, the decision processes involved to produce proper decisions with interacting features of pit limits, lease lives, selection of ore, and methods analyses.

It is hoped that this article has led to a more complete understanding of why you are going to have to pay more for your future feedstocks.

SUGGESTED READINGS

Allen, A. R., 1973, "The Mining and Extraction of Bitumen from the Athabasca Tar Sands," Great Canadian Oil Sands, Ltd., Fort McMurray, Alberta, 24 p.

Carrigy, M. A. (ed.), 1974, "Guide to the Athabasca Oil Sands Area," Alberta Research, Information Series 65, Edmonton, Alberta, 213 p, (collection of 8 articles).

Humphreys, R. D., 1973, "Great Canadian Oil Sands, Ltd., Tar Sands Pioneer," Petroleum Society of CIM, Edmonton, Canada.

Kaminsky, V. P., 1973, "Selection of a Mining Scheme for a Tar Sands Extraction Plant," Canadian Society of Petroleum Geologists, "Oil Sands Symposium," 6 p.

Geothermal Energy 29

L. J. P. MUFFLER and D. E. WHITE 1977

Geothermal energy, in the broadest sense, is the natural heat of the earth. Temperatures in the Earth rise with increasing depth. At the base of the continental crust (25 to 50 kilometers), temperatures range from 200 °C to 1,000 °C; at the center of the Earth (6,731 kilometers), perhaps from 3,500 °C to 4,500 °C. But most of the Earth's heat is far too deeply buried to be tapped by man, even under the most optimistic assumptions of technological development. Although drilling has reached 7.5 kilometers and may some day reach 15 to 20 kilometers, the depths from which heat might be extracted economically are unlikely to be greater than 10 kilometers.

White[1] has calculated that the amount of geothermal heat available in this outer 10 kilometers is approximately 3×10^{26} calories, which is more than 2,000 times the heat represented by the total coal resources of the world.[2] Most of this geothermal energy, however, is far too diffuse ever to be recovered economically. The average heat content of each gram of rock in the outer 10 kilometers of the earth is only 0.3 per cent of the heat obtainable by combusting 1 gram of coal and is less than 0.01 per cent of the heat equivalent of fissionable uranium and thorium contained in 1 gram of average granite. Consequently, most of the heat within the earth, even at depths of less than 10 kilometers, cannot be considered a potential energy resource.

Geothermal energy, however, does have potential economic significance where the heat is concentrated into restricted volumes in a manner analogous to the concentration of valuable metals into ore deposits or of oil into commercial petroleum reservoirs. At present, economically significant concentrations of

1. White, D. E. "Geothermal Energy." *U.S. Geological Survey Circular* 519. 1965. 17 p.
2. Averitt, Paul. "Coal Resources of the United States, January 1, 1967." *U.S. Geological Survey Bulletin 1275*. 1969. 116 p.

Dr. L. J. Patrick Muffler is a geologist for the U.S. Geological Survey, Menlo Park, California 94025; he managed the U.S.G.S. geothermal resource investigations from 1972–1976.

Dr. Donald E. White is a geologist for the U.S. Geological Survey, Menlo Park, California 94025; he managed the U.S.G.S. geothermal resource investigations prior to 1972.

From *The Science Teacher,* Vol. 39, No. 3, pp. 40–43, March 1972. Reprinted with authors' revisions and by permission of the authors and *The Science Teacher.* This article has been updated by the authors for the second edition in March 1977.

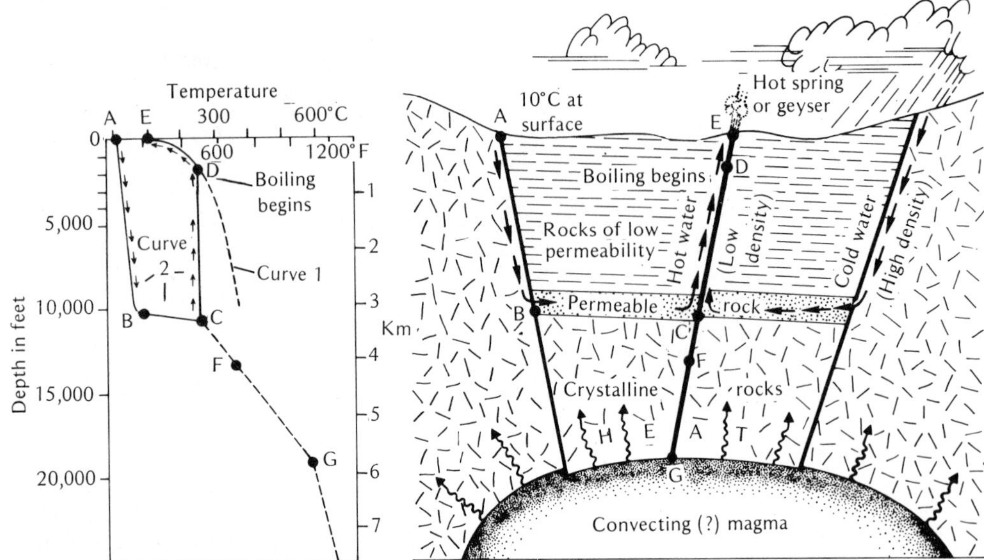

Figure 29-1. Schematic model of a hot-water geothermal system, modified from White.[3,4] Curve 1 shows the boiling point of pure water under pressure exerted by a column of liquid water everywhere at boiling, assuming water level at ground surface. Dissolved salts shift the curve to the right; dissolved gases shift the curve to the left. Curve 2 shows the ground temperature profile of a typical hot-water system.

geothermal energy occur where elevated temperatures (40 °C to more than 380 °C) are found in permeable rocks at shallow depths (less than 3 kilometers). The thermal energy is stored both in the solid rock and in water and steam filling pores and fractures. This water and steam serve to transfer the heat from the rock to a well and thence to the ground surface. Under present technology, rocks with too few pores, or with pores that are not interconnected, do not comprise an economic geothermal reservoir, however hot the rocks may be.

Water in a geothermal system also serves as the medium by which heat is transferred from a deep igneous source to a geothermal reservoir at depths shallow enough to be tapped by drill holes. Geothermal reservoirs are located in the upflowing parts of major water convection systems (Figure 29-1). Cool rain water percolates underground from areas that may comprise tens to thousands of square kilometers and then circulates downward. At depths of 2 to 6 kilometers, the water is heated by contact with hot rock (in turn, probably heated by molten rock). The water expands upon heating and then moves buoyantly upward in a column of relatively restricted cross-sectional area (1 to 50 square kilometers). If the rocks have many interconnected pores or fractures, the heated water rises rapidly to the surface and is dissipated rather than stored. If, however, the upward movement of heated water is impeded by rocks without interconnected pores or fractures, the geothermal energy may be stored in reservoir rocks below the impeding layers. The driving force of this large circulation system is gravity—effective because of the density difference between cold, downward-moving re-

3. White, D. E. "Environment of Generation of Some Base-Metal Ore Deposits." *Economic Geology* 63: 301–335; June–July 1968.
4. White, D. E. "Hydrology, Activity, and Heat Flow of the Steamboat Springs Thermal System, Washoe County, Nevada." *U.S. Geological Survey Professional Paper* 458-C, 1968. 109 p.

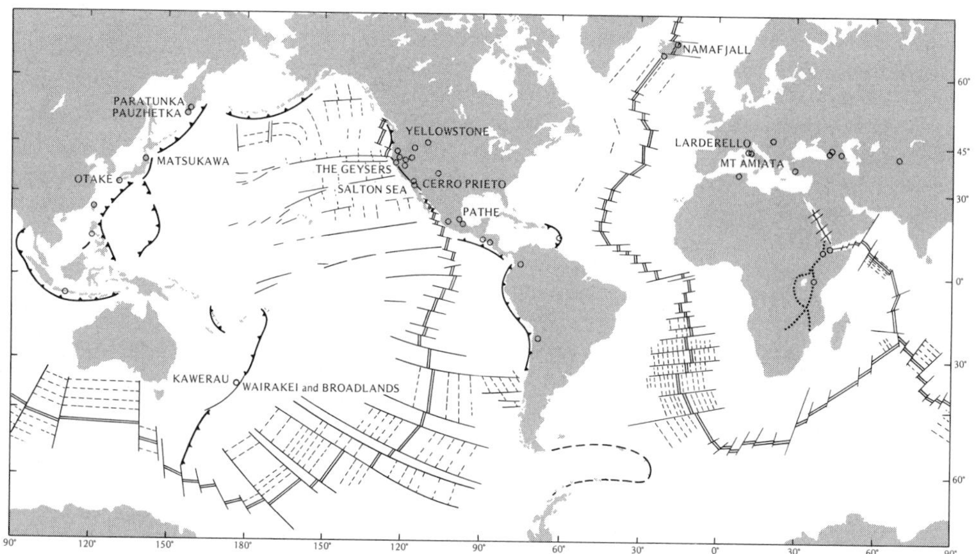

Figure 29-2. World map showing location of major geothermal fields along plate margins. Heavy double lines represent spreading ridges; heavy lines with barbs represent active subduction zones; heavy dotted lines represent rift valleys. Light lines represent transform faults; dashed light lines represent approximate position of magnetic anomalies. (Base map and tectonic features from Coleman, ref. 5, Figure 4.)

charge water and hot, upward-moving geothermal water.

Many investigators in the past considered the water in geothermal systems to be derived from molten rock at depth. Modern studies of hydrogen and oxygen isotopes in geothermal waters, however, indicate that at least 95 per cent of most geothermal fluids must be derived from surface precipitation and that no more than 5 per cent is volcanic steam.

LOCATION OF GEOTHERMAL SYSTEMS

Geothermal reservoirs are the "hot spots" of larger regions where the flow of heat from deep in the earth is one and one-half to perhaps five times the world-wide average of 1.5×10^{-6} calories per square centimeter per second. Such regions of high heat flow commonly are zones of young volcanism and mountain building and are localized along the margins of major crustal plates (Figure 29-2). These margins are zones where either new material from the mantle is being added to the crust (that is, spreading ridges; see Figure 29-3) or where crustal material is being dragged downward and "consumed" in the mantle (subduction zones). In both situations, molten rock is generated and then moves buoyantly upward into the crust. These pods of igneous rock rrovide the heat that is then transferred by conduction to the convecting systems of meteoric water.

Figure 29-2 shows that the geothermal fields presently being exploited or explored occur in three major geologic environments: (a) along spreading ridges, (b) above subduction zones, and (c) along the belt of mountains extending from Italy through Turkey to the Caucasus. Although this last zone is not a modern subduction zone, it is the zone where the African and European plates are in contact, and it appears to have been a subduction zone in the past. Geothermal fields are absent

5. Coleman, R. G. "Plate Tectonic Emplacement of Upper Mantle Peridotites along Continental Edges." *Journal of Geophysical Research* 76: 1212–1222; February 1971.

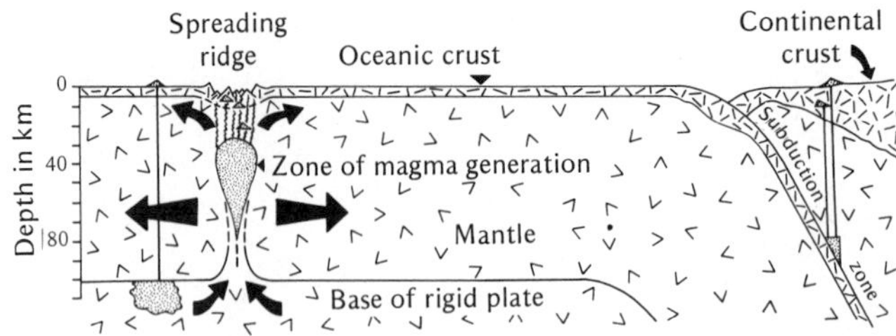

Figure 29-3. Model of development of oceanic crust at spreading ridges and subduction of oceanic crust at consuming plate margins. (Generalized from Coleman, ref. 5, Figure 6.)

from the stable, continental shields, which are characterized by lower-than-average heat flow. Although there are no known shallow geothermal reservoirs in the nonvolcanic continental areas bordering the shields, hot water has been found at depths of 3 to 6 kilometers in the Soviet Union, in Hungary, and on the Gulf Coast of the United States.[6]

USES OF GEOTHERMAL RESOURCES

The primary use of geothermal energy to date is for the generation of electricity. For this purpose, under existing technology, the geothermal reservoir must have a temperature of at least 180 °C, and preferably 200 °C. Geothermal steam, after separation of any associated water (as much as 90 weight per cent of the total effluent), is expanded into a turbine that drives a conventional generator. World electrical capacity from geothermal energy in 1975 was approximately 1,300 megawatts (Table 29-1), or about 0.08 per cent of the total world electrical capacity from all generating modes. Power from favorable geothermal systems is competitive in cost with either fossil fuel or nuclear power. The production of geothermal power is obviously restricted to areas where geothermal energy is found in sufficient quantity. Unlike coal, oil, gas, or uranium, geothermal steam cannot be transported long distances to a generating plant located near the existing load centers.

Geothermal resources have other uses, but to date they have been minor. Geothermal waters as low as 40 °C are used locally for space heating and horticulture. Much of Reykjavik, the capital of Iceland, is heated by geothermal water, as are parts of Rotorua (New Zealand), Boise (Idaho), Klamath Falls (Oregon), and various towns in Hungary and the Soviet Union. Geothermal steam is also used in paper manufacturing at Kawerau, New Zealand, and has potential use for refrigeration. Some geothermal waters contain potentially valuable by-products such as potassium, lithium, calcium, and other metals. Use of geothermal energy to desalt geothermal water itself has been proposed, and the U.S. Bureau of Reclamation and the Office of Saline Water are presently developing a pilot operation for producing fresh water from the geothermal waters of the Imperial Valley, Southern California.

TYPES OF GEOTHERMAL SYSTEMS

There are two major types of geothermal systems: hot-water systems and vapor-dominated ("dry-steam") systems.[7] Among geothermal systems discovered to date, hot-water systems are perhaps twenty times as common as vapor-dominated systems.[8]

Hot-Water Geothermal Systems

Hot-water geothermal systems contain water at temperatures that may be far above surface

6. Jones, P. H. "Geothermal Resources of the Northern Gulf of Mexico Basin." United Nations Symposium on the Development and Utilization of Geothermal Resources, Pisa, Italy, September 1970. Paper I/24.

7. White, D. E., L. J. P. Muffler, and A. H. Truesdell. "Vapor-dominated Hydrothermal Systems Compared with Hot-Water Systems." *Economic Geology* 66: 75–97; January–February 1971.

8. White, D. E. "Geochemistry Applied to the Discovery, Evaluation, and Exploitation of Geothermal Energy Resources." United Nations Symposium on the Development and Utilization of Geothermal Resources, Pisa, Italy, September 1970, Rapporteur's Report, Section V.

Table 29-1. World Geothermal Power Production, May 1975

Country	Field	Electrical Capacity (megawatts) Operating	Under Construction
United States	The Geysers	502	216
Italy	Larderello	380.6	
	Travale	15	
	Monte Amiata	22	
New Zealand	Wairakei	192	
	Kawerau	10	
Japan	Matsukawa	22	
	Otake	13	
	Onuma	10	
	Onikobe	25	
	Hatchobaru		50
	Takinoue		50
Mexico	Pathé	3.5	
	Cerro Prieto	75	
El Salvador	Ahuachapán		90
Iceland	Námafjall	2.5	
	Krafla		55
Philippines	Tiwi		100
Soviet Union	Pauzhetsk	5	
	Paratunka	0.7	
Turkey	Kizildere	0.5	2.5
Total		1,278.8	563.5

From: Muffler, L. J. P., 1976, Summary of Section I: Present Status of Resources Development: Proc. 2nd United Nations Symposium on the Development and Use of Geothermal Resources, San Francisco, Ca., May 1975, p. xxxiii–xliv.

boiling, owing to the effect of pressure on the boiling point of water (curve 1 of Figure 29-1). A typical hot-water system has temperature-depth relations similar to those of curve 2. Little change in temperature occurs as meteoric water descends from A to B, heat is absorbed from B to C, and from C to D the system contains water at nearly constant temperature (the "base temperature"). From D to E pressure has decreased enough for water to boil, and steam and water coexist. In major zones of upflow, coexisting steam and water extend to the surface and are expressed as boiling hot springs and locally as geysers. Geothermal wells, however, are usually sited in nearby cool, stable ground where near-surface temperatures are controlled by conduction of heat through solid rocks; the temperature-depth curve is therefore initially to the left of curve 1 of Figure 29-1.

Water in most hot-water geothermal systems is a dilute solution (1,000 to 30,000 milligrams per liter), containing mostly sodium, potassium, lithium, chloride, bicarbonate, sulfate, borate, and silica. The silica content and the ratio of potassium to sodium are dependent on temperature in the geothermal reservoir, thus allowing prediction of subsurface temperature from chemical analysis of hot springs.[9,10]

In hot-water geothermal systems, only part of the produced fluid is steam and can be used to generate electricity with present technology. For example, water at 250 °C will produce only about 20 weight per cent of steam when the confining pressure is reduced to 6 kilograms per square centimeter, the approx-

9. Ellis, A. J. "Quantitative Interpretation of Chemical Characteristics of Hydrothermal Systems." United Nations Symposium on the Development and Utilization of Geothermal Resources, Pisa, Italy, September 1970. Paper I/11.

10. Fournier, R. O., and J. J. Rowe. "Estimation of Underground Temperatures from the Silica Content of Water from Hot Springs and Wet-Steam Wells." *American Journal of Science* 264: 685–697; 1966.

imate well-head pressure commonly used in geothermal installations. The steam and water at this pressure are mechanically separated before the steam is fed to the turbine.

Some attention is currently being directed toward a heat exchange generating system. Heat in the geothermal water is transferred by a heat exchanger to a low-boiling-point fluid, such as freon or isobutane, which is then expanded into a turbine. The geothermal water is not allowed to boil and is reinjected as water into the ground. If this binary fluid generating technology proves economically feasible, it will allow more complete extraction of heat from geothermal fluids and will allow use of hot-water geothermal systems of lower temperature than are presently required for direct geothermal steam generation.

The major known hot-water geothermal fields are Wairakei (192 megawatts) and Broadlands (100 megawatts proposed) in New Zealand, Cerro Prieto (75 megawatts operating; 200 megawatts proposed) in Mexico, the Salton Sea field in California, and the Yellowstone geyser basins in Wyoming. Although the Yellowstone region is the world's most intensive display of hot-spring and geyser phenomena, the area is permanently withdrawn as a national park and will never be exploited for power.

Whereas the salinities of most hot-water fields are 0.1 to 3 per cent, the Salton Sea geothermal reservoir contains a brine with more than 25 per cent by weight of dissolved solids, mainly chloride, sodium, calcium, and potassium. In addition, the brine is rich in a variety of metals.[3] Although temperatures reach 360 °C, development of the field has been hindered by problems of corrosion, deposition of silica, and disposal of unwanted effluent. Hot, saline brines also occur in pools along the median trench of the Red Sea where geothermal fluids discharge directly onto the sea floor 2 kilometers below sea level.[3]

Vapor-Dominated Geothermal Systems

Vapor-dominated geothermal systems, in contrast to hot-water systems, produce superheated steam with minor amounts of other gases (CO_2, H_2S), but no water. The total fluid can therefore be piped directly to the turbine. Within the vapor-dominated geothermal reservoir, saturated steam and water coexist, with steam being the phase that controls the pressure. With decrease in pressure upon production, heat contained in the rocks dries the fluids first to saturated and then to superheated steam, with as much as 55 °C superheat at a well-head pressure range of 5 to 7 kilograms per square centimeter. Owing to the thermodynamic properties and flow dynamics of steam and water in porous media, vapor-dominated reservoirs are unlikely to exist at pressures much greater than about 34 kilograms per square centimeter and temperatures much above 240 °C.[11] Hot brine probably exists below the vapor-dominated reservoirs at depth, but drill holes are not yet deep enough to confirm the presence of such a brine.

Drilling has demonstrated the existence of only three commercial vapor-dominated systems. Larderello, Italy; The Geysers, California; and probably Matsukawa, Japan. Two small fields in the Monte Amiata region of Italy are marginally commercial. Larderello was the first geothermal field to be exploited, starting in 1904, and is still a large producer of geothermal power (380 megawatts). The Geysers at present produces 502 megawatts, but plants under construction will boost capacity to 718 megawatts, and ultimate potential is in excess of 1,000 megawatts.

THE GEOTHERMAL ENERGY RESOURCE

White[1] estimated that the total stored heat of all geothermal reservoirs to a depth of 10 kilometers was 10^{22} calories. This estimate specifically excluded reservoirs of molten rock, abnormally hot rocks of low permeability, and deep sedimentary basins of near "normal" conductive heat flow, such as the Gulf Coast of the United States or Kazahkstan

11. James, Russell. "Wairakei and Larderello: Geothermal Power Systems Compared." *New Zealand Journal of Science* 11: 706–719; 1968.

in the Soviet Union. The geothermal resources in these environments are at least ten times greater than the resources of the hydrothermal systems, but they are recoverable only at much more than present costs. Should production of these geothermal resources someday become feasible, the potential geothermal resource in all reservoir types would be at least 10^{23} calories, which is approximately equivalent to the heat represented by the world's potential resources of coal.

For a hot-water geothermal system, approximately 1 per cent of the heat stored in the reservoir can be extracted and converted into electricity under present technology. For the far less abundant vapor-dominated geothermal systems, perhaps 2 to 5 per cent of the heat in the reservoir can be extracted and converted to electricity. Therefore, if the use of geothermal energy continues to be restricted primarily to electrical generation by proven techniques, then the potential geothermal resource to 10 kilometers is only about 10^{20} calories. To a depth of 3 kilometers (the deepest well drilled to date for geothermal power), the resource for electrical generation by proven techniques is even less, approximately 2×10^{19} calories.[1] Use of geothermal resources for other than electrical generation (for example, heating, desalination, horticulture) would greatly increase these geothermal resource estimates, perhaps by ten times, but all these uses involve special geographic and economic conditions that to date have been implemented only on a local scale.

Production of electricity from geothermal energy is presently attractive environmentally because no solid atmospheric pollutants are emitted and no radiation hazard is involved. Geothermal generation is not without environmental effects, however. Effluent from either a hot-water or a vapor-dominated system can pollute streams or ground water. Consequently, federal and state regulations require reinjecting objectionable fluids back into a deep reservoir. Thermal pollution is also a problem, particularly in hot-water systems, but it can be solved in part by reinjection of unwanted water and of residual steam condensate. Noise, objectionable gases, visual impact, and subsidence of the land surface due to fluid withdrawal are other problems that are faced in any geothermal energy development.

Geothermal energy is unlikely to supply more than perhaps 10 per cent of domestic or world electrical power demand. In favorable areas, however, geothermal power may be of major importance, particularly in underdeveloped countries that have few other energy resources.

Although geothermal power was produced in Italy as early as 1904 and in New Zealand by 1955, extensive interest in geothermal resources of the United States has developed only in the past ten years. Large areas in the western United States appear to be favorable for geothermal exploration, but knowledge of the nature and extent of our geothermal resources is inadequate. Further investigations are necessary, not only of the distribution and characteristics of geothermal reservoirs, but also of the various ways in which geothermal energy can be used in the most beneficial and least wasteful manner.

SUGGESTED READINGS

Axtmann, Robert C., 1975, Environmental Impact of a Geothermal Power Plant, *Science 187,* No. 4179, March 7, pp. 795–803.

Dermengian, John (Managing Editor), *Geothermal Energy Magazine*—monthly publication on all aspects of geothermal energy.

Eaton, William W., 1975, Geothermal Energy, Energy Research and Development Administration, 42 p.

Kruger, Paul, 1976, Geothermal Energy, *Annual Review of Energy,* Vol. I, pp. 159–182.

Proceedings of the 2nd United Nations Symposium on the Development and Utilization of Geothermal Resources, San Francisco, California, May, 1975, 2,466 p., published in 1976.

U.S. Dept. of the Interior, 1973, Final Environmental Impact Statement for the Geothermal Leasing Program, U.S. Dept. of the Interior, Washington, D.C. (Vol. 1–4).

White, D. E. and D. L. Williams (editors), 1975, Assessment of Geothermal Resources of the United States—1975, *U.S. Geol. Survey Circular* 726, 105 p.

Processing Energy From Waste 30

E. MILTON WILSON AND HARRY M. FREEMAN 1976

Utilizing the waste stream for energy to supplement conventional energy supplies is becoming increasingly attractive as a means of conserving the supply of conventional fuels in the United States. The generation of steam from waste combustion has been practiced in Europe for years; the concept of energy recovery from waste is certainly not new. Until recently, the United States enjoyed relatively low prices of a seemingly inexhaustible supply of fuels, so the concept has not yet been widely adopted here.

The energy situation has now dictated that research and development be done on processes that can effectively utilize waste as an energy source, especially those processes that can transform the wastes into fuel forms that are storeable or transportable. Materials recovery,[1,2] while playing an important role in the over-all economics of a waste processing facility, is not considered here.

ENERGY CONSUMPTION

The Bureau of Mines has forecast that gross U.S. energy consumption through the year 2000 will increase from 73.1 quadrillion BTU consumed in 1974 to 163.4 quadrillion BTU to be consumed in the year 2000, with the percentage contribution of each of the conventional fuel sources changing rather drastically (Figure 30-1). Table 30-1 shows a breakdown in the 1974 consumption to serve as a later guide to the relative contribution that a supplemental source, such as wastes, might make.

Even though nuclear power and oil shale will come to assume more of a contribution to the energy picture by the year 2000, it is obvious that there will have to be a continued reliance upon conventional fossil fuels—coal, petroleum, and natural gas. These presently represent 93 per cent of total energy

E. Milton Wilson is project manager, Systems Division, The Ralph M. Parsons Company, Pasadena, California 91124.

Harry M. Freeman is senior environmental engineer, Fuels Technology Branch, Industrial Environmental Research Laboratory, U.S. Environmental Protection Agency, Cincinnati, Ohio 45268.

From *Environmental Science and Technology*, Vol. 10, No. 5, pp. 430–435, May 1976.

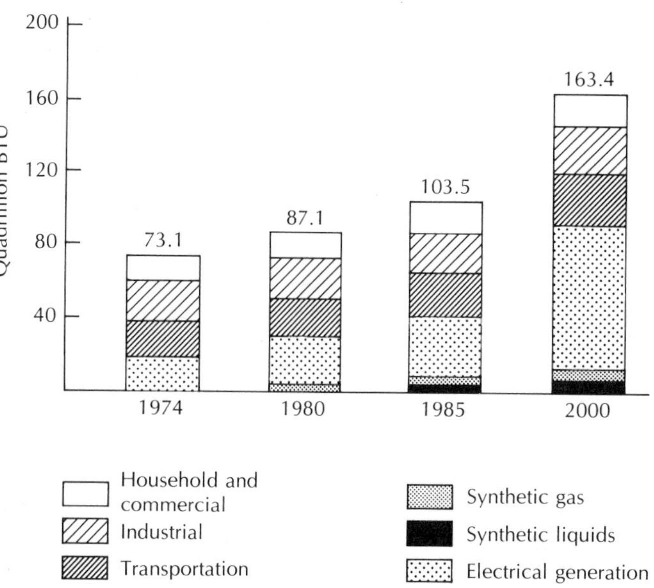

Figure 30-1. United States energy consumption by sector, 1974–2000 (Source: U.S. Bureau of Mines).

consumption. By 2000, even assuming a rapid increase in nuclear capacity, they will still represent a dominant 65 per cent of the total.

WASTE CHARACTERISTICS

The very nature of waste generation and the establishment of its ultimate fate causes serious inaccuracies in any inventory of quantities potentially available for conversion to energy. Even if generating sources and collection organizations were to maintain good records and some form of data reporting system were to be put into effect, the question alone of what makes up "availability" can introduce errors of at least 100 million tons annually.

Studies and data compilation projects are now in progress to more clearly establish the true nature of U.S. wastes. Estimates of quantities that permit an assessment of the role they might offer for the nation's energy needs are presented in Table 30-2. Typical waste heating values range from 3,000 to 10,000 BTU per pound, depending on water content.

CONVERSION PROCESSES

Wastes are generated in solid, liquid, and gaseous forms and the residual energy inherent in them can be recovered from the original

Table 30–1. Major End Users of Energy.[a]

Type of Use	*Percentage of Total Consumption (%)*	*1974 Consumption (Quadrillon BTU)*
Industrial	41.2	30.0
Transportation	25.2	18.4
Residential	19.2	14.0
Commercial	14.4	10.5

[a]Source: Office of Science and Technology (1972).

Table 30–2. United States Waste Quantities Discarded (Millions of Combustible Dry Tons).[a]

Source	*Quantity*
Urban	
Household and municipal	84.2
Sewage solids	6.9
Commercial	31.0
Manufacturing plant wastes	11.8
Demolition	3.8
Manufacturing and processing	
Wood-related wastes	25.7
Textile and fabric wastes	0.3
Non-fabric synthetics	0.4
Food processing solids	0.8
Miscellaneous	0.1
Agricultural	
Animal wastes	206.7
Crop wastes	170.0
Forest and logging residues	25.9
Total	567.6

[a]Source: International Research and Technology Corp.

material or from a conversion product (Table 30-3). The choice depends on the relative amounts of wastes available and the fuel requirement of energy consumers in the region.

At the present time, the great majority of all energy obtained from waste is realized through processes in which no alteration in the original form is required. In many cases, the energy recovery operation has become so routine that the material being used is no longer recognized as waste and would rightfully not be listed on any inventory of residuals.

A prime example is the large quantity of off-gas resulting from a wide variety of chemical processing within industries using petroleum, coal, or secondary products from these fossil fuels. While simultaneously eliminating what otherwise would be a serious source of atmospheric emissions, the fuel-rich gas mixtures are combusted and the resulting high temperatures recovered in waste-heat boilers. Combustible liquid mixtures that cannot be further purified economically are similarly burned for energy recovery.

Because of the extensive European experience with refuse-burning steam generators, municipal solid waste combustion is often the single image formed when waste-to-energy technology is considered. Such on-grate, mass burning water-walled incinerators offer an immediate solution to waste disposal and

Table 30–3. Waste-to-energy Conversion Matrix.

Waste Form	*Using or Derived Form*		
	Solid	*Liquid*	*Gas*
Solid	Direct grate combustion; suspension firing of organic fraction; pelletized organic fraction; low temperature pyrolysis; feedstock for chemical conversion	Flash pyrolysis; fermentation; reaction with carbon monoxide or hydrogen	Pyrolysis; anaerobic digestion; hydrogasification; partial oxidation; water gas reaction
Liquid	Incorporation into porous solid fuel	Liquid incinerator + waste heat boiler	Direct pyrolysis or additive to solid waste pyrolyzer; anaerobic digestion
Gas	Although solid hydrocarbons could be synthesized, there are no practical applications to date	Conversion to methanol or liquid hydrocarbons	Combuster + waste heat boiler; conversion to methane or ammonia

partial energy needs of many municipalities and they will continue to be constructed in the United States and Canada. Their limitations in the over-all waste situation are being increasingly realized, however. Furnace volumes for a given heat release are high; water contents of the fuel reduce thermal efficiencies; fire-side tube wastage is still experienced, and emission control costs can make up a significant fraction of total plant capital.

Initial shredding and component classification of mixed residential/commercial wastes prior to combustion is proving to be of considerable benefit in broadening the utilization of these materials. From the viewpoint of the fuels market, such "front end" processing yields a combustible material for which fairly narrow specifications can be prepared, defining physical properties, heat of combustion, and percentages of water and ash.

Rather minor changes or additions in existing solid fuel combustion equipment will permit ready introduction of this waste fraction into the burning zone, where typically 10 to 20 per cent of the total heat generated is supplied from the refuse-derived fuel and the remainder from finely divided coal. This makes up what has become known as the supplementary fuel concept; it is now practiced by the Union Electric Company and St. Louis, and, was introduced in 1976 by the Commonwealth Edison Company and Chicago.

The isolated organic fraction may also be used as a raw feedstock for chemical conversion processes, although this is essential to only a few schemes, such as in the case of Occidental Research Corporation's pyrolytic oil. Conversion from the original waste form to another can greatly increase the extent of the market in which fuels are a commodity. Not only is the customer base broadened in any locality, but in those areas in which historically or legislatively coal is not used to any great extent, the conversion of solid wastes to either a gas or a liquid permits a user to purchase a fuel that can be directly utilized in existing equipment with only minor alterations.

Transportation costs can often be minimized through waste form conversion, while simultaneously taking advantage of the economies of scale inherent in a large central processing facility.

Such concentration can also be used to advantage with conversion of certain solid wastes to a chemically altered solid. In the system under development by Georgia Tech, for example, high-moisture-content agricultural wastes are converted by means of a mobile pyrolyzer to a practical solid fuel having a heat of combustion in excess of 12,000 BTU per pound, well worth transporting to regional coal users. Principal developmental activities in waste conversion technology rather closely follow the larger efforts now in progress for making clear fuels from coal.[3]

EXISTING AND CANDIDATE SYSTEMS

Since May, 1972, the *City of St. Louis,* the *Union Electric Company,* and the *Environmental Protection Agency* have cooperated in demonstrating the use of refuse-derived fuel (RDF) as a supplemental fuel for utility boilers. In the process, the waste is first shredded into 1½-inch-particles and air-classified to remove heavy non-combustible particles. It is then pneumatically introduced through inlets modified to accept the waste directly into the boilers.

The waste is burned in suspension at temperatures of 2,400 to 2,600 °F. At the rated load, the waste burned is equivalent to 10 per cent of the heat value of the coal and amounts to about 12.5 tons per hour, or 300 tons per day. The efficiency relative to "coal only" firings of the two 125-megawatt boilers that were modified to accept the solid waste supplement has been observed to decline only slightly when the waste is being co-fired with the coal.

The St. Louis project is one of the very few for which air and water emissions have been systematically measured. It has been found that the co-combustion of the wastes and coal:

(1) Results in moderately increased chloride emissions, but does not significantly affect sulfur dioxide, nitrous oxides, or carbon monoxide emissions.

(2) Reduces the collection efficiency of the electrostatic precipitator at loads above 100 megawatts.

(3) Increases the quantity of bottom ash produced by a factor of four to seven.

(4) Increases the water pollution level for 16 of 64 pollutants evaluated so that controls for biochemical oxygen demand (BOD), dissolved oxygen, and suspended solids will probably be required.

The St. Louis project has been one of the more successful demonstrations of a waste-as-fuel technology with some 40,000 tons of wastes having been converted into boiler fuel. As an outgrowth of the project, Union Electric Co. has announced that it will expand the relatively small present operation into an 8,000-ton per day system that will process all of the area's solid waste and convert the combustible fraction into supplementary fuel for several of its existing boilers. Union Electric has estimated that if all of the solid waste in the St. Louis Region were burned as supplementary fuel, it would provide about 5 per cent of the company's annual energy requirement.

The City of Ames, Iowa has begun operating the first non-federally financed, municipally owned, waste-as-fuel system based on the supplementary boiler fuel principle. EPA and ERDA have recently announced programs to evaluate different aspects of the system. The facility, which might be viewed as a second generation St. Louis-type plant, differs from the St. Louis facility in that two of the boilers involved are stoker-fired rather than blower-fired. In the processing plant, the incoming waste is shredded at the rate of 50 tons per hour into 1½-inch particles. Then, the waste is air-classified and transported to a storage area prior to actual firing. The two stoker-fired boilers (7.5 and 12-megawatt rated capacity) were modified to allow shredded refuse to be received on a high velocity stream of air into the front wall of each boiler. The waste feed to the third boiler closely parallels the feed system at St. Louis. It is estimated that the boilers can successfully burn from 10 to 20 per cent refuse fuel.

The Ames unit is presently in its shakedown phase. Since the capacity of the Ames unit is much less than what is actually cited as being the minimum economical size, much national attention is being focused on the project. Should the Ames project prove successful, it will represent a breakthrough regarding the possibilities of using waste as a fuel in smaller communities.

Since 1967, the *Combustion Power Company* (Menlo Park, Calif.) under a series of contracts from the EPA, has been developing a waste-fired gas turbine system for recovering the energy value of solid waste directly as power. At commercial scales the system is to be capable of converting the heating value of 600 tons per day of solid waste into 9 to 12 megawatts of useful electrical power while also recovering secondary materials from the waste stream. Development has progressed to a pilot scale facility capable of converting 100 tons per day of solid waste into energy.

The pilot plant system includes a solid waste processing module and a power module. The solid waste processing module includes two shredders (100 and 75 horsepower), an air classifier, and a materials recovery system. After wastes are shredded and air-classified, the light fraction is pneumatically transported to the shredded waste storage vessel. A material recovery system is used to recover steel and aluminum. A glass-rich fraction and a non-ferrous-rich fraction are also separated and are available for further recovery operations.

The power module consists of a 22 × 9½-foot vertical cylindrical fluidized bed combustor and its feed system, a three-stage hot gas cleaning system, a turbogenerator, and an automatic control system. The separation system consists of two parallel 3-foot cyclones, two parallel 2.5-foot diameter cyclones, and a specially designed granular filter containing aluminum oxide media. A four stage axial flow gas turbine is used to extract energy from the hot gas stream to drive an air compressor and run a 1,000-kilowatt electrical generator. Pilot plant operation is completely automatic from start-up to shutdown.

The plant has been tested using municipal solid wastes, wood waste, and high sulfur coal. Although the system generated power, a severe problem involving the depositing of aluminum particles on the turbine blades led to a modification in the design of the separator system and the addition of the third stage granular filter.

Since April, 1974, the EPA plant has been used by ERDA to burn high sulfur coal. Test results for sulfur dioxide and nitrous oxides emissions have been promising. Future tests will include additional solid waste test burns and combined solid waste and sewage burns by EPA, and high sulfur coal burns by ERDA.

One of the larger waste-to-energy systems utilizing pyrolysis as its integral conversion operation is the *Monsanto Landgard* system recently built by the *City of Baltimore, Md.*[4] This unit, which is supported in part by an EPA Demonstration Grant, is designed to process 1,000 tons per day of typical municipal solid waste by converting the waste into:

(1) A fuel gas that is burned to produce marketable steam.

(2) A glassy aggregate that may be used as an aggregate in concrete.

(3) A carbon char that has possible uses in waste water treatment and soil conditioning. Also, ferrous metals, representing approximately 8 per cent of the waste stream, are removed magnetically. When fully operational, the plant will process approximately half of Baltimore's residential solid waste.

This unit is designed to accept residential and commercial solid wastes, including large household appliances and occasional tires, which are typical to U.S. cities. The plant's ability to process bulky items is a function of its shredder size, not of the pyrolytic process. Although the plant is not designed to accept sewage sludge as fuel, such sludge was pyrolyzed successfully at the pilot scale for the system, and may be used on experimental basis in the commercial scale plant.

Two 900 horsepower shredders are used to mill the wastes into 4-inch diameter particles for feeding into a 2,000-ton capacity storage bin, or directly into the reactor. The reactor is a refractory-lined horizontal rotary kiln that is 19 feet in diameter and 100 feet long, and rotates at approximately two revolutions per minute. The heat required for the pyrolysis reaction is provided by burning a portion of the solid waste feed in an oxygen-starved environment, and by burning 7.1 gallons of No. 2 heating oil per ton of waste. Pyrolysis gases at a controlled temperature of 1,200 °F move counter-current to the waste, and leave the kiln at the feed end.

From the kiln, the gases, which have a heat content of 120 BTU per dry standard cubic foot, go to an afterburner where they are combined with additional air at 1,400 °F. The heat released is directed into two waste heat boilers that generate 200,000 pounds of steam per hour. Waste gas from the boilers are passed through a spray chamber scrubber and, depending on the outcome of tests now underway, may be further passed through a wet electrostatic precipitator. Solid residues from the process are discharged into a quench tank and processed to separate the char and ferrous metals from the largely inert aggregate.

The plant is designed to produce no significant adverse environmental impacts. The emission quality, which is guaranteed by the contractor, will meet the state emission standards for particulates, sulfur dioxide and nitrous oxides. All process waste is to be recycled. The char, which contains about 1 per cent water-soluble materials, will, if disposed of in a properly engineered site, produce no leachate problem.

Construction of the plant is virtually complete; some mechanical modifications to correct problems arising from shakedown operations are still underway. Scale-up problems involving metallic residues in the pyrolysis gas stream and excessive slagging of inerts in the solid discharge streams have necessitated rather substantial changes in the process. The corrective work is to be done in two phases. The first phase will include all of the mechanical modifications, and the second phase will include the additional air pollution control equipment for cleansing the gas streams. Present plans are to have the plant fully operational by 1978.

A process based on a different approach to recovering energy from waste—pyrolyzing the organic fraction of the stream to produce a combustible liquid—is the subject of a demonstration project co-sponsored by the *EPA* and the *San Diego County Department of Sanitation and Flood Control*. The process developed by the Occidental Research Corporation (formerly the Garrett Research and Development Company) is an extension of research work done to liquefy coal, and is designed to recover at least 36 gallons of liquid fuel (equivalent in heating value to 27 gallons of No. 6 fuel oil) from each ton of solid waste processed. The plant is designed to produce 7,200 gallons of pyrolytic oil daily.

In the process feed preparation system, which is the most rigorous reduction system of any waste-to-energy process now under development in the country, the light organic fraction of the waste stream is separated through shredding and air classification. It is then further reduced into extremely fine particles having a normal size of minus 14 mesh (80 per cent of the particles will pass through a screen having 14 openings to the inch). The ferrous metals and glass present in the stream are recovered through magnetic recovery and froth flotation.

The pyrolysis reaction takes place in a vertical stainless steel pipe through which the organic feedstock is blown. As the organic fuel is processing through the reactor, it is mixed with the heated char residues from earlier reactions and is flash-pyrolyzed into a gas and a char mixture. The char is separated from the gas via a cyclone and the gas cooled very quickly in an oil decanter with a mixture of the liquid fuel produced by the plant and No. 2 fuel oil. After cooling, the liquid fuel settles in the base of the decanter.

The remaining gas stream goes through a series of clean-up steps and is compressed for use as a transport medium and as a fuel to preheat various gas streams in the process. The liquid fuel is either stored or passed through a centrifuge if the solid contents are too high.

The process is designed to control atmospheric emissions. Most of the air involved in the process will be recirculated, and exhaust gases from the process heater when released to the atmosphere will be in compliance with Federal, state, and local standards. Only limited test data have been collected on the sulfur dioxide and nitrous oxides emission resulting from the combustion of the pyrolytic oil. In order to assess this impact, the San Diego Gas and Electric Company has proposed a 21-month test program.

In November 1972, the *City of Chicago* initiated a study to establish the best means to enable it to increase its refuse disposal capacity by approximately 25 per cent. Of the more than 20 systems investigated, it was concluded that a supplementary fuel processing plant would offer the most significant advantages based on criteria of economics, resource and energy recovery, environmental impact, and technology. Similar in basic concept to the St. Louis–Union Electric Company developmental project, the Chicago process has taken advantage of the lessons learned there for incorporation of equipment and design features that will assure a supply of high-quality fuel at undoubtedly the lowest level of risk associated with any U.S. waste-to-energy facility. In the fall of 1976, it became the world's largest production plant for fuel from municipal refuse.

The facility is located adjacent to Commonwealth Edison's Crawford generating station, the customer for the supplementary fuel. The plant is presently capable of processing 1,000 tons per day. Raw refuse is reduced to less than 8 inches in diameter in a primary shredder and then separated into two fractions in an air classifier. Ferrous metal is removed from the heavy fraction as the material is discharged from a conveyor over a magnetic drum. Consideration has been given in the design for the possibility of removing materials such as aluminum and glass when these materials become economically recoverable. The light organic fraction is reduced to 1-inch size in a secondary shredder and is then conveyed by means of pneumavic pipeline to storage bins (90,000 and 60,000 cubic feet) on the Edison property. From the bins, the fuel is fed to the tangentially fired furnaces as required.

The *PUROX pyrolysis system* of the Union Carbide Corporation is in the most advanced state of development of any process capable of producing a medium-level heating value fuel gas from a wide variety of wastes. Because there is no nitrogen in the gas, it can be chemically converted to methane, methanol, or ammonia by established technology.

Although the vertical shaft reactor is able to handle municipal refuse as received, the usual preferred mode of operation is to coarsely shred the material to 8-inch maximum size, with 85 per cent less than 3 inch. The ferrous content then can be removed magnetically after air classification. The wet wastes enter the top of the reactor through an airlock. Descending slowly through it, counter-current to hot gases resulting from char combustion at the bottom, they dry and then decompose to synthesis gas, organic liquids, and char. Inorganics melt in the 3,000 °F combustion zone and leave as a molten slag. Oil and tar droplets are scrubbed out by the descending refuse and thus recycled for cracking the gas and char. Relatively pure oxygen produced at an on-site air fractionation plant is passed into the hearth zone to oxidize the char and yield the hot gases. Approximately 0.2 tons of oxygen per ton of wastes is required.

Gas clean-up is accomplished with a spray scrubber, a wet electrostatic precipitator, and a condenser to reduce the moisture content. Further purification when the gas is to be introduced into distribution systems is obtained by compression, cooling, and drying in a glycol absorber. Contaminants measured in the gas indicate hydrochloric acid is less than 1 part per million, nitrous oxides could not be determined at the 1 part per million-sensitivity level, hydrogen sulfide is between 300 and 400 parts per million, and fly ash is typically about 10 parts per million.

Development began in mid-1967. Tests in a 5 ton per day unit at Tarrytown, N.Y., established the basic system parameters, and gases having higher heating values in the range of 300 to 320 BTU per standard cubic foot were obtained. A 200 ton per day demonstration plant became operational in South Charleston, W. Va., in May 1974; it is 30 feet high and has an internal diameter of 10 feet. Extended runs have been made with this commercial-size equipment and 20,270 average cubic foot of 370 BTU per standard cubic foot of gas is produced per ton of refuse. Typical gas composition, by volume, is 50 per cent carbon monoxide, 30 per cent hydrogen gas, 3 per cent methane, 2 per cent mixed carbons, 14 per cent carbon dioxide, and 1 per cent nitrogen plus argon. The 350 ton per day modules under design could each produce 2.62 billion BTU of gas daily.

The *TORRAX pyrolysis system,* now being commercialized by Carborundum Environmental Systems, generates the heat required for the gasification reactions through air oxidation of the pyrolysis char in a vertical shaft furnace. The air is pre-heated to 1,800 to 2,000 °F in heat exchangers and produces a temperature of approximately 3,000 °F in combining with the carbon near the bottom of the reactor. Inorganic components of the waste fed into the top of the pyrolyzer melt to a slag that is quenched to a frit for later disposal or utilization.

Gases are drawn off near the top of the column at slightly subatmospheric pressure and temperatures in the range of 600 to 800 °F. A plug of refuse stands several feet above the product gas outlet, preventing blow-by. If it is desired to isolate a fuel gas having a heating value of approximately 140 BTU per standard cubic foot, the raw mixture is passed through a condenser, a wet electrostatic precipitator, and a water separator. A simplgr mode of operation is to directly introduce the 160 to 170 BTU unpurified gases into a combuster combined with a waste heat boiler.

A 75 ton per day demonstration plant has been built and tested at Orchard Park, N.Y. Basic 300 ton per day modules have been designed that will use 7½-foot diameter reactors. A 200 ton per day unit is now under construction in Luxembourg and a recent order has been received for a similar system for Graase, France. Pre-heating of the combustion air in these systems is accomplished in alternate heating-cooling refractory-filled regenerative heat exchangers by using 15 per cent of the combustor hot flue gases.

The *Georgia Tech Engineering Experimental Station* has been developing a mobile agricultural waste pyrolysis system over the last seven years that offers interesting possibilities for energy production from agricultural and forestry wastes. The concept involves a transportable pyrolytic converter that could be brought to the source of wastes on two standard trailer units and there transform 200 tons per day of wet residues into 45 tons of a dense char-oil fuel similar to powdered coal. Extensive pilot and demonstration testing in units processing 6–50 dry tons per day indicate that the low temperature (800 to 1,400 °F) pyrolysis system is technologically and economically practical.

Wastes are shredded to approximately 1-inch size and dried in a system heated by the combustion of pyrolytic off-gases. A portion of these gases would also be used as a fuel for an internal combustion engine to furnish power to the facility. The waste material pass downward through the stirred reactor, with heat being supplied by internal partial oxidation of the char formed. An air-to-dry-waste mass ratio of 0.3 to 0.4 is typically employed. Pyrolytic oil is separated from the off-gases with a condenser and mixed with the char (40 to 60 ratio) to yield a free-flowing solid having a higher heating value of at least 12,000 BTU per pound. Effluent pollution control would appear to present no particular problem.

ONGOING RESEARCH AND DEVELOPMENT

The EPA and its predecessor agencies have pursued a waste-as-fuel research and demonstration program since the passage of the authorizing legislation in the mid-1960's. This program, which has supported the development of many of the processes discussed in this article, has recently received increased emphasis from the new national focus on energy research and development. The present program is divided into four program areas:

(1) Assessment research and development, studies to evaluate the technological and economic aspects of the various waste-as-fuel options, and studies to determine the environmental impact of those options.

(2) Waste co-combustion with coal, oil, or industrial waste projects to determine the possibilities and potential problem of using waste as a supplement to conventional fuels.

(3) Waste co-combustion with sewage sludge.

(4) Pyrolysis and bioconversion process, projects that explore the chemical and biological conversion of wastes to gases and liquids useful as fuels. A selection of current projects is shown in Table 30-4.

In the "Third Report to Congress—Resource Recovery and Waste Reduction," the EPA estimated that there exists in the nation's most densely populated areas alone enough convertible municipal wastes to provide 1,085 trillion BTU of energy by 1980, or 1.3 per cent of the amount of energy forecast by the Bureau of Mines to be used in that year. This is a significant amount of energy. For example, it is equivalent to 37 per cent of the projected input from the Alaskan pipeline for 1980. It would supply more than the required energy for combined residential cooking and clothes drying needs or 85 per cent of the energy demand of all commercial air conditioning.

Table 30–4. Current EPA Waste-as-fuel Projects.

Project Title	*Contractor/Grantee*	*EPA Project Officer*
Utilization of wastes-as-fossil fuel energy substitutes Contract No. 68-02-2101	The Ralph M. Parsons Co., Pasadena, Calif.	Harry Freeman, IERL-Ci, Cincinnati, Ohio 45268
Pyrolysis of solid waste to generate steam and char EPA Grant No. S-801533	City of Baltimore, Md.	David Sussman, OSWMP, Washington, D.C. 20460
Use of solid waste as a supplementary fuel in coal-fired boilers	City of St. Louis, Mo.	George Huffman, IERL-Ci, Cincinnati, Ohio 45268
Pyrolysis of solid waste to fuel oil and char Grant No. S-801588	San Diego County, Calif.	Steven J. Levy, OSWMP, Washington, D.C. 20460
CPU-400 process	Combustion Power Co., Menlo Park, Calif.	Richard Chapman, IERL-Ci, Cincinnati, Ohio 45268
Environmental assessment of waste-to-energy processes	Not yet scheduled	Harry Freeman, IERL-Ci, Cincinnati, Ohio 45268
Effects of burning densified refuse-derived fuels	Not yet scheduled	Carlton Wiles, MERL, Kirk Stubbs, Cincinnati, Ohio 45268
Pyrolytic conversion of mixed waste to fuel, pilot research and development	Energy Resources Co., Cambridge, Mass.	Richard Chapman, IERL-Ci, Cincinnati, Ohio 45268
Portable pyrolysis of agricultural waste-to-transportable fuels	Dr. John W. Tatom, Georgia Institute of Technology, Engineering Experiment Station	Walter Ilberick, IERL-Ci, Cincinnati, Ohio 45268

Another recent EPA study, "Solid Waste as Fuel for Power Generation," concludes that, even if it is assumed that no conversion plant smaller than 100 tons per day capacity can be justified economically, enough energy could be recovered from the normal solid waste stream to supply up to 3 per cent of the nation's total energy requirement, or enough energy to provide for all of the country's residential and commercial lighting needs. Once a clearer perspective emerges on the true availability of the potentially vast quantities of forestry and agricultural wastes in the United States, these figures could perhaps double or triple.

The conversion of wastes into energy is no longer in the theoretical stages of development, but has moved into the beginning phases of commercial application. Based on energy recovery systems existing or planned at the present time, it is projected in the EPA report to the Congress that by 1980 almost 30 cities and counties around the country should be operating the equivalent of thirty-six 1,000 tons per day plants, recovering an estimated 85 trillion BTU per year.

REFERENCES

1. *Environmental Science and Technology,* May 1972, p.412.
2. *Environmental Science and Technology,* May 1975, p. 423.
3. *Environmental Science and Technology,* January 1976, p. 34.
4. *Environmental Science and Technology,* February 1975, p. 98.

SUGGESTED READINGS

Dupree, W. G., and J. S. Corsentin, 1975, *United States Energy Through the Year 2000 (Revised),* Bureau of Mines, U.S. Department of the Interior.

———, 1975, EPA Wastes as Fuel Research, Development and Demonstration Program Plan, April, U.S. Environmental Protection Agency.

Gibney, Lena C., 1974, Liabilities into Assets, *Environmental Science and Technology 8,* pp. 210–211.

Golueke, Clarence G., and P. H. McGauhey, 1976, Waste Materials, *Annual Review of Energy 1,* pp. 257–277.

Huffman, G. L., 1976, "EPA's Program in Environmental Research in Wastes as Fuels." Paper presented at IGT Symposium on "Clean Fuels from Biomass Sewage, Urban Refuse, and Agricultural Wastes." Orlando, Florida, January 29.

Kasper, William C., 1974, Power from Trash, *Environment 16,* pp. 34–38.

Schwieger, R. G., 1975, Power from Waste, *Power 119,* pp. S·1–S·24.

Wilcox, Denny, 1973, Fuel from City Trash, *Environment 15,* pp. 36–42.

V

CONSERVATION, LIFE-STYLES, AND ENERGY POLICY FOR THE FUTURE

Exxon Corporation drilling platform, 75 miles off the Louisiana coast. If the demand for petroleum products continues to increase, the emphasis in exploration and production drilling will shift to more offshore drilling. (Photo courtesy of Exxon Corporation and the American Petroleum Institute.)

Location of underground natural gas lines. Such pipelines will be able to carry more energy, more economically, than the unsightly, easily damaged overhead lines. (Photo courtesy of D. P. Gregory, Institute of Gas Technology.)

Spoil piles from stripmining of coal in the 1930's, Montana. With no reclamation, the return of natural vegetation has been slow, even after more than 40 years. (Photo courtesy of the Montana Department of State Lands.)

National projections for energy call for the construction of more nuclear power plants similar to this one being constructed some 35 miles south of Miami at Turkey Point, Florida. The two large silo-like buildings house 745-megawatt (electric) power units. (Photo courtesy of J. R. Lennartson, Westinghouse Electric Corporation.)

INTRODUCTION

We have presented the boundary conditions for the energy supply and demand picture, the nature of present fossil fuel- and fission-based energy sources, and the energy alternatives that are being developed to supplant our diminishing conventional resources. The range of response of those examining the energy situation, and the dilemmas it poses, is extremely broad and reflects the backgrounds, values, and world views of the analysts. In this chapter, we present a number of articles illustrating the diversity of responses from a straightforward extrapolation of historical trends to proposals for radical changes in our energy life-styles.

The analyses presented here are intended to be provocative. Many of the conclusions and cause-effect relationships in one analysis directly contradict those in the next, and some are based on obviously questionable assumptions. Each article, however, also contains perceptive insights into the energy problem. The true future, as it unfolds, will undoubtedly contain elements from all these scenarios, and the game the reader should play is to analyze critically the arguments presented and to consider the alternative energy future that seems most likely and/or desirable. If the most likely future does not coincide with the most desirable future, the political process is available to narrow the gap. This political process is now in full swing on both state and national levels. To understand and contribute intelligently to the political debate, it is necessary to visualize the changes in life-style and society that various policy alternatives imply. These articles will assist the reader in this process.

In his analysis, *Economic Growth, Conservation, and Electricity,* Chauncey Starr extrapolates historical trends of the past 85 years to project the energy patterns for the next 25 years. The data he presents provide strong arguments for his recommendations, the heart of which is to increase the supply side of the supply-demand energy picture. His analysis agrees with the following ones on the value of conservation. In his analysis, he also assumes the logic of "social inertia," the habit and spending patterns of millions of Americans and hundreds of electric utilities. Questions on the analysis arise, however, over the omission of energy price factors and recent evidence suggesting that the correlation between GNP and energy consumption can be changed by intelligent planning (e.g., the Swedish example). The crucial test of the analysis will be whether the downturn in energy consumption from 1973–1975 was only a brief fluctuation in a continuing growth trend or a benchmark indicating a fundamental change in energy price structure and the social values affected by it.

Marc Ross and Robert Williams summarize the findings of major conservation studies by the Ford Foundation and the American Physical Society in *The Potential for Fuel Conservation*. The authors make the very useful distinction between quantity and quality of energy in their definitions of "first-law" and "second-law" thermodynamic efficiencies. Implementation of the technical improvements they suggest would provide no change in life-style while reducing the demand for energy by 40 per cent. Such energy thrift would have the effect of moving the clock back 17 years in the upward trend in energy demand. The logic of their scientific arguments is so inescapable and the social benefits of their suggestions so overwhelming that their proposals are already appearing in national energy policy.

In *Energy Strategy: The Industry, Small Business and Public Stakes,* Amory Lovins contrasts the energy alternative proposed by Chauncey Starr, which he identifies as "hard technology," with the "soft technology" energy option he favors. He believes that hard technology—the continued growth scenario—is politically, technically, and economically unworkable, primarily because of the enormous capital investments required. In his analysis, new electrical plants, because of their capital intensive nature, actually *destroy* jobs rather than create them as the conventional wisdom holds. The concept and properties of soft technology are described in very appealing, humanistic terms and are certainly a useful contribution to energy analysis. One cannot help but wonder, however, why, if soft technology is so attractive to every constituency (business people, liberals, conservatives, the religious, and so on), the free market economy (or planned socialist economics, for that matter) have not discovered this fact and generated a multitude of successful soft technology enterprises and new millionaires.

In *A Low Energy Scenario for the United States: 1975–2050,* John Steinhart and his colleagues cast many of the suggestions of Amory Lovins in concrete terms and, combining these with recent demographic trends and the energy efficiency improvements suggested by Ross and Williams, project a scenario with a startling 64 per cent reduction in per capita energy consumption by the year 2050. The scenario is proposed not as a plan, but rather as a feasibility study for the heuristic purpose of stimulating an examination of the basic values shaping our present attitudes toward energy. The policies recommended are designed specifically to alter life-styles in gentle ways—designed not to lower the standard of living but rather provide improved quality of life through a cleaner environment and more rational social patterns. Many of the energy reductions would be achieved through the use of conservation rather than curtailment, and this conservation would be "encouraged" by a rather impressive array of proposed federal legislation. The goals of this program are certainly desirable, and the legislation proposed is a plausible route to the goal. The real issue arises concerning the feasibility of a vast federal bureaucracy to enforce this new "prohibition" (on energy consumption), and the new public morality it represents. In light of the difficulties encountered by the relatively innocuous new gasoline tax proposal, the feasibility of this much more sweeping and all inclusive program seems highly problematic. To the extent that such legislation follows and institutionalizes changing public opinion, however, this scenario offers an intriguing and hopeful prospect for the future.

Glenn Seaborg presents a valuable synthesis of the more attractive features of both the low energy scenario of Lovins and Steinhart and the high technology energy options of Starr in his optimistic perspective, *The Recycle Society of Tomorrow*. He foresees a highly disciplined future society in which cooperation, conservation, and ingenuity are the dominant values. The "use and discard" ethic will have given way to the "conserve and recycle" ethic, with virgin raw materials used only to replace losses in the recycle process. Energy development will have progressed in all the areas previously discussed, with electronic communications relieving the burdens on energy resources that transportation had imposed. Certainly, this steady-state world, even with its tightly controlled social and physical environment, is vastly preferable to the grim social collapse predicted by less optimistic world models. The greatest challenge to our society in facing the limitations of a finite world is to resolve the profound ethical dilemmas involved in such social decisions with compassion and wisdom.

Economic Growth, Conservation, and Electricity 31

CHAUNCEY STARR 1976

OBJECTIVES OF THIS ANALYSIS

The energy issues of any nation are commonly viewed in the context of two time frames—immediate and urgent supply and demand pressures, and future constraints that might warrant initiation of preparatory measures. Although pragmatically these distinctions are blurred over the span of time, it is important to assess future needs as far ahead as is relevant to the ongoing planning of national research and development actions, timing, and priority. As an example of such planning, this article addresses the question of the needs in the United States for electricity a quarter century hence—to the year 2000—a period today's research and development program might influence substantially.

The future needs for so basic a commodity as electricity cannot be predicted with certainty. The best prediction that can be obtained is a reasonable range of outcomes, which may be affected by such societal, economic, and technical trends as can be foreseen. Based on such projections, national choices must be made on the objectives of current programs—such as to provide for a surplus or accept a constrained energy supply or to deplete available cheap fuels now or husband them for the future. Such objectives can be viewed as (a) "imperative" (i.e., essential for national survival), (b) "important" (i.e., needed to maintain national well-being), and (c) "desirable" (i.e., needed to enhance national well-being).

In our society, however, future developments are determined not only by a quantitative assessment of alternatives, but also by public perception, public preferences, and public prejudices. The quality of the national policy debate, arising from the differences in the last three positions, can be enhanced if the

Dr. Chauncey Starr is president of the Electric Power Research Institute. Previously he was dean of the School of Engineering and Applied Science at the University of California at Los Angeles (1967–1973), following a 20-year industrial career, during which he served as vice-president of Rockwell International and president of its Atomic International Division. Dr. Starr is a past vice-president of the National Academy of Engineering, a founder and a past president of the American Nuclear Society, a director of the Atomic Industrial Forum and the American Association for the Advancement of Science, and a former member of the President's Energy Research and Development Council.

Originally presented to the Conference Internationale des Grandes Reseaux Electriques (CIGRE), Paris, France, August 25, 1976.

first item—the quantitative assessment—provides an insight to the probable effect of alternatives. It is in this spirit that the following analysis is presented.

METHODOLOGY

The continuing growth of the U.S. population and its labor force has required a corresponding growth in new jobs. Employment has been a primary goal and independent planning objective of American society. This is exemplified in the Employment Act of 1946 that states it is "the continuing policy and responsibility of the Federal Government . . . to coordinate and utilize all its plans, functions, and resources . . . to promote maximum employment, production, and purchasing power."

After ascertaining the expected population and desired employment level in the year 2000, a projection was made of the output of goods and services (Gross National Product, GNP) for this increased employment level, assuming the continuation of a decreasing work week and a steadily growing productivity. As an extreme contrast to this first case, which assumes a continuation of the historical trend, a hypothetical "no growth" second case was considered; it assumed a freeze on the conditions of 1973 in terms of productivity per employee, i.e., for the year 2000, the 1973 GNP was expanded at exactly the same rate as the increase in employment.

As a first approximation to energy requirements, an empirical historical relationship between GNP and energy was extended to the level of GNP estimated for the year 2000 "historical growth" case. The energy requirement to support the year 2000 GNP was subsequently modified for anticipated societal choices of energy conservation and environmental improvement. This total primary energy need became the year 2000 planning target for societal growth unconstrained by energy availability or a very high relative cost of energy. The interrelated structure of the energy-economic system is illustrated in Figure 31-1. The amount of electricity needed to obtain this energy planning target was calculated by extrapolating the historical trend of the fraction of total primary energy input applied to electricity generation. The potential effect of conservation through technological efficiency improvements was evaluated for three cases. These cases then provided a range of outcomes for the electricity demand from which the most probable demand could be estimated.

Essentially, these steps constitute an approach to a projection based upon historical relationships and identified variations from it. The conservation potential is based upon an analysis of technical feasibility. The price is not considered as an explicit variable in these future relationships, although it is inherent in the conservation treatment and the assumption of historical continuity, which implies that energy will continue as a relatively low-cost item. The relative availability of the necessary resources—fuels, facilities, skills, capital—and the environmental or governmental constraints on their use, will determine pragmatically the market prices and the economic trade-offs in actual choices among alternatives. By including a range of outcomes, which result from wide deviations from the historical relationships, we believe that the study covers the range of possible outcomes and also reveals the comparative importance of the underlying primary technical parameters such as new electricity uses and conservation technology.

EMPLOYMENT

The physical size and societal aspirations of the population provide primary driving forces for the growth of the economic system. For the year 2000, a civilian employment level of 113 million is projected in the United States. This is based on a total population of 263 million (from a replacement fertility rate of 2.1 births per woman) and a 4 per cent unemployment rate. This civilian employment level would be reduced only about 2½ per cent if the very low fertility rate of 1.7 births per woman is assumed, because the labor

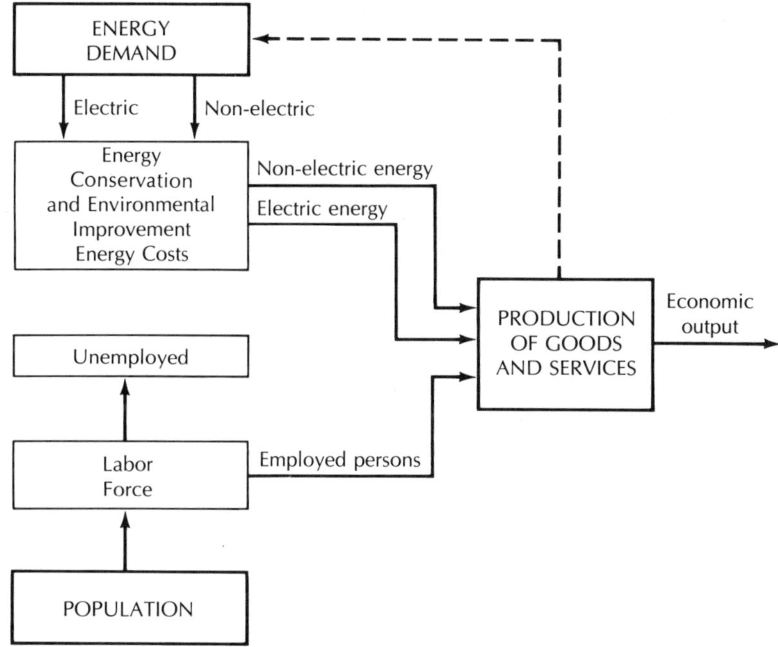

Figure 31-1. Methodology for year 2000 projections. Schematic diagram.

Figure 31-2. United States population, 1890–2050. Projections are based on the fertility rate of 2.1 births per woman, which represents the replacement level.

force available in the year 2000 would be about equivalent to that in existence today. Further, such social trends as the steady increase in the percentage of women who work may somewhat increase adult participation in the labor force above the predicted level by as much as 5 per cent. For these reasons, the projection of 113 million employed in the year 2000 is a reasonable basis for this assessment. These trends are indicated in Figure 31-2.

ECONOMIC GROWTH

The projected growth of the civilian labor force demands related increases in economic growth to create jobs and to maintain full employment. Employment is assumed to be the primary independent planning objective. In the United States, the level of economic activity, as measured by the GNP, depends upon (a) the size of the employed labor force, (b) its annual hours of work, and (c) its productivity or ability to produce marketable goods and services. These relationships are described by the following equation:

$$\text{GNP} = E_m H_y P_r$$

where GNP is dollars per year; E_m is the number of employed persons; H_y is average employee-hours worked per employee-year; and P_r is productivity in dollars per hour per employee. A review of the 80-odd years from

Figure 31-3. Employment and GNP in the United States.

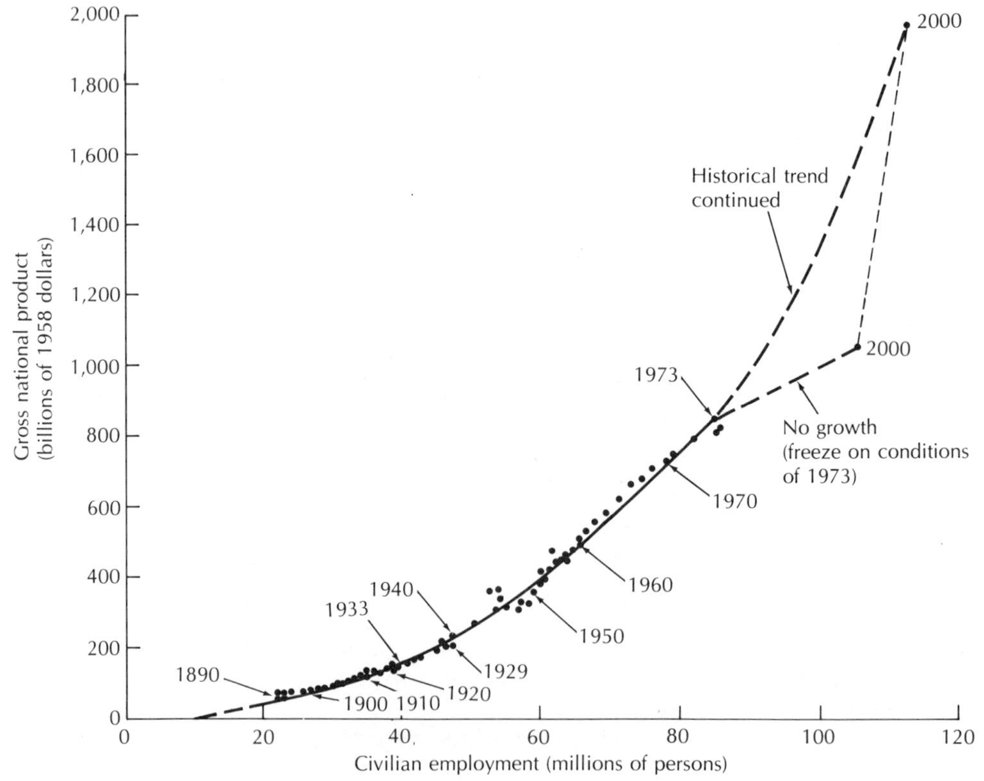

1890 to 1973 shows the output of goods and services in 1973 was nearly 16 times what it was in 1890, and the job was done with only four times as many workers as shown by the curve in Figure 31-3. After accounting for a reduction in the average work week from 54 hours in 1890 (six 9-hour days) to about 40 hours in 1973, one can calculate that the spectacular rise in the GNP per employee was due to a fivefold increase in productivity.

The empirical relationship between GNP and employment over the past 85 years is described by the equation:

$$\text{GNP} = [156 \exp (0.0235E_m)] - 252$$

where GNP is in billions of 1958 dollars and E_m is in millions of persons. Assuming that this relationship properly describes a continuing normal trend, an estimate of the employment level at any future time should provide an estimate of the GNP required to sustain that employment. This equation assumes the continuation of the several trends that are manifested in the historical relationship and is assumed as a reference base. For the year 2000, the employment of 113 million persons, assuming a 4 per cent unemployment rate, would require a GNP of 1,970 billions of 1958 dollars per year.

If a "no growth" situation were postulated by freezing the future GNP per employee (constant productivity and work week) at the 1973 value, the year 2000 GNP would be only 1,050 billions of 1958 dollars per year. Because the 1973 GNP is an integration of old and new productivity patterns and life-styles existing in 1973, freezing the GNP-employment ratio at the 1973 level should correspond to freezing all major societal and industrial patterns, only replicating this mix in the future to handle an increased labor force.

ECONOMIC GROWTH AND ENERGY USE

All energy projections are based on the probable level of output of goods and services of the U.S. economy. This is the quantitative corollary of a perceived future national aspiration of economic welfare and development.

Once a target is set for the GNP, the energy needs of the nation can be roughly estimated. As an empirical approximation (1890–1975), total primary energy consumption tends to follow GNP (Figure 31-4) with a linear relationship described by the equation:

$$E_n = 5 + 0.0833 \text{ GNP}$$

where E_n is total primary energy use is 10^{15} BTU per year (10^{15} BTU = 1 quad; additional energy conversion factors are presented in the Appendix) and GNP is the gross national product in billions of 1958 dollars per year.

This relationship depends on the elemental fact that the combination of labor, raw material, capital equipment, and energy (fuel and solar) creates our goods and services. Fuel energy is a primary input essential to all sectors of the economy; even food production depends heavily on a fuel energy input in addition to that supplied by solar energy. The GNP and energy are thus intrinsically linked.

The empirical relation of GNP and fuel energy can be altered by variations in the historical trends in (a) life-style shifts, i.e., changing the mix of goods and services; (b) changing the mix of factors of production (labor, materials, capital, and energy); and (c) changing the efficiency with which primary energy is converted to end-uses. To project the historical relationship is to assume that these forces will interact in the future as they have in the past. This is an assumption of uncertain validity, but it does provide a basis for an initial analysis.

This historical linear relationship links energy consumption to the productivity of labor and the magnitude of the labor force, as illustrated in Figure 31-5. This occurs despite massive shifts in the labor force from agriculture to the services sector. Figure 31-6 illustrates this changing pattern.

Another fundamental empirical relationship is that of annual total primary energy use and its relationship to employment as shown

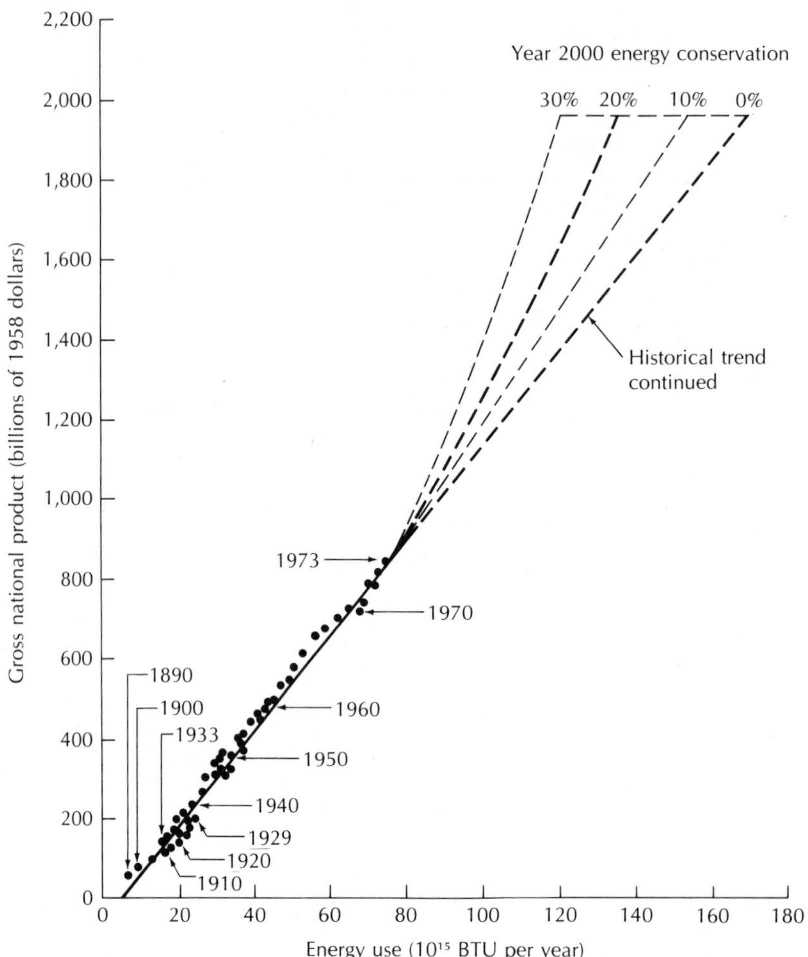

Figure 31-4. The GNP and energy use in the United States.

Figure 31-5. The GNP and energy relationship.

1890 - 1975 STRAIGHT LINE RELATIONSHIP:

$$\text{Energy} = a + b\ \text{GNP}$$

Since

$$\text{Productivity} = \frac{\text{GNP}}{\text{Employee}}$$

Therefore

$$\text{Energy} = a + b\ \text{Employee}\ \left(\frac{\text{GNP}}{\text{Employee}}\right)$$

in Figure 31-7. This relationship is described by the equation:

$$E_n = [13 \exp (0.0235\, E_m)] - 16$$

where E_n is the total primary energy use in 10^{15} BTU per year, and E_m is the number of employed civilians in millions of persons.

On the assumption that this relationship, which has been valid for over three-fourths of

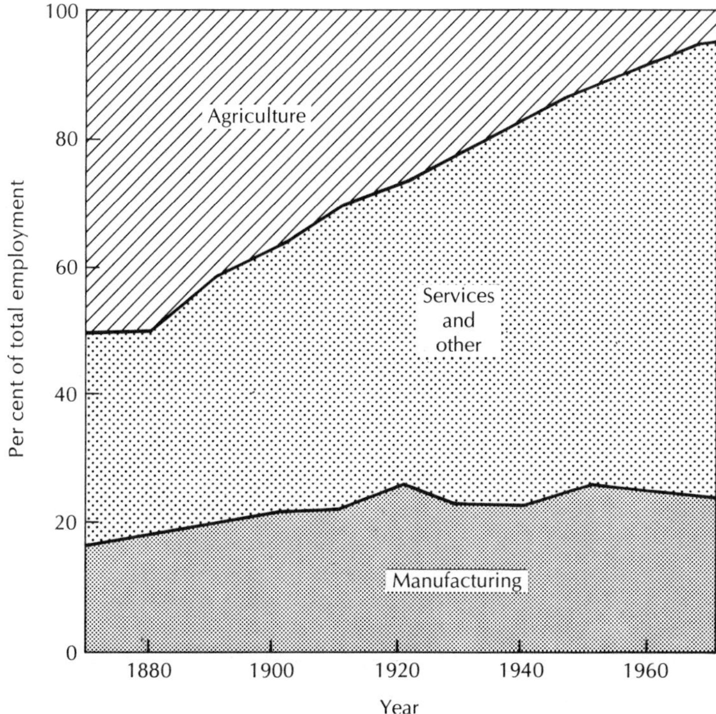

Figure 31-6. Occupational distribution of the employed U.S. labor force.

a century, properly describes a continuing normal trend, a projection of the employment level at any future time should provide an estimate of the total primary energy required to sustain that employment. This estimate serves as a reference base for the consideration of future changes in the historical relationships.

Projections of energy relationships with both GNP and employment have been modified to show a range that includes both a reasonable growth in energy conservation and a moderate degree of energy costs for environmental improvement. In a separate study, it was shown that a reasonable expectation for energy conservation by the year 2000 is about 20 per cent of the unmodified energy projection; similarly, environmental improvement is expected to cost 10 per cent greater energy use by the year 2000. This is illustrated in Figure 31-7.

YEAR 2000 ELECTRICITY PLANNING TARGET

The year 2000 energy requirements associated with the unperturbed continuation of the historical trend would be 170 quadrillion BTU per year. Using this figure as a basis, we can estimate electricity demand by projecting the probable fraction of total energy that is likely to be in the form of electricity. Subsequent modifications can then be made for electricity conservation and for energy costs associated with environmental improvement.

From 1960 to 1973, the energy input to generate electricity as a percent of total energy grew at a compound annual rate of

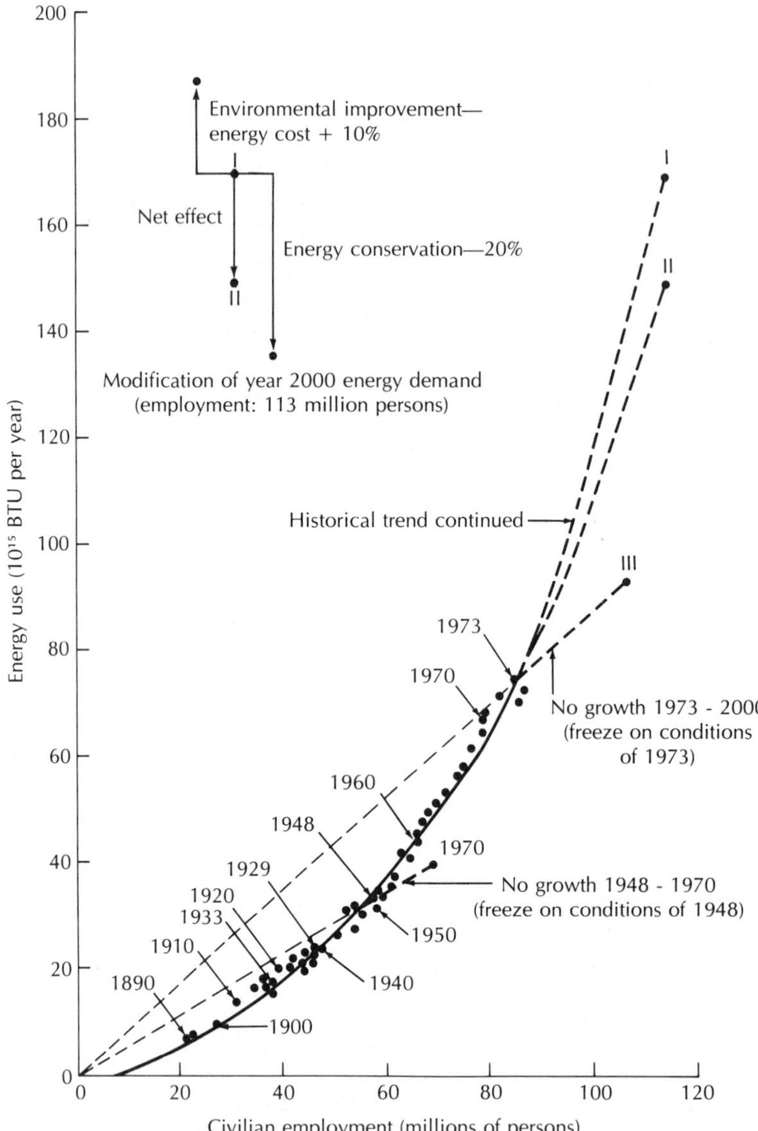

Figure 31-7. Employment and energy use in the United States, 1890–2000.

2.63 per cent per year as shown in Figure 31-8. This, added to the average total energy growth rate of 4.22 per cent per year, gave an electricity growth of 6.85 per cent per year. An extension of the 2.63 per cent per year of fractional increase to the year 2000 indicates that 53 per cent of all primary energy will be used as fuel for the generation of electricity. This extrapolation appears reasonable, although it is not evident how much of the past

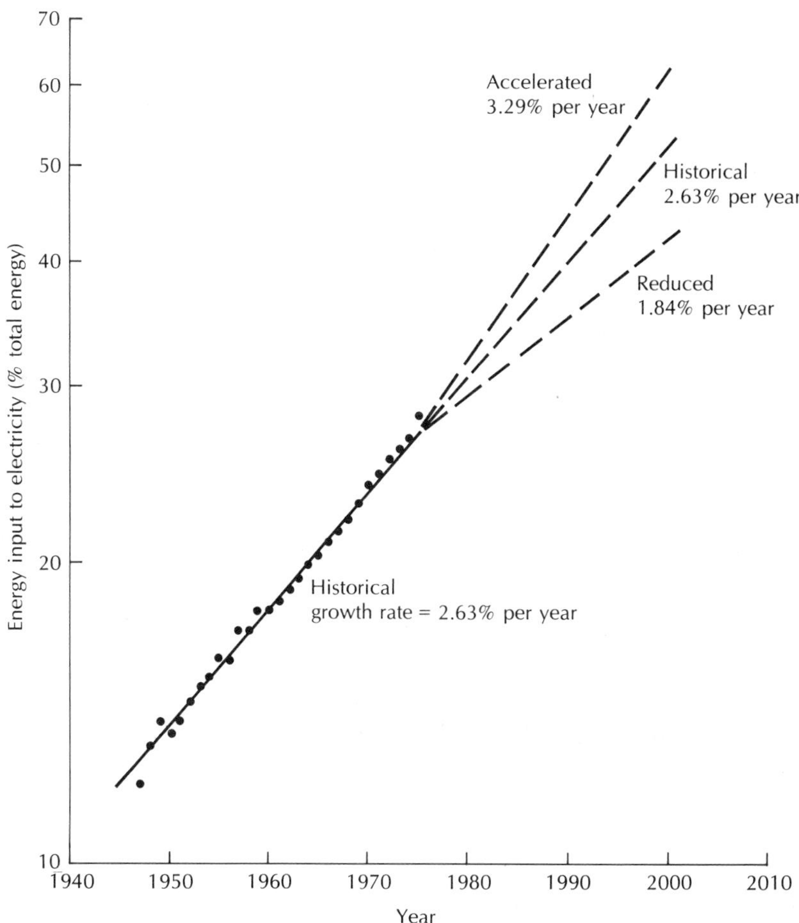

Figure 31-8. Relationship between electricity and total energy in the United States.

growth was cost motivated and how much was due to the utility value of convenience, operational flexibility, uniqueness of application, and other such characteristics of electricity. Although it is recognized that the growth rate of the electric fraction must eventually decrease, because electricity use is still far from saturation, it is assumed that slowing will not occur before the year 2000.

The factors that eventually will affect the energy that will be delivered as electricity are shown in Table 31-1.

Thus, with the year 2000, a total energy demand of 170 quads unperturbed by conservation or environmental costs, and an electric fraction of 53 ± 10 per cent, the projected requirements for electricity range from 7,300 to 10,700 billion kilowatt-hours per year. These projections assume a continuing normal trend of continuing improvement in conversion efficiency (heat rate) from the present average of 10,500 to 10,000 BTU per kilowatt-hour by the year 2000. The energy costs for environmental improvement as-

Table 31–1. Factors Determining Electricity Needs (Growth Rates, Per Cent per Year).

	Historical 1960–1973	*Projected 1973–2000*
1. Total energy	4.22	3.07
2. Electric fraction	2.63	2.63
3. Interfuel substitution		−0.5 to 1.0
4. (a) End-use efficiency improvement (b) Reduced usage (life-style changes) (c) Effect of price on demand		0 to −1.6
Total Electricity Growth Rate	6.85	3.60–6.70

Figure 31-9. Expected distribution of primary energy input in the United States, 1960–2000 (per cent of total energy).

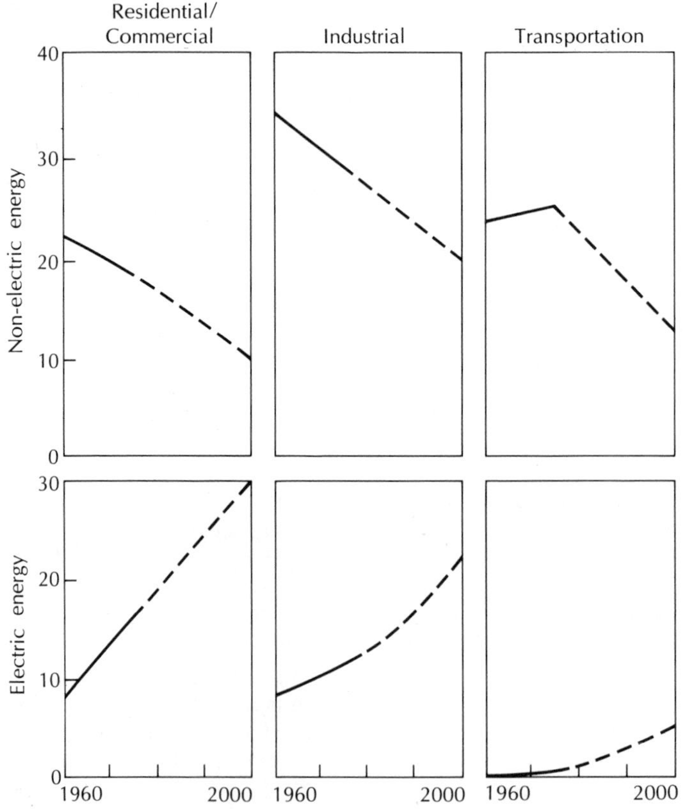

Table 31–2. Year 2000 End-use Conservation Potential (Per Cent Savings).

Conservation Program	*Electric Energy Sector (%)*	*Non-electric Energy Sector (%)*	*Total Energy (%)*
None	0	0	0
Reasonable	17	25	20
Extreme	34	50	40

sociated with electric power generation will increase the year 2000 heat rate to about 11,000 BTU per kilowatt-hour.

The expected distribution of energy by sector is illustrated in Figure 31-9.

The over-all conservation potential for the year 2000 is shown in Table 31-2. As mentioned, the potential for conservation is greater in the nonelectric sector because most electricity-consuming devices are already highly efficient. The size and cost of most electrical equipment is generally determined by the waste heat developed, so efficiency has always been a goal. Sector estimates of the potential are shown in Table 31-3.

A 17 per cent reduction in electricity requirements due to conservation is a reasonable target. Whereas a 34 per cent reduction is theoretically possible, this is considered an extreme case because it implies the universal adoption of, and capital investment in, every possible energy-saving measure—a highly unlikely situation.

The year 2000 electricity demand based on continuing historical growth of total energy and the electricity fraction is summarized in Table 31-4.

The combination of historical shift to electricity as an energy form and a reasonable level of electricity conservation would lead, most likely, to a year 2000 electricity demand of about 7,500 billion kilowatt-hours, which is four times the year 1973 level of 1,856 billion kilowatt-hours. The preceding calculations indicate that the requirement for electricity use grows at an average of 5.3 per cent per year. Since continuing productivity growth may be a necessary basis for continuing public welfare, it is prudent to plan now for a minimum year 2000 target of 7,500 billion kilowatt-hours.

Although significant departures from historically based relationships may occur, it would be unwise to base planning on such assumptions as those involving substantial reduction from historically experienced pro-

Table 31–3. Potential Electricity Savings for the United States.

Sector	*Potential Savings 1975–2000 (% sector electricity use)*	*Sector Importance Year 2000 (% total electricity)*	*Weighted Potential Savings (% total electricity)*
Industry	15–30	40	6–12
Residential and commercial	20–40	50	10–20
Transportation	10–20	10	1–2
Total		100	17–34

Table 31-4. Year 2000 Electricity Demands in the United States on the Basis of Continued Historical Growth for Total Energy.

	Electric Fraction[a]		
Electricity Conservation	*Reduced (43%)*	*Historical (53%)*	*Accelerated (63%)*
None (0)	7,300	9,000	10,700
Reasonable (17%)	6,070	7,500	8,900
Extreme (34%)	4,820	5,950	7,070

[a]Billions of kilowatt-hours per year.

ductivity growth. Planned constraints on electricity supply should not be imposed on the American people. If the United States is to choose a path of lesser growth, this should be a decision reached on the basis of broad national economic policy, with electricity policy tailored accordingly.

Of particular national importance is the role of electricity in the reduction of foreign oil imports. The use of national coal and uranium resources to produce electricity to meet most of the required growth in total energy demand can substantially reduce oil imports as shown in Table 31-5.

The calculations in Table 31-5 are based on the assumption that oil and gas for electricity generation will be limited to 5 quads in the year 2000 and that domestic production of oil and gas in the year 2000 will be the same as current levels. It is evident that increasing electrification works toward important reductions in the need for foreign oil and gas.

Electric power plants will be the only substantial means for converting coal to usable energy by the year 2000. Commercial synthetic oil and gas from coal will only be making a modest contribution at that time because of the lead time required for significant penetration into the national productive capacity. With the first full-scale demonstrations occurring in the mid-1980's, the contribution of such synthetic fuel to the national energy supply will be modest by the year 2000.

Even with the minimum planning target of 7,500 billion kilowatt-hours per year, the

Table 31-5. Potential Impact of Electricity Use on Oil and Gas Import Requirements.

	1973	*2000*			
Electricity (% Total Energy)	26	43		63	
Oil and Gas (10^{15} BTU per Year)		*No Conservation*	*Conservation*	*No Conservation*	*Conservation*
Required: (a) For electricity	7	5	5	5	5
(b) For direct use	50	86	73	52	44
	57	91	78	57	49
Supply: (a) Domestic production	43	43	43	43	43
(b) Imports required	14	48	35	14	6
Total	57	91	78	57	49
Year 2000 imports/Year 1973 imports		3.4	2.5	1.0	0.4

need for imported oil and gas is likely to be 70 per cent greater than 1973 levels. If the national response to the need for conservation is anticipated to be weak, then it would be desirable to implement an intensive electrification program to utilize coal and uranium and plan for a target of 10,700 billion kilowatt-hours per year. This would be the most cautious national policy now.

Any concern with possible overexpansion, as a result of setting too high an achievement target, does not appear to be justified in planning electricity production. The inescapably long time required to accelerate all the components of our national system provides assurance that there will be ample opportunity for continuous assessment and for rescheduling and retargeting as trend factors become more definite. Even if the practicalities of planning and expansion result in some capital facilities being available before they are needed, such a temporary surplus would certainly be only a small per cent of the total and would, in any case, assure the further reduction in consumption of oil and gas by the electric utility sector.

Three major approaches have been considered for reducing our future need for fuels and facilities devoted to the supply of energy. They are *conservation, load management,* and *new energy sources*.

Conservation, the most obvious approach, has been reviewed in the previous section. Load management is a means of improving the use of existing facilities, but except for its secondary effect through reduced future demand for capital equipment and reduced use of inefficient peaking generation, it does not directly reduce total energy input. New energy sources are clearly desirable, but those under development require a substantial lead time to make a significant contribution.

Load management has many desirable operating features and has been a long-time objective of the electric utility industry. Because it usually requires the cooperation of the user (fostered by rate design), and often an increased user investment, it is difficult to accomplish unless energy constraints, costs, or public policy provide the motivation for such procedures. The nontechnical component of load management is the distribution of consumer use to hours when the demand on the electric power system is as uniform over time as possible. The technical component is energy storage—either at the consumer's end or in the power system. Such storage capacity permits the power station to operate more continuously near its optimum output, with the peak demands being reduced or partially met from the storage system. For example, a larger hot water tank in a home would permit heating at night with use during the day. An electrically heated home with a large heat storage block would do the same. Occasional services, such as laundry and dishwashing, could be performed during off hours. To provide consumers with an economic incentive for such adjustments and investments, so-called time-of-day pricing is being investigated and tried by several major utility systems.

Large-scale energy storage systems are a substantial portion of the research and development being undertaken for our electric utility systems. The historically proven method is the use of off-peak power to pump water to high dams and then generate electricity hydraulically when needed. Recent concepts involve compressed gases, storage batteries, and even flywheels. Several of these are in pilot plant or demonstration stages, and one might expect significant use of storage systems by the year 2000.

Recognizing the uncertainty of such projections, it is nevertheless reasonable to assume that the combination of all these approaches will result in moving the present national capacity factor of 50 per cent to some higher value (with probably an upper practical ceiling of about 65 per cent) by the year 2000. About 20 per cent capacity is considered a reasonable stand-by reserve to ensure reliability of service. The actual size of such a reserve could be reduced if plant availability could be improved. If the full impact of such load management could be achieved, it would reduce the projected increase in electric power plants by about one-fourth, a very significant goal for reducing our capital needs.

There are only two new energy sources that conceivably could be significant by year 2000, solar and geothermal stations. Except for dry-steam geothermal energy (a very scarce resource), neither of these resources is yet in a initial commercial stage that would permit a good estimate of their growth. The principal contribution of solar energy during this time period will be in the heating of new residential and commercial buildings; the possible result being a slight reduction in electricity load demand for such purposes (with less effect on stand-by capacity). Solar-generated electricity is very unlikely to be available as a commercial commodity during this period. Geothermal steam-generated electricity is uncertain because of engineering and hydrothermal resource issues. For the purposes of this analysis, however, the optimistic projections of the Energy Research and Development Administration (ERDA) are used for estimating their possible contribution as shown in the following table. Estimates are for solar thermal and geothermal electricity generation capacities in megawatts (electric).

Resource	*1975*	*1980*	*1985*	*2000*
Geothermal	500	1,000	10,000	40,000
Solar thermal	0	10	1,000	50,000

Even with such optimistic assumptions on the contributions of geothermal and solar thermal energy, coal and nuclear plants must provide over 80 per cent of the electricity generated in the year 2000. No forseeable technology can substantially alter this.

Before leaving this question of new energy sources, it would be well to emphasize the lead time required for a new system to make a significant contribution to a large national energy system. As an optimistic example, Figure 31-10 shows a hypothetical growth pattern of a new power option, assuming that it can be first ordered commercially in 1982 and that it accounts for one-half of all new plants ordered in 1993. Even with such a very rapid introduction, it would represent only 8.2 per cent or less of our national electricity

Figure 31-10. Integration rate of new power options. Hypothetical example, assuming a 40-year plant life, a 5.0 per cent capacity growth rate, and a 8-year construction time.

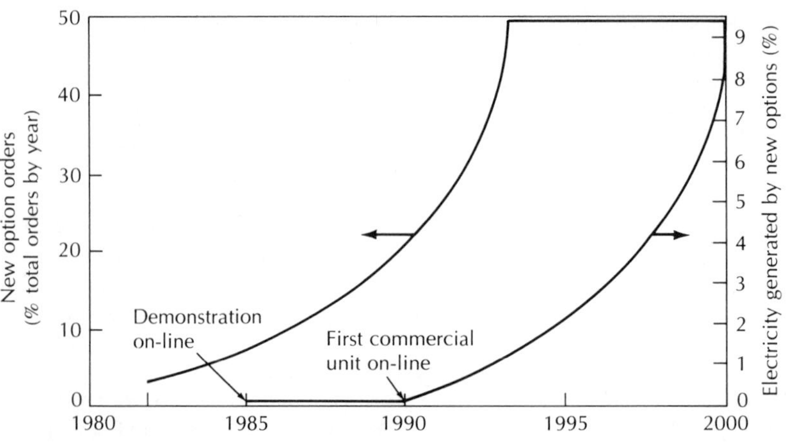

production by the year 2000. This is based on the unlikely assumption that before the first commercial unit ever operates, over 20 per cent of the annual order is for this new plant type. Additionally, assuming a 10-year construction period instead of an 8-year one reduces the year 2000 contribution to 5.3 per cent. The desirability of a diversity of power sources suggests 50 per cent as an upper limit for any single electricity source. These long lead times of 20 years or more for substantial use after development is characteristic of all major innovations.

The year 2000 planning targets for the mix of generating capacity likely to be required are shown in Table 31-6 and Figure 31-11.

From Figure 31-11, we would expect coal development to continue at its historical rate and nuclear power growth to slow somewhat.

Table 31-6. Electricity Needs for Year 2000, Minimum Planning Target.

Energy Source	*1973 Capacity*[a]	*2,000 Capacity*[a]
Coal	167 (39.5)	539 (37.8)
Nuclear	21 (5.0)	539 (37.8)
Oil and gas	172 (40.7)	159 (11.1)
Hydroelectric	62 (14.7)	100 (7.0)
Geothermal	0.5 (0.1)	40 (2.8)
Solar thermal	Nil (Nil)	50 (3.5)
Total	422.5 (100.0)	1427 (100.0)

[a]Capacity in 1,000 megawatts (electric); figures in parentheses are per cent of total.

The assumption that coal-fired and nuclear capacity are equal is arbitrary to some degree, either may increase with a corresponding decrease in the other.

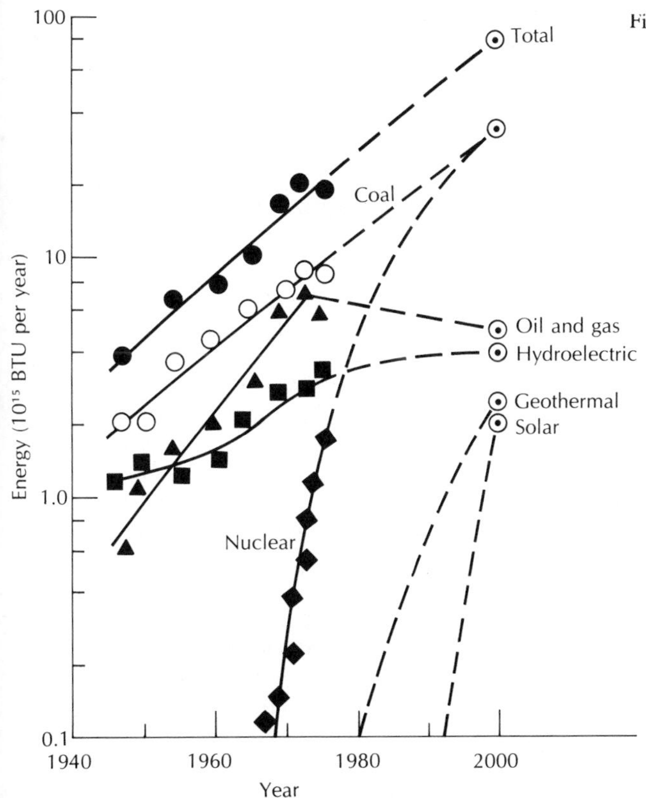

Figure 31-11. Energy input for electricity.

Table 31–7. Estimate of Future Energy Requirements.

	1973	*2000*
Population (millions)	210	263
Employed (millions)	84	113
Energy required (10^{15} BTU per year)		
(a) Historic trend continued	75	170
(b) Reduced for energy conservation		136
(c) Increased for environmental improvement		150

Table 31–9. United States Energy Security Strategy

Short Term (to Year 2000)
- (a) Energy conservation especially in oil and gas
- (b) Increased supplies of readily usable domestic sources—coal and nuclear energy—as electricity

Long Term (Potential beyond Year 2000)
- (a) Explore new energy sources
  1. Solar
  2. Geothermal
  3. Fusion
  4. Others

SUMMARY AND CONCLUSIONS

The energy planning target for the year 2000 is twice the 1973 level of consumption, as shown in Table 31-7. Development of the resources necessary to meet this planning target, as shown in Table 31-8, will require a massive expansion of our use of coal and uranium. Oil and gas usage will increase, but only slowly.

The general conclusions of this study are summarized in Table 31-9. These conclusions are an outgrowth of the following generalizations.

Table 31–8. Estimate of Year 2000 Resource Distribution

Resource	*1973*	*2000*
	(10^{15} BTU per year)	
Electricity		
Coal	8.7	33.0
Nuclear	0.9	33.0
Oil and gas	7.2	5.0
Hydroelectric	2.9	4.0
Geothermal and solar	(neg.)	4.6
Subtotal	19.7	79.6
Direct Fossil Use		
Coal	4.7	9.4
Oil and gas	50.3	61.0
Subtotal	55.0	70.4
Total energy	74.7	150

(1) Societal and economic structures could be substantially and regressively altered by large energy supply constraints, such as might result from very high costs or limited availability. Because of the past availability of energy at relatively low cost, social change has occurred at a rate determined principally by other conditions. It is assumed that maintaining the most of such freedom for future social change and options is desired, even though energy prices are destined to rise for numerous reasons. *Therefore, the national electricity production target should be large enough to avoid forceful constraints on energy use.*

(2) Substantial dependence on foreign fuel sources is undesirable for reasons of national security, balance of payments, and unforseeable costs. The apparently limited availability of oil and gas, and their greater utility as a petrochemical base, airplane and auto fuel, and other unique uses, makes it desirable to minimize their use for future electricity growth. *Therefore, energy options must concentrate on national fuel resources available for this purpose—principally coal and uranium.*

(3) Very long lead times, of the order of decades for various systems, are required to appreciably change the national energy mix—either as to forms of energy supply or to forms of energy use (oil, gas, electricity). The historical "time constant" is in the range of 30 to 50 years for new energy sources to

replace or substantially add to energy supplies. This is the time span usually required for the first feasibility demonstration through commercial development to eventual integration into operating systems on a substantial scale. *Therefore, development of credible technical options must be undertaken decades ahead of a targeted need.*

The Potential for Fuel Conservation 32

MARC H. ROSS AND ROBERT H. WILLIAMS 1977

There is great uncertainty about the capacity of the United States to meet its needs for energy at acceptable social costs in the remaining years of this century. Recent studies suggest that we cannot achieve "energy independence" by 1985 if energy demand continues to increase at historical rates, even if aggressive policies are successful in stimulating new domestic supplies of oil or gas. There is also much concern about the long-term availability of oil and gas. The view of M. King Hubbert (see Article 8, this volume), that domestic oil and gas production can be expected to decline indefinitely, is gaining support, although knowledge of the resource base is so poor that determined exploratory efforts may change the outlook. The use of coal and nuclear fission resources presents other problems. Rapidly increasing capital costs for electric generating plants, quality control problems with nuclear power and continuing uneasiness about its risks, and the controversy over the control of sulfur oxide emissions from coal-fired power plants are some of the more pressing problems facing the electric power industry today. With these problems operating in concert, the potential for the expansion of coal and nuclear power, at least for the next decade, is highly uncertain. New resources, such as synthetics from coal and oil from shale, can contribute little to over-all supply by 1985, and there may be factors (such as water availability) that absolutely limit their development.

This gloomy scenario has led to increasing attention to fuel conservation, more popularly known as "energy conservation," where supply and demand are brought into balance by emphasizing demand reduction rather than supply increases.

To most people, fuel conservation means such near-term austerity policies as 55-miles

Dr. Marc H. Ross is professor of physics at the University of Michigan, Ann Arbor, Michigan 48104.

Dr. Robert H. Williams is a research scientist at the Center for Environmental Studies, Princeton University, Princeton, New Jersey 08540.

From *Technology Review*, Vol. 79, No. 4, pp. 49–57, February 1977. Reprinted by permission of the authors and *Technology Review*. Much of the information in this article is based on a summer study by the American Physical Society and on research conducted for the Energy Policy Project of the Ford Foundation. Dr. Ross was director of the A. P. S. study and Dr. Williams was chief scientist for the Energy Policy Project.

per hour speed limits and lowered thermostats in winter. But several recent studies argue for fuel conservation as a long-term goal—a strategy for simultaneously holding down energy costs, stretching out limited fuel resources, minimizing dependence on foreign energy sources, slowing the introduction of nuclear power to allow time for dealing with unresolved nuclear risks, and protecting the environment. These studies contend that we could reduce our annual growth in energy use from the historical average rate of 3.2 per cent to under 2 per cent. An econometric model by the Ford Foundation's Energy Policy Project suggests that their annual growth rate of 1.8 per cent to the year 2000 could be achieved with little adverse economic effect, and a Conference Board report concludes that historical rates of economic growth could persist over the next decade with energy consumption increasing at perhaps only 1.5 per cent per year.

Such economic studies reflect the growing realization that there is considerable energy "fat" in the U.S. economy today. But these studies do not provide an analytical framework for making quantitative estimates of the potential for fuel conservation.

To assess that potential in quantitative terms, we must answer two questions: What are the real technical possibilities, in both the near and the long term? And what policies are needed to overcome institutional obstacles to the more promising options?

Both of these questions are important. Understanding the technological potential for fuel conservation is essential to establishing realistic goals and priorities. And without effective strategies for overcoming institutional obstacles, conservation goals may never be realized.

In this article, we address primarily the first question, putting forth a framework for estimating the technical potential for fuel conservation. We show that this potential is substantial for both the near and the long term.

The use of energy associated with any product is obtained by multiplying two factors: the demand for the product, and the energy required to provide each unit of the product. In this article, we focus our attention on opportunities for reducing the fuel inputs required to meet existing patterns of consumer demands. Thus, we do not consider here fuel conservation associated with life-style changes.

WE CONSUME "AVAILABLE WORK," NOT ENERGY

To make quantitative estimates of the potential for saving fuel, a measure of energy performance is needed. Thermodynamics provides a useful framework in which to introduce such a measure.

Energy is never created or destroyed; only its form is changed as processes go on. For example, when fuel is burned chemical energy is converted to thermal energy; the total energy in the system is unchanged. The second law of thermodynamics—which implies that the "disorderliness" of a system always increases—tells us that these changes can occur in only one direction, such that energy loses its "quality" or capacity for performing tasks.

The best over-all measure of the capacity for doing any task is *work*—the transfer of the highest quality energy from one system to another. Physicist Willard Gibbs gave us the concept of *available work,* a measurable quantity that takes into account the quality as well as quantity of energy transformed in any process.

Consider two systems in the environment of the Earth. Suppose that a quantity of energy E in one system is transformed so as to do work on the other system. The available work is defined as the theoretical *maximum* amount of work that could be done in this conversion.

If the energy E is of the highest quality then the available work is

$$A = E \qquad (1)$$

The gravitational energy stored in water behind a dam and electrical energy are examples of energy of the highest quality. Chemical energy (as given by the heat of combustion) is also high-quality energy, for which the available work is approximately E (typically about 0.9 E). In general, for the highest quality energies we may interchange the terms "energy" and "available work" without substantial error.

However, if the energy E is thermal energy at fixed temperature T, then the available work A is less than E, or specifically

$$A = E(1 - \frac{T_0}{T}) \tag{2}$$

where T_0 is the temperature of the ambient environment, with both T and T_0 given on the absolute temperature scale (that is, in Celsius units with the zero set at -273 °C).

The efficiency of an energy conversion system is usually defined as the amount of desired energy or work provided by the system, divided by the energy input to the system. Because it is based on the first law of thermodynamics, which holds that energy is neither created nor destroyed, this concept of efficiency is often called the "first-law efficiency." This efficiency concept enables one to keep track of energy flows and is thus useful in comparing devices of a particular type. However, it is wholly inadequate as an indicator of the potential for fuel savings. Several examples illustrate this point.

Household furnaces are typically said to have an efficiency of about 0.6, meaning that 60 per cent of the heat of combustion of the fuel is delivered as useful heat to the house. This measure suggests that a 100 per cent efficient device would be the best possible. But this is incorrect because a heat pump could do better.

A heat pump is simply an air conditioner operating in reverse. It extracts heat energy from the out-of-doors and transfers it at a higher temperature to the interior space, thereby making available as heat more than 100 per cent of the electrical energy it consumes.

Air conditioners are rated by a coefficient of performance (COP), which is the ratio of the heat extracted to the electric input. A typical air conditioner has a $COP = 2$ (a 200 per cent efficiency), a measure that provides no hint of the maximum possible performance—a COP much greater than 2.

In the most modern fossil fuel-fired power plants about 40 per cent of the fuel energy can be converted to electrical energy. In this case the maximum theoretical efficiency is less than 100 per cent, because of the limitations set by the second law of thermodynamics.

In all these examples, the efficiency used is only a partial measure of performance. That is because losses of energy quality, in addition to losses of energy, are inherent to any process. Examples of quality losses are heat flow from higher to lower temperature and the mixing of materials. A more useful measure of efficiency, therefore, would take into account both quantity and quality losses and would show how well a particular energy conversion system performs relative to an ideal one in which there is loss of neither quantity nor quality. The available work concept provides a basis for formulating such an efficiency measure.

The first step in formulating a new efficiency measure is to define the task, such as heating a building, propelling an automobile, or producing steel. The available work consumed in carrying out this task is a direct measure of the expenditure of fuel. In an ideal process this available work would correspond to the absolute minimum expenditure of fuel for the task. But a real process involves losses, so that the actual work consumed, A_{act}, is larger than A_{min}. A suitable measure of efficiency, therefore, is

$$\epsilon \equiv \frac{A_{min}}{A_{act}} \tag{3}$$

This equation for efficiency shows that fuel consumption A_{act} can be reduced either by increasing the efficiency or by modifying the task to be performed (that is, by reducing A_{min}). Because this measure of efficiency shows performance relative to what is possible within the constraints of the second law of thermodynamics, it has been called the "second-law efficiency." In what follows we shall use the term "efficiency" in this sense. This efficiency concept was introduced and applied to a wide range of fuel-consumption activities in a recent American Physical Society study.

The distinction between ϵ and the conventional first-law efficiency can be illustrated with the Carnot engine, an idealized device that makes the fullest use possible of heat E extracted from a reservoir at temperature T. For this engine $A_{act} = A_{min}$ and $\epsilon = 1.0$. In contrast, the first-law efficiency is $A_{min}/E < 1$, suggesting erroneously that this ideal heat engine could be improved upon.

The calculation of A_{min} varies with the task. For a task that involves work W (for example, turning a shaft)

$$A_{min} = W \qquad (4)$$

For the transfer of thermal energy E to a reservoir at temperature $T > T_0$ (for example, heating a room)

$$A_{min} = E(1 - \frac{T_0}{T}) \qquad (5)$$

It is noteworthy that in this particular example the minimum available work is actually less than the amount of heat delivered, because the ideal process for delivering heat involves use of a heat pump that extracts thermal energy from the ambient environment.

Second-law efficiencies for fuel-consuming activities throughout the economy can be calculated using equation (3). The results for some important examples are summarized in Table 32-1, which shows that for most activities second-law efficiencies are less than 10 per cent, clear evidence that energy is being used very inefficiently today. (We usually think of efficiency as the ratio of energy or work provided by a particular device to that which was consumed by it. But this conventional measure is wholly inadequate as an indicator of the potential for fuel savings, hence the authors' emphasis on

Table 32–1. Second-law Efficiencies for Energy-consuming Activities.

Energy-consuming Activities (Current Technology)	*Second-law Efficiency (Per Cent)*
Residential and Commercial	
Space heating:	
Fossil-fuel-fired furnace	5
Electric resistive	2.5
Air conditioning	4.5
Water heating:	
Gas	3
Electric	1.5
Refrigeration	4
Transportation	
Automobile	9
Industrial	
Electric power generation	33
Process-steam production	33
Steel production	23
Aluminum production	13

second-law efficiency, the performance relative to that which is possible for a given task.) For example, the typical household oil-fired furnace has a second-law efficiency of only 5 per cent, compared with its first-law efficiency of 60 per cent. The latter figure, often quoted for household furnaces, gives the misleading impression that only a modest efficiency improvement may be possible, whereas the second-law efficiency correctly indicates a 20-fold maximum potential gain.

How close can we expect efficiencies to approach the ideal limit of $\epsilon = 1$? Examination of experience with high-efficiency systems helps provide insight for making judgments about practical long-term goals. Table 32-1 shows that, contrary to the popular misconception that it is inefficient, electric power generation is one of the more efficient conversion processes in the economy today. (It is only when the power generation system is extended to include especially wasteful uses of electricity that the over-all efficiency is often very low; for example, $\epsilon = 0.025$ for electric resistive space heating.) Furthermore, new fossil-fuel-fired plants achieve

ϵ of up to 0.40, and combined-cycle systems now being developed (the heat from combustion is used first to drive a gas turbine-powered generator and the gas turbine exhaust is then used to make steam for a conventional steam turbine) are expected to achieve efficiencies approaching 0.55. All these energy conversion processes start with fuel combustion, for which $\epsilon = 0.70$; so, in a sense, combined cycles may achieve 0.55 out of a possible 0.70 in efficiency.

These high efficiencies are associated with highly engineered, costly, and rather inflexible devices, and they may not represent a practical goal for most systems. Nevertheless, study of a variety of high-efficiency devices and processes, some described below, suggests that goals for ϵ in the range of 0.2 to 0.5 are reasonable for ultimate practical systems. Values at the high end of this range are more likely to be characteristic of highly engineered devices designed for specialized tasks; values at the low end are more likely for flexible, less sophisticated devices suitable for wide applications.

Here are some examples of how these concepts of energy and efficiency demonstrate opportunities for substantial fuel savings arising from both efficiency improvements and task modifications.

BETTER MILEAGE FOR MODERATE SIZE CARS

Consider first the automobile. The task to be performed is the propulsion of a vehicle of given external characteristics (weight, tires, wind resistance, brakes, and so on) under average driving conditions. The efficiency would be the ratio of the theoretical minimum fuel required to perform this task (A_{min}) to the actual amount required by the vehicle in question (A_{act}).

The theoretical A_{min} for today's average 3,600-pound automobile is about 1,000 BTU per mile. This average automobile actually consumes 9,200 BTU per mile (14 miles per gallon), resulting in an efficiency $\epsilon = 0.11$. The American Physical Society study of energy conservation (see references) identified a series of improvements that could be accomplished with today's technology: a better load-to-engine match could yield an efficiency gain from 0.11 to 0.12; and the use of radial tires, modestly improved streamlining, and a 20 per cent weight reduction would reduce A_{min} to 740 BTU per mile. The combined effect would be to reduce fuel consumption to 6,200 BTU per mile (20 miles per gallon). Further improvements possible over the next few years could boost the efficiency to about 0.17 with a more efficient transmission and an improved engine design (Diesel, Rankine, or Stirling), where further improvements in streamlining, development of a better tire/suspension system, and a further 5 per cent weight reduction could bring A_{min} down to 630 BTU per mile. Such improvements could mean that automobiles of the 1990's would differ little in performance from today's cars but would typically travel 30 to 35 miles on a gallon of fuel. The average weight of these cars would be only 25 per cent less than today's average. (Of course, cars smaller than this with comparable fuel economy are being built with present technology.)

WARMING TO THE CONSERVATION TASK

Potential savings in space heating are immense, because there are opportunities for considerably reducing heat losses (i.e., reducing A_{min}) and because present heating system efficiencies are low.

For average U.S. winter weather, the efficiency ϵ of a typical gas furnace system is 0.05, a figure obtained as follows. The task is taken to be the delivery of heat at 86 °F into the useful space of a given building (with the level of insulation specified). According to equation (5), the minimum available work associated with the delivery of heat E, when the outdoor temperature is 40 °F is $A_{min} = 0.084\,E$. Also, we know that, for a furnace that delivers 60 per cent of the energy content of the fuel to the desired space, $E = 0.6\,A_{act}$. Using equation (3) we thus obtain $\epsilon = 0.05$. With a lower outdoor temperature, the efficiency would be higher.

First consider how to reduce the minimum available work (A_{min}) required to heat a typical house. About 60 per cent of the heat losses are from conduction through walls, roof, windows, and floors. The American Physical Society study estimates that with improved insulation and well designed windows these losses could reasonably be cut to below one-third of present values. The remaining 40 per cent of the heat losses are due to heating and humidification of fresh air; studies have shown that typical rates of air exchange in buildings are unnecessarily high, and it is not unreasonable to reduce the ventilation rate some 80 per cent.

These strategies, which could cut total heat losses nearly fourfold, would involve modest innovations in design and development. Such a fourfold reduction would mean that in many buildings no fuel would be needed on average winter days, when a temperature differential of 30 °F is required between outside and inside, to supplement the heat provided by sunlight through windows, by the lights and appliances, and by the body heat of residents.

On colder days a small heat pump or pumps could be used. If outside air is the heat source for an electrically driven heat pump, the heat pump typically delivers two or three times as much heating as is represented in the electricity consumed (that is, $COP = 2$ to 3). If well or lake water (at, say, 55 °F) is used as a heat source, a COP of 4 is achievable today, corresponding to $\epsilon = 0.10$.

The net effect of thermal tightening of the building shell and of using such an efficient heat pump would be to reduce the primary fuel consumption for space heating to one-eighth of that required for a gas furnace heating a house with insulation characteristic of an average house today.

HIGH-RISE COOLING

Consider a typical new office building in New York City with ten stories and one million square feet of office space. Though the efficiency of air conditioning in a typical new office building in New York City is low [likely to be no more than 0.04 on a hot (90 °F) summer day], the easiest way to achieve fuel savings is by reducing the air-conditioning load—i.e., by reducing A_{min}. In this building, only one-sixth of the air-conditioning load is due to heat conduction from the outside and solar radiation through windows. Over half of the load is due to heat generated by lighting (about 6 watts per square foot) and about one-fifth is due to ventilation (20 cubic feet per minute per person).

It is reasonable to reduce illumination levels to 1.5 watts and ventilation to 5 cubic feet per minute; these efforts to reduce A_{min} would cut the total air-conditioning load by more than 50 per cent. (But at least 10 cubic feet per minute of ventilation per person would be required for a building in which smoking is permitted everywhere. In the case of this office building the extra air-conditioning load associated with smoking requires burning 20 gallons of fuel oil each hour at the power plant.) Among further practical modifications, the most significant would be the use of heat exchangers to recover "cool" from exhausted air. Pursuing all these measures would lead to about a 70 per cent reduction in the air-conditioning load.

An alternative to electric central air conditioning is the heat-driven air conditioner based on desiccation. Such a device, with a $COP = 0.73$, offers the potential of substantial savings if solar energy is used as a partial heat source. The use of sunlight incident on a collector covering the roof of the building as a partial heat source for this device, and the adoption of the load reduction measures considered here, could lead to a system in which the total primary fuel consumption for air conditioning was about one-eighth of that in today's large office building with electric-powered air conditioning.

INDUSTRIAL STEAM PRODUCTION

The first-law efficiency for converting fossil-fuel energy to steam in industry is typically an impressive 0.85, but the second-law efficiency is only 0.33 for steam at 400 °F.

Producing steam by burning fuels wastes available work. This is because the high flame temperatures of fuel combustion (up to about 3,600 °F) represent energy of very high quality, but the temperatures required for industrial process steam are typically 400 °F or lower. Substantial fuel savings can be achieved if the high-quality, high temperature energy available from combustion is first used to make electricity in a heat engine, with the "waste" heat from this device used for low temperature process-steam applications. This "cogeneration" of electricity and process steam is an important application of the more general fuel-saving strategy of "cascading," in which the energy available in combustion is sequentially degraded through a series of uses.

The second-law efficiency for cogeneration is typically between 40 and 45 per cent, compared to about 33 per cent for the separate production of steam and electricity. The resulting savings are actually much more impressive when expressed another way. If only the excess fuel beyond that required for steam generation is allocated to power production, the fuel required to produce a kilowatt-hour of electricity is reduced to about one-half of that required in conventional power plants. The national potential is truly great, since process steam is a major energy-consuming activity in the economy, accounting for about 17 per cent of total energy use.

The most promising application of steam-electricity cogeneration appears to be in industrial plants, where electricity could be produced as a by-product whenever steam is needed. A number of cogeneration technologies could be employed. In a steam-turbine system, steam used to drive the power-generating turbine would be exhausted from the turbine at the desired pressure and (instead of being condensed with cooling water, as at a conventional power plant) delivered to the appropriate industrial process. With a gas-turbine system, the hot gases exhausted from a power-generating turbine would be used to raise steam in a waste heat boiler. The gas-turbine system is the more efficient of the two, typically with $\epsilon = 0.45$ compared to $\epsilon = 0.40$ for a steam-turbine system; in addition, because it produces several times as much electricity for a given steam load, the gas-turbine cogeneration system could yield considerably greater total fuel savings than the steam-turbine system.

Recent studies on the over-all potential for cogeneration have been carried out by Dow Chemical Co. and by Thermo Electron Corp. The latter's study shows that by 1985 electricity amounting to more than 40 per cent of today's U.S. consumption (generated with the equivalent of about 135,000 megawatts (electric) of baseload central station generating capacity) could be produced economically with gas turbines as a by-product of process steam generation at industrial sites. Whereas the gas turbines in most common use today must be fueled with gaseous or liquid fuels, it is likely that over the next decade high-pressure fluidized-bed combustors will be available as an economical method of firing gas turbines directly with coal.

To produce power most economically, an industrial installation that generates electricity as a by-product of process steam production would often produce more electricity than could be consumed on-site. Thus the cogeneration unit should be interconnected with a utility and could substitute for some central-station baseload generating capacity. But such an arrangement is often difficult under existing utility policies. Considerable modification of utilities' transmission, control, and perhaps storage systems may be necessary if interconnected cogeneration capacity is developed on a large scale.

The production of process steam as a by-product of power generation at large central station power plants is an alternative to cogeneration at industrial sites. However, such steam production does not lead to a significant increase in ϵ, since only about 1.5 per cent of the available work originally present in the fuel is discharged in the cooling water, which has an average temperature of about 100 °F. If the waste heat is to be useful for industrial processes, power plant operations would have to be modified to produce heat at more useful temperatures (200 to 400 °F). But this would reduce the electrical output, and this change could lead to a net loss of available work unless essentially all the heat were put to effective use.

Not only are the potential gains of by-product steam generation small, but there are serious implementation difficulties as well. Because it is uneconomic to transport steam long distances, steam-using industries would have to be near the power plants from which their heat is supplied, and this is a condition difficult to fulfill. There is also a serious mismatch in time: large central-station power plants require six to ten years for construction and are designed for a quarter century or more of service. For these reasons, industrial cogeneration is favored.

THE OVER-ALL POTENTIAL OF CONSERVATION

Having considered a number of examples, we now turn to an estimate of the over-all fuel savings potential in the economy through adopting measures to increase ϵ and to decrease A_{min}. We take into account technologies that are either commercial now or are likely to be commercial in the near future, so the estimates we make now are less ambitious than some of the potential savings estimates we have made above. Specifically, we ask what U.S. energy consumption would have been in 1973, had we been a nation of energy thrift.

Our conclusion is that the 1973 living standard of the U.S. could have been provided with about 40 per cent less energy (see Table 32-2). Nearly 60 per cent of the potential savings lies in four areas: space conditioning, the automobile, industrial cogeneration of steam and electricity, and commercial lighting. Whereas total consumption of electricity is reduced by only 30 per cent in the hypothetical energy budget for 1973, central-station power generation is reduced by about 60 per cent because of the large amount of power generated by industrial cogeneration and total energy systems.

It is commonly asserted that the automobile offers the greatest opportunities for fuel conservation. Whereas the time scale for substantial improvements is relatively short for the automobile, the present analysis, which is summarized in Table 32-2 points out that there are comparable fuel-saving opportunities in many cases where low-quality, low-temperature heat is required; these areas make up about 40 per cent of U.S. energy use. In typical residential/commercial low-temperature applications (space conditioning, water heating, refrigeration, and so on), efficiencies now in the range of 2 to 10 per cent can be substantially increased. In industrial applications (e.g., process steam) efficiencies are somewhat higher, but opportunities for fuel savings are still substantial. The summary shows that U.S. energy use in 1973—75 $\times$ 10^{15} BTU—could have been only 44 $\times$ 10^{15} BTU had all the authors' conservation proposals been in place. Note that the potential savings associated with a particular conservation measure in this table sometimes depends on the previously listed measures. For example, the savings associated with a reduced air-conditioning load is affected by the previous assumption that all air conditioners are more efficient.

One way to interpret these results is to note that they set the clock back 17 years on energy consumption. That is, growing at the historical rate from the level of this hypothetical energy budget to the actual 1973 level would require 17 years.

We believe that with an aggressive fuel conservation program the fuel-saving technologies of the general type we propose in this table could in fact be brought into use in the United States within two decades. This strongly suggests the possibility of zero energy growth out to the early 1990's without jeopardizing over-all economic growth. Through fuel conservation efforts, the growth in aggregate demand for products would be compensated for by reductions in the average energy required to provide a unit of product.

Table 32–2. Fuel Conservation by Sector.

		Potential Savings (10^{15} BTU)	*Total Energy Demand in 1973 (10^{15} BTU)*	*Hypothetical Energy Demand with Savings (10^{15} BTU)*
Residential Sector				
Replace resistive (electric) heating with heat pump having COP = 2.5		0.60		
Increase air conditioning COP to 3.6		0.40		
Increase refrigerator efficiency by 30 per cent		0.27		
Reduce water heating fuel requirements by 50 per cent		1.07		
Reduce heat losses by 50 per cent with better insulation, improved windows, and reduced infiltration		3.30		
Reduce air conditioning load by reducing infiltration		0.42		
Introduce total energy systems into half of U.S. multi-family units (15 per cent of all housing units)		0.31		
Use microwave ovens for one-half of cooking		0.25		
Totals		6.62	14.07	7.45
Commercial Sector				
Increase air conditioning COP by 30 per cent		0.37		
Increase refrigeration efficiency by 30 per cent		0.20		
Cut water heating fuel requirements by 50 per cent		0.31		
Reduce building lighting energy by 50 per cent				
Direct savings	0.82			
Increased heating requirements	−0.21			
Reduced air conditioning required	0.34	0.95		
Reduce heating requirements by 50 per cent		2.25		
Reduce air conditioning demand through improved insulation (10 per cent)		0.08		
Reduce air conditioning demand 15 per cent by reducing ventilation rate 50 per cent and by using heat recovery		0.10		
Introduce total energy systems into one-third of all units		0.64		
Use microwave ovens for one-half of cooking		0.06		
Totals		4.96	12.06	7.10
Industrial Sector				
Improve housekeeping measures (better management practices with no changes in capital equipment)		3.85		
Use fossil fuel instead of electric heat in direct heat applications		0.17		
Adopt steam/electric cogeneration for one-half of process steam		2.59		
Use heat recuperators or regenerators in one-half of direct heat applications		0.74		
Generate electricity from bottoming cycles in one-half of direct heat applications		0.49		
Recycle aluminum in urban refuse		0.10		
Recycle iron and steel in urban refuse		0.11		
Use organic wastes in urban refuse for fuel		0.70		
Savings from reduced throughput at petroleum refineries		0.87		
Reduced field and transport losses associated with reduced use of natural gas		0.80		
Totals		10.43	29.65	19.22
Transportation Sector				
Improve automobile fuel economy 150 per cent		5.89		
Emphasize fuel savings in other transportation areas (35 per cent savings)		3.20		
Totals		9.09	18.96	9.87
Grand total		31.10	74.74	43.64

Actually, such a focus on 1973 fuel-use patterns tends in two ways to underestimate potential future fuel savings. First, uses such as residential air conditioning and electric resistive space and industrial heating are major growth areas where savings opportunities are substantial; second, fuel-conserving life-style changes not considered here are already taking place. The growing shift to small cars is an especially important example of such a change.

Our analysis shows that efficiencies of fuel use are in general higher in the industrial sector (with ϵ typically in the range 0.15 to 0.35) than elsewhere. This suggests that long-term fuel savings opportunities, beyond those indicated in Table 32-2, may be limited in the industrial sector, though this observation must be tested through careful analysis of the major industrial processes. Of course, substantial industrial fuel savings over the long term could be realized by shifting the mix of economic output from energy-intensive products to those that require less energy per dollar of value added. Such possibilities have not been taken into account here, where we have estimated potential savings only for the existing pattern of demand for goods and services.

In contrast, because efficiencies are at present so low in the residential, commercial, and transportation sectors, technological innovation in these areas could lead to substantial long-term savings beyond those tabulated, if the appropriate research and development is pursued.

What are the economics of fuel conservation measures? Investments in fuel-saving technology are likely to be costly, but as our supplies of low-cost energy resources diminish these costs may well be less than the costs of increasing our energy supply.

If a particular process requires fuel input at an average rate S_0 (in thermal kilowatts per unit of daily output, say) and costs C_0 (in dollars per unit of daily output), and if the corresponding values for the fuel savings option are S and C, then the capital costs of the conservation option can be expressed as

$$\frac{C-C_0}{S_0-S} \tag{6}$$

in dollars per thermal kilowatt saved. This measure of capital costs can be compared to corresponding costs for energy supply options.

We illustrate this with a few examples. Expressing capital costs as 1974 dollars per thermal kilowatt saved, we find that replacing electric resistive heating plus a central air conditioner with a heat pump ($COP = 2.7$) costs \$50 to \$120 per kilowatt saved; retrofitting a house with insulation and storm windows costs \$450 per kilowatt saved; and the installation of waste-heat recovery units on a heat-treating industrial furnace costs \$100. The extra capital required to save fuel with a cogeneration system is in fact negative, except for very small plants, simply because the cost of a suitably large combined system is less than the cost of separate electricity and process steam generating facilities.

By comparison, a large coal or nuclear power plant, along with the associated transmission and distribution system, today costs \$480 to \$650, respectively, per thermal kilowatt of utilized capacity. Only the home retrofitting example is close in capital costs to these investments required for new capacity; it is, in fact, one of the most capital-intensive conservation options. Insulating *new* homes would certainly require less capital.

These numbers are rough, but they illustrate the kinds of calculations that should be performed. A careful comparison is needed of the capital requirements and the life-cycle costs for all major conservation options and the corresponding costs for conventional practices, taking into account the entire system from resource extraction to the point of end use in each case.

RESEARCH OPPORTUNITIES

Research and development opportunities relating to fuel conservation span a wide range, extending from basic physical research through new or improved devices and mate-

Table 32–3. Agenda for New Research and Development.

Buildings	*Transportation*	*Industry*
	Basic Research	
Physiological requirements for energy services (lighting, space conditioning) as a basis for revising standards	Studies of the combustion process and development of advanced diagnostics	Heat transfer at interfaces
		Two-phase flow
Aerodynamic studies of buildings	Improvement of combustion efficiency through use of emulsions of fuel with water or methanol	Transport in membranes
Heat transfer, at a "micro" level, across various boundaries		Solid electrolytes
		Charge transfer at electrolyte/electrode interfaces
	Improved Devices and Materials	
Thermal diodes (insulation with different heat conductivities in different directions)	Advanced engine cycles (Diesel, Rankine, or Stirling)	Solar-diesel steam generator
Building materials with high specific heats for thermal stability	Battery-electric or hybrid Diesel-electric autos	Modulated capacity compressors for heat pumps and refrigeration
	Continuously variable transmission	
Fuel cells for decentralized power generation	Flywheel storage of braking energy	Materials development for high temperatures
New types of windows to control heat loss and insulation	Absorption air conditioning	
	Analysis and Instrumentation of Existing Processes	
Diagnostic instrumentation for research and inspection (e.g., local heat-flux meter, air exchange meter, local air velocity meter)	Instrumentation for user feedback such as a fuel-flow meter or a specific fuel consumption meter (in gallons of gasoline per ton-mile, say)	Determination of second-law efficiencies of industrial processes
Instrumentation for user feedback (e.g., to signal the consumer when he is consuming electricity at the system peak)	Analysis of energy loss modes (air drag, rolling resistance, braking energy) in different types of trucking	Development of indices measuring energy requirements for various kinds of economic activity
	Systems Analysis	
Designs to take advantage of local natural conditions	Strategies for electrification of transportation that would improve electric load factor	Assessment of decentralized versus centralized power generation
Reassessment of practice for designing baseload energy system conditions	Crashworthiness of lighter cars	Materials recycling and reuse of fabricated items in specific industries
	Trade-offs in function among tires, wheels, and suspension, aimed at decreasing rolling resistance	
Time and zone control of lighting and temperature		Combined electric and heating systems: optimization and development of strategies for integration with utilities

rials and analysis and instrumentation for existing devices and physical systems. There is also a need for better understanding of systems problems and institutional and policy issues. Selected examples of research opportunities in the first few categories are presented in Table 32-3.

Whereas it is true that enormous improvements in fuel utilization could be made using existing technology, fuel conservation in the longer term could be greatly enhanced by better understanding of a large number of technological questions. Most of the topics on this agenda for new research and development were suggested in a study of energy conservation mounted in 1975 by the American Institute of Physics.

It is clear that much technology for fuel conservation is available today but is not being widely used because of institutional obstacles. Better understanding of these problems and assessments of alternative plans for overcoming them should be given close attention in fuel conservation research programs. Among the more general institutional problems, high priority should be given to methods for providing citizens with life-cycle-cost information on energy-related purchases (e.g., heating and cooling systems and those appliances that consume large amounts of energy); new institutional arrangements for financing fuel conservation measures (examples include home insulating services provided by a utility, with financing charges added to the fuel bill, and regulations that require mortgages to cover additional investments needed to minimize life-cycle costs); the relative merits of reliance on energy price, regulations, taxes, and subsidies for achieving fuel conservation goals; the implications for fuel consumption of alternative courses for economic development; and economic (especially employment) implications of fuel-conservation policies.

One especially attractive feature of research on fuel conservation is that it tends to be less costly than research and development on fuel supply. Moreover, with adequate funding, the time required to generate useful results should often be short relative to that for supply-oriented research.

PUTTING CONSERVATION ON THE NATIONAL AGENDA

In the years since the "energy crisis" dramatized the problems of U.S. energy supply, little has been done to implement serious fuel conservation programs in the United States or even to mount a significant research and development program in this area. This inaction no doubt reflects in part a general lack of understanding of what can be achieved with fuel conservation technology to balance energy supply and demand. It also reflects the existence of institutional constraints, which tend to reinforce this limited vision.

The authors are confident that a better understanding of the potential for fuel conservation will lead to a change in this situation. We have shown that the potential based on existing technology is large, and we suggest that substantial further long-term opportunities could arise if the appropriate research and development is pursued. One of the nation's highest priorities should be to make these opportunities evident to political and industrial decisionmakers and to citizens generally.

It appears to us that the physical limitations to fuel conservation are considerably less pressing than many of the public risks and capital cost problems posed by substantial increases in energy supply. Furthermore, if our assessment is correct, a shift in emphasis from energy-supply to fuel-conservation technology will involve a net reduction in capital and very likely an increase in productivity of the economy as a whole.

REFERENCES

Council on Environmental Quality, "National Energy Conservation Program: The 'Half and Half Plan,'" March, 1974.

Energy Policy Project of the Ford Foundation, *A Time to Choose: America's Energy Future,* Ballinger, Cambridge, Mass., 1974.

E. A. Hudson and D. W. Jorgenson, "Economic

Analysis of Alternative Energy Growth Patterns, 1975–2000," a report to the Energy Policy Project, Appendix F in the Ford Foundation Study.

John G. Meyers, "Energy Conservation and Economic Growth: Are they Compatible?" *Conference Board Record,* p. 27, February, 1975.

"Efficient Use of Energy, a Physics Perspective," edited by W. Carnahan, K. W. Ford, A. Prosperetti, G. I. Rochlin, A. H. Rosenfeld, M. H. Ross, J. R. Rothberg, G. W. Seidel, and R. H. Socolow, a report of a 1974 summer study held under the auspices of the American Physical Society, in *Efficient Energy Use,* American Institute of Physics, New York, 1975.

J. H. Keenan, *Thermodynamics,* Wiley, New York, 1948.

E. P. Gyftopoulos, L. J. Lazaridis, and T. F. Widmer, *Potential Fuel Effectiveness in Industry,* a report to the Energy Policy Project of the Ford Foundation, Ballinger, Cambridge, Mass., 1974.

Charles A. Berg, "A Technical Basis for Energy Conservation," *Technology Review,* February, 1974, p. 14, and "Conservation in Industry," *Science,* April 19, 1974, p. 264.

R. H. Williams, ed., *The Energy Conservation Papers,* reports prepared for the Ford Foundation's Energy Policy Project, Ballinger, Cambridge, 1975.

"Energy Industrial Center Study," report to the National Science Foundation by Dow Chemical Co., the Environmental Research Institute of Michigan, Townsend-Greenspan and Co., and Cravath, Swaine, and Moore, June, 1975.

S. E. Nydick et al., "A Study of Inplant Electric Power Generation in Chemical, Petroleum Refining, and Paper and Pulp Industries," draft report prepared for the Federal Energy Administration by Thermo Electron Corp., May, 1976.

SUGGESTED READINGS

Hirst, Eric, 1976, Transportation Energy Conservation Policies, *Science 192,* pp. 15–20.

Hirst, Eric, and John C. Moyers, 1973, Efficiency of Energy Use in the United States, *Science 179,* pp. 1299–1304.

Lincoln, G. A., 1973, Energy Conservation, *Science 180,* pp. 155–161.

Ross, Marc H., and Robert H. Williams, 1976, Energy Efficiency: Our Most Underrated Energy Resource, *Bulletin of the Atomic Scientists 32,* pp. 30–38.

Schipper, Lee, 1976, Raising the Productivity of Energy Utilization, *Annual Review of Energy 1,* pp. 455–517.

Energy Strategy: The Industry, Small Business, and Public Stakes 33

AMORY B. LOVINS 1976

Most people and institutions responsible for past U.S. energy policy consider that the future should be the past writ large: that the current energy problem is how to expand supplies (especially domestic supplies) of energy to meet the extrapolated needs of a dynamic economy. Solutions to this problem have been proposed by, among others, ERDA, FEA, the Department of the Interior, Exxon, and the Edison Electric Institute. A composite of the main elements of their proposals might resemble Figure 33-1. This diagram shows a policy of Strength through Exhaustion—that is, pushing hard on all fuel resources, whether oil, gas, coal, or uranium. Fluid fuels (oil and gas) are obtained from present fields, the Arctic, offshore, and imports. More fluid fuels are synthesized from coal, whose mining is enormously expanded both for that purpose and to supplement vast amounts of nuclear electricity. In essence, more and more remote and fragile places are to be ransacked, at ever greater risk and cost, for increasingly elusive fuels, which are then to be converted into premium forms—fluids and electricity—in ever more costly, complex, gigantic, and centralized plants. As a result, while population rises by less than one-fifth over the next few decades, our use of energy would double and our use of electricity would treble. Not fulfilling such prophecies, it is claimed, would mean massive unemployment, economic depression, and freezing in the dark.

I shall consider in a moment whether such energy growth is necessary. But first let me suggest that it is unwise and unworkable. I do not mean by this that it is *politically* unworkable, though I think that is true: most Americans affected by offshore and Arctic oil operations, coal-stripping, and the plutonium economy have greeted these enterprises with a comprehensive lack of enthusiasm, because they correctly perceive the prohibitive politi-

Amory B. Lovins, a consulting physicist, is British Representative of Friends of the Earth, Limited, London, WIV3DG. His publications include *World Energy Strategies: Facts, Issues and Options* and (with Dr. J. H. Price) *Non-Nuclear Futures: The Case for an Ethical Energy Strategy*, Friends of the Earth/Ballinger, Cambridge, Mass. (1975). His latest books are *Soft Energy Paths: Toward a Durable Peace* (1977) and a supplementary anthology of contextual essays and international soft-path case histories, *Energy In Context* (1977), by the same publisher.

Excerpt from the Senate testimony on "Alternative Long-Range Energy Strategies", as found in the Joint Hearing of the Select Committee on Small Business and the Committee on Interior and Insular Affairs, U.S. Senate, 94th Congress. Reprinted with light editing.

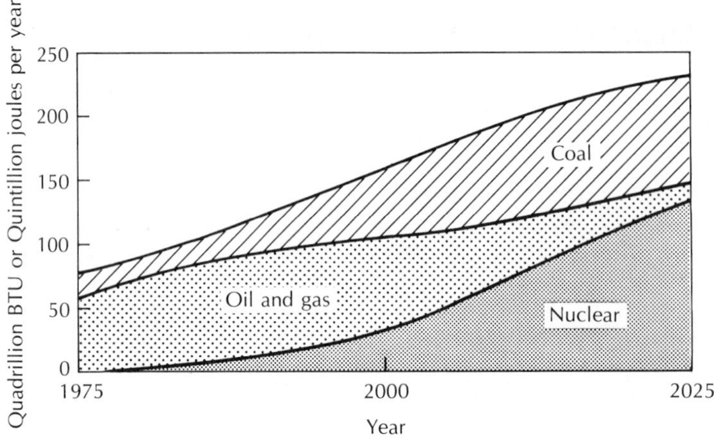

Figure 33-1. An illustrative schematic future for U.S. gross primary energy use.

cal and environmental costs. Nor do I mean that the policy represented by Figure 33-1 is *technically* unworkable, though there is mounting evidence that we lack the skills, industrial capacity, and managerial ability to sustain such rapid expansion of untried and unforgiving technologies. I mean rather that it is *economically* unworkable.

The first six items in Table 33-1 show why. They state the capital investment typically required to build various kinds of complete energy systems to increase delivered energy supplies by the heat equivalent of one barrel of oil per day. As we move from traditional oil and gas and direct-burning coal systems to frontier oil and gas and to synthetic fuels made from coal, the capital intensity of the systems rises by a factor of about ten. As we move from those systems in turn to electrical systems, the capital intensity rises by about a further factor of ten. Such a hundred-fold increase in capital intensity has led many analysts—for example, the Shell Group planners in London—to conclude that no major country outside the Persian Gulf can afford to build these big, complex, high-technology systems on a scale large enough to run a country. The cash flow that electric and synthetic-fuel systems generate is so unsustainable (even for a national treasury) that they are starting to look like future technologies whose time has passed

Because Figure 33-1 relies mainly on the most capital-intensive systems, its first ten years—now through 1985—entail a total capital investment of over one trillion of today's dollars, three-quarters of it for electrification. This sum implies that the energy sector would consume its present quarter of all new private investment in the United States—plus about two-thirds of all the rest. We couldn't even afford to build the things that were supposed to *use* all that energy. Later the burden would grow even heavier.

These astronomical investments would give us so many power stations that, as Professors von Hippel and Williams have shown,[1] we would have to use most of the electricity for very wasteful and economically unjustifiable purposes. Yet because of slow and imperfect substitution of electricity for oil and gas, we would still be seriously short of these indispensable fuels. Even worse, *at least one-half* of our total energy growth in the next few decades would be *lost* in conversions from one kind of energy to another before it ever got to us. The efficiency of the fuel chain would plummet. Serious shortages of capital,

Table 33–1. Approximate Capital Investment (1976 Dollars) Needed to Build an Entire Energy System to Deliver Extra Energy to U.S. Consumers at a Rate Equivalent to One Barrel of Oil per Day (about 67 Kilowatts on an Enthalpic or Heat-supplied Basis).[a]

Traditional direct fossil fuels, 1950s–1960's, or coal, 1970's	$2–3,000[b]
North Sea oil, late 1970's	$10,000
Frontier oil and gas, 1980's	$10–25,000+[b]
Synthetic fuels from coal or unconventional hydrocarbons, 1980's	$20–40,000+
Conventional coal-electric with scrubbers, mid-1980's	$150,000[b]
Nuclear-electric (LWR), mid-1980's	$200–300,000[b]
"Technical fixes" to improve end-use efficiency:	
New commercial buildings	–$3,000[c]
Common industrial and architectural leak-plugging	$0–5,000[c]
Most industrial and architectural heat-recovery systems	$5–15,000[c]
Difficult, extremely thorough building retrofits, worst case	$25,000[c]
Retrofitted 100 per cent solar space heat, mid-1980's, with no backup required, assuming costly traditional flat-plate collectors	$50–70,000[c]
Bioconversion of forestry and agricultural residues, around 1980	$13–20,000
Pyrolysis of municipal wastes, late 1970's	$30,000[d]
Vertical-axis 200-kilowatt-hour (electric), late 1970's	$200,000
Fluidized-bed gas turbine with district heating grid and heat pumps (COP = 2.0), coal-fired, early 1980's	$30,000[c]

[a]The coal-electric, nuclear, and wind systems shown deliver electricity, not heat or fuel. The values given are marginal capital investment to deliver 67 kilowatt-hours regardless of whether it is electric or transient, in accordance with the normal British statistical convention of "heat-supplied basis." As explained in the paper in which these data are derived (A. B. Lovins, "Scale, Centralization, and Electrification in Energy Systems," ORAU symposium "Future Strategies for Energy Development," Oak Ridge, 20-1 October 1976), these data offer a common basis for further computations concerned with specific end-uses. The quality, convenience, reliability, etc., of the form of energy supplied must be taken into account at that time, and this procedure may, for some end-uses, significantly reduce the disparity in capital intensity between electric and other systems. Any attempt, however, to generalize such a result would be invalid and would destroy the universal utility of this data base.

[b]These values can be readily calculated from the data base of the Bechtel Energy Supply Planning Model (1975, updated October 1976).

[c]These values include the capital cost of end-use devices to deliver the desired function.

[d]This value excludes a credit for investment saved in equipment to dispose of the wastes normally and to provide the virgin resources substituted for by those recovered from the wastes.

labor, skills, and materials, as these resources were diverted to the energy sector, would exacerbate inflation. And every "quad" (quadrillion BTU) of primary energy fed into new power stations would *lose* some 75,000 net jobs, because power stations produce fewer jobs per dollar, directly and indirectly, than virtually any other investment in the economy.

The massive diversion of scarce resources into the energy sector would thus worsen, not correct, the economic problems it was intended to prevent. At the same time it would create serious social and political problems. Reallocating scarce resources to priorities that the market is plainly unwilling to support would require a strong central authority with power to override any objections. Political and economic power would concentrate in politically unaccountable oligopolies and bureaucracies. A bureaucratized technical elite, politically remote from energy-users, would operate the complex systems and say who could have how much energy at what price. Centralized energy systems would allocate energy and its side effects to different groups of people at opposite ends of the transmission line or pipeline. As the energy went to Los Angeles or New York and the social costs to Appalachia, Navajo country,

Montana, or the Brooks Range, inequity and alienation would fuel new tensions, pitting region against region, even as a wider and more divisive form of centrifugal politics pitted central siting and regulatory authority against local autonomy.

Energy supplies would depend increasingly on centralized distribution systems vulnerable to disruption by accident or malice. Electrical grids, in particular, distribute a form of energy that cannot readily be stored in bulk, supplied by hundreds of large and precise machines rotating in exact synchrony across a continent, and strung together by a frail network of aerial arteries that can be severed by a rifleman or disconnected by a few strikers. This inherent vulnerability could be reduced only by stringent social controls, similar to those required to protect plutonium from theft, LNG terminals from sabotage, and the whole energy system from dissent. The difficulty, too, of making decisions about compulsory technological hazards that are disputed, unknown, or (often) unknowable would increase the risk that citizens might reject official preferences. Democratic process would thus have to be replaced by elitist technocracy, "we the people" replaced by "we the experts." And over all these structural and political problems would loom the transcendent threat of nuclear violence and coercion in a world dependent on international commerce in atomic bomb materials measured in tens of thousands of bombs' worth per year. The impact of human fallibility and malice on nuclear systems would, I believe, quickly corrode humane values and could destroy humanity itself.

These many side effects of the energy scenario depicted in Figure 33-1 would be even worse in interacting combination than singly. Continued energy waste implies continued U.S. dependence on imported oil, to the detriment of the Third World, Europe, and Japan. We pay for the oil by running down domestic stocks of commodities, which is inflationary; by exporting weapons, which is inflationary, destabilizing, and immoral; and by exporting wheat and soybeans, which inverts Midwestern real-estate markets, makes us mine ground water unsustainably in Kansas, and increases our food prices. Exported American wheat diverts Soviet investment from agriculture into defense, making us increase our own inflationary defense budget, which we have to raise anyhow to defend the sea-lanes to bring in the oil and to defend the Israelis from the arms we sold to the Arabs. Pressures increase for energy- and water-intensive agribusiness, creating yet another spiral by impairing free natural life-support systems and so requiring costly, energy-intensive technical fixes (such as desalination and artificial fertilizers) that increase the stress on remaining natural systems while starving social investments. Poverty and inequity, worsened by the excessive substitution of inanimate energy for people, increase alienation and crime. Priorities in crime control and health care are stalled by the heavy capital demands of the energy sector, which itself contributes to the unemployment and illness at which these social investments were aimed. The drift toward a garrison state at home, and failure to address rational development goals abroad, encourages international distrust and domestic dissent, both entailing further suspicion and repression. Energy-related climatic shifts could jeopardize marginal agriculture, even in our own Midwest, endangering an increasingly fragile world peace.

If it were true, as the proponents of the Figure 33-1 scenario insist that there is no alternative to it, then the prospects for a humane and sustainable energy future would be bleak indeed. But I believe there is another way of looking at the energy problem that can lead us to a very different path: one that is quicker, cheaper, more beneficial to the economy, and politically and environmentally far more attractive. Such an energy path, which I shall call a "soft" path, is illustrated in Figure 33-2. It has three components, which I shall discuss in turn:

(1) greatly increased efficiency in using energy;

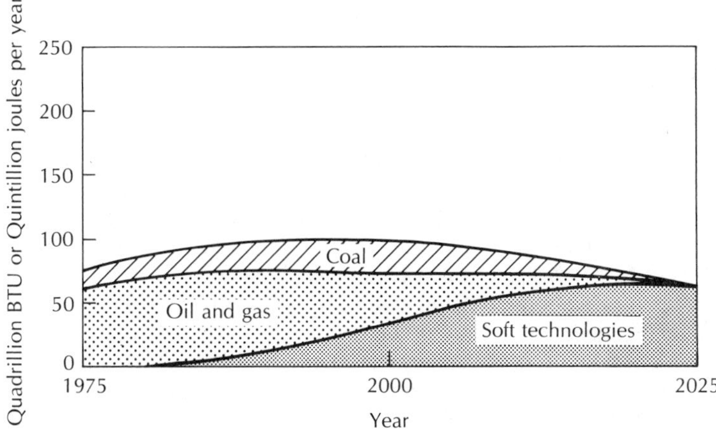

Figure 33-2. An alternate illustrative future for U.S. gross primary energy use.

(2) rapid deployment of "soft" technologies (which I define later); and
(3) the transitional use of fossil fuels.

These three components mesh to make a whole far greater than the sum of its parts: a coherent policy distinguished from the "hard" path of Figure 33-1 not by how much energy we use, but rather by the technical and sociopolitical *structure* of the energy system. This distinction will become clearer shortly.

The hard energy path in Figure 33-1 rests on the belief that the more energy we use, the better off we are. Energy is elevated from a means to an end in itself. In the soft path of Figure 33-2, on the contrary, how much energy we use to accomplish our social goals is considered a measure less of our success than of our failure—just as the amount of traffic we must endure to gain access to places we want to get to is a measure not of well-being but rather of our failure to establish a rational settlement pattern. The cornerstone of Figure 32-2, therefore, is seeking to attain our goals with an elegant frugality of energy and trouble, using our best technologies to wring as much social function as possible from each unit of energy we use.

Many people who have finally learned that energy efficiency does not mean curtailment of functions (that is, that insulating your roof does not mean freezing in the dark) still cling to the bizarre notion that using less energy nevertheless means somehow a loss of prosperity. This idea cannot survive inspection of Table 33-2, which shows how much energy an average person in Denmark used at various times for heating and cooking (over one-half of all end-uses). Looking only at the values for 1900 through 1975, one might be tempted to identify increasing energy use with increasing well-being. But if that were true, the statistics for the years 1800 and 1500 would

Table 33–2. Average Per Capita Primary Energy Consumption in Denmark for Heating and Cooking[a]

Year	*Gigacalories per Year*
ca. 1500	7–15
1800	7
1900	3
1950	7
1975	17

[a]Source: "Energy in Denmark 1990–2005: A Case Study," Report #7, Survey by The Work Group of The International Federation of Institutes for Advanced Study, c/o Sven Bjørnholm, The Niels Bohr Institute, The University of Copenhagen, September 1976.

imply that Danes have only just regained the prosperity they enjoyed in the Middle Ages. Deeper analysis shows what is really happening. In 1500 and 1800, Denmark had a wood and peat economy, and most of the heat went up the chimney rather than into the room or cooking-pot—just as it does in the Third World today. In 1900, Denmark ran on coal, burned efficiently in tight cast-iron stoves. In 1950, Denmark used mainly oil, incurring refinery losses to run inefficient furnaces. In 1975, the further losses of power stations were added as electrification expanded. This example shows that a facile identification of primary energy use with well-being telescopes several complex relationships that must be kept separate. How much primary energy we use—the fuel we take out of the ground—does not tell us how much energy is delivered at the point of end-use, since that depends on how efficient our energy system is. End-use energy, in turn, says nothing about how much function we perform with the energy, for that depends on our end-use efficiency. And how much function we perform says nothing about social welfare, which depends on whether the thing we did was worth doing.

I shall suggest in a moment that a rational energy system can virtually eliminate conversion and distribution losses that rob us of delivered end-use energy. But let me focus first on the efficiency with which that end-use energy can do our tasks for us. There is ample technical evidence that Americans can double this efficiency by about the turn of the century by using only "technical fixes"—that is, measures which (a) are now economic by orthodox criteria, (b) use today's technologies (or, more often, 1920's technologies), and (c) have no significant effect on life-styles. Such measures include thermal insulation, more efficient car engines, heat recovery in industrial processes, and cogeneration of electricity as a by-product of process heat.

Over the 50 years shown in Figure 33-2—long enough to turn over much of the stock of buildings and equipment—we can use technical fixes *alone* to treble or quadruple our end-use efficiency, yielding a convex curve of the type shown despite normally projected growth in population, economic activity, comfort, and equity. People who consider today's values and institutions imperfect are free to obtain the same result by some mix of technical and social changes—perhaps substituting repair and recycling for the throw-away economy, or gradually shifting settlement patterns and concepts of work so as to keep voluntary mobility from being swamped by involuntary traffic. But our end-use efficiency can be improved to and beyond present European levels *entirely* through technical measures if we wish, saving both money and jobs in the process. Table 33-1 shows that conservation is far cheaper than increasing supply. Both technical fixes (such as insulation programs) and shifts toward less energy-intensive consumption patterns produce far more long-term jobs, using existing skills, than alternative supply investments can. Recent input-output studies suggest that conservation programs and shifts of investment from energy-wasting to social programs create anywhere from tens of thousands to nearly a million net jobs per quad saved.

The top curve of Figure 33-2, showing total energy needs of, say, 95 quads in the year 2000, is by no means the lowest that can be realistically considered. Projections are dropping rapidly. Dr. Alvin Weinberg's group at Oak Ridge projects for 2000 a primary energy demand of 101 to 126 quads—the lower value being more likely—even with a modest conservation program. But Dr. Weinberg's end-use energy projections are much *lower* than mine, since he assumes a half-electric economy. Further, a major National Academy of Sciences study is now taking seriously a year-2010 technical-fix projection of around 70 quads of primary energy. One panel is even proposing a value around 40 to 50 quads by assuming some life-style changes that could arguably improve the quality of life far more than the life-style changes of a high-energy path.

The second major component of the soft

path shown in Figure 33-2 is the rapid deployment of soft energy technologies, which I define by five characteristics:

(1) They are diverse. Just as the national budget is paid for by many small tax contributions, so the soft-technology component of energy supply is made up of small contributions by many diverse technologies, each doing what it does best and none trying to be a panacea.

(2) They operate on renewable energy flows—sun, wind, forestry or agricultural wastes, and the like—rather than on depletable fuels.

(3) They are relatively simple and understandable. Like a pocket calculator, they can be highly sophisticated, but are still technologies we can live with, not mysterious giants that are alien and arcane.

(4) They are matched in *scale* to end-use needs.

(5) They are matched in *energy quality* to end-use needs.

These last two points are very important, and I must amplify each in turn.

First, scale: we are used to hearing that energy facilities must be enormous to take advantage of the economies of scale. But we are seldom told about the even greater *dis*-economies of scale. There are at least five main kinds:

(1) Big systems cannot be mass-produced. If we could mass-produce power stations like cars, they would cost less than one-tenth as much as they do now, but we can't.

(2) Big systems, being centralized, require very costly distribution systems. In 1972, out of every dollar that U.S. residential and commercial users of electricity paid to private utilities, only about 31¢ went for electricity; the other 69¢ went for having it delivered. That is a major diseconomy of centralization.

(3) Associated with the distribution system is a pervasive web of energy losses in distribution.

(4) Big energy facilities tend to be much less reliable than small ones, and unreliability is a graver fault in a big than in a small unit, requiring more and costlier reserve capacity. The unreliability of the distribution system compounds this problem, and can make a unit of generating capacity some 2.5 times less reliable (from the user's point of view) if sited in a central power station than if locally sited in a small station.

(5) Big energy facilities take a long time to build and are therefore especially exposed to interest costs, escalation, mistimed demand forecasts, and wage pressure by unions, which know the high cost of delay.

Other diseconomies of large scale, less expressible in economic terms, are also important. For example, big systems entail the high political costs of centrism and vulnerability that I mentioned earlier. Big systems magnify the cost and likelihood of mistakes. Big systems are also too costly and complex for technologists to play with, so an important wellspring of inventiveness and ingenuity is dried up. But even ignoring these qualitative effects, one can use orthodox economics, as I have done in the Oak Ridge paper, to reach a basic and perhaps surprising conclusion: that, in general, soft energy technologies are *cheaper* than the big "hard" energy technologies one would otherwise have to use in the long run to do the same job. Thus, as can be calculated from Table 33-1, a completely solar retrofitted space-heating system, with seasonal heat storage and no backup, has a lower capital cost than a nuclear-electric and heat-pump system to heat the same house; it also has a lower life-cycle cost than a coal-synthetics and furnace system to heat the same house. Making vehicle fuel from forestry and agricultural wastes is generally cheaper than making similar fuels from coal. And so it goes: even using today's rather cumbersome art, the soft technologies compete favorably with their long-run alternatives.

This is not to say that solar heat can always compete with unrealistically cheap gas; but that is irrelevant, for the days of cheap gas are

Table 33-3. Per Cent End-use Energy (Heat-supplied Basis) Classified by Physical Type, *ca.* 1973.

Type	*United States*		*Canada*[a]		*United Kingdom*[a]	
Heat	58%		69%		65%	
Below 100 °C		35%		39%		55%
100 °C and above		23%		30%		10%
Mechanical work	38%		27%		30%	
Vehicles		31%		} 24%		} 27%
Pipelines		3%				
Industrial electric drive		4%		3%		3%
Other electrical	4%		4%		5%	

[a]Preliminary and approximate data; probably within ·5 per cent for Canada and 10 per cent for the United Kingdom.
Source: United States data calculated in A. B. Lovins, "Scale, Centralization, and Electrification in Energy Systems," ORAU symposium "Future Strategies for Energy Development," Oak Ridge, 20-1 October 1976. Canadian data based on sources cited in A. B. Lovins, "Exploring Energy-Efficient Futures for Canada," *Conserver Society Notes* 1, 4, 5–16 (May/June 1976), Science Council of Canada (150 Kent St, Ottawa). British data estiamted by A. B. Lovins from official statistics, including Census of Production data, and consistent with estimates by the Energy Research Group of The Open University (see, *e.g.*, *Energy Policy*, September 1976).

numbered. Congress has already been asked for billions of dollars to subsidize the synthesis of gas from coal at perhaps $25 per barrel equivalent. Of course the soft technologies would have to be financed at the household, neighborhood, or town scale at which they would be built; but capital transfer schemes already in use can give even householders the same kind of access to capital markets that oil majors and utilities now enjoy.

Soft energy technologies are matched to end-use needs not only in scale but also in energy quality. Table 33-3 classifies our end-use needs by physical type. About 58 per cent is in the form of heat, of which 35 per cent is below and 23 per cent above the boiling point of water. A further 38 per cent is mechanical work—31 per cent to move vehicles, 3 per cent to pump fluids through pipelines, and 4 per cent to drive industrial electric motors. The remaining 4 per cent represents *all* lighting, electronics, telecommunications, smelting, electroplating, arc-welding, electric railways, electric drive for home appliances, and all other uses of electricity other than low-grade heating and cooling. Electricity is a very expensive form of energy: Americans already pay typically from $40 to $120 per barrel equivalent for it. The premium applications in which we can get our money's worth out of this special kind of energy total only about 8 per cent of all our end-uses. With improved efficiency, that 8 per cent would shrink to about 5 per cent, which we could cover with our present hydroelectric capacity plus a modest amount of industrial cogeneration. That is, we could advantageously be running this country with no central power stations at all—if we used electricity only for tasks that can use its high quality to advantage, so justifying its high cost in money and fuels. Those limited premium tasks are already far oversupplied, so if we make more electricity we can only use it for inappropriate low-grade purposes. That is rather like cutting butter with a chainsaw—which is inelegant, expensive, messy, and dangerous.

This thermodynamic philosophy saves us energy, money, and trouble by supplying energy only in the quality needed for the task at hand: supplying low temperature heat directly, not as electricity or as a flame temperature of thousands of degrees. Thus, our task is not to find a substitute to produce 1,000-megawatt blocks of electricity if we don't build reactors, but rather to perform directly the tasks we would have performed with the oil and gas for which the reactors were supposed to substitute in the first place. By thus matching energy quality to end-use we can virtually eliminate conversion losses, just as matching scale virtually eliminates distribution losses. These two kinds of losses together make up *more than one-half* of the total energy used at the right-hand end of Figure 33-1, yet are all but absent at the same point in Figure 33-2. Delivered end-use energy is not very different in the two diagrams in the year 2025, but it performs several times as much social function in Figure 33-2 as in Figure 33-1, with a corresponding advantage in conventionally defined social welfare. We would literally be doing better with less energy.

Extremely rapid recent progress in developing soft technologies has produced a wide range of technically mature systems—ones that face no significant technical, economic, environmental, social, or ethical obstacles and require only a modicum of sound product engineering. We already have enough mature soft technologies to meet essentially all our energy needs in about 50 years, using only convenient, reliable systems that are already demonstrated and are already economic or very nearly so. This does not assume cheap photovoltaic systems (which will probably soon be, or may already be, available), nor indeed any other solar-electric technologies. Living within our energy income requires only the appropriate use of straightforward solar heat technologies, organic conversion to clean liquid fuels for vehicles, modest amounts of wind collection (mainly non-electrical), and currently installed hydroelectric capacity.

I believe a *prima facie* case has been made that we already know enough to start planning an orderly transition to essentially complete reliance on soft energy technologies. But this transition, or indeed any other, will take a long time—perhaps 50 years—so we must build a bridge to our energy-income economy by briefly and sparingly using fossil fuels, including modest amounts of coal, to buy time. We know how to do this more cleanly and efficiently than we are doing now, with technologies flexibly designed so that we can plug into the smaller soft technologies as they come along. Simple, flexibly scaled technologies are also rapidly emerging for cleanly extracting premium liquid and gaseous fuels from coal, so filling the real transitional gaps in our fluid-fuel economy with only a temporary (and less than twofold) expansion of coal mining. We can thus squeeze the "oil and gas" wedge in Figure 33-2 from both sides, making its middle section more slender than that of Figure 33-1 and thereby eliminating much medium-term importing and frontier extraction.

Figure 33-2, in summary, shows a different path along which our energy system can evolve from now on. This path does not suggest wiping the slate clean, but rather redirecting our effort at the margin, thus freeing disproportionate resources for other tasks. It does not abolish big technologies, but rather concedes that they have a limited place, which they have long since saturated, and proposes that we can take advantage of the big systems we already have without multiplying them further. Because the long lead time of big systems means that many power stations are now under construction, we can use that backlog, current overcapacity, and the potential for rapid industrial cogeneration to ensure adequate supplies of electricity before improved efficiency starts to bear fruit.

Having these two energy paths before us in outline permits some illuminating comparisons. First, in rates: it appears that the soft and transitional technologies are much quicker to deploy than the big high technologies of Figure 33-1, because the former are so much smaller, simpler, easier to manage, and less dependent on elaborate infrastructure. For fundamental engineering reasons, their lead times are measured in months, not decades. For similar reasons, as I suggested earlier, they are also likely to be substantially cheaper than hard technologies. They are environmentally far more benign, and bypass the risk of major climatic change from burning fossil fuel. And they are more certain to work, since the risk of technical failure in the soft path is distributed among a large number of simple, diverse technologies that are in general already known to work and that require an especially forgiving kind of engineering. The hard energy path, in contrast, puts all its eggs in a few brittle baskets—fast breeder reactors and giant coal-gas plants, for example—which are not here and may or may not work.

Hard and soft technologies have very different implications for technologists. Hard technologies are demanding and frustrating. They are not much fun to do and are therefore unlikely to be done well. Although they strain technology to (and beyond) its limits, the scope they offer for innovation is of a rather narrow, routine sort, and is buried within huge, anonymous research teams. The systems are beyond the developmental reach of all but a few giant corporations, liberally aided by public subsidies, subventions, and bailouts. The disproportionate talent and money devoted to hard technologies gives their proponents disproportionate influence, reinforcing the trend and discouraging good technologists from devoting their careers to soft technologies—which then cannot absorb funds effectively for lack of good people. And once hard technologies are developed, the enormous investments required to tool up to make them effectively exclude small business from the market, thus sacrificing rapid and sustained returns in money, energy, and jobs for all but a small segment of society.

Soft technologies have a completely different character. They are best developed by innovative small businesses and even individuals, for they offer immense scope for basically new ideas. Their challenge lies not in complexity but in simplicity. They permit but do not require mass production, thus encouraging local manufacture, by capital-saving and labor-intensive methods, of equipment adapted to local needs, materials, and skills. Soft technologies are multipurpose and can be integrated with buildings and with transport and food systems, thus saving on infrastructure. Their diversity matches our own pluralism: there is a soft energy system to match any settlement pattern. Soft technologies do not distort political structures or priorities; they improve the quality of work by emphasizing personal ingenuity, responsibility, and craftsmanship; they are inherently nonviolent, and are therefore a livelihood that technologists can have good dreams about.

Soft technologies, unlike hard ones, are compatible with the modern concept of indigenous eco-development in the Third World. They directly meet basic human needs—heating, cooking, lighting, pumping—rather than supplying a costly, high-technology form of energy with imported, capital-intensive, high-technology systems that can only enrich urban elites at the expense of rural villagers. Soft technologies would thus contribute promptly and dramatically to world equity and order. A soft energy path would also do more than a hard path to reduce pressure on world oil and coal markets and to avoid global capital shortages.

An even more important geopolitical side effect of U.S. leadership in a soft energy path is that it promotes a world psychological climate of denuclearization, in which it comes to be viewed as a mark of national immaturity to have or desire either reactors or bombs. Nuclear power programs and their web of knowledge, expectation, and threats are now the main driving force behind proliferation of nuclear weapons. Yet foreign nuclear programs require a domestic political base, both public and private, that does not yet exist and must be borrowed from the United States. Ten years' residence in Europe has led me to the firm political judgment that unilateral U.S. action to encourage soft energy paths at home and abroad, in tandem with new initiatives for nonproliferation and strategic arms reduction, could turn off virtually all foreign nuclear power programs and could thus go very far to put the nuclear genie back into the bottle from which we first coaxed it to emerge. Three decades after we secretly chose a fateful path, which we then tried to force on the world, we can again lead the world by openly choosing, and freely helping others to choose, a path of prudence. But this shift of policy is urgent: we must stop passing the buck before our clients start passing the bombs.

If nuclear power were phased out, here or abroad, but no other policy were changed, the economic, environmental, and sociopolitical costs of centralized electrification would still be intolerable—even with energy conservation. As I suggested earlier, the key distinction between the soft and hard energy paths is in their architecture, the structure of the energy system, rather than in the amount of energy used. Both paths entail difficult social problems of very different kinds: for the hard path, autarchy, centrism, technocracy, and vulnerability; for the soft path, the need to adapt our thinking to use pluralistic consumer choice, participatory local democracy, and resilient design to substitute a myriad small devices and refinements for large, difficult projects under central management. We must choose which of the two kinds of social problems we want. But the problems of the hard path can only be addressed much less pleasantly, less plausibly, and less consistently with traditional values than the more tractable problems of the soft path. The problems of the hard path, too, become steadily harder, whereas those of the soft path become gradually easier.

I believe that to a large extent the soft path would be self-implementing through ordinary market and social processes once we had taken a few important initial steps, including:

(1) Correcting institutional barriers to conservation and soft technologies, such as obsolete building codes and mortgage regulations, lack of capital-transfer schemes, restrictive utility practices, and lack of sound information.

(2) Removing subsidies to conventional fuel and power industries, now estimated at well over $10 billion per year, and vigorously enforcing antitrust laws.

(3) Pricing energy at a level consistent with its long-run replacement cost. I believe this can be done in a way that is both equitable and positively beneficial to the economy, since unrealistically cheap energy is an illusion for which we pay dearly everywhere else in the economy.

I do not pretend that these steps will be easy; only easier than not taking them. Properly handled, though, they can have enormous political appeal, for the soft energy path offers advantages for every constituency: jobs for the unemployed, capital for businesspeople, environmental protection for conservationists, enhanced national security for the military, opportunities for small business to innovate and for big business to recycle itself, exciting technologies for the secular, a rebirth of spiritual values for the religious, world order and equity for globalists, energy independence for isolationists, civil rights for liberals, states' rights for conservatives. Though a hard energy path is consistent with the interests of a few powerful American institutions, a soft path is consistent with far more strands of convergent social change at the grassroots. It goes with, not across, our political grain.

The choice between the soft and hard paths is urgent. Though each path is only illustrative and embraces an infinite spectrum of variations on a theme, there is a deep structural and conceptual dichotomy between them. They are not *technically* incompatible: in principle, nuclear power stations and solar collectors could coexist. But they are *culturally* incompatible: each path entails a certain evolution of social values and perceptions that makes the other kind of world harder to imagine. The two paths are *institutionally* antagonistic: the policy actions, institutions, and political commitments required for each (especially for the hard path) would seriously inhibit the other. And they are *logistically* competitive: every dollar, every bit of sweat and technical talent, every barrel of irreplaceable oil that we devote to the very demanding high technologies is a resource that we cannot use to pursue the elements of a soft path urgently enough to make them work together properly. In this sense, technologies like nuclear power are not only unnecessary but a positive encumbrance, for their resource commitments foreclose other and more attractive options, delaying soft technologies until the fossil fuel bridge has been burned. Thus we must, with due deliberate speed, choose one path or the other, before one has foreclosed the other or before nuclear proliferation has foreclosed both. We should use fossil fuels—thriftily—to capitalize a transition as nearly as possible straight to our ultimate energy-income sources because we won't have another chance to get there.

To fix these ideas more firmly, I should like now to sketch an example from one of the approximately ten other countries in which soft path studies are under way: Canada, whose energy system is strikingly similar to that of the United States. This example comes from a study[2] I did last March in the Canadian Ministry of Energy, Mines, and Resources under the auspices of the Science Council of Canada. The data are theirs, the conclusions my own.

Figure 33-3 shows the approximate structure of energy use in Canada. Use by economic sector and by source broadly resembles our own, except that Canada has proportionately more hydroelectricity. The middle bar, showing the thermodynamic structure of end-use, reveals that, as in the United States, end-use needs are mostly heat (especially at modest temperatures) and liquids. Indeed, the electrical uses other than low-grade heating and cooling are such a small term that, on an aggregated basis, they *and* all high temperature heat could be supplied by present hydroelectricity.

The Canadian Cabinet has approved technical fixes to improve end-use efficiency. The Ministry calculates that these measures, now being implemented, should hold primary energy use for the commercial and transport sectors and for heating houses roughly constant over the next 15 years despite normally projected growth in population and in sectoral economic activity. However, 15 years is really too short a time for these measures to bear much fruit, since it takes much longer to turn over the stock of buildings and equipment. I therefore looked ahead 50 years—about the end of the lifetime of a power station ordered today. I assumed population and economic growth similar to official projections (with minor and unimportant exceptions), plus technical fixes of the moderate, straightforward type already being implemented. The

Figure 33-3. Canadian energy use in 1973 (population, 22 million).

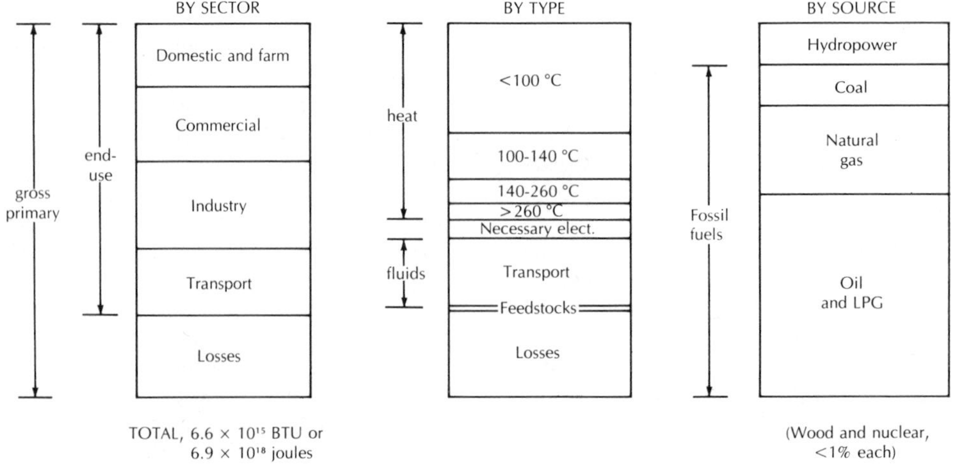

result over 50 years was a shrinkage of per capita primary energy to one-half today's level, or about the present Western European level.

I also applied the same technical fixes not to a standard growth scenario but instead to the per capita activity levels of 1960—which might be a very rough surrogate for a luxurious form of "conserver society." This calculation yielded a further factor-of-two shrinkage, to a quarter of today's level or about the present New Zealand level.

I then returned to my original, higher set of estimates of energy needs for 2025, based on approximately a normal growth projection, and constructed a conservative estimate (exaggerating high-grade needs) of its end-use structure. The result is the middle bar of Figure 33-4, with the current structure on the left for comparison. On the right side of Figure 33-4 I have drawn to the same scale some building-blocks of supply.

The block marked "hydro" is the minimum hydroelectric output already firmly committed for 1985, not counting James Bay. It exceeds the appropriate electrical uses in 2025. Below it is a minor contribution from roughly the present level of rural wood-burning and from pyrolysis, anaerobic digestion, burning energy studies, and so on.

At the lower right in Figure 33-4 I have assumed that 50 years is long enough to meet essentially all low temperature heat needs with solar technologies. These are already technically and economically attractive in Canada, and the real question is not viability but deployment rate. If you think 50 years is not long enough to deploy all those devices, you are free to choose a target date later than 2025 and stretch out the transition. The 50 years is merely a first guess.

On the far right side of Figure 33-4 is a box labeled "liqwood." This is the name and number given by the Canadian Forestry Service to the net amount of fuel alcohols that they think they could sustainably produce from forestry. I suspect that closer ecological study will reduce this estimate, but it is still likely to be larger than the liquid fuel requirement for the transport sector (shown in

Figure 33-4. Canadian energy use projected to 2025 (estimated population, 40 million).

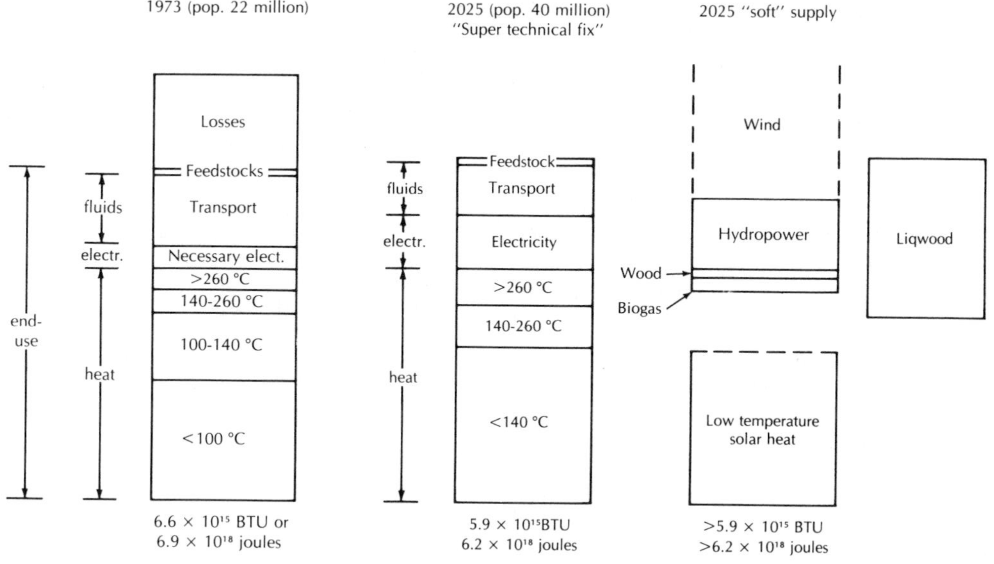

the middle bar), even today (as shown in the left-hand bar).

At the upper right in Figure 33-4 is an open-ended section labeled "wind." It is a very large number, far off-scale. The versatility of wind lets it fit anywhere into the end-use structure—pumping heat, for example, or compressing air to drive industrial machines.

Figure 33-4 suggests on its face that the "hydro" block already committed, plus any two of the other three, will yield *a surplus that matches the structure* of Canadian energy needs in 2025. In practice, one would use a combination of all these sources. The next step in this exercise, which has not yet been done in Canada, is to refine the data, disaggregate by regions, and work backwards from 2025 toward the present to see how to get there. Two things make me expect attractive results. First, such a study has already been done in countries less well placed than Canada, such as Denmark and Japan, and the transition looks quicker and cheaper than present policy. Second, if one pairs off the soft energy supply technologies with the hard technologies that one would otherwise have to use in the long run to do the same job, the soft ones are cheaper; this is also true for the conservation and transitional technologies; so when one adds them all up they should still be cheaper.

The value of thinking backwards in this way from where one wants to be in the long run—the right-hand end of Figure 33-2—is that it reveals the potential for radically different paths that would be completely invisible to anyone who merely worked forwards in time through incremental *adhocracy*. Such a person could only discover, perhaps, in 2010 that we might have gone in a very different direction if we had thought of it in 1980 before it was too late. To avoid such a trap we must be unabashedly normative in exploring our goals, then figure out how to achieve them, rather than blindly extrapolating trend into destiny.

Of course, in this short article, I cannot do justice to the richness of the technical background; but I hope I have conveyed the impression that the basic issues in energy strategy, far from being too complex and technical for ordinary people to understand, are on the contrary too simple and political for experts to understand. I believe that as this nation enters its third century we must concentrate on these simple, yet powerful concepts if we are not only to gain a fuller understanding of the consequences of choice, but also to appreciate the very wide range of choices that is available. Only thus can we learn, as Robert Frost did, that taking the road less traveled by can make all the difference.

REFERENCES

1. Von Hippel, Frank, and Robert H. Williams, 1976, Energy Waste and Nuclear Power Growth, *Bulletin of the Atomic Scientists 32*, pp. 18–21, 48–56.
2. Lovins, Amory B., 1976, Energy Strategy: The Road Not Taken, *Foreign Affairs 55*, pp. 65–90.

SUGGESTED READINGS

Lovins, Amory B., 1975, *World Energy Strategies: Facts, Issues and Options* (Friends of the Earth/Ballinger, Cambridge, Mass.).

Lovins, Amory B., and J. H. Price, 1975, *Non-nuclear Futures: The Case for an Ethical Energy Strategy* (Friends of the Earth/Ballinger, Cambridge, Mass.).

Lovins, Amory B., 1976, Scale, Centralization and Electrification in Energy Systems, *Future Strategies of Energy Development Symposium*, Oak Ridge Associated Universities, October 20–21.

Lovins, Amory B., 1977, *Soft Energy Paths: Toward a Durable Peace* (Friends of the Earth/Ballinger, Cambridge, Mass. and Penguin, United Kingdom).

Lovins, Amory B., 1977, *Energy in Context* (Friends of the Earth/Ballinger, Cambridge, Mass.).

A Low Energy Scenario for the United States: 1975–2050 34

JOHN S. STEINHART, MARK E. HANSON, ROBIN W. GATES, CAREL C. DEWINKEL, KATHLEEN BRIODY, MARK THORNSJO, AND STANLEY KABALA 1977

INTRODUCTION

The scenario outlined in this article is an estimate of the lowest energy use future the authors consider plausible. The plausibility criterion is applied by eliminating those possible futures that require technological miracles, dramatic changes in human behavior, or complete restructuring of national and/or world political groupings. The results indicate that a 64 per cent reduction in U.S. energy use per capita from 1975 levels can be obtained a few decades into the 21st century.

We have attempted to incorporate and extrapolate demographic and settlement relocation trends and to identify some other private trends that might be usefully encouraged. The legislative measures dicussed have been proposed at state or federal levels already, although some may be far from enactment now. The changes of life-style implicit in this scenario combine present trends with subjective estimates of how far they might proceed.

We have tried to point out some of the economic and employment implications of the scenario. Quantitative economic analysis is not attempted because such analysis is very sensitive to the projections of future discount rates and future fuel price increases. Plausible (and published) estimates of these two variables differ sufficiently to produce net discount rates for energy costs (rates of deflated energy cost increase minus discount rate) that are either positive or negative. Resolution of

Original article by Dr. John S. Steinhart and others. Dr. Steinhart is professor of geology and geophysics and environmental studies at The University of Wisconsin-Madison, Madison, Wisconsin 53706.

Mark E. Hanson holds degrees in ecomonics and water resources management and is the author of a number of publications on energy. Robin Gates holds degrees in resource management and public administration and currently works for the Wisconsin Department of Natural Resources. Carel C. DeWinkel holds degrees in physics and civil and environmental engineering and is currently studying wind-electric systems. Kathy Briody is a graduate student in oceanography studying marine policy. She holds a degree in biology. Mark Thornsjo is a graduate in urban and regional planning and is currently employed in utility planning by Northern States Power Company. Stanley Kabala holds a joint degree in urban planning and public administration and is currently a regional planner in Pennsylvania.

This original article is based on a paper titled *A Scenario for Reduced Energy Use and Conservation in the United States: 1975–2050* presented at the American Association for the Advancement of Science Annual Meeting in Denver, Colorado, February 21, 1977.

these differences requires at least some agreement about the quantitative role of energy price increase in general inflationary pressures. These relationships are disputed.

This scenario is not proposed as a plan. It is offered as one of a growing number of such possibilities in the hope that the arena of public discussion may be enlarged.

Any normative scenario of the future assumes a backdrop of world and domestic conditions as the context in which the scenario's plausibility may be tested. No scenario of modest size can hope to describe even the complexity of the present, let alone the complexities of an inherently unknowable future. The result is that a scenario leaves out more of the future conditions than it describes. Although there is no satisfactory escape from the dilemma, it may be useful to the reader to draw attention to some views of the future that are in agreement with this scenario and that have contributed to the views expressed.

The resource pressure outlined by Forrester,[1] Meadows,[2] and Mesarovich, Pestel, and co-workers[3] seems to us to be more or less correct. Critics of the several reports of the Club of Rome have raised valid criticisms of some aspects of this work, but no counter models exist and the basic results still stand. The projections for the United States and the world offered by Watt,[4] Heilbronner,[5] Lovins,[6] (see Article 33, this volume) and Stavrianos[7] and by the Latin American World Model[8] are very close to our own view of the problems faced. Special attention is invited to the difficulties of managing ever-larger, ever-more complex societal and technological systems. Here, our views correspond most closely with those of Vacca.[9]

The problem is to invent the future. Only the most insistent determinists and some mystical and religious groups demand a single, unavoidable future. In the enormous gap between the unavoidable and the miraculous, fall politicians and academics, ordinary people and fortune-tellers, each in their own way trying to estimate something useful about the future in order to reconcile dreams with possibilities. The general agreement on objectives that characterized the industrial world at the end of World War II has vanished as goals were met or abandoned. Little was then heard from the three-fourths of the world that was poor in the 1940's. Now there are many new voices in the world, and some of them command both money and raw materials. Thus, the future is to be invented in the face of many conflicting objectives—about which there is little agreement—and amidst an uncomfortable frequency of political instability. The process is made even more worrisome by the observable tendency of the industrialized nations to support (or even to bring to power) strong central governments for poor nations, even if (one hopes not because) these governments are highly authoritarian, oppressive, and non-representational.

The energy difficulties of the early 1970's have raised the questions of energy and raw material availability in the developed world, and the joint problems of population growth and food supply in the poor nations of the world have provided new visions of the future, most of them conflict-ridden or downright disastrous. Responses to these visions of the future have been very strange. From the economists, in their role as the leading academic contributors to policy discussion, have come rejections but no comprehensive models that show a less destructive future. Calling for more investment in the poor world, many economists show a faith in technological innovation that is far less unanimous among scientists and engineers.

In a world of growing complexity, there is a greater premium than ever on correct estimation of the future. Nearly every major nation has officially sanctioned bodies to produce forecasts, evaluations, policy impact projections, and other types of assessments. What characterizes these efforts above everything else is their operation within the limits of their sponsors. Under these circumstances, it is not surprising to find that the results seldom challenge any existing institutions. Because these analyses are perceived as value free and "hardheaded," the outcome is often given some special weight. Unfortunately, to attain this attention, the analyses are usually restricted to economic assessment, the more obvious deleterious side effects, and measures to mitigate the problems. Despite inevitable caveats about social effects or political problems, these analyses always purport to offer the best (or the least bad) policy recommendations. But, restricted by the methodology and the nature of the charge, the range of options considered is very limited. Analyses by independent groups or individuals are often far less optimistic than official projections, but in the competition for credibility, they may well sacrifice their strongest arguments in efforts to sound unbiased.

A scenario lies somewhere between a forecast and a fantasy. The objective of this scenario is to explore the possibilities of a particular plausible future. The low energy scenario was chosen because it provides the least expensive energy options, but upon further examination was found to have some other interesting and possibly desirable properties. For example, all are aware of the environmental effects of intensive energy use: air pollution, water pollution, land degradation from mining and sprawl, inefficient and occasionally excessive production. All these problems are reduced in proportion to our ability to use less energy more effectively.

There are international implications inherent in this scenario. First, a real reduction in energy use by the industrialized nations may offer the only way to avoid direct confrontation of the rich few with the hopes of the destitute many, and the United States is the leading user of energy. Second, because of sheer economic power and considerable domestic resources, the United States could play an exemplary role—as some U.S. politicians believe we now do. Third, the social conflicts and changes in the United States since the mid-1960's make it possible now—in a way that it was not 20 years ago—for different coalitions and ideals to dominate U.S. policy. Indeed, this scenario incorporates several recent social trends in it, on the theory that it is easiest to persuade people to do something that they already intend to do or are resigned to doing. For example, the U.S. Department of Agriculture notes that in 1976 one-half of all U.S. households attempted to grow some of their own food. Even though the food system requires 16 per cent of all U.S. energy use,[10] no one seems to have considered the possible implications for this major social shift for energy policy. Finally, the idea of central control appears to be weakening both in the United States and in the world. There are now new local and regional disputes and power groups in the United States, and in the world the number of independent and independent-minded voices has increased since World War II. This combination of nationalism at the international level and localism within nations might offer new opportunities for a world with less armed conflict (though with more rhetorical shouting).

OVERVIEW

The scenario described in this article results in an energy use per capita in the year 2050 of 13×10^{10} joules which is 36 per cent of the 1975 United States level of 35×10^{10} joules. To accomplish this end, major changes will be required, but these changes will not lead to a fall in the standard of living. This contrasts with the assertion that further improvement or maintenance of the standard of living is inexorably linked to continued increase in energy use. Dennis Hayes[11] frames the issue this way:

> Curtailment means giving up automobiles; conservation means trading in a seven-mile-per-gallon status symbol for a 40-mile-per-gallon commuter vehicle. Curtailment means a cold house; conservation means a well-insulated house with an efficient heating system.

Although this scenario goes considerably further than Hayes in reducing the use of energy, his distinction is useful.

This analysis takes the traditional sectoral breakdown, residential, commercial, transportation, agricultural, and industrial, and

Table 34–1. Overview of Final Energy Use 1975–2050: Low Energy Scenario.

	1975 Primary[a] Energy per Capita (10^{10} Joules)	*2050 Primary[b] Energy per Capita (10^{10} Joules)*	*Primary Energy Savings per Capita (10^{10} Joules)*	*1975 Total[c] Primary Energy (10^{18} Joules)*	*2050 Total Primary Energy (10^{18} Joules)*
Residential[e]	6.9	2.4	4.5	14.6	6.7
Commercial[e]	5.9	1.8	4.1	12.6	4.9
Transportation	9.2	2.3	6.9	19.6	6.5
Personal	(6.0)	(1.4)	(4.6)	(12.7)	(3.8)
Freight	(3.2)	(1.0)	(2.3)	(6.9)	(2.7)
Industrial[f]	13.0	6.2	6.8	27.6	17
Total[g]	35.0	12	22	74.4	35

[a]Population, 213 × 10^6.
[b]Population, 277 × 10^6. 2050 primary energy per capita is 36 per cent of that of 1975.
[c]News Release March 14, 1977. "Annual U.S. Energy Use Up in 1976," Office of Assistant Director—Fuels, Bureau of Mines, U.S. Department of the Interior.
[d]2050 primary energy is 47 per cent of 1975 primary energy.
[e]The division of energy into residential and commercial from Bureau of Mines figures follows Lovins "Scale, Centralization and Electrification in Energy systems" discussion draft.
[f]Miscellaneous and unaccounted for in Bureau of Mines data included in industrial.
[g]May not total 100 due to rounding.

examines each one for possible energy savings. The posited changes in each sector are described, borrowing from the extensive literature in the field, and aggregated into an over-all sectoral primary energy use estimates as shown in Table 34-1. Energy sources sufficient to meet this level of use throughout the period are exhibited in Figure 34-5. The depletion of petroleum and natural gas, the termination of nuclear power, as well as the implementation of alternative energy sources during the period are outlined.

To bring about these reductions in energy use, changes will have to occur in social and physical institutions and arrangements. These changes will not come from a master plan but from the evolution of tastes, preferences, and organizations. Thus, new community patterns, already emerging in demographic trends, are outlined in the following section. Shifts in the mix of goods and services and employment are described, including the winding down of the automobile, road building, and food processing industries and the rise of the solar energy, mass transit, telecommunications, housing, construction, and health care industries. Shifts in employment patterns, the distribution of work, leisure and income and their meaning are discussed later in this article. These trends anticipate the end of the continued growth of the commodity component of society's output. In any event, endless growth may be neither desirable nor possible.

The final sections treat the policy questions, issues, and measures that are consistent with this scenario as well as the international implications of this scenario.

SETTLEMENT PATTERNS AND CHANGING COMMUNITIES

Many problems of the man-made environment result from sheer size. Getting out of a city of 100,000 is relatively easy even without an automobile; to get beyond the edge of a city of 3 million even with an auto involves a major effort. The air pollution of a city would be less of a problem if it were dispersed over a large area or if cars were restricted—the seriousness of the problem is a function of city size. The magnitude of the problem of solid waste disposal more than doubles with a doubling in the size of a city, not because the volume of waste more than doubles, but because all of it must be hauled further for "disposal." Economies can result from small scale as well as large.

Today's pattern of extremely high and extremely low densities will evolve to a pattern of medium size cities with moderate densities, separated not by suburban sprawl but by farm and forest land. The satisfactory size for such cities would be small enough to avoid megalopolitan diseconomies of scale yet large enough to carry a vigorous industrial and commercial base and sustain a high level of cultural activity.

> Instead of the seemingly endless sprawls we now know, suburbs should be villages, composed of a series of hamlets, closely spaced, that together make up a village and support the services a village can provide. . . . The village may, within its political boundaries, contain, say, 8 square miles, but only 3 square miles should be developed. The average density of the developed area should be 5 dwelling units per acre. The village would have a population, then, of about 35,000. Five square miles should be field and forest, mountain and river. . . . The five square miles should, of course, link up with the open spaces of neighboring villages in a linear fashion which leaves undisturbed and undeveloped the major landscape features, including the principal drainage ways, the ridgelines of hills, and outstanding scenic areas. The village should own all this land. Much of it should be put to agricultural or silvicultural use on a lease basis. . . . Many of the prospects, the striking visual landscapes, may once have been sites for those 1950's-style subdivisions of half-acre, single family houses. They should be razed.[12]

"Impossible to achieve?," asks Charles E. Little after conjuring up this image. Probably so, in terms of the 1950's, 1960's, and 1970's style of development made possible by the private automobile. Probably not, with development to accommodate constrained private transportation.

City planner Patrick Geddes thought that decentralization would be brought about by the development of electricity that would free industry from centralized power facilities. Ralph Borsodi theorized in the 1930's that it could be achieved by the proliferation of power tools that would make possible home-based skilled labor, on the sound but economically heretical assumption that it is more economical to haul machine parts than workmen. Frank Lloyd Wright felt the advent of the automobile would bring it about and designed Broadacre City on that premise. None of the technological innovations that could have been the basis for social innovation halted the trend toward centralization and urbanization. The social, cultural, and economic attraction of the city has overwhelmed any competing considerations. Put simply, modern industrial culture has been rich enough to afford the kind of cities it has, even though there have been simpler and more forthright means of providing for human needs.

The costs of Ward's "unintended city," not planned for human purposes but shaped by the hammers of technology, applied power, the overwhelming drive of self-interest, and the single-minded pursuit of economic gain are now, however, taking their toll in the crime, bankruptcy, blight, and environmental deterioration of cities.[13] The response of modern commerce has been to substitute the blacktop-surrounded, air-conditioned, landscaped mall for the central town square or piazza as a place for people to meet and mingle among shops and fountains. This new town center is now far afield, accessible only by car and stripped of all community functions but the sale of commodities. The energy, environmental, and ultimately financial costs of these changes suggest that a metamorphosis to new settlement patterns has become necessary.

These new forms will be characterized by smaller cities, with present large megalopoles multi-nucleated into communities of human scale such as the "urban villages"—Chelsea, Trastevere, Greenwich—in the 50,000 to 100,000 range of population.[13] The density foreseen is along the lines suggested by Little, roughly five dwelling units per acre.[12] The distribution of the population that we envision is indicative of the form of our future settlements (Table 34-2).

The over-all effect on America's large cities will be the simultaneous implosion and

Table 34–2. United States Demography, 1970 and 2050.

	1970	*2050*
Total U.S. population	203.2 million	277 million[a]
Number of cities > 100,000	156	100
Population (% of total)	56.5 million (38)	20 million (7)
Average population	362,000	200,000
Number of cities > 25,000–100,000	760	1,500
Population in cities (% of total)	34.6 million (17)	79 million (29)
Average population	45,500	53,000
Number of cities 2,500–25,000	5,519	8,000
Population in cities (% of total)	42.4 million (21)	84 million (30)
Average population	7,682	10,000
Rural population (% of total) including urban < 2500 plus unincorporated urban	69.8 million (34)	94 million (34)

[a]Bureau of the Census, Department of Commerce, *Statistical Abstract of the United States, 1977,* U.S. Census, Series II-X projection 1980–2050.

explosion of population, the implosion the result of the loss of automobile as the primary means of city transit and the explosion the reestablishment of distinct—as opposed to megalopolitan—urban areas of reduced size. Urban areas will generally contain 200,000 or fewer residents, a population still manageable in terms of the economics of city operation, full pedestrian and bicycle access to all districts, and accessibility to surrounding food-producing lands.[14] A fundamental aim in the redesign of the urban areas is maximum accessibility as opposed to maximum mobility. As private transportation becomes more and more costly, and as local grocers, butchers, bakers, druggists, jewelers, booksellers, restauranteurs, and clothiers are found to be able to supply most of local residents' needs, the neighborhood and the town will regain their social and community functions. It may be that the parking lots of today's shopping centers will be the sites of tomorrow's housing.

The path of evolution from the present to this future state has been elusive to planners, government officials, and citizenry who have attempted to face the problems of the present patterns of settlement. We believe, however, that the transformation is possible and there is considerable evidence, from recent data on the depopulation of the largest urban areas, that migration out of the largest urban complexes is already occurring.

The history of the United States is sometimes written in terms of population migration and there is no evidence that these migrations have stopped. Figure 34-1 shows the familiar westward and southward migrations. The westward movements continue from our earliest days as a nation. The southward migration, recently popular as a theme for social and political analysts, has continued since 1910 and accelerated since 1940. Superimposed on these changes has been, until recent years, migration from rural areas to cities and from small towns to large metropolitan areas and, within metropolitan areas, movement of residences from city center to suburban areas.

In the years 1970–1974 an unanticipated movement began. Ten of the 13 largest megalopolitan areas (the Standard Consolidated Statistical Areas of the U.S. Census Bureau) exhibited net population migration out of the urban areas. Figure 34-2 shows net migration as a function of city size. From the data, the southern rim urban complexes show net gains or small losses, but it does appear

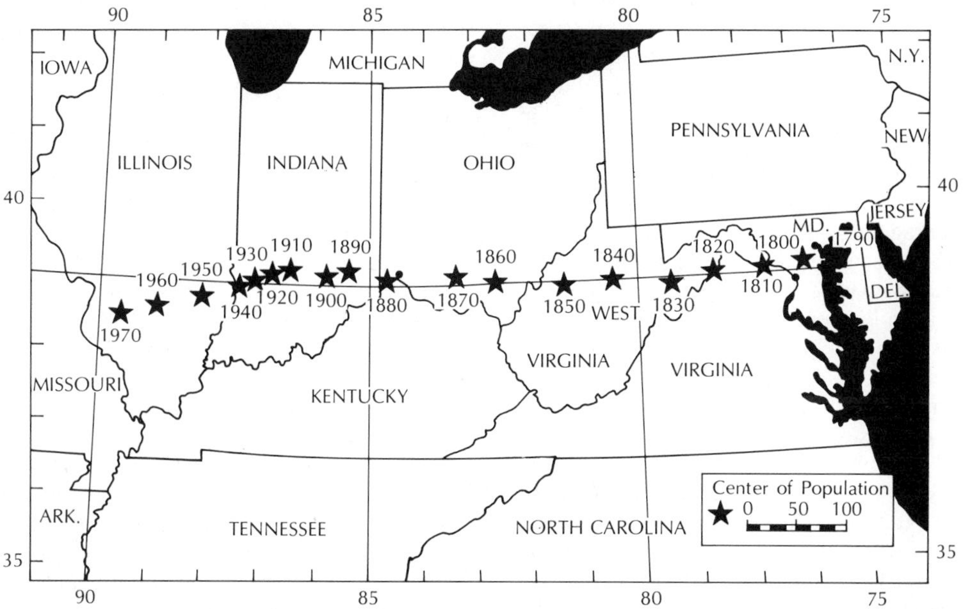

Figure 34-1. Population migration, west and south.

Figure 34-2. Net population migration for the largest megalopoles (Standard Consolidated Statistical Areas), 1970–1974.

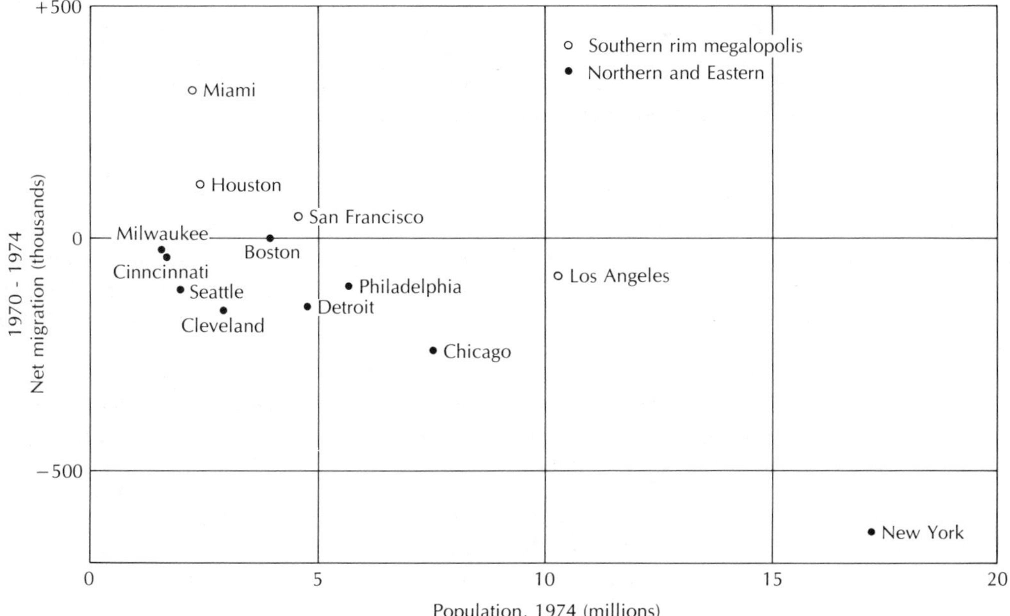

that larger urban areas suffer the most outmigration.

The changes implied by these trends are not predicated on comprehensive planning but on the decision of many people to engage in activities necessitated by the realities of high cost energy. The shifts in settlement patterns set out in Table 34-2 will result from the encouragement of these trends.

The encouragement we envision includes legislative action. These acts will facilitate the abandonment of nonviable populated areas primarily in the megalopli and the construction of viable communities in small cities and rural settlements.[15]

A major step in the process of repopulating rural America will be a National Homestead Lease Act. This act will permit individuals to lease, at no cost, tracts of publically owned land provided the lessee makes his home on the land. Tracts might be 4 to 40 acres in size, depending upon the location. Leases will be renewable indefinitely, as long as the lessee remains living on the tract and cultivates some portion of it. Incentives and/or assistance might be offered at the outset. We estimate that 1 to 4 million people will take advantage of such a program, at a federal cost less than the current federal job programs.[16] If 2 million people took advantage of the program, there is enough public land in unused and abandoned military bases to support the program.

An indication that the United States has been reconsidering the depopulation of its rural areas and the general destruction of rural community life is the restriction of the corporate industrialization of American agriculture embodied in the Family Farm Act of 1974.[17] The Act prohibits any corporation with nonfarm assets of more than 3 million dollars from owning or operating farms. This law comes at a time when American agriculture is on the verge of being captured by corporate interests and provides needed protection for the farmer-owner—with no loss of efficiency. The U.S. Department of Agriculture, usually the ally of large-scale farming, concluded in a 1968 study that the most efficient organization in American agriculture is the one- or two-family farm.[18]

A repopulation of rural American will take some pressure off the largest cities and preserve the desirable aspects of city culture that have been destroyed by urban growth far beyond the human scale. The substantial migration out of urban areas we have included as part of this scenario will leave those who stay behind in possession of cities that could be made very livable.

As a counterpart to the National Homestead Lease Act, Congress will expand the National Urban Homestead Act with the threefold purpose of (a) providing housing for those in the cities who cannot fully afford it; (b) improving the inner cities by putting to use structurally sound buildings now falling into disrepair whose replacement would require impossible amounts of both capital and energy; and (c) accomplishing these things in a way that would increase the independence and equity of the individual involved. The guiding principle of the law is the idea elaborated nearly a decade ago by George Sternlieb, that the basic variable that accounts for differences in the maintenance of slum properties is the factor of ownership.[19] The idea for renewal, tried successfully on a small scale by a number of cities in the 1970's, consists of selling publicly owned (abandoned) dwellings to families for a low price in return for the new owner's agreement to bring the building up to city codes within 18 months and to occupy it for at least 5 years.[20] Because few of the prospective owners will be able to obtain loans to finance the rehabilitation of their buildings, public low-interest loans and loan guarantees will be made available on the basis of maintaining future property values and the income arising from the improvements made. The program could be made to serve the goal of energy conservation. For example, in 1976, the Community Services Administration funded an experimental program in which heavy insulation and a solar water-heating system were installed in an aban-

doned five-story, 11-unit tenement as part of the "sweat equity" renovation of the building by its new owners.

As a necessary complement to the rural repopulation and urban rebuilding in the previous two acts, the National Conurbation Act will provide for the restructuring of present megalopoles. The intent of the Act is to develop a regional pattern of distinct cities and towns intended as no-growth entities including farms and open space as parts of the whole. As people move out, abandoned unsound structures will be demolished with nothing built in their place.[21] What will take place next—in slum neighborhoods out of necessity, in better-off neighborhoods out of frugality or civic pride—is the conversion of these vacant areas into community gardens and orchards. The cities, straining under the loss of tax base as a result of out-migration, will welcome this use of empty lots. After a time, the trend of building rehabilitation, urban open space accrual, and new building construction will lead to multi-nucleated patterns of compact towns and communities on the sites of present-day megalopoles. This planned development with appropriate zoning ordinances will integrate the energy, agricultural, transportational, and recreational needs of a community while avoiding unnecessary transportation of food and materials from distant regions. Zoning in certain areas will allow a mix of commercial and residential uses on the same block, and in the same building complex, so that minimum travel is needed for shopping and going to work.

Thus, we envision recent trends, with the encouragement and structuring from the legislation, leading to a restructuring of settlements.

RESIDENTIAL ENERGY USE

Space and water heating consumes about 75 per cent of the total U.S. energy used in the residential sector. The rest is for cooling, lighting, air conditioning, and the use of a variety of appliances.

As many citizens have noticed in recent years, significant savings in heating fuels can be obtained by changing the allocation of heat to a home both spatially and temperally (zoned control, day and night thermostat setbacks). An estimated 25 per cent of the heating fuels can be saved and often more.[22] We expect this trend of changing behavior during the heating season to continue, since fuel prices are likely to continue to rise.

Major reductions in both heating and cooling requirements can be obtained by retrofitting old buildings and careful design of new buildings. Reducing infiltration, adding insulation, and improving windows of old buildings could result in an average reduction of at least 50 per cent in heating requirements.[23] Renovation of old buildings is consistent with a policy of moderate urban density without autos, since most of the older structures are relatively closely spaced. Up to a 80 per cent reduction in heating needs can be attained for new buildings by building smaller homes and using sound building techniques and correct window placements to gain solar energy.[24,25]

Water-heating devices are very inefficient and can take up to 15 per cent of total residential energy demand. Improved insulation, lower temperature settings, heat recovery from other appliances and reduced hot water use can reduce this energy consumption by 50 per cent or more.[26]

We estimate that the implementation of these measures will decrease the energy consumption per capita for space and water heating to about 30 to 40 per cent of the 1975 level by the year 2050 and in many cases, a smaller percentage. Total residential energy use per capita can, therefore, be reduced by about 50 to 60 per cent by the year 2050. It is worth noting that space and water heating require only relatively low temperature heating devices and can, therefore, be met for a significant part by simple solar (and wind) heating systems.

About 25 per cent of residential energy use is for cooling, refrigeration, air conditioning, and so on. Increasing the efficiency of appliances will have a significant impact. Furthermore, better design of new buildings will make air conditioning unnecessary in a large part of this country by the year 2050. Energy use for home freezers will increase somewhat because of the changing food system. We estimate that energy use for all these devices can be cut by about 50 per cent or about a 10 per cent reduction in total residential energy use. Electricity will continue to be the major form of energy to be used for these tasks, with air conditioning a possible exception.

Energy efficient building codes on the national, state, and local levels, and national and state efficiency standards and labeling laws for energy using equipment, will help bring about these reductions in residential energy use.

The combination of the measures mentioned above will reduce the residential energy use per capita of about 6.9×10^{10} joules in 1975 by 65 per cent to about 2.4×10^{10} joules in the year 2050. Total residential energy use for the year 2050 is estimated at about 6.7×10^{18} joules, of which about 75 per cent or 5.0×10^{18} joules is for space and water heating (low temperature energy needs).

Figure 34-3 shows the space and water-heating demand for *both* the residential and commercial sector over the period 1975–2050 (see Energy Supply).

FOOD AND AGRICULTURE

This scenario includes a regionalization of agriculture as well as changes in the average American diet that will reduce total energy use in food production by 50 per cent over the next 75 years.

Until the 1940's, most regions in the United States produced most of their own food. Specialized, large-scale food production is an invention of the last 25 years. The startling growth in home gardening and local direct-marketing cooperatives in the early 1970's suggest that a trend toward less centralized and specialized food production may already have begun. Large-scale production for export will be with us quite a while, as developing nations struggle with food production. But only by decreasing the energy subsidy to these crops for export can the United States remain competitive as energy prices rise. It is often overlooked that U.S. food is, at present, expensive by world food cost standards (see Article 4, this volume).

The present fossil fuel subsidy to the American food system in the form of gasoline, machinery, fertilizer, and pesticides is 15 calories for every calorie of food energy consumed.[10] As fossil fuels become scarce, agriculture of this intensity will become impossible, not only in the developed nations upon whose agriculture much of the world has come to depend, but also in the less developed countries whose hopes for progress rest on boosting food production with machinery and chemical fertilizer.

The American diet and food system will change over the next 75 years. Beef consumption will be cut by half, and the beef that is eaten will be produced from pasture- and range-fed cattle eating grasses that humans cannot digest instead of from feedlot cattle raised on valuable grain. Swine will be fed poor quality grain and refuse, and land formerly used to grow feed for both cattle and swine will be used to grow grain and beans for human consumption, much of which will be exported. Reducing beef protein intake will mean that protein needs can be made up by other sources. Food such as fish, chicken, eggs, soybeans, and dairy products, which have high protein conversion efficiency and lower energy requirements, will make up the difference.

Fish will be supplied by coastal and local fishing and the extensive use of fish farms. Poultry and egg production will operate on a local basis in a far more energy efficient manner than the current poultry factories are operated. Consumption of dry beans and fresh potatoes, which has declined in the United States in recent decades, will increase, as will the direct consumption of grains. Consumption of fruits and vegetables—90 per cent of

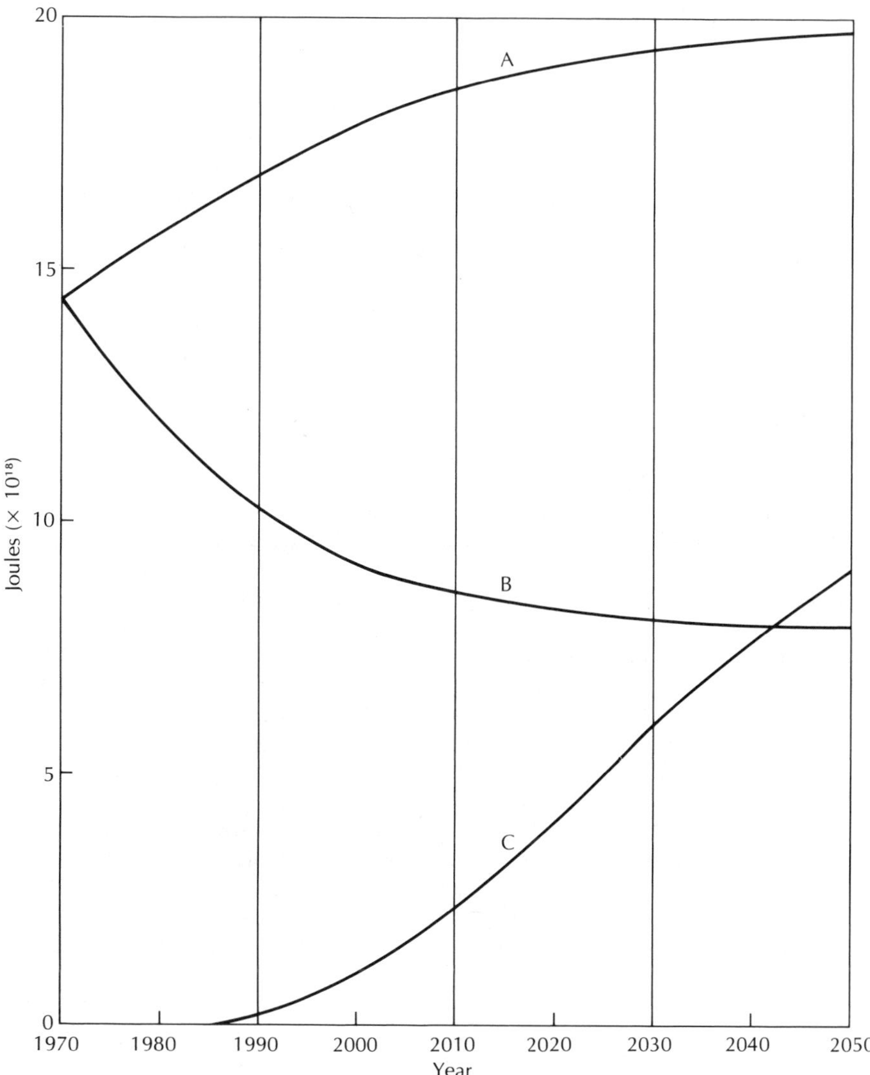

Figure 34-3. Commerical and residential space and water heating projections compared to projections of low temperature energy supplied from solar and wind sources. Curve A, primary fuel demand for commercial and residential space and water heating at 1973 level of consumption; curve B, low energy scenario space and water heating demand; curve C, solar and wind low temperature energy production.

which will be grown and eaten locally—will rise.

Even if direct consumption of grain were to increase to make up for the protein lost due to reduced meat intake, and even if per acre grain production were to drop slightly as a result of the less energy intensive use of chemical fertilizers, there would still be substantially more grain available for export.[27] It is not necessarily the point of this reduction in American meat consumption to provide more grain to feed hungry people around the globe. Such grain surpluses will provide reserves for year-to-year fluctuations in production and aid to famine-stricken areas, but we doubt that enough grain could be freed in this way to supply the world, and we think that, in any case, it would be just one more stop-gap measure to alleviate world hunger until population growth exhausts these grains as well. For Americans, the dietary changes will reflect market responses to escalating prices of energy intensive foods. Maintaining moderate food costs is of considerable interest nationally, even for upper income families who could pay higher prices, if non-food expenditure levels are not to decline drastically as food prices rise.

In addition to the anticipation that the American diet will include a greater proportion of whole grains, dried beans, potatoes, and vegetables generally, we expect that most produce will be grown by the individual or by local gardening co-ops or farmers for local consumption. It is not difficult to imagine a time when lawns will have very nearly disappeared and houses will be surrounded by gardens and orchards tended by city residents, who will gradually come to refuse to pay the high costs of commercially produced produce. We envision the effect of high food prices on suburbs to be quite startling. Areas that now look like green residential deserts will come to resemble the intensely farmed and carefully tended gardens of England or China.

The most fascinating thing about a widespread resurgence of gardening will be the huge amount of food that will be produced by an activity that seems to us today so much like an avocation. Truly, no one should be surprised by the economic value of home gardens. In fact, the U.S. Department of Agriculture has calculated that a family of four could be well fed without animal products by using only one-sixth of an acre. Modern intensive gardening techniques produce still higher produce yields per unit area.

Both the National Conurbation Act and the National Homestead Lease Act support the trends to more local food production and distribution. Energy savings from these measures and agricultural energy saving (see Article 4, this volume, for some specific measures) contribute to the reductions in industrial, residential, commercial, and transportation energy use summarized in Table 34-1. The National Container Act will contribute further savings in the food system (see the following section).

COMMERCIAL ENERGY USE

The characteristics of energy consumption in the commercial sector are similar to those of the residential sector. Space and water heating represent about 75 per cent and air conditioning about 10 per cent of the total commercial energy use, all of which require only low temperature energy sources. Conservation measures and legislation outlined under the residential sector will reduce the commercial energy consumption dramatically. In addition, significant improvements will be made by using "waste" heat generated within buildings. The smaller, nondetached stores and other moderate size commercial buildings will make extensive use of natural ventilation. These changes result in a reduction of about 70 per cent in commercial energy needs for space heating and cooling and water heating, or about a 60 per cent reduction in the total commercial energy use per capita by the year 2050.

Additional energy savings will occur through the use of natural light and reduced lighting standards.[28] Reduced use of lighting for advertising will have the same effect. Furthermore, changes envisioned in the food system will have a significant impact on commercial energy use: phase-out of fast food services and other "junk" commerce, drastically reduced packaging using standard sizes, and more careful display of goods (e.g., no open freezer cases). The popular fact that McDonald's hamburger chain uses enough energy in a year—largely for packaging—to provide electricity for the cities of Pittsburgh, Boston, Washington, and San Francisco illustrates the American penchant for throwaway containers.[29] Now, litter and solid waste simply represent resources not being put to best use. As energy becomes more costly, a society that uses packaging and produces garbage on the scale of the United States will find it necessary to reduce the amount of this waste.

Packaging energy use will decline as disposable paper and plastic containers nearly disappear, as commodities that can be shipped, stored, and merchandised in bulk are handled in bulk lots, and as nonessential junk foods, overprocessed foods, and excessive toiletries and cosmetics nearly vanish. The National Container Act will reduce both wastes and total packaging energy. Litter and solid wastes will cease to be a problem when commercial packaging and containers are designed for nearly complete recycling and reuse. About one-eighth of local trucking is for garbage and trash disposal. A reduction in the amount of trash produced means less trucking.

We estimate that the combination of these measures will reduce the commercial energy use per capita of about 5.9×10^{10} joules in 1975 by about 70 per cent to 1.8×10^{10} joules in the year 2050. Total commercial energy use for the year 2050 is estimated at about 4.9×10^{18} joules of which about 70 per cent or 3.5×10^{18} joules is for space and water heating (low temperature energy needs).

Figure 34-3 displays space and water heating demand (see Energy Supply).

TRANSPORTATION

The transportation energy savings in personal travel and freight in this scenario reduce the per capita direct energy use to 25 per cent of present levels. What is more surprising is that no reductions in social interaction or accessibility will occur. The sources of the energy savings are due to two primary factors. The first is that the redesign of settlements will mean that trips will be far shorter, and the combination of reduced length and provision of alternative modes, including safe walking and bicycle pathways, will markedly reduce the necessity of driving.[31] The second factor is that for the remaining trips that require driving, the vehicles involved will be smaller and far more efficient in terms of energy use per vehicle mile. The same factors apply to freight energy use.

The change foreseen in settlement patterns will not reduce trip-making, but rather reduce the distances spanned and change the mode of the trip.[32] This will be a reversal of trends in social and physical arrangements that began with the widespread ownership of the automobile and the universal willingness to sacrifice 25 to 50 per cent of urban areas to operating and storing the automobile. The pattern of placing numerous competing food and department stores together in shopping centers and malls accessible only by private auto will be replaced by a pattern of decentralized neighborhood stores. Schools and work places will also be decentralized throughout the community. With the emphasis on walking, cycling, traveling by public transportation, far less land will be given over to roadways and parking, and their associated noise and emissions will be reduced. The net effect will be to make the five dwelling units per acre even more spacious than such units are now.

These changes, partially motivated by the increasing cost of operating automobiles, will reduce average annual automobile vehicle miles per capita from 8,000 miles to 3,000 miles. After increased use of other motorized forms of transportation is taken into account, a 50 per cent reduction in energy use is anticipated from these measures.

Precedents for this type of transportation future already exist and others are being developed. In Rotterdam, 43 per cent of all daily trips are by bicycle. The cities of Runcorn, England (population 70,000) and Port

Grimand, France were planned to function without autos; they have bus, bicycle, and pedestrian access exclusively, except for emergency and special delivery vehicles.

This scenario envisions a heavy emphasis on rapid rail systems for intercity travel, especially for travel under 500 miles, to eliminate the least efficient aspects of air travel. Buses and the automobile will still carry a significant part of the load of intercity travel. The requisite interlinking of these modes especially at terminals will be part of the National Transportation Coordination Act. Other acts will include the termination of the Interstate Highway Program (Interstate Highway Termination Act), the termination of air terminal expansion and other airline subsidies (Airline Deregulation Act), and the enforcement of speed limits on auto, air, and truck travel to energy efficient levels.

Complementary legislation will be the Railroad Revitalization Act, which will effect the rebuilding and expansion of most of the existing rail network. This long process will involve some nationalization to provide the requisite capital.

Improvement of personal communications and access will be provided by telecommunications. Many types of present interactions and transactions, which now require large commitments of time and energy in travel, will be met by the rapidly developing telecommunications field.

With automobile passenger and vehicles miles reduced by more than 60 per cent, the next point of focus is the efficiency with which the remaining, still large number of trips are carried out. What is required here is slightly more than has been mandated in the Energy Policy and Conservation Act of 1975: 27.5 miles per gallon for the 1985 new car fleet average.[33] These cars will average 2,200 pounds instead of the current 4,000 pounds; and they will obtain an average gasoline mileage of at least 25 miles per gallon in town, last 20 years or 200,000 miles, and carry the person an average of 3,000 miles per year instead of the current 8,000 miles. These improvements will be mandated in the Fuel Economy Act.

The fuel mix of transportation will shift away from an almost exclusive dependence on petroleum to a mix of electricity, synthetic fuels, hydrogen, and petroleum. Twenty-five per cent of personal travel energy will be electric, mostly for local automobile trips and electrified rail and bus travel. Fifty per cent of freight energy use will be electrified with electric trains on all main rail lines and electric trucks for local delivery.

These changes in vehicle characteristics result in a reduction of over 50 per cent in energy use per vehicle mile. The combined effects of reduced vehicle mileage and improved efficiency result in a 77 per cent reduction in annual personal travel energy use from 6.0×10^{10} joules per capita in 1975 to 1.4×10^{10} joules per capita in 2050.

Similar savings are seen for freight energy use. Since recreation and farm land will separate communities, a large reduction in ton-miles will be due to changes in the agricultural sector resulting from the decentralization and localization of food production and processing (at present about one-half of all trucks haul food and agricultural products). With a trend to more decentralized manufacture in industry and shifts in production noted in the industrial sector, an over-all 50 per cent reduction in ton-miles will occur.

City-wide delivery systems will be required as part of the shift to rail transportation and the decline of centralized shopping centers. Intelligently done, the distribution of goods to neighborhood stores should involve little additional time or cost than delivery to centralized shopping centers. This is especially true given a shift away from cross-country truck delivery of freight, which has allowed direct delivery to the central retailer from producers. This does not occur in rail-supplied cities where local distribution from the city railhead to the various neighborhood outlets is by small trucks.

In addition, we estimate that with the elimination of 90 per cent of all air freight, and with 75 per cent of all truck freight carried shifted to rail carriage, total U.S. freight transportation energy use will be reduced 40 per cent.

The combined effects of reduced ton-mile, modal shifts, and increased modal efficiencies, especially for trucks,[34] will result in a 70 per cent per capita freight energy savings from 3.2×10^{10} to 1.0×10^{10} joules per year in 2050. The total transportation energy use, including freight and personal, in the year 2050 will be 2.3×10^{10} joules per capita resulting in a total of 6.5×10^{18} joules.

INDUSTRY

United States industrial production currently uses 37 per cent of the nation's total energy budget, or 27.6×10^{18} joules annually. This scenario envisions changes in the mix of goods and services produced in the economy. These changes will result in production reductions in certain energy intensive industries (Tables 34-3 and 34-4), which will save 3.8×10^{10} joules per capita or 10.9 per cent of total 1975 energy use.[35] Over-all output of goods, though changing in mix, will cease to grow on a per capita basis.

Table 34-3 summarizes the information from *A Time to Choose*,[36] the report of the Energy Policy Project of the Ford Foundation, to show the effect of changing the output mix and associated cutbacks in production in certain energy intensive sectors. An example of such a cutback in production is a decline in automobile production due to decreased auto ownership and use and greater auto durability. To project the effects of such changes some hypothetical reductions are considered. Each of the energy intensive industries in Table 34-3 is cutback 30 per cent with the exception of food and kindred products and primary metal, which are reduced 50 per cent.

The changes in food and kindred products will primarily occur in the food processing parts of the industry as opposed to primary food production. The change in primary metals will be largely due to the changes in automobile production.

It should be kept in mind that these changes result from production changes, not conservation. Conservation measures are separate measures, which can stand by themselves or can be undertaken in addition to the hypothetical cutbacks. In Table 34-4, it is also assumed that over-all levels of activity in the rest of the economy would remain as they are shown in Table 34-3. Such an assumption cannot be defended except as an heuristic device for interpreting the magnitude of the effects. By the same token, it should be noted that the cutbacks do not take into account secondary effects. With these qualifications, the cutbacks noted will:

(1) Save 29 per cent of manufacturing gross energy consumption or approximately 9.7 per cent of total energy use.

Table 34–3. 1971 Economic Parameters of Energy Intensive Industry.

Energy Intensive Sectors	*Mfg. Gross Energy Consumption (%)*	*U.S. Employment (%)*	*Industrial Production (%)*	*New Plant and Equipment Investment (%)*
Primary metal	26.8	1.6	6.3	3.4
Chemical and allied	17.0	1.1	9.4	4.2
Stone, clay, and glass	7.3	.8	2.9	1.1
Paper and allied products	7.6	.9	3.6	1.5
Food and kindred products	6.3	2.1	9.6	3.3
Subtotal	67.8	7.3	31.8	13.6

Table 34-4. Economic Parameters of Table 34-3 Industries—After Production Change.

Energy Intensive Sectors	*Mfg. Gross Energy Consumption (%)*	*U.S. Employ-ment (%)*	*Indus-trial Pro-duction (%)*	*New Plant and Equipment Investment (%)*
Primary metal	19.3	.8	3.7	1.8
Chemical and allied	16.7	.8	7.7	3.1
Stone, clay, and glass	7.2	.6	2.3	.9
Paper and allied products	7.5	.6	2.9	1.2
Food and kindred products	4.5	1.1	5.6	1.7
Subtotal	55.2	3.8	22.2	8.7

(2) Add 3.4 per cent to unemployment.

(3) Reduce industrial production 12 per cent.

(4) Save or make available 5.5 per cent of new plant and equipment investment capital.

Aside from these changes in industrial production, a significant reduction in industrial energy consumption will be obtained by improved efficiency. Strenuous energy conservation measures will reduce the energy use after the change in production by 3.0×10^{10} joules per capita, an additional 33 per cent. This projection is estimated from data from Ross and Williams,[26] (see also Article 32, this volume), who based their study largely on the concept of second law of thermodynamic efficiency as outlines by the American Physical Society.[37] Higher efficiencies will be obtained by carefully matching the energy quality or temperature of energy supply and demand. The introduction of relatively small-scale, miltipurpose power plants as outlined under Energy Supply, will play a major role. We expect that fuel use taxes will be placed on industries in the near future to discourage the use of oil and natural gas (Depletable Fuels Tax Act), which will make these multi-

Table 34-5. Projected Energy Savings in the Industrial Sector by Conservation Measures, Based on Data from Ross and Williams.[38]

Measures	*Per Cent Reduction*
Good housekeeping measures through industry (except for feedstocks)	13
Fuel instead of electric heat in direct heat applications	.6
Process steam and electric cogeneration	8.7
Heat recuperators or regenerators in 50 per cent of direct heat applications	2.5
Electricity from bottoming cycles in 50 per cent of direct heat applications	1.7
Recycling of iron and steel in urban refuse	.4
Reduced throughput at oil refineries	3.0
Reduced field and transport losses associated with reduced use of natural gas	2.7
Total reduction	*ca.* 33

purpose power plants economically attractive for industry. Table 34-5 shows our estimates of the energy conservation effects in the industrial sector that will be obtained by the year 2050.

The total reduction in industrial energy use due to the change in production and the energy conservation is 6.8×10^{10} joules per capita, which is a 52 per cent reduction from the 1973–1975 level of industrial energy use by the year 2050. Total industrial primary energy use in the year 2050 will be 17×10^{18} joules.

ENERGY SUPPLY

Decreasing per capita energy consumption by 64 per cent postpones but does not solve our energy supply problems. Our increasing population combined with drastically decreasing production of oil and natural gas will put considerable pressure on other energy supplies. In this scenario, solar and wind sources will supply a large fraction of our energy needs. Other alternative supplies such as wood, bio-fuels, geothermal, steam, and so on, will also grow substantially. Less coal, with its associated environmental problems, will be used in the year 2050 and beyond than now.

The 2050 electric generating system will be substantially different than that of today. We envision the decline of the nuclear industry. Due to rising costs and public concern over safety, nuclear power plant construction halts in the mid 1980's, and the breeder reactor fails due to cost, technological problems, and the threat of nuclear proliferation. Solar, wind, water, and geothermal electric generating systems will grow to supply most of the demand for electricity. Marginal cost pricing combined with other load management techniques will be used to tailor the demand curve to follow supply. Daylight peaks may be encouraged to make use of the cheapest solar production stations. As cryogenic storage and electroysis become less expensive, solar energy may assume a base-load function. Hybrid plants, such as coal-solar or coal-wind, will be built, and wind will be used to generate electricity on a centralized as well as a decentralized basis. The trend in coal plants will be toward small (less than 300 megawatts) multi-purpose plants. Industries will generate their own process heat and electricity, selling the excess as district heating expands. The transition to the proposed system will be gradual. As currently operating plants become obsolete, new plants of the types described will take their place. Diverse and innovative electric generation will be the result.

This transition will be facilitated in several ways. We expect to see nuclear construction moratoria and an end to nuclear subsidies and to the federal commercial breeder program. Strong local opposition to nuclear plants is already a frequent occurrence. The cost of solar and wind energy systems, both thermal and electric, will drop as a result of improved techniques and mass production. In some cases, demonstration projects will provide the necessary production demand. A tax and loan guarantee incentive program for the use of renewable (flow) resources on state and federal levels will help this transition. A national strip mining act will set stringent standards for land restoration, so that the continued use of coal will not seriously scar the landscape. Finally, a depletable fuels tax will be levied on most uses of oil and gas as fuels. It will be a progressive tax, increasing steeply for uses for which there are alternatives. The naturally increasing costs of depletable fuels combined with this tax will improve the economic viability of alternative energy sources.

In our scenario, multi-purpose power stations will generally be used in industrial and moderate and high density residential and commercial areas. The industrial sector now consumes about one-third of the electricity generated in the United States. This electricity is mainly used for motors, lighting, and electrolysis (high-quality energy needs). In addition, about 45 per cent of the total industrial energy consumption is used to generate process steam. Electricity could be produced by the industries in combination with steam generation. Gyftopoulos[39] calculated that with the present requirements for process steam, enough electricity could be produced as a by-product to meet not only industrial electricity needs but to have a surplus to sell. The same type of power plant can also supply both electricity and heat to the residential and commercial sectors, where they can be adapted to the energy quality needs of the area. We expect that the general increase in fuel prices will make these small but relatively efficient "total energy systems" cost

Figure 34-4. Projections of total solar energy supply, 1970–2050. Curve A; data from Morrow[46]; curve B data from Business Communication Corp.[45]; curve C, data from Solar Energy Panel[47] (includes wind); curve D, low energy scenario (includes wind).

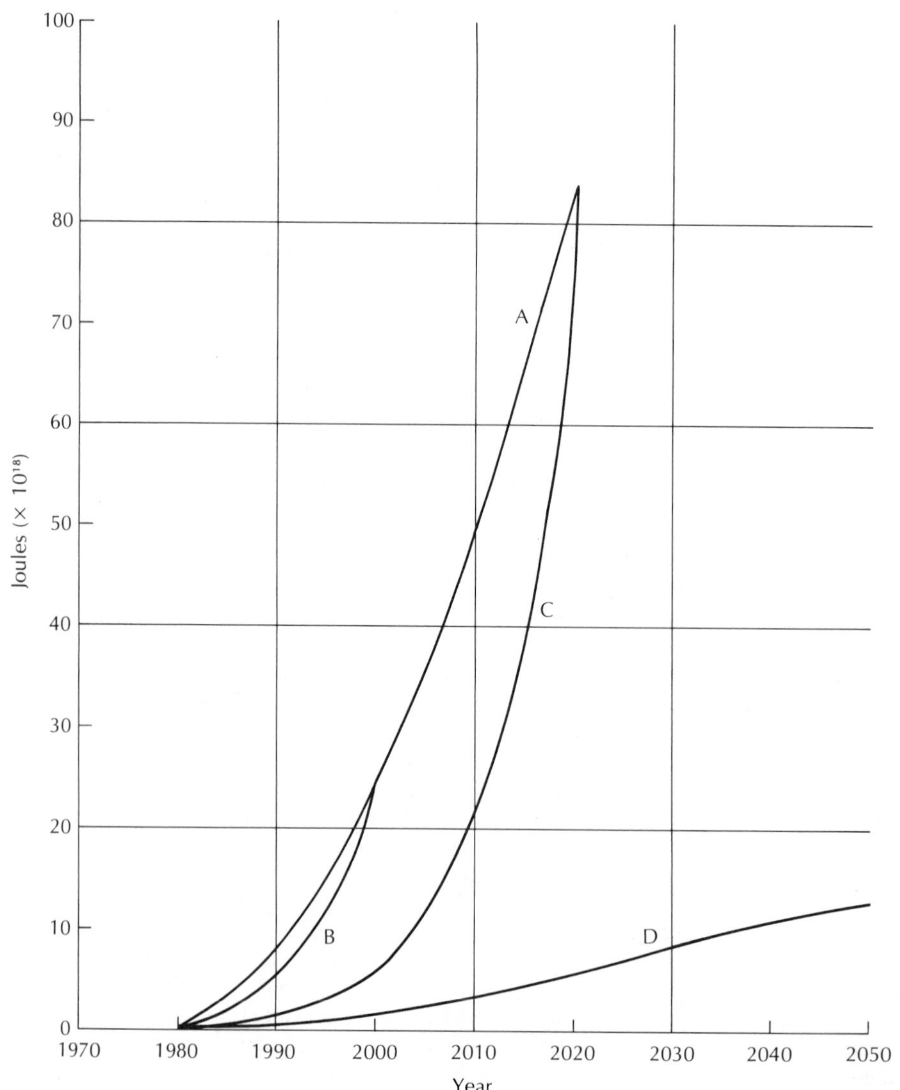

advantageous in the near future. We estimate that coal will be used to fire many of these plants in the industrial sector and some in the residential and commercial sector. Total coal consumption will be slightly lower than the total industrial energy consumption by the year 2050.

Space and water heating by solar energy will be widespread by 2050 and will supply, along with wind energy, most of our low temperature energy needs. The rapid growth in solar heating has already begun. In the last 2 years, the number of firms engaged in solar energy production has grown by one order of magnitude. Figure 34-3 illustrates our space and water heating requirements and our estimate for low temperature solar and wind applications. By the year 2020, nearly all buildings will have solar or wind space and water heating. Approximately 16 per cent of total U.S. energy use is for industrial process heat below 350 °F,[40] which can be easily accommodated by solar and wind technologies.

Central station solar thermal electric generation will be available on a commercial scale by 1985. The early solar plants will most likely be coupled with coal-fired plants. These hybrid plants will eventually give way to solar base-load production when cryogenic storage and electrolysis become economical.

One of the few technological breakthroughs we see in our "future" is the declining cost of photovoltaic cells. We forecast that, by 1990, the cost for photovoltaic electric generation will be $1,000 (in 1976 dollars) per installed kilowatt of capacity—a little less than the current cost for nuclear electric plants. We base our estimate on the current trend in photovoltaic costs and the expected breakthrough in the edge-defined film growth (EFG) production technique of silicon cells and the refinement of gallium arsenide (GaAs) cells that are capable of high efficiencies (20 per cent) in high temperature applications.[41] Table 34-6 shows current and projected photovoltaic costs for panels only. Figure 34-4 is a graph of total solar energy supply projections.

Table 34–6. Photovoltaic Cost Projections.

Year	*Cost per Peak Kilowatt (1976 dollars)*	*References*
1959	200,000	42
1976 (March)	21,000	43
1976 (October)	15,500	43
1979	5,000	43
1986	500	42–44

Wind energy will be utilized in central as well as dispersed applications with the capability of supplying a significant part of the electrical capacity in the year 2050. Included in wind systems are generators ranging in size from a few kilowatts for individual homes to installations of 1 to 2 megawatts connected into electrical grid systems to meet part of the electrical demand. The capital costs per installed kilowatt capacity of wind machines and conventional electric generators are now of the same order of magnitude. Wind electric systems with relatively short-term storage systems or an array of wind machines spread over a large area appear to have approximately the same reliability as large conventional generating units.[48] Wind energy conversion systems will also serve as space heating devices for a large area of the United States, since the seasonal availability of the wind corresponds with space heating needs. Present trends of rapid growth in electric space heating[49] could continue, to some extent, with large wind electric systems, if combined with centrally controlled heat storage devices in individual buildings. In addition, individual wind machines for neighborhoods and small towns will be used as "wind furnaces," without the interconnection with the electric grid. Combinations of these wind thermal and electric systems will also be employed. The economics of wind furnaces appears to be as good as that for solar heating devices. No major technical breakthroughs are needed for large-scale applications of wind energy conversion systems. Table 34-7 illustrates the role of wind energy conversion systems as a major energy source in the future.

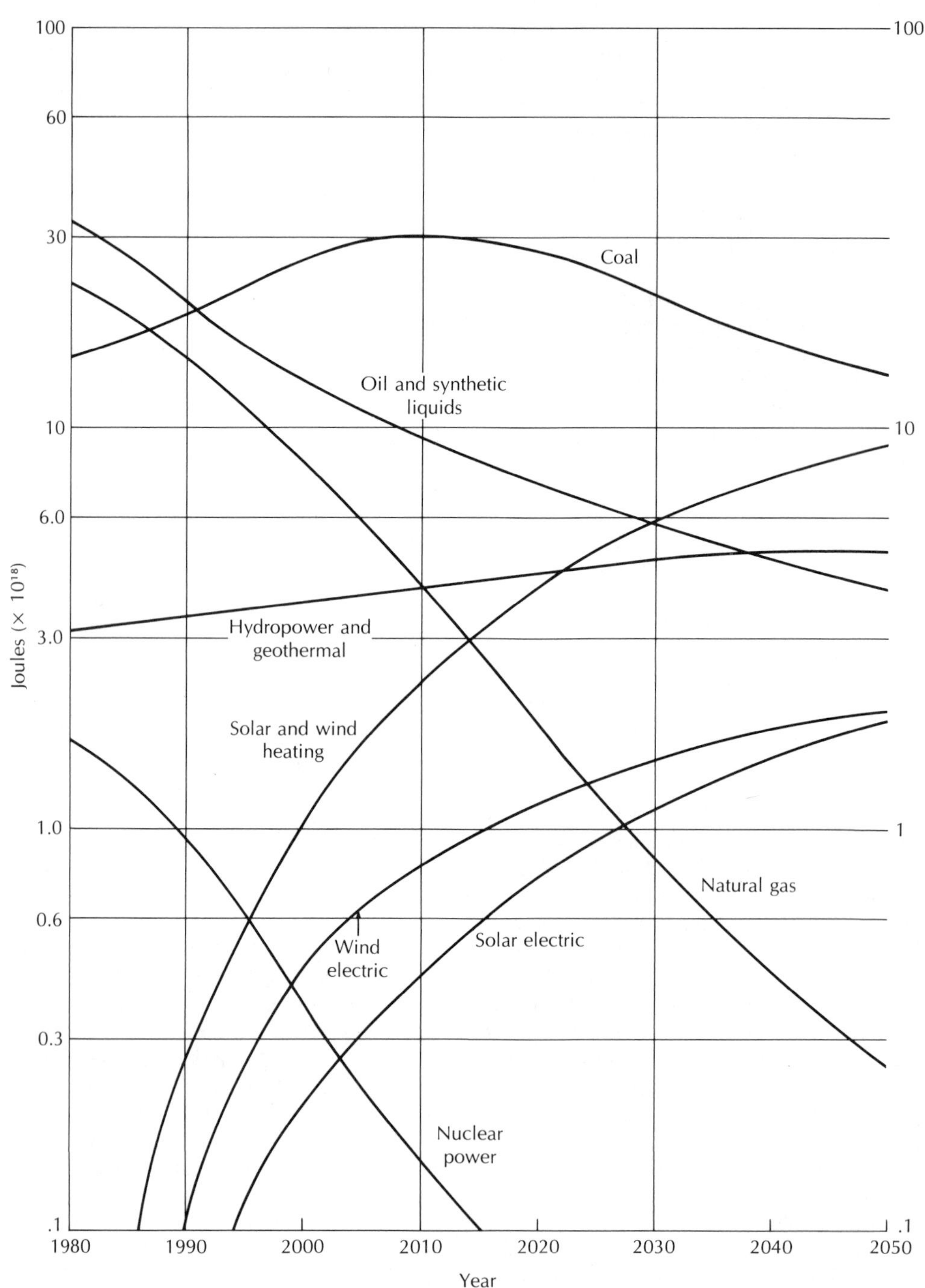

Figure 34-5. Energy supply, 1980–2050.

Table 34–7. Overview of Energy Supply during the Period 1975–2050 (10^{18} joules).

	1975	*1980*	*1990*	*2000*	*2010*	*2020*	*2030*	*2040*	*2050*
Solar electric, including photovoltaic	—	—	—	0.20	0.43	0.80	1.1	1.5	1.9
Wind electric	—	—	0.10	0.44	0.80	1.1	1.5	1.8	2.0
Hydro and geothermal	3.3	3.4	3.5	3.8	4.1	4.4	4.7	4.9	5.0
Solar and wind heating	—	—	0.25	1.0	2.3	4.0	6.0	7.6	9.0
Coal	14.1	15	19	26	27	25	21	17	13
Oil, imported[a]	12.9	12	7.0	2.0	—	—	—	—	—
Oil, domestic	21.4	21	14	11	9.5	7.0	5.5	3.4	2.0
Synthetic liquids[b]	—	—	—	0.10	0.12	0.20	0.50	1.2	2.0
Natural gas	21.1	21	15	8.3	4.0	1.8	0.80	0.44	0.25
Nuclear electric[c] generation	1.6	1.6	0.95	0.37	0.15	—	—	—	—
Total[d]	74.4	74	60	53	48	44	41	38	35

[a]No oil for U.S. import available approximately 10 years after expected world peak production.
[b]Synthetic liquids from coal, oil shale, biological waste (bioconversion), etc. will increasingly be used for transportation, combined with domestic oil.
[c]Last nuclear power plant construction in 1985; approximate lifetime, 30 years.
[d]Figures may not add up because of rounding.

Table 34-7 and Figure 34-5 summarize energy supply in various stages of our scenario. We have separated low and high temperature energy supplies to further illustrate the necessity of thermodynamic matching of supply and demand.

EMPLOYMENT, SOCIAL WELFARE, AND LEISURE TIME

We can be sure that any attempt to control energy consumption by restraining economic output will raise cries of opposition from those concerned with maintaining employment, increasing profits and getting a piece of the economic pie—labor, industry, and the poor, respectively. A clue to a stable employment policy for a time of economic reorganization in response to reduced supplies of energy may be supplied by the example of Sweden. Sweden has been able to "rationalize" its industry, i.e., carry out structural changes in industries and adapt new techniques of production, and by doing so maintain a highly efficient economy. This has been possible, according to Gunnar Myrdal,[50] because its firm national policy of full employment, in the form of guaranteed jobs, effective retraining programs, and smooth relocation of labor, has effectively banished the threat of technological unemployment. Were the United States to take full employment seriously and guarantee jobs to everyone wanting them, the fears of organized labor of economic reorganization could be eased and the transition to a low energy economy made smoother.

We have set the average work week in 1990 at 30 hours to reflect two changes: a 25 per cent decrease in work time for the average individual, accompanied by a 25 per cent decrease in real income that is offset by an increase in (potentially profitable) leisure time. There would then be a 30-hour work week available for a large bloc of the former structurally unemployed, who would fill the work hours left by reduced work time. Reducing average work hours 75 per cent would presumably provide employment opportunities for one new worker in every three now employed, assuming no change in total production and labor productivity. The 1976 labor force of 84 million could thus be expanded by some 28 million, just to maintain current output. The Full Employment Act will provide the needed impetus by establishing a

30-hour work week for federal and state jobs by 1985.

How, it will be asked, can we be so sure that people will agree to lose one-fourth of their income in exchange for more free time? We can't be sure, of course, but we may at least interpret, with Dennis Gabor,[51] the increased and endemic employee absenteeism of recent years as a sign that a significant bloc of people have already reached the point where time off does mean more to them than the dollars they forgo in not going to work. The plain fact is that the opportunity has never before existed except for low-paying part-time jobs. One is expected to work the customary full week or not at all. The increased time available may indeed prove more profitable than the equivalent time spent on the job. Some people will want the unpaid time off not just for leisure, but to be able to have time to perform services for themselves. Conceivably this will result in the service being completed more cheaply than if the person remained on the job during that period and paid for the service. Will the commercial and industrial establishment be able to handle the increased numbers of employees? We believe so, since the 1976 auto worker's contract effectively results in nearly one-fourth of the year as paid time off. The institutionalization of the option to take one's wealth in the form of leisure time and individually performed service time instead of goods may be the way for a society to smooth the transition to a situation of reduced energy availability. Finally, a society that is at last forced to substitute the serious redistribution of wealth for economic growth as a means of eliminating poverty may find a reduction of the average work week that spreads aggregate labor hours among more individuals to be a quite palatable means of redistributing wealth.

Substantial interregional and interindustrial shifts of labor will take place as part of the adjustment to a low-energy society. The transfer of population and industry from the North and Northeast to the South and Southwest will continue (see Settlement Patterns and Changing Communities), bringing the new industrial states into greater prominence. The factors that encouraged this shift—favorable tax structures, lower wage rates, and a generally unorganized labor force[52]—will produce a less than acceptable situation for workers for as long as it takes for union strength to develop and state regulatory authority to be applied. The Appropriate Skills Retraining Act, which provides increased federal support for trade and technical schools teaching needed new skills, will ease this transition. The demand for new housing would provide the opportunity to build good, energy-efficient homes for the influx of workers. At the same time, this drain of people from the older metropolitan areas would reduce the population to provide the opportunity to renovate and rehabilitate the older cities, increasing the demand for the labor of those remaining.

Interindustry shifts of labor will be significant. The housing industry, actively trying to fill the need for energy-efficient dwellings to replace wasteful older buildings, will grow still further in response to the need for building reconstruction, rehabilitation, insulation, and solar retrofitting. In a report prepared for the New York State Legislative Commission on Energy Systems, it was noted that conservation measures will lead to increased employment. By saving 1 million kilowatts (1,000 megawatts) through energy conservation at $300 per kilowatt, the employment level would be 12,000 people on a 30-year cycle, slightly less than a nuclear or coal plant would employ to generate 1,000 megawatts,[53] but significant numbers of people would be employed immediately in the conservation effort. Efforts to conserve energy in existing buildings would employ electricians, carpenters, plasterers, painters, truck drivers, factory workers, engineers, heating, ventilating, and air-conditioning specialists, and other building-trade workers. As the investment per conserved kilowatt increases, so does the employment. It becomes evident that conservation of energy does not reduce employment, as many have claimed, but will instead increase employment.[54]

The rehabilitation of railroads and the construction of mass transit systems will also require an increased labor force. Bezdek and Hannon report the following. Total employment would increase and energy use would decrease if the highway trust fund were reinvested in any of several alternative federal programs; if construction monies were shifted from highways to railroads, the energy required for construction would be reduced by about 62 per cent and employment would increase by 3.2 per cent. Passenger transport by railroad required more labor and less money and energy than transport by automobile in 1963. A similar conclusion was reached in a study substituting buses for automobiles in urban areas.[55] Freight transport by railroad was less expensive in terms of dollars, energy, and labor requirements than was truck transport in 1973. If the monetary savings had been absorbed as a tax and spent on railroad and mass transit construction, about 1.2 million jobs would have been created. Had there been a full shift from intercity car and truck transportation to transportation by railroad, with the savings spent on railroad construction, 2.4 million new jobs could have been created in 1963.[56] This is the trend we envision in railroad and mass tansit requirements.

The manufacture and installation of central as well as single unit solar and wind energy systems will be a burgeoning industry, successfully taking up the slack labor from the declining automobile and fossil fuel industries, the exception among which will be coal, which will grow in the interim to supply that part of electrical demand not met by renewable resources. Wind generators require no fuel but the operation and maintenance of a large wind system would require two to four times the labor force on a continuous basis as would an equivalent nuclear or coal power plant.[54] Increasing reliance upon solar energy is likely to have substantial employment benefits. Even though some of the components will undoubtedly require large production assembly, many of the collectors can be produced locally and certainly installed locally with a relatively small capital investment. The installation of solar systems is a labor intensive process. The FEA's Project Independence Task Force estimates that the solar energy industry could create half a million jobs by the end of this decade.

The need for labor in recycling will increase as this industry expands to handle not only metals and glass but also wood, paper, and cloth containers and to transfer urban sewage sludge to agricultural and silviculutral uses. This new employment will take up the slack created in the throwaway packaging and container industry.

As energy becomes more and more costly, labor will return to agriculture, horticulture, and silviculture, though in new, less physically demanding roles. We noted earlier some of the changes that may take place in an economy working under the new constraints of energy supply and we suspect that the make-up of organized labor will be changed as well.

POLICY IMPLICATIONS AND IMPLEMENTATION

How are the economic and social changes we forecast to come about? Existing trends and logical thinking will not be enough. Public and private policy changes will be necessary. Although government intervention in our lives has come to be resented, we cannot escape the fact that in the complex society in which we find ourselves, it may be a necessary evil. The specific proposed policies we have discussed in the text are summarized in Table 34-8. Many of the necessary measures have already been considered in some form. None require massive political changes, although many will not see an easy passage. No attempt has been made to be all-inclusive in describing policies that would have an impact on energy use. For example, defense pro-

Table 34–8. Policy Directions and Timetable.

Policy Area	*Description*	*Implementation Level*	*Timetable*
Transportation	Railroad Revitalization Act—regulatory reform and partial nationalizaton	National	1978–2000
	Fuel Economy Act—higher fleet mile per gallon requirements, tax penalties for poor economy, and strict speed enforcement	National and state	1976–1985
	Interstate Highway Termination Act—end of federal highway building program; redirection of funds to mass transit and railroads	National	1978–1985
	National Transportation Coordination Act	National	1978–1985
	Airline Deregulation Act	National	1978–1979
Energy and fuel supply	Nuclear power moratoria	National, state, and local	1977–1985
	End of federal nuclear subsidies	National	1977–1985
	Solar and wind incentive programs—tax write-offs, loans, research, product standards, education, and demonstration projects	National and state	1977–1990
	National Stripmining and Restoration Act	National	1977–1980
	Depletable Fuels Tax Act	National	1977–1990
	Synthetic Fuels Standards Act—quality and transportation standards	National	1985–1990
Economic reform	Gross National Product redefinition incorporating externalities	National	1977–1985
	Guaranteed Income Act	National	1980–1985
	Guaranteed Reform Act—effect anti-trust	National	1980–1985
	Corporate Reform Act—effective anti-trust regulations, more progressive income tax, incentives for small businesses	National and state	1978–1985
	World resource price stabilization through "indexing to industrial products and food prices"	International	1980–1990
Energy and resource conservation	Energy efficient building codes	National, state, and local	1977–1980
	Efficiency standards and labeling laws—all energy-using equipment	National and state	1977–1985
	Marginal cost pricing for electricity	National and state	1977–1985
	National Container Act—standard, recyclable containers; state Container Acts	National and state	1977–1985
Industrial	Multi-purpose generation laws—cogeneration and sale of steam, heat, and electricity by industries	National and state	1980–1990
	Utilities cooperation acts—public ownership and energy sales to utilities	National and state	1977–1995
Employment	Full Employment Act—30-hour work week for federal and state jobs	National and state	1980–1985
	Appropriate Skills Retraining Act—increase in federal support for trade and technical schools teaching needed skills	National	1977–1985

Table 34–8 *(continued)*

Policy Area	*Description*	*Implementation Level*	*Timetable*
	Appropriate Technology Act—funding for appropriate technology research and development	National	1977–1985
Land use	National Homestead Leasing Act	National	1980–1985
	National Urban Homestead Act	National	1980–1985
	National Conurbation Act	National	1990–1995
	Mixed use zoning and taxation laws	State and local	1980–1990

grams can be very energy intensive, but they have not been included.

The direct as well as the indirect impact of these policies must be considered. The effect that they will have on our social, economic, and political environment is a crucial question. How is the striving for material gain to be relaxed, and will people acquiesce to high prices and a reduction in material consumption? Why will individuals cease to be acquisitive? We do not suppose that they will, but we suspect that they will accommodate their wants to their diminished means over time. Economic wants are not unlimited, and the premise of the industrial revolution—that wants expand indefinitely—is simply not so. We would like to think that the ''drive beyond consumption'' noted by W. W. Rostow is appearing frequently and that the pursuit of Maslow's ''higher needs'' was the message of the 1960's. All of this would ease our task, but in the end we rely on a conventional mix of economic and legislative measures.

Economic growth has been prescribed as a means of redistributing income and eliminating poverty through the provision of jobs in a bustling economy. Robert Lampmann argued in the late 1960's that economic development had improved the general lot of the poor.[57] But we note that for a significant segment of the population a good part of the time the usual means of securing an income is not effective; there are no jobs. Even in boom times there stubbornly persists a class of ''structurally unemployed'' living on some form of relief, and usually in slums. Adherence to the idea of aggregate economic growth may have its justifications, but belief in its usefulness in alleviating poverty is among the poorest. The ''trickle-down'' theory, if it works at all, is not fast enough or equitable enough to meet the needs of all the people in the short time available to make the transition to a low energy economy. In a future of energy and materials austerity, the sort of GNP growth we as a nation have come to expect will be impossible to maintain and will hardly lend itself to the redistribution of income.

We are more optimistic than Lord Keynes, who noted with dread ''the readjustments of the habits and instincts of the ordinary man, bred into him for countless generations, which he may be asked to discard within a few decades.'' We do not think a calamitous transition is inevitable as long as no individuals or no segments of society are grievously displaced or left destitute and as long as the populace generally feels that everyone is bearing their share of the complications, inconveniences, and troubles of the conversion to a low energy economy. Destitution alone has never been a cause for revolt; history seems to indicate that poverty combined with rising expectations is the formula for revolution. By the same token, a middle class fearful of the loss of jobs and income and led by the proper demagogues to perceive both domestic and foreign ''conspiracies'' causing and profiting from their hardship is the recipe for an ugly strain of fascism. Individual economic security must be assured. Once it has been, the gradual erosion of the "commodity standard of living" will be accommodated in the same way that fiscal inflationary erosion is accommodated now.

The value of a guaranteed annual income (GAI) in a world of limited growth may be greater than any of its early proponents could have suspected. Proponents of the GAI continually explained how it would increase the opportunities for study, social services, and environmental improvement.[58] One can imagine its prospective value as a damper on economic growth. An income program that adequately supplied what we now refer to as necessities, combined with the option of additional work to pay for luxuries, might generate a class of people who would be willing to live at a lower income level and forgo these luxuries if to get them meant more work. The obvious outcome of this is reduced economic demand and reduced energy demand.

If we are able to assure everyone's economic security, what then? We may take some direction from Abraham Maslow's theory of a hierarchy of needs. He believed that as physical needs are met, higher needs such as love, learning, and self-actualization become our driving forces.[59] We have difficulty talking about transcending needs in the United States, a nation at the pinnacle of wealth, while the cities rot, decent housing is not to be found for many, and adults and children suffer from malnutrition and inadequate basic medical care. Our policies must take the inequities of our present society into account. Only when we are all assured of the basics of life may our higher needs be met. In this process our traditional beliefs, economics, and politics may have to change. In this scenario, there is not a cause and effect relationship, but policy does affect values and values affect policy in a process that has already begun.

INTERNATIONAL CONSIDERATIONS

The most obvious international consequence of this scenario is the reduction in a gradual and orderly fashion of U.S. payments for foreign oil imports. Only the increase of arms sales abroad from about 1 billion dollars to more than 10 billion dollars annually (1970 to 1976) has prevented far more serious balance of payment deficits. How long can we or should we be the world's leading arms supplier? The end of U.S. oil imports will come shortly after 2000 (Table 34-7), about the time world oil production is expected to peak and begin to decline (see Article 8, this volume).

Of course, the national security arguments for ending oil imports would be served by this scenario, but we have never been persuaded by these arguments, considering the dependence of the United States on foreign sources for more than 30 critical raw materials.

The non-nuclear future of this scenario offers several international advantages: (a) the effort begun by President Carter to eliminate proliferation of nuclear weapons via nuclear power would be possible without agreements or inspection; (b) the United States, in trying to persuade others to forgo nuclear enrichment technology, would be believable by example; (c) nuclear waste disposal and nuclear accidents would disappear as problems; and (d) the United States could become the leader in solar and wind technologies.

Increasing world oil prices of the early 1970's were an even greater burden to the poor nations of the world than to the United States. With limited foreign exchange and plans for development resting on oil-dependent technology, many poor nations have accumulated growing debts that may threaten the international banking system. At best, plans for development may be delayed by the drain on foreign exchange represented by oil. Are we really helping such nations by urging energy intensive agriculture on them and offering nuclear power plants and other costly and energy intensive technologies to them?

Opinions vary widely about the responsibility of the industrialized world to assist in the development of the Third World, but few would defend policies that inhibit attempts by poor nations to effect their own development. If, as poor nations strive to better their lot, we are perceived as outbidding them for scarce resources, conflict is a likely result. How much better to offer developed solar, wind, and geothermal technologies, which may adapt more easily to labor-rich Third World countries, than to offer capital intensive nuclear plants or oil-dependent machinery. In any case, eliminating U.S. fuel imports will help preserve remaining stocks for developing nations.

We have no illusions about the voluntary redistribution of the wealth of the world, but this scenario offers the chance for a future profitable to both rich and poor. The alternative may mean confrontation between the rich few and the destitute many.

REFERENCES AND NOTES

1. Jay W. Forrester, *World Dynamics* (Cambridge, Mass.: Wright-Allen Press, 1971).
2. Donella H. Meadows, Dennis L. Meadows, Jorgen Randers, and William W. Behrens III, *The Limits to Growth: A Report for the Club of Rome's Project on the Predicament of Mankind* (New York: Universe Books, 1972).
3. Mihajlo Mesarovich and Eduard Pestel, *Mankind at the Turning Point: The Second Report to the Club of Rome* (New York: Dutton, Inc./Reader's Digest Press, 1974).
4. Kenneth E. Watt, *The Titanic Effect* (Stamford, Conn.: Sinauer Associates, Inc., 1974).
5. Robert Heilbronner, *An Inquiry into the Human Prospect* (New York: Norton, 1974).
6. Amory B. Lovins, Energy Strategy: The Road Not Taken, *Foreign Affairs 55,* pp. 65–96 (1976).
7. L. S. Stavrianos, *The Promise of the Coming Dark Age* (San Francisco: W. H. Freeman and Co., 1976).
8. Amilcar Herrera et al., *Catastrophe or New Society: A Latin American World Model* (Ottawa: International Development Research Centre, 1976).
9. Roberto Vacca, *The Coming Dark Age* (Garden City, New York: Anchor Press, 1974).
10. Booz-Allen Associates, *Energy Consumption in the Food System,* Report #13392-007-001 (Washington, D.C.: U.S. Gov't Printing Office, 1976).
11. Dennis Hayes, *The Case for Conservation* (Washington, D.C.: Worldwatch Institute, 1976), p. 9.
12. Charles E. Little, "The Double Standard of Open Space," in *Environmental Quality and Social Justice in Urban America* (Washington, D.C.: The Conservation Foundation, 1975), p. 8.
13. Barbara Ward, *The Home of Man* (New York: Norton, 1976).
14. Daniel Bell, *The Coming of Post Industrial Society: A Venture in Social Forecasting* (New York: Basic Books, 1973).
15. Although we do not foresee the construction of many complete "new towns" on the order of Columbia, Jonathan, or Soul City, we do anticipate the incremental rebuilding of established towns.
16. It should be noted that the U.S. Census data for recent years indicate that the four fastest growth rates in the United States are in rural areas.
17. Walter Goldschmidt, A Tale of Two Towns, in *Food for People, Not for Profit,* edited by Lerza and Jacobson (New York: Random House, 1975), pp. 70–73. See also U.S. Senate Small Business Committee, *Small Business and the Community* (Washington, D.C.: U.S. Gov't Printing Office, 1946).
18. U.S. Department of Agriculture, *Economies of Scale in Farming* (Washington, D.C.: U.S. Gov't. Printing Office, 1968).
19. George Sternlieb, Slum Housing: A Functional Analysis, *Law and Contemporary Problems,* 1966.
20. The abandonment of inner city buildings has been a growing urban problem for some time; one may note that in 1975 some 30,000 buildings were abandoned in New York City alone. Large numbers of these buildings are actually structurally sound but in great need of repair.
21. In the large cities, buildings, and in some cases whole blocks, may be left vacant—much as New York City now has more than 3 square kilometers of vacant office space.
22. D. A. Pilati, *The Energy Conservation Potential of Winter Thermostat Reductions and Night Setback* (Oak Ridge, Tenn.: Oak Ridge National Lab, 1975).
23. Note: percentage reductions by behavioral and structural changes are *not* additive.
24. *A Nation of Energy Efficient Buildings by 1990,* Washington, D.C.: American Institute of Architects, 1975).
25. Raymond W. Bliss, Why Not Just Build the House Right in the First Place, *Bulletin of the Atomic Scientists 32,* pp. 32–40 (1976).
26. Marc H. Ross and Robert H. Williams, Energy Efficiency: Our Most Underrated Energy Resource, *Bulletin of the Atomic Scientists 32,* pp. 30–38 (1976).
27. Dwayne Chapman, An End to Chemical Farming, *Environment,* March, pp. 12–18 (1973).
28. A reduction in energy use for lighting will increase the heating needs, but these needs can generally be met without the use of electricity.
29. Bruce Ingersoll, *Chicago Sun Times,* October 30, 1972. This article reports in some detail Professor Bruce Hannon's study of the McDonald's hamburger chain.

30. Bureau of the Census, Department of Commerce, *Statistical Abstract of the United States, 1977.*
31. Work trips have accounted for the largest share of trips, approzimately 35 per cent, with business 9 per cent, shipping 15 per cent, school 8 per cent, social recreational 20 per cent, and other 13 per cent.
32. Assuming a city of five dwelling units per acre or 10,000 people per square mile with a circular form, the distance from the edge of the city to the center would be 1 mile for a city of 31,000, a 20-minute walk or a 6- to 10-minute bicycle ride. The distance would be 2 miles for a city of 126,000.
33. Fleet averages for recent years have been on the order of 11 to 15 miles per gallon.
34. Cummins Engine Company has estimated that a 25 per cent energy savings is possible with a typical tractor semi-trailer combination. With an appropriate engine, transmission, and axle combination, a total of 35 per cent can be saved.
35. This estimate does not include savings from resulting cutbacks in the energy supply industry.
36. Ford Foundation Energy Policy Project, *A Time to Choose: The Nation's Energy Future* (Cambridge, Mass.: Ballinger, 1974), pp. 140–157.
37. American Physical Society, *Efficient Use of Energy: A physics perspective. A report of the summer study on technical aspects of efficient energy utilization,* In ERDA Authorization-Part I, 1976 and Transition Period Conservation. Hearings before the Subcommittee on Energy Research Development and Demonstration of the Committee on Science and Technology U.S. House of Representatives. Ninety-fourth Congress. Congress, 1st session, Feb 18, 1975.
38. Marc H. Ross and Robert H. Williams, *op. cit.* We assume that these reductions in percentage will be approximately the same for the industrial sector with the proposed changes in industrial production.
39. Elias P. Gyftopoulos et al., *Potential Fuel Effectiveness in Industry. A report to the Energy Policy Project of the Ford Foundation* (Cambridge, Mass: Ballinger, 1974).
40. *Machine Design,* October 7, 1976, p. 4, from ERDA source.
41. Gallium Arsenide Used for Low Cost High Efficiency Solar Cells, *Computer Design,* September, p. 44, (1975).
42. Bruce Chalmers, The Photovoltaic Generation of Electricity, *Scientific American,* October, p. 34, (1976).
43. Cost of Solar Cells Down 26% in Six Months, *Machine Design,* October 7, 1976, p. 10.
44. *Electronics,* April 1, 1976.
45. Business Communications Co., Inc., *Solar Energy: A Realistic Source of Power,* 1975. Includes solar space heating and cooling, solar electric, and solar fuels for transportation and industry.
46. W. E. Morrow, Jr., Solar Energy: Its Time is Near, in *Perspectives on Energy,* edited by Lon C. Ruedisili and Morris W. Firebaugh, Oxford University Press, New York, 1975, p. 336–351. Includes solar heat, solar thermal electric, and electrolysis.
47. Solar Energy Panel, *Solar Energy as a National Energy Source* (NSF/NASA, College Park, Maryland, 1972). Solar heating and cooling, solar electric, and wind electric.
48. Bent Sorensen, *On the Fluctuating Power Generation of Large Wind Energy Converters, with and without Storage* (Copenhagen, Denmark: Niels Bohr Institute, University of Copenhagen, 1976).
49. Fifty per cent of new dwellings in 1976 have electric heating devices. In certain areas of the Midwest, a 15 per cent annual increase in the number of all electric homes is not uncommon.
50. Gunnar Myrdal, Is Sweden Richer than the U.S.?, interview in *Forbes Magazine,* April 1, 1972, p. 23.
51. Dennis Gabor, *The Mature Society* (London: Secker and Warburg, 1972), pp. 10–11.
52. Barbara Koeppel, Something Could be Finer than to be in Carolina, *The Progressive,* June 1976, pp. 20–23.
53. Included is the labor required for maintenance, material processing, component manufacturing, and construction but not mining. Also note that the numbers of jobs apply to one state only and conceivably employment levels nation wide would be 50 times as great.
54. James Monroe et al., *Energy and Employment in New York State, Draft Report: A Report to the New York State Legislative Commission on Energy Systems,* Report ES 119, May 3, 1976.
55. Energy Research Group, *Urban Auto-Bus Substitution: The Dollar, Energy and Employment Impacts* (Report to Energy Policy Project, 1973, 1776 Massachusetts Avenue, NW, Washington D.C., in press), see reference 56.
56. Roger Bezdek, and Bruce Hannon, Energy, Manpower and the Highway Trust Fund, *Science 185,* pp. 669–675 (1974).
57. Robert J. Lampman, as cited in W. W. Heller, Coming to Terms With Growth and the Environment, in *Energy, Economic Growth and the Environment,* edited by S. H. Schurr (Baltimore: Johns Hopkins University Press, 1972).
58. Warren A. Johnson, The Guaranteed Income as an Environmental Measure, in *Economic Growth vs. the Environment,* edited by Warren A. Johnson and John Hardesty (Belmont, Calif.: Wadsworth Publishing Co., 1971).
59. See, for example, Marianne Frankenhauser's, Limits of Tolerance and Quality of Life, paper presented at the symposium *Level of Living—Quality of Life,* held at Biskops—Arno, Sweden in 1974 and published in *Viewpoint* (New York: Swedish Information Service, 1974).

The Recycle Society of Tommorow 35

GLENN T. SEABORG 1974

These days it is difficult enough to forecast what the world will be like next year, let alone predict what kind of a world it may be in 1994. Although I enjoy future forecasting sessions, I cannot help but feel that many of us are projecting the kind of futures we would like to see, knowing that the world could be that way, hoping it will, rather than trying to base our forecasts on that combination of progress and the obstruction to it due to human foibles and follies that inevitably contribute to future conditions.

In the past we physical scientists have been especially prone to the blue skies approach to the future, tending to see the possibilities of gaining and applying new knowledge, of the "technological fix," and of the value of human cooperation. Those in the social and political sciences and in the business world are apt to be a bit more realistic because they deal more directly with the perversity and irrationality of human nature as well as its admirable features.

In recent years we have also seen the rise of forecasting by systems analysts, using elaborate computer models and warning us of total collapse based on the projections of current trends. Their studies offer some serious warnings of what could be. But I am inclined to agree with Rene Dubos' statement that "trend is not destiny."

My own thoughts about where we might be, and might be going, in the 1990's are based on what I consider to be a number of imperatives. That is, I think there are things that will have to happen, conditions that will have to prevail, given the physical limitations we face, but also given man's creativity and will to survive. In other words, sooner or later we will stabilize our population; we will minimize our environmental impact and efficiently manage our use of natural resources; and we will achieve a relatively peaceful world with a more equitable distribution of goods, services and opportunities throughout the world.

Dr. Glenn T. Seaborg is currently University Professor of Chemistry, Lawrence Berkeley Laboratory, University of California. He previously served as chairman of the U.S. Atomic Energy Commission and chancellor of the University of California. He won the Nobel Prize for Chemistry in 1951 as codiscoverer of plutonium and other elements.

From *The Futurist,* Vol. VIII, No. 3, pp. 108–115. Reprinted by permission of the author and *The Futurist.*

The difficulty is not in predicting that we will arrive at these points, or even how we will arrive, but when and how much disruption, deprivation, and destruction will take place in the interim. This, in turn, will depend to a large extent on how quickly we grasp and apply certain principles of constructive human behavior, how we balance self-interest with mutual interest, to what degree and how soon we greatly improve cooperation between people and nations. It will also depend—somewhat fortuitously—on the kind of leadership that rises around the world. That is a most important catalyzing agent over which we seem to have little control.

Bearing all this in mind, I will try to give some approximation of where we might be in 1994—assuming that most things turn out right, that cool heads, kind hearts, and common sense prevail and guide all our other human assets. I will not speculate on what might happen if "the ghost in the machine," as Arthur Koestler refers to man's self-destructive flaws, takes over.

First, let me cover some general conditions that I think will have arrived by 1994, or will be well along in their formation.

TOWARD A "STEADY-STATE" WORLD

Broadly speaking, the 1990's will be a period characterized mainly by the need to stimulate maximum creativity in a tightly controlled social and physical environment. The reason for this is that by the mid-1990's we should be well on our way to making the transition from an "open-ended" world to a "steady-state" one. The United States will be in the forefront of this movement. Others will be following with various degrees of enthusiasm and reluctance, much depending on the sacrifice and cooperation of the advanced nations.

Some of the major characteristics of this transition will be:

(1) *Movement toward a highly disciplined society with behavior self-modified and modified by social conditions*. On the surface, and by the standards of many young people today, it will be a "straight society," but a happier, well adjusted one with a much healthier kind of freedom, as I will explain later.

(2) *Organization of a "recycle society" using all resources with maximum efficiency and effectiveness and a minimum of environmental impact.*

(3) *A mixed energy economy, depending on a combination of several energy sources and technologies and highly conservation conscious*. During this time we will still be searching for the best ways to phase ourselves out of the fossil fuel age.

(4) *Greater progress toward a successful international community spearheaded by the economics of multinational industry, new international trade arrangements that improve the distribution of resources, and a high degree of scientific and technical cooperation.*

Let me elaborate a bit on these characteristics, beginning with a few words about social attitude and behavior, as I believe these will be among the biggest determinants of where we are and where we will be going.

A HIGHLY DISCIPLINED SOCIETY IN THE 1990's?

By the 1990's I suspect we will be a society almost 180 degrees different from what we are today, or some think we will be in the future. I see us in 1994 as a highly disciplined society with behavior self-modified by social and physical conditions already being generated today. The permissiveness, violence, self-indulgence and material extravagance which seem to be some of the earmarks of today will not be characteristic of our 1990 society. In fact, we will have gone through a total reaction to these.

We, therefore, will have a society that on the whole exercises a quiet, non-neurotic self-control, displays a highly cooperative public spirit, has an almost religious attitude toward environmental quality and resource conservation, exercises great care and ingenuity in managing its personal belongings and shows an extraordinary degree of reliability in its work. Furthermore, I see such a society as being mentally and physically healthier and enjoying a greater degree of freedom, even though it will be living in a more crowded, complex environment.

All this will not come about by making everyone subscribe and live up to the Boy Scout oath. I think it will come about as an outgrowth of a number of painful shocks—shocks of recognition, not future shocks—we will undergo over the coming years, one of which we are already getting in our current energy situation. The energy crisis is just the forerunner of a number of situations that we will be facing that will change our attitudes, behavior, and institutions—although I do not in any way minimize its importance or its far-reaching effect on all aspects of our lives. We will face a number of critical materials shortages and some failures in our technological systems that will force us into fairly radical changes in the way we are conducting our lives and managing our society.

My reasons for projecting the "straight society" I have mentioned for the 1990's spring from the series of reactions that the forthcoming shocks will elicit. The reactions will come in sequence but will also widely overlap. The first period will be one mainly emphasizing conservation and cooperation. Of course, there will be some degree of negativism about the noncompliance with the required changes. And there will be those who, with the usual amount of hindsight, blame others for not being able to anticipate current problems.

But by and large, most people will respond postively as they have in the past in the time of crisis. In fact, after the extended period of comparative affluence and self-indulgence most people have enjoyed in this country, we may witness something of a quiet pride and spartan-like spirit in facing some shortages and exercising both the stoicism and ingenuity to face and overcome them. What is important, though, is that the emphasis will shift from stoicism to ingenuity as we come up with new ideas and technologies, to overcome our problems. By the mid-1990's we should be a good way along in this shift, the results of which I will discuss in a moment. But the results of the changes and transitions we face will have left their effect on our society, for we will have realized that we will never again live in a society where so much is taken for granted—where so many apparently "knew the price of everything and the value of nothing." The environmental movement, the energy crisis, and the problems yet to come will have changed all that well before 1990.

Oddly enough, the kind of general outlook that will prevail in 1994 will be a synthesis of ideas coming out of today's low technology communes and high technology industries. We will not see complexity for its own sake. But neither will we be able to maintain the desired quality of life for the number of people present by depending on something akin to handicraft and cottage industry. High technology, much better planned and managed, and important scientific advances will still be the basis for progress.

But that progress will be guided by many of the new values being expressed by young people today. We will be more of a functional and less of a possessive society, more apt to enjoy a less cluttered life, more inclined to share material things and take pleasure in doing so. This will bring us a different kind of freedom, one more closely related to Hegel's definition when he said, "Freedom is the recognition of necessity," but one also allowing more people to "do their own thing" within the framework of a cooperative society.

Let me turn now to some of the physical changes that will be taking place that will accompany these social changes as we move toward and through the 1990's.

HOW THE "RECYCLE SOCIETY" WILL WORK

As I mentioned before, we will be creating a "recycle society." By this I do not mean simply one in which beer cans and Coke bottles are all returned to the supermarket, but one in which virtually all materials used are reused indefinitely and virgin resources become primarily the "make-up" materials to account for the amounts lost in use and production and needed to supplement new production to take care of any new growth that would improve the quality of life.

In such a society the present materials situation is literally reversed; all waste and scrap—what are now called "secondary materials"—become our major resources, and our natural, untapped resources become our backup supplies. This must eventually be the industrial philosophy of a stabilized society and the one toward which we must work.

To many who have not thought about it, this idea may sound simple, or a bit confusing. To many who have given it considerable thought, it can be mind boggling and sound physically and economically impossible, given our current state of industry. And to some it may even appear morally objectionable, given the state of development in many parts of the world. To clarify the concept, let me explain some of the things it will and will not involve.

First, it involves a shift in industry to the design and production of consumer goods that are essentially nonobsolescent. This means that products will be built to be more durable; easily repairable with standardized, replaceable parts; accessible; and able to be repaired with very basic tools. (Along these lines, I understand that at a recent international auto show in Frankfurt, Porsche displayed a car designed to have a twenty-year life, or 200,000 miles—but then quickly assured the industry it had no intentions of putting the car into production!)

In the recycle society, all products and parts will be labeled in such a way that their use, origin and material content can be readily identified; and all will have a regulated trade-in value. Many items of furniture, housewares, appliances, and tools, in addition to their low-maintenance qualities, will be multifunctional, modular, and designed for easy assembly and breakdown to be readily moved and set up in a different location when necessary. Their design and construction will also allow for their reassembly and redesign into essentially new products when their owners have different uses for them or seek a change.

When a consumer (it would be more correct to call him a "user") wishes to replace an item or trade up for something better or different, he can return the old item for the standard trade-in price. All stores will have to accept these trade-ins. They thus will become collection centers as well as selling outlets in the recycle society.

Manufacturers in turn will receive and recondition the used products, use their parts as replacement parts in "new" products, or scrap them for recycled material. Since literally everything will be coded and tagged for material content, much of the high cost of technological materials separation will be eliminated. Materials that were mixtures and alloys would be color coded, magnetically or isotopically tagged to facilitate optical or electromagnetic separation.

Recycling and reprocessing will also apply to software—clothing, bedding, carpeting, and all other textile materials, organic and synthetic, and, of course, to paper products.

The industrial processing aspects of the recycle society may be the easiest to achieve, as there are already one or two major companies that claim the ability to recycle totally the waste products of selected plants without any economic penalty. By 1994 we should also see extensive recycle of organic material from agriculture and forest industries. Animal waste will find many uses as fertilizer, fuel, and feed. Protein will be grown on petroleum waste and extracted from otherwise inedible plants and agricultural products.

PEOPLE WILL BE BETTER OFF IN THE 1990'S

To make the transition to an economic recycle society, much will be required in the way of new legislation, regulation, tax incentives, and other measurers that will make the use of secondary materials more economic than that of virgin resources. The opposite situation prevails today. In addition to the setting up of new methods of marketing and management required to operate a recycle society, there will be the necessity for a longterm consumer education program. A whole new public outlook will have to be acquired.

An entire society reusing and recycling almost all its possessions, especially after an extended era of conspicuous consumption and waste, will take a great deal of pride in a life style that is extremely creative and varied and based on a new degree of human ingenuity and innovation. The "recycle society" of the 1990's will be better off than the affluent society of the 1970's.

Several types of assets will accrue from the movement toward the kind of society I have been describing. One lies in the fact that it will be far less energy-intensive. For example, recycled steel requires 75 per cent less energy than steel made from iron ore; 70 per cent less energy is used in recycling paper than in using virgin pulp; 12 times as much energy is needed to produce primary aluminum as to recover aluminum scrap. A society set up to reuse most of its resources systematically and habitually could effect enormous energy savings.

Perhaps even greater would be the reduction in the environmental impact of a recycle society. This would be true for several reasons. An over-all one is that such a society would have developed by the 1990's an environmental and conservationist ethic, due to the scarcity of resources as well as the new value placed on land, water, and air. We can see this ethic already in the making today. There is some fear that because of our energy crisis we will severely compromise this ethic, or even abandon it. I do not think this will be the case. Rather I believe we will be making substantial sacrifices in the years ahead to change our life style in order to match our economic and environmental needs.

By the 1990's our industrial and power systems will be much more efficient users of energy; hence, they will not be rejecting as great a percentage of waste heat to the environment. In fact, most systems will probably be planned and designed to make maximum use of waste heat, using it for space heating or possibly agriculture or aquaculture. Waste water and sewage water will also be recycled in industrial and perhaps even municipal water systems. What water is returned to the environment will be as clean, if not cleaner, than it was when it entered the man-made system.

It would be foolish to believe that by 1994, even with a recycle society as a reality, we will not still be drawing on a substantial amount of new resources. Even with population growth leveling off and economic growth cooling off we can expect substantial growing demands for new materials resources well into the next century. What this means is that by the 1990's we will have to develop a new level of ingenuity in materials substitution and in what Buckminster Fuller calls "ephemeralization"—the process of doing more with less. Fuller uses as an example of this, the Telstar satellite, which, while weighing only one-tenth of a ton, outperforms 75,000 tons of transatlantic cable.

Communications, of course, have offered the best examples of this "more with less" phenomenon, as in electronics we have seen the size of basic devices reduced by a factor of ten roughly every five years. Today, a single chip of silicon a tenth of an inch square may hold microscopic units that perform the functions of as many as 1,000 separate electronic components. Furthermore, silicon is one of the most abundant substances in the earth's crust.

COMMUNICATIONS MAY SUBSTITUTE FOR TRANSPORTATION

By the 1990's substitution not only in materials but in functions—the way we conduct our business and personal affairs—may vastly alter our lives, effecting many savings in energy and time, and therefore affecting how we otherwise spend our energy and time. For example, communications as a substitution for transportation can effect such savings to a great extent.

Shopping by telephone and having good

home delivery is a very old example of this, one which is largely out of style today. But if one could survey local supermarkets and department stores via videophone and a computer to do some quick comparative shopping and then have the selections delivered, one would have more time, money, and energy (personal and automotive) left for other things. Another aspect of this type of shopping involves a considerable saving in space. A simple warehouse with a small fleet of trucks could service thousands of customers, eliminating the paving over of large parking areas and the operation of an elaborate market.

A society that exercises this option of using communication in place of transportation in many of its activities—whether in shopping, business, or educational activities—can conserve many resources. But it must be one that has learned to substitute other activites for the social and entertainment value that we have come to find in our more random way of life.

In conducting this kind of society, questions that loom larger than those of the technological possibilities are as follows. Assuming a 1994 liberated housewife (if that is not a contradiction in terms) is able to do most of her shopping by video computer and her other chores so efficiently, how will she spend her extra free time? When it is possible to hold national and international conferences via home holography, will we miss the luncheons, banquets, and corridor talk? And what will happen to the Willy Lomans of the world when they can sell their lines long distance in living color, through similar electronic techniques, without covering the territory in person? These are only a sample of the kinds of questions that can be raised when the matter of substituting communication for travel becomes a viable option.

It is possible to speculate that in 1994 we may find a situation in which our working world will be served mainly by communication and public transportation, and the savings from this will allow us to use private transportation in a limited way for recreation and vacations.

WILL URBAN SPRAWL DESTROY THE COUNTRYSIDE?

Much of what I have said to this point will be influenced by, and influence, how we use our space here on Earth—how we manage our land, develop our urban areas, place our industry, locate our power system. Do we build out, up, or down? Do we draw people back into the cities, continue to disperse them around cities, or cluster them in new areas, in new cities around new industries? And how much of a planned, concerted effort do we make to do any of these? We are, in fact, just beginning to take a serious look at land management and the control of our populated areas in this country. In the past we have seen our population explode and implode with both good and bad effects, but certainly without much conscious control on our part.

It is difficult to speculate on how far we will have gone by 1994 in having effected any widespread control or change over today's patterns of growth. Twenty years is not a long time to institute and carry out major changes in land use and population distribution. And yet, unless we do, some of the major effects of the current style of growth could (according to Environmental Protection Agency estimates) lead to some 20 million additional acres being covered by urban sprawl (an area equivalent to New Hampshire, Vermont, Massachusetts, and Rhode Island); more than 3 million acres paved over for highways and airports; and about 5 million acres of agricultural land lost to public facilities, second-home development, and waste control projects. In addition, the approximately 1,000 power stations that may be built by the 1990's, together with their cooling facilities, fuel storage and safety exclusion areas, and right-of-way land for power lines, could require another two to three million acres.

MEASURES TO COUNTER THE DESTRUCTION OF THE COUNTRYSIDE

Much of this is inevitably going to take place before 1994. But I see some of the following as countermeasures and countertrends that may be initiated, or well under way, by the 1990's:

(1) *A large shift toward clustered, attached, and high rise housing surrounded by community-owned open lands.* This planned housing would rise as "new cities" and as neighborhood communities within larger urban areas. It would help eliminate today's suburban sprawl and preserve more open land for recreation, agriculture, or natural reserves.

(2) *Increased use of underground space made possible by advances in excavation technology:* underground shopping centers, warehouses, recreation and entertainment complexes, rapid mass-transit lines, and power and communications cables.

(3) *Offshore power plants with extrahigh voltage, and superconducting transmission cables carrying electricity greater distances inland.* Cables would be underground and might occupy the same rights-of-way as rapid rail transit systems and cable communication systems. In the 1990's such offshore powerplants would be nuclear electric. In the next century they might include nuclear hydrogen-producing plants and solar-powered electric and hydrogen-producing plants.

(4) *Integrated industrial complexes planned to concentrate energy sources, materials, and manufacturing in single locations.* This would reduce long shipments of fuel and material resources, make more efficient use of waste heat and materials, confine and control environmental impact.

IMPROVEMENT IN ENERGY SITUATION BY 1994?

Concerning the energy situation, which is uppermost on people's minds today and will certainly have a major bearing on our future, I believe we will see a turning point in our difficulties by 1994. But the intervening years will necessitate bearing some difficulties and hardships because we have not given ourselves the necessary lead time to make an orderly transition to new energy technologies and resources. There is no doubt that we have been shortsighted and complacent about supplies and have overestimated our ability to develop and shake down new technologies and to get them on line economically.

In the 1990's we will still have a very mixed energy economy. By then, oil and gas will be giving way to coal—but grudgingly, as it will take some time to develop and build economic coal gasification and liquefaction systems. Oil shale may be a significant factor by then. And we may even have found a way to retort the oil from the shale via underground heating and explosives (chemical) to avoid stripping and excavation. We will have a growing amount of electricity in some parts of the country supplied by geothermal energy. Solar energy equipment for home heating and cooling will be prevalent on new single-family dwellings and incentives will be introduced to encourage home owners to retrofit their houses with such equipment if possible. Solar energy may supply a small amount of home use electricity, but the large-scale production of solar electricity may still be a few years off. However, by the 1990's we should see some prototype "solar farms" in the Southwestern United States testing out the economic, large-scale conversion of solar energy.

I am confident that by the 1990's we will be well over the difficulties and resistance facing nuclear power today and that more than a third of our electric power will be generated by nuclear plants. The liquid-metal fast-breeder reactor will have been tested out to everyone's satisfaction by then and coming on line commercially. Other systems, such as the high-temperature gas-cooled reactor, will be adding to our national electric capacity. We may have achieved laboratory success in controlled fusion by 1994 and be building prototype fusion reactors.

We simply must pay the price of pursuing all possibilities in the energy field, and at the same time pursue the energy conservation ethic I mentioned before. Any energy bonuses that would come our way through new breakthroughs would not give us energy to squander but would allow a well-planned, equitable increase in the quality of life on a worldwide basis.

A DESIRABLE FUTURE FOR AN INTERDEPENDENT WORLD

This brings me to my concluding thoughts on 1994, which center on global cooperation. In the midst of an energy crisis aggravated by the withholding of oil as a political weapon, this does not seem to be a popular topic. It is quite natural to want to act from a position of strength. With some sacrifices we can.

And yet, in our immediate reaction to strive for energy self-sufficency, we should not overreact, not delude ourselves into believing that self-sufficiency in energy and other matters is the total solution to national security and well being. This would lead to a dangerous neo-isolationism at a time when we must move in the other direction—toward greater international cooperation, no matter how difficult and painstaking the process seems at some times. The harsh facts are that we live in a highly interdependent world—one in which there will continue to be some hard bargaining but in which cooperation is growing increasingly important.

By 1994, I see the scales tipping more and more in favor of cooperation over competition. My travels over the world in the past dozen years to more than sixty countries—and most recently to the People's Republic of China—have led me to believe that all nations of the world need each other, that all have something to offer, and all could benefit by a greater exchange of human and material resources, of knowledge and goods.

Over the next twenty years we will have to make enormous strides—together—in controlling population, increasing food production, managing our environment, investigating and controlling the resources of the seas, conducting global research, developing methods to reduce the human impact of natural disasters, and generally uplifting the economic conditions of a large number of the world's peoples. There are no alternatives to these measures—except a tremendous increase in human misery that will ultimately affect all the world's peoples.

Forecasting the world of 1994 involves much more than projecting the trends at hand or even reciting the possibilities ahead. That future will be determined in large part by our considering and choosing values, examining and deciding among alternatives, exercising great will and perseverance, and searching for the leadership that will assemble and catalyze the proper resources to construct a chosen future. To the extent that we can do this we will either be drifting toward the world of 1994 or building it. Most likely, we will be doing a little of each, but I hope we will not be trusting to luck that which we could achieve by a new and concerted human effort.

Finally, . .1994 is only twenty years off. We had better get moving!

Appendix

ENERGY DEFINITIONS AND CONVERSION FACTORS

The variety of units and the unclear distinctions between energy and power often prove confusing to students of the energy problem. In this appendix we present a brief introduction to these concepts and a table of conversion factors to assist in energy unit conversions. We use the metric MKS* system of units to present these concepts and the table at the end of the appendix to express British and other energy units in the metric system.

Energy and Power

As an operational concept, *energy is defined as the ability to do work.* Work, in turn, is defined as a force acting through a distance paralled to the force.

$$W = Fd \tag{1}$$

For instance, if we push a stalled car a distance of 10 meters (m) with a force of 500 newtons (nt), we have performed

$$W = 500 \text{ newton} \times 10 \text{ meters} = 5{,}000 \text{nt} \times \text{m}$$

of work. Another name for nt × m is the joule (J). This task required 5,000 J of energy.

*Meter-kilogram-second.

Energy is available in a variety of forms, falling into three general categories of (a) *kinetic energy,* (b) *potential energy,* and (c) *rest-mass energy.*

Kinetic energy is the energy of motion and is expressed mathematically as

$$KE = \tfrac{1}{2} mv^2 \tag{2}$$

where m is the mass of the moving body (kilograms) and v is the velocity of the moving body (meters per second). In the example above, for instance, if the car was initially at rest and there was *no* friction involved (an impossible situation), the work performed on the car would result in 5,000 J of kinetic energy manifested in the final velocity of the car.

There are several forms of *potential energy.* These include the energy stored in a compressed spring, chemical energy stored in fossil fuels, and gravitational energy stored in matter as it is lifted in the earth's gravitational field. For example, as solar energy evaporates water and lifts it high into the mountains, the water accumulates potential energy given by

$$PE = mgh \tag{3}$$

where m is the mass of water (kilograms); g is the acceleration due to gravity (9.8 meters per second squared); and h is the height through which water is raised (meters).

A kilogram of water raised 4,000 meters would store 1 kilogram × 9.8 meters per second squared × 4,000 meters = 39,200 kg × m²/sec² = 39,200 nt × m or 39,200 J of potential energy. This process is the basis for hydroelectric energy.

The third form of energy is *rest-mass energy*. The conversion of mass into energy is the basic process involved in fission reactors and the experimental fusion devices. The sun, in fact, is just one enormous fusion reactor converting part of the mass of hydrogen into heat and radiation energy. The relation governing this conversion is the famous Einstein equation

$$E = mc^2 \tag{4}$$

where m is the mass being converted (kilograms); c is the speed of light (3×10^8 meters per second); and E is the energy released (joules).

For example, if 1 kilogram of reactor fuel is converted to energy, we get

$$\begin{aligned} E &= 1 \times (3 \times 10^8)^2 \text{ joules} \\ &= 9 \times 10^{16} \text{ J} \end{aligned}$$

of energy released. Thus, radioactive isotopes such as deuterium, tritium, uranium-235, and plutonium-239 may be thought of as very concentrated forms of potential energy.

Although energy itself is the fundamental quantity (the quantity we purchase as electricity and gas), a somewhat more intuitive concept is that of *power*. *Power is defined as the time rate of doing work.* It is given by

$$P = W / T \tag{5}$$

where W is work (joules); T is time (seconds); and P is power (watts, where 1 watt = 1 joule per second). Thus, a typical light bulb may be rated at 100 watts (power) and will therefore consume 100 joules of energy every second it burns. The power of motors, both electrical and gasoline powered, is frequently given in horsepower. The conversion factor is 1 horsepower = 746 watts. Therefore a standard U.S. car engine of 300 horsepower would be rated as 223,800 watts or 223.8 kilowatts.

If we know the power rating of a device and the time it operates, we may compute the total energy consumed by rewriting equation (5) as

$$W = PT \tag{6}$$

The 100-watt light left on during 10 hours of darkness would consume 100 watts × 10 hours × 60 minutes per hour × 60 seconds per minutes = 3.6×10^6 watt-seconds = 3.6×10^6 joules of energy. This amount is often expressed as 1,000 watt-hours or 1 kilowatt-hour of energy. The kilowatt-hour is the energy unit used by electric utilities for billing their customers. A kilowatt hour of electrical energy costs in the range of 3 to 6¢, depending on the region of the country.

Other Units and Conversion Factors

For historical reasons or as a matter of convenience a number of other energy units are used. Below, we define some of the more common units and their conversion factors in terms of the kilowatt-hour.

British Thermal Unit (BTU) = the amount of heat energy required to raise the temperature of one pound of water one degree Fahrenheit.

Therm = 100,000 BTU. Widely used in the sale of natural gas energy.

Quad = 10^{15} BTU. Frequently used to display U.S. energy demand of 70 to 85 quad per year for the near future.

Foot-Pound (ft-lb) = the work done by a force of 1 pound acting through a distance of 1 foot.

calorie (also gram-calorie) = the heat energy required to raise the temperature of 1 gram of water one degree Celsius.

Calorie (also kilogram-Calorie) = 1,000 calories. The average adult consumes between 2,000 and 3,000 Calories in food per day.

Electron volt (eV) = the energy change when an electron falls through an electric potential difference of 1 volt. Atomic processes range in energy from several eV to several KeV (1,000 electron volts). Nuclear processes typically occur in the MeV range (million electron volt).

Fossil fuel energy units. Many graphs use units of trillion cubic feet (natural gas), million barrels of oil (or the power equivalent of a million barrels/day = mmb/d), and pounds or tons of coal. Although the energy content of each of these fuels varies, average energy equivalents are given in the following table.

Energy Conversion Table

1kwh = 1 kilowatt-hour

1 kilowatt-hour = 3.60×10^6 joules
1 joule = 2.78×10^{-7} kwh
1 BTU = 2.93×10^{-4} kwh
1 therm = 29.3 kwh
1 quad = 2.93×10^{11} kwh
1 foot-pound = 3.77×10^{-7} kwh
1 calorie = 1.16×10^{-6} kwh
1 Calorie = 1.16×10^{-3} kwh
1 electron volt = 4.45×10^{-26} kwh
1 barrel of oil = 1.65×10^3 kwh
1 gallon of gasoline = 36.7 kwh
1 pound of bituminous coal = 3.84 kwh
1 cubic foot of natural gas = 0.310 kwh